HARPER COLLINS
FRENCH
DICTIONARY

HARPER COLLINS
FRENCH
DICTIONARY

FRENCH · ENGLISH   ENGLISH · FRENCH

HarperResource
An Imprint of HarperCollins*Publishers*

HarperCollins books may be purchased for educational, business, or sales promotional use. For information please write: Special Markets Department, HarperCollins Canada, 55 Avenue Road, Suite 2900, Toronto, Ontario, Canada M5R 3L2

ISBN 0-00-639435-3

The HarperCollins website address is
www.harpercollins.com

The HarperCollins UK website address is
www.**fire**and**water**.com

The HarperCollins Canada website address is
www.harpercanada.com

Harper*Resource* A Division of HarperCollinsPublishers
10 East 53rd Street, New York, N.Y. 10022

first published 1990
second edition 2000

© William Collins Sons & Co. Ltd. 1990
© HarperCollins Publishers 2000

First Harper*Resource* printing: 2000

Typeset by Morton Word Processing Ltd, Scarborough
Printed in the United States of America

HarperResource and colophons are trademarks of HarperCollins*Publishers*

TABLE DES MATIÈRES

CONTENTS

INTRODUCTION

We are delighted you have decided to buy the Collins French Dictionary and hope you will enjoy and benefit from using it at school, at home, on holiday or at work.

This introduction gives you a few tips on how to get the most out of your dictionary — not simply from its comprehensive wordlist but also from the information provided in each entry. This will help you to read and understand modern French, as well as communicate and express yourself in the language.

The Collins French Dictionary begins by listing the abbreviations used in the text and illustrating the sounds shown by the phonetic symbols. You will find French verb tables and English irregular verbs at the back.

USING YOUR COLLINS DICTIONARY

A wealth of information is presented in the dictionary, using various type-faces, sizes of type, symbols, abbreviations and brackets. The conventions and symbols used are explained in the following sections.

Headwords

The words you look up in a dictionary — "headwords" — are listed alpha-betically. They are printed in **bold type** for rapid identification. The two headwords appearing at the top of each page indicate the first and last word dealt with on the page in question.

Information about the usage or form of certain headwords is given in brackets after the phonetic spelling. This usually appears in abbreviated form and in italics (e.g. (*fam*), (*COMM*)).

Where appropriate, words related to headwords are grouped in the same entry (**ronger, rongeur; accept, acceptance**) in a slightly smaller bold type than the headword.

Common expressions in which the headword appears are shown in a different bold roman type (e.g. **avoir du retard**).

Phonetic spellings

The phonetic spelling of each headword (indicating its pronunciation) is given in square brackets immediately after the headword (e.g. **fumer** [fyme]; **knead** [niːd]). A list of these symbols is given on page xi.

Translations

Headword translations are given in ordinary type and, where more than one meaning or usage exists, these are separated by a semi-colon. You will often find other words in italics in brackets before the translations. These offer suggested contexts in which the headword might appear (e.g. **rough** (*voice*) or (*weather*)) or provide synonyms (e.g. **rough** (*violent*)).

"Key" words

Special status is given to certain French and English words which are considered as "key" words in each language. They may, for example, occur very frequently or have several types of usage (e.g. **vouloir, plus; get, that**). A combination of lozenges and numbers helps you to distinguish different parts of speech and different meanings. Further helpful information is provided in brackets and in italics in the relevant language for the user.

Grammatical information

Parts of speech are given in abbreviated form in italics after the phonetic spellings of headwords (e.g. *vt, adv, conj*).

Genders of French nouns are indicated as follows: *nm* for a masculine and *nf* for a feminine noun. Feminine and irregular plural forms of nouns are also shown (**directeur, trice; cheval, aux**).

Adjectives are given in both masculine and feminine forms where these forms are different (e.g. **noir, e**). Clear information is provided where adjectives have an irregular feminine or plural form (e.g. **net, nette**).

INTRODUCTION

Nous sommes très heureux que vous ayez décidé d'acheter le dictionnaire anglais de Collins et espérons que vous aimerez l'utiliser et que vous en tirerez profit au lycée, à la maison, en vacances ou au travail.

Cette introduction a pour but de vous donner quelques conseils sur la meilleure façon d'utiliser au mieux votre dictionnaire, en vous référant non seulement à son importante nomenclature mais aussi aux informations contenues dans chaque entrée. Ceci vous aidera à lire et à comprendre, mais aussi à communiquer et à vous exprimer en anglais contemporain.

Le dictionnaire anglais de Collins commence par la liste des abréviations utilisées dans le texte et par la transcription des sons par des symboles phonétiques. À la fin vous trouverez des tables de verbes français ainsi que la liste des verbes irréguliers en anglais.

COMMENT UTILISER VOTRE DICTIONNAIRE COLLINS

Ce dictionnaire offre une masse d'informations et use de divers formes et tailles de caractères, symboles, abréviations, parenthèses et crochets. Les conventions et symboles utilisés sont expliqués dans les sections qui suivent.

Entrées

Les mots que vous cherchez dans le dictionnaire (les 'entrées') sont classés par ordre alphabétique. Ils sont imprimés en **caractères gras** pour pouvoir être repérés rapidement. Les deux entrées figurant en haut de page indiquent le premier et le dernier mot qui apparaissent sur la page en question.

Des informations sur l'usage ou sur la forme de certaines entrées sont données entre parenthèses, après la transcription phonétique. Ces indications apparaissent sous forme abrégée et en italiques (ex *(fam)*, *(COMM)*).

Dans les cas appropriés, les mots apparentés aux entrées sont regroupés sous la même entrée (**ronger, rongeur; accept, acceptance**) et apparaissent en caractères gras, légèrement plus petits que ceux de l'entrée.

Les expressions courantes dans lesquelles apparaît l'entrée sont indiquées par des caractères romains gras différents (ex **avoir du retard**).

Transcription phonétique

La transcription phonétique de chaque entrée (indiquant sa prononciation) est indiquée entre crochets immédiatement après l'entrée (ex **fumer** [fyme]; **knead** [ni:d]). Une liste de ces symboles figure à la page xi.

Traductions

Les traductions des entrées apparaissent en caractères ordinaires et, lorsque plusieurs sens ou usages coexistent, ces traductions sont séparées par un point-virgule. Vous trouverez souvent entre parenthèses d'autres mots en italiques qui précèdent les traductions. Ces mots fournissent souvent certains des contextes dans lesquels l'entrée est susceptible d'être utilisée (ex **rough** *(voice)* ou *(weather)*) ou offrent des synonymes (ex **rough** *(violent)*).

'Mots-clés'

Une importance particulière est accordée à certains mots français et anglais qui sont considérés comme des "mots-clés" dans chacune des langues. Cela peut être dû à leur utilisation très fréquente ou au fait qu'ils ont divers types d'usages (ex **vouloir, plus; get, that**). Une combinaison de losanges et de chiffres vous aident à distinguer différentes catégories grammaticales et différents sens. D'autres renseignements utiles apparaissent en italiques et entre parenthèses dans la langue de l'utilisateur.

Données grammaticales

Les catégories grammaticales sont données sous forme abrégée et en italiques après la transcription phonétique des entrées (ex *vt, adv, conj*).

Les genres des noms français sont indiqués de la manière suivante: *nm* pour un nom masculin et *nf* pour un nom féminin. Le féminin et le pluriel irréguliers de certains noms sont également indiqués (**directeur, trice; cheval, aux**).

Le masculin et le féminin des adjectif sont indiqués lorsque ces deux formes sont différentes (ex **noir, e**). Lorsque l'adjectif a un féminin ou un pluriel irrégulier, ces formes sont clairement indiquées (ex **net, nette**). Les pluriels irréguliers des noms, et les formes irréguliers des verbes anglais sont indiqués entre parenthèses, avant la catégorie grammaticale (ex **man** ... *(pl* **men***)* *n*; **give** *(pt* **gave**, *pp* **given***)* *vt*).

ABRÉVIATIONS

ABBREVIATIONS

abréviation	ab(b)r	abbreviation
adjectif, locution adjective	adj	adjective, adjectival phrase
adverbe, locution adverbiale	adv	adverb, adverbial phrase
administration	ADMIN	administration
agriculture	AGR	agriculture
anatomie	ANAT	anatomy
architecture	ARCHIT	architecture
article défini	art déf	definite article
article indéfini	art indéf	indefinite article
l'automobile	AUT(O)	the motor car and motoring
aviation, voyages aériens	AVIAT	flying, air travel
biologie	BIO(L)	biology
botanique	BOT	botany
anglais de Grande-Bretagne	BRIT	British English
chimie	CHEM	chemistry
commerce, finance, banque	COMM	commerce, finance, banking
comparatif	compar	comparative
informatique	COMPUT	computing
conjonction	conj	conjunction
construction	CONSTR	building
nom utilisé comme adjectif	cpd	compound element
cuisine, art culinaire	CULIN	cookery
article défini	def art	definite article
déterminant: article; adjectif démonstratif ou indéfini etc	dét	determiner: article, demonstrative etc
diminutif	dimin	diminutive
économie	ECON	economics
électricité, électronique	ELEC	electricity, electronics
exclamation, interjection	excl	exclamation, interjection
féminin	f	feminine
langue familière (! emploi vulgaire)	fam (!)	colloquial usage (! particularly offensive)
emploi figuré	fig	figurative use
(verbe anglais) dont la particule est inséparable du verbe	fus	(phrasal verb) where the particle cannot be separated from main verb
généralement	gén, gen	generally
géographie, géologie	GEO	geography, geology
géométrie	GEOM	geometry
impersonnel	impers	impersonal
article indéfini	indef art	indefinite article
langue familière (! emploi vulgaire)	inf(!)	colloquial usage (! particularly offensive)
infinitif	infin	infinitive
informatique	INFORM	computing
invariable	inv	invariable
irrégulier	irrég, irreg	irregular
domaine juridique	JUR	law
grammaire, linguistique	LING	grammar, linguistics
masculin	m	masculine
mathématiques, algèbre	MATH	mathematics, calculus
médecine	MÉD MED	medical term, medicine

ABRÉVIATIONS

ABBREVIATIONS

masculin ou féminin, suivant le sexe	m/f	masculine or feminine depending on sex
domaine militaire, armée	MIL	military matters
musique	MUS	music
nom	n	noun
navigation, nautisme	NAVIG, NAUT	sailing, navigation
adjectif ou nom numérique	num	numeral adjective or noun
	o.s.	oneself
péjoratif	péj, pej	derogatory, pejorative
photographie	PHOT(O)	photography
physiologie	PHYSIOL	physiology
pluriel	pl	plural
politique	POL	politics
participe passé	pp	past participle
préposition	prép, prep	preposition
pronom	pron	pronoun
psychologie, psychiatrie	PSYCH	psychology, psychiatry
temps du passé	pt	past tense
quelque chose	qch	
quelqu'un	qn	
religions, domaine ecclésiastique	REL	religions, church service
	sb	somebody
enseignement, système scolaire et universitaire	SCOL	schooling, schools and universities
singulier	sg	singular
	sth	something
subjonctif	sub	subjunctive
sujet (grammatical)	su(b)j	(grammatical) subject
superlatif	superl	superlative
techniques, technologie	TECH	technical term, technology
télécommunications	TEL	telecommunications
télévision	TV	television
typographie	TYP(O)	typography, printing
anglais des USA	US	American English
verbe (auxiliaire)	vb (aux)	(auxiliary) verb
verbe intransitif	vi	intransitive verb
verbe transitif	vt	transitive verb
zoologie	ZOOL	zoology
marque déposée	®	registered trademark
indique une équivalence culturelle	≃	introduces a cultural equivalent

TRANSCRIPTION PHONÉTIQUE

CONSONNES

CONSONANTS

NB. **p, b, t, d, k, g** sont suivis d'une aspiration en anglais.

NB. **p, b, t, d, k, g** are not aspirated in French.

poupée	p	*puppy*
bombe	b	*baby*
tente thermal	t	*tent*
dinde	d	*daddy*
coq qui képi	k	*cork kiss chord*
gag bague	g	*gag guess*
sale ce nation	s	*so rice kiss*
zéro rose	z	*cousin buzz*
tache chat	ʃ	*sheep sugar*
gilet juge	ʒ	*pleasure beige*
	tʃ	*church*
	dʒ	*judge general*
fer phare	f	*farm raffle*
valve	v	*very rev*
	θ	*thin maths*
	ð	*that other*
lent salle	l	*little ball*
rare rentrer	ʀ	
	ɹ	*rat rare*
maman femme	m	*mummy comb*
non nonne	n	*no ran*
agneau vigne	ɲ	
	ŋ	*singing bank*
hop!	h	*hat reheat*
yeux paille pied	j	*yet*
nouer oui	w	*wall bewail*
huile lui	ɥ	
	x	*loch*

DIVERS

MISCELLANEOUS

pour l'anglais: le r final se prononce en liaison devant une voyelle	ʳ	in French wordlist: no liaison
pour l'anglais: précède la syllabe accentuée	'	in French transcription: no liaison

PHONETIC TRANSCRIPTION

VOYELLES

NB. La mise en équivalence de certains sons n'indique qu'une ressemblance approximative.

VOWELS

NB. The pairing of some vowel sounds only indicates approximate equivalence.

ici vie lyre	i i:	heel bead
	ɪ	hit pity
jouer été	e	
lait jouet merci	ɛ	set tent
plat amour	a æ	bat apple
bas pâte	ɑ ɑ:	after car calm
	ʌ	fun cousin
le premier	ə	over above
beurre peur		
peu deux	œ ø ə:	urn fern work
or homme	ɔ	wash pot
mot eau gauche	o ɔ:	born cork
genou roue	u	full soot
	u:	boon lewd
rue urne	y	

DIPHTONGUES

DIPHTHONGS

ɪə	beer tier
ɛə	tear fair there
eɪ	date plaice day
aɪ	life buy cry
au	owl foul now
əu	low no
ɔɪ	boil boy oily
uə	poor tour

NASALES

NASAL VOWELS

matin plein	ɛ̃
brun	œ̃
sang an dans	ɑ̃
non pont	ɔ̃

FRANÇAIS – ANGLAIS

FRENCH – ENGLISH

A, a

a [a] *vb voir* **avoir**

MOT-CLÉ

à [a] (*à + le* = **au**, *à + les* = **aux**) *prép* **1**
(*endroit, situation*) at, in; **être à Paris/au
Portugal** to be in Paris/Portugal; **être à la
maison/à l'école** to be at home/at school; **à la
campagne** in the country; **c'est à 10 km/à 20
minutes (d'ici)** it's 10 km/20 minutes away
2 (*direction*) to; **aller à Paris/au Portugal** to
go to Paris/Portugal; **aller à la maison/à
l'école** to go home/to school; **à la campagne**
to the country
3 (*temps*): **à 3 heures/minuit** at 3 o'clock/
midnight; **au printemps/mois de juin** in the
spring/the month of June
4 (*attribution, appartenance*) to; **le livre est à
Paul/à lui/à nous** this book is Paul's/his/ours;
donner qch à qn to give sth to sb
5 (*moyen*) with; **se chauffer au gaz** to have
gas heating; **à bicyclette** on *ou* by bicycle;
à la main/machine by hand/machine
6 (*provenance*) from; **boire à la bouteille** to
drink from the bottle
7 (*caractérisation, manière*): **l'homme aux
yeux bleus** the man with the blue eyes; **à la
russe** the Russian way
8 (*but, destination*): **tasse à café** coffee cup;
maison à vendre house for sale
9 (*rapport, évaluation, distribution*): **100 km/
unités à l'heure** 100 km/units per *ou* an hour;
payé à l'heure paid by the hour; **cinq à six**
five to six

---

abaisser [abese] *vt* to lower, bring down;
(*manette*) to pull down; **s'~** *vi* to go down;
(*fig*) to demean o.s.
abandon [abādɔ̃] *nm* abandoning; giving up;
withdrawal; **être à l'~** to be in a state of
neglect
abandonner [abɑ̃dɔne] *vt* (*personne*) to
abandon; (*projet, activité*) to abandon, give
up; (*SPORT*) to retire *ou* withdraw from;
(*céder*) to surrender; **s'~ à** (*paresse, plaisirs*) to
give o.s. up to
abasourdir [abazurdir] *vt* to stun, stagger
abat-jour [abaʒur] *nm inv* lampshade
abats [aba] *nmpl* (*de bœuf, porc*) offal *sg*; (*de
volaille*) giblets
abattement [abatmã] *nm*: **~ fiscal** ≈ tax

allowance
abattoir [abatwar] *nm* slaughterhouse
abattre [abatr] *vt* (*arbre*) to cut down, fell;
(*mur, maison*) to pull down; (*avion, personne*)
to shoot down; (*animal*) to shoot, kill; (*fig*)
to wear out, tire out; to demoralize; **s'~** *vi* to
crash down; **ne pas se laisser ~** to keep one's
spirits up, not to let things get one down;
s'~ sur to beat down on; (*fig*) to rain down
on
abbaye [abei] *nf* abbey
abbé [abe] *nm* priest; (*d'une abbaye*) abbot
abcès [apsɛ] *nm* abscess
abdiquer [abdike] *vi* to abdicate
abdominaux [abdɔmino] *nmpl*: **faire des ~**
to do exercises for one's abdominals, do
one's abdominals
abeille [abɛj] *nf* bee
aberrant, e [aberɑ̃, ɑ̃t] *adj* absurd
aberration [aberasjɔ̃] *nf* aberration
abêtir [abetir] *vt* to make morons of (*ou* a
moron of)
abîme [abim] *nm* abyss, gulf
abîmer [abime] *vt* to spoil, damage; **s'~** *vi* to
get spoilt *ou* damaged
ablation [ablasjɔ̃] *nf* removal
aboiement [abwamã] *nm* bark, barking
abois [abwa] *nmpl*: **aux ~** at bay
abolir [abɔlir] *vt* to abolish
abominable [abɔminabl] *adj* abominable
abondance [abɔ̃dɑ̃s] *nf* abundance
abondant, e [abɔ̃dɑ̃, ɑ̃t] *adj* plentiful,
abundant, copious; **abonder** *vi* to abound,
be plentiful; **abonder dans le sens de qn** to
concur with sb
abonné, e [abɔne] *nm/f* subscriber; season
ticket holder
abonnement [abɔnmã] *nm* subscription;
(*transports, concerts*) season ticket
abonner [abɔne] *vt*: **s'~ à** to subscribe to,
take out a subscription to
abord [abɔr] *nm*: **au premier ~** at first sight,
initially; **~s** *nmpl* (*environs*) surroundings; **d'~**
first
abordable [abɔrdabl] *adj* (*prix*) reasonable;
(*personne*) approachable
aborder [abɔrde] *vi* to land ♦ *vt* (*sujet,
difficulté*) to tackle; (*personne*) to approach;
(*rivage etc*) to reach
aboutir [abutir] *vi* (*négociations etc*) to

succeed; ~ à to end up at; **n'~ à rien** to come
to nothing

aboyer [abwaje] *vi* to bark

abréger [abreʒe] *vt* to shorten

abreuver [abrœve]: **s'~** *vi* to drink;
abreuvoir *nm* watering place

abréviation [abrevjasjɔ̃] *nf* abbreviation

abri [abri] *nm* shelter; **être à l'~** to be under
cover; **se mettre à l'~** to shelter

abricot [abriko] *nm* apricot

abriter [abrite] *vt* to shelter; **s'~** *vt* to shelter,
take cover

abrupt, e [abrypt] *adj* sheer, steep; (*ton*)
abrupt

abruti, e [abryti] *adj* stunned, dazed ♦ *nm/f*
(*fam*) idiot, moron; **~ de travail** overworked

absence [apsɑ̃s] *nf* absence; (*MÉD*) blackout;
avoir des ~s to have mental blanks

absent, e [apsɑ̃, ɑ̃t] *adj* absent ♦ *nm/f*
absentee; **absenter: s'absenter** *vi* to take
time off work; (*sortir*) to leave, go out

absolu, e [apsɔly] *adj* absolute; **absolument** *adv* absolutely

absorbant, e [apsɔrbɑ̃, ɑ̃t] *adj* absorbent

absorber [apsɔrbe] *vt* to absorb; (*gén MÉD*:
manger, boire) to take

abstenir [apstənir] *vb*: **s'~ de qch/de faire** to
refrain from sth/from doing

abstraction [apstraksjɔ̃] *nf* abstraction

abstrait, e [apstrɛ, ɛt] *adj* abstract

absurde [apsyrd] *adj* absurd

abus [aby] *nm* abuse; **~ de confiance** breach
of trust; **abuser** *vi* to go too far, overstep the
mark; **abuser de** (*duper*) to take advantage
of; **abusif, -ive** *adj* exorbitant; (*punition*)
excessive

acabit [akabi] *nm*: **de cet ~** of that type

académie [akademi] *nf* academy; (*SCOL*:
circonscription) ≈ regional education authority

acajou [akaʒu] *nm* mahogany

acariâtre [akarjɑtr] *adj* cantankerous

accablant, e [akablɑ̃, ɑ̃t] *adj* (*chaleur*)
oppressive; (*témoignage, preuve*) overwhelming

accablement [akabləmɑ̃] *nm* despondency

accabler [akable] *vt* to overwhelm, overcome; **~ qn d'injures** to heap ou shower
abuse on sb

accalmie [akalmi] *nf* lull

accaparer [akapare] *vt* to monopolize; (*suj*:
travail etc) to take up (all) the time ou
attention of

accéder [aksede]: **~ à** *vt* (*lieu*) to reach;
(*accorder: requête*) to grant, accede to

accélérateur [akseleratœr] *nm* accelerator

accélération [akselerasjɔ̃] *nf* acceleration

accélérer [akselere] *vt* to speed up ♦ *vi* to
accelerate

accent [aksɑ̃] *nm* accent; (*PHONÉTIQUE, fig*)

stress; **mettre l'~ sur** (*fig*) to stress; **~ aigu/
grave/circonflexe** acute/grave/circumflex
accent; **accentuer** *vt* (*LING*) to accent; (*fig*)
to accentuate, emphasize; **s'accentuer** *vi* to
become more marked ou pronounced

acceptation [akseptasjɔ̃] *nf* acceptance

accepter [aksepte] *vt* to accept; **~ de faire** to
agree to do

accès [aksɛ] *nm* (*à un lieu*) access; (*MÉD: de
toux*) fit; (: *de fièvre*) bout; **d'~ facile** easily
accessible; **facile d'~** easy to get to; **~ de
colère** fit of anger; **accessible** *adj* accessible;
(*livre, sujet*): **accessible à qn** within the reach
of sb

accessoire [akseswar] *adj* secondary;
incidental ♦ *nm* accessory; (*THÉÂTRE*) prop

accident [aksidɑ̃] *nm* accident; **par ~** by
chance; **~ de la route** road accident; **~ du
travail** industrial injury ou accident;
accidenté, e *adj* damaged; injured; (*relief,
terrain*) uneven; hilly; **accidentel, le** *adj*
accidental

acclamations [aklamasjɔ̃] *nfpl* cheers

acclamer [aklame] *vt* to cheer, acclaim

acclimater [aklimate]: **s'~** *vi* (*personne*) to
adapt (o.s.)

accolade [akɔlad] *nf* (*amicale*) embrace;
(*signe*) brace

accommodant, e [akɔmɔdɑ̃, ɑ̃t] *adj*
accommodating, easy-going

accommoder [akɔmɔde] *vt* (*CULIN*) to
prepare; **s'~ de** *vt* to put up with; (*se
contenter de*) to make do with

accompagnateur, -trice [akɔ̃paɲatœr,
tris] *nm/f* (*MUS*) accompanist; (*de voyage:
guide*) guide; (*de voyage organisé*) courier

accompagner [akɔ̃paɲe] *vt* to accompany,
be ou go ou come with; (*MUS*) to accompany

accompli, e [akɔ̃pli] *adj* accomplished

accomplir [akɔ̃plir] *vt* (*tâche, projet*) to carry
out; (*souhait*) to fulfil; **s'~** *vi* to be fulfilled

accord [akɔr] *nm* agreement; (*entre des
styles, tons etc*) harmony; (*MUS*) chord; **d'~!**
OK!; **se mettre d'~** to come to an agreement;
être d'~ (pour faire qch) to agree (to do) sth

accordéon [akɔrdeɔ̃] *nm* (*MUS*) accordion

accorder [akɔrde] *vt* (*faveur, délai*) to grant;
(*harmoniser*) to match; (*MUS*) to tune; **s'~** *vt*
to get on together; to agree

accoster [akɔste] *vt* (*NAVIG*) to draw
alongside ♦ *vi* to berth

accotement [akɔtmɑ̃] *nm* verge (*BRIT*),
shoulder

accouchement [akuʃmɑ̃] *nm* delivery,
(child)birth; labour

accoucher [akuʃe] *vi* to give birth, have a
baby; **~ d'un garçon** to give birth to a boy;
accoucheur *nm*: (*médecin*) **accoucheur**
obstetrician

accouder [akude]: **s'~** vi to rest one's elbows on/against; **accoudoir** nm armrest

accoupler [akuple] vt to couple; (*pour la reproduction*) to mate; **s'~** vt to mate

accourir [akuʀiʀ] vi to rush ou run up

accoutrement [akutʀəmɑ̃] (*péj*) nm (*tenue*) outfit

accoutumance [akutymɑ̃s] nf (*gén*) adaptation; (*MÉD*) addiction

accoutumé, e [akutyme] adj (*habituel*) customary, usual

accoutumer [akutyme] vt: **s'~ à** to get accustomed ou used to

accréditer [akʀedite] vt (*nouvelle*) to substantiate

accroc [akʀo] nm (*déchirure*) tear; (*fig*) hitch, snag

accrochage [akʀɔʃaʒ] nm (*AUTO*) collision; (*dispute*) clash, brush

accrocher [akʀɔʃe] vt (*fig*) to catch, attract; **s'~** (*se disputer*) to have a clash ou brush; **~ qch à** (*suspendre*) to hang sth (up) on; (*attacher: remorque*) to hitch sth (up) to; **~ qch (à)** (*déchirer*) to catch sth (on); **~ un passant** (*heurter*) to hit a pedestrian; **s'~ à** (*rester pris à*) to catch on; (*agripper, fig*) to hang on ou cling to

accroissement [akʀwasmɑ̃] nm increase

accroître [akʀwatʀ]: **s'~** vi to increase

accroupir [akʀupiʀ]: **s'~** vi to squat, crouch (down)

accru, e [akʀy] pp de **accroître**

accueil [akœj] nm welcome; **comité d'~** reception committee; **accueillir** vt to welcome; (*aller chercher*) to meet, collect

acculer [akyle] vt: **~ qn à** ou **contre** to drive sb back against

accumuler [akymyle] vt to accumulate, amass; **s'~** vi to accumulate; to pile up

accusation [akyzasjɔ̃] nf (*gén*) accusation; (*JUR*) charge; (*partie*): **l'~** the prosecution

accusé, e [akyze] nm/f accused; defendant; **~ de réception** acknowledgement of receipt

accuser [akyze] vt to accuse; (*fig*) to emphasize, bring out; to show; **~ qn de** to accuse sb of; (*JUR*) to charge sb with; **~ réception de** to acknowledge receipt of

acerbe [asɛʀb] adj caustic, acid

acéré, e [asere] adj sharp

acharné, e [aʃaʀne] adj (*efforts*) relentless; (*lutte, adversaire*) fierce, bitter

acharner [aʃaʀne] vb: **s'~ contre** to set o.s. against; (*suj: malchance*) to dog; **s'~ à faire** to try doggedly to do; (*persister*) to persist in doing

achat [aʃa] nm purchase; **faire des ~s** to do some shopping; **faire l'~ de qch** to purchase sth

acheminer [aʃ(ə)mine] vt (*courrier*) to

forward, dispatch; **s'~ vers** to head for

acheter [aʃ(ə)te] vt to buy, purchase; (*soudoyer*) to buy; **~ qch à** (*marchand*) to buy ou purchase sth from; (*ami etc: offrir*) to buy sth for; **acheteur, -euse** nm/f buyer; shopper; (*COMM*) buyer

achever [aʃ(ə)ve] vt to complete, finish; (*blessé*) to finish off; **s'~** vi to end

acide [asid] adj sour, sharp; (*CHIMIE*) acid(ic) ♦ nm (*CHIMIE*) acid; **acidulé, e** adj slightly acid

acier [asje] nm steel; **aciérie** nf steelworks sg

acné [akne] nf acne

acolyte [akɔlit] (*péj*) nm associate

acompte [akɔ̃t] nm deposit

à-côté [akote] nm side-issue; (*argent*) extra

à-coup [aku] nm: **par ~~s** by fits and starts

acoustique [akustik] nf (*d'une salle*) acoustics pl

acquéreur [akeʀœʀ] nm buyer, purchaser

acquérir [akeʀiʀ] vt to acquire

acquis, e [aki, iz] pp de **acquérir** ♦ nm (accumulated) experience; **son aide nous est ~e** we can count on her help

acquit [aki] vb voir **acquérir** ♦ nm (*quittance*) receipt; **par ~ de conscience** to set one's mind at rest

acquitter [akite] vt (*JUR*) to acquit; (*facture*) to pay, settle; **s'~ de** vt (*devoir*) to discharge; (*promesse*) to fulfil

âcre [akʀ] adj acrid, pungent

acrobate [akʀɔbat] nm/f acrobat; **acrobatie** nf acrobatics sg

acte [akt] nm act, action; (*THÉÂTRE*) act; **prendre ~ de** to note, take note of; **faire ~ de candidature** to apply; **faire ~ de présence** to put in an appearance; **~ de naissance** birth certificate

acteur [aktœʀ] nm actor

actif, -ive [aktif, iv] adj active ♦ nm (*COMM*) assets pl; (*fig*): **avoir à son ~** to have to one's credit; **population active** working population

action [aksjɔ̃] nf (*gén*) action; (*COMM*) share; **une bonne ~** a good deed; **actionnaire** nm/f shareholder; **actionner** vt (*mécanisme*) to activate; (*machine*) to operate

activer [aktive] vt to speed up; **s'~** vi to bustle about; to hurry up

activité [aktivite] nf activity; **en ~** (*volcan*) active; (*fonctionnaire*) in active life

actrice [aktʀis] nf actress

actualiser [aktɥalize] vt to bring up to date

actualité [aktɥalite] nf (*d'un problème*) topicality; (*événements*): **l'~** current events; **les ~s** nfpl (*CINÉMA, TV*) the news; **d'~** topical

actuel, le [aktɥɛl] adj (*présent*); (*d'actualité*) topical; **à l'heure ~le** at the present time; **actuellement** adv at present, at the present time

acuité [akцite] nf acuteness
acuponcteur [akypɔ̃ktœʀ] nm acupuncturist
acuponcture [akypɔ̃ktyʀ] nf acupuncture
adaptateur [adaptatœʀ] nm (ÉLEC) adapter
adapter [adapte] vt to adapt; s'~ (à) (suj: personne) to adapt (to); ~ qch à (approprier) to adapt sth to (fit); ~ qch sur/dans/à (fixer) to fit sth on/into/to
additif [aditif] nm additive
addition [adisjɔ̃] nf addition; (au café) bill; **additionner** vt to add (up)
adepte [adɛpt] nm/f follower
adéquat, e [adekwa(t), at] adj appropriate, suitable
adhérent, e [aderɑ̃, ɑ̃t] nm/f member
adhérer [adeʀe]: ~ à vt (coller) to adhere ou stick to; (se rallier à) to join; **adhésif, -ive** adj adhesive, sticky; **ruban adhésif** sticky ou adhesive tape; **adhésion** nf joining; (fait d'être membre) membership; (accord) support
adieu, x [adjø] excl goodbye ♦ nm farewell
adjectif [adʒɛktif] nm adjective
adjoindre [adʒwɛ̃dʀ] vt: ~ qch à to attach sth to; (ajouter) to add sth to; s'~ vt (collaborateur etc) to take on, appoint; **adjoint, e** nm/f assistant; **adjoint au maire** deputy mayor; **directeur adjoint** assistant manager
adjudant [adʒydɑ̃] nm (MIL) warrant officer
adjuger [adʒyʒe] vt (prix, récompense) to award; (lors d'une vente) to auction (off); s'~ vt to take for o.s.
adjurer [adʒyʀe] vt: ~ qn de faire to implore ou beg sb to do
admettre [admɛtʀ] vt (laisser entrer) to admit; (candidat: SCOL) to pass; (tolérer) to allow, accept; (reconnaître) to admit, acknowledge
administrateur, -trice [administʀatœʀ, tʀis] nm/f (COMM) director; (ADMIN) administrator
administration [administʀasjɔ̃] nf administration; l'A~ ≈ the Civil Service
administrer [administʀe] vt (firme) to manage, run; (biens, remède, sacrement etc) to administer
admirable [admiʀabl] adj admirable, wonderful
admirateur, -trice [admiʀatœʀ, tʀis] nm/f admirer
admiration [admiʀasjɔ̃] nf admiration
admirer [admiʀe] vt to admire
admis, e [admi, iz] pp de **admettre**
admissible [admisibl] adj (candidat) eligible; (comportement) admissible, acceptable
admission [admisjɔ̃] nf admission; acknowledgement; **demande d'~** application

for membership
ADN sigle m (= acide désoxyribonucléique) DNA
adolescence [adɔlesɑ̃s] nf adolescence
adolescent, e [adɔlesɑ̃, ɑ̃t] nm/f adolescent, teenager
adonner [adɔne]: s'~ à vt (sport) to devote o.s. to; (boisson) to give o.s. over to
adopter [adɔpte] vt to adopt; **adoptif, -ive** adj (parents) adoptive; (fils, patrie) adopted
adorable [adɔʀabl] adj delightful, adorable
adorer [adɔʀe] vt to adore; (REL) to worship
adosser [adose] vt: ~ qch à ou contre to stand sth against; s'~ à ou contre to lean with one's back against
adoucir [adusiʀ] vt (goût, température) to make milder; (avec du sucre) to sweeten; (peau, voix) to soften; (caractère) to mellow
adresse [adʀɛs] nf (domicile) address; (dextérité) skill, dexterity
adresser [adʀese] vt (lettre: expédier) to send; (: écrire l'adresse sur) to address; (injure, compliments) to address; s'~ à (parler à) to speak to, address; (s'informer auprès de) to go and see; (: bureau) to enquire at; (suj: livre, conseil) to be aimed at; ~ la parole à to speak to, address
adroit, e [adʀwa, wat] adj skilful, skilled
adulte [adylt] nm/f adult, grown-up ♦ adj (chien, arbre) fully-grown, mature; (attitude) adult, grown-up
adultère [adyltɛʀ] nm (acte) adultery
advenir [advəniʀ] vi to happen
adverbe [advɛʀb] nm adverb
adversaire [advɛʀsɛʀ] nm/f (SPORT, gén) opponent, adversary
adverse [advɛʀs] adj opposing
aération [aeʀasjɔ̃] nf airing; (circulation de l'air) ventilation
aérer [aeʀe] vt to air; (fig) to lighten; s'~ vi to get some (fresh) air
aérien, ne [aeʀjɛ̃, jɛn] adj (AVIAT) air cpd, aerial; (câble, métro) overhead; (fig) light; **compagnie ~ne** airline
aéro... [aeʀɔ] préfixe: **aérobic** nm aerobics sg; **aérogare** nf airport (buildings); (en ville) air terminal; **aéroglisseur** nm hovercraft; **Aéronavale** nf ≈ Fleet Air Arm (BRIT), ≈ Naval Air Force (US); **aérophagie** nf (MÉD) wind, aerophagia (MÉD); **aéroport** nm airport; **aéroporté, e** adj airborne, airlifted; **aérosol** nm aerosol
affable [afabl] adj affable
affaiblir [afeblir]: s'~ vi to weaken
affaire [afɛʀ] nf (problème, question) matter; (criminelle, judiciaire) case; (scandaleuse etc) affair; (entreprise) business; (marché, transaction) deal; business no pl; (occasion intéressante) bargain; ~s nfpl (intérêts publics

et privés) affairs; (*activité commerciale*)
business *sg*; (*effets personnels*) things,
belongings; **ce sont mes ~s** (*cela me
concerne*) that's my business; **ça fera l'~** that
will do (nicely); **se tirer d'~** to sort it ou
things out for o.s.; **avoir ~ à** (*être en contact*)
to be dealing with; **les A~s étrangères**
Foreign Affairs; **affairer: s'affairer** *vi* to busy
o.s., bustle about

affaisser [afese]: **s'~** *vi* (*terrain, immeuble*) to
subside, sink; (*personne*) to collapse

affaler [afale] *vb*: **s'~ (dans/sur)** to collapse ou
slump (into/onto)

affamé, e [afame] *adj* starving

affectation [afɛktasjɔ̃] *nf* (*nomination*)
appointment; (*manque de naturel*) affectation

affecter [afɛkte] *vt* to affect; **~ qch à** to
allocate ou allot sth to; **~ qn à** to appoint sb
to; (*diplomate*) to post sb to

affectif, -ive [afɛktif, iv] *adj* emotional

affection [afɛksjɔ̃] *nf* affection; (*mal*)
ailment; **affectionner** *vt* to be fond of;
affectueux, -euse *adj* affectionate

affermir [afɛrmir] *vt* to consolidate,
strengthen; (*muscles*) to tone up

affichage [afiʃaʒ] *nm* billposting;
(*électronique*) display

affiche [afiʃ] *nf* poster; (*officielle*) notice;
(THÉÂTRE) bill

afficher [afiʃe] *vt* (*affiche*) to put up;
(*réunion*) to put up a notice about;
(*électroniquement*) to display; (*fig*) to exhibit,
display; **"défense d'~"** "stick no bills"

affilée [afile]: **d'~** *adv* at a stretch

affiler [afile] *vt* to sharpen

affilier [afilje]: **s'~ à** *vt* (*club, société*) to join

affiner [afine] *vt* to refine

affirmatif, -ive [afirmatif, iv] *adj* affirmative

affirmation [afirmasjɔ̃] *nf* assertion

affirmer [afirme] *vt* to assert

affligé, e [afliʒe] *adj* distressed, grieved; **~ de**
(*maladie, tare*) afflicted with

affliger [afliʒe] *vt* (*peiner*) to distress, grieve

affluence [aflyɑ̃s] *nf* crowds *pl*; **heures d'~**
rush hours; **jours d'~** busiest days

affluent [aflyɑ̃] *nm* tributary

affluer [aflye] *vi* (*secours, biens*) to flood in,
pour in; (*sang*) to rush, flow

affolant, e [afɔlɑ̃, ɑ̃t] *adj* frightening

affolement [afɔlmɑ̃] *nm* panic

affoler [afɔle] *vt* to throw into a panic; **s'~** *vi*
to panic

affranchir [afrɑ̃ʃir] *vt* to put a stamp ou
stamps on; (*à la machine*) to frank (BRIT),
meter (US); (*fig*) to free, liberate;
affranchissement *nm* postage

affréter [afrete] *vt* to charter

affreux, -euse [afrø, øz] *adj* dreadful, awful

affront [afrɔ̃] *nm* affront; **affrontement** *nm*

clash, confrontation

affronter [afrɔ̃te] *vt* to confront, face

affubler [afyble] (*péj*) *vt*: **~ qn de** to rig ou
deck sb out in

affût [afy] *nm*: **à l'~ (de)** (*gibier*) lying in wait
(for); (*fig*) on the look-out (for)

affûter [afyte] *vt* to sharpen, grind

afin [afɛ̃]: **~ que** *conj* so that, in order that;
~ de faire in order to do, so as to do

africain, e [afrikɛ̃, ɛn] *adj, nm/f* African

Afrique [afrik] *nf*: **l'~** Africa; **l'~ du Sud** South
Africa

agacer [agase] *vt* to irritate

âge [ɑʒ] *nm* age; **quel ~ as-tu?** how old are
you?; **prendre de l'~** to be getting on (in
years); **âgé, e** *adj* old, elderly; **âgé de 10 ans**
10 years old

agence [aʒɑ̃s] *nf* agency, office; (*succursale*)
branch; **~ de voyages** travel agency;
~ immobilière estate (BRIT) ou real estate (US)
agent's (office)

agencer [aʒɑ̃se] *vt* to put together; (*local*) to
arrange, lay out

agenda [aʒɛ̃da] *nm* diary

agenouiller [aʒ(ə)nuje]: **s'~** *vi* to kneel
(down)

agent [aʒɑ̃] *nm* (*aussi*: **~ de police**)
policeman; (ADMIN) official, officer;
~ d'assurances insurance broker

agglomération [aglɔmerasjɔ̃] *nf* town;
built-up area; **l'~ parisienne** the urban area of
Paris

aggloméré [aglɔmere] *nm* (*bois*) chipboard

aggraver [agrave]: **s'~** *vi* to worsen

agile [aʒil] *adj* agile, nimble

agir [aʒir] *vi* to act; **il s'agit de** (*ça traite de*) it
is about; (*il est important de*) it's a matter ou
question of

agitation [aʒitasjɔ̃] *nf* (*hustle and*) bustle;
(*trouble*) agitation, excitement; (*politique*)
unrest, agitation

agité, e [aʒite] *adj* fidgety, restless; (*troublé*)
agitated, perturbed; (*mer*) rough

agiter [aʒite] *vt* (*bouteille, chiffon*) to shake;
(*bras, mains*) to wave; (*préoccuper, exciter*) to
perturb; **s'~** *vi* (*enfant, élève*) to fidget

agneau, x [aɲo] *nm* lamb

agonie [agɔni] *nf* mortal agony, death pangs
pl; (*fig*) death throes *pl*

agrafe [agraf] *nf* (*de vêtement*) hook,
fastener; (*de bureau*) staple; **agrafer** *vt* to
fasten; to staple; **agrafeuse** *nf* stapler

agrandir [agrɑ̃dir] *vt* to enlarge; **s'~** *vi* (*ville,
famille*) to grow, expand; (*trou, écart*) to get
bigger; **agrandissement** *nm* (PHOTO)
enlargement

agréable [agreabl] *adj* pleasant, nice

agréé, e [agree] *adj*: **concessionnaire ~**
registered dealer

agréer [agree] vt (*requête*) to accept; ~ à to please, suit; **veuillez** ~ ... (*formule épistolaire*) yours faithfully

agrégation [agregasjɔ̃] nf highest teaching diploma in France; **agrégé, e** nm/f holder of the *agrégation*

agrément [agremã] nm (*accord*) consent, approval; **agrémenter** vt to embellish, adorn

agresser [agrese] vt to attack; **agresseur** nm aggressor, attacker; (*POL, MIL*) aggressor; **agressif, -ive** adj aggressive

agricole [agrikɔl] adj agricultural; **agriculteur** nm farmer; **agriculture** nf agriculture, farming

agripper [agripe] vt to grab, clutch; **s'~ à** to cling (on) to, clutch, grip

agroalimentaire [agroalimãter] nm farm-produce industry

agrumes [agrym] nmpl citrus fruit(s)

aguerrir [agerir] vt to harden

aguets [age] nmpl: **être aux ~** to be on the look out

aguicher [agi[e] vt to entice

ahuri, e [ayri] adj (*stupéfait*) flabbergasted

ai [ɛ] vb voir **avoir**

aide [ɛd] nm/f assistant; carer ♦ nf assistance, help; (*secours financier*) aid; **à l'~ de** (*avec*) with the help ou aid of; **appeler (qn) à l'~** to call for help (from sb); **~ familiale** home help, mother's help; **~ judiciaire** nf legal aid; **~ sociale** nf (*assistance*) state aid; **aide-mémoire** nm inv memoranda pages pl; (*key facts*) handbook; **aide-soignant, e** nm/f auxiliary nurse

aider [ede] vt to help; **s'~ de** (*se servir de*) to use, make use of

aie etc [ɛ] vb voir **avoir**

aïe [aj] excl ouch!

aïeul, e [ajœl] nm/f grandparent, grandfather(-mother)

aïeux [ajø] nmpl grandparents; (*ancêtres*) forebears, forefathers

aigle [ɛgl] nm eagle

aigre [ɛgr] adj sour, sharp; (*fig*) sharp, cutting; **aigre-doux, -ce** adj (*sauce*) sweet and sour; **aigreur** nf sourness; sharpness; **aigreurs d'estomac** heartburn sg; **aigrir** vt (*personne*) to embitter; (*caractère*) to sour

aigu, ë [egy] adj (*objet, douleur*) sharp; (*son, voix*) high-pitched, shrill; (*note*) high(-pitched)

aiguille [egɥij] nf needle; (*de montre*) hand; **~ à tricoter** knitting needle

aiguiller [egɥije] vt (*orienter*) to direct; **aiguilleur du ciel** nm air-traffic controller

aiguillon [egɥijɔ̃] nm (*d'abeille*) sting; **aiguillonner** vt to spur ou goad on

aiguiser [egize] vt to sharpen; (*fig*) to stimulate; (: *sens*) to excite

ail [aj, o] nm garlic

aile [ɛl] nf wing; **aileron** nm (*de requin*) fin; **ailier** nm winger

aille etc [aj] vb voir **aller**

ailleurs [ajœr] adv elsewhere, somewhere else; **partout/nulle part ~** everywhere/nowhere else; **d'~** (*du reste*) moreover, besides; **par ~** (*d'autre part*) moreover, furthermore

aimable [ɛmabl] adj kind, nice

aimant [ɛmã] nm magnet

aimer [eme] vt to love; (*d'amitié, affection, par goût*) to like; (*souhait*): **j'~ais** ... I would like ...; **bien ~ qn/qch** to like sb/sth; **j'~ais mieux faire** I'd much rather do

aine [ɛn] nf groin

aîné, e [ene] adj elder, older; (*le plus âgé*) eldest, oldest ♦ nm/f oldest child ou one, oldest boy ou son/girl ou daughter

ainsi [ɛ̃si] adv (*de cette façon*) like this, in this way, thus; (*ce faisant*) thus ♦ conj thus, so; **~ que** (*comme*) (just) as; (*et aussi*) as well as; **pour ~ dire** so to speak; **et ~ de suite** and so on

aïoli [ajɔli] nm garlic mayonnaise

air [ɛr] nm air; (*mélodie*) tune; (*expression*) look, air; **prendre l'~** to get some (fresh) air; **avoir l'~** (*sembler*) to look, appear; **avoir l'~ de** to look like; **avoir l'~ de faire** to look as though one is doing, appear to be doing; **en l'~** (*promesses*) empty

aisance [ɛzãs] nf ease; (*richesse*) affluence

aise [ɛz] nf comfort; **être à l'~** ou **à son ~** to be comfortable; (*pas embarrassé*) to be at ease; (*financièrement*) to be comfortably off; **se mettre à l'~** to make o.s. comfortable; **être mal à l'~** to be uncomfortable; (*gêné*) to be ill at ease; **en faire à son ~** to do as one likes; **aisé, e** adj easy; (*assez riche*) well-to-do, well-off

aisselle [ɛsɛl] nf armpit

ait [ɛ] vb voir **avoir**

ajonc [aʒɔ̃] nm gorse no pl

ajourner [aʒurne] vt (*réunion*) to adjourn; (*décision*) to defer, postpone

ajouter [aʒute] vt to add

ajusté, e [aʒyste] adj: **bien ~** (*robe etc*) close-fitting

ajuster [aʒyste] vt (*régler*) to adjust; (*vêtement*) to alter; (*coup de fusil*) to aim; (*cible*) to aim at; (*TECH, gén: adapter*): **~ qch à** to fit sth to

alarme [alarm] nf alarm; **donner l'~** to give ou raise the alarm; **alarmer** vt to alarm; **s'alarmer** vi to become alarmed; **alarmiste** adj, nm/f alarmist

album [albɔm] nm album

albumine [albymin] nf albumin; **avoir de l'~**

to suffer from albuminuria

alcool [alkɔl] nm: **l'~** alcohol; **un ~** a spirit, a brandy; **bière sans ~** non-alcoholic ou alcohol-free beer; **~ à brûler** methylated spirits (BRIT), wood alcohol (US); **~ à 90°** surgical spirit; **alcoolique** adj, nm/f alcoholic; **alcoolisé, e** adj alcoholic; **une boisson non alcoolisée** a soft drink; **alcoolisme** nm alcoholism; **alcootest** ® nm Breathalyser ®; (test) breath-test

aléas [alea] nmpl hazards; **aléatoire** adj uncertain; (INFORM) random

alentour [alɑ̃tuʀ] adv around, round about; **~s** nmpl (environs) surroundings; **aux ~s de** in the vicinity ou neighbourhood of, round about; (temps) round about

alerte [alɛʀt] adj agile, nimble; brisk, lively ♦ nf alert; warning; **~ à la bombe** bomb scare; **alerter** vt to alert

algèbre [alʒɛbʀ] nf algebra

Alger [alʒe] n Algiers

Algérie [alʒeʀi] nf: **l'~** Algeria; **algérien, ne** adj Algerian ♦ nm/f: **Algérien, ne** Algerian

algue [alg] nf (gén) seaweed no pl; (BOT) alga

alibi [alibi] nm alibi

aliéné, e [aljene] nm/f insane person, lunatic (péj)

aligner [aliɲe] vt to align, line up; (idées, chiffres) to string together; (adapter): **~ qch sur** to bring sth into alignment with; **s'~** (soldats etc) to line up; **s'~ sur** (POL) to align o.s. on

aliment [alimɑ̃] nm food; **alimentaire** adj: **denrées alimentaires** foodstuffs; **alimentation** nf (commerce) food trade; (magasin) grocery store; (régime) diet; (en eau etc, de moteur) supplying; (INFORM) feed; **alimenter** vt to feed; (TECH): **alimenter (en)** to supply (with); to feed (with); (fig) to sustain, keep going

alinéa [alinea] nm paragraph

aliter [alite]: **s'~** vi to take to one's bed

allaiter [alete] vt to (breast-)feed, nurse; (suj: animal) to suckle

allant [alɑ̃] nm drive, go

alléchant, e [aleʃɑ̃, ɑ̃t] adj (odeur) mouth-watering; (offre) enticing

allécher [aleʃe] vt: **~ qn** to make sb's mouth water; to tempt ou entice sb

allée [ale] nf (de jardin) path; (en ville) avenue, drive; **~s et venues** comings and goings

allégé, e [aleʒe] adj (yaourt etc) low-fat

alléger [aleʒe] vt (voiture) to make lighter; (chargement) to lighten; (souffrance) to alleviate, soothe

allègre [a(l)lɛgʀ] adj lively, cheerful

alléguer [a(l)lege] vt to put forward (as proof ou an excuse)

Allemagne [almaɲ] nf: **l'~** Germany; **allemand, e** adj German ♦ nm/f: **Allemand, e** German ♦ nm (LING) German

aller [ale] nm (trajet) outward journey; (billet: aussi: **~ simple**) single (BRIT) ou one-way (US) ticket ♦ vi (gén) to go; **~ à** (convenir) to suit; (suj: forme, pointure etc) to fit; **~ (bien) avec** (couleurs, style etc) to go (well) with; **je vais y ~/me fâcher** I'm going to go/to get angry; **~ voir** to go and see, go to see; **allez!** come on!; **allons!** come now!; **comment allez-vous?** how are you?; **comment ça va?** how are you?; (affaires etc) how are things?; **il va bien/mal** he's well/not well, he's fine/ill; **ça va bien/mal** (affaires etc) it's going well/not going well; **~ mieux** to be better; **s'en ~** (partir) to be off, go, leave; (disparaître) to go away; **~ retour** return journey (BRIT), round trip; (billet) return (ticket) (BRIT), round trip ticket (US)

allergique [alɛʀʒik] adj: **~ à** allergic to

alliage [aljaʒ] nm alloy

alliance [aljɑ̃s] nf (MIL, POL) alliance; (bague) wedding ring

allier [alje] vt (POL, gén) to ally; (fig) to combine; **s'~** to become allies; to combine

allô [alo] excl hullo, hallo

allocation [alɔkasjɔ̃] nf allowance; **~ (de) chômage** unemployment benefit; **~s familiales** ≈ child benefit

allocution [a(l)lɔkysjɔ̃] nf short speech

allonger [alɔ̃ʒe] vt to lengthen, make longer; (étendre: bras, jambe) to stretch (out); **s'~** vi to get longer; (se coucher) to lie down, stretch out; **~ le pas** to hasten one's step(s)

allouer [alwe] vt to allocate, allot

allumage [alymaʒ] nm (AUTO) ignition

allume-cigare [alymsigaʀ] nm inv cigar lighter

allumer [alyme] vt (lampe, phare, radio) to put ou switch on; (pièce) to put ou switch the light(s) on in; (feu) to light; **s'~** vi (lumière, lampe) to come ou go on

allumette [alymɛt] nf match

allure [alyʀ] nf (vitesse) speed, pace; (démarche) walk; (aspect, air) look; **avoir de l'~** to have style; **à toute ~** at top speed

allusion [a(l)lyzjɔ̃] nf allusion; (sous-entendu) hint; **faire ~ à** to allude ou refer to; to hint at

---

MOT-CLÉ

alors [alɔʀ] adv 1 (à ce moment-là) then, at that time; **il habitait alors à Paris** he lived in Paris at that time

2 (par conséquent) then; **tu as fini? alors je m'en vais** have you finished? I'm going then; **et alors?** so what?

alors que conj 1 (au moment où) when, as; **il est arrivé alors que je partais** he arrived as I

was leaving
2 (*pendant que*) while, when; **alors qu'il était à Paris, il a visité** ... while *ou* when he was in Paris, he visited ...
3 (*tandis que*) whereas, while; **alors que son frère travaillait dur, lui se reposait** while his brother was working hard, HE would rest

alouette [alwɛt] *nf* (sky)lark
alourdir [aluʀdiʀ] *vt* to weigh down, make heavy
aloyau [alwajo] *nm* sirloin
Alpes [alp] *nfpl*: **les ~** the Alps
alphabet [alfabɛ] *nm* alphabet; (*livre*) ABC (book); **alphabétique** *adj* alphabetical; **alphabétiser** *vt* to teach to read and write; (*pays*) to eliminate illiteracy in
alpinisme [alpinism] *nm* mountaineering, climbing; **alpiniste** *nm/f* mountaineer, climber
Alsace [alzas] *nf* Alsace; **alsacien, ne** *adj* Alsatian ♦ *nm/f*: **Alsacien, ne** Alsatian
altérer [alteʀe] *vt* (*vérité*) to distort; **s'~** *vi* to deteriorate
alternateur [altɛʀnatœʀ] *nm* alternator
alternatif, -ive [altɛʀnatif, iv] *adj* alternating; **alternative** *nf* (*choix*) alternative; **alternativement** *adv* alternately; **alterner** *vi* to alternate
Altesse [altɛs] *nf* Highness
altitude [altityd] *nf* altitude, height
alto [alto] *nm* (*instrument*) viola
aluminium [alyminjɔm] *nm* aluminium (*BRIT*), aluminum (*US*)
amabilité [amabilite] *nf* kindness
amadouer [amadwe] *vt* to mollify, soothe
amaigrir [amegʀiʀ] *vt* to make thin(ner); **amaigrissant, e** *adj* (*régime*) slimming
amalgame [amalgam] (*péj*) *nm* (strange) mixture
amande [amɑ̃d] *nf* (*de l'amandier*) almond; **amandier** *nm* almond (tree)
amant [amɑ̃] *nm* lover
amarrer [amaʀe] *vt* (*NAVIG*) to moor; (*gén*) to make fast
amas [amɑ] *nm* heap, pile; **amasser** *vt* to amass; **s'amasser** *vi* (*foule*) to gather
amateur [amatœʀ] *nm* amateur; **en ~** (*péj*) amateurishly; **~ de musique/sport** etc music/ sport etc lover
amazone [amazon] *nf*: **en ~** sidesaddle
ambassade [ɑ̃basad] *nf* embassy; **l'~ de France** the French Embassy; **ambassadeur, -drice** *nm/f* ambassador(-dress)
ambiance [ɑ̃bjɑ̃s] *nf* atmosphere
ambiant, e [ɑ̃bjɑ̃, jɑ̃t] *adj* (*air, milieu*) surrounding; (*température*) ambient
ambigu, ë [ɑ̃bigy] *adj* ambiguous
ambitieux, -euse [ɑ̃bisjø, jøz] *adj*

ambitious
ambition [ɑ̃bisjɔ̃] *nf* ambition
ambulance [ɑ̃bylɑ̃s] *nf* ambulance; **ambulancier, -ière** *nm/f* ambulance man(-woman) (*BRIT*), paramedic (*US*)
ambulant, e [ɑ̃bylɑ̃, ɑ̃t] *adj* travelling, itinerant
âme [ɑm] *nf* soul
amélioration [ameljɔʀasjɔ̃] *nf* improvement
améliorer [ameljɔʀe] *vt* to improve; **s'~** *vi* to improve, get better
aménager [amenaʒe] *vt* (*agencer, transformer*) to fit out; to lay out; (: *quartier, territoire*) to develop; (*installer*) to fix up, put in; **ferme aménagée** converted farmhouse
amende [amɑ̃d] *nf* fine; **faire ~ honorable** to make amends
amener [am(ə)ne] *vt* to bring; (*causer*) to bring about; **s'~** *vi* to show up (*fam*), turn up
amenuiser [amənɥize]: **s'~** *vi* (*chances*) to grow slimmer, lessen
amer, amère [amɛʀ] *adj* bitter
américain, e [ameʀikɛ̃, ɛn] *adj* American ♦ *nm/f*: **A~, e** American
Amérique [ameʀik] *nf*: **l'~** America; **l'~ centrale/latine** Central/Latin America; **l'~ du Nord/du Sud** North/South America
amertume [amɛʀtym] *nf* bitterness
ameublement [amœbləmɑ̃] *nm* furnishing; (*meubles*) furniture
ameuter [amøte] *vt* (*peuple*) to rouse
ami, e [ami] *nm/f* friend; (*amant/maîtresse*) boyfriend/girlfriend ♦ *adj*: **pays/groupe ~** friendly country/group
amiable [amjabl]: **à l'~** *adv* (*JUR*) out of court; (*gén*) amicably
amiante [amjɑ̃t] *nm* asbestos
amical, e, -aux [amikal, o] *adj* friendly; **amicalement** *adv* in a friendly way; (*formule épistolaire*) regards
amidon [amidɔ̃] *nm* starch
amincir [amɛ̃siʀ] *vt*: **~ qn** to make sb thinner *ou* slimmer; (: *suj: vêtement*) to make sb look slimmer
amincissant, e [amɛ̃sisɑ̃, ɑ̃t] *adj*: **régime ~** (slimming) diet; **crème ~e** slimming cream
amiral, -aux [amiʀal, o] *nm* admiral
amitié [amitje] *nf* friendship; **prendre en ~** to befriend; **~s, Christèle** best wishes, Christèle; **présenter ses ~s à qn** to send sb one's best wishes
ammoniaque [amɔnjak] *nf* ammonia (water)
amnistie [amnisti] *nf* amnesty
amoindrir [amwɛ̃dʀiʀ] *vt* to reduce
amollir [amɔliʀ] *vt* to soften
amonceler [amɔ̃s(ə)le] *vt* to pile *ou* heap up; **s'~** *vi* to pile *ou* heap up; (*fig*) to accumulate

amont [amɔ̃]: **en ~** adv upstream

amorce [amɔʀs] nf (sur un hameçon) bait; (explosif) cap; primer; priming; (fig: début) beginning(s), start; **amorcer** vt to start

amorphe [amɔʀf] adj passive, lifeless

amortir [amɔʀtiʀ] vt (atténuer: choc) to absorb, cushion; (bruit, douleur) to deaden; (COMM: dette) to pay off; **~ un achat** to make a purchase pay for itself; **amortisseur** nm shock absorber

amour [amuʀ] nm love; **faire l'~** to make love; **amouracher: s'amouracher de** (péj) vt to become infatuated with; **amoureux, -euse** adj (regard, tempérament) amorous; (vie, problèmes) love cpd; (personne): **amoureux (de qn)** in love (with sb) ♦ nmpl courting couple(s); **amour-propre** nm self-esteem, pride

amovible [amɔvibl] adj removable, detachable

ampère [ɑ̃pɛʀ] nm amp(ere)

amphithéâtre [ɑ̃fiteatʀ] nm amphitheatre; (d'université) lecture hall ou theatre

ample [ɑ̃pl] adj (vêtement) roomy, ample; (gestes, mouvement) broad; (ressources) ample; **amplement** adv: **c'est amplement suffisant** that's more than enough; **ampleur** nf (de dégâts, problème) extent

amplificateur [ɑ̃plifikatœʀ] nm amplifier

amplifier [ɑ̃plifje] vt (fig) to expand, increase

ampoule [ɑ̃pul] nf (électrique) bulb; (de médicament) phial; (aux mains, pieds) blister; **ampoulé, e** (péj) adj pompous, bombastic

amputer [ɑ̃pyte] vt (MÉD) to amputate; (fig) to cut ou reduce drastically

amusant, e [amyzɑ̃, ɑ̃t] adj (divertissant, spirituel) entertaining, amusing; (comique) funny, amusing

amuse-gueule [amyzgœl] nm inv appetizer, snack

amusement [amyzmɑ̃] nm (divertissement) amusement; (jeu etc) pastime, diversion

amuser [amyze] vt (divertir) to entertain, amuse; (égayer, faire rire) to amuse; **s'~** vi (jouer) to play; (se divertir) to enjoy o.s., have fun; (fig) to mess around

amygdale [amidal] nf tonsil

an [ɑ̃] nm year; **avoir quinze ~s** to be fifteen (years old); **le jour de l'~**, **le premier de l'~**, **le nouvel ~** New Year's Day

analogique [analɔʒik] adj (INFORM, montre) analog

analogue [analɔg] adj: **~ (à)** analogous (to), similar (to)

analphabète [analfabɛt] nm/f illiterate

analyse [analiz] nf analysis; (MÉD) test; **analyser** vt to analyse; to test

ananas [anana(s)] nm pineapple

anarchie [anaʀʃi] nf anarchy

anatomie [anatɔmi] nf anatomy

ancêtre [ɑ̃sɛtʀ] nm/f ancestor

anchois [ɑ̃ʃwa] nm anchovy

ancien, ne [ɑ̃sjɛ̃, jɛn] adj old; (de jadis, de l'antiquité) ancient; (précédent, ex-) former, old; (par l'expérience) senior ♦ nm/f (dans une tribu) elder; **~-combattant** ♦ nm war veteran; **anciennement** adv formerly; **ancienneté** nf (ADMIN) (length of) service; (privilèges obtenus) seniority

ancre [ɑ̃kʀ] nf anchor; **jeter/lever l'~** to cast/ weigh anchor; **ancrer** vt (CONSTR: câble etc) to anchor; (fig) to fix firmly

Andorre [ɑ̃dɔʀ] nf Andorra

andouille [ɑ̃duj] nf (CULIN) sausage made of chitterlings; (fam) clot, nit

âne [ɑn] nm donkey, ass; (péj) dunce

anéantir [aneɑ̃tiʀ] vt to annihilate, wipe out; (fig) to obliterate, destroy

anémie [anemi] nf anaemia; **anémique** adj anaemic

ânerie [ɑnʀi] nf stupidity; (parole etc) stupid ou idiotic comment etc

anesthésie [anɛstezi] nf anaesthesia; **faire une ~ locale/générale à qn** to give sb a local/ general anaesthetic

ange [ɑ̃ʒ] nm angel; **être aux ~s** to be over the moon

angélus [ɑ̃ʒelys] nm angelus; (cloches) evening bells pl

angine [ɑ̃ʒin] nf throat infection; **~ de poitrine** angina

anglais, e [ɑ̃glɛ, ɛz] adj English ♦ nm/f: **A~, e** Englishman(-woman) ♦ nm (LING) English; **les A~** the English; **filer à l'~e** to take French leave

angle [ɑ̃gl] nm angle; (coin) corner; **~ droit** right angle

Angleterre [ɑ̃glətɛʀ] nf: **l'~** England

anglo... [ɑ̃glɔ] préfixe Anglo-, anglo(-); **anglophone** adj English-speaking

angoisse [ɑ̃gwas] nf anguish, distress; **angoissé, e** adj (personne) distressed; **angoisser** vt to harrow, cause anguish to ♦ vi to worry, fret

anguille [ɑ̃gij] nf eel

anicroche [anikʀɔʃ] nf hitch, snag

animal, e, -aux [animal, o] adj, nm animal

animateur, -trice [animatœʀ, tʀis] nm/f (de télévision) host; (de groupe) leader, organizer

animation [animasjɔ̃] nf (voir animé) busyness; liveliness; (CINÉMA: technique) animation; **~s culturelles** cultural activities

animé, e [anime] adj (lieu) busy, lively; (conversation, réunion) lively, animated

animer [anime] vt (ville, soirée) to liven up; (mener) to lead; **s'~** vi to liven up

anis [ani(s)] nm (CULIN) aniseed; (BOT) anise

ankyloser [ākiloze]: **s'~** vi to get stiff

anneau, x [ano] nm (de rideau, bague) ring; (de chaîne) link

année [ane] nf year

annexe [anɛks] adj (problème) related; (document) appended; (salle) adjoining ♦ nf (bâtiment) annex(e); (jointe à une lettre) enclosure

anniversaire [aniversɛʀ] nm birthday; (d'un événement, bâtiment) anniversary

annonce [anɔ̃s] nf announcement; (signe, indice) sign; (aussi: ~ publicitaire) advertisement; **les petites ~s** the classified advertisements, the small ads

annoncer [anɔ̃se] vt to announce; (être le signe de) to herald; **s'~ bien/difficile** to look promising/difficult; **annonceur, -euse** nm/f (publicitaire) advertiser; (TV, RADIO: speaker) announcer

annuaire [anɥɛʀ] nm yearbook, annual; **~ téléphonique** (telephone) directory, phone book

annuel, le [anɥɛl] adj annual, yearly

annuité [anɥite] nf annual instalment

annulation [anylasjɔ̃] nf cancellation

annuler [anyle] vt (rendez-vous, voyage) to cancel, call off; (jugement) to quash (BRIT), repeal (US); (MATH, PHYSIQUE) to cancel out

anodin, e [anɔdɛ̃, in] adj (blessure) harmless; (détail) insignificant, trivial

anonymat [anɔnima] nm anonymity

anonyme [anɔnim] adj anonymous; (fig) impersonal

ANPE sigle f (= Agence nationale pour l'emploi) national employment agency

anorak [anɔʀak] nm anorak

anorexie [anɔʀɛksi] nf anorexia

anormal, e, -aux [anɔʀmal, o] adj abnormal

anse [ãs] nf (de panier, tasse) handle

antan [ãtã]: **d'~** adj of long ago

antarctique [ãtaʀktik] adj Antarctic ♦ nm: **l'A~** the Antarctic

antécédents [ãtesedã] nmpl (MÉD etc) past history sg

antenne [ãtɛn] nf (de radio) aerial; (d'insecte) antenna, feeler; (poste avancé) outpost; (petite succursale) sub-branch; **passer à l'~** to go on the air

antérieur, e [ãteʀjœʀ] adj (d'avant) previous, earlier; (de devant) front

anti... [ãti] préfixe anti...; **antialcoolique** adj anti-alcohol; **antiatomique** adj: **abri antiatomique** fallout shelter; **antibiotique** nm antibiotic; **antibrouillard** adj: **phare antibrouillard** fog lamp (BRIT) ou light (US)

anticipation [ãtisipasjɔ̃] nf: **livre/film d'~** science fiction book/film

anticipé, e [ãtisipe] adj: **avec mes remerciements ~s** thanking you in advance ou anticipation

anticiper [ãtisipe] vt (événement, coup) to anticipate, foresee

anti...: anticonceptionnel, le adj contraceptive; **anticorps** nm antibody; **antidote** nm antidote; **antigel** nm antifreeze; **antihistaminique** nm antihistamine

antillais, e [ãtijɛ, ɛz] adj West Indian, Caribbean ♦ nm/f: **A~, e** West Indian, Caribbean

Antilles [ãtij] nfpl: **les ~** the West Indies

antilope [ãtilɔp] nf antelope

anti...: antimite(s) adj, nm: (produit) **antimite(s)** mothproofer; moth repellent; **antipathique** adj unpleasant, disagreeable; **antipelliculaire** adj anti-dandruff

antipodes [ãtipɔd] nmpl (fig): **être aux ~ de** to be the opposite extreme of

antiquaire [ãtikɛʀ] nm/f antique dealer

antique [ãtik] adj antique; (très vieux) ancient, antiquated; **antiquité** nf (objet) antique; **l'Antiquité** Antiquity; **magasin d'antiquités** antique shop

anti...: antirabique adj rabies cpd; **antirouille** adj inv anti-rust cpd; **antisémite** adj anti-Semitic; **antiseptique** adj, nm antiseptic; **antivol** adj, nm: (dispositif) **antivol** anti-theft device

antre [ãtʀ] nm den, lair

anxiété [ãksjete] nf anxiety

anxieux, -euse [ãksjø, jøz] adj anxious, worried

AOC sigle f (= appellation d'origine contrôlée) label guaranteeing the quality of wine

août [u(t)] nm August

apaiser [apeze] vt (colère, douleur) to soothe; (personne) to calm (down), pacify; **s'~** vi (tempête, bruit) to die down, subside; (personne) to calm down

apanage [apanaʒ] nm: **être l'~ de** to be the privilege ou prerogative of

aparté [apaʀte] nm (entretien) private conversation; **en ~** in an aside

apathique [apatik] adj apathetic

apatride [apatʀid] nm/f stateless person

apercevoir [apɛʀsəvwaʀ] vt to see; **s'~ de** vt to notice; **s'~ que** to notice that

aperçu [apɛʀsy] nm (vue d'ensemble) general survey

apéritif [apeʀitif] nm (boisson) aperitif; (réunion) drinks pl

à-peu-près [apøpʀɛ] (péj) nm inv vague approximation

apeuré, e [apœʀe] adj frightened, scared

aphte [aft] nm mouth ulcer

apiculture [apikyltyʀ] nf beekeeping, apiculture

apitoyer [apitwaje] vt to move to pity; **s'~ (sur)** to feel pity (for)

aplanir [aplaniʀ] vt to level; (fig) to smooth away, iron out

aplatir [aplatiʀ] vt to flatten; **s'~** vi to become flatter; (écrasé) to be flattened; **s'~ devant qn** (fig: s'humilier) to crawl to sb

aplomb [aplɔ̃] nm (équilibre) balance, equilibrium; (fig) self-assurance; nerve; **d'~** steady

apogée [apɔʒe] nm (fig) peak, apogee

apologie [apɔlɔʒi] nf vindication, praise

a posteriori [aposteʀjɔʀi] adv after the event

apostrophe [apɔstʀɔf] nf (signe) apostrophe

apostropher [apɔstʀɔfe] vt (interpeller) to shout at, address sharply

apothéose [apɔteoz] nf pinnacle (of achievement); (MUS) grand finale

apôtre [apotʀ] nm apostle

apparaître [apaʀɛtʀ] vi to appear

apparat [apaʀa] nm: **tenue d'~** ceremonial dress

appareil [apaʀɛj] nm (outil, machine) piece of apparatus, device; (électrique, ménager) appliance; (avion) (aero)plane, aircraft inv; (téléphonique) phone; (dentier) brace (BRIT), braces (US); **"qui est à l'~?"** "who's speaking?"; **dans le plus simple ~** in one's birthday suit; **appareiller** vi (NAVIG) to cast off, get under way ♦ vt (assortir) to match up; **appareil(-photo)** nm camera

apparemment [apaʀamã] adv apparently

apparence [apaʀãs] nf appearance; **en ~** apparently

apparent, e [apaʀã, ãt] adj visible; (évident) obvious; (superficiel) apparent

apparenté, e [apaʀãte] adj: ~ **à** related to; (fig) similar to

apparition [apaʀisjɔ̃] nf appearance; (surnaturelle) apparition

appartement [apaʀtəmã] nm flat (BRIT), apartment (US)

appartenir [apaʀtəniʀ]: ~ **à** vt to belong to; **il lui appartient de** it is his duty to

apparu, e [apaʀy] pp de **apparaître**

appât [apa] nm (PÊCHE) bait; (fig) lure, bait; **appâter** vt to lure

appauvrir [apovʀiʀ] vt to impoverish

appel [apɛl] nm call; (nominal) roll call; (: SCOL) register; (MIL: recrutement) call-up; **faire ~ à** (invoquer) to appeal to; (avoir recours à) to call on; (nécessiter) to call for, require; **faire ~** (JUR) to appeal; **faire l'~** to call the roll; to call the register; **sans ~** (fig) final, irrevocable; **~ d'offres** (COMM) invitation to tender; **faire un ~ de phares** to flash one's headlights; **~ (téléphonique)** (tele)phone call

appelé [ap(ə)le] nm (MIL) conscript

appeler [ap(ə)le] vt to call; (faire venir:

médecin etc) to call, send for; **s'~** vi: **elle s'appelle Gabrielle** her name is Gabrielle, she's called Gabrielle; **comment ça s'appelle?** what is it called?; **être appelé à** (fig) to be destined to

appendice [apɛ̃dis] nm appendix; **appendicite** nf appendicitis

appentis [apɑ̃ti] nm lean-to

appesantir [apazɑ̃tiʀ]: **s'~** vi to grow heavier; **s'~ sur** (fig) to dwell on

appétissant, e [apetisɑ̃, ɑ̃t] adj appetizing, mouth-watering

appétit [apeti] nm appetite; **bon ~!** enjoy your meal!

applaudir [aplodiʀ] vt to applaud ♦ vi to applaud, clap; **applaudissements** nmpl applause sg, clapping sg

application [aplikasjɔ̃] nf application

applique [aplik] nf wall lamp

appliquer [aplike] vt to apply; (loi) to enforce; **s'~** vi (élève etc) to apply o.s.; **s'~ à** to apply to

appoint [apwɛ̃] nm (extra) contribution ou help; **chauffage d'~** extra heating

appointements [apwɛ̃tmã] nmpl salary sg

apport [apɔʀ] nm (approvisionnement) supply; (contribution) contribution

apporter [apɔʀte] vt to bring

apposer [apoze] vt (signature) to affix

appréciable [apʀesjabl] adj appreciable

apprécier [apʀesje] vt to appreciate; (évaluer) to estimate, assess

appréhender [apʀeɑ̃de] vt (craindre) to dread; (arrêter) to apprehend; **appréhension** nf apprehension, anxiety

apprendre [apʀɑ̃dʀ] vt to learn; (événement, résultats) to learn of, hear of; ~ **qch à qn** (informer) to tell sb (of) sth; (enseigner) to teach sb sth; ~ **à faire qch** to learn to do sth; ~ **à qn à faire qch** to teach sb to do sth; **apprenti, e** nm/f apprentice; **apprentissage** nm learning; (COMM, SCOL: période) apprenticeship

apprêté, e [apʀete] adj (fig) affected

apprêter [apʀete] vt: **s'~ à faire qch** to get ready to do sth

appris, e [apʀi, iz] pp de **apprendre**

apprivoiser [apʀivwaze] vt to tame

approbation [apʀɔbasjɔ̃] nf approval

approchant, e [apʀɔʃɑ̃, ɑ̃t] adj similar; **quelque chose d'~** something like that

approche [apʀɔʃ] nf approach

approcher [apʀɔʃe] vi to approach, come near ♦ vt to approach; (rapprocher): ~ **qch (de qch)** to bring ou put sth near (to sth); **s'~ de** to approach, go ou come near to; ~ **de** (lieu, but) to draw near to; (quantité, moment) to approach

approfondir [apʀɔfɔ̃diʀ] vt to deepen;

(*question*) to go further into

approprié, e [apRɔpRije] *adj*: ~ (**à**) appropriate (to), suited to

approprier [apRɔpRije]: **s'~** *vt* to appropriate, take over

approuver [apRuve] *vt* to agree with; (*trouver louable*) to approve of

approvisionner [apRɔvizjɔne] *vt* to supply; (*compte bancaire*) to pay funds into; **s'~ en** to stock up with

approximatif, -ive [apRɔksimatif, iv] *adj* approximate, rough; (*termes*) vague

appt *abr* = **appartement**

appui [apɥi] *nm* support; **prendre ~ sur** to lean on; (*objet*) to rest on; **l'~ de la fenêtre** the windowsill, the window ledge; **appui(e)-tête** *nm inv* headrest

appuyer [apɥije] *vt* (*poser*): ~ **qch sur/contre** to lean *ou* rest sth on/against; (*soutenir: personne, demande*) to support, back (up) ♦ *vi*: ~ **sur** (*bouton, frein*) to press, push; (*mot, détail*) to stress, emphasize; **s'~ sur** to lean on; (*fig: compter sur*) to rely on

âpre [apR] *adj* acrid, pungent; ~ **au gain** grasping

après [apRe] *prép* after ♦ *adv* afterwards; **2 heures** ~ 2 hours later; ~ **qu'il est** *ou* **soit parti** after he left; ~ **avoir fait** after having done; **d'~** (*selon*) according to; ~ **coup** after the event, afterwards; ~ **tout** (*au fond*) after all; **et (puis)** ~**?** so what?; **après-demain** *adv* the day after tomorrow; **après-guerre** *nm* post-war years *pl*; **après-midi** *nm ou nf inv* afternoon; **après-rasage** *nm inv* aftershave; **après-shampooing** *nm inv* conditioner; **après-ski** *nm inv* snow boot

à-propos [apRɔpo] *nm* (*d'une remarque*) aptness; **faire preuve d'~~** to show presence of mind

apte [apt] *adj* capable; (*MIL*) fit

aquarelle [akwaRɛl] *nf* watercolour

aquarium [akwaRjɔm] *nm* aquarium

arabe [aRab] *adj* Arabic; (*désert, cheval*) Arabian; (*nation, peuple*) Arab ♦ *nm/f*: **A~** Arab ♦ *nm* (*LING*) Arabic

Arabie [aRabi] *nf*: **l'~ (Saoudite)** Saudi Arabia

arachide [aRaʃid] *nf* (*plante*) groundnut (plant); (*graine*) peanut, groundnut

araignée [aRɛɲe] *nf* spider

arbitraire [aRbitRɛR] *adj* arbitrary

arbitre [aRbitR] *nm* (*SPORT*) referee; (*: TENNIS, CRICKET*) umpire; (*fig*) arbiter, judge; (*JUR*) arbitrator; **arbitrer** *vt* to referee; to umpire; to arbitrate

arborer [aRbɔRe] *vt* to bear, display

arbre [aRbR] *nm* tree; (*TECH*) shaft; ~ **généalogique** family tree

arbuste [aRbyst] *nm* small shrub

arc [aRk] *nm* (*arme*) bow; (*GÉOM*) arc;

(*ARCHIT*) arch; **en ~ de cercle** semi-circular

arcade [aRkad] *nf* arch(way); **~s** *nfpl* (*série*) arcade *sg*, arches

arcanes [aRkan] *nmpl* mysteries

arc-boutant [aRkbutɑ̃] *nm* flying buttress

arceau, x [aRso] *nm* (*métallique etc*) hoop

arc-en-ciel [aRkɑ̃sjɛl] *nm* rainbow

arche [aRʃ] *nf* arch; ~ **de Noé** Noah's Ark

archéologie [aRkeɔlɔʒi] *nf* arch(a)eology; **archéologue** *nm/f* arch(a)eologist

archet [aRʃɛ] *nm* bow

archevêque [aRʃəvɛk] *nm* archbishop

archi... [aRʃi] (*fam*) *préfixe* tremendously; **archicomble** (*fam*) *adj* chock-a-block; **archiconnu, e** (*fam*) *adj* enormously well-known

archipel [aRʃipɛl] *nm* archipelago

architecte [aRʃitɛkt] *nm* architect

architecture [aRʃitɛktyR] *nf* architecture

archives [aRʃiv] *nfpl* (*collection*) archives

arctique [aRktik] *adj* Arctic ♦ *nm*: **l'A~** the Arctic

ardemment [aRdamɑ̃] *adv* ardently, fervently

ardent, e [aRdɑ̃, ɑ̃t] *adj* (*soleil*) blazing; (*amour*) ardent, passionate; (*prière*) fervent

ardeur [aRdœR] *nf* ardour (*BRIT*), ardor (*US*); (*du soleil*) heat

ardoise [aRdwaz] *nf* slate

ardu, e [aRdy] *adj* (*travail*) arduous; (*problème*) difficult

arène [aRɛn] *nf* arena; **~s** *nfpl* (*amphithéâtre*) bull-ring *sg*

arête [aRɛt] *nf* (*de poisson*) bone; (*d'une montagne*) ridge

argent [aRʒɑ̃] *nm* (*métal*) silver; (*monnaie*) money; ~ **de poche** pocket money; ~ **liquide** ready money, (ready) cash; **argenté, e** *adj* (*couleur*) silver, silvery; **en métal argenté** silver-plated; **argenterie** *nf* silverware

argentin, e [aRʒɑ̃tɛ̃, in] *adj* Argentinian, Argentine

Argentine [aRʒɑ̃tin] *nf*: **l'~** Argentina, the Argentine

argile [aRʒil] *nf* clay

argot [aRgo] *nm* slang; **argotique** *adj* slang *cpd*; (*très familier*) slangy

argument [aRgymɑ̃] *nm* argument

argumentaire [aRgymɑ̃tɛR] *nm* sales leaflet

argumenter [aRgymɑ̃te] *vi* to argue

argus [aRgys] *nm* guide to second-hand car etc prices

aride [aRid] *adj* arid

aristocratie [aRistɔkRasi] *nf* aristocracy; **aristocratique** *adj* aristocratic

arithmétique [aRitmetik] *adj* arithmetic(al) ♦ *nf* arithmetic

armateur [aRmatœR] *nm* shipowner

armature [aRmatyR] *nf* framework; (*de tente*

etc) frame; **soutien-gorge à/sans ~** under-wired/unwired bra

arme [aʀm] *nf* weapon; **~s** *nfpl* (*~ment*) weapons, arms; (*blason*) (coat of) arms; **~ à feu** firearm

armée [aʀme] *nf* army; **~ de l'air** Air Force; **~ de terre** Army

armement [aʀməmɑ̃] *nm* (*matériel*) arms *pl*, weapons *pl*

armer [aʀme] *vt* to arm; (*arme à feu*) to cock; (*appareil-photo*) to wind on; **~ qch de** to reinforce sth with; **s'~ de** to arm o.s. with

armistice [aʀmistis] *nm* armistice; **l'A~** ≈ Remembrance (*BRIT*) *ou* Veterans (*US*) Day

armoire [aʀmwaʀ] *nf* (tall) cupboard; (*penderie*) wardrobe (*BRIT*), closet (*US*)

armoiries [aʀmwaʀi] *nfpl* coat *sg* of arms

armure [aʀmyʀ] *nf* armour *no pl*, suit of armour; **armurier** *nm* gunsmith

arnaque [aʀnak] (*fam*) *nf* swindling; **c'est de l'~** it's a rip-off; **arnaquer** (*fam*) *vt* to swindle

aromates [aʀɔmat] *nmpl* seasoning *sg*, herbs (and spices)

aromathérapie [aʀɔmateʀapi] *nf* aromatherapy

aromatisé, e [aʀɔmatize] *adj* flavoured

arôme [aʀom] *nm* aroma

arpenter [aʀpɑ̃te] *vt* (*salle, couloir*) to pace up and down

arpenteur [aʀpɑ̃tœʀ] *nm* surveyor

arqué, e [aʀke] *adj* arched; (*jambes*) bandy

arrache-pied [aʀaʃpje]: **d'~** *adv* relentlessly

arracher [aʀaʃe] *vt* to pull out; (*page etc*) to tear off, tear out; (*légumes, herbe*) to pull up; (*bras etc*) to tear off; **s'~** *vt* (*article recherché*) to fight over; **~ qch à qn** to snatch sth from sb; (*fig*) to wring sth out of sb

arraisonner [aʀezɔne] *vt* (*bateau*) to board and search

arrangeant, e [aʀɑ̃ʒɑ̃, ɑ̃t] *adj* accommodating, obliging

arrangement [aʀɑ̃ʒmɑ̃] *nm* agreement, arrangement

arranger [aʀɑ̃ʒe] *vt* (*gén*) to arrange; (*réparer*) to fix, put right; (*régler: différend*) to settle, sort out; (*convenir à*) to suit, be convenient for; **s'~** *vi* (*se mettre d'accord*) to come to an agreement; **je vais m'~** I'll manage; **ça va s'~** it'll sort itself out

arrestation [aʀestasjɔ̃] *nf* arrest

arrêt [aʀe] *nm* stopping; (*de bus etc*) stop; (*JUR*) judgment, decision; **à l'~** stationary; **tomber en ~ devant** to stop short in front of; **sans ~** (*sans interruption*) non-stop; (*très fréquemment*) continually; **~ de travail** stoppage (of work); **~ maladie** sick leave

arrêté [aʀete] *nm* order, decree

arrêter [aʀete] *vt* to stop; (*chauffage etc*) to

turn off, switch off; (*fixer: date etc*) to appoint, decide on; (*criminel, suspect*) to arrest; **s'~** *vi* to stop; **~ de faire** to stop doing

arrhes [aʀ] *nfpl* deposit *sg*

arrière [aʀjeʀ] *nm* back; (*SPORT*) fullback ♦ *adj inv*: **siège/roue ~** back *ou* rear seat/wheel; **à l'~** behind, at the back; **en ~** behind; (*regarder*) back, behind; (*tomber, aller*) backwards; **arriéré, e** *adj* (*péj*) backward ♦ *nm* (*d'argent*) arrears *pl*; **arrière-goût** *nm* aftertaste; **arrière-grand-mère** *nf* great-grandmother; **arrière-grand-père** *nm* great-grandfather; **arrière-pays** *nm inv* hinterland; **arrière-pensée** *nf* ulterior motive; mental reservation; **arrière-plan** *nm* background; **arrière-saison** *nf* late autumn; **arrière-train** *nm* hindquarters *pl*

arrimer [aʀime] *vt* to secure; (*cargaison*) to stow

arrivage [aʀivaʒ] *nm* consignment

arrivée [aʀive] *nf* arrival; (*ligne d'~*) finish

arriver [aʀive] *vi* to arrive; (*survenir*) to happen, occur; **il arrive à Paris à 8h** he gets to *ou* arrives in Paris at 8; **~ à** (*atteindre*) to reach; **~ à faire qch** to succeed in doing sth; **en ~ à** (*finir par*) to come to; **il arrive que** it happens that; **il lui arrive de faire** he sometimes does; **arriviste** *nm/f* go-getter

arrogance [aʀɔgɑ̃s] *nf* arrogance

arrogant, e [aʀɔgɑ̃, ɑ̃t] *adj* arrogant

arrondir [aʀɔ̃diʀ] *vt* (*forme, objet*) to round; (*somme*) to round off

arrondissement [aʀɔ̃dismɑ̃] *nm* (*ADMIN*) ≈ district

arroser [aʀoze] *vt* to water; (*victoire*) to celebrate (over a drink); (*CULIN*) to baste; **arrosoir** *nm* watering can

arsenal, -aux [aʀsənal, o] *nm* (*NAVIG*) naval dockyard; (*MIL*) arsenal; (*fig*) paraphernalia

art [aʀ] *nm* art

artère [aʀteʀ] *nf* (*ANAT*) artery; (*rue*) main road

arthrite [aʀtʀit] *nf* arthritis

artichaut [aʀtiʃo] *nm* artichoke

article [aʀtikl] *nm* article; (*COMM*) item, article; **à l'~ de la mort** at the point of death; **~s de luxe** luxury goods

articulation [aʀtikylasjɔ̃] *nf* articulation; (*ANAT*) joint

articuler [aʀtikyle] *vt* to articulate

artifice [aʀtifis] *nm* device, trick

artificiel, le [aʀtifisjɛl] *adj* artificial

artisan [aʀtizɑ̃] *nm* artisan, (self-employed) craftsman; **artisanal, e, -aux** *adj* of *ou* made by craftsmen; (*péj*) cottage industry *cpd*; **de fabrication artisanale** home-made; **artisanat** *nm* arts and crafts *pl*

artiste [aʀtist] *nm/f* artist; (*de variétés*) entertainer; (*musicien etc*) performer;

artistique adj artistic

as¹ [a] vb voir **avoir**

as² [as] nm ace

ascendance [asɑ̃dɑ̃s] nf (origine) ancestry

ascendant, e [asɑ̃dɑ̃, ɑ̃t] adj upward ♦ nm influence

ascenseur [asɑ̃sœr] nm lift (BRIT), elevator (US)

ascension [asɑ̃sjɔ̃] nf ascent; (de montagne) climb; **l'A~** (REL) the Ascension

aseptisé, e (péj) adj sanitized

aseptiser [asɛptize] vt (ustensile) to sterilize; (plaie) to disinfect

asiatique [azjatik] adj Asiatic, Asian ♦ nm/f: A~ Asian

Asie [azi] nf: **l'~** Asia

asile [azil] nm (refuge) refuge, sanctuary; (POL): **droit d'~** (political) asylum; **~ (de vieillards)** old people's home

aspect [aspɛ] nm appearance, look; (fig) aspect, side; **à l'~ de** at the sight of

asperge [aspɛrʒ] nf asparagus no pl

asperger [aspɛrʒe] vt to spray, sprinkle

aspérité [asperite] nf bump, protruding bit (of rock etc)

asphalte [asfalt] nm asphalt

asphyxier [asfiksje] vt to suffocate, asphyxiate; (fig) to stifle

aspirateur [aspiratœr] nm vacuum cleaner; **passer l'~** to vacuum

aspirer [aspire] vt (air) to inhale; (liquide) to suck (up); (suj: appareil) to suck up; **~ à** to aspire to

aspirine [aspirin] nf aspirin

assagir [asaʒir]: **s'~** vi to quieten down, settle down

assaillir [asajir] vt to assail, attack

assainir [asenir] vt (logements) to clean up; (eau, air) to purify

assaisonnement [asɛzɔnmɑ̃] nm seasoning

assaisonner [asɛzɔne] vt to season

assassin [asasɛ̃] nm murderer; assassin; **assassiner** vt to murder; (esp POL) to assassinate

assaut [aso] nm assault, attack; **prendre d'~** to storm, assault; **donner l'~** to attack

assécher [aseʃe] vt to drain

assemblage [asɑ̃blaʒ] nm (action) assembling; (de couleurs, choses) collection

assemblée [asɑ̃ble] nf (réunion) meeting; (assistance) gathering; (POL) assembly

assembler [asɑ̃ble] vt (joindre, monter) to assemble, put together; (amasser) to gather (together), collect (together); **s'~** vi to gather

assener, asséner [asene] vt: **~ un coup à qn** to deal sb a blow

assentiment [asɑ̃timɑ̃] nm assent, consent

asseoir [aswar] vt (malade, bébé) to sit up; (personne debout) to sit down; (autorité, réputation) to establish; **s'~** vi to sit (o.s.) down

assermenté, e [asɛrmɑ̃te] adj sworn, on oath

asservir [asɛrvir] vt to subjugate, enslave

assez [ase] adv (suffisamment) enough, sufficiently; (passablement) rather, quite, fairly; **~ de pain/livres** enough ou sufficient bread/books; **vous en avez ~?** have you got enough?; **j'en ai ~!** I've had enough!

assidu, e [asidy] adj (appliqué) assiduous, painstaking; (ponctuel) regular

assied etc [asje] vb voir **asseoir**

assiéger [asjeʒe] vt to besiege

assiérai etc [asjere] vb voir **asseoir**

assiette [asjɛt] nf plate; (contenu) plate(ful); **il n'est pas dans son ~** he's not feeling quite himself; **~ à dessert** dessert plate; **~ anglaise** assorted cold meats; **~ creuse** (soup) dish, soup plate; **~ plate** (dinner) plate

assigner [asiɲe] vt: **~ qch à** (poste, part, travail) to assign sth to

assimiler [asimile] vt to assimilate, absorb; (comparer): **~ qch/qn à** to liken ou compare sth/sb to

assis, e [asi, iz] pp de **asseoir** ♦ adj sitting (down), seated; **assise** nf (fig) basis, foundation; **assises** nfpl (JUR) assizes

assistance [asistɑ̃s] nf (public) audience; (aide) assistance; **enfant de l'A~ publique** child in care

assistant, e [asistɑ̃, ɑ̃t] nm/f assistant; (d'université) probationary lecturer; **~(e) social(e)** social worker

assisté, e [asiste] adj (AUTO) power assisted; **~ par ordinateur** computer-assisted

assister [asiste] vt (aider) to assist; **~ à** (scène, événement) to witness; (conférence, séminaire) to attend, be at; (spectacle, match) to be at, see

association [asɔsjasjɔ̃] nf association

associé, e [asɔsje] nm/f associate; (COMM) partner

associer [asɔsje] vt to associate; **s'~** vi to join together; **s'~ à qn pour faire** to join (forces) with sb to do; **s'~ à** (couleurs, qualités) to be combined with; (opinions, joie de qn) to share in; **~ qn à** (profits) to give sb a share of; (affaire) to make sb a partner in; (joie, triomphe) to include sb in; **~ qch à** (allier à) to combine sth with

assoiffé, e [aswafe] adj thirsty

assombrir [asɔ̃brir] vt to darken; (fig) to fill with gloom

assommer [asɔme] vt (étourdir, abrutir) to knock out, stun

Assomption [asɔ̃psjɔ̃] nf: **l'~** the Assumption

assorti, e [asɔrti] adj matched, matching; (varié) assorted; **~ à** matching; **assortiment**

nm assortment, selection

assortir [asɔʀtiʀ] *vt* to match; ~ qch à to match sth with; ~ qch de to accompany sth with

assoupi, e [asupi] *adj* dozing, sleeping

assoupir [asupiʀ]: s'~ *vi* to doze off

assouplir [asupliʀ] *vt* to make supple; (*fig*) to relax; **assouplissant** *nm* (*fabric*) softener

assourdir [asuʀdiʀ] *vt* (*bruit*) to deaden, muffle; (*suj: bruit*) to deafen

assouvir [asuviʀ] *vt* to satisfy, appease

assujettir [asyʒetiʀ] *vt* to subject

assumer [asyme] *vt* (*fonction, emploi*) to assume, take on

assurance [asyʀɑ̃s] *nf* (*certitude*) assurance; (*confiance en soi*) (self-)confidence; (*contrat*) insurance (policy); (*secteur commercial*) insurance; ~ maladie health insurance; ~ tous risques (*AUTO*) comprehensive insurance; ~s sociales (*BRIT*), ≈ National Insurance (*BRIT*), ≈ Social Security (*US*); **assurance-vie** *nf* life assurance *ou* insurance

assuré, e [asyʀe] *adj* (*certain: réussite, échec*) certain, sure; (*air*) assured; (*pas*) steady ♦ *nm/f* insured (person); **assurément** *adv* assuredly, most certainly

assurer [asyʀe] *vt* (*FIN*) to insure; (*victoire etc*) to ensure; (*frontières, pouvoir*) to make secure; (*service*) to provide, operate; s'~ (contre) to insure o.s. (against); s'~ de/que (*vérifier*) to make sure of/that; s'~ (de) (*aide de qn*) to secure; ~ à qn que to assure sb that; ~ qn de to assure sb of; **assureur** *nm* insurer

asthmatique [asmatik] *adj, nm/f* asthmatic

asthme [asm] *nm* asthma

asticot [astiko] *nm* maggot

astiquer [astike] *vt* to polish, shine

astre [astʀ] *nm* star

astreignant, e [astʀɛɲɑ̃, ɑ̃t] *adj* demanding

astreindre [astʀɛ̃dʀ] *vt*: ~ qn à faire to compel *ou* force sb to do; s'~ *vi*: s'~ à faire to force o.s. to do

astrologie [astʀɔlɔʒi] *nf* astrology

astronaute [astʀonot] *nm/f* astronaut

astronomie [astʀonɔmi] *nf* astronomy

astuce [astys] *nf* shrewdness, astuteness; (*truc*) trick, clever way; **astucieux, -euse** *adj* clever

atelier [atəlje] *nm* workshop; (*de peintre*) studio

athée [ate] *adj* atheistic ♦ *nm/f* atheist

Athènes [atɛn] *n* Athens

athlète [atlɛt] *nm/f* (*SPORT*) athlete; **athlétisme** *nm* athletics *sg*

atlantique [atlɑ̃tik] *adj* Atlantic ♦ *nm*: l'(océan) A~ the Atlantic (Ocean)

atlas [atlɑs] *nm* atlas

atmosphère [atmɔsfɛʀ] *nf* atmosphere

atome [atom] *nm* atom; **atomique** *adj* atomic, nuclear

atomiseur [atɔmizœʀ] *nm* atomizer

atout [atu] *nm* trump; (*fig*) asset

âtre [ɑtʀ] *nm* hearth

atroce [atʀɔs] *adj* atrocious

attabler [atable]: s'~ *vi* to sit down at (the) table

attachant, e [ataʃɑ̃, ɑ̃t] *adj* engaging, lovable, likeable

attache [ataʃ] *nf* clip, fastener; (*fig*) tie

attacher [ataʃe] *vt* to tie up; (*étiquette*) to attach, tie on; (*ceinture*) to fasten ♦ *vi* (*poêle, riz*) to stick; s'~ à (*par affection*) to become attached to; s'~ à faire to endeavour to do; ~ qch à to tie *ou* attach sth to

attaque [atak] *nf* attack; (*cérébrale*) stroke; (*d'épilepsie*) fit; ~ à main armée armed attack

attaquer [atake] *vt* to attack; (*en justice*) to bring an action against, sue ♦ *vi* to attack; s'~ à ♦ *vt* (*personne*) to attack; (*problème*) to tackle

attardé, e [ataʀde] *adj* (*enfant*) backward; (*passants*) late

attarder [ataʀde]: s'~ *vi* to linger

atteindre [atɛ̃dʀ] *vt* to reach; (*blesser*) to hit; (*émouvoir*) to affect; **atteint, e** *adj* (*MÉD*): être atteint de to be suffering from; **atteinte** *nf*: hors d'atteinte out of reach; porter atteinte à to strike a blow at

atteler [at(ə)le] *vt* (*cheval, bœufs*) to hitch up; s'~ à (*travail*) to buckle down to

attelle [atɛl] *nf* splint

attenant, e [at(ə)nɑ̃, ɑ̃t] *adj*: ~ (à) adjoining

attendant [atɑ̃dɑ̃] *adv*: en ~ meanwhile, in the meantime

attendre [atɑ̃dʀ] *vt* (*gén*) to wait for; (*être destiné ou réservé à*) to await, be in store for ♦ *vi* to wait; s'~ à (*ce que*) to expect (that); ~ un enfant to be expecting a baby; ~ de faire/d'être to wait until one does/is; attendez qu'il vienne wait until he comes; ~ qch de to expect sth of

attendrir [atɑ̃dʀiʀ] *vt* to move (to pity); (*viande*) to tenderize; **attendrissant, e** *adj* moving, touching

attendu, e [atɑ̃dy] *adj* (*visiteur*) expected; (*événement*) long-awaited; ~ que considering that, since

attentat [atɑ̃ta] *nm* assassination attempt; ~ à la bombe bomb attack; ~ à la pudeur indecent assault *no pl*

attente [atɑ̃t] *nf* wait; (*espérance*) expectation

attenter [atɑ̃te]: ~ à *vt* (*liberté*) to violate; ~ à la vie de qn to make an attempt on sb's life

attentif, -ive [atɑ̃tif, iv] *adj* (*auditeur*) attentive; (*examen*) careful; ~ à careful to

attention [atɑ̃sjɔ̃] *nf* attention; (*prévenance*)

attention, thoughtfulness no pl; à l'~ de for
the attention of; faire ~ (à) to be careful (of);
faire ~ (à ce) que to be ou make sure that; ~!
carefully, watch out!; **attentionné, e** adj
thoughtful, considerate

atténuer [atenɥe] vt (douleur) to alleviate,
ease; (couleurs) to soften

atterrer [atere] vt to dismay, appal

atterrir [aterir] vi to land; **atterrissage** nm
landing

attestation [atestasjɔ̃] nf certificate

attester [ateste] vt to testify to

attirail [atiraj] (fam) nm gear; (péj)
paraphernalia

attirant, e [atirã, ãt] adj attractive,
appealing

attirer [atire] vt to attract; (appâter) to lure,
entice; ~ qn dans un coin to draw sb into a
corner; ~ l'attention de qn to attract sb's
attention; ~ l'attention de qn sur to draw sb's
attention to; s'~ des ennuis to bring trouble
upon o.s., get into trouble

attiser [atize] vt (feu) to poke (up)

attitré, e [atitre] adj (habituel) regular,
usual; (agréé) accredited

attitude [atityd] nf attitude; (position du
corps) bearing

attouchements [atuʃmɑ̃] nmpl (sexuels)
fondling sg

attraction [atraksjɔ̃] nf (gén) attraction; (de
cabaret, cirque) number

attrait [atre] nm appeal, attraction

attrape-nigaud [atrapnigo] (fam) nm con

attraper [atrape] vt (gén) to catch;
(habitude, amende) to get, pick up; (fam:
duper) to con; se faire ~ (fam) to be told off

attrayant, e [atrejã, ãt] adj attractive

attribuer [atribɥe] vt (prix) to award; (rôle,
tâche) to allocate, assign; (imputer): ~ qch à
to attribute sth to; s'~ vt (s'approprier) to
claim for o.s.; **attribut** nm attribute

attrister [atriste] vt to sadden

attroupement [atrupmɑ̃] nm crowd

attrouper [atrupe]: s'~ vi to gather

au [o] prép +dét = à +le

aubaine [oben] nf godsend

aube [ob] nf dawn, daybreak; à l'~ at dawn
ou daybreak

aubépine [obepin] nf hawthorn

auberge [oberʒ] nf inn; ~ de jeunesse youth
hostel

aubergine [oberʒin] nf aubergine

aubergiste [oberʒist] nm/f inn-keeper,
hotel-keeper

aucun, e [okœ̃, yn] dét no, tournure négative
+any; (positif) any ♦ pron none, tournure
négative +any; any(one); sans ~ doute
without any doubt; plus qu'~ autre more
than any other; ~ des deux neither of the

two; ~ d'entre eux none of them;
aucunement adv in no way, not in the least

audace [odas] nf daring, boldness; (péj)
audacity; **audacieux, -euse** adj daring, bold

au-delà [od(ə)la] adv beyond ♦ nm: l'~ the
hereafter; ~~ de beyond

au-dessous [odsu] adv underneath; below;
~~ de under(neath), below; (limite, somme
etc) below, under; (dignité, condition) below

au-dessus [odsy] adv above; ~~ de above

au-devant [od(ə)vã]: ~~ de prép: aller ~~
~ de (personne, danger) to go (out) and
meet; (souhaits de qn) to anticipate

audience [odjãs] nf audience; (JUR: séance)
hearing

audimat ® [odimat] nm (taux d'écoute)
ratings pl

audio-visuel, le [odjovizɥel] adj audiovisual

auditeur, -trice [oditœr, tris] nm/f listener

audition [odisjɔ̃] nf (ouïe, écoute) hearing;
(JUR: de témoins) examination; (MUS, THÉÂTRE:
épreuve) audition

auditoire [oditwar] nm audience

auge [oʒ] nf trough

augmentation [ɔgmãtasjɔ̃] nf increase;
~ (de salaire) rise (in salary) (BRIT), (pay) raise
(US)

augmenter [ɔgmãte] vt (gén) to increase;
(salaire, prix) to increase, raise, put up;
(employé) to increase the salary of ♦ vi to
increase

augure [ogyr] nm: de bon/mauvais ~ of
good/ill omen; **augurer** vt: augurer bien de
to augur well for

aujourd'hui [oʒurdɥi] adv today

aumône [omon] nf inv alms sg; **aumônier**
nm chaplain

auparavant [oparavã] adv before(hand)

auprès [opre]: ~ de prép next to, close to;
(recourir, s'adresser) to; (en comparaison de)
compared with

auquel [okel] prép +pron = à +lequel

aurai etc [ɔre] vb voir avoir

auréole [ɔreɔl] nf halo; (tache) ring

aurons etc [ɔrɔ̃] vb voir avoir

aurore [ɔrɔr] nf dawn, daybreak

ausculter [ɔskylte] vt to sound (the chest of)

aussi [osi] adv (également) also, too; (de
comparaison) as ♦ conj therefore,
consequently; ~ fort que as strong as; moi ~
me too

aussitôt [osito] adv straight away,
immediately; ~ que as soon as

austère [oster] adj austere

austral, e [ɔstral] adj southern

Australie [ɔstrali] nf: l'~ Australia;
australien, ne adj Australian ♦ nm/f:
Australien, ne Australian

autant [otɑ̃] adv so much; (comparatif):
~ **(que)** as much (as); (nombre) as many
(as); ~ **(de)** so much (ou many); as much (ou
many); ~ **partir** we (ou you etc) may as well
leave; ~ **dire que** ... one might as well say that
...; **pour** ~ for all that; **d'~ plus/mieux (que)** all
the more/the better (since)

autel [otɛl] nm altar

auteur [otœʀ] nm author

authenticité [otɑ̃tisite] nf authenticity

authentique [otɑ̃tik] adj authentic, genuine

auto [oto] nf car

auto...: **autobiographie** nf autobiography;
autobus nm bus; **autocar** nm coach

autochtone [otɔktɔn] nm/f native

auto...: **autocollant, e** adj self-adhesive;
(enveloppe) self-seal ♦ nm sticker; **auto-
couchettes** adj: **train auto-couchettes** car
sleeper train; **autocuiseur** nm pressure
cooker; **autodéfense** nf self-defence;
autodidacte nm/f self-taught person;
auto-école nf driving school; **autographe**
nm autograph

automate [otomat] nm (machine)
(automatic) machine

automatique [otomatik] adj automatic
♦ nm: **l'~** direct dialling; **automatiquement** adv automatically; **automatiser** vt to
automate

automne [otɔn] nm autumn (BRIT), fall (US)

automobile [otomobil] adj motor cpd ♦ nf
(motor) car; **automobiliste** nm/f motorist

autonome [otonom] adj autonomous;
autonomie nf autonomy; (POL) self-
government, autonomy

autopsie [otɔpsi] nf post-mortem
(examination), autopsy

autoradio [otoʀadjo] nm car radio

autorisation [otɔʀizasjɔ̃] nf permission,
authorization; (papiers) permit

autorisé, e [otɔʀize] adj (opinion, sources)
authoritative

autoriser [otɔʀize] vt to give permission for,
authorize; (fig) to allow (of)

autoritaire [otɔʀitɛʀ] adj authoritarian

autorité [otɔʀite] nf authority; **faire** ~ to be
authoritative

autoroute [otoʀut] nf motorway (BRIT),
highway (US); ~ **de l'information** (INFORM)
information superhighway

auto-stop [otostɔp] nm: **faire de l'~~** to
hitch-hike; **prendre qn en ~~** to give sb a lift;
auto-stoppeur, -euse nm/f hitch-hiker

autour [otuʀ] adv around; ~ **de** around; **tout**
~ all around

MOT-CLÉ
---

autre [otʀ] adj **1** (différent) other, different;
je préférerais un autre verre I'd prefer another

ou a different glass
2 (supplémentaire) other; **je voudrais un autre
verre d'eau** I'd like another glass of water
3: **autre chose** something else; **autre part**
somewhere else; **d'autre part** on the other
hand
♦ pron: **un autre** another (one); **nous/vous
autres** us/you; **d'autres** others; **l'autre** the
other (one); **les autres** the others; (autrui)
others; **l'un et l'autre** both of them; **se
détester l'un l'autre/les uns les autres** to hate
each other ou one another; **d'une semaine à
l'autre** from one week to the next;
(incessamment) any week now; **entre autres**
among other things

autrefois [otʀəfwa] adv in the past

autrement [otʀəmɑ̃] adv differently; (d'une
manière différente) in another way; (sinon)
otherwise; ~ **dit** in other words

Autriche [otʀiʃ] nf: **l'~** Austria; **autrichien,
ne** adj Austrian ♦ nm/f: **Autrichien, ne**
Austrian

autruche [otʀyʃ] nf ostrich

autrui [otʀɥi] pron others

auvent [ovɑ̃] nm canopy

aux [o] prép +dét = **à +les**

auxiliaire [ɔksiljɛʀ] adj, nm/f auxiliary

auxquelles [okɛl] prép +pron = **à +lesquelles**

auxquels [okɛl] prép +pron = **à +lesquels**

avachi, e [avaʃi] adj limp, flabby

aval [aval] nm: **en** ~ downstream, downriver

avalanche [avalɑ̃ʃ] nf avalanche

avaler [avale] vt to swallow

avance [avɑ̃s] nf (de troupes etc) advance;
progress; (d'argent) advance; (sur un
concurrent) lead; ~**s** nfpl (amoureuses)
advances; **(être) en** ~ (to be) early; (sur un
programme) (to be) ahead of schedule; **à l'~,
d'~** in advance

avancé, e [avɑ̃se] adj advanced; (travail)
well on, well under way

avancement [avɑ̃smɑ̃] nm (professionnel)
promotion

avancer [avɑ̃se] vi to move forward, advance;
(projet, travail) to make progress; (montre,
réveil) to be fast; to gain ♦ vt to move
forward, advance; (argent) to advance;
(montre, pendule) to put forward; **s'~** vi to
move forward, advance; (fig) to commit o.s.

avant [avɑ̃] prép, adv before ♦ adj inv: **siège/
roue** ~ front seat/wheel ♦ nm (d'un véhicule,
bâtiment) front; (SPORT: joueur) forward;
~ **qu'il (ne) fasse/de faire** before he does/
doing; ~ **tout** (surtout) above all; **à l'~** (dans
un véhicule) in (the) front; **en** ~ forward(s);
en ~ **de** in front of

avantage [avɑ̃taʒ] nm advantage; ~**s sociaux**
fringe benefits; **avantager** vt (favoriser) to

favour; (*embellir*) to flatter; **avantageux, -euse** *adj* (*prix*) attractive

avant...: avant-bras *nm inv* forearm; **avantcoureur** *adj inv*: **signe avantcoureur** advance indication *ou* sign; **avant-dernier, -ière** *adj*, *nm/f* next to last, last but one; **avant-goût** *nm* foretaste; **avant-guerre** *nm* pre-war years; **avant-hier** *adv* the day before yesterday; **avant-première** *nf* (*de film*) preview; **avant-projet** *nm* (preliminary) draft; **avant-propos** *nm* foreword; **avant-veille** *nf*: **l'avant-veille** two days before

avare [avar] *adj* miserly, avaricious ♦ *nm/f* miser; ~ **de** (*compliments etc*) sparing of

avarié, e [avarje] *adj* (*aliment*) rotting

avaries [avari] *nfpl* (*NAVIG*) damage *sg*

avec [avɛk] *prép* with; (*à l'égard de*) to(wards), with; **et ~ ça?** (*dans magasin*) anything else?

avenant, e [av(ə)nɑ̃, ɑ̃t] *adj* pleasant; **à l'~** in keeping

avènement [avɛnmɑ̃] *nm* (*d'un changement*) advent, coming

avenir [avnir] *nm* future; **à l'~** in future; **politicien d'~** politician with prospects *ou* a future

aventure [avɑ̃tyr] *nf* adventure; (*amoureuse*) affair; **aventurer: s'aventurer** *vi* to venture; **aventureux, -euse** *adj* adventurous, venturesome; (*projet*) risky, chancy

avenue [avny] *nf* avenue

avérer [avere]: **s'~** *vb* +*attrib* to prove (to be)

averse [avɛrs] *nf* shower

averti, e [avɛrti] *adj* (well-)informed

avertir [avɛrtir] *vt*: ~ **qn** (**de qch/que**) to warn sb (of sth/that); (*renseigner*) to inform sb (of sth/that); **avertissement** *nm* warning; **avertisseur** *nm* horn, siren

aveu, x [avø] *nm* confession

aveugle [avœgl] *adj* blind ♦ *nm/f* blind man/woman; **aveuglément** *adv* blindly; **aveugler** *vt* to blind

aviateur, -trice [avjatœr, tris] *nm/f* aviator, pilot

aviation [avjasjɔ̃] *nf* aviation; (*sport*) flying; (*MIL*) air force

avide [avid] *adj* eager; (*péj*) greedy, grasping

avilir [avilir] *vt* to debase

avion [avjɔ̃] *nm* (aero)plane (*BRIT*), (air)plane (*US*); **aller (quelque part) en ~** to go (somewhere) by plane, fly (somewhere); **par ~** by airmail; **à réaction** jet (plane)

aviron [avirɔ̃] *nm* oar; (*sport*): **l'~** rowing

avis [avi] *nm* opinion; (*notification*) notice; **à mon ~** in my opinion; **changer d'~** to change one's mind; **jusqu'à nouvel ~** until further notice

avisé, e [avize] *adj* sensible, wise; **bien/mal ~ de** well-/ill-advised to

aviser [avize] *vt* (*informer*): ~ **qn de/que** to advise *ou* inform sb of/that ♦ *vi* to think about things, assess the situation; **nous ~ons sur place** we'll work something out once we're there; **s'~ de qch/que** to become suddenly aware of sth/that; **s'~ de faire** to take it into one's head to do

avocat, e [avɔka, at] *nm/f* (*JUR*) barrister (*BRIT*), lawyer ♦ *nm* (*CULIN*) avocado (pear); ~ **de la défense** counsel for the defence; ~ **général** assistant public prosecutor

avoine [avwan] *nf* oats *pl*

MOT-CLÉ

---

avoir [avwar] *nm* assets *pl*, resources *pl*; (*COMM*) credit
♦ *vt* **1** (*posséder*) to have; **elle a 2 enfants/ une belle maison** she has (got) 2 children/a lovely house; **il a les yeux bleus** he has (got) blue eyes

2 (*âge, dimensions*) to be; **il a 3 ans** he is 3 (years old); **le mur a 3 mètres de haut** the wall is 3 metres high; *voir aussi* **faim**; **peur** *etc*

3 (*fam: duper*) to do, have; **on vous a eu!** you've been done *ou* had!

4: en avoir contre qn to have a grudge against sb; **en avoir assez** to be fed up; **j'en ai pour une demi-heure** it'll take me half an hour
♦ *vb aux* **1** to have; **avoir mangé/dormi** to have eaten/slept

2 (*avoir +à +infinitif*): **avoir à faire qch** to have to do sth; **vous n'avez qu'à lui demander** you only have to ask him
♦ *vb impers* **1**: **il y a** (+ *singulier*) there is; (+ *pluriel*) there are; **qu'y a-t-il?, qu'est-ce qu'il y a?** what's the matter?, what is it?; **il doit y avoir une explication** there must be an explanation; **il n'y a qu'à ... we** (*ou you etc*) will just have to ...

2 (*temporel*): **il y a 10 ans** 10 years ago; **il y a 10 ans/longtemps que je le sais** I've known it for 10 years/a long time; **il y a 10 ans qu'il est arrivé** it's 10 years since he arrived

---

avoisiner [avwazine] *vt* to be near *ou* close to; (*fig*) to border *ou* verge on

avortement [avɔrtəmɑ̃] *nm* abortion

avorter [avɔrte] *vi* (*MÉD*) to have an abortion; (*fig*) to fail

avoué, e [avwe] *adj* avowed ♦ *nm* (*JUR*) ≈ solicitor

avouer [avwe] *vt* (*crime, défaut*) to confess (to); ~ **avoir fait/que** to admit *ou* confess to having done/that

avril [avril] *nm* April

axe [aks] *nm* axis; (*de roue etc*) axle; (*fig*) main line; **axer** *vt*: **axer qch sur** to centre sth on

ayons *etc* [ɛjɔ̃] *vb voir* **avoir**

azote [azɔt] *nm* nitrogen

B, b

baba [baba] *nm*: ~ **au rhum** rum baba

babines [babin] *nfpl* chops

babiole [babjɔl] *nf* (*bibelot*) trinket; (*vétille*) trifle

bâbord [babɔR] *nm*: **à ~** to port, on the port side

baby-foot [babifut] *nm* table football

baby-sitting [babisitiŋ] *nm*: **faire du ~~** to baby-sit

bac [bak] *abr m* = **baccalauréat** ♦ *nm* (*récipient*) tub

baccalauréat [bakalɔRea] *nm* high school diploma

bâche [baʃ] *nf* tarpaulin

bachelier, -ière [baʃəlje, jɛR] *nm/f* holder of the baccalauréat

bâcler [bakle] *vt* to botch (up)

badaud, e [bado, od] *nm/f* idle onlooker, stroller

badigeonner [badiʒɔne] *vt* (*barbouiller*) to daub

badiner [badine] *vi*: ~ **avec qch** to treat sth lightly

baffe [baf] (*fam*) *nf* slap, clout

baffle [bafl] *nm* speaker

bafouer [bafwe] *vt* to deride, ridicule

bafouiller [bafuje] *vi, vt* to stammer

bâfrer [bafRe] (*fam*) *vi* to guzzle

bagages [bagaʒ] *nmpl* luggage *sg*; ~ **à main** hand-luggage

bagarre [bagaR] *nf* fight, brawl; **bagarrer: se bagarrer** *vi* to have a fight *ou* scuffle, fight

bagatelle [bagatɛl] *nf* trifle

bagne [baɲ] *nm* penal colony

bagnole [baɲɔl] (*fam*) *nf* car

bagout [bagu] *nm*: **avoir du ~** to have the gift of the gab

bague [bag] *nf* ring; ~ **de fiançailles** engagement ring

baguette [bagɛt] *nf* stick; (*cuisine chinoise*) chopstick; (*de chef d'orchestre*) baton; (*pain*) stick of (French) bread; ~ **magique** magic wand

baie [bɛ] *nf* (*GÉO*) bay; (*fruit*) berry; ~ (**vitrée**) picture window

baignade [beɲad] *nf* bathing; "~ **interdite**" "no bathing"

baigner [beɲe] *vt* (*bébé*) to bath; **se ~** *vi* to have a swim, go swimming *ou* bathing; **baignoire** *nf* bath(tub)

bail [baj, bo] (*pl* **baux**) *nm* lease

bâillement [bajmɑ̃] *nm* yawn

bâiller [baje] *vi* to yawn; (*être ouvert*) to gape; **bâillonner** *vt* to gag

bain [bɛ̃] *nm* bath; **prendre un ~** to have a bath; **se mettre dans le ~** (*fig*) to get into it *ou* things; ~ **de soleil: prendre un ~ de soleil** to sunbathe; **~s de mer** sea bathing *sg*; **bain-marie** *nm*: **faire chauffer au bain-marie** (*boîte etc*) to immerse in boiling water

baiser [beze] *nm* kiss ♦ *vt* (*main, front*) to kiss; (*fam*) to screw (!)

baisse [bes] *nf* fall, drop; **être en ~** to be falling, be declining

baisser [bese] *vt* to lower; (*radio, chauffage*) to turn down ♦ *vi* to fall, drop, go down; (*vue, santé*) to fail, dwindle; **se ~** *vi* to bend down

bal [bal] *nm* dance; (*grande soirée*) ball; ~ **costumé** fancy-dress ball

balade [balad] (*fam*) *nf* (*à pied*) walk, stroll; (*en voiture*) drive; **balader** (*fam*): **se balader** *vi* to go for a walk *ou* stroll; to go for a drive; **baladeur** *nm* personal stereo, Walkman ®

balafre [balafR] *nf* (*cicatrice*) scar

balai [balɛ] *nm* broom, brush; **balai-brosse** *nm* (long-handled) scrubbing brush

balance [balɑ̃s] *nf* scales *pl*; (*signe*): **la B~** Libra

balancer [balɑ̃se] *vt* to swing; (*fam: lancer*) to fling, chuck; (*: jeter*) to chuck out; **se ~** *vi* to swing, rock; **se ~ de** (*fam*) not to care about; **balançoire** *nf* swing; (*sur pivot*) seesaw

balayer [baleje] *vt* (*feuilles etc*) to sweep up, brush up; (*pièce*) to sweep; (*objections*) to sweep aside; (*suj: radar*) to scan; **balayeur, -euse** *nm/f* roadsweeper

balbutier [balbysje] *vi, vt* to stammer

balcon [balkɔ̃] *nm* balcony; (*THÉÂTRE*) dress circle

baleine [balɛn] *nf* whale

balise [baliz] *nf* (*NAVIG*) beacon; (*marker*) buoy; (*AVIAT*) runway light, beacon; (*AUTO, SKI*) sign, marker; **baliser** *vt* to mark out (with lights etc)

balivernes [balivɛRn] *nfpl* nonsense *sg*

ballant, e [balɑ̃, ɑ̃t] *adj* dangling

balle [bal] *nf* (*de fusil*) bullet; (*de sport*) ball; (*fam: franc*) franc

ballerine [bal(ə)Rin] *nf* (*danseuse*) ballet dancer; (*chaussure*) ballet shoe

ballet [balɛ] *nm* ballet

ballon [balɔ̃] *nm* (*de sport*) ball; (*jouet, AVIAT*) balloon; ~ **de football** football

ballot [balo] *nm* bundle; (*péj*) nitwit

ballottage [balɔtaʒ] *nm* (*POL*) second ballot

ballotter [balɔte] *vt*: **être ballotté** to be thrown about

balnéaire [balneɛR] *adj* seaside *cpd*; **station ~** seaside resort

balourd, e [baluR, uRd] *adj* clumsy

balustrade [balystRad] *nf* railings *pl*, handrail

bambin [bãbɛ̃] nm little child

bambou [bãbu] nm bamboo

ban [bã] nm: **mettre au ~ de** to outlaw from; **~s** nmpl (de mariage) banns

banal, e [banal] adj banal, commonplace; (péj) trite; **banalité** nf banality

banane [banan] nf banana; (sac) waist-bag, bum-bag

banc [bã] nm seat, bench; (de poissons) shoal; **~ d'essai** (fig) testing ground

bancaire [bãkɛʀ] adj banking; (chèque, carte) bank cpd

bancal, e [bãkal] adj wobbly

bandage [bãdaʒ] nm bandage

bande [bãd] nf (de tissu etc) strip; (motif) stripe; (magnétique etc) tape; (groupe) band; (: péj) bunch; **faire ~ à part** to keep to o.s.; **~ dessinée** comic strip; **~ sonore** sound track

bandeau, x [bãdo] nm headband; (sur les yeux) blindfold

bander [bãde] vt (blessure) to bandage; **~ les yeux à qn** to blindfold sb

banderole [bãdʀɔl] nf banner, streamer

bandit [bãdi] nm bandit; **banditisme** nm violent crime, armed robberies pl

bandoulière [bãduljɛʀ] nf: **en ~** (slung ou worn) across the shoulder

banlieue [bãljø] nf suburbs pl; **lignes/ quartiers de ~** suburban lines/areas; **trains de ~** commuter trains

banlieusard, e [bãljøzaʀ, -aʀd(ə)] nm/f (suburban) commuter

bannière [banjɛʀ] nf banner

bannir [baniʀ] vt to banish

banque [bãk] nf bank; (activités) banking; **~ d'affaires** merchant bank; **banqueroute** nf bankruptcy

banquet [bãkɛ] nm dinner; (d'apparat) banquet

banquette [bãkɛt] nf seat

banquier [bãkje] nm banker

banquise [bãkiz] nf ice field

baptême [batɛm] nm christening; baptism; **~ de l'air** first flight

baptiser [batize] vt to baptize, christen

baquet [bakɛ] nm tub, bucket

bar [baʀ] nm bar

baraque [baʀak] nf shed; (fam) house; **baraqué, e** (fam) adj well-built, hefty; **baraquements** nmpl (provisoires) huts

baratin [baʀatɛ̃] (fam) nm smooth talk, patter; **baratiner** vt to chat up

barbare [baʀbaʀ] adj barbaric; **barbarie** nf barbarity

barbe [baʀb] nf beard; **la ~!** (fam) damn it!; **quelle ~!** (fam) what a drag ou bore!; **à la ~ de qn** under sb's nose; **~ à papa** candy-floss (BRIT), cotton candy (US)

barbelé [baʀbəle] adj, nm: (fil de fer) **~** barbed wire no pl

barber [baʀbe] (fam) vt to bore stiff

barbiturique [baʀbityʀik] nm barbiturate

barboter [baʀbɔte] vi (enfant) to paddle

barbouiller [baʀbuje] vt to daub; **avoir l'estomac barbouillé** to feel queasy

barbu, e [baʀby] adj bearded

barda [baʀda] (fam) nm kit, gear

barder [baʀde] (fam) vi: **ça va ~** sparks will fly, things are going to get hot

barème [baʀɛm] nm (SCOL) scale; (table de référence) table

baril [baʀi(l)] nm barrel; (poudre) keg

bariolé, e [baʀjɔle] adj gaudily-coloured

baromètre [baʀɔmɛtʀ] nm barometer

baron, ne [baʀɔ̃] nm/f baron(ess)

baroque [baʀɔk] adj (ART) baroque; (fig) weird

barque [baʀk] nf small boat

barquette [baʀkɛt] nf (pour repas) tray; (pour fruits) punnet

barrage [baʀaʒ] nm dam; (sur route) roadblock, barricade

barre [baʀ] nf bar; (NAVIG) helm; (écrite) line, stroke

barreau, x [baʀo] nm bar; (JUR): **le ~ the** Bar

barrer [baʀe] vt (route etc) to block; (mot) to cross out; (chèque) to cross (BRIT); (NAVIG) to steer; **se ~** (fam) vi to clear off

barrette [baʀɛt] nf (pour cheveux) (hair) slide (BRIT) ou clip (US)

barricader [baʀikade] : **se ~** vi to barricade o.s.

barrière [baʀjɛʀ] nf fence; (obstacle) barrier; (porte) gate

barrique [baʀik] nf barrel, cask

bar-tabac [baʀtaba] nm bar (which sells tobacco and stamps)

bas, basse [bɑ, bɑs] adj low ♦ nm bottom, lower part; (vêtement) stocking ♦ adv low; (parler) softly; **au ~ mot** at the lowest estimate; **en ~** down below; (d'une liste, d'un mur etc) at/to the bottom; (dans une maison) downstairs; **en ~ de** at the bottom of; **un enfant en ~ âge** a young child; **à ~ ...!** down with ...!; **~ morceaux** nmpl (viande) cheap cuts

basané, e [bazane] adj tanned

bas-côté [bakote] nm (de route) verge (BRIT), shoulder (US)

bascule [baskyl] nf: (jeu de) **~** seesaw; (balance à) **~** scales pl; **fauteuil à ~** rocking chair

basculer [baskyle] vi to fall over, topple (over); (benne) to tip up ♦ vt (contenu) to tip out; (benne) to tip up

base [bɑz] nf base; (POL) rank and file; (fondement, principe) basis; **de ~** basic; **à ~ de café** etc coffee etc -based; **~ de données**

database; **baser** vt to base; **se baser sur** vt (preuves) to base one's argument on

bas-fond [bafɔ̃] nm (NAVIG) shallow; **~-s** nmpl (fig) dregs

basilic [bazilik] nm (CULIN) basil

basket [baskɛt] nm trainer (BRIT), sneaker (US); (aussi: **~-ball**) basketball

basque [bask] adj, nm/f Basque

basse [bas] adj voir **bas** ♦ nf (MUS) bass; **basse-cour** nf farmyard

bassin [basɛ̃] nm (pièce d'eau) pond, pool; (de fontaine, GÉO) basin; (ANAT) pelvis; (portuaire) dock

bassine [basin] nf (ustensile) basin; (contenu) bowl(ful)

basson [basɔ̃] nm bassoon

bas-ventre [bavɑ̃tʀ] nm (lower part of the) stomach

bat [ba] vb voir **battre**

bataille [bataj] nf (MIL) battle; (rixe) fight; **batailler** vi to fight

bâtard, e [batar, aʀd] nm/f illegitimate child, bastard (péj)

bateau, x [bato] nm boat, ship; **bateau-mouche** nm passenger pleasure boat (on the Seine)

bâti, e [bati] adj: **bien ~** well-built

batifoler [batifɔle] vi to frolic about

bâtiment [batimɑ̃] nm building; (NAVIG) ship, vessel; (industrie) building trade

bâtir [batiʀ] vt to build

bâtisse [batis] nf building

bâton [batɔ̃] nm stick; **à ~s rompus** informally

bats [ba] vb voir **battre**

battage [bataʒ] nm (publicité) (hard) plugging

battant [batɑ̃, ɑ̃t] nm: **porte à double ~** double door

battement [batmɑ̃] nm (de cœur) beat; (intervalle) interval (between classes, trains); **10 minutes de ~** 10 minutes to spare

batterie [batʀi] nf (MIL, ÉLEC) battery; (MUS) drums pl, drum kit; **~ de cuisine** pots and pans pl, kitchen utensils pl

batteur [batœʀ] nm (MUS) drummer; (appareil) whisk

battre [batʀ] vt to beat; (blé) to thresh; (passer au peigne fin) to scour; (cartes) to shuffle ♦ vi (cœur) to beat; (volets etc) to bang, rattle; **se ~** vi to fight; **~ la mesure** to beat time; **~ son plein** to be at its height, be going full swing; **~ des mains** to clap one's hands

battue [baty] nf (chasse) beat; (policière etc) search, hunt

baume [bom] nm balm

baux [bo] nmpl de **bail**

bavard, e [bavar, aʀd] adj (very) talkative; gossipy; **bavarder** vi to chatter; (commérer)

to gossip; (divulguer un secret) to blab

bave [bav] nf dribble; (de chien etc) slobber; (d'escargot) slime; **baver** vi to dribble; (chien) to slobber; **en baver** (fam) to have a hard time (of it); **baveux, -euse** adj (omelette) runny; **bavoir** nm bib

bavure [bavyʀ] nf smudge; (fig) hitch; (policière etc) blunder

bayer [baje] vi: **~ aux corneilles** to stand gaping

bazar [bazaʀ] nm general store; (fam) jumble; **bazarder** (fam) vt to chuck out

BCBG sigle adj (= bon chic bon genre) preppy, smart and trendy

BD sigle f = **bande dessinée**

bd abr = **boulevard**

béant, e [beɑ̃, ɑ̃t] adj gaping

béat, e [bea, at] adj: **~ d'admiration** struck dumb with admiration; **béatitude** nf bliss

beau (bel), belle [bo, bɛl] (mpl **beaux**) adj beautiful, lovely; (homme) handsome; (femme) beautiful ♦ adv: **il fait beau** the weather's fine; **un ~jour** one (fine) day; **de plus belle** more than ever, even more; **on a ~essayer** however hard we try; **bel et bien** well and truly

┌─────────────────┐
│ **MOT-CLÉ**   │
└─────────────────┘

beaucoup [boku] adv 1 a lot; **il boit beaucoup** he drinks a lot; **il ne boit pas beaucoup** he doesn't drink much ou a lot

2 (suivi de plus, trop etc) much, a lot, far; **il est beaucoup plus grand** he is much ou a lot ou far taller

3: **beaucoup de** (nombre) many, a lot of; (quantité) a lot of; **beaucoup d'étudiants/de touristes** a lot of ou many students/tourists; **beaucoup de courage** a lot of courage; **il n'a pas beaucoup d'argent** he hasn't got much ou at lot of money

4: **de beaucoup** by far

beau...: beau-fils nm son-in-law; (remariage) stepson; **beau-frère** nm brother-in-law; **beau-père** nm father-in-law; (remariage) stepfather

beauté [bote] nf beauty; **de toute ~** beautiful; **finir qch en ~** to complete sth brilliantly

beaux-arts [bozaʀ] nmpl fine arts

beaux-parents [bopaʀɑ̃] nmpl wife's/ husband's family, in-laws

bébé [bebe] nm baby

bec [bɛk] nm beak, bill; (de théière) spout; (de casserole) lip; (fam) mouth; **~ de gaz** (street) gaslamp; **~ verseur** pouring lip

bécane [bekan] (fam) nf bike

bec-de-lièvre [bɛkdəljɛvʀ] nm harelip

bêche [bɛʃ] nf spade; **bêcher** vt to dig

bécoter [bekɔte]: **se ~** vi to smooch

becqueter [bɛkte] (fam) vt to eat
bedaine [bədɛn] nf paunch
bedonnant, e [bədɔnɑ̃, ɑ̃t] adj potbellied
bée [be] adj: **bouche ~** gaping
beffroi [befʀwa] nm belfry
bégayer [begeje] vt, vi to stammer
bègue [bɛg] nm/f: **être ~** to have a stammer
beige [bɛʒ] adj beige
beignet [bɛɲɛ] nm fritter
bel [bɛl] adj voir **beau**
bêler [bele] vi to bleat
belette [bəlɛt] nf weasel
belge [bɛlʒ] adj Belgian ♦ nm/f: **B~** Belgian
Belgique [bɛlʒik] nf: **la ~** Belgium
bélier [belje] nm ram; (signe): **le B~** Aries
belle [bɛl] adj voir **beau** ♦ nf (SPORT) decider;
  belle-fille nf daughter-in-law; (remariage)
  stepdaughter; **belle-mère** nf mother-in-law;
  stepmother; **belle-sœur** nf sister-in-law
belliqueux, -euse [belikø, øz] adj
  aggressive, warlike
belvédère [bɛlvedɛʀ] nm panoramic
  viewpoint (or small building there)
bémol [bemɔl] nm (MUS) flat
bénédiction [benediksjɔ̃] nf blessing
bénéfice [benefis] nm (COMM) profit;
  (avantage) benefit; **bénéficier: bénéficier de**
  vt to enjoy; (situation) to benefit from ou from;
  bénéfique adj beneficial
bénévole [benevɔl] adj voluntary, unpaid
bénin, -igne [benɛ̃, iɲ] adj minor, mild;
  (tumeur) benign
bénir [beniʀ] vt to bless; **bénit, e** adj
  consecrated; **eau bénite** holy water
benjamin, e [bɛ̃ʒamɛ̃, in] nm/f youngest
  child
benne [bɛn] nf skip; (de téléphérique) (cable)
  car; **~ basculante** tipper (BRIT), dump truck
  (US)
BEP sigle m (= brevet d'études professionnelles)
  technical school certificate
béquille [bekij] nf crutch; (de bicyclette)
  stand
berceau, x [bɛʀso] nm cradle, crib
bercer [bɛʀse] vt to rock, cradle; (suj: musique
  etc) to lull; **~ qn de** (promesses etc) to delude
  sb with; **berceuse** nf lullaby
béret (basque) [beʀɛ (bask(ə))] nm beret
berge [bɛʀʒ] nf bank
berger, -ère [bɛʀʒe, ɛʀ] nm/f shep-
  herd(-ess); **~ allemand** alsatian (BRIT), German
  shepherd
berlingot [bɛʀlɛ̃go] nm (bonbon) boiled
  sweet, humbug (BRIT)
berlue [bɛʀly] nf: **j'ai la ~** I must be seeing
  things
berner [bɛʀne] vt to fool
besogne [bəzɔɲ] nf work no pl, job
besoin [bəzwɛ̃] nm need; **avoir ~ de qch/faire**

qch to need sth/to do sth; **au ~** if need be; **le**
  ~ (pauvreté) need, want; **être dans le ~** to be
  in need ou want; **faire ses ~s** to relieve o.s.
bestiaux [bɛstjo] nmpl cattle
bestiole [bɛstjɔl] nf (tiny) creature
bétail [betaj] nm livestock, cattle pl
bête [bɛt] nf animal; (bestiole) insect, creature
  ♦ adj stupid, silly; **il cherche la petite ~** he's
  being pernickety ou overfussy; **~ noire** pet
  hate
bêtement [bɛtmɑ̃] adv stupidly
bêtise [betiz] nf stupidity; (action) stupid
  thing (to say ou do)
béton [betɔ̃] nm concrete; **(en) ~** (alibi,
  argument) cast iron; **~ armé** reinforced
  concrete; **bétonnière** nf cement mixer
betterave [betʀav] nf beetroot (BRIT), beet
  (US); **~ sucrière** sugar beet
beugler [bøgle] vi to low; (radio etc) to blare
  ♦ vt (chanson) to bawl out
Beur [bœʀ] nm/f person of North African origin
  living in France
beurre [bœʀ] nm butter; **beurrer** vt to
  butter; **beurrier** nm butter dish
beuverie [bøvʀi] nf drinking session
bévue [bevy] nf blunder
Beyrouth [beʀut] n Beirut
bi... [bi] préfixe bi..., two-
biais [bjɛ] nm (moyen) device, expedient;
  (aspect) angle; **en ~, de ~** (obliquement) at an
  angle; **par le ~ de** by means of; **biaiser** vi
  (fig) to sidestep the issue
bibelot [biblo] nm trinket, curio
biberon [bibʀɔ̃] nm (feeding) bottle; **nourrir**
  au ~ to bottle-feed
bible [bibl] nf bible
biblio... [bibl] préfixe: **bibliobus** nm mobile
  library van; **bibliographie** nf bibliography;
  bibliothécaire nm/f librarian; **bibliothèque**
  nf library; (meuble) bookcase
bic ® [bik] nm Biro ®
bicarbonate [bikaʀbɔnat] nm: **~ (de soude)**
  bicarbonate of soda
biceps [bisɛps] nm biceps
biche [biʃ] nf doe
bichonner [biʃɔne] vt to pamper
bicolore [bikɔlɔʀ] adj two-coloured
bicoque [bikɔk] (péj) nf shack
bicyclette [bisiklɛt] nf bicycle
bide [bid] (fam) nm (ventre) belly; (THÉÂTRE)
  flop
bidet [bidɛ] nm bidet
bidon [bidɔ̃] nm can ♦ adj inv (fam) phoney
bidonville [bidɔ̃vil] nm shanty town
bidule [bidyl] (fam) nm thingumajig

┌─────────────┐
│ *MOT-CLÉ* │
└─────────────┘

bien [bjɛ̃] nm 1 (avantage, profit): **faire du**
  bien à qn to do sb good; **dire du bien de** to

speak well of; **c'est pour son bien** it's for his own good
2 (*possession, patrimoine*) possession, property; **son bien le plus précieux** his most treasured possession; **avoir du bien** to have property; **biens (de consommation** *etc***)** (consumer *etc*) goods
3 (*moral*): **le bien** good; **distinguer le bien du mal** to tell good from evil
♦ *adv* **1** (*de façon satisfaisante*) well; **elle travaille/mange bien** she works/eats well; **croyant bien faire, je/il ...** thinking I/he was doing the right thing, I/he ...; **c'est bien fait!** it serves him (*ou* her *etc*) right!
2 (*valeur intensive*) quite; **bien jeune** quite young; **bien assez** quite enough; **bien mieux** (very) much better; **j'espère bien y aller** I do hope to go; **je veux bien le faire** (*concession*) I'm quite willing to do it; **il faut bien le faire** it has to be done
3: **bien du temps/des gens** quite a time/a number of people
♦ *adj inv* **1** (*en bonne forme, à l'aise*): **je me sens bien** I feel fine; **je ne me sens pas bien** I don't feel well; **on est bien dans ce fauteuil** this chair is very comfortable
2 (*joli, beau*) good-looking; **tu es bien dans cette robe** you look good in that dress
3 (*satisfaisant*) good; **elle est bien, cette maison/secrétaire** it's a good house/she's a good secretary
4 (*moralement*) right; (: *personne*) good, nice; (*respectable*) respectable; **ce n'est pas bien de ...** it's not right to ...; **elle est bien, cette femme** she's a nice woman, she's a good sort; **des gens biens** respectable people
5 (*en bons termes*): **être bien avec qn** to be on good terms with sb
♦ *préfixe*: **bien-aimé** *adj, nm/f* beloved; **bien-être** *nm* well-being; **bienfaisance** *nf* charity; **bienfaisant, e** *adj* (*chose*) beneficial; **bienfait** *nm* act of generosity, benefaction; (*de la science etc*) benefit; **bienfaiteur, -trice** *nm/f* benefactor/ benefactress; **bien-fondé** *nm* soundness; **bien-fonds** *nm* property; **bienheureux, -euse** *adj* happy; (*REL*) blessed, blest; **bien que** *conj* (al)though; **bien sûr** *adv* certainly

bienséant, e [bjɛ̃seɑ̃, ɑ̃t] *adj* seemly
bientôt [bjɛ̃to] *adv* soon; **à ~ see** you soon
bienveillant, e [bjɛ̃vejɑ̃, ɑ̃t] *adj* kindly
bienvenu, e [bjɛ̃vny] *adj* welcome; **bienvenue** *nf*: **souhaiter la bienvenue à** to welcome; **bienvenue à** welcome to
bière [bjɛʀ] *nf* (*boisson*) beer; (*cercueil*) bier; **~ (à la) pression** draught beer; **~ blonde** lager; **~ brune** brown ale
biffer [bife] *vt* to cross out

bifteck [biftɛk] *nm* steak
bifurquer [bifyʀke] *vi* (*route*) to fork; (*véhicule*) to turn off
bigarré, e [bigaʀe] *adj* multicoloured; (*disparate*) motley
bigorneau, x [bigɔʀno] *nm* winkle
bigot, e [bigo, ɔt] (*péj*) *adj* bigoted
bigoudi [bigudi] *nm* curler
bijou, x [biʒu] *nm* jewel; **bijouterie** *nf* jeweller's (shop); **bijoutier, -ière** *nm/f* jeweller
bikini [bikini] *nm* bikini
bilan [bilɑ̃] *nm* (*fig*) (net) outcome; (: *de victimes*) toll; (*COMM*) balance sheet(s); **un ~ de santé** a (medical) checkup; **faire le ~ de** to assess, review; **déposer son ~** to file a bankruptcy statement
bile [bil] *nf* bile; **se faire de la ~** (*fam*) to worry o.s. sick
bilieux, -euse [biljø, øz] *adj* bilious; (*fig*: *colérique*) testy
bilingue [bilɛ̃g] *adj* bilingual
billard [bijaʀ] *nm* (*jeu*) billiards *sg*; (*table*) billiard table; **~ américain** pool
bille [bij] *nf* (*gén*) ball; (*du jeu de ~s*) marble
billet [bijɛ] *nm* (*aussi*: **~ de banque**) (bank)note; (*de cinéma, de bus etc*) ticket; (*courte lettre*) note; **~ Bige** cheap rail ticket for under-26s; **billetterie** *nf* ticket office; (*distributeur*) ticket machine; (*BANQUE*) cash dispenser
billion [biljɔ̃] *nm* billion (*BRIT*), trillion (*US*)
billot [bijo] *nm* block
bimensuel, le [bimɑ̃sɥɛl] *adj* bimonthly
binette [binɛt] *nf* hoe
bio... [bjɔ] *préfixe* bio...; **biochimie** *nf* biochemistry; **biodiversité** *nf* biodiversity; **bioéthique** *nf* bioethics *sg*; **biographie** *nf* biography; **biologie** *nf* biology; **biologique** *adj* biological; (*produits, aliments*) organic; **biologiste** *nm/f* biologist
Birmanie [biʀmani] *nf* Burma
bis [bis] *adv*: **12 ~ 12a** *ou* A ♦ *excl, nm* encore
bisannuel, le [bizanɥɛl] *adj* biennial
biscornu, e [biskɔʀny] *adj* twisted
biscotte [biskɔt] *nf* toasted bread (*sold in packets*)
biscuit [biskɥi] *nm* biscuit; **~ de savoie** sponge cake
bise [biz] *nf* (*fam*: *baiser*) kiss; (*vent*) North wind; **grosses ~s (de)** (*sur lettre*) love and kisses (from)
bisou [bizu] (*fam*) *nm* kiss
bissextile [bisɛkstil] *adj*: **année ~** leap year
bistouri [bisturi] *nm* lancet
bistro(t) [bistro] *nm* bistro, café
bitume [bitym] *nm* asphalt
bizarre [bizaʀ] *adj* strange, odd
blafard, e [blafaʀ, aʀd] *adj* wan

blague [blag] nf (propos) joke; (farce) trick;
sans ~! no kidding!; **blaguer** vi to joke

blaireau, x [blɛʀo] nm (ZOOL) badger;
(brosse) shaving brush

blairer [blɛʀe] (fam) vt: **je ne peux pas le ~** I
can't bear ou stand him

blâme [blɑm] nm blame; (sanction)
reprimand; **blâmer** vt to blame

blanc, blanche [blɑ̃, blɑ̃ʃ] adj white; (non
imprimé) blank ♦ nm/f white, white
man(-woman) ♦ nm (couleur) white; (espace
non écrit) blank; (aussi: ~ d'œuf) (egg-
)white; (aussi: ~ de poulet) breast, white
meat; (aussi: vin ~) white wine; ~ cassé off-
white; **chèque en ~** blank cheque; **à ~**
(chauffer) white-hot; (tirer, charger) with
blanks; **blanc-bec** nm greenhorn; **blanche**
nf (MUS) minim (BRIT), half-note (US);
blancheur nf whiteness

blanchir [blɑ̃ʃiʀ] vt (gén) to whiten; (linge)
to launder; (CULIN) to blanch; (fig: disculper)
to clear ♦ vi to grow white; (cheveux) to go
white; **blanchisserie** nf laundry

blason [blɑzɔ̃] nm coat of arms

blasphème [blasfɛm] nm blasphemy

blazer [blazɛʀ] nm blazer

blé [ble] nm wheat; ~ **noir** buckwheat

bled [blɛd] (péj) nm hole

blême [blɛm] adj pale

blessant, e [blesɑ̃, ɑ̃t] adj (offensant) hurtful

blessé, e [blese] adj injured ♦ nm/f injured
person, casualty

blesser [blese] vt to injure; (délibérément: MIL
etc) to wound; (offenser) to hurt; **se ~** to
injure o.s.; **se ~ au pied** etc to injure one's
foot etc; **blessure** nf (accidentelle) injury;
(intentionnelle) wound

bleu, e [blø] adj bleu; blue; (bifteck) very rare
♦ nm (couleur) blue; (contusion) bruise;
(vêtement: aussi: ~s) overalls pl; ~ **marine**
navy blue; **bleuet** nm cornflower; **bleuté, e**
adj blue-shaded

blinder [blɛ̃de] vt to armour; (fig) to harden

bloc [blɔk] nm (de pierre etc) block; (de papier
à lettres) pad; (ensemble) group, block; **serré
à ~** tightened right down; **en ~** as a whole;
~ **opératoire** operating ou theatre block;
~ **sanitaire** toilet block; **blocage** nm (des
prix) freezing; (PSYCH) hang-up; **bloc-notes**
nm note pad

blocus [blɔkys] nm blockade

blond, e [blɔ̃, blɔ̃d] adj fair, blond; (sable,
blés) golden; ~ **cendré** ash blond; **blonde** nf
(femme) blonde; (bière) lager; (cigarette)
Virginia cigarette

bloquer [blɔke] vt (passage) to block; (pièce
mobile) to jam; (crédits, compte) to freeze; **se
~** to jam; (PSYCH) to have a mental block

blottir [blɔtiʀ] vi: **se ~** vi to huddle up

blouse [bluz] nf overall

blouson [bluzɔ̃] nm blouson jacket; ~ **noir**
(fig) ≈ rocker

blue-jean [bludʒin] nm (pair of) jeans

bluff [blœf] nm bluff; **bluffer** vi to bluff

bobard [bɔbaʀ] (fam) nm tall story

bobine [bɔbin] nf reel; (ÉLEC) coil

bocal, -aux [bɔkal, o] nm jar

bock [bɔk] nm glass of beer

body [bɔdi] nm body(suit); (SPORT) leotard

bœuf [bœf] nm ox; (CULIN) beef

bof! [bɔf] (fam) excl don't care!; (pas terrible)
nothing special

bohème [bɔɛm] adj happy-go-lucky,
unconventional; **bohémien, ne** nm/f gipsy

boire [bwaʀ] vt to drink; (s'imprégner de) to
soak up; ~ **un coup** (fam) to have a drink

bois [bwa] nm wood; **de ~, en ~** wooden;
boisé, e adj woody, wooded

boisson [bwasɔ̃] nf drink

boîte [bwat] nf box; (fam: entreprise) firm;
aliments en ~ canned ou tinned (BRIT) foods;
~ **aux lettres** letter box; ~ **d'allumettes** box of
matches; (vide) matchbox; ~ **de conserve**
can ou tin (BRIT) (of food); ~ **de nuit** night
club; ~ **de vitesses** gear box; ~ **postale** PO
Box

boiter [bwate] vi to limp; (fig: raisonnement)
to be shaky

boîtier [bwatje] nm case

boive etc [bwav] vb voir **boire**

bol [bɔl] nm bowl; ~ **d'air** a breath of fresh
air; **j'en ai ras le ~** (fam) I'm fed up with this;
avoir du ~ (fam) to be lucky

bolide [bɔlid] nm racing car; **comme un ~** at
top speed, like a rocket

bombardement [bɔ̃baʀdəmɑ̃] nm bombing

bombarder [bɔ̃baʀde] vt to bomb; ~ **qn de**
(cailloux, lettres) to bombard sb with

bombe [bɔ̃b] nf bomb; (atomiseur) (aerosol)
spray; **bombé, e** adj (forme) rounded;
bomber vt: **bomber le torse** to swell out
one's chest

MOT-CLÉ

---

bon, bonne [bɔ̃, bɔn] adj **1** (agréable,
satisfaisant) good; **un bon repas/restaurant** a
good meal/restaurant; **être bon en maths** to
be good at maths

2 (charitable): **être bon (envers)** to be good
(to)

3 (correct) right; **le bon numéro/moment** the
right number/moment

4 (souhaits): **bon anniversaire** happy
birthday; **bon voyage** have a good trip;
bonne chance good luck; **bonne année** happy
New Year; **bonne nuit** good night

5 (approprié, apte): **bon à/pour** fit to/for

6: bon enfant adj inv accommodating, easy-

going; **bonne femme** (*péj*) woman; **de bonne heure** early; **bon marché** adj inv cheap ♦ adv cheap; **bon mot** witticism; **bon sens** common sense; **bon vivant** jovial chap; **bonnes œuvres** charitable works, charities
♦ nm **1** (*billet*) voucher; (*aussi:* **bon cadeau**) gift voucher; **bon d'essence** petrol coupon; **bon du Trésor** Treasury bond
2: **avoir du bon** to have its good points; **pour de bon** for good
♦ adv: **il fait bon** it's *ou* the weather is fine; **sentir bon** to smell good; **tenir bon** to stand firm
♦ excl good!; **ah bon?** really?; *voir aussi* **bonne**

bonbon [bɔ̃bɔ̃] nm (boiled) sweet
bonbonne [bɔ̃bɔn] nf demijohn
bond [bɔ̃] nm leap; **faire un ~** to leap in the air
bondé, e [bɔ̃de] adj packed (full)
bondir [bɔ̃diʀ] vi to leap
bonheur [bɔnœʀ] nm happiness; **porter ~** (**à qn**) to bring (sb) luck; **au petit ~** haphazardly; **par ~** fortunately
bonhomie [bɔnɔmi] nf goodnaturedness
bonhomme [bɔnɔm] (*pl* **bonshommes**) nm fellow; **~ de neige** snowman
bonifier [bɔnifje] vt to improve
boniment [bɔnimɑ̃] nm patter no pl
bonjour [bɔ̃ʒuʀ] excl, nm hello; (*selon l'heure*) good morning/afternoon; **c'est simple comme ~!** it's easy as pie!
bonne [bɔn] adj *voir* **bon** ♦ nf (*domestique*) maid; **bonnement** adv: **tout bonnement** quite simply
bonnet [bɔnɛ] nm hat; (*de soutien-gorge*) cup; **~ de bain** bathing cap
bonshommes [bɔ̃zɔm] nmpl de **bonhomme**
bonsoir [bɔ̃swaʀ] excl good evening
bonté [bɔ̃te] nf kindness no pl
bonus [bɔnys] nm no-claims bonus
bord [bɔʀ] nm (*de table, verre, falaise*) edge; (*de rivière, lac*) bank; (*de route*) side; (**monter**) **à ~** (to go) on board; **jeter par-dessus ~** to throw overboard; **le commandant de/les hommes du ~** the ship's master/crew; **au ~ de la mer** at the seaside; **être au ~ des larmes** to be on the verge of tears
bordeaux [bɔʀdo] nm Bordeaux (wine) ♦ adj inv maroon
bordel [bɔʀdɛl] nm brothel; (*fam!*) bloody mess (!)
bordelais, e [bɔʀdəlɛ, ɛz] adj of *ou* from Bordeaux
border [bɔʀde] vt (*être le long de*) to line; (*qn dans son lit*) to tuck up; (*garnir*): **~ qch de** to edge sth with
bordereau, x [bɔʀdəʀo] nm (*formulaire*) slip
bordure [bɔʀdyʀ] nf border; **en ~ de** on the edge of

borgne [bɔʀɲ] adj one-eyed
borne [bɔʀn] nf boundary stone; (*aussi:* **~ kilométrique**) kilometre-marker; ≈ milestone; **~s** nfpl (*fig*) limits; **dépasser les ~s** to go too far
borné, e [bɔʀne] adj (*personne*) narrow-minded
borner [bɔʀne] vt: **se ~ à faire** (*se contenter de*) to content o.s. with doing; (*se limiter à*) to limit o.s. to doing
bosquet [bɔskɛ] nm grove
bosse [bɔs] nf (*de terrain etc*) bump; (*enflure*) lump; (*du bossu, du chameau*) hump; **avoir la ~ des maths** etc (*fam*) to have a gift for maths etc; **il a roulé sa ~** (*fam*) he's been around
bosser [bɔse] (*fam*) vi (*travailler*) to work; (*travailler dur*) to slave (away)
bossu, e [bɔsy] nm/f hunchback
botanique [bɔtanik] nf botany ♦ adj botanic(al)
botte [bɔt] nf (*soulier*) (high) boot; (*gerbe*): **~ de paille** bundle of straw; **~ de radis** bunch of radishes; **~s de caoutchouc** wellington boots; **botter** vt: **ça me botte** (*fam*) I fancy that
bottin [bɔtɛ̃] nm directory
bottine [bɔtin] nf ankle boot
bouc [buk] nm goat; (*barbe*) goatee; **~ émissaire** scapegoat
boucan [bukɑ̃] (*fam*) nm din, racket
bouche [buʃ] nf mouth; **rester ~ bée** to stand open-mouthed; **le ~ à ~** the kiss of life; **~ d'égout** manhole; **~ d'incendie** fire hydrant; **~ de métro** métro entrance
bouché, e [buʃe] adj (*temps, ciel*) overcast; **c'est ~** there's no future in it
bouchée [buʃe] nf mouthful; **~s à la reine** chicken vol-au-vents
boucher, ère [buʃe] nm/f butcher ♦ vt (*trou*) to fill up; (*obstruer*) to block (up); **se ~** vi (*tuyau etc*) to block up, get blocked up; **j'ai le nez bouché** my nose is blocked; **se ~ le nez** to hold one's nose; **boucherie** nf butcher's (shop); (*fig*) slaughter
bouche-trou [buʃtʀu] nm (*fig*) stop-gap
bouchon [buʃɔ̃] nm stopper; (*de tube*) top; (*en liège*) cork; (*fig: embouteillage*) holdup; (*PÊCHE*) float
boucle [bukl] nf (*forme, figure*) loop; (*objet*) buckle; **~ (de cheveux)** curl; **~ d'oreille** earring
bouclé, e [bukle] adj (*cheveux*) curly
boucler [bukle] vt (*fermer: ceinture etc*) to fasten; (*terminer*) to finish off; (*fam: enfermer*) to shut away; (*quartier*) to seal off ♦ vi to curl
bouclier [buklije] nm shield
bouddhiste [budist] nm/f Buddhist
bouder [bude] vi to sulk ♦ vt to stay away

from
boudin [budɛ̃] nm: **~ (noir)** black pudding;
~ blanc white pudding
boue [bu] nf mud
bouée [bwe] nf buoy; **~ (de sauvetage)**
lifebuoy
boueux, -euse [bwø, øz] adj muddy
bouffe [buf] (fam) nf grub (fam), food
bouffée [bufe] nf (de cigarette) puff; **une
~ d'air pur** a breath of fresh air
bouffer [bufe] (fam) vi to eat
bouffi, e [bufi] adj swollen
bougeoir [buʒwaR] nm candlestick
bougeotte [buʒɔt] nf: **avoir la ~** (fam) to
have the fidgets
bouger [buʒe] vi to move; (dent etc) to be
loose; (s'activer) to get moving ♦ vt to move;
les prix/les couleurs n'ont pas bougé prices/
colours haven't changed
bougie [buʒi] nf candle; (AUTO) spark(ing)
plug
bougon, ne [bugɔ̃, ɔn] adj grumpy
bougonner [bugɔne] vi, vt to grumble
bouillabaisse [bujabɛs] nf type of fish soup
bouillant, e [bujɑ̃, ɑ̃t] adj (qui bout) boiling;
(très chaud) boiling (hot)
bouillie [buji] nf (de bébé) cereal; **en ~** (fig)
crushed
bouillir [bujiR] vi, vt to boil; **~ d'impatience**
to seethe with impatience
bouilloire [bujwaR] nf kettle
bouillon [bujɔ̃] nm (CULIN) stock no pl;
bouillonner vi to bubble; (fig: idées) to
bubble up
bouillotte [bujɔt] nf hot-water bottle
boulanger, -ère [bulɑ̃ʒe, ɛR] nm/f baker;
boulangerie nf bakery; **boulangerie-
pâtisserie** nf baker's and confectioner's
(shop)
boule [bul] nf (gén) ball; **~s** nfpl (jeu) bowls;
se mettre en ~ (fig: fam) to fly off the handle,
to blow one's top; **jouer aux ~s** to play
bowls; **~ de neige** snowball
bouleau, x [bulo] nm (silver) birch
bouledogue [buldɔg] nm bulldog
boulet [bulɛ] nm (aussi: **~ de canon**)
cannonball
boulette [bulɛt] nf (de viande) meatball
boulevard [bulvaR] nm boulevard
bouleversant, e [bulvɛRsɑ̃, ɑ̃t] adj (scène,
récit) deeply moving
bouleversement [bulvɛRsəmɑ̃] nm
upheaval
bouleverser [bulvɛRse] vt (émouvoir) to
overwhelm; (causer du chagrin) to distress;
(pays, vie) to disrupt; (papiers, objets) to turn
upside down
boulon [bulɔ̃] nm bolt
boulot, te [bulo, ɔt] adj plump, tubby ♦ nm

(fam: travail) work
boum [bum] nm bang ♦ nf (fam) party
bouquet [bukɛ] nm (de fleurs) bunch (of
flowers), bouquet; (de persil etc) bunch; **c'est
le ~!** (fam) that takes the biscuit!
bouquin [bukɛ̃] (fam) nm book; **bouquiner**
(fam) vi to read; **bouquiniste** nm/f
bookseller
bourbeux, -euse [buRbø, øz] adj muddy
bourbier [buRbje] nm (quag)mire
bourde [buRd] (fam) nf (erreur) howler;
(gaffe) blunder
bourdon [buRdɔ̃] nm bumblebee;
bourdonner vi to buzz
bourg [buR] nm small market town
bourgeois, e [buRʒwa, waz] (péj) adj ≈
(upper) middle class; **bourgeoisie** nf ≈
upper middle classes pl
bourgeon [buRʒɔ̃] nm bud
Bourgogne [buRgɔɲ] nf: **la ~** Burgundy
♦ nm: **b~** burgundy (wine)
bourguignon, ne [buRgiɲɔ̃, ɔn] adj of ou
from Burgundy, Burgundian
bourlinguer [buRlɛ̃ge] (fam) vi to knock
about a lot, get around a lot
bourrade [buRad] nf shove, thump
bourrage [buRaʒ] nm: **~ de crâne**
brainwashing; (SCOL) cramming
bourrasque [buRask] nf squall
bourratif, -ive [buRatif, iv] (fam) adj filling,
stodgy (pej)
bourré, e [buRe] adj (fam: ivre) plastered,
tanked up (BRIT); (rempli): **~ de** crammed full
of
bourreau, x [buRo] nm executioner; (fig)
torturer; **~ de travail** workaholic
bourrelet [buRlɛ] nm fold ou roll (of flesh)
bourrer [buRe] vt (pipe) to fill; (poêle) to
pack; (valise) to cram (full)
bourrique [buRik] nf (âne) ass
bourru, e [buRy] adj surly, gruff
bourse [buRs] nf (subvention) grant; (porte-
monnaie) purse; **la B~** the Stock Exchange
boursier, -ière [buRsje, jɛR] nm/f (étudiant)
grant holder
boursoufler [buRsufle]: **se ~** vi to swell (up)
bous [bu] vb voir **bouillir**
bousculade [buskylad] nf (hâte) rush;
(cohue) crush; **bousculer** vt (heurter) to
knock into; (fig) to push, rush
bouse [buz] nf dung no pl
bousiller [buzije] (fam) vt (appareil) to
wreck
boussole [busɔl] nf compass
bout [bu] vb voir **bouillir** ♦ nm bit; (d'un bâton
etc) tip; (d'une ficelle, table, rue, période) end;
au ~ de at the end of, after; **pousser qn à ~** to
push sb to the limit; **venir à ~ de** to manage
to finish

boutade [butad] nf quip, sally
boute-en-train [butɑ̃trɛ̃] nm inv (fig) live wire
bouteille [butɛj] nf bottle; (de gaz butane) cylinder
boutique [butik] nf shop
bouton [butɔ̃] nm button; (sur la peau) spot; (BOT) bud; ~ **d'or** buttercup; **boutonner** vt to button up; **boutonnière** nf buttonhole; **bouton-pression** nm press stud
bouture [butyʀ] nf cutting
bovins [bɔvɛ̃] nmpl cattle pl
bowling [buliŋ] nm (tenpin) bowling; (salle) bowling alley
box [bɔks] nm (d'écurie) loose-box; (JUR): ~ **des accusés** dock
boxe [bɔks] nf boxing; **boxeur** nm boxer
boyaux [bwajo] nmpl (viscères) entrails, guts
BP abr = **boîte postale**
bracelet [bʀaslɛ] nm bracelet
braconnier [bʀakɔnje] nm poacher
brader [bʀade] vt to sell off; **braderie** nf cut-price shop/stall
braguette [bʀagɛt] nf fly ou flies pl (BRIT), zipper (US)
brailler [bʀaje] vi to bawl, yell
braire [bʀɛʀ] vi to bray
braise [bʀɛz] nf embers pl
brancard [bʀɑ̃kaʀ] nm (civière) stretcher; **brancardier** nm stretcher-bearer
branchages [bʀɑ̃ʃaʒ] nmpl boughs
branche [bʀɑ̃ʃ] nf branch
branché, e [bʀɑ̃ʃe] (fam) adj trendy
brancher [bʀɑ̃ʃe] vt to connect (up); (en mettant la prise) to plug in
brandir [bʀɑ̃diʀ] vt to brandish
branle [bʀɑ̃l] nm: **mettre en ~** to set in motion; **branle-bas** nm inv commotion
braquer [bʀake] vi (AUTO) to turn (the wheel) ♦ vt (revolver etc): ~ **qch sur** to aim sth at, point sth at; (mettre en colère): ~ **qn** to put sb's back up
bras [bʀa] nm arm; ~ **dessus, ~ dessous** arm in arm; **se retrouver avec qch sur les ~** (fam) to be landed with sth; ~ **droit** (fig) right hand man; ~ **de fer** arm wrestling
brasier [bʀazje] nm blaze, inferno
bras-le-corps [bʀalkɔʀ] adv: **à ~-~-~** (a)round the waist
brassard [bʀasaʀ] nm armband
brasse [bʀas] nf (nage) breast-stroke
brassée [bʀase] nf armful
brasser [bʀase] vt to mix; ~ **l'argent/les affaires** to handle a lot of money/business
brasserie [bʀasʀi] nf (restaurant) café-restaurant; (usine) brewery
brave [bʀav] adj (courageux) brave; (bon, gentil) good, kind
braver [bʀave] vt to defy

bravo [bʀavo] excl bravo ♦ nm cheer
bravoure [bʀavuʀ] nf bravery
break [bʀɛk] nm (AUTO) estate car
brebis [bʀəbi] nf ewe; ~ **galeuse** black sheep
brèche [bʀɛʃ] nf breach, gap; **être toujours sur la ~** (fig) to be always on the go
bredouille [bʀəduj] adj empty-handed
bredouiller [bʀəduje] vi, vt to mumble, stammer
bref, brève [bʀɛf, ɛv] adj short, brief ♦ adv in short; **d'un ton ~** sharply, curtly; **en ~** in short, in brief
Brésil [bʀezil] nm Brazil; **brésilien, -ne** adj Brazilian ♦ nm/f: **Brésilien, ne** Brazilian
Bretagne [bʀətaɲ] nf Brittany
bretelle [bʀətɛl] nf (de vêtement, de sac) strap; (d'autoroute) slip road (BRIT), entrance/exit ramp (US); ~s nfpl (pour pantalon) braces (BRIT), suspenders (US)
breton, ne [bʀətɔ̃, ɔn] adj Breton ♦ nm/f: **B~, ne** Breton
breuvage [bʀœvaʒ] nm beverage, drink
brève [bʀɛv] adj voir bref
brevet [bʀəvɛ] nm diploma, certificate; ~ **(d'invention)** patent; **breveté, e** adj patented
bribes [bʀib] nfpl (de conversation) snatches; **par ~** piecemeal
bricolage [bʀikɔlaʒ] nm: **le ~** do-it-yourself
bricole [bʀikɔl] nf (babiole) trifle
bricoler [bʀikɔle] vi (petits travaux) to do DIY jobs; (passe-temps) to potter about ♦ vt (réparer) to fix up; **bricoleur, -euse** nm/f handyman(-woman), DIY enthusiast
bride [bʀid] nf bridle; **tenir qn en ~** to keep a tight rein on sb
bridé, e [bʀide] adj: **yeux ~s** slit eyes
bridge [bʀidʒ] nm (CARTES) bridge
brièvement [bʀijevmɑ̃] adv briefly
brigade [bʀigad] nf (POLICE) squad; (MIL) brigade; **brigadier** nm sergeant
brigandage [bʀigɑ̃daʒ] nm robbery
briguer [bʀige] vt to aspire to
brillamment [bʀijamɑ̃] adv brilliantly
brillant, e [bʀijɑ̃, ɑ̃t] adj (remarquable) bright; (luisant) shiny, shining
briller [bʀije] vi to shine
brimer [bʀime] vt to bully
brin [bʀɛ̃] nm (de laine, ficelle etc) strand; (fig): **un ~ de** a bit of; ~ **d'herbe** blade of grass; ~ **de muguet** sprig of lily of the valley
brindille [bʀɛ̃dij] nf twig
brio [bʀijo] nm: **avec ~** with panache
brioche [bʀijɔʃ] nf brioche (bun); (fam: ventre) paunch
brique [bʀik] nf brick; (de lait) carton
briquer [bʀike] vt to polish up
briquet [bʀikɛ] nm (cigarette) lighter
brise [bʀiz] nf breeze

briser [bʀize] vt to break; **se ~** vi to break

britannique [bʀitanik] adj British ♦ nm/f: **B~** British person, Briton; **les B~s** the British

brocante [bʀɔkɑ̃t] nf junk, second-hand goods pl; **brocanteur, -euse** nm/f junkshop owner; junk dealer

broche [bʀɔʃ] nf brooch; (CULIN) spit; (MÉD) pin; **à la ~** spit-roasted

broché, e [bʀɔʃe] adj (livre) paper-backed

brochet [bʀɔʃɛ] nm pike inv

brochette [bʀɔʃɛt] nf (ustensile) skewer; (plat) kebab

brochure [bʀɔʃyʀ] nf pamphlet, brochure, booklet

broder [bʀɔde] vt to embroider ♦ vi to embroider the facts; **broderie** nf embroidery

broncher [bʀɔ̃ʃe] vi: **sans ~** without flinching, without turning a hair

bronches [bʀɔ̃ʃ] nfpl bronchial tubes; **bronchite** nf bronchitis

bronze [bʀɔ̃z] nm bronze

bronzer [bʀɔ̃ze] vi to get a tan; **se ~** to sunbathe

brosse [bʀɔs] nf brush; **coiffé en ~** with a crewcut; **~ à cheveux** hairbrush; **~ à dents** toothbrush; **~ à habits** clothesbrush; **brosser** vt (nettoyer) to brush; (fig: tableau etc) to paint; **se brosser les dents** to brush one's teeth

brouette [bʀuɛt] nf wheelbarrow

brouhaha [bʀuaa] nm hubbub

brouillard [bʀujaʀ] nm fog

brouille [bʀuj] nf quarrel

brouiller [bʀuje] vt (œufs, message) to scramble; (idées) to mix up; (rendre trouble) to cloud; (désunir: amis) to set at odds; **se ~** vi (vue) to cloud over; (gens) to fall out

brouillon, ne [bʀujɔ̃, ɔn] adj (sans soin) untidy; (qui manque d'organisation) disorganized ♦ nm draft; (papier) **~** rough paper

broussailles [bʀusaj] nfpl undergrowth sg; **broussailleux, -euse** adj bushy

brousse [bʀus] nf: **la ~** the bush

brouter [bʀute] vi to graze

broutille [bʀutij] nf trifle

broyer [bʀwaje] vt to crush; **~ du noir** to be down in the dumps

bru [bʀy] nf daughter-in-law

brugnon [bʀyɲɔ̃] nm (BOT) nectarine

bruiner [bʀɥine] vb impers: **il bruine** it's drizzling, there's a drizzle

bruire [bʀɥiʀ] vi (feuilles) to rustle

bruit [bʀɥi] nm: **un ~** a noise, a sound; (fig: rumeur) a rumour; **le ~** noise; **sans ~** without a sound, noiselessly; **~ de fond** background noise; **bruitage** nm sound effects pl

brûlant, e [bʀylɑ̃, ɑ̃t] adj burning; (liquide) boiling (hot)

brûlé, e [bʀyle] adj (fig: démasqué) blown ♦ nm: **odeur de ~** smell of burning

brûle-pourpoint [bʀylpuʀpwɛ̃]: **à ~~** adv point-blank

brûler [bʀyle] vt to burn; (suj: eau bouillante) to scald; (consommer: électricité, essence) to use; (feu rouge, signal) to go through ♦ vi to burn; (jeu): **tu brûles!** you're getting hot!; **se ~** to burn o.s.; (s'ébouillanter) to scald o.s.

brûlure [bʀylyʀ] nf (lésion) burn; **~s d'estomac** heartburn sg

brume [bʀym] nf mist; **brumisateur** nm atomizer

brun, e [bʀœ̃, bʀyn] adj (gén, bière) brown; (cheveux, tabac) dark; **elle est ~e** she's got dark hair

brunch [bʀœntʃ] nm brunch

brunir [bʀyniʀ] vi to get a tan

brushing [bʀœʃiŋ] nm blow-dry

brusque [bʀysk] adj abrupt; **brusquer** vt to rush

brut, e [bʀyt] adj (minerai, soie) raw; (diamant) rough; (COMM) gross; (pétrole) crude (oil)

brutal, e, -aux [bʀytal, o] adj brutal; **brutaliser** vt to handle roughly, manhandle

Bruxelles [bʀysɛl] n Brussels

bruyamment [bʀɥijamɑ̃] adv noisily

bruyant, e [bʀɥijɑ̃, ɑ̃t] adj noisy

bruyère [bʀyjɛʀ] nf heather

BTS sigle m (= brevet de technicien supérieur) vocational training certificate taken at the end of a higher education course

bu, e [by] pp de **boire**

buccal, e, -aux [bykal, o] adj: **par voie ~e** orally

bûche [byʃ] nf log; **prendre une ~** (fig) to come a cropper; **~ de Noël** Yule log

bûcher [byʃe] nm (funéraire) pyre; (supplice) stake ♦ vi (fam) to swot (BRIT), slave (away) ♦ vt (fam) to swot up (BRIT), slave away at; **bûcheron** nm woodcutter; **bûcheur, -euse** (fam) adj hard-working

budget [bydʒɛ] nm budget

buée [bɥe] nf (sur une vitre) mist

buffet [byfɛ] nm (meuble) sideboard; (de réception) buffet; **~ (de gare)** (station) buffet, snack bar

buffle [byfl] nm buffalo

buis [bɥi] nm box tree; (bois) box(wood)

buisson [bɥisɔ̃] nm bush

buissonnière [bɥisɔnjɛʀ] adj: **faire l'école ~** to skip school

bulbe [bylb] nm (BOT, ANAT) bulb

Bulgarie [bylgaʀi] nf Bulgaria

bulle [byl] nf bubble

bulletin [byltɛ̃] nm (communiqué, journal) bulletin; (SCOL) report; **~ d'informations** news bulletin; **~ de salaire** pay-slip; **~ (de vote)**

ballot paper; **~ météorologique** weather
report
bureau, x [byʀo] nm (meuble) desk; (pièce,
service) office; (: clientèle) practice; (POL)
exchange office ou bureau; **~ de poste** post
office; **~ de tabac** tobacconist's (shop); **~ de
vote** polling station; **bureaucratie**
[byʀokʀasi] nf bureaucracy
burin [byʀɛ̃] nm cold chisel; (ART) burin
burlesque [byʀlɛsk] adj ridiculous;
(LITTÉRATURE) burlesque
bus¹ [by] vb voir **boire**
bus² [bys] nm bus
busqué, e [byske] adj (nez) hook(ed)
buste [byst] nm (torse) chest; (seins) bust
but¹ [by] vb voir **boire**
but² [by(t)] nm (cible) target; (fig) goal, aim;
(FOOTBALL etc) goal; **de ~ en blanc** point-
blank; **avoir pour ~ de faire** to aim to do;
dans le ~ de with the intention of
butane [bytan] nm (camping) butane; (usage
domestique) Calor gas ®
buté, e [byte] adj stubborn, obstinate
buter [byte] vi: **~ contre** (cogner) to bump
into; (trébucher) to stumble against; **se ~** vi
to get obstinate, dig in one's heels; **~ contre
une difficulté** (fig) to hit a snag
butin [bytɛ̃] nm booty, spoils pl; (d'un vol)
loot
butiner [bytine] vi (abeilles) to gather nectar
butte [byt] nf mound, hillock; **être en ~ à** to
be exposed to
buvais etc [byvɛ] vb voir **boire**
buvard [byvaʀ] nm blotter
buvette [byvɛt] nf bar
buveur, -euse [byvœʀ, øz] nm/f drinker

C, c

c' [s] dét voir **ce**
CA sigle m = **chiffre d'affaires**
ça [sa] pron (pour désigner) this; (: plus loin)
that; (comme sujet indéfini) it; **comment ~ va?**
how are you?; **~ va?** (d'accord?) OK?, all
right?; **où ~?** where's that?; **pourquoi ~?**
why's that?; **qui ~?** who's that?; **~ alors!** well
really!; **~ fait 10 ans (que)** it's 10 years
(since); **c'est ~** that's right; **~ y est** that's it
çà [sa] adv: **~ et là** here and there
cabane [kaban] nf hut, cabin
cabaret [kabaʀɛ] nm night club
cabas [kaba] nm shopping bag
cabillaud [kabijo] nm cod inv
cabine [kabin] nf (de bateau) cabin; (de
piscine etc) cubicle; (de camion, train) cab;
(d'avion) cockpit; **~ d'essayage** fitting room;
~ (téléphonique) call ou (tele)phone box
cabinet [kabinɛ] nm (petite pièce) closet; (de

médecin) surgery (BRIT), office (US); (de
notaire etc) office; (: clientèle) practice; (POL)
Cabinet; **~s** nmpl (w.-c.) toilet sg; **~ d'affaires**
business consultancy; **~ de toilette** toilet
câble [kabl] nm cable
cabosser [kabɔse] vt to dent
cabrer [kabʀe]: **se ~** vi (cheval) to rear up
cabriole [kabʀijɔl] nf: **faire des ~s** to caper
about
cacahuète [kakayɛt] nf peanut
cacao [kakao] nm cocoa
cache [kaʃ] nm mask, card (for masking)
cache-cache [kaʃkaʃ] nm: **jouer à ~~** to play
hide-and-seek
cachemire [kaʃmiʀ] nm cashmere
cache-nez [kaʃne] nm inv scarf, muffler
cacher [kaʃe] vt to hide, conceal; **se ~** vi
(volontairement) to hide; (être caché) to be
hidden ou concealed; **~ qch à qn** to hide ou
conceal sth from sb
cachet [kaʃe] nm (comprimé) tablet; (de la
poste) postmark; (rétribution) fee; (fig) style,
character; **cacheter** vt to seal
cachette [kaʃɛt] nf hiding place; **en ~** on the
sly, secretly
cachot [kaʃo] nm dungeon
cachotterie [kaʃɔtʀi] nf: **faire des ~s** to be
secretive
cactus [kaktys] nm cactus
cadavre [kadavʀ] nm corpse, (dead) body
Caddie ®, **caddy** [kadi] nm (supermarket)
trolley
cadeau, x [kado] nm present, gift; **faire un
~ à qn** to give sb a present ou gift; **faire ~ de
qch à qn** to make a present of sth to sb, give
sb sth as a present
cadenas [kadnɑ] nm padlock
cadence [kadɑ̃s] nf (tempo) rhythm; (de
travail etc) rate; **en ~** rhythmically
cadet, te [kadɛ, ɛt] adj younger; (le plus
jeune) youngest ♦ nm/f youngest child ou
one
cadran [kadʀɑ̃] nm dial; **~ solaire** sundial
cadre [kadʀ] nm frame; (environnement)
surroundings pl ♦ nm/f (ADMIN) managerial
employee, executive; **dans le ~ de** (fig) within
the framework ou context of
cadrer [kadʀe] vi: **~ avec** to tally ou
correspond with ♦ vt to centre
cafard [kafaʀ] nm cockroach; **avoir le ~** (fam)
to be down in the dumps
café [kafe] nm coffee; (bistro) café ♦ adj inv
coffee(-coloured); **~ au lait** white coffee;
~ noir black coffee; **~ tabac** tobacconist's or
newsagent's serving coffee and spirits;
cafetière nf (pot) coffee-pot
cafouiller [kafuje] (fam) vi to get into a
shambles
cage [kaʒ] nf cage; **~ d'escalier** (stair)well;

~ thoracique rib cage
cageot [kaʒo] *nm* crate
cagibi [kaʒibi] (*fam*) *nm* (*débarras*) boxroom
cagnotte [kaɲɔt] *nf* kitty
cagoule [kagul] *nf* (*passe-montagne*) balaclava
cahier [kaje] *nm* notebook; **~ de brouillons** roughbook, jotter; **~ d'exercices** exercise book
cahot [kao] *nm* jolt, bump
caïd [kaid] *nm* big chief, boss
caille [kaj] *nf* quail
cailler [kaje] *vi* (*lait*) to curdle; **ça caille** (*fam*) it's freezing; **caillot** (*blood*) clot
caillou, x [kaju] *nm* (little) stone; **caillouteux, -euse** *adj* (*route*) stony
Caire [kɛʀ] *nm*: **le ~** Cairo
caisse [kes] *nf* box; (*tiroir où l'on met la recette*) till; (*où l'on paye*) cash desk (*BRIT*), check-out; (*de banque*) cashier's desk; **~ d'épargne** savings bank; **~ de retraite** pension fund; **~ enregistreuse** cash register; **caissier, -ière** *nm/f* cashier
cajoler [kaʒɔle] *vt* (*câliner*) to cuddle; (*amadouer*) to wheedle, coax
cake [kɛk] *nm* fruit cake
calandre [kalɑ̃dʀ] *nf* radiator grill
calanque [kalɑ̃k] *nf* rocky inlet
calcaire [kalkɛʀ] *nm* limestone ♦ *adj* (*eau*) hard; (*GÉO*) limestone *cpd*
calciné, e [kalsine] *adj* burnt to ashes
calcul [kalkyl] *nm* calculation; **le ~** (*SCOL*) arithmetic; **~ (biliaire)** (gall)stone; **calculatrice** *nf* calculator; **calculer** *vt* to calculate, work out; **calculette** *nf* pocket calculator
cale [kal] *nf* (*de bateau*) hold; (*en bois*) wedge; **~ sèche** dry dock
calé, e [kale] (*fam*) *adj* clever, bright
caleçon [kalsɔ̃] *nm* (*d'homme*) boxer shorts; (*de femme*) leggings
calembour [kalɑ̃buʀ] *nm* pun
calendrier [kalɑ̃dʀije] *nm* calendar; (*fig*) timetable
calepin [kalpɛ̃] *nm* notebook
caler [kale] *vt* to wedge ♦ *vi* (*moteur, véhicule*) to stall
calfeutrer [kalføtʀe] *vt* to (make) draughtproof; **se ~** *vi* to make o.s. snug and comfortable
calibre [kalibʀ] *nm* calibre
califourchon [kalifuʀʃɔ̃]: **à ~** *adv* astride
câlin, e [kɑlɛ̃, in] *adj* cuddly, cuddlesome; (*regard, voix*) tender; **câliner** *vt* to cuddle
calmant [kalmɑ̃] *nm* tranquillizer, sedative; (*pour la douleur*) painkiller
calme [kalm] *adj* calm, quiet ♦ *nm* calm(ness), quietness; **calmer** *vt* to calm (down); (*douleur, inquiétude*) to ease, soothe; **se calmer** *vi* to calm down

calomnie [kalɔmni] *nf* slander; (*écrite*) libel; **calomnier** *vt* to slander; to libel
calorie [kalɔʀi] *nf* calorie
calotte [kalɔt] *nf* (*coiffure*) skullcap; (*fam*: *gifle*) slap; **~ glaciaire** (*GÉO*) icecap
calquer [kalke] *vt* to trace; (*fig*) to copy exactly
calvaire [kalvɛʀ] *nm* (*croix*) wayside cross, calvary; (*souffrances*) suffering
calvitie [kalvisi] *nf* baldness
camarade [kamaʀad] *nm/f* friend, pal; (*POL*) comrade; **camaraderie** *nf* friendship
cambouis [kɑ̃bwi] *nm* dirty oil *ou* grease
cambrer [kɑ̃bʀe]: **se ~** *vi* to arch one's back
cambriolage [kɑ̃bʀijɔlaʒ] *nm* burglary; **cambrioler** *vt* to burgle (*BRIT*), burglarize (*US*); **cambrioleur, -euse** *nm/f* burglar
camelote [kamlɔt] (*fam*) *nf* rubbish, trash, junk
caméra [kamera] *nf* (*CINÉMA, TV*) camera; (*d'amateur*) cine-camera
caméscope ® [kameskɔp] *nm* camcorder ®
camion [kamjɔ̃] *nm* lorry (*BRIT*), truck; **~ de dépannage** breakdown (*BRIT*) *ou* tow (*US*) truck; **camion-citerne** *nm* tanker; **camionnette** *nf* (small) van; **camionneur** *nm* (*chauffeur*) lorry (*BRIT*) *ou* truck driver; (*entrepreneur*) haulage contractor (*BRIT*), trucker (*US*)
camisole [kamizɔl] *nf*: **~ (de force)** straitjacket
camomille [kamɔmij] *nf* camomile; (*boisson*) camomile tea
camoufler [kamufle] *vt* to camouflage; (*fig*) to conceal, cover up
camp [kɑ̃] *nm* camp; (*fig*) side; **~ de vacances** children's holiday camp (*BRIT*), summer camp (*US*)
campagnard, e [kɑ̃paɲaʀ, aʀd] *adj* country *cpd*
campagne [kɑ̃paɲ] *nf* country, countryside; (*MIL, POL, COMM*) campaign; **à la ~** in the country
camper [kɑ̃pe] *vi* to camp ♦ *vt* to sketch; **se ~ devant** to plant o.s. in front of; **campeur, -euse** *nm/f* camper
camping [kɑ̃piŋ] *nm* camping; (*terrain de*) **~** campsite, camping site; **faire du ~** to go camping; **camping-car** *nm* camper, motorhome (*US*); **camping-gaz** ® *nm inv* camp(ing) stove
Canada [kanada] *nm*: **le ~** Canada; **canadien, ne** *adj* Canadian ♦ *nm/f*: **Canadien, ne** Canadian; **canadienne** *nf* (*veste*) fur-lined jacket
canaille [kanaj] (*péj*) *nf* scoundrel
canal, -aux [kanal, o] *nm* canal; (*naturel*) channel; **canalisation** *nf* (*tuyau*) pipe;

canaliser vt to canalize; (fig) to channel

canapé [kanape] nm settee, sofa

canard [kanaʀ] nm duck; (fam: journal) rag

canari [kanaʀi] nm canary

cancans [kãkã] nmpl (malicious) gossip sg

cancer [kãseʀ] nm cancer; (signe): **le C~** Cancer; **~ de la peau** skin cancer

cancre [kãkʀ] nm dunce

candeur [kãdœʀ] nf ingenuousness, guilelessness

candidat, e [kãdida, at] nm/f candidate; (à un poste) applicant, candidate; **candidature** nf (POL) candidature; (à poste) application; **poser sa candidature à un poste** to apply for a job

candide [kãdid] adj ingenuous, guileless

cane [kan] nf (female) duck

caneton [kantõ] nm duckling

canette [kanɛt] nf (de bière) (flip-top) bottle

canevas [kanva] nm (COUTURE) canvas

caniche [kaniʃ] nm poodle

canicule [kanikyl] nf scorching heat

canif [kanif] nm penknife, pocket knife

canine [kanin] nf canine (tooth)

caniveau, x [kanivo] nm gutter

canne [kan] nf (walking) stick; **~ à pêche** fishing rod; **~ à sucre** sugar cane

cannelle [kanɛl] nf cinnamon

canoë [kanɔe] nm canoe; (sport) canoeing

canon [kanõ] nm (arme) gun; (HISTOIRE) cannon; (d'une arme: tube) barrel; (fig: norme) model; (MUS) canon

canot [kano] nm ding(h)y; **~ de sauvetage** lifeboat; **~ pneumatique** inflatable ding(h)y; **canotier** nm boater

cantatrice [kãtatʀis] nf (opera) singer

cantine [kãtin] nf canteen

cantique [kãtik] nm hymn

canton [kãtõ] nm district consisting of several communes; (en Suisse) canton

cantonade [kãtɔnad]: **à la ~** adv to everyone in general

cantonner [kãtɔne]: **se ~ à** vt to confine o.s. to

cantonnier [kãtɔnje] nm roadmender

canular [kanylaʀ] nm hoax

caoutchouc [kautʃu] nm rubber

cap [kap] nm (GÉO) cape; (promontoire) headland; (fig: tournant) watershed; (NAVIG): **changer de ~** to change course; **mettre le ~ sur** to head ou steer for

CAP sigle m (= Certificat d'aptitude professionnelle) vocational training certificate taken at secondary school

capable [kapabl] adj able, capable; **~ de qch/faire** capable of sth/doing

capacité [kapasite] nf (compétence) ability; (JUR, contenance) capacity

cape [kap] nf cape, cloak; **rire sous ~** to laugh up one's sleeve

CAPES [kapɛs] sigle m (= Certificat d'aptitude pédagogique à l'enseignement secondaire) teaching diploma

capillaire [kapilɛʀ] adj (soins, lotion) hair cpd; (vaisseau etc) capillary

capitaine [kapitɛn] nm captain

capital, e, -aux [kapital, o] adj (œuvre) major; (question, rôle) fundamental ♦ nm capital; (fig) stock; **d'une importance ~e** of capital importance; voir aussi **capitaux**; **~ (social)** authorized capital; **capitale** nf (ville) capital; (lettre) capital (letter); **capitalisme** nm capitalism; **capitaliste** adj, nm/f capitalist; **capitaux** nmpl (fonds) capital sg

capitonné, e [kapitɔne] adj padded

caporal, -aux [kapɔral, o] nm lance corporal

capot [kapo] nm (AUTO) bonnet (BRIT), hood (US)

capote [kapɔt] nf (de voiture) hood (BRIT), top (US); (fam) condom

capoter [kapɔte] vi (négociations) to founder

câpre [kɑpʀ] nf caper

caprice [kapʀis] nm whim, caprice; **faire des ~s** to make a fuss; **capricieux, -euse** adj (fantasque) capricious, whimsical; (enfant) awkward

Capricorne [kapʀikɔʀn] nm: **le ~** Capricorn

capsule [kapsyl] nf (de bouteille) cap; (BOT etc, spatiale) capsule

capter [kapte] vt (ondes radio) to pick up; (fig) to win, capture

captivant, e [kaptivã, ãt] adj captivating

captivité [kaptivite] nf captivity

capturer [kaptyʀe] vt to capture

capuche [kapyʃ] nf hood

capuchon [kapyʃõ] nm hood; (de stylo) cap, top

capucine [kapysin] nf (BOT) nasturtium

caquet [kakɛ] nm: **rabattre le ~ à qn** (fam) to bring sb down a peg or two

caqueter [kakte] vi to cackle

car [kaʀ] nm coach ♦ conj because, for

carabine [kaʀabin] nf rifle

caractère [kaʀaktɛʀ] nm (gén) character; **avoir bon/mauvais ~** to be good-/ill-natured; **en ~s gras** in bold type; **en petits ~s** in small print; **~s d'imprimerie** (block) capitals; **caractériel, le** adj (traits) (of) character; (enfant) emotionally disturbed

caractérisé, e [kaʀakteʀize] adj sheer, downright

caractériser [kaʀakteʀize] vt to be characteristic of

caractéristique [kaʀakteʀistik] adj, nf characteristic

carafe [kaʀaf] nf (pour eau, vin ordinaire)

carafe

caraïbe [kaʀaib] adj Caribbean ♦ n: **les C~s** the Caribbean (Islands)

carambolage [kaʀɑ̃bɔlaʒ] nm multiple crash, pileup

caramel [kaʀamɛl] nm (bonbon) caramel, toffee; (substance) caramel

carapace [kaʀapas] nf shell

caravane [kaʀavan] nf caravan; **caravaning** nm caravanning

carbone [kaʀbɔn] nm carbon; (double) carbon (copy); **carbonique** adj: **gaz carbonique** carbon dioxide; **neige carbonique** dry ice; **carbonisé, e** adj charred

carburant [kaʀbyʀɑ̃] nm (motor) fuel

carburateur [kaʀbyʀatœʀ] nm carburettor

carcan [kaʀkɑ̃] nm (fig) yoke, shackles pl

carcasse [kaʀkas] nf carcass; (de véhicule etc) shell

cardiaque [kaʀdjak] adj cardiac, heart cpd ♦ nm/f heart patient; **être ~** to have heart trouble

cardigan [kaʀdigɑ̃] nm cardigan

cardiologue [kaʀdjɔlɔg] nm/f cardiologist, heart specialist

carême [kaʀɛm] nm: **le C~** Lent

carence [kaʀɑ̃s] nf (manque) deficiency

caresse [kaʀɛs] nf caress

caresser [kaʀese] vt to caress; (animal) to stroke

cargaison [kaʀgɛzɔ̃] nf cargo, freight

cargo [kaʀgo] nm cargo boat, freighter

caricature [kaʀikatyʀ] nf caricature

carie [kaʀi] nf: **la ~** (dentaire) tooth decay; **une ~** a bad tooth

carillon [kaʀijɔ̃] nm (air, de pendule) chimes pl

caritatif, ive [kaʀitatif, iv] adj: **organisation caritative** charity

carnassier, ière [kaʀnasje, jɛʀ] adj carnivorous

carnaval [kaʀnaval] nm carnival

carnet [kaʀnɛ] nm (calepin) notebook; (de tickets, timbres etc) book; **~ de chèques** cheque book; **~ de notes** school report

carotte [kaʀɔt] nf carrot

carpette [kaʀpɛt] nf rug

carré, e [kaʀe] adj square; (fig: franc) straightforward ♦ nm (MATH) square; **mètre/ kilomètre ~** square metre/kilometre

carreau, x [kaʀo] nm (par terre) (floor) tile; (au mur) (wall) tile; (de fenêtre) (window) pane; (motif) check, square; (CARTES: couleur) diamonds pl; **tissu à ~x** checked fabric

carrefour [kaʀfuʀ] nm crossroads sg

carrelage [kaʀlaʒ] nm (sol) (tiled) floor

carrelet [kaʀlɛ] nm (poisson) plaice

carrément [kaʀemɑ̃] adv (franchement) straight out, bluntly; (sans hésiter) straight;

(intensif) completely; **c'est ~ impossible** it's completely impossible

carrière [kaʀjɛʀ] nf (métier) career; (de roches) quarry; **militaire de ~** professional soldier

carrossable [kaʀɔsabl] adj suitable for (motor) vehicles

carrosse [kaʀɔs] nm (horse-drawn) coach

carrosserie [kaʀɔsʀi] nf body, coachwork no pl

carrure [kaʀyʀ] nf build; (fig) stature, calibre

cartable [kaʀtabl] nm satchel, (school)bag

carte [kaʀt] nf (de géographie) map; (marine, du ciel) chart; (d'abonnement, à jouer) card; (au restaurant) menu; (aussi: **~ de visite**) (visiting) card; **à la ~** (au restaurant) à la carte; **donner ~ blanche à qn** to give sb a free rein; **~ bancaire** cash card; **~ de crédit** credit card; **~ d'identité** identity card; **~ de séjour** residence permit; **~ grise** (AUTO) ≈ (car) registration book, logbook; **~ postale** postcard; **~ routière** road map; **~ téléphonique** phonecard

carter [kaʀtɛʀ] nm sump

carton [kaʀtɔ̃] nm (matériau) cardboard; (boîte) (cardboard) box; **faire un ~** (fam) to score a hit; **~ (à dessin)** portfolio; **carton-pâte** nm pasteboard

cartouche [kaʀtuʃ] nf cartridge; (de cigarettes) carton

cas [kɑ] nm case; **ne faire aucun ~ de** to take no notice of; **en aucun ~** on no account; **au ~ où** in case; **en ~ de** in case of, in the event of; **en ~ de besoin** if need be; **en tout ~** in any case, at any rate; **~ de conscience** matter of conscience

casanier, ière [kazanje, jɛʀ] adj stay-at-home

cascade [kaskad] nf waterfall, cascade; (fig) stream, torrent; **cascadeur, euse** nm/f stuntman(-girl)

case [kɑz] nf (hutte) hut; (compartiment) compartment; (sur un formulaire, de mots croisés etc) box

caser [kaze] (fam) vt (placer) to put (away); (loger) to put up; **se ~** vi (se marier) to settle down; (trouver un emploi) to find a (steady) job

caserne [kazɛʀn] nf barracks pl

cash [kaʃ] adv: **payer ~** to pay cash down

casier [kazje] nm (pour courrier) pigeonhole; (compartiment) compartment; (à clef) locker; **~ judiciaire** police record

casino [kazino] nm casino

casque [kask] nm helmet; (chez le coiffeur) (hair-)drier; (pour audition) (head-)phones pl, headset

casquette [kaskɛt] nf cap

cassant, e [kɑsɑ̃, ɑ̃t] adj brittle; (fig: ton)

curt, abrupt
cassation [kɑsasjɔ̃] nf: **cour de ~** final court of appeal
casse [kɑs] (fam) nf (pour voitures): **mettre à la ~** to scrap; (dégâts): **il y a eu de la ~** there were a lot of breakages; **casse-cou** adj inv daredevil, reckless; **casse-croûte** nm inv snack; **casse-noix** nm inv nutcrackers pl; **casse-pieds** (fam) adj inv: **il est casse-pieds** he's a pain in the neck
casser [kɑse] vt to break; (JUR) to quash; **se ~** vi to break; **~ les pieds à qn** (fam: irriter) to get on sb's nerves; **se ~ la tête** (fam) to go to a lot of trouble
casserole [kɑsrɔl] nf saucepan
casse-tête [kɑstɛt] nm inv (difficultés) headache (fig)
cassette [kɑset] nf (bande magnétique) cassette; (coffret) casket
casseur [kɑsœʀ] nm hooligan
cassis [kasis] nm blackcurrant
cassoulet [kasule] nm bean and sausage hot-pot
cassure [kɑsyʀ] nf break, crack
castor [kastɔʀ] nm beaver
castrer [kastʀe] vt (mâle) to castrate; (: cheval) to geld; (femelle) to spay
catalogue [katalɔg] nm catalogue
cataloguer [katalɔge] vt to catalogue, to list; (péj) to put a label on
catalyseur [katalizœʀ] nm catalyst; **catalytique** adj: **pot catalytique** catalytic convertor
catastrophe [katastʀɔf] nf catastrophe, disaster; **catastrophé, e** (fam) adj stunned
catch [katʃ] nm (all-in) wrestling
catéchisme [kateʃism] nm catechism
catégorie [kategɔʀi] nf category; **catégorique** adj categorical
cathédrale [katedʀal] nf cathedral
catholique [katɔlik] adj, nm/f (Roman) Catholic; **pas très ~** a bit shady ou fishy
catimini [katimini]: **en ~** adv on the sly
cauchemar [koʃmaʀ] nm nightmare
cause [koz] nf cause; (JUR) lawsuit, case; **à ~ de** because of, owing to; **pour ~ de** on account of; **(et) pour ~** and for a (very) good reason; **être en ~** (intérêts) to be at stake; **remettre en ~** to challenge; **causer** vt to cause ♦ vi to chat, talk; **causerie** nf (conférence) talk; **causette** nf: **faire la causette** to have a chat
caution [kosjɔ̃] nf guarantee, security; (JUR) bail (bond); (fig) backing, support; **libéré sous ~** released on bail; **cautionner** vt (répondre de) to guarantee; (soutenir) to support
cavalcade [kavalkad] nf (fig) stampede

cavalier, -ière [kavalje, jɛʀ] adj (désinvolte) offhand ♦ nm/f rider; (au bal) partner ♦ nm (ÉCHECS) knight
cave [kav] nf cellar
caveau, x [kavo] nm vault
caverne [kavɛʀn] nf cave
CCP sigle m = compte chèques postaux
CD sigle m (= compact disc) CD
CD-ROM [sedeʀɔm] sigle m CD-ROM
CE n abr f (= Communauté Européenne) EC

MOT-CLÉ

ce, cette [sə, set] (devant nm **cet** + voyelle ou h aspiré; pl **ces**) dét (proximité) this; these pl; (non-proximité) that; those pl; **cette maison(-ci/là)** this/that house; **cette nuit** (qui vient) tonight; (passée) last night
♦ pron **1: c'est** it's ou it is; **c'est un peintre** he's ou he is a painter; **ce sont des peintres** they're ou they are painters; **c'est le facteur** (à la porte) it's the postman; **qui est-ce?** who is it?; (en désignant) who is he/she?; **qu'est-ce?** what is it?
2: ce qui, ce que what; (chose qui): **il est bête, ce qui me chagrine** he's stupid, which saddens me; **tout ce qui bouge** everything that ou which moves; **tout ce que je sais** all I know; **ce dont j'ai parlé** what I talked about; **ce que c'est grand!** it's so big!; voir aussi **-ci**; **est-ce que**; **n'est-ce pas**; **c'est-à-dire**

---

ceci [səsi] pron this
cécité [sesite] nf blindness
céder [sede] vt (donner) to give up ♦ vi (chaise, barrage) to give way; (personne) to give in; **~ à** to yield to, give in to
CEDEX [sedeks] sigle m (= courrier d'entreprise à distribution exceptionnelle) postal service for bulk users
cédille [sedij] nf cedilla
cèdre [sɛdʀ] nm cedar
CEI abr m (= Communauté des États Indépendants) CIS
ceinture [sɛ̃tyʀ] nf belt; (taille) waist; **~ de sécurité** safety ou seat belt
cela [s(ə)la] pron that; (comme sujet indéfini) it; **quand/où ~?** when/where (was that)?
célèbre [selɛbʀ] adj famous; **célébrer** vt to celebrate
céleri [sɛlʀi] nm: **~(-rave)** celeriac; **~ (en branche)** celery
célibat [seliba] nm (homme) bachelorhood; (femme) spinsterhood; (prêtre) celibacy; **célibataire** adj single, unmarried ♦ nm bachelor ♦ nf unmarried woman
celle(s) [sɛl] pron voir **celui**
cellier [selje] nm storeroom (for wine)
cellule [selyl] nf (gén) cell
cellulite [selylit] nf excess fat, cellulite

MOT-CLÉ

celui, celle [səlɥi, sɛl] (*mpl* ceux, *fpl* celles) *pron* 1: **celui-ci/là, celle-ci/là** this one/that one; **ceux-ci, celles-ci** these (ones); **ceux-là, celles-là** those (ones); **celui de mon frère** my brother's; **celui du salon/du dessous** the one in (*ou* from) the lounge/below

2: **celui qui bouge** the one which *ou* that moves; (*personne*) the one who moves; **celui que je vois** the one (which *ou* that) I see; the one (whom) I see; **celui dont je parle** the one I'm talking about

3 (*valeur indéfinie*): **celui qui veut** whoever wants

---

cendre [sɑ̃dʀ] *nf* ash; ~**s** *nfpl* (*d'un défunt*) ashes; **sous la** ~ (*CULIN*) in (the) embers; **cendrier** *nm* ashtray

cène [sɛn] *nf*: **la** ~ (Holy) Communion

censé, e [sɑ̃se] *adj*: **être** ~ **faire** to be supposed to do

censeur [sɑ̃sœʀ] *nm* (*SCOL*) deputy-head (*BRIT*), vice-principal (*US*); (*CINÉMA, POL*) censor

censure [sɑ̃syʀ] *nf* censorship; **censurer** *vt* (*CINÉMA, PRESSE*) to censor; (*POL*) to censure

cent [sɑ̃] *num* a hundred, one hundred; **centaine** *nf*: **une centaine (de)** about a hundred, a hundred or so; **des centaines (de)** hundreds (of); **centenaire** *adj* hundred-year-old ♦ *nm* (*anniversaire*) centenary; **centième** *num* hundredth; **centigrade** *nm* centigrade; **centilitre** *nm* centilitre; **centime** *nm* centime; **centimètre** *nm* centimetre; (*ruban*) tape measure, measuring tape

central, e, -aux [sɑ̃tʀal, o] *adj* central ♦ *nm*: ~ (**téléphonique**) (telephone) exchange; **centrale** *nf* power station

centre [sɑ̃tʀ] *nm* centre; ~ **commercial** shopping centre; **centre-ville** *nm* town centre, downtown (area) (*US*)

centuple [sɑ̃typl] *nm*: **le** ~ **de qch** a hundred times sth; **au** ~ a hundredfold

cep [sɛp] *nm* (vine) stock

cèpe [sɛp] *nm* (edible) boletus

cependant [s(ə)pɑ̃dɑ̃] *adv* however

céramique [seʀamik] *nf* ceramics *sg*

cercle [sɛʀkl] *nm* circle; ~ **vicieux** vicious circle

cercueil [sɛʀkœj] *nm* coffin

céréale [seʀeal] *nf* cereal; ~**s** *nfpl* breakfast cereal

cérémonie [seʀemɔni] *nf* ceremony; **sans** ~ informally

cerf [sɛʀ] *nm* stag

cerfeuil [sɛʀfœj] *nm* chervil

cerf-volant [sɛʀvɔlɑ̃] *nm* kite

cerise [s(ə)ʀiz] *nf* cherry; **cerisier** *nm* cherry (tree)

cerne [sɛʀn] *nm*: **avoir des** ~**s** to have shadows *ou* dark rings under one's eyes

cerner [sɛʀne] *vt* (*MIL etc*) to surround; (*fig: problème*) to delimit, define

certain, e [sɛʀtɛ̃, ɛn] *adj* certain ♦ *dét* certain; **d'un** ~ **âge** past one's prime, not so young; **un** ~ **temps** (quite) some time; ~**s** ♦ *pron* some; **certainement** *adv* (*probablement*) most probably *ou* likely; (*bien sûr*) certainly, of course

certes [sɛʀt] *adv* (*sans doute*) admittedly; (*bien sûr*) of course

certificat [sɛʀtifika] *nm* certificate

certifier [sɛʀtifje] *vt*: ~ **qch à qn** to assure sb of sth; **copie certifiée conforme (à l'original)** certified copy of the original

certitude [sɛʀtityd] *nf* certainty

cerveau, x [sɛʀvo] *nm* brain

cervelas [sɛʀvəla] *nm* saveloy

cervelle [sɛʀvɛl] *nf* (*ANAT*) brain; (*CULIN*) brains

ces [se] *dét voir* **ce**

CES *sigle m* (= Collège d'enseignement secondaire) ≈ (junior) secondary school (*BRIT*)

cesse [sɛs]: **sans** ~ *adv* (*tout le temps*) continually, constantly; (*sans interruption*) continuously; **il n'a eu de** ~ **que** he did not rest until; **cesser** *vt* to stop ♦ *vi* to stop, cease; **cesser de faire** to stop doing; **cessez-le-feu** *nm inv* ceasefire

c'est-à-dire [sɛtadiʀ] *adv* that is (to say)

cet, cette [sɛt] *dét voir* **ce**

ceux [sø] *pron voir* **celui**

CFC *abr* (= chlorofluorocarbon) CFC

CFDT *sigle f* (= Confédération française démocratique du travail) French trade union

CGT *sigle f* (= Confédération générale du travail) French trade union

chacun, e [ʃakœ̃, yn] *pron* each; (*indéfini*) everyone, everybody

chagrin [ʃagʀɛ̃] *nm* grief, sorrow; **avoir du** ~ to be grieved; **chagriner** *vt* to grieve

chahut [ʃay] *nm* uproar; **chahuter** *vt* to rag, bait ♦ *vi* to make an uproar

chaîne [ʃɛn] *nf* chain; (*RADIO, TV: stations*) channel; ~**s** *nfpl* (*AUTO*) (snow) chains; **travail à la** ~ production line work; ~ (**de montage**) production *ou* assembly line; ~ **de montagnes** mountain range; ~ (**hi-fi**) hi-fi system; ~ **laser** CD player; ~ (**stéréo**) stereo (system); **chaînette** *nf* (small) chain

chair [ʃɛʀ] *nf* flesh; **avoir la** ~ **de poule** to have goosepimples *ou* gooseflesh; **bien en** ~ plump, well-padded; **en** ~ **et en os** in the flesh; ~ **à saucisse** sausage meat

chaire [ʃɛʀ] *nf* (*d'église*) pulpit; (*d'université*) chair

chaise [ʃɛz] *nf* chair; ~ **longue** deckchair

châle [ʃɑl] *nm* shawl

chaleur [ʃalœʀ] *nf* heat; (*fig: accueil*) warmth; **chaleureux, -euse** *adj* warm

chaloupe [ʃalup] *nf* launch; (*de sauvetage*) lifeboat

chalumeau, x [ʃalymo] *nm* blowlamp, blowtorch

chalutier [ʃalytje] *nm* trawler

chamailler [ʃamaje]: **se ~** *vi* to squabble, bicker

chambouler [ʃãbule] (*fam*) *vt* to disrupt, turn upside down

chambre [ʃɑ̃bʀ] *nf* bedroom; (*POL, COMM*) chamber; **faire ~ à part** to sleep in separate rooms; **~ à air** (*de pneu*) (inner) tube; **~ à coucher** bedroom; **~ à un lit/deux lits** (*à l'hôtel*) single-/twin-bedded room; **~ d'amis** spare *ou* guest room; **~ noire** (*PHOTO*) dark room; **chambrer** (*vin*) to bring to room temperature

chameau, x [ʃamo] *nm* camel

chamois [ʃamwa] *nm* chamois

champ [ʃɑ̃] *nm* field; **~ de bataille** battlefield; **~ de courses** racecourse; **~ de tir** rifle range

champagne [ʃɑ̃paɲ] *nm* champagne

champêtre [ʃɑ̃pɛtʀ] *adj* country *cpd*, rural

champignon [ʃɑ̃piɲɔ̃] *nm* mushroom; (*terme générique*) fungus; **~ de Paris** button mushroom

champion, ne [ʃɑ̃pjɔ̃, jɔn] *adj, nm/f* champion; **championnat** *nm* championship

chance [ʃɑ̃s] *nf*: **la ~** luck; **~s** *nfpl* (*probabilités*) chances; **avoir de la ~** to be lucky; **il a des ~s de réussir** he's got a good chance of passing

chanceler [ʃɑ̃s(ə)le] *vi* to totter

chancelier [ʃɑ̃səlje] *nm* (*allemand*) chancellor

chanceux, -euse [ʃɑ̃sø, øz] *adj* lucky

chandail [ʃɑ̃daj] *nm* (thick) sweater

Chandeleur [ʃɑ̃dlœʀ] *nf*: **la ~** Candlemas

chandelier [ʃɑ̃dalje] *nm* candlestick

chandelle [ʃɑ̃dɛl] *nf* (tallow) candle; **dîner aux ~s** candlelight dinner

change [ʃɑ̃ʒ] *nm* (*devises*) exchange

changement [ʃɑ̃ʒmɑ̃] *nm* change; **~ de vitesses** gears *pl*

changer [ʃɑ̃ʒe] *vt* (*modifier*) to change, alter; (*remplacer, COMM*) to change ♦ *vi* to change, alter; **se ~** *vi* to change (*o.s.*); **~ de** (*remplacer: adresse, nom, voiture etc*) to change one's; (*échanger: place, train etc*) to change; **~ d'avis** to change one's mind; **~ de vitesse** to change gear

chanson [ʃɑ̃sɔ̃] *nf* song

chant [ʃɑ̃] *nm* song; (*art vocal*) singing; (*d'église*) hymn

chantage [ʃɑ̃taʒ] *nm* blackmail; **faire du ~** to use blackmail

chanter [ʃɑ̃te] *vt, vi* to sing; **si cela lui chante** (*fam*) if he feels like it; **chanteur, -euse** *nm/f* singer

chantier [ʃɑ̃tje] *nm* (building) site; (*sur une route*) roadworks *pl*; **mettre en ~** to put in hand; **~ naval** shipyard

chantilly [ʃɑ̃tiji] *nf voir* **crème**

chantonner [ʃɑ̃tɔne] *vi, vt* to sing to oneself, hum

chanvre [ʃɑ̃vʀ] *nm* hemp

chaparder [ʃapaʀde] (*fam*) *vt* to pinch

chapeau, x [ʃapo] *nm* hat; **~!** well done!

chapelet [ʃaplɛ] *nm* (*REL*) rosary

chapelle [ʃapɛl] *nf* chapel

chapelure [ʃaplyʀ] *nf* (dried) breadcrumbs *pl*

chapiteau, x [ʃapito] *nm* (*de cirque*) marquee, big top

chapitre [ʃapitʀ] *nm* chapter

chaque [ʃak] *dét* each, every; (*indéfini*) every

char [ʃaʀ] *nm* (*MIL*): **~ (d'assaut)** tank; **~ à voile** sand yacht

charabia [ʃaʀabja] (*péj*) *nm* gibberish

charade [ʃaʀad] *nf* riddle; (*mimée*) charade

charbon [ʃaʀbɔ̃] *nm* coal; **~ de bois** charcoal

charcuterie [ʃaʀkytʀi] *nf* (*magasin*) pork butcher's shop and delicatessen; (*produits*) cooked pork meats *pl*; **charcutier, -ière** *nm/f* pork butcher

chardon [ʃaʀdɔ̃] *nm* thistle

charge [ʃaʀʒ] *nf* (*fardeau*) load, burden; (*explosif, ÉLEC, MIL, JUR*) charge; (*rôle, mission*) responsibility; **~s** *nfpl* (*du loyer*) service charges; **à la ~ de** (*dépendant de*) dependent upon; (*aux frais de*) chargeable to; **prendre en ~** to take charge of; (*suj: véhicule*) to take on; (*dépenses*) to take care of; **~s sociales** social security contributions

chargé, e [ʃaʀʒe] *adj* (*emploi du temps, journée*) full, heavy

chargement [ʃaʀʒəmɑ̃] *nm* (*objets*) load

charger [ʃaʀʒe] *vt* (*voiture, fusil, caméra*) to load; (*batterie*) to charge ♦ *vi* (*MIL etc*) to charge; **se ~ de** *vt* to see to; **~ qn de (faire) qch** to put sb in charge of (doing) sth

chariot [ʃaʀjo] *nm* trolley; (*charrette*) waggon

charité [ʃaʀite] *nf* charity

charmant, e [ʃaʀmɑ̃, ɑ̃t] *adj* charming

charme [ʃaʀm] *nm* charm; **charmer** *vt* to charm

charnel, le [ʃaʀnɛl] *adj* carnal

charnière [ʃaʀnjɛʀ] *nf* hinge; (*fig*) turning-point

charnu, e [ʃaʀny] *adj* fleshy

charpente [ʃaʀpɑ̃t] *nf* frame(work); **charpentier** *nm* carpenter

charpie [ʃaʀpi] *nf*: **en ~** (*fig*) in shreds *ou* ribbons

charrette [ʃaʀɛt] *nf* cart

charrier [ʃaʀje] *vt* (*entraîner: fleuve*) to carry

(along); (*transporter*) to cart, carry

charrue [ʃaʀy] nf plough (BRIT), plow (US)

charter [ʃaʀtɛʀ] nm (*vol*) charter flight

chasse [ʃas] nf hunting; (*au fusil*) shooting; (*poursuite*) chase; (*aussi*: ~ d'eau) flush; ~ **gardée** private hunting grounds pl; **prendre en** ~ to give chase to; **tirer la** ~ (d'eau) to flush the toilet, pull the chain; ~ **à courre** hunting; **chasse-neige** nm inv snowplough (BRIT), snowplow (US); **chasser** vt to hunt; (*expulser*) to chase away ou out, drive away ou out; **chasseur, -euse** nm/f hunter ♦ nm (*avion*) fighter

châssis [ʃasi] nm (AUTO) chassis; (*cadre*) frame

chat [ʃa] nm cat

châtaigne [ʃatɛɲ] nf chestnut; **châtaignier** nm chestnut (tree)

châtain [ʃatɛ̃] adj inv (*cheveux*) chestnut (brown); (*personne*) chestnut-haired

château, x [ʃato] nm (*forteresse*) castle; (*résidence royale*) palace; (*manoir*) mansion; ~ **d'eau** water tower; ~ **fort** stronghold, fortified castle

châtier [ʃatje] vt to punish; **châtiment** nm punishment

chaton [ʃatɔ̃] nm (ZOOL) kitten

chatouiller [ʃatuje] vt to tickle; **chatouilleux, -euse** adj ticklish; (*fig*) touchy, over-sensitive

chatoyer [ʃatwaje] vi to shimmer

châtrer [ʃatʀe] vt (*mâle*) to castrate; (: *cheval*) to geld; (*femelle*) to spay

chatte [ʃat] nf (she-)cat

chaud, e [ʃo, ʃod] adj (*gén*) warm; (*très* ~) hot; **il fait** ~ it's warm; it's hot; **avoir** ~ to be warm; to be hot; **ça me tient** ~ it keeps me warm; **rester au** ~ to stay in the warm

chaudière [ʃodjɛʀ] nf boiler

chaudron [ʃodʀɔ̃] nm cauldron

chauffage [ʃofaʒ] nm heating; ~ **central** central heating

chauffard [ʃofaʀ] nm (*péj*) reckless driver

chauffe-eau [ʃofo] nm inv water-heater

chauffer [ʃofe] vt to heat ♦ vi to heat up, warm up; (*trop* ~: *moteur*) to overheat; **se** ~ vi (*au soleil*) to warm o.s

chauffeur [ʃofœʀ] nm driver; (*privé*) chauffeur

chaume [ʃom] nm (*du toit*) thatch; **chaumière** nf (thatched) cottage

chaussée [ʃose] nf road(way)

chausse-pied [ʃospje] nm shoe-horn

chausser [ʃose] vt (*bottes, skis*) to put on; (*enfant*) to put shoes on; ~ **du 38/42** to take size 38/42

chaussette [ʃosɛt] nf sock

chausson [ʃosɔ̃] nm slipper; (*de bébé*) bootee; ~ (**aux pommes**) (apple) turnover

chaussure [ʃosyʀ] nf shoe; ~s **à talon** high-heeled shoes; ~s **de marche** walking shoes/boots; ~s **de ski** ski boots

chauve [ʃov] adj bald; **chauve-souris** nf bat

chauvin, e [ʃovɛ̃, in] adj chauvinistic

chaux [ʃo] nf lime; **blanchi à la** ~ whitewashed

chavirer [ʃaviʀe] vi to capsize

chef [ʃɛf] nm head, leader; (*de cuisine*) chef; ~ **d'accusation** charge; ~ **d'entreprise** company head; ~ **d'état** head of state; ~ **de famille** head of the family; ~ **de gare** station master; ~ **d'orchestre** conductor; ~ **de service** department head; **chef-d'œuvre** nm masterpiece; **chef-lieu** nm county town

chemin [ʃ(ə)mɛ̃] nm path; (*itinéraire, direction, trajet*) way; **en** ~ on the way; ~ **de fer** railway (BRIT), railroad (US); **par** ~ **de fer** by rail

cheminée [ʃ(ə)mine] nf chimney; (*à l'intérieur*) chimney piece, fireplace; (*de bateau*) funnel

cheminement [ʃ(ə)minmɑ̃] nm progress

cheminot [ʃ(ə)mino] nm railwayman

chemise [ʃ(ə)miz] nf shirt; (*dossier*) folder; ~ **de nuit** nightdress

chemisier [ʃ(ə)mizje, jɛʀ] nm blouse

chenal, -aux [ʃənal, o] nm channel

chêne [ʃɛn] nm oak (tree); (*bois*) oak

chenil [ʃ(ə)nil] nm kennels pl

chenille [ʃ(ə)nij] nf (ZOOL) caterpillar

chèque [ʃɛk] nm cheque (BRIT), check (US); ~ **sans provision** bad cheque; ~ **de voyage** traveller's cheque; **chéquier** [ʃekje] nm cheque book

cher, -ère [ʃɛʀ] adj (*aimé*) dear; (*coûteux*) expensive, dear ♦ adv: **ça coûte** ~ it's expensive

chercher [ʃɛʀʃe] vt to look for; (*gloire etc*) to seek; **aller** ~ to go for, go and fetch; ~ **à faire** to try to do; **chercheur, -euse** nm/f researcher, research worker

chère [ʃɛʀ] adj voir **cher**

chéri, e [ʃeʀi] adj beloved, dear; (**mon**) ~ darling

chérir [ʃeʀiʀ] vt to cherish

cherté [ʃɛʀte] nf: **la** ~ **de la vie** the high cost of living

chétif, -ive [ʃetif, iv] adj (*enfant*) puny

cheval, -aux [ʃ(ə)val, o] nm horse; (AUTO): ~ (**vapeur**) horsepower no pl; **faire du** ~ to ride; **à** ~ on horseback; **à** ~ **sur** astride; (*fig*) overlapping; ~ **de course** racehorse

chevalet [ʃ(ə)valɛ] nm easel

chevalier [ʃ(ə)valje] nm knight

chevalière [ʃ(ə)valjɛʀ] nf signet ring

chevalin, e [ʃ(ə)valɛ̃, in] adj: **boucherie ~e** horse-meat butcher's

chevaucher [ʃ(ə)voʃe] vi (*aussi*: **se** ~) to overlap (each other) ♦ vt to be astride, straddle

chevaux [ʃəvo] nmpl de **cheval**

chevelu, e [ʃəv(ə)ly] (péj) adj long-haired

chevelure [ʃəv(ə)lyʀ] nf hair no pl

chevet [ʃ(ə)vε] nm: **au ~ de** qn at sb's bedside; **lampe de ~** bedside lamp

cheveu, x [ʃ(ə)vø] nm hair; **~x** nmpl (chevelure) hair sg; **avoir les ~x courts** to have short hair

cheville [ʃ(ə)vij] nf (ANAT) ankle; (de bois) peg; (pour une vis) plug

chèvre [ʃεvʀ] nf (she-)goat

chevreau, x [ʃəvʀo] nm kid

chèvrefeuille [ʃεvʀəfœj] nm honeysuckle

chevreuil [ʃəvʀœj] nm roe deer inv; (CULIN) venison

chevronné, e [ʃəvʀɔne] adj seasoned

MOT-CLÉ
---

chez [ʃe] prép **1** (à la demeure de) at; (: direction) to; **chez qn** at/to sb's house ou place; **chez moi** at home; (direction) home

2 (+profession) at; (: direction) to; **chez le boulanger/dentiste** at ou to the baker's/dentist's

3 (dans le caractère, l'œuvre de) in; **chez les renards/Racine** in foxes/Racine

---

chez-soi [ʃeswa] nm inv home

chic [ʃik] adj inv chic, smart; (fam: généreux) nice, decent ♦ nm stylishness; **~ (alors)!** (fam) great!; **avoir le ~ de** to have the knack of

chicane [ʃikan] nf (querelle) squabble; **chicaner** vi (ergoter) to quibble; **chicaner sur** to quibble about

chiche [ʃiʃ] adj niggardly, mean ♦ excl (à un défi) you're on!

chichis [ʃiʃi] (fam) nmpl fuss sg

chicorée [ʃikɔʀe] nf (café) chicory; (salade) endive

chien [ʃjε̃] nm dog; **~ de garde** guard dog; **chien-loup** nm wolfhound

chiendent [ʃjε̃dɑ̃] nm couch grass

chienne [ʃjεn] nf dog, bitch

chier [ʃje] (fam!) vi to crap (!)

chiffon [ʃifɔ̃] nm (piece of) rag; **chiffonner** vt to crumple; (fam: tracasser) to concern

chiffre [ʃifʀ] nm (représentant un nombre) figure, numeral; (montant, total) total, sum; **en ~s ronds** in round figures; **~ d'affaires** turnover; **chiffrer** vt (dépense) to put a figure to, assess; (message) to (en)code, cipher; **se chiffrer à** to add up to, amount to

chignon [ʃiɲɔ̃] nm chignon, bun

Chili [ʃili] nm: **le ~** Chile; **chilien, ne** adj Chilean ♦ nm/f: **Chilien, ne** Chilean

chimie [ʃimi] nf chemistry; **chimique** adj chemical; **produits chimiques** chemicals

chimpanzé [ʃε̃pɑ̃ze] nm chimpanzee

Chine [ʃin] nf: **la ~** China; **chinois, e** adj Chinese ♦ nm/f: **Chinois, e** Chinese ♦ nm (LING) Chinese

chiot [ʃjo] nm pup(py)

chiper [ʃipe] (fam) vt to pinch

chipoter [ʃipɔte] (fam) vi (ergoter) to quibble

chips [ʃips] nfpl crisps (BRIT), (potato) chips (US)

chiquenaude [ʃiknod] nf flick, flip

chirurgical, e, -aux [ʃiʀyʀʒikal, o] adj surgical

chirurgie [ʃiʀyʀʒi] nf surgery; **~ esthétique** plastic surgery; **chirurgien, ne** nm/f surgeon

chlore [klɔʀ] nm chlorine

choc [ʃɔk] nm (heurt) impact, shock; (collision) crash; (moral) shock; (affrontement) clash

chocolat [ʃɔkɔla] nm chocolate; **~ au lait** milk chocolate; **~ (chaud)** hot chocolate

chœur [kœʀ] nm (chorale) choir; (OPÉRA, THÉÂTRE) chorus; **en ~** in chorus

choisir [ʃwaziʀ] vt to choose, select

choix [ʃwa] nm choice, selection; **avoir le ~** to have the choice; **premier ~** (COMM) class one; **de ~** choice, selected; **au ~** as you wish

chômage [ʃomaʒ] nm unemployment; **mettre au ~** to make redundant, put out of work; **être au ~** to be unemployed ou out of work; **chômeur, -euse** nm/f unemployed person

chope [ʃɔp] nf tankard

choper [ʃɔpe] (fam) vt (objet, maladie) to catch

choquer [ʃɔke] vt (offenser) to shock; (deuil) to shake

chorale [kɔʀal] nf choir

choriste [kɔʀist] nm/f choir member; (OPÉRA) chorus member

chose [ʃoz] nf thing; **c'est peu de ~** it's nothing (really)

chou, x [ʃu] nm cabbage; **mon petit ~** (my) sweetheart; **~ à la crème** choux bun; **~x de Bruxelles** Brussels sprouts; **chouchou, te** (fam) nm/f darling; (SCOL) teacher's pet; **choucroute** nf sauerkraut

chouette [ʃwεt] nf owl ♦ adj (fam) great, smashing

chou-fleur [ʃuflœʀ] nm cauliflower

choyer [ʃwaje] vt (dorloter) to cherish; (: excessivement) to pamper

chrétien, ne [kʀetjε̃, jεn] adj, nm/f Christian

Christ [kʀist] nm: **le ~** Christ; **christianisme** nm Christianity

chrome [kʀom] nm chromium; **chromé, e** adj chromium-plated

chronique [kʀɔnik] adj chronic ♦ nf (de journal) column, page; (historique) chronicle; (RADIO, TV): **la ~ sportive** the sports review

chronologique [kʀɔnɔlɔʒik] adj chronological

chronomètre [kʀɔnɔmɛtʀ] nm stopwatch; **chronométrer** vt to time

chrysanthème [kʀizɑ̃tɛm] nm. chrysanthème

chuchotement [ʃyʃɔtmɑ̃] nm whisper

chuchoter [ʃyʃɔte] vt, vi to whisper

chut [ʃyt] excl sh!

chute [ʃyt] nf fall; (déchet) scrap; **faire une ~ (de 10 m)** to fall (10 m); **~ (d'eau)** waterfall; **la ~ des cheveux** hair loss; **~ libre** free fall; **~s de pluie/neige** rain/snowfalls

Chypre [ʃipʀ] nm/f Cyprus

-ci [si] adv voir **par ♦ dét**: **ce garçon-~/-là** this/that boy; **ces femmes-~/-là** these/those women

cible [sibl] nf target

ciboulette [sibulɛt] nf (small) chive

cicatrice [sikatʀis] nf scar; **cicatriser** vt to heal

ci-contre [sikɔ̃tʀ] adv opposite

ci-dessous [sidəsu] adv below

ci-dessus [sidəsy] adv above

cidre [sidʀ] nm cider

Cie abr (= compagnie) Co.

ciel [sjɛl] nm sky; (REL) heaven; **cieux** nmpl (REL) heaven sg; **à ~ ouvert** open-air; (mine) open-cast

cierge [sjɛʀʒ] nm candle

cieux [sjø] nmpl de **ciel**

cigale [sigal] nf cicada

cigare [sigaʀ] nm cigar

cigarette [sigaʀɛt] nf cigarette

ci-gît [siʒi] adv +vb here lies

cigogne [sigɔɲ] nf stork

ci-inclus, e [siɛ̃kly, yz] adj, adv enclosed

ci-joint, e [siʒwɛ̃, ɛ̃t] adj, adv enclosed

cil [sil] nm (eye)lash

cime [sim] nf top; (montagne) peak

ciment [simɑ̃] nm cement

cimetière [simtjɛʀ] nm cemetery; (d'église) churchyard

cinéaste [sineast] nm/f film-maker

cinéma [sinema] nm cinema; **cinématographique** adj film cpd, cinema cpd

cinglant, e [sɛ̃glɑ̃, ɑ̃t] adj (remarque) biting

cinglé, e [sɛ̃gle] (fam) adj crazy

cinq [sɛ̃k] num five; **cinquantaine** nf: **une cinquantaine (de)** about fifty; **avoir la cinquantaine** (âge) to be around fifty; **cinquante** num fifty; **cinquantenaire** adj, nm/f fifty-year-old; **cinquième** num fifth

cintre [sɛ̃tʀ] nm coat-hanger

cintré, e [sɛ̃tʀe] adj (chemise) fitted

cirage [siʀaʒ] nm (shoe) polish

circonflexe [siʀkɔ̃flɛks] adj: **accent ~** circumflex accent

circonscription [siʀkɔ̃skʀipsjɔ̃] nf district; **~ électorale** (d'un député) constituency

circonscrire [siʀkɔ̃skʀiʀ] vt (sujet) to define, delimit; (incendie) to contain

circonstance [siʀkɔ̃stɑ̃s] nf circumstance; (occasion) occasion; **~s atténuantes** mitigating circumstances

circuit [siʀkɥi] nm (ÉLEC, TECH) circuit; (trajet) tour, (round) trip

circulaire [siʀkylɛʀ] adj, nf circular

circulation [siʀkylasjɔ̃] nf circulation; (AUTO): **la ~** (the) traffic

circuler [siʀkyle] vi (sang, devises) to circulate; (véhicules) to drive (along); (passants) to walk along; (train, bus) to run; **faire ~** (nouvelle) to spread (about), circulate; (badauds) to move on

cire [siʀ] nf wax; **ciré** nm oilskin; **cirer** vt to wax, polish

cirque [siʀk] nm circus; (fig) chaos, bedlam; **quel ~!** what a carry-on!

cisaille(s) [sizaj] nf(pl) (gardening) shears pl

ciseau, x [sizo] nm: **~ (à bois)** chisel; **~x** nmpl (paire de ~x) (pair of) scissors

ciseler [siz(ə)le] vt to chisel, carve

citadin, e [sitadɛ̃, in] nm/f city dweller

citation [sitasjɔ̃] nf (d'auteur) quotation; (JUR) summons sg

cité [site] nf town; (plus grande) city; **~ universitaire** students' residences pl

citer [site] vt (un auteur) to quote (from); (nommer) to name; (JUR) to summon

citerne [sitɛʀn] nf tank

citoyen, ne [sitwajɛ̃, jɛn] nm/f citizen

citron [sitʀɔ̃] nm lemon; **~ vert** lime; **citronnade** nf still lemonade

citrouille [sitʀuj] nf pumpkin

civet [sivɛ] nm: **~ de lapin** rabbit stew

civière [sivjɛʀ] nf stretcher

civil, e [sivil] adj (mariage, poli) civil; (non militaire) civilian; **en ~** in civilian clothes; **dans le ~** in civilian life

civilisation [sivilizasjɔ̃] nf civilization

clair, e [klɛʀ] adj light; (pièce) light, bright; (eau, son, fig) clear ♦ adv: **voir ~** to see clearly; **tirer qch au ~** to clear sth up, clarify sth; **mettre au ~** (notes etc) to tidy up; **~ de lune ♦** nm moonlight; **clairement** adv clearly

clairière [klɛʀjɛʀ] nf clearing

clairon [klɛʀɔ̃] nm bugle; **claironner** vt (fig) to trumpet, shout from the rooftops

clairsemé, e [klɛʀsəme] adj sparse

clairvoyant, e [klɛʀvwajɑ̃, ɑ̃t] adj perceptive, clear-sighted

clandestin, e [klɑ̃dɛstɛ̃, in] adj clandestine, secret; (mouvement) underground; (travailleur) illegal; **passager ~** stowaway

clapier [klapje] nm (rabbit) hutch

clapoter [klapɔte] vi to lap

claque [klak] nf (gifle) slap; **claquer** vi

(*porte*) to bang, slam; (*fam: mourir*) to snuff it ♦ *vt* (*porte*) to slam, bang; (*doigts*) to snap; (*fam: dépenser*) to blow; **il claquait des dents** his teeth were chattering; **être claqué** (*fam*) to be dead tired; **se claquer un muscle** to pull *ou* strain a muscle; **claquettes** *nfpl* tap-dancing *sg*; (*chaussures*) flip-flops

clarinette [klaʀinɛt] *nf* clarinet

clarté [klaʀte] *nf* (*luminosité*) brightness; (*d'un son, de l'eau*) clearness; (*d'une explication*) clarity

classe [klɑs] *nf* class; (*SCOL: local*) class(room); (: *leçon, élèves*) class; **aller en ~** to go to school; **classement** *nm* (*rang: SCOL*) placing; (: *SPORT*) placing; (*liste: SCOL*) class list (in order of merit); (: *SPORT*) placings *pl*

classer [klɑse] *vt* (*idées, livres*) to classify; (*papiers*) to file; (*candidat, concurrent*) to grade; (*JUR: affaire*) to close; **se ~ premier/ dernier** to come first/last; (*SPORT*) to finish first/last; **classeur** *nm* (*cahier*) file

classique [klɑsik] *adj* classical; (*sobre: coupe etc*) classic(al); (*habituel*) standard, classic

clause [kloz] *nf* clause

clavecin [klav(ə)sɛ̃] *nm* harpsichord

clavicule [klavikyl] *nf* collarbone

clavier [klavje] *nm* keyboard

clé [kle] *nf* key; (*MUS*) clef; (*de mécanicien*) spanner (*BRIT*), wrench (*US*); **prix ~s en main** (*d'une voiture*) on-the-road price; **~ anglaise** (monkey) wrench; **~ de contact** ignition key

clef [kle] *nf* = **clé**

clément, e [klemã, ãt] *adj* (*temps*) mild; (*indulgent*) lenient

clerc [klɛʀ] *nm*: **~ de notaire** solicitor's clerk

clergé [klɛʀʒe] *nm* clergy

cliché [kliʃe] *nm* (*fig*) cliché; (*négatif*) negative; (*photo*) print

client, e [klijã, klijãt] *nm/f* (*acheteur*) customer, client; (*d'hôtel*) guest, patron; (*du docteur*) patient; (*de l'avocat*) client; **clientèle** *nf* (*du magasin*) customers *pl*, clientèle; (*du docteur, de l'avocat*) practice

cligner [kliɲe] *vi*: **~ des yeux** to blink (one's eyes); **~ de l'œil** to wink; **clignotant** *nm* (*AUTO*) indicator; **clignoter** *vi* (*étoiles etc*) to twinkle; (*lumière*) to flicker

climat [klima] *nm* climate

climatisation [klimatizasjɔ̃] *nf* air conditioning; **climatisé, e** *adj* air-conditioned

clin d'œil [klɛ̃dœj] *nm* wink; **en un ~** in a flash

clinique [klinik] *nf* private hospital

clinquant, e [klɛ̃kɑ̃, ɑ̃t] *adj* flashy

clip [klip] *nm* (*boucle d'oreille*) clip-on; (*vidéo*) **~ (pop)** video

cliqueter [klik(ə)te] *vi* (*ferraille*) to jangle;

(*clés*) to jingle

clochard, e [klɔʃaʀ, aʀd] *nm/f* tramp

cloche [klɔʃ] *nf* (*d'église*) bell; (*fam*) clot; **cloche-pied: à cloche-pied** *adv* on one leg, hopping (along); **clocher** *nm* church tower; (*en pointe*) steeple ♦ *vi* (*fam*) to be *ou* go wrong; **de clocher** (*péj*) parochial

cloison [klwazɔ̃] *nf* partition (wall)

cloître [klwatʀ] *nm* cloister; **cloîtrer** *vt*: **se cloîtrer** to shut o.s. up *ou* away

cloque [klɔk] *nf* blister

clore [klɔʀ] *vt* to close; **clos, e** *adj voir* **maison; huis**

clôture [klotyʀ] *nf* closure; (*barrière*) enclosure; **clôturer** *vt* (*terrain*) to enclose; (*débats*) to close

clou [klu] *nm* nail; **~s** *nmpl* (*passage ~té*) pedestrian crossing; **pneus à ~s** studded tyres; **le ~ du spectacle** the highlight of the show; **~ de girofle** clove; **clouer** *vt* to nail down *ou* up; **clouer le bec à qn** (*fam*) to shut sb up

clown [klun] *nm* clown

club [klœb] *nm* club

CNRS *sigle m* (= *Centre nationale de la recherche scientifique*) ≈ SERC (*BRIT*), ≈ NSF (*US*)

coaguler [kɔagyle] *vt, vi* (*aussi*: **se ~**: *sang*) to coagulate

coasser [kɔase] *vi* to croak

cobaye [kɔbaj] *nm* guinea-pig

coca [kɔka] *nm* Coke ®

cocaïne [kɔkain] *nf* cocaine

cocasse [kɔkas] *adj* comical, funny

coccinelle [kɔksinɛl] *nf* ladybird (*BRIT*), ladybug (*US*)

cocher [kɔʃe] *vt* to tick off

cochère [kɔʃɛʀ] *adj f*: **porte ~** carriage entrance

cochon, ne [kɔʃɔ̃, ɔn] *nm* pig ♦ *adj* (*fam*) dirty, smutty; **~ d'Inde** guinea pig; **cochonnerie** (*fam*) *nf* (*saleté*) filth; (*marchandise*) rubbish, trash

cocktail [kɔktɛl] *nm* cocktail; (*réception*) cocktail party

coco [kɔko] *nm voir* **noix**

cocorico [kɔkɔʀiko] *excl, nm* cock-a-doodle-do

cocotier [kɔkɔtje] *nm* coconut palm

cocotte [kɔkɔt] *nf* (*en fonte*) casserole; **~ (minute)** pressure cooker; **ma ~** (*fam*) sweetie (*pie*)

cocu [kɔky] (*fam*) *nm* cuckold

code [kɔd] *nm* code ♦ *adj*: **phares ~s** dipped lights; **se mettre en ~(s)** to dip one's (head)lights; **~ à barres** bar code; **~ civil** Common Law; **~ de la route** highway code; **~ pénal** penal code; **~ postal** (*numéro*) post (*BRIT*) *ou* zip (*US*) code

cœur [kœʀ] nm heart; (CARTES: couleur) hearts pl; (: carte) heart; **avoir bon ~** to be kind-hearted; **avoir mal au ~** to feel sick; **en avoir le ~ net** to be clear in one's own mind (about it); **par ~** by heart; **de bon ~** willingly; **cela lui tient à ~** that's (very) close to his heart

coffre [kɔfʀ] nm (meuble) chest; (d'auto) boot (BRIT), trunk (US); **coffre(-fort)** nm safe; **coffret** nm casket

cognac [kɔɲak] nm brandy, cognac

cogner [kɔɲe] vi to knock; **se ~ la tête** to bang one's head

cohérent, e [kɔeʀɑ̃, ɑ̃t] adj coherent, consistent

cohorte [kɔɔʀt] nf troop

cohue [kɔy] nf crowd

coi, coite [kwa, kwat] adj: **rester ~** to remain silent

coiffe [kwaf] nf headdress

coiffé, e [kwafe] adj: **bien/mal ~** with tidy/untidy hair

coiffer [kwafe] vt (fig: surmonter) to cover, top; **se ~** vi to do one's hair; **~ qn** to do sb's hair; **coiffeur, -euse** nm/f hairdresser; **coiffeuse** nf (table) dressing table; **coiffure** nf (cheveux) hairstyle, hairdo; (art): **la coiffure** hairdressing

coin [kwɛ̃] nm corner; (pour ~cer) wedge; **l'épicerie du ~** the local grocer; **dans le ~** (aux alentours) in the area, around about; (habiter) locally; **je ne suis pas du ~** I'm not from here; **au ~ du feu** by the fireside; **regard en ~** sideways glance

coincé, e [kwɛ̃se] adj stuck, jammed; (fig: inhibé) inhibited, hung up (fam)

coincer [kwɛ̃se] vt to jam; (fam: attraper) to pinch

coïncidence [kɔɛ̃sidɑ̃s] nf coincidence

coïncider [kɔɛ̃side] vi to coincide

coing [kwɛ̃] nm quince

col [kɔl] nm (de chemise) collar; (encolure, cou) neck; (de montagne) pass; **~ de l'utérus** cervix; **~ roulé** polo-neck

colère [kɔlɛʀ] nf anger; **une ~ a** fit of anger; **(se mettre) en ~** (to get) angry; **coléreux, -euse** adj, **colérique** adj quick-tempered, irascible

colifichet [kɔlifiʃɛ] nm trinket

colimaçon [kɔlimasɔ̃] nm: **escalier en ~** spiral staircase

colin [kɔlɛ̃] nm hake

colique [kɔlik] nf diarrhoea

colis [kɔli] nm parcel

collaborateur, -trice [kɔ(l)labɔʀatœʀ, tʀis] nm/f (aussi POL) collaborator; (d'une revue) contributor

collaborer [kɔ(l)labɔʀe] vi to collaborate; **~ à** to collaborate on; (revue) to contribute to

collant, e [kɔlɑ̃, ɑ̃t] adj sticky; (robe etc)

clinging, skintight; (péj) clinging ♦ nm (bas) tights pl; (de danseur) leotard

collation [kɔlasjɔ̃] nf light meal

colle [kɔl] nf glue; (à papiers peints) (wallpaper) paste; (fam: devinette) teaser, riddle; (SCOL: fam) detention

collecte [kɔlɛkt] nf collection; **collectif, -ive** adj collective; (visite, billet) group cpd

collection [kɔlɛksjɔ̃] nf collection; (ÉDITION) series; **collectionner** vt to collect; **collectionneur, -euse** nm/f collector

collectivité [kɔlɛktivite] nf group; **~s locales** (ADMIN) local authorities

collège [kɔlɛʒ] nm (école) (secondary) school; (assemblée) body; **collégien** nm schoolboy; **collégienne** nf schoolgirl

collègue [kɔ(l)lɛg] nm/f colleague

coller [kɔle] vt (papier, timbre) to stick (on); (affiche) to stick up; (enveloppe) to stick down; (morceaux) to stick ou glue together; (fam: mettre, fourrer) to stick, shove; (SCOL: fam) to keep in ♦ vi (être collant) to be sticky; (adhérer) to stick; **~ à** to stick to; **être collé à un examen** (fam) to fail an exam

collet [kɔlɛ] nm (piège) snare, noose; (cou): **prendre qn au ~** to grab sb by the throat

collier [kɔlje] nm (bijou) necklace; (de chien, TECH) collar

collimateur [kɔlimatœʀ] nm: **avoir qn/qch dans le ~** (fig) to have sb/sth in one's sights

colline [kɔlin] nf hill

collision [kɔlizjɔ̃] nf collision, crash; **entrer en ~ (avec)** to collide (with)

colloque [kɔ(l)lɔk] nm symposium

collyre [kɔliʀ] nm eye drops

colmater [kɔlmate] vt (fuite) to seal off; (brèche) to plug, fill in

colombe [kɔlɔ̃b] nf dove

Colombie [kɔlɔ̃bi] nf: **la ~** Colombia

colon [kɔlɔ̃] nm settler

colonel [kɔlɔnɛl] nm colonel

colonie [kɔlɔni] nf colony; **~ (de vacances)** holiday camp (for children)

colonne [kɔlɔn] nf column; **se mettre en ~ par deux** to get into twos; **~ (vertébrale)** spine, spinal column

colorant [kɔlɔʀɑ̃, ɑ̃t] nm colouring

colorer [kɔlɔʀe] vt to colour

colorier [kɔlɔʀje] vt to colour (in)

coloris [kɔlɔʀi] nm colour, shade

colporter [kɔlpɔʀte] vt to hawk, peddle

colza [kɔlza] nm rape(seed)

coma [kɔma] nm coma; **être dans le ~** to be in a coma

combat [kɔ̃ba] nm fight, fighting no pl; **~ de boxe** boxing match; **combattant** nm: **ancien combattant** war veteran; **combattre** vt to fight; (épidémie, ignorance) to combat, fight against

combien [kɔ̃bjɛ̃] adv (quantité) how much; (nombre) how many; ~ **de** (quantité) how much; (nombre) how many; ~ **de temps** how long; ~ **ça coûte/pèse?** how much does it cost/weigh?; **on est le ~ aujourd'hui?** (fam) what's the date today?

combinaison [kɔ̃binezɔ̃] nf combination; (astuce) device, scheme; (de femme) slip; (de plongée) wetsuit; (bleu de travail) boiler suit (BRIT), coveralls pl (US)

combine [kɔ̃bin] nf trick; (péj) scheme, fiddle (BRIT)

combiné [kɔ̃bine] nm (aussi: ~ **téléphonique**) receiver

combiner [kɔ̃bine] vt (grouper) to combine; (plan, horaire) to work out, devise

comble [kɔ̃bl] adj (salle) packed (full) ♦ nm (du bonheur, plaisir) height; ~**s** nmpl (CONSTR) attic sg, loft sg; **c'est le ~!** that beats everything!

combler [kɔ̃ble] vt (trou) to fill in; (besoin, lacune) to fill; (déficit) to make good; (satisfaire) to fulfil

combustible [kɔ̃bystibl] nm fuel

comédie [kɔmedi] nf comedy; (fig) playacting no pl; **faire la ~** (fam) to make a fuss; ~ **musicale** musical; **comédien, ne** nm/f actor(-tress)

comestible [kɔmɛstibl] adj edible

comique [kɔmik] adj (drôle) comical; (THÉÂTRE) comic ♦ nm (artiste) comic, comedian

comité [kɔmite] nm committee; ~ **d'entreprise** works council

commandant [kɔmɑ̃dɑ̃] nm (gén) commander, commandant; (NAVIG, AVIAT) captain

commande [kɔmɑ̃d] nf (COMM) order; ~**s** nfpl (AVIAT etc) controls; **sur** ~ to order; **commandement** nm command; (REL) commandment; **commander** vt (COMM) to order; (diriger, ordonner) to command; **commander à qn de faire** to command ou order sb to do

commando [kɔmɑ̃do] nm commando (squad)

comme [kɔm] prép 1 (comparaison) like; **tout comme son père** just like his father; **fort comme un bœuf** as strong as an ox; **joli comme tout** ever so pretty
2 (manière) like; **faites-le comme ça** do it like this, do it this way; **comme ci, comme ça** so-so, middling
3 (en tant que) as a; **donner comme prix** to give as a prize; **travailler comme secrétaire** to work as a secretary
♦ conj 1 (ainsi que) as; **elle écrit comme elle parle** she writes as she talks; **comme si** as if
2 (au moment où, alors que) as; **il est parti comme j'arrivais** he left as I arrived
3 (parce que, puisque) as; **comme il était en retard, il ... as** he was late, he ...
♦ adv: **comme il est fort/c'est bon!** he's so strong/it's so good!

commémorer [kɔmemɔre] vt to commemorate

commencement [kɔmɑ̃smɑ̃] nm beginning, start

commencer [kɔmɑ̃se] vt, vi to begin, start; ~ **à ou de faire** to begin ou start doing

comment [kɔmɑ̃] adv how; ~**?** (que dites-vous) pardon?

commentaire [kɔmɑ̃tɛr] nm (remarque) comment, remark; (exposé) commentary

commenter [kɔmɑ̃te] vt (jugement, événement) to comment (up)on; (RADIO, TV: match, manifestation) to cover

commérages [kɔmeraʒ] nmpl gossip sg

commerçant, e [kɔmɛrsɑ̃, ɑ̃t] nm/f shopkeeper, trader

commerce [kɔmɛrs] nm (activité) trade, commerce; (boutique) business; **commercial, e, -aux** adj commercial, trading; (péj) commercial; **les commerciaux** the sales people; **commercialiser** vt to market

commère [kɔmɛr] nf gossip

commettre [kɔmɛtr] vt to commit

commis [kɔmi] nm (de magasin) (shop) assistant; (de banque) clerk

commissaire [kɔmisɛr] nm (de police) ≈ (police) superintendent; **commissaire-priseur** nm auctioneer; **commissariat** nm police station

commission [kɔmisjɔ̃] nf (comité, pourcentage) commission; (message) message; (course) errand; ~**s** nfpl (achats) shopping sg

commode [kɔmɔd] adj (pratique) convenient, handy; (facile) easy; (personne): **pas ~** awkward (to deal with) ♦ nf chest of drawers; **commodité** nf convenience

commotion [kɔmosjɔ̃] nf: ~ **(cérébrale)** concussion; **commotionné, e** adj shocked, shaken

commun, e [kɔmœ̃, yn] adj common; (pièce) communal, shared; (effort) joint; **ça sort du ~** it's out of the ordinary; **le ~ des mortels** the common run of people; **en ~ (faire)** jointly; **mettre en ~** to pool, share; voir aussi **communs**

communauté [kɔmynote] nf community

commune [kɔmyn] nf (ADMIN) commune, ~ district; (: urbaine) ≈ borough

communicatif, -ive [kɔmynikatif, iv] adj

(*rire*) infectious; (*personne*) communicative

communication [kɔmynikasjɔ̃] *nf* communication; **~** (**téléphonique**) (telephone) call

communier [kɔmynje] *vi* (*REL*) to receive communion

communion [kɔmynjɔ̃] *nf* communion

communiquer [kɔmynike] *vt* (*nouvelle, dossier*) to pass on, convey; (*peur etc*) to communicate ♦ *vi* to communicate; **se ~ à** (*se propager*) to spread to

communisme [kɔmynism] *nm* communism; **communiste** *adj, nm/f* communist

communs [kɔmœ̃] *nmpl* (*bâtiments*) outbuildings

commutateur [kɔmytatœʀ] *nm* (*ÉLEC*) (change-over) switch, commutator

compact, e [kɔpakt] *adj* (*dense*) dense; (*appareil*) compact

compagne [kɔpaɲ] *nf* companion

compagnie [kɔpaɲi] *nf* (*firme, MIL*) company; **tenir ~ à qn** to keep sb company; **fausser ~ à qn** to give sb the slip, slip *ou* sneak away from sb; **~ aérienne** airline (company)

compagnon [kɔpaɲɔ̃] *nm* companion

comparable [kɔparabl] *adj*: **~ (à)** comparable (to)

comparaison [kɔparezɔ̃] *nf* comparison

comparaître [kɔparetr] *vi*: **~ (devant)** to appear (before)

comparer [kɔpare] *vt* to compare; **~ qch/qn à ou et** (*pour choisir*) to compare sth/sb with *ou* and; (*pour établir une similitude*) to compare sth/sb to

compartiment [kɔpartimɑ̃] *nm* compartment

comparution [kɔparysjɔ̃] *nf* (*JUR*) appearance

compas [kɔpa] *nm* (*GÉOM*) (pair of) compasses *pl*; (*NAVIG*) compass

compatible [kɔpatibl] *adj* compatible

compatir [kɔpatir] *vi* to sympathize

compatriote [kɔpatrijɔt] *nm/f* compatriot

compensation [kɔpɑ̃sasjɔ̃] *nf* compensation

compenser [kɔpɑ̃se] *vt* to compensate for, make up for

compère [kɔpɛʀ] *nm* accomplice

compétence [kɔpetɑ̃s] *nf* competence

compétent, e [kɔpetɑ̃, ɑ̃t] *adj* (*apte*) competent, capable

compétition [kɔpetisjɔ̃] *nf* (*gén*) competition; (*SPORT: épreuve*) event; **la ~ automobile** motor racing

complainte [kɔplɛ̃t] *nf* lament

complaire [kɔplɛʀ]: **se ~** *vi*: **se ~ dans** to take pleasure in

complaisance [kɔplɛzɑ̃s] *nf* kindness;

pavillon de ~ flag of convenience

complaisant, e [kɔplɛzɑ̃, ɑ̃t] *adj* (*aimable*) kind, obliging

complément [kɔplemɑ̃] *nm* complement; (*reste*) remainder; **~ d'information** (*ADMIN*) supplementary *ou* further information; **complémentaire** *adj* complementary; (*additionnel*) supplementary

complet, -ète [kɔplɛ, ɛt] *adj* complete; (*plein: hôtel etc*) full ♦ *nm* (*aussi*: **~-veston**) suit; **pain ~** wholemeal bread; **complètement** *adv* completely; **compléter** *vt* (*porter à la quantité voulue*) to complete; (*augmenter: connaissances, études*) to complement, supplement; (: *garde-robe*) to add to; **se compléter** (*caractères*) to complement one another

complexe [kɔplɛks] *adj, nm* complex; **complexé, e** *adj* mixed-up, hung-up

complication [kɔplikasjɔ̃] *nf* complexity, intricacy; (*difficulté, ennui*) complication

complice [kɔplis] *nm* accomplice; **complicité** *nf* complicity

compliment [kɔplimɑ̃] *nm* (*louange*) compliment; **~s** *nmpl* (*félicitations*) congratulations

compliqué, e [kɔplike] *adj* complicated, complex; (*personne*) complicated

compliquer [kɔplike] *vt* to complicate; **se ~** to become complicated

complot [kɔplo] *nm* plot

comportement [kɔpɔrtəmɑ̃] *nm* behaviour

comporter [kɔpɔrte] *vt* (*consister en*) to consist of, comprise; (*inclure*) to have; **se ~** *vi* to behave

composant [kɔpozɑ̃] *nm*, **composante** [kɔpozɑ̃t] *nf* component

composé [kɔpoze] *nm* compound

composer [kɔpoze] *vt* (*musique, texte*) to compose; (*mélange, équipe*) to make up; (*numéro*) to dial; (*constituer*) to make up, form ♦ *vi* (*transiger*) to come to terms; **se ~ de** to be composed of, be made up of; **compositeur, -trice** *nm/f* (*MUS*) composer; **composition** *nf* composition; (*SCOL*) test

composter [kɔpɔste] *vt* (*billet*) to punch

compote [kɔpɔt] *nf* stewed fruit *no pl*; **~ de pommes** stewed apples

compréhensible [kɔpreɑ̃sibl] *adj* comprehensible; (*attitude*) understandable

compréhensif, -ive [kɔpreɑ̃sif, iv] *adj* understanding

comprendre [kɔprɑ̃dr] *vt* to understand; (*se composer de*) to comprise, consist of

compresse [kɔprɛs] *nf* compress

compression [kɔpresjɔ̃] *nf* compression; (*de personnes*) reduction

comprimé [kɔprime] *nm* tablet

comprimer [kɔprime] *vt* to compress; (*fig*:

crédit etc) to reduce, cut down
compris, e [kɔ̃pʀi, iz] *pp de* **comprendre**
♦ *adj* (*inclus*) included; ~ **entre** (*situé*)
contained between; **l'électricité ~e/non ~e,**
y/non ~ **l'électricité** including/excluding
electricity; **100 F tout** ~ 100 F all inclusive *ou*
all-in
compromettre [kɔ̃pʀɔmɛtʀ] *vt* to
compromise; **compromis** *nm* compromise
comptabilité [kɔ̃tabilite] *nf* (*activité*)
accounting, accountancy; (*comptes*) accounts
pl, books pl; (*service*) accounts office
comptable [kɔ̃tabl] *nm/f* accountant
comptant [kɔ̃tɑ̃] *adv*: **payer** ~ to pay cash;
acheter ~ to buy for cash
compte [kɔ̃t] *nm* count; (*total, montant*)
count, (right) number; (*bancaire, facture*)
account; ~**s** *nmpl* (FINANCE) accounts, books;
(*fig*) explanation *sg*; **en fin de** ~ all things
considered; **s'en tirer à bon** ~ to get off
lightly; **pour le** ~ **de** on behalf of; **pour son
propre** ~ for one's own benefit; **tenir** ~ **de** to
take account of; **travailler à son** ~ to work for
oneself; **rendre** ~ **(à qn) de qch** to give (sb)
an account of sth; *voir aussi* **rendre** ~ **à
rebours** countdown; ~ **chèques postaux** Post
Office account; ~ **courant** current account; ~
rendu account, report; (*de film, livre*)
review; **compte-gouttes** *nm inv* dropper
compter [kɔ̃te] *vt* to count; (*facturer*) to
charge for; (*avoir à son actif, comporter*) to
have; (*prévoir*) to allow, reckon; (*penser,
espérer*): ~ **réussir** to expect to succeed ♦ *vi*
to count; (*être économe*) to economize;
(*figurer*): ~ **parmi** to be *ou* rank among; ~
sur to count (up)on; ~ **avec qch/qn** to reckon
with *ou* take account of sth/sb; **sans** ~ **que**
besides which
compteur [kɔ̃tœʀ] *nm* meter; ~ **de vitesse**
speedometer
comptine [kɔ̃tin] *nf* nursery rhyme
comptoir [kɔ̃twaʀ] *nm* (*de magasin*) counter;
(*bar*) bar
compulser [kɔ̃pylse] *vt* to consult
comte [kɔ̃t] *nm* count; **comtesse** *nf*
countess
con, ne [kɔ̃, kɔn] (*fam!*) *adj* damned *ou*
bloody (BRIT) stupid (*!*)
concéder [kɔ̃sede] *vt* to grant; (*défaite,
point*) to concede
concentré, e [kɔ̃sɑ̃tʀe] *adj* (*lait*) condensed
♦ *nm*: ~ **de tomates** tomato purée
concentrer [kɔ̃sɑ̃tʀe] *vt* to concentrate; **se** ~
vi to concentrate
concept [kɔ̃sɛpt] *nm* concept
conception [kɔ̃sɛpsjɔ̃] *nf* conception; (*d'une
machine etc*) design; (*d'un problème, de la
vie*) approach
concerner [kɔ̃sɛʀne] *vt* to concern; **en ce**

qui me **concerne** as far as I am concerned
concert [kɔ̃sɛʀ] *nm* concert; **de** ~ (*décider*)
unanimously; **concerter: se concerter** *vi* to
put their *etc* heads together
concession [kɔ̃sesjɔ̃] *nf* concession;
concessionnaire *nm/f* agent, dealer
concevoir [kɔ̃s(ə)vwaʀ] *vt* (*idée, projet*) to
conceive (of); (*comprendre*) to understand;
(*enfant*) to conceive; **bien/mal conçu** well-/
badly-designed
concierge [kɔ̃sjɛʀʒ] *nm/f* caretaker
conciliabules [kɔ̃siljabyl] *nmpl* (private)
discussions, confabulations
concilier [kɔ̃silje] *vt* to reconcile; **se** ~ *vt* to
win over
concis, e [kɔ̃si, iz] *adj* concise
concitoyen, ne [kɔ̃sitwajɛ̃, jɛn] *nm/f* fellow
citizen
concluant, e [kɔ̃klyɑ̃, ɑ̃t] *adj* conclusive
conclure [kɔ̃klyʀ] *vt* to conclude;
conclusion *nf* conclusion
conçois *etc* [kɔ̃swa] *vb voir* **concevoir**
concombre [kɔ̃kɔ̃bʀ] *nm* cucumber
concorder [kɔ̃kɔʀde] *vi* to tally, agree
concourir [kɔ̃kuʀiʀ] *vi* (SPORT) to compete;
~ **à** (*effet etc*) to work towards
concours [kɔ̃kuʀ] *nm* competition; (SCOL)
competitive examination; (*assistance*) aid,
help; ~ **de circonstances** combination of
circumstances; ~ **hippique** horse show
concret, -ète [kɔ̃kʀɛ, ɛt] *adj* concrete
concrétiser [kɔ̃kʀetize]: **se** ~ *vi* to
materialize
conçu, e [kɔ̃sy] *pp de* **concevoir**
concubinage [kɔ̃kybinaʒ] *nm* (JUR)
cohabitation
concurrence [kɔ̃kyʀɑ̃s] *nf* competition; **faire**
~ **à** to be in competition with; **jusqu'à** ~ **de**
up to
concurrent, e [kɔ̃kyʀɑ̃, ɑ̃t] *nm/f* (SPORT,
ÉCON etc) competitor; (SCOL) candidate
condamner [kɔ̃dɑne] *vt* (*blâmer*) to
condemn; (JUR) to sentence; (*porte,
ouverture*) to fill in, block up; ~ **qn à 2 ans de
prison** to sentence sb to 2 years' imprison-
onment
condensation [kɔ̃dɑ̃sasjɔ̃] *nf* condensation
condenser [kɔ̃dɑ̃se] *vt* to condense; **se** ~ *vi*
to condense
condisciple [kɔ̃disipl] *nm/f* fellow student
condition [kɔ̃disjɔ̃] *nf* condition; ~**s** *nfpl*
(*tarif, prix*) terms; (*circonstances*) conditions;
à ~ **de** *ou* **que** provided that; **conditionnel,
le** *nm* conditional (tense)
conditionnement [kɔ̃disjɔnmɑ̃] *nm*
(*emballage*) packaging
conditionner [kɔ̃disjɔne] *vt* (*déterminer*) to
determine; (COMM: *produit*) to package; **air
conditionné** air conditioning

condoléances [kɔ̃dɔleɑ̃s] *nfpl* condolences
conducteur, -trice [kɔ̃dyktœʀ, tʀis] *nm/f* driver ♦ *nm* (*ÉLEC etc*) conductor
conduire [kɔ̃dɥiʀ] *vt* to drive; (*délégation, troupeau*) to lead; **se ~** *vi* to behave; **~ à** to lead to; **~ qn quelque part** to take sb somewhere; **~** to drive sb somewhere
conduite [kɔ̃dɥit] *nf* (*comportement*) behaviour; (*d'eau, de gaz*) pipe; **sous la ~ de** led by; **~ à gauche** left-hand drive
cône [kon] *nm* cone
confection [kɔ̃fɛksjɔ̃] *nf* (*fabrication*) making; (*COUTURE*): **la ~** the clothing industry
confectionner [kɔ̃fɛksjɔne] *vt* to make
conférence [kɔ̃feʀɑ̃s] *nf* conference; (*exposé*) lecture; **~ de presse** press conference; **conférencier, -ière** *nm/f* speaker, lecturer
confesser [kɔ̃fese] *vt* to confess; **se ~** *vi* (*REL*) to go to confession; **confession** *nf* confession; (*culte: catholique etc*) denomination
confiance [kɔ̃fjɑ̃s] *nf* (*en l'honnêteté de qn*) confidence, trust; (*en la valeur de qch*) faith; **avoir ~ en** to have confidence ou faith in, trust; **faire ~ à qn** to trust sb; **mettre qn en ~** to win sb's trust; **~ en soi** self-confidence
confiant, e [kɔ̃fjɑ̃, jɑ̃t] *adj* confident; trusting
confidence [kɔ̃fidɑ̃s] *nf* confidence; **confidentiel, le** *adj* confidential
confier [kɔ̃fje] *vt*: **~ à qn** (*objet, travail*) to entrust to sb; (*secret, pensée*) to confide to sb; **se ~ à qn** to confide in sb
confins [kɔ̃fɛ̃] *nmpl*: **aux ~ de** on the borders of
confirmation [kɔ̃fiʀmasjɔ̃] *nf* confirmation
confirmer [kɔ̃fiʀme] *vt* to confirm
confiserie [kɔ̃fizʀi] *nf* (*magasin*) confectioner's ou sweet shop; **~s** *nfpl* (*bonbons*) confectionery *sg*
confisquer [kɔ̃fiske] *vt* to confiscate
confit, e [kɔ̃fi, it] *adj*: **fruits ~s** crystallized fruits ♦ *nm*: **~ d'oie** conserve of goose
confiture [kɔ̃fityʀ] *nf* jam; **~ d'oranges** (orange) marmalade
conflit [kɔ̃fli] *nm* conflict
confondre [kɔ̃fɔ̃dʀ] *vt* (*jumeaux, faits*) to confuse, mix up; (*témoin, menteur*) to confound; **se ~** *vi* to merge; **se ~ en excuses** to apologize profusely; **confondu, e** *adj* (*stupéfait*) speechless, overcome
conforme [kɔ̃fɔʀm] *adj*: **~ à** (*loi, règle*) in accordance with; **conformément** *adv*: **conformément à** in accordance with; **conformer** *vt*: **se conformer à** to conform to
confort [kɔ̃fɔʀ] *nm* comfort; **tout ~** (*COMM*) with all modern conveniences; **confortable** *adj* comfortable

confrère [kɔ̃fʀɛʀ] *nm* colleague
confronter [kɔ̃fʀɔ̃te] *vt* to confront
confus, e [kɔ̃fy, yz] *adj* (*vague*) confused; (*embarrassé*) embarrassed; **confusion** *nf* (*voir confus*) confusion; embarrassment; (*voir confondre*) confusion, mixing up
congé [kɔ̃ʒe] *nm* (*vacances*) holiday; **en ~** on holiday; **semaine de ~** week off; **prendre ~ de qn** to take one's leave of sb; **donner son ~ à** to give in one's notice to; **~ de maladie** sick leave; **~ de maternité** maternity leave; **~s payés** paid holiday
congédier [kɔ̃ʒedje] *vt* to dismiss
congélateur [kɔ̃ʒelatœʀ] *nm* freezer
congeler [kɔ̃ʒ(ə)le] *vt* to freeze; **les produits congelés** frozen foods
congestion [kɔ̃ʒɛstjɔ̃] *nf* congestion; **~ cérébrale** stroke; **congestionner** *vt* (*rue*) to congest; (*visage*) to flush
congrès [kɔ̃gʀɛ] *nm* congress
conifère [kɔnifɛʀ] *nm* conifer
conjecture [kɔ̃ʒɛktyʀ] *nf* conjecture
conjoint, e [kɔ̃ʒwɛ̃, wɛ̃t] *adj* joint ♦ *nm/f* spouse
conjonction [kɔ̃ʒɔ̃ksjɔ̃] *nf* (*LING*) conjunction
conjonctivite [kɔ̃ʒɔ̃ktivit] *nf* conjunctivitis
conjoncture [kɔ̃ʒɔ̃ktyʀ] *nf* circumstances *pl*; **la ~ actuelle** the present (economic) situation
conjugaison [kɔ̃ʒygɛzɔ̃] *nf* (*LING*) conjugation
conjuguer [kɔ̃ʒyge] *vt* (*LING*) to conjugate; (*efforts etc*) to combine
conjuration [kɔ̃ʒyʀasjɔ̃] *nf* conspiracy
conjurer [kɔ̃ʒyʀe] *vt* (*sort, maladie*) to avert; (*implorer*) to beseech, entreat
connaissance [kɔnesɑ̃s] *nf* (*savoir*) knowledge *no pl*; (*personne connue*) acquaintance; **être sans ~** to be unconscious; **perdre/reprendre ~** to lose/regain consciousness; **à ma/sa ~** to (the best of) my/his knowledge; **faire la ~ de qn** to meet sb
connaisseur [kɔnesœʀ, øz] *nm* connoisseur
connaître [kɔnɛtʀ] *vt* to know; (*éprouver*) to experience; (*avoir: succès*) to have, enjoy; **~ de nom/vue** to know by name/sight; **ils se sont connus à Genève** they (first) met in Geneva; **s'y ~ en qch** to know a lot about sth
connecter [kɔnɛkte] *vt* to connect
connerie [kɔnʀi] *nf* (*fam!*) stupid thing (to do/say)
connu, e [kɔny] *adj* (*célèbre*) well-known
conquérir [kɔ̃keʀiʀ] *vt* to conquer; **conquête** *nf* conquest
consacrer [kɔ̃sakʀe] *vt* (*employer*) to devote, dedicate; (*REL*) to consecrate
conscience [kɔ̃sjɑ̃s] *nf* conscience; **avoir/prendre ~ de** to be/become aware of; **perdre ~** to lose consciousness; **avoir bonne/mauvaise ~** to have a clear/guilty conscience;

consciencieux, -euse adj conscientious; **conscient, e** adj conscious

conscrit [kɔ̃skʀi] nm conscript

consécutif, -ive [kɔ̃sekytif, iv] adj consecutive; ~ **à** following upon

conseil [kɔ̃sɛj] nm (avis) piece of advice; (assemblée) council; **des ~s** advice; **prendre ~ (auprès de qn)** to take advice (from sb); ~ **d'administration** board (of directors); **le ~ des ministres** ≈ the Cabinet; ~ **municipal** town council

conseiller, -ère [kɔ̃seje, ɛʀ] nm/f adviser ♦ vt (personne) to advise; (méthode, action) to recommend, advise; ~ **à qn de** to advise sb to; ~ **municipal** town councillor

consentement [kɔ̃sɑ̃tmɑ̃] nm consent

consentir [kɔ̃sɑ̃tiʀ] vt to agree, consent

conséquence [kɔ̃sekɑ̃s] nf consequence; **en ~** (donc) consequently; (de façon appropriée) accordingly; **conséquent, e** adj logical, rational; (fam: important) substantial; **par conséquent** consequently

conservateur, -trice [kɔ̃sɛʀvatœʀ, tʀis] nm/f (POL) conservative; (de musée) curator ♦ nm (pour aliments) preservative

conservatoire [kɔ̃sɛʀvatwaʀ] nm academy

conserve [kɔ̃sɛʀv] nf (gén pl) canned ou tinned (BRIT) food; **en ~** canned, tinned (BRIT)

conserver [kɔ̃sɛʀve] vt (faculté) to retain, keep; (amis, livres) to keep; (préserver, aussi CULIN) to preserve

considérable [kɔ̃sideʀabl] adj considerable, significant, extensive

considération [kɔ̃sideʀasjɔ̃] nf consideration; (estime) esteem

considérer [kɔ̃sideʀe] vt to consider; ~ **qch comme** to regard sth as

consigne [kɔ̃siɲ] nf (de gare) left luggage (office) (BRIT), checkroom (US); (ordre, instruction) instructions pl; ~ **(automatique)** left-luggage locker; **consigner** vt (note, pensée) to record; (punir: élève) to put in detention; (COMM) to put a deposit on

consistant, e [kɔ̃sistɑ̃, ɑ̃t] adj (mélange) thick; (repas) solid

consister [kɔ̃siste] vi: ~ **en/à faire** to consist of/in doing

consœur [kɔ̃sœʀ] nf (lady) colleague

consoler [kɔ̃sɔle] vt to console

consolider [kɔ̃sɔlide] vt to strengthen; (fig) to consolidate

consommateur, -trice [kɔ̃sɔmatœʀ, tʀis] nm/f (ÉCON) consumer; (dans un café) customer

consommation [kɔ̃sɔmasjɔ̃] nf (boisson) drink; (ÉCON) consumption

consommer [kɔ̃sɔme] vt (suj: personne) to eat ou drink, consume; (: voiture, machine) to use, consume; (mariage) to consummate

♦ vi (dans un café) to (have a) drink

consonne [kɔ̃sɔn] nf consonant

conspirer [kɔ̃spiʀe] vi to conspire

constamment [kɔ̃stamɑ̃] adv constantly

constant, e [kɔ̃stɑ̃, ɑ̃t] adj constant; (personne) steadfast

constat [kɔ̃sta] nm (de police, d'accident) report; ~ **(à l')amiable** jointly-agreed statement for insurance purposes; ~ **d'échec** acknowledgement of failure

constatation [kɔ̃statasjɔ̃] nf (observation) (observed) fact, observation

constater [kɔ̃state] vt (remarquer) to note; (ADMIN, JUR: attester) to certify

consterner [kɔ̃stɛʀne] vt to dismay

constipé, e [kɔ̃stipe] adj constipated

constitué, e [kɔ̃stitɥe] adj: ~ **de** made up ou composed of

constituer [kɔ̃stitɥe] vt (équipe) to set up; (dossier, collection) to put together; (suj: éléments: composer) to make up, constitute; (représenter, être) to constitute; **se ~ prisonnier** to give o.s. up; **constitution** nf (composition) composition, make-up; (santé, POL) constitution

constructeur [kɔ̃stʀyktœʀ] nm manufacturer, builder

constructif, -ive [kɔ̃stʀyktif, iv] adj constructive

construction [kɔ̃stʀyksjɔ̃] nf construction, building

construire [kɔ̃stʀɥiʀ] vt to build, construct

consul [kɔ̃syl] nm consul; **consulat** nm consulate

consultant, e [kɔ̃syltɑ̃, ɑ̃t] adj, nm consultant

consultation [kɔ̃syltasjɔ̃] nf consultation; ~**s** nfpl (POL) talks; **heures de ~** (MÉD) surgery (BRIT) ou office (US) hours

consulter [kɔ̃sylte] vt to consult ♦ vi (médecin) to hold surgery (BRIT), be in (the office) (US); **se ~** vi to confer

consumer [kɔ̃syme] vt to consume; **se ~** vi to burn

contact [kɔ̃takt] nm contact; **au ~ de** (air, peau) on contact with; (gens) through contact with; **mettre/couper le ~** (AUTO) to switch on/off the ignition; **entrer en** ou **prendre ~ avec** to get in touch ou contact with; **contacter** vt to contact, get in touch with

contagieux, -euse [kɔ̃taʒjø, jøz] adj infectious; (par le contact) contagious

contaminer [kɔ̃tamine] vt to contaminate

conte [kɔ̃t] nm tale; ~ **de fées** fairy tale

contempler [kɔ̃tɑ̃ple] vt to contemplate, gaze at

contemporain, e [kɔ̃tɑ̃pɔʀɛ̃, ɛn] adj, nm/f contemporary

contenance [kɔ̃t(ə)nɑ̃s] nf (d'un récipient) capacity; (attitude) bearing, attitude; **perdre ~** to lose one's composure

conteneur [kɔ̃t(ə)nœʀ] nm container

contenir [kɔ̃t(ə)niʀ] vt to contain; (avoir une capacité de) to hold; **se ~** vi to contain o.s.

content, e [kɔ̃tɑ̃, ɑ̃t] adj pleased, glad; **~ de** pleased with; **contenter** vt to satisfy, please; **se contenter de** to content o.s. with

contentieux [kɔ̃tɑ̃sjø] nm (COMM) litigation; (service) litigation department

contenu [kɔ̃t(ə)ny] nm (d'un récipient) contents pl; (d'un texte) content

conter [kɔ̃te] vt to recount, relate

contestable [kɔ̃tɛstabl] adj questionable

contestation [kɔ̃tɛstasjɔ̃] nf (POL) protest

conteste [kɔ̃tɛst]: **sans ~** adv unquestionably, indisputably; **contester** vt to question, contest ♦ vi (POL, gén) to protest, rebel (against established authority)

contexte [kɔ̃tɛkst] nm context

contigu, ë [kɔ̃tigy] adj: **~ (à)** adjacent (to)

continent [kɔ̃tinɑ̃] nm continent

continu, e [kɔ̃tiny] adj continuous; **faire la journée ~e** to work without taking a full lunch break; (courant) **~ direct** current, DC

continuel, le [kɔ̃tinɥɛl] adj (qui se répète) constant, continual; (continu) continuous

continuer [kɔ̃tinɥe] vt (travail, voyage etc) to continue (with), carry on (with), go on (with); (prolonger: alignement, rue) to continue ♦ vi (vie, bruit) to continue, go on; **~ à** ou **de faire** to go on ou continue doing

contorsionner [kɔ̃tɔʀsjɔne]: **se ~** vi to contort o.s., writhe about

contour [kɔ̃tuʀ] nm outline, contour; **contourner** vt to go round; (difficulté) to get round

contraceptif, -ive [kɔ̃tʀasɛptif, iv] adj, nm contraceptive; **contraception** nf contraception

contracté, e [kɔ̃tʀakte] adj tense

contracter [kɔ̃tʀakte] vt (muscle etc) to tense, contract; (maladie, dette) to contract; (assurance) to take out; **se ~** vi (muscles) to contract

contractuel, le [kɔ̃tʀaktɥɛl] nm/f (agent) traffic warden

contradiction [kɔ̃tʀadiksjɔ̃] nf contradiction; **contradictoire** adj contradictory, conflicting

contraignant, e [kɔ̃tʀɛɲɑ̃, ɑ̃t] adj restricting

contraindre [kɔ̃tʀɛ̃dʀ] vt: **~ qn à faire** to compel sb to do; **contrainte** nf constraint

contraire [kɔ̃tʀɛʀ] adj, nm opposite; **~ à** contrary to; **au ~** on the contrary

contrarier [kɔ̃tʀaʀje] vt (personne: irriter) to annoy; (fig: projets) to thwart, frustrate; **contrariété** nf annoyance

contraste [kɔ̃tʀast] nm contrast

contrat [kɔ̃tʀa] nm contract; **~ de travail** employment contract

contravention [kɔ̃tʀavɑ̃sjɔ̃] nf parking ticket

contre [kɔ̃tʀ] prép against; (en échange) (in exchange) for; **par ~** on the other hand

contrebande [kɔ̃tʀəbɑ̃d] nf (trafic) contraband, smuggling; (marchandise) contraband, smuggled goods pl; **faire la ~ de** to smuggle; **contrebandier, -ière** nm/f smuggler

contrebas [kɔ̃tʀəbɑ]: **en ~** adv (down) below

contrebasse [kɔ̃tʀəbas] nf (double) bass

contre...: **contrecarrer** vt to thwart; **contrecœur**: **à contrecœur** adv (be)grudgingly, reluctantly; **contrecoup** nm repercussions pl; **contredire** vt (personne) to contradict; (faits) to refute

contrée [kɔ̃tʀe] nf (région) region; (pays) land

contrefaçon [kɔ̃tʀəfasɔ̃] nf forgery

contrefaire [kɔ̃tʀəfɛʀ] vt (document, signature) to forge, counterfeit

contre...: **contre-indication** (pl contre-indications) nf (MÉD) contra-indication; **"contre-indication en cas d'eczéma"** "should not be used by people with eczema"; **contre-indiqué, e** adj (MÉD) contra-indicated; (déconseillé) unadvisable, ill-advised; **contre-jour**: **à contre-jour** adv against the sunlight

contremaître [kɔ̃tʀəmɛtʀ] nm foreman

contrepartie [kɔ̃tʀəpaʀti] nf: **en ~** in return

contre-pied [kɔ̃tʀəpje] nm: **prendre le ~~ de** (opinion) to take the opposing view of; (action) to take the opposite course to

contre-plaqué [kɔ̃tʀəplake] nm plywood

contrepoids [kɔ̃tʀəpwa] nm counterweight, counterbalance

contrepoison [kɔ̃tʀəpwazɔ̃] nm antidote

contrer [kɔ̃tʀe] vt to counter

contresens [kɔ̃tʀəsɑ̃s] nm (erreur) misinterpretation; (de traduction) mistranslation; **à ~** the wrong way

contretemps [kɔ̃tʀətɑ̃] nm hitch; **à ~** (fig) at an inopportune moment

contrevenir [kɔ̃tʀəv(ə)niʀ] vt: **~ à** vt to contravene

contribuable [kɔ̃tʀibɥabl] nm/f taxpayer

contribuer [kɔ̃tʀibɥe] vt: **~ à** vt to contribute towards; **contribution** nf contribution; **contributions directes/indirectes** direct/indirect taxation; **mettre à contribution** to call upon

contrôle [kɔ̃tʀol] nm checking no pl, check; (des prix) monitoring, control; (test) test, examination; **perdre le ~ de** (véhicule) to lose control of; **~ continu** (SCOL) continuous assessment; **~ d'identité** identity check

contrôler [kɔ̃trole] vt (vérifier) to check; (surveiller: opérations) to supervise; (: prix) to monitor, control; (maîtriser, COMM: firme) to control; **se ~** vi to control o.s.; **contrôleur, -euse** nm/f (de train) (ticket) inspector; (de bus) (bus) conductor(-tress)

contrordre [kɔ̃trɔrdr] nm: **sauf ~** unless otherwise directed

controversé, e [kɔ̃trɔvɛrse] adj (personnage, question) controversial

contusion [kɔ̃tyzjɔ̃] nf bruise, contusion

convaincre [kɔ̃vɛ̃kr] vt: **~ qn (de qch)** to convince sb (of sth); **~ qn (de faire)** to persuade sb (to do)

convalescence [kɔ̃valesãs] nf convalescence

convenable [kɔ̃vnabl] adj suitable; (assez bon, respectable) decent

convenance [kɔ̃vnãs] nf: **à ma/votre ~** to my/your liking; **~s** nfpl (normes sociales) proprieties

convenir [kɔ̃vnir] vi to be suitable; **~ à** to suit; **~ de** (bien-fondé de qch) to admit (to), acknowledge; (date, somme etc) to agree upon; **~ que** (admettre) to admit that; **~ de faire** to agree to do

convention [kɔ̃vɑ̃sjɔ̃] nf convention; **~s** nfpl (convenances) convention sg; **~ collective** (ÉCON) collective agreement; **conventionné, e** adj (ADMIN) applying charges laid down by the state

convenu, e [kɔ̃vny] pp de **convenir** ♦ adj agreed

conversation [kɔ̃vɛrsasjɔ̃] nf conversation

convertir [kɔ̃vɛrtir] vt: **~ qn (à)** to convert sb (to); **se ~ (à)** to be converted (to); **~ qch en** to convert sth into

conviction [kɔ̃viksjɔ̃] nf conviction

convienne etc [kɔ̃vjɛn] vb voir **convenir**

convier [kɔ̃vje] vt: **~ qn à** (dîner etc) to (cordially) invite sb to

convive [kɔ̃viv] nm/f guest (at table)

convivial, e, -aux [kɔ̃vivjal, jo] adj (INFORM) user-friendly

convocation [kɔ̃vɔkasjɔ̃] nf (document) notification to attend; (: JUR) summons sg

convoi [kɔ̃vwa] nm convoy; (train) train

convoiter [kɔ̃vwate] vt to covet

convoquer [kɔ̃vɔke] vt (assemblée) to convene; (subordonné) to summon; (candidat) to ask to attend

convoyeur [kɔ̃vwajœr] nm: **~ de fonds** security guard

coopération [kɔɔperasjɔ̃] nf co-operation; (ADMIN): **la C~** ≈ Voluntary Service Overseas (BRIT), ≈ Peace Corps (US)

coopérer [kɔɔpere] vi: **~ (à)** to co-operate (in)

coordonnées [kɔɔrdɔne] nfpl: **donnez-moi vos ~** (fam) can I have your details please?

coordonner [kɔɔrdɔne] vt to coordinate

copain [kɔpɛ̃] (fam) nm mate, pal; (petit ami) boyfriend

copeau, x [kɔpo] nm shaving

copie [kɔpi] nf copy; (SCOL) script, paper; **copier** vt, vi to copy; **copier sur** to copy from; **copieur** nm (photo)copier

copieux, -euse [kɔpjø, jøz] adj copious

copine [kɔpin] (fam) nf mate, pal; (petite amie) girlfriend

copropriété [kɔprɔprijete] nf co-ownership, joint ownership

coq [kɔk] nm cock, rooster; **coq-à-l'âne** nm inv abrupt change of subject

coque [kɔk] nf (de noix, mollusque) shell; (de bateau) hull; **à la ~** (CULIN) (soft-)boiled

coquelicot [kɔkliko] nm poppy

coqueluche [kɔklyʃ] nf whooping-cough

coquet, te [kɔkɛ, ɛt] adj appearance-conscious; (logement) smart, charming

coquetier [kɔk(ə)tje] nm egg-cup

coquillage [kɔkijaʒ] nm (mollusque) shellfish inv; (coquille) shell

coquille [kɔkij] nf shell; (TYPO) misprint; **~ St Jacques** scallop

coquin, e [kɔkɛ̃, in] adj mischievous, roguish; (polisson) naughty

cor [kɔr] nm (MUS) horn; (MÉD): **~ (au pied)** corn

corail, -aux [kɔraj, o] nm coral no pl

Coran [kɔrɑ̃] nm: **le ~** the Koran

corbeau, x [kɔrbo] nm crow

corbeille [kɔrbɛj] nf basket; **~ à papier** waste paper basket ou bin

corbillard [kɔrbijar] nm hearse

corde [kɔrd] nf rope; (de violon, raquette) string; **usé jusqu'à la ~** threadbare; **~ à linge** washing ou clothes line; **~ à sauter** skipping rope; **~s vocales** vocal cords

cordée [kɔrde] nf (d'alpinistes) rope, roped party

cordialement [kɔrdjalmɑ̃] adv (formule épistolaire) (kind) regards

cordon [kɔrdɔ̃] nm cord, string; **~ ombilical** umbilical cord; **~ sanitaire/de police** sanitary/police cordon

cordonnerie [kɔrdɔnri] nf shoe repairer's (shop); **cordonnier** nm shoe repairer

Corée [kɔre] nf: **la ~ du Sud/du Nord** South/North Korea

coriace [kɔrjas] adj tough

corne [kɔrn] nf horn; (de cerf) antler

cornée [kɔrne] nf cornea

corneille [kɔrnɛj] nf crow

cornemuse [kɔrnəmyz] nf bagpipes pl

cornet [kɔrnɛ] nm (paper) cone; (de glace) cornet, cone

corniche [kɔrniʃ] nf (route) coast road

cornichon [kɔrniʃɔ̃] nm gherkin

Cornouailles [kɔrnwaj] nf Cornwall
corporation [kɔrpɔrasjɔ̃] nf corporate body
corporel, le [kɔrpɔrɛl] adj bodily; (punition) corporal
corps [kɔr] nm body; **à ~ perdu** headlong; **prendre ~** to take shape; **~ à ~** ♦ adv hand-to-hand ♦ nm clinch; **le ~ électoral** the electorate; **le ~ enseignant** the teaching profession
corpulent, e [kɔrpylɑ̃, ɑ̃t] adj stout
correct, e [kɔrɛkt] adj correct; (fam: acceptable: salaire, hôtel) reasonable, decent; **correcteur, -trice** nm/f (SCOL) examiner; **correction** nf (voir corriger) correction; (voir correct) correctness; (coups) thrashing; **correctionnel, le** adj (JUR): **tribunal correctionnel** ≈ criminal court
correspondance [kɔrɛspɔ̃dɑ̃s] nf correspondence; (de train, d'avion) connection; **cours par ~** correspondence course; **vente par ~** mail-order business
correspondant, e [kɔrɛspɔ̃dɑ̃, ɑ̃t] nm/f correspondent; (TÉL) person phoning (ou being phoned)
correspondre [kɔrɛspɔ̃dr] vi to correspond, tally; **~ à** to correspond to; **~ avec qn** to correspond with sb
corrida [kɔrida] nf bullfight
corridor [kɔridɔr] nm corridor
corrigé [kɔriʒe] nm (SCOL: d'exercise) correct version
corriger [kɔriʒe] vt (devoir) to correct; (punir) to thrash; **~ qn de** (défaut) to cure sb of
corroborer [kɔrɔbɔre] vt to corroborate
corrompre [kɔrɔ̃pr] vt to corrupt; (acheter: témoin etc) to bribe
corruption [kɔrypsjɔ̃] nf corruption; (de témoins) bribery
corsage [kɔrsaʒ] nm bodice; (chemisier) blouse
corsaire [kɔrsɛr] nm pirate
corse [kɔrs] adj, nm/f Corsican ♦ nf: **la C~** Corsica
corsé, e [kɔrse] adj (café) full-flavoured; (sauce) spicy; (problème) tough
corset [kɔrsɛ] nm corset
cortège [kɔrtɛʒ] nm procession
cortisone [kɔrtizɔn] nf cortisone
corvée [kɔrve] nf chore, drudgery no pl
cosmétique [kɔsmetik] nm beauty care product
cosmopolite [kɔsmɔpɔlit] adj cosmopolitan
cossu, e [kɔsy] adj (maison) opulent(-looking)
costaud, e [kɔsto, od] (fam) adj strong, sturdy
costume [kɔstym] nm (d'homme) suit; (de théâtre) costume; **costumé, e** adj dressed

up; **bal costumé** fancy dress ball
cote [kɔt] nf (en Bourse) quotation; **~ d'alerte** danger ou flood level
côte [kot] nf (rivage) coast(line); (pente) hill; (ANAT) rib; (d'un tricot, tissu) rib, ribbing no pl; **~ à ~** side by side; **la C~ (d'Azur)** the (French) Riviera
coté, e [kɔte] adj: **être bien ~** to be highly rated
côté [kote] nm (gén) side; (direction) way, direction; **de chaque ~ (de)** on each side (of); **de tous les ~s** from all directions; **de quel ~ est-il parti?** which way did he go?; **de ce/de l'autre** ~ this/the other way; **du ~ de** (provenance) from; (direction) towards; (proximité) near; **de ~** (regarder) sideways; (mettre) aside; **mettre de l'argent de ~** to save some money; **à ~** (right) nearby; (voisins) next door; **à ~ de** beside, next to; (en comparaison) compared to; **être aux ~s de** to be by the side of
coteau, x [kɔto] nm hill
côtelette [kotlɛt] nf chop
côtier, -ière [kotje, jɛr] adj coastal
cotisation [kɔtizasjɔ̃] nf subscription, dues pl; (pour une pension) contributions pl
cotiser [kɔtize] vi: **~ (à)** to pay contributions (to); **se ~** vi to club together
coton [kɔtɔ̃] nm cotton; **~ hydrophile** cotton wool (BRIT), absorbent cotton (US); **Coton-Tige** ® nm cotton bud
côtoyer [kotwaje] vt (fréquenter) to rub shoulders with
cou [ku] nm neck
couchant [kuʃɑ̃] adj: **soleil ~** setting sun
couche [kuʃ] nf layer; (de peinture, vernis) coat; (de bébé) nappy (BRIT), diaper (US); **~ d'ozone** ozone layer; **~s sociales** social levels ou strata
couché, e [kuʃe] adj lying down; (au lit) in bed
coucher [kuʃe] nm (du soleil) setting ♦ vt (personne) to put to bed; (: loger) to put up; (objet) to lay on its side ♦ vi to sleep; **se ~** vi (pour dormir) to go to bed; (pour se reposer) to lie down; (soleil) to set; **~ de soleil** sunset
couchette [kuʃɛt] nf couchette; (pour voyageur, sur bateau) berth
coucou [kuku] nm cuckoo
coude [kud] nm (ANAT) elbow; (de tuyau, de la route) bend; **~ à ~** shoulder to shoulder, side by side
coudre [kudr] vt (bouton) to sew on ♦ vi to sew
couenne [kwan] nf (de lard) rind
couette [kwɛt] nf duvet, quilt; **~s** nfpl (cheveux) bunches
couffin [kufɛ̃] nm Moses basket
couler [kule] vi to flow, run; (fuir: stylo,

récipient) to leak; (*nez*) to run; (*sombrer: bateau*) to sink ♦ *vt* (*cloche, sculpture*) to cast; (*bateau*) to sink; (*faire échouer: personne*) to bring down

couleur [kulœʀ] *nf* colour (BRIT), color (US); (CARTES) suit; **film/télévision en ~s** colo(u)r film/television

couleuvre [kulœvʀ] *nf* grass snake

coulisse [kulis] *nf:* **~s** ♦ *nfpl* (THÉÂTRE) wings; (*fig*): **dans les ~s** behind the scenes; **coulisser** *vi* to slide, run

couloir [kulwaʀ] *nm* corridor, passage; (*d'avion*) aisle; (*de bus*) gangway; **~ aérien/de navigation** air/shipping lane

coup [ku] *nm* (*heurt, choc*) knock; (*affectif*) blow, shock; (*agressif*) blow; (*avec arme à feu*) shot; (*de l'horloge*) stroke; (*tennis, golf*) stroke; (*boxe*) blow; (*fam: fois*) time; **~ de coude** nudge (with the elbow); **~ de tonnerre** clap of thunder; **~ de sonnette** ring of the bell; **donner un ~ de balai** to give the floor a sweep; **boire un ~** (*fam*) to have a drink; **être dans le ~** to be in on it; **du ~ ...** as a result; **d'un seul ~** (*subitement*) suddenly; (*à la fois*) at one go; **du premier ~** first time; **du même ~** at the same time; **à tous les ~s** (*fam*) every time; **tenir le ~** to hold out; **après ~** afterwards; **à ~ sûr** definitely, without fail; **~ sur ~** in quick succession; **sur le ~** outright; **sous le ~ de** (*surprise etc*) under the influence of; **en ~ de vent** in a tearing hurry; **~ de chance** stroke of luck; **~ de couteau** stab (of a knife); **~ d'État** coup; **~ de feu** shot; **~ de fil** (*fam*) phone call; **~ de frein** (sharp) braking *no pl*; **~ de main: donner un ~ de main à qn** to give sb a (helping) hand; **~ d'œil** glance; **~ de pied** kick; **~ de poing** punch; **~ de soleil** sunburn *no pl*; **~ de téléphone** phone call; **~ de tête** (*fig*) (sudden) impulse

coupable [kupabl] *adj* guilty ♦ *nm/f* (*gén*) culprit; (*JUR*) guilty party

coupe [kup] *nf* (*verre*) goblet; (*à fruits*) dish; (SPORT) cup; (*de cheveux, de vêtement*) cut; (*graphique, plan*) (cross) section

coupe-papier [kuppapje] *nm inv* paper knife

couper [kupe] *vt* to cut; (*retrancher*) to cut (out); (*route, courant*) to cut off; (*appétit*) to take away; (*vin à table*) to dilute ♦ *vi* to cut; (*prendre un raccourci*) to take a short-cut; **se ~** *vi* (*se blesser*) to cut o.s.; **~ la parole à qn** to cut sb short

couple [kupl] *nm* couple

couplet [kuplɛ] *nm* verse

coupole [kupɔl] *nf* dome

coupon [kupɔ̃] *nm* (*ticket*) coupon; (*reste de tissu*) remnant; **coupon-réponse** *nm* reply coupon

coupure [kupyʀ] *nf* cut; (*billet de banque*) note; (*de journal*) cutting; **~ de courant**

power cut

cour [kuʀ] *nf* (*de ferme, jardin*) (court)yard; (*d'immeuble*) back yard; (JUR, *royale*) court; **faire la ~ à qn** to court sb; **~ d'assises** court of assizes; **~ de récréation** playground; **~ martiale** court-martial

courage [kuʀaʒ] *nm* courage, bravery; **courageux, -euse** *adj* brave, courageous

couramment [kuʀamɑ̃] *adv* commonly; (*parler*) fluently

courant, e [kuʀɑ̃, ɑ̃t] *adj* (*fréquent*) common; (COMM, *gén: normal*) standard; (*en cours*) current ♦ *nm* current; (*fig*) movement; (: *d'opinion*) trend; **être au ~ (de)** (*fait, nouvelle*) to know (about); **mettre qn au ~ (de)** to tell sb (about); (*nouveau travail etc*) to teach sb the basics (of); **se tenir au ~ (de)** (*techniques etc*) to keep o.s. up-to-date (on); **dans le ~ de** (*pendant*) in the course of; **le 10 ~** (COMM) the 10th inst.; **~ d'air** draught; **~ électrique** (electric) current, power

courbature [kuʀbatyʀ] *nf* ache

courbe [kuʀb] *adj* curved ♦ *nf* curve; **courber** *vt* to bend; **se courber** *vi* (*personne*) to bend (down), stoop

coureur, -euse [kuʀœʀ, øz] *nm/f* (SPORT) runner (*ou* driver); (*péj*) womanizer; manhunter; **~ automobile** racing driver

courge [kuʀʒ] *nf* (CULIN) marrow; **courgette** *nf* courgette (BRIT), zucchini (US)

courir [kuʀiʀ] *vi* to run ♦ *vt* (SPORT: *épreuve*) to compete in; (*risque*) to run; (*danger*) to face; **~ les magasins** to go round the shops; **le bruit court que** the rumour is going round that

couronne [kuʀɔn] *nf* crown; (*de fleurs*) wreath, circlet

courons *etc* [kuʀɔ̃] *vb voir* **courir**

courrier [kuʀje] *nm* mail, post; (*lettres à écrire*) letters *pl*; **~ électronique** E-mail

courroie [kuʀwa] *nf* strap; (TECH) belt

courrons *etc* [kuʀɔ̃] *vb voir* **courir**

cours [kuʀ] *nm* (*leçon*) class; (: *particulier*) lesson; (*série de leçons, cheminement*) course; (*écoulement*) flow; (COMM: *de devises*) rate; (: *de denrées*) price; **donner libre ~ à** to give free expression to; **avoir ~** (SCOL) to have a class *ou* lecture; **en ~** (*année*) current; (*travaux*) in progress; **en ~ de route** on the way; **au ~ de** in the course of, during; **~ d'eau** waterway; **~ du soir** night school; **~ intensif** crash course

course [kuʀs] *nf* running; (SPORT: *épreuve*) race; (*d'un taxi*) journey, trip; (*commission*) errand; **~s** *nfpl* (*achats*) shopping *sg*; **faire des ~s** to do some shopping

court, e [kuʀ, kuʀt(ə)] *adj* short ♦ *adv* short ♦ *nm:* **~ (de tennis)** (tennis) court; **à ~ de** short of; **prendre qn de ~** to catch sb unawares; **court-circuit** *nm* short-circuit

courtier, -ère [kuʀtje, jɛʀ] nm/f broker
courtiser [kuʀtize] vt to court, woo
courtois, e [kuʀtwa, waz] adj courteous;
courtoisie nf courtesy
couru, e [kuʀy] pp de **courir**
cousais etc [kuze] vb voir **coudre**
couscous [kuskus] nm couscous
cousin, e [kuzɛ̃, in] nm/f cousin
coussin [kusɛ̃] nm cushion
cousu, e [kuzy] pp de **coudre**
coût [ku] nm cost; **le ~ de la vie** the cost of
living; **coûtant** adj m: **au prix coûtant** at
cost price
couteau, x [kuto] nm knife
coûter [kute] vt, vi to cost; **combien ça coûte?**
how much is it?, what does it cost?; **coûte
que coûte** at all costs; **coûteux, -euse** adj
costly, expensive
coutume [kutym] nf custom
couture [kutyʀ] nf sewing; (profession)
dressmaking; (points) seam; **couturier** nm
fashion designer; **couturière** nf dressmaker
couvée [kuve] nf brood, clutch
couvent [kuvɑ̃] nm (de sœurs) convent; (de
frères) monastery
couver [kuve] vt to hatch; (maladie) to be
coming down with ♦ vi (feu) to smoulder;
(révolte) to be brewing
couvercle [kuvɛʀkl] nm lid; (de bombe
aérosol etc, qui se visse) cap, top
couvert, e [kuvɛʀ, ɛʀt] pp de **couvrir** ♦ adj
(ciel) overcast ♦ nm place setting; (place à
table) place; **~s** nmpl (ustensiles) cutlery sg;
~ de covered with ou in; **mettre le ~** to lay
the table
couverture [kuvɛʀtyʀ] nf blanket; (de livre,
assurance, fig) cover; (presse) coverage;
~ chauffante electric blanket
couveuse [kuvøz] nf (de maternité)
incubator
couvre-feu [kuvʀəfø] nm curfew
couvre-lit [kuvʀəli] nm bedspread
couvreur [kuvʀœʀ] nm roofer
couvrir [kuvʀiʀ] vt to cover; **se ~** vi
(s'habiller) to cover up; (se coiffer) to put on
one's hat; (ciel) to cloud over
cow-boy [kɔbɔj] nm cowboy
crabe [kʀab] nm crab
cracher [kʀaʃe] vi, vt to spit
crachin [kʀaʃɛ̃] nm drizzle
crack [kʀak] nm (fam: as) ace
craie [kʀɛ] nf chalk
craindre [kʀɛ̃dʀ] vt to fear, be afraid of; (être
sensible à: chaleur, froid) to be easily
damaged by
crainte [kʀɛ̃t] nf fear; **de ~ de/que** for fear of/
that; **craintif, -ive** adj timid
cramoisi, e [kʀamwazi] adj crimson
crampe [kʀɑ̃p] nf cramp

crampon [kʀɑ̃pɔ̃] nm (de chaussure de
football) stud; (de chaussure de course) spike;
(d'alpinisme) crampon; **cramponner** vb: **se
cramponner (à)** to hang ou cling on (to)
cran [kʀɑ̃] nm (entaille) notch; (de courroie)
hole; (fam: courage) guts pl; **~ d'arrêt** safety
catch
crâne [kʀɑn] nm skull
crâner [kʀɑne] (fam) vi to show off
crapaud [kʀapo] nm toad
crapule [kʀapyl] nf villain
craquement [kʀakmɑ̃] nm crack, snap; (du
plancher) creak, creaking no pl
craquer [kʀake] vi (bois, plancher) to creak;
(fil, branche) to snap; (couture) to come
apart; (fig: accusé) to break down; (: fam) to
crack up ♦ vt (allumette) to strike; **j'ai craqué**
(fam) I couldn't resist it
crasse [kʀas] nf grime, filth; **crasseux,
-euse** adj grimy, filthy
cravache [kʀavaʃ] nf (riding) crop
cravate [kʀavat] nf tie
crawl [kʀol] nm crawl; **dos ~é** backstroke
crayon [kʀɛjɔ̃] nm pencil; **~ à bille** ball-point
pen; **~ de couleur** crayon, colouring pencil;
crayon-feutre (pl crayons-feutres) nm felt(-
tip) pen
créancier, -ière [kʀeɑ̃sje, jɛʀ] nm/f creditor
création [kʀeasjɔ̃] nf creation
créature [kʀeatyʀ] nf creature
crèche [kʀɛʃ] nf (de Noël) crib; (garderie)
crèche, day nursery
crédit [kʀedi] nm (gén) credit; **~s** nmpl
(fonds) funds; **payer/acheter à ~** to pay/buy
on credit ou on easy terms; **faire ~ à qn** to
give sb credit; **créditer** vt: **créditer un
compte (de)** to credit an account (with)
crédule [kʀedyl] adj credulous, gullible
créer [kʀee] vt to create
crémaillère [kʀemajɛʀ] nf: **pendre la ~** to
have a house-warming party
crématoire [kʀematwaʀ] adj: **four ~**
crematorium
crème [kʀɛm] nf cream; (entremets) cream
dessert ♦ adj inv cream(-coloured); **un (café)
~** = a white coffee; **~ anglaise** (egg) custard;
~ chantilly whipped cream; **~ fouettée**
= crème chantilly; **crémerie** nf dairy;
crémeux, -euse adj creamy
créneau, x [kʀeno] nm (de fortification)
crenel(le); (dans marché) gap, niche; (AUTO):
faire un ~ to reverse into a parking space
(between two cars alongside the kerb)
crêpe [kʀɛp] nf (galette) pancake ♦ nm (tissu)
crêpe; **crêpé, e** adj (cheveux) backcombed;
crêperie nf pancake shop ou restaurant
crépiter [kʀepite] vi (friture) to sputter,
splutter; (fire) to crackle
crépu, e [kʀepy] adj frizzy, fuzzy

crépuscule [kʀepyskyl] *nm* twilight, dusk
cresson [kʀesɔ̃] *nm* watercress
crête [kʀɛt] *nf* (*de coq*) comb; (*de vague, montagne*) crest
creuser [kʀøze] *vt* (*trou, tunnel*) to dig; (*sol*) to dig a hole in; (*fig*) to go (deeply) into; **ça creuse** that gives you a real appetite; **se ~ la cervelle** (*fam*) to rack one's brains
creux, -euse [kʀø, kʀøz] *adj* hollow ♦ *nm* hollow; **heures creuses** slack periods; (*électricité, téléphone*) off-peak periods; **avoir un ~** (*fam*) to be hungry
crevaison [kʀəvezɔ̃] *nf* puncture
crevasse [kʀəvas] *nf* (*dans le sol, la peau*) crack; (*de glacier*) crevasse
crevé, e [kʀəve] (*fam*) *adj* (*fatigué*) all in, exhausted
crever [kʀəve] *vt* (*ballon*) to burst ♦ *vi* (*pneu*) to burst; (*automobiliste*) to have a puncture (*BRIT*) *ou* a flat (tire) (*US*); (*fam*) to die
crevette [kʀəvɛt] *nf*: **~ (rose)** prawn; **~ grise** shrimp
cri [kʀi] *nm* cry, shout; (*d'animal: spécifique*) cry, call; **c'est le dernier ~** (*fig*) it's the latest fashion
criant, e [kʀijɑ̃, kʀijɑ̃t] *adj* (*injustice*) glaring
criard, e [kʀijaʀ, kʀijaʀd] *adj* (*couleur*) garish, loud; (*voix*) yelling
crible [kʀibl] *nm* riddle; **passer qch au ~** (*fig*) to go over sth with a fine-tooth comb; **criblé, e** *adj*: **criblé de** riddled with; (*de dettes*) crippled with
cric [kʀik] *nm* (*AUTO*) jack
crier [kʀije] *vi* (*pour appeler*) to shout, cry (out); (*de douleur etc*) to scream, yell ♦ *vt* (*injure*) to shout (out), yell (out)
crime [kʀim] *nm* crime; (*meurtre*) murder; **criminel, le** *nm/f* criminal; (*assassin*) murderer
crin [kʀɛ̃] *nm* (*de cheval*) hair *no pl*
crinière [kʀinjɛʀ] *nf* mane
crique [kʀik] *nf* creek, inlet
criquet [kʀikɛ] *nm* grasshopper
crise [kʀiz] *nf* crisis; (*MÉD*) attack; (*: d'épilepsie*) fit; **piquer une ~ de nerfs** to go hysterical; **~ cardiaque** heart attack; **~ de foie** bilious attack
crisper [kʀispe] *vt* (*poings*) to clench; **se ~** *vi* (*visage*) to tense; (*personne*) to get tense
crisser [kʀise] *vi* (*neige*) to crunch; (*pneu*) to screech
cristal, -aux [kʀistal, o] *nm* crystal; **cristallin, e** *adj* crystal-clear
critère [kʀiteʀ] *nm* criterion
critiquable [kʀitikabl] *adj* open to criticism
critique [kʀitik] *adj* critical ♦ *nm/f* (*de théâtre, musique*) critic ♦ *nf* criticism; (*THÉÂTRE etc: article*) review
critiquer [kʀitike] *vt* (*dénigrer*) to criticize;

(*évaluer*) to assess, examine (critically)
croasser [kʀɔase] *vi* to caw
Croatie [kʀɔasi] *nf* Croatia
croc [kʀo] *nm* (*dent*) fang; (*de boucher*) hook; **croc-en-jambe** *nm*: **faire un croc-en-jambe à qn** to trip sb up
croche [kʀɔʃ] *nf* (*MUS*) quaver (*BRIT*), eighth note (*US*); **croche-pied** *nm* = **croc-en-jambe**
crochet [kʀɔʃɛ] *nm* hook; (*détour*) detour; (*TRICOT: aiguille*) crochet hook; (*: technique*) crochet; **vivre aux ~s de qn** to live *ou* sponge off sb
crochu, e [kʀɔʃy] *adj* (*nez*) hooked; (*doigts*) claw-like
crocodile [kʀɔkɔdil] *nm* crocodile
croire [kʀwaʀ] *vt* to believe; **se ~ fort** to think one is strong; **~ que** to believe *ou* think that; **~ à, ~ en** to believe in
crois [kʀwa] *vb voir* **croître**
croisade [kʀwazad] *nf* crusade
croisé, e [kʀwaze] *adj* (*veste*) double-breasted
croisement [kʀwazmɑ̃] *nm* (*carrefour*) crossroads *sg*; (*BIO*) crossing; (*: résultat*) crossbreed
croiser [kʀwaze] *vt* (*personne, voiture*) to pass; (*route*) to cross, cut across; (*BIO*) to cross; **se ~** *vi* (*personnes, véhicules*) to pass each other; (*routes, lettres*) to cross; (*regards*) to meet; **~ les jambes/bras** to cross one's legs/fold one's arms
croisière [kʀwazjɛʀ] *nf* cruise
croissance [kʀwasɑ̃s] *nf* growth
croissant [kʀwasɑ̃] *nm* (*à manger*) croissant; (*motif*) crescent
croître [kʀwatʀ] *vi* to grow
croix [kʀwa] *nf* cross; **~ gammée** swastika; **la C~ Rouge** the Red Cross
croque-monsieur [kʀɔkməsjø] *nm inv* toasted ham and cheese sandwich
croquer [kʀɔke] *vt* (*manger*) to crunch; (*: fruit*) to munch; (*dessiner*) to sketch; **chocolat à ~** plain dessert chocolate
croquis [kʀɔki] *nm* sketch
cross [kʀɔs] *nm*: **faire du ~ (à pied)** to do cross-country running
crosse [kʀɔs] *nf* (*de fusil*) butt; (*de revolver*) grip
crotte [kʀɔt] *nf* droppings *pl*; **crotté, e** *adj* muddy, mucky; **crottin** *nm* dung, manure; (*fromage*) (small round) cheese (*made of goat's milk*)
crouler [kʀule] *vi* (*s'effondrer*) to collapse; (*être délabré*) to be crumbling
croupe [kʀup] *nf* rump; **en ~** pillion
croupir [kʀupiʀ] *vi* to stagnate
croustillant, e [kʀustijɑ̃, ɑ̃t] *adj* crisp
croûte [kʀut] *nf* crust; (*du fromage*) rind; (*MÉD*) scab; **en ~** (*CULIN*) in pastry

croûton [kʀutɔ̃] nm (CULIN) crouton; (bout du pain) crust, heel

croyable [kʀwajabl] adj credible

croyant, e [kʀwajɑ̃, ɑ̃t] nm/f believer

CRS sigle fpl (= Compagnies républicaines de sécurité) state security police force ♦ sigle m member of the CRS

cru, e [kʀy] pp de **croire** ♦ adj (non cuit) raw; (lumière, couleur) harsh; (paroles) crude ♦ nm (vignoble) vineyard; (vin) wine; **un grand ~ a** great vintage; **jambon ~** Parma ham

crû [kʀy] pp de **croître**

cruauté [kʀyote] nf cruelty

cruche [kʀyʃ] nf pitcher, jug

crucifix [kʀysifi] nm crucifix; **crucifixion** nf crucifixion

crudités [kʀydite] nfpl (CULIN) salads

crue [kʀy] nf (inondation) flood

cruel, le [kʀyɛl] adj cruel

crus etc [kʀy] vb voir **croire**; **croître**

crûs etc [kʀy] vb voir **croître**

crustacés [kʀystase] nmpl shellfish

Cuba [kyba] nf Cuba; **cubain, e** adj Cuban ♦ nm/f: **Cubain, e** Cuban

cube [kyb] nm cube; (jouet) brick; **mètre ~** cubic metre; **2 au ~** 2 cubed

cueillette [kœjɛt] nf picking; (quantité) crop, harvest

cueillir [kœjiʀ] vt (fruits, fleurs) to pick, gather; (fig) to catch

cuiller [kɥijɛʀ], **cuillère** [kɥijɛʀ] nf spoon; **~ à café** coffee spoon; (CULIN) teaspoonful; **~ à soupe** soup-spoon; (CULIN) tablespoonful; **cuillerée** nf spoonful

cuir [kɥiʀ] nm leather; **~ chevelu** scalp

cuire [kɥiʀ] vt (aliments) to cook; (au four) to bake ♦ vi to cook; **bien cuit** (viande) well done; **trop cuit** overdone

cuisant, e [kɥizɑ̃, ɑ̃t] adj (douleur) stinging; (fig: souvenir, échec) bitter

cuisine [kɥizin] nf (pièce) kitchen; (art culinaire) cookery, cooking; (nourriture) cooking, food; **faire la ~** to cook; **cuisiné, e** adj: **plat cuisiné** ready-made meal ou dish; **cuisiner** vt to cook; (fam) to grill ♦ vi to cook; **cuisinier, -ière** nm/f cook; **cuisinière** nf (poêle) cooker

cuisse [kɥis] nf thigh; (CULIN) leg

cuisson [kɥisɔ̃] nf cooking

cuit, e [kɥi, kɥit] pp de **cuire**

cuivre [kɥivʀ] nm copper; **les ~s** (MUS) the brass

cul [ky] (fam!) nm arse (!)

culbute [kylbyt] nf somersault; (accidentelle) tumble, fall

culminant, e [kylminɑ̃, ɑ̃t] adj: **point ~** highest point

culminer [kylmine] vi to reach its highest point

culot [kylo] (fam) nm (effronterie) cheek

culotte [kylɔt] nf (de femme) knickers pl (BRIT), panties pl

culpabilité [kylpabilite] nf guilt

culte [kylt] nm (religion) religion; (hommage, vénération) worship; (protestant) service

cultivateur, -trice [kyltivatœʀ, tʀis] nm/f farmer

cultivé, e [kyltive] adj (personne) cultured, cultivated

cultiver [kyltive] vt to cultivate; (légumes) to grow, cultivate

culture [kyltyʀ] nf cultivation; (connaissances etc) culture; **les ~s intensives** intensive farming; **~ physique** physical training; **culturel, le** adj cultural; **culturisme** nm body-building

cumin [kymɛ̃] nm cumin

cumuler [kymyle] vt (emplois) to hold concurrently; (salaires) to draw concurrently

cupide [kypid] adj greedy, grasping

cure [kyʀ] nf (MÉD) course of treatment

curé [kyʀe] nm parish priest

cure-dent [kyʀdɑ̃] nm toothpick

cure-pipe [kyʀpip] nm pipe cleaner

curer [kyʀe] vt to clean out

curieusement [kyʀjøzmɑ̃] adv curiously

curieux, -euse [kyʀjø, jøz] adj (indiscret) curious, inquisitive; (étrange) strange, curious ♦ nmpl (badauds) onlookers; **curiosité** nf curiosity; (site) unusual feature

curriculum vitae [kyʀikylɔmvite] nm inv curriculum vitae

curseur [kyʀsœʀ] nm (INFORM) cursor

cutané, e [kytane] adj skin

cuti-réaction [kytiʀeaksjɔ̃] nf (MÉD) skin-test

cuve [kyv] nf vat; (à mazout etc) tank

cuvée [kyve] nf vintage

cuvette [kyvɛt] nf (récipient) bowl, basin; (GÉO) basin

CV sigle m (AUTO) = **cheval vapeur**; (COMM) = **curriculum vitae**

cyanure [sjanyʀ] nm cyanide

cyclable [siklabl] adj: **piste ~** cycle track

cycle [sikl] nm cycle; **cyclisme** nm cycling; **cycliste** nm/f cyclist ♦ adj cycle cpd; **coureur cycliste** racing cyclist

cyclomoteur [siklomɔtœʀ] nm moped

cyclone [siklon] nm hurricane

cygne [siɲ] nm swan

cylindre [silɛ̃dʀ] nm cylinder; **cylindrée** nf (AUTO) (cubic) capacity

cymbale [sɛ̃bal] nf cymbal

cynique [sinik] adj cynical

cystite [sistit] nf cystitis

D, d

d' [d] prép voir **de**

dactylo [daktilo] nf (aussi: ~**graphe**) typist; (aussi: ~**graphie**) typing; **dactylographier** vt to type (out)

dada [dada] nm hobby-horse

daigner [deɲe] vt to deign

daim [dɛ̃] nm (fallow) deer inv; (cuir suédé) suede

dalle [dal] nf paving stone, slab

daltonien, ne [daltɔnjɛ̃, jɛn] adj colour-blind

dam [dɑ̃] nm: **au grand ~ de** much to the detriment (ou annoyance) of

dame [dam] nf lady; (CARTES, ÉCHECS) queen; **~s** nfpl (jeu) draughts sg (BRIT), checkers sg (US)

damner [dɑne] vt to damn

dancing [dɑ̃siŋ] nm dance hall

Danemark [danmark] nm Denmark

danger [dɑ̃ʒe] nm danger; **dangereux, -euse** adj dangerous

danois, e [danwa, waz] adj Danish ♦ nm/f: **D~, e Dane** ♦ nm (LING) Danish

dans [dɑ̃] prép **1** (position) in; (à l'intérieur de) inside; **c'est dans le tiroir/le salon** it's in the drawer/lounge; **dans la boîte** in ou inside the box; **marcher dans la ville** to walk about the town

2 (direction) into; **elle a couru dans le salon** she ran into the lounge

3 (provenance) out of, from; **je l'ai pris dans le tiroir/salon** I took it out of ou from the drawer/lounge; **boire dans un verre** to drink out of ou from a glass

4 (temps) in; **dans 2 mois** in 2 months, in 2 months' time

5 (approximation) about; **dans les 20 F** about 20F

danse [dɑ̃s] nf: **la ~** dancing; **une ~** a dance; **la ~ classique** ballet; **danser** vi, vt to dance; **danseur, -euse** nm/f ballet dancer; (au bal etc) dancer; (: cavalier) partner

dard [dar] nm (d'animal) sting

date [dat] nf date; **de longue ~** longstanding; **~ de naissance** date of birth; **~ de péremption** expiry date; **~ limite** deadline; **dater** vt, vi to date; **dater de** to date from; **à dater de** (as) from

datte [dat] nf date

dauphin [dofɛ̃] nm (ZOOL) dolphin

davantage [davɑ̃taʒ] adv more; (plus longtemps) longer; **~ de** more

de, d' [də] (de + le = **du**, de + les = **des**) prép **1** (appartenance) of; **le toit de la maison** the roof of the house; **la voiture d'Elisabeth/de mes parents** Elizabeth's/my parents' car

2 (provenance) from; **il vient de Londres** he comes from London; **elle est sortie du cinéma** she came out of the cinema

3 (caractérisation, mesure): **un mur de brique/bureau d'acajou** a brick wall/mahogany desk; **un billet de 50 F** a 50F note; **une pièce de 2 m de large** ou **large de 2 m** a room 2m wide, a 2m-wide room; **un bébé de 10 mois** a 10-month-old baby; **12 mois de crédit/travail** 12 months' credit/work; **augmenter de 10 F** to increase by 10F; **de 14 à 18** from 14 to 18

♦ **dét 1** (phrases affirmatives) some (souvent omis); **du vin, de l'eau, des pommes** (some) wine, (some) water, (some) apples; **des enfants sont venus** some children came; **pendant des mois** for months

2 (phrases interrogatives et négatives) any; **a-t-il du vin?** has he got any wine?; **il n'a pas de pommes/d'enfants** he hasn't (got) any apples/children, he has no apples/children

dé [de] nm (à jouer) die ou dice; (aussi: ~ **à coudre**) thimble

dealer [dilœr] (fam) nm (drug) pusher

déambuler [deãbyle] vi to stroll about

débâcle [debakl] nf rout

déballer [debale] vt to unpack

débandade [debɑ̃dad] nf (dispersion) scattering

débarbouiller [debarbuje] vt to wash; **se ~** vi to wash (one's face)

débarcadère [debarkadɛr] nm wharf

débardeur [debardœr] nm (maillot) tank top

débarquer [debarke] vt to unload, land ♦ vi to disembark; (fig: fam) to turn up

débarras [debara] nm (pièce) lumber room; (placard) junk cupboard; **bon ~!** good riddance!; **débarrasser** vt to clear; **se débarrasser de** vt to get rid of; **débarrasser qn de** (vêtements, paquets) to relieve sb of

débat [deba] nm discussion, debate; **débattre** vt to discuss, debate; **se débattre** vi to struggle

débaucher [debofe] vt (licencier) to lay off, dismiss; (entraîner) to lead astray, debauch

débile [debil] (fam) adj (idiot) dim-witted

débit [debi] nm (d'un liquide, fleuve) flow; (d'un magasin) turnover (of goods); (élocution) delivery; (bancaire) debit; **~ de boissons** drinking establishment; **~ de tabac** tobacconist's; **débiter** vt (compte) to debit;

(*couper: bois, viande*) to cut up; (*péj: dire*) to churn out; **débiteur, -trice** *nm/f* debtor ♦ *adj* in debit; (*compte*) debit *cpd*

déblayer [debleje] *vt* to clear

débloquer [debloke] *vt* (*prix, crédits*) to free

déboires [debwar] *nmpl* setbacks

déboiser [debwaze] *vt* to deforest

déboîter [debwate] *vt* (*AUTO*) to pull out; **se ~ le genou** *etc* to dislocate one's knee *etc*

débonnaire [deboner] *adj* easy-going, good-natured

débordé, e [deborde] *adj*: **être ~ (de)** (*travail, demandes*) to be snowed under (with)

déborder [deborde] *vi* to overflow; (*lait etc*) to boil over; **~ (de) qch** (*dépasser*) to extend beyond sth

débouché [debuʃe] *nm* (*pour vendre*) outlet; (*perspective d'emploi*) opening

déboucher [debuʃe] *vt* (*évier, tuyau etc*) to unblock; (*bouteille*) to uncork ♦ *vi*: **~ de** to emerge from; **~ sur** (*études*) to lead on to

débourser [deburse] *vt* to pay out

déboussolé, e [debusole] (*fam*) *adj* disorientated

debout [d(ə)bu] *adv*: **être ~** (*personne*) to be standing, stand; (: *levé, éveillé*) to be up; **se mettre ~** to stand up; **se tenir ~** to stand; **~!** stand up!; (*du lit*) get up!; **cette histoire ne tient pas ~** this story doesn't hold water

déboutonner [debutɔne] *vt* to undo, unbutton

débraillé, e [debraje] *adj* slovenly, untidy

débrancher [debrɑ̃ʃe] *vt* to disconnect; (*appareil électrique*) to unplug

débrayage [debrejaʒ] *nm* (*AUTO*) clutch; **débrayer** *vi* (*AUTO*) to declutch; (*cesser le travail*) to stop work

débris [debri] *nmpl* fragments; **des ~ de verre** bits of glass

débrouillard, e [debrujar, ard] (*fam*) *adj* smart, resourceful

débrouiller [debruje] *vt* to disentangle, untangle; **se ~** *vi* to manage; **débrouillez-vous** you'll have to sort things out yourself

début [deby] *nm* beginning, start; **~s** *nmpl* (*de carrière*) début *sg*; **~ juin** in early June; **débutant, e** *nm/f* beginner, novice; **débuter** *vi* to begin, start; (*faire ses débuts*) to start out

deçà [dəsa]: **en ~ de** *prép* this side of

décadence [dekadɑ̃s] *nf* decline

décaféiné, e [dekafeine] *adj* decaffeinated

décalage [dekalaʒ] *nm* gap; **~ horaire** time difference

décaler [dekale] *vt* to shift

décalquer [dekalke] *vt* to trace

décamper [dekɑ̃pe] (*fam*) *vi* to clear out *ou* off

décaper [dekape] *vt* (*surface peinte*) to strip

décapiter [dekapite] *vt* to behead; (*par accident*) to decapitate

décapotable [dekapɔtabl] *adj* convertible

décapsuleur [dekapsylœr] *nm* bottle-opener

décarcasser: **se ~** (*fam*) *vi* to flog o.s. to death

décédé, e [desede] *adj* deceased

décéder [desede] *vi* to die

déceler [des(ə)le] *vt* (*trouver*) to discover, detect

décembre [desɑ̃br] *nm* December

décemment [desamɑ̃] *adv* decently

décennie [deseni] *nf* decade

décent, e [desɑ̃, ɑ̃t] *adj* decent

déception [desɛpsjɔ̃] *nf* disappointment

décerner [deserne] *vt* to award

décès [desɛ] *nm* death

décevant, e [des(ə)vɑ̃, ɑ̃t] *adj* disappointing

décevoir [des(ə)vwar] *vt* to disappoint

déchaîner [deʃene] *vt* (*violence*) to unleash; (*enthousiasme*) to arouse; **se ~** (*tempête*) to rage; (*personne*) to fly into a rage

déchanter [deʃɑ̃te] *vi* to become disillusioned

décharge [deʃarʒ] *nf* (*dépôt d'ordures*) rubbish tip *ou* dump; (*électrique*) electrical discharge; **décharger** *vt* (*marchandise, véhicule*) to unload; (*tirer*) to discharge; **se décharger** *vi* (*batterie*) to go flat; **décharger qn de** (*responsabilité*) to release sb from

décharné, e [deʃarne] *adj* emaciated

déchausser [deʃose] *vt* (*skis*) to take off; **se ~** *vi* to take off one's shoes; (*dent*) to come *ou* work loose

déchéance [deʃeɑ̃s] *nf* (*physique*) degeneration; (*morale*) decay

déchet [deʃɛ] *nm* (*reste*) scrap; **~s** *nmpl* (*ordures*) refuse *sg*, rubbish *sg*; **~s nucléaires** nuclear waste

déchiffrer [deʃifre] *vt* to decipher

déchiqueter [deʃik(ə)te] *vt* to tear *ou* pull to pieces

déchirant, e [deʃirɑ̃, ɑ̃t] *adj* heart-rending

déchirement [deʃirmɑ̃] *nm* (*chagrin*) wrench, heartbreak; (*gén pl: conflit*) rift, split

déchirer [deʃire] *vt* to tear; (*en morceaux*) to tear up; (*arracher*) to tear out; (*fig: conflit*) to tear (apart); **se ~** *vi* to tear, rip; **se ~ un muscle** to tear a muscle

déchirure [deʃiryr] *nf* (*accroc*) tear, rip; **~ musculaire** torn muscle

déchoir [deʃwar] *vi* (*personne*) to lower o.s., demean o.s.

déchu, e [deʃy] *adj* (*roi*) deposed

décidé, e [deside] *adj* (*personne, air*) determined; **c'est ~** it's decided; **décidément** *adv* really

décider [deside] vt: ~ qch to decide on sth; **se ~ (à faire)** to decide (to do), make up one's mind; **se ~ pour** to decide on ou in favour of; ~ **de faire/que** to decide to do/that; ~ **qn (à faire qch)** to persuade sb (to do sth)

décimal, e, -aux [desimal, o] adj decimal; **décimale** nf decimal

décimètre [desimɛtʀ] nm decimetre

décisif, -ive [desizif, iv] adj decisive

décision [desizjɔ̃] nf decision

déclaration [deklaʀasjɔ̃] nf declaration; (discours: POL etc) statement; ~ **(d'impôts)** ≈ tax return

déclarer [deklaʀe] vt to declare; (décès, naissance) to register; **se ~** vi (feu) to break out

déclencher [deklɑ̃ʃe] vt (mécanisme etc) to release; (sonnerie) to set off; (attaque, grève) to launch; (provoquer) to trigger off; **se ~** vi (sonnerie) to go off

déclic [deklik] nm (bruit) click

décliner [dekline] vi to decline ♦ vt (invitation) to decline; (nom, adresse) to state

décocher [dekɔʃe] vt (coup de poing) to throw; (flèche, regard) to shoot

décoiffer [dekwafe] vt: ~ **qn** to mess up sb's hair; **je suis toute décoiffée** my hair is in a real mess

déçois etc [deswa] vb voir **décevoir**

décollage [dekɔlaʒ] nm (AVIAT) takeoff

décoller [dekɔle] vt to unstick ♦ vi (avion) to take off; **se ~** vi to come unstuck

décolleté, e [dekɔlte] adj low-cut ♦ nm low neck(line); (plongeant) cleavage

décolorer [dekɔlɔʀe]: **se ~** vi to fade; **se faire ~ les cheveux** to have one's hair bleached

décombres [dekɔ̃bʀ] nmpl rubble sg, debris sg

décommander [dekɔmɑ̃de] vt to cancel; **se ~** vi to cry off

décomposé, e [dekɔ̃poze] adj (pourri) decomposed; (visage) haggard, distorted

décompte [dekɔ̃t] nm deduction; (facture) detailed account

déconcerter [dekɔ̃sɛʀte] vt to disconcert, confound

déconfit, e [dekɔ̃fi, it] adj crestfallen

décongeler [dekɔ̃ʒ(ə)le] vt to thaw

déconner [dekɔne] (fam) vi to talk rubbish

déconseiller [dekɔ̃seje] vt: ~ **qch (à qn)** to advise (sb) against sth; **c'est déconseillé** it's not recommended

décontracté, e [dekɔ̃tʀakte] adj relaxed, laid-back (fam)

décontracter [dekɔ̃tʀakte]: **se ~** vi to relax

déconvenue [dekɔ̃v(ə)ny] nf disappointment

décor [dekɔʀ] nm décor; (paysage) scenery;

~**s** nmpl (THÉÂTRE) scenery sg, décor sg; (CINÉMA) set sg; **décorateur** nm (interior) decorator; **décoration** nf decoration; **décorer** vt to decorate

décortiquer [dekɔʀtike] vt to shell; (fig: texte) to dissect

découcher [dekuʃe] vi to spend the night away from home

découdre [dekudʀ]: **se ~** vi to come unstitched

découler [dekule] vi: ~ **de** to ensue ou follow from

découper [dekupe] vt (papier, tissu etc) to cut up; (viande) to carve; (article) to cut out; **se ~ sur** to stand out against

décourager [dekuʀaʒe] vt to discourage; **se ~** vi to lose heart, become discouraged

décousu, e [dekuzy] adj unstitched; (fig) disjointed, disconnected

découvert, e [dekuvɛʀ, ɛʀt] adj (tête) bare, uncovered; (lieu) open, exposed ♦ nm (bancaire) overdraft; **découverte** nf discovery; **faire la découverte de** to discover

découvrir [dekuvʀiʀ] vt to discover; (enlever ce qui couvre) to uncover; (dévoiler) to reveal; **se ~** vi (chapeau) to take off one's hat; (vêtement) to take something off; (ciel) to clear

décret [dekʀɛ] nm decree; **décréter** vt to decree

décrié, e [dekʀije] adj disparaged

décrire [dekʀiʀ] vt to describe

décrocher [dekʀɔʃe] vt (détacher) to take down; (téléphone) to take off the hook; (: pour répondre) to lift the receiver; (fam: contrat etc) to get, land ♦ vi (fam: abandonner) to drop out; (: cesser d'écouter) to switch off

décroître [dekʀwatʀ] vi to decrease, decline

décrypter [dekʀipte] vt to decipher

déçu, e [desy] pp de **décevoir**

décupler [dekyple] vt, vi to increase tenfold

dédaigner [dedeɲe] vt to despise, scorn; (négliger) to disregard, spurn; **dédaigneux, -euse** adj scornful, disdainful; **dédain** nm scorn, disdain

dédale [dedal] nm maze

dedans [dədɑ̃] adv inside; (pas en plein air) indoors, inside ♦ nm inside; **au ~** inside

dédicacer [dedikase] vt: ~ **(à qn)** to sign (for sb), autograph (for sb)

dédier [dedje] vt to dedicate

dédire [dediʀ]: **se ~** vi to go back on one's word, retract

dédommagement [dedɔmaʒmɑ̃] nm compensation

dédommager [dedɔmaʒe] vt: ~ **qn (de)** to compensate sb (for)

dédouaner [dedwane] vt to clear through

customs

dédoubler [deduble] vt (classe, effectifs) to split (into two)

déduire [deduiʀ] vt: ~ qch (de) (ôter) to deduct sth (from); (conclure) to deduce ou infer sth (from)

déesse [dɛɛs] nf goddess

défaillance [defajɑ̃s] nf (syncope) blackout; (fatigue) (sudden) weakness no pl; (technique) fault, failure; ~ cardiaque heart failure

défaillir [defajiʀ] vi to feel faint; (mémoire etc) to fail

défaire [defɛʀ] vt to undo; (installation) to take down, dismantle; se ~ vi to come undone; se ~ de to get rid of

défait, e [defɛ, ɛt] adj (visage) haggard, ravaged; **défaite** nf defeat

défalquer [defalke] vt to deduct

défaut [defo] nm (moral) fault, failing, defect; (tissu) fault, flaw; (manque, carence): ~ de shortage of; **prendre qn en ~** to catch sb out; **faire ~** (manquer) to be lacking; **à ~ de** for lack ou want of

défavorable [defavɔʀabl] adj unfavourable (BRIT), unfavorable (US)

défavoriser [defavɔʀize] vt to put at a disadvantage

défection [defɛksjɔ̃] nf defection, failure to give support

défectueux, -euse [defɛktɥø, øz] adj faulty, defective

défendre [defɑ̃dʀ] vt to defend; (interdire) to forbid; **se ~** vi to defend o.s.; ~ **à qn de faire** to forbid sb sth/to do; **il se défend** (fam: se débrouille) he can hold his own; **se ~ de/ contre** (se protéger) to protect o.s. from/ against; **se ~ de** (se garder de) to refrain from

défense [defɑ̃s] nf defence; (d'éléphant etc) tusk; **"~ de fumer"** "no smoking"

déférer [defeʀe] vt (JUR) to refer; ~ **à** (requête, décision) to defer to

déferler [defɛʀle] vi (vagues) to break; (fig: foule) to surge

défi [defi] nm challenge; **lancer un ~ à qn** to challenge sb; **sur un ton de ~** defiantly

déficit [defisit] nm (COMM) deficit; **déficitaire** adj in deficit

défier [defje] vt (provoquer) to challenge; (mort, autorité) to defy

défigurer [defigyʀe] vt to disfigure

défilé [defile] nm (GÉO) (narrow) gorge ou pass; (soldats) parade; (manifestants) procession, march; ~ **de mode** fashion parade

défiler [defile] vi (troupes) to march past; (sportifs) to parade; (manifestants) to march; (visiteurs) to pour, stream; **se ~** vi: **il s'est défilé** (fam) he wriggled out of it

définir [definiʀ] vt to define

définitif, -ive [definitif, iv] adj (final) final, definitive; (pour longtemps) permanent, definitive; (refus) definite; **définitive** nf: **en définitive** eventually; (somme toute) in fact; **définitivement** adv (partir, s'installer) for good

défoncer [defɔ̃se] vt (porte) to smash in ou down; **se ~** (fam) vi (travailler) to work like a dog; (drogué) to get high

déformer [defɔʀme] vt to put out of shape; (pensée, fait) to distort; **se ~** vi to lose its shape

défraîchir [defʀeʃiʀ]: **se ~** vi to fade

défricher [defʀiʃe] vt to clear (for cultivation)

défunt, e [defœ̃, œ̃t] nm/f deceased

dégagé, e [degaʒe] adj (route, ciel) clear; **sur un ton ~** casually

dégagement [degaʒmɑ̃] nm: **voie de ~** slip road

dégager [degaʒe] vt (exhaler) to give off; (délivrer) to free, extricate; (désencombrer) to clear; (isoler: idée, aspect) to bring out; **se ~** vi (passage, ciel) to clear

dégarnir [degaʀniʀ] vt (vider) to empty, clear; **se ~** vi (tempes, crâne) to go bald

dégâts [dega] nmpl damage sg

dégel [deʒɛl] nm thaw; **dégeler** vt to thaw (out)

dégénérer [deʒeneʀe] vi to degenerate

dégingandé, e [deʒɛ̃gɑ̃de] adj gangling

dégivrer [deʒivʀe] vt (frigo) to defrost; (vitres) to de-ice

dégonflé, e [degɔ̃fle] adj (pneu) flat

dégonfler [degɔ̃fle] vt (pneu, ballon) to let down, deflate; **se ~** vi (fam) to chicken out

dégouliner [deguline] vi to trickle, drip

dégourdi, e [deguʀdi] adj smart, resourceful

dégourdir [deguʀdiʀ] vt: **se ~ les jambes** to stretch one's legs (fig)

dégoût [degu] nm disgust, distaste; **dégoûtant, e** adj disgusting; **dégoûté, e** adj disgusted; **dégoûté de** sick of; **dégoûter** vt to disgust; **dégoûter qn de qch** to put sb off sth

dégrader [degʀade] vt (MIL: officier) to degrade; (abîmer) to damage, deface; **se ~** vi (relations, situation) to deteriorate

dégrafer [degʀafe] vt to unclip, unhook

degré [dəgʀe] nm degree

dégressif, -ive [degʀesif, iv] adj on a decreasing scale

dégringoler [degʀɛ̃gɔle] vi to tumble (down)

dégrossir [degʀosiʀ] vt (fig: projet) to work out roughly

déguenillé, e [deg(ə)nije] adj ragged, tattered

déguerpir [degɛʀpiʀ] vi to clear off

dégueulasse [degœlas] (fam) adj disgusting

dégueuler [degœle] (fam) vi to throw up

déguisement [degizmɑ̃] nm (pour s'amuser) fancy dress

déguiser [degize]: **se ~** vi (se costumer) to dress up; (pour tromper) to disguise o.s.

dégustation [degystasjɔ̃] nf (de fromages etc) sampling; **~ de vins** wine-tasting session

déguster [degyste] vt (vins) to taste; (fromages etc) to sample; (savourer) to enjoy, savour

dehors [dəɔʀ] adv outside; (en plein air) outdoors ♦ nm outside ♦ nmpl (apparences) appearances; **mettre** ou **jeter ~** (expulser) to throw out; **au ~** outside; **au ~ de** outside; **en ~ de** (hormis) apart from

déjà [deʒa] adv already; (auparavant) before, already

déjeuner [deʒœne] vi to (have) lunch; (le matin) to have breakfast ♦ nm lunch

déjouer [deʒwe] vt (complot) to foil

delà [dəla] adv: **en ~ (de)**, **au ~ (de)** beyond

délabrer [delabʀe]: **se ~** vi to fall into decay, become dilapidated

délacer [delase] vt (chaussures) to undo

délai [dele] nm (attente) waiting period; (sursis) extension (of time); (temps accordé) time limit; **sans ~** without delay; **dans les ~s** within the time limit

délaisser [delese] vt to abandon, desert

délasser [delɑse] vt to relax; **se ~** vi to relax

délavé, e [delave] adj faded

délayer [deleje] vt (CULIN) to mix (with water etc); (peinture) to thin down

delco [dɛlko] nm (AUTO) distributor

délecter [delɛkte]: **se ~** vi to revel ou delight in

délégué, e [delege] nm/f representative

déléguer [delege] vt to delegate

délibéré, e [delibeʀe] adj (conscient) deliberate

délibérer [delibeʀe] vi to deliberate

délicat, e [delika, at] adj delicate; (plein de tact) tactful; (attention) thoughtful; **délicatement** adv delicately; (avec douceur) gently

délice [delis] nm delight

délicieux, -euse [delisjø, jøz] adj (au goût) delicious; (sensation) delightful

délimiter [delimite] vt (terrain) to delimit, demarcate

délinquance [delɛ̃kɑ̃s] nf criminality; **délinquant, e** adj, nm/f delinquent

délirant, e [deliʀɑ̃, ɑ̃t] (fam) adj wild

délirer [deliʀe] vi to be delirious; **tu délires!** (fam) you're crazy!

délit [deli] nm (criminal) offence

délivrer [delivʀe] vt (prisonnier) to (set) free,

release; (passeport) to issue

déloger [delɔʒe] vt (objet coincé) to dislodge

déloyal, e, -aux [delwajal, o] adj (ami) disloyal; (procédé) unfair

deltaplane [dɛltaplan] nm hang-glider

déluge [delyʒ] nm (pluie) downpour; (biblique) Flood

déluré, e [delyʀe] (péj) adj forward, pert

demain [d(ə)mɛ̃] adv tomorrow

demande [d(ə)mɑ̃d] nf (requête) request; (revendication) demand; (d'emploi) application; (ÉCON): **la ~** demand; **"~s d'emploi"** (annonces) "situations wanted"; **~ en mariage** proposal of marriage

demandé, e [d(ə)mɑ̃de] adj (article etc): **très ~** (very) much in demand

demander [d(ə)mɑ̃de] vt to ask for; (chemin, heure etc) to ask; (nécessiter) to require, demand; **se ~ si/pourquoi** etc to wonder whether/why etc; **~ qch à qn** to ask sb for sth; **~ un service à qn** to ask sb a favour; **~ à qn de faire** to ask sb to do; **demandeur, -euse** nm/f: **demandeur d'emploi** job-seeker

démangeaison [demɑ̃ʒezɔ̃] nf itching; **avoir des ~s** to be itching

démanger [demɑ̃ʒe] vi to itch

démanteler [demɑ̃t(ə)le] vt to break up

démaquillant [demakijɑ̃] nm make-up remover

démaquiller [demakije] vt: **se ~** to remove one's make-up

démarche [demaʀʃ] nf (allure) gait, walk; (intervention) step; (fig: intellectuelle) thought processes pl; **faire les ~s nécessaires (pour obtenir qch)** to take the necessary steps (to obtain sth)

démarcheur, -euse [demaʀʃœʀ. øz] nm/f (COMM) door-to-door salesman(-woman)

démarque [demaʀk] nf (article) markdown

démarrage [demaʀaʒ] nm start

démarrer [demaʀe] vi (conducteur) to start (up); (véhicule) to move off; (travaux) to get moving; **démarreur** nm (AUTO) starter

démêlant [demɛlɑ̃] nm conditioner

démêler [demele] vt to untangle; **démêlés** nmpl problems

déménagement [demenaʒmɑ̃] nm move; **camion de ~** removal van

déménager [demenaʒe] vt (meubles) to (re)move ♦ vi to move (house); **déménageur** nm removal man

démener [dem(ə)ne]: **se ~** vi (se dépenser) to exert o.s.; (pour obtenir qch) to go to great lengths

dément, e [demɑ̃, ɑ̃t] adj (fou) mad, crazy; (fam) brilliant, fantastic

démentiel, le [demɑ̃sjɛl] adj insane

démentir [demɑ̃tiʀ] vt to refute; **~ que** to deny that

démerder [demɛʀde] (fam): **se ~** vi to sort things out for o.s.

démesuré, e [dem(ə)zyʀe] adj immoderate

démettre [demɛtʀ] vt: **~ qn de** (fonction, poste) to dismiss sb from; **se ~ l'épaule** etc to dislocate one's shoulder etc

demeurant [d(ə)mœʀɑ̃]: **au ~** adv for all that

demeure [d(ə)mœʀ] nf residence; **demeurer** vi (habiter) to live; (rester) to remain

demi, e [dəmi] adj half ♦ nm (bière) ≈ half-pint (0,25 litres) ♦ préfixe: **~...** half-, semi..., demi-; **trois heures/bouteilles et ~es** three and a half hours/bottles, three hours/bottles and a half; **il est 2 heures et ~e/midi et ~** it's half past 2/half past 12; **à ~** half-; **à la ~e** (heure) on the half-hour; **demi-cercle** nm semicircle; **en demi-cercle** adj semicircular ♦ adv in a half circle; **demi-douzaine** nf half-dozen, half a dozen; **demi-finale** nf semifinal; **demi-frère** nm half-brother; **demi-heure** nf half-hour, half an hour; **demi-journée** nf half-day, half a day; **demi-litre** nm half-litre, half a litre; **demi-livre** nf half-pound, half a pound; **demi-mot** adv: **à demi-mot** without having to spell things out; **demi-pension** nf (à l'hôtel) half-board; **demi-pensionnaire** nm/f: **être demi-pensionnaire** to take school lunches; **demi-place** nf half-fare

démis, e [demi, iz] adj (épaule etc) dislocated

demi-sel [dəmisɛl] adj inv (beurre, fromage) slightly salted

demi-sœur [dəmisœʀ] nf half-sister

démission [demisjɔ̃] nf resignation; **donner sa ~** to give ou hand in one's notice; **démissionner** vi to resign

demi-tarif [dəmitaʀif] nm half-price; **voyager à ~~** to travel half-fare

demi-tour [dəmituʀ] nm about-turn; **faire ~~** to turn (and go) back

démocratie [demɔkʀasi] nf democracy; **démocratique** adj democratic

démodé, e [demɔde] adj old-fashioned

demoiselle [d(ə)mwazɛl] nf (jeune fille) young lady; (célibataire) single lady, maiden lady; **~ d'honneur** bridesmaid

démolir [demɔliʀ] vt to demolish

démon [demɔ̃] nm (enfant turbulent) devil, demon; **le D~** the Devil

démonstration [demɔ̃stʀasjɔ̃] nf demonstration

démonté, e [demɔ̃te] adj (mer) raging, wild

démonter [demɔ̃te] vt (machine etc) to take down, dismantle

démontrer [demɔ̃tʀe] vt to demonstrate

démordre [demɔʀdʀ] vi: **ne pas ~ de** to

refuse to give up, stick to

démouler [demule] vt to turn out

démuni, e [demyni] adj (sans argent) impoverished; **~ de** without

démunir [demyniʀ] vt: **~ qn de** to deprive sb of; **se ~ de** to part with, give up

dénaturer [denatyʀe] vt (goût) to alter; (pensée, fait) to distort

dénicher [denife] (fam) vt (objet) to unearth; (restaurant etc) to discover

dénier [denje] vt to deny

dénigrer [denigʀe] vt to denigrate, run down

dénivellation [denivelasjɔ̃] nf (pente) slope

dénombrer [denɔ̃bʀe] vt to count

dénomination [denɔminasjɔ̃] nf designation, appellation

dénommé, e [denɔme] adj: **un ~ Dupont** a certain Mr Dupont

dénoncer [denɔ̃se] vt to denounce

dénouement [denumɑ̃] nm outcome

dénouer [denwe] vt to unknot, undo; **se ~** vi (nœud) to come undone

dénoyauter [denwajote] vt to stone

denrée [dɑ̃ʀe] nf: **~s (alimentaires)** foodstuffs

dense [dɑ̃s] adj dense; **densité** nf density

dent [dɑ̃] nf tooth; **~ de lait/sagesse** milk/ wisdom tooth; **dentaire** adj dental

dentelé, e [dɑ̃t(ə)le] adj jagged, indented

dentelle [dɑ̃tɛl] nf lace no pl

dentier [dɑ̃tje] nm denture

dentifrice [dɑ̃tifʀis] nm toothpaste

dentiste [dɑ̃tist] nm/f dentist

dentition [dɑ̃tisjɔ̃] nf teeth

dénuder [denyde] vt to bare

dénué, e [denye] adj: **~ de** devoid of; **dénuement** nm destitution

déodorant [deɔdɔʀɑ̃] nm deodorant

déontologie [deɔ̃tɔlɔʒi] nf code of practice

dépannage [depanaʒ] nm: **service de ~** (AUTO) breakdown service

dépanner [depane] vt (voiture, télévision) to fix, repair; (fig) to bail out, help out; **dépanneuse** nf breakdown lorry (BRIT), tow truck (US)

dépareillé, e [depaʀeje] adj (collection, service) incomplete; (objet) odd

départ [depaʀ] nm departure; (SPORT) start; **au ~** at the start; **la veille de son ~** the day before he leaves/left

départager [depaʀtaʒe] vt to decide between

département [depaʀtəmɑ̃] nm department

dépassé, e [depɑse] adj superseded, outmoded; **il est complètement ~** he's completely out of his depth, he can't cope

dépasser [depɑse] vt (véhicule, concurrent) to overtake; (endroit) to pass, go past; (somme, limite) to exceed; (fig: en beauté etc) to surpass, outshine ♦ vi (jupon etc) to show

dépaysé, e [depeize] adj disoriented

dépaysement [depeizmɑ̃] nm (changement) change of scenery

dépecer [depəse] vt to joint, cut up

dépêche [depɛʃ] nf dispatch

dépêcher [depeʃe]: **se ~** vi to hurry

dépeindre [depɛ̃dʀ] vt to depict

dépendance [depɑ̃dɑ̃s] nf dependence; (bâtiment) outbuilding

dépendre [depɑ̃dʀ]: **~ de** vt to depend on; (financièrement etc) to be dependent on

dépens [depɑ̃] nmpl: **aux ~ de** at the expense of

dépense [depɑ̃s] nf spending no pl, expense, expenditure no pl; **dépenser** vt to spend; (énergie) to expend, use up; **se dépenser** vi to exert o.s.; **dépensier, -ière** adj: **il est dépensier** he's a spendthrift

dépérir [depeʀiʀ] vi (personne) to waste away; (plante) to wither

dépêtrer [depetʀe] vt: **se ~ de** to extricate o.s. from

dépeupler [depœple]: **se ~** vi to become depopulated

dépilatoire [depilatwaʀ] adj depilatory, hair-removing

dépister [depiste] vt to detect; (voleur) to track down

dépit [depi] nm vexation, frustration; **en ~ de** in spite of; **en ~ du bon sens** contrary to all good sense; **dépité, e** adj vexed, frustrated

déplacé, e [deplase] adj (propos) out of place, uncalled-for

déplacement [deplasmɑ̃] nm (voyage) trip, travelling no pl

déplacer [deplase] vt (table, voiture) to move, shift; **se ~** vi to move; (voyager) to travel; **se ~ une vertèbre** to slip a disc

déplaire [deplɛʀ] vt: **ça me déplaît** I don't like this, I dislike this; **se ~** vi to be unhappy; **déplaisant, e** adj disagreeable

dépliant [deplijɑ̃] nm leaflet

déplier [deplije] vt to unfold

déplorer [deplɔʀe] vt to deplore

déployer [deplwaje] vt (carte) to open out; (ailes) to spread; (troupes) to deploy

déporter [depɔʀte] vt (exiler) to deport; (dévier) to carry off course

déposer [depoze] vt (gén: mettre, poser) to lay ou put down; (à la banque, à la consigne) to deposit; (passager) to drop (off), set down; (roi) to depose; (plainte) to lodge; (marque) to register; **se ~** vi to settle; **dépositaire** nm/f (COMM) agent; **déposition** nf statement

dépôt [depo] nm (à la banque, sédiment) deposit; (entrepôt) warehouse, store

dépotoir [depɔtwaʀ] nm dumping ground, rubbish dump

dépouiller [depuje] vt (documents) to go through, peruse; **~ qn/qch de** to strip sb/sth of; **~ le scrutin** to count the votes

dépourvu, e [depuʀvy] adj: **~ de** lacking in, without; **prendre qn au ~** to catch sb unprepared

déprécier [depʀesje]: **se ~** vi to depreciate

dépression [depʀesjɔ̃] nf depression; **~ (nerveuse)** breakdown

déprimant, e [depʀimɑ̃, ɑ̃t] adj depressing

déprimer [depʀime] vi to be/get depressed

MOT-CLÉ

depuis [dəpɥi] prép **1** (point de départ dans le temps) since; **il habite Paris depuis 1983/l'an dernier** he has been living in Paris since 1983/last year; **depuis quand le connaissez-vous?** how long have you known him?

2 (temps écoulé) for; **il habite Paris depuis 5 ans** he has been living in Paris for 5 years; **je le connais depuis 3 ans** I've known him for 3 years

3 (lieu): **il a plu depuis Metz** it's been raining since Metz; **elle a téléphoné depuis Valence** she rang from Valence

4 (quantité, rang) from; **depuis les plus petits jusqu'aux plus grands** from the youngest to the oldest

♦ adv (temps) since (then); **je ne lui ai pas parlé depuis** I haven't spoken to him since (then) **depuis que** conj (ever) since; **depuis qu'il m'a dit ça** (ever) since he said that to me

---

député, e [depyte] nm/f (POL) ≈ Member of Parliament (BRIT), ≈ Member of Congress (US)

députer [depyte] vt to delegate

déraciner [deʀasine] vt to uproot

dérailler [deʀaje] vi (train) to be derailed; **faire ~** to derail

déraisonner [deʀɛzɔne] vi to talk nonsense, rave

dérangement [deʀɑ̃ʒmɑ̃] nm (gêne) trouble; (gastrique etc) disorder; **en ~** (téléphone, machine) out of order

déranger [deʀɑ̃ʒe] vt (personne) to trouble, bother; (projets) to disrupt, upset; (objets, vêtements) to disarrange; **se ~** vi: **surtout ne vous dérangez pas pour moi** please don't put yourself out on my account; **est-ce que cela vous dérange si ...?** do you mind if ...?

déraper [deʀape] vi (voiture) to skid; (personne, semelles) to slip

dérégler [deʀegle] vt (mécanisme) to put out of order; (estomac) to upset

dérider [deʀide]: **se ~** vi to brighten up

dérision [deʀizjɔ̃] nf: **tourner en ~** to deride; **dérisoire** adj derisory

dérive [deʀiv] *nf:* **aller à la ~** (*NAVIG, fig*) to drift

dérivé, e [deʀive] *nm* (*TECH*) by-product

dériver [deʀive] *vt* (*MATH*) to derive; (*cours d'eau etc*) to divert ♦ *vi* (*bateau*) to drift; **~ de** to derive from

dermatologue [dɛʀmatɔlɔg] *nm/f* dermatologist

dernier, -ière [dɛʀnje, jɛʀ] *adj* last; (*le plus récent*) latest, last; **lundi/le mois ~** last Monday/month; **c'est le ~ cri** it's the very latest thing; **en ~** last; **ce ~** the latter; **dernièrement** *adv* recently

dérobé, e [deʀɔbe] *adj:* **à la ~e** surreptitiously

dérober [deʀɔbe] *vt* to steal; **se ~** *vi* (*s'esquiver*) to slip away; **se ~ à** (*justice, regards*) to hide from; (*obligation*) to shirk

dérogation [deʀɔgasjɔ̃] *nf* (special) dispensation

déroger [deʀɔʒe] : **~ à** *vt* to go against, depart from

dérouiller [deʀuje] *vt:* **se ~ les jambes** to stretch one's legs (*fig*)

déroulement [deʀulmɑ̃] *nm* (*d'une opération etc*) progress

dérouler [deʀule] *vt* (*ficelle*) to unwind; **se ~** *vi* (*avoir lieu*) to take place; (*se passer*) to go (off); **tout s'est déroulé comme prévu** everything went as planned

dérouter [deʀute] *vt* (*avion, train*) to reroute, divert; (*étonner*) to disconcert, throw (out)

derrière [dɛʀjɛʀ] *adv, prép* behind ♦ *nm* (*d'une maison*) back; (*postérieur*) behind, bottom; **les pattes de ~** the back *ou* hind legs; **par ~** from behind; (*fig*) behind one's back

des [de] *dét voir de* ♦ *prép* +*dét* = **de +les**

dès [dɛ] *prép* from; **~ que** as soon as; **~ son retour** as soon as he was (*ou* is) back

désabusé, e [dezabyze] *adj* disillusioned

désaccord [dezakɔʀ] *nm* disagreement; **désaccordé, e** *adj* (*MUS*) out of tune

désaffecté, e [dezafɛkte] *adj* disused

désagréable [dezagʀeabl] *adj* unpleasant

désagréger [dezagʀeʒe] : **se ~** *vi* to disintegrate, break up

désagrément [dezagʀemɑ̃] *nm* annoyance, trouble *no pl*

désaltérer [dezaltere] *vt:* **se ~** to quench one's thirst

désapprobateur, -trice [dezapʀɔbatœʀ, tʀis] *adj* disapproving

désapprouver [dezapʀuve] *vt* to disapprove of

désarmant, e [dezaʀmɑ̃, ɑ̃t] *adj* disarming

désarroi [dezaʀwa] *nm* disarray

désastre [dezastʀ] *nm* disaster; **désastreux, -euse** *adj* disastrous

désavantage [dezavɑ̃taʒ] *nm* disadvantage;

désavantager *vt* to put at a disadvantage

descendre [desɑ̃dʀ] *vt* (*escalier, montagne*) to go (*ou* come) down; (*valise, paquet*) to take *ou* get down; (*étagère etc*) to lower; (*fam: abattre*) to shoot down ♦ *vi* to go (*ou* come) down; (*passager: s'arrêter*) to get out, alight; **~ à pied/en voiture** to walk/drive down; **~ du train** to get out of *ou* get off the train; **~ de cheval** to dismount; **~ à l'hôtel** to stay at a hotel

descente [desɑ̃t] *nf* descent, going down; (*chemin*) way down; (*SKI*) downhill (race); **~ de lit** bedside rug; **~ (de police)** (police) raid

description [dɛskʀipsjɔ̃] *nf* description

désemparé, e [dezɑ̃paʀe] *adj* bewildered, distraught

désemplir [dezɑ̃pliʀ] *vi:* **ne pas ~** to be always full

déséquilibre [dezekilibʀ] *nm* (*position*): **en ~** unsteady; (*fig: des forces, du budget*) imbalance; **déséquilibré, e** *nm/f* (*PSYCH*) unbalanced person; **déséquilibrer** *vt* to throw off balance

désert, e [dezɛʀ, ɛʀt] *adj* deserted ♦ *nm* desert; **déserter** *vi, vt* to desert; **désertique** *adj* desert *cpd*

désespéré, e [dezɛspeʀe] *adj* desperate

désespérer [dezɛspeʀe] *vi:* **~ (de)** to despair (of); **désespoir** *nm* despair; **en désespoir de cause** in desperation

déshabiller [dezabije] *vt* to undress; **se ~** *vi* to undress (o.s.)

déshériter [dezeʀite] *vt* to disinherit; **déshérités** *nmpl:* **les déshérités** the underprivileged

déshonneur [dezɔnœʀ] *nm* dishonour

déshydraté, e [dezidʀate] *adj* dehydrated

desiderata [dezideʀata] *nmpl* requirements

désigner [dezine] *vt* (*montrer*) to point out, indicate; (*dénommer*) to denote; (*candidat etc*) to name

désinfectant, e [dezɛ̃fɛktɑ̃, ɑ̃t] *adj, nm* disinfectant

désinfecter [dezɛ̃fɛkte] *vt* to disinfect

désintégrer [dezɛ̃tegʀe] : **se ~** *vi* to disintegrate

désintéressé, e [dezɛ̃teʀese] *adj* disinterested, unselfish

désintéresser [dezɛ̃teʀese] *vt:* **se ~ (de)** to lose interest (in)

désintoxication [dezɛ̃tɔksikasjɔ̃] *nf:* **faire une cure de ~** to undergo treatment for alcoholism (*ou* drug addiction)

désinvolte [dezɛ̃vɔlt] *adj* casual, off-hand; **désinvolture** *nf* casualness

désir [deziʀ] *nm* wish; (*sensuel*) desire; **désirer** *vt* to want, wish for; (*sexuellement*) to desire; **je désire ...** (*formule de politesse*) |

would like ...

désister [dezistə]: se ~ vi to stand down, withdraw

désobéir [dezɔbeiʀ] vi: ~ (à qn/qch) to disobey (sb/sth); **désobéissant, e** adj disobedient

désobligeant, e [dezɔbliʒɑ̃, ɑ̃t] adj disagreeable

désodorisant [dezɔdɔʀizɑ̃] nm air freshener, deodorizer

désœuvré, e [dezœvʀe] adj idle

désolé, e [dezɔle] adj (paysage) desolate; **je suis ~** I'm sorry

désoler [dezɔle] vt to distress, grieve

désopilant, e [dezɔpilɑ̃, ɑ̃t] adj hilarious

désordonné, e [dezɔʀdɔne] adj untidy

désordre [dezɔʀdʀ] nm disorder(liness), untidiness; (anarchie) disorder; **en ~** in a mess, untidy

désorienté, e [dezɔʀjɑ̃te] adj disorientated

désormais [dezɔʀmɛ] adv from now on

désossé, e [dezɔse] adj (viande) boned

desquelles [dekɛl] prép +pron = de +lesquelles

desquels [dekɛl] prép +pron = de +lesquels

desséché, e [desefe] adj dried up

dessécher [desefe]: se ~ vi to dry out

dessein [desɛ̃] nm: à ~ intentionally, deliberately

desserrer [deseʀe] vt to loosen; (frein) to release

dessert [desɛʀ] nm dessert, pudding

desserte [desɛʀt] nf (table) side table; (transport): **la ~ du village est assurée par autocar** there is a coach service to the village

desservir [desɛʀviʀ] vt (ville, quartier) to serve; (débarrasser): ~ (la table) to clear the table

dessin [desɛ̃] nm (œuvre, art) drawing; (motif) pattern, design; **~ animé** cartoon (film); **~ humoristique** cartoon; **dessinateur, -trice** nm/f drawer; (de bandes dessinées) cartoonist; (industriel) draughtsman(-woman) (BRIT), draftsman(-woman) (US); **dessiner** vt to draw; (concevoir) to design

dessous [d(ə)su] adv underneath, beneath ♦ nm underside ♦ nmpl (sous-vêtements) underwear sg; **en ~, par ~** underneath; **au- ~ (de)** below; (peu digne de) beneath; **avoir le ~** to get the worst of it; **les voisins du ~** the downstairs neighbours; **dessous-de-plat** nm inv tablemat

dessus [d(ə)sy] adv on top; (collé, écrit) on it ♦ nm top; **en ~** above; **par ~** ♦ adv over it ♦ prép over; **au-~ (de)** above; **avoir le ~** to get the upper hand; **dessus-de-lit** nm inv bedspread

destin [destɛ̃] nm fate; (avenir) destiny

destinataire [destinatɛʀ] nm/f (POSTES) addressee; (d'un colis) consignee

destination [destinasjɔ̃] nf (lieu) destination; (usage) purpose; **à ~ de** bound for, travelling to

destinée [destine] nf fate; (existence, avenir) destiny

destiner [destine] vt: ~ qch à qn (envisager de donner) to intend sb to have sth; (adresser) to intend sth for sb; **être destiné à** (usage) to be meant for

désuet, -ète [dezɥɛ, ɛt] adj outdated, outmoded

détachant [detaʃɑ̃] nm stain remover

détachement [detaʃmɑ̃] nm detachment

détacher [detaʃe] vt (enlever) to detach, remove; (délier) to untie; (ADMIN): ~ qn (auprès de ou à) to post sb (to); se ~ vi (se séparer) to come off; (: page) to come out; (se défaire) to come undone; **se ~ sur** to stand out against; **se ~ de** (se désintéresser) to grow away from

détail [detaj] nm detail; (COMM): **le ~** retail; **en ~** in detail; **au ~** (COMM) retail; **détaillant** nm retailer; **détaillé, e** adj (plan, explications) detailed; (facture) itemized; **détailler** vt (expliquer) to explain in detail

détaler [detale] (fam) vi (personne) to take off

détartrant [detaʀtʀɑ̃] nm scale remover

détaxé, e [detakse] adj: **produits ~s** tax-free goods

détecter [detɛkte] vt to detect

détective [detɛktiv] nm: ~ **(privé)** private detective

déteindre [detɛ̃dʀ] vi (au lavage) to run, lose its colour

détendre [detɑ̃dʀ] vt (corps, esprit) to relax; se ~ vi (ressort) to lose its tension; (personne) to relax

détenir [det(ə)niʀ] vt (record, pouvoir, secret) to hold; (prisonnier) to detain, hold

détente [detɑ̃t] nf relaxation

détention [detɑ̃sjɔ̃] nf (d'armes) possession; (captivité) detention; ~ **préventive** custody

détenu, e [det(ə)ny] nm/f prisoner

détergent [detɛʀʒɑ̃] nm detergent

détériorer [deteʀjɔʀe] vt to damage; se ~ vi to deteriorate

déterminé, e [detɛʀmine] adj (résolu) determined; (précis) specific, definite

déterminer [detɛʀmine] vt (fixer) to determine; **se ~ à faire qch** to make up one's mind to do sth

déterrer [deteʀe] vt to dig up

détestable [detɛstabl] adj foul, detestable

détester [detɛste] vt to hate, detest

détonner [detɔne] vi (fig) to clash

détour [detuʀ] nm detour; (tournant) bend,

curve; **ça vaut le ~** it's worth the trip; **sans ~** (*fig*) plainly

détourné, e [deturne] *adj* (*moyen*) roundabout

détournement [deturnəmā] *nm:* **~ d'avion** hijacking

détourner [deturne] *vt* to divert; (*par la force*) to hijack; (*yeux, tête*) to turn away; (*de l'argent*) to embezzle; **se ~** *vi* to turn away

détracteur, -trice [detraktœr, tris] *nm/f* disparager, critic

détraquer [detrake] *vt* to put out of order; (*estomac*) to upset; **se ~** *vi* (*machine*) to go wrong

détrempé, e [detrãpe] *adj* (*sol*) sodden, waterlogged

détresse [detrɛs] *nf* distress

détriment [detrimã] *nm:* **au ~ de** to the detriment of

détritus [detrity(s)] *nmpl* rubbish *sg*, refuse *sg*

détroit [detrwa] *nm* strait

détromper [detrɔ̃pe] *vt* to disabuse

détruire [detrɥir] *vt* to destroy

dette [det] *nf* debt

DEUG [dœg] *sigle m* (= *diplôme d'études universitaires générales*) diploma taken after 2 years at university

deuil [dœj] *nm* (*perte*) bereavement; (*période*) mourning; **être en ~** to be in mourning

deux [dø] *num* two; **tous les ~** both; **ses ~ mains** both his hands, his two hands; **~ fois** twice; **deuxième** *num* second; **deuxièmement** *adv* secondly; **deux-pièces** *nm inv* (*tailleur*) two-piece suit; (*de bain*) two-piece (swimsuit); (*appartement*) two-roomed flat (*BRIT*) *ou* apartment (*US*); **deux-points** *nm inv* colon *sg*; **deux-roues** *nm inv* two-wheeled vehicle

devais *etc* [dəvɛ] *vb voir* **devoir**

dévaler [devale] *vt* to hurtle down

dévaliser [devalize] *vt* to rob, burgle

dévaloriser [devalɔrize] *vt* to depreciate; **se ~** *vi* to depreciate

dévaluation [devalɥasjɔ̃] *nf* devaluation

devancer [d(ə)vɑ̃se] *vt* (*coureur, rival*) to get ahead of; (*arriver*) to arrive before; (*prévenir: questions, désirs*) to anticipate

devant [d(ə)vɑ̃] *adv* in front; (*à distance: en avant*) ahead ♦ *prép* in front of; (*en avant*) ahead of; (*avec mouvement: passer*) past; (*en présence de*) before, in front of; (*étant donné*) in view of ♦ *nm* front; **prendre les ~s** to make the first move; **les pattes de ~** the front legs, the forelegs; **par ~** (*boutonner*) at the front; (*entrer*) the front way; **aller au-~ de qn** to go out to meet sb; **aller au-~ de** (*désirs de qn*) to anticipate

devanture [d(ə)vɑ̃tyr] *nf* (*étalage*) display;

(*vitrine*) (shop) window

déveine [devɛn] (*fam*) *nf* rotten luck *no pl*

développement [dev(ə)lɔpmã] *nm* development; **pays en voie de ~** developing countries

développer [dev(ə)lɔpe] *vt* to develop; **se ~** *vi* to develop

devenir [dəv(ə)nir] *vb +attrib* to become; **que sont-ils devenus?** what has become of them?

dévergondé, e [devɛrgɔ̃de] *adj* wild, shameless

déverser [devɛrse] *vt* (*liquide*) to pour (out); (*ordures*) to tip (out); **se ~ dans** (*fleuve*) to flow into

dévêtir [devetir]: **se ~** *vi* to undress

devez *etc* [dəve] *vb voir* **devoir**

déviation [devjasjɔ̃] *nf* (*AUTO*) diversion (*BRIT*), detour (*US*)

devienne *etc* [dəvjɛn] *vb voir* **devenir**

dévier [devje] *vt* (*fleuve, circulation*) to divert; (*coup*) to deflect ♦ *vi* to veer (off course)

devin [dəvɛ̃] *nm* soothsayer, seer

deviner [d(ə)vine] *vt* to guess; (*apercevoir*) to distinguish; **devinette** *nf* riddle

devins *etc* [dəvɛ̃] *vb voir* **devenir**

devis [d(ə)vi] *nm* estimate, quotation

dévisager [devizaʒe] *vt* to stare at

devise [dəviz] *nf* (*formule*) motto, watchword; **~s** *nfpl* (*argent*) currency *sg*

deviser [dəvize] *vi* to converse

dévisser [devise] *vt* to unscrew, undo

dévoiler [devwale] *vt* to unveil

devoir [d(ə)vwar] *nm* duty; (*SCOL*) homework *no pl*; (: *en classe*) exercise ♦ *vt* (*argent, respect*): **~ qch (à qn)** to owe (sb) sth; (+*infin: obligation*): **il doit le faire** he has to do it, he must do it; (: *intention*): **le nouveau centre commercial doit ouvrir en mai** the new shopping centre is due to open in May; (: *probabilité*): **il doit être tard** it must be late

dévolu [devɔly] *nm:* **jeter son ~ sur** to fix one's choice on

dévorer [devɔre] *vt* to devour

dévot, e [devo, ɔt] *adj* devout, pious; **dévotion** *nf* devoutness

dévoué, e [devwe] *adj* devoted

dévouement [devumã] *nm* devotion

dévouer [devwe]: **se ~** *vi* (*se sacrifier*): **se ~ (pour)** to sacrifice o.s. (for); (*se consacrer*): **se ~ à** to devote *ou* dedicate o.s. to

dévoyé, e [devwaje] *adj* delinquent

devrai *etc* [dəvre] *vb voir* **devoir**

diabète [djabɛt] *nm* diabetes *sg*; **diabétique** *nm/f* diabetic

diable [djabl] *nm* devil

diabolo [djabɔlo] *nm* (*boisson*) lemonade with fruit cordial

diagnostic [djagnɔstik] *nm* diagnosis *sg*; **diagnostiquer** *vt* to diagnose

diagonal, e, -aux [djagɔnal, o] *adj* diagonal; **diagonale** *nf* diagonal; **en diagonale** diagonally

diagramme [djagʀam] *nm* chart, graph

dialecte [djalɛkt] *nm* dialect

dialogue [djalɔg] *nm* dialogue

diamant [djamɑ̃] *nm* diamond

diamètre [djamɛtʀ] *nm* diameter

diapason [djapazɔ̃] *nm* tuning fork

diaphragme [djafʀagm] *nm* diaphragm

diapo [djapo] (*fam*) *nf* slide

diapositive [djapozitiv] *nf* transparency, slide

diarrhée [djaʀe] *nf* diarrhoea

dictateur [diktatœʀ] *nm* dictator; **dictature** *nf* dictatorship

dictée [dikte] *nf* dictation

dicter [dikte] *vt* to dictate

dictionnaire [diksjɔnɛʀ] *nm* dictionary

dicton [diktɔ̃] *nm* saying, dictum

dièse [djɛz] *nm* sharp

diesel [djezɛl] *nm* diesel ♦ *adj inv* diesel

diète [djɛt] *nf* (*jeûne*) starvation diet; (*régime*) diet; **diététique** *adj*: **magasin diététique** health food shop

dieu, x [djø] *nm* god; **D~** God; **mon D~!** good heavens!

diffamation [difamasjɔ̃] *nf* slander; (*écrite*) libel

différé [difeʀe] *nm* (*TV*): **en ~** (pre-)recorded

différemment [difeʀamɑ̃] *adv* differently

différence [difeʀɑ̃s] *nf* difference; **à la ~ de** unlike; **différencier** *vt* to differentiate; **différend** *nm* difference (of opinion), disagreement

différent, e [difeʀɑ̃, ɑ̃t] *adj* (*dissemblable*) different; **~ de** different from; (*divers*) different, various

différer [difeʀe] *vt* to postpone, put off ♦ *vi*: **~ (de)** to differ (from)

difficile [difisil] *adj* difficult; (*exigeant*) hard to please; **difficilement** *adv* with difficulty

difficulté [difikylte] *nf* difficulty; **en ~** (*bateau, alpiniste*) in difficulties

difforme [difɔʀm] *adj* deformed, misshapen

diffuser [difyze] *vt* (*chaleur*) to diffuse; (*émission, musique*) to broadcast; (*nouvelle*) to circulate; (*COMM*) to distribute

digérer [diʒeʀe] *vt* to digest; (*fam: accepter*) to stomach, put up with; **digestif** *nm* (after-dinner) liqueur; **digestion** *nf* digestion

digne [diɲ] *adj* dignified; **~ de** worthy of; **~ de foi** trustworthy; **dignité** *nf* dignity

digue [dig] *nf* dike, dyke

dilapider [dilapide] *vt* to squander

dilemme [dilɛm] *nm* dilemma

dilettante [diletɑ̃t] *nm/f*: **faire qch en ~** to dabble in sth

diligence [diliʒɑ̃s] *nf* stagecoach

diluer [dilɥe] *vt* to dilute

diluvien, ne [dilyvjɛ̃, jɛn] *adj*: **pluie ~ne** torrential rain

dimanche [dimɑ̃ʃ] *nm* Sunday

dimension [dimɑ̃sjɔ̃] *nf* (*grandeur*) size; (~s) dimensions

diminué, e [diminɥe] *adj*: **il est très ~ depuis son accident** he's not at all the man he was since his accident

diminuer [diminɥe] *vt* to reduce, decrease; (*ardeur etc*) to lessen; (*dénigrer*) to belittle ♦ *vi* to decrease, diminish; **diminutif** *nm* (*surnom*) pet name; **diminution** *nf* decreasing, diminishing

dinde [dɛ̃d] *nf* turkey

dindon [dɛ̃dɔ̃] *nm* turkey

dîner [dine] *nm* dinner ♦ *vi* to have dinner

dingue [dɛ̃g] (*fam*) *adj* crazy

dinosaure [dinɔzɔʀ] *nm* dinosaur

diplomate [diplɔmat] *adj* diplomatic ♦ *nm* diplomat; (*fig*) diplomatist; **diplomatie** *nf* diplomacy

diplôme [diplom] *nm* diploma; **avoir des ~s** to have qualifications; **diplômé, e** *adj* qualified

dire [diʀ] *nm*: **au ~ de** according to ♦ *vt* to say; (*secret, mensonge, heure*) to tell; **~ qch à qn** to tell sb sth; **~ à qn qu'il fasse** *ou* **de faire** to tell sb to do; **~ on dit que** they say that; **ceci dit** that being said; **si cela lui dit** (*plaire*) if he fancies it; **que dites-vous de** (*penser*) what do you think of; **on dirait que** it looks (*ou* sounds *etc*) as if; **dis/dites** (**donc**)**!** I say!

direct, e [diʀɛkt] *adj* direct ♦ *nm* (*TV*): **en ~** live; **directement** *adv* directly

directeur, -trice [diʀɛktœʀ, tʀis] *nm/f* (*d'entreprise*) director; (*de service*) manager(-eress); (*d'école*) head(teacher) (*BRIT*), principal (*US*)

direction [diʀɛksjɔ̃] *nf* (*sens*) direction; (*d'entreprise*) management; (*AUTO*) steering; **"toutes ~s"** "all routes"

dirent [diʀ] *vb voir* **dire**

dirigeant, e [diʀiʒɑ̃, ɑ̃t] *adj* (*classe*) ruling ♦ *nm/f* (*d'un parti etc*) leader

diriger [diʀiʒe] *vt* (*entreprise*) to manage, run; (*véhicule*) to steer; (*orchestre*) to conduct; (*recherches, travaux*) to supervise; **se ~** (*s'orienter*) to find one's way; **se ~ vers** *ou* **sur** to make *ou* head for

dis *etc* [di] *vb voir* **dire**

discernement [disɛʀnəmɑ̃] *nm* (*bon sens*) discernment, judgement

discerner [disɛʀne] *vt* to discern, make out

discipline [disiplin] *nf* discipline; **discipliner** *vt* to discipline

discontinu, e [diskɔ̃tiny] *adj* intermittent

discontinuer [diskɔ̃tinɥe] vi: **sans ~** without stopping, without a break

discordant, e [diskɔʀdɑ̃, ɑ̃t] adj discordant

discothèque [diskɔtɛk] nf (boîte de nuit) disco(thèque)

discours [diskuʀ] nm speech

discret, -ète [diskʀɛ, ɛt] adj discreet; (parfum, maquillage) unobtrusive; **discrétion** nf discretion; **à discrétion** as much as one wants

discrimination [diskʀiminasjɔ̃] nf discrimination; **sans ~** indiscriminately

disculper [diskylpe] vt to exonerate

discussion [diskysjɔ̃] nf discussion

discutable [diskytabl] adj debatable

discuté, e [diskyte] adj controversial

discuter [diskyte] vt (débattre) to discuss; (contester) to question, dispute ♦ vi to talk; (protester) to argue; **~ de** to discuss

dise etc [diz] vb voir **dire**

diseuse [dizøz] nf: **~ de bonne aventure** fortuneteller

disgracieux, -euse [disgʀasjø, jøz] adj ungainly, awkward

disjoindre [disʒwɛ̃dʀ] vt to take apart; **se ~** vi to come apart

disjoncteur [disʒɔ̃ktœʀ] nm (ÉLEC) circuit breaker

disloquer [dislɔke]: **se ~** vi (parti, empire) to break up

disons [dizɔ̃] vb voir **dire**

disparaître [dispaʀɛtʀ] vi to disappear; (se perdre: traditions etc) to die out; **faire ~** (tache) to remove; (douleur) to get rid of

disparition [dispaʀisjɔ̃] nf disappearance; **espèce en voie de ~** endangered species

disparu, e [dispaʀy] nm/f missing person ♦ adj: **être porté ~** to be reported missing

dispensaire [dispɑ̃sɛʀ] nm community clinic

dispenser [dispɑ̃se] vt: **~ qn de** to exempt sb from; **se ~ de** vt (corvée) to get out of

disperser [dispɛʀse] vt to scatter; **se ~** vi to break up

disponibilité [dispɔnibilite] nf availability; **disponible** adj available

dispos [dispo] adj m: **(frais et) ~** fresh (as a daisy)

disposé, e [dispoze] adj: **bien/mal ~** (humeur) in a good/bad mood; **~ à** (prêt à) willing ou prepared to

disposer [dispoze] vt to arrange ♦ vi: **vous pouvez ~** you may leave; **~ de** to have (at one's disposal); **se ~ à faire** to prepare to do, be about to do

dispositif [dispozitif] nm device; (fig) system, plan of action

disposition [dispozisjɔ̃] nf (arrangement) arrangement, layout; (humeur) mood; **prendre ses ~s** to make arrangements; **avoir**

des ~s pour la musique etc to have a special aptitude for music etc; **à la ~ de qn** at sb's disposal; **je suis à votre ~** I am at your service

disproportionné, e [dispʀɔpɔʀsjɔne] adj disproportionate, out of all proportion

dispute [dispyt] nf quarrel, argument; **disputer** vt (match) to play; (combat) to fight; **se disputer** vi to quarrel

disquaire [diskɛʀ] nm/f record dealer

disqualifier [diskalifje] vt to disqualify

disque [disk] nm (MUS) record; (forme, pièce) disc; (SPORT) discus; **~ compact** compact disc; **~ dur** hard disk; **disquette** nf floppy disk, diskette

disséminer [disemine] vt to scatter

disséquer [diseke] vt to dissect

dissertation [disɛʀtasjɔ̃] nf (SCOL) essay

dissimuler [disimyle] vt to conceal

dissipé, e [disipe] adj (élève) undisciplined, unruly

dissiper [disipe] vt to dissipate; (fortune) to squander; **se ~** vi (brouillard) to clear, disperse

dissolvant [disɔlvɑ̃] nm nail polish remover

dissonant, e [disɔnɑ̃, ɑ̃t] adj discordant

dissoudre [disudʀ] vt to dissolve; **se ~** vi to dissolve

dissuader [disɥade] vt: **~ qn de faire** to dissuade sb from doing; **dissuasion** nf: **force de dissuasion** deterrent power

distance [distɑ̃s] nf distance; (fig: écart) gap; **à ~ at** ou from a distance; **distancer** vt to outdistance

distant, e [distɑ̃, ɑ̃t] adj (réservé) distant; **~ de** (lieu) far away from

distendre [distɑ̃dʀ]: **se ~** vi to distend

distillerie [distilʀi] nf distillery

distinct, e [distɛ̃(kt), ɛ̃kt] adj distinct; **distinctement** adv distinctly, clearly; **distinctif, -ive** adj distinctive

distingué, e [distɛ̃ge] adj distinguished

distinguer [distɛ̃ge] vt to distinguish

distraction [distʀaksjɔ̃] nf (inattention) absent-mindedness; (passe-temps) distraction, entertainment

distraire [distʀɛʀ] vt (divertir) to entertain, divert; (déranger) to distract; **se ~** vi to amuse ou enjoy o.s.; **distrait, e** adj absent-minded

distrayant, e [distʀɛjɑ̃, ɑ̃t] adj entertaining

distribuer [distʀibɥe] vt to distribute, hand out; (CARTES) to deal (out); (courrier) to deliver; **distributeur** nm (COMM) distributor; (automatique) (vending) machine; (: de billets) (cash) dispenser; **distribution** nf distribution; (postale) delivery; (choix d'acteurs) casting, cast

dit, e [di, dit] pp de **dire** ♦ adj (fixé): **le jour ~** the arranged day; (surnommé): **X, ~ Pierrot** X, known as Pierrot

dites [dit] *vb voir* **dire**
divaguer [divage] *vi* to ramble; (*fam*) to rave
divan [divã] *nm* divan
diverger [diverʒe] *vi* to diverge
divers, e [diver, ers] *adj* (*varié*) diverse, varied; (*différent*) different, various; **~es personnes** various *ou* several people
diversifier [diversifje] *vt* to vary
diversité [diversite] *nf* (*variété*) diversity
divertir [divertir]: **se ~** *vi* to amuse *ou* enjoy o.s.; **divertissement** *nm* distraction, entertainment
divin, e [divɛ̃, in] *adj* divine
diviser [divize] *vt* to divide; **division** *nf* division
divorce [divɔrs] *nm* divorce; **divorcé, e** *nm/f* divorcee; **divorcer** *vi* to get a divorce, get divorced
divulguer [divylge] *vt* to divulge, disclose
dix [dis] *num* ten; **dixième** *num* tenth
dizaine [dizen] *nf*: **une ~ (de)** about ten, ten or so
do [do] *nm* (*note*) C; (*en chantant la gamme*) do(h)
docile [dɔsil] *adj* docile
dock [dɔk] *nm* dock; **docker** *nm* docker
docteur [dɔktœr] *nm* doctor; **doctorat** *nm* doctorate; **doctoresse** *nf* lady doctor
doctrine [dɔktrin] *nf* doctrine
document [dɔkymã] *nm* document; **documentaire** *adj, nm* documentary; **documentaliste** *nm/f* (SCOL) librarian; **documentation** *nf* documentation, literature; **documenter** *vt*: **se documenter (sur)** to gather information (on)
dodo [dodo] *nm* (*langage enfantin*): **aller faire ~** to go to beddy-byes
dodu, e [dody] *adj* plump
dogue [dɔg] *nm* mastiff
doigt [dwa] *nm* finger; **à deux ~s de** within an inch of; **~ de pied** toe; **doigté** *nm* (MUS) fingering; (*fig: habileté*) diplomacy, tact
doit *etc* [dwa] *vb voir* **devoir**
doléances [dɔleãs] *nfpl* grievances
dollar [dɔlar] *nm* dollar
domaine [dɔmen] *nm* estate, property; (*fig*) domain, field
domestique [dɔmestik] *adj* domestic ♦ *nm/f* servant, domestic; **domestiquer** *vt* to domesticate
domicile [dɔmisil] *nm* home, place of residence; **à ~** at home; **livrer à ~** to deliver; **domicilié, e** *adj*: **"domicilié à ..."** "address ..."
dominant, e [dɔminã, ãt] *adj* (*opinion*) predominant
dominer [dɔmine] *vt* to dominate; (*sujet*) to master; (*surpasser*) to outclass, surpass; (*surplomber*) to tower above, dominate ♦ *vi*

to be in the dominant position; **se ~** *vi* to control o.s.
domino [dɔmino] *nm* domino
dommage [dɔmaʒ] *nm*: **~s** (*dégâts*) damage *no pl*; **c'est ~!** what a shame!; **c'est ~ que** it's a shame *ou* pity that; **dommages-intérêts** *nmpl* damages
dompter [dɔ̃(p)te] *vt* to tame; **dompteur, -euse** *nm/f* trainer
DOM-TOM [dɔmtɔm] *sigle m* (= *départements et territoires d'outre-mer*) French overseas departments and territories
don [dɔ̃] *nm* gift; (*charité*) donation; **avoir des ~s pour** to have a gift *ou* talent for; **elle a le ~ de m'énerver** she's got a knack of getting on my nerves
donc [dɔ̃k] *conj* therefore, so; (*après une digression*) so, then
donjon [dɔ̃ʒɔ̃] *nm* keep
donné, e [dɔne] *adj* (*convenu: lieu, heure*) given; (*pas cher: fam*): **c'est ~** it's a gift; **étant ~ ... given ...**; **données** *nfpl* data
donner [dɔne] *vt* to give; (*vieux habits etc*) to give away; (*spectacle*) to put on; **~ qch à qn** to give sb sth, give sth to sb; **~ sur** (*suj: fenêtre, chambre*) to look (out) onto; **ça donne soif/faim** it makes you feel thirsty/hungry; **se ~ à fond** to give one's all; **se ~ du mal** to take (great) trouble; **s'en ~ à cœur joie** (*fam*) to have a great time

---

┌─────────────┐
│ *MOT-CLÉ* │
└─────────────┘

dont [dɔ̃] *pron relatif* **1** (*appartenance: objets*) whose, of which; (*appartenance: êtres animés*) whose; **la maison dont le toit est rouge** the house the roof of which is red, the house whose roof is red; **l'homme dont je connais la sœur** the man whose sister I know
2 (*parmi lesquel(le)s*): **2 livres, dont l'un est ...** 2 books, one of which is ...; **il y avait plusieurs personnes, dont Gabrielle** there were several people, among them Gabrielle; **10 blessés, dont 2 grièvement** 10 injured, 2 of them seriously
3 (*complément d'adjectif, de verbe*): **le fils dont il est si fier** the son he's so proud of; **ce dont je parle** what I'm talking about

---

doré, e [dɔre] *adj* golden; (*avec dorure*) gilt, gilded
dorénavant [dɔrenavã] *adv* henceforth
dorer [dɔre] *vt* to gild; (*faire*) **~** (CULIN) to brown
dorloter [dɔrlɔte] *vt* to pamper
dormir [dɔrmir] *vi* to sleep; (*être endormi*) to be asleep
dortoir [dɔrtwar] *nm* dormitory
dorure [dɔryr] *nf* gilding
dos [do] *nm* back; (*de livre*) spine; **"voir au ~"**

"see over"; **de ~** from the back
dosage [dozaʒ] *nm* mixture
dose [doz] *nf* dose; **doser** *vt* to measure out;
il faut savoir doser ses efforts you have to be
able to pace yourself
dossard [dosar] *nm* number (*worn by
competitor*)
dossier [dosje] *nm* (*documents*) file; (*de
chaise*) back; (*PRESSE*) feature; **un ~ scolaire** a
school report
dot [dɔt] *nf* dowry
doter [dɔte] *vt*: **~ de** to equip with
douane [dwan] *nf* customs *pl*; (**droits de**) **~**
(customs) duty; **douanier, -ière** *adj*
customs *cpd* ♦ *nm* customs officer
double [dubl] *adj, adv* double ♦ *nm* (*2 fois
plus*): **le ~ (de)** twice as much (*ou* many)
(as); (*autre exemplaire*) duplicate, copy;
(*sosie*) double; (*TENNIS*) doubles *sg*; **en
~ (exemplaire)** in duplicate; **faire ~ emploi** to
be redundant
doubler [duble] *vt* (*multiplier par 2*) to
double; (*vêtement*) to line; (*dépasser*) to
overtake, pass; (*film*) to dub; (*acteur*) to
stand in for ♦ *vi* to double
doublure [dublyr] *nf* lining; (*CINÉMA*) stand-
in
douce [dus] *adj voir* **doux; douceâtre** *adj*
sickly sweet; **doucement** *adv* gently;
(*lentement*) slowly; **doucereux, -euse** (*péj*)
adj sugary; **douceur** *nf* softness; (*de
quelqu'un*) gentleness; (*de climat*) mildness
douche [duʃ] *nf* shower; **doucher: se
doucher** *vi* to have *ou* take a shower
doudoune [dudun] *nf* padded jacket
doué, e [dwe] *adj* gifted, talented; **être
~ pour** to have a gift for
douille [duj] *nf* (*ÉLEC*) socket
douillet, te [dujɛ, ɛt] *adj* cosy; (*péj: à la
douleur*) soft
douleur [dulœr] *nf* pain; (*chagrin*) grief,
distress; **douloureux, -euse** *adj* painful
doute [dut] *nm* doubt; **sans ~** no doubt;
(*probablement*) probably; **sans aucun ~**
without a doubt; **douter** *vt* to doubt; **douter
de** (*sincérité de qn*) to have (one's) doubts
about; (*réussite*) to be doubtful of; **se douter
de qch/que** to suspect sth/that; **je m'en
doutais** I suspected as much; **douteux,
-euse** *adj* (*incertain*) doubtful; (*péj*)
dubious-looking
Douvres [duvr] *n* Dover
doux, douce [du, dus] *adj* soft; (*sucré*)
sweet; (*peu fort: moutarde, clément: climat*)
mild; (*pas brusque*) gentle
douzaine [duzɛn] *nf* (*12*) dozen; (*environ
12*): **une ~ (de)** a dozen or so, twelve or so
douze [duz] *num* twelve; **douzième** *num*
twelfth

doyen, ne [dwajɛ̃, jɛn] *nm/f* (*en âge*) most
senior member; (*de faculté*) dean
dragée [draʒe] *nf* sugared almond
dragon [dragɔ̃] *nm* dragon
draguer [drage] *vt* (*rivière*) to dredge; (*fam*)
to try to pick up
dramatique [dramatik] *adj* dramatic;
(*tragique*) tragic ♦ *nf* (*TV*) (television) drama
dramaturge [dramatyrʒ] *nm* dramatist,
playwright
drame [dram] *nm* drama
drap [dra] *nm* (*de lit*) sheet; (*tissu*) woollen
fabric
drapeau, x [drapo] *nm* flag
drap-housse [draus] *nm* fitted sheet
dresser [drese] *vt* (*mettre vertical, monter*) to
put up, erect; (*liste*) to draw up; (*animal*) to
train; **se ~** *vi* (*obstacle*) to stand; (*personne*)
to draw o.s. up; **~ qn contre qn** to set sb
against sb; **~ l'oreille** to prick up one's ears
drogue [drɔg] *nf* drug; **la ~** drugs *pl*;
drogué, e *nm/f* drug addict; **droguer** *vt*
(*victime*) to drug; **se droguer** *vi* (*aux
stupéfiants*) to take drugs; (*péj: de
médicaments*) to dose o.s. up; **droguerie** *nf*
hardware shop; **droguiste** *nm* keeper/owner
of a hardware shop
droit, e [drwa, drwat] *adj* (*non courbe*)
straight; (*vertical*) upright, straight; (*fig:
loyal*) upright, straight(forward); (*opposé à
gauche*) right, right-hand ♦ *adv* straight ♦ *nm*
(*prérogative*) right; (*taxe*) duty, tax; (: *d'inscription*) fee; (*JUR*): **le ~** law; **avoir le ~ de** to
be allowed to; **avoir ~ à** to be entitled to;
être dans son ~ to be within one's rights; **à ~e**
on the right; (*direction*) (to the) right; **~s
d'auteur** royalties; **~s de l'homme** human
rights; **~s d'inscription** enrolment fee; **droite**
nf (*POL*): **la droite** the right (wing); **droitier,
-ière** *nm/f* right-handed person; **droiture** *nf*
uprightness, straightness
drôle [drol] *adj* funny; **une ~ d'idée** a funny
idea; **drôlement** (*fam*) *adv* (*très*) terribly,
awfully
dromadaire [drɔmadɛr] *nm* dromedary
dru, e [dry] *adj* (*cheveux*) thick, bushy;
(*pluie*) heavy
du [dy] *dét voir* **de** ♦ *prép* +*dét* = **de + le**
dû, due [dy] *vb voir* **devoir** ♦ *adj* (*somme*)
owing, owed; (*causé par*): **~ à** due to ♦ *nm*
due
duc [dyk] *nm* duke; **duchesse** *nf* duchess
dûment [dymɑ̃] *adv* duly
dune [dyn] *nf* dune
Dunkerque [dœ̃kɛrk] *n* Dunkirk
duo [dɥo] *nm* (*MUS*) duet
dupe [dyp] *nf* dupe ♦ *adj*: **(ne pas) être ~ de**
(not) to be taken in by
duplex [dyplɛks] *nm* (*appartement*) split-level

apartment, duplex

duplicata [dyplikata] *nm* duplicate

duquel [dykɛl] *prép +pron* = **de +lequel**

dur, e [dyʀ] *adj* (*pierre, siège, travail, problème*) hard; (*voix, climat*) harsh; (*sévère*) hard, harsh; (*cruel*) hard(-hearted); (*porte, col*) stiff; (*viande*) tough ♦ *adv* hard ♦ *nm* (*fam: meneur*) tough nut; **~ d'oreille** hard of hearing

durant [dyʀɑ̃] *prép* (*au cours de*) during; (*pendant*) for; **des mois ~** for months

durcir [dyʀsiʀ] *vt, vi* to harden; **se ~** *vi* to harden

durée [dyʀe] *nf* length; (*d'une pile etc*) life; **de courte ~** (*séjour*) short

durement [dyʀmɑ̃] *adv* harshly

durer [dyʀe] *vi* to last

dureté [dyʀte] *nf* hardness; harshness; stiffness; toughness

durit ® [dyʀit] *nf* (car radiator) hose

dus *etc* [dy] *vb voir* **devoir**

duvet [dyvɛ] *nm* down; (*sac de couchage*) down-filled sleeping bag

dynamique [dinamik] *adj* dynamic; **dynamisme** *nm* dynamism

dynamite [dinamit] *nf* dynamite

dynamo [dinamo] *nf* dynamo

dysenterie [disɑ̃tʀi] *nf* dysentery

dyslexie [dislɛksi] *nf* dyslexia, word-blindness

E, e

eau, x [o] *nf* water; **~x** *nfpl* (*MÉD*) waters; **prendre l'~** to leak, let in water; **tomber à l'~** (*fig*) to fall through; **~ courante** running water; **~ de Javel** bleach; **~ de toilette** toilet water; **~ douce** fresh water; **~ gazeuse** sparkling (mineral) water; **~ minérale** mineral water; **~ plate** still water; **~ potable** drinking water; **eau-de-vie** *nf* brandy; **eau-forte** *nf* etching

ébahi, e [ebai] *adj* dumbfounded

ébattre [ebatʀ]: **s'~** *vi* to frolic

ébaucher [eboʃe] *vt* to sketch out, outline; **s'~** *vi* to take shape

ébène [ebɛn] *nf* ebony; **ébéniste** *nm* cabinetmaker

éberlué, e [ebɛʀlɥe] *adj* astounded

éblouir [ebluiʀ] *vt* to dazzle

éborgner [ebɔʀɲe] *vt* to blind in one eye

éboueur [ebwœʀ] *nm* dustman (*BRIT*), garbageman (*US*)

ébouillanter [ebujɑ̃te] *vt* to scald; (*CULIN*) to blanch

éboulement [ebulmɑ̃] *nm* rock fall

ébouler [ebule]: **s'~** *vi* to crumble, collapse; **éboulis** *nmpl* fallen rocks

ébouriffé, e [ebuʀife] *adj* tousled

ébranler [ebʀɑ̃le] *vt* to shake; (*affaiblir*) to weaken; **s'~** *vi* (*partir*) to move off

ébrécher [ebʀeʃe] *vt* to chip

ébriété [ebʀijete] *nf*: **en état d'~** in a state of intoxication

ébrouer [ebʀue]: **s'~** *vi* to shake o.s.

ébruiter [ebʀɥite] *vt* to spread, disclose

ébullition [ebylisjɔ̃] *nf* boiling point

écaille [ekaj] *nf* (*de poisson*) scale; (*matière*) tortoiseshell; **écailler** *vt* (*poisson*) to scale; **s'écailler** *vi* to flake ou peel (off)

écarlate [ekaʀlat] *adj* scarlet

écarquiller [ekaʀkije] *vt*: **~ les yeux** to stare wide-eyed

écart [ekaʀ] *nm* gap; **à l'~** out of the way; **à l'~ de** away from; **faire un ~** (*voiture*) to swerve; **~ de conduite** misdemeanour

écarté, e [ekaʀte] *adj* (*lieu*) out-of-the-way, remote; (*ouvert*): **les jambes ~es** legs apart; **les bras ~s** arms outstretched

écarter [ekaʀte] *vt* (*séparer*) to move apart, separate; (*éloigner*) to push back, move away; (*ouvrir: bras, jambes*) to spread, open; (: *rideau*) to draw (back); (*éliminer: candidat, possibilité*) to dismiss; **s'~** *vi* to part; (*s'éloigner*) to move away; **s'~ de** to wander from

écervelé, e [esɛʀvəle] *adj* scatterbrained, featherbrained

échafaud [eʃafo] *nm* scaffold

échafaudage [eʃafodaʒ] *nm* scaffolding

échafauder [eʃafode] *vt* (*plan*) to construct

échalote [eʃalɔt] *nf* shallot

échancrure [eʃɑ̃kʀyʀ] *nf* (*de robe*) scoop neckline

échange [eʃɑ̃ʒ] *nm* exchange; **en ~ de** in exchange ou return for; **échanger** *vt*: **échanger qch (contre)** to exchange sth (for); **échangeur** *nm* (*AUTO*) interchange

échantillon [eʃɑ̃tijɔ̃] *nm* sample

échappement [eʃapmɑ̃] *nm* (*AUTO*) exhaust

échapper [eʃape]: **~ à** *vt* (*gardien*) to escape (from); (*punition, péril*) to escape; **s'~** *vi* to escape; **~ à qn** (*détail, sens*) to escape sb; (*objet qu'on tient*) to slip out of sb's hands; **laisser ~** (*cri etc*) to let out; **l'~ belle** to have a narrow escape

écharde [eʃaʀd] *nf* splinter (of wood)

écharpe [eʃaʀp] *nf* scarf; **avoir le bras en ~** to have one's arm in a sling

échasse [eʃas] *nf* stilt

échassier [eʃasje] *nm* wader

échauffer [eʃofe] *vt* (*moteur*) to overheat; **s'~** *vi* (*SPORT*) to warm up; (*dans la discussion*) to become heated

échéance [eʃeɑ̃s] *nf* (*d'un paiement: date*) settlement date; (*fig*) deadline; **à brève ~** in the short term; **à longue ~** in the long run

échéant [eʃeɑ̃]: **le cas ~** *adv* if the case arises

échec [eʃɛk] nm failure; (ÉCHECS): ~ **et mat/au roi** checkmate/check; ~**s** nmpl (jeu) chess sg; **tenir en ~ ~** to hold in check

échelle [eʃɛl] nf ladder; (fig, d'une carte) scale

échelon [eʃ(ə)lɔ̃] nm (d'échelle) rung; (ADMIN) grade; **échelonner** vt to space out

échevelé, e [eʃəv(ə)le] adj tousled, dishevelled

échine [eʃin] nf backbone, spine

échiquier [eʃikje] nm chessboard

écho [eko] nm echo; **échographie** nf: **passer une échographie** to have a scan

échoir [eʃwaR] vi (dette) to fall due; (délais) to expire; ~ **à** to fall to

échouer [eʃwe] vi to fail; **s'~** vi to run aground

échu, e [eʃy] pp de **échoir**

éclabousser [eklabuse] vt to splash

éclair [eklɛR] nm (d'orage) flash of lightning, lightning no pl; (gâteau) éclair

éclairage [eklɛRaʒ] nm lighting

éclaircie [eklɛRsi] nf bright interval

éclaircir [eklɛRsiR] vt to lighten; (fig: mystère) to clear up; (: point) to clarify; **s'~** vi (ciel) to clear; **s'~ la voix** to clear one's throat; **éclaircissement** nm (sur un point) clarification

éclairer [eklɛRe] vt (lieu) to light (up); (personne: avec une lampe etc) to light the way for; (fig: problème) to shed light on ♦ vi: ~ **mal/bien** to give a poor/good light; **s'~ à la bougie** to use candlelight

éclaireur, -euse [eklɛRœR, øz] nm/f (scout) (boy) scout/(girl) guide ♦ nm (MIL) scout

éclat [ekla] nm (de bombe, de verre) fragment; (du soleil, d'une couleur etc) brightness, brilliance; (d'une cérémonie) splendour; (scandale): **faire un ~** to cause a commotion; ~**s de voix** shouts; ~ **de rire** roar of laughter

éclatant, e [eklatɑ̃, ɑ̃t] adj brilliant

éclater [eklate] vi (pneu) to burst; (bombe) to explode; (guerre) to break out; (groupe, parti) to break up; ~ **en sanglots/de rire** to burst out sobbing/laughing

éclipser [eklipse]: **s'~** vi to slip away

éclore [eklɔR] vi (œuf) to hatch; (fleur) to open (out)

écluse [eklyz] nf lock

écœurant, e [ekœRɑ̃, ɑ̃t] adj (gâteau etc) sickly; (fig) sickening

écœurer [ekœRe] vt: ~ **qn** (nourriture) to make sb feel sick; (conduite, personne) to disgust sb

école [ekɔl] nf school; **aller à l'~** to go to school; ~ **maternelle/primaire** nursery/primary school; ~ **publique** state school; **écolier, -ière** nm/f schoolboy(-girl)

écologie [ekɔlɔʒi] nf ecology; **écologique** adj environment-friendly; **écologiste** nm/f ecologist

éconduire [ekɔ̃dɥiR] vt to dismiss

économe [ekɔnɔm] adj thrifty ♦ nm/f (de lycée etc) bursar (BRIT), treasurer (US)

économie [ekɔnɔmi] nf economy; (gain: d'argent, de temps etc) saving; (science) economics sg; ~**s** nfpl (pécule) savings; **économique** adj (avantageux) economical; (ÉCON) economic; **économiser** vt, vi to save

écoper [ekɔpe] vi to bale out; ~ **de 3 ans de prison** (fig: fam) to get sentenced to 3 years

écorce [ekɔRs] nf bark; (de fruit) peel

écorcher [ekɔRʃe] vt: **s'~ le genou/la main** to graze one's knee/one's hand; **écorchure** nf graze

écossais, e [ekɔsɛ, ɛz] adj Scottish ♦ nm/f: **É~, e** Scot

Écosse [ekɔs] nf: **l'~** Scotland

écosser [ekɔse] vt to shell

écoulement [ekulmɑ̃] nm (d'eau) flow

écouler [ekule] vt (marchandise) to sell; **s'~** (eau) to flow (out); (jours, temps) to pass (by)

écourter [ekuRte] vt to curtail, cut short

écoute [ekut] nf (RADIO, TV): **temps/heure d'~** listening (ou viewing) time/hour; **rester à l'~ (de)** to stay tuned in (to); ~**s téléphoniques** phone tapping sg

écouter [ekute] vt to listen to; **écouteur** nm (TÉL) receiver; (RADIO) headphones pl, headset

écoutille [ekutij] nf hatch

écran [ekRɑ̃] nm screen; **petit ~** television; ~ **total** sunblock

écrasant, e [ekRazɑ̃, ɑ̃t] adj overwhelming

écraser [ekRaze] vt to crush; (piéton) to run over; **s'~ (au sol)** to crash; **s'~ contre** to crash into

écrémé, e [ekReme] adj (lait) skimmed

écrevisse [ekRəvis] nf crayfish inv

écrier [ekRije]: **s'~** vi to exclaim

écrin [ekRɛ̃] nm case, box

écrire [ekRiR] vt to write; **s'~** to write to each other; **ça s'écrit comment?** how is it spelt?; **écrit** nm (examen) written paper; **par écrit** in writing

écriteau, x [ekRito] nm notice, sign

écriture [ekRityR] nf writing; **l'É~, les É~s** the Scriptures

écrivain [ekRivɛ̃] nm writer

écrou [ekRu] nm nut

écrouer [ekRue] vt to imprison

écrouler [ekRule]: **s'~** vi to collapse

écru, e [ekRy] adj (couleur) off-white, écru

ECU [eky] sigle m ECU

écueil [ekœj] nm reef; (fig) pitfall

éculé, e [ekyle] adj (chaussure) down-at-heel; (fig: péj) hackneyed

écume [ekym] nf foam; **écumer** vt (CULIN) to skim; **écumoire** nf skimmer

écureuil [ekyRœj] nm squirrel

écurie [ekyʀi] *nf* stable

écusson [ekysɔ̃] *nm* badge

écuyer, -ère [ekɥije, jeʀ] *nm/f* rider

eczéma [egzema] *nm* eczema

édenté, e [edɑ̃te] *adj* toothless

EDF *sigle f* (= *Électricité de France*) national electricity company

édifice [edifis] *nm* edifice, building

édifier [edifje] *vt* to build, erect; (*fig*) to edify

Édimbourg [edɛ̃buʀ] *n* Edinburgh

éditer [edite] *vt* (*publier*) to publish; (*annoter*) to edit; **éditeur, -trice** *nm/f* publisher; **édition** *nf* edition; (*industrie du livre*) publishing

édredon [edʀədɔ̃] *nm* eiderdown

éducateur, -trice [edykatœʀ, tʀis] *nm/f* teacher; (*in special school*) instructor

éducatif, -ive [edykatif, iv] *adj* educational

éducation [edykasjɔ̃] *nf* education; (*familiale*) upbringing; (*manières*) (good) manners *pl*; ~ **physique** physical education

édulcorant [edylkɔʀɑ̃] *nm* sweetener

éduquer [edyke] *vt* to educate; (*élever*) to bring up

effacé, e [efase] *adj* unassuming

effacer [efase] *vt* to erase, rub out; **s'~** *vi* (*inscription etc*) to wear off; (*pour laisser passer*) to step aside

effarant, e [efaʀɑ̃, ɑ̃t] *adj* alarming

effarer [efaʀe] *vt* to alarm

effaroucher [efaʀuʃe] *vt* to frighten *ou* scare away

effectif, -ive [efektif, iv] *adj* real ♦ *nm* (SCOL) (*pupil*) numbers *pl*; (*entreprise*) staff, workforce; **effectivement** *adv* (*réellement*) actually, really; (*en effet*) indeed

effectuer [efektɥe] *vt* (*opération*) to carry out; (*trajet*) to make

efféminé, e [efemine] *adj* effeminate

effervescent, e [efɛʀvesɑ̃, ɑ̃t] *adj* effervescent

effet [efɛ] *nm* effect; (*impression*) impression; **~s** *nmpl* (*vêtements etc*) things; **faire ~** (*médicament*) to take effect; **faire bon/mauvais ~ sur qn** to make a good/bad impression on sb; **en ~** indeed; **~ de serre** greenhouse effect

efficace [efikas] *adj* (*personne*) efficient; (*action, médicament*) effective; **efficacité** *nf* efficiency; effectiveness

effilocher [efilɔʃe] **s'~** *vi* to fray

efflanqué, e [eflɑ̃ke] *adj* emaciated

effleurer [eflœʀe] *vt* to brush (against); (*sujet*) to touch upon; (*suj: idée, pensée*): **ça ne m'a pas effleuré** it didn't cross my mind

effluves [eflyv] *nmpl* exhalation(s)

effondrer [efɔ̃dʀe] **s'~** *vi* to collapse

efforcer [efɔʀse] **s'~ de** *vt*: **s'~ de faire** to try hard to do

effort [efɔʀ] *nm* effort

effraction [efʀaksjɔ̃] *nf*: **s'introduire par ~ dans** to break into

effrayant, e [efʀejɑ̃, ɑ̃t] *adj* frightening

effrayer [efʀeje] *vt* to frighten, scare

effréné, e [efʀene] *adj* wild

effriter [efʀite] **s'~** *vi* to crumble

effroi [efʀwa] *nm* terror, dread *no pl*

effronté, e [efʀɔ̃te] *adj* cheeky

effroyable [efʀwajabl] *adj* horrifying, appalling

effusion [efyzjɔ̃] *nf* effusion; **sans ~ de sang** without bloodshed

égal, e, -aux [egal, o] *adj* equal; (*constant: vitesse*) steady ♦ *nm/f* equal; **être ~ à** (*prix, nombre*) to be equal to; **ça lui est ~** it's all the same to him, he doesn't mind; **sans ~** matchless, unequalled; **d'~ à ~** as equals;

également *adv* equally; (*aussi*) too, as well; **égaler** *vt* to equal; **égaliser** *vt* (*sol, salaires*) to level (out); (*chances*) to equalize ♦ *vi* (SPORT) to equalize; **égalité** *nf* equality; **être à égalité** to be level

égard [egaʀ] *nm*: **~s** consideration *sg*; **à cet ~** in this respect; **par ~ pour** out of consideration for; **à l'~ de** towards

égarement [egaʀmɑ̃] *nm* distraction

égarer [egaʀe] *vt* to mislay; **s'~** *vi* to get lost, lose one's way; (*objet*) to go astray

égayer [egeje] *vt* to cheer up; (*pièce*) to brighten up

églantine [eglɑ̃tin] *nf* wild *ou* dog rose

églefin [egləfɛ̃] *nm* haddock

église [egliz] *nf* church; **aller à l'~** to go to church

égoïsme [egɔism] *nm* selfishness; **égoïste** *adj* selfish

égorger [egɔʀʒe] *vt* to cut the throat of

égosiller [egozije]: **s'~** *vi* to shout o.s. hoarse

égout [egu] *nm* sewer

égoutter [egute] *vi* to drip; **s'~** *vi* to drip; **égouttoir** *nm* draining board; (*mobile*) draining rack

égratigner [egʀatiɲe] *vt* to scratch; **égratignure** *nf* scratch

Égypte [eʒipt] *nf*: **l'~** Egypt; **égyptien, ne** *adj* Egyptian ♦ *nm/f*: **Égyptien, ne** Egyptian

eh [e] *excl* hey!; **~ bien** well

éhonté, e [eɔ̃te] *adj* shameless, brazen

éjecter [eʒɛkte] *vt* (TECH) to eject; (*fam*) to kick *ou* chuck out

élaborer [elabɔʀe] *vt* to elaborate; (*projet, stratégie*) to work out; (*rapport*) to draft

élan [elɑ̃] *nm* (ZOOL) elk, moose; (SPORT) run up; (*fig: de tendresse etc*) surge; **prendre de l'~** to gather speed

élancé, e [elɑ̃se] *adj* slender

élancement [elɑ̃smɑ̃] *nm* shooting pain

élancer [elɑ̃se]: **s'~** *vi* to dash, hurl o.s.

élargir [elaʀʒiʀ] vt to widen; s'~ vi to widen; (vêtement) to stretch

élastique [elastik] adj elastic ♦ nm (de bureau) rubber band; (pour la couture) elastic no pl

électeur, -trice [elɛktœʀ, tʀis] nm/f elector, voter

élection [elɛksjɔ̃] nf election

électorat [elɛktɔʀa] nm electorate

électricien, ne [elɛktʀisjɛ̃, jɛn] nm/f electrician

électricité [elɛktʀisite] nf electricity; allumer/éteindre l'~ to put on/off the light

électrique [elɛktʀik] adj electric(al)

électrocuter [elɛktʀɔkyte] vt to electrocute

électroménager [elɛktʀomenaʒe] adj, nm: appareils ~s, l'~ domestic (electrical) appliances

électronique [elɛktʀɔnik] adj electronic ♦ nf electronics sg

électrophone [elɛktʀɔfɔn] nm record player

élégance [elegɑ̃s] nf elegance

élégant, e [elegɑ̃, ɑ̃t] adj elegant

élément [elemɑ̃] nm element; (pièce) component, part; ~s de cuisine kitchen units; **élémentaire** adj elementary

éléphant [elefɑ̃] nm elephant

élevage [el(ə)vaʒ] nm breeding; (de bovins) cattle rearing; truite d'~ farmed trout

élévation [elevasjɔ̃] nf (hausse) rise

élevé, e [el(ə)ve] adj high; bien/mal ~ well-/ill-mannered

élève [elɛv] nm/f pupil

élever [el(ə)ve] vt (enfant) to bring up, raise; (animaux) to breed; (hausser: taux, niveau) to raise; (édifier: monument) to put up, erect; s'~ vi (avion) to go up; (niveau, température) to rise; s'~ à (suj: frais, dégâts) to amount to, add up to; s'~ contre qch to rise up against sth; ~ la voix to raise one's voice; **éleveur, -euse** nm/f breeder

élimé, e [elime] adj threadbare

éliminatoire [eliminatwaʀ] nf (SPORT) heat

éliminer [elimine] vt to eliminate

élire [eliʀ] vt to elect

elle [ɛl] pron (sujet) she; (: chose) it; (complément) her; it; ~s (sujet) they; (complément) them; ~-même herself; itself; ~s-mêmes themselves; voir aussi **il**

élocution [elɔkysjɔ̃] nf delivery; défaut d'~ speech impediment

éloge [elɔʒ] nm (gén no pl) praise; faire l'~ de to praise; **élogieux, -euse** adj laudatory, full of praise

éloigné, e [elwaɲe] adj distant, far-off; (parent) distant; **éloignement** nm (distance, aussi fig) distance

éloigner [elwaɲe] vt (échéance) to put off, postpone; (soupçons, danger) to ward off; (objet): ~ qch (de) to move ou take sth away (from); (personne): ~ qn (de) to take sb away ou remove sb (from); s'~ (de) (personne) to go away (from); (véhicule) to move away (from); (affectivement) to become estranged (from); ne vous éloignez pas! don't go far away!

élu, e [ely] pp de **élire** ♦ nm/f (POL) elected representative

éluder [elyde] vt to evade

Élysée [elize] nm: (le palais de) l'~ the Élysée Palace (the French president's residence)

émacié, e [emasje] adj emaciated

émail, -aux [emaj, o] nm enamel

émaillé, e [emaje] adj (fig): ~ de dotted with

émanciper [emɑ̃sipe] s'~ vi (fig) to become emancipated ou liberated

émaner [emane]: ~ de vt to come from

emballage [ɑ̃balaʒ] nm (papier) wrapping; (boîte) packaging

emballer [ɑ̃bale] vt to wrap (up); (dans un carton) to pack (up); (fig: fam) to thrill (to bits); s'~ vi (moteur) to race; (cheval) to bolt; (fig: personne) to get carried away

embarcadère [ɑ̃baʀkadɛʀ] nm wharf, pier

embarcation [ɑ̃baʀkasjɔ̃] nf (small) boat, (small) craft inv

embardée [ɑ̃baʀde] nf: faire une ~ to swerve

embarquement [ɑ̃baʀkəmɑ̃] nm (de passagers) boarding; (de marchandises) loading

embarquer [ɑ̃baʀke] vt (personne) to embark; (marchandise) to load; (fam) to cart off ♦ vi (passager) to board; s'~ vi to board; s'~ dans (affaire, aventure) to embark upon

embarras [ɑ̃baʀa] nm (gêne) embarrassment; mettre qn dans l'~ to put sb in an awkward position; vous n'avez que l'~ du choix the only problem is choosing

embarrassant, e [ɑ̃baʀasɑ̃, ɑ̃t] adj embarrassing

embarrasser [ɑ̃baʀase] vt (encombrer) to clutter (up); (gêner) to hinder, hamper; ~ qn to put sb in an awkward position; s'~ de to burden o.s. with

embauche [ɑ̃boʃ] nf hiring; **embaucher** vt to take on, hire

embaumer [ɑ̃bome] vt: ~ la lavande etc to be fragrant with (the scent of) lavender etc

embellie [ɑ̃beli] nf brighter period

embellir [ɑ̃beliʀ] vt to make more attractive; (une histoire) to embellish ♦ vi to grow lovelier ou more attractive

embêtements [ɑ̃bɛtmɑ̃] nmpl trouble sg

embêter [ɑ̃bete] vt to bother; s'~ vi (s'ennuyer) to be bored

emblée [ɑ̃ble]: d'~ adv straightaway

embobiner [ɑ̃bɔbine] vt (fam) to get round

emboîter [ɑ̃bwate] vt to fit together;

s'~ (dans) to fit (into); **~ le pas à qn** to follow in sb's footsteps

embonpoint [ɑ̃bɔ̃pwɛ̃] nm stoutness

embouchure [ɑ̃buʃyʀ] nf (GÉO) mouth

embourber [ɑ̃buʀbe]: **s'~** vi to get stuck in the mud

embourgeoiser [ɑ̃buʀʒwaze]: **s'~** vi to become middle-class

embouteillage [ɑ̃butejaʒ] nm traffic jam

emboutir [ɑ̃butiʀ] vt (heurter) to crash into, ram

embranchement [ɑ̃bʀɑ̃ʃmɑ̃] nm (routier) junction

embraser [ɑ̃bʀaze]: **s'~** vi to flare up

embrassades [ɑ̃bʀasad] nfpl hugging and kissing

embrasser [ɑ̃bʀase] vt to kiss; (sujet, période) to embrace, encompass; **s'~** to kiss (each other)

embrasure [ɑ̃bʀazyʀ] nf: **dans l'~ de la porte** in the door(way)

embrayage [ɑ̃bʀejaʒ] nm clutch

embrayer [ɑ̃bʀeje] vi (AUTO) to let in the clutch

embrocher [ɑ̃bʀɔʃe] vt to put on a spit

embrouiller [ɑ̃bʀuje] vt to muddle up; (fils) to tangle (up); **s'~** vi (personne) to get in a muddle

embruns [ɑ̃bʀœ̃] nmpl sea spray sg

embryon [ɑ̃bʀijɔ̃] nm embryo

embûches [ɑ̃byʃ] nfpl pitfalls, traps

embué, e [ɑ̃bye] adj misted up

embuscade [ɑ̃byskad] nf ambush

éméché, e [emeʃe] adj tipsy, merry

émeraude [em(ə)ʀod] nf emerald

émerger [emeʀʒe] vi to emerge; (faire saillie, aussi fig) to stand out

émeri [em(ə)ʀi] nm: **toile ou papier ~** emery paper

émerveillement [emeʀvejmɑ̃] nm wonder

émerveiller [emeʀveje] vt to fill with wonder; **s'~ de** to marvel at

émettre [emetʀ] vt (son, lumière) to give out, emit; (message etc: RADIO) to transmit; (billet, timbre, emprunt) to issue; (hypothèse, avis) to voice, put forward ♦ vi to broadcast

émeus etc [emø] vb voir **émouvoir**

émeute [emøt] nf riot

émietter [emjete] vt to crumble

émigrer [emigʀe] vi to emigrate

émincer [emɛ̃se] vt to cut into thin slices

éminent, e [eminɑ̃, ɑ̃t] adj distinguished

émission [emisjɔ̃] nf (RADIO, TV) programme, broadcast; (d'un message) transmission; (de timbre) issue

emmagasiner [ɑ̃magazine] vt (amasser) to store up

emmanchure [ɑ̃mɑ̃ʃyʀ] nf armhole

emmêler [ɑ̃mele] vt to tangle (up); (fig) to

muddle up; **s'~** vi to get in a tangle

emménager [ɑ̃menaʒe] vi to move in; **~ dans** to move into

emmener [ɑ̃m(ə)ne] vt to take (with one); (comme otage, capture) to take away; **~ qn au cinéma** to take sb to the cinema

emmerder [ɑ̃mɛʀde] vt (fam!) to bug, bother; **s'~** vi to be bored stiff

emmitoufler [ɑ̃mitufle]: **s'~** vi to wrap up (warmly)

émoi [emwa] nm commotion

émotif, -ive [emɔtif, iv] adj emotional

émotion [emosjɔ̃] nf emotion

émousser [emuse] vt to blunt; (fig) to dull

émouvoir [emuvwaʀ] vt to move; **s'~** vi to be moved; (s'indigner) to be roused

empailler [ɑ̃paje] vt to stuff

empaqueter [ɑ̃pakte] vt to parcel up

emparer [ɑ̃paʀe]: **s'~ de** vt (objet) to seize, grab; (comme otage, MIL) to seize; (suj: peur etc) to take hold of

empâter [ɑ̃pɑte]: **s'~** vi to thicken out

empêchement [ɑ̃pɛʃmɑ̃] nm (unexpected) obstacle, hitch

empêcher [ɑ̃peʃe] vt to prevent; **~ qn de faire** to prevent ou stop sb (from) doing; **il n'empêche que** nevertheless; **il n'a pas pu s'~ de rire** he couldn't help laughing

empereur [ɑ̃pʀœʀ] nm emperor

empester [ɑ̃peste] vt to stink, reek

empêtrer [ɑ̃petʀe] vt: **s'~ dans** (fils etc) to get tangled up in

emphase [ɑ̃faz] nf pomposity, bombast

empiéter [ɑ̃pjete] vi: **~ sur** to encroach upon

empiffrer [ɑ̃pifʀe]: **s'~** (fam) vi to stuff o.s.

empiler [ɑ̃pile] vt to pile (up)

empire [ɑ̃piʀ] nm empire; (fig) influence

empirer [ɑ̃piʀe] vi to worsen, deteriorate

emplacement [ɑ̃plasmɑ̃] nm site

emplettes [ɑ̃plɛt] nfpl shopping sg

emplir [ɑ̃pliʀ] vt to fill; **s'~ (de)** to fill (with)

emploi [ɑ̃plwa] nm use; (COMM, ÉCON) employment; (poste) job, situation; **mode d'~** directions for use; **~ du temps** timetable, schedule

employé, e [ɑ̃plwaje] nm/f employee; **~ de bureau** office employee ou clerk

employer [ɑ̃plwaje] vt to use; (ouvrier, main-d'œuvre) to employ; **s'~ à faire** to apply ou devote o.s. to doing; **employeur, -euse** nm/f employer

empocher [ɑ̃pɔʃe] vt to pocket

empoigner [ɑ̃pwaɲe] vt to grab

empoisonner [ɑ̃pwazɔne] vt to poison; (empester: air, pièce) to stink out; (fam): **~ qn** to drive sb mad

emporté, e [ɑ̃pɔʀte] adj quick-tempered

emporter [ɑ̃pɔʀte] vt to take (with one); (en dérobant ou enlevant, emmener: blessés, voyageurs) to take away; (entraîner) to carry away; **s'~** vi (de colère) to lose one's temper; **l'~ (sur)** to get the upper hand (of); **plats à ~** take-away meals

empreint, e [ɑ̃pʀɛ̃, ɛ̃t] adj: **~ de** (regret, jalousie) marked with; **empreinte** nf: **empreinte (de pas)** footprint; **empreinte (digitale)** fingerprint

empressé, e [ɑ̃pʀese] adj attentive

empressement [ɑ̃pʀesmɑ̃] nm (hâte) eagerness

empresser [ɑ̃pʀese] **s'~** vi: **s'~ auprès de qn** to surround sb with attentions; **s'~ de faire** (se hâter) to hasten to do

emprise [ɑ̃pʀiz] nf hold, ascendancy

emprisonnement [ɑ̃pʀizɔnmɑ̃] nm imprisonment

emprisonner [ɑ̃pʀizɔne] vt to imprison

emprunt [ɑ̃pʀœ̃] nm loan

emprunté, e [ɑ̃pʀœ̃te] adj (fig) ill-at-ease, awkward

emprunter [ɑ̃pʀœ̃te] vt to borrow; (itinéraire) to take, follow

ému, e [emy] pp de **émouvoir ♦** adj (gratitude) touched; (compassion) moved

---

MOT-CLÉ

en [ɑ̃] prép **1** (endroit, pays) in; (direction) to; **habiter en France/ville** to live in France/town; **aller en France/ville** to go to France/town
2 (moment, temps) in; **en été/juin** in summer/June
3 (moyen) by; **en avion/taxi** by plane/taxi
4 (composition) made of; **c'est en verre** it's (made of) glass; **un collier en argent** a silver necklace
5 (description, état): **une femme (habillée) en rouge** a woman (dressed) in red; **peindre qch en rouge** to paint sth red; **en T/étoile** T/star-shaped; **en chemise/chaussettes** in one's shirt-sleeves/socks; **en soldat** as a soldier; **cassé en plusieurs morceaux** broken into several pieces; **en réparation** being repaired, under repair; **en vacances** on holiday; **en deuil** in mourning; **le même en plus grand** the same but ou only bigger
6 (avec gérondif) while, on, by; **en dormant** while sleeping, as one sleeps; **en sortant** on going out, as he etc went out; **sortir en courant** to run out

♦ pron **1** (indéfini): **j'en ai/veux** I have/want some; **en as-tu?** have you got any?; **je n'en veux pas** I don't want any; **j'en ai 2** I've got 2; **combien y en a-t-il?** how many (of them) are there?; **j'en ai assez** I've got enough (of it ou them); (j'en ai marre) I've had enough
2 (provenance) from there; **j'en viens** I've come from there
3 (cause): **il en est malade/perd le sommeil**

he is ill/can't sleep because of it
4 (complément de nom, d'adjectif, de verbe): **j'en connais les dangers** I know its ou the dangers; **j'en suis fier/ai besoin** I am proud of it/need it

---

ENA [ena] sigle f (= École Nationale d'Administration) one of the Grandes Écoles

encadrement [ɑ̃kadʀəmɑ̃] nm (cadres) managerial staff

encadrer [ɑ̃kadʀe] vt (tableau, image) to frame; (fig: entourer) to surround; (personnel, soldats etc) to train

encaissé, e [ɑ̃kese] adj (vallée) steep-sided; (rivière) with steep banks

encaisser [ɑ̃kese] vt (chèque) to cash; (argent) to collect; (fam: coup, défaite) to take

encart [ɑ̃kaʀ] nm insert

en-cas [ɑ̃ka] nm snack

encastré, e [ɑ̃kastʀe] adj: **four ~** built-in oven

enceinte [ɑ̃sɛ̃t] adj f: **~ (de 6 mois)** (6 months) pregnant **♦** nf (mur) wall; (espace) enclosure; (aussi: **~ acoustique**) (loud)speaker

encens [ɑ̃sɑ̃] nm incense

encercler [ɑ̃sɛʀkle] vt to surround

enchaîner [ɑ̃ʃene] vt to chain up; (mouvements, séquences) to link (together) **♦** vi to carry on

enchanté, e [ɑ̃ʃɑ̃te] adj (ravi) delighted; (magique) enchanted; **~ (de faire votre connaissance)** pleased to meet you

enchantement [ɑ̃ʃɑ̃tmɑ̃] nm delight; (magie) enchantment

enchère [ɑ̃ʃɛʀ] nf bid; **mettre/vendre aux ~s** to put up for (sale by)/sell by auction

enchevêtrer [ɑ̃ʃ(ə)vetʀe]: **s'~** vi to get in a tangle

enclencher [ɑ̃klɑ̃ʃe] vt (mécanisme) to engage; **s'~** vi to engage

enclin, e [ɑ̃klɛ̃, in] adj: **~ à** inclined ou prone to

enclos [ɑ̃klo] nm enclosure

enclume [ɑ̃klym] nf anvil

encoche [ɑ̃kɔʃ] nf notch

encoignure [ɑ̃kɔɲyʀ] nf corner

encolure [ɑ̃kɔlyʀ] nf (cou) neck

encombrant, e [ɑ̃kɔ̃bʀɑ̃, ɑ̃t] adj cumbersome, bulky

encombre [ɑ̃kɔ̃bʀ]: **sans ~** adv without mishap ou incident; **encombrement** nm: **être pris dans un encombrement** to be stuck in a traffic jam

encombrer [ɑ̃kɔ̃bʀe] vt to clutter (up); (gêner) to hamper; **s'~ de** (bagages etc) to load ou burden o.s. with

encontre [ɑ̃kɔ̃tʀ]: **à l'~ de** prép against,

counter to

MOT-CLÉ
---

encore [ãkɔʀ] adv **1** (continuation) still; **il y travaille encore** he's still working on it; **pas encore** not yet
2 (de nouveau) again; **j'irai encore demain** I'll go again tomorrow; **encore une fois** (once) again; **encore deux jours** two more days
3 (intensif) even, still; **encore plus fort/mieux** even louder/better, louder/better still
4 (restriction) even so ou then, only; **encore pourrais-je le faire si ...** even so, I might be able to do it if ...; **si encore** if only
encore que conj although

encouragement [ãkuʀaʒmã] nm encouragement
encourager [ãkuʀaʒe] vt to encourage
encourir [ãkuʀiʀ] vt to incur
encrasser [ãkʀase] vt to make filthy
encre [ãkʀ] nf ink; **encrier** nm inkwell
encroûter [ãkʀute]: **s'~** (fam) vi (fig) to get into a rut, get set in one's ways
encyclopédie [ãsiklɔpedi] nf encyclopaedia
endetter [ãdete]: **s'~** vi to get into debt
endiablé, e [ãdjable] adj (danse) furious
endimanché, e [ãdimãʃe] adj in one's Sunday best
endive [ãdiv] nf chicory no pl
endoctriner [ãdɔktʀine] vt to indoctrinate
endommager [ãdɔmaʒe] vt to damage
endormi, e [ãdɔʀmi] adj asleep
endormir [ãdɔʀmiʀ] vt to put to sleep; (suj: chaleur etc) to send to sleep; (MÉD: dent, nerf) to anaesthetize; (fig: soupçons) to allay; **s'~** vi to fall asleep, go to sleep
endosser [ãdose] vt (responsabilité) to take, shoulder; (chèque) to endorse; (uniforme, tenue) to put on, don
endroit [ãdʀwa] nm place; (opposé à l'envers) right side; **à l'~** (vêtement) the right way out; (objet posé) the right way round
enduire [ãdɥiʀ] vt to coat
enduit [ãdɥi] nm coating
endurance [ãdyʀãs] nf endurance
endurant, e [ãdyʀã, ãt] adj tough, hardy
endurcir [ãdyʀsiʀ]: **s'~** vi (physiquement) to become tougher; (moralement) to become hardened
endurer [ãdyʀe] vt to endure, bear
énergétique [enɛʀʒetik] adj (aliment) energy-giving
énergie [enɛʀʒi] nf (PHYSIQUE) energy; (TECH) power; (morale) vigour, spirit; **énergique** adj energetic, vigorous; (mesures) drastic, stringent
énervant, e [enɛʀvã, ãt] adj irritating, annoying

énerver [enɛʀve] vt to irritate, annoy; **s'~** vi to get excited, get worked up
enfance [ãfãs] nf childhood
enfant [ãfã] nm/f child; **~ de chœur** nm (REL) altar boy; **enfantillage** (péj) nm childish behaviour no pl; **enfantin, e** adj (puéril) childlike; (langage, jeu etc) children's cpd
enfer [ãfɛʀ] nm hell
enfermer [ãfɛʀme] vt to shut up; (à clef, interner) to lock up
enfiévré, e [ãfjevʀe] adj feverish
enfiler [ãfile] vt (vêtement) to slip on, slip into; (perles) to string; (aiguille) to thread
enfin [ãfɛ̃] adv at last; (en énumérant) lastly; (toutefois) still; (pour conclure) in a word; (somme toute) after all
enflammer [ãflame]: **s'~** vi to catch fire; (MÉD) to become inflamed
enflé, e [ãfle] adj swollen
enfler [ãfle] vi to swell (up)
enfoncer [ãfõse] vt (clou) to drive in; (faire pénétrer): **~ qch dans** to push (ou drive) sth into; (forcer: porte) to break open; **s'~** vi to sink; **s'~ dans** to sink into; (forêt, ville) to disappear into
enfouir [ãfwiʀ] vt (dans le sol) to bury; (dans un tiroir etc) to tuck away
enfourcher [ãfuʀʃe] vt to mount
enfreindre [ãfʀɛ̃dʀ] vt to infringe, break
enfuir [ãfɥiʀ]: **s'~** vi to run away ou off
enfumer [ãfyme] vt (pièce) to fill with smoke
engageant, e [ãgaʒã, ãt] adj attractive, appealing
engagement [ãgaʒmã] nm commitment
engager [ãgaʒe] vt (embaucher) to take on; (: artiste) to engage; (commencer) to start; (lier) to bind, commit; (impliquer) to involve; (investir) to invest, lay out; (inciter) to urge; (introduire: clé) to insert; **s'~** vi (promettre) to commit o.s.; (MIL) to enlist; (débuter: conversation etc) to start (up); **s'~ à faire** to undertake to do; **s'~ dans** (rue, passage) to turn into; (fig: affaire, discussion) to enter into, embark on
engelures [ãʒlyʀ] nfpl chilblains
engendrer [ãʒãdʀe] vt to breed, create
engin [ãʒɛ̃] nm machine; (outil) instrument; (AUT) vehicle; (AVIAT) aircraft inv
englober [ãglɔbe] vt to include
engloutir [ãglutiʀ] vt to swallow up
engoncé, e [ãgõse] adj: **~ dans** cramped in
engorger [ãgɔʀʒe] vt to obstruct, block
engouement [ãgumã] nm (sudden) passion
engouffrer [ãgufʀe] vt to swallow up, devour; **s'~ dans** to rush into
engourdir [ãguʀdiʀ] vt to numb; (fig) to dull, blunt; **s'~** vi to go numb
engrais [ãgʀɛ] nm manure; **~ (chimique)**

(chemical) fertilizer

engraisser [ɑ̃ɡʀese] vt to fatten (up)

engrenage [ɑ̃ɡʀənaʒ] nm gears pl, gearing; (fig) chain

engueuler [ɑ̃ɡœle] (fam) vt to bawl at

enhardir [ɑ̃ardiʀ]: **s'~** vi to grow bolder

énigme [enigm] nf riddle

enivrer [ɑ̃nivʀe] vt: **s'~** to get drunk

enjambée [ɑ̃ʒɑ̃be] nf stride

enjamber [ɑ̃ʒɑ̃be] vt to stride over

enjeu, x [ɑ̃ʒø] nm stakes pl

enjôler [ɑ̃ʒole] vt to coax, wheedle

enjoliver [ɑ̃ʒɔlive] vt to embellish; **enjoliveur** nm (AUTO) hub cap

enjoué, e [ɑ̃ʒwe] adj playful

enlacer [ɑ̃lase] vt (étreindre) to embrace, hug

enlaidir [ɑ̃lediʀ] vt to make ugly ♦ vi to become ugly

enlèvement [ɑ̃levmɑ̃] nm (rapt) abduction, kidnapping

enlever [ɑ̃l(ə)ve] vt (ôter: gén) to remove; (: vêtement, lunettes) to take off; (emporter: ordures etc) to take away; (kidnapper) to abduct, kidnap; (obtenir: prix, contrat) to win; (prendre): **~ qch à qn** to take sth (away) from sb

enliser [ɑ̃lize]: **s'~** vi to sink, get stuck

enneigé, e [ɑ̃neʒe] adj (route, maison) snowed-up; (paysage) snowy

ennemi, e [enmi] adj hostile; (MIL) enemy cpd ♦ nm/f enemy

ennui [ɑ̃nɥi] nm (lassitude) boredom; (difficulté) trouble no pl; **avoir des ~s** to have problems; **ennuyer** vt to bother; (lasser) to bore; **s'ennuyer** vi to be bored; **ennuyeux, -euse** adj boring, tedious; (embêtant) annoying

énoncé [enɔ̃se] nm (de problème) terms pl

énoncer [enɔ̃se] vt (faits) to set out, state

enorgueillir [ɑ̃nɔʀɡœjiʀ]: **s'~ de** vt to pride o.s. on

énorme [enɔʀm] adj enormous, huge; **énormément** adv enormously; **énormément de neige/gens** an enormous amount of snow/number of people; **énormité** nf (propos) outrageous remark

enquérir [ɑ̃keʀiʀ]: **s'~ de** vt to inquire about

enquête [ɑ̃kɛt] nf (de journaliste, de police) investigation; (judiciaire, administrative) inquiry; (sondage d'opinion) survey; **enquêter** vi to investigate

enquiers etc [ɑ̃kje] vb voir **enquérir**

enquiquiner [ɑ̃kikine] (fam) vt to annoy, irritate, bother

enraciné, e [ɑ̃ʀasine] adj deep-rooted

enragé, e [ɑ̃ʀaʒe] adj (MÉD) rabid, with rabies; (fig) fanatical

enrageant, e [ɑ̃ʀaʒɑ̃, ɑ̃t] adj infuriating

enrager [ɑ̃ʀaʒe] vi to be in a rage

enrayer [ɑ̃ʀeje] vt to check, stop

enregistrement [ɑ̃ʀ(ə)ʒistʀəmɑ̃] nm recording; **~ des bagages** (à l'aéroport) baggage check-in

enregistrer [ɑ̃ʀ(ə)ʒistʀe] vt (MUS etc) to record; (fig: mémoriser) to make a mental note of; (bagages: à l'aéroport) to check in

enrhumer [ɑ̃ʀyme] vt: **s'~, être enrhumé** to catch a cold

enrichir [ɑ̃ʀiʃiʀ] vt to make rich(er); (fig) to enrich; **s'~** vi to get rich(er)

enrober [ɑ̃ʀɔbe] vt: **~ qch de** to coat sth with

enrôler [ɑ̃ʀole] vt to enlist; **s'~ (dans)** to enlist (in)

enrouer [ɑ̃ʀwe]: **s'~** vi to go hoarse

enrouler [ɑ̃ʀule] vt (fil, corde) to wind (up)

ensanglanté, e [ɑ̃sɑ̃ɡlɑ̃te] adj covered with blood

enseignant, e [ɑ̃sɛɲɑ̃, ɑ̃t] nm/f teacher

enseigne [ɑ̃sɛɲ] nf sign; **~ lumineuse** neon sign

enseignement [ɑ̃sɛɲ(ə)mɑ̃] nm teaching; (ADMIN) education

enseigner [ɑ̃sɛɲe] vt, vi to teach; **~ qch à qn** to teach sb sth

ensemble [ɑ̃sɑ̃bl] adv together ♦ nm (groupement) set; (vêtements) outfit; (totalité): **l'~ du/de la** the whole ou entire; (unité, harmonie) unity; **impression/idée d'~** overall ou general impression/idea; **dans l'~** (en gros) on the whole

ensemencer [ɑ̃s(ə)mɑ̃se] vt to sow

ensevelir [ɑ̃səv(ə)liʀ] vt to bury

ensoleillé, e [ɑ̃sɔleje] adj sunny

ensommeillé, e [ɑ̃sɔmeje] adj drowsy

ensorceler [ɑ̃sɔʀsəle] vt to enchant, bewitch

ensuite [ɑ̃sɥit] adv then, next; (plus tard) afterwards, later

ensuivre [ɑ̃sɥivʀ]: **s'~** vi to follow, ensue; **et tout ce qui s'ensuit** and all that goes with it

entaille [ɑ̃taj] nf cut; (sur un objet) notch

entamer [ɑ̃tame] vt (pain, bouteille) to start; (hostilités, pourparlers) to open

entasser [ɑ̃tase] vt (empiler) to pile up, heap up; **s'~** vi (s'amonceler) to pile up; **s'~ dans** (personnes) to cram into

entendre [ɑ̃tɑ̃dʀ] vt to hear; (comprendre) to understand; (vouloir dire) to mean; **s'~** vi (sympathiser) to get on; (se mettre d'accord) to agree; **j'ai entendu dire que** I've heard (it said) that

entendu, e [ɑ̃tɑ̃dy] adj (réglé) agreed; (au courant: air) knowing; (**c'est**) **~** all right, agreed; **bien ~** of course

entente [ɑ̃tɑ̃t] nf understanding; (accord, traité) agreement; **à double ~** (sens) with a double meaning

entériner [ɑ̃teʀine] vt to ratify, confirm

enterrement [ɑ̃tɛʀmɑ̃] nm (cérémonie)

funeral, burial

enterrer [ɑ̃teʀe] vt to bury

entêtant, e [ɑ̃tetɑ̃, ɑ̃t] adj heady

entêté, e [ɑ̃tete] adj stubborn

en-tête [ɑ̃tɛt] nm heading; **papier à ~-~** headed notepaper

entêter [ɑ̃tete]: **s'~** vi: **s'~ (à faire)** to persist (in doing)

enthousiasme [ɑ̃tuzjasm] nm enthusiasm; **enthousiasmer** vt to fill with enthusiasm; **s'enthousiasmer (pour qch)** to get enthusiastic (about sth); **enthousiaste** adj enthusiastic

enticher [ɑ̃tiʃe]: **s'~ de** vt to become infatuated with

entier, -ère [ɑ̃tje, jɛʀ] adj whole; (total: satisfaction etc) complete; (fig: caractère) unbending ♦ nm (MATH) whole; **en ~** totally; **lait ~** full-cream milk; **entièrement** adv entirely, wholly

entonner [ɑ̃tɔne] vt (chanson) to strike up

entonnoir [ɑ̃tɔnwaʀ] nm funnel

entorse [ɑ̃tɔʀs] nf (MÉD) sprain; (fig): **~ au règlement** infringement of the rule

entortiller [ɑ̃tɔʀtije] vt (enrouler) to twist, wind; (fam: cajoler) to get round

entourage [ɑ̃tuʀaʒ] nm circle; (famille) circle of family/friends; (ce qui enclôt) surround

entourer [ɑ̃tuʀe] vt to surround; (apporter son soutien à) to rally round; **~ de** to surround with

entracte [ɑ̃tʀakt] nm interval

entraide [ɑ̃tʀɛd] nf mutual aid; **s'~r** vi to help each other

entrain [ɑ̃tʀɛ̃] nm spirit; **avec/sans ~** spiritedly/half-heartedly

entraînement [ɑ̃tʀɛnmɑ̃] nm training

entraîner [ɑ̃tʀene] vt (charrier) to carry ou drag along; (TECH) to drive; (emmener: personne) to take (off); (influencer) to lead; (SPORT) to train; (impliquer) to entail; **s'~** vi (SPORT) to train; **s'~ à qch/à faire** to train o.s. for sth/to do; **~ qn à faire** (inciter) to lead sb to do; **entraîneur, -euse** nm/f (SPORT) coach, trainer ♦ nm (HIPPISME) trainer

entraver [ɑ̃tʀave] vt (action, progrès) to hinder

entre [ɑ̃tʀ] prép between; (parmi) among(st); **l'un d'~ eux/nous** one of them/us; **~ eux** among(st) themselves; **entrebâillé, e** adj half-open, ajar; **entrechoquer: s'entrechoquer** vi to knock ou bang together; **entrecôte** nf entrecôte ou rib steak; **entrecouper** vt: **entrecouper qch de** to intersperse sth with; **entrecroiser: s'entrecroiser** vi to intertwine

entrée [ɑ̃tʀe] nf entrance; (accès: au cinéma etc) admission; (billet) (admission) ticket; (CULIN) first course

entre...: entrefaites: sur ces entrefaites adv at this juncture; **entrefilet** nm paragraph (short article); **entrejambes** nm crotch; **entrelacer** vt to intertwine; **entremêler: s'entremêler** vi to become entangled; **entremets** nm (cream) dessert; **entremise** nf intervention; **par l'entremise de** through

entreposer [ɑ̃tʀəpoze] vt to store, put into storage

entrepôt [ɑ̃tʀəpo] nm warehouse

entreprenant, e [ɑ̃tʀəpʀənɑ̃, ɑ̃t] adj (actif) enterprising; (trop galant) forward

entreprendre [ɑ̃tʀəpʀɑ̃dʀ] vt (se lancer dans) to undertake; (commencer) to begin ou start (upon)

entrepreneur [ɑ̃tʀəpʀənœʀ, øz] nm: **~ (en bâtiment)** (building) contractor

entreprise [ɑ̃tʀəpʀiz] nf (société) firm, concern; (action) undertaking, venture

entrer [ɑ̃tʀe] vi to go (ou come) in, enter ♦ vt (INFORM) to enter, input; **(faire) ~ qch dans** to get sth into; **~ dans** (gén) to enter; (pièce) to go (ou come) into, enter; (club) to join; (heurter) to run into; **~ à l'hôpital** to go into hospital; **faire ~** (visiteur) to show in

entresol [ɑ̃tʀəsɔl] nm mezzanine

entre-temps [ɑ̃tʀətɑ̃] adv meanwhile

entretenir [ɑ̃tʀət(ə)niʀ] vt to maintain; (famille, maîtresse) to support, keep; **~ qn (de)** to speak to sb (about)

entretien [ɑ̃tʀətjɛ̃] nm maintenance; (discussion) discussion, talk; (pour un emploi) interview

entrevoir [ɑ̃tʀəvwaʀ] vt (à peine) to make out; (brièvement) to catch a glimpse of

entrevue [ɑ̃tʀəvy] nf (audience) interview

entrouvert, e [ɑ̃tʀuvɛʀ, ɛʀt] adj half-open

énumérer [enymeʀe] vt to list, enumerate

envahir [ɑ̃vaiʀ] vt to invade; (suj: inquiétude, peur) to come over; **envahissant, e** (péj) adj (personne) interfering, intrusive

enveloppe [ɑ̃v(ə)lɔp] nf (de lettre) envelope; (crédits) budget; **envelopper** vt to wrap; (fig) to envelop, shroud

envenimer [ɑ̃v(ə)nime] vt to aggravate

envergure [ɑ̃vɛʀgyʀ] nf (fig) scope; (personne) calibre

enverrai etc [ɑ̃veʀe] vb voir **envoyer**

envers [ɑ̃vɛʀ] prép towards, to ♦ nm other side; (d'une étoffe) wrong side; **à l'~** (verticalement) upside down; (pull) back to front; (chaussettes) inside out

envie [ɑ̃vi] nf (sentiment) envy; (souhait) desire, wish; **avoir ~ de (faire)** to feel like (doing); (plus fort) to want (to do); **avoir ~ que** to wish that; **cette glace me fait ~** I fancy some of that ice cream; **envier** vt to envy; **envieux, -euse** adj envious

environ [ɑ̃viʀɔ̃] adv: **~ 3 h/2 km** (around)

about 3 o'clock/2 km; *voir aussi* **environs**

environnant, e [ãvirɔnã, ãt] *adj*
surrounding

environnement [ãvirɔnmã] *nm*
environment

environs [ãvirɔ̃] *nmpl* surroundings; **aux
~ de** (round) about

envisager [ãvizaʒe] *vt* to contemplate,
envisage; **~ de faire** to consider doing

envoi [ãvwa] *nm* (*paquet*) parcel,
consignment; **coup d'~** (*SPORT*) kick-off

envoler [ãvɔle]: **s'~** *vi* (*oiseau*) to fly away *ou*
off; (*avion*) to take off; (*papier, feuille*) to
blow away; (*fig*) to vanish (into thin air)

envoûter [ãvute] *vt* to bewitch

envoyé, e [ãvwaje] *nm/f* (*POL*) envoy;
(*PRESSE*) correspondent

envoyer [ãvwaje] *vt* to send; (*lancer*) to hurl,
throw; (*expédier*) to send for; **~ promener qn**
(*fam*) to send sb packing

épagneul, e [epaɲœl] *nm/f* spaniel

épais, se [epɛ, ɛs] *adj* thick; **épaisseur** *nf*
thickness

épancher [epɑ̃ʃe]: **s'~** *vi* to open one's heart

épanouir [epanwir]: **s'~** *vi* (*fleur*) to bloom,
open out; (*visage*) to light up; (*personne*) to
blossom

épargne [eparɲ] *nf* saving

épargner [eparɲe] *vt* to save; (*ne pas tuer ou
endommager*) to spare ♦ *vi* to save; **~ qch à
qn** to spare sb sth

éparpiller [eparpije] *vt* to scatter; **s'~** *vi* to
scatter; (*fig*) to dissipate one's efforts

épars, e [epar, ars] *adj* scattered

épatant, e [epatã, ãt] (*fam*) *adj* super

épater [epate] (*fam*) *vt* (*étonner*) to amaze;
(*impressionner*) to impress

épaule [epol] *nf* shoulder

épauler [epole] *vt* (*aider*) to back up,
support; (*arme*) to raise (to one's shoulder)
♦ *vi* to (take) aim

épaulette [epolɛt] *nf* (*MIL*) epaulette;
(*rembourrage*) shoulder pad

épave [epav] *nf* wreck

épée [epe] *nf* sword

épeler [ep(ə)le] *vt* to spell

éperdu, e [epɛrdy] *adj* distraught,
overcome; (*amour*) passionate

éperon [eprɔ̃] *nm* spur

épervier [epɛrvje] *nm* sparrowhawk

épi [epi] *nm* (*de blé, d'orge*) ear; (*de maïs*) cob

épice [epis] *nf* spice

épicé, e [epise] *adj* spicy

épicer [epise] *vt* to spice

épicerie [episri] *nf* grocer's shop; (*denrées*)
groceries *pl*; **~ fine** delicatessen; **épicier,
-ière** *nm/f* grocer

épidémie [epidemi] *nf* epidemic

épiderme [epidɛrm] *nm* skin

épier [epje] *vt* to spy on, watch closely

épilepsie [epilɛpsi] *nf* epilepsy

épiler [epile] *vt* (*jambes*) to remove the hair
from; (*sourcils*) to pluck

épilogue [epilɔg] *nm* (*fig*) conclusion,
dénouement; **épiloguer** *vi*: **épiloguer sur** to
hold forth on

épinards [epinar] *nmpl* spinach *sg*

épine [epin] *nf* thorn, prickle; (*d'oursin etc*)
spine; **~ dorsale** backbone; **épineux, -euse**
adj thorny

épingle [epɛ̃gl] *nf* pin; **~ à cheveux** hairpin;
~ de nourrice *ou* **de sûreté** safety pin;
épingler *vt* (*badge, décoration*): **épingler qch
sur** to pin sth on(to); (*fam*) to catch, nick

épique [epik] *adj* epic

épisode [epizɔd] *nm* episode; **film/roman à
~s** serial; **épisodique** *adj* occasional

éploré, e [eplɔre] *adj* tearful

épluche-légumes [eplyʃlegym] *nm inv*
(potato) peeler

éplucher [eplyʃe] *vt* (*fruit, légumes*) to peel;
(*fig*) to go over with a fine-tooth comb;
épluchures *nfpl* peelings

éponge [epɔ̃ʒ] *nf* sponge; **éponger** *vt*
(*liquide*) to mop up; (*surface*) to sponge;
(*fig: déficit*) to soak up

épopée [epɔpe] *nf* epic

époque [epɔk] *nf* (*de l'histoire*) age, era; (*de
l'année, la vie*) time; **d'~** (*meuble*) period *cpd*

époumoner [epumɔne]: **s'~** *vi* to shout o.s.
hoarse

épouse [epuz] *nf* wife; **épouser** *vt* to marry

épousseter [epuste] *vt* to dust

époustouflant, e [epustuflã, ãt] (*fam*) *adj*
staggering, mind-boggling

épouvantable [epuvãtabl] *adj* appalling,
dreadful

épouvantail [epuvãtaj] *nm* scarecrow

épouvante [epuvãt] *nf* terror; **film d'~** horror
film; **épouvanter** *vt* to terrify

époux [epu] *nm* husband ♦ *nmpl* (married)
couple

éprendre [eprɑ̃dr]: **s'~ de** *vt* to fall in love
with

épreuve [eprœv] *nf* (*d'examen*) test;
(*malheur, difficulté*) trial, ordeal; (*PHOTO*)
print; (*TYPO*) proof; (*SPORT*) event; **à toute ~**
unfailing; **mettre à l'~** to put to the test

épris, e [epri, iz] *pp de* **éprendre**

éprouvant, e [epruvã, ãt] *adj* trying,
testing

éprouver [epruve] *vt* (*tester*) to test;
(*marquer, faire souffrir*) to afflict, distress;
(*ressentir*) to experience

éprouvette [epruvɛt] *nf* test tube

épuisé, e [epɥize] *adj* exhausted; (*livre*) out
of print; **épuisement** *nm* exhaustion

épuiser [epɥize] *vt* (*fatiguer*) to exhaust,

wear *ou* tire out; **s'~** *vi* to wear *ou* tire o.s. out, exhaust o.s.

épuisette [epɥizɛt] *nf* shrimping net

épurer [epyre] *vt* (*liquide*) to purify; (*parti etc*) to purge

équateur [ekwatœʀ] *nm* equator; (**la république de**) **l'É~** Ecuador

équation [ekwasjɔ̃] *nf* equation

équerre [ekɛʀ] *nf* (*à dessin*) (set) square

équilibre [ekilibʀ] *nm* balance; **garder/perdre l'~** to keep/lose one's balance; **être en ~** to be balanced; **équilibré, e** *adj* well-balanced; **équilibrer** *vt* to balance; **s'équilibrer** *vi* (*poids*) to balance; (*fig: défauts etc*) to balance each other out

équipage [ekipaʒ] *nm* crew

équipe [ekip] *nf* team

équipé, e [ekipe] *adj*: **bien/mal ~** well-/poorly-equipped; **équipée** *nf* escapade

équipement [ekipmɑ̃] *nm* equipment; **~s** *nmpl* (*installations*) amenities, facilities

équiper [ekipe] *vt* to equip; **~ qn/qch de** to equip sb/sth with

équipier, -ière [ekipje, jɛʀ] *nm/f* team member

équitable [ekitabl] *adj* fair

équitation [ekitasjɔ̃] *nf* (horse-)riding; **faire de l'~** to go riding

équivalent, e [ekivalɑ̃, ɑ̃t] *adj, nm* equivalent

équivaloir [ekivalwaʀ]: **~ à** *vt* to be equivalent to

équivoque [ekivɔk] *adj* equivocal, ambiguous; (*louche*) dubious ♦ *nf* (*incertitude*) doubt

érable [eʀabl] *nm* maple

érafler [eʀafle] *vt* to scratch; **éraflure** *nf* scratch

éraillé, e [eʀaje] *adj* (*voix*) rasping

ère [ɛʀ] *nf* era; **en l'an 1050 de notre ~** in the year 1050 A.D.

érection [eʀɛksjɔ̃] *nf* erection

éreinter [eʀɛ̃te] *vt* to exhaust, wear out; (*critiquer*) to pull to pieces

ériger [eʀiʒe] *vt* (*monument*) to erect

ermite [ɛʀmit] *nm* hermit

éroder [eʀɔde] *vt* to erode

érotique [eʀɔtik] *adj* erotic

errer [eʀe] *vi* to wander

erreur [eʀœʀ] *nf* mistake, error; **faire ~** to be mistaken; **par ~** by mistake; **~ judiciaire** miscarriage of justice

érudit, e [eʀydi, it] *adj* erudite, learned

éruption [eʀypsjɔ̃] *nf* eruption; (*MÉD*) rash

es [ɛ] *vb voir* **être**

ès [ɛs] *prép*: **licencié ~ lettres/sciences** ≈ Bachelor of Arts/Science

escabeau, x [ɛskabo] *nm* (*tabouret*) stool; (*échelle*) stepladder

escadron [ɛskadʀɔ̃] *nm* squadron

escalade [ɛskalad] *nf* climbing *no pl*; (*POL etc*) escalation; **escalader** *vt* to climb

escale [ɛskal] *nf* (*NAVIG: durée*) call; (*endroit*) port of call; (*AVIAT*) stop(over); **faire ~ à** (*NAVIG*) to put in at; (*AVIAT*) to stop over at; **vol sans ~** nonstop flight

escalier [ɛskalje] *nm* stairs *pl*; **dans l'~** on the stairs; **~ roulant** escalator

escamoter [ɛskamɔte] *vt* (*esquiver*) to get round, evade; (*faire disparaître*) to conjure away

escapade [ɛskapad] *nf*: **faire une ~** to go on a jaunt; (*s'enfuir*) to run away *ou* off

escargot [ɛskaʀgo] *nm* snail

escarpé, e [ɛskaʀpe] *adj* steep

escarpin [ɛskaʀpɛ̃] *nm* low-fronted shoe, court shoe (*BRIT*)

escient [esjɑ̃] *nm*: **à bon ~** advisedly

esclaffer [ɛsklafe]: **s'~** *vi* to guffaw

esclandre [ɛsklɑ̃dʀ] *nm* scene, fracas

esclavage [ɛsklavaʒ] *nm* slavery

esclave [ɛsklav] *nm/f* slave

escompte [ɛskɔ̃t] *nm* discount; **escompter** *vt* (*fig*) to expect

escorte [ɛskɔʀt] *nf* escort; **escorter** *vt* to escort

escrime [ɛskʀim] *nf* fencing

escrimer [ɛskʀime]: **s'~** *vi*: **s'~ à faire** to wear o.s. out doing

escroc [ɛskʀo] *nm* swindler, conman; **escroquer** [ɛskʀɔke] *vt*: **escroquer qch (à qn)** to swindle sth (out of sb); **escroquerie** *nf* swindle

espace [ɛspas] *nm* space

espacer *vt* to space out; **s'~** *vi* (*visites etc*) to become less frequent

espadon [ɛspadɔ̃] *nm* swordfish *inv*

espadrille [ɛspadʀij] *nf* rope-soled sandal

Espagne [ɛspaɲ] *nf*: **l'~** Spain; **espagnol, e** *adj* Spanish ♦ *nm/f*: **Espagnol, e** Spaniard ♦ *nm* (*LING*) Spanish

escouade [ɛskwad] *nf* squad

espèce [ɛspɛs] *nf* (*BIO, BOT, ZOOL*) species *inv*; (*gén: sorte*) sort, kind, type; (*péj*): **~ de maladroit!** you clumsy oaf!; **~s** *nfpl* (*COMM*) cash *sg*; **en ~** in cash

espérance [ɛspeʀɑ̃s] *nf* hope; **~ de vie** life expectancy

espérer [ɛspeʀe] *vt* to hope for; **j'espère (bien)** I hope so; **~ que/faire** to hope that/to do

espiègle [ɛspjɛgl] *adj* mischievous

espion, ne [ɛspjɔ̃, jɔn] *nm/f* spy; **espionnage** *nm* espionage, spying; **espionner** *vt* to spy (up)on

esplanade [ɛsplanad] *nf* esplanade

espoir [ɛspwaʀ] *nm* hope

esprit [ɛspʀi] *nm* (*intellect*) mind; (*humour*)

wit; (*mentalité, d'une loi etc, fantôme etc*) spirit; **faire de l'~** to try to be witty; **reprendre ses ~s** to come to; **perdre l'~** to lose one's mind

esquimau, de, x [ɛskimo, od] *adj* Eskimo ♦ *nm/f:* **E~, de** Eskimo ♦ *nm:* **E~** ® ice lolly (*BRIT*), popsicle (*US*)

esquinter [ɛskɛ̃te] (*fam*) *vt* to mess up

esquisse [ɛskis] *nf* sketch; **esquisser** *vt* to sketch; **esquisser un sourire** to give a vague smile

esquiver [ɛskive] *vt* to dodge; **s'~** *vi* to slip away

essai [ese] *nm* (*tentative*) attempt, try; (*de produit*) testing; (*RUGBY*) try; (*LITTÉRATURE*) essay; **~s** *nmpl* (*AUTO*) trials; **~ gratuit** (*COMM*) free trial; **à l'~** on a trial basis

essaim [esɛ̃] *nm* swarm

essayer [eseje] *vt* to try; (*vêtement, chaussures*) to try (on); (*méthode, voiture*) to try (out) ♦ *vi* to try; **~ de faire** to try *ou* attempt to do

essence [esɑ̃s] *nf* (*de voiture*) petrol (*BRIT*), gas(oline) (*US*); (*extrait de plante*) essence; (*espèce: d'arbre*) species *inv*

essentiel, le [esɑ̃sjɛl] *adj* essential; **c'est l'~** (*ce qui importe*) that's the main thing; **l'~ de** the main part of

essieu, x [esjø] *nm* axle

essor [esɔʀ] *nm* (*de l'économie etc*) rapid expansion

essorer [esɔʀe] *vt* (*en tordant*) to wring (out); (*par la force centrifuge*) to spin-dry; **essoreuse** *nf* spin-dryer

essouffler [esufle]: **s'~** *vi* to get out of breath

essuie-glace [esɥiglas] *nm inv* windscreen (*BRIT*) *ou* windshield (*US*) wiper

essuyer [esɥije] *vt* to wipe; (*fig: échec*) to suffer; **s'~** *vi* (*après le bain*) to dry o.s.; **~ la vaisselle** to dry up

est¹ [ɛ] *vb voir* **être**

est² [ɛst] *nm* east ♦ *adj inv* east; (*région*) east(ern); **à l'~** in the east; (*direction*) to the east, east(wards); **à l'~ de** (to the) east of

estampe [ɛstɑ̃p] *nf* print, engraving

est-ce que [ɛska] *adv:* **~ c'est cher/c'était bon?** is it expensive/was it good?; **quand est-ce qu'il part?** when does he leave?, when is he leaving?; *voir aussi* **que**

esthéticienne [ɛstetisjɛn] *nf* beautician

esthétique [ɛstetik] *adj* attractive

estimation [ɛstimasjɔ̃] *nf* valuation; (*chiffre*) estimate

estime [ɛstim] *nf* esteem, regard; **estimer** *vt* (*respecter*) to esteem; (*expertiser: bijou etc*) to value; (*évaluer: coût etc*) to assess, estimate; (*penser*): **estimer que/être** to consider that/o.s. to be

estival, e, -aux [ɛstival, o] *adj* summer *cpd*

estivant, e [ɛstivɑ̃, ɑ̃t] *nm/f* (summer) holiday-maker

estomac [ɛstɔma] *nm* stomach

estomaqué, e [ɛstɔmake] (*fam*) *adj* flabbergasted

estomper [ɛstɔ̃pe]: **s'~** *vi* (*sentiments*) to soften; (*contour*) to become blurred

estrade [ɛstʀad] *nf* platform, rostrum

estragon [ɛstʀagɔ̃] *nm* tarragon

estuaire [ɛstɥɛʀ] *nm* estuary

et [e] *conj* and; **~ lui?** what about him?; **~ alors!** so what!

étable [etabl] *nf* cowshed

établi [etabli] *nm* (work)bench

établir [etabliʀ] *vt* (*papiers d'identité, facture*) to make out; (*liste, programme*) to draw up; (*entreprise*) to set up; (*réputation, usage, fait, culpabilité*) to establish; **s'~** *vi* to be established; **s'~ (à son compte)** to set up in business; **s'~ à/près de** to settle in/near

établissement [etablismɑ̃] *nm* (*entreprise, institution*) establishment; **~ scolaire** school, educational establishment

étage [etaʒ] *nm* (*d'immeuble*) storey, floor; **à l'~** upstairs; **au 2ème ~** on the 2nd (*BRIT*) *ou* 3rd (*US*) floor

étagère [etaʒɛʀ] *nf* (*rayon*) shelf; (*meuble*) shelves *pl*

étai [ete] *nm* stay, prop

étain [etɛ̃] *nm* pewter *no pl*

étais *etc* [etɛ] *vb voir* **être**

étal [etal] *nm* stall

étalage [etalaʒ] *nm* display; (*devanture*) display window; **faire ~ de** to show off, parade

étaler [etale] *vt* (*carte, nappe*) to spread (out); (*peinture*) to spread; (*échelonner: paiements, vacances*) to spread, stagger; (*marchandises*) to display; (*connaissances*) to parade; **s'~** *vi* (*liquide*) to spread out; (*fam*) to fall flat on one's face; **s'~ sur** (*suj: paiements etc*) to be spread out over

étalon [etalɔ̃] *nm* (*cheval*) stallion

étanche [etɑ̃ʃ] *adj* (*récipient*) watertight; (*montre, vêtement*) waterproof; **étancher** *vt:* **étancher sa soif** to quench one's thirst

étang [etɑ̃] *nm* pond

étant [etɑ̃] *vb voir* **être; donné**

étape [etap] *nf* stage; (*lieu d'arrivée*) stopping place; (: *CYCLISME*) staging point

état [eta] *nm* (*POL, condition*) state; **en mauvais ~** in poor condition; **en ~ (de marche)** in (working) order; **remettre en ~** to repair; **hors d'~** out of order; **être en ~/hors d'~ de faire** to be in a/in no fit state to do; **être dans tous ses ~s** to be in a state; **faire ~ de** (*alléguer*) to put forward; **l'É~** the State; **~ civil** civil status; **~ des lieux** inventory of fixtures; **étatiser** *vt*

to bring under state control; **état-major** nm
(MIL) staff; **États-Unis** nmpl: **les États-Unis**
the United States

étau, x [eto] nm vice (BRIT), vise (US)

étayer [eteje] vt to prop ou shore up

etc. [etsetera] adv etc

et c(a)etera [etsetera] adv et cetera, and so
on

été [ete] pp de être ♦ nm summer

éteindre [etɛ̃dʀ] vt (lampe, lumière, radio) to
turn ou switch off; (cigarette, feu) to put out,
extinguish; **s'~** vi (feu, lumière) to go out;
(mourir) to pass away; **éteint, e** adj (fig)
lacklustre, dull; (volcan) extinct

étendard [etɑ̃daʀ] nm standard

étendre [etɑ̃dʀ] vt (pâte, liquide) to spread;
(carte etc) to spread out; (linge) to hang up;
(bras, jambes) to stretch out; (fig: agrandir)
to extend; **s'~** vi (augmenter, se propager) to
spread; (terrain, forêt etc) to stretch;
(s'allonger) to stretch out; (se coucher) to lie
down; (fig: expliquer) to elaborate

étendu, e [etɑ̃dy] adj extensive; **étendue** nf
(d'eau, de sable) stretch, expanse;
(importance) extent

éternel, le [etɛʀnɛl] adj eternal

éterniser [etɛʀnize]: **s'~** vi to last for ages;
(visiteur) to stay for ages

éternité [etɛʀnite] nf eternity; **ça a duré une
~** it lasted for ages

éternuement [etɛʀnymɑ̃] nm sneeze

éternuer [etɛʀnɥe] vi to sneeze

êtes [ɛt(z)] vb voir être

éthique [etik] adj ethical

ethnie [ɛtni] nf ethnic group

éthylisme [etilism] nm alcoholism

étiez [etje] vb voir être

étinceler [etɛ̃s(ə)le] vi to sparkle

étincelle [etɛ̃sɛl] nf spark

étiqueter [etik(ə)te] vt to label

étiquette [etiket] nf label; (protocole): **l'~**
etiquette

étirer [etiʀe]: **s'~** vi (personne) to stretch;
(convoi, route): **s'~ sur** to stretch out over

étoffe [etɔf] nf material, fabric

étoffer [etɔfe] vt to fill out; **s'~** vi to fill out

étoile [etwal] nf star; **à la belle ~** in the open;
~ de mer starfish; **~ filante** shooting star;
étoilé, e adj starry

étonnant, e [etɔnɑ̃, ɑ̃t] adj amazing

étonnement [etɔnmɑ̃] nm surprise,
amazement

étonner [etɔne] vt to surprise, amaze;
s'~ que/de to be amazed that/at; **cela m'~ait
(que)** (j'en doute) I'd be very surprised (if)

étouffant, e [etufɑ̃, ɑ̃t] adj stifling

étouffée [etufe]: **à l'~** adv (CULIN: légumes)
steamed; (: viande) braised

étouffer [etufe] vt to suffocate; (bruit) to

muffle; (scandale) to hush up ♦ vi to
suffocate; **s'~** vi (en mangeant etc) to choke;
on étouffe it's stifling

étourderie [etuʀdəʀi] nf (caractère) absent-
mindedness no pl; (faute) thoughtless
blunder

étourdi, e [etuʀdi] adj (distrait)
scatterbrained, heedless

étourdir [etuʀdiʀ] vt (assommer) to stun,
daze; (griser) to make dizzy ou giddy;
étourdissement nm dizzy spell

étourneau, x [etuʀno] nm starling

étrange [etʀɑ̃ʒ] adj strange

étranger, -ère [etʀɑ̃ʒe, ɛʀ] adj foreign; (pas
de la famille, non familier) strange ♦ nm/f
foreigner; stranger ♦ nm: **à l'~** abroad

étrangler [etʀɑ̃gle] vt to strangle; **s'~** vi (en
mangeant etc) to choke

MOT-CLÉ

être [ɛtʀ] nm being; **être humain** human being
♦ vb +attrib 1 (état, description) to be; **il est
instituteur** he is ou he's a teacher; **vous êtes
grand/intelligent/fatigué** you are ou you're
tall/clever/tired

2 (+à: appartenir) to be; **le livre est à Paul**
the book is Paul's ou belongs to Paul; **c'est à
moi/eux** it is ou it's mine/theirs

3 (+de: provenance): **il est de Paris** he is from
Paris; (: appartenance): **il est des nôtres** he is
one of us

4 (date): **nous sommes le 10 janvier** it's the
10th of January (today)

♦ vi to be; **je ne serai pas ici demain** I won't
be here tomorrow

♦ vb aux 1 to have; to be; **être arrivé/allé** to
have arrived/gone; **il est parti** he has left, he
has gone

2 (forme passive) to be; **être fait par** to be
made by; **il a été promu** he has been
promoted

3 (+à: obligation): **c'est à réparer** it needs
repairing; **c'est à essayer** it should be tried

♦ vb impers 1: **il est +adjectif** it is +adjective; **il
est impossible de le faire** it's impossible to do
it

2 (heure, date): **il est 10 heures, c'est 10
heures** it is ou it's 10 o'clock

3 (emphatique): **c'est moi** it's me; **c'est à lui
de le faire** it's up to him to do it

étreindre [etʀɛ̃dʀ] vt to clutch, grip;
(amoureusement, amicalement) to embrace;
s'~ vi to embrace

étrenner [etʀene] vt to use (ou wear) for the
first time; **étrennes** nfpl Christmas box sg

étrier [etʀije] nm stirrup

étriqué, e [etʀike] adj skimpy

étroit, e [etʀwa, wat] adj narrow; (vêtement)

tight; (*fig*: *liens, collaboration*) close; **à l'~**
cramped; **~ d'esprit** narrow-minded

étude [etyd] *nf* studying; (*ouvrage, rapport*)
study; (SCOL: *salle de travail*) study room; **~s**
nfpl (SCOL) studies; **être à l'~** (*projet etc*) to be
under consideration; **faire des ~s (de droit/
médecine)** to study (law/medicine)

étudiant, e [etydjā, jāt] *nm/f* student

étudier [etydje] *vt, vi* to study

étui [etɥi] *nm* case

étuve [etyv] *nf* steamroom

étuvée [etyve] : **à l'~** *adv* braised

eu, eue [y] *pp de* avoir

euh [ø] *excl* er

Europe [ørɔp] *nf*: **l'~** Europe; **européen, ne**
adj European ♦ *nm/f*: **Européen, ne** European

eus *etc* [y] *vb voir* avoir

eux [ø] *pron* (*sujet*) they; (*objet*) them

évacuer [evakɥe] *vt* to evacuate

évader [evade]: **s'~** *vi* to escape

évaluer [evalɥe] *vt* (*expertiser*) to appraise,
evaluate; (*juger approximativement*) to
estimate

évangile [evāʒil] *nm* gospel

évanouir [evanwiʀ]: **s'~** *vi* to faint;
(*disparaître*) to vanish, disappear;
évanouissement *nm* (*syncope*) fainting fit

évaporer [evapɔʀe]: **s'~** *vi* to evaporate

évasé, e [evaze] *adj* (*manches, jupe*) flared

évasif, -ive [evazif, iv] *adj* evasive

évasion [evazjɔ̃] *nf* escape

évêché [eveʃe] *nm* bishop's palace

éveil [evɛj] *nm* awakening; **être en ~** to be
alert; **éveillé, e** *adj* awake; (*vif*) alert, sharp;
éveiller *vt* to (a)waken; (*soupçons etc*) to
arouse; **s'éveiller** *vi* to (a)waken; (*fig*) to be
aroused

événement [evɛnmā] *nm* event

éventail [evātaj] *nm* fan; (*choix*) range

éventaire [evātɛʀ] *nm* stall, stand

éventer [evāte] *vt* (*secret*) to uncover; **s'~** *vi*
(*parfum*) to go stale

éventualité [evātɥalite] *nf* eventuality;
possibility; **dans l'~ de** in the event of

éventuel, le [evātɥel] *adj* possible;
éventuellement *adv* possibly

évêque [evɛk] *nm* bishop

évertuer [evɛʀtɥe]: **s'~** *vi*: **s'~ à faire** to try
very hard to do

éviction [eviksjɔ̃] *nf* (*de locataire*) eviction

évidemment [evidamā] *adv* (*bien sûr*) of
course; (*certainement*) obviously

évidence [evidās] *nf* obviousness; (*fait*)
obvious fact; **de toute ~** quite obviously *ou*
evidently; **être en ~** to be clearly visible;
mettre en ~ (*fait*) to highlight; (*personne*) to
bring to the fore; **évident, e** *adj* obvious,
evident; **ce n'est pas évident!** (*fam*) it's not
that easy!

évider [evide] *vt* to scoop out

évier [evje] *nm* (kitchen) sink

évincer [evɛ̃se] *vt* to oust

éviter [evite] *vt* to avoid; **~ de faire** to avoid
doing; **~ qch à qn** to spare sb sth

évolué, e [evɔlɥe] *adj* advanced

évoluer [evɔlɥe] *vi* (*enfant, maladie*) to
develop; (*situation, moralement*) to evolve,
develop; (*aller et venir*) to move about;
évolution *nf* development, evolution

évoquer [evɔke] *vt* to call to mind, evoke;
(*mentionner*) to mention

ex... [ɛks] *préfixe* ex-

exact, e [ɛgza(kt), ɛgzakt] *adj* exact; (*correct*)
correct; (*ponctuel*) punctual; **l'heure ~e** the
right *ou* exact time; **exactement** *adv* exactly

ex aequo [ɛgzeko] *adj* equally placed; **arriver
~** to finish neck and neck

exagéré, e [ɛgzaʒeʀe] *adj* (*prix etc*) excessive

exagérer [ɛgzaʒeʀe] *vt* to exaggerate ♦ *vi* to
exaggerate; (*abuser*) to go too far

exalter [ɛgzalte] *vt* (*enthousiasmer*) to excite,
elate

examen [ɛgzamɛ̃] *nm* examination; (SCOL)
exam, examination; **à l'~** under consideration

examinateur, -trice [ɛgzaminatœʀ, tʀis]
nm/f examiner

examiner [ɛgzamine] *vt* to examine

exaspérant, e [ɛgzaspeʀā, āt] *adj*
exasperating

exaspérer [ɛgzaspeʀe] *vt* to exasperate

exaucer [ɛgzose] *vt* (*vœu*) to grant

excédent [ɛksedā] *nm* surplus; **en ~** surplus;
~ de bagages excess luggage

excéder [ɛksede] *vt* (*dépasser*) to exceed;
(*agacer*) to exasperate

excellent, e [ɛkselā, āt] *adj* excellent

excentrique [ɛksātʀik] *adj* eccentric

excepté, e [ɛksɛpte] *adj, prép*: **les élèves ~s,
~ les élèves** except for the pupils

exception [ɛksɛpsjɔ̃] *nf* exception; **à l'~ de**
except for, with the exception of; **d'~**
(*mesure, loi*) special, exceptional;
exceptionnel, le *adj* exceptional;
exceptionnellement *adv* exceptionally

excès [ɛksɛ] *nm* surplus ♦ *nmpl* excesses; **faire
des ~** to overindulge; **~ de vitesse** speeding

excessif, -ive [ɛksesif, iv] *adj* excessive

excitant, e [ɛksitā, āt] *adj* exciting ♦ *nm*
stimulant; **excitation** *nf* (*état*) excitement

exciter [ɛksite] *vt* to excite; (*suj: café etc*) to
stimulate; **s'~** *vi* to get excited

exclamation [ɛksklamasjɔ̃] *nf* exclamation

exclamer [ɛksklame]: **s'~** *vi* to exclaim

exclure [ɛksklyʀ] *vt* (*faire sortir*) to expel; (*ne
pas compter*) to exclude, leave out; (*rendre
impossible*) to exclude, rule out; **il est exclu
que** it's out of the question that ...; **il n'est
pas exclu que ...** it's not impossible that ...;

exclusif, -ive [ɛksklyzif, iv] adj exclusive; **exclusion** nf exclusion; **à l'exclusion de** with the exclusion ou exception of; **exclusivité** nf (COMM) exclusive rights pl; **film passant en exclusivité à** film showing only at

excursion [ɛkskyrsjɔ̃] nf (en autocar) excursion, trip; (à pied) walk, hike

excuse [ɛkskyz] nf excuse; **~s** nfpl (regret) apology sg, apologies; **excuser** vt to excuse; **s'excuser (de)** to apologize (for); **"excusez-moi"** "I'm sorry"; (pour attirer l'attention) "excuse me"

exécrable [ɛgzekrabl] adj atrocious

exécuter [ɛgzekyte] vt (tuer) to execute; (tâche etc) to execute, carry out; (MUS: jouer) to perform, execute; **s'~** vi to comply; **exécutif, -ive** adj, nm (POL) executive; **exécution** nf execution; **mettre à exécution** to carry out

exemplaire [ɛgzɑ̃plɛr] nm copy

exemple [ɛgzɑ̃pl] nm example; **par ~** for instance, for example; **donner l'~** to set an example

exempt, e [ɛgzɑ̃, ɑ̃(p)t] adj: **~ de** (dispensé de) exempt from; (sans) free from

exercer [ɛgzɛrse] vt (pratiquer) to exercise, practise; (influence, contrôle) to exert; (former) to exercise, train; **s'~** vi (sportif, musicien) to practise

exercice [ɛgzɛrsis] nm exercise

exhaustif, -ive [ɛgzostif, iv] adj exhaustive

exhiber [ɛgzibe] vt (montrer: papiers, certificat) to present, produce; (péj) to display, flaunt; **s'~** vi to parade; (suj: exhibitionniste) to expose o.s; **exhibitionniste** [ɛgzibisjɔnist] nm/f flasher

exhorter [ɛgzɔrte] vt to urge

exigeant, e [ɛgziʒɑ̃, ɑ̃t] adj demanding; (péj) hard to please

exigence [ɛgziʒɑ̃s] nf demand, requirement

exiger [ɛgziʒe] vt to demand, require

exigu, ë [ɛgzigy] adj cramped, tiny

exil [ɛgzil] nm exile; **exiler** vt to exile; **s'exiler** vi to go into exile

existence [ɛgzistɑ̃s] nf existence

exister [ɛgziste] vi to exist; **il existe un/des** there is a/are (some)

exonérer [ɛgzɔnere] vt: **~ de** to exempt from

exorbitant, e [ɛgzɔrbitɑ̃, ɑ̃t] adj exorbitant

exorbité, e [ɛgzɔrbite] adj: **yeux ~s** bulging eyes

exotique [ɛgzɔtik] adj exotic; **yaourt aux fruits ~s** tropical fruit yoghurt

expatrier [ɛkspatrije] vt: **s'~** to leave one's country

expectative [ɛkspɛktativ] nf: **être dans l'~** to be still waiting

expédient [ɛkspedjɑ̃, jɑ̃t] (péj) nm: **vivre d'~s** to live by one's wits

expédier [ɛkspedje] vt (lettre, paquet) to send; (troupes) to dispatch; (fam: travail etc) to dispose of, dispatch; **expéditeur, -trice** nm/f sender; **expédition** nf sending; (scientifique, sportive, MIL) expedition

expérience [ɛksperjɑ̃s] nf (de la vie) experience; (scientifique) experiment

expérimenté, e [ɛksperimɑ̃te] adj experienced

expérimenter [ɛksperimɑ̃te] vt to test out, experiment with

expert, e [ɛkspɛr, ɛrt] adj, nm expert; **expert-comptable** nm ≈ chartered accountant (BRIT), ≈ certified public accountant (US)

expertise [ɛkspɛrtiz] nf (évaluation) expert evaluation

expertiser [ɛkspɛrtize] vt (objet de valeur) to value; (voiture accidentée etc) to assess damage to

expier [ɛkspje] vt to expiate, atone for

expirer [ɛkspire] vi (prendre fin, mourir) to expire; (respirer) to breathe out

explicatif, -ive [ɛksplikatif, iv] adj explanatory

explication [ɛksplikasjɔ̃] nf explanation; (discussion) discussion; (dispute) argument; **~ de texte** (SCOL) critical analysis

explicite [ɛksplisit] adj explicit

expliquer [ɛksplike] vt to explain; **s'~** to explain (o.s.); **s'~ avec qn** (discuter) to explain o.s. to sb; **son erreur s'explique** one can understand his mistake

exploit [ɛksplwa] nm exploit, feat; **exploitant, e** nm/f: **exploitant (agricole)** farmer

exploitation nf exploitation; (d'une entreprise) running; **~ agricole** farming concern; **exploiter** vt (personne, don) to exploit; (entreprise, ferme) to run, operate; (mine) to exploit, work

explorer [ɛksplɔre] vt to explore

exploser [ɛksploze] vi to explode, blow up; (engin explosif) to go off; (personne: de colère) to flare up; **explosif, -ive** adj, nm explosive; **explosion** nf explosion

exportateur, -trice [ɛkspɔrtatœr, tris] adj export cpd, exporting ♦ nm exporter

exportation [ɛkspɔrtasjɔ̃] nf (action) exportation; (produit) export

exporter [ɛkspɔrte] vt to export

exposant [ɛkspozɑ̃] nm exhibitor

exposé, e [ɛkspoze] nm talk ♦ adj: **~ au sud** facing south

exposer [ɛkspoze] vt (marchandise) to display; (peinture) to exhibit, show; (parler de) to explain, set out; (mettre en danger, orienter, PHOTO) to expose; **exposition** nf (manifestation) exhibition; (PHOTO) exposure

exprès¹ [ɛksprɛ] adv (délibérément) on purpose; (spécialement) specially

exprès², -esse [ɛksprɛs] adj (ordre, défense) express, formal ♦ adj inv (PTT) express ♦ adv express

express [ɛksprɛs] adj, nm: (café) ~ espresso (coffee); (train) ~ fast train

expressément [ɛksprɛsemã] adv (spécialement) specifically

expressif, -ive [ɛksprɛsif, iv] adj expressive

expression [ɛksprɛsjɔ̃] nf expression

exprimer [ɛksprime] vt (sentiment, idée) to express; (jus, liquide) to press out; s'~ vi (personne) to express o.s

exproprier [ɛksprɔprije] vt to buy up by compulsory purchase, expropriate

expulser [ɛkspylse] vt to expel; (locataire) to evict; (SPORT) to send off

exquis, e [ɛkski, iz] adj exquisite

extase [ɛkstaz] nf ecstasy; **extasier**: **s'extasier sur** vt to go into raptures over

extension [ɛkstãsjɔ̃] nf (fig) extension

exténuer [ɛkstenɥe] vt to exhaust

extérieur, e [ɛksterjœr] adj (porte, mur etc) outer, outside; (au dehors: escalier, w.-c.) outside; (commerce) foreign; (influences) external; (apparent: calme, gaieté etc) surface cpd ♦ nm (d'une maison, d'un récipient etc) outside, exterior; (apparence) exterior; à l'~ outside; (à l'étranger) abroad; **extérieurement** adv on the outside; (en apparence) on the surface

exterminer [ɛkstɛrmine] vt to exterminate, wipe out

externat [ɛkstɛrna] nm day school

externe [ɛkstɛrn] adj external, outer ♦ nm/f (MÉD) non-resident medical student (BRIT), extern (US); (SCOL) day pupil

extincteur [ɛkstɛ̃ktœr] nm (fire) extinguisher

extinction [ɛkstɛ̃ksjɔ̃] nf: ~ **de voix** loss of voice

extorquer [ɛkstɔrke] vt to extort

extra [ɛkstra] adj inv first-rate; (fam) fantastic ♦ nm inv extra help

extrader [ɛkstrade] vt to extradite

extraire [ɛkstrɛr] vt to extract; **extrait** nm extract

extraordinaire [ɛkstraɔrdinɛr] adj extraordinary; (POL: mesures etc) special

extravagant, e [ɛkstravagã, ãt] adj extravagant

extraverti, e [ɛkstravɛrti] adj extrovert

extrême [ɛkstrɛm] adj, nm extreme; **extrêmement** adv extremely; **extrême-onction** nf last rites pl; **Extrême-Orient** nm Far East

extrémité [ɛkstremite] nf end; (situation) straits pl, plight; (geste désespéré) extreme action; ~s nfpl (pieds et mains) extremities

exubérant, e [ɛgzyberã, ãt] adj exuberant

exutoire [ɛgzytwar] nm outlet, release

F, f

F abr = **franc**

fa [fa] nm inv (MUS) F; (en chantant la gamme) fa

fable [fabl] nf fable

fabricant [fabrikã, ãt] nm manufacturer

fabrication [fabrikasjɔ̃] nf manufacture

fabrique [fabrik] nf factory; **fabriquer** vt to make; (industriellement) to manufacture; (fig): **qu'est-ce qu'il fabrique?** (fam) what is he doing?

fabulation [fabylasjɔ̃] nf fantasizing

fac [fak] (fam) abr f (SCOL) = **faculté**

façade [fasad] nf front, façade

face [fas] nf face; (fig: aspect) side ♦ adj: **le côté ~** heads; **en ~ de** opposite; (fig) in front of; **de ~** (voir) face on; **~ à** facing; (fig) faced with, in the face of; **faire ~ à** to face; **~ à ~** adv facing each other ♦ nm inv encounter

fâché, e [faʃe] adj angry; (désolé) sorry

fâcher [faʃe] vt to anger; **se ~** vi to get angry; **se ~ avec** (se brouiller) to fall out with

fâcheux, -euse [faʃø, øz] adj unfortunate, regrettable

facile [fasil] adj easy; (caractère) easy-going; **facilement** adv easily

facilité nf easiness; (disposition, don) aptitude; **facilités de paiement** easy terms; **faciliter** vt to make easier

façon [fasɔ̃] nf (manière) way; (d'une robe etc) making-up, cut; ~s nfpl (péj) fuss sg; **de ~ à/à ce que** so as to/that; **de toute ~** anyway, in any case; **façonner** [fasɔne] vt (travailler: matière) to shape, fashion

facteur, -trice [faktœr] nm/f postman(-woman) (BRIT), mailman(-woman) (US) ♦ nm (MATH, fig: élément) factor

factice [faktis] adj artificial

faction [faksjɔ̃] nf faction; **être de ~** to be on guard (duty)

facture [faktyr] nf (à payer: gén) bill; invoice; **facturer** vt to invoice

facultatif, -ive [fakyltatif, iv] adj optional

faculté [fakylte] nf (intellectuelle, d'université) faculty; (pouvoir, possibilité) power

fade [fad] adj insipid

fagot [fago] nm bundle of sticks

faible [fɛbl] adj weak; (voix, lumière, vent) faint; (rendement, revenu) low ♦ nm (pour quelqu'un) weakness, soft spot; **faiblesse** nf weakness; **faiblir** vi to weaken; (lumière) to dim; (vent) to drop

faïence [fajãs] nf earthenware no pl

faignant, e [fɛɲã, ãt] nm/f = **fainéant, e**

faille [faj] *vb voir* **faillir** ♦ *nf* (*GÉO*) fault; (*fig*) flaw, weakness

faillir [fajiʀ] *vi*: **j'ai failli tomber** I almost *ou* very nearly fell

faillite [fajit] *nf* bankruptcy

faim [fɛ̃] *nf* hunger; **avoir ~** to be hungry; **rester sur sa ~** (*aussi fig*) to be left wanting more

fainéant, e [feneɑ̃, ɑ̃t] *nm/f* idler, loafer

MOT-CLÉ
---

faire [fɛʀ] *vt* **1** (*fabriquer, être l'auteur de*) to make; **faire du vin/une offre/un film** to make wine/an offer/a film; **faire du bruit** to make a noise
2 (*effectuer: travail, opération*) to do; **que faites-vous?** (*quel métier etc*) what do you do?; (*quelle activité: au moment de la question*) what are you doing?; **faire la lessive** to do the washing
3 (*études*) to do; (*sport, musique*) to play; **faire du droit/du français** to do law/French; **faire du rugby/piano** to play rugby/the piano
4 (*simuler*): **faire le malade/l'ignorant** to act the invalid/the fool
5 (*transformer, avoir un effet sur*): **faire de qn un frustré/avocat** to make sb frustrated/a lawyer; **ça ne me fait rien** (*m'est égal*) I don't care *ou* mind; (*me laisse froid*) it has no effect on me; **ça ne fait rien** it doesn't matter; **faire que** (*impliquer*) to mean that
6 (*calculs, prix, mesures*): **2 et 2 font 4** 2 and 2 are *ou* make 4; **ça fait 10 m/15 F** it's 10 m/ 15F; **je vous le fais 10 F** I'll let you have it for 10F
7: **qu'a-t-il fait de sa valise?** what has he done with his case?
8: **ne faire que**: **il ne fait que critiquer** (*sans cesse*) all he (ever) does is criticize; (*seulement*) he's only criticizing
9 (*dire*) to say; **"vraiment?" fit-il** "really?" he said
10 (*maladie*) to have; **faire du diabète** to have diabetes *sg*
♦ *vi* **1** (*agir, s'y prendre*) to act, do; **il faut faire vite** we (*ou* you etc) must act quickly; **comment a-t-il fait pour?** how did he manage to?; **faites comme chez vous** make yourself at home
2 (*paraître*) to look; **faire vieux/démodé** to look old/old-fashioned; **ça fait bien** it looks good
♦ *vb substitut* to do; **ne le casse pas comme je l'ai fait** don't break it as I did; **je peux le voir? - faites!** can I see it? - please do!
♦ *vb impers* **1**: **il fait beau** *etc* the weather is fine *etc*; *voir aussi* **jour**; **froid** *etc*
2 (*temps écoulé, durée*): **ça fait 2 ans qu'il est parti** it's 2 years since he left; **ça fait 2 ans**

qu'il y est he's been there for 2 years
♦ *vb semi-aux* **1**: **faire +infinitif** (*action directe*) to make; **faire tomber/bouger qch** to make sth fall/move; **faire démarrer un moteur/ chauffer de l'eau** to start up an engine/heat some water; **cela fait dormir** it makes you sleep; **faire travailler les enfants** to make the children work *ou* get the children to work
2 (*indirectement, par un intermédiaire*): **faire réparer qch** to get *ou* have sth repaired; **faire punir les enfants** to have the children punished; **se faire** *vi* **1** (*vin, fromage*) to mature
2: **cela se fait beaucoup/ne se fait pas** it's done a lot/not done
3: **se faire +nom ou pron**: **se faire une jupe** to make o.s. a skirt; **se faire des amis** to make friends; **se faire du souci** to worry; **il ne s'en fait pas** he doesn't worry
4: **se faire +adj** (*devenir*): **se faire vieux** to be getting old; (*délibérément*): **se faire beau** to do o.s. up
5: **se faire à** (*s'habituer*) to get used to; **je n'arrive pas à me faire à la nourriture/au climat** I can't get used to the food/climate
6: **se faire +infinitif**: **se faire examiner la vue/ opérer** to have one's eyes tested/to have an operation; **se faire couper les cheveux** to get one's hair cut; **il va se faire tuer/punir** he's going to get himself killed/get (himself) punished; **il s'est fait aider** he got somebody to help him; **il s'est fait aider par Simon** he got Simon to help him; **se faire faire un vêtement** to get a garment made for o.s.
7 (*impersonnel*): **comment se fait-il/faisait-il que?** how is it/was it that?

---

faire-part [fɛʀpaʀ] *nm inv* announcement (*of birth, marriage etc*)

faisable [fazabl] *adj* feasible

faisan, e [fəzɑ̃, an] *nm/f* pheasant; **faisandé, e** *adj* high (*bad*)

faisceau, x [fɛso] *nm* (*de lumière etc*) beam

faisons [fəzɔ̃] *vb voir* **faire**

fait, e [fɛ, fɛt] *adj* (*mûr: fromage, melon*) ripe ♦ *nm* (*événement*) event, occurrence; (*réalité, donnée*) fact; **être au ~ (de)** to be informed (of); **au ~** (*à propos*) by the way; **en venir au ~** to get to the point; **du ~ de ceci/qu'il a menti** because of *ou* on account of this/his having lied; **de ce ~** for this reason; **en ~** in fact; **prendre qn sur le ~** to catch sb in the act; **~ divers** news item

faîte [fɛt] *nm* top; (*fig*) pinnacle, height

faites [fɛt] *vb voir* **faire**

faitout [fɛtu] *nm*, **fait-tout** [fɛtu] *nm inv* stewpot

falaise [falɛz] *nf* cliff

falloir [falwaʀ] *vb impers*: **il faut qu'il parte/a**

fallu qu'il parte (*obligation*) he has to *ou* must leave/had to leave; **il a fallu le faire** it had to be done; **il faut faire attention** you have to be careful; **il me faudrait 100 F** I would need 100 F; **il vous faut tourner à gauche après l'église** you have to turn left past the church; **nous avons ce qu'il (nous) faut** we have what we need; **s'en ~: il s'en est fallu de 100 F/5 minutes** we/they *etc* were 100 F short/5 minutes late (*ou* early); **il s'en faut de beaucoup qu'il soit** he is far from being; **il s'en est fallu de peu que cela n'arrive** it very nearly happened

falsifier [falsifje] *vt* to falsify, doctor

famé, e [fame] *adj*: **mal ~** disreputable, of ill repute

famélique [famelik] *adj* half-starved

fameux, -euse [famø, øz] *adj* (*illustre*) famous; (*bon: repas, plat etc*) first-rate, first-class; (*valeur intensive*) real, downright

familial, e, -aux [familjal, jo] *adj* family *cpd*

familiarité [familjaʀite] *nf* familiarity; **~s** *nfpl* (*privautés*) familiarities

familier, -ère [familje, jeʀ] *adj* (*connu*) familiar; (*atmosphère*) informal, friendly; (*LING*) informal, colloquial ♦ *nm* regular (*visitor*)

famille [famij] *nf* family; **il a de la ~ à Paris** he has relatives in Paris

famine [famin] *nf* famine

fanatique [fanatik] *adj* fanatical ♦ *nm/f* fanatic; **fanatisme** *nm* fanaticism

faner [fane]: **se ~** *vi* to fade

fanfare [fɑ̃faʀ] *nf* (*orchestre*) brass band; (*musique*) fanfare

fanfaron, ne [fɑ̃faʀɔ̃, ɔn] *nm/f* braggart

fantaisie [fɑ̃tezi] *nf* (*spontanéité*) fancy, imagination; (*caprice*) whim ♦ *adj*: **bijou ~** costume jewellery; **fantaisiste** (*péj*) *adj* unorthodox, eccentric

fantasme [fɑ̃tasm] *nm* fantasy

fantasque [fɑ̃task] *adj* whimsical, capricious

fantastique [fɑ̃tastik] *adj* fantastic

fantôme [fɑ̃tom] *nm* ghost, phantom

faon [fɑ̃] *nm* fawn

farce [faʀs] *nf* (*viande*) stuffing; (*blague*) (practical) joke; (*THÉÂTRE*) farce; **farcir** *vt* (*viande*) to stuff

fardeau, x [faʀdo] *nm* burden

farder [faʀde]: **se ~** *vi* to make (o.s.) up

farfelu, e [faʀfəly] *adj* hare-brained

farine [faʀin] *nf* flour; **farineux, -euse** *adj* (*sauce, pomme*) floury

farouche [faʀuʃ] *adj* (*timide*) shy, timid

fart [faʀt] *nm* (ski) wax

fascicule [fasikyl] *nm* volume

fascination [fasinasjɔ̃] *nf* fascination

fasciner [fasine] *vt* to fascinate

fascisme [faʃism] *nm* fascism

fasse *etc* [fas] *vb voir* **faire**

faste [fast] *nm* splendour

fastidieux, -euse [fastidjø, jøz] *adj* tedious, tiresome

fastueux, -euse [fastɥø, øz] *adj* sumptuous, luxurious

fatal, e [fatal] *adj* fatal; (*inévitable*) inevitable; **fatalité** *nf* (*destin*) fate; (*coïncidence*) fateful coincidence

fatidique [fatidik] *adj* fateful

fatigant, e [fatigɑ̃, ɑ̃t] *adj* tiring; (*agaçant*) tiresome

fatigue [fatig] *nf* tiredness, fatigue; **fatigué, e** *adj* tired; **fatiguer** *vt* to tire, make tired; (*fig: agacer*) to annoy ♦ *vi* (*moteur*) to labour, strain; **se fatiguer** to get tired

fatras [fatʀa] *nm* jumble, hotchpotch

faubourg [fobuʀ] *nm* suburb

fauché, e [foʃe] (*fam*) *adj* broke

faucher [foʃe] *vt* (*herbe*) to cut; (*champs, blés*) to reap; (*fig: véhicule*) to mow down; (*fam: voler*) to pinch

faucille [fosij] *nf* sickle

faucon [fokɔ̃] *nm* falcon, hawk

faudra [fodʀa] *vb voir* **falloir**

faufiler [fofile]: **se ~** *vi*: **se ~ dans** to edge one's way into; **se ~ parmi/entre** to thread one's way among/between

faune [fon] *nf* (*ZOOL*) wildlife, fauna

faussaire [fosɛʀ] *nm* forger

fausse [fos] *adj voir* **faux**; **faussement** *adv* (*accuser*) wrongly, wrongfully; (*croire*) falsely

fausser [fose] *vt* (*objet*) to bend, buckle; (*fig*) to distort; **~ compagnie à qn** to give sb the slip

faut [fo] *vb voir* **falloir**

faute [fot] *nf* (*erreur*) mistake, error; (*mauvaise action*) misdemeanour; (*FOOTBALL etc*) offence; (*TENNIS*) fault; **c'est de sa/ma ~** it's his/my fault; **être en ~** to be in the wrong; **~ de** (*temps, argent*) for *ou* through lack of; **sans ~** without fail; **~ de frappe** typing error; **~ de goût** error of taste; **~ professionnelle** professional misconduct *no pl*

fauteuil [fotœj] *nm* armchair; **~ roulant** wheelchair

fauteur [fotœʀ] *nm*: **~ de troubles** trouble-maker

fautif, -ive [fotif, iv] *adj* (*responsable*) at fault, in the wrong; (*incorrect*) incorrect, inaccurate; **il se sentait ~** he felt guilty

fauve [fov] *nm* wildcat ♦ *adj* (*couleur*) fawn

faux¹ [fo] *nf* scythe

faux², fausse [fo, fos] *adj* (*inexact*) wrong; (*voix*) out of tune; (*billet*) fake, forged; (*sournois, postiche*) false ♦ *adv* (*MUS*) out of tune ♦ *nm* (*copie*) fake, forgery; (*opposé au vrai*): **le ~** falsehood; **faire ~ bond à qn** to stand sb up; **fausse alerte** false alarm; **fausse**

couche miscarriage; **~ frais** *nmpl* extras, incidental expenses; **~ pas** tripping *no pl*; *(fig)* faux pas; **~ témoignage** *(délit)* perjury; **faux-filet** *nm* sirloin; **faux-monnayeur** *nm* counterfeiter, forger

faveur [favœʀ] *nf* favour; **traitement de ~** preferential treatment; **en ~ de** in favour of

favorable [favɔʀabl] *adj* favourable

favori, te [favɔʀi, it] *adj, nm/f* favourite

favoriser [favɔʀize] *vt* to favour

fax [faks] *nm* fax; **faxer** *vt* to fax

FB *abr* (= *franc belge*) BF

fébrile [febʀil] *adj* feverish, febrile

fécond, e [fekɔ̃, ɔ̃d] *adj* fertile; **féconder** *vt* to fertilize; **fécondité** *nf* fertility

fécule [fekyl] *nf* potato flour; **féculent** *nm* starchy food

fédéral, e, -aux [fedeʀal, o] *adj* federal

fée [fe] *nf* fairy; **féerique** *adj* magical, fairytale *cpd*

feignant, e [fɛɲɑ̃, ɑ̃t] *nm/f* = **fainéant, e**

feindre [fɛ̃dʀ] *vt* to feign; **~ de faire** to pretend to do

feinte [fɛ̃t] *nf* (*SPORT*) dummy

fêler [fele] *vt* to crack

félicitations [felisitasjɔ̃] *nfpl* congratulations

féliciter [felisite] *vt*: **~ qn (de)** to congratulate sb (on)

félin, e [felɛ̃, in] *nm* (big) cat

fêlure [felyʀ] *nf* crack

femelle [fəmɛl] *adj, nf* female

féminin, e [feminɛ̃, in] *adj* feminine; *(sexe)* female; *(équipe, vêtements etc)* women's ♦ *nm* (*LING*) feminine; **féministe** [feminist] *adj* feminist

femme [fam] *nf* woman; *(épouse)* wife; **~ au foyer** housewife; **~ de chambre** chambermaid; **~ de ménage** cleaning lady

fémur [femyʀ] *nm* femur, thighbone

fendre [fɑ̃dʀ] *vt* *(couper en deux)* to split; *(fissurer)* to crack; *(traverser: foule, air)* to cleave through; **se ~** *vi* to crack

fenêtre [f(ə)nɛtʀ] *nf* window

fenouil [fənuj] *nm* fennel

fente [fɑ̃t] *nf* *(fissure)* crack; *(de boîte à lettres etc)* slit

féodal, e, -aux [feɔdal, o] *adj* feudal

fer [fɛʀ] *nm* iron; **~ à cheval** horseshoe; **~ (à repasser)** iron; **~ forgé** wrought iron

ferai *etc* [faʀe] *vb voir* **faire**

fer-blanc [fɛʀblɑ̃] *nm* tin(plate)

férié, e [feʀje] *adj*: **jour ~** public holiday

ferions *etc* [faʀjɔ̃] *vb voir* **faire**

ferme [fɛʀm] *adj* firm ♦ *adv* *(travailler etc)* hard ♦ *nf* *(exploitation)* farm; *(maison)* farmhouse

fermé, e [fɛʀme] *adj* closed, shut; *(gaz, eau etc)* off; *(fig: milieu)* exclusive

fermenter [fɛʀmɑ̃te] *vi* to ferment

fermer [fɛʀme] *vt* to close, shut; *(cesser l'exploitation de)* to close down, shut down; *(eau, électricité, robinet)* to put off, turn off; *(aéroport, route)* to close ♦ *vi* to close, shut; *(magasin: definitivement)* to close down, shut down; **se ~** *vi* to close, shut

fermeté [fɛʀməte] *nf* firmness

fermeture [fɛʀmətyʀ] *nf* closing; *(dispositif)* catch; **heures de ~** closing times; **~ éclair** ® zip (fastener) (*BRIT*), zipper (*US*)

fermier [fɛʀmje, jɛʀ] *nm* farmer; **fermière** *nf* woman farmer; *(épouse)* farmer's wife

fermoir [fɛʀmwaʀ] *nm* clasp

féroce [feʀɔs] *adj* ferocious, fierce

ferons [fəʀɔ̃] *vb voir* **faire**

ferraille [feʀaj] *nf* scrap iron; **mettre à la ~** to scrap

ferrer [feʀe] *vt* *(cheval)* to shoe

ferronnerie [feʀɔnʀi] *nf* ironwork

ferroviaire [feʀɔvjɛʀ] *adj* rail(way) *cpd* (*BRIT*), rail(road) *cpd* (*US*)

ferry(boat) [feʀe(bot)] *nm* ferry

fertile [fɛʀtil] *adj* fertile; **~ en incidents** eventful, packed with incidents

féru, e [feʀy] *adj*: **~ de** with a keen interest in

fervent, e [fɛʀvɑ̃, ɑ̃t] *adj* fervent

fesse [fɛs] *nf* buttock; **fessée** *nf* spanking

festin [fɛstɛ̃] *nm* feast

festival [fɛstival] *nm* festival

festivités [fɛstivite] *nfpl* festivities

festoyer [fɛstwaje] *vi* to feast

fêtard [fɛtaʀ, aʀd] *(fam)* *nm* high liver, merry-maker

fête [fɛt] *nf* *(religieuse)* feast; *(publique)* holiday; *(réception)* party; *(kermesse)* fête, fair; *(du nom)* feast day, name day; **faire la ~** to live it up; **faire ~ à qn** to give sb a warm welcome; **les ~s (de fin d'année)** the festive season; **la salle des ~s** the village hall; **~ foraine** (fun) fair; **fêter** *vt* to celebrate; *(personne)* to have a celebration for

feu, x [fø] *nm* *(gén)* fire; *(signal lumineux)* light; *(de cuisinière)* ring; **~x** *nmpl* (*AUTO*) (traffic) lights; **au ~!** *(incendie)* fire!; **à ~ doux/vif** over a slow/brisk heat; **à petit ~** (*CULIN*) over a gentle heat; *(fig)* slowly; **faire ~** to fire; **prendre ~** to catch fire; **mettre le ~ à** to set fire to; **faire du ~** to make a fire; **avez-vous du ~?** *(pour cigarette)* have you (got) a light?; **~ arrière** rear light; **~ d'artifice** *(spectacle)* fireworks *pl*; **~ de joie** bonfire; **~ rouge/vert/orange** red/green/amber (*BRIT*) *ou* yellow (*US*) light; **~x de brouillard** fog-lamps; **~x de croisement** dipped (*BRIT*) *ou* dimmed (*US*) headlights; **~x de position** sidelights; **~x de route** headlights

feuillage [fœjaʒ] *nm* foliage, leaves *pl*

feuille [fœj] *nf* *(d'arbre)* leaf; *(de papier)* sheet; **~ de maladie** medical expenses claim

form; ~ **de paie** pay slip
feuillet [fœjɛ] *nm* leaf
feuilleté, e [fœjte] *adj:* **pâte** ~ flaky pastry
feuilleter [fœjte] *vt (livre)* to leaf through
feuilleton [fœjtɔ̃] *nm* serial
feutre [føtʀ] *nm* felt; *(chapeau)* felt hat; *(aussi:* **stylo-**~) felt-tip pen; **feutré, e** *adj (atmosphère)* muffled
fève [fɛv] *nf* broad bean
février [fevʀije] *nm* February
FF *abr (= franc français)* FF
fiable [fjabl] *adj* reliable
fiançailles [fjɑ̃sɑj] *nfpl* engagement *sg*
fiancé, e [fjɑ̃se] *nm/f* fiancé(e) ♦ *adj:* **être** ~ **(à)** to be engaged *(to)*
fiancer [fjɑ̃se]: **se** ~ *vi* to become engaged
fibre [fibʀ] *nf* fibre; ~ **de verre** fibreglass, glass fibre
ficeler [fis(ə)le] *vt* to tie up
ficelle [fisɛl] *nf* string *no pl; (morceau)* piece *ou* length of string
fiche [fiʃ] *nf (pour fichier)* (index) card; *(formulaire)* form; *(ÉLEC)* plug
ficher [fiʃe] *vt (dans un fichier)* to file; *(POLICE)* to put on file; *(fam: faire)* to do; *(: donner)* to give; *(: mettre)* to stick *ou* shove; **se** ~ **de** *(fam: se gausser)* to make fun of; **fiche-(moi) le camp** *(fam)* clear off; **fiche-moi la paix** *(fam)* leave me alone; **je m'en fiche!** *(fam)* I don't care!
fichier [fiʃje] *nm* file
fichu, e [fiʃy] *pp de* ficher *(fam)* ♦ *adj (fam: fini, inutilisable)* bust, done for; *(: intensif)* wretched, darned ♦ *nm (foulard)* (head)scarf; **mal** ~ *(fam)* feeling lousy
fictif, -ive [fiktif, iv] *adj* fictitious
fiction [fiksjɔ̃] *nf* fiction; *(fait imaginé)* invention
fidèle [fidɛl] *adj* faithful ♦ *nm/f (REL):* **les** ~**s** *(à l'église)* the congregation *sg;* **fidélité** *nf* fidelity
fier¹ [fje]: **se** ~ **à** *vt* to trust
fier², fière [fjɛʀ] *adj* proud; **fierté** *nf* pride
fièvre [fjɛvʀ] *nf* fever; **avoir de la** ~**/39 de** ~ to have a high temperature/a temperature of 39°C; **fiévreux, -euse** *adj* feverish
figé, e [fiʒe] *adj (manières)* stiff; *(société)* rigid; *(sourire)* set
figer [fiʒe]: **se** ~ *vi (huile)* to congeal; *(personne)* to freeze
fignoler [fiɲɔle] *(fam) vt* to polish up
figue [fig] *nf* fig; **figuier** *nm* fig tree
figurant, e [figyʀɑ̃, ɑ̃t] *nm/f (THÉÂTRE)* walk-on; *(CINÉMA)* extra
figure [figyʀ] *nf (visage)* face; *(forme, personnage)* figure; *(illustration)* picture, diagram
figuré, e [figyʀe] *adj (sens)* figurative
figurer [figyʀe] *vi* to appear ♦ *vt* to represent;

se ~ **que** to imagine that
fil [fil] *nm (brin, fig: d'une histoire)* thread; *(électrique)* wire; *(d'un couteau)* edge; **au** ~ **des années** with the passing of the years; **au** ~ **de l'eau** with the stream *ou* current; **coup de** ~ *(fam)* phone call; ~ **à coudre** (sewing) thread; ~ **de fer** wire; ~ **de fer barbelé** barbed wire
filament [filamɑ̃] *nm (ÉLEC)* filament
filandreux, -euse [filɑ̃dʀø, øz] *adj* stringy
filature [filatyʀ] *nf (fabrique)* mill; *(policière)* shadowing *no pl*, tailing *no pl*
file [fil] *nf* line; *(AUTO)* lane; **en** ~ **indienne** in single file; **à la** ~ *(d'affilée)* in succession; ~ *(d'attente)* queue *(BRIT)*, line *(US)*
filer [file] *vt (tissu, toile)* to spin; *(prendre en filature)* to shadow, tail; *(fam: donner):* ~ **qch à qn** to slip sb sth ♦ *vi (bas)* to run; *(aller vite)* to fly past; *(fam: partir)* to make *ou* be off; ~ **doux** to toe the line
filet [filɛ] *nm* net; *(CULIN)* fillet; *(d'eau, de sang)* trickle; ~ *(à provisions)* string bag
filiale [filjal] *nf (COMM)* subsidiary
filière [filjɛʀ] *nf (carrière)* path; **suivre la** ~ *(dans sa carrière)* to work one's way up *(through the hierarchy)*
filiforme [filifɔʀm] *adj* spindly
filigrane [filigʀan] *nm (d'un billet, timbre)* watermark
fille [fij] *nf* girl; *(opposé à fils)* daughter; **vieille** ~ old maid; **fillette** *nf* (little) girl
filleul, e [fijœl] *nm/f* godchild, godson/daughter
film [film] *nm (pour photo)* (roll of) film; *(œuvre)* film, picture, movie; ~ **d'épouvante** horror film; ~ **policier** thriller
filon [filɔ̃] *nm* vein, lode; *(fig)* lucrative line, money spinner
fils [fis] *nm* son; ~ **à papa** daddy's boy
filtre [filtʀ] *nm* filter; **filtrer** *vt* to filter; *(fig: candidats, visiteurs)* to screen
fin¹ [fɛ̃] *nf* end; ~**s** *nfpl (but)* ends; **prendre** ~ to come to an end; **mettre** ~ **à** to put an end to; **à la** ~ in the end, eventually; **en** ~ **de compte** in the end; **sans** ~ endless; ~ **juin** the end of June
fin², e [fɛ̃, fin] *adj (papier, couche, fil)* thin; *(cheveux, visage)* fine; *(taille)* neat, slim; *(esprit, remarque)* subtle ♦ *adv (couper)* finely; ~ **prêt** quite ready; ~**es herbes** mixed herbs
final, e [final, o] *adj* final ♦ *nm (MUS)* finale; **finale** *nf* final; **quarts de finale** quarter finals; **finalement** *adv* finally, in the end; *(après tout)* after all
finance [finɑ̃s] *nf:* ~**s** *nfpl (situation)* finances; *(activités)* finance *sg;* **moyennant** ~ for a fee; **financer** *vt* to finance; **financier, -ière** *adj* financial

finaud, e [fino, od] *adj* wily
finesse [fines] *nf* thinness; (*raffinement*)
　fineness; (*subtilité*) subtlety
fini, e [fini] *adj* finished; (*MATH*) finite ♦ *nm*
　(*d'un objet manufacturé*) finish
finir [finir] *vt* to finish ♦ *vi* to finish, end;
　~ **par faire** to end up *ou* finish up doing; ~ **de**
　faire to finish doing; (*cesser*) to stop doing; **il**
　finit par m'agacer he's beginning to get on
　my nerves; **en ~ avec** to be *ou* have done
　with; **il va mal ~** he will come to a bad end
finition [finisjɔ̃] *nf* (*résultat*) finish
finlandais, e [fɛ̃lɑ̃dɛ, ɛz] *adj* Finnish ♦ *nm/f*:
　F~, e Finn
Finlande [fɛ̃lɑ̃d] *nf*: **la ~** Finland
fiole [fjɔl] *nf* phial
firme [firm] *nf* firm
fis [fi] *vb voir* **faire**
fisc [fisk] *nm* tax authorities *pl*; **fiscal, e, -aux**
　adj tax *cpd*, fiscal; **fiscalité** *nf* tax system
fissure [fisyr] *nf* crack; **fissurer** *vt* to crack;
　se fissurer *vi* to crack
fiston [fistɔ̃] (*fam*) *nm* son, lad
fit [fi] *vb voir* **faire**
fixation [fiksasjɔ̃] *nf* (*attache*) fastening;
　(*PSYCH*) fixation
fixe [fiks] *adj* fixed; (*emploi*) steady, regular
　♦ *nm* (*salaire*) basic salary; **à heure ~** at a set
　time; **menu à prix ~** set menu
fixé, e [fikse] *adj*: **être ~ (sur)** (*savoir à quoi*
　s'en tenir) to have made up one's mind
　(about)
fixer [fikse] *vt* (*attacher*): ~ **qch (à/sur)** to fix
　ou fasten sth (to/onto); (*déterminer*) to fix,
　set; (*regarder*) to stare at; **se ~** *vi* (*s'établir*) to
　settle down; **se ~ sur** (*suj: attention*) to focus
　on
flacon [flakɔ̃] *nm* bottle
flageoler [flaʒɔle] *vi* (*jambes*) to sag
flageolet [flaʒɔle] *nm* (*CULIN*) dwarf kidney
　bean
flagrant, e [flagrɑ̃, ɑ̃t] *adj* flagrant, blatant;
　en ~ délit in the act
flair [flɛr] *nm* sense of smell; (*fig*) intuition;
　flairer *vt* (*humer*) to sniff (at); (*détecter*) to
　scent
flamand, e [flamɑ̃, ɑ̃d] *adj* Flemish ♦ *nm*
　(*LING*) Flemish ♦ *nm/f*: F~, e Fleming; **les F~s**
　the Flemish
flamant [flamɑ̃] *nm* flamingo
flambant [flɑ̃bɑ̃, ɑ̃t] *adv*: ~ **neuf** brand new
flambé, e [flɑ̃be] *adj* (*CULIN*) flambé
flambeau, x [flɑ̃bo] *nm* (*flaming*) torch
flambée [flɑ̃be] *nf* blaze; (*fig: des prix*)
　explosion
flamber [flɑ̃be] *vi* to blaze (up)
flamboyer [flɑ̃bwaje] *vi* to blaze (up)
flamme [flam] *nf* flame; (*fig*) fire, fervour; **en**
　~s on fire, ablaze

flan [flɑ̃] *nm* (*CULIN*) custard tart *ou* pie
flanc [flɑ̃] *nm* side; (*MIL*) flank
flancher [flɑ̃ʃe] (*fam*) *vi* to fail, pack up
flanelle [flanɛl] *nf* flannel
flâner [flɑne] *vi* to stroll; **flânerie** *nf* stroll
flanquer [flɑ̃ke] *vt* to flank; (*fam: mettre*) to
　chuck, shove; (: *jeter*): ~ **par terre/à la porte**
　to fling to the ground/chuck out
flaque [flak] *nf* (*d'eau*) puddle; (*d'huile, de*
　sang etc) pool
flash [flaʃ] (*pl* **~es**) *nm* (*PHOTO*) flash;
　~ (**d'information**) newsflash
flasque [flask] *adj* flabby
flatter [flate] *vt* to flatter; **se ~ de qch** to pride
　o.s. on sth; **flatterie** *nf* flattery *no pl*;
　flatteur, -euse *adj* flattering
fléau, x [fleo] *nm* scourge
flèche [flɛʃ] *nf* arrow; (*de clocher*) spire;
　monter en ~ (*fig*) to soar, rocket; **partir en ~**
　to be off like a shot; **fléchette** *nf* dart
fléchir [fleʃir] *vt* (*corps, genou*) to bend; (*fig*)
　to sway, weaken ♦ *vi* to weaken, flag
flemmard, e [flemar, ard] (*fam*) *nm/f*
　lazybones *sg*, loafer
flemme [flem] (*fam*) *nf* laziness; **j'ai la ~ de**
　faire I can't be bothered doing it
flétrir [fletrir] *vt*: **se ~** *vi* to wither
fleur [flœr] *nf* flower; (*d'un arbre*) blossom;
　en ~ (*arbre*) in blossom; **à ~s** flowery
fleuri, e [flœri] *adj* (*jardin*) in flower *ou*
　bloom; (*tissu, papier*) flowery
fleurir [flœrir] *vi* (*rose*) to flower; (*arbre*) to
　blossom; (*fig*) to flourish ♦ *vt* (*tombe*) to put
　flowers on; (*chambre*) to decorate with
　flowers
fleuriste [flœrist] *nm/f* florist
fleuve [flœv] *nm* river
flexible [fleksibl] *adj* flexible
flic [flik] (*fam: péj*) *nm* cop
flipper [flipœr] *nm* pinball (machine)
flirter [flœrte] *vi* to flirt
flocon [flɔkɔ̃] *nm* flake
flopée [flɔpe] (*fam*) *nf*: **une ~ de** loads of,
　masses of
floraison [flɔrezɔ̃] *nf* flowering
flore [flɔr] *nf* flora
florissant, e [flɔrisɑ̃, ɑ̃t] *adj* (*économie*)
　flourishing
flot [flo] *nm* flood, stream; **~s** *nmpl* (*de la mer*)
　waves; **être à ~** (*NAVIG*) to be afloat; **entrer à**
　~s to stream *ou* pour in
flottant, e [flɔtɑ̃, ɑ̃t] *adj* (*vêtement*) loose
flotte [flɔt] *nf* (*NAVIG*) fleet; (*fam: eau*) water;
　(: *pluie*) rain
flottement [flɔtmɑ̃] *nm* (*fig*) wavering,
　hesitation
flotter [flɔte] *vi* to float; (*nuage, odeur*) to
　drift; (*drapeau*) to fly; (*vêtements*) to hang
　loose; (*fam: pleuvoir*) to rain; **faire ~** to float;

flotteur nm float

flou, e [flu] adj fuzzy, blurred; (fig) woolly, vague

fluctuation [flyktɥasjɔ̃] nf fluctuation

fluet, te [flɥɛ, ɛt] adj thin, slight

fluide [flɥid] adj fluid; (circulation etc) flowing freely ♦ nm fluid

fluor [flyɔʀ] nm: **dentifrice au ~** fluoride toothpaste

fluorescent, e [flyɔʀesɑ̃, ɑ̃t] adj fluorescent

flûte [flyt] nf flute; (verre) flute glass; (pain) long loaf; **~! drat it!; ~ à bec** recorder

flux [fly] nm incoming tide; (écoulement) flow; **le ~ et le reflux** the ebb and flow

FM sigle f (= fréquence modulée) FM

foc [fɔk] nm jib

foi [fwa] nf faith; **digne de ~** reliable; **être de bonne/mauvaise ~** to be sincere/insincere; **ma ~ ... well ...**

foie [fwa] nm liver; **crise de ~** stomach upset

foin [fwɛ̃] nm hay; **faire du ~** (fig: fam) to kick up a row

foire [fwaʀ] nf fair; (fête foraine) (fun) fair; **faire la ~** (fig: fam) to whoop it up; **~ (exposition)** trade fair

fois [fwa] nf time; **une/deux ~** once/twice; **2 ~ 2** 2 times 2; **une ~** (passé) once; (futur) sometime; **une ~ pour toutes** once and for all; **une ~ que** once; **des ~** (parfois) sometimes; **à la ~** (ensemble) at once

foison [fwazɔ̃] nf: **à ~** in plenty; **foisonner** vi to abound

fol [fɔl] adj voir **fou**

folie [fɔli] nf (d'une décision, d'un acte) madness, folly; (état) madness, insanity; **la ~ des grandeurs** delusions of grandeur; **faire des ~s** (en dépenses) to be extravagant

folklorique [fɔlklɔʀik] adj folk cpd; (fam) weird

folle [fɔl] adj, nf voir **fou**; **follement** adv (très) madly, wildly

foncé, e [fɔ̃se] adj dark

foncer [fɔ̃se] vi to go darker; (fam: aller vite) to tear ou belt along; **~ sur** to charge at

foncier, -ère [fɔ̃sje, jɛʀ] adj (honnêteté etc) basic, fundamental; (COMM) real estate cpd

fonction [fɔ̃ksjɔ̃] nf function; (emploi, poste) post, position; **~s** nfpl (professionnelles) duties; **voiture de ~** company car; **en ~ de** (par rapport à) according to; **faire ~ de** to serve as; **la ~ publique** the state ou civil (BRIT) service; **fonctionnaire** nm/f state employee, local authority employee; (dans l'administration) ≈ civil servant; **fonctionner** vi to work, function

fond [fɔ̃] nm (d'un récipient, trou) bottom; (d'une salle, scène) back; (d'un tableau, décor) background; (opposé à la forme) content; (SPORT): **le ~** long distance (running); **au ~ de** at the bottom of; at the back of; **à ~** (connaître, soutenir) thoroughly; (appuyer, visser) right down ou home; **à ~ (de train)** (fam) full tilt; **dans le ~, au ~** (en somme) basically, really; **de ~ en comble** from top to bottom; voir aussi **fonds**; **~ de teint** foundation (cream)

fondamental, e, -aux [fɔ̃damɑ̃tal, o] adj fundamental

fondant, e [fɔ̃dɑ̃, ɑ̃t] adj (neige) melting; (poire) that melts in the mouth

fondateur, -trice [fɔ̃datœʀ, tʀis] nm/f founder

fondation [fɔ̃dasjɔ̃] nf founding; (établissement) foundation; **~s** nfpl (d'une maison) foundations

fondé, e [fɔ̃de] adj (accusation etc) well-founded; **être ~ à** to have grounds for ou good reason to

fondement [fɔ̃dmɑ̃] nm: **sans ~** (rumeur etc) groundless, unfounded

fonder [fɔ̃de] vt to found; (fig) to base; **se ~ sur** (suj: personne) to base o.s. on

fonderie [fɔ̃dʀi] nf smelting works sg

fondre [fɔ̃dʀ] vt (aussi: **faire ~**) to melt; (dans l'eau) to dissolve; (fig: mélanger) to merge, blend ♦ vi (à la chaleur) to melt; (dans l'eau) to dissolve; (fig) to melt away; (se précipiter): **~ sur** to swoop down on; **~ en larmes** to burst into tears

fonds [fɔ̃] nm (COMM): **~ (de commerce)** business ♦ nmpl (argent) funds

fondu, e [fɔ̃dy] adj (beurre, neige) melted; (métal) molten; **fondue** nf (CULIN) fondue

font [fɔ̃] vb voir **faire**

fontaine [fɔ̃tɛn] nf fountain; (source) spring

fonte [fɔ̃t] nf melting; (métal) cast iron; **la ~ des neiges** (the spring) thaw

foot [fut] (fam) nm football

football [futbol] nm football, soccer; **footballeur** nm footballer

footing [futiŋ] nm jogging; **faire du ~** to go jogging

for [fɔʀ] nm: **dans son ~ intérieur** in one's heart of hearts

forain, e [fɔʀɛ̃, ɛn] adj fairground cpd ♦ nm (marchand) stallholder; (acteur) fairground entertainer

forçat [fɔʀsa] nm convict

force [fɔʀs] nf strength; (PHYSIQUE, MÉCANIQUE) force; **~s** nfpl (physiques) strength sg; (MIL) forces; **à ~ d'insister** by dint of insisting; as he (ou l etc) kept on insisting; **de ~** forcibly, by force; **les ~s de l'ordre** the police

forcé, e [fɔʀse] adj forced; **c'est ~** (fam) it's inevitable; **forcément** adv inevitably; **pas forcément** not necessarily

forcené, e [fɔʀsəne] nm/f maniac

forcer [fɔʀse] vt to force; (voix) to strain ♦ vi

(*SPORT*) to overtax o.s.; ~ **la dose** (*fam*) to overdo it; **se ~ (à faire)** to force o.s. (to do)

forcir [fɔʀsiʀ] *vi* (*grossir*) to broaden out

forer [fɔʀe] *vt* to drill, bore

forestier, -ère [fɔʀɛstje, jɛʀ] *adj* forest *cpd*

forêt [fɔʀɛ] *nf* forest

forfait [fɔʀfɛ] *nm* (*COMM*) all-in deal *ou* price; **forfaitaire** *adj* inclusive

forge [fɔʀʒ] *nf* forge, smithy; **forger** *vt* to forge; (*fig: prétexte*) to contrive, make up; **forgeron** *nm* (black)smith

formaliser [fɔʀmalize]: **se ~** *vi*: **se ~ (de)** to take offence (at)

formalité [fɔʀmalite] *nf* formality; **simple ~** mere formality

format [fɔʀma] *nm* size; **formater** *vt* (*disque*) to format

formation [fɔʀmasjɔ̃] *nf* (*développement*) forming; (*apprentissage*) training; **~ permanente** continuing education; **~ professionnelle** vocational training

forme [fɔʀm] *nf* (*gén*) form; (*d'un objet*) shape, form; **~s** *nfpl* (*bonnes manières*) proprieties; (*d'une femme*) figure *sg*; **être en ~** (*SPORT etc*) to be on form; **en bonne et due ~** in due form

formel, le [fɔʀmɛl] *adj* (*catégorique*) definite, positive; **formellement** *adv* (*absolument*) positively; **formellement interdit** strictly forbidden

former [fɔʀme] *vt* to form; (*éduquer*) to train; **se ~** *vi* to form

formidable [fɔʀmidabl] *adj* tremendous

formulaire [fɔʀmylɛʀ] *nm* form

formule [fɔʀmyl] *nf* (*gén*) formula; (*expression*) phrase; **~ de politesse** polite phrase; (*en fin de lettre*) letter ending; **formuler** *vt* (*émettre: désir*) to formulate

fort, e [fɔʀ, fɔʀt] *adj* strong; (*intensité, rendement*) high, great; (*corpulent*) stout; (*doué*) good, able ♦ *adv* (*serrer, frapper*) hard; (*parler*) loud(ly); (*beaucoup*) greatly, very much; (*très*) very ♦ *nm* (*édifice*) fort; (*point ~*) strong point, forte; **~e tête** rebel; **forteresse** *nf* stronghold

fortifiant [fɔʀtifjɑ̃, jɑ̃t] *nm* tonic

fortifier [fɔʀtifje] *vt* to strengthen, fortify

fortiori [fɔʀsjɔʀi]: **à ~** *adv* all the more so

fortuit, e [fɔʀtɥi, it] *adj* fortuitous, chance *cpd*

fortune [fɔʀtyn] *nf* fortune; **faire ~** to make one's fortune; **de ~** makeshift; **fortuné, e** *adj* wealthy

fosse [fos] *nf* (*grand trou*) pit; (*tombe*) grave

fossé [fose] *nm* ditch; (*fig*) gulf, gap

fossette [fosɛt] *nf* dimple

fossile [fosil] *nm* fossil

fossoyeur [foswajœʀ] *nm* gravedigger

fou (fol), folle [fu, fɔl] *adj* mad; (*déréglé*

etc) wild, erratic; (*fam: extrême, très grand*) terrific, tremendous ♦ *nm/f* madman(-woman) ♦ *nm* (*du roi*) jester; **être ~ de** to be mad *ou* crazy about; **avoir le ~ rire** to have the giggles

foudre [fudʀ] *nf*: **la ~** lightning

foudroyant, e [fudʀwajɑ̃, ɑ̃t] *adj* (*progrès*) lightning *cpd*; (*succès*) stunning; (*maladie, poison*) violent

foudroyer [fudʀwaje] *vt* to strike down; **être foudroyé** to be struck by lightning; **~ qn du regard** to glare at sb

fouet [fwɛ] *nm* whip; (*CULIN*) whisk; **de plein ~** (*se heurter*) head on; **fouetter** *vt* to whip; (*crème*) to whisk

fougère [fuʒɛʀ] *nf* fern

fougue [fug] *nf* ardour, spirit; **fougueux, -euse** *adj* fiery

fouille [fuj] *nf* search; **~s** *nfpl* (*archéologiques*) excavations; **fouiller** *vt* to search; (*creuser*) to dig ♦ *vi* to rummage; **fouillis** *nm* jumble, muddle

fouiner [fwine] (*péj*) *vi*: **~ dans** to nose around *ou* about in

foulard [fulaʀ] *nm* scarf

foule [ful] *nf* crowd; **la ~** crowds *pl*; **une ~ de** masses of

foulée [fule] *nf* stride

fouler [fule] *vt* to press; (*sol*) to tread upon; **se ~ la cheville** to sprain one's ankle; **ne pas se ~** not to overexert o.s.; **il ne se foule pas** he doesn't put himself out; **foulure** *nf* sprain

four [fuʀ] *nm* oven; (*de potier*) kiln; (*THÉÂTRE: échec*) flop

fourbe [fuʀb] *adj* deceitful

fourbu, e [fuʀby] *adj* exhausted

fourche [fuʀʃ] *nf* pitchfork

fourchette [fuʀʃɛt] *nf* fork; (*STATISTIQUE*) bracket, margin

fourgon [fuʀgɔ̃] *nm* van; (*RAIL*) wag(g)on; **fourgonnette** *nf* (small) van

fourmi [fuʀmi] *nf* ant; **~s** *nfpl* (*fig*) pins and needles; **fourmilière** *nf* ant-hill; **fourmiller** *vi* to swarm

fournaise [fuʀnɛz] *nf* blaze; (*fig*) furnace, oven

fourneau, x [fuʀno] *nm* stove

fournée [fuʀne] *nf* batch

fourni, e [fuʀni] *adj* (*barbe, cheveux*) thick; (*magasin*): **bien ~ (en)** well stocked (with)

fournir [fuʀniʀ] *vt* to supply; (*preuve, exemple*) to provide, supply; (*effort*) to put in; **fournisseur, -euse** *nm/f* supplier; **fourniture** *nf* supply(ing); **fournitures scolaires** school stationery

fourrage [fuʀaʒ] *nm* fodder

fourré, e [fuʀe] *adj* (*bonbon etc*) filled; (*manteau etc*) fur-lined ♦ *nm* thicket

fourrer [fuʀe] (*fam*) *vt* to stick, shove; **se**

~ dans/sous to get into/under; **fourre-tout**
nm inv (sac) holdall; (fig) rag-bag
fourrière [furjɛr] nf pound
fourrure [furyr] nf fur; (sur l'animal) coat
fourvoyer [furvwaje]: se ~ vi to go astray,
stray
foutre [futr] (fam!) vt = **ficher**; **foutu, e**
(fam!) adj = **fichu, e**
foyer [fwaje] nm (maison) home; (famille)
family; (de cheminée) hearth; (de jeunes etc)
(social) club; (résidence) hostel; (salon)
foyer; **lunettes à double** ~ bi-focal glasses
fracas [fraka] nm (d'objet qui tombe) crash;
fracassant, e adj (succès) thundering;
fracasser vt to smash
fraction [fraksjɔ̃] nf fraction; **fractionner** vt
to divide (up), split (up)
fracture [fraktyr] nf fracture; ~ **du crâne**
fractured skull; **fracturer** vt (coffre, serrure)
to break open; (os, membre) to fracture
fragile [fraʒil] adj fragile, delicate; (fig) frail;
fragilité nf fragility
fragment [fragmā] nm (d'un objet)
fragment, piece
fraîche [frɛʃ] adj voir **frais**; **fraîcheur** nf
coolness; (d'un aliment) freshness; **fraîchir** vi
to get cooler; (vent) to freshen
frais, fraîche [frɛ, frɛʃ] adj fresh; (froid)
cool ♦ adv (récemment) newly, fresh(ly)
♦ nm: **mettre au** ~ to put in a cool place
♦ nmpl (gén) expenses; (COMM) costs; **il fait** ~
it's cool; **servir** ~ serve chilled; **prendre le** ~
to take a breath of cool air; **faire des** ~ to go to
a lot of expense; ~ **de scolarité** school fees
(BRIT), tuition (US); ~ **généraux** overheads
fraise [frɛz] nf strawberry; ~ **des bois** wild
strawberry
framboise [frābwaz] nf raspberry
franc, franche [frā, frāʃ] adj (personne)
frank, straightforward; (visage) open; (net:
refus) clear; (: coupure) clean; (intensif)
downright ♦ nm franc
français, e [frāsɛ, ɛz] adj French ♦ nm/f: F~,
e Frenchman(-woman) ♦ nm (LING) French;
les F~ the French
France [frās] nf: **la** ~ France
franche [frāʃ] adj voir **franc**; **franchement**
adv frankly; (nettement) definitely; (tout à
fait: mauvais etc) downright
franchir [frāʃir] vt (obstacle) to clear, get
over; (seuil, ligne, rivière) to cross; (distance)
to cover
franchise [frāʃiz] nf frankness; (douanière)
exemption; (ASSURANCES) excess
franc-maçon [frāmasɔ̃] nm freemason
franco [frāko] adv (COMM): ~ **(de port)**
postage paid
francophone [frākɔfɔn] adj French-speaking
franc-parler [frāparle] nm inv

outspokenness; **avoir son** ~-~ to speak one's
mind
frange [frāʒ] nf fringe
frangipane [frāʒipan] nf almond paste
franquette [frākɛt]: **à la bonne** ~ adv
without any fuss
frappant, e [frapā, āt] adj striking
frappé, e [frape] adj iced
frapper [frape] vt to hit, strike; (étonner) to
strike; ~ **dans ses mains** to clap one's hands;
frappé de stupeur dumbfounded
frasques [frask] nfpl escapades
fraternel, le [fratɛrnɛl] adj brotherly,
fraternal; **fraternité** nf brotherhood
fraude [frod] nf fraud; (SCOL) cheating;
passer qch en ~ to smuggle sth in (ou out);
~ **fiscale** tax evasion; **frauder** vi, vt to cheat;
frauduleux, -euse adj fraudulent
frayer [freje] vt to open up, clear ♦ vi to
spawn; **se** ~ **un chemin dans la foule** to force
one's way through the crowd
frayeur [frejœr] nf fright
fredonner [frədɔne] vt to hum
freezer [frizœr] nm freezing compartment
frein [frɛ̃] nm brake; **mettre un** ~ **à** (fig) to
curb, check; ~ **à main** handbrake; **freiner** vi
to brake ♦ vt (progrès etc) to check
frêle [frɛl] adj frail, fragile
frelon [frəlɔ̃] nm hornet
frémir [fremir] vi (de peur, d'horreur) to
shudder; (de colère) to shake; (feuillage) to
quiver
frêne [frɛn] nm ash
frénétique [frenetik] adj frenzied, frenetic
fréquemment [frekamā] adv frequently
fréquent, e [frekā, āt] adj frequent
fréquentation [frekātasjɔ̃] nf frequenting;
~**s** nfpl (relations) company sg
fréquenté, e [frekāte] adj: **très** ~ (very)
busy; **mal** ~ patronized by disreputable
elements
fréquenter [frekāte] vt (lieu) to frequent;
(personne) to see; **se** ~ to see each other
frère [frɛr] nm brother
fresque [frɛsk] nf (ART) fresco
fret [frɛ(t)] nm freight
frétiller [fretije] vi (poisson) to wriggle
fretin [frətɛ̃] nm: **menu** ~ small fry
friable [frijabl] adj crumbly
friand, e [frijā, frijād] adj: ~ **de** very fond of
♦ nm: ~ **au fromage** cheese puff
friandise [frijādiz] nf sweet
fric [frik] (fam) nm cash, bread
friche [friʃ]: **en** ~ adj, adv (lying) fallow
friction [friksjɔ̃] nf (massage) rub, rub-down;
(TECH, fig) friction; **frictionner** vt to rub
(down)
frigidaire ® [friʒidɛr] nm refrigerator
frigide [friʒid] adj frigid

frigo [fʀigo] (fam) nm fridge

frigorifié, e [fʀigɔʀifje] (fam) adj: être ~ to be frozen stiff

frigorifique [fʀigɔʀifik] adj refrigerating

frileux, -euse [fʀilø, øz] adj sensitive to (the) cold

frime [fʀim] (fam) nf: c'est de la ~ it's a lot of eyewash, it's all put on; **frimer** (fam) vi to show off

frimousse [fʀimus] nf (sweet) little face

fringale [fʀɛ̃gal] (fam) nf: avoir la ~ to be ravenous

fringant, e [fʀɛ̃gɑ̃, ɑ̃t] adj dashing

fringues [fʀɛ̃g] (fam) nfpl clothes

fripé, e [fʀipe] adj crumpled

fripon, ne [fʀipɔ̃, ɔn] adj roguish, mischievous ♦ nm/f rascal, rogue

fripouille [fʀipuj] nf scoundrel

frire [fʀiʀ] vt, vi: **faire ~** to fry

frisé, e [fʀize] adj (cheveux) curly; (personne) curly-haired

frisson [fʀisɔ̃] nm (de froid) shiver; (de peur) shudder; **frissonner** vi (de fièvre, froid) to shiver; (d'horreur) to shudder

frit, e [fʀi, fʀit] pp de **frire**; **frite** nf: (pommes) frites chips (BRIT), French fries; **friteuse** nf chip pan; **friture** nf (huile) (deep) fat; (plat): **friture (de poissons)** fried fish

frivole [fʀivɔl] adj frivolous

froid, e [fʀwa, fʀwad] adj, nm cold; **il fait ~** it's cold; **avoir/prendre ~** to be/catch cold; **être en ~ avec** to be on bad terms with; **froidement** adv (accueillir) coldly; (décider) coolly

froideur [fʀwadœʀ] nf coldness

froisser [fʀwase] vt to crumple (up), crease; (fig) to hurt, offend; **se ~** vi to crumple, crease; (personne) to take offence; **se ~ un muscle** to strain a muscle

frôler [fʀole] vt to brush against; (suj: projectile) to skim past; (fig) to come very close to

fromage [fʀɔmaʒ] nm cheese; **~ blanc** soft white cheese

froment [fʀɔmɑ̃] nm wheat

froncer [fʀɔ̃se] vt to gather; **~ les sourcils** to frown

frondaisons [fʀɔ̃dɛzɔ̃] nfpl foliage sg

front [fʀɔ̃] nm forehead, brow; (MIL) front; **de ~** (se heurter) head-on; (rouler) together (i.e. 2 or 3 abreast); (simultanément) at once; **faire ~ à** to face up to

frontalier, -ère [fʀɔ̃talje, jɛʀ] adj border cpd, frontier cpd

frontière [fʀɔ̃tjɛʀ] nf frontier, border

frotter [fʀɔte] vi to rub, scrape ♦ vt to rub; (pommes de terre, plancher) to scrub; **~ une allumette** to strike a match

fructifier [fʀyktifje] vi to yield a profit

fructueux, -euse [fʀyktɥø, øz] adj fruitful

frugal, e, -aux [fʀygal, o] adj frugal

fruit [fʀɥi] nm fruit gen no pl; **~ de la passion** passion fruit; **~s de mer** seafood(s); **~s secs** dried fruit sg; **fruité, e** adj fruity; **fruitier, -ère** adj: **arbre fruitier** fruit tree

fruste [fʀyst] adj unpolished, uncultivated

frustrer [fʀystʀe] vt to frustrate

FS abr (= franc suisse) SF

fuel(-oil) [fjul(ɔjl)] nm fuel oil; (domestique) heating oil

fugace [fygas] adj fleeting

fugitif, -ive [fyʒitif, iv] adj (fugace) fleeting ♦ nm/f fugitive

fugue [fyg] nf: **faire une ~** to run away, abscond

fuir [fɥiʀ] vt to flee from; (éviter) to shun ♦ vi to run away; (gaz, robinet) to leak

fuite [fɥit] nf flight; (écoulement, divulgation) leak; **être en ~** to be on the run; **mettre en ~** to put to flight

fulgurant, e [fylgyʀɑ̃, ɑ̃t] adj lightning cpd, dazzling

fulminer [fylmine] vi to thunder forth

fumé, e [fyme] adj (CULIN) smoked; (verre) tinted; **fumée** nf smoke

fumer [fyme] vi to smoke; (soupe) to steam ♦ vt to smoke

fûmes etc [fym] vb voir **être**

fumet [fymɛ] nm aroma

fumeur, -euse [fymœʀ, øz] nm/f smoker

fumeux, -euse [fymø, øz] (péj) adj woolly, hazy

fumier [fymje] nm manure

fumiste [fymist] nm/f (péj: paresseux) shirker

funèbre [fynɛbʀ] adj funeral cpd; (fig: atmosphère) gloomy

funérailles [fyneʀaj] nfpl funeral sg

funeste [fynɛst] adj (erreur) disastrous

fur [fyʀ]: **au ~ et à mesure** adv as one goes along; **au ~ et à mesure que** as

furet [fyʀɛ] nm ferret

fureter [fyʀ(ə)te] (péj) vi to, nose about

fureur [fyʀœʀ] nf fury; **être en ~** to be infuriated; **faire ~** to be all the rage

furibond, e [fyʀibɔ̃, ɔ̃d] adj furious

furie [fyʀi] nf fury; (femme) shrew, vixen; **en ~** (mer) raging; **furieux, -euse** adj furious

furoncle [fyʀɔ̃kl] nm boil

furtif, -ive [fyʀtif, iv] adj furtive

fus [fy] vb voir **être**

fusain [fyzɛ̃] nm (ART) charcoal

fuseau, x [fyzo] nm (pour filer) spindle; (pantalon) (ski) pants; **~ horaire** time zone

fusée [fyze] nf rocket; **~ éclairante** flare

fuser [fyze] vi (rires etc) to burst forth

fusible [fyzibl] nm (ÉLEC: fil) fuse wire; (: fiche) fuse

fusil [fyzi] nm (de guerre, à canon rayé) rifle, gun; (de chasse, à canon lisse) shotgun, gun; **fusillade** nf gunfire no pl, shooting no pl; **fusiller** vt to shoot; **fusil-mitrailleur** nm machine gun

fusionner [fyzjɔne] vi to merge

fut [fy] vb voir **être**

fût [fy] vb voir **être** ♦ nm (tonneau) barrel, cask

futé, e [fyte] adj crafty; **Bison ~** ® TV and radio traffic monitoring service

futile [fytil] adj futile; frivolous

futur, e [fytyʀ] adj, nm future

fuyant, e [fɥijã, ãt] vb voir **fuir** ♦ adj (regard etc) evasive; (lignes etc) receding

fuyard, e [fɥijaʀ, aʀd] nm/f runaway

G, g

gâcher [gɑʃe] vt (gâter) to spoil; (gaspiller) to waste; **gâchis** nm waste no pl

gadoue [gadu] nf sludge

gaffe [gaf] nf blunder; **faire ~** (fam) to be careful

gage [gaʒ] nm (dans un jeu) forfeit; (fig: de fidélité, d'amour) token

gageure [gaʒyʀ] nf: **c'est une ~** it's attempting the impossible

gagnant, e [gaɲã, ãt] nm/f winner

gagne-pain [gaɲpɛ̃] nm inv job

gagner [gaɲe] vt to win; (somme d'argent, revenu) to earn; (aller vers, atteindre) to reach; (envahir: sommeil, peur) to overcome; (: mal) to spread to ♦ vi to win; (fig) to gain; **~ du temps/de la place** to gain time/save space; **~ sa vie** to earn one's living

gai, e [ge] adj cheerful; (un peu ivre) merry; **gaiement** adv cheerfully; **gaieté** nf cheerfulness; **de gaieté de cœur** with a light heart

gaillard [gajaʀ, aʀd] nm (strapping) fellow

gain [gɛ̃] nm (revenu) earnings pl; (bénéfice: gén pl) profits pl

gaine [gɛn] nf (corset) girdle; (fourreau) sheath

gala [gala] nm official reception; **de ~** (soirée etc) gala

galant, e [galã, ãt] adj (courtois) courteous, gentlemanly; (entreprenant) flirtatious, gallant; (scène, rendez-vous) romantic

galère [galɛʀ] nf galley; **quelle ~!** (fam) it's a real grind!; **galérer** (fam) vi to slog away, work hard; (rencontrer les difficultés) to have a hassle

galerie [galʀi] nf gallery; (THÉÂTRE) circle; (de voiture) roof rack; (fig: spectateurs) audience; **~ de peinture** (private) art gallery; **~ marchande** shopping arcade

galet [galɛ] nm pebble

galette [galɛt] nf flat cake; **~ des Rois** cake eaten on Twelfth Night

galipette [galipɛt] nf somersault

Galles [gal] nfpl: **le pays de ~** Wales; **gallois, e** adj Welsh ♦ nm/f: **Gallois, e** Welshman(-woman) ♦ nm (LING) Welsh

galon [galɔ̃] nm (MIL) stripe; (décoratif) piece of braid

galop [galo] nm gallop; **galoper** vi to gallop

galopin [galɔpɛ̃] nm urchin, ragamuffin

gambader [gãbade] vi (animal, enfant) to leap about

gambas [gãbas] nfpl Mediterranean prawns

gamin, e [gamɛ̃, in] nm/f kid ♦ adj childish

gamme [gam] nf (MUS) scale; (fig) range

gammé, e [game] adj: **croix ~e** swastika

gang [gãg] nm (de criminels) gang

gant [gã] nm glove; **~ de toilette** face flannel (BRIT), face cloth

garage [gaʀaʒ] nm garage; **garagiste** nm/f garage owner; (employé) garage mechanic

garantie [gaʀɑ̃ti] nf guarantee; **(bon de) ~** guarantee ou warranty slip

garantir [gaʀɑ̃tiʀ] vt to guarantee

garce [gaʀs] (fam) nf bitch

garçon [gaʀsɔ̃] nm boy; (célibataire): **vieux ~** bachelor; (serveur): **~ (de café)** waiter; **~ de courses** messenger; **~ d'honneur** best man; **garçonnière** nf bachelor flat

garde [gaʀd(ə)] nm (de prisonnier) guard; (de domaine etc) warden; (soldat, sentinelle) guardsman ♦ nf (soldats) guard; **de ~** on duty; **monter la ~** to stand guard; **mettre en ~** to warn; **prendre ~ (à)** to be careful (of); **~ champêtre** nm rural policeman; **~ du corps** nm bodyguard; **~ des enfants** nf (après divorce) custody of the children; **~ à vue** nf (JUR) ≈ police custody; **garde-à-vous** nm: **être/se mettre au garde-à-vous** to be at/stand to attention; **garde-barrière** nm/f level-crossing keeper; **garde-boue** nm inv mudguard; **garde-chasse** nm game-keeper; **garde-malade** nf home nurse; **garde-manger** nm inv (armoire) meat safe; (pièce) pantry, larder

garder [gaʀde] vt (conserver) to keep; (surveiller: enfants) to look after; (: immeuble, lieu, prisonnier) to guard; **se ~** vi (aliment: se conserver) to keep; **se ~ de faire** to be careful not to do; **~ le lit/la chambre** to stay in bed/indoors; **pêche/chasse gardée** private fishing/hunting (ground)

garderie [gaʀdəʀi] nf day nursery, crèche

garde-robe [gaʀdəʀɔb] nf wardrobe

gardien, ne [gaʀdjɛ̃, jɛn] nm/f (garde) guard; (de prison) warder; (de domaine, réserve) warden; (de musée etc) attendant; (de phare, cimetière) keeper; (d'immeuble) caretaker; (fig) guardian; **~ de but**

goalkeeper; **~ de la paix** policeman; **~ de nuit** night watchman

gare [gaʀ] nf station; **~ routière** bus station

garer [gaʀe] vt to park; **se ~** vi to park

gargariser [gaʀgaʀize]: **se ~** vi to gargle

gargote [gaʀgɔt] nf cheap restaurant

gargouille [gaʀguj] nf gargoyle

gargouiller [gaʀguje] vi to gurgle

garnement [gaʀnəmã] nm rascal, scallywag

garni, e [gaʀni] adj (plat) served with vegetables (and chips or rice etc)

garnison [gaʀnizɔ̃] nf garrison

garniture [gaʀnityʀ] nf (CULIN) vegetables pl; **~ de frein** brake lining

gars [gɑ] (fam) nm guy

Gascogne [gaskɔɲ] nf Gascony; **le golfe de ~** the Bay of Biscay

gas-oil [gazɔjl] nm diesel (oid)

gaspiller [gaspije] vt to waste

gastronome [gastʀɔnɔm] nm/f gourmet; **gastronomie** nf gastronomy; **gastronomique** adj gastronomic

gâteau, x [gato] nm cake; **~ sec** biscuit

gâter [gate] vt to spoil; **se ~** vi (dent, fruit) to go bad; (temps, situation) to change for the worse

gâterie [gatʀi] nf little treat

gâteux, -euse [gatø, øz] adj senile

gauche [goʃ] adj left, left-hand; (maladroit) awkward, clumsy ♦ nf (POL) left (wing); **le bras ~** the left arm; **le côté ~** the left-hand side; **à ~** on the left; (direction) (to the) left; **gaucher, -ère** adj left-handed; **gauchiste** nm/f leftist

gaufre [gofʀ] nf waffle

gaufrette [gofʀɛt] nf wafer

gaulois, e [golwa, waz] adj Gallic ♦ nm/f: **G~, e** Gaul

gaver [gave] vt to force-feed; **se ~ de** to stuff o.s. with

gaz [gaz] nm inv gas

gaze [gaz] nf gauze

gazer [gaze] (fam) vi: **ça gaze?** how's things?

gazette [gazɛt] nf news sheet

gazeux, -euse [gazø, øz] adj (boisson) fizzy; (eau) sparkling

gazoduc [gazodyk] nm gas pipeline

gazon [gazɔ̃] nm (herbe) grass; (pelouse) lawn

gazouiller [gazuje] vi to chirp; (enfant) to babble

geai [ʒɛ] nm jay

géant, e [ʒeã, ãt] adj gigantic; (COMM) giant-size ♦ nm/f giant

geindre [ʒɛ̃dʀ] vi to groan, moan

gel [ʒɛl] nm frost

gélatine [ʒelatin] nf gelatine

gelée [ʒ(ə)le] nf jelly; (gel) frost

geler [ʒ(ə)le] vt, vi to freeze; **il gèle** it's freezing

gélule [ʒelyl] nf (MÉD) capsule

gelures [ʒəlyʀ] nfpl frostbite sg

Gémeaux [ʒemo] nmpl: **les ~** Gemini

gémir [ʒemiʀ] vi to groan, moan

gênant, e [ʒɛnã, ãt] adj (irritant) annoying; (embarrassant) embarrassing

gencive [ʒãsiv] nf gum

gendarme [ʒãdaʀm] nm gendarme; **gendarmerie** nf military police force in countryside and small towns; their police station or barracks

gendre [ʒãdʀ] nm son-in-law

gêné, e [ʒene] adj embarrassed

gêner [ʒene] vt (incommoder) to bother; (encombrer) to be in the way; (embarrasser) to make sb feel ill-at-ease; **~ qn** to make sb feel ill-at-ease

général, e, -aux [ʒeneʀal, o] adj, nm general; **en ~** usually, in general; **générale** nf: (répétition) générale final dress rehearsal; **généralement** adv generally; **généraliser** vt, vi to generalize; **se généraliser** vi to become widespread; **généraliste** nm/f general practitioner, G.P.

génération [ʒeneʀasjɔ̃] nf generation

généreux, -euse [ʒeneʀø, øz] adj generous

générique [ʒeneʀik] nm (CINÉMA) credits pl

générosité [ʒeneʀozite] nf generosity

genêt [ʒ(ə)nɛ] nm broom no pl (shrub)

génétique [ʒenetik] adj genetic

Genève [ʒ(ə)nɛv] n Geneva

génial, e, -aux [ʒenjal, jo] adj of genius; (fam: formidable) fantastic, brilliant

génie [ʒeni] nm genius; (MIL): **le ~** the Engineers pl; **~ civil** civil engineering

genièvre [ʒ(ə)njɛvʀ] nm juniper

génisse [ʒenis] nf heifer

génital, e, -aux [ʒenital, o] adj genital; **les parties ~es** the genitals

génoise [ʒenwaz] nf sponge cake

genou, x [ʒ(ə)nu] nm knee; **à ~x** on one's knees; **se mettre à ~x** to kneel down

genre [ʒãʀ] nm kind, type, sort; (LING) gender; **avoir bon ~** to look a nice sort; **avoir mauvais ~** to be coarse-looking; **ce n'est pas son ~** it's not like him

gens [ʒã] nmpl (f in some phrases) people pl

gentil, le [ʒãti, ij] adj kind; (enfant: sage) good; (endroit etc) nice; **gentillesse** nf kindness; **gentiment** adv kindly

géographie [ʒeɔgʀafi] nf geography

geôlier [ʒolje, jeʀ] nm jailer

géologie [ʒeɔlɔʒi] nf geology

géomètre [ʒeɔmɛtʀ] nm/f (arpenteur) (land) surveyor

géométrie [ʒeɔmetʀi] nf geometry; **géométrique** adj geometric

géranium [ʒeʀanjɔm] nm geranium

gérant, e [ʒeʀã, ãt] nm/f manager(-eress)

gerbe [ʒɛʀb] nf (de fleurs) spray; (de blé)

sheaf

gercé, e [ʒɛʀse] *adj* chapped

gerçure [ʒɛʀsyʀ] *nf* crack

gérer [ʒeʀe] *vt* to manage

germain, e [ʒɛʀmɛ̃, ɛn] *adj*: **cousin ~** first cousin

germe [ʒɛʀm] *nm* germ; **germer** *vi* to sprout; (*semence*) to germinate

geste [ʒɛst] *nm* gesture

gestion [ʒɛstjɔ̃] *nf* management

ghetto [geto] *nm* ghetto

gibet [ʒibɛ] *nm* gallows *pl*

gibier [ʒibje] *nm* (*animaux*) game

giboulée [ʒibule] *nf* sudden shower

gicler [ʒikle] *vi* to spurt, squirt

gifle [ʒifl] *nf* slap (in the face); **gifler** *vt* to slap (in the face)

gigantesque [ʒigɑ̃tɛsk] *adj* gigantic

gigogne [ʒigɔɲ] *adj*: **lits ~s** truckle (*BRIT*) ou trundle beds

gigot [ʒigo] *nm* leg (of mutton *ou* lamb)

gigoter [ʒigɔte] *vi* to wriggle (about)

gilet [ʒilɛ] *nm* waistcoat; (*pull*) cardigan; **~ de sauvetage** life jacket

gin [dʒin] *nm* gin; **~-tonic** gin and tonic

gingembre [ʒɛ̃ʒɑ̃bʀ] *nm* ginger

girafe [ʒiʀaf] *nf* giraffe

giratoire [ʒiʀatwaʀ] *adj*: **sens ~** roundabout

girofle [ʒiʀɔfl] *nf*: **clou de ~** clove

girouette [ʒiʀwɛt] *nf* weather vane *ou* cock

gitan, e [ʒitɑ̃, an] *nm/f* gipsy

gîte [ʒit] *nm* (*maison*) home; (*abri*) shelter; **~** (*rural*) holiday cottage *ou* apartment

givre [ʒivʀ] *nm* (hoar) frost; **givré, e** *adj* covered in frost; (*fam*: fou) nuts; **orange givrée** orange sorbet (*served in peel*)

glace [glas] *nf* ice; (*crème glacée*) ice cream; (*miroir*) mirror; (*de voiture*) window

glacé, e [glase] *adj* (*mains, vent, pluie*) freezing; (*lac*) frozen; (*boisson*) iced

glacer [glase] *vt* to freeze; (*gâteau*) to ice; (*fig*): **~ qn** (*intimider*) to chill sb; (*paralyser*) to make sb's blood run cold

glacial, e [glasjal, jo] *adj* icy

glacier [glasje] *nm* (*GÉO*) glacier; (*marchand*) ice-cream maker

glacière [glasjɛʀ] *nf* icebox

glaçon [glasɔ̃] *nm* icicle; (*pour boisson*) ice cube

glaïeul [glajœl] *nm* gladiolus

glaise [glɛz] *nf* clay

gland [glɑ̃] *nm* acorn; (*décoration*) tassel

glande [glɑ̃d] *nf* gland

glander [glɑ̃de] (*fam*) *vi* to fart around (*!*)

glauque [glok] *adj* dull blue-green

glissade [glisad] *nf* (*par jeu*) slide; (*chute*) slip; **faire des ~s sur la glace** to slide on the ice

glissant, e [glisɑ̃, ɑ̃t] *adj* slippery

glissement [glismɑ̃] *nm*: **~ de terrain** landslide

glisser [glise] *vi* (*avancer*) to glide *ou* slide along; (*coulisser, tomber*) to slide; (*déraper*) to slip; (*être glissant*) to be slippery ♦ *vt* to slip; **se ~ dans** to slip into

global, e, -aux [glɔbal, o] *adj* overall

globe [glɔb] *nm* globe

globule [glɔbyl] *nm* (*du sang*) corpuscle

globuleux, -euse [glɔbylø, øz] *adj*: **yeux ~** protruding eyes

gloire [glwaʀ] *nf* glory; **glorieux, -euse** *adj* glorious

glousser [gluse] *vi* to cluck; (*rire*) to chuckle; **gloussement** *nm* cluck; chuckle

glouton, ne [glutɔ̃, ɔn] *adj* gluttonous

gluant, e [glyɑ̃, ɑ̃t] *adj* sticky, gummy

glucose [glykoz] *nm* glucose

glycine [glisin] *nf* wisteria

goal [gol] *nm* goalkeeper

GO *sigle* (= *grandes ondes*) LW

gobelet [gɔblɛ] *nm* (*en étain, verre, argent*) tumbler; (*d'enfant, de pique-nique*) beaker; (*à dés*) cup

gober [gɔbe] *vt* to swallow (whole)

godasse [gɔdas] (*fam*) *nf* shoe

godet [gɔdɛ] *nm* pot

goéland [gɔelɑ̃] *nm* (sea)gull

goélette [gɔelɛt] *nf* schooner

gogo [gɔgo]: **à ~** *adv* galore

goguenard, e [gɔg(ə)naʀ, aʀd] *adj* mocking

goinfre [gwɛ̃fʀ] *nm* glutton

golf [gɔlf] *nm* golf; (*terrain*) golf course

golfe [gɔlf] *nm* gulf; (*petit*) bay

gomme [gɔm] *nf* (*à effacer*) rubber (*BRIT*), eraser; **gommer** *vt* to rub out (*BRIT*), erase

gond [gɔ̃] *nm* hinge; **sortir de ses ~s** (*fig*) to fly off the handle

gondoler [gɔ̃dɔle]: **se ~** *vi* (*planche*) to warp; (*métal*) to buckle

gonflé, e [gɔ̃fle] *adj* swollen; **il est ~** (*fam*: courageux) he's got some nerve; (*impertinent*) he's got a nerve

gonfler [gɔ̃fle] *vt* (*pneu, ballon*: en soufflant) to blow up; (: *avec une pompe*) to pump up; (*nombre, importance*) to inflate ♦ *vi* to swell (up); (*CULIN*: *pâte*) to rise; **gonfleur** *nm* pump

gonzesse [gɔ̃zɛs] (*fam*) *nf* chick, bird (*BRIT*)

goret [gɔʀɛ] *nm* piglet

gorge [gɔʀʒ] *nf* (*ANAT*) throat; (*vallée*) gorge

gorgé, e [gɔʀʒe] *adj*: **~ de** filled with; (*eau*) saturated with; **gorgée** *nf* (*petite*) sip; (*grande*) gulp

gorille [gɔʀij] *nm* gorilla; (*fam*) bodyguard

gosier [gozje] *nm* throat

gosse [gɔs] (*fam*) *nm/f* kid

goudron [gudʀɔ̃] *nm* tar; **goudronner** *vt* to tar(mac) (*BRIT*), asphalt (*US*)

gouffre [gufʀ] nm abyss, gulf

goujat [guʒa] nm boor

goulot [gulo] nm neck; **boire au ~** to drink from the bottle

goulu, e [guly] adj greedy

gourd, e [guʀ, guʀd] adj numb (with cold)

gourde [guʀd] nf (*récipient*) flask; (*fam*) (clumsy) clot *ou* oaf ♦ adj oafish

gourdin [guʀdɛ̃] nm club, bludgeon

gourer [guʀe] (*fam*): **se ~** vi to boob

gourmand, e [guʀmɑ̃, ɑ̃d] adj greedy; **gourmandise** [guʀmɑ̃diz] nf greed; (*bonbon*) sweet

gourmet [guʀmɛ] nm gourmet

gourmette [guʀmɛt] nf chain bracelet

gousse [gus] nf: **~ d'ail** clove of garlic

goût [gu] nm taste; **avoir bon ~** to taste good; **de bon ~** tasteful; **de mauvais ~** tasteless; **prendre ~ à** to develop a taste *ou* a liking for

goûter [gute] vt (*essayer*) to taste; (*apprécier*) to enjoy ♦ vi to have (afternoon) tea ♦ nm (afternoon) tea

goutte [gut] nf drop; (*MÉD*) gout; (*alcool*) brandy; **tomber ~ à ~** to drip; **goutte-à-goutte** nm (*MÉD*) drip

gouttelette [gut(ə)lɛt] nf droplet

gouttière [gutjɛʀ] nf gutter

gouvernail [guvɛʀnaj] nm rudder; (*barre*) helm, tiller

gouvernante [guvɛʀnɑ̃t] nf governess

gouvernement [guvɛʀnəmɑ̃] nm government

gouverner [guvɛʀne] vt to govern

grabuge [gʀaby3] (*fam*) nm mayhem

grâce [gʀas] nf (*charme*) grace; (*faveur*) favour; (*jur: pardon*) ~s nfpl (*REL*) grace sg; **faire ~ à qn de qch** to spare sb sth; **rendre ~(s) à** to give thanks to; **demander ~** to beg for mercy; **à ~** thanks to; **gracier** vt to pardon; **gracieux, -euse** adj graceful

grade [gʀad] nm rank; **monter en ~** to be promoted

gradin [gʀadɛ̃] nm tier; step; **~s** nmpl (*de stade*) terracing sg

gradué, e [gʀadɥe] adj: **verre ~** measuring jug

graduel, le [gʀadɥɛl] adj gradual

graduer [gʀadɥe] vt (*effort etc*) to increase gradually; (*règle, verre*) to graduate

graffiti [gʀafiti] nmpl graffiti

grain [gʀɛ̃] nm (*gén*) grain; (*NAVIG*) squall; **~ de beauté** beauty spot; **~ de café** coffee bean; **~ de poivre** peppercorn; **~ de poussière** speck of dust; **~ de raisin** grape

graine [gʀɛn] nf seed

graissage [gʀesa3] nm lubrication, greasing

graisse [gʀɛs] nf fat; (*lubrifiant*) grease; **graisser** vt to lubricate, grease; (*tacher*) to make greasy; **graisseux, -euse** adj greasy

grammaire [gʀa(m)mɛʀ] nf grammar; **grammatical, e, -aux** adj grammatical

gramme [gʀam] nm gramme

grand, e [gʀɑ̃, gʀɑ̃d] adj (*haut*) tall; (*gros, vaste, large*) big, large; (*long*) long; (*plus âgé*) big; (*adulte*) grown-up; (*sens abstraits*) great ♦ adv: **~ ouvert** wide open; **au ~ air** in the open (air); **les ~s blessés** the severely injured; **~ ensemble** housing scheme; **~ magasin** department store; **~e personne** grown-up; **~e surface** hypermarket; **~es écoles** prestige schools of university level; **~es lignes** (*RAIL*) main lines; **~es vacances** summer holidays; **grand-chose** [gʀɑ̃foz] nm/f inv: **pas grand-chose** not much; **Grande-Bretagne** nf (Great) Britain; **grandeur** nf (*dimension*) size; **grandeur nature** life-size; **grandiose** adj imposing; **grandir** vi to grow ♦ vt: **grandir qn** (suj: *vêtement, chaussure*) to make sb look taller; **grand-mère** nf grandmother; **grand-messe** nf high mass; **grand-peine**: **à grand-peine** adv with difficulty; **grand-père** nm grandfather; **grand-route** nf main road; **grands-parents** nmpl grandparents

grange [gʀɑ̃3] nf barn

granit(e) [gʀanit] nm granite

graphique [gʀafik] adj graphic ♦ nm graph

grappe [gʀap] nf cluster; **~ de raisin** bunch of grapes

gras, se [gʀɑ, gʀɑs] adj (*viande, soupe*) fatty; (*personne*) fat; (*surface, main*) greasy; (*plaisanterie*) coarse; (*TYPO*) bold ♦ nm (*CULIN*) fat; **faire la ~se matinée** to have a lie-in (*BRIT*), sleep late (*US*); **grassement** adv: **grassement payé** handsomely paid; **grassouillet, te** adj podgy, plump

gratifiant, e [gʀatifjɑ̃, jɑ̃t] adj gratifying, rewarding

gratin [gʀatɛ̃] nm (*plat*) cheese-topped dish; (*croûte*) cheese topping; **gratiné, e** adj (*CULIN*) au gratin

gratis [gʀatis] adv free

gratitude [gʀatityd] nf gratitude

gratte-ciel [gʀatsjɛl] nm inv skyscraper

gratte-papier [gʀatpapje] (*péj*) nm inv penpusher

gratter [gʀate] vt (*avec un outil*) to scrape; (*enlever: avec un outil*) to scrape off; (: *avec un ongle*) to scratch; (*enlever avec un ongle*) to scratch off ♦ vi (*irriter*) to be scratchy; (*démanger*) to itch; **se ~** to scratch (o.s.)

gratuit, e [gʀatɥi, ɥit] adj (*entrée, billet*) free; (*fig*) gratuitous

gravats [gʀava] nmpl rubble sg

grave [gʀav] adj (*maladie, accident*) serious, bad; (*sujet, problème*) serious, grave; (*air*) grave, solemn; (*voix, son*) deep, low-pitched; **gravement** adv seriously; (*parler, regarder*)

gravely
graver [gʀave] vt to engrave
gravier [gʀavje] nm gravel no pl; **gravillons** nmpl loose chippings ou gravel sg
gravir [gʀaviʀ] vt to climb (up)
gravité [gʀavite] nf (de maladie, d'accident) seriousness; (de sujet, problème) gravity
graviter [gʀavite] vi to revolve
gravure [gʀavyʀ] nf engraving; (reproduction) print
gré [gʀe] nm: **de bon ~** willingly; **contre le ~ de qn** against sb's will; **de son (plein) ~** of one's own free will; **bon ~ mal ~** like it or not; **de ~ ou de force** whether one likes it or not; **savoir ~ à qn de qch** to be grateful to sb for sth
grec, grecque [gʀɛk] adj Greek; (classique: vase etc) Grecian ♦ nm/f: **G~, Grecque** Greek ♦ nm (LING) Greek
Grèce [gʀɛs] nf: **la ~** Greece
greffe [gʀɛf] nf (BOT, MÉD: de tissu) graft; (MÉD: d'organe) transplant; **greffer** vt (BOT, MÉD: tissu) to graft; (MÉD: organe) to transplant
greffier [gʀefje, jɛʀ] nm clerk of the court
grêle [gʀɛl] adj (very) thin ♦ nf hail; **grêler** vb impers: **il grêle** it's hailing; **grêlon** nm hailstone
grelot [gʀəlo] nm little bell
grelotter [gʀəlɔte] vi to shiver
grenade [gʀənad] nf (explosive) grenade; (BOT) pomegranate; **grenadine** nf grenadine
grenat [gʀəna] adj inv dark red
grenier [gʀənje] nm attic; (de ferme) loft
grenouille [gʀənuj] nf frog
grès [gʀɛ] nm sandstone; (poterie) stoneware
grésiller [gʀezije] vi to sizzle; (RADIO) to crackle
grève [gʀɛv] nf (d'ouvriers) strike; (plage) shore; **se mettre en/faire ~** to go on/be on strike; **~ de la faim** hunger strike; **~ du zèle** work-to-rule (BRIT), slowdown (US); **~ sauvage** wildcat strike
gréviste [gʀevist] nm/f striker
gribouiller [gʀibuje] vt to scribble, scrawl
grièvement [gʀijɛvmã] adv seriously
griffe [gʀif] nf claw; (de couturier) label; **griffer** vt to scratch
griffonner [gʀifɔne] vt to scribble
grignoter [gʀiɲɔte] vt (personne) to nibble at; (souris) to gnaw at ♦ vi to nibble
gril [gʀil] nm steak ou grill pan; **faire cuire au ~** to grill; **grillade** nf (viande etc) grill
grillage [gʀijaʒ] nm (treillis) wire netting; (clôture) wire fencing
grille [gʀij] nf (clôture) wire fence; (portail) (metad) gate; (d'égout) (metad) grate; (fig) grid
grille-pain [gʀijpɛ̃] nm inv toaster

griller [gʀije] vt (pain) to toast; (viande) to grill; (fig: ampoule etc) to blow; **faire ~** toast; to grill; (châtaignes) to roast; **~ un feu rouge** to jump the lights
grillon [gʀijɔ̃] nm cricket
grimace [gʀimas] nf grimace; (pour faire rire): **faire des ~s** to pull ou make faces
grimper [gʀɛ̃pe] vi, vt to climb
grincer [gʀɛ̃se] vi (objet métallique) to grate; (plancher, porte) to creak; **~ des dents** to grind one's teeth
grincheux, -euse [gʀɛ̃ʃø, øz] adj grumpy
grippe [gʀip] nf flu, influenza; **grippé, e** adj: **être grippé** to have flu
gris, e [gʀi, gʀiz] adj grey; (ivre) tipsy
grisaille [gʀizaj] nf greyness, dullness
griser [gʀize] vt to intoxicate
grisonner [gʀizɔne] vi to be going grey
grisou [gʀizu] nm firedamp
grive [gʀiv] nf thrush
grivois, e [gʀivwa, waz] adj saucy
Groenland [gʀɔenlãd] nm Greenland
grogner [gʀɔɲe] vi to growl; (fig) to grumble; **grognon, ne** adj grumpy
groin [gʀwɛ̃] nm snout
grommeler [gʀɔm(ə)le] vi to mutter to o.s.
gronder [gʀɔ̃de] vi to rumble; (fig: révolte) to be brewing ♦ vt to scold; **se faire ~** to get a telling-off
groom [gʀum] nm bellboy
gros, se [gʀo, gʀos] adj big, large; (obèse) fat; (travaux, dégâts) extensive; (épais) thick; (rhume, averse) heavy ♦ adv: **risquer/gagner ~** to risk/win a lot ♦ nm/f fat man/woman ♦ nm (COMM): **le ~** the wholesale business; **prix de ~** wholesale price; **par ~ temps/grosse mer** in rough weather/heavy seas; **en ~** roughly; (COMM) wholesale; **~ lot** jackpot; **~ mot** coarse word; **~ plan** (PHOTO) close-up; **~ sel** cooking salt; **~ titre** headline; **~se caisse** big drum
groseille [gʀozɛj] nf: **~ (rouge/blanche)** red/white currant; **~ à maquereau** gooseberry
grosse [gʀos] adj voir gros; **grossesse** nf pregnancy; **grosseur** nf size; (tumeur) lump
grossier, -ière [gʀosje, jɛʀ] adj coarse; (insolent) rude; (dessin) rough; (travail) roughly done; (imitation, instrument) crude; (évident: erreur) gross; **grossièrement** adv (sommairement) roughly; (vulgairement) coarsely; **grossièretés** nfpl: **dire des grossièretés** to use coarse language
grossir [gʀosiʀ] vi (personne) to put on weight ♦ vt (exagérer) to exaggerate; (au microscope) to magnify; (suj: vêtement): **~ qn** to make sb look fatter
grossiste [gʀosist] nm/f wholesaler
grosso modo [gʀosomɔdo] adv roughly
grotesque [gʀɔtɛsk] adj (extravagant)

grotesque; (*ridicule*) ludicrous

grotte [gʀɔt] *nf* cave

grouiller [gʀuje] *vi*: ~ **de** to be swarming with; **se ~** (*fam*) ♦ *vi* to get a move on; **grouillant, e** *adj* swarming

groupe [gʀup] *nm* group; **le ~ des 7** Group of 7; **~ sanguin** blood group; **groupement** *nm* (*action*) grouping; (*groupe*) group; **grouper** *vt* to group; **se grouper** *vi* to gather

grue [gʀy] *nf* crane

grumeaux [gʀymo] *nmpl* lumps

guenilles [gənij] *nfpl* rags

guenon [gənɔ̃] *nf* female monkey

guépard [gepaʀ] *nm* cheetah

guêpe [gɛp] *nf* wasp

guêpier [gepje] *nm* (*fig*) trap

guère [gɛʀ] *adv* (*avec adjectif, adverbe*): **ne ... ~** hardly; (*avec verbe*): **ne ... ~** (*pas beaucoup*) *tournure négative +much*; (*pas souvent*) hardly ever; (*pas longtemps*) *tournure négative +(very)* long; **il n'y a ~ que/de** there's hardly anybody (*ou* anything) but/hardly any; **ce n'est ~ difficile** it's hardly difficult; **nous n'avons ~ de temps** we have hardly any time

guéridon [geʀidɔ̃] *nm* pedestal table

guérilla [geʀija] *nf* guerrilla warfare

guérillero [geʀijeʀo] *nm* guerrilla

guérir [geʀiʀ] *vt* (*personne, maladie*) to cure; (*membre, plaie*) to heal ♦ *vi* (*malade, maladie*) to be cured; (*blessure*) to heal; **guérison** *nf* (*de maladie*) curing; (*de membre, plaie*) healing; (*de malade*) recovery; **guérisseur, -euse** *nm/f* healer

guerre [gɛʀ] *nf* war; **~ civile** civil war; **en ~** at war; **faire la ~ à** to wage war against; **guerrier, -ière** *adj* warlike ♦ *nm/f* warrior

guet [gɛ] *nm*: **faire le ~** to be on the watch *ou* look-out; **guet-apens** [getapɑ̃] *nm* ambush; **guetter** *vt* (*épier*) to watch (intently); (*attendre*) to watch (out) for; (*hostilement*) to be lying in wait for

gueule [gœl] *nf* (*d'animal*) mouth; (*fam: figure*) face; (: *bouche*) mouth; **ta ~!** (*fam*) shut up!; **~ de bois** (*fam*) hangover; **gueuler** (*fam*) *vi* to bawl; **gueuleton** (*fam*) *nm* blow-out

gui [gi] *nm* mistletoe

guichet [giʃɛ] *nm* (*de bureau, banque*) counter; **les ~s** (*à la gare, au théâtre*) the ticket office *sg*; **~ automatique** cash dispenser (*BRIT*), automatic telling machine (*US*)

guide [gid] *nm* guide ♦ *nf* (*éclaireuse*) girl guide; **guider** *vt* to guide

guidon [gidɔ̃] *nm* handlebars *pl*

guignol [giɲɔl] *nm* ≈ Punch and Judy show; (*fig*) clown

guillemets [gijmɛ] *nmpl*: **entre ~** in inverted commas

guillotiner [gijɔtine] *vt* to guillotine

guindé, e [gɛ̃de] *adj* (*personne, air*) stiff, starchy; (*style*) stilted

guirlande [giʀlɑ̃d] *nf* (*fleurs*) garland; **~ de Noël** tinsel garland; **~ lumineuse** string of fairy lights; **~ de papier** paper chain

guise [giz] *nf*: **à votre ~** as you wish *ou* please; **en ~ de** by way of

guitare [gitaʀ] *nf* guitar

gym [ʒim] *nf* (*exercices*) gym; **gymnase** *nm* gym(nasium); **gymnaste** *nm/f* gymnast; **gymnastique** *nf* gymnastics *sg*; (*au réveil etc*) keep-fit exercises *pl*

gynécologie [ʒinekɔlɔʒi] *nf* gynaecology; **gynécologique** *adj* gynaecological; **gynécologue** *nm/f* gynaecologist

H, h

habile [abil] *adj* skilful; (*malin*) clever; **habileté** [abilte] *nf* skill, skilfulness; cleverness

habillé, e [abije] *adj* dressed; (*chic*) dressy

habillement [abijmɑ̃] *nm* clothes *pl*

habiller [abije] *vt* to dress; (*fournir en vêtements*) to clothe; **s'~** *vi* to dress (o.s.); (*se déguiser, mettre des vêtements chic*) to dress up

habit [abi] *nm* outfit; **~s** *nmpl* (*vêtements*) clothes; **~ (de soirée)** evening dress; (*pour homme*) tails *pl*

habitant, e [abitɑ̃, ɑ̃t] *nm/f* inhabitant; (*d'une maison*) occupant; **loger chez l'~** to stay with the locals

habitation [abitasjɔ̃] *nf* house; **~s à loyer modéré** (block of) council flats

habiter [abite] *vt* to live in ♦ *vi*: **~ à/dans** to live in

habitude [abityd] *nf* habit; **avoir l'~ de faire** to be in the habit of doing; (*expérience*) to be used to doing; **d'~** usually; **comme d'~** as usual

habitué, e [abitɥe] *nm/f* (*de maison*) regular visitor; (*de café*) regular (customer)

habituel, le [abitɥɛl] *adj* usual

habituer [abitɥe] *vt*: **~ qn à** to get sb used to; **s'~ à** to get used to

'hache [ʼaʃ] *nf* axe

'hacher [ʼaʃe] *vt* (*viande*) to mince; (*persil*) to chop; **'hachis** *nm* mince *no pl*; **hachis Parmentier** ≈ shepherd's pie

'hachisch [ʼaʃiʃ] *nm* hashish

'hachoir [ʼaʃwaʀ] *nm* (*couteau*) chopper; (*appareil*) (meat) mincer; (*planche*) chopping board

'hagard, e [ʼagaʀ, aʀd] *adj* wild, distraught

'haie [ʼɛ] *nf* hedge; (*SPORT*) hurdle

'haillons [ʼajɔ̃] *nmpl* rags

'haine [ʼɛn] *nf* hatred

'**haïr** ['aiʀ] vt to detest, hate

'**hâlé, e** ['ɑle] adj (sun)tanned, sunburnt

haleine [alɛn] nf breath; **hors d'~** out of breath; **tenir en ~** (attention) to hold spellbound; (incertitude) to keep in suspense; **de longue ~** long-term

'**haleter** ['alte] vt to pant

'**hall** ['ol] nm hall

'**halle** ['al] nf (covered) market; **~s** nfpl (d'une grande ville) central food market sg

'**hallucinant, e** [alysinɑ̃, ɑ̃t] adj staggering

hallucination [alysinasjɔ̃] nf hallucination

'**halte** ['alt] nf stop, break; (endroit) stopping place ♦ excl stop!; **faire ~** to stop

haltère [altɛʀ] nm dumbbell, barbell; **~s** nmpl: (**poids et) ~s** (activité) weightlifting sg; **haltérophilie** nf weightlifting

'**hamac** ['amak] nm hammock

'**hamburger** ['ɑ̃buʀgœʀ] nm hamburger

'**hameau, x** ['amo] nm hamlet

hameçon [amsɔ̃] nm (fish) hook

'**hanche** ['ɑ̃ʃ] nf hip

'**hand-ball** ['ɑ̃dbal] nm handball

'**handicapé, e** ['ɑ̃dikape] nm/f physically (ou mentally) handicapped person; **~ moteur** spastic

'**hangar** ['ɑ̃gaʀ] nm shed; (AVIAT) hangar

'**hanneton** ['ɑ̃tɔ̃] nm cockchafer

'**hanter** ['ɑ̃te] vt to haunt

'**hantise** ['ɑ̃tiz] nf obsessive fear

'**happer** ['ape] vt to snatch; (suj: train etc) to hit

'**haras** ['aʀɑ] nm stud farm

'**harassant, e** ['aʀasɑ̃, ɑ̃t] adj exhausting

'**harcèlement** ['aʀsɛlmɑ̃] nm harassment; **~ sexuel** sexual harassment

'**harceler** ['aʀsəle] vt to harass; **~ qn de questions** to plague sb with questions

'**hardi, e** ['aʀdi] adj bold, daring

'**hareng** ['aʀɑ̃] nm herring

'**hargne** ['aʀɲ] nf aggressiveness; '**hargneux, -euse** adj aggressive

'**haricot** ['aʀiko] nm bean; **~ blanc** haricot bean; **~ vert** green bean; **~ rouge** kidney bean

harmonica [aʀmɔnika] nm mouth organ

harmonie [aʀmɔni] nf harmony; **harmonieux, -euse** adj harmonious; (couleurs, couple) well-matched

'**harnacher** ['aʀnaʃe] vt to harness

'**harnais** ['aʀnɛ] nm harness

'**harpe** ['aʀp] nf harp

'**harponner** ['aʀpɔne] vt to harpoon; (fam) to collar

'**hasard** ['azaʀ] nm: **le ~** chance, fate; **un ~** a coincidence; **au ~** (aller) aimlessly; (choisir) at random; **par ~** by chance; **à tout ~** (en cas de besoin) just in case; (en espérant trouver ce qu'on cherche) on the off chance (BRIT);

'**hasarder** vt (mot) to venture; **se hasarder à faire** to risk doing

'**hâte** ['ɑt] nf haste; **à la ~** hurriedly, hastily; **en ~** posthaste, with all possible speed; **avoir ~ de** to be eager ou anxious to; '**hâter** vt to hasten; **se hâter** vi to hurry; '**hâtif, -ive** adj (travail) hurried; (décision, jugement) hasty

'**hausse** ['os] nf rise, increase; **être en ~** to be going up; '**hausser** vt to raise; **hausser les épaules** to shrug (one's shoulders)

'**haut, e** ['o, 'ot] adj high; (grand) tall ♦ adv high ♦ nm top (part); **de 3 m ~** 3 m high, 3 m in height; **des ~s et des bas** ups and downs; **en ~ lieu** in high places; **à ~e voix, (tout)** aloud, out loud; **du ~ de** from the top of; **de ~ en bas** from top to bottom; **plus ~** higher up, further up; (dans un texte) above; (parler) louder; **en ~** (être/aller) at/to the top; (dans une maison) upstairs; **en ~ de** at the top of

'**hautain, e** ['otɛ̃, ɛn] adj haughty

'**hautbois** ['obwa] nm oboe

'**haut-de-forme** ['odfɔʀm] nm top hat

'**hauteur** ['otœʀ] nf height; **à la ~ de** (accident) near; (fig: tâche, situation) equal to; **à la ~** (fig) up to it

'**haut...:** '**haut-fourneau** nm blast ou smelting furnace; '**haut-le-cœur** nm inv retch, heave; '**haut-parleur** nm (loud)speaker

'**havre** ['avʀ] nm haven

'**Haye** ['ɛ] nf: **la ~** the Hague

'**hayon** ['ejɔ̃] nm hatchback

hebdo [ebdo] (fam) nm weekly

hebdomadaire [ebdɔmadɛʀ] adj, nm weekly

hébergement [ebɛʀʒəmɑ̃] nm accommodation

héberger [ebɛʀʒe] vt (touristes) to accommodate, lodge; (amis) to put up; (réfugiés) to take in

hébété, e [ebete] adj dazed

hébreu, x [ebʀø] adj m, nm Hebrew

hécatombe [ekatɔ̃b] nf slaughter

hectare [ɛktaʀ] nm hectare

'**hein** ['ɛ̃] excl eh?

'**hélas** ['elɑs] excl alas! ♦ adv unfortunately

'**héler** ['ele] vt to hail

hélice [elis] nf propeller

hélicoptère [elikɔptɛʀ] nm helicopter

helvétique [ɛlvetik] adj Swiss

hématome [ematom] nm nasty bruise

hémicycle [emisikl] nm (POL): **l'~ ≈** the benches (of the Commons) (BRIT); **≈** the floor (of the House of Representatives) (US)

hémisphère [emisfɛʀ] nm: **l'~ nord/sud** the northern/southern hemisphere

hémorragie [emɔʀaʒi] nf bleeding no pl, haemorrhage

hémorroïdes [emɔʀɔid] *nfpl* piles, haemorrhoids

'**hennir** ['eniʀ] *vi* to neigh, whinny; '**hennissement** *nm* neigh, whinny

hépatite [epatit] *nf* hepatitis

herbe [ɛʀb] *nf* grass; (*CULIN, MÉD*) herb; ~s **de Provence** mixed herbs; **en** ~ unripe; (*fig*) budding; **herbicide** *nm* weed-killer; **herboriste** *nm/f* herbalist

'**hère** ['ɛʀ] *nm*: **pauvre** ~ poor wretch

héréditaire [eʀeditɛʀ] *adj* hereditary

'**hérisser** ['eʀise] *vt*: ~ **qn** (*fig*) to ruffle sb; **se** ~ *vi* to bristle, bristle up; '**hérisson** *nm/f* hedgehog

héritage [eʀitaʒ] *nm* inheritance; (*coutumes, système*) heritage, legacy

hériter [eʀite] *vi*: ~ **de qch (de qn)** to inherit sth (from sb); **héritier, -ière** [eʀitje, jɛʀ] *nm/f* heir(-ess)

hermétique [ɛʀmetik] *adj* airtight; watertight; (*fig: obscur*) abstruse; (: *impénétrable*) impenetrable

hermine [ɛʀmin] *nf* ermine

'**hernie** ['ɛʀni] *nf* hernia

héroïne [eʀɔin] *nf* heroine; (*drogue*) heroin

héroïque [eʀɔik] *adj* heroic

'**héron** ['eʀɔ̃] *nm* heron

'**héros** ['eʀo] *nm* hero

hésitant, e [ezitɑ̃, ɑ̃t] *adj* hesitant

hésitation [ezitasjɔ̃] *nf* hesitation

hésiter [ezite] *vi*: ~ (**à faire**) to hesitate (to do)

hétéroclite [eteʀɔklit] *adj* heterogeneous; (*objets*) sundry

hétérogène [eteʀɔʒɛn] *adj* heterogeneous

hétérosexuel, le [eteʀɔsɛkɥɛl] *adj* heterosexual

'**hêtre** ['ɛtʀ] *nm* beech

heure [œʀ] *nf* hour; (*SCOL*) period; (*moment*) time; **c'est l'**~ it's time; **quelle** ~ **est-il?** what time is it?; **2** ~**s (du matin)** 2 o'clock (in the morning); **être à l'**~ to be on time; (*montre*) to be right; **mettre à l'**~ to set right; **à une** ~ **avancée (de la nuit)** at a late hour of the night; **à toute** ~ at any time; **24** ~**s sur 24** round the clock, 24 hours a day; **à l'**~ **qu'il est** at this time (of day); **by now**; **sur l'**~ at once; ~ **de pointe** rush hour; (*téléphone*) peak period; ~ **d'affluence** rush hour; ~**s creuses** slack periods; (*pour électricité, téléphone etc*) off-peak periods; ~**s supplémentaires** overtime *sg*

heureusement [œʀøzmɑ̃] *adv* (*par bonheur*) fortunately, luckily

heureux, -euse [œʀø, øz] *adj* happy; (*chanceux*) lucky, fortunate

'**heurter** ['œʀte] *vt* (*mur*) to strike, hit; (*personne*) to collide with; **se** ~ **à** *vt* (*fig*) to come up against

'**heurts** ['œʀ] *nmpl* (*fig*) clashes

hexagone [ɛgzagɔn] *nm* hexagon; (*la France*) France (*because of its shape*)

hiberner [ibɛʀne] *vi* to hibernate

'**hibou, x** ['ibu] *nm* owl

'**hideux, -euse** ['idø, øz] *adj* hideous

hier [jɛʀ] *adv* yesterday; ~ **soir** last night, yesterday evening; **toute la journée d'**~ all day yesterday; **toute la matinée d'**~ all yesterday morning

'**hiérarchie** ['jeʀaʀʃi] *nf* hierarchy

'**hi-fi** ['ifi] *adj inv* hi-fi ♦ *nf* hi-fi

hilare [ilaʀ] *adj* mirthful

hindou, e [ɛ̃du] *adj* Hindu ♦ *nm/f*: **H~, e** Hindu

hippique [ipik] *adj* equestrian, horse *cpd*; **un club** ~ a riding centre; **un concours** ~ a horse show; **hippisme** *nm* (horse)riding

hippodrome [ipɔdʀom] *nm* racecourse

hippopotame [ipɔpɔtam] *nm* hippopotamus

hirondelle [iʀɔ̃dɛl] *nf* swallow

hirsute [iʀsyt] *adj* (*personne*) shaggy-haired; (*barbe*) shaggy; (*tête*) tousled

'**hisser** ['ise] *vt* to hoist, haul up; **se** ~ *vi* to heave o.s. up

histoire [istwaʀ] *nf* (*science, événements*) history; (*anecdote, récit, mensonge*) story; (*affaire*) business *no pl*; ~**s** *nfpl* (*chichis*) fuss *no pl*; (*ennuis*) trouble *sg*; **historique** *adj* historical; (*important*) historic

'**hit-parade** ['itpaʀad] *nm*: **le** ~-~ the charts

hiver [ivɛʀ] *nm* winter; **hivernal, e, -aux** *adj* winter *cpd*; (*glacial*) wintry; **hiverner** *vi* to winter

HLM *nm ou f* (= *habitation à loyer modéré*) council flat; **des HLM** council housing

'**hobby** ['ɔbi] *nm* hobby

'**hocher** ['ɔʃe] *vt*: ~ **la tête** to nod; (*signe négatif ou dubitatif*) to shake one's head

'**hochet** ['ɔʃɛ] *nm* rattle

'**hockey** ['ɔkɛ] *nm*: ~ (**sur glace/gazon**) (ice/ field) hockey

'**hold-up** ['ɔldœp] *nm inv* hold-up

'**hollandais, e** ['ɔlɑ̃dɛ, ɛz] *adj* Dutch ♦ *nm* (*LING*) Dutch ♦ *nm/f*: **H~, e** Dutchman(-woman); **les H~** the Dutch

'**Hollande** ['ɔlɑ̃d] *nf*: **la** ~ Holland

'**homard** ['ɔmaʀ] *nm* lobster

homéopathique [ɔmeɔpatik] *adj* homoeopathic

homicide [ɔmisid] *nm* murder; ~ **involontaire** manslaughter

hommage [ɔmaʒ] *nm* tribute; ~**s** *nmpl*: **présenter ses** ~**s** to pay one's respects; **rendre** ~ **à** to pay tribute ou homage to

homme [ɔm] *nm* man; ~ **d'affaires** businessman; ~ **d'État** statesman; ~ **de main** hired man; ~ **de paille** stooge; ~ **politique**

politician; **homme-grenouille** nm frogman
homo...: homogène adj homogeneous;
homologue nm/f counterpart;
homologué, e adj (SPORT) ratified; (tarif)
authorized; **homonyme** nm (LING)
homonym; (d'une personne) namesake;
homosexuel, le adj homosexual
'**Hongrie** ['ɔ̃gʀi] nf: **la ~** Hungary;
'**hongrois, e** adj Hungarian ♦ nm/f:
Hongrois, e Hungarian ♦ nm (LING) Hungarian
honnête [ɔnɛt] adj (intègre) honest; (juste,
satisfaisant) fair; (honnêtement) adv
honestly; **honnêteté** nf honesty
honneur [ɔnœʀ] nm honour; (mérite) credit;
en l'~ de in honour of; (événement) on the
occasion of; **faire ~ à** (engagements) to
honour; (famille) to be a credit to; (fig: repas
etc) to do justice to
honorable [ɔnɔʀabl] adj worthy,
honourable; (suffisant) decent
honoraire [ɔnɔʀɛʀ] adj honorary; **professeur
~** professor emeritus; **honoraires** [ɔnɔʀɛʀ]
nmpl fees pl
honorer [ɔnɔʀe] vt to honour; (estimer) to
hold in high regard; (faire honneur à) to do
credit to; **honorifique** [ɔnɔʀifik] adj
honorary
'**honte** ['ɔ̃t] nf shame; **avoir ~ de** to be
ashamed of; **faire ~ à qn** to make sb (feel)
ashamed; '**honteux, -euse** adj ashamed;
(conduite, acte) shameful, disgraceful
hôpital, -aux [ɔpital, o] nm hospital
'**hoquet** ['ɔkɛ] nm: **avoir le ~** to have (the)
hiccoughs; '**hoqueter** vi to hiccough
horaire [ɔʀɛʀ] adj hourly ♦ nm timetable,
schedule; **~s** nmpl (d'employé) hours;
~ souple flexitime
horizon [ɔʀizɔ̃] nm horizon
horizontal, e, -aux [ɔʀizɔ̃tal, o] adj
horizontal
horloge [ɔʀlɔʒ] nf clock; **l'~ parlante** the
speaking clock; **horloger, -ère** nm/f
watchmaker; clockmaker
'**hormis** ['ɔʀmi] prép save
horoscope [ɔʀɔskɔp] nm horoscope
horreur [ɔʀœʀ] nf horror; **quelle ~!** how
awful!; **avoir ~ de** to loathe ou detest;
horrible adj horrible; **horrifier** vt to horrify
horripiler [ɔʀipile] vt to exasperate
'**hors** ['ɔʀ] prép: **~ de** out of; **~ pair**
outstanding; **~ de propos** inopportune; **être
~ de soi** to be beside o.s.; **~ d'usage** out of
service; '**hors-bord** nm inv speedboat (with
outboard motor); '**hors-d'œuvre** nm inv hors
d'œuvre; '**hors-jeu** nm inv offside; '**hors-
la-loi** nm inv outlaw; '**hors-taxe** adj
(boutique, articles) duty-free
hortensia [ɔʀtɑ̃sja] nm hydrangea
hospice [ɔspis] nm (de vieillards) home

hospitalier, -ière [ɔspitalje, jɛʀ] adj
(accueillant) hospitable; (MÉD: service, centre)
hospital cpd
hospitaliser [ɔspitalize] vt to take/send to
hospital, hospitalize
hospitalité [ɔspitalite] nf hospitality
hostie [ɔsti] nf host (REL)
hostile [ɔstil] adj hostile; **hostilité** nf hostility
hosto [ɔsto] (fam) nm hospital
hôte [ot] nm (maître de maison) host; (invité)
guest
hôtel [otɛl] nm hotel; **aller à l'~** to stay in a
hotel; **~ de ville** town hall; **~ (particulier)**
(private) mansion; **hôtelier, -ière** adj hotel
cpd ♦ nm/f hotelier; **hôtellerie** nf hotel
business
hôtesse [otɛs] nf hostess; **~ de l'air** air
stewardess; **~ (d'accueil)** receptionist
'**hotte** ['ɔt] nf (panier) basket (carried on the
back); **~ aspirante** cooker hood
'**houblon** ['ublɔ̃] nm (BOT) hop; (pour la
bière) hops pl
'**houille** ['uj] nf coal; **~ blanche** hydroelectric
power
'**houle** ['ul] nf swell; '**houleux, -euse** adj
stormy
'**houligan** ['uligɑ̃] nm hooligan
'**hourra** ['uʀa] excl hurrah!
'**houspiller** ['uspije] vt to scold
'**housse** ['us] nf cover
'**houx** ['u] nm holly
'**hublot** ['yblo] nm porthole
'**huche** ['yʃ] nf: **~ à pain** bread bin
'**huer** ['ɥe] vt to boo
huile [ɥil] nf oil; **~ solaire** suntan oil; **huiler** vt
to oil; **huileux, -euse** adj oily
huis [ɥi] nm: **à ~ clos** in camera
huissier [ɥisje] nm usher; (JUR) ≈ bailiff
'**huit** ['ɥi(t)] num eight; **samedi en ~** a week
on Saturday; **dans ~ jours** in a week;
'**huitaine** nf: **une huitaine (de jours)** a week
or so; '**huitième** num eighth
huître [ɥitʀ] nf oyster
humain, e [ymɛ̃, ɛn] adj human;
(compatissant) humane ♦ nm human
(being); **humanitaire** adj humanitarian;
humanité nf humanity
humble [œ̃bl] adj humble
humecter [ymɛkte] vt to dampen
'**humer** ['yme] vt (plat) to smell; (parfum) to
inhale
humeur [ymœʀ] nf mood; **de bonne/
mauvaise ~** in a good/bad mood
humide [ymid] adj damp; (main, yeux)
moist; (climat, chaleur) humid; (saison, route)
wet
humilier [ymilje] vt to humiliate
humilité [ymilite] nf humility, humbleness
humoristique [ymɔʀistik] adj humorous

humour [ymur] nm humour; **avoir de l'~** to have a sense of humour; **~ noir** black humour

'huppé, e ['ype] (fam) adj posh

'hurlement ['yrləmã] nm howling no pl, howl, yelling no pl, yell

'hurler ['yrle] vi to howl, yell

hurluberlu [yrlybɛrly] (péj) nm crank

'hutte ['yt] nf hut

hybride [ibrid] adj, nm hybrid

hydratant, e [idratã, ãt] adj (crème) moisturizing

hydraulique [idrolik] adj hydraulic

hydravion [idravjɔ̃] nm seaplane

- **hydrogène** [idrɔʒɛn] nm hydrogen

hydroglisseur [idrɔglisœr] nm hydroplane

hyène [jɛn] nf hyena

hygiénique [iʒenik] adj hygienic

hymne [imn] nm hymn; **~ national** national anthem

hypermarché [ipɛrmarʃe] nm hypermarket

hypermétrope [ipɛrmetrɔp] adj long-sighted

hypertension [ipɛrtãsjɔ̃] nf high blood pressure

hypnose [ipnoz] nf hypnosis; **hypnotiser** vt to hypnotize; **hypnotiseur** nm hypnotist

hypocrisie [ipɔkrizi] nf hypocrisy; **hypocrite** adj hypocritical

hypothèque [ipɔtɛk] nf mortgage

hypothèse [ipɔtɛz] nf hypothesis

hystérique [isterik] adj hysterical

I, i

iceberg [ajsbɛrg] nm iceberg

ici [isi] adv here; **jusqu'~** as far as this; (temps) so far; **d'~ demain** by tomorrow; **d'~ là** by then, in the meantime; **d'~ peu** before long

icône [ikon] nf icon

idéal, e, -aux [ideal, o] adj ideal ♦ nm ideal; **idéaliste** adj idealistic ♦ nm/f idealist

idée [ide] nf idea; **avoir dans l'~ que** to have an idea that; **~ fixe** obsession; **~ reçue** generally accepted idea; **~s noires** black ou dark thoughts

identifier [idãtifje] vt to identify; **s'~ à** (héros etc) to identify with

identique [idãtik] adj: **~ (à)** identical (to)

identité [idãtite] nf identity

idiot, e [idjo, idjɔt] adj idiotic ♦ nm/f idiot; **idiotie** nf idiotic thing

idole [idɔl] nf idol

if [if] nm yew

igloo [iglu] nm igloo

ignare [iɲar] adj ignorant

ignifugé, e [iɲifyʒe] adj fireproof

ignoble [iɲɔbl] adj vile

ignorant, e [iɲɔrã, ãt] adj ignorant

ignorer [iɲɔre] vt not to know; (personne) to ignore

il [il] pron he; (animal, chose, en tournure impersonnelle) it; **~s** they; voir aussi **avoir**

île [il] nf island; **l'~ Maurice** Mauritius; **les ~s anglo-normandes** the Channel Islands; **les ~s Britanniques** the British Isles

illégal, e, -aux [i(l)legal, o] adj illegal

illégitime [i(l)leʒitim] adj illegitimate

illettré, e [i(l)letre] adj, nm/f illiterate

illimité, e [i(l)limite] adj unlimited

illisible [i(l)lizibl] adj illegible; (roman) unreadable

illogique [i(l)lɔʒik] adj illogical

illumination [i(l)lyminasjɔ̃] nf illumination; (idée) flash of inspiration

illuminer [i(l)lymine] vt to light up; (monument, rue: pour une fête) to illuminate; (: au moyen de projecteurs) to floodlight

illusion [i(l)lyzjɔ̃] nf illusion; **se faire des ~s** to delude o.s.; **faire ~** to delude ou fool people; **illusionniste** nm/f conjuror

illustration [i(l)lystrasjɔ̃] nf illustration

illustre [i(l)lystr] adj illustrious

illustré, e [i(l)lystre] adj illustrated ♦ nm comic

illustrer [i(l)lystre] vt to illustrate; **s'~** to become famous, win fame

îlot [ilo] nm small island, islet

ils [il] pron voir **il**

image [imaʒ] nf (gén) picture; (métaphore) image; **~ de marque** brand image; (fig) public image; **imagé, e** adj (texte) full of imagery; (langage) colourful

imaginaire [imaʒinɛr] adj imaginary

imagination [imaʒinasjɔ̃] nf imagination; **avoir de l'~** to be imaginative

imaginer [imaʒine] vt to imagine; (inventer: expédient) to devise, think up; **s'~** vt (se figurer: scène etc) to imagine, picture; **s'~ que** to imagine that

imbattable [ɛ̃batabl] adj unbeatable

imbécile [ɛ̃besil] adj idiotic ♦ nm/f idiot; **imbécillité** nf idiocy; (action) idiotic thing; (film, livre, propos) rubbish

imbiber [ɛ̃bibe] vt to soak; **s'~ de** to become saturated with

imbu, e [ɛ̃by] adj: **~ de** full of

imbuvable [ɛ̃byvabl] adj undrinkable; (personne: fam) unbearable

imitateur, -trice [imitatœr, tris] nm/f (gén) imitator; (MUSIC-HALL) impersonator

imitation [imitasjɔ̃] nf imitation; (de personnalité) impersonation

imiter [imite] vt to imitate; (contrefaire) to forge; (ressembler à) to look like

immaculé, e [imakyle] adj (linge, surface, réputation) spotless; (blancheur) immaculate

immangeable [ɛ̃mãʒabl] adj inedible

immatriculation [imatrikylasjɔ̃] nf registration

immatriculer [imatrikyle] vt to register; **faire/se faire ~** to register

immédiat, e [imedja, jat] adj immediate ♦ nm: **dans l'~** for the time being; **immédiatement** adv immediately

immense [i(m)mɑ̃s] adj immense

immerger [imɛrʒe] vt to immerse, submerge

immeuble [imœbl] nm building; (à usage d'habitation) block of flats

immigration [imigrasjɔ̃] nf immigration

immigré, e [imigre] nm/f immigrant

imminent, e [iminɑ̃, ɑ̃t] adj imminent

immiscer [imise]: **s'~** vi: **s'~ dans** to interfere in ou with

immobile [i(m)mɔbil] adj still, motionless

immobilier, -ière [imɔbilje, jɛr] adj property cpd ♦ nm: **l'~** the property business

immobiliser [imɔbilize] vt (gén) to immobilize; (circulation, véhicule, affaires) to bring to a standstill; **s'~** (personne) to stand still; (machine, véhicule) to come to a halt

immonde [i(m)mɔ̃d] adj foul

immoral, e, -aux [i(m)mɔral, o] adj immoral

immortel, le [imɔrtɛl] adj immortal

immuable [imɥabl] adj unchanging

immunisé, e [im(m)ynize] adj: **~ contre** immune to

immunité [imynite] nf immunity

impact [ɛ̃pakt] nm impact

impair, e [ɛ̃pɛr] adj odd ♦ nm faux pas, blunder

impardonnable [ɛ̃pardɔnabl] adj unpardonable, unforgivable

imparfait, e [ɛ̃parfɛ, ɛt] adj imperfect

impartial, e, -aux [ɛ̃parsjal, jo] adj impartial, unbiased

impasse [ɛ̃pas] nf dead end, cul-de-sac; (fig) deadlock

impassible [ɛ̃pasibl] adj impassive

impatience [ɛ̃pasjɑ̃s] nf impatience

impatient, e [ɛ̃pasjɑ̃, jɑ̃t] adj impatient; **impatienter: s'impatienter** vi to get impatient

impeccable [ɛ̃pekabl] adj (parfait) perfect; (propre) impeccable; (fam) smashing

impensable [ɛ̃pɑ̃sabl] adj (événement hypothétique) unthinkable; (événement qui a eu lieu) unbelievable

imper [ɛ̃pɛr] (fam) nm raincoat

impératif, -ive [ɛ̃peratif, iv] adj imperative ♦ nm (LING) imperative; **~s** nmpl (exigences: d'une fonction, d'une charge) requirements; (: de la mode) demands

impératrice [ɛ̃peratris] nf empress

imperceptible [ɛ̃pɛrsɛptibl] adj imperceptible

impérial, e, -aux [ɛ̃perjal, jo] adj imperial; **impériale** nf top deck

impérieux, -euse [ɛ̃perjø, jøz] adj (caractère, ton) imperious; (obligation, besoin) pressing, urgent

impérissable [ɛ̃perisabl] adj undying

imperméable [ɛ̃pɛrmeabl] adj waterproof; (fig): **~ à** impervious to ♦ nm raincoat

impertinent, e [ɛ̃pɛrtinɑ̃, ɑ̃t] adj impertinent

imperturbable [ɛ̃pɛrtyrbabl] adj (personne, caractère) unperturbable; (sang-froid, gaieté, sérieux) unshakeable

impétueux, -euse [ɛ̃petɥø, øz] adj impetuous

impitoyable [ɛ̃pitwajabl] adj pitiless, merciless

implanter [ɛ̃plɑ̃te]: **s'~** vi to be set up

impliquer [ɛ̃plike] vt to imply; **~ qn (dans)** to implicate sb (in)

impoli, e [ɛ̃pɔli] adj impolite, rude

impopulaire [ɛ̃pɔpylɛr] adj unpopular

importance [ɛ̃pɔrtɑ̃s] nf importance; **sans ~** unimportant

important, e [ɛ̃pɔrtɑ̃, ɑ̃t] adj important; (en quantité: somme, retard) considerable, sizeable; (: dégâts) extensive; (péj: airs, ton) self-important ♦ nm: **l'~** the important thing

importateur, -trice [ɛ̃pɔrtatœr, tris] nm/f importer

importation [ɛ̃pɔrtasjɔ̃] nf importation; (produit) import

importer [ɛ̃pɔrte] vt (COMM) to import; (maladies, plantes) to introduce ♦ vi (être important) to matter; **il importe qu'il fasse** it is important that he should do; **peu m'importe** (je n'ai pas de préférence) I don't mind; (je m'en moque) I don't care; **peu importe (que)** it doesn't matter (if); voir aussi **n'importe**

importun, e [ɛ̃pɔrtœ̃, yn] adj irksome, importunate; (arrivée, visite) inopportune, ill-timed ♦ nm intruder; **importuner** vt to bother

imposable [ɛ̃pozabl] adj taxable

imposant, e [ɛ̃pozɑ̃, ɑ̃t] adj imposing

imposer [ɛ̃poze] vt (taxer) to tax; **s'~** (être nécessaire) to be imperative; **~ qch à qn** to impose sth on sb; **en ~ à** to impress; **s'~ comme** to emerge as; **s'~ par** to win recognition through

impossibilité [ɛ̃pɔsibilite] nf impossibility; **être dans l'~ de faire qch** to be unable to do sth

impossible [ɛ̃pɔsibl] adj impossible; **il m'est ~ de le faire** it is impossible for me to do it, I can't possibly do it; **faire l'~** to do one's utmost

imposteur [ɛ̃pɔstœr] nm impostor

impôt [ɛ̃po] nm tax; **~s** nmpl (*contributions*) (income) tax sg; **payer 1000 F d'~s** to pay 1,000F in tax; **~ foncier** land tax; **~ sur le chiffre d'affaires** corporation (*BRIT*) ou corporate (*US*) tax; **~ sur le revenu** income tax

impotent, e [ɛ̃pɔtɑ̃, ɑ̃t] adj disabled

impraticable [ɛ̃pratikabl] adj (*projet*) impracticable, unworkable; (*piste*) impassable

imprécis, e [ɛ̃presi, iz] adj imprecise

imprégner [ɛ̃preɲe] vt (*tissu*) to impregnate; (*lieu, air*) to fill; **s'~ de** (*fig*) to absorb

imprenable [ɛ̃prənabl] adj (*forteresse*) impregnable; **vue ~** unimpeded outlook

imprésario [ɛ̃presarjo] nm manager

impression [ɛ̃presjɔ̃] nf impression; (*d'un ouvrage, tissu*) printing; **faire bonne ~** to make a good impression; **impressionnant, e** adj (*imposant*) impressive; (*bouleversant*) upsetting; **impressionner** vt (*frapper*) to impress; (*bouleverser*) to upset

imprévisible [ɛ̃previzibl] adj unforeseeable

imprévoyant, e [ɛ̃prevwajɑ̃, ɑ̃t] adj lacking in foresight; (*en matière d'argent*) improvident

imprévu, e [ɛ̃prevy] adj unforeseen, unexpected ♦ nm (*incident*) unexpected incident; **des vacances pleines d'~** holidays full of surprises; **en cas d'~** if anything unexpected happens; **sauf ~** unless anything unexpected crops up

imprimante [ɛ̃primɑ̃t] nf printer

imprimé [ɛ̃prime] nm (*formulaire*) printed form; (*POSTES*) printed matter no pl; (*tissu*) printed fabric; **~ à fleur** floral print

imprimer [ɛ̃prime] vt (*tissu*) to print; (*publier*) to publish; **imprimerie** nf printing; (*établissement*) printing works sg; **imprimeur** nm printer

impromptu, e [ɛ̃prɔ̃pty] adj (*repas, discours*) impromptu; (*départ*) sudden; (*visite*) surprise

impropre [ɛ̃prɔpr] adj inappropriate; **~ à** unfit for

improviser [ɛ̃provize] vt, vi to improvise

improviste [ɛ̃provist]: **à l'~** adv unexpectedly, without warning

imprudence [ɛ̃prydɑ̃s] nf (*d'une personne, d'une action*) carelessness no pl; (*d'une remarque*) imprudence no pl; **commettre une ~** to do something foolish

imprudent, e [ɛ̃prydɑ̃, ɑ̃t] adj (*conducteur, geste, action*) careless; (*remarque*) unwise, imprudent; (*projet*) foolhardy

impudent, e [ɛ̃pydɑ̃, ɑ̃t] adj impudent

impudique [ɛ̃pydik] adj shameless

impuissant, e [ɛ̃pɥisɑ̃, ɑ̃t] adj helpless; (*sans effet*) ineffectual; (*sexuellement*)

impotent

impulsif, -ive [ɛ̃pylsif, iv] adj impulsive

impulsion [ɛ̃pylsjɔ̃] nf (*ÉLEC, instinct*) impulse; (*élan, influence*) impetus

impunément [ɛ̃pynemɑ̃] adv with impunity

inabordable [inabɔrdabl] adj (*cher*) prohibitive

inacceptable [inakseptabl] adj unacceptable

inaccessible [inaksesibl] adj inaccessible

inachevé, e [inaʃ(ə)ve] adj unfinished

inactif, -ive [inaktif, iv] adj inactive; (*remède*) ineffective; (*BOURSE: marché*) slack ♦ nm: **les ~s** the non-working population

inadapté, e [inadapte] adj (*gén*) **~ à** not adapted to, unsuited to; (*PSYCH*) maladjusted

inadéquat, e [inadekwa(t), kwat] adj inadequate

inadmissible [inadmisibl] adj inadmissible

inadvertance [inadvɛrtɑ̃s]: **par ~** adv inadvertently

inaltérable [inalterabl] adj (*matière*) stable; (*fig*) unfailing; **~ à** unaffected by

inanimé, e [inanime] adj (*matière*) inanimate; (*évanoui*) unconscious; (*sans vie*) lifeless

inanition [inanisjɔ̃] nf: **tomber d'~** to faint with hunger (and exhaustion)

inaperçu, e [inapɛrsy] adj: **passer ~** to go unnoticed

inapte [inapt] adj: **~ à** incapable of; (*MIL*) unfit for

inattaquable [inatakabl] adj (*texte, preuve*) irrefutable

inattendu, e [inatɑ̃dy] adj unexpected

inattentif, -ive [inatɑ̃tif, iv] adj inattentive; **~ à** (*dangers, détails*) heedless of; **inattention** nf: **faute d'inattention** careless mistake

inauguration [inogyrasjɔ̃] nf inauguration

inaugurer [inogyre] vt (*monument*) to unveil; (*exposition, usine*) to open; (*fig*) to inaugurate

inavouable [inavwabl] adj shameful; (*bénéfices*) undisclosable

incalculable [ɛ̃kalkylabl] adj incalculable

incandescence [ɛ̃kɑ̃desɑ̃s] nf: **porter à ~** to heat white-hot

incapable [ɛ̃kapabl] adj incapable; **~ de faire** incapable of doing; (*empêché*) unable to do

incapacité [ɛ̃kapasite] nf (*incompétence*) incapability; (*impossibilité*) incapacity; **dans l'~ de faire** unable to do

incarcérer [ɛ̃karsere] vt to incarcerate, imprison

incarné, e [ɛ̃karne] adj (*ongle*) ingrown

incarner [ɛ̃karne] vt to embody, personify; (*THÉÂTRE*) to play

incassable [ɛ̃kasabl] adj unbreakable

incendiaire [ɛ̃sɑ̃djɛr] adj incendiary; (*fig:*

discours) inflammatory

incendie [ɛ̃sɑ̃di] *nm* fire; ~ **criminel** arson *no pl*; ~ **de forêt** forest fire; **incendier** *vt* (*mettre le feu à*) to set fire to, set alight; (*brûler complètement*) to burn down; **se faire incendier** (*fam*) to get a rocket

incertain, e [ɛ̃sɛʀtɛ̃, ɛn] *adj* uncertain; (*temps*) unsettled; (*imprécis: contours*) indistinct, blurred; **incertitude** *nf* uncertainty

incessamment [ɛ̃sesamɑ̃] *adv* very shortly

incident [ɛ̃sidɑ̃, ɑ̃t] *nm* incident; ~ **de parcours** minor hitch *ou* setback; ~ **technique** technical difficulties *pl*

incinérer [ɛ̃sineʀe] *vt* (*ordures*) to incinerate; (*mort*) to cremate

incisive [ɛ̃siziv] *nf* incisor

inciter [ɛ̃site] *vt*: ~ **qn à** (**faire**) **qch** to encourage sb to do sth; (*à la révolte etc*) to incite sb to do sth

inclinable [ɛ̃klinabl] *adj*: **siège à dossier** ~ reclining seat

inclinaison [ɛ̃klinɛzɔ̃] *nf* (*déclivité: d'une route etc*) incline; (: *d'un toit*) slope; (*état penché*) tilt

inclination [ɛ̃klinasjɔ̃] *nf* (*penchant*) inclination; ~ **de** (**la**) **tête** nod (of the head); ~ (**de buste**) bow

incliner [ɛ̃kline] *vt* (*pencher*) to tilt ♦ *vi*: ~ **à qch/à faire** to incline towards sth/doing; **s'~** (*devant*) to bow (before); (*céder*) to give in *ou* cave in (to); ~ **la tête** to give a slight bow

inclure [ɛ̃klyʀ] *vt* to include; (*joindre à un envoi*) to enclose; **jusqu'au 10 mars inclus** until 10th March inclusive

incognito [ɛ̃kɔnito] *adv* incognito ♦ *nm*: **garder l'~** to remain incognito

incohérent, e [ɛ̃kɔeʀɑ̃, ɑ̃t] *adj* (*comportement*) inconsistent; (*geste, langage, texte*) incoherent

incollable [ɛ̃kɔlabl] *adj* (*riz*) non-stick; **il est ~** (*fam*) he's got all the answers

incolore [ɛ̃kɔlɔʀ] *adj* colourless

incommoder [ɛ̃kɔmɔde] *vt* (*chaleur, odeur*): ~ **qn** to bother sb

incomparable [ɛ̃kɔ̃paʀabl] *adj* incomparable

incompatible [ɛ̃kɔ̃patibl] *adj* incompatible

incompétent, e [ɛ̃kɔ̃petɑ̃, ɑ̃t] *adj* incompetent

incomplet, -ète [ɛ̃kɔ̃plɛ, ɛt] *adj* incomplete

incompréhensible [ɛ̃kɔ̃pʀeɑ̃sibl] *adj* incomprehensible

incompris, e [ɛ̃kɔ̃pʀi, iz] *adj* misunderstood

inconcevable [ɛ̃kɔ̃s(ə)vabl] *adj* inconceivable

inconciliable [ɛ̃kɔ̃siljabl] *adj* irreconcilable

inconditionnel, le [ɛ̃kɔ̃disjɔnɛl] *adj* unconditional; (*partisan*) unquestioning ♦ *nm/f* (*d'un homme politique*) ardent supporter; (*d'un écrivain, d'un chanteur*)

ardent admirer; (*d'une activité*) fanatic

inconfort [ɛ̃kɔ̃fɔʀ] *nm* discomfort; **inconfortable** *adj* uncomfortable

incongru, e [ɛ̃kɔ̃gʀy] *adj* unseemly

inconnu, e [ɛ̃kɔny] *adj* unknown ♦ *nm/f* stranger ♦ *nm*: **l'~** the unknown; **inconnue** *nf* unknown factor

inconsciemment [ɛ̃kɔ̃sjamɑ̃] *adv* unconsciously

inconscient, e [ɛ̃kɔ̃sjɑ̃, jɑ̃t] *adj* unconscious; (*irréfléchi*) thoughtless, reckless; (*sentiment*) subconscious ♦ *nm* (*PSYCH*): **l'~** the unconscious; ~ **de** unaware of

inconsidéré, e [ɛ̃kɔ̃sideʀe] *adj* ill-considered

inconsistant, e [ɛ̃kɔ̃sistɑ̃, ɑ̃t] *adj* (*fig*) flimsy, weak

inconsolable [ɛ̃kɔ̃sɔlabl] *adj* inconsolable

incontestable [ɛ̃kɔ̃tɛstabl] *adj* indisputable

incontinent, e [ɛ̃kɔ̃tinɑ̃, ɑ̃t] *adj* incontinent

incontournable [ɛ̃kɔ̃tuʀnabl] *adj* unavoidable

incontrôlable [ɛ̃kɔ̃tʀolabl] *adj* unverifiable; (*irrépressible*) uncontrollable

inconvenant, e [ɛ̃kɔ̃v(ə)nɑ̃, ɑ̃t] *adj* unseemly, improper

inconvénient [ɛ̃kɔ̃venjɑ̃] *nm* disadvantage, drawback; **si vous n'y voyez pas d'~** if you have no objections

incorporer [ɛ̃kɔʀpɔʀe] *vt*: ~ (**à**) to mix in (with); ~ (**dans**) (*paragraphe etc*) to incorporate (in); (*MIL: appeler*) to recruit (into); **il a très bien su s'~ à notre groupe** he was very easily incorporated into our group

incorrect, e [ɛ̃kɔʀɛkt] *adj* (*impropre, inconvenant*) improper; (*défectueux*) faulty; (*inexact*) incorrect; (*impoli*) impolite; (*déloyal*) underhand

incorrigible [ɛ̃kɔʀiʒibl] *adj* incorrigible

incrédule [ɛ̃kʀedyl] *adj* incredulous; (*REL*) unbelieving

increvable [ɛ̃kʀəvabl] (*fam*) *adj* tireless

incriminer [ɛ̃kʀimine] *vt* (*personne*) to incriminate; (*action, conduite*) to bring under attack; (*bonne foi, honnêteté*) to call into question

incroyable [ɛ̃kʀwajabl] *adj* incredible

incruster [ɛ̃kʀyste] *vt* (*ART*) to inlay; **s'~** *vi* (*invité*) to take root

inculpé, e [ɛ̃kylpe] *nm/f* accused

inculper [ɛ̃kylpe] *vt*: ~ (**de**) to charge (with)

inculquer [ɛ̃kylke] *vt*: ~ **qch à** to inculcate sth in *ou* instil sth into

inculte [ɛ̃kylt] *adj* uncultivated; (*esprit, peuple*) uncultured

Inde [ɛ̃d] *nf*: **l'~** India

indécent, e [ɛ̃desɑ̃, ɑ̃t] *adj* indecent

indéchiffrable [ɛ̃deʃifʀabl] *adj* indecipherable

indécis, e [ɛ̃desi, iz] *adj* (*par nature*)

indecisive; (*temporairement*) undecided

indéfendable [ɛ̃defɑ̃dabl] *adj* indefensible

indéfini, e [ɛ̃defini] *adj* (*imprécis, incertain*) undefined; (*illimité,* LING) indefinite;
indéfiniment *adv* indefinitely;
indéfinissable *adj* indefinable

indélébile [ɛ̃delebil] *adj* indelible

indélicat, e [ɛ̃delika, at] *adj* tactless

indemne [ɛ̃dɛmn] *adj* unharmed;
indemniser *vt*: **indemniser qn (de)** to compensate sb (for)

indemnité [ɛ̃dɛmnite] *nf* (*dédommagement*) compensation *no pl*; (*allocation*) allowance;
indemnité de licenciement redundancy payment

indépendamment [ɛ̃depɑ̃damɑ̃] *adv* independently; **~ de** (*abstraction faite de*) irrespective of; (*en plus de*) over and above

indépendance [ɛ̃depɑ̃dɑ̃s] *nf* independence

indépendant, e [ɛ̃depɑ̃dɑ̃, ɑ̃t] *adj* independent; **~ de** independent of

indescriptible [ɛ̃deskriptibl] *adj* indescribable

indésirable [ɛ̃dezirabl] *adj* undesirable

indestructible [ɛ̃destryktibl] *adj* indestructible

indétermination [ɛ̃detɛrminasjɔ̃] *nf* (*irrésolution: chronique*) indecision; (*: temporaire*) indecisiveness

indéterminé, e [ɛ̃detɛrmine] *adj* (*date, cause, nature*) unspecified; (*forme, longueur, quantité*) indeterminate

index [ɛ̃dɛks] *nm* (*doigt*) index finger; (*d'un livre etc*) index; **mettre à l'~** to blacklist;
indexé, e *adj* (ÉCON): **indexé (sur)** index-linked (to)

indic [ɛ̃dik] (*fam*) *nm* (POLICE) grass

indicateur [ɛ̃dikatœr] *nm* (POLICE) informer; (TECH) gauge, indicator

indicatif, -ive [ɛ̃dikatif, iv] *adj*: **à titre ~** for (your) information ♦ *nm* (LING) indicative; (RADIO) theme *ou* signature tune; (TÉL) dialling code

indication [ɛ̃dikasjɔ̃] *nf* indication; (*renseignement*) information *no pl*; **~s** *nfpl* (*directives*) instructions

indice [ɛ̃dis] *nm* (*marque, signe*) indication, sign; (POLICE: *lors d'une enquête*) clue; (JUR: *présomption*) piece of evidence; (SCIENCE, ÉCON, TECH) index

indicible [ɛ̃disibl] *adj* inexpressible

indien, ne [ɛ̃djɛ̃, jɛn] *adj* Indian ♦ *nm/f*: **I~, ne** Indian

indifféremment [ɛ̃diferamɑ̃] *adv* (*sans distinction*) equally (well)

indifférence [ɛ̃diferɑ̃s] *nf* indifference

indifférent, e [ɛ̃diferɑ̃, ɑ̃t] *adj* (*peu intéressé*) indifferent; **ça m'est ~** it doesn't matter to me; **elle m'est ~e** I am indifferent

to her

indigence [ɛ̃diʒɑ̃s] *nf* poverty

indigène [ɛ̃diʒɛn] *adj* native, indigenous; (*des gens du pays*) local ♦ *nm/f* native

indigeste [ɛ̃diʒɛst] *adj* indigestible

indigestion [ɛ̃diʒɛstjɔ̃] *nf* indigestion *no pl*

indigne [ɛ̃diɲ] *adj* unworthy

indigner [ɛ̃diɲe] *vt*: **s'~ (de ou contre)** to get indignant (at)

indiqué, e [ɛ̃dike] *adj* (*date, lieu*) agreed; (*traitement*) appropriate; (*conseillé*) advisable

indiquer [ɛ̃dike] *vt* (*suj: pendule, aiguille*) to show; (*: étiquette, panneau*) to show, indicate; (*renseigner sur*) to point out, tell; (*déterminer: date, lieu*) to give, state; (*signaler, dénoter*) to indicate, point to; **~ qch/qn à qn** (*montrer du doigt*) to point sth/sb out to sb; (*faire connaître: médecin, restaurant*) to tell sb of sth/sb

indirect, e [ɛ̃dirɛkt] *adj* indirect

indiscipliné, e [ɛ̃disipline] *adj* undisciplined

indiscret, -ète [ɛ̃diskrɛ, ɛt] *adj* indiscreet

indiscutable [ɛ̃diskytabl] *adj* indisputable

indispensable [ɛ̃dispɑ̃sabl] *adj* indispensable, essential

indisposé, e [ɛ̃dispoze] *adj* indisposed

indisposer [ɛ̃dispoze] *vt* (*incommoder*) to upset; (*déplaire à*) to antagonize; (*énerver*) to irritate

indistinct, e [ɛ̃distɛ̃(kt), ɛ̃kt] *adj* indistinct;
indistinctement *adv* (*voir, prononcer*) indistinctly; (*sans distinction*) indiscriminately

individu [ɛ̃dividy] *nm* individual; **individuel, le** *adj* (*gén*) individual; (*responsabilité, propriété, liberté*) personal; **chambre individuelle** single room; **maison individuelle** detached house

indolore [ɛ̃dɔlɔr] *adj* painless

indomptable [ɛ̃dɔ̃(p)tabl] *adj* untameable; (*fig*) invincible

Indonésie [ɛ̃dɔnezi] *nf* Indonesia

indu, e [ɛ̃dy] *adj*: **à une heure ~e** at some ungodly hour

induire [ɛ̃dɥir] *vt*: **~ qn en erreur** to lead sb astray, mislead sb

indulgent, e [ɛ̃dylʒɑ̃, ɑ̃t] *adj* (*parent, regard*) indulgent; (*juge, examinateur*) lenient

industrialisé, e [ɛ̃dystrijalize] *adj* industrialized

industrie [ɛ̃dystri] *nf* industry; **industriel, le** *adj* industrial ♦ *nm* industrialist

inébranlable [inebrɑ̃labl] *adj* (*masse, colonne*) solid; (*personne, certitude, foi*) unshakeable

inédit, e [inedi, it] *adj* (*correspondance, livre*) hitherto unpublished; (*spectacle, moyen*) novel, original; (*film*) unreleased

ineffaçable [inefasabl] *adj* indelible

inefficace [inefikas] *adj* (*remède, moyen*)

ineffective; (*machine, employé*) inefficient

inégal, e, -aux [inegal, o] *adj* unequal;
(*irrégulier*) uneven; **inégalable** *adj*
matchless; **inégalé, e** *adj* (*record*)
unequalled; (*beauté*) unrivalled; **inégalité** *nf*
inequality

inépuisable [inepɥizabl] *adj* inexhaustible

inerte [inɛʀt] *adj* (*immobile*) lifeless; (*sans
réaction*) passive

inespéré, e [inɛspeʀe] *adj* unexpected,
unhoped-for

inestimable [inɛstimabl] *adj* priceless; (*fig:
bienfait*) invaluable

inévitable [inevitabl] *adj* unavoidable; (*fatal,
habituel*) inevitable

inexact, e [inɛgza(kt), akt] *adj* inaccurate

inexcusable [inɛkskyzabl] *adj* unforgivable

inexplicable [inɛksplikabl] *adj* inexplicable

in extremis [inɛkstʀemis] *adv* at the last
minute ♦ *adj* last-minute

infaillible [ɛ̃fajibl] *adj* infallible

infâme [ɛ̃fɑm] *adj* vile

infarctus [ɛ̃faʀktys] *nm*: ~ **(du myocarde)**
coronary (thrombosis)

infatigable [ɛ̃fatigabl] *adj* tireless

infect, e [ɛ̃fɛkt] *adj* (*personne*)
obnoxious; (*temps*) foul

infecter [ɛ̃fɛkte] *vt* (*atmosphère, eau*) to
contaminate; (*MÉD*) to infect; **s'~** to become
infected *ou* septic; **infection** *nf* infection;
(*puanteur*) stench

inférieur, e [ɛ̃feʀjœʀ] *adj* lower; (*en qualité,
intelligence*) inferior; ~ **à** (*somme, quantité*)
less *ou* smaller than; (*moins bon que*) inferior
to

infernal, e, -aux [ɛ̃fɛʀnal, o] *adj*
(*insupportable: chaleur, rythme*) infernal;
(: *enfant*) horrid; (*satanique, effrayant*)
diabolical

infidèle [ɛ̃fidɛl] *adj* unfaithful

infiltrer [ɛ̃filtʀe] *vb*: **s'~ dans** to get into;
(*liquide*) to seep through; (*fig: groupe,
ennemi*) to infiltrate

infime [ɛ̃fim] *adj* minute, tiny

infini, e [ɛ̃fini] *adj* infinite ♦ *nm* infinity; **à l'~**
endlessly; **infiniment** *adv* infinitely; **infinité**
nf: **une infinité de** an infinite number of

infinitif [ɛ̃finitif, iv] *nm* infinitive

infirme [ɛ̃fiʀm] *adj* disabled ♦ *nm/f* disabled
person

infirmerie [ɛ̃fiʀməʀi] *nf* medical room

infirmier, -ière [ɛ̃fiʀmje] *nm/f* nurse;
infirmière chef sister

infirmité [ɛ̃fiʀmite] *nf* disability

inflammable [ɛ̃flamabl] *adj* (in)flammable

inflation [ɛ̃flasjɔ̃] *nf* inflation

infliger [ɛ̃fliʒe] *vt*: ~ **qch (à qn)** to inflict sth
(on sb); (*amende, sanction*) to impose sth
(on sb)

influençable [ɛ̃flɥɑ̃sabl] *adj* easily influenced

influence [ɛ̃flɥɑ̃s] *nf* influence; **influencer** *vt*
to influence; **influent, e** *adj* influential

informateur, -trice [ɛ̃fɔʀmatœʀ, tʀis] *nm/f*
(*POLICE*) informer

informaticien, ne [ɛ̃fɔʀmatisjɛ̃, jɛn] *nm/f*
computer scientist

information [ɛ̃fɔʀmasjɔ̃] *nf* (*renseignement*)
piece of information; (*PRESSE, TV: nouvelle*)
item of news; (*diffusion de renseignements ,
INFORM*) information; (*JUR*) inquiry,
investigation; **~s** *nfpl* (*TV*) news *sg*

informatique [ɛ̃fɔʀmatik] *nf* (*technique*)
data processing; (*science*) computer science
♦ *adj* computer *cpd*; **informatiser** *vt* to
computerize

informe [ɛ̃fɔʀm] *adj* shapeless

informer [ɛ̃fɔʀme] *vt*: ~ **qn (de)** to inform sb
(of); **s'~ (de/si)** to inquire *ou* find out
(about/whether *ou* if)

infos [ɛ̃fo] *nfpl*: **les** ~ the news *sg*

infraction [ɛ̃fʀaksjɔ̃] *nf* offence; ~ **à** violation
ou breach of; **être en** ~ to be in breach of the
law

infranchissable [ɛ̃fʀɑ̃ʃisabl] *adj* impassable;
(*fig*) insuperable

infrarouge [ɛ̃fʀaʀuʒ] *adj* infrared

infrastructure [ɛ̃fʀastʀyktyʀ] *nf* (*AVIAT, MIL*)
ground installations *pl*; (*ÉCON: touristique etc*)
infrastructure

infuser [ɛ̃fyze] *vt, vi* (*thé*) to brew; (*tisane*) to
infuse; **infusion** *nf* (*tisane*) herb tea

ingénier [ɛ̃ʒenje]: **s'~** *vi*: **s'~ à faire** to strive
to do

ingénierie [ɛ̃ʒeniʀi] *nf* engineering;
~ **génétique** genetic engineering

ingénieur [ɛ̃ʒenjœʀ] *nm* engineer; **ingénieur
du son** sound engineer

ingénieux, -euse [ɛ̃ʒenjø, jøz] *adj*
ingenious, clever

ingénu, e [ɛ̃ʒeny] *adj* ingenuous, artless

ingérer [ɛ̃ʒeʀe] *vb*: **s'~ dans** to interfere in

ingrat, e [ɛ̃gʀa, at] *adj* (*personne*) ungrateful;
(*travail, sujet*) thankless; (*visage*)
unprepossessing

ingrédient [ɛ̃gʀedjɑ̃] *nm* ingredient

ingurgiter [ɛ̃gyʀʒite] *vt* to swallow

inhabitable [inabitabl] *adj* uninhabitable

inhabité, e [inabite] *adj* uninhabited

inhabituel, le [inabitɥɛl] *adj* unusual

inhibition [inibisjɔ̃] *nf* inhibition

inhumain, e [inymɛ̃, ɛn] *adj* inhuman

inhumation [inymasjɔ̃] *nf* burial

inhumer [inyme] *vt* to inter, bury

inimaginable [inimaʒinabl] *adj*
unimaginable

ininterrompu, e [inɛ̃teʀɔ̃py] *adj* (*file, série*)
unbroken; (*flot, vacarme*) uninterrupted,
non-stop; (*effort*) unremitting, continuous;

(suite, ligne) unbroken
initial, e, -aux [inisjal, jo] adj initial;
initiale nf initial; **initialiser** vt to initialize
initiation [inisjasjɔ̃] nf: ~ à introduction to
initiative [inisjativ] nf initiative
initier [inisje] vt: ~ qn à to initiate sb into;
(faire découvrir: art, jeu) to introduce sb to
injecté, e [ɛ̃ʒɛkte] adj: **yeux ~s de sang**
bloodshot eyes
injecter [ɛ̃ʒɛkte] vt to inject; **injection** nf
injection; **à injection** (AUTO) fuel injection
cpd
injure [ɛ̃ʒyʀ] nf insult, abuse no pl; **injurier**
vt to insult, abuse; **injurieux, -euse** adj
abusive, insulting
injuste [ɛ̃ʒyst] adj unjust, unfair; **injustice**
nf injustice
inlassable [ɛ̃lɑsabl] adj tireless
inné, e [i(n)ne] adj innate, inborn
innocent, e [inɔsɑ̃, ɑ̃t] adj innocent;
innocenter vt to clear, prove innocent
innombrable [i(n)nɔ̃bʀabl] adj innumerable
innommable [i(n)nɔmabl] adj unspeakable
innover [inɔve] vi to break new ground
inoccupé, e [inɔkype] adj unoccupied
inodore [inɔdɔʀ] adj (gaz) odourless; (fleur)
scentless
inoffensif, -ive [inɔfɑ̃sif, iv] adj harmless,
innocuous
inondation [inɔ̃dasjɔ̃] nf flood
inonder [inɔ̃de] vt to flood; ~ **de** to flood
with
inopiné, e [inɔpine] adj unexpected; (mort)
sudden
inopportun, e [inɔpɔʀtœ̃, yn] adj ill-timed,
untimely
inoubliable [inublijabl] adj unforgettable
inouï, e [inwi] adj unheard-of, extraordinary
inox [inɔks] nm stainless steel
inqualifiable [ɛ̃kalifjabl] adj unspeakable
inquiet, -ète [ɛ̃kjɛ, ɛ̃kjɛt] adj anxious;
inquiétant, e adj worrying, disturbing;
inquiéter vt to worry; **s'inquiéter** (de) to worry;
s'inquiéter de to worry about; (s'enquérir de)
to inquire about; **inquiétude** nf anxiety
insaisissable [ɛ̃sezisabl] adj (fugitif, ennemi)
elusive; (différence, nuance) imperceptible
insalubre [ɛ̃salybʀ] adj insalubrious
insatisfaisant, e [ɛ̃satisfəzɑ̃, ɑ̃t] adj
unsatisfactory
insatisfait, e [ɛ̃satisfɛ, ɛt] adj (non comblé)
unsatisfied; (mécontent) dissatisfied
inscription [ɛ̃skʀipsjɔ̃] nf inscription;
(immatriculation) enrolment
inscrire [ɛ̃skʀiʀ] vt (marquer: sur son calepin
etc) to note ou write down; (: sur un mur,
une affiche etc) to write; (: dans la pierre, le
métal) to inscribe; (mettre: sur une liste, un
budget etc) to put down; **s'~** (pour une excur-

sion etc) to put one's name down; **s'~** (à)
(club, parti) to join; (université) to register ou
enrol (at); (examen, concours) to register
(for); ~ **qn à** (club, parti) to enrol sb at
insecte [ɛ̃sɛkt] nm insect; **insecticide** nm
insecticide
insensé, e [ɛ̃sɑ̃se] adj mad
insensibiliser [ɛ̃sɑ̃sibilize] vt to anaesthetize
insensible [ɛ̃sɑ̃sibl] adj (nerf, membre)
numb; (dur, indifférent) insensitive
inséparable [ɛ̃sepaʀabl] adj inseparable
♦ nm: ~**s** (oiseaux) lovebirds
insigne [ɛ̃siɲ] nm (d'un parti, club) badge;
(d'une fonction) insignia ♦ adj distinguished
insignifiant, e [ɛ̃siɲifjɑ̃, jɑ̃t] adj
insignificant; trivial
insinuer [ɛ̃sinɥe] vt to insinuate; **s'~ dans**
(fig) to worm one's way into
insipide [ɛ̃sipid] adj insipid
insister [ɛ̃siste] vi to insist; (continuer à
sonner) to keep on trying; ~ **sur** (détail, sujet)
to lay stress on
insolation [ɛ̃sɔlasjɔ̃] nf (MÉD) sunstroke no pl
insolent, e [ɛ̃sɔlɑ̃, ɑ̃t] adj insolent
insolite [ɛ̃sɔlit] adj strange, unusual
insomnie [ɛ̃sɔmni] nf insomnia no pl
insonoriser [ɛ̃sɔnɔʀize] vt to soundproof
insouciant, e [ɛ̃susjɑ̃, jɑ̃t] adj carefree; ~ **du
danger** heedless of (the) danger
insoumis, e [ɛ̃sumi, iz] adj (caractère,
enfant) rebellious, refractory; (contrée, tribu)
unsubdued
insoupçonnable [ɛ̃supsɔnabl] adj
unsuspected; (personne) above suspicion
insoupçonné, e [ɛ̃supsɔne] adj unsuspected
insoutenable [ɛ̃sut(ə)nabl] adj (argument)
untenable; (chaleur) unbearable
inspecter [ɛ̃spɛkte] vt to inspect;
inspecteur, -trice nm/f inspector;
inspecteur d'Académie (regional) director of
education; **inspecteur des finances** ≈ tax
inspector (BRIT), ≈ Internal Revenue Service
agent (US); **inspection** nf inspection
inspirer [ɛ̃spiʀe] vt (gén) to inspire ♦ vi
(aspirer) to breathe in; **s'~ de** (suj: artiste) to
draw one's inspiration from
instable [ɛ̃stabl] adj unstable; (meuble,
équilibre) unsteady; (temps) unsettled
installation [ɛ̃stalasjɔ̃] nf installation; ~**s** nfpl
facilities
installer [ɛ̃stale] vt (loger, placer) to put;
(meuble, gaz, électricité) to put in; (rideau,
étagère, tente) to put up; (appartement) to fit
out; **s'~** (s'établir: artisan, dentiste etc) to set
o.s. up; (se loger) to settle; (emménager) to
settle in; (sur un siège, à un emplacement) to
settle (down); (fig: maladie, grève) to take a
firm hold
instance [ɛ̃stɑ̃s] nf (ADMIN: autorité) author-

ity; **affaire en ~** matter pending; **être en ~ de divorce** to be awaiting a divorce

instant [ɛ̃stɑ̃] *nm* moment, instant; **dans un ~** in a moment; **à l'~** this instant; **pour l'~** for the moment, for the time being

instantané, e [ɛ̃stɑ̃tane] *adj* (*lait, café*) instant; (*explosion, mort*) instantaneous ♦ *nm* snapshot

instar [ɛ̃staʀ]: **à l'~ de** *prép* following the example of, like

instaurer [ɛ̃stɔʀe] *vt* to institute; (*couvre-feu*) to impose

instinct [ɛ̃stɛ̃] *nm* instinct; **instinctivement** *adv* instinctively

instit [ɛ̃stit] (*fam*) *nm/f* (primary school) teacher

instituer [ɛ̃stitɥe] *vt* to establish

institut [ɛ̃stity] *nm* institute; **~ de beauté** beauty salon; **Institut universitaire de technologie** ≈ polytechnic

instituteur, -trice [ɛ̃stitytœʀ, tʀis] *nm/f* (primary school) teacher

institution [ɛ̃stitysjɔ̃] *nf* institution; (*collège*) private school

instructif, -ive [ɛ̃stʀyktif, iv] *adj* instructive

instruction [ɛ̃stʀyksjɔ̃] *nf* (*enseignement, savoir*) education; (*JUR*) (preliminary) investigation and hearing; **~s** *nfpl* (*ordres, mode d'emploi*) instructions; **~ civique** civics *sg*

instruire [ɛ̃stʀɥiʀ] *vt* (*élèves*) to teach; (*recrues*) to train; (*JUR: affaire*) to conduct the investigation for; **s'~** to educate o.s.; **instruit, e** *adj* educated

instrument [ɛ̃stʀymɑ̃] *nm* instrument; **~ à cordes/vent** stringed/wind instrument; **~ de mesure** measuring instrument; **~ de musique** musical instrument; **~ de travail** (working) tool

insu [ɛ̃sy] *nm*: **à l'~ de qn** without sb knowing (it)

insubmersible [ɛ̃sybmɛʀsibl] *adj* unsinkable

insuffisant, e [ɛ̃syfizɑ̃, ɑ̃t] *adj* (*en quantité*) insufficient; (*en qualité*) inadequate; (*sur une copie*) poor

insulaire [ɛ̃sylɛʀ] *adj* island *cpd*; (*attitude*) insular

insuline [ɛ̃sylin] *nf* insulin

insulte [ɛ̃sylt] *nf* insult; **insulter** *vt* to insult

insupportable [ɛ̃sypɔʀtabl] *adj* unbearable

insurger [ɛ̃syʀʒe] *vb*: **s'~ (contre)** to rise up *ou* rebel (against)

insurmontable [ɛ̃syʀmɔ̃tabl] *adj* (*difficulté*) insuperable; (*aversion*) unconquerable

insurrection [ɛ̃syʀɛksjɔ̃] *nf* insurrection

intact, e [ɛ̃takt] *adj* intact

intangible [ɛ̃tɑ̃ʒibl] *adj* intangible; (*principe*) inviolable

intarissable [ɛ̃taʀisabl] *adj* inexhaustible

intégral, e, -aux [ɛ̃tegʀal, o] *adj* complete; **texte ~** unabridged version; **bronzage ~** all-over suntan; **intégralement** *adv* in full; **intégralité** *nf* whole; **dans son intégralité** in full; **intégrant, e** *adj*: **faire partie intégrante de** to be an integral part of

intègre [ɛ̃tegʀ] *adj* upright

intégrer [ɛ̃tegʀe] *vt*: **bien s'~** to integrate well

intégrisme [ɛ̃tegʀism] *nm* fundamentalism

intellectuel, le [ɛ̃telɛktɥel] *adj* intellectual ♦ *nm/f* intellectual; (*péj*) highbrow

intelligence [ɛ̃teliʒɑ̃s] *nf* intelligence; (*compréhension*): **l'~ de** the understanding of; (*complicité*): **regard d'~** glance of complicity; (*accord*): **vivre en bonne ~ avec qn** to be on good terms with sb

intelligent, e [ɛ̃teliʒɑ̃, ɑ̃t] *adj* intelligent

intelligible [ɛ̃teliʒibl] *adj* intelligible

intempéries [ɛ̃tɑ̃peʀi] *nfpl* bad weather *sg*

intempestif, -ive [ɛ̃tɑ̃pestif, iv] *adj* untimely

intenable [ɛ̃t(ə)nabl] *adj* (*chaleur*) unbearable

intendant, e [ɛ̃tɑ̃dɑ̃] *nm/f* (*MIL*) quartermaster; (*SCOL*) bursar

intense [ɛ̃tɑ̃s] *adj* intense; **intensif, -ive** *adj* intensive; **un cours intensif** a crash course

intenter [ɛ̃tɑ̃te] *vt*: **~ un procès contre** *ou* **à** to start proceedings against

intention [ɛ̃tɑ̃sjɔ̃] *nf* intention; (*JUR*) intent; **avoir l'~ de faire** to intend to do; **à l'~ de** for; (*renseignement*) for the benefit of; (*film, ouvrage*) aimed at; **à cette ~** with this aim in view; **intentionné, e** *adj*: **bien intentionné** well-meaning *ou* -intentioned; **mal intentionné** ill-intentioned

interactif, -ive [ɛ̃teʀaktif, iv] *adj* (*COMPUT*) interactive

intercalaire [ɛ̃teʀkalɛʀ] *nm* divider

intercaler [ɛ̃teʀkale] *vt* to insert

intercepter [ɛ̃teʀsɛpte] *vt* to intercept; (*lumière, chaleur*) to cut off

interchangeable [ɛ̃teʀʃɑ̃ʒabl] *adj* interchangeable

interclasse [ɛ̃teʀklɑs] *nm* (*SCOL*) break (between classes)

interdiction [ɛ̃teʀdiksjɔ̃] *nf* ban; **~ de stationner** no parking; **~ de fumer** no smoking

interdire [ɛ̃teʀdiʀ] *vt* to forbid; (*ADMIN*) to ban, prohibit; (: *journal, livre*) to ban; **~ à qn de faire** to forbid sb to do; (*suj: empêchement*) to prevent sb from doing

interdit, e [ɛ̃teʀdi, it] *adj* (*stupéfait*) taken aback

intéressant, e [ɛ̃teʀesɑ̃, ɑ̃t] *adj* interesting; (*avantageux*) attractive

intéressé, e [ɛ̃teʀese] *adj* (*parties*) involved, concerned; (*amitié, motifs*) self-interested

intéresser [ɛ̃terese] vt (captiver) to interest; (toucher) to be of interest to; (ADMIN: concerner) to affect, concern; **s'~ à** to be interested in

intérêt [ɛ̃terɛ] nm interest; (égoïsme) self-interest; **tu as ~ à accepter** it's in your interest to accept; **tu as ~ à te dépêcher** you'd better hurry

intérieur, e [ɛ̃terjœr] adj (mur, escalier, poche) inside; (commerce, politique) domestic; (cour, calme, vie) inner; (navigation) inland ♦ nm (d'une maison, d'un récipient etc) inside; (d'un pays, aussi décor, mobilier) interior; **à l'~ (de)** inside; **intérieurement** adv inwardly

intérim [ɛ̃terim] nm interim period; **faire de l'~** to temp; **assurer l'~ (de)** to deputize (for); **par ~** interim

intérimaire [ɛ̃terimɛr] adj (directeur, ministre) acting; (secrétaire, personnel) temporary ♦ nm/f (secrétaire) temporary secretary, temp (BRIT)

interlocuteur, -trice [ɛ̃terlɔkytœr, tris] nm/f speaker; **son ~** the person he was speaking to

interloquer [ɛ̃terlɔke] vt to take aback

intermède [ɛ̃termɛd] nm interlude

intermédiaire [ɛ̃termedjɛr] adj intermediate; (solution) temporary ♦ nm/f intermediary; (COMM) middleman; **sans ~** directly; **par l'~ de** through

interminable [ɛ̃terminabl] adj endless

intermittence [ɛ̃termitɑ̃s] nf: **par ~** sporadically, intermittently

internat [ɛ̃terna] nm (SCOL) boarding school

international, e, -aux [ɛ̃ternasjɔnal, o] adj, nm/f international

interne [ɛ̃tern] adj internal ♦ nm/f (SCOL) boarder; (MÉD) houseman

interner [ɛ̃terne] vt (POL) to intern; (MÉD) to confine to a mental institution

Internet [ɛ̃ternɛt] nm Internet

interpeller [ɛ̃terpale] vt (appeler) to call out to; (apostropher) to shout at; (POLICE, POL) to question; (concerner) to concern

interphone [ɛ̃terfɔn] nm intercom; (d'immeuble) entry phone

interposer [ɛ̃terpoze] vt: **s'~** to intervene; **par personnes interposées** through a third party

interprétation [ɛ̃terpretasjɔ̃] nf interpretation

interprète [ɛ̃terpret] nm/f interpreter; (porte-parole) spokesperson

interpréter [ɛ̃terprete] vt to interpret; (jouer) to play; (chanter) to sing

interrogateur, -trice [ɛ̃terɔgatœr, tris] adj questioning, inquiring

interrogatif, -ive [ɛ̃terɔgatif, iv] adj (LING) interrogative

interrogation [ɛ̃terɔgasjɔ̃] nf question; (action) questioning; (SCOL) (written ou oral) test

interrogatoire [ɛ̃terɔgatwar] nm (POLICE) questioning no pl; (JUR, aussi fig) cross-examination

interroger [ɛ̃terɔʒe] vt to question; (INFORM) to consult; (SCOL) to test

interrompre [ɛ̃terɔ̃pr] vt (gén) to interrupt; (négociations) to break off; (match) to stop; **s'~** to break off; **interrupteur** nm switch; **interruption** nf interruption; (pause) break; **sans interruption** without stopping

intersection [ɛ̃terseksjɔ̃] nf intersection

interstice [ɛ̃terstis] nm crack; (de volet) slit

interurbain, e [ɛ̃teryrbɛ̃, ɛn] adj (TÉL) long-distance

intervalle [ɛ̃terval] nm (espace) space; (de temps) interval; **à deux jours d'~** two days apart

intervenir [ɛ̃tervənir] vi (gén) to intervene; **~ auprès de qn** to intervene with sb

intervention [ɛ̃tervɑ̃sjɔ̃] nf intervention; (discours) speech; **intervention chirurgicale** (surgical) operation

intervertir [ɛ̃tervertir] vt to invert (the order of), reverse

interview [ɛ̃tervju] nf interview

intestin [ɛ̃testɛ̃, in] nm intestine

intime [ɛ̃tim] adj intimate; (vie) private; (conviction) inmost; (dîner, cérémonie) quiet ♦ nm/f close friend; **un journal ~** a diary

intimider [ɛ̃timide] vt to intimidate

intimité [ɛ̃timite] nf: **dans l'~** in private; (sans formalités) with only a few friends, quietly

intitulé, e [ɛ̃tityle] adj entitled

intolérable [ɛ̃tɔlerabl] adj intolerable

intox [ɛ̃tɔks] (fam) nf brainwashing

intoxication [ɛ̃tɔksikasjɔ̃] nf: **~ alimentaire** food poisoning

intoxiquer [ɛ̃tɔksike] vt to poison; (fig) brainwash

intraduisible [ɛ̃traduizibl] adj untranslatable; (fig) inexpressible

intraitable [ɛ̃tretabl] adj inflexible, uncompromising

intransigeant, e [ɛ̃trɑ̃ziʒɑ̃, ɑ̃t] adj intransigent

intransitif, -ive [ɛ̃trɑ̃zitif, iv] adj (LING) intransitive

intrépide [ɛ̃trepid] adj dauntless

intrigue [ɛ̃trig] nf (scénario) plot; **intriguer** vt to puzzle, intrigue

intrinsèque [ɛ̃trɛ̃sɛk] adj intrinsic

introduction [ɛ̃trɔdyksjɔ̃] nf introduction

introduire [ɛ̃trɔdɥir] vt to introduce; (visiteur) to show in; (aiguille, clef): **~ qch dans** to insert ou introduce sth into; **s'~ (dans)** to get in(to); (dans un groupe) to get o.s. accepted (into)

introuvable [ɛ̃truvabl] *adj* which cannot be found; (COMM) unobtainable

introverti, e [ɛ̃trɔvɛrti] *nm/f* introvert

intrus, e [ɛ̃try, yz] *nm/f* intruder

intrusion [ɛ̃tryzjɔ̃] *nf* intrusion

intuition [ɛ̃tɥisjɔ̃] *nf* intuition

inusable [inyzabl] *adj* hard-wearing

inusité, e [inyzite] *adj* rarely used

inutile [inytil] *adj* useless; (*superflu*) unnecessary; **inutilement** *adv* unnecessarily; **inutilisable** *adj* unusable

invalide [ɛ̃valid] *adj* disabled ♦ *nm:* ~ **de guerre** disabled ex-serviceman

invariable [ɛ̃varjabl] *adj* invariable

invasion [ɛ̃vazjɔ̃] *nf* invasion

invectiver [ɛ̃vɛktive] *vt* to hurl abuse at

invendable [ɛ̃vɑ̃dabl] *adj* unsaleable; (COMM) unmarketable; **invendus** *nmpl* unsold goods

inventaire [ɛ̃vɑ̃tɛr] *nm* inventory; (COMM: *liste*) stocklist; (: *opération*) stocktaking *no pl*

inventer [ɛ̃vɑ̃te] *vt* to invent; (*subterfuge*) to devise, invent; (*histoire, excuse*) to make up, invent; **inventeur** *nm* inventor; **inventif, -ive** *adj* inventive; **invention** *nf* invention

inverse [ɛ̃vɛrs] *adj* opposite ♦ *nm* opposite; **dans l'ordre** ~ in the reverse order; **en sens** ~ in (*ou* from) the opposite direction; **dans le sens** ~ **des aiguilles d'une montre** anticlockwise; **tu t'es trompé, c'est l'**~ **you've** got it wrong, it's the other way round; **inversement** *adv* conversely; **inverser** *vt* to invert, reverse; (ÉLEC) to reverse

investigation [ɛ̃vɛstigasjɔ̃] *nf* investigation

investir [ɛ̃vɛstir] *vt* to invest; **investissement** *nm* investment; **investiture** *nf* nomination

invétéré, e [ɛ̃vetere] *adj* inveterate

invisible [ɛ̃vizibl] *adj* invisible

invitation [ɛ̃vitasjɔ̃] *nf* invitation

invité, e [ɛ̃vite] *nm/f* guest

inviter [ɛ̃vite] *vt* to invite

invivable [ɛ̃vivabl] *adj* unbearable

involontaire [ɛ̃vɔlɔ̃tɛr] *adj* (*mouvement*) involuntary; (*insulte*) unintentional; (*complice*) unwitting

invoquer [ɛ̃vɔke] *vt* (*Dieu, muse*) to call upon, invoke; (*prétexte*) to put forward (as an excuse); (*loi, texte*) to refer to

invraisemblable [ɛ̃vrɛsɑ̃blabl] *adj* (*fait, nouvelle*) unlikely, improbable; (*insolence, habit*) incredible

iode [jɔd] *nm* iodine

irai *etc* [ire] *vb voir* aller

Irak [irak] *nm* Iraq; **irakien, ne** *adj* Iraqi ♦ *nm/f:* **Irakien, ne** Iraqi

Iran [irɑ̃] *nm* Iran; **iranien, ne** *adj* Iranian ♦ *nm/f:* **Iranien, ne** Iranian

irascible [irasibl] *adj* short-tempered

irions *etc* [irjɔ̃] *vb voir* aller

iris [iris] *nm* iris

irlandais, e [irlɑ̃dɛ, ɛz] *adj* Irish ♦ *nm/f:* **Irlandais, e** Irishman(-woman); **les Irlandais** the Irish

Irlande [irlɑ̃d] *nf* Ireland; ~ **du Nord** Northern Ireland; **la République d'**~ the Irish Republic

ironie [irɔni] *nf* irony; **ironique** *adj* ironical; **ironiser** *vi* to be ironical

irons *etc* [irɔ̃] *vb voir* aller

irradier [iradje] *vt* to irradiate

irraisonné, e [irɛzɔne] *adj* irrational

irrationnel, le [irasjɔnɛl] *adj* irrational

irréalisable [irealizabl] *adj* unrealizable; (*projet*) impracticable

irrécupérable [irekyperabl] *adj* beyond repair; (*personne*) beyond redemption

irréductible [iredyktibl] *adj* (*volonté*) indomitable; (*ennemi*) implacable

irréel, le [ireɛl] *adj* unreal

irréfléchi, e [irefleʃi] *adj* thoughtless

irrégularité [iregylarite] *nf* irregularity; (*de travail, d'effort, de qualité*) unevenness *no pl*

irrégulier, -ière [iregylje, jɛr] *adj* irregular (*travail, effort, qualité*) uneven; (*élève, athlète*) erratic

irrémédiable [iremedjabl] *adj* irreparable

irremplaçable [irɑ̃plasabl] *adj* irreplaceable

irréparable [ireparabl] *adj* (*objet*) beyond repair; (*dommage etc*) irreparable

irréprochable [ireprɔʃabl] *adj* irreproachable, beyond reproach; (*tenue*) impeccable

irrésistible [irezistibl] *adj* irresistible; (*besoin, désir, preuve, logique*) compelling; (*amusant*) hilarious

irrésolu, e [irezɔly] *adj* (*personne*) irresolute (*problème*) unresolved

irrespectueux, -euse [irɛspɛktɥø, øz] *adj* disrespectful

irrespirable [irɛspirabl] *adj* unbreathable; (*fig*) oppressive

irresponsable [irɛspɔ̃sabl] *adj* irresponsible

irriguer [irige] *vt* to irrigate

irritable [iritabl] *adj* irritable

irriter [irite] *vt* to irritate

irruption [irypsjɔ̃] *nf:* **faire** ~ (**chez qn**) to burst in (on sb)

Islam [islam] *nm* Islam; **islamique** *adj* Islamic; **islamiste** *adj* (*militant*) Islamic; (*mouvement*) Islamic fundamentalist ♦ *nm/f* Islamic fundamentalist

Islande [islɑ̃d] *nf* Iceland

isolant, e [izɔlɑ̃, ɑ̃t] *adj* insulating; (*insonorisant*) soundproofing

isolation [izɔlasjɔ̃] *nf* insulation

isolé, e [izɔle] *adj* isolated; (*contre le froid*) insulated

isoler [izɔle] *vt* to isolate; *(prisonnier)* to put in solitary confinement; *(ville)* to cut off, isolate; *(contre le froid)* to insulate; **s'~** *vi* to isolate o.s.; **isoloir** [izɔlwaʀ] *nm* polling booth

Israël [israɛl] *nm* Israel; **israélien, ne** *adj* Israeli ♦ *nm/f*: **Israélien, ne** Israeli; **israélite** *adj* Jewish ♦ *nm/f*: **Israélite** Jew (Jewess)

issu, e [isy] *adj*: **~ de** *(né de)* descended from; *(résultant de)* stemming from; **issue** *nf* *(ouverture, sortie)* exit; *(solution)* way out, solution; *(dénouement)* outcome; **à l'issue de** at the conclusion *ou* close of; **voie sans issue** dead end; **issue de secours** emergency exit

Italie [itali] *nf* Italy; **italien, ne** *adj* Italian ♦ *nm/f*: **Italien, ne** Italian ♦ *nm* (LING) Italian

italique [italik] *nm*: **en ~** in italics

itinéraire [itineʀɛʀ] *nm* itinerary, route; **~ bis** diversion

IUT *sigle m* = **Institut universitaire de technologie**

IVG *sigle f* (= interruption volontaire de grossesse) abortion

ivoire [ivwaʀ] *nm* ivory

ivre [ivʀ] *adj* drunk; **~ de** *(colère, bonheur)* wild with; **ivresse** *nf* drunkenness; **ivrogne** *nm/f* drunkard

J, j

j' [ʒ] *pron voir* **je**

jacasser [ʒakase] *vi* to chatter

jacinthe [ʒasɛ̃t] *nf* hyacinth

jadis [ʒadis] *adv* long ago

jaillir [ʒajiʀ] *vi* *(liquide)* to spurt out; *(cris, responses)* to burst forth

jais [ʒɛ] *nm* jet; **(d'un noir) de ~** jet-black

jalousie [ʒaluzi] *nf* jealousy; *(store)* slatted blind

jaloux, -ouse [ʒalu, uz] *adj* jealous

jamais [ʒamɛ] *adv* never; *(sans négation)* ever; **ne ... ~** never; **à ~** for ever

jambe [ʒɑ̃b] *nf* leg

jambon [ʒɑ̃bɔ̃] *nm* ham; **~ blanc** boiled *ou* cooked ham; **jambonneau, x** *nm* knuckle of ham

jante [ʒɑ̃t] *nf* (wheel) rim

janvier [ʒɑ̃vje] *nm* January

Japon [ʒapɔ̃] *nm* Japan; **japonais, e** *adj* Japanese ♦ *nm/f*: **Japonais, e** Japanese ♦ *nm* (LING) Japanese

japper [ʒape] *vi* to yap, yelp

jaquette [ʒakɛt] *nf* *(de cérémonie)* morning coat

jardin [ʒaʀdɛ̃] *nm* garden; **~ d'enfants** nursery school; **jardinage** *nm* gardening; **jardiner** *vi* to do some gardening; **jardinier, -ière** *nm/f* gardener; **jardinière** *nf* planter; *(de fenêtre)* window box; **jardinière de légumes** mixed vegetables

jargon [ʒaʀgɔ̃] *nm* *(baragouin)* gibberish; *(langue professionnelle)* jargon

jarret [ʒaʀɛ] *nm* back of knee; (CULIN) knuckle, shin

jarretelle [ʒaʀtɛl] *nf* suspender (BRIT), garter (US)

jarretière [ʒaʀtjɛʀ] *nf* garter

jaser [ʒaze] *vi* *(médire)* to gossip

jatte [ʒat] *nf* basin, bowl

jauge [ʒoʒ] *nf* *(instrument)* gauge; **~ d'essence** petrol gauge; **~ d'huile** (oil) dipstick

jaune [ʒon] *adj, nm* yellow ♦ *adv* (fam): **rire ~** to laugh on the other side of one's face; **~ d'œuf** (egg) yolk; **jaunir** *vi, vt* to turn yellow; **jaunisse** *nf* jaundice

Javel [ʒavɛl] *nf voir* **eau**

javelot [ʒavlo] *nm* javelin

J.-C. *abr* = **Jésus-Christ**

je, j' [ʒə] *pron* I

jean [dʒin] *nm* jeans *pl*

Jésus-Christ [ʒezykʀi(st)] *n* Jesus Christ; **600 avant/après ~-~** *ou* **J.-C.** 600 B.C./A.D.

jet¹ [ʒɛ] *nm* *(lancer: action)* throwing *no pl*; *(: résultat)* throw; *(jaillissement: d'eaux)* jet; *(: de sang)* spurt; **~ d'eau** spray

jet² [dʒɛt] *nm* *(avion)* jet

jetable [ʒ(ə)tabl] *adj* disposable

jetée [ʒəte] *nf* jetty; *(grande)* pier

jeter [ʒ(ə)te] *vt* *(gén)* to throw; *(se défaire de)* to throw away *ou* out; **se ~ dans** to flow into; **~ qch à qn** to throw sth to sb; *(de façon agressive)* to throw sth at sb; **~ un coup d'œil (à)** to take a look (at); **~ un sort à qn** to cast a spell on sb; **se ~ sur qn** to rush at sb

jeton [ʒ(ə)tɔ̃] *nm* *(au jeu)* counter; *(de téléphone)* token

jette *etc* [ʒɛt] *vb voir* **jeter**

jeu, x [ʒø] *nm* *(divertissement, TECH: d'une pièce)* play; *(TENNIS: partie, FOOTBALL etc: façon de jouer)* game; *(THÉÂTRE etc)* acting; *(série d'objets, jouet)* set; *(CARTES)* hand; *(au casino)*: **le ~** gambling; **être en ~** to be at stake; **entrer/mettre en ~** to come/bring into play; **~ de cartes** pack of cards; **~ d'échecs** chess set; **~ de hasard** game of chance; **~ de mots** pun; **~ de société** parlour game; **~ télévisé** television quiz; **~ vidéo** video game

jeudi [ʒødi] *nm* Thursday

jeûn [ʒœ̃]: **à ~** *adv* on an empty stomach; **être à ~** to have eaten nothing; **rester à ~** not to eat anything

jeune [ʒœn] *adj* young; **les ~s** young people; **~ fille** girl; **~ homme** young man; **~s mariés** newly-weds

jeûne [ʒøn] *nm* fast

jeunesse [ʒœnɛs] *nf* youth; *(aspect)*

youthfulness

joaillerie [ʒɔajʀi] nf jewellery; (magasin) jeweller's; **joaillier, -ière** nm/f jeweller

jogging [dʒɔgin] nm jogging; (survêtement) tracksuit; **faire du ~** to go jogging

joie [ʒwa] nf joy

joindre [ʒwɛ̃dʀ] vt to join; (à une lettre): **~ qch à** to enclose sth with; (contacter) to contact, get in touch with; **se ~ à** to join; **~ les mains** to put one's hands together

joint, e [ʒwɛ̃, ɛ̃t] adj: **pièce ~e** enclosure ♦ nm joint; (ligne) join; **~ de culasse** cylinder head gasket; **~ de robinet** washer

joli, e [ʒɔli] adj pretty, attractive; **c'est du ~!** (ironique) that's very nice!; **c'est bien ~, mais ...** that's all very well but ...

jonc [ʒɔ̃] nm (bul)rush

jonction [ʒɔ̃ksjɔ̃] nf junction

jongleur, -euse [ʒɔ̃glœʀ, øz] nm/f juggler

jonquille [ʒɔ̃kij] nf daffodil

Jordanie [ʒɔʀdani] nf: **la ~** Jordan

joue [ʒu] nf cheek

jouer [ʒwe] vt to play; (somme d'argent, réputation) to stake, wager; (simuler: sentiment) to affect, feign ♦ vi to play; (THÉÂTRE, CINÉMA) to act; (au casino) to gamble; (bois, porte: se voiler) to warp; (clef, pièce: avoir du jeu) to be loose; **~ sur** (miser) to gamble on; **~ de** (MUS) to play; **~ à** (jeu, sport, roulette) to play; **~ un tour à qn** to play a trick on sb; **~ serré** to play a close game; **~ la comédie** to put on an act; **bien joué!** well done!; **on joue Hamlet au théâtre X** Hamlet is on at the X theatre

jouet [ʒwe] nm toy; **être le ~ de** (illusion etc) to be the victim of

joueur, -euse [ʒwœʀ, øz] nm/f player; **être beau ~** to be a good loser

joufflu, e [ʒufly] adj chubby-cheeked

joug [ʒu] nm yoke

jouir [ʒwiʀ] vi (sexe: fam) to come ♦ vt: **~ de** to enjoy; **jouissance** nf pleasure; (JUR) use

joujou [ʒuʒu] (fam) nm toy

jour [ʒuʀ] nm day; (opposé à la nuit) day, daytime; (clarté) daylight; (fig: aspect) light; (ouverture) gap; **au ~ le ~** from day to day; **de nos ~s** these days; **du ~ au lendemain** overnight; **voir le ~** to be born; **au grand ~** (fig) in the open; **mettre au ~** to disclose; **mettre à ~** to update; **donner le ~ à** to give birth to; **il fait ~** it's daylight; **au grand ~** holiday; **~ de fête** holiday; **~ ouvrable** weekday, working day

journal, -aux [ʒuʀnal, o] nm (news)paper; (spécialisé) journal; (intime) diary; **~ de bord** log; **~ télévisé** television news sg

journalier, -ière [ʒuʀnalje, jɛʀ] adj daily; (banal) everyday

journalisme [ʒuʀnalism] nm journalism;

journaliste nm/f journalist

journée [ʒuʀne] nf day; **faire la ~ continue** to work over lunch

journellement [ʒuʀnɛlmɑ̃] adv daily

joyau, x [ʒwajo] nm gem, jewel

joyeux, -euse [ʒwajø, øz] adj joyful, merry; **~ Noël!** merry Christmas!; **~ anniversaire!** happy birthday!

jubiler [ʒybile] vi to be jubilant, exult

jucher [ʒyʃe] vt, vi to perch

judas [ʒyda] nm (trou) spy-hole

judiciaire [ʒydisjɛʀ] adj judicial

judicieux, -euse [ʒydisjø, jøz] adj judicious

judo [ʒydo] nm judo

juge [ʒyʒ] nm judge; **~ d'instruction** examining (BRIT) ou committing (US) magistrate; **~ de paix** justice of the peace; **~ de touche** linesman

jugé [ʒyʒe]: **au ~** adv by guesswork

jugement [ʒyʒmɑ̃] nm judgment; (JUR: au pénal) sentence; (: au civil) decision

jugeote [ʒyʒɔt] (fam) nf commonsense

juger [ʒyʒe] vt to judge; (estimer) to consider; **~ qn/qch satisfaisant** to consider sb/sth (to be) satisfactory; **~ bon de faire** to see fit to do; **~ de** to appreciate

juif, -ive [ʒɥif, ʒɥiv] adj Jewish ♦ nm/f: **J~, ive** Jew (Jewess)

juillet [ʒɥijɛ] nm July

juin [ʒɥɛ̃] nm June

jumeau, -elle, x [ʒymo, ɛl] adj, nm/f twin

jumeler [ʒym(ə)le] vt to twin

jumelle [ʒymɛl] adj, nf voir **jumeau**; **~s** nfpl (appareil) binoculars

jument [ʒymɑ̃] nf mare

jungle [ʒœ̃gl] nf jungle

jupe [ʒyp] nf skirt

jupon [ʒypɔ̃] nm waist slip

juré, e [ʒyʀe] nm/f juror

jurer [ʒyʀe] vt (obéissance etc) to swear, vow ♦ vi (dire des jurons) to swear, curse; (dissoner): **~ (avec)** to clash (with); **~ de faire/que** to swear to do/that; **~ de qch** (s'en porter garant) to swear to sth

juridique [ʒyʀidik] adj legal

juron [ʒyʀɔ̃] nm curse, swearword

jury [ʒyʀi] nm jury; (ART, SPORT) panel of judges; (SCOL) board of examiners

jus [ʒy] nm juice; (de viande) gravy, (meat) juice; **~ de fruit** fruit juice

jusque [ʒysk]: **jusqu'à** prép (endroit) as far as, (up) to; (moment) until, till; (limite) up to; **~ sur/dans** up to; (y compris) even on/in; **jusqu'à ce que** until; **jusqu'à présent** so far; **jusqu'où?** how far?

justaucorps [ʒystokɔʀ] nm leotard

juste [ʒyst] adj (équitable) just, fair; (légitime) just; (exact) right; (pertinent) apt; (étroit) tight; (insuffisant) on the short side ♦ adv rightly, correctly; (*chanter*) in tune; (*exactement, seulement*) just; **~ assez/au-dessus** just enough/above; **au ~** exactly; **le ~ milieu** the happy medium; **c'était ~** it was a close thing; **justement** *adv* justly; (*précisément*) just, precisely; **justesse** *nf* (*précision*) accuracy; (*d'une remarque*) aptness; (*d'une opinion*) soundness; **de justesse** only just

justice [ʒystis] *nf* (*équité*) fairness, justice; (ADMIN) justice; **rendre ~ à qn** to do sb justice; **justicier, -ière** *nm/f* righter of wrongs

justificatif, -ive [ʒystifikatif, iv] *adj* (*document*) supporting; **pièce justificative** written proof

justifier [ʒystifje] *vt* to justify; **~ de** to prove

juteux, -euse [ʒytø, øz] *adj* juicy

juvénile [ʒyvenil] *adj* youthful

K, k

K [ka] *nm* (INFORM) K

kaki [kaki] *adj inv* khaki

kangourou [kɑ̃guʀu] *nm* kangaroo

karaté [kaʀate] *nm* karate

karting [kaʀtiŋ] *nm* go-carting, karting

kascher [kaʃɛʀ] *adj* kosher

kayak [kajak] *nm* canoe, kayak; **faire du ~** to go canoeing

képi [kepi] *nm* kepi

kermesse [kɛʀmɛs] *nf* fair; (*fête de charité*) bazaar, (charity) fête

kidnapper [kidnape] *vt* to kidnap

kilo [kilo] *nm* = **kilogramme**

kilo...: kilogramme *nm* kilogramme; **kilométrage** *nm* number of kilometres travelled, ≈ mileage; **kilomètre** *nm* kilometre; **kilométrique** *adj* (*distance*) in kilometres

kinésithérapeute [kinezite ʀapøt] *nm/f* physiotherapist

kiosque [kjɔsk] *nm* kiosk, stall; **~ à musique** bandstand

kir [kiʀ] *nm* kir (*white wine with blackcurrant liqueur*)

kit [kit] *nm*: **en ~** in kit form

kiwi [kiwi] *nm* kiwi

klaxon [klaksɔn] *nm* horn; **klaxonner** *vi, vt* to hoot (BRIT), honk (US)

km *abr* = **kilomètre**

km/h *abr* (= *kilomètres/heure*) ≈ mph

K.-O. (*fam*) *adj inv* shattered, knackered

k-way ® [kawe] *nm* (*lightweight nylon*) cagoule

kyste [kist] *nm* cyst

L, l

l' [l] *art déf voir* **le**

la [la] *art déf voir* **le** ♦ *nm* (MUS) A; (*en chantant la gamme*) la

là [la] *adv* there; (*ici*) here; (*dans le temps*) then; **elle n'est pas ~** she isn't here; **c'est ~ que** this is where; **~ où** where; **de ~** (*fig*) hence; **par ~** (*fig*) by that; *voir aussi* **-ci**; **ce**; **celui**; **là-bas** *adv* there

label [label] *nm* stamp, seal

labeur [labœʀ] *nm* toil *no pl*, toiling *no pl*

labo [labo] (*fam*) *nm* (= *laboratoire*) lab

laboratoire [labɔʀatwaʀ] *nm* laboratory; **~ de langues** language laboratory

laborieux, -euse [labɔʀjø, jøz] *adj* (*tâche*) laborious

labour [labuʀ] *nm* ploughing *no pl*; **~s** *nmpl* (*champs*) ploughed fields; **cheval de ~** plough- *ou* cart-horse; **labourer** *vt* to plough

labyrinthe [labiʀɛ̃t] *nm* labyrinth, maze

lac [lak] *nm* lake

lacer [lase] *vt* to lace *ou* do up

lacérer [laseʀe] *vt* to tear to shreds

lacet [lase] *nm* (*de chaussure*) lace; (*de route*) sharp bend; (*piège*) snare

lâche [lɑʃ] *adj* (*poltron*) cowardly; (*desserré*) loose, slack ♦ *nm/f* coward

lâcher [lɑʃe] *vt* to let go of; (*ce qui tombe, abandonner*) to drop; (*oiseau, animal: libérer*) to release, set free; (*fig: mot, remarque*) to let slip, come out with ♦ *vi* (*freins*) to fail; **~ les amarres** (NAVIG) to cast off (the moorings); **~ prise** to let go

lâcheté [lɑʃte] *nf* cowardice

lacrymogène [lakʀimɔʒɛn] *adj*: **gaz ~** teargas

lacté, e [lakte] *adj* (*produit, régime*) milk *cpd*

lacune [lakyn] *nf* gap

là-dedans [ladədɑ̃] *adv* inside (there), in it; (*fig*) in that

là-dessous [ladsu] *adv* underneath, under there; (*fig*) behind that

là-dessus [ladsy] *adv* on there; (*fig: sur ces mots*) at that point; (: *à ce sujet*) about that

ladite [ladit] *dét voir* **ledit**

lagune [lagyn] *nf* lagoon

là-haut [lao] *adv* up there

laïc [laik] *adj, nm/f* = **laïque**

laid, e [lɛ, lɛd] *adj* ugly; **laideur** *nf* ugliness *no pl*

lainage [lɛnaʒ] *nm* (*vêtement*) woollen garment; (*étoffe*) woollen material

laine [lɛn] *nf* wool

laïque [laik] *adj* lay, civil; (SCOL) state *cpd* ♦ *nm/f* layman(-woman)

laisse [lɛs] *nf* (*de chien*) lead, leash; **tenir en ~**

to keep on a lead *ou* leash

laisser [lese] *vt* to leave ♦ *vb aux*: ~ **qn faire** to let sb do; **se ~ aller** to let o.s. go; **laisse-toi faire** let me (*ou* him *etc*) do it; **laisser-aller** *nm* carelessness, slovenliness; **laissez-passer** *nm inv* pass

lait [le] *nm* milk; **frère/sœur de ~** foster brother/sister; ~ **condensé/concentré** evaporated/condensed milk; ~ **démaquillant** cleansing milk; **laitage** *nm* dairy product; **laiterie** *nf* dairy; **laitier, -ière** *adj* dairy *cpd* ♦ *nm/f* milkman (dairywoman).

laiton [letɔ̃] *nm* brass

laitue [lety] *nf* lettuce

laïus [lajys] (*péj*) *nm* spiel

lambeau, x [lɑ̃bo] *nm* scrap; **en ~x** in tatters, tattered

lambris [lɑ̃bʀi] *nm* panelling *no pl*

lame [lam] *nf* blade; (*vague*) wave; (*lamelle*) strip; ~ **de fond** ground swell *no pl*; ~ **de rasoir** razor blade; **lamelle** *nf* thin strip *ou* blade

lamentable [lamɑ̃tabl] *adj* appalling

lamenter [lamɑ̃te] *vb*: **se ~ (sur)** to moan (over)

lampadaire [lɑ̃padɛʀ] *nm* (*de salon*) standard lamp; (*dans la rue*) street lamp

lampe [lɑ̃p] *nf* lamp; (*TECH*) valve; ~ **à souder** blowlamp; ~ **de chevet** bedside lamp; ~ **de poche** torch (*BRIT*), flashlight (*US*)

lampion [lɑ̃pjɔ̃] *nm* Chinese lantern

lance [lɑ̃s] *nf* spear; ~ **d'incendie** fire hose

lancée [lɑ̃se] *nf*: **être/continuer sur sa ~** to be under way/keep going

lancement [lɑ̃smɑ̃] *nm* launching

lance-pierres [lɑ̃spjɛʀ] *nm inv* catapult

lancer [lɑ̃se] *nm* (*SPORT*) throwing *no pl*, throw ♦ *vt* to throw; (*émettre, projeter*) to throw out, send out; (*produit, fusée, bateau, artiste*) to launch; (*injure*) to hurl, fling; **se ~** *vi* (*prendre de l'élan*) to build up speed; (*se précipiter*): **se ~ sur** *ou* **contre** to rush at; **se ~ dans** (*discussion*) to launch into; (*aventure*) to embark on; ~ **qch à qn** to throw sth to sb; (*de façon agressive*) to throw sth at sb; ~ **du poids** putting the shot

lancinant, e [lɑ̃sinɑ̃, ɑ̃t] *adj* (*douleur*) shooting

landau [lɑ̃do] *nm* pram (*BRIT*), baby carriage (*US*)

lande [lɑ̃d] *nf* moor

langage [lɑ̃gaʒ] *nm* language

langouste [lɑ̃gust] *nf* crayfish *inv*; **langoustine** *nf* Dublin Bay prawn

langue [lɑ̃g] *nf* (*ANAT, CULIN*) tongue; (*LING*) language; **tirer la ~ (à)** to stick out one's tongue (at); **de ~ française** French-speaking; ~ **maternelle** native language, mother tongue; ~ **vivante/étrangère** modern/foreign language

langueur [lɑ̃gœʀ] *nf* languidness

languir [lɑ̃giʀ] *vi* to languish; (*conversation*) to flag; **faire ~ qn** to keep sb waiting

lanière [lanjɛʀ] *nf* (*de fouet*) lash; (*de sac, bretelle*) strap

lanterne [lɑ̃tɛʀn] *nf* (*portable*) lantern; (*électrique*) light, lamp; (*de voiture*) (side)light

laper [lape] *vt* to lap up

lapidaire [lapidɛʀ] *adj* (*fig*) terse

lapin [lapɛ̃] *nm* rabbit; (*peau*) rabbitskin; (*fourrure*) cony; **poser un ~ à qn** (*fam*) to stand sb up

Laponie [lapɔni] *nf* Lapland

laps [laps] *nm*: ~ **de temps** space of time, time *no pl*

laque [lak] *nf* (*vernis*) lacquer; (*pour cheveux*) hair spray

laquelle [lakɛl] *pron voir* **lequel**

larcin [laʀsɛ̃] *nm* theft

lard [laʀ] *nm* (*bacon*) (streaky) bacon; (*graisse*) fat

lardon [laʀdɔ̃] *nm*: **~s** chopped bacon

large [laʀʒ] *adj* wide, broad; (*fig*) generous ♦ *adv*: **calculer/voir ~** to allow extra/think big ♦ *nm* (*largeur*): **5 m de ~** 5 m wide *ou* in width; (*mer*): **le ~** the open sea; **au ~ de** off; ~ **d'esprit** broad-minded; **largement** *adv* widely; (*de loin*) greatly; (*au moins*) easily; (*généreusement*) generously; **c'est largement suffisant** that's ample; **largesse** *nf* generosity; **largesses** *nfpl* liberalities; **largeur** *nf* (*qu'on mesure*) width; (*impression visuelle*) wideness, width; (*d'esprit*) broadness

larguer [laʀge] *vt* to drop; ~ **les amarres** to cast off (the moorings)

larme [laʀm] *nf* tear; (*fam: goutte*) drop; **en ~s** in tears; **larmoyer** *vi* (*yeux*) to water; (*se plaindre*) to whimper

larvé, e [laʀve] *adj* (*fig*) latent

laryngite [laʀɛ̃ʒit] *nf* laryngitis

las, lasse [lɑ, lɑs] *adj* weary

laser [lazɛʀ] *nm*: (*rayon*) ~ laser (beam); **chaîne ~** compact disc (player); **disque ~** compact disc

lasse [lɑs] *adj voir* **las**

lasser [lɑse] *vt* to weary, tire; **se ~ de** *vt* to grow weary *ou* tired of

latéral, e, -aux [lateʀal, o] *adj* side *cpd*, lateral

latin, e [latɛ̃, in] *adj* Latin ♦ *nm/f*: **L~, e** Latin ♦ *nm* (*LING*) Latin

latitude [latityd] *nf* latitude

latte [lat] *nf* lath, slat; (*de plancher*) board

lauréat, e [lɔʀea, at] *nm/f* winner

laurier [lɔʀje] *nm* (*BOT*) laurel; (*CULIN*) bay leaves *pl*

lavable [lavabl] *adj* washable

lavabo [lavabo] *nm* washbasin; **~s** *nmpl* (*toilettes*) toilet *sg*

lavage [lavaʒ] *nm* washing *no pl*, wash; **~ de cerveau** brainwashing *no pl*

lavande [lavɑ̃d] *nf* lavender

lave [lav] *nf* lava *no pl*

lave-linge [lavlɛ̃ʒ] *nm inv* washing machine

laver [lave] *vt* to wash; (*tache*) to wash off; se **~** *vi* to have a wash, wash; se **~ les mains/dents** to wash one's hands/clean one's teeth; **~ qn de** (*accusation*) to clear sb of; **laverie** *nf*: **laverie (automatique)** launderette;

lavette *nf* dish cloth; (*fam*) drip; **laveur, -euse** *nm/f* cleaner; **lave-vaisselle** *nm inv* dishwasher; **lavoir** *nm* wash house; (*évier*) sink

laxatif, -ive [laksatif, iv] *adj, nm* laxative

layette [lɛjɛt] *nf* baby clothes

MOT-CLÉ
---

le [lə], **la, l'** (*pl* **les**) *art déf* **1** le; le **livre/la pomme/l'arbre** the book/the apple/the tree; **les étudiants** the students

2 (*noms abstraits*): **le courage/l'amour/la jeunesse** courage/love/youth

3 (*indiquant la possession*): **se casser la jambe** *etc* to break one's leg *etc*; **levez la main** put your hand up; **avoir les yeux gris/le nez rouge** to have grey eyes/a red nose

4 (*temps*): **le matin/soir** in the morning/evening; mornings/evenings; **le jeudi** *etc* (*d'habitude*) on Thursdays *etc*; (*ce jeudi-là* etc) on (the) Thursday

5 (*distribution, évaluation*) a, an; **10 F le mètre/kilo** 10F a *ou* per metre/kilo; **le tiers/quart de** a third/quarter of

♦ *pron* **1** (*personne: mâle*) him; (*personne: femelle*) her; (: *pluriel*) them; **je le/la/les vois** I can see him/her/them

2 (*animal, chose: singulier*) it; (: *pluriel*) them; **je le** (*ou* **la**) **vois** I can see it; **je les vois** I can see them

3 (*remplaçant une phrase*): **je ne le savais pas** I didn't know (about it); **il était riche et ne l'est plus** he was once rich but no longer is

---

lécher [leʃe] *vt* to lick; (*laper: lait, eau*) to lick *ou* lap up; **lèche-vitrines** *nm*: **faire du lèche-vitrines** to go window-shopping

leçon [l(ə)ɔ̃] *nf* lesson; **faire la ~ à** (*fig*) to give a lecture to; **~s de conduite** driving lessons

lecteur, -trice [lɛktœʀ, tʀis] *nm/f* reader; (*d'université*) foreign language assistant ♦ *nm* (*TECH*): **~ de cassettes/CD** cassette/CD player; **~ de disquette** disk drive

lecture [lɛktyʀ] *nf* reading

ledit [lədi], **ladite** (*mpl* **lesdits**, *fpl* **lesdites**) *dét* the aforesaid

légal, e, -aux [legal, o] *adj* legal; **légaliser** *vt* to legalize; **légalité** *nf* law

légendaire [leʒɑ̃dɛʀ] *adj* legendary

légende [leʒɑ̃d] *nf* (*mythe*) legend; (*de carte, plan*) key; (*de dessin*) caption

léger, -ère [leʒe, ɛʀ] *adj* light; (*bruit, retard*) slight; (*personne: superficiel*) thoughtless; (: *volage*) free and easy; **à la légère** (*parler, agir*) rashly, thoughtlessly; **légèrement** *adv* (*s'habiller, bouger*) lightly; (*un peu*) slightly; **manger légèrement** to eat a light meal; **légèreté** *nf* lightness; (*d'une remarque*) flippancy

législatif, -ive [leʒislatif, iv] *adj* legislative; **législatives** *nfpl* general election *sg*

légitime [leʒitim] *adj* (*JUR*) lawful, legitimate; (*fig*) rightful, legitimate; **en état de ~ défense** in self-defence

legs [lɛg] *nm* legacy

léguer [lege] *vt*: **~ qch à qn** (*JUR*) to bequeath sth to sb

légume [legym] *nm* vegetable

lendemain [lɑ̃dmɛ̃] *nm*: **le ~** the next *ou* following day; **le ~ matin/soir** the next *ou* following morning/evening; **le ~ de** the day after

lent, e [lɑ̃, lɑ̃t] *adj* slow; **lentement** *adv* slowly; **lenteur** *nf* slowness *no pl*

lentille [lɑ̃tij] *nf* (*OPTIQUE*) lens *sg*; (*CULIN*) lentil

léopard [leɔpaʀ] *nm* leopard

lèpre [lɛpʀ] *nf* leprosy

MOT-CLÉ
---

lequel, laquelle [ləkɛl, lakɛl] (*mpl* **lesquels**, *fpl* **lesquelles**) (*à + lequel* = **auquel**, *de + lequel* = **duquel** *etc*) *pron* **1** (*interrogatif*) which, which one

2 (*relatif: personne: sujet*) who; (: *objet, après préposition*) whom; (: *chose*) which

♦ *adj*: **auquel cas** in which case

---

les [le] *dét voir* **le**

lesbienne [lɛsbjɛn] *nf* lesbian

lesdites [ledit], **lesdits** [ledi] *dét pl voir* **ledit**

léser [leze] *vt* to wrong

lésiner [lezine] *vi*: **ne pas ~ sur les moyens** (*pour mariage etc*) to push the boat out

lésion [lezjɔ̃] *nf* lesion, damage *no pl*

lesquelles, lesquels [lekɛl] *pron pl voir* **lequel**

lessive [lesiv] *nf* (*poudre*) washing powder; (*linge*) washing *no pl*, wash; **lessiver** *vt* to wash; (*fam: fatiguer*) to tire out, exhaust

lest [lɛst] *nm* ballast

leste [lɛst] *adj* sprightly, nimble

lettre [lɛtʀ] *nf* letter; **~s** *nfpl* (*littérature*) literature *sg*; (*SCOL*) arts (subjects); **à la ~**

literally; **en toutes ~s** in full
leucémie [løsemi] nf leukaemia

MOT-CLÉ
---

leur [lœʀ] adj possessif their; **leur maison** their
house; **leurs amis** their friends
♦ pron **1** (objet indirect) (to) them; **je leur ai
dit la vérité** I told them the truth; **je le leur ai
donné** I gave it to them, I gave them it
2 (possessif): **le(la) leur, les leurs** theirs

---

leurre [lœʀ] nm (fig: illusion) delusion;
(: duperie) deception; **leurrer** vt to delude,
deceive
leurs [lœʀ] adj voir **leur**
levain [ləvɛ̃] nm leaven
levé, e [ləve] adj: **être ~** to be up; **levée** nf
(POSTES) collection
lever [l(ə)ve] vt (vitre, bras etc) to raise;
(soulever de terre, supprimer: interdiction,
siège) to lift; (impôts, armée) to levy ♦ vi to
rise ♦ nm: **au ~** on getting up; **se ~** vi to get
up; (soleil) to rise; (jour) to break;
(brouillard) to lift; **~ de soleil** sunrise; **~ du
jour** daybreak
levier [ləvje] nm lever
lèvre [lɛvʀ] nf lip
lévrier [levʀije] nm greyhound
levure [l(ə)vyʀ] nf yeast; **~ chimique** baking
powder
lexique [leksik] nm vocabulary; (glossaire)
lexicon
lézard [lezaʀ] nm lizard
lézarde [lezaʀd] nf crack
liaison [ljɛzɔ̃] nf (rapport) connection;
(transport) link; (amoureuse) affair;
(PHONÉTIQUE) liaison; **entrer/être en ~ avec** to
get/be in contact with
liane [ljan] nf creeper
liant, e [ljɑ̃, ljɑ̃t] adj sociable
liasse [ljas] nf wad, bundle
Liban [libɑ̃] nm: **le ~** (the) Lebanon;
libanais, e adj Lebanese ♦ nm/f: **Libanais, e**
Lebanese
libeller [libele] vt (chèque, mandat): **~ (au
nom de)** to make out (to); (lettre) to word
libellule [libelyl] nf dragonfly
libéral, e, -aux [liberal, o] adj, nm/f liberal;
profession ~e (liberal) profession
libérer [libere] vt (délivrer) to free, liberate;
(relâcher: prisonnier) to discharge, release;
(: d'inhibitions) to liberate; (gaz) to release;
se ~ vi (de rendez-vous) to get out of previous
engagements
liberté [libɛʀte] nf freedom; (loisir) free time;
~s nfpl (privautés) liberties; **mettre/être en ~**
to set/be free; **en ~ provisoire/surveillée/
conditionnelle** on bail/probation/parole
libraire [libʀɛʀ] nm/f bookseller

librairie [libʀɛʀi] nf bookshop
libre [libʀ] adj free; (route, voie) clear; (place,
salle) free; (ligne) not engaged; (SCOL) non-
state; **~ de qch/de faire** free from sth/to do;
~ arbitre free will; **libre-échange** nm free
trade; **libre-service** nm self-service store
Libye [libi] nf: **la ~** Libya
licence [lisɑ̃s] nf (permis) permit; (diplôme)
degree; (liberté) liberty; **licencié, e** nm/f
(SCOL): **licencié ès lettres/en droit** ≈ Bachelor
of Arts/Law
licenciement [lisɑ̃simɑ̃] nm redundancy
licencier [lisɑ̃sje] vt (débaucher) to make
redundant, lay off; (renvoyer) to dismiss
licite [lisit] adj lawful
lie [li] nf dregs pl, sediment
lié, e [lje] adj: **très ~ avec** very friendly with ou
close to
liège [ljɛʒ] nm cork
lien [ljɛ̃] nm (corde, fig: affectif) bond;
(rapport) link, connection; **~ de parenté**
family tie
lier [lje] vt (attacher) to tie up; (joindre) to link
up; (fig: unir, engager) to bind; **se ~ avec** to
make friends with; **~ qch à** to tie ou link sth
to; **~ conversation avec** to strike up a
conversation with
lierre [ljɛʀ] nm ivy
liesse [ljes] nf: **être en ~** to be celebrating ou
jubilant
lieu, x [ljø] nm place; **~x** nmpl (locaux)
premises; (endroit: d'un accident etc) scene
sg; **en ~ sûr** in a safe place; **en premier ~** in
the first place; **en dernier ~** lastly; **avoir ~** to
take place; **tenir ~ de** to serve as; **donner ~ à**
to give rise to; **au ~ de** instead of; **lieu-dit**
(pl **lieux-dits**) nm locality
lieutenant [ljøt(ə)nɑ̃] nm lieutenant
lièvre [ljɛvʀ] nm hare
ligament [ligamɑ̃] nm ligament
ligne [liɲ] nf (gén) line; (TRANSPORTS: liaison)
service; (: trajet) route; (silhouette) figure;
entrer en ~ de compte to come into it
lignée [liɲe] nf line, lineage
ligoter [ligɔte] vt to tie up
ligue [lig] nf league; **liguer** vt: **se liguer
contre** (fig) to combine against
lilas [lila] nm lilac
limace [limas] nf slug
limande [limɑ̃d] nf dab
lime [lim] nf file; **~ à ongles** nail file; **limer** vt
to file
limier [limje] nm bloodhound; (détective)
sleuth
limitation [limitasjɔ̃] nf: **~ de vitesse** speed
limit
limite [limit] nf (de terrain) boundary; (partie
ou point extrême) limit; **vitesse/charge ~;**
maximum speed/load; **cas ~** borderline case;

date ~ deadline; **limiter** vt (restreindre) to
limit, restrict; (délimiter) to border;
limitrophe adj border cpd
limoger [limɔʒe] vt to dismiss
limon [limɔ̃] nm silt
limonade [limɔnad] nf lemonade
lin [lɛ̃] nm (tissu) linen
linceul [lɛ̃sœl] nm shroud
linge [lɛ̃ʒ] nm (serviettes etc) linen; (lessive)
washing; (aussi: ~ de corps) underwear;
lingerie nf lingerie, underwear
lingot [lɛ̃go] nm ingot
linguistique [lɛ̃gɥistik] adj linguistic ♦ nf
linguistics sg
lion, ne [ljɔ̃, ljɔn] nm/f lion (lioness); (signe):
le L~ Leo; **lionceau, x** nm lion cub
liqueur [likœʀ] nf liqueur
liquidation [likidasjɔ̃] nf (vente) sale
liquide [likid] adj liquid ♦ nm liquid; (COMM):
en ~ in ready money ou cash; **liquider** vt to
liquidate; (COMM: articles) to clear, sell off;
liquidités nfpl (COMM) liquid assets
lire [liʀ] nf (monnaie) lira ♦ vt, vi to read
lis [lis] nm = **lys**
lisible [lizibl] adj legible
lisière [lizjɛʀ] nf (de forêt) edge
lisons [lizɔ̃] vb voir **lire**
lisse [lis] adj smooth
liste [list] nf list; **faire la ~ de** to list;
~ **électorale** electoral roll; **listing** nm
(INFORM) printout
lit [li] nm bed; **petit ~, lit à une place** single
bed; **grand ~, lit à deux places** double bed;
faire son ~ to make one's bed; **aller/se mettre
au ~** to go to/get into bed; ~ **de camp**
campbed; ~ **d'enfant** cot (BRIT), crib (US)
literie [litʀi] nf bedding, bedclothes pl
litière [litjɛʀ] nf litter
litige [litiʒ] nm dispute
litre [litʀ] nm litre
littéraire [liteʀɛʀ] adj literary ♦ nm/f arts
student; **elle est très ~** (she's very literary)
littéral, e, -aux [liteʀal, o] adj literal
littérature [liteʀatyʀ] nf literature
littoral, -aux [litɔʀal, o] nm coast
liturgie [lityʀʒi] nf liturgy
livide [livid] adj livid, pallid
livraison [livʀɛzɔ̃] nf delivery
livre [livʀ] nm book ♦ nf (poids, monnaie)
pound; ~ **de bord** logbook; ~ **de poche**
paperback
livré, e [livʀe] adj: ~ **à soi-même** left to o.s.
ou one's own devices; **livrée** nf livery
livrer [livʀe] vt (COMM) to deliver; (otage,
coupable) to hand over; (secret, information)
to give away; **se ~ à** (se confier) to confide in;
(se rendre, s'abandonner) to give o.s. up to;
(faire: pratiques, actes) to indulge in;
(enquête) to carry out

livret [livʀɛ] nm booklet; (d'opéra) libretto;
~ **de caisse d'épargne** (savings) bank-book;
~ **de famille** (official) family record book;
~ **scolaire** (school) report book
livreur, -euse [livʀœʀ, øz] nm/f delivery
boy ou man/girl ou woman
local, e, -aux [lɔkal] adj local ♦ nm (salle)
premises pl; voir aussi **locaux; localiser** vt
(repérer) to locate, place; (limiter) to confine;
localité nf locality
locataire [lɔkatɛʀ] nm/f tenant; (de chambre)
lodger
location [lɔkasjɔ̃] nf (par le locataire, le
loueur) renting; (par le propriétaire) renting
out, letting; (THÉÂTRE) booking office; "~ **de
voitures**" "car rental"; **habiter en ~** to live in
rented accommodation; **prendre une ~ (pour
les vacances)** to rent a house etc (for the
holidays)
locaux [lɔko] nmpl premises
locomotive [lɔkɔmɔtiv] nf locomotive,
engine
locution [lɔkysjɔ̃] nf phrase
loge [lɔʒ] nf (THÉÂTRE: d'artiste) dressing room;
(: de spectateurs) box; (de concierge, franc-
maçon) lodge
logement [lɔʒmɑ̃] nm accommodation no pl
(BRIT), accommodations pl (US); (appartement) flat (BRIT), apartment (US);
(hébergement) housing no pl
loger [lɔʒe] vt to accommodate ♦ vi to live; **se
~ dans** (suj: balle, flèche) to lodge itself in;
trouver à se ~ to find accommodation;
logeur, -euse nm/f landlord(-lady)
logiciel [lɔʒisjɛl] nm software
logique [lɔʒik] adj logical ♦ nf logic
logis [lɔʒi] nm abode, dwelling
logo [lɔgo] nm logo
loi [lwa] nf law; **faire la ~** to lay down the law
loin [lwɛ̃] adv far; (dans le temps: futur) a long
way off; (: passé) a long time ago; **plus ~**
further; ~ **de** far from; **au ~** far off; **de ~** from
a distance; (fig: de beaucoup) by far
lointain, e [lwɛ̃tɛ̃, ɛn] adj faraway, distant;
(dans le futur, passé) distant; (cause, parent)
remote, distant ♦ nm: **dans le ~** in the
distance
loir [lwaʀ] nm dormouse
loisir [lwaziʀ] nm: **heures de ~** spare time; **~s**
nmpl (temps libre) leisure sg; (activités) leisure
activities; **avoir le ~ de faire** to have the time
ou opportunity to do; **à ~** at leisure
londonien, ne [lɔ̃dɔnjɛ̃, jɛn] adj London
cpd, of London ♦ nm/f: **L~, ne** Londoner
Londres [lɔ̃dʀ] n London
long, longue [lɔ̃, lɔ̃g] adj long ♦ adv: **en
savoir ~** to know a great deal ♦ nm: **de 3 m
de ~** 3 m long, 3 m in length; **ne pas faire
~ feu** not to last long; **(tout) le ~ de** (all)

along; **tout au ~ de** (*année, vie*) throughout; **de ~ en large** (*marcher*) to and fro, up and down; *voir aussi* **longue**

longer [lɔ̃ʒe] *vt* to go (*ou* walk *ou* drive) along(side); (*suj: mur, route*) to border

longiligne [lɔ̃ʒiliɲ] *adj* long-limbed

longitude [lɔ̃ʒityd] *nf* longitude

longtemps [lɔ̃tɑ̃] *adv* (for) a long time, (for) long; **avant ~** before long; **pour** *ou* **pendant ~** for a long time; **mettre ~ à faire** to take a long time to do

longue [lɔ̃g] *adj voir* **long ♦** *nf*: **à la ~** in the end; **longuement** *adv* (*longtemps*) for a long time; (*en détail*) at length

longueur [lɔ̃gœʀ] *nf* length; **~s** *nfpl* (*fig: d'un film etc*) tedious parts; **en ~** lengthwise; **tirer en ~** to drag on; **à ~ de journée** all day long; **~ d'onde** wavelength

longue-vue [lɔ̃gvy] *nf* telescope

look [luk] (*fam*) *nm* look, image

lopin [lɔpɛ̃] *nm*: **~ de terre** patch of land

loque [lɔk] *nf* (*personne*) wreck; **~s** *nfpl* (*habits*) rags

loquet [lɔkɛ] *nm* latch

lorgner [lɔʀɲe] *vt* to eye; (*fig*) to have one's eye on

lors [lɔʀ]: **~ de** *prép* at the time of; during

lorsque [lɔʀsk] *conj* when, as

losange [lɔzɑ̃ʒ] *nm* diamond

lot [lo] *nm* (*part*) share; (*de ~erie*) prize; (*fig: destin*) fate, lot; (*COMM, INFORM*) batch; **le gros ~** the jackpot

loterie [lɔtʀi] *nf* lottery

loti, e [lɔti] *adj*: **bien/mal ~** well-/badly off

lotion [losjɔ̃] *nf* lotion

lotissement [lɔtismɑ̃] *nm* housing development; (*parcelle*) plot, lot

loto [lɔto] *nm* lotto

lotte [lɔt] *nf* monkfish

louable [lwabl] *adj* commendable

louanges [lwɑ̃ʒ] *nfpl* praise *sg*

loubard [lubaʀ] (*fam*) *nm* lout

louche [luʃ] *adj* shady, fishy, dubious **♦** *nf* ladle; **loucher** *vi* to squint

louer [lwe] *vt* (*maison: suj: propriétaire*) to let, rent (out); (*: locataire*) to rent; (*voiture etc: entreprise*) to hire out (*BRIT*), rent (out); (*: locataire*) to hire, rent; (*réserver*) to book; (*faire l'éloge de*) to praise; **"à ~"** "to let" (*BRIT*), "for rent" (*US*)

loup [lu] *nm* wolf

loupe [lup] *nf* magnifying glass

louper [lupe] (*fam*) *vt* (*manquer*) to miss; (*examen*) to flunk

lourd, e [luʀ, luʀd] *adj, adv* heavy; **~ de** (*conséquences, menaces*) charged with; **il fait ~** the weather is close, it's sultry; **lourdaud, e** (*péj*) *adj* clumsy; **lourdement** *adv* heavily; **lourdeur** *nf* weight; **lourdeurs d'estomac**

indigestion

loutre [lutʀ] *nf* otter

louveteau, x [luv(ə)to] *nm* wolf-cub; (*scout*) cub (*scout*)

louvoyer [luvwaje] *vi* (*fig*) to hedge, evade the issue

loyal, e, -aux [lwajal, o] *adj* (*fidèle*) loyal, faithful; (*fair-play*) fair; **loyauté** *nf* loyalty, faithfulness; fairness

loyer [lwaje] *nm* rent

lu, e [ly] *pp de* **lire**

lubie [lybi] *nf* whim, craze

lubrifiant [lybʀifjɑ̃, jɑ̃t] *nm* lubricant

lubrifier [lybʀifje] *vt* to lubricate

lubrique [lybʀik] *adj* lecherous

lucarne [lykaʀn] *nf* skylight

lucide [lysid] *adj* lucid; (*accidenté*) conscious

lucratif, -ive [lykʀatif, iv] *adj* lucrative, profitable; **à but non ~** non profit-making

lueur [lɥœʀ] *nf* (*pâle*) (faint) light; (*chatoyante*) glimmer *no pl*; (*fig*) glimmer; gleam

luge [lyʒ] *nf* sledge (*BRIT*), sled (*US*)

lugubre [lygybʀ] *adj* gloomy, dismal

MOT-CLÉ

lui [lɥi] *pron* **1** (*objet indirect: mâle*) (to) him; (*: femelle*) (to) her; (*: chose, animal*) (to) it; **je lui ai parlé** I have spoken to him (*ou* to her); **il lui a offert un cadeau** he gave him (*ou* her) a present

2 (*après préposition, comparatif: personne*) him; (*: chose, animal*) it; **elle est contente de lui** she is pleased with him; **je la connais mieux que lui** I know her better than he does; I know her better than him

3 (*sujet, forme emphatique*) he; **lui, il est à Paris** HE is in Paris

4: **lui-même** himself; itself

---

luire [lɥiʀ] *vi* to shine; (*en rougeoyant*) to glow

lumière [lymjɛʀ] *nf* light; **mettre en ~** (*fig*) to highlight; **~ du jour** daylight

luminaire [lyminɛʀ] *nm* lamp, light

lumineux, -euse [lyminø, øz] *adj* luminous; (*éclairé*) illuminated; (*ciel, couleur*) bright; (*rayon*) of light, light *cpd*; (*fig: regard*) radiant

lunatique [lynatik] *adj* whimsical, temperamental

lundi [lœ̃di] *nm* Monday; **~ de Pâques** Easter Monday

lune [lyn] *nf* moon; **~ de miel** honeymoon

lunette [lynɛt] *nf*: **~s** *nfpl* glasses, spectacles; (*protectrices*) goggles; **~ arrière** (*AUTO*) rear window; **~s de soleil** sunglasses

lus *etc* [ly] *vb voir* **lire**

lustre [lystʀ] *nm* (*de plafond*) chandelier; (*fig:*

éclat) lustre; **lustrer** vt to shine
lut [ly] vb voir **lire**
luth [lyt] nm lute
lutin [lytɛ̃] nm imp, goblin
lutte [lyt] nf (conflit) struggle; (sport)
wrestling; **lutter** vi to fight, struggle
luxe [lyks] nm luxury; **de ~** luxury cpd
Luxembourg [lyksɑ̃buʀ] nm: **le ~**
Luxembourg
luxer [lykse] vt: **se ~ l'épaule** to dislocate
one's shoulder
luxueux, -euse [lyksɥø, øz] adj luxurious
luxure [lyksyʀ] nf lust
luxuriant, e [lyksyʀjɑ̃, jɑ̃t] adj luxuriant
lycée [lise] nm secondary school; **lycéen, ne**
nm/f secondary school pupil
lyophilisé, e [ljɔfilize] adj (café) freeze-dried
lyrique [liʀik] adj lyrical; (OPÉRA) lyric; **artiste**
~ opera singer
lys [lis] nm lily

M, m

M abr = **Monsieur**
m' [m] pron voir **me**
ma [ma] adj voir **mon**
macaron [makaʀɔ̃] nm (gâteau) macaroon;
(insigne) (round) badge
macaronis [makaʀɔni] nmpl macaroni sg
macédoine [masedwan] nf: **~ de fruits** fruit
salad; **~ de légumes** mixed vegetables
macérer [maseʀe] vi, vt to macerate; (dans
du vinaigre) to pickle
mâcher [maʃe] vt to chew; **ne pas ~ ses mots**
not to mince one's words
machin [maʃɛ̃] (fam) nm thing(umajig)
machinal, e, -aux [maʃinal, o] adj
mechanical, automatic; **machinalement** adv
mechanically, automatically
machination [maʃinasjɔ̃] nf frame-up
machine [maʃin] nf machine; (locomotive)
engine; **~ à écrire** typewriter; **~ à laver/coudre**
washing/sewing machine; **~ à sous** fruit
machine
macho [matʃo] (fam) nm male chauvinist
mâchoire [maʃwaʀ] nf jaw
mâchonner [maʃɔne] vt to chew (at)
maçon [masɔ̃] nm builder; (poseur de briques)
bricklayer; **maçonnerie** nf (murs) brickwork;
(pierres) masonry, stonework
maculer [makyle] vt to stain
Madame [madam] (pl **Mesdames**) nf: **~ X**
Mrs X; **occupez-vous de ~/Monsieur/**
Mademoiselle please serve this lady/
gentleman/(young) lady; **bonjour ~/**
Monsieur/Mademoiselle good morning; (ton
déférent) good morning Madam/Sir/Madam;
(le nom est connu) good morning Mrs/Mr/

Miss X; **~/Monsieur/Mademoiselle!** (pour
appeler) Madam/Sir/Miss!; **~/Monsieur/**
Mademoiselle (sur lettre) Dear Madam/Sir/
Madam; **chère ~/cher Monsieur/chère**
Mademoiselle Dear Mrs/Mr/Miss X;
Mesdames Ladies
madeleine [madlɛn] nf madeleine; small
sponge cake
Mademoiselle [madmwazɛl] (pl
Mesdemoiselles) nf Miss; voir aussi **Madame**
madère [madɛʀ] nm Madeira (wine)
magasin [magazɛ̃] nm (boutique) shop;
(entrepôt) warehouse; **en ~** (COMM) in stock
magazine [magazin] nm magazine
Maghreb [magʀɛb] nm: **le ~** North Africa;
maghrébin, e adj North African ♦ nm/f:
Maghrébin, e North African
magicien, ne [maʒisjɛ̃, jɛn] nm/f magician
magie [maʒi] nf magic; **magique** adj magic;
(enchanteur) magical
magistral, e, -aux [maʒistʀal, o] adj
(œuvre, adresse) masterly; (ton) authoritative;
cours ~ lecture
magistrat [maʒistʀa] nm magistrate
magnat [magna] nm tycoon
magnétique [maɲetik] adj magnetic
magnétiser [maɲetize] vt to magnetize;
(fig) to mesmerize, hypnotize
magnétophone [maɲetɔfɔn] nm tape
recorder; **~ à cassettes** cassette recorder
magnétoscope [maɲetɔskɔp] nm video-
tape recorder
magnifique [maɲifik] adj magnificent
magot [mago] (fam) nm (argent) pile (of
money); (économies) nest egg
magouille [maguj] (fam) nf scheming;
magouiller (fam) vi to scheme
magret [magʀɛ] nm: **~ de canard** duck
steaklet
mai [mɛ] nm May
maigre [mɛgʀ] adj (very) thin, skinny;
(viande) lean; (fromage) low-fat; (végétation)
thin, sparse; (fig) poor, meagre, skimpy;
jours ~s days of abstinence, fish days;
maigreur nf thinness; **maigrir** vi to get
thinner, lose weight; **maigrir de 2 kilos** to lose
2 kilos
maille [maj] nf stitch; **avoir ~ à partir avec qn**
to have a brush with sb; **~ à l'endroit/à**
l'envers plain/purl stitch
maillet [majɛ] nm mallet
maillon [majɔ̃] nm link
maillot [majo] nm (aussi: **~ de corps**) vest;
(de sportif) jersey; **~ de bain** swimsuit;
(d'homme) bathing trunks pl
main [mɛ̃] nf hand; **à la ~** in one's hand; **se**
donner la ~ to hold hands; **donner ou tendre**
la ~ à qn to hold out one's hand to sb; **serrer**
la ~ à qn to shake hands with sb; **sous la ~** to

ou at hand; **à remettre en ~s propres** to be delivered personally; **mettre la dernière ~ à** to put the finishing touches to; **se faire/perdre la ~** to get one's hand in/lose one's touch; **avoir qch bien en ~** to have (got) the hang of sth; **main-d'œuvre** *nf* manpower, labour; **main-forte** *nf*: **prêter main-forte à qn** to come to sb's assistance; **mainmise** *nf* (*fig*): **mainmise sur** complete hold on

maint, e [mɛ̃, mɛ̃t] *adj* many a; **~s** many; **à ~es reprises** time and (time) again

maintenant [mɛ̃t(ə)nɑ̃] *adv* now; (*actuellement*) nowadays

maintenir [mɛ̃t(ə)niʀ] *vt* (*retenir, soutenir*) to support; (*contenir: foule etc*) to hold back; (*conserver, affirmer*) to maintain; **se ~** *vi* (*prix*) to keep steady; (*amélioration*) to persist

maintien [mɛ̃tjɛ̃] *nm* (*sauvegarde*) maintenance; (*attitude*) bearing

maire [mɛʀ] *nm* mayor; **mairie** *nf* (*bâtiment*) town hall; (*administration*) town council

mais [mɛ] *conj* but; **~ non!** of course not!; **~ enfin** but after all; (*indignation*) look here!

maïs [mais] *nm* maize (*BRIT*), corn (*US*)

maison [mɛzɔ̃] *nf* house; (*chez-soi*) home; (*COMM*) firm ♦ *adj inv* (*CULIN*) home-made; (*fig*) in-house, own; **à la ~** at home; (*direction*) home; **~ close** *ou* **de passe** brothel; **~ de repos** convalescent home; **~ de santé** mental home; **~ des jeunes** ≈ youth club; **~ mère** parent company; **maisonnée** *nf* household, family; **maisonnette** *nf* small house, cottage

maître, -esse [mɛtʀ, mɛtʀɛs] *nm/f* master (mistress); (*SCOL*) teacher, schoolmaster(-mistress) ♦ *nm* (*peintre etc*) master; (*titre*): **M~ Maître**, *term of address gen for a barrister* ♦ *adj* (*principal, essentiel*) main; **être ~ de** (*soi, situation*) to be in control of; **une maîtresse femme** a managing woman; **~ chanteur** blackmailer; **~ d'école** schoolmaster; **~ d'hôtel** (*domestique*) butler; (*d'hôtel*) head waiter; **~ nageur** lifeguard; **maîtresse** *nf* (*amante*) mistress; **maîtresse (d'école)** teacher, (school)mistress; **maîtresse de maison** hostess; (*ménagère*) housewife

maîtrise [mɛtʀiz] *nf* (*aussi*: **~ de soi**) self-control, self-possession; (*habileté*) skill, mastery; (*suprématie*) mastery, command; (*diplôme*) ≈ master's degree; **maîtriser** *vt* (*cheval, incendie*) to (bring under) control; (*sujet*) to master; (*émotion*) to control, master; **se maîtriser** to control o.s.

maïzena ® [maizena] *nf* cornflour

majestueux, -euse [maʒɛstɥø, øz] *adj* majestic

majeur, e [maʒœʀ] *adj* (*important*) major; (*JUR*) of age ♦ *nm* (*doigt*) middle finger; **en ~e partie** for the most part; **la ~e partie de** most of

majoration [maʒɔʀasjɔ̃] *nf* rise, increase

majorer [maʒɔʀe] *vt* to increase

majoritaire [maʒɔʀitɛʀ] *adj* majority *cpd*

majorité [maʒɔʀite] *nf* (*gén*) majority; (*parti*) party in power; **en ~** mainly

majuscule [maʒyskyl] *adj, nf*: **(lettre) ~** capital (letter)

mal [mal, mo] (*pl* **maux**) *nm* (*opposé au bien*) evil; (*tort, dommage*) harm; (*douleur physique*) pain, ache; (*~adie*) illness, sickness *no pl* ♦ *adv* badly ♦ *adj* bad, wrong; **être ~ à l'aise** to be uncomfortable; **être ~ avec qn** to be on bad terms with sb; **il a ~ compris** he misunderstood; **dire/penser du ~ de** to speak/think ill of; **ne voir aucun ~ à** to see no harm in, see nothing wrong in; **faire ~ à qn** to hurt sb; **se faire ~** to hurt o.s.; **se donner du ~ pour faire qch** to go to a lot of trouble to do sth; **ça fait ~** it hurts; **j'ai ~ au dos** my back hurts; **avoir ~ à la tête/à la gorge/aux dents** to have a headache/a sore throat/toothache; **avoir le ~ du pays** to be homesick; *voir aussi* **cœur**; **maux**; **~ de mer** seasickness; **~ en point** in a bad state

malade [malad] *adj* ill, sick; (*poitrine, jambe*) bad; (*plante*) diseased ♦ *nm/f* invalid, sick person; (*à l'hôpital etc*) patient; **tomber ~** to fall ill; **être ~ du cœur** to have heart trouble *ou* a bad heart; **~ mental** mentally sick *ou* ill person; **maladie** *nf* (*spécifique*) disease, illness; (*mauvaise santé*) illness, sickness; **maladif, -ive** *adj* sickly; (*curiosité, besoin*) pathological

maladresse [maladʀɛs] *nf* clumsiness *no pl*; (*gaffe*) blunder

maladroit, e [maladʀwa, wat] *adj* clumsy

malaise [malɛz] *nm* (*MÉD*) feeling of faintness; (*fig*) uneasiness, malaise; **avoir un ~** to feel faint

malaisé, e [maleze] *adj* difficult

malaria [malaʀja] *nf* malaria

malaxer [malakse] *vt* (*pétrir*) to knead; (*mélanger*) to mix

malchance [malʃɑ̃s] *nf* misfortune, ill luck *no pl*; **par ~** unfortunately; **malchanceux, -euse** *adj* unlucky

mâle [mɑl] *adj* (*aussi ÉLEC, TECH*) male; (*viril: voix, traits*) manly ♦ *nm* male

malédiction [malediksjɔ̃] *nf* curse

mal...: **malencontreux, -euse** *adj* unfortunate, untoward; **mal-en-point** *adj inv* in a sorry state; **malentendant, e** *nm/f*: **les malentendants** the hard of hearing; **malentendu** *nm* misunderstanding; **malfaçon** *nf* fault; **malfaisant, e** *adj* evil, harmful; **malfaiteur** *nm* lawbreaker, criminal; (*voleur*) burglar, thief; **malfamé, e** *adj* disreputable

malgache [malgaʃ] *adj* Madagascan,
Malagasy ♦ *nm/f:* **M~** Madagascan, Malagasy
♦ *nm* (*LING*) Malagasy

malgré [malgre] *prép* in spite of, despite;
~ tout all the same

malhabile [malabil] *adj* clumsy, awkward

malheur [malœr] *nm* (*situation*) adversity,
misfortune; (*événement*) misfortune; (: *très
grave*) disaster, tragedy; **faire un ~** to be a
smash hit; **malheureusement** *adv*
unfortunately; **malheureux, -euse** *adj*
(*triste*) unhappy, miserable; (*infortuné,
regrettable*) unfortunate; (*malchanceux*)
unlucky; (*insignifiant*) wretched ♦ *nm/f* poor
soul; **les malheureux** the destitute

malhonnête [malɔnɛt] *adj* dishonest;
malhonnêteté *nf* dishonesty

malice [malis] *nf* mischievousness;
(*méchanceté*): **par ~** out of malice *ou* spite;
sans ~ guileless; **malicieux, -euse** *adj*
mischievous

malin, -igne [malɛ̃, maliɲ] *adj* (*futé*: *f gén*:
~e) smart, shrewd; (*MÉD*) malignant

malingre [malɛ̃gr] *adj* puny

malle [mal] *nf* trunk; **mallette** *nf* (*small*)
suitcase; (*porte-documents*) attaché case

malmener [malməne] *vt* to manhandle; (*fig*)
to give a rough handling to

malodorant, e [malɔdɔrɑ̃, ɑ̃t] *adj* foul- *ou*
ill-smelling

malotru [malɔtry] *nm* lout, boor

malpoli, e [malpɔli] *adj* impolite

malpropre [malprɔpr] *adj* dirty

malsain, e [malsɛ̃, ɛn] *adj* unhealthy

malt [malt] *nm* malt

Malte [malt] *nf* Malta

maltraiter [maltrete] *vt* to manhandle, ill-
treat

malveillance [malvejɑ̃s] *nf* (*animosité*) ill
will; (*intention de nuire*) malevolence

malversation [malvɛrsasjɔ̃] *nf*
embezzlement

maman [mamɑ̃] *nf* mum(my), mother

mamelle [mamɛl] *nf* teat

mamelon [mam(ə)lɔ̃] *nm* (*ANAT*) nipple

mamie [mami] *nf* (*fam*) granny

mammifère [mamifɛr] *nm* mammal

mammouth [mamut] *nm* mammoth

manche [mɑ̃ʃ] *nf* (*de vêtement*) sleeve; (*d'un
jeu, tournoi*) round; (*GÉO*): **la M~** the Channel
♦ *nm* (*d'outil, casserole*) handle; (*de pelle,
pioche etc*) shaft; **à ~s courtes/longues** short-
/long-sleeved

manchette [mɑ̃ʃɛt] *nf* (*de chemise*) cuff;
(*coup*) forearm blow; (*titre*) headline

manchot [mɑ̃ʃo, ɔt] *nm* one-armed man;
armless man; (*ZOOL*) penguin

mandarine [mɑ̃darin] *nf* mandarin
(orange), tangerine

mandat [mɑ̃da] *nm* (*postal*) postal *ou* money
order; (*d'un député etc*) mandate;
(*procuration*) power of attorney, proxy;
(*POLICE*) warrant; **~ d'arrêt** warrant for arrest;
mandataire *nm/f* (*représentant*)
representative; (*JUR*) proxy

manège [manɛʒ] *nm* riding school; (*à la
foire*) roundabout, merry-go-round; (*fig*)
game, ploy

manette [manɛt] *nf* lever, tap; **~ de jeu**
joystick

mangeable [mɑ̃ʒabl] *adj* edible, eatable

mangeoire [mɑ̃ʒwar] *nf* trough, manger

manger [mɑ̃ʒe] *vt* to eat; (*ronger: suj: rouille
etc*) to eat into *ou* away ♦ *vi* to eat; **donner à
~ à** (*enfant*) to feed; **mangeur, -euse** *nm/f*
eater; **gros mangeur** big eater

mangue [mɑ̃g] *nf* mango

maniable [manjabl] *adj* (*outil*) handy;
(*voiture, voilier*) easy to handle

maniaque [manjak] *adj* finicky, fussy ♦ *nm/f*
(*méticuleux*) fusspot; (*fou*) maniac

manie [mani] *nf* (*tic*) odd habit; (*obsession*)
mania; **avoir la ~ de** to be obsessive about

manier [manje] *vt* to handle

manière [manjɛr] *nf* (*façon*) way, manner;
~s *nfpl* (*attitude*) manners; (*chichis*) fuss *sg*;
de ~ à so as to; **de cette ~** in this way *ou*
manner; **d'une certaine ~** in a way; **de toute ~**
in any case

maniéré, e [manjere] *adj* affected

manif [manif] *nf* (*fam*) ref demo

manifestant, e [manifestɑ̃, ɑ̃t] *nm/f*
demonstrator

manifestation [manifestasjɔ̃] *nf* (*de joie,
mécontentement*) expression, demonstration;
(*symptôme*) outward sign; (*culturelle etc*)
event; (*POL*) demonstration

manifeste [manifest] *adj* obvious, evident
♦ *nm* manifesto; **manifester** *vt* (*volonté,
intentions*) to show, indicate; (*joie, peur*) to
express, show ♦ *vi* to demonstrate; **se
manifester** *vi* (*émotion*) to show *ou* express
itself; (*difficultés*) to arise; (*symptômes*) to
appear

manigance [manigɑ̃s] *nf* scheme;
manigancer *vt* to plot

manipulation [manipylasjɔ̃] *nf* handling;
(*POL, génétique*) manipulation

manipuler [manipyle] *vt* to handle; (*fig*) to
manipulate

manivelle [manivɛl] *nf* crank

mannequin [mankɛ̃] *nm* (*COUTURE*) dummy;
(*MODE*) model

manœuvre [manœvr] *nf* (*gén*) manoeuvre
(*BRIT*), maneuver (*US*) ♦ *nm* labourer;
manœuvrer *vt* to manoeuvre (*BRIT*),
maneuver (*US*); (*levier, machine*) to operate
♦ *vi* to manoeuvre

manoir [manwaʀ] *nm* manor *ou* country house

manque [mɑ̃k] *nm* (*insuffisance*): ~ **de** lack of; (*vide*) emptiness, gap; (*MÉD*) withdrawal; **être en état de** ~ to suffer withdrawal symptoms

manqué, e [mɑ̃ke] *adj* failed; **garçon** ~ tomboy

manquer [mɑ̃ke] *vi* (*faire défaut*) to be lacking; (*être absent*) to be missing; (*échouer*) to fail ♦ *vt* to miss ♦ *vb impers*: **il (nous) manque encore 100 F** we are still 100 F short; **il manque des pages (au livre)** there are some pages missing (from the book); **il/cela me manque** I miss him/this; ~ **à** (*règles etc*) to be in breach of, fail to observe; ~ **de** to lack; **je ne ~ai pas de le lui dire** I'll be sure to tell him; **il a manqué (de) se tuer** he very nearly got killed

mansarde [mɑ̃saʀd] *nf* attic; **mansardé, e** *adj*: **chambre mansardée** attic room

manteau, x [mɑ̃to] *nm* coat

manucure [manykyʀ] *nf* manicurist

manuel, le [manɥɛl] *adj* manual ♦ *nm* (*ouvrage*) manual, handbook

manufacture [manyfaktyʀ] *nf* factory; **manufacturé, e** *adj* manufactured

manuscrit, e [manyskʀi, it] *adj* handwritten ♦ *nm* manuscript

manutention [manytɑ̃sjɔ̃] *nf* (*COMM*) handling

mappemonde [mapmɔ̃d] *nf* (*plane*) map of the world; (*sphère*) globe

maquereau, x [makʀo] *nm* (*ZOOL*) mackerel *inv*; (*fam*) pimp

maquette [makɛt] *nf* (*à échelle réduite*) (scale) model; (*d'une page illustrée*) paste-up

maquillage [makijaʒ] *nm* making up; (*crème etc*) make-up

maquiller [makije] *vt* (*personne, visage*) to make up; (*truquer: passeport, statistique*) to fake; (: *voiture volée*) to do over (*respray etc*); **se** ~ *vi* to make up (one's face)

maquis [maki] *nm* (*GÉO*) scrub; (*MIL*) maquis, underground fighting *no pl*

maraîcher, -ère [maʀeʃe, ɛʀ] *adj*: **cultures maraîchères** market gardening *sg* ♦ *nm/f* market gardener

marais [maʀɛ] *nm* marsh, swamp

marasme [maʀasm] *nm* stagnation, slump

marathon [maʀatɔ̃] *nm* marathon

maraudeur [maʀodœʀ, øz] *nm* prowler

marbre [maʀbʀ] *nm* marble

marc [maʀ] *nm* (*de raisin, pommes*) marc; ~ **de café** coffee grounds *pl ou* dregs *pl*

marchand, e [maʀʃɑ̃, ɑ̃d] *nm/f* shopkeeper, tradesman(-woman); (*au marché*) stallholder; (*de vins, charbon*) merchant ♦ *adj*: **prix/valeur ~(e)** market price/value; **~(e) de fruits** fruiterer (*BRIT*), fruit seller (*US*); **~(e) de journaux** newsagent; **~(e) de légumes** greengrocer (*BRIT*), produce dealer (*US*); **~(e) de poissons** fishmonger; **marchander** *vi* to bargain, haggle; **marchandise** *nf* goods *pl*, merchandise *no pl*

marche [maʀʃ] *nf* (*d'escalier*) step; (*activité*) walking; (*promenade, trajet, allure*) walk; (*démarche*) walk, gait; (*MIL etc*) march; (*fonctionnement*) running; (*des événements*) course; **dans le sens de la** ~ (*RAIL*) facing the engine; **en** ~ (*monter etc*) while the vehicle is moving *ou* in motion; **mettre en** ~ to start; **se mettre en** ~ (*personne*) to get moving; (*machine*) to start; **être en état de** ~ to be in working order; ~ **à suivre** (*correct*) procedure; ~ **arrière** reverse (gear); **faire** ~ **arrière** to reverse; (*fig*) to backtrack, backpedal

marché [maʀʃe] *nm* market; (*transaction*) bargain, deal; **faire du** ~ **noir** to buy and sell on the black market; ~ **aux puces** flea market; **M~ commun** Common Market

marchepied [maʀʃəpje] *nm* (*RAIL*) step

marcher [maʀʃe] *vi* to walk; (*MIL*) to march; (*aller: voiture, train, affaires*) to go; (*prospérer*) to go well; (*fonctionner*) to work, run; (*fam: consentir*) to go along, agree; (: *croire naïvement*) to be taken in; **faire** ~ **qn** (*taquiner*) to pull sb's leg; (*tromper*) to lead sb up the garden path; **marcheur, -euse** *nm/f* walker

mardi [maʀdi] *nm* Tuesday; **M~ gras** Shrove Tuesday

mare [maʀ] *nf* pond; (*flaque*) pool

marécage [maʀekaʒ] *nm* marsh, swamp; **marécageux, -euse** *adj* marshy

maréchal, -aux [maʀeʃal, o] *nm* marshal; **maréchal-ferrant** [maʀeʃalfɛʀɑ̃, maʀefo-] (*pl* **maréchaux-ferrants**) *nm* blacksmith, farrier

marée [maʀe] *nf* tide; (*poissons*) fresh (sea) fish; ~ **haute/basse** high/low tide; ~ **montante/descendante** rising/ebb tide; ~ **noire** oil slick

marelle [maʀɛl] *nf* hopscotch

margarine [maʀgaʀin] *nf* margarine

marge [maʀʒ] *nf* margin; **en** ~ **de** (*fig*) on the fringe of; ~ **bénéficiaire** profit margin

marginal, e, -aux [maʀʒinal, o] *nm/f* (*original*) eccentric; (*déshérité*) dropout

marguerite [maʀgəʀit] *nf* marguerite, (oxeye) daisy; (*d'imprimante*) daisy-wheel

mari [maʀi] *nm* husband

mariage [maʀjaʒ] *nm* marriage; (*noce*) wedding; ~ **civil/religieux** registry office (*BRIT*) *ou* civil/church wedding

marié, e [maʀje] *adj* married ♦ *nm* (bride)groom; **les ~s** the bride and groom; **les (jeunes) ~s** the newly-weds; **mariée** *nf* bride

marier [maʀje] *vt* to marry; (*fig*) to blend; **se ~ vr** to get married; **se ~ (avec)** to marry

marin, e [maʀɛ̃, in] *adj* sea *cpd*, marine ♦ *nm* sailor

marine [maʀin] *adj voir* **marin** ♦ *adj inv* navy (blue) ♦ *nm* (MIL) marine ♦ *nf* navy; **~ de guerre** navy; **~ marchande** merchant navy

mariner [maʀine] *vt*: **faire ~** to marinade

marionnette [maʀjɔnɛt] *nf* puppet

maritalement [maʀitalmɑ̃] *adv*: **vivre ~** to live as husband and wife

maritime [maʀitim] *adj* sea *cpd*, maritime

mark [maʀk] *nm* mark

marmelade [maʀmәlad] *nf* stewed fruit, compote; **~ d'oranges** marmalade

marmite [maʀmit] *nf* (cooking-)pot

marmonner [maʀmɔne] *vt, vi* to mumble, mutter

marmot [maʀmo] (*fam*) *nm* kid

marmotter [maʀmɔte] *vt* to mumble

Maroc [maʀɔk] *nm*: **le ~** Morocco; **marocain, e** [maʀɔkɛ̃, ɛn] *adj* Moroccan ♦ *nm/f*: **Marocain, e** Moroccan

maroquinerie [maʀɔkinʀi] *nf* (*articles*) fine leather goods *pl*; (*boutique*) shop selling fine leather goods

marquant, e [maʀkɑ̃, ɑ̃t] *adj* outstanding

marque [maʀk] *nf* mark; (COMM: *de nourriture*) brand; (: *de voiture, produits manufacturés*) make; (*de disques*) label; **de ~** (*produits*) high-class; (*visiteur etc*) distinguished, well-known; **une grande ~ de vin** a well-known brand of wine; **~ de fabrique** trademark; **~ déposée** registered trademark

marquer [maʀke] *vt* to mark; (*inscrire*) to write down; (*bétail*) to brand; (SPORT: *but etc*) to score; (: *joueur*) to mark; (*accentuer: taille etc*) to emphasize; (*manifester: refus, intérêt*) to show ♦ *vi* (*événement*) to stand out, be outstanding; (SPORT) to score

marqueterie [maʀkɛtʀi] *nf* inlaid work, marquetry

marquis [maʀki] *nm* marquis, marquess; **marquise** *nf* marchioness; (*auvent*) glass canopy ou awning

marraine [maʀɛn] *nf* godmother

marrant, e [maʀɑ̃, ɑ̃t] (*fam*) *adj* funny

marre [maʀ] (*fam*) *adv*: **en avoir ~ de** to be fed up with

marrer [maʀe]: **se ~** (*fam*) *vi* to have a (good) laugh

marron [maʀɔ̃] *nm* (*fruit*) chestnut ♦ *adj inv* brown; **~s glacés** candied chestnuts; **marronnier** *nm* chestnut (tree)

mars [maʀs] *nm* March

Marseille [maʀsɛj] *n* Marseilles

marsouin [maʀswɛ̃] *nm* porpoise

marteau, x [maʀto] *nm* hammer; **être ~** (*fam*) to be nuts; **marteau-piqueur** *nm* pneumatic drill

marteler [maʀtәle] *vt* to hammer

martien, ne [maʀsjɛ̃, jɛn] *adj* Martian, of ou from Mars

martyr, e [maʀtiʀ] *nm/f* martyr; **martyre** *nm* martyrdom; (*fig: sens affaibli*) agony, torture; **martyriser** *vt* (REL) to martyr; (*fig*) to bully; (*enfant*) to batter, beat

marxiste [maʀksist] *adj, nm/f* Marxist

mascara [maskaʀa] *nm* mascara

masculin, e [maskylɛ̃, in] *adj* masculine; (*sexe, population*) male; (*équipe, vêtements*) men's; (*viril*) manly ♦ *nm* masculine; **masculinité** *nf* masculinity

masochiste [mazɔʃist] *adj* masochistic

masque [mask] *nm* mask; **masquer** *vt* (*cacher: paysage, porte*) to hide, conceal; (*dissimuler: vérité, projet*) to mask, obscure

massacre [masakʀ] *nm* massacre, slaughter; **massacrer** *vt* to massacre, slaughter; (*fam: texte etc*) to murder

massage [masaʒ] *nm* massage

masse [mas] *nf* mass; (ÉLEC) earth; (*maillet*) sledgehammer; (*péj*): **la ~** the masses *pl*; **une ~ de** (*fam*) masses ou loads of; **en ~** *adv* (*acheter*) in bulk; (*en foule*) en masse ♦ *adj* (*exécutions, production*) mass *cpd*

masser [mase] *vt* (*assembler: gens*) to gather; (*pétrir*) to massage; **se ~** *vi* (*foule*) to gather; **masseur, -euse** *nm/f* masseur(-euse)

massif, -ive [masif, iv] *adj* (*porte*) solid, massive; (*visage*) heavy, large; (*bois, or*) solid; (*dose*) massive; (*déportations etc*) mass *cpd* ♦ *nm* (*montagneux*) massif; (*de fleurs*) clump, bank

massue [masy] *nf* club, bludgeon

mastic [mastik] *nm* (*pour vitres*) putty; (*pour fentes*) filler

mastiquer [mastike] *vt* (*aliment*) to chew, masticate

mat, e [mat] *adj* (*couleur, métal*) mat(t); (*bruit, son*) dull ♦ *adj inv* (ÉCHECS): **être ~** to be checkmate

mât [mɑ] *nm* (NAVIG) mast; (*poteau*) pole, post

match [matʃ] *nm* match; **faire ~ nul** to draw; **~ aller** first leg; **~ retour** second leg, return match

matelas [mat(ə)la] *nm* mattress; **~ pneumatique** air bed ou mattress; **matelassé, e** *adj* (*vêtement*) padded; (*tissu*) quilted

matelot [mat(ə)lo] *nm* sailor, seaman

mater [mate] *vt* (*personne*) to bring to heel, subdue; (*révolte*) to put down

matérialiser [mateʀjalize]: **se ~** *vi* to materialize

matérialiste [mateʀjalist] adj materialistic

matériaux [mateʀjo] nmpl material(s)

matériel, le [mateʀjɛl] adj material ♦ nm equipment no pl; (de camping etc) gear no pl; (INFORM) hardware

maternel, le [matɛʀnɛl] adj (amour, geste) motherly, maternal; (grand-père, oncle) maternal; **maternelle** nf (aussi: **école maternelle**) (state) nursery school

maternité [matɛʀnite] nf (établissement) maternity hospital; (état de mère) motherhood, maternity; (grossesse) pregnancy; **congé de ~** maternity leave

mathématique [matematik] adj mathematical; **mathématiques** nfpl (science) mathematics sg

maths [mat] (fam) nfpl maths

matière [matjɛʀ] nf matter; (COMM, TECH) material, matter no pl; (fig: d'un livre etc) subject matter, material; (SCOL) subject; **en ~ de** as regards; **~s grasses** fat content sg; **~s premières** raw materials

matin [matɛ̃] nm, adv morning; **du ~ au soir** from morning till night; **de bon ou grand ~** early in the morning; **matinal, e, -aux** adj (toilette, gymnastique) morning cpd; **être matinal** (personne) to be up early; to be an early riser; **matinée** nf morning; (spectacle) matinée

matou [matu] nm tom(cat)

matraque [matʀak] nf (de policier) truncheon (BRIT), billy (US)

matricule [matʀikyl] nm (MIL) regimental number; (ADMIN) reference number

matrimonial, e, -aux [matʀimɔnjal, jo] adj marital, marriage cpd

maudire [modiʀ] vt to curse; **maudit, e** (fam) adj (satané) blasted, confounded

maugréer [mogʀee] vi to grumble

maussade [mosad] adj sullen; (temps) gloomy

mauvais, e [mɔvɛ, ɛz] adj bad; (faux): **le ~ numéro/moment** the wrong number/moment; (méchant, malveillant) malicious, spiteful; **il fait ~** the weather is bad; **la mer est ~e** the sea is rough; **~ plaisant** hoaxer; **~e herbe** weed; **~e langue** gossip, scandalmonger (BRIT); **~e passe** bad patch

mauve [mov] adj mauve

maux [mo] nmpl de **mal**; **~ de ventre** stomachache sg

maximum [maksimɔm] adj, nm maximum; **au ~** (le plus possible) as much as one can; (tout au plus) at the (very) most ou maximum; **faire le ~** to do one's level best

mayonnaise [majɔnɛz] nf mayonnaise

mazout [mazut] nm (fuel) oil

Me abr = **Maître**

me, m' [m(ə)] pron (direct: téléphoner, attendre etc) me; (indirect: parler, donner etc) (to) me; (réfléchi) myself

mec [mɛk] (fam) nm bloke, guy

mécanicien, ne [mekanisjɛ̃, jɛn] nm/f mechanic; (RAIL) (train ou engine) driver

mécanique [mekanik] adj mechanical ♦ nf (science) mechanics sg; (mécanisme) mechanism; **ennui ~** engine trouble no pl

mécanisme [mekanism] nm mechanism

méchamment [meʃamɑ̃] adv nastily, maliciously, spitefully

méchanceté [meʃɑ̃ste] nf nastiness, maliciousness; **dire des ~s à qn** to say spiteful things to sb

méchant, e [meʃɑ̃, ɑ̃t] adj nasty, malicious, spiteful; (enfant: pas sage) naughty; (animal) vicious

mèche [mɛʃ] nf (de cheveux) lock; (de lampe, bougie) wick; (d'un explosif) fuse; **de ~ avec** in league with

méchoui [meʃwi] nm barbecue of a whole roast sheep

méconnaissable [mekɔnɛsabl] adj unrecognizable

méconnaître [mekɔnɛtʀ] vt (ignorer) to be unaware of; (mésestimer) to misjudge

mécontent, e [mekɔ̃tɑ̃, ɑ̃t] adj: **~ (de)** discontented ou dissatisfied ou displeased (with); (contrarié) annoyed (at); **mécontentement** nm dissatisfaction, discontent, displeasure; (irritation) annoyance

médaille [medaj] nf medal

médaillon [medajɔ̃] nm (bijou) locket

médecin [med(ə)sɛ̃] nm doctor; **~ légiste** forensic surgeon

médecine [med(ə)sin] nf medicine

média [medja] nmpl: **les ~** the media; **médiatique** adj media cpd; **médiatisé, e** adj reported in the media; **ce procès a été très médiatisé** (péj) this trial was turned into a media event

médical, e, -aux [medikal, o] adj medical; **passer une visite ~e** to have a medical

médicament [medikamɑ̃] nm medicine, drug

médiéval, e, -aux [medjeval, o] adj medieval

médiocre [medjɔkʀ] adj mediocre, poor

médire [mediʀ] vi: **~ de** to speak ill of; **médisance** nf scandalmongering (BRIT)

méditer [medite] vi to meditate

Méditerranée [mediteʀane] nf: **la (mer) ~** the Mediterranean (Sea); **méditerranéen, ne** adj Mediterranean ♦ nm/f: **Méditerranéen, ne** native ou inhabitant of a Mediterranean country

méduse [medyz] nf jellyfish

meeting [mitiŋ] nm (POL, SPORT) rally

méfait [mefɛ] nm (faute) misdemeanour,

wrongdoing; **~s** *nmpl* (*ravages*) ravages, damage *sg*

méfiance [mefjɑ̃s] *nf* mistrust, distrust

méfiant, e [mefjɑ̃, jɑ̃t] *adj* mistrustful, distrustful

méfier [mefje]: **se ~** *vi* to be wary; to be careful; **se ~ de** to mistrust, be wary of

mégarde [megaʀd] *nf*: **par ~** (*accidentellement*) accidentally; (*par erreur*) by mistake

mégère [meʒɛʀ] *nf* shrew

mégot [mego] (*fam*) *nm* cigarette end

meilleur, e [mɛjœʀ] *adj, adv* better ♦ *nm*: **le ~** the best; **le ~ des deux** the better of the two; **~ marché** (*inv*) cheaper; **meilleure** *nf*: **la meilleure** the best (one)

mélancolie [melɑ̃kɔli] *nf* melancholy, gloom; **mélancolique** *adj* melancholic, melancholy

mélange [melɑ̃ʒ] *nm* mixture; **mélanger** *vt* to mix; (*vins, couleurs*) to blend; (*mettre en désordre*) to mix up, muddle (up)

mélasse [melas] *nf* treacle, molasses *sg*

mêlée [mele] *nf* mêlée, scramble; (*RUGBY*) scrum(mage)

mêler [mele] *vt* (*unir*) to mix; (*embrouiller*) to muddle (up), mix up; **se ~** *vi* to mix, mingle; **se ~ à** (*personne: se joindre à*) to join; (: *s'associer à*) to mix with; **se ~ de** (*suj: personne*) to meddle with, interfere in; **mêle-toi de ce qui te regarde!** mind your own business!

mélodie [melɔdi] *nf* melody; **mélodieux, -euse** *adj* melodious

melon [m(ə)lɔ̃] *nm* (*BOT*) (honeydew) melon; (*aussi: chapeau ~*) bowler (hat)

membre [mɑ̃bʀ] *nm* (*ANAT*) limb; (*personne, pays, élément*) member ♦ *adj* member *cpd*

mémé [meme] (*fam*) *nf* granny

MOT-CLÉ

même [mɛm] *adj* **1** (*avant le nom*) same; **en même temps** at the same time

2 (*après le nom: renforcement*): **il est la loyauté même** he is loyalty itself; **ce sont ses paroles/celles-là mêmes** they are his very words/the very ones

♦ *pron*: **le(la) même** the same one

♦ *adv* **1** (*renforcement*): **il n'a même pas pleuré** he didn't even cry; **même lui l'a dit** even HE said it; **ici même** at this very place

2: **à même**: **à même la bouteille** straight from the bottle; **à même la peau** next to the skin; **être à même de faire** to be in a position to do, be able to do

3: **de même**: **faire de même** to do likewise; **lui de même** so does (*ou* did *ou* is) he; **de même que** just as; **il en va de même pour** the same goes for

---

mémo [memo] (*fam*) *nm* memo

mémoire [memwaʀ] *nf* memory ♦ *nm* (*SCOL*) dissertation, paper; **~s** *nmpl* (*souvenirs*) memoirs; **à la ~ de** to the *ou* in memory of; **de ~** from memory; **~ morte/vive** (*INFORM*) ROM/RAM

mémorable [memɔʀabl] *adj* memorable, unforgettable

menace [mənas] *nf* threat; **menacer** *vt* to threaten

ménage [menaʒ] *nm* (*travail*) housekeeping, housework; (*couple*) (married) couple; (*famille, ADMIN*) household; **faire le ~** to do the housework; **ménagement** *nm* care and attention; **ménager, -ère** *adj* household *cpd*, domestic ♦ *vt* (*traiter: personne*) to handle with tact; (*utiliser*) to use sparingly; (*prendre soin de*) to take (great) care of, look after; (*organiser*) to arrange; **ménager qch à qn** (*réserver*) to have sth in store for sb; **ménagère** *nf* housewife

mendiant, e [mɑ̃djɑ̃, jɑ̃t] *nm/f* beggar

mendier [mɑ̃dje] *vi* to beg ♦ *vt* to beg (for)

mener [m(ə)ne] *vt* to lead; (*enquête*) to conduct; (*affaires*) to manage ♦ *vi*: **~ à/dans** (*emmener*) to take to/into; **~ qch à bien** to see sth through (to a successful conclusion), complete sth successfully

meneur, -euse [mənœʀ, øz] *nm/f* leader; (*péj*) agitator

méningite [menɛ̃ʒit] *nf* meningitis *no pl*

ménopause [menopoz] *nf* menopause

menottes [mənɔt] *nfpl* handcuffs

mensonge [mɑ̃sɔ̃ʒ] *nm* lie; (*action*) lying *no pl*; **mensonger, -ère** *adj* false

mensualité [mɑ̃sɥalite] *nf* (*traite*) monthly payment

mensuel, le [mɑ̃sɥɛl] *adj* monthly

mensurations [mɑ̃syʀasjɔ̃] *nfpl* measurements

mental, e, -aux [mɑ̃tal, o] *adj* mental; **mentalité** *nf* mentality

menteur, -euse [mɑ̃tœʀ, øz] *nm/f* liar

menthe [mɑ̃t] *nf* mint

mention [mɑ̃sjɔ̃] *nf* (*annotation*) note, comment; (*SCOL*) grade; **~ bien** *etc* ≈ grade B *etc* (*ou* upper 2nd class *etc*) pass (*BRIT*), ≈ pass with (high) honors (*US*); (*ADMIN*): **"rayer les ~s inutiles"** "delete as appropriate"; **mentionner** *vt* to mention

mentir [mɑ̃tiʀ] *vi* to lie

menton [mɑ̃tɔ̃] *nm* chin

menu, e [məny] *adj* (*personne*) slim, slight; (*frais, difficulté*) minor ♦ *adv* (*couper, hacher*) very fine ♦ *nm* menu; **~ touristique/ gastronomique** economy/gourmet's menu

menuiserie [mənɥizʀi] *nf* (*métier*) joinery, carpentry; (*passe-temps*) woodwork; **menuisier** *nm* joiner, carpenter

méprendre [mepʀɑ̃dʀ]: **se ~** vi: **se ~ sur** to be mistaken (about)

mépris [mepʀi] nm (dédain) contempt, scorn; **au ~ de** regardless of, in defiance of; **méprisable** adj contemptible, despicable; **méprisant, e** adj scornful; **méprise** nf mistake, error; **mépriser** vt to scorn, despise; (gloire, danger) to scorn, spurn

mer [mɛʀ] nf sea; (marée) tide; **en ~** at sea; **en haute** ou **pleine ~** off shore, on the open sea; **la ~ du Nord/Rouge** the North/Red Sea

mercenaire [mɛʀsənɛʀ] nm mercenary, hired soldier

mercerie [mɛʀsəʀi] nf (boutique) haberdasher's shop (BRIT), notions store (US)

merci [mɛʀsi] excl thank you ♦ nf: **à la ~ de qn/qch** at sb's mercy/the mercy of sth; **~ beaucoup** thank you very much; **~ de** thank you for; **sans ~** merciless(ly)

mercredi [mɛʀkʀədi] nm Wednesday

mercure [mɛʀkyʀ] nm mercury

merde [mɛʀd] (fam!) nf shit (!) ♦ excl (bloody) hell (!)

mère [mɛʀ] nf mother; **~ célibataire** unmarried mother

merguez [mɛʀgɛz] nf merguez sausage (type of spicy sausage from N Africa)

méridional, e, -aux [meʀidjɔnal, o] adj southern ♦ nm/f Southerner

meringue [məʀɛ̃g] nf meringue

mérite [meʀit] nm merit; **avoir du ~ (à faire qch)** to deserve credit (for doing sth); **mériter** vt to deserve

merlan [mɛʀlɑ̃] nm whiting

merle [mɛʀl] nm blackbird

merveille [mɛʀvɛj] nf marvel, wonder; **faire ~** to work wonders; **à ~** perfectly, wonderfully; **merveilleux, -euse** adj marvellous, wonderful

mes [me] adj voir **mon**

mésange [mezɑ̃ʒ] nf tit(mouse)

mésaventure [mezavɑ̃tyʀ] nf misadventure, misfortune

Mesdames [medam] nfpl de **Madame**

Mesdemoiselles [medmwazɛl] nfpl de **Mademoiselle**

mesquin, e [mɛskɛ̃, in] adj mean, petty; **mesquinerie** nf meanness; (procédé) mean trick

message [mesaʒ] nm message; **messager, -ère** nm/f messenger

messe [mes] nf mass

Messieurs [mesjø] nmpl de **Monsieur**

mesure [m(ə)zyʀ] nf (évaluation, dimension) measurement; (récipient) measure; (MUS: cadence) time, tempo; (: division) bar; (retenue) moderation; (disposition) measure, step; **sur ~** (costume) made-to-measure; **dans**

la ~ où insofar as, inasmuch as; **à ~ que** as; **être en ~ de** to be in a position to; **dans une certaine ~** to a certain extent

mesurer [məzyʀe] vt to measure; (juger) to weigh up, assess; (modérer: ses paroles etc) to moderate; **se ~ avec** to have a confrontation with; **il mesure 1 m 80** he's 1 m 80 tall

met [me] vb voir **mettre**

métal, -aux [metal, o] nm metal; **métallique** adj metallic

météo [meteo] nf (bulletin) weather report

météorologie [meteɔʀɔlɔʒi] nf meteorology

méthode [metɔd] nf method; (livre, ouvrage) manual, tutor

méticuleux, -euse [metikylø, øz] adj meticulous

métier [metje] nm (profession: gén) job; (: manuel) trade; (artisanal) craft; (technique, expérience) (acquired) skill ou technique; (aussi: **~ à tisser**) (weaving) loom; **avoir du ~** to have practical experience

métis, se [metis] adj, nm/f half-caste, half-breed

métrage [metʀaʒ] nm: **long/moyen/court ~** full-length/medium-length/short film

mètre [mɛtʀ] nm metre; (règle) (metre) rule; (ruban) tape measure; **métrique** adj metric

métro [metʀo] nm underground (BRIT), subway

métropole [metʀɔpɔl] nf (capitale) metropolis; (pays) home country

mets [me] nm dish

metteur [metœʀ] nm: **~ en scène** (THÉÂTRE) producer; (CINÉMA) director

---

MOT-CLÉ

---

mettre [mɛtʀ] vt **1** (placer) to put; **mettre en bouteille/en sac** to bottle/put in bags ou sacks; **mettre en charge (pour)** to charge (with), indict (for)

2 (vêtements: revêtir) to put on; (: porter) to wear; **mets ton gilet** put your cardigan on; **je ne mets plus mon manteau** I no longer wear my coat

3 (faire fonctionner: chauffage, électricité) to put on; (: réveil, minuteur) to set; (installer: gaz, eau) to put in, lay on; **mettre en marche** to start up

4 (consacrer): **mettre du temps à faire qch** to take time to do sth ou over sth

5 (noter, écrire) to say, put (down); **qu'est-ce qu'il a mis sur la carte?** what did he say ou write on the card?; **mettez au pluriel** ... put ... into the plural

6 (supposer): **mettons que ...** let's suppose ou say that ...

7: y mettre du sien to pull one's weight

se mettre vi **1** (se placer): **vous pouvez vous**

mettre là you can sit (*ou* stand) there; **où ça se met?** where does it go?; **se mettre au lit** to get into bed; **se mettre au piano** to sit down at the piano; **se mettre de l'encre sur les doigts** to get ink on one's fingers
2 (*s'habiller*): **se mettre en maillot de bain** to get into *ou* put on a swimsuit; **n'avoir rien à se mettre** to have nothing to wear
3: **se mettre à** to begin, start; **se mettre à faire** to begin *ou* start doing *ou* to do; **se mettre au piano** to start learning the piano; **se mettre au travail/à l'étude** to get down to work/one's studies

meuble [mœbl] *nm* piece of furniture; **des ~s** furniture; **meublé** *nm* furnished flatlet (*BRIT*) *ou* room; **meubler** *vt* to furnish
meugler [møgle] *vi* to low, moo
meule [møl] *nf* (*de foin, blé*) stack; (*de fromage*) round; (*à broyer*) millstone
meunier [mønje, jɛʀ] *nm* miller; **meunière** *nf* miller's wife
meure *etc* [mœʀ] *vb voir* **mourir**
meurtre [mœʀtʀ] *nm* murder; **meurtrier, -ière** *adj* (*arme etc*) deadly; (*fureur, instincts*) murderous ♦ *nm/f* murderer(-eress)
meurtrir [mœʀtʀiʀ] *vt* to bruise; (*fig*) to wound; **meurtrissure** *nf* bruise
meus *etc* [mœ] *vb voir* **mouvoir**
meute [møt] *nf* pack
mexicain, e [mɛksikɛ̃, ɛn] *adj* Mexican ♦ *nm/f*: **M~, e** Mexican
Mexico [mɛksiko] *n* Mexico City
Mexique [mɛksik] *nm*: **le ~** Mexico
Mgr *abr* = **Monseigneur**
mi [mi] *nm* (*MUS*) E; (*en chantant la gamme*) mi ♦ *préfixe*: **~...** half(-); mid-; **à la ~-janvier** in mid-January; **à ~-hauteur** halfway up; **mi-bas** *nm inv* knee sock
miauler [mjole] *vi* to mew
miche [miʃ] *nf* round *ou* cob loaf
mi-chemin [miʃmɛ̃]: **à ~~** *adv* halfway, midway
mi-clos, e [miklo, kloz] *adj* half-closed
micro [mikʀo] *nm* mike, microphone; (*INFORM*) micro
microbe [mikʀɔb] *nm* germ, microbe
micro...: **micro-onde** *nf*: **four à micro-ondes** microwave oven; **micro-ordinateur** *nm* microcomputer; **microscope** *nm* microscope; **microscopique** *adj* microscopic
midi [midi] *nm* midday, noon; (*moment du déjeuner*) lunchtime; (*sud*) south; **à ~** at 12 (o'clock) *ou* midday *ou* noon; **le M~** the South (of France), the Midi
mie [mi] *nf* crumb (of the loaf)
miel [mjɛl] *nm* honey; **mielleux, -euse** *adj* (*personne*) unctuous, syrupy
mien, ne [mjɛ̃, mjɛn] *pron*: **le(la) ~(ne), les**

~(ne)s mine; **les ~s** my family
miette [mjɛt] *nf* (*de pain, gâteau*) crumb; (*fig: de la conversation etc*) scrap; **en ~s** in pieces *ou* bits

mieux [mjø] *adv* **1** (*d'une meilleure façon*): **mieux (que)** better (than); **elle travaille/mange mieux** she works/eats better; **elle va mieux** she is better
2 (*de la meilleure façon*) best; **ce que je sais le mieux** what I know best; **les livres les mieux faits** the best made books
3: **de mieux en mieux** better and better
♦ *adj* **1** (*plus à l'aise, en meilleure forme*) better; **se sentir mieux** to feel better
2 (*plus satisfaisant*) better; **c'est mieux ainsi** it's better like this; **c'est le mieux des deux** it's the better of the two; **le(la) mieux, les mieux** the best; **demandez-lui, c'est le mieux** ask him, it's the best thing
3 (*plus joli*) better-looking
4: **au mieux** at best; **au mieux avec** on the best of terms with; **pour le mieux** for the best
♦ *nm* **1** (*progrès*) improvement
2: **de mon/ton mieux** as best I/you can (*ou* could); **faire de son mieux** to do one's best

mièvre [mjɛvʀ] *adj* mawkish (*BRIT*), sickly sentimental
mignon, ne [miɲɔ̃, ɔn] *adj* sweet, cute
migraine [migʀɛn] *nf* headache; (*MÉD*) migraine
mijoter [miʒɔte] *vt* to simmer; (*préparer avec soin*) to cook lovingly; (*fam: tramer*) to plot, cook up ♦ *vi* to simmer
mil [mil] *num* = **mille**
milieu, x [miljø] *nm* (*centre*) middle; (*BIO, GÉO*) environment; (*entourage social*) milieu; (*provenance*) background; (*pègre*): **le ~** the underworld; **au ~ de** in the middle of; **au beau ou en plein ~ (de)** right in the middle (of); **un juste ~** a happy medium
militaire [militɛʀ] *adj* military, army *cpd* ♦ *nm* serviceman
militant, e [militɑ̃, ɑ̃t] *adj, nm/f* militant
militer [milite] *vi* to be a militant
mille [mil] *num* a *ou* one thousand ♦ *nm* (*mesure*): **~ (marin)** nautical mile; **mettre dans le ~** (*fig*) to be bang on target; **millefeuille** *nm* cream *ou* vanilla slice; **millénaire** *nm* millennium ♦ *adj* thousand-year-old; (*fig*) ancient; **mille-pattes** *nm inv* centipede
millésimé, e [milezime] *adj* vintage *cpd*
millet [mijɛ] *nm* millet
milliard [miljaʀ] *nm* milliard, thousand million (*BRIT*), billion (*US*); **milliardaire** *nm/f* multimillionaire (*BRIT*), billionaire (*US*)

millier [milje] *nm* thousand; **un ~ (de)** a thousand or so, about a thousand; **par ~s** in (their) thousands, by the thousand

milligramme [miligram] *nm* milligramme

millimètre [milimɛtʀ] *nm* millimetre

million [miljɔ̃] *nm* million; **deux ~s de** two million; **millionnaire** *nm/f* millionaire

mime [mim] *nm/f* (*acteur*) mime(r) ♦ *nm* (*art*) mime, miming; **mimer** *vt* to mime; (*singer*) to mimic, take off

mimique [mimik] *nf* (*grimace*) (funny) face; (*signes*) gesticulations *pl*, sign language *no pl*

minable [minabl] *adj* (*décrépit*) shabby(-looking); (*médiocre*) pathetic

mince [mɛ̃s] *adj* thin; (*personne, taille*) slim, slender; (*fig: profit, connaissances*) slight, small, weak ♦ *excl:* **~ alors!** drat it!, darn it! (*US*); **minceur** *nf* thinness; (*d'une personne*) slimness, slenderness; **mincir** *vi* to get slimmer

mine [min] *nf* (*physionomie*) expression, look; (*allure*) exterior, appearance; (*de crayon*) lead; (*gisement, explosif, fig: source*) mine; **avoir bonne ~** (*personne*) to look well; (*ironique*) to look an utter idiot; **avoir mauvaise ~** to look unwell *ou* poorly; **faire ~ de faire** to make a pretence of doing; **~ de rien** although you wouldn't think so

miner [mine] *vt* (*saper*) to undermine, erode; (*MIL*) to mine

minerai [minʀe] *nm* ore

minéral, e, -aux [mineʀal, o] *adj, nm* mineral

minéralogique [mineʀalɔʒik] *adj:* **numéro ~** registration number

minet, te [minɛ, ɛt] *nm/f* (*chat*) pussy-cat; (*péj*) young trendy

mineur, e [minœʀ] *adj* minor ♦ *nm/f* (*JUR*) minor, person under age ♦ *nm* (*travailleur*) miner

miniature [minjatyʀ] *adj, nf* miniature

minibus [minibys] *nm* minibus

mini-cassette [minikaset] *nf* cassette (recorder)

minier, -ière [minje, jɛʀ] *adj* mining

mini-jupe [miniʒyp] *nf* mini-skirt

minime [minim] *adj* minor, minimal

minimiser [minimize] *vt* to minimize; (*fig*) to play down

minimum [minimɔm] *adj, nm* minimum; **au ~** (*au moins*) at the very least

ministère [ministɛʀ] *nm* (*aussi REL*) ministry; (*cabinet*) government

ministre [ministʀ] *nm* (*aussi REL*) minister

Minitel ® [minitel] *nm* videotext terminal and service

minoritaire [minɔʀitɛʀ] *adj* minority

minorité [minɔʀite] *nf* minority; **être en ~** to be in the *ou* a minority

minuit [minɥi] *nm* midnight

minuscule [minyskyl] *adj* minute, tiny ♦ *nf:* (**lettre**) **~** small letter

minute [minyt] *nf* minute; **à la ~** (just) this instant; (*faire*) there and then; **minuter** *vt* to time; **minuterie** *nf* time switch

minutieux, -euse [minysjø, jøz] *adj* (*personne*) meticulous; (*travail*) minutely detailed

mirabelle [miʀabel] *nf* (cherry) plum

miracle [miʀakl] *nm* miracle

mirage [miʀaʒ] *nm* mirage

mire [miʀ] *nf:* **point de ~** (*fig*) focal point

miroir [miʀwaʀ] *nm* mirror

miroiter [miʀwate] *vi* to sparkle, shimmer; **faire ~ qch à qn** to paint sth in glowing colours for sb, dangle sth in front of sb's eyes

mis, e [mi, miz] *pp de* **mettre** ♦ *adj:* **bien ~** well-dressed

mise [miz] *nf* (*argent: au jeu*) stake; (*tenue*) clothing, attire; **être de ~** to be acceptable *ou* in season; **~ au point** (*fig*) clarification; **~ de fonds** capital outlay; **~ en examen** charging, indictment; **~ en plis** set; **~ en scène** production

miser [mize] *vt* (*enjeu*) to stake, bet; **~ sur** (*cheval, numéro*) to bet on; (*fig*) to bank *ou* count on

misérable [mizeʀabl] *adj* (*lamentable, malheureux*) pitiful, wretched; (*pauvre*) poverty-stricken; (*insignifiant, mesquin*) miserable ♦ *nm/f* wretch

misère [mizeʀ] *nf* (extreme) poverty, destitution; **~s** *nfpl* (*malheurs*) woes, miseries; (*ennuis*) little troubles; **salaire de ~** starvation wage

missile [misil] *nm* missile

mission [misjɔ̃] *nf* mission; **partir en ~** (*ADMIN, POL*) to go on an assignment; **missionnaire** *nm/f* missionary

mit [mi] *vb voir* **mettre**

mité, e [mite] *adj* moth-eaten

mi-temps [mitɑ̃] *nf inv* (*SPORT: période*) half; (*: pause*) half-time; **à ~** part-time

miteux, -euse [mitø, øz] *adj* (*lieu*) seedy

mitigé, e [mitiʒe] *adj:* **sentiments ~s** mixed feelings

mitonner [mitɔne] *vt* to cook with loving care; (*fig*) to cook up quietly

mitoyen, ne [mitwajɛ̃, jɛn] *adj* (*mur*) common, party cpd

mitrailler [mitʀaje] *vt* to machine-gun; (*fig*) to pelt, bombard; (*: photographier*) to take shot after shot of; **mitraillette** *nf* submachine gun; **mitrailleuse** *nf* machine gun

mi-voix [mivwa]: **à ~~** *adv* in a low *ou* hushed voice

mixage [miksaʒ] *nm* (*CINÉMA*) (sound)

mixing
mixer [miksœr] *nm* (*food*) mixer
mixte [mikst] *adj* (*gén*) mixed; (*SCOL*) mixed, coeducational
mixture [mikstyʀ] *nf* mixture; (*fig*) concoction
Mlle (*pl* **Mlles**) *abr* = **Mademoiselle**
MM *abr* = **Messieurs**
Mme (*pl* **Mmes**) *abr* = **Madame**
mobile [mɔbil] *adj* mobile; (*pièce de machine*) moving ♦ *nm* (*motif*) motive; (*œuvre d'art*) mobile
mobilier, -ière [mɔbilje, jeʀ] *nm* furniture
mobiliser [mɔbilize] *vt* to mobilize
mocassin [mɔkasɛ̃] *nm* moccasin
moche [mɔʃ] (*fam*) *adj* (*laid*) ugly; (*mauvais*) rotten
modalité [mɔdalite] *nf* form, mode; **~s de paiement** methods of payment
mode [mɔd] *nf* fashion ♦ *nm* (*manière*) form, mode; **à la ~** fashionable, in fashion; **~ d'emploi** directions *pl* (for use)
modèle [mɔdɛl] *adj, nm* model; (*qui pose*) sitter; **~ déposé** registered design; **~ réduit** small-scale model; **modeler** *vt* to model
modem [mɔdɛm] *nm* modem
modéré, e [mɔdeʀe] *adj, nm/f* moderate
modérer [mɔdeʀe] *vt* to moderate; **se ~** *vi* to restrain o.s.
moderne [mɔdɛʀn] *adj* modern ♦ *nm* (*style*) modern style; (*meubles*) modern furniture; **moderniser** *vt* to modernize
modeste [mɔdɛst] *adj* modest; **modestie** *nf* modesty
modifier [mɔdifje] *vt* to modify, alter; **se ~** *vi* to alter
modique [mɔdik] *adj* modest
modiste [mɔdist] *nf* milliner
moelle [mwal] *nf* marrow; **~ épinière** spinal cord
moelleux, -euse [mwalø, øz] *adj* soft; (*gâteau*) light and moist
mœurs [mœʀ] *nfpl* (*conduite*) morals; (*manières*) manners; (*pratiques sociales, mode de vie*) habits
mohair [mɔɛʀ] *nm* mohair
moi [mwa] *pron* me; (*emphatique*): **~, je ...** for my part, I ...; **I myself ...; à ~** mine; **moi-même** *pron* myself; (*emphatique*) I myself
moindre [mwɛ̃dʀ] *adj* lesser; lower; **le(la) ~, les ~s** the least, the slightest; **merci – c'est la ~ des choses!** thank you – it's a pleasure!
moine [mwan] *nm* monk, friar
moineau, x [mwano] *nm* sparrow

MOT-CLÉ

moins [mwɛ̃] *adv* **1** (*comparatif*): **moins (que)** less (than); **moins grand que** less tall than, not as tall as; **moins je travaille, mieux je me**

porte the less I work, the better I feel
2 (*superlatif*): **le moins** (the) least; **c'est ce que j'aime le moins** it's what I like (the) least; **le(la) moins doué(e)** the least gifted; **au moins, du moins** at least; **pour le moins** at the very least
3: **moins de** (*quantité*) less (than); (*nombre*) fewer (than); **moins de sable/d'eau** less sand/water; **moins de livres/gens** fewer books/people; **moins de 2 ans** less than 2 years; **moins de midi** not yet midday
4: **de moins, en moins: 100 F/3 jours de moins** 100F/3 days less; **3 livres en moins** 3 books fewer; **3 livres too few; de l'argent en moins** less money; **le soleil en moins** but for the sun, minus the sun; **de moins en moins** less and less
5: **à moins de, à moins que** unless; **à moins de faire** unless we do (*ou* he does *etc*); **à moins que tu ne fasses** unless you do; **à moins d'un accident** barring any accident
♦ *prép*: **4 moins 2** 4 minus 2; **il est moins 5** it's 5 to; **il fait moins 5** it's 5 (degrees) below (freezing), it's minus 5

mois [mwa] *nm* month
moisi [mwazi] *nm* mould, mildew; **odeur de ~** musty smell; **moisir** *vi* to go mouldy; **moisissure** *nf* mould *no pl*
moisson [mwasɔ̃] *nf* harvest; **moissonner** *vt* to harvest, reap; **moissonneuse** *nf* (*machine*) harvester
moite [mwat] *adj* sweaty, sticky
moitié [mwatje] *nf* half; **la ~ half; la ~ de** half (of); **la ~ du temps** half the time; **à la ~ de** halfway through; **à ~** (*avant le verbe*) half; (*avant l'adjectif*) half-; **à ~ prix** (at) half-price; **~ moitié** half-and-half
moka [mɔka] *nm* coffee gateau
mol [mɔl] *adj voir* **mou**
molaire [mɔlɛʀ] *nf* molar
molester [mɔleste] *vt* to manhandle, maul (about)
molle [mɔl] *adj voir* **mou**; **mollement** *adv* (*péj: travailler*) sluggishly; (*protester*) feebly
mollet [mɔlɛ] *nm* calf ♦ *adj m*: **œuf ~** soft-boiled egg
molletonné, e [mɔltɔne] *adj* (*gants etc*) fleece-lined
mollir [mɔliʀ] *vi* (*fléchir*) to relent; (*substance*) to go soft
mollusque [mɔlysk] *nm* mollusc
môme [mom] (*fam*) *nm/f* (*enfant*) brat
moment [mɔmɑ̃] *nm* moment; **ce n'est pas le ~** this is not the (right) time; **pour un bon ~** for a good while; **pour le ~** for the moment, for the time being; **au ~ de** at the time of; **au ~ où** just as; **à tout ~** (*peut arriver etc*) at any

time ou moment; (*constamment*) constantly, continually; **en ce ~** at the moment; at present; **sur le ~** at the time; **par ~s** now and then, at times; **du ~ où** ou **que** seeing that, since; **momentané, e** *adj* temporary, momentary; **momentanément** *adv* (*court instant*) for a short while

momie [mɔmi] *nf* mummy

mon, ma [mɔ̃, ma] (*pl* **mes**) *adj* my

Monaco [mɔnako] *nm* Monaco

monarchie [mɔnaʀʃi] *nf* monarchy

monastère [mɔnastɛʀ] *nm* monastery

monceau, x [mɔ̃so] *nm* heap

mondain, e [mɔ̃dɛ̃, ɛn] *adj* (*vie*) society *cpd*

monde [mɔ̃d] *nm* world; (*haute société*): **le ~** (high) society; **il y a du ~** (*beaucoup de gens*) there are a lot of people; (*quelques personnes*) there are some people; **beaucoup/peu de ~** many/few people; **mettre au ~** to bring into the world; **pas le moins du ~** not in the least; **se faire un ~ de qch** to make a great deal of fuss about sth; **mondial, e, -aux** *adj* (*population*) world *cpd*; (*influence*) world-wide; **mondialement** *adv* throughout the world

monégasque [mɔnegask] *adj* Monegasque, of ou from Monaco

monétaire [mɔnetɛʀ] *adj* monetary

moniteur, -trice [mɔnitœʀ, tʀis] *nm/f* (*SPORT*) instructor(-tress); (*de colonie de vacances*) supervisor ♦ *nm* (*écran*) monitor

monnaie [mɔnɛ] *nf* (*ÉCON, gén: moyen d'échange*) currency; (*petites pièces*): **avoir de la ~** to have (some) change; **une pièce de ~** a coin; **faire de la ~** to get (some) change; **avoir/faire la ~ de 20 F** to have change of/get change for 20 F; **rendre à qn la ~ (sur 20 F)** to give sb the change (out of ou from 20 F); **monnayer** *vt* to convert into cash; (*talent*) to capitalize on

monologue [mɔnɔlɔg] *nm* monologue, soliloquy; **monologuer** *vi* to soliloquize

monopole [mɔnɔpɔl] *nm* monopoly

monotone [mɔnɔtɔn] *adj* monotonous

Monsieur [masjø] (*pl* **Messieurs**) *titre* Mr ♦ *nm* (*homme quelconque*): **un/le m~** a/the gentleman; **~, ...** (*en tête de lettre*) Dear Sir, ...; *voir aussi* **Madame**

monstre [mɔ̃stʀ] *nm* monster ♦ *adj* (*fam: colossal*) monstrous; **un travail ~** a fantastic amount of work; **monstrueux, -euse** *adj* monstrous

mont [mɔ̃] *nm*: **par ~s et par vaux** up hill and down dale; **le M~ Blanc** Mont Blanc

montage [mɔ̃taʒ] *nm* (*assemblage: d'appareil*) assembly; (*PHOTO*) photomontage; (*CINÉMA*) editing

montagnard, e [mɔ̃taɲaʀ, aʀd] *adj* mountain *cpd* ♦ *nm/f* mountain-dweller

montagne [mɔ̃taɲ] *nf* (*cime*) mountain; (*région*): **la ~** the mountains *pl*; **~s russes** big dipper *sg*, switchback *sg*; **montagneux, -euse** *adj* mountainous; (*basse montagne*) hilly

montant, e [mɔ̃tɑ̃, ɑ̃t] *adj* rising; **pull à col ~** high-necked jumper ♦ *nm* (*somme, total*) (sum) total, (total) amount; (*de fenêtre*) upright; (*de lit*) post

monte-charge [mɔ̃tʃaʀʒ] *nm inv* goods lift, hoist

montée [mɔ̃te] *nf* (*des prix, hostilités*) rise; (*escalade*) climb; (*côte*) hill; **au milieu de la ~** halfway up

monter [mɔ̃te] *vt* (*escalier, côte*) to go (ou come) up; (*valise, paquet*) to take (ou bring) up; (*étagère*) to raise; (*tente, échafaudage*) to put up; (*machine*) to assemble; (*CINÉMA*) to edit; (*THÉÂTRE*) to put on, stage; (*société etc*) to set up ♦ *vi* to go (ou come) up; (*prix, niveau, température*) to go up, rise; (*passager*) to get on; **se ~ à** (*frais etc*) to add up to, come to; **~ à pied** to walk up, go up on foot; **~ dans le train/l'avion** to get into the train/plane, board the train/plane; **~ sur** to climb up onto; **~ à cheval** (*faire du cheval*) to ride, go riding

montre [mɔ̃tʀ] *nf* watch; **contre la ~** (*SPORT*) against the clock; **montre-bracelet** *nf* wristwatch

montrer [mɔ̃tʀe] *vt* to show; **~ qch à qn** to show sb sth

monture [mɔ̃tyʀ] *nf* (*cheval*) mount; (*de lunettes*) frame; (*d'une bague*) setting

monument [mɔnymɑ̃] *nm* monument; **~ aux morts** war memorial

moquer [mɔke]: **se ~ de** *vt* to make fun of, laugh at; (*fam: se désintéresser de*) not to care about; (*tromper*): **se ~ de qn** to take sb for a ride; **moquerie** *nf* mockery

moquette [mɔket] *nf* fitted carpet

moqueur, -euse [mɔkœʀ, øz] *adj* mocking

moral, e, -aux [mɔʀal, o] *adj* moral ♦ *nm* morale; **avoir le ~** (*fam*) to be in good spirits; **avoir le ~ à zéro** (*fam*) to be really down; **morale** *nf* (*mœurs*) morals *pl*; (*valeurs*) moral standards *pl*, morality; (*d'une fable etc*) moral; **faire la morale à** to lecture, preach at; **moralité** *nf* morality; (*d'une histoire*) moral

morceau, x [mɔʀso] *nm* piece, bit; (*d'une œuvre*) passage, extract; (*MUS*) piece; (*CULIN: de viande*) cut; (*de sucre*) lump; **mettre en ~x** to pull to pieces ou bits; **manger un ~** to have a bite (to eat)

morceler [mɔʀsəle] *vt* to break up, divide up

mordant, e [mɔʀdɑ̃, ɑ̃t] *adj* (*ton, remarque*) scathing, cutting; (*ironie, froid*) biting ♦ *nm* (*style*) bite, punch

mordiller [mɔʀdije] *vt* to nibble at, chew at

mordre [mɔʀdʀ] vt to bite ♦ vi (poisson) to
bite; ~ **sur** (fig) to go over into, overlap into;
~ **à l'hameçon** to bite, rise to the bait

mordu, e [mɔʀdy] (fam) nm/f enthusiast;
un ~ de jazz a jazz fanatic

morfondre [mɔʀfɔ̃dʀ]: **se ~** vi to mope

morgue [mɔʀg] nf (arrogance) haughtiness;
(lieu: de la police) morgue; (: à l'hôpital)
mortuary

morne [mɔʀn] adj dismal, dreary

morose [mɔʀoz] adj sullen, morose

mors [mɔʀ] nm bit

morse [mɔʀs] nm (ZOOL) walrus; (TÉL) Morse
(code)

morsure [mɔʀsyʀ] nf bite

mort¹ [mɔʀ] nf death

mort², e [mɔʀ, mɔʀt] pp de **mourir** ♦ adj
dead ♦ nm/f (défunt) dead man/woman;
(victime): **il y a eu plusieurs ~s** several people
were killed, there were several killed; ~ **de
peur/fatigue** frightened to death/dead tired

mortalité [mɔʀtalite] nf mortality, death rate

mortel, le [mɔʀtɛl] adj (poison etc) deadly,
lethal; (accident, blessure) fatal; (silence,
ennemi) deadly; (péché) mortal; (fam:
ennuyeux) deadly boring

mortier [mɔʀtje] nm (gén) mortar

mort-né, e [mɔʀne] adj (enfant) stillborn

mortuaire [mɔʀtɥeʀ] adj: **avis ~** death
announcement

morue [mɔʀy] nf (ZOOL) cod inv

mosaïque [mɔzaik] nf mosaic

Moscou [mɔsku] n Moscow

mosquée [mɔske] nf mosque

mot [mo] nm word; (message) line, note; ~
à ~ word for word; ~ **d'ordre** watchword;
~ **de passe** password; **~s croisés** crossword
(puzzle) sg

motard [mɔtaʀ, aʀd] nm biker; (policier)
motorcycle cop

motel [mɔtɛl] nm motel

moteur, -trice [mɔtœʀ, tʀis] adj (ANAT,
PHYSIOL) motor; (TECH) driving; (AUTO): **à 4
roues motrices** 4-wheel drive ♦ nm engine,
motor; **à ~** power-driven, motor cpd

motif [mɔtif] nm (cause) motive; (décoratif)
design, pattern, motif; **sans ~** groundless

motivation [mɔtivasjɔ̃] nf motivation

motiver [mɔtive] vt to motivate; (justifier) to
justify, account for

moto [mɔto] nf (motor)bike; **motocycliste**
nm/f motorcyclist

motorisé, e [mɔtɔʀize] adj (personne)
having transport ou a car

motrice [mɔtʀis] adj voir **moteur**

motte [mɔt] nf: ~ **de terre** lump of earth, clod
(of earth); ~ **de beurre** lump of butter

mou (mol), molle [mu, mɔl] adj soft;
(personne) lethargic; (protestations) weak

♦ nm: **avoir du mou** to be slack

moucharder [muʃaʀde] (fam) vt (SCOL) to
sneak on; (POLICE) to grass on

mouche [muʃ] nf fly

moucher [muʃe]: **se ~** vi to blow one's nose

moucheron [muʃʀɔ̃] nm midge

mouchoir [muʃwaʀ] nm handkerchief,
hanky; ~ **en papier** tissue, paper hanky

moudre [mudʀ] vt to grind

moue [mu] nf pout; **faire la ~** to pout; (fig) to
pull a face

mouette [mwɛt] nf (sea)gull

moufle [mufl] nf (gant) mitt(en)

mouillé, e [muje] adj wet

mouiller [muje] vt (humecter) to wet,
moisten; (tremper): ~ **qn/qch** to make sb/sth
wet ♦ vi (NAVIG) to lie ou be at anchor; **se ~**
to get wet; (fam: prendre des risques) to
commit o.s.

moulant, e [mulɑ̃, ɑ̃t] adj figure-hugging

moule [mul] nf mussel ♦ nm (CULIN) mould;
~ **à gâteaux** ♦ nm cake tin (BRIT) ou pan (US)

moulent [mul] vb voir **moudre**; **mouler**

mouler [mule] vt (suj: vêtement) to hug, fit
closely round

moulin [mulɛ̃] nm mill; ~ **à café/à poivre**
coffee/pepper mill; ~ **à légumes** (vegetable)
shredder; ~ **à paroles** (fig) chatterbox; ~ **à
vent** windmill

moulinet [mulinɛ] nm (de canne à pêche)
reel; (mouvement): **faire des ~s avec qch** to
whirl sth around

moulinette ® [mulinɛt] nf (vegetable)
shredder

moulu, e [muly] pp de **moudre**

mourant, e [muʀɑ̃, ɑ̃t] adj dying

mourir [muʀiʀ] vi to die; (civilisation) to die
out; ~ **de froid/faim** to die of exposure/
hunger; ~ **de faim/d'ennui** (fig) to be
starving/be bored to death; ~ **d'envie de faire**
to be dying to do

mousse [mus] nf (BOT) moss; (de savon)
lather; (écume: sur eau, bière) froth, foam;
(CULIN) mousse ♦ nm (NAVIG) ship's boy; ~ **à
raser** shaving foam

mousseline [muslin] nf muslin; **pommes ~**
mashed potatoes

mousser [muse] vi (bière, détergent) to foam;
(savon) to lather; **mousseux, -euse** adj
frothy ♦ nm: **(vin) mousseux** sparkling wine

mousson [musɔ̃] nf monsoon

moustache [mustaʃ] nf moustache; **~s** nfpl
(du chat) whiskers pl; **moustachu, e** adj
with a moustache

moustiquaire [mustikɛʀ] nf mosquito net

moustique [mustik] nm mosquito

moutarde [mutaʀd] nf mustard

mouton [mutɔ̃] nm sheep inv; (peau)
sheepskin; (CULIN) mutton

mouvement [muvmɑ̃] nm movement; (fig: impulsion) gesture; **avoir un bon ~** to make a nice gesture; **en ~** in motion; on the move; **mouvementé, e** adj (vie, poursuite) eventful; (réunion) turbulent

mouvoir [muvwaʀ]: **se ~** vi to move

moyen, ne [mwajɛ̃, jɛn] adj average; (tailles, prix) medium; (de grandeur moyenne) medium-sized ♦ nm (façon) means sg, way; **~s** nmpl (capacités) means; **très ~** (résultats) pretty poor; **je n'en ai pas les ~s** I can't afford it; **au ~ de** by means of; **par tous les ~s** by every possible means, every possible way; **par ses propres ~s** all by oneself; **~ âge** Middle Ages; **~ de transport** means of transport

moyennant [mwajenɑ̃] prép (somme) for; (service, conditions) in return for; (travail, effort) with

moyenne [mwajɛn] nf average; (MATH) mean; (SCOL: à l'examen) pass mark; **en ~** on (an) average; **~ d'âge** average age

Moyen-Orient [mwajɛnɔʀjɑ̃] nm: **le ~-~** the Middle East

moyeu, x [mwajø] nm hub

MST sigle f (= maladie sexuellement transmissible) STD

mû, mue [my] pp de **mouvoir**

muer [mɥe] vi (oiseau, mammifère) to moult; (serpent) to slough; (jeune garçon): **il mue** his voice is breaking; **se ~ en** to transform into

muet, te [mɥe, mɥɛt] adj dumb; (fig): **~ d'admiration** etc speechless with admiration etc; (CINÉMA) silent ♦ nm/f mute

mufle [myfl] nm muzzle; (fam: goujat) boor

mugir [myʒiʀ] vi (taureau) to bellow; (vache) to low; (fig) to howl

muguet [mygɛ] nm lily of the valley

mule [myl] nf (ZOOL) (she-)mule

mulet [mylɛ] nm (ZOOL) (he-)mule

multinationale [myltinasjɔnal] nf multinational

multiple [myltipl] adj multiple, numerous; (varié) many, manifold; **multiplication** nf multiplication; **multiplier** vt to multiply; **se multiplier** vi to multiply

municipal, e, -aux [mynisipal, o] adj (élections, stade) municipal; (conseil) town cpd; **piscine/bibliothèque ~e** public swimming pool/library; **municipalité** nf (ville) municipality; (conseil) town council

munir [myniʀ] vt: **~ qch de** to equip sth with; **se ~ de** to arm o.s. with

munitions [mynisjɔ̃] nfpl ammunition sg

mur [myʀ] nm wall; **~ du son** sound barrier

mûr, e [myʀ] adj ripe; (personne) mature

muraille [myʀaj] nf (high) wall

mural, e, -aux [myʀal, o] adj wall cpd; (art) mural

mûre [myʀ] nf blackberry

muret [myʀɛ] nm low wall

mûrir [myʀiʀ] vi (fruit, blé) to ripen; (abcès) to come to a head; (fig: idée, personne) to mature ♦ vt (projet) to nurture; (personne) to (make) mature

murmure [myʀmyʀ] nm murmur; **murmurer** vi to murmur

muscade [myskad] nf (aussi: **noix (de) ~**) nutmeg

muscat [myska] nm (raisins) muscat grape; (vin) muscatel (wine)

muscle [myskl] nm muscle; **musclé, e** adj muscular; (fig) strong-arm

museau, x [myzo] nm muzzle; (CULIN) brawn

musée [myze] nm museum; (de peinture) art gallery

museler [myz(ə)le] vt to muzzle; **muselière** nf muzzle

musette [myzɛt] nf (sac) lunchbag

musical, e, o [myzikal, o] adj musical

music-hall [myzikol] nm (salle) variety theatre; (genre) variety

musicien, ne [myzisjɛ̃, jɛn] adj musical ♦ nm/f musician

musique [myzik] nf music; **~ d'ambiance** background music

musulman, e [myzylmɑ̃, an] adj, nm/f Moslem, Muslim

mutation [mytasjɔ̃] nf (ADMIN) transfer

muter [myte] vt to transfer, move

mutilé, e [mytile] nm/f disabled person (through loss of limbs)

mutiler [mytile] vt to mutilate, maim

mutin, e [mytɛ̃, in] adj (air, ton) mischievous, impish ♦ nm/f (MIL, NAVIG) mutineer; **mutinerie** nf mutiny

mutisme [mytism] nm silence

mutuel, le [mytɥɛl] adj mutual; **mutuelle** nf voluntary insurance premiums for back-up health cover

myope [mjɔp] adj short-sighted

myosotis [mjɔzɔtis] nm forget-me-not

myrtille [miʀtij] nf bilberry

mystère [mistɛʀ] nm mystery; **mystérieux, -euse** adj mysterious

mystifier [mistifje] vt to fool

mythe [mit] nm myth

mythologie [mitɔlɔʒi] nf mythology

N, n

n' [n] adv voir **ne**

nacre [nakʀ] nf mother of pearl

nage [naʒ] nf swimming; (manière) style of swimming, stroke; **traverser/s'éloigner à la ~** to swim across/away; **en ~** bathed in sweat; **nageoire** nf fin; **nager** vi to swim; **nageur,**

-euse *nm/f* swimmer

naguère [nagɛʀ] *adv* formerly

naïf, -ive [naif, naiv] *adj* naïve

nain, e [nɛ̃, nɛn] *nm/f* dwarf

naissance [nɛsɑ̃s] *nf* birth; **donner ~ à** to give birth to; *(fig)* to give rise to

naître [nɛtʀ] *vi* to be born; *(fig)*: **~ de** to arise from, be born out of; **il est né en 1960** he was born in 1960; **faire ~** *(fig)* to give rise to, arouse

naïve [naiv] *adj voir* **naïf**

naïveté [naivte] *nf* naïvety

nana [nana] *(fam) nf (fille)* chick, bird *(BRIT)*

nantir [nɑ̃tiʀ] *vt*: **~ qn de** to provide sb with; **les nantis** *(péj)* the well-to-do

nappe [nap] *nf* tablecloth; *(de pétrole, gaz)* layer; **~ phréatique** ground water; **napperon** *nm* table-mat

naquit *etc* [naki] *vb voir* **naître**

narcodollars [naʀkodɔlaʀ] *nmpl* drug money *sg*

narguer [naʀge] *vt* to taunt

narine [naʀin] *nf* nostril

narquois, e [naʀkwa, waz] *adj* mocking

natal, e [natal] *adj* native; **natalité** *nf* birth rate

natation [natasjɔ̃] *nf* swimming

natif, -ive [natif, iv] *adj* native

nation [nasjɔ̃] *nf* nation; **national, e, -aux** *adj* national; **nationale** *nf*: *(route)* **nationale** ≈ A road *(BRIT)*, ≈ state highway *(US)*; **nationaliser** *vt* to nationalize; **nationalisme** *nm* nationalism; **nationalité** *nf* nationality

natte [nat] *nf (cheveux)* plait; *(tapis)* mat

naturaliser [natyʀalize] *vt* to naturalize

nature [natyʀ] *nf* nature ♦ *adj, adv (CULIN)* plain, without seasoning or sweetening; *(café, thé)* black, without sugar; *(yaourt)* natural; **payer en ~** to pay in kind; **~ morte** still-life; **naturel, le** *adj (gén, aussi enfant)* natural ♦ *nm (absence d'affectation)* naturalness; *(caractère)* disposition, nature; **naturellement** *adv* naturally; *(bien sûr)* of course

naufrage [nofʀaʒ] *nm* (ship)wreck; **faire ~** to be shipwrecked

nauséabond, e [nozeabɔ̃, ɔ̃d] *adj* foul

nausée [noze] *nf* nausea

nautique [notik] *adj* nautical, water *cpd*; **sports ~s** water sports

naval, e [naval] *adj* naval; *(industrie)* shipbuilding

navet [navɛ] *nm* turnip; *(péj: film)* rubbishy film

navette [navɛt] *nf* shuttle; **faire la ~ (entre)** to go to and fro *ou* shuttle (between)

navigateur [navigatœʀ, tʀis] *nm (NAVIG)* seafarer

navigation [navigasjɔ̃] *nf* navigation, sailing

naviguer [navige] *vi* to navigate, sail

navire [naviʀ] *nm* ship

navrer [navʀe] *vt* to upset, distress; **je suis navré** I'm so sorry

ne, n' [n(ə)] *adv voir* **pas; plus; jamais** *etc*; *(sans valeur négative: non traduit)*: **c'est plus loin que je ~ le croyais** it's further than I thought

né, e [ne] *pp (voir* **naître)**: **~ en 1960** born in 1960; **~e Scott** née Scott

néanmoins [neɑ̃mwɛ̃] *adv* nevertheless

néant [neɑ̃] *nm* nothingness; **réduire à ~** to bring to nought; *(espoir)* to dash

nécessaire [neseseʀ] *adj* necessary ♦ *nm* necessary; *(sac)* kit; **je vais faire le ~** I'll see to it; **~ de couture** sewing kit; **nécessité** *nf* necessity; **nécessiter** *vt* to require

nécrologique [nekʀɔlɔʒik] *adj*: **rubrique ~** obituary column

nectar [nɛktaʀ] *nm* nectar

néerlandais, e [neɛʀlɑ̃dɛ, ɛz] *adj* Dutch

nef [nɛf] *nf (d'église)* nave

néfaste [nefast] *adj (nuisible)* harmful; *(funeste)* ill-fated

négatif, -ive [negatif, iv] *adj* negative ♦ *nm (PHOTO)* negative

négligé, e [negliʒe] *adj (en désordre)* slovenly ♦ *nm (tenue)* negligee

négligeable [negliʒabl] *adj* negligible

négligent, e [negliʒɑ̃, ɑ̃t] *adj* careless, negligent

négliger [negliʒe] *vt (tenue)* to be careless about; *(avis, précautions)* to disregard; *(épouse, jardin)* to neglect; **~ de faire** to fail to do, not bother to do

négoce [negɔs] *nm* trade

négociant [negɔsjɑ̃, jɑ̃t] *nm* merchant

négociation [negɔsjasjɔ̃] *nf* negotiation

négocier [negɔsje] *vi, vt* to negotiate

nègre [nɛgʀ] *(péj) nm (écrivain)* ghost (writer)

neige [nɛʒ] *nf* snow; **neiger** *vi* to snow

nénuphar [nenyfaʀ] *nm* water-lily

néon [neɔ̃] *nm* neon

néo-zélandais, e [neozelɑ̃dɛ, ɛz] *adj* New Zealand *cpd* ♦ *nm/f*: **N~-Z~, e** New Zealander

nerf [nɛʀ] *nm* nerve; **être sur les ~s** to be all keyed up; **allons, du ~!** come on, buck up!; **nerveux, -euse** *adj* nervous; *(irritable)* touchy, nervy; *(voiture)* nippy, responsive; **nervosité** *nf* excitability, tenseness; *(irritabilité passagère)* irritability, nerviness

nervure [nɛʀvyʀ] *nf* vein

n'est-ce pas [nɛspa] *adv* isn't it?, won't you? *etc, selon le verbe qui précède*

net, nette [nɛt] *adj (sans équivoque, distinct)* clear; *(évident: amélioration, différence)* marked, distinct; *(propre)* neat, clean;

(COMM: prix, salaire) net ♦ adv (refuser) flatly ♦ nm: **mettre au ~** to copy out; **s'arrêter ~** to stop dead; **nettement** adv clearly, distinctly; (incontestablement) decidedly, distinctly; **netteté** nf clearness

nettoyage [netwajaʒ] nm cleaning; **~ à sec** dry cleaning

nettoyer [netwaje] vt to clean

neuf¹ [nœf] num nine

neuf², neuve [nœf, nœv] adj new ♦ nm: **remettre à ~** to do up (as good as new), refurbish; **quoi de ~?** what's new?

neutre [nøtʀ] adj neutral; (LING) neuter

neuve [nœv] adj voir **neuf²**

neuvième [nœvjɛm] num ninth

neveu, x [n(ə)vø] nm nephew

névrosé, e [nevʀoze] adj, nm/f neurotic

nez [ne] nm nose; **~ à ~** avec face to face with; **avoir du ~** to have flair

ni [ni] conj: **~ ... ~** neither ... nor; **je n'aime ~ les lentilles ~ les épinards** I like neither lentils nor spinach; **il n'a dit ~ oui ~ non** he didn't say either yes or no; **elles ne sont venues ~ l'une ~ l'autre** neither of them came

niais, e [njɛ, njɛz] adj silly, thick

niche [niʃ] nf (du chien) kennel; (de mur) recess, niche; **nicher** vi to nest

nid [ni] nm nest; **~ de poule** pothole

nièce [njɛs] nf niece

nier [nje] vt to deny

nigaud, e [nigo, od] nm/f booby, fool

Nil [nil] nm: **le ~** the Nile

n'importe [nɛ̃pɔʀt] adv: **~ qui/quoi/où** anybody/anything/anywhere; **~ quand** any time; **~ quel/quelle** any; **~ lequel/laquelle** any (one); **~ comment** (sans soin) carelessly

niveau, x [nivo] nm level; (des élèves, études) standard; **~ de vie** standard of living

niveler [niv(ə)le] vt to level

NN abr (= nouvelle norme) revised standard of hotel classification

noble [nɔbl] adj noble; **noblesse** nf nobility; (d'une action etc) nobleness

noce [nɔs] nf wedding; (gens) wedding party (ou guests pl); **faire la ~** (fam) to go on a binge

nocif, -ive [nɔsif, iv] adj harmful, noxious

nocturne [nɔktyʀn] adj nocturnal ♦ nf late-night opening

Noël [nɔɛl] nm Christmas

nœud [nø] nm knot; (ruban) bow; **~ papillon** bow tie

noir, e [nwaʀ] adj black; (obscur, sombre) dark ♦ nm/f black man/woman ♦ nm: **dans le ~** in the dark; **travail au ~** moonlighting; **travailler au ~** to work on the side; **noircir** vt, vi to blacken; **noire** nf (MUS) crotchet, quarter note (US)

noisette [nwazɛt] nf hazelnut

noix [nwa] nf walnut; (CULIN): **une ~ de beurre** a knob of butter; **~ de cajou** cashew nut; **~ de coco** coconut; **à la ~** (fam) worthless

nom [nɔ̃] nm name; (LING) noun; **~ de famille** surname; **~ de jeune fille** maiden name; **~ déposé** trade name; **~ propre** proper noun

nomade [nɔmad] nm/f nomad

nombre [nɔ̃bʀ] nm number; **venir en ~** to come in large numbers; **depuis ~ d'années** for many years; **au ~ de mes amis** among my friends; **nombreux, -euse** adj many, numerous; (avec nom sg: foule etc) large; **peu nombreux** few

nombril [nɔ̃bʀi(l)] nm navel

nommer [nɔme] vt to name; (élire) to appoint, nominate; **se ~: il se nomme Pascal** his name's Pascal, he's called Pascal

non [nɔ̃] adv (réponse) no; (avec loin, sans, seulement) not; **~ (pas) que** not that; **moi ~ plus** neither do I, I don't either; **c'est bon ~?** (exprimant le doute) it's good, isn't it?

non-alcoolisé, e [nɔ̃alkɔlize] adj non-alcoholic

nonante [nɔnɑ̃t] (BELGIQUE, SUISSE) num ninety

non-fumeur [nɔ̃fymœʀ, øz] nm non-smoker

non-sens [nɔ̃sɑ̃s] nm absurdity

nonchalant, e [nɔ̃ʃalɑ̃, ɑ̃t] adj nonchalant

nord [nɔʀ] nm North ♦ adj northern; north; **au ~** (situation) in the north; (direction) to the north; **au ~ de** (to the) north of; **nord-est** nm North-East; **nord-ouest** nm North-West

normal, e, -aux [nɔʀmal, o] adj normal; **c'est tout à fait ~** it's perfectly natural; **vous trouvez ça ~?** does it seem right to you?; **normale** nf: **la normale** the norm, the average; **normalement** adv (en général) normally

normand, e [nɔʀmɑ̃, ɑ̃d] adj of Normandy

Normandie [nɔʀmɑ̃di] nf Normandy

norme [nɔʀm] nf norm; (TECH) standard

Norvège [nɔʀvɛʒ] nf Norway; **norvégien, ne** [nɔʀveʒjɛ̃, ɛn] adj Norwegian ♦ nm/f: **Norvégien, ne** Norwegian ♦ nm (LING) Norwegian

nos [no] adj voir **notre**

nostalgie [nɔstalʒi] nf nostalgia; **nostalgique** adj nostalgic

notable [nɔtabl] adj (fait) notable, noteworthy; (marqué) noticeable, marked ♦ nm prominent citizen

notaire [nɔtɛʀ] nm solicitor

notamment [nɔtamɑ̃] adv in particular, among others

note [nɔt] nf (écrite, MUS) note; (SCOL) mark (BRIT), grade; (facture) bill; **~ de service** memorandum

noté, e [nɔte] adj: **être bien/mal ~** (employé etc) to have a good/bad record

noter [nɔte] vt (écrire) to write down;

(*remarquer*) to note, notice; (*devoir*) to mark, grade

notice [nɔtis] nf summary, short article; (*brochure*) leaflet, instruction book

notifier [nɔtifje] vt: ~ qch à qn to notify sb of sth, notify sth to sb

notion [nosjɔ̃] nf notion, idea

notoire [nɔtwaʀ] adj widely known; (*en mal*) notorious

notre [nɔtʀ] (*pl* **nos**) adj our

nôtre [notʀ] pron: **le ~, la ~, les ~s** ours ♦ adj ours; **les ~s** ours; (*alliés etc*) our own people; **soyez des ~s** join us

nouer [nwe] vt to tie, knot; (*fig: alliance etc*) to strike up

noueux, -euse [nwø, øz] adj gnarled

nouilles [nuj] nfpl noodles

nourrice [nuʀis] nf (*gardienne*) child-minder

nourrir [nuʀiʀ] vt to feed; (*fig: espoir*) to harbour, nurse; **se ~** to eat; **se ~ de** to feed (o.s.) on; **nourrissant, e** adj nourishing, nutritious; **nourrisson** nm (*unweaned*) infant; **nourriture** nf food

nous [nu] pron (*sujet*) we; (*objet*) us; **nous-mêmes** pron ourselves

nouveau (nouvel), -elle, x [nuvo, nuvɛl] adj new ♦ nm: **y a-t-il du ~?** is there anything new on this? ♦ nm/f new pupil (*ou* employee); **de ~, à ~** again; **~ venu, nouvelle venue** newcomer; **~x mariés** newly-weds; **nouveau-né, e** nm/f newborn baby; **nouveauté** nf novelty; (*objet*) new thing ou article

nouvel [nuvɛl] adj voir **nouveau; N~ An** New Year

nouvelle [nuvɛl] adj voir **nouveau** ♦ nf (*piece of*) news sg; (*LITTÉRATURE*) short story; **les ~s** the news; **je suis sans ~s de lui** I haven't heard from him; **Nouvelle-Calédonie** nf New Caledonia; **nouvellement** adv recently, newly; **Nouvelle-Zélande** nf New Zealand

novembre [nɔvɑ̃bʀ] nm November

novice [nɔvis] adj inexperienced

noyade [nwajad] nf drowning no pl

noyau, x [nwajo] nm (*de fruit*) stone; (*BIO, PHYSIQUE*) nucleus; (*fig: centre*) core; **noyauter** vt (*POL*) to infiltrate

noyer [nwaje] nm walnut (tree); (*bois*) walnut ♦ vt to drown; (*moteur*) to flood; **se ~** vi to be drowned, drown; (*suicide*) to drown o.s.

nu, e [ny] adj naked; (*membres*) naked, bare; (*pieds, mains, chambre, fil électrique*) bare ♦ nm (*ART*) nude; **tout ~** stark naked; **se mettre ~** to strip; **mettre à ~** to bare

nuage [nɥaʒ] nm cloud; **nuageux, -euse** adj cloudy

nuance [nɥɑ̃s] nf (*de couleur, sens*) shade; **il y a une ~ (entre)** there's a slight difference

(between); **nuancer** vt (*opinion*) to bring some reservations ou qualifications to

nucléaire [nykleeʀ] adj nuclear ♦ nm: **le ~** nuclear energy

nudiste [nydist] nm/f nudist

nuée [nɥe] nf: **une ~ de** a cloud ou host ou swarm of

nues [ny] nfpl: **tomber des ~** to be taken aback; **porter qn aux ~** to praise sb to the skies

nuire [nɥiʀ] vi to be harmful; **~ à** to harm, do damage to; **nuisible** adj harmful; **animal nuisible** pest

nuit [nɥi] nf night; **il fait ~** it's dark; **cette ~** (*hier*) last night; (*aujourd'hui*) tonight; **~ blanche** sleepless night

nul, nulle [nyl] adj (*aucun*) no; (*minime*) nil, non-existent; (*non valable*) null; (*péj*) useless, hopeless ♦ pron none, no one; **match** ou **résultat ~** draw; **~le part** nowhere; **nullement** adv by no means; **nullité** nf (*personne*) nonentity

numérique [nymeʀik] adj numerical; (*affichage*) digital

numéro [nymeʀo] nm number; (*spectacle*) act, turn; (*PRESSE*) issue, number; **~ de téléphone** (tele)phone number; **~ vert** ≈ freefone ® number (*BRIT*), ≈ toll-free number (*US*); **numéroter** vt to number

nu-pieds [nypje] adj inv, adv barefoot

nuque [nyk] nf nape of the neck

nu-tête [nytɛt] adj inv, adv bareheaded

nutritif, -ive [nytʀitif, iv] adj (*besoins, valeur*) nutritional; (*nourrissant*) nutritious

nylon [nilɔ̃] nm nylon

O, o

oasis [ɔazis] nf oasis

obéir [ɔbeiʀ] vi to obey; **~ à** to obey; **obéissance** nf obedience; **obéissant, e** adj obedient

obèse [ɔbɛz] adj obese; **obésité** nf obesity

objecter [ɔbʒɛkte] vt (*prétexter*) to plead, put forward as an excuse; **~ (à qn) que** to object (to sb) that; **objecteur** nm: **objecteur de conscience** conscientious objector

objectif, -ive [ɔbʒɛktif, iv] adj objective ♦ nm objective; (*PHOTO*) lens sg, objective; **objectivité** nf objectivity

objection [ɔbʒɛksjɔ̃] nf objection

objet [ɔbʒɛ] nm object; (*d'une discussion, recherche*) subject; **être** ou **faire l'~ de** (*discussion*) to be the subject of; (*soins*) to be given ou shown; **sans ~** purposeless; groundless; **~ d'art** objet d'art; **~s trouvés** lost property sg (*BRIT*), lost-and-found sg (*US*); **~s de valeur** valuables

obligation [ɔbligasjɔ̃] nf obligation; (COMM) bond, debenture; **obligatoire** adj compulsory, obligatory; **obligatoirement** adv necessarily; (fam: sans aucun doute) inevitably

obligé, e [ɔbliʒe] adj (redevable): être très ~ à qn to be most obliged to sb

obligeance [ɔbliʒɑ̃s] nf: avoir l'~ de ... to be kind ou good enough to ...; **obligeant, e** adj (personne) obliging, kind

obliger [ɔbliʒe] vt (contraindre): ~ qn à faire to force ou oblige sb to do; je suis bien obligé I have to

oblique [ɔblik] adj oblique; en ~ diagonally; **obliquer** vi: obliquer vers to turn off towards

oblitérer [ɔblitere] vt (timbre-poste) to cancel

obnubiler [ɔbnybile] vt to obsess

obscène [ɔpsɛn] adj obscene

obscur, e [ɔpskyr] adj dark; (méconnu) obscure; **obscurcir** vt to darken; (fig) to obscure; **s'obscurcir** vi to grow dark; **obscurité** nf darkness; **dans l'obscurité** in the dark, in darkness

obsédé, e [ɔpsede] nm/f: un ~ (sexuel) a sex maniac

obséder [ɔpsede] vt to obsess, haunt

obsèques [ɔpsɛk] nfpl funeral sg

observateur, -trice [ɔpsɛrvatœr, tris] adj observant, perceptive ♦ nm/f observer

observation [ɔpsɛrvasjɔ̃] nf observation; (d'un règlement etc) observance; (reproche) reproof; être en ~ (MÉD) to be under observation

observatoire [ɔpsɛrvatwar] nm observatory

observer [ɔpsɛrve] vt (regarder) to observe, watch; (scientifiquement; aussi règlement etc) to observe; (surveiller) to watch; (remarquer) to observe, notice; **faire ~ qch à qn** (dire) to point out sth to sb

obsession [ɔpsesjɔ̃] nf obsession

obstacle [ɔpstakl] nm obstacle; (ÉQUITATION) jump, hurdle; **faire ~ à** (projet) to hinder, put obstacles in the path of

obstiné, e [ɔpstine] adj obstinate

obstiner [ɔpstine]: **s'~** vi to insist, dig one's heels in; **s'~ à faire** to persist (obstinately) in doing

obstruer [ɔpstrye] vt to block, obstruct

obtenir [ɔptənir] vt to obtain, get; (résultat) to achieve, obtain; ~ de pouvoir faire to obtain permission to do

obturateur [ɔptyratœr, tris] nm (PHOTO) shutter

obus [ɔby] nm shell

occasion [ɔkazjɔ̃] nf (aubaine, possibilité) opportunity; (circonstance) occasion; (COMM: article non neuf) secondhand buy; (: acquisition avantageuse) bargain; **à plusieurs ~s** on several occasions; **à l'~** sometimes, on

occasions; **d'~** secondhand; **occasionnel, le** adj (non régulier) occasional; **occasionnellement** adv occasionally, from time to time

occasionner [ɔkazjɔne] vt to cause

occident [ɔksidɑ̃] nm: l'O~ the West; **occidental, e, -aux** adj western; (POL) Western ♦ nm/f Westerner

occupation [ɔkypasjɔ̃] nf occupation

occupé, e [ɔkype] adj (personne) busy; (place, sièges) taken; (toilettes) engaged; (ligne) engaged (BRIT), busy (US); (MIL, POL) occupied

occuper [ɔkype] vt to occupy; (poste) to hold; **s'~ de** (être responsable de) to be in charge of; (se charger de: affaire) to take charge of, deal with; (: clients etc) to attend to; **s'~ (à qch)** to occupy o.s. ou keep o.s. busy (with sth)

occurrence [ɔkyrɑ̃s] nf: **en l'~** in this case

océan [ɔseɑ̃] nm ocean

octante [ɔktɑ̃t] adj (regional) eighty

octet [ɔktɛ] nm byte

octobre [ɔktɔbr] nm October

octroyer [ɔktrwaje]: **s'~** vt (vacances etc) to treat o.s. to

oculiste [ɔkylist] nm/f eye specialist

odeur [ɔdœr] nf smell

odieux, -euse [ɔdjø, jøz] adj hateful

odorant, e [ɔdɔrɑ̃, ɑ̃t] adj sweet-smelling, fragrant

odorat [ɔdɔra] nm (sense of) smell

œil [œj] nm (pl yeux) nm eye; **à l'œil** (fam) for free; **à l'œil nu** with the naked eye; **tenir qn à l'œil** to keep an eye ou a watch on sb; **avoir l'œil à** to keep an eye on; **fermer les yeux (sur)** (fig) to turn a blind eye (to); **voir qch d'un bon/mauvais œil** to look on sth favourably/unfavourably

œillères [œjɛr] nfpl blinkers (BRIT), blinders (US)

œillet [œjɛ] nm (BOT) carnation

œuf [œf, œf ø] nm egg; **œuf à la coque/sur le plat/dur** boiled/fried/hard-boiled egg; **œuf de Pâques** Easter egg; **œufs brouillés** scrambled eggs

œuvre [œvr] nf (tâche) task, undertaking; (livre, tableau etc) work; (ensemble de la production artistique) works pl ♦ nm (CONSTR): **le gros œuvre** the shell; (bienfaisance) charity; **mettre en œuvre** (moyens) to make use of; **œuvre d'art** work of art

offense [ɔfɑ̃s] nf insult; **offenser** vt to offend, hurt

offert, e [ɔfɛr, ɛrt] pp de **offrir**

office [ɔfis] nm (agence) bureau, agency; (REL) service ♦ nm ou nf (pièce) pantry; **faire ~ de** to act as; **d'~** automatically; **~ du**

tourisme tourist bureau
officiel, le [ɔfisjɛl] adj, nm/f official
officier [ɔfisje] nm officer
officieux, -euse [ɔfisjø, jøz] adj unofficial
offrande [ɔfrɑ̃d] nf offering
offre [ɔfr] nf offer; (aux enchères) bid;
(ADMIN: soumission) tender; (ÉCON): **l'~ et la
demande** supply and demand; **"~s d'emploi**
"situations vacant"; **~ d'emploi** job advertised
offrir [ɔfrir] vt: **~ (à qn)** to offer (to sb); (faire
cadeau de) to give (to sb) **s'~** vt (vacances,
voiture) to treat o.s. to; **~ (à qn) de faire qch**
to offer to do sth (for sb); **~ à boire à qn**
(chez soi) to offer sb a drink
offusquer [ɔfyske] vt to offend
oie [wa] nf (ZOOL) goose
oignon [ɔɲɔ̃] nm onion; (de tulipe etc) bulb
oiseau, x [wazo] nm bird; **~ de proie** bird of
prey
oisif, -ive [wazif, iv] adj idle
oléoduc [ɔleɔdyk] nm (oil) pipeline
olive [ɔliv] nf (BOT) olive; **olivier** nm olive
(tree)
OLP sigle f (= Organisation de libération de la
Palestine) PLO
olympique [ɔlɛ̃pik] adj Olympic
ombragé, e [ɔ̃braʒe] adj shaded, shady;
ombrageux, -euse (personne) touchy,
easily offended
ombre [ɔ̃br] nf (espace non ensoleillé) shade;
(~ portée, tache) shadow; **à l'~** in the shade;
dans l'~ (fig) in the dark; **~ à paupières**
eyeshadow; **ombrelle** nf parasol, sunshade
omelette [ɔmlɛt] nf omelette; **~ norvégienne**
baked Alaska
omettre [ɔmɛtr] vt to omit, leave out
omnibus [ɔmnibys] nm slow ou stopping
train
omoplate [ɔmɔplat] nf shoulder blade

MOT-CLÉ
---

on [ɔ̃] pron **1** (indéterminé) you, one; **on peut
le faire ainsi** you ou one can do it like this, it
can be done like this
2 (quelqu'un): **on les a attaqués** they were
attacked; **on vous demande au téléphone**
there's a phone call for you, you're wanted
on the phone
3 (nous) we; **on va y aller demain** we're
going tomorrow
4 (les gens) they; **autrefois, on croyait ...** they
used to believe ...
5: on ne peut plus
♦ adv: **on ne peut plus stupide** as stupid as
can be

---

oncle [ɔ̃kl] nm uncle
onctueux, -euse [ɔ̃ktɥø, øz] adj creamy,
smooth

onde [ɔ̃d] nf wave; **sur les ~s** on the radio; **sur
~s courtes** on short wave sg; **moyennes/
longues ~s** medium/long wave sg
ondée [ɔ̃de] nf shower
on-dit [ɔ̃di] nm inv rumour
onduler [ɔ̃dyle] vi to undulate; (cheveux) to
wave
onéreux, -euse [ɔnerø, øz] adj costly
ongle [ɔ̃gl] nm nail
ont [ɔ̃] vb voir **avoir**
ONU sigle f (= Organisation des Nations Unies)
UN
onze [ɔ̃z] num eleven; **onzième** num
eleventh
OPA sigle f = offre publique d'achat
opaque [ɔpak] adj opaque
opéra [ɔpera] nm opera; (édifice) opera house
opérateur, -trice [ɔperatœr, tris] nm/f
operator; **~ (de prise de vues)** cameraman
opération [ɔperasjɔ̃] nf operation; (COMM)
dealing
opératoire [ɔperatwar] adj (choc etc) post-
operative
opérer [ɔpere] vt (personne) to operate on;
(faire, exécuter) to carry out, make ♦ vi
(remède: faire effet) to act, work; (MÉD) to
operate; **s'~** vi (avoir lieu) to occur, take
place; **se faire ~** to have an operation
opérette [ɔperɛt] nf operetta, light opera
ophtalmologiste [ɔftalmɔlɔʒist] nm/f
ophthalmologist, optician
opiner [ɔpine] vi: **~ de la tête** to nod assent
opinion [ɔpinjɔ̃] nf opinion; **l'~ (publique)**
public opinion
opportun, e [ɔpɔrtœ̃, yn] adj timely,
opportune; **opportuniste** nm/f opportunist
opposant, e [ɔpozɑ̃, ɑ̃t] nm/f opponent
opposé, e [ɔpoze] adj (direction) opposite;
(faction) opposing; (opinions, intérêts)
conflicting; (contre): **~ à** opposed to, against
♦ nm: **l'~** the other ou opposite side (ou
direction); (contraire) the opposite; **à l'~** (fig)
on the other hand; **à l'~ de** (fig) contrary to,
unlike
opposer [ɔpoze] vt (personnes, équipes) to
oppose; (couleurs) to contrast; **s'~** vi (équipes)
to confront each other; (opinions) to conflict;
(couleurs, styles) to contrast; **s'~ à** (interdire)
to oppose; **~ qch à** (comme obstacle, défense)
to set sth against; (comme objection) to put
sth forward against
opposition [ɔpozisjɔ̃] nf opposition; **par ~ à**
as opposed to, in contrast with; **entrer en
~ avec** to come into conflict with; **faire ~ à un
chèque** to stop a cheque
oppressant, e [ɔpresɑ̃, ɑ̃t] adj oppressive
oppresser [ɔprese] vt to oppress;
oppression nf oppression
opprimer [ɔprime] vt to oppress

opter [ɔpte] vi: ~ **pour** to opt for

opticien, ne [ɔptisjɛ̃, jɛn] nm/f optician

optimisme [ɔptimism] nm optimism; **optimiste** nm/f optimist ♦ adj optimistic

option [ɔpsjɔ̃] nf option; **matière à ~** (SCOL) optional subject

optique [ɔptik] adj (nerf) optic; (verres) optical ♦ nf (fig: manière de voir) perspective

opulent, e [ɔpylɑ̃, ɑ̃t] adj wealthy, opulent; (formes, poitrine) ample, generous

or [ɔR] nm gold ♦ conj now, but; **en ~** (objet) gold cpd; **une affaire en ~** a real bargain; **il croyait gagner ~ il a perdu** he was sure he would win and yet he lost

orage [ɔRaʒ] nm (thunder)storm; **orageux, -euse** adj stormy

oral, e, -aux [ɔRal, o] adj, nm oral; **par voie ~e** (MÉD) orally

orange [ɔRɑ̃ʒ] nf orange ♦ adj inv orange; **orangeade** nf orangeade; **orangé, e** adj orangey, orange-coloured; **oranger** nm orange tree

orateur [ɔRatœR, tRis] nm speaker

orbite [ɔRbit] nf (ANAT) (eye-)socket; (PHYSIQUE) orbit

orchestre [ɔRkɛstR] nm orchestra; (de jazz) band; (places) stalls pl (BRIT), orchestra (US); **orchestrer** vt to orchestrate

orchidée [ɔRkide] nf orchid

ordinaire [ɔRdinɛR] adj ordinary; (qualité) standard; (péj: commun) common ♦ nm ordinary; (menus) everyday fare ♦ nf (essence) ≈ two-star (petrol) (BRIT), ≈ regular gas (US); **d'~** usually, normally; **comme à l'~** as usual

ordinateur [ɔRdinatœR] nm computer

ordonnance [ɔRdɔnɑ̃s] nf (MÉD) prescription; (MIL) orderly, batman (BRIT)

ordonné, e [ɔRdɔne] adj tidy, orderly

ordonner [ɔRdɔne] vt (agencer) to organize, arrange; (donner un ordre): **~ à qn de faire** to order sb to do; (REL) to ordain; (MÉD) to prescribe

ordre [ɔRdR] nm order; (propreté et soin) orderliness, tidiness; (nature): **d'~ pratique** of a practical nature; **~s** nmpl (REL) holy orders; **mettre en ~** to tidy (up), put in order; **à l'~ de qn** payable to sb; **être aux ~s de qn/ sous les ~s de qn** to be at sb's disposal/under sb's command; **jusqu'à nouvel ~** until further notice; **de premier ~** first-rate; **~ du jour** (d'une réunion) agenda; **à l'~ du jour** (fig) topical

ordure [ɔRdyR] nf filth no pl; **~s** nfpl (balayures, déchets) rubbish sg, refuse sg; **~s ménagères** household refuse

oreille [ɔRɛj] nf ear; **avoir de l'~** to have a good ear (for music)

oreiller [ɔReje] nm pillow

oreillons [ɔRɛjɔ̃] nmpl mumps sg

ores [ɔR]: **d'~ et déjà** adv already

orfèvrerie [ɔRfɛvRaRi] nf goldsmith's (ou silversmith's) trade; (ouvrage) gold (ou silver) plate

organe [ɔRgan] nm organ; (porte-parole) representative, mouthpiece

organigramme [ɔRganigRam] nm (tableau hiérarchique) organization chart; (schéma) flow chart

organique [ɔRganik] adj organic

organisateur, -trice [ɔRganizatœR, tRis] nm/f organizer

organisation [ɔRganizasjɔ̃] nf organization

organiser [ɔRganize] vt to organize; (mettre sur pied: service etc) to set up; **s'~** to get organized

organisme [ɔRganism] nm (BIO) organism; (corps, ADMIN) body

organiste [ɔRganist] nm/f organist

orgasme [ɔRgasm] nm orgasm, climax

orge [ɔRʒ] nf barley

orgue [ɔRg] nm organ; **~s** nfpl (MUS) organ sg

orgueil [ɔRgœj] nm pride; **orgueilleux, -euse** adj proud

Orient [ɔRjɑ̃] nm: **l'~** the East, the Orient; **oriental, e, -aux** adj (langue, produit) oriental; (frontière) eastern

orientation [ɔRjɑ̃tasjɔ̃] nf (de recherches) orientation; (d'une maison etc) aspect; (d'un journal) leanings pl; **avoir le sens de l'~** to have a (good) sense of direction; **~ professionnelle** careers advisory service

orienté, e [ɔRjɑ̃te] adj (fig: article, journal) slanted; **bien/mal ~** (appartement) well/badly positioned; **~ au sud** facing south, with a southern aspect

orienter [ɔRjɑ̃te] vt (tourner: antenne) to direct, turn; (personne, recherches) to direct; (fig: élève) to orientate; **s'~** (se repérer) to find one's bearings; **s'~ vers** (fig) to turn towards

origan [ɔRigɑ̃] nm oregano

originaire [ɔRiʒinɛR] adj: **être ~ de** to be a native of

original, e, -aux [ɔRiʒinal, o] adj original; (bizarre) eccentric ♦ nm/f eccentric ♦ nm (document etc, ART) original

origine [ɔRiʒin] nf origin; **dès l'~** at ou from the outset; **à l'~** originally; **originel, le** adj original

orme [ɔRm] nm elm

ornement [ɔRnəmɑ̃] nm ornament

orner [ɔRne] vt to decorate, adorn

ornière [ɔRnjɛR] nf rut

orphelin, e [ɔRfəlɛ̃, in] adj orphan(ed) ♦ nm/f orphan; **~ de père/mère** fatherless/ motherless; **orphelinat** nm orphanage

orteil [ɔRtɛj] nm toe; **gros ~** big toe

orthographe [ɔʀtɔgʀaf] nf spelling

ortie [ɔʀti] nf (stinging) nettle

os [ɔs] nm bone; **tomber sur un ~** (fam) to hit a snag

osciller [ɔsile] vi (au vent etc) to rock; (fig): **~ entre** to waver ou fluctuate between

osé, e [oze] adj daring, bold

oseille [ozɛj] nf sorrel

oser [oze] vi, vt to dare; **~ faire** to dare (to) do

osier [ozje] nm willow; **d'~, en ~** wicker(work)

ossature [ɔsatyʀ] nf (ANAT) frame, skeletal structure; (fig) framework

osseux, -euse [ɔsø, øz] adj bony; (tissu, maladie, greffe) bone cpd

ostensible [ɔstɑ̃sibl] adj conspicuous

otage [ɔtaʒ] nm hostage; **prendre qn comme ~ to** take sb hostage

OTAN sigle f (= Organisation du traité de l'Atlantique Nord) NATO

otarie [ɔtaʀi] nf sea-lion

ôter [ote] vt to remove; (soustraire) to take away; **~ qch à qn** to take sth (away) from sb; **~ qch de** to remove sth from

otite [ɔtit] nf ear infection

ou [u] conj or; **~ ... ~** either ... or; **~ bien** or (else)

---

où [u] pron relatif **1** (position, situation) where, that (souvent omis); **la chambre où il était** the room (that) he was in, the room where he was; **la ville où je l'ai rencontré** the town where I met him; **la pièce d'où il est sorti** the room he came out of; **le village d'où je viens** the village I come from; **les villes par où il est passé** the towns he went through

2 (temps, état) that (souvent omis); **le jour où il est parti** the day (that) he left; **au prix où c'est** at the price it is

♦ adv **1** (interrogation) where; **où est-il/va-t-il?** where is he/is he going?; **par où?** which way?; **d'où vient que ...?** how come ...?

2 (position) where; **où que l'on aille** wherever you go

---

ouate [wat] nf cotton wool (BRIT), cotton (US)

oubli [ubli] nm (acte): **l'~ de** forgetting; (trou de mémoire) lapse of memory; (négligence) omission, oversight; **tomber dans l'~** to sink into oblivion

oublier [ublije] vt to forget; (laisser quelque part: chapeau etc) to leave behind; (ne pas voir: erreurs etc) to miss

oubliettes [ublijet] nfpl dungeon sg

ouest [wɛst] nm west ♦ adj inv west; (région) western; **à l'~** in the west; (direction) (to the) west, westwards; **à l'~ de** (to the) west of

ouf [uf] excl phew!

oui [wi] adv yes

ouï-dire [widiʀ]: **par ~~** adv by hearsay

ouïe [wi] nf hearing; **~s** nfpl (de poisson) gills

ouille [uj] excl ouch!

ouragan [uʀagɑ̃] nm hurricane

ourlet [uʀlɛ] nm hem

ours [uʀs] nm bear; **~ brun/blanc** brown/polar bear; **~ (en peluche)** teddy (bear)

oursin [uʀsɛ̃] nm sea urchin

ourson [uʀsɔ̃] nm (bear-)cub

ouste [ust] excl hop it!

outil [uti] nm tool; **outiller** vt to equip

outrage [utʀaʒ] nm insult; **~ à la pudeur** indecent conduct no pl; **outrager** vt to offend gravely

outrance [utʀɑ̃s]: **à ~** adv excessively, to excess

outre [utʀ] prép besides ♦ adv: **passer ~ à** to disregard, take no notice of; **en ~** besides, moreover; **~ mesure** to excess; (manger, boire) immoderately; **outre-Atlantique** adv across the Atlantic; **outre-Manche** adv across the Channel; **outre-mer** adv overseas; **outrepasser** vt to go beyond, exceed

ouvert, e [uvɛʀ, ɛʀt] pp de **ouvrir** ♦ adj open; (robinet, gaz etc) on; **ouvertement** adv openly; **ouverture** nf opening; (MUS) overture; **ouverture d'esprit** open-mindedness

ouvrable [uvʀabl] adj: **jour ~** working day, weekday

ouvrage [uvʀaʒ] nm (tâche, de tricot etc) work no pl; (texte, livre) work; **ouvragé, e** adj finely embroidered (ou worked ou carved)

ouvre-boîte(s) [uvʀǝbwat] nm inv tin (BRIT) ou can opener

ouvre-bouteille(s) [uvʀǝbutɛj] nm inv bottle-opener

ouvreuse [uvʀøz] nf usherette

ouvrier, -ière [uvʀije, ijɛʀ] nm/f worker ♦ adj working-class; (conflit) industrial; (mouvement) labour cpd; **classe ouvrière** working class

ouvrir [uvʀiʀ] vt (gén) to open; (brèche, passage, MÉD: abcès) to open up; (commencer l'exploitation de, créer) to open (up); (eau, électricité, chauffage, robinet) to turn on ♦ vi to open; to open up; **s'~** vi to open; **s'~ à qn** to open one's heart to sb; **~ l'appétit à qn** to whet sb's appetite

ovaire [ɔvɛʀ] nm ovary

ovale [ɔval] adj oval

ovni [ɔvni] sigle m (= objet volant non identifié) UFO

oxyder [ɔkside]: **s'~** vi to become oxidized

oxygène [ɔksiʒɛn] nm oxygen

oxygéné, e [ɔksiʒene] adj: **eau ~e** hydrogen peroxide

oxygéner [ɔksiʒene]: **s'~** (fam) vi to get

some fresh air

ozone [ozon] *nf* ozone; **la couche d'~** the ozone layer

P, p

pacifique [pasifik] *adj* peaceful ♦ *nm*: **le P~, l'océan P~** the Pacific (Ocean)

pacotille [pakɔtij] *nf* cheap junk; **bijoux de ~** cheap(-jack) jewellery

pack [pak] *nm* pack

pacte [pakt] *nm* pact, treaty

pagaie [page] *nf* paddle

pagaille [pagaj] *nf* mess, shambles *sg*

pagayer *vi* to paddle

page [paʒ] *nf* page ♦ *nm* page (boy); **à la ~** *(fig)* up-to-date

paiement [pɛmɑ̃] *nm* payment

païen, ne [pajɛ̃, pajɛn] *adj, nm/f* pagan, heathen

paillasson [pajasɔ̃] *nm* doormat

paille [pɑj] *nf* straw

paillettes [pɑjɛt] *nfpl* *(décoratives)* sequins, spangles

pain [pɛ̃] *nm* *(substance)* bread; *(unité)* loaf (of bread); *(morceau)*: **~ de savon** *etc* bar of soap *etc*; **~ au chocolat** chocolate-filled pastry; **~ aux raisins** currant bun; **~ bis/complet** brown/wholemeal *(BRIT)* ou wholewheat *(US)* bread; **~ d'épice** gingerbread; **~ de mie** sandwich loaf; **~ grillé** toast

pair, e [pɛʀ] *adj (nombre)* even ♦ *nm* peer; **aller de ~** to go hand in hand ou together; **jeune fille au ~** au pair; **paire** *nf* pair

paisible [pezibl] *adj* peaceful, quiet

paître [pɛtʀ] *vi* to graze

paix [pɛ] *nf* peace; **faire/avoir la ~** to make/ have peace; **fiche-lui la ~!** *(fam)* leave him alone!

Pakistan [pakistɑ̃] *nm*: **le ~** Pakistan

palace [palas] *nm* luxury hotel

palais [palɛ] *nm* palace; *(ANAT)* palate

pâle [pɑl] *adj* pale; **bleu ~** pale blue

Palestine [palɛstin] *nf*: **la ~** Palestine

palet [palɛ] *nm* disc; *(HOCKEY)* puck

paletot [palto] *nm* (thick) cardigan

palette [palɛt] *nf* *(de peintre)* palette; *(produits)* range

pâleur [pɑlœʀ] *nf* paleness

palier [palje] *nm* *(d'escalier)* landing; *(fig)* level, plateau; **par ~s** in stages

pâlir [pɑliʀ] *vi* to turn ou go pale; *(couleur)* to fade

palissade [palisad] *nf* fence

pallier [palje]: **~ à** *vt* to offset, make up for

palmarès [palmaʀɛs] *nm* record (of achievements); *(SPORT)* list of winners

palme [palm] *nf* *(de plongeur)* flipper;

palmé, e *adj (pattes)* webbed

palmier [palmje] *nm* palm tree; *(gâteau)* heart-shaped biscuit made of flaky pastry

pâlot, te [palo, ɔt] *adj* pale, peaky

palourde [paluʀd] *nf* clam

palper [palpe] *vt* to feel, finger

palpitant, e [palpitɑ̃, ɑ̃t] *adj* thrilling

palpiter [palpite] *vi (cœur, pouls)* to beat; *(: plus fort)* to pound, throb

paludisme [palydism] *nm* malaria

pamphlet [pɑ̃flɛ] *nm* lampoon, satirical tract

pamplemousse [pɑ̃pləmus] *nm* grapefruit

pan [pɑ̃] *nm* section, piece ♦ *excl* bang!

panache [panaʃ] *nm* plume; *(fig)* spirit, panache

panaché, e [panaʃe] *adj*: **glace ~e** mixed-flavour ice cream ♦ *nm (bière)* shandy

pancarte [pɑ̃kaʀt] *nf* sign, notice

pancréas [pɑ̃kʀeas] *nm* pancreas

pané, e [pane] *adj* fried in breadcrumbs

panier [panje] *nm* basket; **mettre au ~** to chuck away; **~ à provisions** shopping basket; **panier-repas** *nm* packed lunch

panique [panik] *nf, adj* panic; **paniquer** *vi* to panic

panne [pan] *nf* breakdown; **être/tomber en ~** to have broken down/break down; **être en ~ d'essence** ou **sèche** to have run out of petrol *(BRIT)* ou gas *(US)*; **~ d'électricité** ou **de courant** power ou electrical failure

panneau, x [pano] *nm (écriteau)* sign, notice; **~ d'affichage** notice board; **~ de signalisation** roadsign

panoplie [panɔpli] *nf (jouet)* outfit; *(fig)* array

panorama [panɔʀama] *nm* panorama

panse [pɑ̃s] *nf* paunch

pansement [pɑ̃smɑ̃] *nm* dressing, bandage; **~ adhésif** sticking plaster

panser [pɑ̃se] *vt (plaie)* to dress, bandage; *(bras)* to put a dressing on, bandage; *(cheval)* to groom

pantalon [pɑ̃talɔ̃] *nm* trousers *pl*, pair of trousers; **~ de ski** ski pants *pl*

panthère [pɑ̃tɛʀ] *nf* panther

pantin [pɑ̃tɛ̃] *nm* puppet

pantois [pɑ̃twa] *adj m*: **rester ~** to be flabbergasted

pantoufle [pɑ̃tufl] *nf* slipper

paon [pɑ̃] *nm* peacock

papa [papa] *nm* dad(dy)

pape [pap] *nm* pope

paperasse [papʀas] *(péj)* *nf* bumf *no pl*, papers *pl*; **paperasserie** *(péj)* *nf* paperwork *no pl*; *(tracasserie)* red tape *no pl*

papeterie [papetʀi] *nf (magasin)* stationer's (shop)

papi *nm (fam)* granddad

papier [papje] *nm* paper; *(article)* article; **~s**

nmpl (*aussi:* **~s d'identité**) (identity) papers; **~ à lettres** writing paper, notepaper; **~ carbone** carbon paper; **~ (d')aluminium** aluminium (*BRIT*) *ou* aluminum (*US*) foil, tinfoil; **~ de verre** sandpaper; **~ hygiénique** *ou* **de toilette** toilet paper; **~ journal** newspaper; **~ peint** wallpaper

papillon [papijɔ̃] *nm* butterfly; (*fam:* contravention) (parking) ticket; **~ de nuit** moth

papillote [papijɔt] *nf:* **en ~** cooked in tinfoil

papoter [papɔte] *vi* to chatter

paquebot [pak(ə)bo] *nm* liner

pâquerette [pakrɛt] *nf* daisy

Pâques [pak] *nm, nfpl* Easter

paquet [pakɛ] *nm* packet, (*colis*) parcel; (*fig: tas*): **~ de pile** *ou* heap of; **paquet-cadeau** *nm:* **faites-moi un paquet-cadeau** gift-wrap it for me

par [paʀ] *prép* by; **finir** *etc* **~** to end *etc* with; **~ amour** out of love; **passer ~ Lyon/la côte** to go via *ou* through Lyons/along the coast; **~ la fenêtre** (*jeter, regarder*) out of the window; **3 ~ jour/personne** 3 a *ou* per day/head; **2 ~ 2** in twos; **~ ici** this way; (*dans le coin*) round here; **~-ci, ~-là** here and there; **~ temps de pluie** in wet weather

parabolique [paʀabɔlik] *adj:* **antenne ~** parabolic *ou* dish aerial

parachever [paʀaʃ(ə)ve] *vt* to perfect

parachute [paʀaʃyt] *nm* parachute; **parachutiste** *nm/f* parachutist; (*MIL*) paratrooper

parade [paʀad] *nf* (*spectacle, défilé*) parade; (*ESCRIME, BOXE*) parry

paradis [paʀadi] *nm* heaven, paradise

paradoxe [paʀadɔks] *nm* paradox

paraffine [paʀafin] *nf* paraffin

parages [paʀaʒ] *nmpl:* **dans les ~ (de)** in the area *ou* vicinity (of)

paragraphe [paʀagʀaf] *nm* paragraph

paraître [paʀɛtʀ] *vb +attrib* to seem, look, appear ♦ *vi* to appear; (*être visible*) to show; (*PRESSE, ÉDITION*) to be published, come out, appear ♦ *vb impers:* **il paraît que** it seems *ou* appears that, they say that; **chercher à ~** to show off

parallèle [paʀalɛl] *adj* parallel; (*non officiel*) unofficial ♦ *nm* (*comparaison*): **faire un ~ entre** to draw a parallel between ♦ *nf* parallel (line)

paralyser [paʀalize] *vt* to paralyse

paramédical, e, -aux [paʀamedikal, o] *adj:* **personnel ~** paramedics *pl*, paramedical workers *pl*

paraphrase [paʀafʀɑz] *nf* paraphrase

parapluie [paʀaplɥi] *nm* umbrella

parasite [paʀazit] *nm* parasite; **~s** *nmpl* (*TÉL*) interference *sg*

parasol [paʀasɔl] *nm* parasol, sunshade

paratonnerre [paʀatɔnɛʀ] *nm* lightning conductor

paravent [paʀavɑ̃] *nm* folding screen

parc [paʀk] *nm* (public) park, gardens *pl*; (*de château etc*) grounds *pl*; (*d'enfant*) playpen; (*ensemble d'unités*) stock; (*de voitures etc*) fleet; **~ d'attractions** theme park; **~ de stationnement** car park

parcelle [paʀsɛl] *nf* fragment, scrap; (*de terrain*) plot, parcel

parce que [paʀsk(ə)] *conj* because

parchemin [paʀʃəmɛ̃] *nm* parchment

parcmètre [paʀkmɛtʀ] *nm* parking meter

parcourir [paʀkuʀiʀ] *vt* (*trajet, distance*) to cover; (*article, livre*) to skim *ou* glance through; (*lieu*) to go all over, travel up and down; (*suj: frisson*) to run through

parcours [paʀkuʀ] *nm* (*trajet*) journey; (*itinéraire*) route

par-derrière [paʀdɛʀjɛʀ] *adv* round the back; **dire du mal de qn ~~** to speak ill of sb behind his back

par-dessous [paʀd(ə)su] *prép, adv* under(neath)

pardessus [paʀdəsy] *nm* overcoat

par-dessus [paʀd(ə)sy] *prép* over (the top of) ♦ *adv* over (the top); **~~ le marché** on top of all that; **~~ tout** above all; **en avoir ~~ la tête** to have had enough

par-devant [paʀd(ə)vɑ̃] *adv* (*passer*) round the front

pardon [paʀdɔ̃] *nm* forgiveness *no pl* ♦ *excl* sorry!; (*pour interpeller etc*) excuse me!; **demander ~ à qn (de)** to apologize to sb (for); **je vous demande ~** I'm sorry; (*pour interpeller*) excuse me; **pardonner** *vt* to forgive; **pardonner qch à qn** to forgive sb for sth

pare...: **pare-balles** *adj inv* bulletproof; **pare-brise** *nm inv* windscreen (*BRIT*), windshield (*US*); **pare-chocs** *nm inv* bumper

paré, e [paʀe] *adj* ready, all set

pareil, le [paʀɛj] *adj* (*identique*) the same, alike; (*similaire*) similar; (*tel*): **un courage/livre ~** such courage/a book, courage/a book like this; **de ~s livres** such books; **ne pas avoir son(sa) ~(le)** to be second to none; **~ à** the same as; (*similaire*) similar to; **sans ~** unparalleled, unequalled

parent, e [paʀɑ̃, ɑ̃t] *nm/f:* **un(e) ~(e)** a relative *ou* relation; **~s** *nmpl* (*père et mère*) parents; **parenté** *nf* (*lien*) relationship

parenthèse [paʀɑ̃tɛz] *nf* (*ponctuation*) bracket, parenthesis; (*digression*) parenthesis, digression; **entre ~s** in brackets; (*fig*) incidentally

parer [paʀe] *vt* to adorn; (*éviter*) to ward off; **~ au plus pressé** to attend to the most urgent things first

paresse [paʀɛs] *nf* laziness; **paresseux, -euse** *adj* lazy

parfaire [paʀfɛʀ] *vt* to perfect

parfait, e [paʀfɛ, ɛt] *adj* perfect ♦ *nm* (LING) perfect (tense); **parfaitement** *adv* perfectly ♦ *excl* (most) certainly

parfois [paʀfwa] *adv* sometimes

parfum [paʀfœ̃] *nm* (*produit*) perfume, scent; (*odeur: de fleur*) scent, fragrance; (*goût*) flavour; **parfumé, e** *adj* (*fleur, fruit*) fragrant; (*femme*) perfumed; **parfumé au café** coffee-flavoured; **parfumer** *vt* (*suj: odeur, bouquet*) to perfume; (*crème, gâteau*) to flavour; **parfumerie** *nf* (*produits*) perfumes *pl*; (*boutique*) perfume shop

pari [paʀi] *nm* bet; **parier** *vt* to bet

Paris [paʀi] *n* Paris; **parisien, ne** *adj* Parisian; (GÉO, ADMIN) Paris *cpd* ♦ *nm/f*: **Parisien, ne** Parisian

parjure [paʀʒyʀ] *nm* perjury

parking [paʀkiŋ] *nm* (*lieu*) car park

parlant, e [paʀlɑ̃, ɑ̃t] *adj* (*regard*) eloquent; (CINÉMA) talking; **les chiffres sont ~s** the figures speak for themselves

parlement [paʀləmɑ̃] *nm* parliament; **parlementaire** *adj* parliamentary ♦ *nm/f* member of parliament; **parlementer** *vi* to negotiate, parley

parler [paʀle] *vi* to speak, talk; (*avouer*) to talk; **~ (à qn) de** to talk ou speak (to sb) about; **~ le/en français** to speak French/in French; **~ affaires** to talk business; **sans ~ de** (*fig*) not to mention, to say nothing of; **tu parles!** (*fam: bien sûr*) you bet!

parloir [paʀlwaʀ] *nm* (*de prison, d'hôpital*) visiting room

parmi [paʀmi] *prép* among(st)

paroi [paʀwa] *nf* wall; (*cloison*) partition; **~ rocheuse** rock face

paroisse [paʀwas] *nf* parish

parole [paʀɔl] *nf* (*faculté*): **la ~** speech; (*mot, promesse*) word; **~s** *nfpl* (MUS) words, lyrics; **tenir ~** to keep one's word; **prendre la ~** to speak; **demander la ~** to ask for permission to speak; **je te crois sur ~** I'll take your word for it

parquer [paʀke] *vt* (*voiture, matériel*) to park; (*bestiaux*) to pen (in ou up)

parquet [paʀkɛ] *nm* (*parquet*) floor; (JUR): **le ~** the Public Prosecutor's department

parrain [paʀɛ̃] *nm* godfather; **parrainer** *vt* (*suj: entreprise*) to sponsor

pars [paʀ] *vb voir* **partir**

parsemer [paʀsəme] *vt* (*suj: feuilles, papiers*) to be scattered over; **~ qch de** to scatter sth with

part [paʀ] *nf* (*qui revient à qn*) share; (*fraction, ~ie*) part; **prendre ~ à** (*débat etc*) to take part

in; (*soucis, douleur de qn*) to share in; **faire ~ de qch à qn** to announce sth to sb, inform sb of sth; **pour ma ~** as for me, as far as I'm concerned; **à ~ entière** full; **de la ~ de** (*au nom de*) on behalf of; (*donné par*) from; **de toute(s) ~(s)** from all sides ou quarters; **de ~ et d'autre** on both sides, on either side; **d'une ~ ... d'autre ~** on the one hand ... on the other hand; **d'autre ~** (*de plus*) moreover; **à ~** ♦ *adv* (*séparément*) separately; (*de côté*) aside ♦ *prép* apart from, except for; **faire la ~ des choses** to make allowances

partage [paʀtaʒ] *nm* (*fractionnement*) dividing up; (*répartition*) sharing (out) *no pl*, share-out

partager [paʀtaʒe] *vt* to share; (*distribuer, répartir*) to share (out); (*morceler, diviser*) to divide (up); **se ~** *vt* (*héritage etc*) to share between themselves (*ou* ourselves)

partance [paʀtɑ̃s]: **en ~** *adv*: **en ~ pour** (bound) for

partenaire [paʀtənɛʀ] *nm/f* partner

parterre [paʀtɛʀ] *nm* (*de fleurs*) (flower) bed; (THÉÂTRE) stalls *pl*

parti [paʀti] *nm* (POL) party; (*décision*) course of action; (*personne à marier*) match; **tirer ~ de** to take advantage of, turn to good account; **prendre ~ (pour/contre)** to take sides *ou* a stand (for/against); **~ pris** bias

partial, e, -aux [paʀsjal, jo] *adj* biased, partial

participant, e [paʀtisipɑ̃, ɑ̃t] *nm/f* participant; (*à un concours*) entrant

participation [paʀtisipasjɔ̃] *nf* participation; (*financière*) contribution

participer [paʀtisipe]: **~ à** *vt* (*course, réunion*) to take part in; (*frais etc*) to contribute to; (*chagrin, succès de qn*) to share (in)

particularité [paʀtikylaʀite] *nf* (*distinctive*) characteristic

particulier, -ière [paʀtikylje, jɛʀ] *adj* (*spécifique*) particular; (*spécial*) special, particular; (*personnel, privé*) private; (*étrange*) peculiar, odd ♦ *nm* (*individu*: ADMIN) private individual; **~ à** peculiar to; **en ~** (*surtout*) in particular, particularly; (*en privé*) in private; **particulièrement** *adv* particularly

partie [paʀti] *nf* (*gén*) part; (JUR etc: *protagonistes*) party; (*de cartes, tennis etc*) game; **une ~ de pêche** a fishing party ou trip; **en ~** partly, in part; **faire ~ de** (*suj: chose*) to be part of; **prendre qn à ~** to take sb to task; **en grande ~** largely, in the main; **~ civile** (JUR) party claiming damages in a criminal case

partiel, le [paʀsjɛl] *adj* partial ♦ *nm* (SCOL) class exam

partir [paʀtiʀ] *vi* (*gén*) to go; (*quitter*) to go, leave; (*tache*) to go, come out; **~ de** (*lieu*: *quitter*) to leave; (: *commencer à*) to start from; **à ~ de** from

partisan, e [paʀtizɑ̃, an] *nm/f* partisan
♦ *adj*: **être ~ de qch/de faire** to be in favour of sth/doing

partition [paʀtisjɔ̃] *nf* (*MUS*) score

partout [paʀtu] *adv* everywhere; **~ où il allait** everywhere ou wherever he went

paru [paʀy] *pp de* **paraître**

parure [paʀyʀ] *nf* (*bijoux etc*) finery *no pl*; jewellery *no pl*; (*assortiment*) set

parution [paʀysjɔ̃] *nf* publication

parvenir [paʀvəniʀ]: **~ à** *vt* (*atteindre*) to reach; (*réussir*): **~ à faire** to manage to do, succeed in doing; **~ à ses fins** to achieve one's ends

pas¹ [pɑ] *nm* (*enjambée, DANSE*) step; (*allure, mesure*) pace; (*bruit*) (foot)step; (*trace*) footprint; **~ à ~** step by step; **au ~** at walking pace; **faire les cent ~** to pace up and down; **faire les premiers ~** to make the first move; **sur le ~ de la porte** on the doorstep

┌─────────────────────────────────────┐
│ MOT-CLÉ │
└─────────────────────────────────────┘

pas² [pɑ] *adv* **1** (*en corrélation avec ne, non etc*) not; **il ne pleure pas** he does not ou doesn't cry; **he's not** ou **isn't crying**; **il n'a pas pleuré/ne pleurera pas** he did not ou didn't/ will not ou won't cry; **ils n'ont pas de voiture/d'enfants** they haven't got a car/any children, they have no car/children; **il m'a dit de ne pas le faire** he told me not to do it; **non pas que ...** not that ...

2 (*employé sans ne etc*): **pas moi** not me; not I, I don't (ou can't *etc*); **une pomme pas mûre** an apple which isn't ripe; **pas plus tard qu'hier** only yesterday; **pas du tout** not at all

3: **pas mal** not bad; not badly; **pas mal de** quite a lot of

└─────────────────────────────────────┘

passage [pɑsaʒ] *nm* (*fait de passer*) voir **passer**; (*lieu, prix de la traversée, extrait*) passage; (*chemin*) way; **de ~** (*touristes*) passing through; **~ à niveau** level crossing; **~ clouté** pedestrian crossing; **"~ interdit"** "no entry"; **~ souterrain** subway (*BRIT*), underpass

passager, -ère [pɑsaʒe, ɛʀ] *adj* passing
♦ *nm/f* passenger; **~ clandestin** stowaway

passant, e [pɑsɑ̃, ɑ̃t] *adj* (*rue, endroit*) busy
♦ *nm/f* passer-by; **en ~** in passing

passe¹ [pɑs] *nf* (*SPORT, NAVIG*) pass; **être en ~ de faire** to be on the way to doing; **être dans une mauvaise ~** to be going through a rough patch

passe² [pɑs] *nm* (*~-partout*) master ou skeleton key

passé, e [pɑse] *adj* (*révolu*) past; (*dernier: semaine etc*) last; (*couleur*) faded ♦ *prép* after
♦ *nm* past; (*LING*) past (tense); **~ de mode** out of fashion; **~ composé** perfect (tense);

~ simple past historic

passe-partout [pɑspaʀtu] *nm inv* master ou skeleton key ♦ *adj inv* all-purpose

passeport [pɑspɔʀ] *nm* passport

passer [pɑse] *vi* (*aller*) to go; (*voiture, piétons: défiler*) to pass (by), go by; (*facteur, laitier etc*) to come, call; (*pour rendre visite*) to call ou drop in; (*film, émission*) to be on; (*temps, jours*) to pass, go by; (*couleur*) to fade; (*mode*) to die out; (*douleur*) to pass, go away; (*SCOL*) to go up (to the next class) ♦ *vt* (*frontière, rivière etc*) to cross; (*douane*) to go through; (*examen*) to sit, take; (*visite médicale etc*) to have; (*journée, temps*) to spend; (*enfiler: vêtement*) to slip on; (*film, pièce*) to show, put on; (*disque*) to play, put on; (*marché, accord*) to agree on; **se ~** *vi* (*avoir lieu: scène, action*) to take place; (*se dérouler: entretien etc*) to go; (*s'écouler: semaine etc*) to pass, go by; (*arriver*): **que s'est-il passé?** what happened?; **~ qch à qn** (*sel etc*) to pass sth to sb; (*prêter*) to lend sb sth; (*lettre, message*) to pass sth on to sb; (*tolérer*) to let sb get away with sth; **~ par** to go through; **~ avant qch/qn** (*fig*) to come before sth/sb; **~ un coup de fil à qn** (*fam*) to give sb a ring; **laisser ~** (*air, lumière, personne*) to let through; (*occasion*) to let slip, miss; (*erreur*) to overlook; **~ la seconde** (*AUTO*) to change into second; **~ le balai/ l'aspirateur** to sweep up/hoover; **je vous passe M. X** (*je vous mets en communication avec lui*) I'm putting you through to Mr X; (*je lui passe l'appareil*) here is Mr X, I'll hand you over to Mr X; **se ~ de** to go ou do without

passerelle [pɑsʀɛl] *nf* footbridge; (*de navire, avion*) gangway

passe-temps [pɑstɑ̃] *nm inv* pastime

passible [pɑsibl] *adj*: **~ de** liable to

passif, -ive [pasif, iv] *adj* passive

passion [pɑsjɔ̃] *nf* passion; **passionnant, e** *adj* fascinating; **passionné, e** *adj* (*personne*) passionate; (*récit*) impassioned; **être passionné de** to have a passion for;

passionner *vt* (*personne*) to fascinate, grip; **se passionner pour** (*sport*) to have a passion for

passoire [pɑswaʀ] *nf* sieve; (*à légumes*) colander; (*à thé*) strainer

pastèque [pastɛk] *nf* watermelon

pasteur [pastœʀ] *nm* (*protestant*) minister, pastor

pasteurisé, e [pastœʀize] *adj* pasteurized

pastille [pastij] *nf* (*à sucer*) lozenge, pastille

patate [patat] *nf* (*fam: pomme de terre*) spud; **~ douce** sweet potato

patauger [patoʒe] *vi* to splash about

pâte [pɑt] *nf* (*à tarte*) pastry; (*à pain*) dough; (*à frire*) batter; **~s** *nfpl* (*macaroni etc*) pasta *sg;* ~ **à modeler** modelling clay, Plasticine ® (*BRIT*); ~ **brisée** shortcrust pastry; ~ **d'amandes** almond paste; ~ **de fruits** crystallized fruit *no pl;* ~ **feuilletée** puff *ou* flaky pastry

pâté [pate] *nm (charcuterie)* pâté; *(tache)* ink blot; *(de sable)* sandpie; ~ **de maisons** block (of houses); ~ **en croûte** ≈ pork pie

pâtée [pate] *nf* mash, feed

patente [patɑ̃t] *nf (COMM)* trading licence

paternel, le [patɛʀnɛl] *adj (amour, soins)* fatherly; *(ligne, autorité)* paternal

pâteux, -euse [patø, øz] *adj* pasty; *(langue)* coated

pathétique [patetik] *adj* moving

patience [pasjɑ̃s] *nf* patience

patient, e [pasjɑ̃, jɑ̃t] *adj, nm/f* patient; **patienter** *vi* to wait

patin [patɛ̃] *nm* skate; *(sport)* skating; ~**s (à glace)** (ice) skates; ~**s à roulettes** roller skates

patinage [patinaʒ] *nm* skating

patiner [patine] *vi* to skate; *(roue, voiture)* to spin; **se** ~ *vi (meuble, cuir)* to acquire a sheen; **patineur, -euse** *nm/f* skater; **patinoire** *nf* skating rink, (ice) rink

pâtir [patiʀ]: ~ **de** *vt* to suffer because of

pâtisserie [patisʀi] *nf (boutique)* cake shop; *(gâteau)* cake, pastry; *(à la maison)* pastry-*ou* cake-making, baking; **pâtissier, -ière** *nm/f* pastrycook

patois [patwa, waz] *nm* dialect, patois

patraque [patʀak] *(fam) adj* peaky, off-colour

patrie [patʀi] *nf* homeland

patrimoine [patʀimwan] *nm (culture)* heritage

patriotique [patʀijɔtik] *adj* patriotic

patron, ne [patʀɔ̃, ɔn] *nm/f* boss; *(REL)* patron saint ♦ *nm (COUTURE)* pattern; **patronat** *nm* employers *pl;* **patronner** *vt* to sponsor, support

patrouille [patʀuj] *nf* patrol

patte [pat] *nf (jambe)* leg; *(pied: de chien, chat)* paw; *(: d'oiseau)* foot

pâturage [patyʀaʒ] *nm* pasture

paume [pom] *nf* palm

paumé, e [pome] *(fam) nm/f* drop-out

paumer [pome] *(fam) vt* to lose

paupière [popjɛʀ] *nf* eyelid

pause [poz] *nf (arrêt)* break; *(en parlant, MUS)* pause

pauvre [povʀ] *adj* poor; **pauvreté** *nf (état)* poverty

pavaner [pavane]: **se** ~ *vi* to strut about

pavé, e [pave] *adj (cour)* paved; *(chaussée)* cobbled ♦ *nm (bloc)* paving stone; cobblestone

pavillon [pavijɔ̃] *nm (de banlieue)* small (detached) house, pavilion; *(drapeau)* flag

pavoiser [pavwaze] *vi (fig)* to rejoice, exult

pavot [pavo] *nm* poppy

payant, e [pejɑ̃, ɑ̃t] *adj (spectateurs etc)* paying; *(fig: entreprise)* profitable; *(effort)* which pays off; **c'est** ~ you have to pay, there is a charge

paye [pɛj] *nf* pay, wages *pl*

payer [peje] *vt (créancier, employé, loyer)* to pay; *(achat, réparations, fig: faute)* to pay for ♦ *vi* to pay; *(métier)* to be well-paid; *(tactique etc)* to pay off; **il me l'a fait** ~ **10 F** he charged me 10 F for it; ~ **qch à qn** to buy sth for sb, buy sb sth; **se** ~ **la tête de qn** *(fam)* to take the mickey out of sb

pays [pei] *nm* country; *(région)* region; **du** ~ local

paysage [peizaʒ] *nm* landscape

paysan, ne [peizɑ̃, an] *nm/f* farmer; *(péj)* peasant ♦ *adj (agricole)* farming; *(rural)* country

Pays-Bas [peiba] *nmpl:* **les** ~~ the Netherlands

PC *nm (INFORM)* PC ♦ *sigle m* = **parti communiste**

P.D.G. *sigle m* = **président directeur général**

péage [peaʒ] *nm* toll; *(endroit)* tollgate

peau, x [po] *nf* skin; *(cuir)* leather; **gants de** ~ fine leather gloves; **être bien/mal dans sa** ~ to be quite at ease/ill-at-ease; ~ **de chamois** *(chiffon)* chamois leather, shammy; **Peau-Rouge** *nm/f* Red Indian, redskin

pêche [pɛʃ] *nf (sport, activité)* fishing; *(poissons pêchés)* catch; *(fruit)* peach; ~ **à la ligne** *(en rivière)* angling

péché [peʃe] *nm* sin

pécher [peʃe] *vi (REL)* to sin

pêcher [peʃe] *nm* peach tree ♦ *vi* to go fishing ♦ *vt (attraper)* to catch; *(être pêcheur de)* to fish for

pécheur, -eresse [peʃœʀ, peʃʀɛs] *nm/f* sinner

pêcheur [peʃœʀ] *nm* fisherman; *(à la ligne)* angler

pécule [pekyl] *nm* savings *pl,* nest egg

pédagogie [pedagɔʒi] *nf* educational methods *pl,* pedagogy; **pédagogique** *adj* educational

pédale [pedal] *nf* pedal

pédalo [pedalo] *nm* pedal-boat

pédant, e [pedɑ̃, ɑ̃t] *(péj) adj* pedantic

pédestre [pedɛstʀ] *adj:* **randonnée** ~ ramble; **sentier** ~ pedestrian footpath

pédiatre [pedjatʀ] *nm/f* paediatrician, child specialist

pédicure [pedikyʀ] *nm/f* chiropodist

pègre [pɛgʀ] *nf* underworld

peignais *etc* [pɛɲɛ] *vb voir* **peindre; peigner**

peigne [pɛɲ] *nm* comb; **peigner** *vt* to comb (the hair of); **se peigner** *vi* to comb one's hair

peignoir *nm* dressing gown; **peignoir de bain**

bathrobe
peindre [pɛ̃dʀ] vt to paint; (fig) to portray, depict

peine [pɛn] nf (affliction) sorrow, sadness no pl; (mal, effort) trouble no pl, effort; (difficulté) difficulty; (JUR) sentence; **avoir de la ~** to be sad; **faire de la ~ à qn** to distress ou upset sb; **prendre la ~ de faire** to go to the trouble of doing; **se donner de la ~** to make an effort; **ce n'est pas la ~ de faire** there's no point in doing, it's not worth doing; **à ~** scarcely, hardly, barely; **à ~ ... que** hardly ... than; **~ capitale** ou **de mort** capital punishment, death sentence; **peiner** vi (personne) to work hard; (moteur, voiture) to labour ♦ vt to grieve, sadden

peintre [pɛ̃tʀ] nm painter; **~ en bâtiment** house painter

peinture [pɛ̃tyʀ] nf painting; (matière) paint; (surfaces peintes: aussi: **~s**) paintwork; **"~ fraîche"** "wet paint"

péjoratif, -ive [peʒɔʀatif, iv] adj pejorative, derogatory

pelage [pəlaʒ] nm coat, fur

pêle-mêle [pɛlmɛl] adv higgledy-piggledy

peler [pəle] vt, vi to peel

pèlerin [pɛlʀɛ̃] nm pilgrim

pèlerinage [pɛlʀinaʒ] nm pilgrimage

pelle [pɛl] nf shovel; (d'enfant, de terrassier) spade

pellicule [pelikyl] nf film; **~s** nfpl (MÉD) dandruff sg

pelote [p(ə)lɔt] nf (de fil, laine) ball

peloton [p(ə)lɔtɔ̃] nm group, squad; (CYCLISME) pack; **~ d'exécution** firing squad

pelotonner [p(ə)lɔtɔne]: **se ~** vi to curl (o.s.) up

pelouse [p(ə)luz] nf lawn

peluche [p(ə)lyʃ] nf: (animal en) **~** fluffy animal, soft toy; **chien/lapin en ~** fluffy dog/rabbit

pelure [p(ə)lyʀ] nf peeling, peel no pl

pénal, e, -aux [penal, o] adj penal; **pénalité** nf penalty

penaud, e [pəno, od] adj sheepish, contrite

penchant [pɑ̃ʃɑ̃] nm (tendance) tendency, propensity; (faible) liking, fondness

pencher [pɑ̃ʃe] vi to tilt, lean over ♦ vt to tilt; **se ~** vi to lean over; (se baisser) to bend down; **se ~ sur** (fig: problème) to look into; **~ pour** to be inclined to favour

pendaison [pɑ̃dɛzɔ̃] nf hanging

pendant [pɑ̃dɑ̃] prép (au cours de) during; (indique la durée) for; **~ que** while

pendentif [pɑ̃dɑ̃tif] nm pendant

penderie [pɑ̃dʀi] nf wardrobe

pendre [pɑ̃dʀ] vt, vi to hang; **se ~** (se suicider) to hang o.s.; **~ la crémaillère** to have a house-warming party

pendule [pɑ̃dyl] nf clock ♦ nm pendulum

pénétrer [penetʀe] vi, vt to penetrate; **~ dans** to enter

pénible [penibl] adj (travail) hard; (sujet) painful; (personne) tiresome; **péniblement** adv with difficulty

péniche [peniʃ] nf barge

pénicilline [penisilin] nf penicillin

péninsule [penɛ̃syl] nf peninsula

pénis [penis] nm penis

pénitence [penitɑ̃s] nf (peine) penance; (repentir) penitence; **pénitencier** nm penitentiary

pénombre [penɔ̃bʀ] nf (faible clarté) half-light; (obscurité) darkness

pensée [pɑ̃se] nf thought; (démarche, doctrine) thinking no pl; (fleur) pansy; **en ~** in one's mind

penser [pɑ̃se] vi, vt to think; **~ à** (ami, vacances) to think of ou about; (réfléchir à: problème, offre) to think about ou over; (prévoir) to think of; **faire ~ à** to remind one of; **~ faire qch** to be thinking of doing sth, intend to do sth; **pensif, -ive** adj pensive, thoughtful

pension [pɑ̃sjɔ̃] nf (allocation) pension; (prix du logement) board and lodgings, bed and board; (école) boarding school; **~ alimentaire** (de divorcée) maintenance allowance, alimony; **~ complète** full board; **~ (de famille)** boarding house, guesthouse; **pensionnaire** nm/f (SCOL) boarder; **pensionnat** nm boarding school

pente [pɑ̃t] nf slope; **en ~** sloping

Pentecôte [pɑ̃tkot] nf: **la ~** Whitsun (BRIT), Pentecost

pénurie [penyʀi] nf shortage

pépé [pepe] (fam) nm grandad

pépin [pepɛ̃] nm (BOT: graine) pip; (ennui) snag, hitch

pépinière [pepinjɛʀ] nf nursery

perçant, e [pɛʀsɑ̃, ɑ̃t] adj (cri) piercing, shrill; (regard) piercing

percée [pɛʀse] nf (trouée) opening; (MIL, technologique) breakthrough

perce-neige [pɛʀsɑneʒ] nf inv snowdrop

percepteur [pɛʀsɛptœʀ, tʀis] nm tax collector

perception [pɛʀsɛpsjɔ̃] nf perception; (bureau) tax office

percer [pɛʀse] vt to pierce; (ouverture etc) to make; (mystère, énigme) to penetrate ♦ vi to break through; **perceuse** nf drill

percevoir [pɛʀsəvwaʀ] vt (distinguer) to perceive, detect; (taxe, impôt) to collect; (revenu, indemnité) to receive

perche [pɛʀʃ] nf (bâton) pole

percher [pɛʀʃe] vt, vi to perch; **se ~** vi to perch; **perchoir** nm perch

perçois etc [pɛʀswa] vb voir **percevoir**
percolateur [pɛʀkɔlatœʀ] nm percolator
perçu, e [pɛʀsy] pp de **percevoir**
percussion [pɛʀkysjɔ̃] nf percussion
percuter [pɛʀkyte] vt to strike; (suj: véhicule) to crash into
perdant, e [pɛʀdɑ̃, ɑ̃t] nm/f loser
perdre [pɛʀdʀ] vt to lose; (gaspiller: temps, argent) to waste; (personne: moralement etc) to ruin ♦ vi to lose; (sur une vente etc) to lose out; se ~ vi (s'égarer) to get lost, lose one's way; (denrées) to go to waste
perdrix [pɛʀdʀi] nf partridge
perdu, e [pɛʀdy] pp de **perdre** ♦ adj (isolé) out-of-the-way; (COMM: emballage) non-returnable; (malade): **il est ~** there's no hope left for him; **à vos moments ~s** in your spare time
père [pɛʀ] nm father; **~ de famille** father; **le ~ Noël** Father Christmas
perfection [pɛʀfɛksjɔ̃] nf perfection; **à la ~** to perfection; **perfectionné, e** adj sophisticated; **perfectionner** vt to improve, perfect
perforatrice [pɛʀfɔʀatʀis] nf (de bureau) punch
perforer [pɛʀfɔʀe] vt (poinçonner) to punch
performant, e [pɛʀfɔʀmɑ̃, ɑ̃t] adj: **très ~** high-performance cpd
perfusion [pɛʀfyzjɔ̃] nf: **faire une ~ à qn** to put sb on a drip
péricliter [peʀiklite] vi to collapse
péril [peʀil] nm peril
périmé, e [peʀime] adj (ADMIN) out-of-date, expired
périmètre [peʀimɛtʀ] nm perimeter
période [peʀjɔd] nf period; **périodique** adj periodic ♦ nm periodical
péripéties [peʀipesi] nfpl events, episodes
périphérique [peʀifeʀik] adj (quartiers) outlying ♦ nm (AUTO) ring road
périple [peʀipl] nm journey
périr [peʀiʀ] vi to die, perish
périssable [peʀisabl] adj perishable
perle [pɛʀl] nf pearl; (de plastique, métal, sueur) bead
permanence [pɛʀmanɑ̃s] nf permanence; (local) (duty) office; **assurer une ~** (service public, bureaux) to operate ou maintain a basic service; **être de ~** to be on call ou duty; **en ~** continuously
permanent, e [pɛʀmanɑ̃, ɑ̃t] adj permanent; (spectacle) continuous; **permanente** nf perm
perméable [pɛʀmeabl] adj (terrain) permeable; **~ à** (fig) receptive ou open to
permettre [pɛʀmɛtʀ] vt to allow, permit; **~ à qn de faire/qch** to allow sb to do/sth; **se ~ de faire** to take the liberty of doing

permis [pɛʀmi, iz] nm permit, licence; **~ de chasse** hunting permit; **~ (de conduire)** (driving) licence (BRIT), (driver's) license (US); **~ de construire** planning permission (BRIT), building permit (US); **~ de séjour** residence permit; **~ de travail** work permit
permission [pɛʀmisjɔ̃] nf permission; (MIL) leave; **avoir la ~ de faire** to have permission to do; **en ~** on leave
permuter [pɛʀmyte] vt to change around, permutate ♦ vi to change, swap
Pérou [peʀu] nm Peru
perpétuel, le [pɛʀpetɥɛl] adj perpetual; **perpétuité** nf: **à perpétuité** for life; **être condamné à perpétuité** to receive a life sentence
perplexe [pɛʀplɛks] adj perplexed, puzzled
perquisitionner [pɛʀkizisjɔne] vi to carry out a search
perron [pɛʀɔ̃] nm steps pl (leading to entrance)
perroquet [pɛʀɔkɛ] nm parrot
perruche [pɛʀyʃ] nf budgerigar (BRIT), budgie (BRIT), parakeet (US)
perruque [pɛʀyk] nf wig
persan, e [pɛʀsɑ̃, an] adj Persian
persécuter [pɛʀsekyte] vt to persecute
persévérer [pɛʀseveʀe] vi to persevere
persiennes [pɛʀsjɛn] nfpl shutters
persil [pɛʀsi] nm parsley
Persique [pɛʀsik] adj: **le golfe ~** the (Persian) Gulf
persistant, e [pɛʀsistɑ̃, ɑ̃t] adj persistent
persister [pɛʀsiste] vi to persist; **~ à faire qch** to persist in doing sth
personnage [pɛʀsɔnaʒ] nm (individu) character, individual; (célébrité) important person; (de roman, film) character; (PEINTURE) figure
personnalité [pɛʀsɔnalite] nf personality; (personnage) prominent figure
personne [pɛʀsɔn] nf person ♦ pron nobody, no one; (avec négation en anglais) anybody, anyone; **~s** nfpl (gens) people pl; **il n'y a ~** there's nobody there, there isn't anybody there; **~ âgée** elderly person; **personnel, le** adj personal; (égoïste) selfish ♦ nm staff, personnel; **personnellement** adv personally
perspective [pɛʀspɛktiv] nf (ART) perspective; (vue) view; (point de vue) viewpoint, angle; (chose envisagée) prospect; **en ~** in prospect
perspicace [pɛʀspikas] adj clear-sighted, gifted with (ou showing) insight; **perspicacité** nf clear-sightedness
persuader [pɛʀsɥade] vt: **~ qn (de faire)** to persuade sb (to do); **persuasif, -ive** adj persuasive
perte [pɛʀt] nf loss; (de temps) waste; (fig:

morale) ruin; **à ~ de vue** as far as the eye can (*ou* could) see; **~s blanches** (vaginal) discharge *sg*

pertinemment [pɛʀtinamɑ̃] *adv* (*savoir*) full well

pertinent, e [pɛʀtinɑ̃, ɑ̃t] *adj* apt, relevant

perturbation [pɛʀtyʀbasjɔ̃] *nf*: **~ (atmosphérique)** atmospheric disturbance

perturber [pɛʀtyʀbe] *vt* to disrupt; (*PSYCH*) to perturb, disturb

pervers, e [pɛʀvɛʀ, ɛʀs] *adj* perverted

pervertir [pɛʀvɛʀtiʀ] *vt* to pervert

pesant, e [pəzɑ̃, ɑ̃t] *adj* heavy; (*fig: présence*) burdensome

pèse-personne [pɛzpɛʀsɔn] *nm* (bathroom) scales *pl*

peser [pəze] *vt* to weigh ♦ *vi* to weigh; (*fig: avoir de l'importance*) to carry weight; **~ lourd** to be heavy

pessimisme [pesimism] *nm* pessimism

pessimiste [pesimist] *adj* pessimistic ♦ *nm/f* pessimist

peste [pɛst] *nf* plague

pester [pɛste] *vi*: **~ contre** to curse

pétale [petal] *nm* petal

pétanque [petɑ̃k] *nf* type of bowls

pétarader [petaʀade] *vi* to backfire

pétard [petaʀ] *nm* banger (*BRIT*), firecracker

péter [pete] *vi* (*fam: casser*) to bust; (*fam!*) to fart (!)

pétillant, e [petijɑ̃, ɑ̃t] *adj* (*eau etc*) sparkling

pétiller [petije] *vi* (*feu*) to crackle; (*champagne*) to bubble; (*yeux*) to sparkle

petit, e [p(ə)ti, it] *adj* small; (*avec nuance affective*) little; (*voyage*) short, little; (*bruit etc*) faint, slight; **~s** *nmpl* (*d'un animal*) young *pl*; **les tout~s** the little ones, the tiny tots; **~ à ~** bit by bit, gradually; **~(e) ami(e)** boyfriend/girlfriend; **~ déjeuner** breakfast; **~ pain** (bread) roll; **les ~es annonces** the small ads; **~s pois** garden peas; **petite-fille** *nf* granddaughter; **petit-fils** *nm* grandson

pétition [petisjɔ̃] *nf* petition

petits-enfants [pətizɑ̃fɑ̃] *nmpl* grandchildren

petit-suisse [pətisɥis] (*pl* **~s-~s**) *nm* small individual pot of cream cheese

pétrin [petʀɛ̃] *nm* (*fig*): **dans le ~** (*fam*) in a jam *ou* fix

pétrir [petʀiʀ] *vt* to knead

pétrole [petʀɔl] *nm* oil; (*pour lampe, réchaud etc*) paraffin (oil); **pétrolier, -ière** *nm* oil tanker

─── MOT-CLÉ ───

peu [pø] *adv* **1** (*modifiant verbe, adjectif, adverbe*): **il boit peu** he doesn't drink (very) much; **il est peu bavard** he's not very

talkative; **peu avant/après** shortly before/afterwards

2 (*modifiant nom*): **peu de: peu de gens/d'arbres** few *ou* not (very) many people/trees; **il a peu d'espoir** he hasn't (got) much hope, he has little hope; **pour peu de temps** for (only) a short while

3: **peu à peu** little by little; **à peu près** just about, more or less; **à peu près 10 kg/10 F** approximately 10 kg/10F

♦ *nm* **1**: **le peu de gens qui** the few people who; **le peu de sable qui** what little sand, the little sand which

2: **un peu** a little; **un petit peu** a little bit; **un peu d'espoir** a little hope

♦ *pron*: **peu le savent** few know (it); **avant** *ou* **sous peu** shortly, before long; **de peu** (only) just

───────────────

peuple [pœpl] *nm* people; **peupler** *vt* (*pays, région*) to populate; (*étang*) to stock; (*suj: hommes, poissons*) to inhabit

peuplier [pøplije] *nm* poplar (tree)

peur [pœʀ] *nf* fear; **avoir ~** (**de/de faire/que**) to be frightened *ou* afraid (of/of doing/that); **faire ~ à** to frighten; **de ~ de/que** for fear of/that; **peureux, -euse** *adj* fearful, timorous

peut [pø] *vb voir* **pouvoir**

peut-être [pøtɛtʀ] *adv* perhaps, maybe; **~-~ que** perhaps, maybe; **~-~ bien qu'il fera/est** he may well do/be

peux *etc* [pø] *vb voir* **pouvoir**

phare [faʀ] *nm* (*en mer*) lighthouse; (*de véhicule*) headlight; **~s de recul** reversing lights

pharmacie [faʀmasi] *nf* (*magasin*) chemist's (*BRIT*), pharmacy; (*de salle de bain*) medicine cabinet; **pharmacien, ne** *nm/f* pharmacist, chemist (*BRIT*)

phénomène [fenɔmɛn] *nm* phenomenon

philatélie [filateli] *nf* philately, stamp collecting

philosophe [filɔzɔf] *nm/f* philosopher ♦ *adj* philosophical

philosophie [filɔzɔfi] *nf* philosophy

phobie [fɔbi] *nf* phobia

phonétique [fɔnetik] *nf* phonetics *sg*

phoque [fɔk] *nm* seal

phosphorescent, e [fɔsfɔʀesɑ̃, ɑ̃t] *adj* luminous

photo [fɔto] *nf* photo(graph); **prendre en ~** to take a photo of; **faire de la ~** to take photos; **~ d'identité** passport photograph; **photocopie** *nf* photocopy; **photocopier** *vt* to photocopy; **photocopieuse** *nf* photocopier; **photographe** *nm/f* photographer; **photographie** *nf* (*technique*) photography; (*cliché*) photograph; **photographier** *vt* to photograph

phrase [fʀɑz] nf sentence
physicien, ne [fizisjɛ̃, jɛn] nm/f physicist
physionomie [fizjɔnɔmi] nf face
physique [fizik] adj physical ♦ nm physique
♦ nf physics sg; **au ~** physically;
physiquement adv physically
piailler [pjaje] vi to squawk
pianiste [pjanist] nm/f pianist
piano [pjano] nm piano; **pianoter** vi to tinkle
away (at the piano)
pic [pik] nm (instrument) pick(axe);
(montagne) peak; (ZOOL) woodpecker; **à ~**
vertically; (fig: tomber, arriver) just at the
right time
pichet [piʃɛ] nm jug
picorer [pikɔʀe] vt to peck
picoter [pikɔte] vt (suj: oiseau) to peck ♦ vi
(irriter) to smart, prickle
pie [pi] nf magpie
pièce [pjɛs] nf (d'un logement) room;
(THÉÂTRE) play; (de machine) part; (de
monnaie) coin; (document) document;
(fragment, de collection) piece; **dix francs ~**
ten francs each; **vendre à la ~** to sell
separately; **travailler à la ~** to do piecework;
un maillot une ~ a one-piece swimsuit; **un
deux~s cuisine** a two-room(ed) flat (BRIT) ou
apartment (US) with kitchen; **~ à conviction**
exhibit; **~ d'identité: avez-vous une
~ d'identité?** have you got any (means of)
identification?; **~ montée** tiered cake; **~s
détachées** spares, (spare) parts; **~s
justificatives** supporting documents
pied [pje] nm foot; (de table) leg; (de lampe)
base; **à ~** on foot; **au ~ de la lettre** literally;
avoir ~ to be able to touch the bottom, not
to be out of one's depth; **avoir le ~ marin** to
be a good sailor; **sur ~** (debout, rétabli) up
and about; **mettre sur ~** (entreprise) to set
up; **c'est le ~** (fam) it's brilliant; **mettre les ~s
dans le plat** (fam) to put one's foot in it; **il se
débrouille comme un ~** (fam) he's completely
useless; **pied-noir** nm Algerian-born
Frenchman
piège [pjɛʒ] nm trap; **prendre au ~** to trap;
piéger vt (avec une bombe) to booby-trap;
lettre/voiture piégée letter-/car-bomb
pierre [pjɛʀ] nf stone; **~ précieuse** precious
stone, gem; **~ tombale** tombstone;
pierreries nfpl gems, precious stones
piétiner [pjetine] vi (trépigner) to stamp
(one's foot); (fig) to be at a standstill ♦ vt to
trample on
piéton, ne [pjetɔ̃, ɔn] nm/f pedestrian;
piétonnier, -ière adj: **rue ou zone
piétonnière** pedestrian precinct
pieu, x [pjø] nm post; (pointu) stake
pieuvre [pjœvʀ] nf octopus
pieux, -euse [pjø, pjøz] adj pious

piffer [pife] (fam) vt: **je ne peux pas le ~** I
can't stand him
pigeon [piʒɔ̃] nm pigeon
piger [piʒe] (fam) vi, vt to understand
pigiste [piʒist] nm/f freelance(r)
pignon [piɲɔ̃] nm (de mur) gable
pile [pil] nf (tas) pile; (ÉLEC) battery ♦ adv
(fam: s'arrêter etc) dead; **à deux heures ~** at
two on the dot; **jouer à ~ ou face** to toss up
(for it); **~ ou face?** heads or tails?
piler [pile] vt to crush, pound
pilier [pilje] nm pillar
piller [pije] vt to pillage, plunder, loot
pilote [pilɔt] nm pilot; (de voiture) driver
♦ adj pilot cpd; **~ de course** racing driver;
~ de ligne/d'essai/de chasse airline/test/
fighter pilot; **piloter** vt (avion) to pilot, fly;
(voiture) to drive
pilule [pilyl] nf pill; **prendre la ~** to be on the
pill
piment [pimɑ̃] nm (aussi: **~ rouge**) chilli;
(fig) spice, piquancy; **~ doux** pepper,
capsicum; **pimenté, e** adj (plat) hot, spicy
pimpant, e [pɛ̃pɑ̃, ɑ̃t] adj spruce
pin [pɛ̃] nm pine
pinard [pinaʀ] (fam) nm (cheap) wine, plonk
(BRIT)
pince [pɛ̃s] nf (outil) pliers pl; (de homard,
crabe) pincer, claw; (COUTURE: pli) dart; **~ à
épiler** tweezers pl; **~ à linge** clothes peg (BRIT)
ou pin (US)
pincé, e [pɛ̃se] adj (air) stiff
pinceau, x [pɛ̃so] nm (paint)brush
pincée [pɛ̃se] nf: **une ~ de** a pinch of
pincer [pɛ̃se] vt to pinch; (fam) to nab
pinède [pinɛd] nf pinewood, pine forest
pingouin [pɛ̃gwɛ̃] nm penguin
ping-pong ® [piŋpɔ̃g] nm table tennis
pingre [pɛ̃gʀ] adj niggardly
pinson [pɛ̃sɔ̃] nm chaffinch
pintade [pɛ̃tad] nf guinea-fowl
pioche [pjɔʃ] nf pickaxe; **piocher** vt to dig
up (with a pickaxe); **piocher dans** (le tas, ses
économies) to dig into
pion [pjɔ̃] nm (ÉCHECS) pawn; (DAMES) piece;
(SCOL) supervisor
pionnier [pjɔnje] nm pioneer
pipe [pip] nf pipe; **fumer la ~** to smoke a pipe
pipeau, x [pipo] nm (reed-)pipe
piquant, e [pikɑ̃, ɑ̃t] adj (barbe, rosier etc)
prickly; (saveur, sauce) hot, pungent; (détail)
titillating; (froid) biting ♦ nm (épine) thorn,
prickle; (fig) spiciness, spice
pique [pik] nf pike; (fig) cutting remark ♦ nm
(CARTES) spades pl
pique-nique [piknik] nm picnic; **pique-
niquer** vi to have a picnic
piquer [pike] vt (suj: guêpe, fumée, orties) to
sting; (: moustique) to bite; (: barbe) to

prick; (: *froid*) to bite; (*MÉD*) to give a jab to; (: *chien, chat*) to put to sleep; (*intérêt*) to arouse; (*fam: voler*) to pinch ♦ vi (*avion*) to go into a dive; **se ~** (*avec une aiguille*) to prick o.s.; (*dans les orties*) to get stung; (*suj: toxicomane*) to shoot up; **~ une colère** to fly into a rage

piquet [pikɛ] *nm* (*pieu*) post, stake; (*de tente*) peg; **~ de grève** (strike-)picket

piqûre [pikyʀ] *nf* (*d'épingle*) prick; (*d'ortie*) sting; (*de moustique*) bite; (*MÉD*) injection, shot (*US*); **faire une ~ à qn** to give sb an injection

pirate [piʀat] *nm, adj* pirate; **~ de l'air** hijacker

pire [piʀ] *adj* worse; (*superlatif*): **le(la) ~ ...** the worst ... ♦ *nm*: **le ~ (de)** the worst (of); **au ~** at (the very) worst

pis [pi] *nm* (*de vache*) udder; (*pire*): **le ~** the worst ♦ *adj, adv* worse; **de mal en ~** from bad to worse

piscine [pisin] *nf* (swimming) pool; **~ couverte** indoor (swimming) pool

pissenlit [pisɑ̃li] *nm* dandelion

pistache [pistaʃ] *nf* pistachio (nut)

piste [pist] *nf* (*d'un animal, sentier*) track, trail; (*indice*) lead; (*de stade*) track; (*de cirque*) ring; (*de danse*) floor; (*de patinage*) rink; (*de ski*) run; (*AVIAT*) runway; **~ cyclable** cycle track

pistolet [pistɔlɛ] *nm* (*arme*) pistol, gun; (*à peinture*) spray gun; **pistolet-mitrailleur** *nm* submachine gun

piston [pistɔ̃] *nm* (*TECH*) piston; **avoir du ~** (*fam*) to have friends in the right places; **pistonner** *vt* (*candidat*) to pull strings for

piteux, -euse [pitø, øz] *adj* pitiful, sorry (*avant le nom*)

pitié [pitje] *nf* pity; **il me fait ~** I feel sorry for him; **avoir ~ de** (*compassion*) to pity, feel sorry for; (*merci*) to have pity ou mercy on

pitoyable [pitwajabl] *adj* pitiful

pitre [pitʀ] *nm* clown; **pitrerie** *nf* tomfoolery *no pl*

pittoresque [pitɔʀɛsk] *adj* picturesque

pivot [pivo] *nm* pivot; **pivoter** *vi* to revolve; (*fauteuil*) to swivel

P.J. *sigle f* (= *police judiciaire*) ≈ CID (*BRIT*), ≈ FBI (*US*)

placard |plakaʀ| *nm* (*armoire*) cupboard; (*affiche*) poster, notice

place [plas] *nf* (*emplacement, classement*) place; (*de ville, village*) square; (*espace libre*) room, space; (*de parking*) space; (*siège: de train, cinéma, voiture*) seat; (*emploi*) job; (*mettre*) in its place; **sur ~** on the spot; **faire ~ à** to give way to; **ça prend de la ~** it takes up a lot of room ou space; **à la ~ de** in place of, instead of; **à ta ~ ...** if I were you ...; **se mettre à la ~ de qn** to put o.s. in sb's place ou

in sb's shoes

placé, e [plase] *adj*: **être bien/mal ~** (*spectateur*) to have a good/a poor seat; (*concurrent*) to be in a good/bad position; **il est bien ~ pour le savoir** he is in a position to know

placement [plasmɑ̃] *nm* (*FINANCE*) investment; **bureau de ~** employment agency

placer [plase] *vt* to place; (*convive, spectateur*) to seat; (*argent*) to place, invest; **il n'a pas pu ~ un mot** he couldn't get a word in; **se ~ au premier rang** to go and stand (ou sit) in the first row

plafond [plafɔ̃] *nm* ceiling

plage [plaʒ] *nf* beach

plagiat [plaʒja] *nm* plagiarism

plaid [plɛd] *nm* (*tartan*) car rug

plaider [plede] *vi* (*avocat*) to plead ♦ *vt* to plead; **~ pour** (*fig*) to speak for; **plaidoyer** *nm* (*JUR*) speech for the defence; (*fig*) plea

plaie [plɛ] *nf* wound

plaignant, e [plɛɲɑ̃, ɑ̃t] *nm/f* plaintiff

plaindre [plɛ̃dʀ] *vt* to pity, feel sorry for; **se ~** *vi* (*gémir*) to moan; (*protester*): **se ~ (à qn) (de)** to complain (to sb) (about); (*souffrir*): **se ~ de** to complain of

plaine [plɛn] *nf* plain

plain-pied [plɛ̃pje] *adv*: **de ~~ (avec)** on the same level (as)

plainte [plɛ̃t] *nf* (*gémissement*) moan, groan; (*doléance*) complaint; **porter ~** to lodge a complaint

plaire [plɛʀ] *vi* to be a success, be successful; **ça plaît beaucoup aux jeunes** it's very popular with young people; **~ à: cela me plaît** I like it; **se ~ quelque part** to like being somewhere ou like it somewhere; **j'irai si ça me plaît** I'll go if I feel like it; **s'il vous plaît** please

plaisance [plɛzɑ̃s] *nf* (*aussi*: **navigation de ~**) (pleasure) sailing, yachting

plaisant, e [plɛzɑ̃, ɑ̃t] *adj* pleasant; (*histoire, anecdote*) amusing

plaisanter [plɛzɑ̃te] *vi* to joke; **plaisanterie** *nf* joke

plaise *etc* [plɛz] *vb voir* **plaire**

plaisir [pleziʀ] *nm* pleasure; **faire ~ à qn** (*délibérément*) to be nice to sb, please sb; **ça me fait ~** I like (doing) it; **j'espère que ça te fera ~** I hope you'll like it; **pour le ~** for pleasure

plaît [plɛ] *vb voir* **plaire**

plan, e [plɑ̃, an] *adj* flat ♦ *nm* plan; (*fig*) level, plane; (*CINÉMA*) shot; **au premier/second ~** in the foreground/middle distance; **à l'arrière ~** in the background; **rester en ~** (*fam*) to be left stranded; **laisser en ~** (*fam: travail*) to drop, abandon; **~ d'eau** lake

planche [plɑ̃ʃ] *nf* (*pièce de bois*) plank, (wooden) board; (*illustration*) plate; **~ à**

repasser ironing board; ~ **à roulettes** skateboard; ~ **à voile** (*sport*) windsurfing

plancher [plɑ̃ʃe] *nm* floor; floorboards *pl* ♦ *vi* (*fam*) to work hard

planer [plane] *vi* to glide; (*fam: rêveur*) to have one's head in the clouds; ~ **sur** (*fig: danger*) to hang over

planète [planɛt] *nf* planet

planeur [planœʀ] *nm* glider

planification [planifikasjɔ̃] *nf* (*economic*) planning

planifier [planifje] *vt* to plan

planning [planiŋ] *nm* programme, schedule

planque [plɑ̃k] *nf* (*fam*) (*emploi peu fatigant*) cushy (*BRIT*) *ou* easy number; (*cachette*) hiding place

plant [plɑ̃] *nm* seedling, young plant

plante [plɑ̃t] *nf* plant; ~ **d'appartement** house *ou* pot plant; ~ **des pieds** sole (of the foot)

planter [plɑ̃te] *vt* (*plante*) to plant; (*enfoncer*) to hammer *ou* drive in; (*tente*) to put up, pitch; (*fam: personne*) to dump; **se** ~ (*fam: se tromper*) to get it wrong

plantureux, -euse [plɑ̃tyʀø, øz] *adj* copious, lavish; (*femme*) buxom

plaque [plak] *nf* plate; (*de verglas, d'eczéma*) patch; (*avec inscription*) plaque; ~ **chauffante** hotplate; ~ **de chocolat** bar of chocolate; ~ (**minéralogique** *ou* **d'immatriculation**) number (*BRIT*) *ou* license (*US*) plate; ~ **tournante** (*fig*) centre

plaqué, e [plake] *adj*: ~ **or/argent** gold-/silver-plated

plaquer [plake] *vt* (*aplatir*): ~ **qch sur** *ou* **contre** to make sth stick *ou* cling to; (*RUGBY*) to bring down; (*fam: laisser tomber*) to drop

plaquette [plakɛt] *nf* (*de chocolat*) bar; (*beurre*) pack(et); ~ **de frein** brake pad

plastique [plastik] *adj, nm* plastic; **plastiquer** *vt* to blow up (*with a plastic bomb*)

plat, e [pla, -at] *adj* flat; (*cheveux*) straight; (*style*) flat, dull ♦ *nm* (*récipient, CULIN*) dish; (*d'un repas*) course; **à** ~ **ventre** face down; **à** ~ (*pneu, batterie*) flat; (*fam: personne*) dead beat; ~ **cuisiné** pre-cooked meal; ~ **de résistance** main course; ~ **du jour** dish of the day

platane [platan] *nm* plane tree

plateau, x [plato] *nm* (*support*) tray; (*GÉO*) plateau; (*CINÉMA*) set; ~ **de fromages** cheeseboard

plate-bande [platbɑ̃d] *nf* flower bed

plate-forme [platfɔʀm] *nf* platform; ~~ **de forage/pétrolière** drilling/oil rig

platine [platin] *nm* platinum ♦ *nf* (*d'un tourne-disque*) turntable

plâtre [plɑtʀ] *nm* (*matériau*) plaster; (*statue*) plaster statue; (*MÉD*) (plaster) cast; **avoir un**

bras dans le ~ to have an arm in plaster

plein, e [plɛ̃, plɛn] *adj* full ♦ *nm*: **faire le** ~ (**d'essence**) to fill up (with petrol); **à** ~**es mains** (*ramasser*) in handfuls; **à** ~ **temps** full-time; **en** ~ **air** in the open air; **en** ~ **soleil** in direct sunlight; **en** ~**e nuit/rue** in the middle of the night/street; **en** ~ **jour** in broad daylight

pleurer [plœʀe] *vi* to cry; (*yeux*) to water ♦ *vt* to mourn (for); ~ **sur** to lament (over), to bemoan

pleurnicher [plœʀniʃe] *vi* to snivel, whine

pleurs [plœʀ] *nmpl*: **en** ~ in tears

pleut [plø] *vb voir* **pleuvoir**

pleuvoir [pløvwaʀ] *vb impers* to rain ♦ *vi* (*coups*) to rain down; (*critiques, invitations*) to shower down; **il pleut** it's raining

pli [pli] *nm* fold; (*de jupe*) pleat; (*de pantalon*) crease; **prendre le** ~ **de faire** to get into the habit of doing; **un mauvais** ~ a bad habit

pliant, e [plijɑ̃, plijɑ̃t] *adj* folding

plier [plije] *vt* to fold; (*pour ranger*) to fold up; (*genou, bras*) to bend ♦ *vi* to bend; (*fig*) to yield; **se** ~ **à** to submit to

plinthe [plɛ̃t] *nf* skirting board

plisser [plise] *vt* (*jupe*) to put pleats in; (*yeux*) to screw up; (*front*) to crease

plomb [plɔ̃] *nm* (*métal*) lead; (*d'une cartouche*) (lead) shot; (*PÊCHE*) sinker; (*ÉLEC*) fuse; **sans** ~ (*essence etc*) unleaded

plombage [plɔ̃baʒ] *nm* (*de dent*) filling

plomberie [plɔ̃bʀi] *nf* plumbing

plombier [plɔ̃bje] *nm* plumber

plonge [plɔ̃ʒ] *nf* washing-up

plongeant, e [plɔ̃ʒɑ̃, ɑ̃t] *adj* (*vue*) from above; (*décolleté*) plunging

plongée [plɔ̃ʒe] *nf* (*SPORT*) diving *no pl*; (*sans scaphandre*) skin diving; ~ **sous-marine** diving

plongeoir [plɔ̃ʒwaʀ] *nm* diving board

plongeon [plɔ̃ʒɔ̃] *nm* dive

plonger [plɔ̃ʒe] *vi* to dive ♦ *vt*: ~ **qch dans** to plunge sth into; **se** ~ **dans** (*études, lecture*) to bury *ou* immerse o.s. in; **plongeur** *nm* diver

ployer [plwaje] *vt, vi* to bend

plu [ply] *pp de* **plaire**; **pleuvoir**

pluie [plɥi] *nf* rain

plume [plym] *nf* feather; (*pour écrire*) (pen) nib; (*fig*) pen

plupart [plypaʀ]: **la** ~ *pron* the majority, most (of them); **la** ~ **des** most, the majority of; **la** ~ **du temps/d'entre nous** most of the time/of us; **pour la** ~ for the most part, mostly

pluriel [plyʀjɛl] *nm* plural

plus¹ [ply] *vb voir* **plaire**

MOT-CLÉ
---

plus² [ply] *adv* **1** (*forme négative*): **ne ... plus** no more, no longer; **je n'ai plus d'argent** I've got no more money *ou* no money left; **il ne**

travaille plus he's no longer working, he doesn't work any more

2 (comparatif) more, ...+er; (superlatif): **le plus** the most, the ...+est; **plus grand/ intelligent (que)** bigger/more intelligent (than); **le plus grand/intelligent** the biggest/ most intelligent; **tout au plus** at the very most **3** (davantage) more; **il travaille plus (que)** he works more (than); **plus il travaille, plus il est heureux** the more he works, the happier he is; **plus de pain** more bread; **plus de 10 personnes** more than 10 people, over 10 people; **3 heures de plus que** 3 hours more than; **de plus** what's more, moreover; **3 kilos en plus** 3 kilos more; **en plus de** in addition to; **de plus en plus** more and more; **plus ou moins** more or less; **ni plus ni moins** no more, no less

♦ prép: **4 plus 2** 4 plus 2

plusieurs [plyzjœʀ] dét, pron several; **ils sont ~** there are several of them

plus-value [plyvaly] nf (bénéfice) surplus

plut [ply] vb voir **plaire**

plutôt [plyto] adv rather; **je préfère ~ celui-ci** I'd rather have this one; **~ que (de) faire** rather than ou instead of doing

pluvieux, -euse [plyvjø, jøz] adj rainy, wet

PME sigle f (= petite(s) et moyenne(s) entreprise(s)) small business(es)

PMU sigle m (= Pari mutuel urbain) system of betting on horses; (café) betting agency

PNB sigle m (= produit national brut) GNP

pneu [pnø] nm tyre (BRIT), tire (US)

pneumonie [pnømɔni] nf pneumonia

poche [pɔʃ] nf pocket; (sous les yeux) bag, pouch; **argent de ~** pocket money

pocher [pɔʃe] vt (CULIN) to poach

pochette [pɔʃɛt] nf (d'aiguilles etc) case; (mouchoir) breast pocket handkerchief; (sac à main) clutch bag; **~ de disque** record sleeve

poêle [pwal] nm stove ♦ nf: **~ (à frire)** frying pan

poème [pɔɛm] nm poem

poésie [pɔezi] nf (poème) poem; (art): **la ~** poetry

poète [pɔɛt] nm poet

poids [pwa] nm weight; (SPORT) shot; **vendre au ~** to sell by weight; **prendre du ~** to put on weight; **~ lourd** (camion) lorry (BRIT), truck (US)

poignant, e [pwaɲɑ̃, ɑ̃t] adj poignant

poignard [pwaɲaʀ] nm dagger; **poignarder** vt to stab, knife

poigne [pwaɲ] nf grip; **avoir de la ~** (fig) to rule with a firm hand

poignée [pwaɲe] nf (de sel etc, fig) handful; (de couvercle, porte) handle; **~ de main** handshake

poignet [pwaɲɛ] nm (ANAT) wrist; (de chemise) cuff

poil [pwal] nm (ANAT) hair; (de pinceau, brosse) bristle; (de tapis) strand; (pelage) coat; **à ~** (fam) starkers; **au ~** (fam) hunky-dory; **poilu, e** adj hairy

poinçon [pwɛ̃sɔ̃] nm (marque) hallmark; **poinçonner** vt (bijou) to hallmark; (billet) to punch

poing [pwɛ̃] nm fist; **coup de ~** punch

point [pwɛ̃] nm point; (endroit) spot; (marque, signe) dot; (: de ponctuation) full stop, period (US); (COUTURE, TRICOT) stitch ♦ adv = **pas²**; **faire le ~** (fig) to take stock (of the situation); **sur le ~ de faire** (just) about to do; **à tel ~ que** so much so that; **mettre au ~** (procédé) to develop; (affaire) to settle; **à ~** (CULIN: viande) medium; **à ~ (nommé)** just at the right time; **deux ~s** colon; **~ (de côté)** stitch (pain); **~ d'exclamation/d'interrogation** exclamation/question mark; **~ de repère** landmark; (dans le temps) point of reference; **~ de suture** (MÉD) stitch; **~ de vente** retail outlet; **~ de vue** viewpoint; (fig: opinion) point of view; **~ d'honneur: mettre un ~ d'honneur à faire qch** to make it a point of honour to do sth; **~ faible/fort** weak/strong point; **~ noir** blackhead; **~s de suspension** suspension points

pointe [pwɛ̃t] nf point; (clou) tack; (fig): **une ~ de** a hint of; **être à la ~ de** (fig) to be in the forefront of; **sur la ~ des pieds** on tiptoe; **en ~** pointed, tapered; **de ~** (technique etc) leading; **heures de ~** peak hours

pointer [pwɛ̃te] vt (diriger: canon, doigt): **~ sur qch** to point at sth ♦ vi (employé) to clock in

pointillé [pwɛ̃tije] nm (trait) dotted line

pointilleux, -euse [pwɛ̃tijø, øz] adj particular, pernickety

pointu, e [pwɛ̃ty] adj pointed; (voix) shrill; (analyse) precise

pointure [pwɛ̃tyʀ] nf size

point-virgule [pwɛ̃viʀgyl] nm semi-colon

poire [pwaʀ] nf pear; (fam: péj) mug

poireau, x [pwaʀo] nm leek

poireauter [pwaʀote] vi (fam) to be left kicking one's heels

poirier [pwaʀje] nm pear tree

pois [pwa] nm (BOT) pea; (sur une étoffe) dot, spot; **~ chiche** chickpea; **à ~** (cravate etc) spotted, polka-dot cpd

poison [pwazɔ̃] nm poison

poisse [pwas] (fam) nf rotten luck

poisseux, -euse [pwasø, øz] adj sticky

poisson [pwasɔ̃] nm fish gén inv; **les P~s** (signe) Pisces; **~ d'avril!** April fool!; **~ rouge** goldfish; **poissonnerie** nf fish-shop; **poissonnier, -ière** nm/f fishmonger (BRIT), fish merchant (US)

poitrine [pwatʀin] nf chest; (seins) bust, bosom; (CULIN) breast

poivre [pwavʀ] nm pepper

poivron [pwavʀɔ̃] nm pepper, capsicum

polaire [pɔlɛʀ] adj polar

polar [pɔlaʀ] (fam) nm detective novel

pôle [pol] nm (GÉO, ÉLEC) pole

poli, e [pɔli] adj polite; (lisse) smooth

police [pɔlis] nf police; ~ **d'assurance** insurance policy; ~ **judiciaire** ≈ Criminal Investigation Department (BRIT), ≈ Federal Bureau of Investigation (US), ~ **secours** ≈ emergency services pl (BRIT), ≈ paramedics pl (US); **policier, -ière** adj police cpd ♦ nm policeman; (aussi: **roman policier**) detective novel

polio [pɔljo] nf polio

polir [pɔliʀ] vt to polish

polisson, ne [pɔlisɔ̃, ɔn] nm/f (enfant) (little) rascal

politesse [pɔlitɛs] nf politeness

politicien, ne [pɔlitisjɛ̃, jɛn] (péj) nm/f politician

politique [pɔlitik] adj political ♦ nf politics sg; (mesures, méthode) policies pl

pollen [pɔlɛn] nm pollen

polluant, e [pɔlɥɑ̃, ɑ̃t] adj polluting; **produit** ~ pollutant

polluer [pɔlɥe] vt to pollute; **pollution** nf pollution

polo [pɔlo] nm (chemise) polo shirt

Pologne [pɔlɔɲ] nf: **la** ~ Poland; **polonais, e** adj Polish ♦ nm/f: **Polonais, e** Pole ♦ nm (LING) Polish

poltron, ne [pɔltʀɔ̃, ɔn] adj cowardly

polycopier [pɔlikɔpje] vt to duplicate

Polynésie [pɔlinezi] nf: **la** ~ Polynesia

polyvalent, e [pɔlivalɑ̃, ɑ̃t] adj (rôle) varied; (salle) multi-purpose

pommade [pɔmad] nf ointment, cream

pomme [pɔm] nf apple; **tomber dans les** ~**s** (fam) to pass out; ~ **d'Adam** Adam's apple; ~ **de pin** pine ou fir cone; ~ **de terre** potato

pommeau, x [pɔmo] nm (boule) knob; (de selle) pommel

pommette [pɔmɛt] nf cheekbone

pommier [pɔmje] nm apple tree

pompe [pɔ̃p] nf pump; (faste) pomp (and ceremony); ~ **à essence** petrol pump; ~**s funèbres** funeral parlour sg, undertaker's sg; **pomper** vt to pump; (aspirer) to pump up; (absorber) to soak up

pompeux, -euse [pɔ̃pø, øz] adj pompous

pompier [pɔ̃pje] nm fireman

pompiste [pɔ̃pist] nm/f petrol (BRIT) ou gas (US) pump attendant

poncer [pɔ̃se] vt to sand (down)

ponctuation [pɔ̃ktɥasjɔ̃] nf punctuation

ponctuel, le [pɔ̃ktɥɛl] adj punctual

pondéré, e [pɔ̃deʀe] adj level-headed, composed

pondre [pɔ̃dʀ] vt to lay

poney [pɔnɛ] nm pony

pont [pɔ̃] nm bridge; (NAVIG) deck; **faire le** ~ to take the extra day off; ~ **suspendu** suspension bridge; **pont-levis** nm drawbridge

pop [pɔp] adj inv pop

populace [pɔpylas] (péj) nf rabble

populaire [pɔpylɛʀ] adj popular; (manifestation) mass cpd; (milieux, quartier) working-class; (expression) vernacular

popularité [pɔpylaʀite] nf popularity

population [pɔpylasjɔ̃] nf population; ~ **active** working population

populeux, -euse [pɔpylø, øz] adj densely populated

porc [pɔʀ] nm pig; (CULIN) pork

porcelaine [pɔʀsəlɛn] nf porcelain, china; piece of china(ware)

porc-épic [pɔʀkepik] nm porcupine

porche [pɔʀʃ] nm porch

porcherie [pɔʀʃəʀi] nf pigsty

pore [pɔʀ] nm pore

porno [pɔʀno] adj porno ♦ nm porn

port [pɔʀ] nm harbour, port; (ville) port; (de l'uniforme etc) wearing; (pour lettre) postage; (pour colis, aussi: posture) carriage; ~ **de pêche/de plaisance** fishing/sailing harbour

portable [pɔʀtabl] nm (COMPUT) laptop (computer)

portail [pɔʀtaj] nm gate

portant, e [pɔʀtɑ̃, ɑ̃t] adj: **bien/mal** ~ in good/poor health

portatif, -ive [pɔʀtatif, iv] adj portable

porte [pɔʀt] nf door; (de ville, jardin) gate; **mettre à la** ~ to throw out; ~ **à** ~ nm door-to-door selling; ~ **d'entrée** front door; **porte-avions** nm inv aircraft carrier; **porte-bagages** nm inv luggage rack; **porte-bonheur** nm inv lucky charm; **porte-clefs** nm inv key ring; **porte-documents** nm inv attaché ou document case

porté, e [pɔʀte] adj: **être** ~ **à faire** to be inclined to do; **être** ~ **sur qch** to be keen on sth; **portée** nf (d'une arme) range; (fig: effet) impact, import; (: capacité) scope, capability; (de chatte etc) litter; (MUS) stave, staff; **à/hors de portée (de)** within/out of reach (of); **à portée de (la) main** within (arm's) reach; **à la portée de qn** (fig) at sb's level, within sb's capabilities

porte...: porte-fenêtre nf French window; **portefeuille** nm wallet; **portemanteau, x** nm (cintre) coat hanger; (au mur) coat rack; **porte-monnaie** nm inv purse; **porte-parole** nm inv spokesman

porter [pɔʀte] vt to carry; (sur soi: vêtement, barbe, bague) to wear; (fig: responsabilité etc) to bear, carry; (inscription, nom, fruits) to bear; (coup) to deal; (attention) to turn; (apporter): ~ qch à qn to take sth to sb ♦ vi (voix) to carry; (coup, argument) to hit home; se ~ vi (se sentir): se ~ bien/mal to be well/unwell; ~ sur (recherches) to be concerned with; se faire ~ malade to report sick

porteur, euse [pɔʀtœʀ, øz] nm (de bagages) porter; (de chèque) bearer

porte-voix [pɔʀtəvwa] nm inv megaphone

portier [pɔʀtje] nm doorman

portière [pɔʀtjɛʀ] nf door

portillon [pɔʀtijɔ̃] nm gate

portion [pɔʀsjɔ̃] nf (part) portion, share; (partie) portion, section

porto [pɔʀto] nm port (wine)

portrait [pɔʀtʀɛ] nm (peinture) portrait; (photo) photograph; **portrait-robot** nm Identikit ® ou photo-fit ® picture

portuaire [pɔʀtɥɛʀ] adj port cpd, harbour cpd

portugais, e [pɔʀtygɛ, ɛz] adj Portuguese ♦ nm/f: P~, e Portuguese ♦ nm (LING) Portuguese

Portugal [pɔʀtygal] nm: le ~ Portugal

pose [poz] nf (de moquette) laying; (attitude, d'un modèle) pose; (PHOTO) exposure

posé, e [poze] adj serious

poser [poze] vt to put; (installer: moquette, carrelage) to lay; (rideaux, papier peint) to hang; (question) to ask; (principe, conditions) to lay ou set down; (problème) to formulate; (difficulté) to pose ♦ vi (modèle) to pose; se ~ vi (oiseau, avion) to land; (question) to arise; ~ qch (sur) (déposer) to put sth down (on); ~ qch sur/quelque part (placer) to put sth on/somewhere; ~ sa candidature à un poste to apply for a post

positif, -ive [pozitif, iv] adj positive

position [pozisjɔ̃] nf position; prendre ~ (fig) to take a stand

posologie [pozɔlɔʒi] nf dosage

posséder [posede] vt to own, possess; (qualité, talent) to have, possess; (sexuellement) to possess; **possession** nf ownership no pl, possession

possibilité [posibilite] nf possibility; ~s nfpl (potentiel) potential sg

possible [posibl] adj possible; (projet, entreprise) feasible ♦ nm: faire son ~ to do all one can, do one's utmost; le plus/moins de livres ~ as many/few books as possible; le plus vite ~ as quickly as possible; dès que ~ as soon as possible

postal, e, -aux [postal, o] adj postal

poste [post] nf (service) post, postal service; (administration, bureau) post office ♦ nm (fonction, MIL) post; (TÉL) extension; (de radio etc) set; mettre à la ~ to post; ~ (de police) nm police station; ~ de secours nm first-aid post; ~ restante nf poste restante (BRIT), general delivery (US)

poster¹ [poste] vt to post

poster² [pɔstɛʀ] nm poster

postérieur, e [posteʀjœʀ] adj (date) later; (partie) back ♦ nm (fam) behind

posthume [postym] adj posthumous

postulant, e [postylɑ̃, ɑ̃t] nm/f applicant

postuler [postyle] vi: ~ à ou pour un emploi to apply for a job

posture [postyʀ] nf position

pot [po] nm (en verre) jar; (en terre) pot; (en plastique, carton) carton; (en métal) tin; (fam: chance) luck; avoir du ~ (fam) to be lucky; boire ou prendre un ~ (fam) to have a drink; petit ~ (pour bébé) (jar of) baby food; ~ catalytique catalytic converter; ~ d'échappement exhaust pipe; ~ de fleurs plant pot, flowerpot; (plante) pot plant

potable [potabl] adj: eau (non) ~ (non-)drinking water

potage [potaʒ] nm soup; **potager, -ère** adj: (jardin) potager kitchen ou vegetable garden

pot-au-feu [potofø] nm inv (beef) stew

pot-de-vin [podvɛ̃] nm bribe

pote [pot] nm (fam) nm pal

poteau, x [poto] nm post; ~ indicateur signpost

potelé, e [pɔt(ə)le] adj plump, chubby

potence [potɑ̃s] nf gallows sg

potentiel, le [potɑ̃sjɛl] adj, nm potential

poterie [potʀi] nf pottery; (objet) piece of pottery

potier [pɔtje, jɛʀ] nm potter

potins [pɔtɛ̃] nmpl gossip sg

potiron [pɔtiʀɔ̃] nm pumpkin

pou, x [pu] nm louse

poubelle [pubɛl] nf (dust)bin

pouce [pus] nm thumb

poudre [pudʀ] nf powder; (fard) (face) powder; (explosif) gunpowder; en ~: café en ~ instant coffee; lait en ~ dried ou powdered milk; **poudreuse** nf powder snow; **poudrier** nm (powder) compact

pouffer [pufe] vi: ~ (de rire) to burst out laughing

poulailler [pulaje] nm henhouse

poulain [pulɛ̃] nm foal; (fig) protégé

poule [pul] nf hen; (CULIN) (boiling) fowl

poulet [pulɛ] nm chicken; (fam) cop

poulie [puli] nf pulley

pouls [pu] nm pulse; prendre le ~ de qn to feel sb's pulse

poumon [pumɔ̃] nm lung

poupe [pup] nf stern; en ~ astern

poupée [pupe] nf doll

pouponnière [pupɔnjɛʀ] nf crèche, day nursery

pour [puʀ] prép for ♦ nm: **le ~ et le contre** the pros and cons; **~ faire** (so as) to do, in order to do; **~ avoir fait** for having done; **~ que** so that, in order that; **~ 100 francs d'essence** 100 francs' worth of petrol; **~ cent** per cent; **~ ce qui est de** as for

pourboire [puʀbwaʀ] nm tip

pourcentage [puʀsɑ̃taʒ] nm percentage

pourchasser [puʀʃase] vt to pursue

pourparlers [puʀpaʀle] nmpl talks, negotiations

pourpre [puʀpʀ] adj crimson

pourquoi [puʀkwa] adv, conj why ♦ nm inv: **le ~ (de)** the reason (for)

pourrai etc [puʀe] vb voir **pouvoir**

pourri, e [puʀi] adj rotten

pourrir [puʀiʀ] vi to rot; (fruit) to go rotten ou bad ♦ vt to rot; (fig) to spoil thoroughly; **pourriture** nf rot

pourrons etc [puʀɔ̃] vb voir **pouvoir**

poursuite [puʀsɥit] nf pursuit, chase; **~s** nfpl (JUR) legal proceedings

poursuivre [puʀsɥivʀ] vt to pursue, chase (after); (obséder) to haunt; (JUR) to bring proceedings against, prosecute; (: au civil) to sue; (but) to strive towards; (continuer: études etc) to carry on with, continue; **se ~** vi to go on, continue

pourtant [puʀtɑ̃] adv yet; **c'est ~ facile** (and) yet it's easy

pourtour [puʀtuʀ] nm perimeter

pourvoir [puʀvwaʀ] vt: **~ qch/qn de** to equip sth/sb with ♦ vi: **à** to provide for; **pourvoyeur** nm supplier; **pourvu, e** adj: **pourvu de** equipped with; **pourvu que** (si) provided that, so long as; (espérons que) let's hope (that)

pousse [pus] nf growth; (bourgeon) shoot

poussé, e [puse] adj (enquête) exhaustive; (études) advanced; **poussée** nf thrust; (d'acné) eruption; (fig: prix) upsurge

pousser [puse] vt to push; (émettre: cri, soupir) to give; (stimuler: élève) to urge on; (poursuivre: études, discussion) to carry on (further) ♦ vi to push; (croître) to grow; **se ~** vi to move over; **~ qn à** (inciter) to urge ou press sb to; (acculer) to drive sb to; **faire ~** (plante) to grow

poussette [puset] nf push chair (BRIT), stroller (US)

poussière [pusjɛʀ] nf dust; **poussiéreux, -euse** adj dusty

poussin [pusɛ̃] nm chick

poutre [putʀ] nf beam

MOT-CLÉ
---

pouvoir [puvwaʀ] nm power; (POL: dirigeants): **le pouvoir** those in power; **les**

pouvoirs publics the authorities; **pouvoir d'achat** purchasing power

♦ vb semi-aux **1** (être en état de) can, be able to; **je ne peux pas le réparer** I can't ou I am not able to repair it; **déçu de ne pas pouvoir le faire** disappointed not to be able to do it

2 (avoir la permission) can, may, be allowed to; **vous pouvez aller au cinéma** you can ou may go to the pictures

3 (probabilité, hypothèse) may, might, could; **il a pu avoir un accident** he may ou might ou could have had an accident; **il aurait pu le dire!** he might ou could have said (so)!

♦ vb impers may, might, could; **il peut arriver que** it may ou might ou could happen that

♦ vt can, be able to; **j'ai fait tout ce que j'ai pu** I did all I could; **je n'en peux plus** (épuisé) I'm exhausted; (à bout) I can't take any more; **se pouvoir** vi: **il se peut que** it may ou might be that; **cela se pourrait** that's quite possible

---

prairie [pʀeʀi] nf meadow

praline [pʀalin] nf sugared almond

praticable [pʀatikabl] adj passable, practicable

pratiquant, e [pʀatikɑ̃, ɑ̃t] nm/f (regular) churchgoer

pratique [pʀatik] nf practice ♦ adj practical; **pratiquement** adv (pour ainsi dire) practically, virtually; **pratiquer** vt to practise; (l'équitation, la pêche) to go in for; (le golf, football) to play; (intervention, opération) to carry out

pré [pʀe] nm meadow

préalable [pʀealabl] adj preliminary; **au ~** beforehand

préambule [pʀeɑ̃byl] nm preamble; (fig) prelude; **sans ~** straight away

préau [pʀeo] nm (SCOL) covered playground

préavis [pʀeavi] nm notice

précaution [pʀekosjɔ̃] nf precaution; **avec ~** cautiously; **par ~** as a precaution

précédemment [pʀesedamɑ̃] adv before, previously

précédent, e [pʀesedɑ̃, ɑ̃t] adj previous ♦ nm precedent

précéder [pʀesede] vt to precede

précepteur, -trice [pʀeseptœʀ, tʀis] nm/f (private) tutor

prêcher [pʀeʃe] vt to preach

précieux, -euse [pʀesjø, jøz] adj precious; (aide, conseil) invaluable

précipice [pʀesipis] nm drop, chasm

précipitamment [pʀesipitamɑ̃] adv hurriedly, hastily

précipitation [pʀesipitasjɔ̃] nf (hâte) haste; **~s** nfpl (pluie) rain sg

précipité, e [presipite] *adj* hurried, hasty
précipiter [presipite] *vt* (*hâter: départ*) to
hasten; (*faire tomber*): **~ qn/qch du haut de**
to throw *ou* hurl sb/sth off *ou* from; **se ~** *vi* to
speed up; **se ~ sur/vers** to rush at/towards
précis, e [presi, iz] *adj* precise; (*mesures*)
accurate, precise; **à 4 heures ~es** at 4 o'clock
sharp; **précisément** *adv* precisely; **préciser**
vt (*expliquer*) to be more specific about,
clarify; (*spécifier*) to state, specify; **se préciser**
vi to become clear(er); **précision** *nf*
precision; (*détail*) point *ou* detail; **demander
des précisions** to ask for further explanation
précoce [prekɔs] *adj* early; (*enfant*)
precocious
préconçu, e [prekɔsy] *adj* preconceived
préconiser [prekɔnize] *vt* to advocate
prédécesseur [predesesœr] *nm*
predecessor
prédilection [predilɛksjɔ̃] *nf*: **avoir une
~ pour** to be partial to
prédire [predir] *vt* to predict
prédominer [predɔmine] *vi* to predominate
préface [prefas] *nf* preface
préfecture [prefɛktyr] *nf* prefecture; **~ de
police** police headquarters *pl*
préférable [preferabl] *adj* preferable
préféré, e [prefere] *adj*, *nm/f* favourite
préférence [preferãs] *nf* preference; **de ~**
preferably
préférer [prefere] *vt*: **~ qn/qch (à)** to prefer
sb/sth (to), like sb/sth better (than); **~ faire**
to prefer to do; **je ~ais du thé** I would rather
have tea, I'd prefer tea
préfet [prefɛ] *nm* prefect
préhistorique [preistɔrik] *adj* prehistoric
préjudice [preʒydis] *nm* (*matériel*) loss;
(*moral*) harm *no pl*; **porter ~ à** to harm, be
detrimental to; **au ~ de** at the expense of
préjugé [preʒyʒe] *nm* prejudice; **avoir un
~ contre** to be prejudiced *ou* biased against
préjuger [preʒyʒe]: **~ de** *vt* to prejudge
prélasser [prelase]: **se ~** to lounge
prélèvement [prelɛvmã] *nm* (*montant*)
deduction; **faire un ~ de sang** to take a blood
sample
prélever [prel(ə)ve] *vt* (*échantillon*) to take;
~ (sur) (*montant*) to deduct (from); (*argent:
sur son compte*) to withdraw (from)
prématuré, e [prematyre] *adj* premature
♦ *nm* premature baby
premier, -ière [prəmje, jɛr] *adj* first; (*rang*)
front; (*fig: objectif*) basic; **le ~ venu** the first
person to come along; **de ~ ordre** first-rate;
P~ Ministre Prime Minister; **première** *nf*
(*SCOL*) lower sixth form; (*THÉÂTRE*) first night;
(*AUTO*) first (gear); (*AVIAT, RAIL etc*) first class;
(*CINÉMA*) première; (*exploit*) first; **premièrement** *adv* firstly

prémonition [premɔnisjɔ̃] *nf* premonition
prémunir [premynir]: **se ~** *vi*: **se ~ contre** to
guard against
prenant, e [prənã, ãt] *adj* absorbing,
engrossing
prénatal, e [prenatal] *adj* (*MÉD*) antenatal
prendre [prãdr] *vt* to take; (*repas*) to have;
(*se procurer*) to get; (*malfaiteur, poisson*) to
catch; (*passager*) to pick up; (*personnel*) to
take on; (*traiter: personne*) to handle; (*voix,
ton*) to put on; (*ôter*): **~ qch à** to take sth
from; (*coincer*): **se ~ les doigts dans** to get
one's fingers caught in ♦ *vi* (*liquide, ciment*)
to set; (*greffe, vaccin*) to take; (*feu: foyer*) to
go; (*se diriger*): **~ à gauche** to turn (to the)
left; (*froid*) to catch cold; **se ~ pour** to think
one is; **s'en ~ à** to attack; **se ~ d'amitié pour**
to befriend; **s'y ~** (*procéder*) to set about it
preneur, oz [prənœr, øz] *nm*: **être/trouver ~** to
be willing to buy/find a buyer
preniez [prənje] *vb voir* **prendre**
prenne *etc* [prɛn] *vb voir* **prendre**
prénom [prenɔ̃] *nm* first *ou* Christian name
préoccupation [preɔkypasjɔ̃] *nf* (*souci*)
concern; (*idée fixe*) preoccupation
préoccuper [preɔkype] *vt* (*inquiéter*) to
worry; (*absorber*) to preoccupy; **se ~ de** to be
concerned with
préparatifs [preparatif] *nmpl* preparations
préparation [preparasjɔ̃] *nf* preparation
préparer [prepare] *vt* to prepare; (*café, thé*)
to make; (*examen*) to prepare for; (*voyage,
entreprise*) to plan; **se ~** *vi* (*orage, tragédie*) to
brew, be in the air; **~ qch à qn** (*surprise etc*)
to have sth in store for sb; **se ~ (à qch/faire)**
to prepare (o.s.) *ou* get ready (for sth/to do)
prépondérant, e [prepɔ̃derã, ãt] *adj*
major, dominating
préposé, e [prepoze] *nm/f* employee;
(*facteur*) postman
préposition [prepozisjɔ̃] *nf* preposition
près [prɛ] *adv* near, close; **~ de** near (to),
close to; (*environ*) nearly, almost; **de ~**
closely; **à 5 kg ~** to within about 5 kg; **à cela
~ que** apart from the fact that; **il n'est pas à
10 minutes ~** he can spare 10 minutes
présage [prezaʒ] *nm* omen; **présager** *vt* to
foresee
presbyte [prɛsbit] *adj* long-sighted
presbytère [prɛsbitɛr] *nm* presbytery
prescription [prɛskripsjɔ̃] *nf* prescription
prescrire [prɛskrir] *vt* to prescribe
présence [prezãs] *nf* presence; (*au bureau, à
l'école*) attendance
présent, e [prezã, ãt] *adj*, *nm* present; **à
~ (que)** now (that)
présentation [prezãtasjɔ̃] *nf* presentation;
(*de nouveau venu*) introduction; (*allure*)
appearance; **faire les ~s** to do the

introductions

présenter [pʀezɑ̃te] *vt* to present; (*excuses, condoléances*) to offer; (*invité, conférencier*): ~ **qn (à)** to introduce sb (to) ♦ *vi*: ~ **bien** to have a pleasing appearance; **se** ~ *vi* (*occasion*) to arise; **se** ~ **à** (*examen*) to sit; (*élection*) to stand at, run for

préservatif [pʀezɛʀvatif, iv] *nm* sheath, condom

préserver [pʀezɛʀve] *vt*: ~ **de** (*protéger*) to protect from

président [pʀezidɑ̃] *nm* (POL) president; (*d'une assemblée*, COMM) chairman; ~ **directeur général** chairman and managing director; **présidentielles** *nfpl* presidential elections

présider [pʀezide] *vt* to preside over; (*dîner*) to be the guest of honour at

présomptueux, -euse [pʀezɔ̃ptɥø, øz] *adj* presumptuous

presque [pʀɛsk] *adv* almost, nearly; ~ **personne** hardly anyone; ~ **rien** hardly anything; ~ **pas** hardly (at all); ~ **pas (de)** hardly any

presqu'île [pʀɛskil] *nf* peninsula

pressant, e [pʀesɑ̃, ɑ̃t] *adj* urgent

presse [pʀɛs] *nf* press; (*affluence*): **heures de** ~ busy times

pressé, e [pʀese] *adj* in a hurry; (*travail*) urgent; **orange** ~**e** freshly-squeezed orange juice

pressentiment [pʀesɑ̃timɑ̃] *nm* foreboding, premonition

pressentir [pʀesɑ̃tiʀ] *vt* to sense

presse-papiers [pʀɛspapje] *nm inv* paperweight

presser [pʀese] *vt* (*fruit, éponge*) to squeeze; (*bouton*) to press; (*allure*) to speed up; (*inciter*): ~ **qn de faire** to urge *ou* press sb to do ♦ *vi* to be urgent; **se** ~ *vi* (*se hâter*) to hurry (up); **se** ~ **contre qn** to squeeze up against sb; **rien ne presse** there's no hurry

pressing [pʀesiŋ] *nm* (*magasin*) dry-cleaner's

pression [pʀesjɔ̃] *nf* pressure; (*bouton*) press stud; (*fam: bière*) draught beer; **faire** ~ **sur** to put pressure on; ~ **artérielle** blood pressure

prestance [pʀɛstɑ̃s] *nf* presence, imposing bearing

prestataire [pʀɛstatɛʀ] *nm/f* supplier

prestation [pʀɛstasjɔ̃] *nf* (*allocation*) benefit; (*d'une entreprise*) service provided; (*d'un artiste*) performance

prestidigitateur, -trice [pʀɛstidiʒitatœʀ, tʀis] *nm/f* conjurer

prestige [pʀɛstiʒ] *nm* prestige; **prestigieux, -euse** *adj* prestigious

présumer [pʀezyme] *vt*: ~ **que** to presume *ou* assume that

prêt, e [pʀɛ, pʀɛt] *adj* ready ♦ *nm* (*somme*) loan; **prêt-à-porter** *nm* ready-to-wear *ou* off-the-peg (BRIT) clothes *pl*

prétendre [pʀetɑ̃dʀ] *vt* (*affirmer*): ~ **que** to claim that; (*avoir l'intention de*): ~ **faire qch** to mean *ou* intend to do sth; **prétendu, e** *adj* (*supposé*) so-called

prétentieux, -euse [pʀetɑ̃sjø, jøz] *adj* pretentious

prétention [pʀetɑ̃sjɔ̃] *nf* claim; (*vanité*) pretentiousness; ~**s** *nfpl* (*salaire*) expected salary

prêter [pʀete] *vt* (*livres, argent*): ~ **qch (à)** to lend sth (to); (*supposer*): ~ **à qn** (*caractère, propos*) to attribute to sb; **se** ~ **à** to lend o.s. (*ou* itself) to; (*manigances etc*) to go along with; ~ **à** (*critique, commentaires etc*) to be open to, give rise to; ~ **attention à** to pay attention to; ~ **serment** to take the oath

prétexte [pʀetɛkst] *nm* pretext, excuse; **sous aucun** ~ on no account; **prétexter** *vt* to give as a pretext *ou* an excuse

prêtre [pʀɛtʀ] *nm* priest

preuve [pʀœv] *nf* proof; (*indice*) proof, evidence *no pl*; **faire** ~ **de** to show; **faire ses** ~**s** to prove o.s. (*ou* itself)

prévaloir [pʀevalwaʀ] *vi* to prevail

prévenant, e [pʀev(ə)nɑ̃, ɑ̃t] *adj* thoughtful, kind

prévenir [pʀev(ə)niʀ] *vt* (*éviter: catastrophe etc*) to avoid, prevent; (*anticiper: désirs, besoins*) to anticipate; ~ **qn (de)** (*avertir*) to warn sb (about); (*informer*) to tell *ou* inform sb (about)

préventif, -ive [pʀevɑ̃tif, iv] *adj* preventive

prévention [pʀevɑ̃sjɔ̃] *nf* prevention; ~ **routière** road safety

prévenu, e [pʀev(ə)ny] *nm/f* (JUR) defendant, accused

prévision [pʀevizjɔ̃] *nf*: ~**s** predictions; (ÉCON) forecast *sg*; **en** ~ **de** in anticipation of; ~**s météorologiques** weather forecast *sg*

prévoir [pʀevwaʀ] *vt* (*anticiper*) to foresee; (*s'attendre à*) to expect, reckon on; (*organiser: voyage etc*) to plan; (*envisager*) to allow; **comme prévu** as planned; **prévoyant, e** *adj* gifted with (*ou* showing) foresight; **prévu, e** *pp* de **prévoir**

prier [pʀije] *vi* to pray ♦ *vt* (*Dieu*) to pray to; (*implorer*) to beg; (*demander*): ~ **qn de faire** to ask sb to do; **se faire** ~ to need coaxing *ou* persuading; **je vous en prie** (*allez-y*) please do; (*de rien*) don't mention it; **prière** *nf* prayer; **"prière de ..."** "please ..."

primaire [pʀimɛʀ] *adj* primary ♦ *nm* (SCOL) primary education

prime [pʀim] *nf* (*bonus*) bonus; (*subvention*) premium; (COMM: *cadeau*) free gift; (ASSURANCES, BOURSE) premium ♦ *adj*: **de** ~ **abord** at first glance; **primer** *vt*

(*récompenser*) to award a prize to ♦ *vi* to dominate; to be most important
primeurs [primœr] *nfpl* early fruits and vegetables
primevère [primvɛr] *nf* primrose
primitif, -ive [primitif, iv] *adj* primitive; (*originel*) original
primordial, e, -iaux [primɔrdjal, jo] *adj* essential
prince [prɛ̃s] *nm* prince; **princesse** *nf* princess
principal, e, -aux [prɛ̃sipal, o] *adj* principal, main ♦ *nm* (SCOL) principal, head(master); (*essentiel*) main thing
principe [prɛ̃sip] *nm* principle; **par ~** on principle; **en ~** (*habituellement*) as a rule; (*théoriquement*) in principle
printemps [prɛ̃tɑ̃] *nm* spring
priorité [prijɔrite] *nf* priority; (AUTO) right of way; **~ à droite** right of way to vehicles coming from the right
pris, e [pri, priz] *pp de* prendre ♦ *adj* (*place*) taken; (*mains*) full; (*personne*) busy; **avoir le nez/la gorge ~(e)** to have a stuffy nose/a hoarse throat; **être ~ de panique** to be panic-stricken
prise [priz] *nf* (*d'une ville*) capture; (PÊCHE, CHASSE) catch; (*point d'appui ou pour empoigner*) hold; (ÉLEC: *fiche*) plug; (: *femelle*) socket; **être aux ~s avec** to be grappling with; **~ de conscience** awareness, realization; **~ de contact** (*rencontre*) initial meeting, first contact; **~ de courant** power point; **~ de sang** blood test; **~ de vue** (*photo*) shot; **~ multiple** adaptor
priser [prize] *vt* (*estimer*) to prize, value
prison [prizɔ̃] *nf* prison; **aller/être en ~** to go to/be in prison ou jail; **prisonnier, -ière** *nm/f* prisoner ♦ *adj* captive
prit [pri] *vb voir* **prendre**
privé, e [prive] *adj* private ♦ *nm* (COMM) private sector; **en ~** in private
priver [prive] *vt*: **~ qn de** to deprive sb of; **se ~ de** to go ou do without
privilège [privilɛʒ] *nm* privilege
prix [pri] *nm* price; (*récompense, SCOL*) prize; **hors de ~** exorbitantly priced; **à aucun ~** not at any price; **à tout ~** at all costs; **~ d'achat/de vente/de revient** purchasing/selling/cost price
probable [prɔbabl] *adj* likely, probable; **probablement** *adv* probably
probant, e [prɔbɑ̃, ɑ̃t] *adj* convincing
problème [prɔblɛm] *nm* problem
procédé [prɔsede] *nm* (*méthode*) process; (*comportement*) behaviour *no pl*
procéder [prɔsede] *vi* to proceed; (*moralement*) to behave; **~ à** to carry out
procès [prɔsɛ] *nm* trial; (*poursuites*) proceedings *pl*; **être en ~ avec** to be involved

in a lawsuit with
processus [prɔsesys] *nm* process
procès-verbal, -aux [prɔsɛvɛrbal, o] *nm* (*de réunion*) minutes *pl*; (*aussi*: **P.V.**) parking ticket
prochain, e [prɔʃɛ̃, ɛn] *adj* next; (*proche*: *départ, arrivée*) impending ♦ *nm* fellow man; **la ~e fois/semaine ~e** next time/week; **prochainement** *adv* soon, shortly
proche [prɔʃ] *adj* nearby; (*dans le temps*) imminent; (*parent, ami*) close; **~s** *nmpl* (*parents*) close relatives; **être ~ (de)** to be near, be close (to); **le P~ Orient** the Middle East
proclamer [prɔklame] *vt* to proclaim
procuration [prɔkyrasjɔ̃] *nf* proxy
procurer [prɔkyre] *vt*: **~ qch à qn** (*fournir*) to obtain sth for sb; (*causer*: *plaisir etc*) to bring sb sth; **se ~** *vt* to get; **procureur** *nm* public prosecutor
prodige [prɔdiʒ] *nm* marvel, wonder; (*personne*) prodigy; **prodiguer** *vt* (*soins, attentions*): **prodiguer qch à qn** to give sb sth
producteur, -trice [prɔdyktœr, tris] *nm/f* producer
productif, -ive [prɔdyktif, iv] *adj* productive
production [prɔdyksjɔ̃] *nf* production; (*rendement*) output
productivité [prɔdyktivite] *nf* productivity
produire [prɔdɥir] *vt* to produce; **se ~** *vi* (*événement*) to happen, occur; (*acteur*) to perform, appear
produit [prɔdɥi] *nm* product; **~ chimique** chemical; **~ d'entretien** cleaning product; **~ national brut** gross national product; **~s alimentaires** foodstuffs
prof [prɔf] (*fam*) *nm* teacher
profane [prɔfan] *adj* (REL) secular ♦ *nm/f* layman(-woman)
proférer [prɔfere] *vt* to utter
professeur [prɔfesœr] *nm* teacher; (*de faculté*) (university) lecturer; (: *titulaire d'une chaire*) professor
profession [prɔfesjɔ̃] *nf* occupation; **~ libérale** (liberal) profession; **sans ~** unemployed; **professionnel, le** *adj, nm/f* professional
profil [prɔfil] *nm* profile; **de ~** in profile
profit [prɔfi] *nm* (*avantage*) benefit, advantage; (COMM, FINANCE) profit; **au ~ de** in aid of; **tirer ~ de** to profit from; **profitable** *adj* (*utile*) beneficial; (*lucratif*) profitable; **profiter** *vi*: **profiter de** (*situation, occasion*) to take advantage of; (*vacances, jeunesse etc*) to make the most of
profond, e [prɔfɔ̃, ɔ̃d] *adj* deep; (*sentiment, intérêt*) profound; **profondément** *adv* deeply; **il dort profondément** he is sound

asleep; **profondeur** *nf* depth
progéniture [prɔʒenityr] *nf* offspring *inv*
programme [prɔgram] *nm* programme;
(*SCOL*) syllabus, curriculum; (*INFORM*)
program; **programmer** *vt* (*émission*) to
schedule; (*INFORM*) to program;
programmeur, -euse *nm/f* programmer
progrès [prɔgrɛ] *nm* progress *no pl*; **faire des
~** to make progress; **progresser** *vi* to
progress; **progressif, -ive** *adj* progressive
prohiber [prɔibe] *vt* to prohibit, ban
proie [prwa] *nf* prey *no pl*
projecteur [prɔʒɛktœr] *nm* (*pour film*)
projector; (*de théâtre, cirque*) spotlight
projectile [prɔʒɛktil] *nm* missile
projection [prɔʒɛksjɔ̃] *nf* projection;
(*séance*) showing
projet [prɔʒɛ] *nm* plan; (*ébauche*) draft; **~ de
loi** bill; **projeter** *vt* (*envisager*) to plan; (*film,
photos*) to project; (*ombre, lueur*) to throw,
cast; (*jeter*) to throw up (*ou* off *ou* out)
prolétaire [prɔletɛr] *adj, nmf* proletarian
prolongement [prɔlɔ̃ʒmɑ̃] *nm* extension;
dans le ~ de running on from
prolonger [prɔlɔ̃ʒe] *vt* (*débat, séjour*) to
prolong; (*délai, billet, rue*) to extend; **se ~** *vi*
to go on
promenade [prɔmnad] *nf* walk (*ou* drive
ou ride); **faire une ~** to go for a walk; **une
~ en voiture/à vélo** a drive/(bicycle) ride
promener [prɔmne] *vt* (*chien*) to take out
for a walk; (*doigts, regard*): **~ qch sur** to run
sth over; **se ~** *vi* to go for (*ou* be out for) a
walk
promesse [prɔmɛs] *nf* promise
promettre [prɔmɛtr] *vt* to promise ♦ *vi* to
be *ou* look promising; **~ à qn de faire** to
promise sb that one will do
promiscuité [prɔmiskɥite] *nf* (*chambre*)
lack of privacy
promontoire [prɔmɔ̃twar] *nm* headland
promoteur, -trice [prɔmɔtœr, tris] *nm/f*:
~ (immobilier) property developer (*BRIT*), real
estate promoter (*US*)
promotion [prɔmosjɔ̃] *nf* promotion; **en ~**
on special offer
promouvoir [prɔmuvwar] *vt* to promote
prompt, e [prɔ̃(pt), prɔ̃(p)t] *adj* swift, rapid
prôner [prone] *vt* (*préconiser*) to advocate
pronom [prɔnɔ̃] *nm* pronoun
prononcer [prɔnɔ̃se] *vt* to pronounce; (*dire*)
to utter; (*discours*) to deliver; **se ~** *vi* to be
pronounced; **se ~ (sur)** (*se décider*) to reach a
decision (on *ou* about), give a verdict (on);
prononciation *nf* pronunciation
pronostic [prɔnɔstik] *nm* (*MÉD*) prognosis;
(*fig: aussi: ~s*) forecast
propagande [prɔpagɑ̃d] *nf* propaganda
propager [prɔpaʒe] *vt* to spread; **se ~** *vi* to

spread
prophète [prɔfɛt] *nm* prophet
prophétie [prɔfesi] *nf* prophecy
propice [prɔpis] *adj* favourable
proportion [prɔpɔrsjɔ̃] *nf* proportion;
toute(s) ~(s) gardée(s) making due
allowance(s)
propos [prɔpo] *nm* (*intention*) intention, aim;
(*sujet*): **à quel ~?** what about? ♦ *nmpl*
(*paroles*) talk *no pl*, remarks; **à ~ de** about,
regarding; **à tout ~** for the slightest thing *ou*
reason; **à ~** by the way; (*opportunément*) at
the right moment
proposer [prɔpoze] *vt* to propose; **~ qch (à
qn)** (*suggérer*) to suggest sth (to sb), propose
sth (to sb); (*offrir*) to offer (sb) sth; **se ~** to
offer one's services; **se ~ de faire** to intend *ou*
propose to do; **proposition** (*suggestion*) *nf*
proposal, suggestion; (*LING*) clause
propre [prɔpr] *adj* clean; (*net*) neat, tidy;
(*possessif*) own; (*sens*) literal; (*particulier*):
~ à peculiar to; (*approprié*): **~ à** suitable for
♦ *nm*: **recopier au ~** to make a fair copy of;
proprement *adv* (*avec propreté*) cleanly; **le
village proprement dit** the village itself; **à
proprement parler** strictly speaking; **propreté**
nf cleanliness
propriétaire [prɔprijetɛr] *nm/f* owner;
(*pour le locataire*) landlord(-lady)
propriété [prɔprijete] *nf* property; (*droit*)
ownership
propulser [prɔpylse] *vt* to propel
proroger [prɔrɔʒe] *vt* (*prolonger*) to extend
proscrire [prɔskrir] *vt* (*interdire*) to ban,
prohibit
prose [proz] *nf* (*style*) prose
prospecter [prɔspɛkte] *vt* to prospect;
(*COMM*) to canvass
prospectus [prɔspɛktys] *nm* leaflet
prospère [prɔspɛr] *adj* prosperous;
prospérer *vi* to prosper
prosterner [prɔstɛrne]: **se ~** *vi* to bow low,
prostrate o.s.
prostituée [prɔstitɥe] *nf* prostitute
prostitution [prɔstitysjɔ̃] *nf* prostitution
protecteur, -trice [prɔtɛktœr, tris] *adj*
protective; (*air, ton: péj*) patronizing ♦ *nm/f*
protector
protection [prɔtɛksjɔ̃] *nf* protection; (*d'un
personnage influent: aide*) patronage
protéger [prɔteʒe] *vt* to protect; **se ~ de** *ou*
contre to protect o.s. from
protéine [prɔtein] *nf* protein
protestant, e [prɔtɛstɑ̃, ɑ̃t] *adj, nm/f*
Protestant
protestation [prɔtɛstasjɔ̃] *nf* (*plainte*)
protest
protester [prɔtɛste] *vi*: **~ (contre)** to protest
(against *ou* about); **~ de** (*son innocence*) to

protest
prothèse [pʀɔtɛz] *nf*: ~ **dentaire** denture
protocole [pʀɔtɔkɔl] *nm* (*fig*) etiquette
proue [pʀu] *nf* bow(s *pl*), prow
prouesse [pʀuɛs] *nf* feat
prouver [pʀuve] *vt* to prove
provenance [pʀɔv(ə)nɑ̃s] *nf* origin; **avion en ~ de** plane (arriving) from
provenir [pʀɔv(ə)niʀ]: ~ **de** *vt* to come from
proverbe [pʀɔvɛʀb] *nm* proverb
province [pʀɔvɛ̃s] *nf* province
proviseur [pʀɔvizœʀ] *nm* ≈ head(teacher) (*BRIT*), ≈ principal (*US*)
provision [pʀɔvizjɔ̃] *nf* (*réserve*) stock, supply; **~s** *nfpl* (*vivres*) provisions, food *no pl*
provisoire [pʀɔvizwaʀ] *adj* temporary; **provisoirement** *adv* temporarily
provocant, e [pʀɔvɔkɑ̃, ɑ̃t] *adj* provocative
provoquer [pʀɔvɔke] *vt* (*défier*) to provoke; (*causer*) to cause, bring about; (*inciter*): ~ **qn à** to incite sb to
proxénète [pʀɔksenet] *nm* procurer
proximité [pʀɔksimite] *nf* nearness, closeness; (*dans le temps*) imminence, closeness; **à ~** near *ou* close by; **à ~ de** near (to), close to
prudemment [pʀydamɑ̃] *adv* carefully; wisely, sensibly
prudence [pʀydɑ̃s] *nf* carefulness; **avec ~** carefully; **par ~** as a precaution
prudent, e [pʀydɑ̃, ɑ̃t] *adj* (*pas téméraire*) careful; (: *en général*) safety-conscious; (*sage, conseillé*) wise, sensible; **c'est plus ~** it's wiser
prune [pʀyn] *nf* plum
pruneau, x [pʀyno] *nm* prune
prunelle [pʀynel] *nf* (*BOT*) sloe; **il y tient comme à la ~ de ses yeux** he treasures *ou* cherishes it
prunier [pʀynje] *nm* plum tree
PS *sigle m* = **parti socialiste**
psaume [psom] *nm* psalm
pseudonyme [psødɔnim] *nm* (*gén*) fictitious name; (*d'écrivain*) pseudonym, pen name
psychanalyse [psikanaliz] *nf* psychoanalysis
psychiatre [psikjatʀ] *nm/f* psychiatrist; **psychiatrique** *adj* psychiatric
psychique [psiʃik] *adj* psychological
psychologie [psikɔlɔʒi] *nf* psychology; **psychologique** *adj* psychological; **psychologue** *nm/f* psychologist
P.T.T. *sigle fpl* = **Postes, Télécommunications et Télédiffusion**
pu [py] *pp de* **pouvoir**
puanteur [pɥɑ̃tœʀ] *nf* stink, stench
pub [pyb] *nf* (*fam*: *annonce*) ad, advert; (*pratique*) advertising
public, -ique [pyblik] *adj* public; (*école, instruction*) state *cpd* ♦ *nm* public;

(*assistance*) audience; **en ~** in public
publicitaire [pyblisitɛʀ] *adj* advertising *cpd*; (*film*) publicity *cpd*
publicité [pyblisite] *nf* (*méthode, profession*) advertising; (*annonce*) advertisement; (*révélations*) publicity
publier [pyblije] *vt* to publish
publique [pyblik] *adj voir* **public**
puce [pys] *nf* flea; (*INFORM*) chip; **carte à ~** smart card; **~s** *nfpl* (*marché*) flea market *sg*
pudeur [pydœʀ] *nf* modesty; **pudique** *adj* (*chaste*) modest; (*discret*) discreet
puer [pɥe] (*péj*) *vi* to stink
puéricultrice [pɥeʀikyltʀis] *nf* p(a)ediatric nurse
puéril, e [pɥeʀil] *adj* childish
puis [pɥi] *vb voir* **pouvoir** ♦ *adv* then
puiser [pɥize] *vt*: ~ (**dans**) to draw (from)
puisque [pɥisk] *conj* since
puissance [pɥisɑ̃s] *nf* power; **en ~** ♦ *adj* potential
puissant, e [pɥisɑ̃, ɑ̃t] *adj* powerful
puisse *etc* [pɥis] *vb voir* **pouvoir**
puits [pɥi] *nm* well
pull(-over) [pyl(ɔvɛʀ)] *nm* sweater
pulluler [pylyle] *vi* to swarm
pulpe [pylp] *nf* pulp
pulvérisateur [pylveʀizatœʀ] *nm* spray
pulvériser [pylveʀize] *vt* to pulverize; (*liquide*) to spray
punaise [pynez] *nf* (*ZOOL*) bug; (*clou*) drawing pin (*BRIT*), thumbtack (*US*)
punch¹ [pɔ̃ʃ] *nm* (*boisson*) punch
punch² [pœnʃ] *nm* (*BOXE, fig*) punch
punir [pyniʀ] *vt* to punish; **punition** *nf* punishment
pupille [pypij] *nf* (*ANAT*) pupil ♦ *nm/f* (*enfant*) ward
pupitre [pypitʀ] *nm* (*SCOL*) desk
pur, e [pyʀ] *adj* pure; (*vin*) undiluted; (*whisky*) neat; **en ~e perte** to no avail; **c'est de la folie ~e** it's sheer madness; **purement** *adv* purely
purée [pyʀe] *nf*: ~ (**de pommes de terre**) mashed potatoes *pl*; ~ **de marrons** chestnut purée
purgatoire [pyʀgatwaʀ] *nm* purgatory
purger [pyʀʒe] *vt* (*MÉD, POL*) to purge; (*JUR: peine*) to serve
purin [pyʀɛ̃] *nm* liquid manure
pur-sang [pyʀsɑ̃] *nm inv* thoroughbred
pus [py] *nm* pus
putain [pytɛ̃] (*fam!*) *nf* whore (!)
puzzle [pœzl] *nm* jigsaw (puzzle)
P.-V. *sigle m* = **procès-verbal**
pyjama [piʒama] *nm* pyjamas *pl* (*BRIT*), pajamas *pl* (*US*)
pyramide [piʀamid] *nf* pyramid
Pyrénées [piʀene] *nfpl*: **les ~** the Pyrenees

Q, q

QI sigle m (= quotient intellectuel) IQ
quadragénaire [k(w)adraʒenɛʀ] nm/f
man/woman in his/her forties
quadriller [kadʀije] vt (POLICE) to keep under
tight control
quadruple [k(w)adʀypl] nm: **le ~ de** four
times as much as; **quadruplés, -ées** nm/fpl
quadruplets, quads
quai [ke] nm (de port) quay; (de gare)
platform; **être à ~** (navire) to be alongside
qualification [kalifikasjɔ̃] nf (aptitude)
qualification
qualifié, e [kalifje] adj qualified; (main
d'œuvre) skilled
qualifier [kalifje] vt to qualify; **se ~** vi to
qualify; **~ qch/qn de** to describe sth/sb as
qualité [kalite] nf quality
quand [kɑ̃] conj, adv when; **~ je serai riche**
when I'm rich; **~ même** all the same;
~ même, il exagère really, he overdoes it!;
~ bien même even though
quant [kɑ̃]: **~ à** prép (pour ce qui est de) as
for, as to; (au sujet de) regarding; **quant-à-
soi** nm: **rester sur son quant-à-soi** to remain
aloof
quantité [kɑ̃tite] nf quantity, amount;
(grand nombre): **une** ou **des ~(s) de** a great
deal of
quarantaine [kaʀɑ̃tɛn] nf (MÉD) quarantine;
avoir la ~ (âge) to be around forty; **une
~ (de)** forty or so, about forty
quarante [kaʀɑ̃t] num forty
quart [kaʀ] nm (fraction) quarter;
(surveillance) watch; **un ~ de vin** a quarter
litre of wine; **le ~ de** a quarter of; **~ d'heure**
quarter of an hour; **~s de finale** quarter
finals
quartier [kaʀtje] nm (de ville) district, area;
(de bœuf) quarter; (de fruit) piece; **cinéma de
~** local cinema; **avoir ~ libre** (fig) to be free;
~ général headquarters pl
quartz [kwaʀts] nm quartz
quasi [kazi] adv almost, nearly; **quasiment**
adv almost, nearly; **quasiment jamais** hardly
ever
quatorze [katɔʀz] num fourteen
quatre [katʀ] num four; **à ~ pattes** on all
fours; **se mettre en ~ pour qn** to go out of
one's way for sb; **~ à ~** (monter, descendre)
four at a time; **quatre-quarts** nm inv pound
cake; **quatre-vingt-dix** num ninety;
quatre-vingts num eighty; **quatre-vingt-
un** num eighty-one; **quatrième** num fourth
♦ nf (SCOL) third form ou year
quatuor [kwatyɔʀ] nm quartet(te)

que [kə] conj **1** (introduisant complétive) that;
il sait que tu es là he knows (that) you're
here; **je veux que tu acceptes** I want you to
accept; **il a dit que oui** he said he would (ou
it was etc)
2 (reprise d'autres conjonctions): **quand il
rentrera et qu'il aura mangé** when he gets
back and (when) he has eaten; **si vous y
allez ou que vous ...** if you go there or if
you ...
3 (en tête de phrase: hypothèse, souhait etc):
qu'il le veuille ou non whether he likes it or
not; **qu'il fasse ce qu'il voudra!** let him do as
he pleases!
4 (après comparatif) than, as; voir aussi **plus;
aussi; autant** etc
5 (seulement): **ne ... que** only; **il ne boit que
de l'eau** he only drinks water
♦ adv (exclamation): **qu'il** ou **qu'est-ce
qu'il est bête/court vite!** he's so silly!/he
runs°so fast!; **que de livres!** what a lot of
books!
♦ pron **1** (relatif: personne) whom; (: chose)
that, which; **l'homme que je vois** the man
(whom) I see; **le livre que tu vois** the book
(that ou which) you see; **un jour que j'étais ...**
a day when I was ...
2 (interrogatif: chose) what; **que fais-tu?,** qu'est-ce
que tu fais? what are you doing?; **qu'est-ce
que c'est?** what is it?, what's that?; **que faire?**
what can one do?

Québec [kebɛk] n: **le ~** Quebec
québécois, e [kebekwa, -waz] adj Quebec
♦ nm/f: **Québécois, e** Quebecker ♦ nm (LING)
Quebec French

quel, quelle [kɛl] adj **1** (interrogatif:
personne) who; (: chose) what; which; **quel
est cet homme?** who is this man?; **quel est ce
livre?** what is this book?; **quel livre/homme?**
what book/man?; (parmi un certain choix)
which book/man?; **quels acteurs préférez-
vous?** which actors do you prefer?; **dans
quels pays êtes-vous allé?** which ou what
countries did you go to?
2 (exclamatif): **quelle surprise!** what a
surprise!
3: quel que soit le coupable whoever is guilty;
quel que soit votre avis whatever your
opinion

quelconque [kɛlkɔ̃k] adj (indéfini): **un ami/
prétexte** ~ some friend/pretext or other;
(médiocre: repas) indifferent, poor; (laid:
personne) plain-looking

MOT-CLÉ
---

quelque [kɛlk] *adj* **1** some; a few; (*tournure
interrogative*) any; **quelque espoir** some hope;
il a quelques amis he has a few *ou* some
friends; **a-t-il quelques amis?** has he any
friends?; **les quelques livres qui** the few books
which; **20 kg et quelque(s)** a bit over 20 kg
**2: quelque ... que: quelque livre qu'il
choisisse** whatever (*ou* whichever) book he
chooses
3: quelque chose something; (*tournure interrogative*) anything; **quelque chose d'autre** something else; anything else; **quelque part** somewhere; anywhere; **en quelque sorte** as it were
♦ *adv* **1** (*environ*): **quelque 100 mètres** some 100
metres
2: quelque peu rather, somewhat

quelquefois [kɛlkəfwa] *adv* sometimes
quelques-uns, -unes [kɛlkəzœ̃, yn] *pron* a
few, some
quelqu'un [kɛlkœ̃] *pron* someone,
somebody; (+*tournure interrogative*) anyone,
anybody; **~ d'autre** someone *ou* somebody
else; (+ *tournure interrogative*) anybody else
quémander [kemɑ̃de] *vt* to beg for
qu'en dira-t-on [kɑ̃diratɔ̃] *nm inv*: **le ~ ~-
~-~** gossip, what people say
querelle [kəʀɛl] *nf* quarrel; **quereller: se
quereller** *vi* to quarrel
qu'est-ce que [kɛskə] *voir* **que**
qu'est-ce qui [kɛski] *voir* **qui**
question [kɛstjɔ̃] *nf* question; (*fig*) matter,
issue; **il a été ~ de** we (*ou* they) spoke about;
de quoi est-il ~? what is it about?; **il n'en est
pas ~** there's no question of it; **hors de ~** out
of the question; **remettre en ~** to question;
questionner *vt* to question
quête [kɛt] *nf* collection; (*recherche*) quest,
search; **faire la ~** (*à l'église*) to take the
collection; (*artiste*) to pass the hat round
quetsche [kwɛtʃ] *nf* kind of dark-red plum
queue [kø] *nf* tail; (*fig: du classement*)
bottom; (: *de poêle*) handle; (: *de fruit,
feuille*) stalk; (: *de train, colonne, file*) rear;
faire la ~ to queue (up) (*BRIT*), line up (*US*);
~ de cheval ponytail; **~ de poisson** (*AUT*): **faire
une ~ de poisson à qn** to cut in front of sb
qui [ki] *pron* (*personne*) who; (+*prép*) whom;
(*chose, animal*) which, that; **qu'est-ce ~ est
sur la table?** what is on the table?; **~ est-ce que?**
who?; **~ est-ce que?** who?; **à ~ est ce sac?**
whose bag is this?; **à ~ parlais-tu?** who were
you talking to?, to whom were you talking?;
amenez ~ vous voulez bring who you like;
~ que ce soit whoever it may be
quiconque [kikɔ̃k] *pron* (*celui qui*) whoever,
anyone who; (*n'importe qui*) anyone,

anybody
quiétude [kjetyd] *nf*: **en toute ~** in complete
peace
quille [kij] *nf*: (**jeu de**) **~s** skittles *sg* (*BRIT*),
bowling (*US*)
quincaillerie [kɛ̃kɑjʀi] *nf* (*ustensiles*)
hardware; (*magasin*) hardware shop;
quincaillier, -ière *nm/f* hardware dealer
quinquagénaire [kɛ̃kaʒenɛʀ] *nm/f* man/
woman in his/her fifties
quintal, -aux [kɛ̃tal, o] *nm* quintal (*100 kg*)
quinte [kɛ̃t] *nf*: **~ (de toux)** coughing fit
quintuple [kɛ̃typl] *nm*: **le ~ de** five times as
much as; **quintuplés, -ées** *nm/fpl*
quintuplets, quins
quinzaine [kɛ̃zɛn] *nf*: **une ~ (de)** about
fifteen, fifteen or so; **une ~ (de jours)** a
fortnight (*BRIT*), two weeks
quinze [kɛ̃z] *num* fifteen; **dans ~ jours** in a
fortnight('s time), in two weeks(' time)
quiproquo [kipʀɔko] *nm* misunderstanding
quittance [kitɑ̃s] *nf* (*reçu*) receipt
quitte [kit] *adj*: **être ~ envers qn** to be no
longer in sb's debt; (*fig*) to be quits with sb;
~ à faire even if it means doing
quitter [kite] *vt* to leave; (*vêtement*) to take
off; **se ~** *vi* (*couples, interlocuteurs*) to part; **ne
quittez pas** (*au téléphone*) hold the line
qui-vive [kiviv] *nm*: **être sur le ~~** to be on
the alert
quoi [kwa] *pron* (*interrogatif*) what; **~ de neuf?**
what's the news?; **as-tu de ~ écrire?** have you
anything to write with?; **~ qu'il arrive**
whatever happens; **~ qu'il en soit** be that as it
may; **~ que ce soit** anything at all; **"il n'y a
pas de ~"** "(please) don't mention it"; **il n'y a
pas de ~ rire** there's nothing to laugh about;
à ~ bon? what's the use?; **en ~ puis-je vous
aider?** how can I help you?
quoique [kwak] *conj* (al)though
quote-part [kɔtpaʀ] *nf* share
quotidien, ne [kɔtidjɛ̃, jɛn] *adj* daily; (*banal*) everyday ♦ *nm* (*journal*) daily (paper)

R, r

r. *abr* = **route; rue**
rab [ʀab] (*fam*) *nm* (*nourriture*) extra; **est-ce
qu'il y a du ~?** is there any extra (left)?
rabâcher [ʀabaʃe] *vt* to keep on repeating
rabais [ʀabɛ] *nm* reduction, discount;
rabaisser *vt* (*dénigrer*) to belittle; (*rabattre:
prix*) to reduce
rabat-joie [ʀabaʒwa] *nm inv* killjoy
rabattre [ʀabatʀ] *vt* (*couvercle, siège*) to pull
down; (*déduire*) to reduce; **se ~** *vi* (*se
refermer: couvercle*) to fall shut; (*véhicule,
coureur*) to cut in; **se ~ sur** to fall back on

rabbin [Rabɛ̃] nm rabbi
râblé, e [Rable] adj stocky
rabot [Rabo] nm plane
rabougri, e [RabugRi] adj stunted
rabrouer [RabRue] vt to snub
racaille [Rakaj] (péj) nf rabble, riffraff
raccommoder [Rakɔmɔde] vt to mend,
repair; **se ~** vi (fam) to make it up
raccompagner [Rakɔ̃paɲe] vt to take ou see
back
raccord [RakɔR] nm link; (retouche) touch up;
raccorder vt to join (up), link up; (suj: pont
etc) to connect, link
raccourci [RakuRsi] nm short cut
raccourcir [RakuRsiR] vt to shorten ♦ vi
(jours) to grow shorter, draw in
raccrocher [RakRɔʃe] vt (tableau) to hang
back up; (récepteur) to put down ♦ vi (TÉL)
to hang up, ring off; **se ~ à** vt to cling to,
hang on to
race [Ras] nf race; (d'animaux, fig) breed; **de
~** purebred, pedigree
rachat [Raʃa] nm buying; (du même objet)
buying back
racheter [Raʃ(ə)te] vt (article perdu) to buy
another; (après avoir vendu) to buy back;
(d'occasion) to buy; (COMM: part, firme) to
buy up; (davantage): **~ du lait/3 œufs** to buy
more milk/another 3 eggs ou 3 more eggs;
se ~ vi (fig) to make amends
racial, e, -aux [Rasjal, jo] adj racial
racine [Rasin] nf root; **~ carrée/cubique**
square/cube root
raciste [Rasist] adj, nm/f raci(al)ist
racket [Raket] nm racketeering no pl
raclée [Rɑkle] (fam) nf hiding, thrashing
racler [Rɑkle] vt (surface) to scrape; **se ~ la
gorge** to clear one's throat
racoler [Rakɔle] vt (suj: prostituée) to solicit;
(: parti, marchand) to tout for
racontars [Rakɔ̃taR] nmpl story, lie
raconter [Rakɔ̃te] vt: (à qn) (décrire) to
relate (to sb), tell (sb) about; (dire de
mauvaise foi) to tell (sb); **~ une histoire** to tell
a story
racorni, e [RakɔRni] adj hard(ened)
radar [RadaR] nm radar
rade [Rad] nf (natural) harbour; **rester en ~**
(fig) to be left stranded
radeau, x [Rado] nm raft
radiateur [RadjatœR] nm radiator, heater;
(AUTO) radiator; **~ électrique/à gaz** electric/
gas heater ou fire
radiation [Radjasjɔ̃] nf (PHYSIQUE) radiation
radical, e, -aux [Radikal, o] adj radical
radier [Radje] vt to strike off
radieux, -euse [Radjø, jøz] adj radiant
radin, e [Radɛ̃, in] (fam) adj stingy
radio [Radjo] nf radio; (MÉD) X-ray ♦ nm radio

operator; **à la ~** on the radio; **radioactif,
-ive** adj radioactive; **radiocassette** nm
cassette radio, radio cassette player;
radiodiffuser vt to broadcast; **radio-
graphie** nf radiography; (photo) X-ray
photograph; **radiophonique** adj radio cpd;
radio-réveil (pl radios-réveils) nm radio
alarm clock
radis [Radi] nm radish
radoter [Radɔte] vi to ramble on
radoucir [RadusiR]: **se ~** vi (temps) to
become milder; (se calmer) to calm down
rafale [Rafal] nf (vent) gust (of wind); (tir)
burst of gunfire
raffermir [RafɛRmiR] vt to firm up; **se ~** vi
(fig: autorité, prix) to strengthen
raffiner [Rafine] vt to refine; **raffinerie** nf
refinery
raffoler [Rafɔle]: **~ de** vt to be very keen on
rafistoler [Rafistɔle] (fam) vt to patch up
rafle [Rafl] nf (de police) raid; **rafler** (fam) vt
to swipe, nick
rafraîchir [RafreʃiR] vt (atmosphère,
température) to cool (down); (aussi: **mettre à
~**) to chill; (fig: rénover) to brighten up; **se ~**
vi (temps) to grow cooler; (en se lavant) to
freshen up; (en buvant) to refresh o.s.;
rafraîchissant, e adj refreshing;
rafraîchissement nm (boisson) cool drink;
rafraîchissements nmpl (boissons, fruits etc)
refreshments
rage [Raʒ] nf (MÉD): **la ~** rabies; (fureur) rage,
fury; **faire ~** to rage; **~ de dents** (raging)
toothache
ragot [Rago] (fam) nm malicious gossip no pl
ragoût [Ragu] nm stew
raide [Rɛd] adj stiff; (câble) taut, tight;
(escarpé) steep; (droit: cheveux) straight;
(fam: sans argent) flat broke; (osé) daring,
bold ♦ adv (en pente) steeply; **~ mort** stone
dead; **raidir** vt (muscles) to stiffen; **se raidir**
vi (tissu) to stiffen; (personne) to tense up;
(: se préparer moralement) to brace o.s.; (fig:
position) to harden; **raideur** nf (rigidité)
stiffness; **avec raideur** (répondre) stiffly,
abruptly
raie [Rɛ] nf (ZOOL) skate, ray; (rayure) stripe;
(des cheveux) parting
raifort [RefɔR] nm horseradish
rail [Rɑj] nm rail; (chemins de fer) railways pl;
par ~ by rail
railler [Rɑje] vt to scoff at, jeer at
rainure [RenyR] nf groove
raisin [Rezɛ̃] nm (aussi: **~s**) grapes pl; **~s secs**
raisins
raison [Rezɔ̃] nf reason; **avoir ~** to be right;
donner ~ à qn to agree with sb; (événement)
to prove sb right; **perdre la ~** to become
insane; **~ de plus** all the more reason; **à plus**

forte ~ all the more so; **en ~ de** because of; **à ~ de** at the rate of; **sans ~** for no reason;
raisonnable adj reasonable, sensible

raisonnement [rɛzɔnmã] nm (façon de réfléchir) reasoning; (argumentation) argument

raisonner [rɛzɔne] vi (penser) to reason; (argumenter, discuter) to argue ♦ vt (personne) to reason with

rajeunir [raʒœniʀ] vt (suj: coiffure, robe): ~ **qn** to make sb look younger; (fig: personnel) to inject new blood into ♦ vi to become (ou look) younger

rajouter [raʒute] vt to add

rajuster [raʒyste] vt (vêtement) to straighten, tidy; (salaires) to adjust

ralenti [ralɑ̃ti] nm: **au ~** (fig) at a slower pace; **tourner au ~** (AUTO) to tick over (AUTO), idle

ralentir [ralɑ̃tiʀ] vt to slow down

râler [rɑle] vi to groan; (fam) to grouse, moan (and groan)

rallier [ralje] vt (rejoindre) to rejoin; (gagner à sa cause) to win over; **se ~ à** (avis) to come over ou round to

rallonge [ralɔ̃ʒ] nf (de table) (extra) leaf

rallonger [ralɔ̃ʒe] vt to lengthen

rallye [rali] nm rally; (POL) march

ramassage [ramasaʒ] nm: ~ **scolaire** school bus service

ramassé, e [ramase] adj (trapu) squat

ramasser [ramase] vt (objet tombé ou par terre, fam) to pick up; (recueillir: copies, ordures) to collect; (récolter) to gather; **se ~** vi (sur soi-même) to huddle up; **ramassis** (péj) nm (de voyous) bunch; (d'objets) jumble

rambarde [ʀɑ̃baʀd] nf guardrail

rame [ram] nf (aviron) oar; (de métro) train; (de papier) ream

rameau, x [ramo] nm (small) branch; **les R~x** (REL) Palm Sunday sg

ramener [ram(ə)ne] vt to bring back; (reconduire) to take back; ~ **qch à** (réduire à) to reduce sth to

ramer [rame] vi to row

ramollir [ramɔliʀ] vt to soften; **se ~** vi to go soft

ramoner [ramɔne] vt to sweep

rampe [ʀɑ̃p] nf (d'escalier) banister(s pl); (dans un garage) ramp; (THÉÂTRE): **la ~** the footlights pl; ~ **de lancement** launching pad

ramper [ʀɑ̃pe] vi to crawl

rancard [ʀɑ̃kaʀ] (fam) nm (rendez-vous) date

rancart [ʀɑ̃kaʀ] nm: **mettre au ~** (fam) to scrap

rance [ʀɑ̃s] adj rancid

rancœur [ʀɑ̃kœʀ] nf rancour

rançon [ʀɑ̃sɔ̃] nf ransom

rancune [ʀɑ̃kyn] nf grudge, rancour; **garder**

~ **à qn (de qch)** to bear sb a grudge (for sth); **sans ~!** no hard feelings!; **rancunier, -ière** adj vindictive, spiteful

randonnée [ʀɑ̃dɔne] nf ride; (pédestre) walk, ramble; (: en montagne) hike, hiking no pl

rang [ʀɑ̃] nm (rangée) row; (grade, classement) rank; ~**s** nmpl (MIL) ranks; **se mettre en ~s** to get into ou form rows; **au premier ~** in the first row; (fig) ranking first

rangé, e [ʀɑ̃ʒe] adj (vie) well-ordered; (personne) steady

rangée [ʀɑ̃ʒe] nf row

ranger [ʀɑ̃ʒe] vt (mettre de l'ordre dans) to tidy up; (classer, grouper) to order, arrange; (mettre à sa place) to put away; (fig: classer): ~ **qn/qch parmi** to rank sb/sth among; **se ~** vi (véhicule, conducteur) to pull over ou in; (piéton) to step aside; (s'assagir) to settle down; **se ~ à** (avis) to come round to

ranimer [ranime] vt (personne) to bring round; (douleur, souvenir) to revive; (feu) to rekindle

rap [ʀap] nm rap (music)

rapace [rapas] nm bird of prey

râpe [ʀɑp] nf (CULIN) grater; **râper** vt (CULIN) to grate

rapetisser [ʀap(ə)tise] vt to shorten

rapide [rapid] adj fast; (prompt: coup d'œil, mouvement) quick ♦ nm express (train); (de cours d'eau) rapid; **rapidement** adv fast; quickly

rapiécer [rapjese] vt to patch

rappel [ʀapɛl] nm (THÉÂTRE) curtain call; (MÉD: vaccination) booster; (deuxième avis) reminder; **rappeler** vt to call back; (ambassadeur, MIL) to recall; (faire se souvenir): **rappeler qch à qn** to remind sb of sth; **se rappeler** vt (se souvenir de) to remember, recall

rapport [ʀapɔʀ] nm (lien, analogie) connection; (compte rendu) report; (profit) yield, return; ~**s** nmpl (entre personnes, pays) relations; **avoir ~ à** to have something to do with; **être/se mettre en ~ avec qn** to be/get in touch with sb; **par ~ à** in relation to; ~**s (sexuels)** (sexual) intercourse sg

rapporter [ʀapɔʀte] vt (rendre, ramener) to bring back; (bénéfice) to yield, bring in; (mentionner, répéter) to report ♦ vi (investissement) to give a good return ou yield; (: activité) to be very profitable; **se ~ à** (correspondre à) to relate to; **rapporteur, -euse** nm/f (péj) telltale ♦ nm (GÉOM) protractor

rapprochement [ʀapʀɔʃmã] nm (de nations) reconciliation; (rapport) parallel

rapprocher [ʀapʀɔʃe] vt (deux objets) to bring closer together; (fig: ennemis, partis etc) to bring together; (comparer) to establish a

parallel between; (chaise d'une table): ~ qch
(de) to bring sth closer (to); se ~ vi to draw
closer ou nearer; se ~ de to come closer to;
(présenter une analogie avec) to be close to

rapt [Rapt] nm abduction

raquette [Raket] nf (de tennis) racket; (de
ping-pong) bat

rare [RQR] adj rare; **se faire** ~ to become
scarce; **rarement** adv rarely, seldom

ras, e [Ra, Raz] adj (poil, herbe) short; (tête)
close-cropped ♦ adv short; **en ~e campagne**
in open country; **à** ~ **bords** to the brim; **en
avoir** ~ **le bol** (fam) to be fed up; ~ **du cou**
♦ adj (pull, robe) crew-neck

rasade [Razad] nf glassful

raser [Raze] vt (barbe, cheveux) to shave off;
(menton, personne) to shave; (fam: ennuyer)
to bore; (démolir) to raze (to the ground);
(frôler) to graze, skim; **se** ~ vi to shave; (fam)
to be bored (to tears); **rasoir** nm razor

rassasier [Rasazje] vt: **être rassasié** to have
eaten one's fill

rassemblement [Rasãbləmã] nm (groupe)
gathering; (POL) union

rassembler [Rasãble] vt (réunir) to
assemble, gather; (documents, notes) to
gather together, collect; **se** ~ vi to gather

rassis, e [Rasi, iz] adj (pain) stale

rassurer [RasyRe] vt to reassure; **se** ~ vi to
reassure o.s.; **rassure-toi** don't worry

rat [Ra] nm rat

rate [Rat] nf spleen

raté, e [Rate] adj (tentative) unsuccessful,
failed ♦ nm/f (fam: personne) failure

râteau, x [Rato] nm rake

rater [Rate] vi (affaire, projet etc) to go wrong,
fail ♦ vt (fam: cible, train, occasion) to miss;
(plat) to spoil; (fam: examen) to fail

ration [Rasjɔ̃] nf ration

ratisser [Ratise] vt (allée) to rake; (feuilles) to
rake up; (suj: armée, police) to comb

RATP sigle f (= Régie autonome des transports
parisiens) Paris transport authority

rattacher [Rataʃe] vt (animal, cheveux) to tie
up again; (fig: relier): ~ qch à to link sth with

rattrapage [RatRapaʒ] nm: **cours de** ~
remedial class

rattraper [RatRape] vt (fugitif) to recapture;
(empêcher de tomber) to catch (hold of);
(atteindre, rejoindre) to catch up with;
(réparer: erreur) to make up for; **se** ~ vi to
make up for it; **se** ~ (à) (se raccrocher) to stop
o.s. falling (by catching hold of)

rature [RatyR] nf deletion, erasure

rauque [Rok] adj (voix) hoarse

ravages [Ravaʒ] nmpl: **faire des** ~ to wreak
havoc

ravaler [Ravale] vt (mur, façade) to restore;
(déprécier) to lower

ravi, e [Ravi] adj: **être** ~ **de/que** to be
delighted with/that

ravigoter [Ravigɔte] (fam) vt to buck up

ravin [Ravɛ̃] nm gully, ravine

ravir [RaviR] vt (enchanter) to delight; **à** ~ adv
beautifully

raviser [Ravize]: **se** ~ vi to change one's mind

ravissant, e [Ravisã, ãt] adj delightful

ravisseur, -euse [RavisœR, øz] nm/f
abductor, kidnapper

ravitaillement [Ravitajmã] nm (réserves)
supplies pl

ravitailler [Ravitaje] vt (en vivres,
ammunitions) to provide with fresh supplies;
(avion) to refuel; **se** ~ vi to get fresh supplies;
(avion) to refuel

raviver [Ravive] vt (feu, douleur) to revive;
(couleurs) to brighten up

rayé, e [Reje] adj (à rayures) striped

rayer [Reje] vt (érafler) to scratch; (barrer) to
cross out; (d'une liste) to cross off

rayon [Rejɔ̃] nm (de soleil etc) ray; (GÉOM)
radius; (de roue) spoke; (étagère) shelf; (de
grand magasin) department; **dans un** ~ **de**
within a radius of; ~ **de soleil** sunbeam; ~**s X**
X-rays

rayonnement [Rejɔnmã] nm (fig: d'une
culture) influence

rayonner [Rejɔne] vi (fig) to shine forth;
(personne: de joie, de beauté) to be radiant;
(touriste) to go touring (from one base)

rayure [RejyR] nf (motif) stripe; (éraflure)
scratch; **à** ~**s** striped

raz-de-marée [Radmare] nm inv tidal wave

ré [Re] nm (MUS) D; (en chantant la gamme) re

réacteur [Reaktœr] nm (d'avion) jet engine;
(nucléaire) reactor

réaction [Reaksjɔ̃] nf reaction

réadapter [Readapte]: **se** ~ (**à**) vi to readjust
(to)

réagir [ReaʒiR] vi to react

réalisateur, -trice [RealizatœR, tRis] nm/f
(TV, CINÉMA) director

réalisation [Realizasjɔ̃] nf realization;
(cinéma) production; **en cours de** ~ under
way

réaliser [Realize] vt (projet, opération) to carry
out, realize; (rêve, souhait) to realize, fulfil;
(exploit) to achieve; (film) to produce; (se
rendre compte de) to realize; **se** ~ vi to be
realized

réaliste [Realist] adj realistic

réalité [Realite] nf reality; **en** ~ in (actual)
fact; **dans la** ~ in reality

réanimation [Reanimasjɔ̃] nf resuscitation;
service de ~ intensive care unit

rébarbatif, -ive [RebaRbatif, iv] adj
forbidding

rebattu, e [R(ə)baty] adj hackneyed

rebelle [ʀəbɛl] nm/f rebel ♦ adj (troupes) rebel; (enfant) rebellious; (mèche etc) unruly

rebeller [ʀ(ə)bele]: se ~ vi to rebel

rebondi, e [ʀ(ə)bɔ̃di] adj (joues) chubby

rebondir [ʀ(ə)bɔ̃diʀ] vi (ballon: au sol) to bounce; (: contre un mur) to rebound; (fig) to get moving again; **rebondissement** nm new development

rebord [ʀ(ə)bɔʀ] nm edge; le ~ de la fenêtre the windowsill

rebours [ʀ(ə)buʀ]: à ~ adv the wrong way

rebrousser [ʀ(ə)bʀuse] vt: ~ chemin to turn back

rebut [ʀəby] nm: mettre au ~ to scrap; **rebutant, e** adj off-putting; **rebuter** vt to put off

récalcitrant, e [ʀekalsitʀɑ̃, ɑ̃t] adj refractory

recaler [ʀ(ə)kale] vt (SCOL) to fail; se faire ~ to fail

récapituler [ʀekapityle] vt to recapitulate, sum up

receler [ʀ(ə)səle] vt (produit d'un vol) to receive; (fig) to conceal; **receleur, -euse** nm/f receiver

récemment [ʀesamɑ̃] adv recently

recensement [ʀ(ə)sɑ̃smɑ̃] nm (population) census

recenser [ʀ(ə)sɑ̃se] vt (population) to take a census of; (inventorier) to list

récent, e [ʀesɑ̃, ɑ̃t] adj recent

récépissé [ʀesepise] nm receipt

récepteur [ʀeseptœʀ, tʀis] nm receiver

réception [ʀesepsjɔ̃] nf receiving no pl; (accueil) reception, welcome; (bureau) reception desk; (réunion mondaine) reception, party; **réceptionniste** nm/f receptionist

recette [ʀ(ə)sɛt] nf recipe; (COMM) takings pl; ~s nfpl (COMM: rentrées) receipts

receveur, -euse [ʀ(ə)səvœʀ, øz] nm/f (des contributions) tax collector; (des postes) postmaster(-mistress)

recevoir [ʀ(ə)səvwaʀ] vt to receive; (client, patient) to see; être reçu (à un examen) to pass

rechange [ʀ(ə)fɑ̃ʒ]: de ~ adj (pièces, roue) spare; (fig: solution) alternative; des vêtements de ~ a change of clothes

réchapper [ʀefape]: ~ de ou à vt (accident, maladie) to come through

recharge [ʀ(ə)faʀʒ] nf refill; **rechargeable** adj (stylo etc) refillable; **recharger** vt (stylo) to refill; (batterie) to recharge

réchaud [ʀefo] nm (portable) stove

réchauffer [ʀefofe] vt (plat) to reheat; (mains, personne) to warm; se ~ vi (température) to get warmer; (personne) to warm o.s. (up)

rêche [ʀɛʃ] adj rough

recherche [ʀ(ə)fɛʀʃ] nf (action) search;

(raffinement) studied elegance; (scientifique etc): la ~ research; ~s nfpl (de la police) investigations; (scientifiques) research sg; la ~ de the search for; être à la ~ de qch to be looking for sth

recherché, e [ʀ(ə)fɛʀfe] adj (rare, demandé) much sought-after; (raffiné: style) mannered; (: tenue) elegant

rechercher [ʀ(ə)fɛʀfe] vt (objet égaré, personne) to look for; (causes, nouveau procédé) to try to find; (bonheur, compliments) to seek

rechigner [ʀ(ə)fine] vi: ~ à faire qch to balk ou jib at doing sth

rechute [ʀ(ə)fyt] nf (MÉD) relapse

récidiver [ʀesidive] vi to commit a subsequent offence; (fig) to do it again

récif [ʀesif] nm reef

récipient [ʀesipjɑ̃] nm container

réciproque [ʀesipʀɔk] adj reciprocal

récit [ʀesi] nm story; **récital** nm recital; **réciter** vt to recite

réclamation [ʀeklamasjɔ̃] nf complaint; ~s nfpl (bureau) complaints department sg

réclame [ʀeklam] nf ad, advert(isement); en ~ on special offer; **réclamer** vt to ask for; (revendiquer) to claim, demand ♦ vi to complain

réclusion [ʀeklyzjɔ̃] nf imprisonment

recoin [ʀəkwɛ̃] nm nook, corner

reçois etc [ʀəswa] vb voir recevoir

récolte [ʀekɔlt] nf harvesting, gathering; (produits) harvest, crop; **récolter** vt to harvest, gather (in); (fig) to collect

recommandé [ʀ(ə)kɔmɑ̃de] nm (POSTES): en ~ by registered mail

recommander [ʀ(ə)kɔmɑ̃de] vt to recommend; (POSTES) to register

recommencer [ʀ(ə)kɔmɑ̃se] vt (reprendre: lutte, séance) to resume, start again; (refaire: travail, explications) to start afresh, start (over) again ♦ vi to start again; (récidiver) to do it again

récompense [ʀekɔ̃pɑ̃s] nf reward; (prix) award; **récompenser** vt: **récompenser qn** (de ou pour) to reward sb (for)

réconcilier [ʀekɔ̃silje] vt to reconcile; se ~ (avec) to be reconciled (with)

reconduire [ʀ(ə)kɔ̃dɥiʀ] vt (raccompagner) to take ou see back; (renouveler) to renew

réconfort [ʀekɔ̃fɔʀ] nm comfort; **réconforter** vt (consoler) to comfort

reconnaissance [ʀ(ə)kɔnɛsɑ̃s] nf (gratitude) gratitude, gratefulness; (action de reconnaître) recognition; (MIL) reconnaissance, recce; **reconnaissant, e** adj grateful

reconnaître [ʀ(ə)kɔnɛtʀ] vt to recognize; (MIL: lieu) to reconnoitre; (JUR: enfant, torts) to acknowledge; **~ que** to admit *ou* acknowledge that; **reconnu, e** *adj* (*indiscuté, connu*) recognized

reconstituant, e [R(ə)kɔ̃stitɥɑ̃, ɑ̃t] *adj* (*aliment, régime*) strength-building

reconstituer [R(ə)kɔ̃stitɥe] *vt* (*événement, accident*) to reconstruct; (*fresque, vase brisé*) to piece together, reconstitute

reconstruction [R(ə)kɔ̃stRyksjɔ̃] *nf* rebuilding

reconstruire [R(ə)kɔ̃stRɥiR] *vt* to rebuild

reconvertir [R(ə)kɔ̃veRtiR] *vt*: **se ~ dans** *vr* (*un métier, une branche*) to go into

record [R(ə)kɔR] *nm, adj* record

recoupement [R(ə)kupmɑ̃] *nm*: **par ~** by cross-checking

recouper [R(ə)kupe]: **se ~** *vi* (*témoignages*) to tie *ou* match up

recourber [R(ə)kuRbe]: **se ~** *vi* to curve (up), bend (up)

recourir [R(ə)kuRiR]: **~ à** *vt* (*ami, agence*) to turn *ou* appeal to; (*force, ruse, emprunt*) to resort to

recours [R(ə)kuR] *nm*: **avoir ~ à = recourir à; en dernier ~** as a last resort

recouvrer [R(ə)kuvRe] *vt* (*vue, santé etc*) to recover, regain

recouvrir [R(ə)kuvRiR] *vt* (*couvrir à nouveau*) to re-cover; (*couvrir entièrement, aussi fig*) to cover

récréation [RekReasjɔ̃] *nf* (*SCOL*) break

récrier [RekRije]: **se ~** *vi* to exclaim

récriminations [RekRiminasjɔ̃] *nfpl* remonstrations, complaints

recroqueviller [R(ə)kRɔk(ə)vije]: **se ~** *vi* (*personne*) to huddle up

recrudescence [R(ə)kRydesɑ̃s] *nf* fresh outbreak

recrue [RəkRy] *nf* recruit

recruter [R(ə)kRyte] *vt* to recruit

rectangle [Rɛktɑ̃gl] *nm* rectangle; **rectangulaire** *adj* rectangular

rectificatif [Rɛktifikatif, iv] *nm* correction

rectifier [Rɛktifje] *vt* (*calcul, adresse, paroles*) to correct; (*erreur*) to rectify

rectiligne [Rɛktiliɲ] *adj* straight

recto [Rɛkto] *nm* front (of a page); **~ verso** on both sides (of the page)

reçu, e [R(ə)sy] *pp de* **recevoir** ♦ *adj* (*candidat*) successful; (*admis, consacré*) accepted ♦ *nm* (*COMM*) receipt

recueil [Rəkœj] *nm* collection; **recueillir** *vt* to collect; (*voix, suffrages*) to win; (*accueillir: réfugiés, chat*) to take in; **se recueillir** *vi* to gather one's thoughts, meditate

recul [R(ə)kyl] *nm* (*éloignement*) distance; (*déclin*) decline; **être en ~** to be on the decline; **avec du ~** with hindsight; **avoir un mouvement de ~** to recoil; **prendre du ~** to

stand back; **reculé, e** *adj* remote; **reculer** *vi* to move back, back away; (*AUTO*) to reverse, back (up); (*fig*) to (be on the) decline ♦ *vt* to move back; (*véhicule*) to reverse, back (up); (*date, décision*) to postpone; **reculons: à reculons** *adv* backwards

récupérer [RekypeRe] *vt* to recover, get back; (*heures de travail*) to make up; (*déchets*) to salvage ♦ *vi* to recover

récurer [RekyRe] *vt* to scour

récuser [Rekyze] *vt* to challenge; **se ~** *vi* to decline to give an opinion

reçut [Rəsy] *vb voir* **recevoir**

recycler [R(ə)sikle] *vt* (*TECH*) to recycle; **se ~** *vi* to retrain

rédacteur, -trice [RedaktœR, tRis] *nm/f* (*journaliste*) writer; subeditor; (*d'ouvrage de référence*) editor, compiler; **~ en chef** chief editor

rédaction [Redaksjɔ̃] *nf* writing; (*rédacteurs*) editorial staff; (*SCOL: devoir*) essay, composition

redemander [Rədmɑ̃de] *vt* (*une nouvelle fois*) to ask again for; (*davantage*) to ask for more of

redescendre [R(ə)desɑ̃dR] *vi* to go back down ♦ *vt* (*pente etc*) to go down

redevance [R(ə)dəvɑ̃s] *nf* (*TÉL*) rental charge; (*TV*) licence fee

rédiger [Rediʒe] *vt* to write; (*contrat*) to draw up

redire [R(ə)diR] *vt* to repeat; **trouver à ~ à** to find fault with

redonner [R(ə)dɔne] *vt* (*rendre*) to give back; (*resservir: nourriture*) to give more

redoubler [R(ə)duble] *vi* (*tempête, violence*) to intensify; (*SCOL*) to repeat a year; **~ de patience/prudence** to be doubly patient/careful

redoutable [R(ə)dutabl] *adj* formidable, fearsome

redouter [R(ə)dute] *vt* to dread

redressement [R(ə)dRɛsmɑ̃] *nm* (*économique*) recovery

redresser [R(ə)dRese] *vt* (*relever*) to set upright; (*pièce tordue*) to straighten out; (*situation, économie*) to put right; **se ~** *vi* (*personne*) to sit (*ou* stand) up (straight); (*économie*) to recover

réduction [Redyksjɔ̃] *nf* reduction

réduire [RedɥiR] *vt* to reduce; (*prix, dépenses*) to cut, reduce; **se ~ à** (*revenir à*) to boil down to; **réduit** *nm* (*pièce*) tiny room

rééducation [Reedykasjɔ̃] *nf* (*d'un membre*) re-education; (*de délinquants, d'un blessé*) rehabilitation

réel, le [Reɛl] *adj* real; **réellement** *adv* really

réexpédier [Rekspedje] *vt* (*à l'envoyeur*) to return, send back; (*au destinataire*) to send on, forward

refaire [R(ə)fɛR] vt to do again; (faire de nouveau: sport) to take up again; (réparer, restaurer) to do up

réfection [Refɛksjɔ̃] nf repair

réfectoire [RefɛktwaR] nm refectory

référence [Referɑ̃s] nf reference; **~s** nfpl (recommandations) reference sg

référer [RefeRe]: **se ~ à** vt to refer to

refermer [R(ə)fɛRme] vt to close ou shut again; **se ~** vi (porte) to close ou shut (again)

refiler [R(ə)file] vi (fam) to palm off

réfléchi, e [Refleʃi] adj (caractère) thoughtful; (action) well-thought-out; (LING) reflexive; **c'est tout ~** my mind's made up

réfléchir [RefleʃiR] vt to reflect ♦ vi to think; **~ à** to think about

reflet [R(ə)flɛ] nm reflection; (sur l'eau etc) sheen no pl, glint; **refléter** vt to reflect; **se refléter** vi to be reflected

réflexe [Reflɛks] nm, adj reflex

réflexion [Reflɛksjɔ̃] nf (de la lumière etc) reflection; (fait de penser) thought; (remarque) remark; **~ faite, à la ~** on reflection

refluer [R(ə)flye] vi to flow back; (foule) to surge back

reflux [Rəfly] nm (de la mer) ebb

réforme [RefɔRm] nf reform; (REL): **la R~** the Reformation; **réformer** vt to reform; (MIL) to declare unfit for service

refouler [R(ə)fule] vt (envahisseurs) to drive back; (larmes) to force back; (désir, colère) to repress

refrain [R(ə)fRɛ̃] nm refrain, chorus

refréner [RəfRene] vt, **réfréner** [RefRene] vt to curb, check

réfrigérateur [RefRizeRatœR] nm refrigerator, fridge

refroidir [R(ə)fRwadiR] vt to cool; (fig: personne) to put off ♦ vi to cool (down); **se ~** vi (temps) to get cooler ou colder; (fig: ardeur) to cool (off); **refroidissement** nm (grippe etc) chill

refuge [R(ə)fyʒ] nm refuge; **réfugié, e** adj, nm/f refugee; **réfugier: se réfugier** vi to take refuge

refus [R(ə)fy] nm refusal; **ce n'est pas de ~** I won't say no, it's welcome; **refuser** vt to refuse; (SCOL: candidat) to fail; **refuser qch à qn** to refuse sb sth; **se refuser à faire** to refuse to do

réfuter [Refyte] vt to refute

regagner [R(ə)ɡaɲe] vt (faveur) to win back; (lieu) to get back to

regain [Rəɡɛ̃] nm (renouveau): **un ~ de** renewed +nom

régal [Reɡal] nm treat; **régaler: se régaler** vi to have a delicious meal; (fig) to enjoy o.s.

regard [R(ə)ɡaR] nm (coup d'œil) look, glance; (expression) look (in one's eye); **au ~ de** (loi, morale) from the point of view of; **en ~ de** in comparison with

regardant, e [R(ə)ɡaRdɑ̃, ɑ̃t] adj (économe) tight-fisted; **peu ~ (sur)** very free (about)

regarder [R(ə)ɡaRde] vt to look at; (film, télévision, match) to watch; (concerner) to concern ♦ vi to look; **ne pas ~ à la dépense** to spare no expense; **~ qn/qch comme** to regard sb/sth as

régie [Reʒi] nf (COMM, INDUSTRIE) state-owned company; (THÉÂTRE, CINÉMA) production; (RADIO, TV) control room

regimber [R(ə)ʒɛ̃be] vi to balk, jib

régime [Reʒim] nm (POL) régime; (MÉD) diet; (ADMIN: carcéral, fiscal etc) system; (de bananes, dattes) bunch; **se mettre au/suivre un ~** to go on/be on a diet

régiment [Reʒimɑ̃] nm regiment

région [Reʒjɔ̃] nf region; **régional, e, -aux** adj regional

régir [ReʒiR] vt to govern

régisseur [ReʒisœR] nm (d'un domaine) steward; (CINÉMA, TV) assistant director; (THÉÂTRE) stage manager

registre [RəʒistR] nm register

réglage [Reɡlaʒ] nm adjustment

règle [Reɡl] nf (instrument) ruler; (loi) rule; **~s** nfpl (menstruation) period sg; **en ~** (papiers d'identité) in order; **en ~ générale** as a (general) rule

réglé, e [Reɡle] adj (vie) well-ordered; (arrangé) settled

règlement [Reɡləmɑ̃] nm (paiement) settlement; (arrêté) regulation; (règles, statuts) regulations pl, rules pl; **~ de compte(s)** settling of old scores; **réglementaire** adj conforming to the regulations; (tenue) regulation cpd; **réglementation** nf (règles) regulations; **réglementer** vt to regulate

régler [Reɡle] vt (conflit, facture) to settle; (personne) to settle up with; (mécanisme, machine) to regulate, adjust; (thermostat etc) to set, adjust

réglisse [Reɡlis] nf liquorice

règne [Rɛɲ] nm (d'un roi etc, fig) reign; **régner** vi (roi) to rule, reign; (fig) to reign

regorger [R(ə)ɡɔRʒe] vi: **~ de** to overflow with, be bursting with

regret [R(ə)ɡRɛ] nm regret; **à ~** with regret; **sans ~** with no regrets; **regrettable** adj regrettable; **regretter** vt to regret; (personne) to miss; **je regrette mais ...** I'm sorry but ...

regrouper [R(ə)ɡRupe] vt (grouper) to group together; (contenir) to include, comprise; **se ~** vi to gather (together)

régulier, -ière [ʀegylje, jɛʀ] adj (gén) regular; (vitesse, qualité) steady; (égal: couche, ligne) even, (TRANSPORTS: ligne, service), scheduled, regular; (légal) lawful, in order; (honnête) straight, on the level; **régulièrement** adv regularly; (uniformément) evenly

rehausser [ʀəose] vt (relever) to heighten, raise; (fig: souligner) to set off, enhance

rein [ʀɛ̃] nm kidney; ~s nmpl (dos) back sg

reine [ʀɛn] nf queen

reine-claude [ʀɛnklod] nf greengage

réinsertion [ʀeɛ̃sɛʀsjɔ̃] nf (de délinquant) reintegration, rehabilitation

réintégrer [ʀeɛ̃tegʀe] vt (lieu) to return to; (fonctionnaire) to reinstate

rejaillir [ʀəʒajiʀ] vi to splash up; ~ sur (fig: scandale) to rebound on; (: gloire) to be reflected on

rejet [ʀəʒɛ] nm rejection; **rejeter** vt (relancer) to throw back; (écarter) to reject; (déverser) to throw out, discharge; (vomir) to bring ou throw up; **rejeter la responsabilité de qch sur qn** to lay the responsibility for sth at sb's door

rejoindre [ʀəʒwɛ̃dʀ] vt (famille, régiment) to rejoin, return to; (lieu) to get (back) to; (suj: route etc) to meet, join; (rattraper) to catch up (with); **se ~** vi to meet; **je te rejoins à la gare** I'll see ou meet you at the station

réjouir [ʀeʒwiʀ] vt to delight; **se ~ (de)** vi to be delighted (about); **réjouissances** nfpl (fête) festivities

relâche [ʀəlɑʃ] nm ou nf: **sans ~** without respite ou a break; **relâché, e** adj loose, lax; **relâcher** vt (libérer) to release; (desserrer) to loosen; **se relâcher** vi (discipline) to become slack ou lax; (élève etc) to slacken off

relais [ʀəlɛ] nm (SPORT): **(course de) ~** relay (race); **prendre le ~ (de)** to take over (from); **~ routier** ≈ transport café (BRIT), ≈ truck stop (US)

relancer [ʀəlɑ̃se] vt (balle) to throw back; (moteur) to restart; (fig) to boost, revive; (harceler): ~ **qn** to pester sb

relatif, -ive [ʀəlatif, iv] adj relative

relation [ʀəlasjɔ̃] nf (rapport) relation(ship); (connaissance) acquaintance; ~s nfpl (rapports) relations; (connaissances) connections; **être/entrer en ~(s) avec** to be/ get in contact with

relaxe [ʀəlaks] (fam) adj (tenue) informal; (personne) relaxed; **relaxer: se relaxer** vi to relax

relayer [ʀəleje] vt (collaborateur, coureur etc) to relieve; **se ~** vi (dans une activité) to take it in turns

reléguer [ʀəlege] vt to relegate

relent(s) [ʀəlɑ̃] nm(pl) (foul) smell

relevé, e [ʀəl(ə)ve] adj (manches) rolled-up; (sauce) highly-seasoned ♦ nm (de compteur) reading; (bancaire) statement

relève [ʀəlɛv] nf (personne) relief; **prendre la ~** to take over

relever [ʀəl(ə)ve] vt (meuble) to stand up again; (personne tombée) to help up; (vitre, niveau de vie) to raise; (col) to turn up; (style) to elevate; (plat, sauce) to season; (sentinelle, équipe) to relieve; (fautes) to pick out; (défi) to accept, take up; (noter: adresse etc) to take down, note; (: plan) to sketch; (compteur) to read; (ramasser: cahiers) to collect, take in; **se ~** vi (se remettre debout) to get up; ~ **de** (maladie) to be recovering from; (être du ressort de) to be a matter for; (fig) to pertain to; ~ **qn de** (fonctions) to relieve sb of

relief [ʀəljɛf] nm relief; **mettre en ~** (fig) to bring out, highlight

relier [ʀəlje] vt to link up; (livre) to bind; ~ **qch à** to link sth to

religieuse [ʀəliʒjøz] nf nun; (gâteau) cream bun

religieux, -euse [ʀəliʒjø, jøz] adj religious ♦ nm monk

religion [ʀəliʒjɔ̃] nf religion

relire [ʀəliʀ] vt (à nouveau) to reread, read again; (vérifier) to read over

reliure [ʀəljyʀ] nf binding

reluire [ʀəlɥiʀ] vi to gleam

remanier [ʀəmanje] vt to reshape, recast; (POL) to reshuffle

remarquable [ʀəmaʀkabl] adj remarkable

remarque [ʀəmaʀk] nf remark; (écrite) note

remarquer [ʀəmaʀke] vt (voir) to notice; **se ~** vi to be noticeable; **faire ~ (à qn) que** to point out (to sb) that; **faire ~ qch (à qn)** to point sth out (to sb); **remarquez, ...** mind you ...; **se faire ~** to draw attention to o.s.

rembourrer [ʀɑ̃buʀe] vt to stuff

remboursement [ʀɑ̃buʀsəmɑ̃] nm (de dette, d'emprunt) repayment; (de frais) refund; **rembourser** vt to pay back, repay; (frais, billet etc) to refund; **se faire rembourser** to get a refund

remède [ʀəmɛd] nm (médicament) medicine; (traitement, fig) remedy, cure

remémorer [ʀəmemɔʀe]: **se ~** vt to recall, recollect

remerciements [ʀəmɛʀsimɑ̃] nmpl thanks

remercier [ʀəmɛʀsje] vt to thank; (congédier) to dismiss; ~ **qn de/d'avoir fait** to thank sb for/for having done

remettre [ʀəmɛtʀ] vt (replacer) to put back; (vêtement) to put back on; (ajouter) to add; (ajourner) to postpone sth (until); **se ~** vi: **se ~ (de)** to recover (from); ~ **qch à qn** (donner: lettre, clé etc) to hand over sth to sb; (: prix, décoration) to present sb with sth; **se ~ à faire qch** to start doing sth again

remise [ʀ(ə)miz] *nf* (*rabais*) discount; (*local*) shed; **~ de peine** reduction of sentence; **~ en jeu** (*FOOTBALL*) throw-in

remontant [ʀ(ə)mɔ̃tɑ̃, ɑ̃t] *nm* tonic, pick-me-up

remonte-pente [ʀ(ə)mɔ̃tpɑ̃t] *nm* ski-lift

remonter [ʀ(ə)mɔ̃te] *vi* to go back up; (*prix, température*) to go up again ♦ *vt* (*pente*) to go up; (*fleuve*) to sail (*ou* swim *etc*) up; (*manches, pantalon*) to roll up; (*col*) to turn up; (*niveau, limite*) to raise; (*fig: personne*) to buck up; (*qch de démonté*) to put back together, reassemble; (*montre*) to wind up; **~ le moral à qn** to raise sb's spirits; **~ à** (*dater de*) to date *ou* go back to

remontrance [ʀ(ə)mɔ̃trɑ̃s] *nf* reproof, reprimand

remontrer [ʀ(ə)mɔ̃tre] *vt* (*fig*): **en ~ à** to prove one's superiority over

remords [ʀ(ə)mɔr] *nm* remorse *no pl*; **avoir des ~** to feel remorse

remorque [ʀ(ə)mɔrk] *nf* trailer; **remorquer** *vt* to tow; **remorqueur** *nm* tug(boat)

remous [ʀəmu] *nm* (*d'un navire*) (back)wash *no pl*; (*de rivière*) swirl, eddy ♦ *nmpl* (*fig*) stir *sg*

remparts [ʀɑ̃par] *nmpl* walls, ramparts

remplaçant, e [ʀɑ̃plasɑ̃, ɑ̃t] *nm/f* replacement, stand-in; (*SCOL*) supply teacher

remplacement [ʀɑ̃plasmɑ̃] *nm* replacement; **faire des ~s** (*professeur*) to do supply teaching; (*secrétaire*) to temp

remplacer [ʀɑ̃plase] *vt* to replace; **~ qch/qn par** to replace sth/sb with

rempli, e [ʀɑ̃pli] *adj* (*emploi du temps*) full, busy; **~ de** full of, filled with

remplir [ʀɑ̃plir] *vt* to fill (up); (*questionnaire*) to fill out *ou* up; (*obligations, fonction, condition*) to fulfil; **se ~** *vi* to fill up

remporter [ʀɑ̃pɔrte] *vt* (*marchandise*) to take away; (*fig*) to win, achieve

remuant, e [ʀəmɥɑ̃, ɑ̃t] *adj* restless

remue-ménage [ʀ(ə)mymenaʒ] *nm inv* commotion

remuer [ʀəmɥe] *vt* to move; (*café, sauce*) to stir ♦ *vi* to move; **se ~** *vi* to move; (*fam: s'activer*) to get a move on

rémunérer [ʀemynere] *vt* to remunerate

renard [ʀ(ə)nar] *nm* fox

renchérir [ʀɑ̃ferir] *vi* (*fig*): **~ (sur)** (*en paroles*) to add something (to)

rencontre [ʀɑ̃kɔ̃tr] *nf* meeting; (*imprévue*) encounter; **aller à la ~ de qn** to go and meet sb; **rencontrer** *vt* to meet; (*mot, expression*) to come across; (*difficultés*) to meet with; **se rencontrer** *vi* to meet

rendement [ʀɑ̃dmɑ̃] *nm* (*d'un travailleur,*

d'une machine) output; (*d'un champ*) yield

rendez-vous [ʀɑ̃devu] *nm* appointment; (*d'amoureux*) date; (*lieu*) meeting place; **donner ~~ à qn** to arrange to meet sb; **avoir/prendre ~~ (avec)** to have/make an appointment (with)

rendre [ʀɑ̃dr] *vt* (*restituer*) to give back, return; (*invitation*) to return, repay; (*vomir*) to bring up; (*exprimer, traduire*) to render; (*faire devenir*): **~ qn célèbre/qch possible** to make sb famous/sth possible; **se ~** *vi* (*capituler*) to surrender, give o.s. up; (*aller*): **se ~ quelque part** to go somewhere; **~ la monnaie à qn** to give sb his change; **se ~ compte de qch** to realize sth

rênes [ʀɛn] *nfpl* reins

renfermé, e [ʀɑ̃fɛrme] *adj* (*fig*) withdrawn ♦ *nm*: **sentir le ~** to smell stuffy

renfermer [ʀɑ̃fɛrme] *vt* to contain

renflouer [ʀɑ̃flue] *vt* to refloat; (*fig*) to set back on its (*ou* his/her *etc*) feet

renfoncement [ʀɑ̃fɔ̃smɑ̃] *nm* recess

renforcer [ʀɑ̃fɔrse] *vt* to reinforce; **renfort: renforts** *nmpl* reinforcements; **à grand renfort de** with a great deal of

renfrogné, e [ʀɑ̃frɔɲe] *adj* sullen

rengaine [ʀɑ̃gɛn] (*péj*) *nf* old tune

renier [ʀənje] *vt* (*personne*) to disown, repudiate; (*foi*) to renounce

renifler [ʀ(ə)nifle] *vi, vt* to sniff

renne [ʀɛn] *nm* reindeer *inv*

renom [ʀənɔ̃] *nm* reputation; (*célébrité*) renown; **renommé, e** *adj* celebrated, renowned; **renommée** *nf* fame

renoncer [ʀ(ə)nɔ̃se]: **~ à** *vt* to give up; **~ à faire** to give up the idea of doing

renouer [ʀənwe] *vt*: **~ avec** (*habitude*) to take up again

renouvelable [ʀ(ə)nuv(ə)labl] *adj* (*énergie etc*) renewable

renouveler [ʀ(ə)nuv(ə)le] *vt* to renew; (*exploit, méfait*) to repeat; **se ~** *vi* (*incident*) to recur, happen again; **renouvellement** *nm* (*remplacement*) renewal

rénover [ʀenɔve] *vt* (*immeuble*) to renovate, do up; (*quartier*) to redevelop

renseignement [ʀɑ̃sɛɲmɑ̃] *nm* information *no pl*, piece of information; **(bureau des) ~s** information office

renseigner [ʀɑ̃seɲe] *vt*: **~ qn (sur)** to give information to sb (about); **se ~** *vi* to ask for information, make inquiries

rentabilité [ʀɑ̃tabilite] *nf* profitability

rentable [ʀɑ̃tabl] *adj* profitable

rente [ʀɑ̃t] *nf* private income; (*pension*) pension

rentrée [ʀɑ̃tre] *nf*: **~ (d'argent)** cash *no pl* coming in; **la ~ (des classes)** the start of the new school year

rentrer [Rɑ̃tRe] vi (*revenir chez soi*) to go (*ou* come) (back) home; (*entrer de nouveau*) to go (*ou* come) back in; (*entrer*) to go (*ou* come) in; (*air, clou: pénétrer*) to go in; (*revenu*) to come in ♦ vt to bring in; (*mettre à l'abri: animaux etc*) to bring in; (: *véhicule*) to put away; (*chemise dans pantalon etc*) to tuck in; (*griffes*) to draw in; ~ **le ventre** to pull in one's stomach; ~ **dans** (*heurter*) to crash into; ~ **dans l'ordre** to be back to normal; ~ **dans ses frais** to recover one's expenses

renverse [Rɑ̃vERs]: **à la** ~ adv backwards

renverser [Rɑ̃vERse] vt (*faire tomber: chaise, verre*) to knock over, overturn; (*liquide, contenu*) to spill, upset; (*piéton*) to knock down; (*retourner*) to turn upside down; (: *ordre des mots etc*) to reverse; (*fig: gouvernement etc*) to overthrow; (*fam: stupéfier*) to bowl over; **se** ~ vi (*verre, vase*) to fall over; (*contenu*) to spill

renvoi [Rɑ̃vwa] nm (*d'employé*) dismissal; (*d'élève*) expulsion; (*référence*) cross-reference; (*éructation*) belch; **renvoyer** vt to send back; (*congédier*) to dismiss; (*élève: définitivement*) to expel; (*lumière*) to reflect; (*ajourner*): **renvoyer qch** (à) to put sth off *ou* postpone sth (until)

repaire [R(ə)pER] nm den

répandre [RepɑdR] vt (*renverser*) to spill; (*étaler, diffuser*) to spread; (*odeur*) to give off; **se** ~ vi to spill; (*se propager*) to spread; **répandu, e** adj (*opinion, usage*) widespread

réparation [RepaRasjɔ̃] nf repair

réparer [RepaRe] vt to repair; (*fig: offense*) to make up for, atone for; (: *oubli, erreur*) to put right

repartie [Reparti] nf retort; **avoir de la** ~ to be quick at repartee

repartir [R(ə)paRtiR] vi to leave again; (*voyageur*) to set off again; (*fig*) to get going again; ~ **à zéro** to start from scratch (again)

répartir [RepartiR] vt (*pour attribuer*) to share out; (*pour disperser, disposer*) to divide up; (*poids*) to distribute; **se** ~ vt (*travail, rôles*) to share out between themselves; **répartition** nf (*des richesses etc*) distribution

repas [R(ə)pɑ] nm meal

repassage [R(ə)pasaʒ] nm ironing

repasser [R(ə)pase] vi to come (*ou* go) back ♦ vt (*vêtement, tissu*) to iron; (*examen*) to retake, resit; (*film*) to show again; (*leçon: revoir*) to go over (again)

repêcher [R(ə)peʃe] vt to fish out; (*candidat*) to pass (*by inflating marks*)

repentir [RəpɑtiR] nm repentance; **se** ~ vi to repent; **se** ~ **d'avoir fait qch** (*regretter*) to regret having done sth

répercussions [RepERkysjɔ̃] nfpl (*fig*) repercussions

répercuter [RepERkyte]: **se** ~ vi (*bruit*) to reverberate; (*fig*): **se** ~ **sur** to have repercussions on

repère [R(ə)pER] nm mark; (*monument, événement*) landmark

repérer [R(ə)peRe] vt (*fam: erreur, personne*) to spot; (: *endroit*) to locate; **se** ~ vi to find one's way about

répertoire [RepERtwaR] nm (*liste*) (alphabetical) list; (*carnet*) index notebook; (*d'un artiste*) repertoire

répéter [Repete] vt to repeat; (*préparer: leçon*) to learn, go over; (*THÉÂTRE*) to rehearse; **se** ~ vi (*redire*) to repeat o.s.; (*se reproduire*) to be repeated, recur

répétition [Repetisjɔ̃] nf repetition; (*THÉÂTRE*) rehearsal

répit [Repi] nm respite

replier [R(ə)plije] vt (*rabattre*) to fold down *ou* over; **se** ~ vi (*troupes, armée*) to withdraw, fall back; (*sur soi-même*) to withdraw into o.s.

réplique [Replik] nf (*repartie, fig*) reply; (*THÉÂTRE*) line; (*copie*) replica; **répliquer** vi to reply; (*riposter*) to retaliate

répondeur [RepɔdœR, øz] nm: ~ **automatique** (*TÉL*) answering machine

répondre [RepɔdR] vi to answer, reply; (*freins*) to respond; ~ **à** to reply to, answer; (*affection, salut*) to return; (*provocation*) to respond to; (*correspondre à: besoin*) to answer; (: *conditions*) to meet; (: *description*) to match; (*avec impertinence*): ~ **à qn** to answer sb back; ~ **de** to answer for

réponse [Repɔ̃s] nf answer, reply; **en** ~ **à** in reply to

reportage [R(ə)pɔRtaʒ] nm report; ~ **en direct** (*live*) commentary

reporter[1] [RəpɔRtER] nm reporter

reporter[2] [RəpɔRte] vt (*ajourner*): ~ **qch** (à) to postpone sth (until); (*transférer*): ~ **qch sur** to transfer sth to; **se** ~ **à** (*époque*) to think back to; (*document*) to refer to

repos [R(ə)po] nm rest; (*tranquillité*) peace (and quiet); (*MIL*): ~! stand at ease!; **ce n'est pas de tout** ~! it's no picnic!

reposant, e [R(ə)pozɑ̃, ɑ̃t] adj restful

reposer [R(ə)poze] vt (*verre, livre*) to put down; (*délasser*) to rest ♦ vi: **laisser** ~ (*pâte*) to leave to stand; **se** ~ vi to rest; **se** ~ **sur qn** to rely on sb; ~ **sur** (*fig*) to rest on

repoussant, e [R(ə)pusɑ̃, ɑ̃t] adj repulsive

repousser [R(ə)puse] vi to grow again ♦ vt to repel, repulse; (*offre*) to turn down, reject; (*personne*) to push back; (*différer*) to put back

reprendre [R(ə)prɑdR] vt (*objet prêté, donné*) to take back; (*prisonnier, ville*) to recapture; (*firme, entreprise*) to take over; (*le* *travail*) to resume; (*emprunter: argument, idée*) to take up, use; (*refaire: article etc*) to go over again; (*vêtement*) to alter; (*réprimander*) to tell off; (*corriger*) to correct; (*chercher*): **je viendrai te ~ à 4 h** I'll come and fetch you at 4; (*se resservir de*): **~ du pain/un œuf** to take (*ou* eat) more bread/another egg ♦ *vi* (*classes, pluie*) to start (up) again; (*activités, travaux, combats*) to resume, start (up) again; (*affaires*) to pick up; (*dire*): **reprit-il** he went on; **se ~** *vi* (*se resaisir*) to recover; **~ des forces** to recover one's strength; **~ courage** to take new heart; **~ la route** to set off again; **~ haleine** *ou* **son souffle** to get one's breath back

représailles [R(ə)prezajj] *nfpl* reprisals

représentant, e [R(ə)prezɑ̃tɑ̃, ɑ̃t] *nm/f* representative

représentation [R(ə)prezɑ̃tasjɔ̃] *nf* (*symbole, image*) representation; (*spectacle*) performance

représenter [R(ə)prezɑ̃te] *vt* to represent; (*donner: pièce, opéra*) to perform; **se ~** *vt* (*se figurer*) to imagine

répression [Represjɔ̃] *nf* repression

réprimer [Reprime] *vt* (*émotions*) to suppress; (*peuple etc*) to repress

repris [R(ə)pri, iz] *nm*: **~ de justice** ex-prisoner, ex-convict

reprise [R(ə)priz] *nf* (*recommencement*) resumption; (*économique*) recovery; (*TV*) repeat; (*COMM*) trade-in, part exchange; (*raccommodage*) mend; **à plusieurs ~s** on several occasions

repriser [R(ə)prize] *vt* (*chaussette, lainage*) to darn; (*tissu*) to mend

reproche [R(ə)prɔʃ] *nf* (*remontrance*) reproach; **faire des ~s à qn** to reproach sb; **sans ~(s)** beyond reproach; **reprocher** *vt*: **reprocher qch à qn** to reproach *ou* blame sb for sth; **reprocher qch à** (*critiquer*) to have sth against

reproduction [R(ə)prɔdyksjɔ̃] *nf* reproduction

reproduire [R(ə)prɔdɥir] *vt* to reproduce; **se ~** *vi* (*BIO*) to reproduce; (*recommencer*) to recur, re-occur

réprouver [Repruve] *vt* to reprove

reptile [Reptil] *nm* reptile

repu, e [Rəpy] *adj* satisfied, sated

république [Repyblik] *nf* republic

répugnant, e [Repyɲɑ̃, ɑ̃t] *adj* disgusting

répugner [Repyɲe]: **~ à** *vt*: **~ à qn** to repel *ou* disgust sb; **~ à faire** to be loath *ou* reluctant to do

réputation [Repytasjɔ̃] *nf* reputation; **réputé, e** *adj* renowned

requérir [RəkeriR] *vt* (*nécessiter*) to require, call for

requête [Rəkɛt] *nf* request

requin [Rəkɛ̃] *nm* shark

requis, e [Rəki, iz] *adj* required

RER *sigle m* (= *réseau express régional*) Greater Paris high-speed train service

rescapé, e [Rɛskape] *nm/f* survivor

rescousse [Rɛskus] *nf*: **aller à la ~ de qn** to go to sb's aid *ou* rescue

réseau, x [Rezo] *nm* network

réservation [RezɛRvasjɔ̃] *nf* booking, reservation

réserve [RezɛRv] *nf* (*retenue*) reserve; (*entrepôt*) storeroom; (*restriction, d'Indiens*) reservation; (*de pêche, chasse*) preserve; **de ~** (*provisions etc*) in reserve

réservé, e [RezɛRve] *adj* reserved; **chasse/pêche ~e** private hunting/fishing

réserver [RezɛRve] *vt* to reserve; (*chambre, billet etc*) to book, reserve; (*fig: destiner*) to have in store; (*garder*): **~ qch pour/à** to keep *ou* save sth for

réservoir [RezɛRvwaR] *nm* tank

résidence [Rezidɑ̃s] *nf* residence; **~ secondaire** second home; **résidentiel, le** *adj* residential; **résider** *vi*: **résider à/dans/en** to reside in; **résider dans** (*fig*) to lie in

résidu [Rezidy] *nm* residue *no pl*

résigner [Reziɲe]: **se ~** *vi* (**à qch/à faire**) to resign o.s. (to sth/to doing)

résilier [Rezilje] *vt* to terminate

résistance [Rezistɑ̃s] *nf* resistance; (*de réchaud, bouilloire: fil*) element

résistant, e [Rezistɑ̃, ɑ̃t] *adj* (*personne*) robust, tough; (*matériau*) strong, hard-wearing

résister [Reziste] *vi* to resist; **~ à** (*assaut, tentation*) to resist; (*supporter: gel etc*) to withstand; (*désobéir à*) to stand up to, oppose

résolu, e [Rezɔly] *pp de* **résoudre** ♦ *adj*: **être ~ à qch/faire** to be set upon sth/doing

résolution [Rezɔlysjɔ̃] *nf* (*fermeté, décision*) resolution; (*d'un problème*) solution

résolve *etc* [Rezɔlv] *vb voir* **résoudre**

résonner [Rezɔne] *vi* (*cloche, pas*) to reverberate, resound; (*salle*) to be resonant

résorber [RezɔRbe]: **se ~** *vi* (*fig: chômage*) to be reduced; (: *déficit*) to be absorbed

résoudre [RezudR] *vt* to solve; **se ~ à faire** to bring o.s. to do

respect [Rɛspɛ] *nm* respect; **tenir en ~** to keep at bay; **respecter** *vt* to respect; **respectueux, -euse** *adj* respectful

respiration [Rɛspirasjɔ̃] *nf* breathing *no pl*

respirer [Rɛspire] *vi* to breathe; (*fig: se détendre*) to get one's breath; (: *se rassurer*) to breathe again ♦ *vt* to breathe (in), inhale; (*manifester: santé, calme etc*) to exude

resplendir [Rɛsplɑ̃diR] *vi* to shine; (*fig*):

~ **(de)** to be radiant (with)

responsabilité [Respɔ̃sabilite] *nf*
responsibility; (*légale*) liability

responsable [Respɔ̃sabl] *adj* responsible
♦ *nm/f* (*coupable*) person responsible;
(*personne compétente*) person in charge; (*de
parti, syndicat*) official; ~ **de** responsible for

resquiller [Reskije] (*fam*) *vi* to get in without
paying; (*ne pas faire la queue*) to jump the
queue

ressaisir [R(ə)seziR]: **se** ~ *vi* to regain one's
self-control

ressasser [R(ə)sase] *vt* to keep going over

ressemblance [R(ə)sɑ̃blɑ̃s] *nf* resemblance,
similarity, likeness

ressemblant, e [R(ə)sɑ̃blɑ̃, ɑ̃t] *adj*
(*portrait*) lifelike, true to life

ressembler [R(ə)sɑ̃ble]: ~ **à** *vt* to be like,
resemble; (*visuellement*) to look like; **se** ~ *vi*
to be like (*ou* look) alike

ressemeler [R(ə)səm(ə)le] *vt* to (re)sole

ressentiment [R(ə)sɑ̃timɑ̃] *nm* resentment

ressentir [R(ə)sɑ̃tiR] *vt* to feel

resserrer [R(ə)seRe] *vt* (*nœud, boulon*) to
tighten (up); (*fig: liens*) to strengthen

resservir [R(ə)seRviR] *vi* to do *ou* serve
again; **se** ~ *vi* to help o.s. again

ressort [RəsɔR] *nm* (*pièce*) spring; (*énergie*)
spirit; (*recours*): **en dernier** ~ as a last resort;
(*compétence*): **être du** ~ **de** to fall within the
competence of

ressortir [RəsɔRtiR] *vi* to go (*ou* come) out
(again); (*contraster*) to stand out; ~ **de** to
emerge from; **faire** ~ (*fig: souligner*) to bring
out

ressortissant, e [R(ə)sɔRtisɑ̃, ɑ̃t] *nm/f*
national

ressources [R(ə)suRs] *nfpl* (*moyens*)
resources

ressusciter [Resysite] *vt* to revive, bring
back ♦ *vi* to rise (from the dead)

restant, e [Restɑ̃, ɑ̃t] *adj* remaining ♦ *nm*: **le**
~ **(de)** the remainder (of); **un** ~ **de** (*de trop*)
some left-over

restaurant [RestɔRɑ̃] *nm* restaurant

restauration [RestɔRasjɔ̃] *nf* restoration;
(*hôtellerie*) catering; ~ **rapide** fast food

restaurer [RestɔRe] *vt* to restore; **se** ~ *vi* to
have something to eat

reste [Rest] *nm* (*restant*): **le** ~ **(de)** the rest
(of); (*de trop*): **un** ~ **(de)** some left-over; ~**s**
nmpl (*nourriture*) left-overs; (*d'une cité etc,
dépouille mortelle*) remains; **du** ~, **au** ~ besides,
moreover

rester [Reste] *vi* to stay, remain; (*subsister*) to
remain, be left; (*durer*) to last, live on ♦ *vb
impers*: **il reste du pain/2 œufs** there's some
bread/there are 2 eggs left (over); **restons-en
là** let's leave it at that; **il me reste assez de**

temps I have enough time left; **il ne me reste
plus qu'à ...** I've just got to ...

restituer [Restitɥe] *vt* (*objet, somme*): ~ **qch
(à qn)** to return sth (to sb)

restreindre [RestRɛ̃dR] *vt* to restrict, limit

restriction [RestRiksjɔ̃] *nf* restriction

résultat [Rezylta] *nm* result; (*d'examen,
d'élection*) results *pl*

résulter [Rezylte]: ~ **de** *vt* to result from, be
the result of

résumé [Rezyme] *nm* summary, résumé

résumer [Rezyme] *vt* (*texte*) to summarize;
(*récapituler*) to sum up

résurrection [RezyRɛksjɔ̃] *nf* resurrection

rétablir [RetabliR] *vt* to restore, re-establish;
se ~ *vi* (*guérir*) to recover; (*silence, calme*) to
return, be restored; **rétablissement** *nm*
restoring; (*guérison*) recovery

retaper [R(ə)tape] (*fam*) *vt* (*maison, voiture
etc*) to do up; (*revigorer*) to buck up

retard [R(ə)taR] *nm* (*d'une personne attendue*)
lateness *no pl*; (*sur l'horaire, un programme*)
delay; (*fig: scolaire, mental etc*) back-
wardness; **en** ~ **(de 2 heures)** (2 hours) late;
avoir du ~ to be late; (*sur un programme*)
to be behind (schedule); **prendre du**
~ (*train, avion*) to be delayed; **sans** ~ without
delay

retardataire [R(ə)taRdatɛR] *nmf* latecomer

retardement [R(ə)taRdəmɑ̃]: **à** ~ *adj*
delayed action *cpd*; **bombe à** ~ time bomb

retarder [R(ə)taRde] *vt* to delay; (*montre*) to
put back ♦ *vi* (*montre*) to be slow; ~ **qn
(d'une heure)** (*sur un horaire*) to delay sb (an
hour); ~ **qch (de 2 jours)** (*départ, date*) to put
sth back (2 days)

retenir [Rət(ə)niR] *vt* (*garder, retarder*) to
keep, detain; (*maintenir: objet qui glisse, fig:
colère, larmes*) to hold back; (*se rappeler*) to
retain; (*réserver*) to reserve; (*accepter:
proposition etc*) to accept; (*fig: empêcher
d'agir*): ~ **qn (de faire)** to hold sb back (from
doing); (*prélever*): ~ **qch (sur)** to deduct sth
(from); **se** ~ *vi* (*se raccrocher*): **se** ~ **à** to hold
onto; (*se contenir*): **se** ~ **de faire** to restrain
o.s. from doing; ~ **son souffle** to hold one's
breath

retentir [R(ə)tɑ̃tiR] *vi* to ring out; (*salle*):
~ **de** to ring *ou* resound with; **retentissant,
e** *adj* resounding; **retentissement** *nm*
repercussion

retenu, e [Rət(ə)ny] *adj* (*place*) reserved;
(*personne: empêché*) held up; **retenue** *nf*
(*prélèvement*) deduction; (*SCOL*) detention;
(*modération*) (self-)restraint

réticence [Retisɑ̃s] *nf* hesitation, reluctance
no pl; **réticent, e** *adj* hesitant, reluctant

rétine [Retin] *nf* retina

retiré, e [R(ə)tiRe] *adj* (*vie*) secluded; (*lieu*)

remote

retirer [ʀ(ə)tiʀe] vt (vêtement, lunettes) to take off, remove; (argent, plainte) to withdraw; (reprendre: bagages, billets) to collect, pick up; (extraire): ~ **qch de** to take sth out of, remove sth from

retombées [ʀətɔ̃be] nfpl (radioactives) fallout sg; (fig: répercussions) effects

retomber [ʀ(ə)tɔ̃be] vi (à nouveau) to fall again; (atterrir: après un saut etc) to land; (échoir): ~ **sur qn** to fall on sb

rétorquer [ʀetɔʀke] vt: ~ (**à qn**) **que** to retort (to sb) that

retouche [ʀ(ə)tuʃ] nf (sur vêtement) alteration; **retoucher** vt (photographie) to touch up; (texte, vêtement) to alter

retour [ʀ(ə)tuʀ] nm return; **au** ~ (en route) on the way back; **à mon** ~ when I get/got back; **être de** ~ (**de**) to be back (from); **par** ~ **du courrier** by return of post

retourner [ʀ(ə)tuʀne] vt (dans l'autre sens: matelas, crêpe etc) to turn (over); (: sac, vêtement) to turn inside out; (fam: bouleverser) to shake; (renvoyer, restituer): ~ **qch à qn** to return sth to sb ♦ vi (aller, revenir): ~ **quelque part/à** to go back ou return somewhere/to; **se** ~ vi (tourner la tête) to turn round; ~ **à** (état, activité) to return to, go back to; **se** ~ **contre** (fig) to turn against

retrait [ʀ(ə)tʀɛ] nm (d'argent) withdrawal; **en** ~ set back; ~ **du permis** (**de conduire**) disqualification from driving (BRIT), revocation of driver's license (US)

retraite [ʀ(ə)tʀɛt] nf (d'un employé) retirement; (revenu) pension; (d'une armée, REL) retreat; **prendre sa** ~ to retire; ~ **anticipée** early retirement; **retraité, e** adj retired ♦ nm/f pensioner

retrancher [ʀ(ə)tʀɑ̃ʃe] vt (nombre, somme): ~ **qch de** to take ou deduct sth from; **se** ~ **derrière/dans** to take refuge behind/in

retransmettre [ʀ(ə)tʀɑ̃smɛtʀ] vt (RADIO) to broadcast; (TV) to show

rétrécir [ʀetʀesiʀ] vt (vêtement) to take in ♦ vi to shrink

rétribution [ʀetʀibysjɔ̃] nf payment

rétro [ʀetʀo] adj inv: **la mode** ~ the nostalgia vogue

rétrograde [ʀetʀɔgʀad] adj reactionary, backward-looking

rétroprojecteur [ʀetʀopʀɔʒɛktœʀ] nm overhead projector

rétrospective [ʀetʀɔspɛktiv] nf retrospective exhibition/season; **rétrospectivement** adv in retrospect

retrousser [ʀ(ə)tʀuse] vt to roll up

retrouvailles [ʀ(ə)tʀuvaj] nfpl reunion sg

retrouver [ʀ(ə)tʀuve] vt (fugitif, objet perdu) to find; (calme, santé) to regain; (revoir) to

see again; (rejoindre) to meet (again), join; **se** ~ vi to meet; (s'orienter) to find one's way; **se** ~ **quelque part** to find o.s. somewhere; **s'y** ~ (y voir clair) to make sense of sth; (rentrer dans ses frais) to break even

rétroviseur [ʀetʀɔvizœʀ] nm (rear-view) mirror

réunion [ʀeynjɔ̃] nf (séance) meeting

réunir [ʀeyniʀ] vt (rassembler) to gather together; (inviter: amis, famille) to have round, have in; (cumuler: qualités etc) to combine; (rapprocher: ennemis) to bring together (again), reunite; (rattacher: parties) to join (together); **se** ~ vi (se rencontrer) to meet

réussi, e [ʀeysi] adj successful

réussir [ʀeysiʀ] vi to succeed, be successful; (à un examen) to pass ♦ vt to make a success of; ~ **à faire** to succeed in doing; ~ **à qn** (être bénéfique à) to agree with sb; **réussite** nf success; (CARTES) patience

revaloir [ʀ(ə)valwaʀ] vt: **je vous revaudrai cela** I'll repay you some day; (en mal) I'll pay you back for this

revanche [ʀ(ə)vɑ̃ʃ] nf revenge; (sport) revenge match; **en** ~ on the other hand

rêve [ʀɛv] nm dream; **de** ~ dream cpd; **faire un** ~ to have a dream

revêche [ʀəvɛʃ] adj surly, sour-tempered

réveil [ʀevɛj] nm waking up no pl; (fig) awakening; (pendule) alarm (clock); **au** ~ on waking (up); **réveille-matin** nm inv alarm clock; **réveiller** vt (personne) to wake up; (fig) to awaken, revive; **se réveiller** vi to wake up

réveillon [ʀevɛjɔ̃] nm Christmas Eve; (de la Saint-Sylvestre) New Year's Eve; **réveillonner** vi to celebrate Christmas Eve (ou New Year's Eve)

révélateur, -trice [ʀevelatœʀ, tʀis] adj: ~ (**de qch**) revealing (sth)

révéler [ʀevele] vt to reveal; **se** ~ vi to be revealed, reveal itself ♦ vb +attrib: **se** ~ **difficile/aisé** to prove difficult/easy

revenant, e [ʀ(ə)vənɑ̃, ɑ̃t] nm/f ghost

revendeur, -euse [ʀ(ə)vɑ̃dœʀ, øz] nm/f (détaillant) retailer; (de drogue) (drug-)dealer

revendication [ʀ(ə)vɑ̃dikasjɔ̃] nf claim, demand

revendiquer [ʀ(ə)vɑ̃dike] vt to claim, demand; (responsabilité) to claim

revendre [ʀ(ə)vɑ̃dʀ] vt (d'occasion) to resell; (détailler) to sell; **à** ~ (en abondance) to spare

revenir [ʀəv(ə)niʀ] vi to come back; (coûter): ~ **cher/à 100 F** (**à qn**) to cost (sb) a lot/100 F; ~ **à** (reprendre: études, projet) to return to, go back to; (équivaloir à) to amount to; ~ **à qn** (part, honneur) to go to sb, be sb's; (souvenir, nom) to come back to sb; ~ **sur** (question, *sujet*) to go back over; (*engagement*) to go back on; **~ à soi** to come round; **n'en pas ~: je n'en reviens pas** I can't get over it; **~ sur ses pas** to retrace one's steps; **cela revient à dire que/au même** it amounts to saying that/the same thing; **faire ~** (*CULIN*) to brown

revenu [ʀəv(ə)ny] *nm* income; **~s** *nmpl* income *sg*

rêver [ʀeve] *vi, vt* to dream; **~ de/à** to dream of

réverbère [ʀevεʀbεʀ] *nm* street lamp *ou* light; **réverbérer** *vt* to reflect

révérence [ʀeveʀɑ̃s] *nf* (*salut*) bow; (: *de femme*) curtsey

rêverie [ʀεvʀi] *nf* daydreaming *no pl*, daydream

revers [ʀ(ə)vεʀ] *nm* (*de feuille, main*) back; (*d'étoffe*) wrong side; (*de pièce, médaille*) back, reverse; (*TENNIS, PING-PONG*) backhand; (*de veste*) lapel; (*fig: échec*) setback

revêtement [ʀ(ə)vεtmɑ̃] *nm* (*des sols*) flooring; (*de chaussée*) surface

revêtir [ʀ(ə)vetiʀ] *vt* (*habit*) to don, put on; (*prendre: importance, apparence*) to take on; **~ qch de** to cover sth with

rêveur, -euse [ʀεvœʀ, øz] *adj* dreamy
♦ *nm/f* dreamer

revient [ʀəvjε̃] *vb voir* revenir

revigorer [ʀ(ə)vigɔʀe] *vt* (*air frais*) to invigorate, brace up; (*repas, boisson*) to revive, buck up

revirement [ʀ(ə)viʀmɑ̃] *nm* change of mind; (*d'une situation*) reversal

réviser [ʀevize] *vt* to revise; (*machine*) to overhaul, service

révision [ʀevizjɔ̃] *nf* revision; (*de voiture*) servicing *no pl*

revivre [ʀ(ə)vivʀ] *vi* (*reprendre des forces*) to come alive again ♦ *vt* (*épreuve, moment*) to relive

revoir [ʀəvwaʀ] *vt* to see again; (*réviser*) to revise ♦ *nm*: **au ~** goodbye

révoltant, e [ʀevɔltɑ̃, ɑ̃t] *adj* revolting, appalling

révolte [ʀevɔlt] *nf* rebellion, revolt

révolter [ʀevɔlte] *vt* to revolt; **se ~ (contre)** to rebel (against); **ça me révolte (de voir que ...)** I'm revolted *ou* appalled (to see that ...)

révolu, e [ʀevɔly] *adj* past; (*ADMIN*): **âgé de 18 ans ~s** over 18 years of age

révolution [ʀevɔlysjɔ̃] *nf* revolution; **révolutionnaire** *adj, nm/f* revolutionary

revolver [ʀevɔlvεʀ] *nm* gun; (*à barillet*) revolver

révoquer [ʀevɔke] *vt* (*fonctionnaire*) to dismiss; (*arrêt, contrat*) to revoke

revue [ʀ(ə)vy] *nf* review; (*périodique*) review, magazine; (*de music-hall*) variety show; **passer en ~** (*mentalement*) to go through

rez-de-chaussée [ʀed(ə)ʃose] *nm inv* ground floor

RF *sigle f* = **République française**

Rhin [ʀε̃] *nm* Rhine

rhinocéros [ʀinɔseʀɔs] *nm* rhinoceros

Rhône [ʀon] *nm* Rhone

rhubarbe [ʀybaʀb] *nf* rhubarb

rhum [ʀɔm] *nm* rum

rhumatisme [ʀymatism] *nm* rheumatism *no pl*

rhume [ʀym] *nm* cold; **~ de cerveau** head cold; **le ~ des foins** hay fever

ri [ʀi] *pp de* rire

riant, e [ʀ(i)jɑ̃, ʀ(i)jɑ̃t] *adj* smiling, cheerful

ricaner [ʀikane] *vi* (*avec méchanceté*) to snigger; (*bêtement*) to giggle

riche [ʀiʃ] *adj* rich; (*personne, pays*) rich, wealthy; **~ en** rich in; **richesse** *nf* wealth; (*fig: de sol, musée etc*) richness; **richesses** *nfpl* (*ressources, argent*) wealth *sg*; (*fig: trésors*) treasures

ricochet [ʀikɔʃε] *nm*: **faire des ~s** to skip stones; **par ~** (*fig*) as an indirect result

rictus [ʀiktys] *nm* grin

ride [ʀid] *nf* wrinkle

rideau, x [ʀido] *nm* curtain; **~ de fer** (*boutique*) metal shutter(s)

rider [ʀide] *vt* to wrinkle; **se ~** *vi* to become wrinkled

ridicule [ʀidikyl] *adj* ridiculous ♦ *nm*: **le ~** ridicule; **ridiculiser: se ridiculiser** *vi* to make a fool of o.s.

MOT-CLÉ

rien [ʀjε̃] *pron* **1**: **(ne) ... rien** nothing; *tournure negative + anything*; **qu'est-ce que vous avez? – rien** what have you got? – nothing; **il a rien dit/fait** he said/did nothing; he hasn't said/done anything; **il n'a rien** (*n'est pas blessé*) he's all right; **de rien!** not at all!
2 (*quelque chose*): **a-t-il jamais rien fait pour nous?** has he ever done anything for us?
3: **rien de: rien d'intéressant** nothing interesting; **rien d'autre** nothing else; **rien du tout** nothing at all
4: **rien que** just, only; nothing but; **rien que pour lui faire plaisir** only *ou* just to please him; **rien que la vérité** nothing but the truth; **rien que cela** that alone
♦ *nm*: **un petit rien** (*cadeau*) a little something; **des riens** trivia *pl*; **un rien de** a hint of; **en un rien de temps** in no time at all

---

rieur, -euse [ʀ(i)jœʀ, ʀ(i)jøz] *adj* cheerful

rigide [ʀiʒid] *adj* stiff; (*fig*) rigid; strict

rigole [ʀigɔl] *nf* (*conduit*) channel

rigoler [ʀigɔle] *vi* (*fam: rire*) to laugh; (*s'amuser*) to have (some) fun; (*plaisanter*) to be joking *ou* kidding; **rigolo, -ote** (*fam*) *adj* funny ♦ nm/f comic; (péj) fraud, phoney

rigoureusement [ʀiguʀøzmɑ̃] adv (vrai) absolutely; (interdit) strictly

rigoureux, -euse [ʀiguʀø, øz] adj rigorous; (hiver) hard, harsh

rigueur [ʀigœʀ] nf rigour; **être de ~** to be the rule; **à la ~** at a pinch; **tenir ~ à qn de qch** to hold sth against sth

rillettes [ʀijɛt] nfpl potted meat (made from pork or goose)

rime [ʀim] nf rhyme

rinçage [ʀɛ̃saʒ] nm rinsing (out); (opération) rinse

rincer [ʀɛ̃se] vt to rinse; (récipient) to rinse out

ring [ʀiŋ] nm (boxing) ring

ringard, e [ʀɛ̃gaʀ, aʀd] (fam) adj old-fashioned

rions [ʀiɔ̃] vb voir rire

riposter [ʀipɔste] vi to retaliate ♦ vt: **~ que** to retort that

rire [ʀiʀ] vi to laugh; (se divertir) to have fun ♦ nm sg **le ~** laughter; **~ de** to laugh at; **pour ~** (pas sérieusement) for a joke ou a laugh

risée [ʀize] nf: **être la ~ de** to be the laughing stock of

risible [ʀizibl] adj laughable

risque [ʀisk] nm risk; **le ~** danger; **à ses ~s et périls** at his own risk; **risqué, e** adj risky; (plaisanterie) risqué, daring; **risquer** vt to risk; (allusion, question) to venture, hazard; **ça ne risque rien** it's quite safe; **risquer de: il risque de se tuer** he could get himself killed; **ce qui risque de se produire** what might ou could well happen; **il ne risque pas de recommencer** there's no chance of him doing that again; **se risquer à faire** (tenter) to venture ou dare to do

rissoler [ʀisɔle] vi, vt: **(faire) ~** to brown

ristourne [ʀistuʀn] nf discount

rite [ʀit] nm rite; (fig) ritual

rivage [ʀivaʒ] nm shore

rival, e, -aux [ʀival, o] adj, nm/f rival; **rivaliser** vi: **rivaliser avec** (personne) to rival, vie with; **rivalité** nf rivalry

rive [ʀiv] nf shore; (de fleuve) bank; **riverain, e** nm/f riverside (ou lakeside) resident; (d'une route) local resident

rivet [ʀivɛ] nm rivet

rivière [ʀivjɛʀ] nf river

rixe [ʀiks] nf brawl, scuffle

riz [ʀi] nm rice; **rizière** nf paddy-field, ricefield

RMI sigle m (= revenu minimum d'insertion) ≈ income support (BRIT), welfare (US)

RN sigle f = route nationale

robe [ʀɔb] nf dress; (de juge) robe; (pelage) coat; **~ de chambre** dressing gown; **~ de soirée/de mariée** evening/wedding dress

robinet [ʀɔbinɛ] nm tap

robot [ʀɔbo] nm robot

robuste [ʀɔbyst] adj robust, sturdy; **robustesse** nf robustness, sturdiness

roc [ʀɔk] nm rock

rocade [ʀɔkad] nf bypass

rocaille [ʀɔkaj] nf loose stones pl; (jardin) rockery, rock garden

roche [ʀɔʃ] nf rock

rocher [ʀɔʃe] nm rock

rocheux, -euse [ʀɔʃø, øz] adj rocky

rodage [ʀɔdaʒ] nm: **en ~** running in

roder [ʀɔde] vt (AUTO) to run in

rôder [ʀode] vi to roam about; (de façon suspecte) to lurk (about ou around); **rôdeur, -euse** nm/f prowler

rogne [ʀɔɲ] (fam) nf: **être en ~** to be in a temper

rogner [ʀɔɲe] vt to clip; **~ sur** (fig) to cut down ou back on

rognons [ʀɔɲɔ̃] nmpl (CULIN) kidneys

roi [ʀwa] nm king; **la fête des R~s, les R~s** Twelfth Night

rôle [ʀol] nm role, part

romain, e [ʀɔmɛ̃, ɛn] adj Roman ♦ nm/f: **R~, e** Roman

roman, e [ʀɔmɑ̃, an] adj (ARCHIT) Romanesque ♦ nm novel; **~ d'espionnage** spy novel ou story; **~ policier** detective story

romance [ʀɔmɑ̃s] nf ballad

romancer [ʀɔmɑ̃se] vt (agrémenter) to romanticize; **romancier, -ière** nm/f novelist; **romanesque** (amours, aventures) storybook cpd; (sentimental: personne) romantic

roman-feuilleton [ʀɔmɑ̃fœjtɔ̃] nm serialized novel

romanichel, le [ʀɔmaniʃɛl] (péj) nm/f gipsy

romantique [ʀɔmɑ̃tik] adj romantic

romarin [ʀɔmaʀɛ̃] nm rosemary

rompre [ʀɔ̃pʀ] vt to break; (entretien, fiançailles) to break off ♦ vi (fiancés) to break it off; **se ~** vi to break; **rompu, e** adj (fourbu) exhausted

ronces [ʀɔ̃s] nfpl brambles

ronchonner [ʀɔ̃ʃɔne] (fam) vi to grouse, grouch

rond, e [ʀɔ̃, ʀɔ̃d] adj round; (joues, mollets) well-rounded; (fam: ivre) tight ♦ nm (cercle) ring; (fam: sou): **je n'ai plus un ~** I haven't a penny left; **en ~** (s'asseoir, danser) in a ring; **ronde** nf (gén: de surveillance) rounds pl, patrol; (danse) round (dance); (MUS) semibreve (BRIT), whole note (US); **à la ronde** (alentour): **à 10 km à la ronde** for 10 km round; **rondelet, te** adj plump

rondelle [ʀɔ̃dɛl] nf (tranche) slice, round; (TECH) washer

rondement [ʀɔ̃dmɑ̃] adv (efficacement)

briskly

rondin [ʀɔ̃dɛ̃] nm log

rond-point [ʀɔ̃pwɛ̃] nm roundabout

ronflant, e [ʀɔ̃flɑ̃, ɑ̃t] (péj) adj high-flown, grand

ronflement [ʀɔ̃fləmɑ̃] nm snore, snoring

ronfler [ʀɔ̃fle] vi to snore; (moteur, poêle) to hum

ronger [ʀɔ̃ʒe] vt to gnaw (at); (suj: vers, rouille) to eat into; **se ~ les ongles** to bite one's nails; **se ~ les sangs** to worry o.s. sick; **rongeur** nm rodent

ronronner [ʀɔ̃ʀɔne] vi to purr

rosace [ʀozas] nf (vitrail) rose window

rosbif [ʀɔsbif] nm: **du ~** roasting beef; (cuit) roast beef

rose [ʀoz] nf rose ♦ adj pink

rosé, e [ʀoze] adj pinkish; (vin) **~ rosé**

roseau, x [ʀozo] nm reed

rosée [ʀoze] nf dew

rosette [ʀozɛt] nf (nœud) bow

rosier [ʀozje] nm rosebush, rose tree

rosse [ʀɔs] (fam) adj nasty, vicious

rossignol [ʀɔsiɲɔl] nm (ZOOL) nightingale

rot [ʀo] nm belch; (de bébé) burp

rotatif, -ive [ʀɔtatif, iv] adj rotary

rotation [ʀɔtasjɔ̃] nf rotation

roter [ʀɔte] (fam) vi to burp, belch

rôti [ʀoti] nm: **du ~** roasting meat; (cuit) roast meat; **~ de bœuf/porc** joint of beef/pork

rotin [ʀɔtɛ̃] nm rattan (cane); **fauteuil en ~** cane (arm)chair

rôtir [ʀotiʀ] vi, vt (aussi: **faire ~**) to roast; **rôtisserie** nf (restaurant) steakhouse; (traiteur) roast meat shop; **rôtissoire** nf (roasting) spit

rotule [ʀɔtyl] nf kneecap

roturier, -ière [ʀɔtyʀje, jɛʀ] nm/f commoner

rouage [ʀwaʒ] nm cog(wheel), gearwheel; **les ~s de l'État** the wheels of State

roucouler [ʀukule] vi to coo

roue [ʀu] nf wheel; **~ de secours** spare wheel

roué, e [ʀwe] adj wily

rouer [ʀwe] vt: **~ qn de coups** to give sb a thrashing

rouge [ʀuʒ] adj, nm/f red ♦ nm red; (vin) **~** red wine; **sur la liste** ~ ex-directory (BRIT), unlisted (US); **passer au ~** (signal) to go red; (automobiliste) to go through a red light; **~** (à lèvres) lipstick; **rouge-gorge** nm robin (redbreast)

rougeole [ʀuʒɔl] nf measles sg

rougeoyer [ʀuʒwaje] vi to glow red

rouget [ʀuʒɛ] nm mullet

rougeur [ʀuʒœʀ] nf redness; (MÉD: tache) red blotch

rougir [ʀuʒiʀ] vi to turn red; (de honte, timidité) to blush, flush; (de plaisir, colère) to

flush

rouille [ʀuj] nf rust; **rouillé, e** adj rusty; **rouiller** vt to rust ♦ vi to rust, go rusty; **se rouiller** vi to rust

roulant, e [ʀulɑ̃, ɑ̃t] adj (meuble) on wheels; (tapis etc) moving; **escalier ~** escalator

rouleau, x [ʀulo] nm roll; (à mise en plis, à peinture, vague) roller; **~ à pâtisserie** rolling pin

roulement [ʀulmɑ̃] nm (rotation) rotation; (bruit) rumbling no pl, rumble; **travailler par ~** to work on a rota (BRIT) ou rotation (US) basis; **~ (à billes)** ball bearings pl; **~ de tambour** drum roll

rouler [ʀule] vt to roll; (papier, tapis) to roll up; (CULIN: pâte) to roll out; (fam: duper) to do, con ♦ vi (bille, boule) to roll; (voiture, train) to go, run; (automobiliste) to drive; (bateau) to roll; **se ~ dans** (boue) to roll in; (couverture) to roll o.s. (up) in

roulette [ʀulɛt] nf (de table, fauteuil) castor; (de dentiste) drill; (jeu) roulette; **à ~s** on castors; **ça a marché comme sur des ~s** (fam) it went off very smoothly

roulis [ʀuli] nm roll(ing)

roulotte [ʀulɔt] nf caravan

roumain, e [ʀumɛ̃, ɛn] adj Rumanian ♦ nm/ f: **R~, e** Rumanian

Roumanie [ʀumani] nf Rumania

rouquin, e [ʀukɛ̃, in] (péj) nm/f redhead

rouspéter [ʀuspete] (fam) vi to moan

rousse [ʀus] adj voir roux

roussir [ʀusiʀ] vt to scorch ♦ vi (CULIN): **faire ~** to brown

route [ʀut] nf road; (fig: chemin) way; (itinéraire, parcours) route; (fig: voie) road, path; **il y a 3h de ~** it's a 3-hour ride ou journey; **en ~** on the way; **mettre en ~** to start up; **se mettre en ~** to set off; **~ nationale** ≈ A road (BRIT), ≈ state highway (US); **routier, -ière** adj road cpd ♦ nm (camionneur) (long-distance) lorry (BRIT) ou truck (US) driver; (restaurant) ≈ transport café (BRIT), ≈ truck stop (US)

routine [ʀutin] nf routine; **routinier, -ière** (péj) adj (activité) humdrum; (personne) addicted to routine

rouvrir [ʀuvʀiʀ] vt, vi to reopen, open again; **se ~** vi to reopen, open again

roux, rousse [ʀu, ʀus] adj red; (personne) red-haired ♦ nm/f redhead

royal, e, -aux [ʀwajal, o] adj royal; (cadeau etc) fit for a king

royaume [ʀwajom] nm kingdom; (fig) realm; **le R~-Uni** the United Kingdom

royauté [ʀwajote] nf (régime) monarchy

RPR sigle m: **Rassemblement pour la République** French right-wing political party

ruban [ʀybɑ̃] nm ribbon; **~ adhésif** adhesive

tape
rubéole [ʀybeɔl] *nf* German measles *sg*, rubella
rubis [ʀybi] *nm* ruby
rubrique [ʀybʀik] *nf* (*titre, catégorie*) heading; (*PRESSE: article*) column
ruche [ʀyʃ] *nf* hive
rude [ʀyd] *adj* (*au toucher*) rough; (*métier, tâche*) hard, tough; (*climat*) severe, harsh; (*bourru*) harsh, rough; (*fruste: manières*) rugged, tough; (*fam: fameux*) jolly good; **rudement** (*fam*) *adv* (*très*) terribly
rudimentaire [ʀydimɑ̃tɛʀ] *adj* rudimentary, basic
rudiments [ʀydimɑ̃] *nmpl*: **avoir des ~ d'anglais** to have a smattering of English
rudoyer [ʀydwaje] *vt* to treat harshly
rue [ʀy] *nf* street
ruée [ʀɥe] *nf* rush
ruelle [ʀɥɛl] *nf* alley(-way)
ruer [ʀɥe] *vi* (*cheval*) to kick out; **se ~** *vi*: **se ~ sur** to pounce on; **se ~ vers/dans/hors de** to rush *ou* dash towards/into/out of
rugby [ʀygbi] *nm* rugby (football)
rugir [ʀyʒiʀ] *vi* to roar
rugueux, -euse [ʀygø, øz] *adj* rough
ruine [ʀɥin] *nf* ruin; **ruiner** *vt* to ruin; **ruineux, -euse** *adj* ruinous
ruisseau, x [ʀɥiso] *nm* stream, brook
ruisseler [ʀɥis(ə)le] *vi* to stream
rumeur [ʀymœʀ] *nf* (*nouvelle*) rumour; (*bruit confus*) rumbling
ruminer [ʀymine] *vt* (*herbe*) to ruminate; (*fig*) to ruminate on *ou* over, chew over
rupture [ʀyptyʀ] *nf* (*séparation, désunion*) break-up, split; (*de négociations etc*) breakdown; (*de contrat*) breach; (*dans continuité*) break
rural, e, -aux [ʀyʀal, o] *adj* rural, country *cpd*
ruse [ʀyz] *nf*: **la ~** cunning, craftiness; (*pour tromper*) trickery; **une ~** a trick, a ruse; **rusé, e** *adj* cunning, crafty
russe [ʀys] *adj* Russian ♦ *nm/f*: **R~** Russian ♦ *nm* (*LING*) Russian
Russie [ʀysi] *nf*: **la ~** Russia
rustine ® [ʀystin] *nf* rubber repair patch (*for bicycle tyre*)
rustique [ʀystik] *adj* rustic
rustre [ʀystʀ] *nm* boor
rutilant, e [ʀytilɑ̃, ɑ̃t] *adj* gleaming
rythme [ʀitm] *nm* rhythm; (*vitesse*) rate; (: *de la vie*) pace, tempo; **rythmé, e** *adj* rhythmic(al)

S, s

s' [s] *pron voir* **se**
sa [sa] *adj voir* **son¹**
SA *sigle* (= société anonyme) ≈ Ltd (*BRIT*), ≈ Inc. (*US*)
sable [sɑbl] *nm* sand; **~s mouvants** quicksand(s)
sablé [sɑble] *nm* shortbread biscuit
sabler [sɑble] *vt* (*contre le verglas*) to grit; **~ le champagne** to drink champagne
sablier [sɑblije] *nm* hourglass; (*de cuisine*) egg timer
sablonneux, -euse [sɑblɔnø, øz] *adj* sandy
saborder [sabɔʀde] *vt* (*navire*) to scuttle; (*fig: projet*) to put paid to, scupper
sabot [sabo] *nm* clog; (*de cheval*) hoof; **~ de frein** brake shoe
saboter [sabɔte] *vt* to sabotage; (*bâcler*) to make a mess of, botch
sac [sak] *nm* bag; (*à charbon etc*) sack; **~ à dos** rucksack; **~ à main** handbag; **~ de couchage** sleeping bag; **~ de voyage** travelling bag; **~ poubelle** bin liner
saccadé, e [sakade] *adj* jerky; (*respiration*) spasmodic
saccager [sakaʒe] *vt* (*piller*) to sack; (*dévaster*) to create havoc in
saccharine [sakaʀin] *nf* saccharin
sacerdoce [sasɛʀdɔs] *nm* priesthood; (*fig*) calling, vocation
sache *etc* [saʃ] *vb voir* **savoir**
sachet [saʃɛ] *nm* (small) bag; (*de sucre, café*) sachet; **du potage en ~** packet soup; **~ de thé** tea bag
sacoche [sakɔʃ] *nf* (*gén*) bag; (*de bicyclette*) saddlebag
sacquer [sake] (*fam*) *vt* (*employé*) to fire; (*détester*): **je ne peux pas le ~** I can't stand him
sacre [sakʀ] *nm* (*roi*) coronation
sacré, e [sakʀe] *adj* sacred; (*fam: satané*) blasted; (: *fameux*): **un ~ toupé** a heck of a cheek
sacrement [sakʀəmɑ̃] *nm* sacrament
sacrifice [sakʀifis] *nm* sacrifice; **sacrifier** *vt* to sacrifice
sacristie [sakʀisti] *nf* (*catholique*) sacristy; (*protestante*) vestry
sadique [sadik] *adj* sadistic
safran [safʀɑ̃] *nm* saffron
sage [saʒ] *adj* wise; (*enfant*) good
sage-femme [saʒfam] *nf* midwife
sagesse [saʒɛs] *nf* wisdom
Sagittaire [saʒitɛʀ] *nm*: **le ~** Sagittarius
Sahara [saaʀa] *nm*: **le ~** the Sahara (desert)
saignant, e [sɛɲɑ̃, ɑ̃t] *adj* (*viande*) rare

saignée [seɲe] nf (fig) heavy losses pl
saigner [seɲe] vi to bleed ♦ vt to bleed; (animal) to kill (by bleeding); ~ **du nez** to have a nosebleed
saillie [saji] nf (sur un mur etc) projection
saillir [sajiʀ] vi to project, stick out; (veine, muscle) to bulge
sain, e [sɛ̃, sɛn] adj healthy; ~ **d'esprit** sound in mind, sane; ~ **et sauf** safe and sound, unharmed
saindoux [sɛ̃du] nm lard
saint, e [sɛ̃, sɛ̃t] adj holy ♦ nm/f saint; **le S~ Esprit** the Holy Spirit ou Ghost; **la S~e Vierge** the Blessed Virgin; **la S~-Sylvestre** New Year's Eve; **sainteté** nf holiness
sais etc [sɛ] vb voir **savoir**
saisi, e [sezi] adj: ~ **de panique** panic-stricken; **être** ~ **(par le froid)** to be struck by the sudden cold
saisie nf seizure; ~**e (de données)** (data) capture
saisir [seziʀ] vt to take hold of, grab; (fig: occasion) to seize; (comprendre) to grasp; (entendre) to get, catch; (données) to capture; (CULIN) to fry quickly; (JUR: biens, publication) to seize; **se** ~ **de** vt to seize; **saisissant, e** adj startling, striking
saison [sɛzɔ̃] nf season; **morte** ~ slack season; **saisonnier, -ière** adj seasonal
sait [sɛ] vb voir **savoir**
salade [salad] nf (BOT) lettuce etc; (CULIN) (green) salad; (fam: confusion) tangle, muddle; ~ **composée** mixed salad; ~ **de fruits** fruit salad; **saladier** nm (salad) bowl
salaire [salɛʀ] nm (annuel, mensuel) salary; (hebdomadaire, journalier) pay, wages pl; ~ **minimum interprofessionnel de croissance** index-linked guaranteed minimum wage
salarié, e [salaʀje] nm/f salaried employee; wage-earner
salaud [salo] (fam!) nm sod (!), bastard (!)
sale [sal] adj dirty, filthy; (fam: mauvais) nasty
salé, e [sale] adj (mer, goût) salty; (CULIN: amandes, beurre etc) salted; (: gâteaux) savoury; (fam: grivois) spicy; (: facture) steep
saler [sale] vt to salt
saleté [salte] nf (état) dirtiness; (crasse) dirt, filth; (tache etc) dirt no pl; (fam: méchanceté) dirty trick; (: camelote) rubbish no pl; (: obscénité) filthy thing (to say)
salière [saljɛʀ] nf saltcellar
salin, e [salɛ̃, in] adj saline
salir [saliʀ] vt to (make) dirty; (fig: quelqu'un) to soil the reputation of; **se** ~ vi to get dirty; **salissant, e** adj (tissu) which shows the dirt; (travail) dirty, messy
salle [sal] nf room; (d'hôpital) ward; (de restaurant) dining room; (d'un cinéma) auditorium; (: public) audience; ~ **à manger**

dining room; ~ **d'attente** waiting room; ~ **de bain(s)** bathroom; ~ **de classe** classroom; ~ **de concert** concert hall; ~ **d'eau** shower-room; ~ **d'embarquement** (à l'aéroport) departure lounge; ~ **de jeux** (pour enfants) playroom; ~ **d'opération** (d'hôpital) operating theatre; ~ **de séjour** living room; ~ **des ventes** saleroom
salon [salɔ̃] nm lounge, sitting room; (mobilier) lounge suite; (exposition) exhibition, show; ~ **de coiffure** hairdressing salon; ~ **de thé** tearoom
salope [salɔp] (fam!) nf bitch (!); **saloperie** (fam!) nf (action) dirty trick; (chose sans valeur) rubbish no pl
salopette [salɔpɛt] nf dungarees pl; (d'ouvrier) overall(s)
salsifis [salsifi] nm salsify
salubre [salybʀ] adj healthy, salubrious
saluer [salɥe] vt (pour dire bonjour, fig) to greet; (pour dire au revoir) to take one's leave; (MIL) to salute
salut [saly] nm (geste) wave; (parole) greeting; (MIL) salute; (sauvegarde) safety; (REL) salvation ♦ excl (fam: bonjour) hi (there); (: au revoir) see you, bye
salutations [salytasjɔ̃] nfpl greetings; **Veuillez agréer, Monsieur, mes** ~ **distinguées** yours faithfully
samedi [samdi] nm Saturday
SAMU [samy] sigle m (= service d'assistance médicale d'urgence) ≈ ambulance (service) (BRIT), ≈ paramedics pl (US)
sanction [sɑ̃ksjɔ̃] nf sanction; **sanctionner** vt (loi, usage) to sanction; (punir) to punish
sandale [sɑ̃dal] nf sandal
sandwich [sɑ̃dwi(t)ʃ] nm sandwich
sang [sɑ̃] nm blood; **en** ~ covered in blood; **se faire du mauvais** ~ to fret, get in a state; **sang-froid** nm calm, sangfroid; **de sang-froid** in cold blood; **sanglant, e** adj bloody
sangle [sɑ̃gl] nf strap
sanglier [sɑ̃glije] nm (wild) boar
sanglot [sɑ̃glo] nm sob; **sangloter** vi to sob
sangsue [sɑ̃sy] nf leech
sanguin, e [sɑ̃gɛ̃, in] adj blood cpd; **sanguinaire** adj bloodthirsty
sanitaire [sanitɛʀ] adj health cpd; ~**s** nmpl (lieu) bathroom sg
sans [sɑ̃] prép without; **un pull** ~ **manches** a sleeveless jumper; ~ **faute** without fail; ~ **arrêt** without a break; ~ **ça** (fam) otherwise; ~ **qu'il s'en aperçoive** without him ou his noticing; **sans-abri** nmpl homeless; **sans-emploi** nm/f inv unemployed person; **les sans-emploi** the unemployed; **sans-gêne** adj inv inconsiderate
santé [sɑ̃te] nf health; **en bonne** ~ in good health; **boire à la** ~ **de qn** to drink (to) sb's

health; **à ta/votre ~!** cheers!

saoudien, ne [saudjɛ̃, jɛn] *adj* Saudi Arabian ♦ *nm/f:* **S~, ne** Saudi Arabian

saoul, e [su, sul] *adj* = **soûl**

saper [sape] *vt* to undermine, sap

sapeur-pompier [sapœʀpɔ̃pje] *nm* fireman

saphir [safiʀ] *nm* sapphire

sapin [sapɛ̃] *nm* fir (tree); (*bois*) fir; **~ de Noël** Christmas tree

sarcastique [saʀkastik] *adj* sarcastic

sarcler [saʀkle] *vt* to weed

Sardaigne [saʀdɛɲ] *nf:* **la ~** Sardinia

sardine [saʀdin] *nf* sardine

sarrasin [saʀazɛ̃] *nm* buckwheat

SARL *sigle f* (= *société à responsabilité limitée*) ≈ plc (*BRIT*) ≈ Inc. (*US*)

sas [sɑs] *nm* (*de sous-marin, d'engin spatial*) airlock; (*d'écluse*) lock

satané, e [satane] (*fam*) *adj* confounded

satellite [satelit] *nm* satellite

satin [satɛ̃] *nm* satin

satire [satiʀ] *nf* satire; **satirique** *adj* satirical

satisfaction [satisfaksjɔ̃] *nf* satisfaction

satisfaire [satisfɛʀ] *vt* to satisfy; **~ à** (*conditions*) to meet; **satisfaisant, e** *adj* (*acceptable*) satisfactory; **satisfait, e** *adj* satisfied; **satisfait de** happy *ou* satisfied with

saturer [satyʀe] *vt* to saturate

sauce [sos] *nf* sauce; (*avec un rôti*) gravy; **saucière** *nf* sauceboat

saucisse [sosis] *nf* sausage

saucisson [sosisɔ̃] *nm* (slicing) sausage

sauf, sauve [sof, sov] *adj* unharmed, unhurt; (*fig: honneur*) intact, saved ♦ *prép* except; **laisser la vie sauve à qn** to spare sb's life; **~ si** (*à moins que*) unless; **~ erreur** if I'm not mistaken; **~ avis contraire** unless you hear to the contrary

sauge [soʒ] *nf* sage

saugrenu, e [soɡʀəny] *adj* preposterous

saule [sol] *nm* willow (tree)

saumon [somɔ̃] *nm* salmon *inv*

saumure [somyʀ] *nf* brine

saupoudrer [supudʀe] *vt:* **~ qch de** to sprinkle sth with

saur [sɔʀ] *adj m:* **hareng ~** smoked *ou* red herring, kipper

saurai *etc* [sɔʀe] *vb voir* **savoir**

saut [so] *nm* jump; (*discipline sportive*) jumping; **faire un ~ chez qn** to pop over to sb's (place); **~ à l'élastique** bungee jumping; **~ à la perche** pole vaulting; **~ en hauteur/ longueur** high/long jump; **~ périlleux** somersault

saute [sot] *nf:* **~ d'humeur** sudden change of mood

sauter [sote] *vi* to jump, leap; (*exploser*) to blow up, explode; (: *fusibles*) to blow; (*se détacher*) to pop out (*ou* off) ♦ *vt* to jump

(over), leap (over); (*fig: omettre*) to skip, miss (out); **faire ~** to blow up; (*CULIN*) to sauté; **~ au cou de qn** to fly into sb's arms; **~ sur une occasion** to jump at an opportunity; **~ aux yeux** to be (quite) obvious

sauterelle [sotʀɛl] *nf* grasshopper

sautiller [sotije] *vi* (*oiseau*) to hop; (*enfant*) to skip

sauvage [sovaʒ] *adj* (*gén*) wild; (*peuplade*) savage; (*farouche: personne*) unsociable; (*barbare*) wild, savage; (*non officiel*) unauthorized, unofficial; **faire du camping ~** to camp in the wild ♦ *nm/f* savage; (*timide*) unsociable type

sauve [sov] *adj f voir* **sauf**

sauvegarde [sovɡaʀd] *nf* safeguard; (*INFORM*) backup; **sauvegarder** *vt* to safeguard; (*INFORM: enregistrer*) to save; (: *copier*) to back up

sauve-qui-peut [sovkipø] *excl* run for your life!

sauver [sove] *vt* to save; (*porter secours à*) to rescue; (*récupérer*) to salvage, rescue; **se ~** *vi* (*s'enfuir*) to run away; (*fam: partir*) to be off; **sauvetage** *nm* rescue; **sauveteur** *nm* rescuer; **sauvette: à la sauvette** *adv* (*se marier etc*) hastily, hurriedly; **sauveur** *nm* saviour (*BRIT*), savior (*US*)

savais *etc* [save] *vb voir* **savoir**

savamment [savamɑ̃] *adv* (*avec érudition*) learnedly; (*habilement*) skilfully, cleverly

savant, e [savɑ̃, ɑ̃t] *adj* scholarly, learned ♦ *nm* scientist

saveur [savœʀ] *nf* flavour; (*fig*) savour

savoir [savwaʀ] *vt* to know; (*être capable de*): **il sait nager** he can swim ♦ *nm* knowledge; **se ~** *vi* (*être connu*) to be known; **à ~ that** is, namely; **faire ~ qch à qn** to let sb know sth; **pas que je sache** not as far as I know

savon [savɔ̃] *nm* (*produit*) soap; (*morceau*) bar of soap; (*fam*): **passer un ~ à qn** to give sb a good dressing-down; **savonner** *vt* to soap; **savonnette** *nf* bar of soap

savons [savɔ̃] *vb voir* **savoir**

savourer [savuʀe] *vt* to savour; **savoureux, -euse** *adj* tasty; (*fig: anecdote*) spicy, juicy

saxo(phone) [saksɔ(fɔn)] *nm* sax(ophone)

scabreux, -euse [skabʀø, øz] *adj* risky; (*indécent*) improper, shocking

scandale [skɑ̃dal] *nm* scandal; (*tapage*): **faire un ~** to make a scene, create a disturbance; **faire ~** to scandalize people; **scandaleux, -euse** *adj* scandalous, outrageous

scandinave [skɑ̃dinav] *adj* Scandinavian ♦ *nm/f:* **S~** Scandinavian

Scandinavie [skɑ̃dinavi] *nf* Scandinavia

scaphandre [skafɑ̃dʀ] *nm* (*de plongeur*) diving suit

scarabée [skaʀabe] *nm* beetle

scarlatine [skaʁlatin] *nf* scarlet fever
scarole [skaʁɔl] *nf* endive
sceau, x [so] *nm* seal
scélérat, e [seleʁa, at] *nm/f* villain
sceller [sele] *vt* to seal
scénario [senaʁjo] *nm* scenario
scène [sɛn] *nf* (*gén*) scene; (*estrade, fig:
théâtre*) stage; **entrer en ~** to come on stage;
mettre en ~ (*THÉÂTRE*) to stage; (*CINÉMA*) to
direct; **~ de ménage** domestic scene
sceptique [sɛptik] *adj* sceptical
schéma [ʃema] *nm* (*diagramme*) diagram,
sketch; **schématique** *adj* diagrammatic(al),
schematic; (*fig*) oversimplified
sciatique [sjatik] *nf* sciatica
scie [si] *nf* saw; **~ à métaux** hacksaw
sciemment [sjamã] *adv* knowingly
science [sjãs] *nf* science; (*savoir*) knowledge;
~s naturelles (*SCOL*) natural science *sg*,
biology *sg*; **~s po** political science *ou* studies
pl; **science-fiction** *nf* science fiction;
scientifique *adj* scientific ♦ *nm/f* scientist;
(*étudiant*) science student
scier [sje] *vt* to saw; (*retrancher*) to saw off;
scierie *nf* sawmill
scinder [sɛ̃de] *vt* to split up; **se ~** *vi* to split up
scintiller [sɛ̃tije] *vi* to sparkle; (*étoile*) to
twinkle
scission [sisjɔ̃] *nf* split
sciure [sjyʁ] *nf*: **~ (de bois)** sawdust
sclérose [skleʁoz] *nf*: **~ en plaques** multiple
sclerosis
scolaire [skɔlɛʁ] *adj* school *cpd*; **scolariser**
vt to provide with schooling/schools;
scolarité *nf* schooling
scooter [skutœʁ] *nm* (motor) scooter
score [skɔʁ] *nm* score
scorpion [skɔʁpjɔ̃] *nm* (*signe*): **le S~** Scorpio
Scotch ® [skɔtʃ] *nm* adhesive tape
scout, e [skut] *adj, nm* scout
script [skʁipt] *nm* (*écriture*) printing; (*CINÉMA*)
(shooting) script
scrupule [skʁypyl] *nm* scruple
scruter [skʁyte] *vt* to scrutinize; (*l'obscurité*)
to peer into
scrutin [skʁytɛ̃] *nm* (*vote*) ballot; (*ensemble
des opérations*) poll
sculpter [skylte] *vt* to sculpt; (*bois*) to carve;
sculpteur *nm* sculptor; **sculpture** *nf*
sculpture; **sculpture sur bois** wood carving
SDF *sigle m* (= *sans domicile fixe*) homeless
person; **les SDF** the homeless

--- MOT-CLÉ ---

se [sə], **s'** *pron* **1** (*emploi réfléchi*) oneself;
(: *masc*) himself; (: *fém*) herself; (: *sujet non
humain*) itself; (: *pl*) themselves; **se voir
comme l'on est** to see o.s. as one is
2 (*réciproque*) one another, each other; **ils**

s'aiment they love one another *ou* each other
3 (*passif*): **cela se répare facilement** it is easily
repaired
4 (*possessif*): **se casser la jambe/laver les
mains** to break one's leg/wash one's hands

--- ⌐ ---

séance [seãs] *nf* (*d'assemblée*) meeting,
session; (*de tribunal*) sitting, session;
(*musicale, CINÉMA, THÉÂTRE*) performance;
~ tenante forthwith
seau, x [so] *nm* bucket, pail
sec, sèche [sɛk, sɛʃ] *adj* dry; (*raisins, figues*)
dried; (*cœur: insensible*) hard, cold ♦ *nm*:
tenir au ~ to keep in a dry place ♦ *adv* hard;
je le bois ~ I drink it straight *ou* neat; **à ~**
(*puits*) dried up
sécateur [sekatœʁ] *nm* secateurs *pl* (*BRIT*),
shears *pl*
sèche [sɛʃ] *adj f voir* **sec**; **sèche-cheveux** *nm
inv* hair-drier; **sèche-linge** *nm inv* tumble
dryer; **sèchement** *adv* (*répondre*) drily
sécher [seʃe] *vt* to dry; (*dessécher: peau, blé*)
to dry (out); (: *étang*) to dry up; (*fam:
cours*) to skip ♦ *vi* to dry; to dry out; to dry
up; (*fam: candidat*) to be stumped; **se ~**
(*après le bain*) to dry o.s.; **sécheresse** *nf*
dryness; (*absence de pluie*) drought; **séchoir**
nm drier
second, e [s(ə)gɔ̃, ɔ̃d] *adj* second ♦ *nm*
(*assistant*) second in command; (*NAVIG*) first
mate; **voyager en ~e** to travel second-class;
secondaire *adj* secondary; **seconde** *nf*
second; **seconder** *vt* to assist
secouer [s(ə)kwe] *vt* to shake; (*passagers*) to
rock; (*traumatiser*) to shake (up); **se ~** *vi*
(*fam: faire un effort*) to shake o.s. up; (: *se
dépêcher*) to get a move on
secourir [s(ə)kuʁiʁ] *vt* (*venir en aide à*) to
assist, aid; **secourisme** *nm* first aid;
secouriste *nmf* first-aid worker
secours [s(ə)kuʁ] *nm* help, aid, assistance
♦ *nmpl* aid *sg*; **au ~!** help!; **appeler au ~** to
shout *ou* call for help; **porter ~ à qn** to give sb
assistance, help sb; **les premiers ~** first aid *sg*
secousse [s(ə)kus] *nf* jolt, bump; (*électrique*)
shock; (*fig: psychologique*) jolt, shock;
~ sismique earth tremor
secret, -ète [sɔkʁe, ɛt] *adj* secret; (*fig:
renfermé*) reticent, reserved ♦ *nm* secret;
(*discrétion absolue*): **le ~** secrecy
secrétaire [s(ə)kʁetɛʁ] *nm/f* secretary ♦ *nm*
(*meuble*) writing desk; **~ de direction** private
ou personal secretary; **~ d'État** junior minister;
~ général (*COMM*) company secretary;
secrétariat *nm* (*profession*) secretarial work;
(*bureau*) office; (: *d'organisation inter-
nationale*) secretariat
secteur [sɛktœʁ] *nm* sector; (*zone*) area;
(*ÉLEC*): **branché sur ~** plugged into the mains

(supply)

section [sɛksjɔ̃] nf section; (*de parcours d'autobus*) fare stage; (*MIL: unité*) platoon; **sectionner** vt to sever

Sécu [seky] abr f = **sécurité sociale**

séculaire [sekylɛʀ] adj (*très vieux*) age-old

sécuriser [sekyʀize] vt to give (a feeling of) security to

sécurité [sekyʀite] nf (*absence de danger*) safety; (*absence de troubles*) security; **système de ~** security system; **être en ~** to be safe; **la ~ routière** road safety; **la ~ sociale** ≈ (the) Social Security (*BRIT*), ≈ Welfare (*US*)

sédentaire [sedɑ̃tɛʀ] adj sedentary

séduction [sedyksjɔ̃] nf seduction; (*charme, attrait*) appeal, charm

séduire [sedɥiʀ] vt to charm; (*femme: abuser de*) to seduce; **séduisant, e** adj (*femme*) seductive; (*homme, offre*) very attractive

ségrégation [segʀegasjɔ̃] nf segregation

seigle [sɛgl] nm rye

seigneur [sɛɲœʀ] nm lord

sein [sɛ̃] nm breast; (*entrailles*) womb; **au ~ de** (*équipe, institution*) within

séisme [seism] nm earthquake

seize [sɛz] num sixteen; **seizième** num sixteenth

séjour [seʒuʀ] nm stay; (*pièce*) living room; **séjourner** vi to stay

sel [sɛl] nm salt; (*fig: piquant*) spice

sélection [selɛksjɔ̃] nf selection; **sélectionner** vt to select

self-service [sɛlfsɛʀvis] adj, nm self-service

selle [sɛl] nf saddle; **~s** nfpl (*MÉD*) stools; **seller** vt to saddle

sellette [sɛlɛt] nf: **être sur la ~** to be in the hot seat

selon [s(ə)lɔ̃] prép according to; (*en se conformant à*) in accordance with; **~ que** according to whether; **~ moi** as I see it

semaine [s(ə)mɛn] nf week; **en ~** during the week, on weekdays

semblable [sɑ̃blabl] adj similar; (*de ce genre*) : **de ~s mésaventures** such mishaps ♦ nm fellow creature ou man; **~ à** similar to, like

semblant [sɑ̃blɑ̃] nm: **un ~ de ...** a semblance of ...; **faire ~ (de faire)** to pretend (to do)

sembler [sɑ̃ble] vb +attrib to seem ♦ vb impers: **il semble (bien) que/inutile de** it (really) seems ou appears that/useless to; **il me semble que** it seems to me that; **comme bon lui semble** as he sees fit

semelle [s(ə)mɛl] nf sole; (*intérieure*) insole, inner sole

semence [s(ə)mɑ̃s] nf (*graine*) seed

semer [s(ə)me] vt to sow; (*fig: éparpiller*) to scatter; (: *confusion*) to spread; (*fam:*

poursuivants) to lose, shake off; **semé de** (*difficultés*) riddled with

semestre [s(ə)mɛstʀ] nm half-year; (*SCOL*) semester

séminaire [seminɛʀ] nm seminar

semi-remorque [səmiʀəmɔʀk] nm articulated lorry (*BRIT*), semi(trailer) (*US*)

semoule [s(ə)mul] nf semolina

sempiternel, le [sɑ̃pitɛʀnɛl] adj eternal, never-ending

sénat [sena] nm senate; **sénateur** nm senator

sens [sɑ̃s] nm (*PHYSIOL, instinct*) sense; (*signification*) meaning, sense; (*direction*) direction; **à mon ~** to my mind; **dans le ~ des aiguilles d'une montre** clockwise; **~ dessus dessous** upside down; **~ interdit** one-way street; **~ unique** one-way street

sensation [sɑ̃sasjɔ̃] nf sensation; **à ~** (*péj*) sensational; **faire ~** to cause ou create a sensation; **sensationnel, le** adj (*fam*) fantastic, terrific

sensé, e [sɑ̃se] adj sensible

sensibiliser [sɑ̃sibilize] vt: **~ qn à** to make sb sensitive to

sensibilité [sɑ̃sibilite] nf sensitivity

sensible [sɑ̃sibl] adj sensitive; (*aux sens*) perceptible; (*appréciable: différence, progrès*) appreciable, noticeable; **sensiblement** adv (*à peu près*): **ils sont sensiblement du même âge** they are approximately the same age; **sensiblerie** nf sentimentality

sensuel, le [sɑ̃sɥel] adj (*personne*) sensual; (*musique*) sensuous

sentence [sɑ̃tɑ̃s] nf (*jugement*) sentence

sentier [sɑ̃tje] nm path

sentiment [sɑ̃timɑ̃] nm feeling; **sentimental, e, -aux** adj sentimental; (*vie, aventure*) love cpd

sentinelle [sɑ̃tinɛl] nf sentry

sentir [sɑ̃tiʀ] vt (*par l'odorat*) to smell; (*par le goût*) to taste; (*au toucher, fig*) to feel; (*répandre une odeur de*) to smell of; (: *ressemblance*) to smell like ♦ vi to smell; **~ mauvais** to smell bad; **se ~ bien** to feel good; **se ~ mal** (*être indisposé*) to feel unwell ou ill; **se ~ le courage/la force de faire** to feel brave/strong enough to do; **il ne peut pas le ~** (*fam*) he can't stand him

séparation [sepaʀasjɔ̃] nf separation; (*cloison*) division, partition

séparé, e [sepaʀe] adj (*distinct*) separate; (*époux*) separated; **séparément** adv separately

séparer [sepaʀe] vt to separate; (*désunir*) to drive apart; (*détacher*): **~ qch de** to pull sth (off) from; **se ~** vi (*époux, amis*) to separate, part; (*se diviser: route etc*) to divide; **se ~ de** (*époux*) to separate ou part from; (*employé,* *objet personnel*) to part with

sept [sɛt] *num* seven; **septante** (*BELGIQUE, SUISSE*) *adj inv* seventy

septembre [sɛptãbʀ] *nm* September

septennat [sɛptena] *nm* seven year term of office (*of French President*)

septentrional, e, -aux [sɛptãtʀijɔnal, o] *adj* northern

septicémie [sɛptisemi] *nf* blood poisoning, septicaemia

septième [sɛtjɛm] *num* seventh

septique [sɛptik] *adj*: **fosse ~** septic tank

sépulture [sepyltyʀ] *nf* (*tombeau*) burial place, grave

séquelles [sekɛl] *nfpl* after-effects; (*fig*) aftermath *sg*

séquestrer [sekɛstʀe] *vt* (*personne*) to confine illegally; (*biens*) to impound

serai *etc* [sʀe] *vb voir* **être**

serein, e [sʀɛ̃, ɛn] *adj* serene

serez [sʀe] *vb voir* **être**

sergent [sɛʀʒã] *nm* sergeant

série [seʀi] *nf* series *inv*; (*de clés, casseroles, outils*) set; (*catégorie: SPORT*) rank; **en ~** in quick succession; (*COMM*) mass *cpd*; **hors ~** (*COMM*) custom-built

sérieusement [seʀjøzmã] *adv* seriously

sérieux, -euse [seʀjø, jøz] *adj* serious; (*élève, employé*) reliable, responsible; (*client, maison*) reliable, dependable ♦ *nm* seriousness; (*d'une entreprise etc*) reliability; **garder son ~** to keep a straight face; **prendre qch/qn au ~** to take sth/sb seriously

serin [s(ə)ʀɛ̃] *nm* canary

seringue [s(ə)ʀɛ̃g] *nf* syringe

serions [sʀjɔ̃] *vb voir* **être**

serment [sɛʀmã] *nm* (*juré*) oath; (*promesse*) pledge, vow

sermon [sɛʀmɔ̃] *nm* sermon

séronégatif, -ive [seʀonegatif, iv] *adj* (*MÉD*) HIV negative

séropositif, -ive [seʀopozitif, iv] *adj* (*MÉD*) HIV positive

serpent [sɛʀpã] *nm* snake; **serpenter** *vi* to wind

serpillière [sɛʀpijɛʀ] *nf* floorcloth

serre [sɛʀ] *nf* (*AGR*) greenhouse; **~s** *nfpl* (*griffes*) claws, talons

serré, e [seʀe] *adj* (*habits*) tight; (*fig: lutte, match*) tight, close-fought; (*passagers etc*) (tightly) packed; (*réseau*) dense; **avoir le cœur ~** to have a heavy heart

serrer [seʀe] *vt* (*tenir*) to grip *ou* hold tight; (*comprimer, coincer*) to squeeze; (*poings, mâchoires*) to clench; (*suj: vêtement*) to be too tight for; (*ceinture, nœud, vis*) to tighten ♦ *vi*: **~ à droite** to keep *ou* get over to the right; **se ~** *vi* (*se rapprocher*) to squeeze up; **se ~ contre qn** to huddle up to sb; **~ la main**

à qn to shake sb's hand; **~ qn dans ses bras** to hug sb, clasp sb in one's arms

serrure [seʀyʀ] *nf* lock; **serrurier** *nm* locksmith

sert *etc* [sɛʀ] *vb voir* **servir**

servante [sɛʀvãt] *nf* (*maid*)servant

serveur, -euse [sɛʀvœʀ, øz] *nm/f* waiter (waitress)

serviable [sɛʀvjabl] *adj* obliging, willing to help

service [sɛʀvis] *nm* service; (*assortiment de vaisselle*) set, service; (*bureau: de la vente etc*) department, section; (*travail*) duty; **premier ~** (*série de repas*) first sitting; **être de ~** to be on duty; **faire le ~** to serve; **rendre un ~ à qn** to do sb a favour; (*objet: s'avérer utile*) to come in useful *ou* handy for sb; **mettre en ~** to put into service *ou* operation; **~ compris/non compris** service included/not included; **hors ~** out of order; **~ après-vente** after-sales service; **~ d'ordre** police (*ou* stewards) in charge of maintaining order; **~ militaire** military service; **~s secrets** secret service *sg*

serviette [sɛʀvjɛt] *nf* (*de table*) (table) napkin, serviette; (*de toilette*) towel; (*porte-documents*) briefcase; **~ hygiénique** sanitary towel

servir [sɛʀviʀ] *vt* to serve; (*au restaurant*) to wait on; (*au magasin*) to serve, attend to ♦ *vi* (*TENNIS*) to serve; (*CARTES*) to deal; **se ~** *vi* (*prendre d'un plat*) to help o.s.; **vous êtes servi?** are you being served?; **~ à qn** (*diplôme, livre*) to be of use to sb; **~ à qch/faire** (*outil etc*) to be used for sth/doing; **ça ne sert à rien** it's no use; (**~ à qn**) **de** to serve as (for sb); **se ~ de** (*plat*) to help o.s. to; (*voiture, outil, relations*) to use

serviteur [sɛʀvitœʀ] *nm* servant

ses [se] *adj voir* **son¹**

set [sɛt] *nm*: **~ (de table)** tablemat, place mat

seuil [sœj] *nm* doorstep; (*fig*) threshold

seul, e [sœl] *adj* (*sans compagnie*) alone; (*unique*): **un ~ livre** only one book, a single book ♦ *adv* (*vivre*) alone, on one's own ♦ *nm, nf*: **il en reste un(e) ~(e)** there's only one left; **le ~ livre** the only book; **parler tout ~** to talk to oneself; **faire qch (tout) ~** to do sth (all) on one's own *ou* (all) by oneself; **à lui (tout) ~** single-handed, on his own; **se sentir ~** to feel lonely; **seulement** *adv* only; **non seulement ... mais aussi** *ou* **encore** not only ... but also

sève [sɛv] *nf* sap

sévère [sevɛʀ] *adj* severe

sévices [sevis] *nmpl* (physical) cruelty *sg*, ill treatment *sg*

sévir [seviʀ] *vi* (*punir*) to use harsh measures, crack down; (*suj: fléau*) to rage, be rampant

sevrer [səvʀe] *vt* (*enfant etc*) to wean

sexe [sɛks] nm sex; (*organes génitaux*) genitals, sex organs; **sexuel, le** adj sexual

seyant, e [sejɑ̃, ɑ̃t] adj becoming

shampooing [ʃɑ̃pwɛ̃] nm shampoo

short [ʃɔʀt] nm (pair of) shorts pl

---

si [si] nm (MUS) B; (*en chantant la gamme*) ti
♦ adv **1** (*oui*) yes
2 (*tellement*) so; **si gentil/rapidement** so kind/fast; **(tant et) si bien que** so much so that; **si rapide qu'il soit** however fast he may be
♦ conj if; **si tu veux** if you want; **je me demande si** I wonder if ou whether; **si seulement** if only

---

Sicile [sisil] nf: **la ~** Sicily

SIDA [sida] sigle m (= *syndrome immuno-déficitaire acquis*) AIDS sg

sidéré, e [sideʀe] adj staggered

sidérurgie [sideʀyʀʒi] nf steel industry

siècle [sjɛkl] nm century

siège [sjɛʒ] nm seat; (*d'entreprise*) head office; (*d'organisation*) headquarters pl; (MIL) siege; **~ social** registered office; **siéger** vi to sit

sien, ne [sjɛ̃, sjɛn] pron: **le(la) ~(ne), les ~(ne)s** (*homme*) his; (*femme*) hers; (*chose, animal*) its; **les ~s** (*sa famille*) one's family; **faire des ~nes** (*fam*) to be up to one's (usual) tricks

sieste [sjɛst] nf (afternoon) snooze ou nap; **faire la ~** to have a snooze ou nap

sifflement [siflǝmɑ̃] nm: **un ~** a whistle

siffler [sifle] vi (*gén*) to whistle; (*en respirant*) to wheeze; (*serpent, vapeur*) to hiss ♦ vt (*chanson*) to whistle; (*chien etc*) to whistle for; (*fille*) to whistle at; (*pièce, orateur*) to hiss, boo; (*fin du match, départ*) to blow one's whistle for; (*fam: verre*) to guzzle

sifflet [sifle] nm whistle; **coup de ~** whistle

siffloter [siflɔte] vi, vt to whistle

sigle [sigl] nm acronym

signal, -aux [siɲal, o] nm signal; (*indice, écriteau*) sign; **donner le ~ de** to give the signal for; **~ d'alarme** alarm signal; **signaux (lumineux)** (AUTO) traffic signals; **signalement** nm description, particulars pl

signaler [siɲale] vt to indicate; (*personne: faire un signe*) to signal; (*vol, perte*) to report; (*faire remarquer*): **~ qch à qn/(à qn) que** to point out sth to sb/(to sb) that; **se ~ (par)** to distinguish o.s. (by)

signature [siɲatyʀ] nf signature; (*action*) signing

signe [siɲ] nm sign; (TYPO) mark; **faire un ~ de la main** to give a sign with one's hand; **faire ~ à qn** (*fig: contacter*) to get in touch with sb; **faire ~ à qn d'entrer** to motion (to)

sb to come in; **signer** vt to sign; **se signer** vi to cross o.s.

significatif, -ive [siɲifikatif, iv] adj significant

signification [siɲifikasjɔ̃] nf meaning

signifier [siɲifje] vt (*vouloir dire*) to mean; (*faire connaître*): **~ qch (à qn)** to make sth known (to sb)

silence [silɑ̃s] nm silence; (MUS) rest; **garder le ~** to keep silent, say nothing; **silencieux, -euse** adj quiet, silent ♦ nm silencer

silex [silɛks] nm flint

silhouette [silwɛt] nf outline, silhouette; (*lignes, contour*) outline; (*allure*) figure

silicium [silisjɔm] nm silicon

sillage [sijaʒ] nm wake

sillon [sijɔ̃] nm furrow; (*de disque*) groove; **sillonner** vt to criss-cross

simagrées [simagʀe] nfpl fuss sg

similaire [similɛʀ] adj similar; **similicuir** nm imitation leather; **similitude** nf similarity

simple [sɛ̃pl] adj simple; (*non multiple*) single; **~ messieurs** nm (TENNIS) men's singles sg; **~ soldat** private

simplicité [sɛ̃plisite] nf simplicity

simplifier [sɛ̃plifje] vt to simplify

simulacre [simylakʀ] nm (*péj*): **un ~ de** a pretence of

simuler [simyle] vt to sham, simulate

simultané, e [simyltane] adj simultaneous

sincère [sɛ̃sɛʀ] adj sincere; **sincèrement** adv sincerely; (*pour parler franchement*) honestly, really; **sincérité** nf sincerity

sine qua non [sinekwanɔn] adj: **condition ~** indispensable condition

singe [sɛ̃ʒ] nm monkey; (*de grande taille*) ape; **singer** vt to ape, mimic; **singeries** nfpl antics

singulariser [sɛ̃gylaʀize]: **se ~** vi to call attention to o.s.

singularité [sɛ̃gylaʀite] nf peculiarity

singulier, -ière [sɛ̃gylje, jɛʀ] adj remarkable, singular ♦ nm singular

sinistre [sinistʀ] adj sinister ♦ nm (*incendie*) blaze; (*catastrophe*) disaster; (ASSURANCES) damage (*giving rise to a claim*); **sinistré, e** adj disaster-stricken ♦ nm/f disaster victim

sinon [sinɔ̃] conj (*autrement, sans quoi*) otherwise, or else; (*sauf*) except, other than; (*si ce n'est*) if not

sinueux, -euse [sinɥø, øz] adj winding

sinus [sinys] nm (ANAT) sinus; (GÉOM) sine; **sinusite** nf sinusitis

siphon [sifɔ̃] nm (*tube, d'eau gazeuse*) siphon; (*d'évier etc*) U-bend

sirène [siʀɛn] nf siren; **~ d'alarme** fire alarm; (*en temps de guerre*) air-raid siren

sirop [siʀo] nm (*à diluer: de fruit etc*) syrup; (*pharmaceutique*) syrup, mixture; **~ pour la**

toux cough mixture
siroter [siʀɔte] vt to sip
sismique [sismik] adj seismic
site [sit] nm (paysage, environnement) setting; (d'une ville etc: emplacement) site; ~ (pittoresque) beauty spot; ~s touristiques places of interest
sitôt [sito] adv: ~ parti as soon as he etc had left; ~ que as soon as; pas de ~ not for a long time
situation [sitɥasjɔ̃] nf situation; (d'un édifice, d'une ville) position, location; ~ de famille marital status
situé, e [sitɥe] adj situated
situer [sitɥe] vt to site, situate; (en pensée) to set, place; se ~ vi to be situated
six [sis] num six; **sixième** num sixth ♦ nf (SCOL) first form
Skaï ® [skaj] nm Leatherette ®
ski [ski] nm (objet) ski; (sport) skiing; **faire du** ~ to ski; ~ **de fond** cross-country skiing; ~ **nautique** water-skiing; ~ **de piste** downhill skiing; ~ **de randonnée** cross-country skiing; **skier** vi to ski; **skieur, -euse** nm/f skier
slip [slip] nm (sous-vêtement) pants pl, briefs pl; (de bain: d'homme) trunks pl; (: du bikini) (bikini) briefs pl
slogan [slɔgɑ̃] nm slogan
SMIC [smik] sigle m = **salaire minimum interprofessionnel de croissance**
smicard, e [smikaʀ, aʀd] (fam) nm/f minimum wage earner
smoking [smɔkiŋ] nm dinner ou evening suit
SNCF sigle f (= Société nationale des chemins de fer français) French railways
snob [snɔb] adj snobbish ♦ nm/f snob; **snobisme** nm snobbery, snobbishness
sobre [sɔbʀ] adj (personne) temperate, abstemious; (élégance, style) sober
sobriquet [sɔbʀikɛ] nm nickname
social, e, -aux [sɔsjal, jo] adj social
socialisme [sɔsjalism] nm socialism; **socialiste** nm/f socialist
société [sɔsjete] nf society; (sportive) club; (COMM) company; **la ~ de consommation** the consumer society; ~ **anonyme** ≈ limited (BRIT) ou incorporated (US) company
sociologie [sɔsjɔlɔʒi] nf sociology
socle [sɔkl] nm (de colonne, statue) plinth, pedestal; (de lampe) base
socquette [sɔkɛt] nf ankle sock
sœur [sœʀ] nf sister; (religieuse) nun, sister
soi [swa] pron oneself; **en** ~ (intrinsèquement) in itself; **cela va de** ~ that ou it goes without saying; **soi-disant** adj inv so-called ♦ adv supposedly
soie [swa] nf silk; **soierie** nf (tissu) silk
soif [swaf] nf thirst; **avoir** ~ to be thirsty; **donner** ~ **à qn** to make sb thirsty

soigné, e [swaɲe] adj (tenue) well-groomed, neat; (travail) careful, meticulous
soigner [swaɲe] vt (malade, maladie: suj: docteur) to treat; (suj: infirmière, mère) to nurse, look after; (travail, détails) to take care over; (jardin, invités) to look after; **soigneux, -euse** adj (propre) tidy, neat; (appliqué) painstaking, careful
soi-même [swamɛm] pron oneself
soin [swɛ̃] nm (application) care; (propreté, ordre) tidiness, neatness; ~s nmpl (à un malade, blessé) treatment sg, medical attention sg; (hygiène) care sg; **prendre** ~ **de** to take care of, look after; **prendre** ~ **de faire** to take care to do; **les premiers** ~s first aid sg
soir [swaʀ] nm evening; **ce** ~ this evening, tonight; **demain** ~ tomorrow evening, tomorrow night; **soirée** nf evening; (réception) party
soit [swa] vb voir être ♦ conj (à savoir) namely; (ou): ~ ... ~ either ... or ♦ adv so be it, very well; ~ **que** ... ~ **que** ou **ou que** whether ... or whether
soixantaine [swasɑ̃tɛn] nf: **une** ~ (de) sixty or so, about sixty; **avoir la** ~ (âge) to be around sixty
soixante [swasɑ̃t] num sixty; **soixante-dix** num seventy
soja [sɔʒa] nm soya; (graines) soya beans pl; **germes de** ~ beansprouts
sol [sɔl] nm ground; (de logement) floor; (AGR) soil; (MUS) G; (: en chantant la gamme) so(h)
solaire [sɔlɛʀ] adj (énergie etc) solar; (crème etc) sun cpd
soldat [sɔlda] nm soldier
solde [sɔld] nf pay ♦ nm (COMM) balance; ~s nm ou f pl (articles) sale goods; (vente) sales; **en** ~ at sale price; **solder** vt (marchandise) to sell at sale price, sell off; **se solder par** (fig) to end in; **article soldé (à) 10 F** item reduced to 10 F
sole [sɔl] nf sole inv (fish)
soleil [sɔlɛj] nm sun; (lumière) sun(light); (temps ensoleillé) sun(shine); **il fait du** ~ it's sunny; **au** ~ in the sun
solennel, le [sɔlanɛl] adj solemn
solfège [sɔlfɛʒ] nm musical theory
solidaire [sɔlidɛʀ] adj: **être** ~s to show solidarity, stand ou stick together; **être** ~ **de** (collègues) to stand by; **solidarité** nf solidarity; **par solidarité (avec)** in sympathy (with)
solide [sɔlid] adj solid; (mur, maison, meuble) solid, sturdy; (connaissances, argument) sound; (personne, estomac) robust, sturdy ♦ nm solid
soliste [sɔlist] nm/f soloist
solitaire [sɔlitɛʀ] adj (sans compagnie) solitary, lonely; (lieu) lonely ♦ nm/f (ermite)

recluse; (*fig*: *ours*) loner
solitude [sɔlityd] *nf* loneliness; (*tranquillité*)
solitude
solive [sɔliv] *nf* joist
solliciter [sɔlisite] *vt* (*personne*) to appeal to;
(*emploi, faveur*) to seek
sollicitude [sɔlisityd] *nf* concern
soluble [sɔlybl] *adj* soluble
solution [sɔlysjɔ̃] *nf* solution; **~ de facilité**
easy way out
solvable [sɔlvabl] *adj* solvent
sombre [sɔ̃bʀ] *adj* dark; (*fig*) gloomy;
sombrer *vi* (*bateau*) to sink; **sombrer dans**
(*misère, désespoir*) to sink into
sommaire [sɔmɛʀ] *adj* (*simple*) basic;
(*expéditif*) summary ♦ *nm* summary
sommation [sɔmasjɔ̃] *nf* (*JUR*) summons *sg*;
(*avant de faire feu*) warning
somme [sɔm] *nf* (*MATH*) sum; (*quantité*)
amount; (*argent*) sum, amount ♦ *nm*: **faire
un ~** to have a (short) nap; **en ~** all in all;
~ toute all in all
sommeil [sɔmɛj] *nm* sleep; **avoir ~** to be
sleepy; **sommeiller** *vi* to doze
sommer [sɔme] *vt*: **~ qn de faire** to
command *ou* order sb to do
sommes [sɔm] *vb voir* **être**
sommet [sɔmɛ] *nm* top; (*d'une montagne*)
summit, top; (*fig*: *de la perfection, gloire*)
height
sommier [sɔmje] *nm* (*bed*) base
somnambule [sɔmnɑ̃byl] *nm/f* sleepwalker
somnifère [sɔmnifɛʀ] *nm* sleeping drug *no
pl* (*ou* pill)
somnoler [sɔmnɔle] *vi* to doze
somptueux, -euse [sɔ̃ptɥø, øz] *adj*
sumptuous
son¹, sa [sɔ̃, sa] (*pl* **ses**) *adj* (*antécédent
humain*: *mâle*) his; (: *femelle*) her; (: *valeur
indéfinie*) one's, his/her; (*antécédent non
humain*) its
son² [sɔ̃] *nm* sound; (*de blé*) bran
sondage [sɔ̃daʒ] *nm*: **~ (d'opinion)** (opinion)
poll
sonde [sɔ̃d] *nf* (*NAVIG*) lead *ou* sounding line;
(*MÉD*) probe; (*TECH*: *de forage*) borer, driller
sonder [sɔ̃de] *vt* (*NAVIG*) to sound; (*TECH*) to
bore, drill; (*fig*: *personne*) to sound out; **~ le
terrain** (*fig*) to test the ground
songe [sɔ̃ʒ] *nm* dream; **songer** *vi*: **songer à**
(*penser à*) to think over; (*envisager*) to
consider, think of; **songer que** to think that;
songeur, -euse *adj* pensive
sonnant, e [sɔnɑ̃, ɑ̃t] *adj*: **à 8 heures ~es** on
the stroke of 8
sonné, e [sɔne] *adj* (*fam*) cracked; **il est midi
~** it's gone twelve
sonner [sɔne] *vi* to ring ♦ *vt* (*cloche*) to ring;
(*glas, tocsin*) to sound; (*portier, infirmière*) to

ring for; **~ faux** (*instrument*) to sound out of
tune; (*rire*) to ring false
sonnerie [sɔnʀi] *nf* (*son*) ringing; (*sonnette*)
bell; **~ d'alarme** alarm bell
sonnette [sɔnɛt] *nf* bell; **~ d'alarme** alarm
bell
sono [sɔno] *abr f* = **sonorisation**
sonore [sɔnɔʀ] *adj* (*voix*) sonorous, ringing;
(*salle*) resonant; (*film, signal*) sound *cpd*;
sonorisation *nf* (*équipement*: *de salle de
conférences*) public address system, P.A.
system; (: *de discothèque*) sound system;
sonorité *nf* (*de piano, violon*) tone; (*d'une
salle*) acoustics *pl*
sont [sɔ̃] *vb voir* **être**
sophistiqué, e [sɔfistike] *adj* sophisticated
sorbet [sɔʀbɛ] *nm* water ice, sorbet
sorcellerie [sɔʀsɛlʀi] *nf* witchcraft *no pl*
sorcier [sɔʀsje] *nm* sorcerer; **sorcière** *nf*
witch *ou* sorceress
sordide [sɔʀdid] *adj* (*lieu*) squalid; (*action*)
sordid
sornettes [sɔʀnɛt] *nfpl* twaddle *sg*
sort [sɔʀ] *nm* (*destinée*) fate; (*condition*) lot;
(*magique*) curse, spell; **tirer au ~** to draw lots
sorte [sɔʀt] *nf* sort, kind; **de la ~** in that way;
de (telle) ~ que so that; **en quelque ~** in a
way; **faire en ~ que** to see to it that
sortie [sɔʀti] *nf* (*issue*) way out, exit;
(*remarque drôle*) sally; (*promenade*) outing;
(*le soir*: *au restaurant etc*) night out; (*COMM*:
d'un disque) release; (: *d'un livre*) publication;
(: *d'un modèle*) launching; **~s** *nfpl* (*COMM*:
somme) items of expenditure, outgoings;
~ de bain (*vêtement*) bathrobe; **~ de secours**
emergency exit
sortilège [sɔʀtilɛʒ] *nm* (*magic*) spell
sortir [sɔʀtiʀ] *vi* (*gén*) to come out; (*partir, se
promener, aller au spectacle*) to go out;
(*numéro gagnant*) to come up ♦ *vt* (*gén*) to
take out; (*produit, modèle*) to bring out;
(*fam*: *dire*) to come out with; **~ avec qn** to be
going out with sb; **s'en ~** (*malade*) to pull
through; (*d'une difficulté etc*) to get through;
~ de (*endroit*) to go (*ou* come) out of, leave;
(*provenir de*) to come from; (*compétence*) to
be outside
sosie [sozi] *nm* double
sot, sotte [so, sɔt] *adj* silly, foolish ♦ *nm/f*
fool; **sottise** *nf* (*caractère*) silliness,
foolishness; (*action*) silly *ou* foolish thing
sou [su] *nm*: **près de ses ~s** tight-fisted; **sans
le ~** penniless
soubresaut [subʀəso] *nm* start; (*cahot*) jolt
souche [suʃ] *nf* (*d'arbre*) stump; (*de carnet*)
counterfoil (*BRIT*), stub
souci [susi] *nm* (*inquiétude*) worry;
(*préoccupation*) concern; (*BOT*) marigold; **se
faire du ~** to worry; **soucier: se soucier de** *vt*

to care about; **soucieux, -euse** adj concerned, worried

soucoupe [sukup] nf saucer; **~ volante** flying saucer

soudain, e [sudɛ̃, ɛn] adj (douleur, mort) sudden ♦ adv suddenly, all of a sudden

soude [sud] nf soda

souder [sude] vt (avec fil à ~) to solder; (par soudure autogène) to weld; (fig) to bind together

soudoyer [sudwaje] (péj) vt to bribe

soudure [sudyʀ] nf soldering; welding; (joint) soldered joint; weld

souffert, e [sufɛʀ, ɛʀt] pp de **souffrir**

souffle [sufl] nm (en expirant) breath; (en soufflant) puff, blow; (respiration) breathing; (d'explosion, de ventilateur) blast; (du vent) blowing; **être à bout de ~** to be out of breath; **un ~ d'air** a breath of air

soufflé, e [sufle] adj (fam: stupéfié) staggered ♦ nm (CULIN) soufflé

souffler [sufle] vi (gén) to blow; (haleter) to puff (and blow) ♦ vt (feu, bougie) to blow out; (chasser: poussière etc) to blow away; (TECH: verre) to blow; (dire): **~ qch à qn** to whisper sth to sb; **soufflet** nm (instrument) bellows pl; (gifle) slap (in the face); **souffleur** nm (THÉÂTRE) prompter

souffrance [sufʀɑ̃s] nf suffering; **en ~** (affaire) pending

souffrant, e [sufʀɑ̃, ɑ̃t] adj unwell

souffre-douleur [sufʀədulœʀ] nm inv butt, underdog

souffrir [sufʀiʀ] vi to suffer, be in pain ♦ vt to suffer, endure; (supporter) to bear, stand; **~ de** (maladie, froid) to suffer from; **elle ne peut pas le ~** she can't stand ou bear him

soufre [sufʀ] nm sulphur

souhait [swɛ] nm wish; **tous nos ~s de** good wishes ou our best wishes for; **à vos ~s!** bless you!; **souhaitable** adj desirable

souhaiter [swɛte] vt to wish for; **~ la bonne année à qn** to wish sb a happy New Year; **~ que** to hope that

souiller [suje] vt to dirty, soil; (fig: réputation etc) to sully, tarnish

soûl, e [su, sul] adj drunk ♦ nm: **tout son ~** to one's heart's content

soulagement [sulaʒmɑ̃] nm relief

soulager [sulaʒe] vt to relieve

soûler [sule] vt: **~ qn** to get sb drunk; (suj: boisson) to make sb drunk; (fig) to make sb's head spin ou reel; **se ~** vi to get drunk

soulever [sul(ə)ve] vt to lift; (poussière) to send up; (enthousiasme) to arouse; (question, débat) to raise; **se ~** vi (peuple) to rise up; (personne couchée) to lift o.s. up

soulier [sulje] nm shoe

souligner [suliɲe] vt to underline; (fig) to emphasize, stress

soumettre [sumɛtʀ] vt (pays) to subject, subjugate; (rebelle) to put down, subdue; **se ~ (à)** to submit (to); **~ qch à qn** (projet etc) to submit sth to sb

soumis, e [sumi, iz] adj submissive; **soumission** nf submission

soupape [supap] nf valve

soupçon [supsɔ̃] nm suspicion; (petite quantité): **un ~ de** a hint ou touch of; **soupçonner** vt to suspect; **soupçonneux, -euse** adj suspicious

soupe [sup] nf soup

souper [supe] vi to have supper ♦ nm supper

soupeser [supəze] vt to weigh in one's hand(s); (fig) to weigh up

soupière [supjɛʀ] nf (soup) tureen

soupir [supiʀ] nm sigh; **pousser un ~ de soulagement** to heave a sigh of relief

soupirail, -aux [supiʀaj, o] nm (small) basement window

soupirer [supiʀe] vi to sigh

souple [supl] adj supple; (fig: règlement, caractère) flexible; (: démarche, taille) lithe, supple; **souplesse** nf suppleness; (de caractère) flexibility

source [suʀs] nf (point d'eau) spring; (d'un cours d'eau, fig) source; **de bonne ~** on good authority

sourcil [suʀsi] nm (eye)brow; **sourciller** vi: **sans sourciller** without turning a hair ou batting an eyelid

sourd, e [suʀ, suʀd] adj deaf; (bruit) muffled; (douleur) dull ♦ nm/f deaf person; **faire la ~e oreille** to turn a deaf ear; **sourdine** nf (MUS) mute; **en sourdine** softly, quietly; **sourd-muet, sourde-muette** adj deaf-and-dumb ♦ nm/f deaf-mute

souriant, e [suʀjɑ̃, ɑ̃t] adj cheerful

souricière [suʀisjɛʀ] nf mousetrap; (fig) trap

sourire [suʀiʀ] nm smile ♦ vi to smile; **~ à qn** to smile at sb; (fig: plaire à) to appeal to sb; (suj: chance) to smile on sb; **garder le ~** to keep smiling

souris [suʀi] nf mouse

sournois, e [suʀnwa, waz] adj deceitful, underhand

sous [su] prép under; **~ la pluie** in the rain; **~ terre** underground; **~ peu** shortly, before long; **sous-bois** nm inv undergrowth

souscrire [suskʀiʀ]: **~ à** vt to subscribe to

sous...: **sous-directeur, -trice** nm/f assistant manager(-manageress); **sous-entendre** vt to imply, infer; **sous-entendu, e** adj implied ♦ nm innuendo, insinuation; **sous-estimer** vt to underestimate; **sous-jacent, e** adj underlying; **sous-louer** vt to sublet; **sous-marin, e** adj (flore, faune) submarine; (pêche) underwater ♦ nm submarine; **sous-officier** nm ≈ non-commissioned officer (N.C.O.); **sous-produit** nm by-product; **sous-pull** nm thin poloneck jersey; **soussigné, e** adj: **je soussigné** I the undersigned; **sous-sol** nm basement; **sous-titre** nm subtitle

soustraction [sustraksjɔ̃] nf subtraction

soustraire [sustrɛr] vt to subtract, take away; (dérober): ~ **qch à qn** to remove sth from sb; **se** ~ **à** (autorité etc) to elude, escape from

sous...: sous-traitant nm sub-contractor; **sous-traiter** vt to sub-contract; **sous-vêtements** nmpl underwear sg

soutane [sutan] nf cassock, soutane

soute [sut] nf hold

soutenir [sut(ə)nir] vt to support; (assaut, choc) to stand up to, withstand; (intérêt, effort) to keep up; (assurer): ~ **que** to maintain that; **soutenu, e** adj (efforts) sustained, unflagging; (style) elevated

souterrain, e [sutɛrɛ̃, ɛn] adj underground ♦ nm underground passage

soutien [sutjɛ̃] nm support; **soutien-gorge** nm bra

soutirer [sutire] vt: ~ **qch à qn** to squeeze ou get sth out of sb

souvenir [suv(ə)nir] nm (réminiscence) memory; (objet) souvenir ♦ vb: **se** ~ **de** ♦ vt to remember; **se** ~ **que** to remember that; **en** ~ **de** in memory ou remembrance of

souvent [suvɑ̃] adv often; **peu** ~ seldom, infrequently

souverain, e [suv(ə)rɛ̃, ɛn] nm/f sovereign, monarch

soyeux, -euse [swajø, øz] adj silky

soyons etc [swajɔ̃] vb voir **être**

spacieux, -euse [spasjø, jøz] adj spacious, roomy

spaghettis [spageti] nmpl spaghetti sg

sparadrap [sparadra] nm sticking plaster (BRIT), Bandaid ® (US)

spatial, e, -aux [spasjal, jo] adj (AVIAT) space cpd

speaker, ine [spikœr, krin] nm/f announcer

spécial, e, -aux [spesjal, jo] adj special; (bizarre) peculiar; **spécialement** adv especially, particularly; (tout exprès) specially; **spécialiser: se spécialiser** vi to specialize; **spécialiste** nm/f specialist; **spécialité** nf speciality; (branche) special field

spécifier [spesifje] vt to specify, state

spécimen [spesimɛn] nm specimen

spectacle [spɛktakl] nm (scène) sight; (représentation) show; (industrie) show business; **spectaculaire** adj spectacular

spectateur, -trice [spɛktatœr, tris] nm/f (CINÉMA etc) member of the audience; (SPORT) spectator; (d'un événement) onlooker, witness

spéculer [spekyle] vi to speculate

spéléologie [speleɔlɔʒi] nf potholing

sperme [spɛrm] nm semen, sperm

sphère [sfɛr] nf sphere

spirale [spiral] nf spiral

spirituel, le [spirityɛl] adj spiritual; (fin, piquant) witty

splendide [splɑ̃did] adj splendid

sponsoriser [spɔ̃sɔrize] vt to sponsor

spontané, e [spɔ̃tane] adj spontaneous; **spontanéité** nf spontaneity

sport [spɔr] nm sport ♦ adj inv (vêtement) casual; **faire du** ~ to do sport; ~**s d'hiver** winter sports; **sportif, -ive** adj (journal, association, épreuve) sports cpd; (allure, démarche) athletic; (attitude, esprit) sporting

spot [spɔt] nm (lampe) spot(light); (annonce): ~ **(publicitaire)** commercial (break)

square [skwar] nm public garden(s)

squelette [skəlɛt] nm skeleton; **squelettique** adj scrawny

stabiliser [stabilize] vt to stabilize

stable [stabl] adj stable, steady

stade [stad] nm (SPORT) stadium; (phase, niveau) stage

stage [staʒ] nm (cours) training course; ~ **de formation (professionnelle)** vocational (training) course; ~ **de perfectionnement** advanced training course; **stagiaire** nm/f, adj trainee

stagner [stagne] vi to stagnate

stalle [stal] nf stall, box

stand [stɑ̃d] nm (d'exposition) stand; (de foire) stall; ~ **de tir** (à la foire, SPORT) shooting range

standard [stɑ̃dar] adj inv standard ♦ nm switchboard; **standardiste** nm/f switchboard operator

standing [stɑ̃diŋ] nm standing; **de grand** ~ luxury

starter [starter] nm (AUTO) choke

station [stasjɔ̃] nf station; (de bus) stop; (de villégiature) resort; ~ **balnéaire** seaside resort; ~ **de ski** ski resort; ~ **de taxis** taxi rank (BRIT) ou stand (US); **stationnement** nm parking; **stationner** vi to park; **station-service** nf service station

statistique [statistik] nf (science) statistics sg; (rapport, étude) statistic ♦ adj statistical

statue [staty] nf statue

statu quo [statykwo] nm status quo

statut [staty] nm status; ~**s** nmpl (JUR, ADMIN) statutes; **statutaire** adj statutory

Sté abr = **société**

steak [stɛk] nm steak; ~ **haché** hamburger

sténo(dactylo) [steno(daktilo)] nf shorthand typist (BRIT), stenographer (US)

sténo(graphie) [steno(grafi)] nf shorthand

stéréo [stereo] adj stereo

stérile [steril] *adj* sterile

stérilet [sterilɛ] *nm* coil, loop

stériliser [sterilize] *vt* to sterilize

stigmates [stigmat] *nmpl* scars, marks

stimulant [stimylɑ̃] *nm* (*fig*) stimulus, incentive; (*physique*) stimulant

stimuler [stimyle] *vt* to stimulate

stipuler [stipyle] *vt* to stipulate

stock [stɔk] *nm* stock; **stocker** *vt* to stock

stop [stɔp] *nm* (*AUTO: écriteau*) stop sign; (: *feu arrière*) brake-light; **faire du ~** (*fam*) to hitch(hike); **stopper** *vt, vi* to stop, halt

store [stɔʀ] *nm* blind; (*de magasin*) shade, awning

strabisme [strabism] *nm* squinting

strapontin [strapɔ̃tɛ̃] *nm* jump *ou* foldaway seat

stratégie [strateʒi] *nf* strategy; **stratégique** *adj* strategic

stress [strɛs] *nm* stress; **stressant, e** *adj* stressful; **stresser** *vt*: **stresser qn** to make sb (feel) tense

strict, e [strikt] *adj* strict; (*tenue, décor*) severe, plain; **le ~ nécessaire/minimum** the bare essentials/minimum

strident, e [stridɑ̃, ɑ̃t] *adj* shrill, strident

strophe [strɔf] *nf* verse, stanza

structure [stryktyr] *nf* structure

studieux, -euse [stydjø, jøz] *adj* studious

studio [stydjo] *nm* (*logement*) (one-roomed) flatlet (*BRIT*) *ou* apartment (*US*); (*d'artiste, TV etc*) studio

stupéfait, e [stypefɛ, ɛt] *adj* astonished

stupéfiant [stypefjɑ̃, jɑ̃t] *adj* (*étonnant*) stunning, astounding ♦ *nm* (*MÉD*) drug, narcotic

stupéfier [stypefje] *vt* (*étonner*) to stun, astonish

stupeur [stypœʀ] *nf* astonishment

stupide [stypid] *adj* stupid; **stupidité** *nf* stupidity; (*parole, acte*) stupid thing (to do *ou* say)

style [stil] *nm* style

stylé, e [stile] *adj* well-trained

styliste [stilist] *nm/f* designer

stylo [stilo] *nm*: **~ (à encre)** (fountain) pen; **~ (à) bille** ball-point pen; **~-feutre** felt-tip pen

su, e [sy] *pp de* **savoir** ♦ *nm*: **au ~ de** with the knowledge of

suave [sɥav] *adj* sweet

subalterne [sybaltɛrn] *adj* (*employé, officier*) junior; (*rôle*) subordinate, subsidiary ♦ *nm/f* subordinate

subconscient [sypkɔ̃sjɑ̃] *nm* subconscious

subir [sybir] *vt* (*affront, dégâts*) to suffer; (*opération, châtiment*) to undergo

subit, e [sybi, it] *adj* sudden; **subitement** *adv* suddenly, all of a sudden

subjectif, -ive [sybʒɛktif, iv] *adj* subjective

subjonctif [sybʒɔ̃ktif] *nm* subjunctive

subjuguer [sybʒyge] *vt* to captivate

submerger [sybmɛrʒe] *vt* to submerge; (*fig*) to overwhelm

subordonné, e [sybɔrdɔne] *adj, nm/f* subordinate

subrepticement [sybrɛptismɑ̃] *adv* surreptitiously

subside [sybzid] *nm* grant

subsidiaire [sybzidjɛr] *adj*: **question ~** deciding question

subsister [sybziste] *vi* (*rester*) to remain, subsist; (*survivre*) to live on

substance [sypstɑ̃s] *nf* substance

substituer [sypstitɥe] *vt*: **~ qn/qch à** to substitute sb/sth for; **se ~ à qn** (*évincer*) to substitute o.s. for sb

substitut [sypstity] *nm* (*succédané*) substitute

subterfuge [sybtɛrfyʒ] *nm* subterfuge

subtil, e [sybtil] *adj* subtle

subtiliser [sybtilize] *vt*: **~ qch (à qn)** to spirit sth away (from sb)

subvenir [sybvənir]: **~ à** *vt* to meet

subvention [sybvɑ̃sjɔ̃] *nf* subsidy, grant; **subventionner** *vt* to subsidize

suc [syk] *nm* (*BOT*) sap; (*de viande, fruit*) juice

succédané [syksedane] *nm* substitute

succéder [syksede]: **~ à** *vt* to succeed; **se ~** *vi* (*accidents, années*) to follow one another

succès [syksɛ] *nm* success; **avoir du ~** to be a success, be successful; **à ~** successful; **~ de librairie** bestseller; **~ (féminins)** conquests

successif, -ive [syksesif, iv] *adj* successive

successeur [syksesœr] *nm* successor

succession [syksesjɔ̃] *nf* (*série, POL*) succession; (*JUR: patrimoine*) estate, inheritance

succomber [sykɔ̃be] *vi* to die, succumb; (*fig*): **~ à** to succumb to

succulent, e [sykylɑ̃, ɑ̃t] *adj* (*repas, mets*) delicious

succursale [sykyrsal] *nf* branch

sucer [syse] *vt* to suck; **sucette** *nf* (*bonbon*) lollipop; (*de bébé*) dummy (*BRIT*), pacifier (*US*)

sucre [sykr] *nm* (*substance*) sugar; (*morceau*) lump of sugar, sugar lump *ou* cube; **~ d'orge** barley sugar; **~ en morceaux/en poudre** lump/caster sugar; **~ glace/roux** icing/brown sugar; **sucré, e** *adj* (*produit alimentaire*) sweetened; (*au goût*) sweet; **sucrer** *vt* (*thé, café*) to sweeten, put sugar in; **sucreries** *nfpl* (*bonbons*) sweets, sweet things; **sucrier** *nm* (*récipient*) sugar bowl

sud [syd] *nm*: **le ~** the south ♦ *adj inv* south; (*côte*) south, southern; **au ~** (*situation*) in the south; (*direction*) to the south; **au ~ de** (to the) south of; **sud-africain, e** *adj* South

African ♦ *nm/f*: **Sud-Africain, e** South African;
sud-américain, e *adj* South American
♦ *nm/f*: **Sud-Américain, e** South American;
sud-est *nm, adj inv* south-east; **sud-ouest**
nm, adj inv south-west

Suède [sɥɛd] *nf*: **la ~** Sweden; **suédois, e**
adj Swedish ♦ *nm/f*: **Suédois, e** Swede ♦ *nm*
(*LING*) Swedish

suer [sɥe] *vi* to sweat; (*suinter*) to ooze;
sueur *nf* sweat; **en sueur** sweating, in a
sweat; **donner des sueurs froids à qn** to put
sb in(to) a cold sweat

suffire [sɥfiʀ] *vi* (*être assez*): **~ (à qn/pour
qch/pour faire)** to be enough *ou* sufficient
(for sb/for sth/to do); **il suffit d'une
négligence ...** it only takes one act of
carelessness ...; **il suffit qu'on oublie pour que
...** one only needs to forget for ...; **ça suffit!**
that's enough!

suffisamment [sɥfizamɑ̃] *adv* sufficiently,
enough; **~ de** sufficient, enough

suffisant, e [sɥfizɑ̃, ɑ̃t] *adj* sufficient;
(*résultats*) satisfactory; (*vaniteux*) self-
important, bumptious

suffixe [sɥfiks] *nm* suffix

suffoquer [sɥfɔke] *vt* to choke, suffocate;
(*stupéfier*) to stagger, astound ♦ *vi* to choke,
suffocate

suffrage [sɥfʀaʒ] *nm* (*POL*: *voix*) vote

suggérer [sɥgʒeʀe] *vt* to suggest;
suggestion *nf* suggestion

suicide [sɥisid] *nm* suicide; **suicider: se
suicider** *vi* to commit suicide

suie [sɥi] *nf* soot

suinter [sɥɛ̃te] *vi* to ooze

suis [sɥi] *vb voir* **être**; **suivre**

suisse [sɥis] *adj* Swiss ♦ *nm*: **S~** Swiss *pl inv*
♦ *nf*: **la S~** Switzerland; **la S~ romande/
allemande** French-speaking/German-speaking
Switzerland; **Suissesse** *nf* Swiss (woman *ou*
girl)

suite [sɥit] *nf* (*continuation*: *d'énumération
etc*) rest, remainder; (: *de feuilleton*)
continuation; (: *film etc sur le même thème*)
sequel; (*série*) series, succession;
(*conséquence*) result; (*ordre, liaison logique*)
coherence; (*appartement , MUS*) suite;
(*escorte*) retinue, suite; **~s** *nfpl* (*d'une maladie
etc*) effects; **prendre la ~ de** (*directeur etc*) to
succeed, take over from; **donner ~ à** (*requête,
projet*) to follow up; **faire ~ à** to follow;
(faisant) ~ à votre lettre du ... further to your
letter of the ...; **de ~** (*d'affilée*) in succession;
(*immédiatement*) at once; **par la ~** afterwards,
subsequently; **à la ~** one after the other; **à la
~ de** (*derrière*) behind; (*en conséquence de*)
following

suivant, e [sɥivɑ̃, ɑ̃t] *adj* next, following
♦ *prép* (*selon*) according to; **au ~!** next!

suivi, e [sɥivi] *adj* (*effort, qualité*) consistent;
(*cohérent*) coherent; **très/peu ~** (*cours*) well-/
poorly-attended

suivre [sɥivʀ] *vt* (*gén*) to follow; (*SCOL*: *cours*)
to attend; (*comprendre*) to keep up with;
(*COMM*: *article*) to continue to stock ♦ *vi* to
follow; (*élève*: *assimiler*) to keep up; **se ~** *vi*
(*accidents etc*) to follow one after the other;
faire ~ (*lettre*) to forward; **"à ~"** "to be
continued"

sujet, te [syʒɛ, ɛt] *adj*: **être ~ à** (*vertige etc*)
to be liable *ou* subject to ♦ *nm/f* (*d'un
souverain*) subject ♦ *nm* subject; **au ~ de**
about; **~ de conversation** topic *ou* subject of
conversation; **~ d'examen** (*SCOL*) examination
question

summum [sɔ(m)mɔm] *nm*: **le ~ de** the
height of

super [sypɛʀ] (*fam*) *adj inv* terrific, great,
fantastic, super

superbe [sypɛʀb] *adj* magnificent, superb

super(carburant) [sypɛʀ(kaʀbyʀɑ̃)] *nm* ≈
4-star petrol (*BRIT*), ≈ high-octane gasoline
(*US*)

supercherie [sypɛʀʃəʀi] *nf* trick

supérette [sypeʀɛt] *nf* (*COMM*) minimarket,
superette (*US*)

superficie [sypɛʀfisi] *nf* (*surface*) area

superficiel, le [sypɛʀfisjɛl] *adj* superficial

superflu, e [sypɛʀfly] *adj* superfluous

supérieur, e [sypeʀjœʀ] *adj* (*lèvre, étages,
classes*) upper; (*plus élevé*: *température,
niveau, enseignement*): **~ (à)** higher (than);
(*meilleur*: *qualité, produit*): **~ (à)** superior (to);
(*excellent, hautain*) superior ♦ *nm, nf*
superior; **supériorité** *nf* superiority

superlatif [sypɛʀlatif] *nm* superlative

supermarché [sypɛʀmaʀʃe] *nm* supermarket

superposer [sypɛʀpoze] *vt* (*faire chevaucher*)
to superimpose; **lits superposés** bunk beds

superproduction [sypɛʀpʀɔdyksjɔ̃] *nf*
(*film*) spectacular

superpuissance [sypɛʀpɥisɑ̃s] *nf* superpower

superstitieux, -euse [sypɛʀstisjø, jøz] *adj*
superstitious

superviser [sypɛʀvize] *vt* to supervise

supplanter [syplɑ̃te] *vt* to supplant

suppléance [sypleɑ̃s] *nf*: **faire des ~s**
(*professeur*) to do supply teaching;
suppléant, e *adj* (*professeur*) supply *cpd*;
(*juge, fonctionnaire*) deputy *cpd* ♦ *nm/f*
(*professeur*) supply teacher

suppléer [syplee] *vt* (*ajouter*: *mot manquant
etc*) to supply, provide; (*compenser*: *lacune*)
to fill in; **~ à** to make up for

supplément [syplemɑ̃] *nm* supplement; (*de
frites etc*) extra portion; **un ~ de travail** extra
ou additional work; **payer un ~** to pay an

additional charge; **le vin est en ~** wine is extra; **supplémentaire** adj additional, further; (train, bus) relief cpd, extra

supplications [syplikasjɔ̃] nfpl pleas, entreaties

supplice [syplis] nm torture no pl

supplier [syplije] vt to implore, beseech

support [sypɔʀ] nm support; (publicitaire) medium; (audio-visuel) aid

supportable [sypɔʀtabl] adj (douleur) bearable

supporter¹ [sypɔʀtɛʀ] nm supporter, fan

supporter² [sypɔʀte] vt (conséquences, épreuve) to bear, endure; (défauts, personne) to put up with; (suj: chose: chaleur etc) to withstand; (: personne: chaleur, vin) to be able to take

supposer [sypoze] vt to suppose; (impliquer) to presuppose; **à ~ que** supposing (that)

suppositoire [sypozitwaʀ] nm suppository

suppression [sypʀesjɔ̃] nf (voir supprimer) cancellation; removal; deletion

supprimer [sypʀime] vt (congés, service d'autobus etc) to cancel; (emplois, privilèges, témoin gênant) to do away with; (cloison, cause, anxiété) to remove; (clause, mot) to delete

suprême [sypʀɛm] adj supreme

sur [syʀ] prép **1** (position) on; (par-dessus) over; (au-dessus) above; **pose-le sur la table** put it on the table; **je n'ai pas d'argent sur moi** I haven't any money on me

2 (direction) towards; **en allant sur Paris** going towards Paris; **sur votre droite** on ou to your right

3 (à propos de) on, about; **un livre/une conférence sur Balzac** a book/lecture on ou about Balzac

4 (proportion, mesures) out of, by; **un sur 10** one in 10; (SCOL) one out of 10; **4 m sur 2** 4 m by 2

sur ce adv hereupon

sûr, e [syʀ] adj sure, certain; (digne de confiance) reliable; (sans danger) safe; (diagnostic, goût) reliable; **le plus ~ est de** the safest thing is to; **~ de soi** self-confident; **~ et certain** absolutely certain

surcharge [syʀʃaʀʒ] nf (de passagers, marchandises) excess load; **surcharger** vt to overload

surchoix [syʀʃwa] adj inv top-quality

surclasser [syʀklase] vt to outclass

surcroît [syʀkʀwa] nm: **un ~ de** additional +nom; **par** ou **de ~** moreover; **en ~** in addition

surdité [syʀdite] nf deafness

surélever [syʀel(ə)ve] vt to raise, heighten

sûrement [syʀmɑ̃] adv (certainement) certainly; (sans risques) safely

surenchère [syʀɑ̃ʃɛʀ] nf (aux enchères) higher bid; **surenchérir** vi to bid higher; (fig) to try and outbid each other

surent [syʀ] vb voir **savoir**

surestimer [syʀɛstime] vt to overestimate

sûreté [syʀte] nf (sécurité) safety; (exactitude: de renseignements etc) reliability; (d'un geste) steadiness; **mettre en ~** to put in a safe place; **pour plus de ~** as an extra precaution, to be on the safe side

surf [sœʀf] nm surfing

surface [syʀfas] nf surface; (superficie) surface area; **une grande ~** a supermarket; **faire ~** to surface; **en ~** near the surface; (fig) superficially

surfait, e [syʀfɛ, ɛt] adj overrated

surgelé, e [syʀʒale] adj (deep-)frozen ♦ nm: **les ~s** (deep-)frozen food

surgir [syʀʒiʀ] vi to appear suddenly; (fig: problème, conflit) to arise

sur...: surhumain, e adj superhuman; **sur-le-champ** adv immediately; **surlendemain** nm: **le surlendemain (soir)** two days later (in the evening); **le surlendemain de** two days after; **surmenage** nm overwork(ing); **surmener: se surmener** vi to overwork

surmonter [syʀmɔ̃te] vt (vaincre) to overcome; (être au-dessus de) to top

surnaturel, le [syʀnatyʀɛl] adj, nm supernatural

surnom [syʀnɔ̃] nm nickname

surnombre [syʀnɔ̃bʀ] nm: **être en ~** to be too many (ou one too many)

surpeuplé, e [syʀpœple] adj overpopulated

sur-place [syʀplas] nm: **faire du ~~** to mark time

surplomber [syʀplɔ̃be] vt, vi to overhang

surplus [syʀply] nm (COMM) surplus; (reste): **~ de bois** wood left over

surprenant, e [syʀpʀənɑ̃, ɑ̃t] adj amazing

surprendre [syʀpʀɑ̃dʀ] vt (étonner) to surprise; (tomber sur: intrus etc) to catch; (entendre) to overhear

surpris, e [syʀpʀi, iz] adj: **~ (de/que)** surprised (at/that); **surprise** nf surprise; **faire une surprise à qn** to give sb a surprise; **surprise-partie** nf party

surréservation [syʀʀezɛʀvasjɔ̃] nf double booking, overbooking

sursaut [syʀso] nm start, jump; **~ de** (énergie, indignation) sudden fit ou burst of; **en ~** with a start; **sursauter** vi to (give a) start, jump

sursis [syʀsi] nm (JUR: gén) suspended sentence; (fig) reprieve

surtaxe [syʀtaks] nf surcharge

surtout [syʀtu] adv (avant tout, d'abord) above all; (spécialement, particulièrement) especially; **~, ne dites rien!** whatever you do don't say anything!; **~ pas!** certainly *ou* definitely not!; **~ que ...** especially as ...

surveillance [syʀvɛjɑ̃s] *nf* watch; (*POLICE, MIL*) surveillance; **sous ~ médicale** under medical supervision

surveillant, e [syʀvɛjɑ̃, ɑ̃t] *nm/f* (*de prison*) warder; (*SCOL*) monitor

surveiller [syʀveje] *vt* (*enfant, élèves, bagages*) to watch, keep an eye on; (*prisonnier, suspect*) to keep (a) watch on; (*territoire, bâtiment*) to (keep) watch over; (*travaux, cuisson*) to supervise; (*SCOL: examen*) to invigilate; **~ son langage/sa ligne** to watch one's language/figure

survenir [syʀvəniʀ] *vi* (*incident, retards*) to occur, arise; (*événement*) to take place

survêt(ement) [syʀvɛt(mɑ̃)] *nm* tracksuit

survie [syʀvi] *nf* survival; **survivant, e** *nm/f* survivor; **survivre** *vi* to survive; **survivre à** (*accident etc*) to survive

survoler [syʀvɔle] *vt* to fly over; (*fig: livre*) to skim through

survolté, e [syʀvɔlte] *adj* (*fig*) worked up

sus [sy(s)]: **en ~ de** *prép* in addition to, over and above; **en ~** in addition

susceptible [syseptibl] *adj* touchy, sensitive; **~ de faire** (*hypothèse*) liable to do

susciter [sysite] *vt* (*admiration*) to arouse; (*ennuis*) **~ (à qn)** to create (for sb)

suspect, e [syspɛ(kt), ɛkt] *adj* suspicious; (*témoignage, opinions*) suspect ♦ *nm/f* suspect; **suspecter** *vt* to suspect; (*honnêteté de qn*) to question, have one's suspicions about

suspendre [syspɑ̃dʀ] *vt* (*accrocher: vêtement*): **~ qch (à)** to hang sth up (on); (*interrompre, démettre*) to suspend; **se ~ à** to hang from

suspendu, e [syspɑ̃dy] *adj* (*accroché*): **~ à** hanging on (*ou* from); (*perché*): **~ au-dessus de** suspended over

suspens [syspɑ̃]: **en ~** *adv* (*affaire*) in abeyance; **tenir en ~** to keep in suspense

suspense [syspɛns, syspɑ̃s] *nm* suspense

suspension [syspɑ̃sjɔ̃] *nf* suspension; (*lustre*) light fitting *ou* fitment

sut [sy] *vb voir* **savoir**

suture [sytyʀ] *nf* (*MÉD*): **point de ~** stitch

svelte [svɛlt] *adj* slender, svelte

SVP *abr* (= *s'il vous plaît*) please

sweat-shirt [switʃœʀt] (*pl* **~~s**) *nm* sweatshirt

syllabe [si(l)lab] *nf* syllable

symbole [sɛ̃bɔl] *nm* symbol; **symbolique** *adj* symbolic(al); (*geste, offrande*) token *cpd*; **symboliser** *vt* to symbolize

symétrique [simetʀik] *adj* symmetrical

sympa [sɛ̃pa] (*fam*) *adj inv* nice; **sois ~,**

prête-le moi be a pal and lend it to me

sympathie [sɛ̃pati] *nf* (*inclination*) liking; (*affinité*) friendship; (*condoléances*) sympathy; **j'ai beaucoup de ~ pour lui** I like him a lot; **sympathique** *adj* nice, friendly

sympathisant, e [sɛ̃patizɑ̃, ɑ̃t] *nm/f* sympathizer

sympathiser [sɛ̃patize] *vi* (*voisins etc*): **s'entendre** to get on (*BRIT*) *ou* along (*US*) (well)

symphonie [sɛ̃fɔni] *nf* symphony

symptôme [sɛ̃ptom] *nm* symptom

synagogue [sinagɔg] *nf* synagogue

syncope [sɛ̃kɔp] *nf* (*MÉD*) blackout; **tomber en ~** to faint, pass out

syndic [sɛ̃dik] *nm* (*d'immeuble*) managing agent

syndical, e, -aux [sɛ̃dikal, o] *adj* (trade) union *cpd*; **syndicaliste** *nm/f* trade unionist

syndicat [sɛ̃dika] *nm* (*d'ouvriers, employés*) (trade) union; **~ d'initiative** tourist office; **syndiqué, e** *adj* belonging to a (trade) union; **syndiquer: se syndiquer** *vi* to form a trade union; (*adhérer*) to join a trade union

synonyme [sinɔnim] *adj* synonymous ♦ *nm* synonym; **~ de** synonymous with

syntaxe [sɛ̃taks] *nf* syntax

synthèse [sɛ̃tɛz] *nf* synthesis

synthétique [sɛ̃tetik] *adj* synthetic

Syrie [siʀi] *nf*: **la ~** Syria

systématique [sistematik] *adj* systematic

système [sistɛm] *nm* system; **~ D** (*fam*) resourcefulness

T, t

t' [t] *pron voir* **te**

ta [ta] *adj voir* **ton**[1]

tabac [taba] *nm* tobacco; (*magasin*) tobacconist's (shop); **~ blond/brun** light/dark tobacco

tabagisme [tabaʒism] *nm*: **~ passif** passive smoking

tabasser [tabase] (*fam*) *vt* to beat up

table [tabl] *nf* table; **à ~!** dinner etc is ready!; **se mettre à ~** to sit down to eat; **mettre la ~** to lay the table; **faire ~ rase de** to make a clean sweep of; **~ à repasser** ironing board; **~ de cuisson** (*à l'électricité*) hotplate; (*au gaz*) gas ring; **~ de nuit** *ou* **de chevet** bedside table; **~ des matières** (table of) contents *pl*; **~ d'orientation** viewpoint indicator; **~ roulante** trolley

tableau, x [tablo] *nm* (*peinture*) painting; (*reproduction, fig*) picture; (*panneau*) board; (*schéma*) table, chart; **~ d'affichage** notice board; **~ de bord** dashboard; (*AVIAT*) instrument panel; **~ noir** blackboard

tabler [table] vi: ~ **sur** to bank on

tablette [tablɛt] nf (*planche*) shelf; ~ **de chocolat** bar of chocolate

tableur [tablœʀ] nm spreadsheet

tablier [tablije] nm apron

tabou [tabu] nm taboo

tabouret [tabuʀɛ] nm stool

tac [tak] nm: **il m'a répondu du ~ au ~** he answered me right back

tache [taʃ] nf (*saleté*) stain, mark; (*ART, de couleur, lumière*) spot; ~ **de rousseur** freckle

tâche [taʃ] nf task

tacher [taʃe] vt to stain, mark

tâcher [taʃe] vi: ~ **de faire** to try *ou* endeavour to do

tacheté, e [taʃte] adj spotted

tacot [tako] (*péj*) nm banger (*BRIT*), (old) heap

tact [takt] nm tact; **avoir du ~** to be tactful

tactique [taktik] adj tactical ♦ nf (*technique*) tactics sg; (*plan*) tactic

taie [tɛ] nf: ~ (**d'oreiller**) pillowslip, pillowcase

taille [taj] nf cutting; (*d'arbre etc*) pruning; (*milieu du corps*) waist; (*hauteur*) height; (*grandeur*) size; **de ~ à faire** capable of doing; **de ~** sizeable; **taille-crayon(s)** nm pencil sharpener

tailler [taje] vt (*pierre, diamant*) to cut; (*arbre, plante*) to prune; (*vêtement*) to cut out; (*crayon*) to sharpen

tailleur [tajœʀ] nm (*couturier*) tailor; (*vêtement*) suit; **en ~** (*assis*) cross-legged

taillis [taji] nm copse

taire [tɛʀ] vi: **faire ~ qn** to make sb be quiet; **se ~** vi to be silent *ou* quiet

talc [talk] nm talc, talcum powder

talent [talɑ̃] nm talent

talkie-walkie [tokiwoki] nm walkie-talkie

taloche [talɔʃ] (*fam*) nf clout, cuff

talon [talɔ̃] nm heel; (*de chèque, billet*) stub, counterfoil (*BRIT*); ~**s plats/aiguilles** flat/stiletto heels

talonner [talɔne] vt (*suivre*) to follow hot on the heels of; (*harceler*) to hound

talus [taly] nm embankment

tambour [tɑ̃buʀ] nm (*MUS, aussi*) drum; (*musicien*) drummer; (*porte*) revolving door(s pl); **tambourin** nm tambourine; **tambouriner** vi to drum; **tambouriner à/sur** to drum on

tamis [tami] nm sieve

Tamise [tamiz] nf: **la ~** the Thames

tamisé, e [tamize] adj (*fig*) subdued, soft

tampon [tɑ̃pɔ̃] nm (*de coton, d'ouate*) wad, pad; (*amortisseur*) buffer; (*bouchon*) plug, stopper; (*cachet, timbre*) stamp; (*mémoire*) ~ (*INFORM*) buffer; ~ (**hygiénique**) tampon; **tamponner** vt (*timbres*) to stamp; (*heurter*) to crash *ou* ram into; **tamponneuse** adj f:

autos tamponneuses dodgems

tandem [tɑ̃dɛm] nm tandem

tandis [tɑ̃di]: ~ **que** conj while

tanguer [tɑ̃ge] vi to pitch (and toss)

tanière [tanjɛʀ] nf lair, den

tanné, e [tane] adj weather-beaten

tanner [tane] vt to tan; (*fam: harceler*) to badger

tant [tɑ̃] adv so much; ~ **de** (*sable, eau*) so much; (*gens, livres*) so many; ~ **que** as long as; (*autant que*) as much as; ~ **mieux** that's great; (*avec une certaine réserve*) so much the better; ~ **pis** too bad; (*conciliant*) never mind

tante [tɑ̃t] nf aunt

tantôt [tɑ̃to] adv (*parfois*): ~ ... ~ **now** ... now; (*cet après-midi*) this afternoon

taon [tɑ̃] nm horsefly

tapage [tapaʒ] nm uproar, din

tapageur, -euse [tapaʒœʀ, øz] adj noisy; (*voyant*) loud, flashy

tape [tap] nf slap

tape-à-l'œil [tapalœj] adj inv flashy, showy

taper [tape] vt (*porte*) to bang, slam; (*enfant*) to slap; (*dactylographier*) to type (out); (*fam: emprunter*): ~ **qn de 10 F** to touch sb for 10 F ♦ vi (*soleil*) to beat down; **se ~** vt (*repas*) to put away; (*fam: corvée*) to get landed with; ~ **sur qn** to thump sb; (*fig*) to run sb down; ~ **sur un clou** to hit a nail; ~ **sur la table** to bang on the table; ~ **à** (*porte etc*) to knock on; ~ **dans** (*se servir*) to dig into; ~ **des mains/pieds** to clap one's hands/stamp one's feet; ~ (**à la machine**) to type; **se ~ un travail** (*fam*) to land o.s. a job

tapi, e [tapi] adj (*blotti*) crouching; (*caché*) hidden away

tapis [tapi] nm carpet; (*petit*) rug; **mettre sur le ~** (*fig*) to bring up for discussion; ~ **de bain** bath mat; ~ **de sol** (*de tente*) groundsheet; ~ **roulant** (*pour piétons*) moving walkway; (*pour bagages*) carousel

tapisser [tapise] vt (*avec du papier peint*) to paper; (*recouvrir*): ~ **qch (de)** to cover sth (with); **tapisserie** nf (*tenture, broderie*) tapestry; (*papier peint*) wallpaper; **tapissier, -ière** nm/f: **tapissier-décorateur** interior decorator

tapoter [tapɔte] vt (*joue, main*) to pat; (*objet*) to tap

taquin, e [takɛ̃, in] adj teasing; **taquiner** vt to tease

tarabiscoté, e [taʀabiskɔte] adj over-ornate, fussy

tard [taʀ] adv late; **plus ~** later (on); **au plus ~** at the latest; **sur le ~** late in life

tarder [taʀde] vi (*chose*) to be a long time coming; (*personne*): ~ **à faire** to delay doing; **il me tarde d'être** I am longing to be; **sans (plus) ~** without (further) delay

tardif, -ive [taʀdif, iv] *adj* late

taré, e [taʀe] *nm/f* cretin

tarif [taʀif] *nm*: ~ **des consommations** price list; ~**s postaux/douaniers** postal/customs rates; ~ **des taxis** taxi fares; ~ **plein/réduit** (*train*) full/reduced fare; (*téléphone*) peak/off-peak rate

tarir [taʀiʀ] *vi* to dry up, run dry

tarte [taʀt] *nf* tart; ~ **aux fraises** strawberry tart; ~ **Tatin** ≈ apple upside-down tart

tartine [taʀtin] *nf* slice of bread; ~ **de miel** slice of bread and honey; **tartiner** *vt* to spread; **fromage à tartiner** cheese spread

tartre [taʀtʀ] *nm* (*des dents*) tartar; (*de bouilloire*) fur, scale

tas [ta] *nm* heap, pile; (*fig*): **un ~ de** heaps of, lots of; **en ~** in a heap *ou* pile; **formé sur le ~** trained on the job

tasse [tas] *nf* cup; ~ **à café** coffee cup

tassé, e [tase] *adj*: **bien ~** (*café etc*) strong

tasser [tase] *vt* (*terre, neige*) to pack down; (*entasser*): ~ **qch dans** to cram sth into; **se ~** *vi* (*se serrer*) to squeeze up; (*s'affaisser*) to settle; (*fig*) to settle down

tata [tata] *nf* auntie

tâter [tate] *vt* to feel; (*fig*) to try out; **se ~** (*hésiter*) to be in two minds; ~ **de** (*prison etc*) to have a taste of

tatillon, ne [tatijɔ̃, ɔn] *adj* pernickety

tâtonnement [tatɔnmɑ̃] *nm*: **par ~s** (*fig*) by trial and error

tâtonner [tatɔne] *vi* to grope one's way along

tâtons [tatɔ̃]: **à ~** *adv*: **chercher/avancer à ~** to grope around for/advance one's way forward

tatouage [tatwaʒ] *nm* tattoo

tatouer [tatwe] *vt* to tattoo

taudis [todi] *nm* hovel, slum

taule [tol] (*fam*) *nf* nick (*fam*), prison

taupe [top] *nf* mole

taureau, x [tɔʀo] *nm* bull; (*signe*): **le T~** Taurus

tauromachie [tɔʀɔmaʃi] *nf* bullfighting

taux [to] *nm* rate; (*d'alcool*) level; ~ **de change** exchange rate; ~ **d'intérêt** interest rate

taxe [taks] *nf* tax; (*douanière*) duty; **toutes ~s comprises** inclusive of tax; **la boutique hors ~s** the duty free shop; ~ **à la valeur ajoutée** value added tax

taxer [takse] *vt* (*personne*) to tax; (*produit*) to put a tax on, tax

taxi [taksi] *nm* taxi; (*chauffeur: fam*) taxi driver

Tchécoslovaquie [tʃekɔslɔvaki] *nf* Czechoslovakia; **tchèque** *adj* Czech ♦ *nm/f*: **Tchèque** Czech ♦ *nm* (*LING*) Czech; **la République tchèque** the Czech Republic

te, t' [tə] *pron* you; (*réfléchi*) yourself

technicien, ne [tɛknisjɛ̃, jɛn] *nm/f* technician

technico-commercial, e, -aux [tɛknikokɔmɛʀsjal, jo] *adj*: **agent ~-~** sales technician

technique [tɛknik] *adj* technical ♦ *nf* technique; **techniquement** *adv* technically

technologie [tɛknɔlɔʒi] *nf* technology; **technologique** *adj* technological

teck [tɛk] *nm* teak

tee-shirt [tiʃœʀt] *nm* T-shirt, tee-shirt

teignais *etc* [tɛɲɛ] *vb voir* **teindre**

teindre [tɛ̃dʀ] *vt* to dye; **se ~ les cheveux** to dye one's hair; **teint, e** *adj* dyed ♦ *nm* (*du visage*) complexion; (*momentané*) colour ♦ *nf* shade; **grand teint** colourfast

teinté, e [tɛ̃te] *adj*: ~ **de** (*fig*) tinged with

teinter [tɛ̃te] *vt* (*verre, papier*) to tint; (*bois*) to stain

teinture [tɛ̃tyʀ] *nf* dye; ~ **d'iode** tincture of iodine; **teinturerie** *nf* dry cleaner's; **teinturier** *nm* dry cleaner

tel, telle [tɛl] *adj* (*pareil*) such; (*comme*): ~ **un/des ...** like a/like ...; (*indéfini*) such-and-such a; (*intensif*): **un ~/de tels ...** such (a)/such ...; **rien de ~** nothing like it; ~ **que** like, such as; ~ **quel** as it is ou stands (*ou* was *etc*); **venez ~ jour** come on such-and-such a day

télé [tele] (*fam*) *nf* TV

télé...: **télécabine** *nf* (*benne*) cable car; **télécarte** *nf* phonecard; **télécommande** *nf* remote control; **télécopie** *nf* fax; **envoyer qch par télécopie** to fax sth; **télécopieur** *nm* fax machine; **télédistribution** *nf* cable TV; **téléférique** *nm* = **téléphérique**; **télégramme** *nm* telegram; **télégraphier** *vt* to telegraph, cable; **téléguider** *vt* to radio-control; **télématique** *nf* telematics *sg*; **téléobjectif** *nm* telephoto lens *sg*; **télépathie** *nf* telepathy; **téléphérique** *nm* cable car

téléphone [telefɔn] *nm* telephone; **avoir le ~** to be on the (tele)phone; **au ~** on the phone; ~ **mobile** mobile phone; ~ **rouge** hot line; ~ **sans fil** cordless (tele)phone; ~ **de voiture** car phone; **téléphoner** *vi* to make a phone call; **téléphoner à** to phone, call up; **téléphonique** *adj* (tele)phone *cpd*

télescope [teleskɔp] *nm* telescope

télescoper [teleskɔpe] *vt* to smash up; **se ~** (*véhicules*) to concertina

télé...: **téléscripteur** *nm* teleprinter; **télésiège** *nm* chairlift; **téléski** *nm* ski-tow; **téléspectateur, -trice** *nm/f* (television) viewer; **télévente** *nf* telesales; **téléviseur** *nm* television set; **télévision** *nf* television; **à la télévision** on television

télex [telɛks] *nm* telex

telle [tɛl] *adj voir* **tel**; **tellement** *adv* (*tant*) so much; (*si*) so; **tellement de** (*sable, eau*) so much; (*gens, livres*) so many; **il s'est endormi**

téméraire → térébenthine

194

tellement il était fatigué he was so tired (that) he fell asleep; **pas tellement** not (all) that much; not (all) that +*adjectif*

téméraire [temeʀɛʀ] *adj* reckless, rash; **témérité** *nf* recklessness, rashness

témoignage [temwaɲaʒ] *nm* (*JUR: déclaration*) testimony *no pl*, evidence *no pl*; (*rapport, récit*) account; (*fig: d'affection etc: cadeau*) token, mark; (: *geste*) expression

témoigner [temwaɲe] *vt* (*intérêt, gratitude*) to show ♦ *vi* (*JUR*) to testify, give evidence; **~ de** to bear witness to, testify to

témoin [temwɛ̃] *nm* witness ♦ *adj*: **appartement ~** show flat (*BRIT*); **être ~ de** to witness; **~ oculaire** eyewitness

tempe [tɑ̃p] *nf* temple

tempérament [tɑ̃peʀamɑ̃] *nm* temperament, disposition; **à ~** (*vente*) on deferred (payment) terms; (*achat*) by instalments, hire purchase *cpd*

température [tɑ̃peʀatyʀ] *nf* temperature; **avoir** *ou* **faire de la ~** to be running *ou* have a temperature

tempéré, e [tɑ̃peʀe] *adj* temperate

tempête [tɑ̃pɛt] *nf* storm; **~ de sable/neige** sand/snowstorm

temple [tɑ̃pl] *nm* temple; (*protestant*) church

temporaire [tɑ̃pɔʀɛʀ] *adj* temporary

temps [tɑ̃] *nm* (*atmosphérique*) weather; (*durée*) time; (*époque*) time, times *pl*; (*LING*) tense; (*MUS*) beat; (*TECH*) stroke; **un ~ de chien** (*fam*) rotten weather; **quel ~ fait-il?** what's the weather like?; **il fait beau/mauvais ~** the weather is fine/bad; **avoir le ~/pas le ~** to have time/plenty of time; **en ~ de paix/guerre** in peacetime/wartime; **en ~ utile** *ou* **voulu** in due time *ou* course; **ces derniers ~** lately; **dans quelque ~** in a (little) while; **de ~ en ~, de ~ à autre** from time to time; **à ~** (*partir, arriver*) in time; **à ~ complet, à plein ~** full-time; **à ~ partiel** part-time; **dans le ~** at one time; **~ d'arrêt** pause, halt; **~ mort** (*COMM*) slack period

tenable [t(ə)nabl] *adj* bearable

tenace [tənas] *adj* persistent

tenailler [tənɑje] *vt* (*fig*) to torment

tenailles [tənɑj] *nfpl* pincers

tenais *etc* [t(ə)nɛ] *vb voir* **tenir**

tenancier, -ière [tənɑ̃sje] *nm/f* manager/manageress

tenant, e [tənɑ̃, ɑ̃t] *nm/f* (*SPORT*): **~ du titre** title-holder

tendance [tɑ̃dɑ̃s] *nf* tendency; (*opinions*) leanings *pl*, sympathies *pl*; (*évolution*) trend; **avoir ~ à** to have a tendency to, tend to

tendeur [tɑ̃dœʀ] *nm* (*attache*) elastic strap

tendre [tɑ̃dʀ] *adj* tender; (*bois, roche, couleur*) soft ♦ *vt* (*élastique, peau*) to stretch; (*corde*) to tighten; (*muscle*) to tense; (*fig*:

piège) to set, lay; (*donner*): **~ qch à qn** to hold sth out to sb; (*offrir*) to offer sb sth; **se ~** *vi* (*corde*) to tighten; (*relations*) to become strained; **~ à qch/à faire** to tend towards sth/to do; **~ l'oreille** to prick up one's ears; **~ la main/le bras** to hold out one's hand/stretch out one's arm; **tendrement** *adv* tenderly; **tendresse** *nf* tenderness

tendu, e [tɑ̃dy] *pp de* **tendre** ♦ *adj* (*corde*) tight; (*muscles*) tensed; (*relations*) strained

ténèbres [tenɛbʀ] *nfpl* darkness *sg*

teneur [tənœʀ] *nf* content; (*d'une lettre*) terms *pl*, content

tenir [t(ə)niʀ] *vt* to hold; (*magasin, hôtel*) to run; (*promesse*) to keep ♦ *vi* to hold; (*neige, gel*) to last; **se ~** *vi* (*avoir lieu*) to be held, take place; (*être: personne*) to stand; **~ à** (*personne, objet*) to be attached to; (*réputation*) to care about; **~ à faire** to be determined to do; **~ de** (*ressembler à*) to take after; **ça ne tient qu'à lui** it is entirely up to him; **~ qn pour** to regard sb as; **~ qch de qn** (*histoire*) to have heard *ou* learnt sth from sb; (*qualité, défaut*) to have inherited *ou* got sth from sb; **~ dans** to fit into; **~ compte de qch** to take sth into account; **~ les comptes** to keep the books; **~ bon** to stand fast; **~ le coup** to hold out; **~ au chaud** to keep hot; **tiens/tenez, voilà le stylo** there's the pen!; **tiens, voilà Alain!** look, here's Alain!; **tiens?** (*surprise*) really?; **se ~ droit** to stand (*ou* sit) up straight; **bien se ~** to behave well; **se ~ à qch** to hold on to sth; **s'en ~ à qch** to confine o.s. to sth

tennis [tenis] *nm* tennis; (*court*) tennis court ♦ *nm* *ou* f *pl* (*aussi*: **chaussures de ~**) tennis *ou* gym shoes; **~ de table** table tennis; **tennisman** *nm* tennis player

tension [tɑ̃sjɔ̃] *nf* tension; (*MÉD*) blood pressure; **avoir de la ~** to have high blood pressure

tentation [tɑ̃tasjɔ̃] *nf* temptation

tentative [tɑ̃tativ] *nf* attempt

tente [tɑ̃t] *nf* tent

tenter [tɑ̃te] *vt* (*éprouver, attirer*) to tempt; (*essayer*): **~ qch/de faire** to attempt *ou* try sth/to do; **~ sa chance** to try one's luck

tenture [tɑ̃tyʀ] *nf* hanging

tenu, e [t(ə)ny] *pp de* **tenir** ♦ *adj* (*maison, comptes*): **bien ~** well-kept; (*obligé*): **~ de faire** obliged to do ♦ *nf* (*vêtements*) clothes *pl*; (*comportement*) (good) manners *pl*, good behaviour; (*d'une maison*) upkeep; **en petite ~e** scantily dressed *ou* clad; **~e de route** (*AUTO*) road-holding; **~e de soirée** evening dress

ter [tɛʀ] *adj*: **16** ~ 16b *ou* B

térébenthine [teʀebɑ̃tin] *nf*: **(essence de) ~** (oil of) turpentine

Tergal ® [tɛʀgal] nm Terylene ®
terme [tɛʀm] nm term; (fin) end; **à court/ long ~** ♦ adj short-/long-term ♦ adv in the short/long term; **avant ~** (MÉD) prematurely; **mettre un ~ à** to put an end ou a stop to; **en bons ~s** on good terms
terminaison [tɛʀminɛzɔ̃] nf (LING) ending
terminal [tɛʀminal, o] nm terminal; **terminale** nf (SCOL) ≈ sixth form ou year (BRIT), ≈ twelfth grade (US)
terminer [tɛʀmine] vt to finish; **se ~** vi to end
terne [tɛʀn] adj dull
ternir [tɛʀniʀ] vt to dull; (fig) to sully, tarnish; **se ~** vi to become dull
terrain [teʀɛ̃] nm (gén, aussi ÉLEC) ground; (COMM: étendue de terre) land no pl; (parcelle) plot (of land); (à bâtir) site; **sur le ~** (fig) on the field; **~ d'aviation** airfield; **~ de camping** campsite; **~ de football/rugby** football/rugby pitch (BRIT) ou field (US); **~ de golf** golf course; **~ de jeu** games field; (pour les petits) playground; **~ de sport** sports ground; **~ vague** waste ground no pl
terrasse [teʀas] nf terrace; **à la ~** (café) outside; **terrasser** vt (adversaire) to floor; (suj: maladie etc) to strike down
terre [tɛʀ] nf (gén, aussi ÉLEC) earth; (substance) soil, earth; (opposé à mer) land no pl; (contrée) land; **~s** nfpl (terrains) lands, land sg; **en ~** (pipe, poterie) clay cpd; **à ~** ou **par ~** (mettre, être, s'asseoir) on the ground (ou floor); (jeter, tomber) to the ground, down; **~ à ~** adj inv down-to-earth; **~ cuite** terracotta; **la ~ ferme** dry land; **~ glaise** clay
terreau [teʀo] nm compost
terre-plein [tɛʀplɛ̃] nm platform; (sur chaussée) central reservation
terrer [teʀe] vi: **se ~** vi to hide away
terrestre [teʀɛstʀ] adj (surface) earth's, of the earth; (BOT, ZOOL, MIL) land cpd; (REL) earthly
terreur [teʀœʀ] nf terror no pl
terrible [teʀibl] adj terrible, dreadful; (fam) terrific; **pas ~** nothing special
terrien, ne [teʀjɛ̃, jɛn] adj: **propriétaire ~** landowner ♦ nm/f (non martien etc) earthling
terrier [teʀje] nm burrow, hole; (chien) terrier
terrifier [teʀifje] vt to terrify
terrine [teʀin] nf (récipient) terrine; (CULIN) pâté
territoire [teʀitwaʀ] nm territory
terroir [teʀwaʀ] nm: **accent du ~** country accent
terroriser [teʀɔʀize] vt to terrorize
terrorisme [teʀɔʀism] nm terrorism; **terroriste** nm/f terrorist
tertiaire [tɛʀsjɛʀ] adj tertiary ♦ nm (ÉCON) service industries pl

tertre [tɛʀtʀ] nm hillock, mound
tes [te] adj voir **ton**[1]
tesson [tesɔ̃] nm: **~ de bouteille** piece of broken bottle
test [tɛst] nm test
testament [tɛstamɑ̃] nm (JUR) will; (REL) Testament; (fig) legacy
tester [tɛste] vt to test
testicule [tɛstikyl] nm testicle
tétanos [tetanos] nm tetanus
têtard [tetaʀ] nm tadpole
tête [tɛt] nf head; (cheveux) hair no pl; (visage) face; **de ~** adj (wagon etc) front cpd ♦ adv (calculer) in one's head, mentally; **tenir ~ à qn** to stand up to sb; **la ~ en bas** with one's head down; **la ~ la première** (tomber) headfirst; **faire une ~** (FOOTBALL) to head the ball; **faire la ~** (fig) to sulk; **en ~** at the front; (SPORT) in the lead; **à la ~ de** at the head of; **à ~ reposée** in a more leisurely moment; **n'en faire qu'à sa ~** to do as one pleases; **en avoir par-dessus la ~** to be fed up; **en ~ à ~** in private, alone together; **de la ~ aux pieds** from head to toe; **~ de lecture** (playback) head; **~ de liste** (POL) chief candidate; **~ de série** (TENNIS) seeded player, seed; **tête-à-queue** nm inv: **faire un tête-à-queue** to spin round
téter [tete] vt: **~ (sa mère)** to suck at one's mother's breast, feed
tétine [tetin] nf teat; (sucette) dummy (BRIT), pacifier (US)
têtu, e [tety] adj stubborn, pigheaded
texte [tɛkst] nm text; (morceau choisi) passage
textile [tɛkstil] adj textile cpd ♦ nm textile; **le ~** the textile industry
texto [tɛksto] (fam) adj word for word
texture [tɛkstyʀ] nf texture
thaïlandais, e [tajlɑ̃dɛ, ɛz] adj Thai ♦ nm/f: **T~, e** Thai
Thaïlande [tajlɑ̃d] nf Thailand
TGV sigle m (= train à grande vitesse) high-speed train
thé [te] nm tea; **~ au citron** lemon tea; **~ au lait** tea with milk; **prendre le ~** to have tea; **faire le ~** to make the tea
théâtral, e, -aux [teɑtʀal, o] adj theatrical
théâtre [teɑtʀ] nm theatre; (péj: simulation) playacting; (fig: lieu): **le ~ de** the scene of; **faire du ~** to act
théière [tejɛʀ] nf teapot
thème [tɛm] nm theme; (SCOL: traduction) prose (composition)
théologie [teɔlɔʒi] nf theology
théorie [teɔʀi] nf theory; **théorique** adj theoretical
thérapie [teʀapi] nf therapy
thermal, e, -aux [tɛʀmal, o] adj: **station ~e** spa; **cure ~e** water cure

thermes [tɛʀm] nmpl thermal baths

thermomètre [tɛʀmɔmɛtʀ] nm thermometer

thermos ® [tɛʀmos] nm ou nf: (**bouteille**) ~ vacuum ou Thermos ® flask

thermostat [tɛʀmɔsta] nm thermostat

thèse [tɛz] nf thesis

thon [tɔ̃] nm tuna (fish)

thym [tɛ̃] nm thyme

tibia [tibja] nm shinbone, tibia; (partie antérieure de la jambe) shin

tic [tik] nm tic, (nervous) twitch; (de langage etc) mannerism

ticket [tikɛ] nm ticket; ~ **de caisse** receipt; ~ **de quai** platform ticket

tic-tac [tiktak] nm ticking; **faire** ~~ to tick

tiède [tjɛd] adj lukewarm; (vent, air) mild, warm; **tiédir** vi to cool; (se réchauffer) to grow warmer

tien, ne [tjɛ̃, tjɛn] pron: **le(la)** ~**(ne)**, **les** ~**(ne)s** yours; **à la** ~**ne!** cheers!

tiens [tjɛ̃] vb, excl voir **tenir**

tierce [tjɛʀs] adj voir **tiers**

tiercé [tjɛʀse] nm system of forecast betting giving first 3 horses

tiers, tierce [tjɛʀ, tjɛʀs] adj third ♦ nm (JUR) third party; (fraction) third; **le** ~ **monde** the Third World

tifs [tif] (fam) nmpl hair

tige [tiʒ] nf stem; (baguette) rod

tignasse [tiɲas] (péj) nf mop of hair

tigre [tigʀ] nm tiger; **tigresse** nf tigress; **tigré, e** adj (rayé) striped; (tacheté) spotted; (chat) tabby

tilleul [tijœl] nm lime (tree), linden (tree); (boisson) lime(-blossom) tea

timbale [tɛ̃bal] nf (metal) tumbler; ~**s** nfpl (MUS) timpani, kettledrums

timbre [tɛ̃bʀ] nm (tampon) stamp; (aussi: ~ **poste**) (postage) stamp; (MUS: de voix, instrument) timbre, tone

timbré, e [tɛ̃bʀe] (fam) adj cracked

timide [timid] adj shy; (timoré) timid; **timidement** adv shyly; **timidité** nf shyness; timidity

tins etc [tɛ̃] vb voir **tenir**

tintamarre [tɛ̃tamaʀ] nm din, uproar

tinter [tɛ̃te] vi to ring, chime; (argent, clefs) to jingle

tique [tik] nf (parasite) tick

tir [tiʀ] nm (sport) shooting; (fait ou manière de ~er) firing no pl; (rafale) fire; (stand) shooting gallery; **à l'arc** archery; ~ **au pigeon** clay pigeon shooting

tirage [tiʀaʒ] nm (action) printing; (PHOTO) print; (de livre: nombre d'exemplaires) (print) run; (: édition) edition; (de loterie) draw; **par** ~ **au sort** by drawing lots

tirailler [tiʀaje] vt: **être tiraillé entre** to be torn between

tire [tiʀ] nf: **vol à la** ~ pickpocketing

tiré, e [tiʀe] adj (traits) drawn; ~ **par les cheveux** far-fetched

tire-au-flanc [tiʀoflɑ̃] (péj) nm inv skiver

tire-bouchon [tiʀbuʃɔ̃] nm corkscrew

tirelire [tiʀliʀ] nf moneybox

tirer [tiʀe] vt (gén) to pull; (extraire): ~ **qch de** to take ou pull sth out of; (trait, rideau, carte, conclusion, chèque) to draw; (langue) to stick out; (en faisant feu: balle, coup) to fire; (: animal) to shoot; (journal, livre, photo) to print; (FOOTBALL: corner etc) to take ♦ vi (faire feu) to fire; (faire du tir, FOOTBALL) to shoot; **se** ~ vi (fam) to push off; **s'en** ~ (éviter le pire) to get off; (survivre) to pull through; (se débrouiller) to manage; ~ **sur** (corde) to pull on ou at; (faire feu sur) to shoot ou fire at; (pipe) to draw on; (approcher de: couleur) to verge ou border on; ~ **qn de** (embarras etc) to help ou get sb out of; ~ **à l'arc/la carabine** to shoot with a bow and arrow/with a rifle; ~ **à sa fin** to be drawing to a close; ~ **qch au clair** to clear sth up; ~ **au sort** to draw lots; ~ **parti de** to take advantage of; ~ **profit de** to profit from

tiret [tiʀɛ] nm dash

tireur [tiʀœʀ] nm gunman; ~ **d'élite** marksman

tiroir [tiʀwaʀ] nm drawer; **tiroir-caisse** nm till

tisane [tizan] nf herb tea

tisonnier [tizɔnje] nm poker

tisser [tise] vt to weave; **tisserand** nm weaver

tissu [tisy] nm fabric, material, cloth no pl; (ANAT, BIO) tissue; **tissu-éponge** nm (terry) towelling no pl

titre [titʀ] nm (gén) title; (de journal) headline; (diplôme) qualification; (COMM) security; **en** ~ (champion) official; **à juste** ~ rightly; **à quel** ~? on what grounds?; **à aucun** ~ on no account; **au même** ~ **(que)** in the same way (as); **à** ~ **d'information** for (your) information; **à** ~ **gracieux** free of charge; **à** ~ **d'essai** on a trial basis; **à** ~ **privé** in a private capacity; ~ **de propriété** title deed; ~ **de transport** ticket

tituber [titybe] vi to stagger (along)

titulaire [titylɛʀ] adj (ADMIN) with tenure ♦ nm/f (de permis) holder

toast [tost] nm slice ou piece of toast; (de bienvenue) (welcoming) toast; **porter un** ~ **à qn** to propose ou drink a toast to sb

toboggan [tɔbɔɡɑ̃] nm slide; (AUTO) flyover

toc [tɔk] excl: ~, **toc** knock knock ♦ nm: **en** ~ fake

tocsin [tɔksɛ̃] nm alarm (bell)

toge [tɔʒ] nf toga; (de juge) gown
tohu-bohu [tɔybɔy] nm hubbub
toi [twa] pron you
toile [twal] nf (tableau) canvas; **de** ou **en ~**
  (pantalon) cotton; (sac) canvas; **~ cirée**
  oilcloth; **~ d'araignée** cobweb; **~ de fond** (fig)
  backdrop
toilette [twalɛt] nf (habits) outfit; **~s** nfpl
  (w.-c.) toilet sg; **faire sa ~** to have a wash,
  get washed; **articles de ~** toiletries
toi-même [twamɛm] pron yourself
toiser [twaze] vt to eye up and down
toison [twazɔ̃] nf (de mouton) fleece
toit [twa] nm roof; **~ ouvrant** sunroof
toiture [twatyʀ] nf roof
tôle [tol] nf (plaque) steel ou iron sheet;
  ~ ondulée corrugated iron
tolérable [tɔleʀabl] adj tolerable
tolérant, e [tɔleʀɑ̃, ɑ̃t] adj tolerant
tolérer [tɔleʀe] vt to tolerate; (ADMIN: hors
  taxe etc) to allow
tollé [tɔ(l)le] nm outcry
tomate [tɔmat] nf tomato; **~s farcies** stuffed
  tomatoes
tombe [tɔ̃b] nf (sépulture) grave; (avec
  monument) tomb
tombeau, x [tɔ̃bo] nm tomb
tombée [tɔ̃be] nf: **à la ~ de la nuit** at nightfall
tomber [tɔ̃be] vi to fall; (fièvre, vent) to drop;
  laisser ~ (objet) to drop; (personne) to let
  down; (activité) to give up; **laisse ~!** forget
  it!; **faire ~** to knock over; **~ sur** (rencontrer) to
  bump into; **~ de fatigue/sommeil** to drop
  from exhaustion/be falling asleep on one's
  feet; **ça tombe bien** that's come at the right
  time; **il est bien tombé** he's been lucky; **~ à
  l'eau** (projet) to fall through; **~ en panne** to
  break down
tombola [tɔ̃bɔla] nf raffle
tome [tɔm] nm volume
ton¹, ta [tɔ̃, ta] (pl **tes**) adj your
ton² [tɔ̃] nm (gén) tone; (couleur) shade, tone;
  de bon ~ in good taste
tonalité [tɔnalite] nf (au téléphone) dialling
  tone
tondeuse [tɔ̃døz] nf (à gazon) (lawn)
  mower; (du coiffeur) clippers pl; (pour
  les moutons) shears pl
tondre [tɔ̃dʀ] vt (pelouse, herbe) to mow;
  (haie) to cut, clip; (mouton, toison) to shear;
  (cheveux) to crop
tongs [tɔ̃g] nfpl flip-flops
tonifier [tɔnifje] vt (peau, organisme) to tone
  up
tonique [tɔnik] adj fortifying ♦ nm tonic
tonne [tɔn] nf metric ton, tonne
tonneau, x [tɔno] nm (à vin, cidre) barrel;
  faire des ~x (voiture, avion) to roll over
tonnelle [tɔnɛl] nf bower, arbour

tonner [tɔne] vi to thunder; **il tonne** it is
  thundering, there's some thunder
tonnerre [tɔnɛʀ] nm thunder
tonton [tɔ̃tɔ̃] nm uncle
tonus [tɔnys] nm energy
top [tɔp] nm: **au 3ème ~** at the 3rd stroke
topinambour [tɔpinɑ̃buʀ] nm Jerusalem
  artichoke
topo [tɔpo] (fam) nm rundown; **c'est le même
  ~** it's the same old story
toque [tɔk] nf (de fourrure) fur hat; **~ de
  cuisinier** chef's hat; **~ de jockey/juge**
  jockey's/judge's cap
toqué, e [tɔke] (fam) adj cracked
torche [tɔʀʃ] nf torch
torchon [tɔʀʃɔ̃] nm cloth; (à vaisselle) tea
  towel ou cloth
tordre [tɔʀdʀ] vt (chiffon) to wring; (barre,
  fig: visage) to twist; **se ~** vi: **se ~ le poignet/la
  cheville** to twist one's wrist/ankle; **se ~ de
  douleur/rire** to be doubled up with pain/
  laughter; **tordu, e** adj bent; (fig) crazy
tornade [tɔʀnad] nf tornado
torpille [tɔʀpij] nf torpedo
torréfier [tɔʀefje] vt to roast
torrent [tɔʀɑ̃] nm mountain stream
torsade [tɔʀsad] nf: **un pull à ~s** a cable
  sweater
torse [tɔʀs] nm chest; (ANAT, SCULPTURE) torso;
  ~ nu stripped to the waist
tort [tɔʀ] nm (défaut) fault; **~s** nmpl (JUR) fault
  sg; **avoir ~** to be wrong; **être dans son ~** to
  be in the wrong; **donner ~ à qn** to lay the
  blame on sb; **causer du ~ à** to harm; **à ~**
  wrongly; **à ~ et à travers** wildly
torticolis [tɔʀtikɔli] nm stiff neck
tortiller [tɔʀtije] vt to twist; (moustache) to
  twirl; **se ~** vi to wriggle; (en dansant) to
  wiggle
tortionnaire [tɔʀsjɔnɛʀ] nm torturer
tortue [tɔʀty] nf tortoise; (d'eau douce)
  terrapin; (d'eau de mer) turtle
tortueux, -euse [tɔʀtɥø, øz] adj (rue)
  twisting; (fig) tortuous
torture [tɔʀtyʀ] nf torture; **torturer** vt to
  torture; (fig) to torment
tôt [to] adv early; **~ ou tard** sooner or later; **si
  ~** so early; (déjà) so soon; **plus ~** earlier; **au
  plus ~** at the earliest; **il eut ~ fait de faire** he
  soon did
total, e, -aux [tɔtal, o] adj, nm total; **au ~** in
  total; (fig) on the whole; **faire le ~** to work
  out the total; **totalement** adv totally;
  totaliser vt to total; **totalitaire** adj
  totalitarian; **totalité** nf: **la totalité de** all (of);
  the whole **~sg**; **en totalité** entirely
toubib [tubib] (fam) nm doctor
touchant, e [tuʃɑ̃, ɑ̃t] adj touching
touche [tuʃ] nf (de piano, de machine à écrire)

key; (de téléphone) button; (PEINTURE etc) stroke, touch; (fig: de nostalgie) touch; (FOOTBALL: aussi: **remise en ~**) throw-in; (aussi: **ligne de ~**) touch-line

toucher [tuʃe] nm touch ♦ vt to touch; (palper) to feel; (atteindre: d'un coup de feu etc) to hit; (concerner) to concern, affect; (contacter) to reach, contact; (recevoir: récompense) to receive, get; (: salaire) to draw, get; (: chèque) to cash; **se ~** (être en contact) to touch; **au ~** to the touch; **~ à** to touch; (concerner) to have to do with, concern; **je vais lui en ~ un mot** I'll have a word with him about it; **~ à sa fin** to be drawing to a close

touffe [tuf] nf tuft

touffu, e [tufy] adj thick, dense

toujours [tuʒuR] adv always; (encore) still; (constamment) forever; **~ plus** more and more; **pour ~** forever; **~ est-il que** the fact remains that; **essaie ~** (you can) try anyway

toupet [tupɛ] (fam) nm cheek

toupie [tupi] nf (spinning) top

tour [tuR] nf tower; (immeuble) high-rise block (BRIT) ou building (US); (ÉCHECS) castle, rook ♦ nm (excursion) trip; (à pied) stroll, walk; (en voiture) run, ride; (SPORT: aussi: **~ de piste**) lap; (d'être servi ou de jouer etc) turn; (de roue etc) revolution; (POL: aussi: **~ de scrutin**) ballot; (ruse, de prestidigitation) trick; (de forme) wheel; (à bois, métaux) lathe; (circonférence): **de 3 m de ~** 3 m round, with a circumference ou girth of 3 m; **faire le ~ de** to go round; (à pied) to walk round; **c'est au ~ de Renée** it's Renée's turn; **à ~ de rôle, ~ à ~** in turn; **~ de chant** nm song recital; **~ de contrôle** nf control tower; **~ de garde** nm spell of duty; **~ d'horizon** nm (fig) general survey; **~ de taille/tête** nm waist/head measurement; **un 33 ~s** an LP; **un 45 ~s** a single

tourbe [tuRb] nf peat

tourbillon [tuRbijɔ̃] nm whirlwind; (d'eau) whirlpool; (fig) whirl, swirl; **tourbillonner** vi to whirl (round)

tourelle [tuRɛl] nf turret

tourisme [tuRism] nm tourism; **agence de ~** tourist agency; **faire du ~** to go touring; (en ville) to go sightseeing; **touriste** nm/f tourist; **touristique** adj tourist cpd; (région) touristic

tourment [tuRmɑ̃] nm torment; **tourmenter** vt to torment; **se tourmenter** vi to fret, worry o.s.

tournage [tuRnaʒ] nm (CINÉMA) shooting

tournant [tuRnɑ̃] nm (de route) bend; (fig) turning point

tournebroche [tuRnəbRɔʃ] nm roasting spit

tourne-disque [tuRnədisk] nm record player

tournée [tuRne] nf (du facteur etc) round; (d'artiste, politicien) tour; (au café) round (of drinks)

tournemain [tuRnəmɛ̃]: **en un ~** adv (as) quick as a flash

tourner [tuRne] vt to turn; (sauce, mélange) to stir; (CINÉMA: faire les prises de vues) to shoot; (: produire) to make ♦ vi to turn; (moteur) to run; (taximètre) to tick away; (lait etc) to turn (sour); **se ~** vi to turn round; **mal ~** to go wrong; **~ autour de** to go round; (péj) to hang round; **~ à/en** to turn into; **~ à gauche/droite** to turn left/right; **~ le dos à** to turn one's back on; to have one's back to; **~ de l'œil** to pass out; **se ~ vers** to turn towards; (fig) to turn to

tournesol [tuRnəsɔl] nm sunflower

tournevis [tuRnəvis] nm screwdriver

tourniquet [tuRnikɛ] nm (pour arroser) sprinkler; (portillon) turnstile; (présentoir) revolving stand

tournoi [tuRnwa] nm tournament

tournoyer [tuRnwaje] vi to swirl (round)

tournure [tuRnyR] nf (LING) turn of phrase; (évolution): **la ~ de qch** the way sth is developing; **~ d'esprit** turn ou cast of mind; **la ~ des événements** the turn of events

tourte [tuRt] nf pie

tourterelle [tuRtəRɛl] nf turtledove

tous [tu] adj, pron voir **tout**

Toussaint [tusɛ̃] nf: **la ~** All Saints' Day

tousser [tuse] vi to cough

MOT-CLÉ

---

tout, e [tu, tut] (mpl **tous**, fpl **toutes**) adj **1** (avec article singulier) all; **tout le lait** all the milk; **toute la nuit** all night, the whole night; **tout le livre** the whole book; **tout un pain** a whole loaf; **tout le temps** all the time; the whole time; **c'est tout le contraire** it's quite the opposite

2 (avec article pluriel) every, all; **tous les livres** all the books; **toutes les nuits** every night; **toutes les fois** every time; **toutes les trois/deux semaines** every third/other ou second week, every three/two weeks; **tous les deux** both ou each of us (ou them ou you); **toutes les trois** all three of us (ou them ou you)

3 (sans article): **à tout âge** at any age; **pour toute nourriture, il avait ...** his only food was ...

♦ pron everything, all; **il a tout fait** he's done everything; **je les vois tous** I can see them all ou all of them; **nous y sommes tous allés** all of us went, we all went; **en tout** in all; **tout ce qu'il sait** all he knows

♦ nm whole; **le tout** all of it (ou them); **le tout est de ...** the main thing is to ...; **pas du tout** not at all

♦ *adv* **1** (*très, complètement*) very; **tout près** very near; **le tout premier** the very first; **tout seul** all alone; **le livre tout entier** the whole book; **tout en haut** right at the top; **tout droit** straight ahead

2: tout en while; **tout en travaillant** while working, as he *etc* works

3: tout d'abord first of all; **tout à coup** suddenly; **tout à fait** absolutely; **tout à l'heure** a short while ago; (*futur*) in a short while, shortly; **à tout à l'heure!** see you later!; **tout de même** all the same; **tout le monde** everybody; **tout de suite** immediately, straight away; **tout terrain** *ou* **tous terrains** all-terrain

toutefois [tutfwa] *adv* however

toutes [tut] *adj, pron voir* **tout**

toux [tu] *nf* cough

toxicomane [tɔksikɔman] *nm/f* drug addict

toxique [tɔksik] *adj* toxic

trac [trak] *nm* (*au théâtre, en public*) stage fright; (*aux examens*) nerves *pl*; **avoir le ~** (*au théâtre, en public*) to have stage fright; (*aux examens*) to be feeling nervous

tracasser [trakase] *vt* to worry, bother; **se ~** to worry

trace [tras] *nf* (*empreintes*) tracks *pl*; (*marques, aussi fig*) mark; (*quantité infime, indice, vestige*) trace; **~s de pas** footprints

tracé [trase] *nm* (*parcours*) line; (*plan*) layout

tracer [trase] *vt* to draw; (*piste*) to open up

tract [trakt] *nm* tract, pamphlet

tractations [traktasjɔ̃] *nfpl* dealings, bargaining *sg*

tracteur [traktœr] *nm* tractor

traction [traksjɔ̃] *nf:* **~ avant/arrière** front-wheel/rear-wheel drive

tradition [tradisjɔ̃] *nf* tradition; **traditionnel, le** *adj* traditional

traducteur, -trice [tradyktœr, tris] *nm/f* translator

traduction [tradyksjɔ̃] *nf* translation

traduire [tradɥir] *vt* to translate; (*exprimer*) to convey; **~ qn en justice** to bring sb before the courts

trafic [trafik] *nm* traffic; **~ d'armes** arms dealing; **trafiquant, e** *nm/f* trafficker; (*d'armes*) dealer; **trafiquer** (*péj*) *vt* (*vin*) to doctor; (*moteur, document*) to tamper with

tragédie [traʒedi] *nf* tragedy; **tragique** *adj* tragic

trahir [trair] *vt* to betray; **trahison** *nf* betrayal; (*JUR*) treason

train [trɛ̃] *nm* (*RAIL*) train; (*allure*) pace; **être en ~ de faire qch** to be doing sth; **mettre qn en ~** to put sb in good spirits; **se sentir en ~** to feel in good form; **~ d'atterrissage** undercarriage; **~ de vie** style of living; **~ électrique** (*jouet*) (electric) train set; **~-**

autos-couchettes car-sleeper train

traîne [trɛn] *nf* (*de robe*) train; **être à la ~** to lag behind

traîneau, x [trɛno] *nm* sleigh, sledge

traînée [trene] *nf* trail; (*sur un mur, dans le ciel*) streak; (*péj*) slut

traîner [trene] *vt* (*remorque*) to pull; (*enfant, chien*) to drag *ou* trail along ♦ *vi* (*robe, manteau*) to trail; (*être en désordre*) to lie around; (*aller lentement*) to dawdle (along); (*vagabonder, agir lentement*) to hang about; (*durer*) to drag on; **se ~** *vi* to drag o.s. along; **~ les pieds** to drag one's feet

train-train [trɛ̃trɛ̃] *nm* humdrum routine

traire [trɛr] *vt* to milk

trait [trɛ] *nm* (*ligne*) line; (*de dessin*) stroke; (*caractéristique*) feature, trait; **~s** *nmpl* (*du visage*) features; **d'un ~** (*boire*) in one gulp; **de ~** (*animal*) draught; **avoir ~ à** to concern; **~ d'union** hyphen

traitant, e [trɛtɑ̃, ɑ̃t] *adj* (*shampooing*) medicated; **votre médecin ~** your usual *ou* family doctor

traite [trɛt] *nf* (*COMM*) draft; (*AGR*) milking; **d'une ~** without stopping; **la ~ des noirs** the slave trade

traité [trɛte] *nm* treaty

traitement [trɛtmɑ̃] *nm* treatment; (*salaire*) salary; **~ de données** data processing; **~ de texte** word processing; (*logiciel*) word processing package

traiter [trɛte] *vt* to treat; (*qualifier*): **~ qn d'idiot** to call sb a fool ♦ *vi* to deal; **~ de** to deal with

traiteur [trɛtœr] *nm* caterer

traître, -esse [trɛtr, trɛtrɛs] *adj* (*dangereux*) treacherous ♦ *nm* traitor

trajectoire [traʒɛktwar] *nf* path

trajet [traʒɛ] *nm* (*parcours, voyage*) journey; (*itinéraire*) route; (*distance à parcourir*) distance

trame [tram] *nf* (*de tissu*) weft; (*fig*) framework; **usé jusqu'à la ~** threadbare

tramer [trame] *vt*: **il se trame quelque chose** there's something brewing

trampoline [trɑ̃pɔlin] *nm* trampoline

tramway [tramwɛ] *nm* tram(way); (*voiture*) tram(car) (*BRIT*), streetcar (*US*)

tranchant, e [trɑ̃ʃɑ̃, ɑ̃t] *adj* sharp; (*fig*) peremptory ♦ *nm* (*d'un couteau*) cutting edge; (*de la main*) edge; **à double ~** double-edged

tranche [trɑ̃ʃ] *nf* (*morceau*) slice; (*arête*) edge; **~ d'âge/de salaires** age/wage bracket

tranché, e [trɑ̃ʃe] *adj* (*couleurs*) distinct; (*opinions*) clear-cut; **tranchée** *nf* trench

trancher [trɑ̃ʃe] *vt* to cut, sever ♦ *vi* to take a decision; **~ avec** to contrast sharply with

tranquille [trɑ̃kil] *adj* quiet; (*rassuré*) easy in

one's mind, with one's mind at rest; **se tenir ~** (*enfant*) to be quiet; **laisse-moi/laisse-ça ~** leave me/it alone; **avoir la conscience ~** to have a clear conscience; **tranquillisant** *nm* tranquillizer; **tranquillité** *nf* peace (and quiet); (*d'esprit*) peace of mind

transat [trɑ̃zat] *nm* deckchair

transborder [trɑ̃sbɔrde] *vt* to tran(s)ship

transcription [trɑ̃skripsjɔ̃] *nf* transcription; (*copie*) transcript

transférer [trɑ̃sfere] *vt* to transfer; **transfert** *nm* transfer

transformation [trɑ̃sfɔrmasjɔ̃] *nf* change; transformation; alteration; (*RUGBY*) conversion

transformer [trɑ̃sfɔrme] *vt* to change; (*radicalement*) to transform; (*vêtement*) to alter; (*matière première, appartement, RUGBY*) to convert; (**se**) **~ en** to turn into

transfusion [trɑ̃sfyzjɔ̃] *nf*: **~ sanguine** blood transfusion

transgresser [trɑ̃sɡrese] *vt* to contravene

transi, e [trɑ̃zi] *adj* numb (with cold), chilled to the bone

transiger [trɑ̃ziʒe] *vi* to compromise

transit [trɑ̃zit] *nm* transit; **transiter** *vi* to pass in transit

transitif, -ive [trɑ̃zitif, iv] *adj* transitive

transition [trɑ̃zisjɔ̃] *nf* transition; **transitoire** *adj* transitional

translucide [trɑ̃slysid] *adj* translucent

transmettre [trɑ̃smetr] *vt* (*passer*): **~ qch à qn** to pass sth on to sb; (*TECH, TÉL, MÉD*) to transmit; (*TV, RADIO: retransmettre*) to broadcast; **transmission** *nf* transmission

transparent, e [trɑ̃sparɑ̃, ɑ̃t] *adj* transparent

transpercer [trɑ̃sperse] *vt* (*froid, pluie*) to go through, pierce; (*balle*) to go through

transpiration [trɑ̃spirasjɔ̃] *nf* perspiration

transpirer [trɑ̃spire] *vi* to perspire

transplanter [trɑ̃splɑ̃te] *vt* (*MÉD, BOT*) to transplant; **transplantation** *nf* (*MÉD*) transplant

transport [trɑ̃spɔr] *nm* transport; **~s en commun** public transport *sg*; **transporter** *vt* to carry, move; (*COMM*) to transport, convey; **transporteur** *nm* haulage contractor (*BRIT*), trucker (*US*)

transvaser [trɑ̃svaze] *vt* to decant

transversal, e, -aux [trɑ̃sversal, o] *adj* (*rue*) which runs across; **coupe ~e** cross section

trapèze [trapez] *nm* (*au cirque*) trapeze

trappe [trap] *nf* trap door

trapu, e [trapy] *adj* squat, stocky

traquenard [traknar] *nm* trap

traquer [trake] *vt* to track down; (*harceler*) to hound

traumatiser [tromatize] *vt* to traumatize

travail, -aux [travaj] *nm* (*gén*) work; (*tâche, métier*) work *no pl*, job; (*ÉCON, MÉD*) labour; **être sans ~** (*employé*) to be out of work *ou* unemployed; *voir aussi* **travaux**; **~ (au) noir** moonlighting

travailler [travaje] *vi* to work; (*bois*) to warp ♦ *vt* (*bois, métal*) to work; (*objet d'art, discipline*) to work on; **cela te travaille** it is on his mind; **travailleur, -euse** *adj* hardworking ♦ *nm/f* worker; **travailliste** *adj* ≈ Labour *cpd*

travaux [travo] *nmpl* (*de réparation, agricoles etc*) work *sg*; (*sur route*) roadworks *pl*; (*de construction*) building (work); **travaux des champs** farmwork *sg*; **travaux dirigés** (*SCOL*) tutorial; **travaux forcés** hard labour *sg*; **travaux manuels** (*SCOL*) handicrafts; **travaux ménagers** housework *sg*; **travaux pratiques** (*SCOL*) practical work; (*en laboratoire*) lab work

travers [traver] *nm* fault, failing; **en ~ (de)** across; **au ~ (de)/à ~** through; **de ~** (*nez, bouche*) crooked; (*chapeau*) askew; **comprendre de ~** to misunderstand; **regarder de ~** (*fig*) to look askance at

traverse [travers] *nf* (*de voie ferrée*) sleeper; **chemin de ~** shortcut

traversée [traverse] *nf* crossing

traverser [traverse] *vt* (*gén*) to cross; (*ville, tunnel, aussi: percer, fig*) to go through; (*suj: ligne, trait*) to run across

traversin [traversɛ̃] *nm* bolster

travesti [travesti] *nm* transvestite

trébucher [trebyʃe] *vi*: **~ (sur)** to stumble (over), trip (against)

trèfle [trefl] *nm* (*BOT*) clover; (*CARTES: couleur*) clubs *pl*; (: *carte*) club

treille [trej] *nf* vine arbour

treillis [treji] *nm* (*métallique*) wire-mesh

treize [trez] *num* thirteen; **treizième** *num* thirteenth

tréma [trema] *nm* diaeresis

tremblement [trɑ̃bləmɑ̃] *nm*: **~ de terre** earthquake

trembler [trɑ̃ble] *vi* to tremble, shake; **~ de** (*froid, fièvre*) to shiver *ou* tremble with; (*peur*) to shake *ou* tremble with; **~ pour qn** to fear for sb

trémousser [tremuse]: **se ~** *vi* to jig about, wriggle about

trempe [trɑ̃p] *nf* (*fig*): **de cette/sa ~** of this/his calibre

trempé, e [trɑ̃pe] *adj* soaking (wet), drenched; (*TECH*) tempered

tremper [trɑ̃pe] *vt* to soak, drench; (*aussi:* **faire ~, mettre à ~**) to soak; (*plonger*): **~ qch dans** to dip sth in(to) ♦ *vi* to soak; (*fig*): **~ dans** to be involved *ou* have a hand in; **se ~** *vi* to have a quick dip; **trempette** *nf*: **faire**

trempette to go paddling

tremplin [trɑ̃plɛ̃] nm springboard; (SKI) ski-jump

trentaine [trɑ̃tɛn] nf: **une ~ (de)** thirty or so, about thirty; **avoir la ~ (âge)** to be around thirty

trente [trɑ̃t] num thirty; **être/se mettre sur son ~ et un** to be wearing/put on one's Sunday best; **trentième** num thirtieth

trépidant, e [trepidɑ̃, ɑ̃t] adj (fig: rythme) pulsating; (: vie) hectic

trépied [trepje] nm tripod

trépigner [trepiɲe] vi to stamp (one's feet)

très [trɛ] adv very; much +pp, highly +pp

trésor [trezɔr] nm treasure; **T~ (public)** public revenue; **trésorerie** nf (gestion) accounts pl; (bureaux) accounts department; **difficultés de trésorerie** cash problems, shortage of cash ou funds; **trésorier, -ière** nm/f treasurer

tressaillir [tresajir] vi to shiver, shudder

tressauter [tresote] vi to start, jump

tresse [trɛs] nf braid, plait; **tresser** vt (cheveux) to braid, plait; (fil, jonc) to plait; (corbeille) to weave; (corde) to twist

tréteau, x [treto] nm trestle

treuil [trœj] nm winch

trêve [trɛv] nf (MIL, POL) truce; (fig) respite; **~ de ...** enough of this ...

tri [tri] nm: **faire le ~ (de)** to sort out; **le (bureau de) ~ (POSTES)** the sorting office

triangle [trijɑ̃gl] nm triangle; **triangulaire** adj triangular

tribord [tribɔr] nm: **à ~** to starboard, on the starboard side

tribu [triby] nf tribe

tribunal, -aux [tribynal, o] nm (JUR) court; (MIL) tribunal

tribune [tribyn] nf (estrade) platform, rostrum; (débat) forum; (d'église, de tribunal) gallery; (de stade) stand

tribut [triby] nm tribute

tributaire [tribytɛr] adj: **être ~ de** to be dependent on

tricher [triʃe] vi to cheat; **tricheur, -euse** nm/f cheat(er)

tricolore [trikɔlɔr] adj three-coloured; (français) red, white and blue

tricot [triko] nm (technique, ouvrage) knitting no pl; (vêtement) jersey, sweater; **~ de peau** vest; **tricoter** vt to knit

trictrac [triktrak] nm backgammon

tricycle [trisikl] nm tricycle

triennal, e, -aux [trijenal, o] adj three-year

trier [trije] vt to sort out; (POSTES, fruits) to sort

trimestre [trimɛstr] nm (SCOL) term; (COMM) quarter; **trimestriel, le** adj quarterly; (SCOL) end-of-term

tringle [trɛ̃gl] nf rod

trinquer [trɛ̃ke] vi to clink glasses

triomphe [trijɔ̃f] nm triumph; **triompher** vi to triumph, win; **triompher de** to triumph over, overcome

tripes [trip] nfpl (CULIN) tripe sg

triple [tripl] adj triple ♦ nm: **le ~ (de)** (comparaison) three times as much (as); **en ~ exemplaire** in triplicate; **tripler** vi, vt to triple, treble

triplés, -ées [triple] nm/fpl triplets

tripoter [tripɔte] vt to fiddle with

triste [trist] adj sad; (couleur, temps, journée) dreary; (péj): **~ personnage/affaire** sorry individual/affair; **tristesse** nf sadness

trivial, e, -aux [trivjal, jo] adj coarse, crude; (commun) mundane

troc [trɔk] nm barter

troène [trɔɛn] nm privet

trognon [trɔɲɔ̃] nm (de fruit) core; (de légume) stalk

trois [trwa] num three; **troisième** num third; **trois quarts** nmpl: **les trois quarts de** three-quarters of

trombe [trɔ̃b] nf: **des ~s d'eau** a downpour; **en ~** like a whirlwind

trombone [trɔ̃bɔn] nm (MUS) trombone; (de bureau) paper clip

trompe [trɔ̃p] nf (d'éléphant) trunk; (MUS) trumpet, horn

tromper [trɔ̃pe] vt to deceive; (vigilance, poursuivants) to elude; **se ~** vi to make a mistake, be mistaken; **se ~ de voiture/jour** to take the wrong car/get the day wrong; **se ~ de 3 cm/20 F** to be out by 3 cm/20 F; **tromperie** nf deception, trickery no pl

trompette [trɔ̃pɛt] nf trumpet; **en ~ (nez)** turned-up

trompeur, -euse [trɔ̃pœr, øz] adj deceptive

tronc [trɔ̃] nm (BOT, ANAT) trunk; (d'église) collection box

tronçon [trɔ̃sɔ̃] nm section; **tronçonner** vt to saw up

trône [tron] nm throne

trop [tro] adv (+vb) too much; (+adjectif, adverbe) too; **~ (nombreux)** too many; **~ peu (nombreux)** too few; **~ (souvent)** too often; **~ (longtemps)** (for) too long; **~ de (nombre)** too many; (quantité) too much; **de ~, en ~**: **des livres en ~** a few books too many; **du lait en ~** too much milk; **3 livres/3 F de ~** 3 books too many/3 F too much

tropical, e, -aux [trɔpikal, o] adj tropical

tropique [trɔpik] nm tropic

trop-plein [troplɛ̃] nm (tuyau) overflow ou outlet (pipe); (liquide) overflow

troquer [trɔke] vt: **~ qch contre** to barter ou trade sth for; (fig) to swap sth for

trot [tro] nm trot; **trotter** vi to trot

trotteuse [tʀɔtøz] nf (sweep) second hand
trottinette [tʀɔtinɛt] nf (child's) scooter
trottoir [tʀɔtwaʀ] nm pavement; **faire le ~**
(péj) to walk the streets; **~ roulant** moving
walkway, travellator
trou [tʀu] nm hole; (fig) gap; (COMM) deficit;
~ d'air air pocket; **~ d'ozone** ozone hole; **le
~ de la serrure** the keyhole; **~ de mémoire**
blank, lapse of memory
troublant, e [tʀublɑ̃, ɑ̃t] adj disturbing
trouble [tʀubl] adj (liquide) cloudy; (image,
photo) blurred; (affaire) shady, murky ♦ nm
agitation; **~s** nmpl (POL) disturbances,
troubles, unrest sg; (MÉD) trouble sg,
disorders; **trouble-fête** nm spoilsport
troubler [tʀuble] vt to disturb; (liquide) to
make cloudy; (intriguer) to bother; **se ~** vi
(personne) to become flustered ou confused
trouer [tʀue] vt to make a hole (ou holes) in
trouille [tʀuj] (fam) nf: **avoir la ~** to be
scared to death
troupe [tʀup] nf troop; **~ (de théâtre)**
(theatrical) company
troupeau, x [tʀupo] nm (de moutons) flock;
(de vaches) herd
trousse [tʀus] nf case, kit; (d'écolier) pencil
case; **aux ~s de** (fig) on the heels ou tail of;
~ à outils toolkit; **~ de toilette** toilet bag
trousseau, x [tʀuso] nm (de mariée)
trousseau; **~ de clefs** bunch of keys
trouvaille [tʀuvaj] nf find
trouver [tʀuve] vt to find; (rendre visite):
aller/venir ~ qn to go/come and see sb; **se ~**
vi (être) to be; **je trouve que** I find ou think
that; **~ à boire/critiquer** to find something to
drink/criticize; **se ~ bien** to feel well; **se ~ mal**
to pass out
truand [tʀyɑ̃] nm gangster; **truander** vt: **se
faire truander** to be swindled
truc [tʀyk] nm (astuce) way, trick; (de cinéma,
prestidigitateur) trick, effect; (chose) thing,
thingumajig; **avoir le ~** to have the knack
truelle [tʀyɛl] nf trowel
truffe [tʀyf] nf truffle; (nez) nose
truffé, e [tʀyfe] adj: **~ de** (fig) peppered
with; (fautes) riddled with; (pièges) bristling
with
truie [tʀɥi] nf sow
truite [tʀɥit] nf trout inv
truquage [tʀykaʒ] nm special effects
truquer [tʀyke] vt (élections, serrure, dés) to
fix
TSVP sigle (= tournez svp) PTO
TTC sigle (= toutes taxes comprises) inclusive of
tax
tu¹ [ty] pron you
tu², e [ty] pp de **taire**
tuba [tyba] nm (MUS) tuba; (SPORT) snorkel
tube [tyb] nm tube; (chanson) hit

tuberculose [tybɛʀkyloz] nf tuberculosis
tuer [tɥe] vt to kill; **se ~** vi to be killed;
(suicide) to kill o.s.; **tuerie** nf slaughter no pl
tue-tête [tytɛt]: **à ~~** adv at the top of one's
voice
tueur [tɥœʀ] nm killer; **~ à gages** hired killer
tuile [tɥil] nf tile; (fam) spot of bad luck, blow
tulipe [tylip] nf tulip
tuméfié, e [tymefje] adj puffed-up, swollen
tumeur [tymœʀ] nf growth, tumour
tumulte [tymylt] nm commotion;
tumultueux, -euse adj stormy, turbulent
tunique [tynik] nf tunic
Tunisie [tynizi] nf: **la ~** Tunisia; **tunisien, ne**
adj Tunisian ♦ nm/f: **Tunisien, ne** Tunisian
tunnel [tynɛl] nm tunnel; **le ~ sous la Manche**
the Channel Tunnel
turbulences [tyʀbylɑ̃s] nfpl (AVIAT)
turbulence sg
turbulent, e [tyʀbylɑ̃, ɑ̃t] adj boisterous,
unruly
turc, turque [tyʀk] adj Turkish ♦ nm/f: **T~,
-que** Turk/Turkish woman ♦ nm (LING) Turkish
turf [tyʀf] nm racing; **turfiste** nm/f racegoer
Turquie [tyʀki] nf: **la ~** Turkey
turquoise [tyʀkwaz] nf turquoise ♦ adj inv
turquoise
tus etc [ty] vb voir **taire**
tutelle [tytɛl] nf (JUR) guardianship; (POL)
trusteeship; **sous la ~ de** (fig) under the
supervision of
tuteur [tytœʀ] nm (JUR) guardian; (de plante)
stake, support
tutoyer [tytwaje] vt: **~ qn** to address sb as
"tu"
tuyau, x [tɥijo] nm pipe; (flexible) tube;
(fam) tip; **~ d'arrosage** hosepipe;
~ d'échappement exhaust pipe; **tuyauterie**
nf piping no pl
TVA sigle f (= taxe à la valeur ajoutée) VAT
tympan [tɛ̃pɑ̃] nm (ANAT) eardrum
type [tip] nm type; (fam) chap, guy ♦ adj
typical, classic
typé, e [tipe] adj ethnic
typique [tipik] adj typical
tyran [tiʀɑ̃] nm tyrant; **tyrannique** adj
tyrannical
tzigane [dzigan] adj gipsy, tzigane

U, u

UEM sigle f (= union économique et monétaire)
EMU
ulcère [ylsɛʀ] nm ulcer; **ulcérer** vt (fig) to
sicken, appal
ultérieur, e [ylteʀjœʀ] adj later, subsequent;
remis à une date ~e postponed to a later
date; **ultérieurement** adv later,

subsequently

ultime [yltim] *adj* final

ultra... [yltʁa] *préfixe:* **~moderne/-rapide** ultra-modern/-fast

---
MOT-CLÉ
---

un, une [œ̃, yn] *art indéf* a; *(devant voyelle)* an; **un garçon/vieillard** a boy/an old man; **une fille** a girl

♦ *pron* one; **l'un des meilleurs** one of the best; **l'un ..., l'autre** (the) one ..., the other; **les uns ..., les autres** some ..., others; **l'un et l'autre** both (of them); **l'un ou l'autre** either (of them); **l'un l'autre, les uns les autres** each other, one another; **pas un seul** not a single one; **un par un** one by one

♦ *num* one; **une pomme seulement** one apple only

---

unanime [ynanim] *adj* unanimous; **unanimité** *nf:* **à l'unanimité** unanimously

uni, e [yni] *adj (ton, tissu)* plain; *(surface)* smooth, even; *(famille)* close(-knit); *(pays)* united

unifier [ynifje] *vt* to unite, unify

uniforme [ynifɔʁm] *adj* uniform; *(surface, ton)* even ♦ *nm* uniform; **uniformiser** *vt (systèmes)* to standardize

union [ynjɔ̃] *nf* union; **~ de consommateurs** consumers' association; **U~ européenne** European Union; **U~ soviétique** Soviet Union

unique [ynik] *adj (seul)* only; *(exceptionnel)* unique; *(le même):* **un prix/système ~** a single price/system; **fils/fille ~** only son/daughter, only child; **sens ~** one-way street; **uniquement** *adv* only, solely; *(juste)* only, merely

unir [yniʁ] *vt (nations)* to unite; *(en mariage)* to unite, join together; **s'~** *vi* to unite; *(en mariage)* to be joined together

unitaire [ynitɛʁ] *adj:* **prix ~** unit price

unité [ynite] *nf* unit; *(harmonie, cohésion)* unity

univers [ynivɛʁ] *nm* universe; **universel, le** *adj* universal

universitaire [ynivɛʁsitɛʁ] *adj* university *cpd;* *(diplôme, études)* academic, university *cpd* ♦ *nm/f* academic

université [ynivɛʁsite] *nf* university

urbain, e [yʁbɛ̃, ɛn] *adj* urban, city *cpd,* town *cpd;* **urbanisme** *nm* town planning

urgence [yʁʒɑ̃s] *nf* urgency; *(MÉD etc)* emergency; **d'~** *adj* emergency *cpd* ♦ *adv* as a matter of urgency; **(service des) ~s** casualty

urgent, e [yʁʒɑ̃, ɑ̃t] *adj* urgent

urine [yʁin] *nf* urine; **urinoir** *nm* (public) urinal

urne [yʁn] *nf (électorale)* ballot box; *(vase)* urn

urticaire [yʁtikɛʁ] *nf* nettle rash

us [ys] *nmpl:* **~ et coutumes** (habits and) customs

USA *sigle mpl:* **les USA** the USA

usage [yzaʒ] *nm (emploi, utilisation)* use; *(coutume)* custom; **à l'~** with use; **à l'~ de** *(pour)* for (use of); **hors d'~** out of service; **à ~ interne** *(MÉD)* to be taken; **à ~ externe** *(MÉD)* for external use only; **usagé, e** *adj (usé)* worn; **usager, -ère** *nm/f* user

usé, e [yze] *adj* worn; *(banal: argument etc)* hackneyed

user [yze] *vt (outil)* to wear down; *(vêtement)* to wear out; *(matière)* to wear away; *(consommer: charbon etc)* to use; **s'~** *vi (tissu, vêtement)* to wear out; **~ de** *(moyen, procédé)* to use, employ; *(droit)* to exercise

usine [yzin] *nf* factory

usité, e [yzite] *adj* common

ustensile [ystɑ̃sil] *nm* implement; **~ de cuisine** kitchen utensil

usuel, le [yzɥɛl] *adj* everyday, common

usure [yzyʁ] *nf* wear

utérus [yteʁys] *nm* uterus, womb

utile [ytil] *adj* useful

utilisation [ytilizasjɔ̃] *nf* use

utiliser [ytilize] *vt* to use

utilitaire [ytilitɛʁ] *adj* utilitarian

utilité [ytilite] *nf* usefulness *no pl;* **de peu d'~** of little use *ou* help

utopie [ytɔpi] *nf* utopia

V, v

va [va] *vb voir* aller

vacance [vakɑ̃s] *nf (ADMIN)* vacancy; **~s** *nfpl* holiday(s *pl*), vacation *sg;* **les grandes ~s** the summer holidays; **prendre des/ses ~s** to take a holiday/one's holiday(s); **aller en ~s** to go on holiday; **vacancier, -ière** *nm/f* holiday-maker

vacant, e [vakɑ̃, ɑ̃t] *adj* vacant

vacarme [vakaʁm] *nm (bruit)* racket

vaccin [vaksɛ̃] *nm* vaccine; *(opération)* vaccination; **vaccination** *nf* vaccination; **vacciner** *vt* to vaccinate; **être vacciné contre qch** *(fam)* to be cured of sth

vache [vaʃ] *nf (ZOOL)* cow; *(cuir)* cowhide ♦ *adj (fam)* rotten, mean; **vachement** *(fam) adv (très)* really; *(pleuvoir, travailler)* a hell of a lot; **vacherie** *nf (action)* dirty trick; *(remarque)* nasty remark

vaciller [vasije] *vi* to sway, wobble; *(bougie, lumière)* to flicker; *(fig)* to be failing, falter

va-et-vient [vaevjɛ̃] *nm inv (de personnes, véhicules)* comings and goings *pl,* to-ings and fro-ings *pl*

vagabond [vagabɔ̃] *nm (rôdeur)* tramp,

vagrant; (*voyageur*) wanderer; **vagabonder**
vi to roam, wander

vagin [vaʒɛ̃] *nm* vagina

vague [vag] *nf* wave ♦ *adj* vague; (*regard*)
faraway; (*manteau, robe*) loose(-fitting);
(*quelconque*): **un ~ bureau/cousin** some
office/cousin or other; **~ de fond** ground
swell; **~ de froid** cold spell

vaillant, e [vajɑ̃, ɑ̃t] *adj* (*courageux*) gallant;
(*robuste*) hale and hearty

vaille [vaj] *vb voir* **valoir**

vain, e [vɛ̃, vɛn] *adj* vain; **en ~** in vain

vaincre [vɛ̃kʁ] *vt* to defeat; (*fig*) to conquer,
overcome; **vaincu, e** *nm/f* defeated party;
vainqueur *nm* victor; (*SPORT*) winner

vais [vɛ] *vb voir* **aller**

vaisseau, x [vɛso] *nm* (*ANAT*) vessel; (*NAVIG*)
ship, vessel; **~ spatial** spaceship

vaisselier [vɛsalje] *nm* dresser

vaisselle [vɛsɛl] *nf* (*service*) crockery; (*plats
etc à laver*) (dirty) dishes *pl*; **faire la ~** to do
the washing-up (*BRIT*) ou the dishes

val [val, vo] (*pl* **vaux** ou **~s**) *nm* valley

valable [valabl] *adj* valid; (*acceptable*)
decent, worthwhile

valent *etc* [val] *vb voir* **valoir**

valet [valɛ] *nm* manservant; (*CARTES*) jack

valeur [valœʁ] *nf* (*gén*) value; (*mérite*) worth,
merit; (*COMM: titre*) security; **mettre en ~**
(*détail*) to highlight; (*objet décoratif*) to show
off to advantage; **avoir de la ~** to be valuable;
sans ~ worthless; **prendre de la ~** to go up ou
gain in value

valide [valid] *adj* (*en bonne santé*) fit;
(*valable*) valid; **valider** *vt* to validate

valions [valjɔ̃] *vb voir* **valoir**

valise [valiz] *nf* (suit)case; **faire ses ~s** to pack
one's bags

vallée [vale] *nf* valley

vallon [valɔ̃] *nm* small valley; **vallonné, e** *adj*
hilly

valoir [valwaʁ] *vi* (*être valable*) to hold, apply
♦ *vt* (*prix, valeur, effort*) to be worth;
(*causer*): **~ qch à qn** to earn sb sth; **se ~** *vi* to
be of equal merit; (*péj*) to be two of a kind;
faire ~ (*droits, prérogatives*) to assert; **faire
~ que** to point out that; **à ~ sur** to be
deducted from; **vaille que vaille** somehow or
other; **cela ne me dit rien qui vaille** I don't like
the look of it at all; **ce climat ne me vaut rien**
this climate doesn't suit me; **~ le coup** ou **la
peine** to be worth the trouble ou worth it;
~ mieux: il vaut mieux se taire it's better to
say nothing; **ça ne vaut rien** it's worthless;
que vaut ce candidat? how good is this
applicant?

valse [vals] *nf* waltz

valu, e [valy] *pp de* **valoir**

vandalisme [vɑ̃dalism] *nm* vandalism

vanille [vanij] *nf* vanilla

vanité [vanite] *nf* vanity; **vaniteux, -euse**
adj vain, conceited

vanne [van] *nf* gate; (*fig*) joke

vannerie [vanʁi] *nf* basketwork

vantard, e [vɑ̃taʁ, aʁd] *adj* boastful

vanter [vɑ̃te] *vt* to speak highly of, praise; **se
~** *vi* to boast, brag; **se ~ de** to pride o.s. on;
(*péj*) to boast of

vapeur [vapœʁ] *nf* steam; (*émanation*)
vapour, fumes *pl*; **~s** *nfpl* (*bouffées*) vapours;
à ~ steam-powered, steam *cpd*; **cuit à la ~**
steamed; **vaporeux, -euse** *adj* (*flou*) hazy,
misty; (*léger*) filmy; **vaporisateur** *nm* spray;
vaporiser *vt* (*parfum etc*) to spray

varappe [vaʁap] *nf* rock climbing

vareuse [vaʁøz] *nf* (*blouson*) pea jacket;
(*d'uniforme*) tunic

variable [vaʁjabl] *adj* variable; (*temps,
humeur*) changeable; (*divers: résultats*) varied,
various

varice [vaʁis] *nf* varicose vein

varicelle [vaʁisɛl] *nf* chickenpox

varié, e [vaʁje] *adj* varied; (*divers*) various

varier [vaʁje] *vi* to vary; (*temps, humeur*) to
change ♦ *vt* to vary; **variété** *nf* variety;
variétés *nfpl*: **spectacle/émission de variétés**
variety show

variole [vaʁjɔl] *nf* smallpox

vas [va] *vb voir* **aller**

vase [vaz] *nm* vase ♦ *nf* silt, mud; **vaseux,
-euse** *adj* silty, muddy; (*fig: confus*) woolly,
hazy; (: *fatigué*) woozy

vasistas [vazistas] *nm* fanlight

vaste [vast] *adj* vast, immense

vaudrai *etc* [vodʁe] *vb voir* **valoir**

vaurien, ne [voʁjɛ̃, jɛn] *nm/f* good-for-
nothing

vaut [vo] *vb voir* **valoir**

vautour [votuʁ] *nm* vulture

vautrer [votʁe] *vb*: **se ~ dans/sur** to wallow
in/sprawl on

vaux [vo] *nmpl de* **val** ♦ *vb voir* **valoir**

va-vite [vavit]: **à la ~~** *adv* in a rush ou hurry

veau, x [vo] *nm* (*ZOOL*) calf; (*CULIN*) veal;
(*peau*) calfskin

vécu, e [veky] *pp de* **vivre**

vedette [vədɛt] *nf* (*artiste etc*) star; (*canot*)
motor boat; (*police*) launch

végétal, e, -aux [veʒetal, o] *adj* vegetable
♦ *nm* vegetable, plant; **végétalien, ne** *adj,
nm/f* vegan

végétarien, ne [veʒetaʁjɛ̃, jɛn] *adj, nm/f*
vegetarian

végétation [veʒetasjɔ̃] *nf* vegetation; **~s** *nfpl*
(*MÉD*) adenoids

véhicule [veikyl] *nm* vehicle; **~ utilitaire**
commercial vehicle

veille [vɛj] *nf* (*état*) wakefulness; (*jour*): **la**

~ **(de)** the day before; **la ~ au soir** the previous evening; **à la ~ de** on the eve of; **la ~ de Noël** Christmas Eve; **la ~ du jour de l'An** New Year's Eve

veillée [veje] *nf (soirée)* evening; *(réunion)* evening gathering; ~ *(funèbre)* wake

veiller [veje] *vi* to stay up ♦ *vt (malade, mort)* to watch over, sit up with; ~ **à** to attend to, see to; ~ **à ce que** to make sure that; ~ **sur** to watch over; **veilleur** *nm*: **veilleur de nuit** night watchman; **veilleuse** *nf (lampe)* night light; *(AUTO)* sidelight; *(flamme)* pilot light

veinard, e [venar, ard] *nm/f* lucky devil

veine [ven] *nf (ANAT, du bois etc)* vein; *(filon)* vein, seam; *(fam: chance)*: **avoir de la ~** to be lucky

véliplanchiste [veliplɑ̃ʃist] *nm/f* windsurfer

vélo [velo] *nm* bike, cycle; **faire du ~** to go cycling; ~ **tout-terrain** mountain bike; **vélomoteur** *nm* moped

velours [v(ə)luʀ] *nm* velvet; ~ **côtelé** corduroy; **velouté, e** *adj* velvety ♦ *nm*: **velouté de tomates** cream of tomato soup

velu, e [vəly] *adj* hairy

venais *etc* [vəne] *vb voir* **venir**

venaison [vənɛzɔ̃] *nf* venison

vendange [vɑ̃dɑ̃ʒ] *nf (aussi:* **~s)** grape harvest; **vendanger** *vi* to harvest the grapes

vendeur, -euse [vɑ̃dœʀ, øz] *nm/f* shop assistant ♦ *nm (JUR)* vendor, seller; ~ **de journaux** newspaper seller

vendre [vɑ̃dʀ] *vt* to sell; ~ **qch à qn** to sell sb sth; **"à ~"** "for sale"

vendredi [vɑ̃dʀədi] *nm* Friday; **V~ saint** Good Friday

vénéneux, -euse [venenø, øz] *adj* poisonous

vénérien, ne [veneʀjɛ̃, jɛn] *adj* venereal

vengeance [vɑ̃ʒɑ̃s] *nf* vengeance *no pl*, revenge *no pl*

venger [vɑ̃ʒe] *vt* to avenge; **se ~** *vi* to avenge o.s.; **se ~ de qch** to avenge o.s. for sth, take one's revenge for sth; **se ~ de qn** to take revenge on sb; **se ~ sur** to take revenge on

venimeux, -euse [vənimø, øz] *adj* poisonous, venomous; *(fig: haineux)* venomous, vicious

venin [vənɛ̃] *nm* venom, poison

venir [v(ə)niʀ] *vi* to come; ~ **de** to come from; ~ **de faire**: **je viens d'y aller/de le voir** I've just been there/seen him; **s'il vient à pleuvoir** if it should rain; **j'en viens à croire que** I have come to believe that; **faire ~** *(docteur, plombier)* to call (out)

vent [vɑ̃] *nm* wind; **il y a du ~** it's windy; **c'est du ~** it's all hot air; **au ~** to windward; **sous le ~** to leeward; **avoir le ~ debout/arrière** to head into the wind/have the wind astern; **dans le ~** *(fam)* trendy

vente [vɑ̃t] *nf* sale; **la ~** *(activité)* selling; *(secteur)* sales *pl*; **mettre en ~** *(produit)* to put on sale; *(maison, objet personnel)* to put up for sale; ~ **aux enchères** auction sale; ~ **de charité** jumble sale

venteux, -euse [vɑ̃tø, øz] *adj* windy

ventilateur [vɑ̃tilatœʀ] *nm* fan

ventiler [vɑ̃tile] *vt* to ventilate

ventouse [vɑ̃tuz] *nf (de caoutchouc)* suction pad

ventre [vɑ̃tʀ] *nm (ANAT)* stomach; *(légèrement péj)* belly; *(utérus)* womb; **avoir mal au ~** to have stomach ache *(BRIT)* ou a stomach ache *(US)*

ventriloque [vɑ̃tʀilɔk] *nm/f* ventriloquist

venu, e [v(ə)ny] *pp de* **venir** ♦ *adj*: **bien ~** timely; **mal ~** out of place; **être mal ~ à** ou **de faire** to have no grounds for doing, be in no position to do

ver [veʀ] *nm* worm; *(des fruits etc)* maggot; *(du bois)* woodworm *no pl; voir aussi* **vers**; ~ **à soie** silkworm; ~ **de terre** earthworm; ~ **luisant** glow-worm; ~ **solitaire** tapeworm

verbaliser [veʀbalize] *vi (POLICE)* to book ou report an offender

verbe [veʀb] *nm* verb

verdâtre [veʀdɑtʀ] *adj* greenish

verdict [veʀdik(t)] *nm* verdict

verdir [veʀdiʀ] *vi, vt* to turn green; **verdure** *nf* greenery

véreux, -euse [veʀø, øz] *adj* worm-eaten; *(malhonnête)* shady, corrupt

verge [veʀʒ] *nf (ANAT)* penis

verger [veʀʒe] *nm* orchard

verglacé, e [veʀglase] *adj* icy, iced-over

verglas [veʀgla] *nm* (black) ice

vergogne [veʀgɔɲ]: **sans ~** *adv* shamelessly

véridique [veʀidik] *adj* truthful

vérification [veʀifikasjɔ̃] *nf (action)* checking *no pl; (contrôle)* check

vérifier [veʀifje] *vt* to check; *(corroborer)* to confirm, bear out

véritable [veʀitabl] *adj* real; *(ami, amour)* true

vérité [veʀite] *nf* truth; **en ~** really, actually

vermeil, le [veʀmɛj] *adj* ruby red

vermine [veʀmin] *nf* vermin *pl*

vermoulu, e [veʀmuly] *adj* worm-eaten

verni, e [veʀni] *adj (fam)* lucky; **cuir ~** patent leather

vernir [veʀniʀ] *vt (bois, tableau, ongles)* to varnish; *(poterie)* to glaze

vernis [veʀni] *nm (enduit)* varnish; glaze; *(fig)* veneer; ~ **à ongles** nail polish ou varnish; **vernissage** *nm (d'une exposition)* preview

vérole [veʀɔl] *nf (variole)* smallpox

verrai *etc* [veʀe] *vb voir* **voir**

verre [veʀ] *nm* glass; *(de lunettes)* lens *sg*; **boire** ou **prendre un ~** to have a drink;

~ dépoli frosted glass; **~s de contact** contact lenses; **verrerie** nf (fabrique) glassworks sg; (activité) glass-making; (objets) glassware; **verrière** nf (paroi vitrée) glass wall; (toit vitré) glass roof

verrons etc [ver5] vb voir **voir**

verrou [veru] nm (targette) bolt; **mettre qn sous les ~s** to put sb behind bars; **verrouillage** nm locking; **verrouillage centralisé** central locking; **verrouiller** vt (porte) to bolt; (ordinateur) to lock

verrue [very] nf wart

vers [ver] nm line ♦ nmpl (poésie) verse sg ♦ prép (en direction de) toward(s); (près de) around (about); (temporel) about, around

versant [versɑ̃] nm slopes pl, side

versatile [versatil] adj fickle, changeable

verse [vers]: **à ~** adv: **il pleut à ~** it's pouring (with rain)

Verseau [verso] nm: **le ~** Aquarius

versement [versəmɑ̃] nm payment; **en 3 ~s** in 3 instalments

verser [verse] vt (liquide, grains) to pour; (larmes, sang) to shed; (argent) to pay ♦ vi (véhicule) to overturn; (fig): **~ dans** to lapse into

verset [verse] nm verse

version [versjɔ̃] nf version; (SCOL) translation (into the mother tongue); **film en ~ originale** film in the original language

verso [verso] nm back; **voir au ~** see over(leaf)

vert, e [ver, vert] adj green; (vin) young; (vigoureux) sprightly ♦ nm green

vertèbre [vertebr] nf vertebra

vertement [vertəmɑ̃] adv (réprimander) sharply

vertical, e, -aux [vertikal, o] adj vertical; **verticale** nf vertical; **à la verticale** vertically; **verticalement** adv vertically

vertige [vertiʒ] nm (peur du vide) vertigo; (étourdissement) dizzy spell; (fig) fever; **vertigineux, -euse** adj breathtaking

vertu [verty] nf virtue; **en ~ de** in accordance with; **vertueux, -euse** adj virtuous

verve [verv] nf witty eloquence; **être en ~** to be in brilliant form

verveine [verven] nf (BOT) verbena, vervain; (infusion) verbena tea

vésicule [vezikyl] nf vesicle; **~ biliaire** gall-bladder

vessie [vesi] nf bladder

veste [vest] nf jacket; **~ droite/croisée** single-/double-breasted jacket

vestiaire [vestjer] nm (au théâtre etc) cloakroom; (de stade etc) changing-room (BRIT), locker-room (US)

vestibule [vestibyl] nm hall

vestige [vestiʒ] nm relic; (fig) vestige; **~s** nmpl (de ville) remains

vestimentaire [vestimɑ̃ter] adj (détail) of dress; (élégance) sartorial; **dépenses ~s** clothing expenditure

veston [vestɔ̃] nm jacket

vêtement [vetmɑ̃] nm garment, item of clothing; **~s** nmpl clothes

vétérinaire [veteriner] nm/f vet, veterinary surgeon

vêtir [vetir] vt to clothe, dress

veto [veto] nm veto; **opposer un ~ à** to veto

vêtu, e [vety] pp de **vêtir**

vétuste [vetyst] adj ancient, timeworn

veuf, veuve [vœf, vœv] adj widowed ♦ nm widower

veuille [vœj] vb voir **vouloir**

veuillez [vœje] vb voir **vouloir**

veule [vøl] adj spineless

veuve [vœv] nf widow

veux [vø] vb voir **vouloir**

vexant, e [veksɑ̃, ɑ̃t] adj (contrariant) annoying; (blessant) hurtful

vexation [veksasjɔ̃] nf humiliation

vexer [vekse] vt: **~ qn** to hurt sb's feelings; **se ~ vi** to be offended

viable [vjabl] adj viable; (économie, industrie etc) sustainable

viaduc [vjadyk] nm viaduct

viager, -ère [vjaʒe, er] adj: **rente viagère** life annuity

viande [vjɑ̃d] nf meat

vibrer [vibre] vi to vibrate; (son, voix) to be vibrant; (fig) to be stirred; **faire ~** to (cause to) vibrate; (fig) to stir, thrill

vice [vis] nm vice; (défaut) fault ♦ préfixe: **~...** vice-; **~ de forme** legal flaw ou irregularity

vichy [viʃi] nm (toile) gingham

vicié, e [visje] adj (air) polluted, tainted; (JUR) invalidated

vicieux, -euse [visjø, øz] adj (pervers) lecherous; (rétif) unruly ♦ nm/f lecher

vicinal, e, -aux [visinal, o] adj: **chemin ~** by-road, byway

victime [viktim] nf victim; (d'accident) casualty

victoire [viktwar] nf victory

victuailles [viktɥaj] nfpl provisions

vidange [vidɑ̃ʒ] nf (d'un fossé, réservoir) emptying; (AUTO) oil change; (de lavabo: bonde) waste outlet; **~s** nfpl (matières) sewage sg; **vidanger** vt to empty

vide [vid] adj empty ♦ nm (PHYSIQUE) vacuum; (espace) (empty) space, gap; (futilité, néant) void; **avoir peur du ~** to be afraid of heights; **emballé sous ~** vacuum packed; **à ~** (sans occupants) empty; (sans charge) unladen

vidéo [video] nf video ♦ adj: **cassette ~** video cassette; **jeu ~** video game; **vidéoclip** nm music video; **vidéoclub** nm video shop

vide-ordures [vidɔʀdyʀ] nm inv (rubbish) chute

vidéothèque [videotɛk] nf video library

vide-poches [vidpɔʃ] nm inv tidy; (AUTO) glove compartment

vider [vide] vt to empty; (CULIN: volaille, poisson) to gut, clean out; **se ~** vi to empty; **~ les lieux** to quit ou vacate the premises; **videur** nm (de boîte de nuit) bouncer

vie [vi] nf life; **être en ~** to be alive; **sans ~** lifeless; **à ~** for life

vieil [vjɛj] adj m voir **vieux**; **vieillard** nm old man; **les vieillards** old people, the elderly; **vieille** adj, nf voir **vieux**; **vieilleries** nfpl old things; **vieillesse** nf old age; **vieillir** vi (prendre de l'âge) to grow old; (population, vin) to age; (doctrine, auteur) to become dated ♦ vt to age; **vieillissement** nm growing old; ageing

Vienne [vjɛn] nf Vienna

viens [vjɛ̃] vb voir **venir**

vierge [vjɛʀʒ] adj virgin; (page) clean, blank ♦ nf virgin; (signe): **la V~** Virgo

Vietnam, Viet-Nam [vjɛtnam] nm Vietnam; **vietnamien, ne** adj Vietnamese ♦ nm/f: **Vietnamien, ne** Vietnamese

vieux (vieil), vieille [vjø, vjɛj] adj old ♦ nm/f old man (woman) ♦ nmpl old people; **mon ~/ma vieille** (fam) old man/girl; **prendre un coup de ~** to put years on; **vieille fille** spinster; **~ garçon** bachelor; **~ jeu** adj inv old-fashioned

vif, vive [vif, viv] adj (animé) lively; (alerte, brusque, aigu) sharp; (lumière, couleur) bright; (air) crisp; (vent, émotion) keen; (fort: regret, déception) great, deep; (vivant): **brûlé ~** burnt alive; **de vive voix** personally; **avoir l'esprit ~** to be quick-witted; **piquer qn au ~** to cut sb to the quick; **à ~** (plaie) open; **avoir les nerfs à ~** to be on edge

vigne [viɲ] nf (plante) vine; (plantation) vineyard; **vigneron** nm wine grower

vignette [viɲɛt] nf (ADMIN) ≈ (road) tax disc (BRIT), ≈ license plate sticker (US); (de médicament) price label (used for reimbursement)

vignoble [viɲɔbl] nm (plantation) vineyard; (vignes d'une région) vineyards pl

vigoureux, -euse [viguʀø, øz] adj vigorous, robust

vigueur [vigœʀ] nf vigour; **entrer en ~** to come into force; **en ~** current

vil, e [vil] adj vile, base

vilain, e [vilɛ̃, ɛn] adj (laid) ugly; (affaire, blessure) nasty; (pas sage: enfant) naughty

villa [villa] nf (detached) house; **~ en multipropriété** time-share villa

village [vilaʒ] nm village; **villageois, e** adj village cpd ♦ nm/f villager

ville [vil] nf town; (importante) city; (administration): **la ~** ≈ the Corporation; ≈ the (town) council; **~ d'eaux** spa

villégiature [vi(l)leʒjatyʀ] nf holiday; (lieu de) ~ (holiday) resort

vin [vɛ̃] nm wine; **avoir le ~ gai** to get happy after a few drinks; **~ d'honneur** reception (with wine and snacks); **~ de pays** local wine; **~ ordinaire** table wine

vinaigre [vinɛgʀ] nm vinegar; **vinaigrette** nf vinaigrette, French dressing

vindicatif, -ive [vɛ̃dikatif, iv] adj vindictive

vineux, -euse [vinø, øz] adj win(e)y

vingt [vɛ̃] num twenty; **vingtaine** nf: **une vingtaine (de)** about twenty, twenty or so; **vingtième** num twentieth

vinicole [vinikɔl] adj wine cpd, wine-growing

vins etc [vɛ̃] vb voir **venir**

vinyle [vinil] nm vinyl

viol [vjɔl] nm (d'une femme) rape; (d'un lieu sacré) violation

violacé, e [vjɔlase] adj purplish, mauvish

violemment [vjɔlamɑ̃] adv violently

violence [vjɔlɑ̃s] nf violence

violent, e [vjɔlɑ̃, ɑ̃t] adj violent; (remède) drastic

violer [vjɔle] vt (femme) to rape; (sépulture, loi, traité) to violate

violet, te [vjɔlɛ, ɛt] adj, nm purple, mauve; **violette** nf (fleur) violet

violon [vjɔlɔ̃] nm violin; (fam: prison) lock-up; **~ d'Ingres** hobby; **violoncelle** nm cello; **violoniste** nm/f violinist

vipère [vipɛʀ] nf viper, adder

virage [viʀaʒ] nm (d'un véhicule) turn; (d'une route, piste) bend

virée [viʀe] nf trip; (à pied) walk; (longue) walking tour; (dans les cafés) tour

virement [viʀmɑ̃] nm (COMM) transfer

virent [viʀ] vb voir **voir**

virer [viʀe] vt (COMM): **~ qch (sur)** to transfer sth (into); (fam: expulser): **~ qn** to kick sb out ♦ vi to turn; (CHIMIE) to change colour; **~ de bord** to tack

virevolter [viʀvɔlte] vi to twirl around

virgule [viʀgyl] nf comma; (MATH) point

viril, e [viʀil] adj (propre à l'homme) masculine; (énergique, courageux) manly, virile

virtuel, le [viʀtɥɛl] adj potential; (théorique) virtual

virtuose [viʀtɥoz] nm/f (MUS) virtuoso; (gén) master

virus [viʀys] nm virus

vis¹ [vi] vb voir **voir; vivre**

vis² [vi] nf screw

visa [viza] nm (sceau) stamp; (validation de passeport) visa

visage [vizaʒ] nm face

vis-à-vis [vizavi] *prép*: ~-~-~ **de qn** to(wards) sb; **en** ~-~-~ facing each other

viscéral, e, -aux [viseʀal, o] *adj* (*fig*) deep-seated, deep-rooted

visées [vize] *nfpl* (*intentions*) designs

viser [vize] *vi* to aim ♦ *vt* to aim at; (*concerner*) to be aimed ou directed at; (*apposer un visa sur*) to stamp, visa; ~ **à qch/faire** to aim at sth/at doing ou to do; **viseur** *nm* (*d'arme*) sights *pl*; (*PHOTO*) viewfinder

visibilité [vizibilite] *nf* visibility

visible [vizibl] *adj* visible; (*disponible*): **est-il ~?** can he see me?, will he see visitors?

visière [vizjɛʀ] *nf* (*de casquette*) peak; (*qui s'attache*) eyeshade

vision [vizjɔ̃] *nf* vision; (*sens*) (eye)sight, vision; (*fait de voir*): **la ~ de** the sight of; **visionneuse** *nf* viewer

visite [vizit] *nf* visit; ~ **médicale** medical examination; ~ **accompagnée** ou **guidée** guided tour; **faire une ~ à qn** to call on sb, pay sb a visit; **rendre ~ à qn** to visit sb, pay sb a visit; **être en ~** (**chez qn**) to be visiting (sb); **avoir de la ~** to have visitors; **heures de ~** (*hôpital, prison*) visiting hours

visiter [vizite] *vt* to visit; **visiteur, -euse** *nm/f* visitor

vison [vizɔ̃] *nm* mink

visser [vise] *vt*: ~ **qch** (*fixer, serrer*) to screw sth on

visuel, le [vizɥɛl] *adj* visual

vit [vi] *vb voir* **voir; vivre**

vital, e, -aux [vital, o] *adj* vital

vitamine [vitamin] *nf* vitamin

vite [vit] *adv* (*rapidement*) quickly, fast; (*sans délai*) quickly; (*sous peu*) soon; ~! quick!; **faire ~** to be quick; **le temps passe ~** time flies

vitesse [vites] *nf* speed; (*AUTO: dispositif*) gear; **prendre de la ~** to pick up speed; **à toute ~** at full ou top speed; **en ~** (*rapidement*) quickly; (*en hâte*) in a hurry

viticole [vitikɔl] *adj* wine *cpd*, wine-growing; **viticulteur** *nm* wine grower

vitrage [vitʀaʒ] *nm*: **double ~** double glazing

vitrail, -aux [vitʀaj, o] *nm* stained-glass window

vitre [vitʀ] *nf* (*window*) pane; (*de portière, voiture*) window; **vitré, e** *adj* glass *cpd*; **vitrer** *vt* to glaze; **vitreux, -euse** *adj* (*terne*) glassy

vitrine [vitʀin] *nf* (*shop*) window; (*petite armoire*) display cabinet; **en ~** in the window; ~ **publicitaire** display case, showcase

vivable [vivabl] *adj* (*personne*) livable-with; (*maison*) fit to live in

vivace [vivas] *adj* (*arbre, plante*) hardy; (*fig*) indestructible, inveterate

vivacité [vivasite] *nf* liveliness, vivacity

vivant, e [vivɑ̃, ɑ̃t] *adj* (*qui vit*) living, alive; (*animé*) lively; (*preuve, exemple*) living ♦ *nm*: **du ~ de qn** in sb's lifetime; **les ~s** the living

vive [viv] *adj voir* **vif** ♦ *vb voir* **vivre** ♦ *excl*: ~ **le roi!** long live the king!; **vivement** *adv* deeply ♦ *excl*: **vivement les vacances!** roll on the holidays!

vivier [vivje] *nm* (*étang*) fish tank; (*réservoir*) fishpond

vivifiant, e [vivifjɑ̃, jɑ̃t] *adj* invigorating

vivions [vivjɔ̃] *vb voir* **vivre**

vivoter [vivɔte] *vi* (*personne*) to scrape a living, get by; (*fig: affaire etc*) to struggle along

vivre [vivʀ] *vi, vt* to live; (*période*) to live through; ~ **de** to live on; **il vit encore** he is still alive; **se laisser ~** to take life as it comes; **ne plus ~** (*être anxieux*) to live on one's nerves; **il a vécu** (*eu une vie aventureuse*) he has seen life; **être facile à ~** to be easy to get on with; **faire ~ qn** (*pourvoir à sa subsistance*) to provide (a living) for sb; **vivres** *nmpl* provisions, food supplies

vlan [vlɑ̃] *excl* wham!, bang!

VO [veo] *nf*: **film en ~** film in the original version; **en ~ sous-titrée** in the original version with subtitles

vocable [vɔkabl] *nm* term

vocabulaire [vɔkabylɛʀ] *nm* vocabulary

vocation [vɔkasjɔ̃] *nf* vocation, calling

vociférer [vɔsifeʀe] *vi, vt* to scream

vœu, x [vø] *nm* wish; (*promesse*) vow; **faire ~ de** to take a vow of; **tous nos ~x de bonne année, meilleurs ~x** best wishes for the New Year

vogue [vɔg] *nf* fashion, vogue

voguer [vɔge] *vi* to sail

voici [vwasi] *prép* (*pour introduire, désigner*) here is +*sg*, here are +*pl*; **et ~ que ...** and now it (*ou* he) ...; *voir aussi* **voilà**

voie [vwa] *nf* way; (*RAIL*) track, line; (*AUTO*) lane; **être en bonne ~** to be going well; **mettre qn sur la ~** to put sb on the right track; **pays en ~ de développement** developing country; **être en ~ d'achèvement/de rénovation** to be nearing completion/in the process of renovation; **par ~ buccale** *ou* **orale** orally; **à ~ étroite** narrow-gauge; ~ **d'eau** (*NAVIG*) leak; ~ **de garage** (*RAIL*) siding; ~ **ferrée** track; railway line; **la ~ publique** the public highway

voilà [vwala] *prép* (*en désignant*) there is +*sg*, there are +*pl*; **les ~** *ou* **voici** here *ou* there they are; **en ~** *ou* **voici un** here's one, there's one; **voici mon frère et ~ ma sœur** this is my brother and that's my sister; ~ *ou* **voici deux ans** two years ago; ~ *ou* **voici deux ans que** it's two years since; **et ~!** there we are!; ~ **tout** that's all; ~ *ou* **voici** (*en offrant etc*) there *ou* here you are; **tiens!** ~ **Paul** look!

there's Paul

voile [vwal] *nm* veil; (*tissu léger*) net ♦ *nf* sail; (*sport*) sailing; **voiler** *vt* to veil; (*fausser: roue*) to buckle; (: *bois*) to warp; **se voiler** *vi* (*lune, regard*) to mist over; (*voix*) to become husky; (*roue, disque*) to buckle; (*planche*) to warp; **voilier** *nm* sailing ship; (*de plaisance*) sailing boat; **voilure** *nf* (*de voilier*) sails *pl*

voir [vwaʀ] *vi, vt* to see; **se** ~ *vt* (*être visible*) to show; (*se fréquenter*) to see each other; (*se produire*) to happen; **se ~ critiquer/ transformer** to be criticized/transformed; **cela se voit** (*c'est visible*) that's obvious, it shows; **faire ~ qch à qn** to show sb sth; **en faire ~ à qn** (*fig*) to give sb a hard time; **ne pas pouvoir ~ qn** not to be able to stand sb; **voyons!** let's see now; (*indignation etc*) come on!; **avoir quelque chose à ~ avec** to have something to do with

voire [vwaʀ] *adv* even

voisin, e [vwazɛ̃, in] *adj* (*proche*) neighbouring; (*contigu*) next; (*ressemblant*) connected ♦ *nm/f* neighbour; **voisinage** *nm* (*proximité*) proximity; (*environs*) vicinity; (*quartier, voisins*) neighbourhood

voiture [vwatyʀ] *nf* car; (*wagon*) coach, carriage; ~ **de course** racing car; ~ **de sport** sports car

voix [vwa] *nf* voice; (*POL*) vote; **à haute** ~ aloud; **à** ~ **basse** in a low voice; **à 2/4** ~ (*MUS*) in 2/4 parts; **avoir** ~ **au chapitre** to have a say in the matter

vol [vɔl] *nm* (*d'oiseau, d'avion*) flight; (*larcin*) theft; ~ **régulier** scheduled flight; **à** ~ **d'oiseau** as the crow flies; **au** ~: **attraper qch au** ~ to catch sth as it flies past; **en** ~ in flight; ~ **à main armée** armed robbery; ~ **à voile** gliding; ~ **libre** hang-gliding

volage [vɔlaʒ] *adj* fickle

volaille [vɔlaj] *nf* (*oiseaux*) poultry *pl*; (*viande*) poultry *no pl*; (*oiseau*) fowl

volant, e [vɔlɑ̃, ɑ̃t] *adj voir* **feuille** *etc* ♦ *nm* (*d'automobile*) (steering) wheel; (*de commande*) wheel; (*objet lancé*) shuttlecock; (*bande de tissu*) flounce

volcan [vɔlkɑ̃] *nm* volcano

volée [vɔle] *nf* (*TENNIS*) volley; **à la** ~: **rattraper à la** ~ to catch in mid-air; **à toute** ~ (*sonner les cloches*) vigorously; (*lancer un projectile*) with full force; ~ **de coups/de flèches** volley of blows/arrows

voler [vɔle] *vi* (*avion, oiseau, fig*) to fly; (*voleur*) to steal ♦ *vt* (*objet*) to steal; (*personne*) to rob; ~ **qch à qn** to steal sth from sb; **il ne l'a pas volé!** he asked for it!

volet [vɔle] *nm* (*de fenêtre*) shutter; (*de feuillet, document*) section

voleur, -euse [vɔlœʀ, øz] *nm/f* thief ♦ *adj* thieving; **"au** ~**!"** "stop thief!"

volière [vɔljeʀ] *nf* aviary

volley [vɔle] *nm* volleyball

volontaire [vɔlɔ̃teʀ] *adj* (*acte, enrôlement, prisonnier*) voluntary; (*oubli*) intentional; (*caractère, personne: décidé*) self-willed ♦ *nm/f* volunteer

volonté [vɔlɔ̃te] *nf* (*faculté de vouloir*) will; (*énergie, fermeté*) will(power); (*souhait, désir*) wish; **à** ~ as much as one likes; **bonne** ~ goodwill, willingness; **mauvaise** ~ lack of goodwill, unwillingness

volontiers [vɔlɔ̃tje] *adv* (*avec plaisir*) willingly, gladly; (*habituellement, souvent*) readily, willingly; **voulez-vous boire quelque chose? -** ~! would you like something to drink? - yes, please!

volt [vɔlt] *nm* volt

volte-face [vɔltəfas] *nf inv*: **faire** ~-~ to turn round

voltige [vɔltiʒ] *nf* (*ÉQUITATION*) trick riding; (*au cirque*) acrobatics *sg*; **voltiger** *vi* to flutter (about)

volubile [vɔlybil] *adj* voluble

volume [vɔlym] *nm* volume; (*GÉOM: solide*) solid; **volumineux, -euse** *adj* voluminous, bulky

volupté [vɔlypte] *nf* sensual delight *ou* pleasure

vomi [vɔmi] *nm* vomit; **vomir** *vi* to vomit, be sick ♦ *vt* to vomit, bring up; (*fig*) to belch out, spew out; (*exécrer*) to loathe, abhor; **vomissements** *nmpl*: **être pris de vomissements** to (suddenly) start vomiting

vont [vɔ̃] *vb voir* **aller**

vorace [vɔras] *adj* voracious

vos [vo] *adj voir* **votre**

vote [vɔt] *nm* vote; ~ **par correspondance/ procuration** postal/proxy vote; **voter** *vi* to vote ♦ *vt* (*projet de loi*) to vote for; (*loi, réforme*) to pass

votre [vɔtʀ] (*pl* **vos**) *adj* your

vôtre [votʀ] *pron*: **le** ~, **la** ~, **les** ~**s** yours; **les** ~**s** (*fig*) your family *ou* folks; **à la** ~ (*toast*) your (good) health!

voudrai *etc* [vudʀe] *vb voir* **vouloir**

voué, e [vwe] *adj*: ~ **à** doomed to

vouer [vwe] *vt*: ~ **qch à** (*Dieu, un saint*) to dedicate sth to; ~ **sa vie à** (*étude, cause etc*) to devote one's life to; ~ **une amitié éternelle à qn** to vow undying friendship to sb

┌─────────────┐
│ MOT-CLÉ │
└─────────────┘

vouloir [vulwaʀ] *nm*: **le bon vouloir de qn** sb's goodwill; sb's pleasure
♦ *vt* **1** (*exiger, désirer*) to want; **vouloir faire/ que qn fasse** to want to do/sb to do; **voulez-vous du thé?** would you like *ou* do you want some tea?; **que me veut-il?** what does he want with me?; **sans le vouloir**

(*involontairement*) without meaning to, unintentionally; **je voudrais ceci/faire** I would ou I'd like this/to do
2 (*consentir*): **je veux bien** (*bonne volonté*) I'll be happy to; (*concession*) fair enough, that's fine; **oui, si on veut** (*en quelque sorte*) yes, if you like; **veuillez attendre** please wait; **veuillez agréer ...** (*formule épistolaire*) yours faithfully
3: **en vouloir à qn** to bear sb a grudge; **s'en vouloir (de)** to be annoyed with o.s. (for); **il en veut à mon argent** he's after my money
4: **vouloir de: l'entreprise ne veut plus de lui** the firm doesn't want him any more; **elle ne veut pas de son aide** she doesn't want his help
5: **vouloir dire** to mean

voulu, e [vuly] adj (*requis*) required, requisite; (*délibéré*) deliberate, intentional; voir aussi **vouloir**

vous [vu] pron you; (*objet indirect*) (to) you; (*réfléchi: sg*) yourself; (: *pl*) yourselves; (*réciproque*) each other; **~-même** yourself; **~-mêmes** yourselves

voûte [vut] nf vault; **voûter: se voûter** vi (*dos, personne*) to become stooped

vouvoyer [vuvwaje] vt: **~ qn** to address sb as "vous"

voyage [vwajaʒ] nm journey, trip; (*fait de ~r*): **le ~** travel(ling); **partir/être en ~** to go off/be away on a journey ou trip; **faire bon ~** to have a good journey; **~ d'agrément/d'affaires** pleasure/business trip; **~ de noces** honeymoon; **~ organisé** package tour

voyager [vwajaʒe] vi to travel; **voyageur, -euse** nm/f traveller; (*passager*) passenger

voyant, e [vwajã, ãt] adj (*couleur*) loud, gaudy ♦ nm (*signal*) (warning) light; **voyante** nf clairvoyante

voyelle [vwajɛl] nf vowel

voyons etc [vwajɔ̃] vb voir **voir**

voyou [vwaju] nm hooligan

vrac [vʀak]: **en ~** adv (*au détail*) loose; (*en gros*) in bulk; (*en désordre*) in a jumble

vrai, e [vʀɛ] adj (*véridique: récit, faits*) true; (*non factice, authentique*) real; **à ~ dire** to tell the truth; **vraiment** adv really; **vraisemblable** adj likely; (*excuse*) convincing; **vraisemblablement** adv probably; **vraisemblance** nf likelihood; (*romanesque*) verisimilitude

vrille [vʀij] nf (*de plante*) tendril; (*outil*) gimlet; (*spirale*) spiral; (AVIAT) spin

vrombir [vʀɔ̃biʀ] vi to hum

VRP sigle m (= voyageur, représentant, placier) sales rep (fam)

VTT sigle m (= vélo tout-terrain) mountain bike

vu, e [vy] pp de **voir** ♦ adj: **bien/mal ~** (fig: *personne*) popular/unpopular; (: *chose*) approved/disapproved of ♦ prép (*en raison de*) in view of; **~ que** in view of the fact that

vue [vy] nf (*fait de voir*): **la ~ de** the sight of; (*sens, faculté*) (eye)sight; (*panorama, image, photo*) view; **~s** nfpl (*idées*) views; (*dessein*) designs; **hors de ~** out of sight; **avoir en ~** to have in mind; **tirer à ~** to shoot on sight; **à ~ d'œil** visibly; **de ~** by sight; **perdre de ~** to lose sight of; **en ~** (*visible*) in sight; (*célèbre*) in the public eye; **en ~ de faire** with a view to doing

vulgaire [vylgɛʀ] adj (*grossier*) vulgar, coarse; (*ordinaire*) commonplace, mundane; (*péj: quelconque*): **de ~s touristes** common tourists; (BOT, ZOOL: *non latin*) common; **vulgariser** vt to popularize

vulnérable [vylneʀabl] adj vulnerable

W, w

wagon [vagɔ̃] nm (*de voyageurs*) carriage; (*de marchandises*) truck, wagon; **wagon-lit** nm sleeper, sleeping car; **wagon-restaurant** nm restaurant ou dining car

wallon, ne [walɔ̃, ɔn] adj Walloon

waters [watɛʀ] nmpl toilet sg

watt [wat] nm watt

WC sigle mpl (= water-closet(s)) toilet

week-end [wikɛnd] nm weekend

western [wɛstɛʀn] nm western

whisky [wiski] (pl whiskies) nm whisky

X, x

xénophobe [gzenɔfɔb] adj xenophobic ♦ nm/f xenophobe

xérès [gzeʀɛs] nm sherry

xylophone [gzilɔfɔn] nm xylophone

Y, y

y [i] adv (*à cet endroit*) there; (*dessus*) on it (ou them); (*dedans*) in it (ou them) ♦ pron (*about ou on ou of*) it (*d'après le verbe employé*); **j'~ pense** I'm thinking about it; **ça ~ est!** that's it!; voir aussi **aller**; **avoir**

yacht [jɔt] nm yacht

yaourt [jauʀt] nm yoghourt; **~ nature/aux fruits** plain/fruit yogurt

yeux [jø] nmpl de **œil**

yoga [jɔga] nm yoga

yoghourt [jɔguʀt] nm = **yaourt**

yougoslave [jugɔslav] (HISTOIRE) adj Yugoslav(ian) ♦ nm/f: **Y~** Yugoslav

Yougoslavie [jugɔslavi] (*HISTOIRE*)
nf Yugoslavia

Z, z

zapper [zape] *vi* to zap

zapping [zapiŋ] *nm*: **faire du ~** to flick
through the channels

zèbre [zɛbʀ(ə)] *nm* (*ZOOL*) zebra; **zébré, e**
adj striped, streaked

zèle [zɛl] *nm* zeal; **faire du ~** (*péj*) to be over-
zealous; **zélé, e** *adj* zealous

zéro [zeʀo] *nm* zero, nought (*BRIT*); **au-
dessous de ~** below zero (Centigrade) *ou*
freezing; **partir de ~** to start from scratch;
trois (buts) à ~ 3 (goals to) nil

zeste [zɛst] *nm* peel, zest

zézayer [zezeje] *vi* to have a lisp

zigzag [zigzag] *nm* zigzag; **zigzaguer** *vi* to
zigzag

zinc [zɛ̃g] *nm* (*CHIMIE*) zinc

zizanie [zizani] *nf*: **semer la ~** to stir up ill-
feeling

zizi [zizi] *nm* (*langage enfantin*) willy

zodiaque [zɔdjak] *nm* zodiac

zona [zona] *nm* shingles *sg*

zone [zon] *nf* zone, area; **~ bleue** ≈ restricted parking area; **~ industrielle** industrial
estate

zoo [zo(o)] *nm* zoo

zoologie [zɔɔlɔʒi] *nf* zoology; **zoologique**
adj zoological

zut [zyt] *excl* dash (it)! (*BRIT*), nuts! (*US*)

ENGLISH – FRENCH
ANGLAIS – FRANÇAIS

A, a

A [eɪ] n (MUS) la m

a [eɪ, ə] (*before vowel or silent h: an*) *indef art* **1** un(e); **a book** un livre; **an apple** une pomme; **she's a doctor** elle est médecin
2 (*instead of the number "one"*) un(e); **a year ago** il y a un an; **a hundred/thousand** *etc* **pounds** cent/mille *etc* livres
3 (*in expressing ratios, prices etc*): **3 a day/ week** 3 par jour/semaine; **10 km an hour** 10 km à l'heure; **30p a kilo** 30p le kilo

A.A. n abbr = **Alcoholics Anonymous**; (BRIT: *Automobile Association*) ≈ TCF m
A.A.A. (US) n abbr (= American Automobile Association) ≈ TCF m
aback [ə'bæk] adv: **to be taken ~** être stupéfait(e), être déconcentané(e)
abandon [ə'bændən] vt abandonner
abate [ə'beɪt] vi s'apaiser, se calmer
abbey ['æbɪ] n abbaye f
abbot ['æbət] n père supérieur
abbreviation [əbriːvɪ'eɪʃən] n abréviation f
abdicate ['æbdɪkeɪt] vt, vi abdiquer
abdomen ['æbdəmen] n abdomen m
abduct [æb'dʌkt] vt enlever
aberration [æbə'reɪʃən] n anomalie f
abide [ə'baɪd] vt: **I can't ~ it/him** je ne peux pas le souffrir or supporter; **~ by** vt fus observer, respecter
ability [ə'bɪlɪtɪ] n compétence f; capacité f; (*skill*) talent m
abject ['æbdʒɛkt] adj (*poverty*) sordide; (*apology*) plat(e)
ablaze [ə'bleɪz] adj en feu, en flammes
able ['eɪbl] adj capable, compétent(e); **to be ~ to do sth** être capable de faire qch, pouvoir faire qch; **~-bodied** adj robuste; **ably** adv avec compétence or talent, habilement
abnormal [æb'nɔːməl] adj anormal(e)
aboard [ə'bɔːd] adv à bord ♦ prep à bord de
abode [ə'bəud] n (LAW): **of no fixed ~** sans domicile fixe
abolish [ə'bɔlɪʃ] vt abolir
aborigine [æbə'rɪdʒɪnɪ] n aborigène m/f
abort [ə'bɔːt] vt faire avorter; **~ion** n avortement m; **to have an ~ion** se faire avorter; **~ive** adj manqué(e)

about [ə'baut] adv **1** (*approximately*) environ, à peu près; **about a hundred/thousand** *etc* environ cent/mille *etc*, une centaine/un millier *etc*; **it takes about 10 hours** ça prend environ or à peu près 10 heures; **at about 2 o'clock** vers 2 heures; **I've just about finished** j'ai presque fini
2 (*referring to place*) çà et là, de côté et d'autre; **to run about** courir çà et là; **to walk about** se promener, aller et venir
3: **to be about to do sth** être sur le point de faire qch
♦ prep **1** (*relating to*) au sujet de, à propos de; **a book about London** un livre sur Londres; **what is it about?** de quoi s'agit-il?; **we talked about it** nous en avons parlé; **what or how about doing this?** et si nous faisions ceci?
2 (*referring to place*) dans; **to walk about the town** se promener dans la ville

about-face [ə'baut'feɪs] n demi-tour m
about-turn [ə'baut'tɜːn] n (MIL) demi-tour m; (*fig*) volte-face f
above [ə'bʌv] adv au-dessus ♦ prep au-dessus de; (*more*) plus de; **mentioned ~** mentionné ci-dessus; **~ all** par-dessus tout, surtout; **~board** adj franc (franche); honnête
abrasive [ə'breɪzɪv] adj abrasif(-ive); (*fig*) caustique, agressif(-ive)
abreast [ə'brɛst] adv de front; **to keep ~ of** se tenir au courant de
abroad [ə'brɔːd] adv à l'étranger
abrupt [ə'brʌpt] adj (*steep, blunt*) abrupt(e); (*sudden, gruff*) brusque; **~ly** adv (*speak, end*) brusquement
abscess ['æbsɪs] n abcès m
absence ['æbsəns] n absence f
absent ['æbsənt] adj absent(e); **~ee** [æbsən'tiː] n absent(e); (*habitual*) absentéiste m/f; **~-minded** adj distrait(e)
absolute ['æbsəluːt] adj absolu(e); **~ly** [æbsə'luːtlɪ] adv absolument
absolve [əb'zɔlv] vt: **to ~ sb (from)** (*blame, responsibility, sin*) absoudre qn (de)
absorb [əb'zɔːb] vt absorber; **to be ~ed in a book** être plongé(e) dans un livre; **~ent cotton** (US) n coton m hydrophile

abstain [əb'steɪn] vi: to ~ (from) s'abstenir (de)

abstract ['æbstrækt] adj abstrait(e)

absurd [əb'səːd] adj absurde

abundant [ə'bʌndənt] adj abondant(e)

abuse [n ə'bjuːs, vb ə'bjuːz] n abus m; (insults) insultes fpl, injures fpl ♦ vt abuser de; (insult) insulter; **abusive** [ə'bjuːsɪv] adj grossier(-ère), injurieux(-euse)

abysmal [ə'bɪzməl] adj exécrable; (ignorance etc) sans bornes

abyss [ə'bɪs] n abîme m, gouffre m

AC abbr (= alternating current) courant alternatif

academic [ækə'demɪk] adj universitaire; (person: scholarly) intellectuel(le); (pej: issue) oiseux(-euse), purement théorique ♦ n universitaire m/f; ~ **year** n année f universitaire

academy [ə'kædəmɪ] n (learned body) académie f; (school) collège m; ~ **of music** conservatoire m

accelerate [æk'seləreɪt] vt, vi accélérer; **accelerator** n accélérateur m

accent ['æksənt] n accent m

accept [ək'sept] vt accepter; **~able** adj acceptable; **~ance** n acceptation f

access ['ækses] n accès m; (LAW: in divorce) droit m de visite; **~ible** [æk'sesəbl] adj accessible

accessory [æk'sesərɪ] n accessoire m

accident ['æksɪdənt] n accident m; (chance) hasard m; **by** ~ accidentellement; par hasard; **~al** [æksɪ'dentl] adj accidentel(le); **~ally** [æksɪ'dentəlɪ] adv accidentellement; ~ **insurance** n assurance f accident; **~-prone** adj sujet(te) aux accidents

acclaim [ə'kleɪm] n acclamations fpl ♦ vt acclamer

accommodate [ə'kɔmədeɪt] vt loger, recevoir; (oblige, help) obliger; (car etc) contenir; **accommodating** adj obligeant(e), arrangeant(e); **accommodation** [əkɔmə'deɪʃən] (US **accommodations**) n logement m

accompany [ə'kʌmpənɪ] vt accompagner

accomplice [ə'kʌmplɪs] n complice m/f

accomplish [ə'kʌmplɪʃ] vt accomplir; **~ment** n accomplissement m; réussite f; (skill: gen pl) talent m

accord [ə'kɔːd] n accord m ♦ vt accorder; **of his own** ~ de son plein gré; **~ance** [ə'kɔːdəns] n: **in ~ance with** conformément à; **~ing:** **~ing to** prep selon; **~ingly** adv en conséquence

accordion [ə'kɔːdɪən] n accordéon m

account [ə'kaunt] n (COMM) compte m; (report) compte rendu; récit m; **~s** npl (COMM) comptabilité f, comptes; **of no** ~ sans

importance; **on** ~ en acompte; **on no** ~ en aucun cas; **on** ~ **of** à cause de; **to take into** ~, **take** ~ **of** tenir compte de; ~ **for** vt fus expliquer, rendre compte de; **~able** adj: **~able (to)** responsable (devant); **~ancy** n comptabilité f; **~ant** n comptable m/f; ~ **number** n (at bank etc) numéro m de compte

accrued interest [ə'kruːd-] n intérêt m cumulé

accumulate [ə'kjuːmjuleɪt] vt accumuler, amasser ♦ vi s'accumuler, s'amasser

accuracy ['ækjurəsɪ] n exactitude f, précision f

accurate ['ækjurɪt] adj exact(e), précis(e); **~ly** adv avec précision

accusation [ækju'zeɪʃən] n accusation f

accuse [ə'kjuːz] vt: to ~ **sb (of sth)** accuser qn (de qch); **the ~d** l'accusé(e)

accustom [ə'kʌstəm] vt accoutumer, habituer; **~ed** adj (usual) habituel(le); (in the habit): **~ed to** habitué(e) or accoutumé(e) à

ace [eɪs] n as m

ache [eɪk] n mal m, douleur f ♦ vi (yearn): to ~ **to do sth** mourir d'envie de faire qch; **my head ~s** j'ai mal à la tête

achieve [ə'tʃiːv] vt (aim) atteindre; (victory, success) remporter, obtenir; **~ment** n exploit m, réussite f

acid ['æsɪd] adj acide ♦ n acide m; ~ **rain** n pluies fpl acides

acknowledge [ək'nɔlɪdʒ] vt (letter: also: ~ **receipt of**) accuser réception de; (fact) reconnaître; **~ment** n (of letter) accusé m de réception

acne ['æknɪ] n acné f

acorn ['eɪkɔːn] n gland m

acoustic [ə'kuːstɪk] adj acoustique; **~s** n, npl acoustique f

acquaint [ə'kweɪnt] vt: to ~ **sb with sth** mettre qn au courant de qch; **to be ~ed with** connaître; **~ance** n connaissance f

acquire [ə'kwaɪə*] vt acquérir

acquit [ə'kwɪt] vt acquitter; to ~ **o.s. well** bien se comporter, s'en tirer très honorablement

acre ['eɪkə*] n acre f (= 4047 m²)

acrid ['ækrɪd] adj âcre

acrobat ['ækrəbæt] n acrobate m/f

across [ə'krɔs] prep (on the other side) de l'autre côté de; (crosswise) en travers de ♦ adv de l'autre côté; en travers; **to run/swim** ~ traverser en courant/à la nage; ~ **from** en face de

acrylic [ə'krɪlɪk] adj acrylique

act [ækt] n acte m, action f; (of play) acte; (in music-hall etc) numéro m; (LAW) loi f ♦ vi agir; (THEATRE) jouer; (pretend) jouer la comédie ♦ vt (part) jouer, tenir; **in the ~ of** en train de; **to ~ as** servir de; **~ing** adj suppléant(e), par intérim ♦ n (*activity*): **to do some ~ing** faire du théâtre (*or* du cinéma)

action ['ækʃən] n action f; (*MIL*) combat(s) m(pl); **out of ~** hors de combat; (*machine*) hors d'usage; **to take ~** agir, prendre des mesures; **~ replay** n (*TV*) ralenti m

activate ['æktɪveɪt] vt (*mechanism*) actionner, faire fonctionner

active ['æktɪv] adj actif(-ive); (*volcano*) en activité; **~ly** adv activement; **activity** [æk'tɪvɪtɪ] n activité f; **activity holiday** n vacances actives

actor ['æktər] n acteur m

actress ['æktrɪs] n actrice f

actual ['æktjuəl] adj réel(le), véritable; **~ly** adv (*really*) réellement, véritablement; (*in fact*) en fait

acute [ə'kjuːt] adj aigu(ë); (*mind, observer*) pénétrant(e), perspicace

ad [æd] n abbr = **advertisement**

A.D. adv abbr (= *anno Domini*) ap. J.-C.

adamant ['ædəmənt] adj inflexible

adapt [ə'dæpt] vt adapter ♦ vi: **to ~ (to)** s'adapter (à); **~able** adj (*device*) adaptable; (*person*) qui s'adapte facilement; **~er, ~or** n (*ELEC*) adaptateur m

add [æd] vt ajouter; (*figures: also:* **to ~ up**) additionner ♦ vi: **to ~ to** (*increase*) ajouter à, accroître

adder ['ædər] n vipère f

addict ['ædɪkt] n intoxiqué(e); (*fig*) fanatique m/f; **~ed** [ə'dɪktɪd] adj: **to be ~ed to** (*drugs, drink etc*) être adonné(e) à; (*fig: football etc*) être un(e) fanatique de; **~ion** n (*MED*) dépendance f; **~ive** adj qui crée une dépendance

addition [ə'dɪʃən] n addition f; (*thing added*) ajout m; **in ~** de plus; de surcroît; **in ~ to** en plus de; **~al** adj supplémentaire

additive ['ædɪtɪv] n additif m

address [ə'drɛs] n adresse f; (*talk*) discours m, allocution f ♦ vt adresser; (*speak to*) s'adresser à; **to ~ (o.s. to) a problem** s'attaquer à un problème

adept ['ædɛpt] adj: **~ at** expert(e) à or en

adequate ['ædɪkwɪt] adj adéquat(e); suffisant(e)

adhere [əd'hɪər] vi: **to ~ to** adhérer à; (*fig: rule, decision*) se tenir à

adhesive [əd'hiːzɪv] n adhésif m; **~ tape** n (*BRIT*) ruban adhésif; (*US: MED*) sparadrap m

ad hoc [æd'hɔk] adj improvisé(e), ad hoc

adjacent [ə'dʒeɪsənt] adj: **~ (to)** adjacent (à)

adjective ['ædʒɛktɪv] n adjectif m

adjoining [ə'dʒɔɪnɪŋ] adj voisin(e), adjacent(e), attenant(e)

adjourn [ə'dʒəːn] vt ajourner ♦ vi suspendre la séance; clore la session

adjust [ə'dʒʌst] vt (*machine*) ajuster, régler;

(*prices, wages*) rajuster ♦ vi: **to ~ (to)** s'adapter (à); **~able** adj réglable; **~ment** n (*PSYCH*) adaptation f; (*to machine*) ajustage m, réglage m; (*of prices, wages*) rajustement m

ad-lib [æd'lɪb] vt, vi improviser; **ad lib** adv à volonté, à loisir

administer [əd'mɪnɪstər] vt administrer; (*justice*) rendre; **administration** [ədmɪnɪs'treɪʃən] n administration f; **administrative** [əd'mɪnɪstrətɪv] adj administratif(-ive)

admiral ['ædmərəl] n amiral m; **A~ty** ['ædmərəltɪ] (*BRIT*) n: **the A~ty** le ministère m de la Marine

admire [əd'maɪər] vt admirer

admission [əd'mɪʃən] n admission f; (*to exhibition, night club etc*) entrée f; (*confession*) aveu m; **~ charge** n droits mpl d'admission

admit [əd'mɪt] vt laisser entrer; admettre; (*agree*) reconnaître, admettre; **~ to** vt fus reconnaître, avouer; **~tance** n admission f, (droit m d')entrée f; **~tedly** adv il faut admettre

ado [ə'duː] n: **without (any) more ~** sans plus de cérémonies

adolescence [ædəu'lɛsns] n adolescence f; **adolescent** adj, n adolescent(e)

adopt [ə'dɔpt] vt adopter; **~ed** adj adoptif(-ive), adopté(e); **~ion** n adoption f

adore [ə'dɔːr] vt adorer

adorn [ə'dɔːn] vt orner

Adriatic (Sea) [eɪdrɪ'ætɪk-] n Adriatique f

adrift [ə'drɪft] adv à la dérive

adult ['ædʌlt] n adulte m/f ♦ adj adulte; (*literature, education*) pour adultes

adultery [ə'dʌltərɪ] n adultère m

advance [əd'vɑːns] n avance f ♦ adj: **~ booking** réservation f ♦ vt avancer ♦ vi avancer, s'avancer; **~ notice** avertissement m; **to make ~s (to sb)** faire des propositions (à qn); (*amorously*) faire des avances (à qn); **in ~** à l'avance, d'avance; **~d** adj avancé(e); (*SCOL: studies*) supérieur(e)

advantage [əd'vɑːntɪdʒ] n (*also TENNIS*) avantage m; **to take ~ of** (*person*) exploiter

advent ['ædvənt] n avènement m, venue f; **A~** Avent m

adventure [əd'vɛntʃər] n aventure f

adverb ['ædvəːb] n adverbe m

adverse ['ædvəːs] adj défavorable, contraire

advert ['ædvəːt] (*BRIT*) n abbr = **advertisement**

advertise ['ædvətaɪz] vi, vt faire de la publicité (pour); (*in classified ads etc*) mettre une annonce (pour vendre); **to ~ for** (*staff, accommodation*) faire paraître une annonce pour trouver; **~ment** [əd'vəːtɪsmənt] n (*COMM*) réclame f, publicité f; (*in classified ads*) annonce f; **advertising** n publicité f

advice [əd'vaɪs] n conseils mpl; (notification) avis m; **piece of ~** conseil; **to take legal ~** consulter un avocat

advisable [əd'vaɪzəbl] adj conseillé(e), indiqué(e)

advise [əd'vaɪz] vt conseiller; **to ~ sb of sth** aviser or informer qn de qch; **to ~ against sth/doing sth** déconseiller qch/conseiller de ne pas faire qch; **~r, advisor** n conseiller(-ère); **advisory** adj consultatif(-ive)

advocate [n 'ædvəkɪt, vb 'ædvəkeɪt] n (upholder) défenseur m, avocat(e); (LAW) avocat(e) ♦ vt recommander, prôner

Aegean (Sea) [iː'dʒiːən-] n (mer f) Égée f

aerial ['ɛərɪəl] n antenne f ♦ adj aérien(ne)

aerobics [ɛə'rəubɪks] n aérobic m

aeroplane ['ɛərəpleɪn] (BRIT) n avion m

aerosol ['ɛərəsɔl] n aérosol m

aesthetic [iːs'θetɪk] adj esthétique

afar [ə'fɑːr] adv: **from ~** de loin

affair [ə'fɛər] n affaire f; (also: **love ~**) liaison f; aventure f

affect [ə'fekt] vt affecter; (disease) atteindre; **~ed** adj affecté(e); **~ion** n affection f; **~ionate** adj affectueux(-euse)

affinity [ə'fɪnɪtɪ] n (bond, rapport): **to have an ~ with/for** avoir une affinité avec/pour

afflict [ə'flɪkt] vt affliger

affluence ['æfluəns] n abondance f, opulence f

affluent ['æfluənt] adj (person, family, surroundings) aisé(e), riche; **the ~ society** la société d'abondance

afford [ə'fɔːd] vt se permettre; (provide) fournir, procurer

afloat [ə'fləut] adj, adv à flot; **to stay ~** surnager

afoot [ə'fut] adv: **there is something ~** il se prépare quelque chose

afraid [ə'freɪd] adj effrayé(e); **to be ~ of** or **to** avoir peur de; **I am ~ that ...** je suis désolé(e), mais ...; **I am ~ so/not** hélas oui/non

Africa ['æfrɪkə] n Afrique f; **~n** adj africain(e) ♦ n Africain(e)

after ['ɑːftər] prep, adv après ♦ conj après que, après avoir or être +pp; **what/who are you ~?** que/qui cherchez-vous?; **~ he left/having done** après qu'il fut parti/après avoir fait; **ask ~ him** demandez de ses nouvelles; **to name sb ~ sb** donner à qn le nom de qn; **twenty ~ eight** (US) huit heures vingt; **~ all** après tout; **~ you!** après vous, Monsieur (or Madame etc); **~effects** npl (of disaster, radiation, drink etc) répercussions fpl; (of illness) séquelles fpl, suites fpl; **~math** n conséquences fpl, suites fpl; **~noon** n après-midi m or f; **~s** (inf) n (dessert) dessert m; **~-sales service** (BRIT) n (for car, washing machine etc) service m après-vente; **~-shave** (lotion) n after-shave m; **~sun** n après-soleil m inv; **~thought** n: **I had an ~thought** il m'est venu une idée après coup; **~wards** (US **afterward**) adv après

again [ə'gen] adv de nouveau; encore (une fois); **to do sth ~** refaire qch; **not ... ~** ne ... plus; **~ and ~** à plusieurs reprises

against [ə'genst] prep contre; (compared to) par rapport à

age [eɪdʒ] n âge m ♦ vi vieillir; **it's been ~s since** ça fait une éternité que ... ne; **he is 20 years of ~** il a 20 ans; **to come of ~** atteindre sa majorité; **~d** [adj eɪdʒd, npl 'eɪdʒɪd] adj: **~d 10** âgé(e) de 10 ans ♦ npl: **the ~d** les personnes âgées; **~ group** n tranche f d'âge; **~ limit** n limite f d'âge

agency ['eɪdʒənsɪ] n agence f; (government body) organisme m, office m

agenda [ə'dʒendə] n ordre m du jour

agent ['eɪdʒənt] n agent m, représentant m; (firm) concessionnaire m

aggravate ['ægrəveɪt] vt aggraver; (annoy) exaspérer

aggressive [ə'gresɪv] adj agressif(-ive)

agitate ['ædʒɪteɪt] vt (person) agiter, émouvoir, troubler ♦ vi: **to ~ for/against** faire campagne pour/contre

AGM n abbr (= annual general meeting) AG f

ago [ə'gəu] adv: **2 days ~** il y a deux jours; **not long ~** il n'y a pas longtemps; **how long ~?** il y a combien de temps (de cela)?

agony ['ægənɪ] n (pain) douleur f atroce; **to be in ~** souffrir le martyre

agree [ə'griː] vt (price) convenir de ♦ vi: **to ~ with** (person) être d'accord avec; (statements etc) concorder avec; (LING) s'accorder avec; **to ~ to do** accepter de or consentir à faire; **to ~ to sth** consentir à qch; **to ~ that** (admit) convenir or reconnaître que; **garlic doesn't ~ with me** je ne supporte pas l'ail; **~able** adj agréable; (willing) consentant(e), d'accord; **~d** adj (time, place) convenu(e); **~ment** n accord m; **in ~ment** d'accord

agricultural [ægrɪ'kʌltʃərəl] adj agricole

agriculture ['ægrɪkʌltʃər] n agriculture f

aground [ə'graund] adv: **to run ~** échouer, s'échouer

ahead [ə'hed] adv (in front: of position, place) devant; (: at the head) en avant; (look, plan, think) en avant; **~ of** devant; (fig: schedule etc) en avance sur; **~ of time** en avance; **go right** or **straight ~** allez tout droit; **go ~!** (fig: permission) allez-y!

aid [eɪd] n aide f; (device) appareil m ♦ vt aider; **in ~ of** en faveur de; see also **hearing**

aide [eɪd] n (person) aide mf, assistant(e)

AIDS [eɪdz] n abbr (= acquired immune deficiency syndrome) SIDA m; **AIDS-related deficiency syndrome**

adj associé(e) au sida

aim [eɪm] *vt*: **to ~ sth (at)** (*gun, camera*) braquer or pointer qch (sur); (*missile*) lancer qch (à or contre or en direction de); (*blow*) allonger qch (à); (*remark*) destiner or adresser qch (à) ♦ *vi* (*also*: **to take ~**) viser ♦ *n* but *m*; (*skill*): **his ~ is bad** il vise mal; **to ~ at** viser; (*fig*) viser (à); **to ~ to do** avoir l'intention de faire; **~less** *adj* sans but

ain't [eɪnt] (*inf*) = **am not; aren't; isn't**

air [ɛəʳ] *n* air *m* ♦ *vt* (*room, bed, clothes*) aérer; (*grievances, views, ideas*) exposer, faire connaître ♦ *cpd* (*currents, attack etc*) aérien(ne); **to throw sth into the ~** jeter qch en l'air; **by ~** (*travel*) par avion; **to be on the ~** (*RADIO, TV: programme*) être diffusé(e); (: *station*) diffuser; **~bed** *n* matelas *m* pneumatique; **~-conditioned** *adj* climatisé(e); **~ conditioning** *n* climatisation *f*; **~craft** *n inv* avion *m*; **~craft carrier** *n* porte-avions *m inv*; **~field** *n* terrain *m* d'aviation; **A~ Force** *n* armée *f* de l'air; **~ freshener** *n* désodorisant *m*; **~gun** *n* fusil *m* à air comprimé; **~ hostess** *n* (*BRIT*) hôtesse *f* de l'air; **~ letter** *n* (*BRIT*) aérogramme *m*; **~lift** *n* pont aérien; **~line** *n* ligne aérienne, compagnie *f* d'aviation; **~liner** *n* avion *m* de ligne; **~mail** *n*: **by ~mail** par avion; **~ mile** *n* air mile *m*; **~plane** *n* (*US*) avion *m*; **~port** *n* aéroport *m*; **~ raid** *n* attaque or raid aérien(ne); **~sick** *adj*: **to be ~sick** avoir le mal de l'air; **~tight** *adj* hermétique; **~-traffic controller** *n* aiguilleur *m* du ciel; **~y** *adj* bien aéré(e); (*manners*) dégagé(e)

aisle [aɪl] *n* (*of church*) allée centrale; nef latérale; (*of theatre etc*) couloir *m*, passage *m*, allée; **~ seat** *n* place *f* côté couloir

ajar [əˈdʒɑːʳ] *adj* entrouvert(e)

akin [əˈkɪn] *adj*: **~ to** (*similar*) qui tient de or ressemble à

alarm [əˈlɑːm] *n* alarme *f* ♦ *vt* alarmer; **~ call** *n* coup de fil pour réveiller; **~ clock** *n* réveille-matin *m inv*, réveil *m*

alas [əˈlæs] *excl* hélas!

album [ˈælbəm] *n* album *m*

alcohol [ˈælkəhɔl] *n* alcool *m*; **~-free** *adj* sans alcool; **~ic** [ælkəˈhɔlɪk] *adj* alcoolique ♦ *n* alcoolique *m/f*; **A~ics Anonymous** Alcooliques anonymes

ale [eɪl] *n* bière *f*

alert [əˈləːt] *adj* alerte, vif (vive); vigilant(e) ♦ *n* alerte *f* ♦ *vt* alerter; **on the ~** sur le qui-vive; (*MIL*) en état d'alerte

algebra [ˈældʒɪbrə] *n* algèbre *f*

Algeria [ælˈdʒɪərɪə] *n* Algérie *f*

alias [ˈeɪlɪəs] *adv* alias ♦ *n* faux nom, nom d'emprunt; (*writer*) pseudonyme *m*

alibi [ˈælɪbaɪ] *n* alibi *m*

alien [ˈeɪlɪən] *n* étranger(-ère); (*from outer space*) extraterrestre *mf* ♦ *adj*: **~ (to)** étranger(-ère) (à)

alight [əˈlaɪt] *adj, adv* en feu ♦ *vi* mettre pied à terre; (*passenger*) descendre

alike [əˈlaɪk] *adj* semblable, pareil(le) ♦ *adv* de même; **to look ~** se ressembler

alimony [ˈælɪmənɪ] *n* (*payment*) pension *f* alimentaire

alive [əˈlaɪv] *adj* vivant(e); (*lively*) plein(e) de vie

╔══════════════╗
║ *KEYWORD* ║
╚══════════════╝

all [ɔːl] *adj* (*singular*) tout(e); (*plural*) tous (toutes); **all day** toute la journée; **all night** toute la nuit; **all men** tous les hommes; **all five** tous les cinq; **all the food** toute la nourriture; **all the books** tous les livres; **all the time** tout le temps; **all his life** toute sa vie ♦ *pron* **1** tout; **I ate it all, I ate all of it** j'ai tout mangé; **all of us went** nous y sommes tous allés; **all of the boys went** tous les garçons y sont allés

2 (*in phrases*): **above all** surtout, par-dessus tout; **after all** après tout; **not at all** (*in answer to question*) pas du tout; (*in answer to thanks*) je vous en prie!; **I'm not at all tired** je ne suis pas du tout fatigué(e); **anything at all will do** n'importe quoi fera l'affaire; **all in all** tout bien considéré, en fin de compte ♦ *adv*: **all alone** tout(e) seul(e); **it's not as hard as all that** ce n'est pas si difficile que ça; **all the more/the better** d'autant plus/mieux; **all but** presque, pratiquement; **the score is 2 all** le score est de 2 partout

allege [əˈledʒ] *vt* alléguer, prétendre; **~dly** [əˈledʒɪdlɪ] *adv* à ce que l'on prétend, paraît-il

allegiance [əˈliːdʒəns] *n* allégeance *f*, fidélité *f*, obéissance *f*

allergic [əˈləːdʒɪk] *adj*: **~ to** allergique à

allergy [ˈælədʒɪ] *n* allergie *f*

alleviate [əˈliːvɪeɪt] *vt* soulager, adoucir

alley [ˈælɪ] *n* ruelle *f*

alliance [əˈlaɪəns] *n* alliance *f*

allied [ˈælaɪd] *adj* allié(e)

all-in [ˈɔːlɪn] (*BRIT*) *adj* (*also adv*: *charge*) tout compris

all-night [ˈɔːlˈnaɪt] *adj* ouvert(e) or qui dure toute la nuit

allocate [ˈæləkeɪt] *vt* (*share out*) répartir, distribuer; **to ~ sth to** (*duties*) assigner or attribuer qch à; (*sum, time*) allouer qch à

allot [əˈlɔt] *vt*: **to ~ (to)** (*money*) répartir (entre), distribuer (à); (*time*) allouer (à); **~ment** *n* (*share*) part *f*; (*garden*) lopin *m* de terre (*loué à la municipalité*)

all-out [ˈɔːlaut] *adj* (*effort etc*) total(e) ♦ *adv*: **all out** à fond

allow [əˈlau] vt (*practice, behaviour*) permettre, autoriser; (*sum to spend etc*) accorder; allouer; (*sum, time estimated*) compter, prévoir; (*claim, goal*) admettre; (*concede*): **to ~ that** convenir que; **to ~ sb to do** permettre à qn de faire, autoriser qn à faire; **he is ~ed to ...** on lui permet de ...; **~ for** vt fus tenir compte de; **~ance** [əˈlauəns] n (*money received*) allocation f; subside m; indemnité f; (*TAX*) somme f déductible du revenu imposable, abattement m; **to make ~ances for** tenir compte de

alloy [ˈælɔɪ] n alliage m

all: **~ right** adv (*feel, work*) bien; (*as answer*) d'accord; **~-rounder** n: **to be a good ~-rounder** être doué(e) en tout; **~-time** adj (*record*) sans précédent, absolu(e)

ally [n ˈælaɪ, vb əˈlaɪ] n allié m ♦ vt: **to ~ o.s. with** s'allier avec

almighty [ɔːlˈmaɪtɪ] adj tout-puissant; (*tremendous*) énorme

almond [ˈɑːmənd] n amande f

almost [ˈɔːlməust] adv presque

alone [əˈləun] adj, adv seul(e); **to leave sb ~** laisser qn tranquille; **to leave sth ~** ne pas toucher à qch; **let ~ ...** sans parler de ...; encore moins ...

along [əˈlɒŋ] prep le long de ♦ adv: **is he coming ~ with us?** vient-il avec nous?; **he was hopping/limping ~** il avançait en sautillant/boitant; **~ with** (*together with: person*) en compagnie de; (: *thing*) avec, en plus de; **all ~** (*all the time*) depuis le début; **~side** prep le long de; à côté de ♦ adv bord à bord

aloof [əˈluːf] adj distant(e) ♦ adv: **to stand ~** se tenir à distance or à l'écart

aloud [əˈlaud] adv à haute voix

alphabet [ˈælfəbɛt] n alphabet m; **~ical** [ælfəˈbɛtɪkl] adj alphabétique

alpine [ˈælpaɪn] adj alpin(e), alpestre

Alps [ælps] npl: **the ~** les Alpes fpl

already [ɔːlˈrɛdɪ] adv déjà

alright [ˈɔːlˈraɪt] (*BRIT*) adv = **all right**

Alsatian [ælˈseɪʃən] (*BRIT*) n (*dog*) berger allemand

also [ˈɔːlsəu] adv aussi

altar [ˈɔltəʳ] n autel m

alter [ˈɔltəʳ] vt, vi changer

alternate [adj ɔlˈtɜːnɪt, vb ˈɔltəneɪt] adj alterné(e), alternant(e), alternatif(-ive) ♦ vi alterner; **on ~ days** un jour sur deux, tous les deux jours; **alternating current** n courant alternatif

alternative [ɔlˈtɜːnətɪv] adj (*solutions*) possible, au choix; (*plan*) autre, de rechange; (*lifestyle etc*) parallèle ♦ n (*choice*) alternative f; (*other possibility*) solution f de remplacement or de rechange, autre possibilité f; **an ~ comedian** un nouveau comique; **~ medicine** médecines fpl parallèles or douces; **~ly** adv: **~ly one could** une autre or l'autre solution serait de, on pourrait aussi

alternator [ˈɔltəneɪtəʳ] n (*AUT*) alternateur m

although [ɔːlˈðəu] conj bien que +sub

altitude [ˈæltɪtjuːd] n altitude f

alto [ˈæltəu] n (*female*) contralto m; (*male*) haute-contre f

altogether [ɔːltəˈgɛðəʳ] adv entièrement, tout à fait; (*on the whole*) tout compte fait; (*in all*) en tout

aluminium [æljuˈmɪnɪəm] (*BRIT*), **aluminum** [əˈluːmɪnəm] (*US*) n aluminium m

always [ˈɔːlweɪz] adv toujours

Alzheimer's (disease) [ˈæltshaɪməz-] n maladie f d'Alzheimer

am [æm] vb see **be**

a.m. adv abbr (= *ante meridiem*) du matin

amalgamate [əˈmælgəmeɪt] vt, vi fusionner

amateur [ˈæmətəʳ] n amateur m; **~ish** (*pej*) adj d'amateur

amaze [əˈmeɪz] vt stupéfier; **to be ~d (at)** être stupéfait(e) (de); **~ment** n stupéfaction f, stupeur f; **amazing** adj étonnant(e); exceptionnel(le)

ambassador [æmˈbæsədəʳ] n ambassadeur m

amber [ˈæmbəʳ] n ambre m; **at ~** (*BRIT: AUT*) à l'orange

ambiguous [æmˈbɪgjuəs] adj ambigu(ë)

ambition [æmˈbɪʃən] n ambition f; **ambitious** adj ambitieux(-euse)

ambulance [ˈæmbjuləns] n ambulance f

ambush [ˈæmbuʃ] n embuscade f ♦ vt tendre une embuscade à

amenable [əˈmiːnəbl] adj: **~ to** (*advice etc*) disposé(e) à écouter

amend [əˈmɛnd] vt (*law*) amender; (*text*) corriger; **to make ~s** réparer ses torts, faire amende honorable

amenities [əˈmiːnɪtɪz] npl aménagements mpl, équipements mpl

America [əˈmɛrɪkə] n Amérique f; **~n** adj américain(e) ♦ n Américain(e)

amiable [ˈeɪmɪəbl] adj aimable, affable

amicable [ˈæmɪkəbl] adj amical(e); (*LAW*) à l'amiable

amid(st) [əˈmɪd(st)] prep parmi, au milieu de

amiss [əˈmɪs] adj, adv: **there's something ~** il y a quelque chose qui ne va pas or qui cloche; **to take sth ~** prendre qch mal or de travers

ammonia [əˈməunɪə] n (*gas*) ammoniac m; (*liquid*) ammoniaque f

ammunition [æmjuˈnɪʃən] n munitions fpl

amok [əˈmɔk] adv: **to run ~** être pris(e) d'un accès de folie furieuse

among(st) [əˈmʌŋ(st)] prep parmi, entre

amorous [ˈæmərəs] adj amoureux(-euse)

amount [ə'maunt] n (sum) somme f, montant m; (quantity) quantité f, nombre m ♦ vi: **to ~ to** (total) s'élever à; (be same as) équivaloir à, revenir à

amp(ere) ['æmp(ɛəʳ)] n ampère m

ample ['æmpl] adj ample; spacieux(-euse); (enough): **this is ~** c'est largement suffisant; **to have ~ time/room** avoir bien assez de temps/place

amplifier ['æmplɪfaɪəʳ] n amplificateur m

amuse [ə'mju:z] vt amuser, divertir; **~ment** n amusement m; **~ment arcade** n salle f de jeu; **~ment park** n parc m d'attractions

an [æn, ən] indef art see **a**

anaemic [ə'ni:mɪk] (US **anemic**) adj anémique

anaesthetic [ænɪs'θetɪk] (US **anesthetic**) n anesthésique m

analog(ue) ['ænələg] adj (watch, computer) analogique

analyse ['ænəlaɪz] (US **analyze**) vt analyser; **analysis** [ə'næləsɪs] (pl **analyses**) n analyse f; **analyst** ['ænəlɪst] n (POL etc) spécialiste m/f; (US) psychanalyste m/f

analyze ['ænəlaɪz] (US) vt = **analyse**

anarchist ['ænəkɪst] n anarchiste m/f

anarchy ['ænəkɪ] n anarchie f

anatomy [ə'nætəmɪ] n anatomie f

ancestor ['ænsɪstəʳ] n ancêtre m, aïeul m

anchor ['æŋkəʳ] n ancre f ♦ vi (also: **to drop ~**) jeter l'ancre, mouiller ♦ vt mettre à l'ancre; (fig): **to ~ sth to** fixer qch à

anchovy ['æntʃəvɪ] n anchois m

ancient ['eɪnʃənt] adj ancien(ne), antique; (person) d'un âge vénérable; (car) antédiluvien(ne)

ancillary [æn'sɪlərɪ] adj auxiliaire

and [ænd] conj et; **~ so on** et ainsi de suite; **try ~ come** tâchez de venir; **he talked ~ talked** il n'a pas arrêté de parler; **better ~ better** de mieux en mieux

anew [ə'nju:] adv à nouveau

angel ['eɪndʒəl] n ange m

anger ['æŋgəʳ] n colère f

angina [æn'dʒaɪnə] n angine f de poitrine

angle ['æŋgl] n angle m; **from their ~** de leur point de vue

angler ['æŋgləʳ] n pêcheur(-euse) à la ligne

Anglican ['æŋglɪkən] adj, n anglican(e)

angling ['æŋglɪŋ] n pêche f à la ligne

Anglo- ['æŋgləʊ] prefix anglo(-)

angrily ['æŋgrɪlɪ] adv avec colère

angry ['æŋgrɪ] adj en colère, furieux(-euse); (wound) enflammé(e); **to be ~ with sb/at sth** être furieux contre qn/de qch; **to get ~ se** fâcher, se mettre en colère

anguish ['æŋgwɪʃ] n (mental) angoisse f

animal ['ænɪməl] n animal m ♦ adj animal(e)

animate [vb 'ænɪmeɪt, adj 'ænɪmɪt] vt animer

♦ adj animé(e), vivant(e); **~d** adj animé(e)

aniseed ['ænɪsi:d] n anis m

ankle ['æŋkl] n cheville f; **~ sock** n socquette f

annex [n 'ænɛks, vb ə'nɛks] n (BRIT: **~e**) annexe f ♦ vt annexer

anniversary [ænɪ'vɜːsərɪ] n anniversaire m

announce [ə'nauns] vt annoncer; (birth, death) faire part de; **~ment** n annonce f; (for births etc: in newspaper) avis m de faire-part; (: letter, card) faire-part m; **~r** n (RADIO, TV: between programmes) speaker(ine)

annoy [ə'nɔɪ] vt agacer, ennuyer, contrarier; **don't get ~ed!** ne vous fâchez pas!; **~ance** n mécontentement m, contrariété f; **~ing** adj agaçant(e), contrariant(e)

annual ['ænjuəl] adj annuel(le) ♦ n (BOT) plante annuelle; (children's book) album m

annul [ə'nʌl] vt annuler

annum ['ænəm] n see **per**

anonymous [ə'nɔnɪməs] adj anonyme

anorak ['ænəræk] n anorak m

anorexia [ænə'rɛksɪə] n (also: **~ nervosa**) anorexie f

another [ə'nʌðəʳ] adj: **~ book** (one more) un autre livre, encore un livre, un livre de plus; (a different one) un autre livre ♦ pron un(e) autre, encore un(e), un(e) de plus; see also **one**

answer ['ɑːnsəʳ] n réponse f; (to problem) solution f ♦ vi répondre ♦ vt (reply to) répondre à; (problem) résoudre; (prayer) exaucer; **in ~ to your letter** en réponse à votre lettre; **to ~ the phone** répondre (au téléphone); **to ~ the bell** or **the door** aller or venir ouvrir (la porte); **~ back** vi répondre, répliquer; **~ for** vt fus (person) répondre de, se porter garant de; (crime, one's actions) être responsable de; **~ to** vt fus (description) répondre or correspondre à; **~able** adj: **~able (to sb/for sth)** responsable (devant qn/de qch); **~ing machine** n répondeur m automatique

ant [ænt] n fourmi f

antagonism [æn'tægənɪzəm] n antagonisme m

antagonize [æn'tægənaɪz] vt éveiller l'hostilité de, contrarier

Antarctic [ænt'ɑːktɪk] n: **the ~** l'Antarctique m

antenatal ['æntɪ'neɪtl] adj prénatal(e); **~ clinic** n service m de consultation prénatale

anthem ['ænθəm] n: **national ~** hymne national

anti: **~-aircraft** adj (missile) anti-aérien(ne); **~biotic** ['æntɪbaɪ'ɔtɪk] n antibiotique m; **~body** n anticorps m

anticipate [æn'tɪsɪpeɪt] vt s'attendre à; prévoir; (wishes, request) aller au devant de,

devancer
anticipation [æntɪsɪ'peɪʃən] n attente f; **in ~**
par anticipation, à l'avance
anticlimax ['æntɪ'klaɪmæks] n déception f,
douche froide (fam)
anticlockwise ['æntɪ'klɔkwaɪz] adj, adv
dans le sens inverse des aiguilles d'une
montre
antics ['æntɪks] npl singeries fpl
antifreeze ['æntɪfriːz] n antigel m
antihistamine ['æntɪ'hɪstəmɪn] n
antihistaminique m
antiquated ['æntɪkweɪtɪd] adj vieilli(e),
suranné(e), vieillot(te)
antique [æn'tiːk] n objet m d'art ancien,
meuble ancien or d'époque, antiquité f ♦ adj
ancien(ne); **~ dealer** n antiquaire m;
~ shop n magasin m d'antiquités
anti- **~-Semitism** ['æntɪ'semɪtɪzəm] n
antisémitisme m; **~septic** [æntɪ'septɪk] n
antiseptique m; **~social** ['æntɪ'səuʃəl] adj peu
liant(e), sauvage, insociable; (against society)
antisocial(e)
antlers ['æntləz] npl bois mpl, ramure f
anvil ['ænvɪl] n enclume f
anxiety [æŋ'zaɪətɪ] n anxiété f; (keenness):
~ to do grand désir or impatience f de faire
anxious ['æŋkʃəs] adj anxieux(-euse),
angoissé(e); (worrying: time, situation)
inquiétant(e); (keen): **~ to do/that** qui tient
beaucoup à faire/à ce que; impatient(e) de
faire/que

KEYWORD

any ['enɪ] adj **1** (in questions etc: singular) du,
de l', de la; (: plural) des; **have you any
butter/children/ink?** avez-vous du beurre/des
enfants/de l'encre?
2 (with negative) de, d'; **I haven't any
money/books** je n'ai pas d'argent/de livres
3 (no matter which) n'importe quel(le);
choose any book you like vous pouvez choisir
n'importe quel livre
4 (in phrases): **in any case** de toute façon;
any day now d'un jour à l'autre; **at any
moment** à tout moment, d'un instant à
l'autre; **at any rate** en tout cas
♦ pron **1** (in questions etc) en; **have you got
any?** est-ce que vous en avez?; **can any of
you sing?** est-ce que parmi vous il y en a qui
savent chanter?
2 (with negative) en; **I haven't any (of them)**
je n'en ai pas, je n'en ai aucun
3 (no matter which one(s)) n'importe lequel
(or laquelle); **take any of those books (you
like)** vous pouvez prendre n'importe lequel
de ces livres
♦ adv **1** (in questions etc): **do you want any
more soup/sandwiches?** voulez-vous encore

de la soupe/des sandwichs?; **are you feeling
any better?** est-ce que vous vous sentez
mieux?
2 (with negative): **I can't hear him any more**
je ne l'entends plus; **don't wait any longer**
n'attendez pas plus longtemps

any: **~body** pron n'importe qui; (in
interrogative sentences) quelqu'un; (in
negative sentences) personne; **~how** adv (at any rate) de
toute façon, quand même; (haphazard)
n'importe comment; **~one** pron = **anybody**;
~thing pron n'importe quoi, quelque chose,
ne ... rien; **~way** adv de toute façon;
~where adv n'importe où, quelque part; **I
don't see him ~where** je ne le vois nulle part
apart [ə'pɑːt] adv (to one side) à part; de
côté; à l'écart; (separately) séparément; **10
miles ~** à 10 miles l'un de l'autre; **to take ~**
démonter; **~ from** à part, excepté
apartheid [ə'pɑːteɪt] n apartheid m
apartment [ə'pɑːtmənt] n (US) appartement
m, logement m; (room) chambre f;
~ building (US) n immeuble m; (divided
house) maison divisée en appartements
ape [eɪp] n (grand) singe ♦ vt singer
apéritif [ə'perɪtiːf] n apéritif m
aperture ['æpətʃuə'] n orifice m, ouverture f;
(PHOT) ouverture (du diaphragme)
APEX ['eɪpeks] n abbr (AVIAT) (= advance
purchase excursion) APEX m
apologetic [əpɔlə'dʒetɪk] adj (tone, letter)
d'excuse; (person): **to be ~** s'excuser
apologize [ə'pɔlədʒaɪz] vi: **to ~ (for sth to
sb)** s'excuser (de qch auprès de qn),
présenter des excuses (à qn pour qch)
apology [ə'pɔlədʒɪ] n excuses fpl
apostle [ə'pɔsl] n apôtre m
apostrophe [ə'pɔstrəfɪ] n apostrophe f
appalling [ə'pɔːlɪŋ] adj épouvantable;
(stupidity) consternant(e)
apparatus [æpə'reɪtəs] n appareil m,
dispositif m; (in gymnasium) agrès mpl; (of
government) dispositif m
apparel [ə'pærəl] (US) n habillement m
apparent [ə'pærənt] adj apparent(e); **~ly**
adv apparemment
appeal [ə'piːl] vi (LAW) faire or interjeter appel
♦ n appel m; (request) prière f; appel m;
(charm) attrait m, charme m; **to ~** for lancer
un appel pour; **to ~ to** (beg) faire appel à;
(be attractive) plaire à; **it doesn't ~ to me** cela
ne m'attire pas; **~ing** adj (attractive)
attrayant(e)
appear [ə'pɪə'] vi apparaître, se montrer;
(LAW) comparaître; (publication) paraître,
sortir, être publié(e); (seem) paraître,
sembler; **it would ~ that** il semble que; **to ~ in**

Hamlet jouer dans Hamlet; **to ~ on TV** passer à la télé; **~ance** n apparition f; parution f; (look, aspect) apparence f, aspect m

appease [əˈpiːz] vt apaiser, calmer

appendicitis [əpendɪˈsaɪtɪs] n appendicite f

appendix [əˈpendɪks] (pl **appendices**) n appendice m

appetite [ˈæpɪtaɪt] n appétit m; **appetizer** n amuse-gueule m; (drink) apéritif m

applaud [əˈplɔːd] vt, vi applaudir

applause [əˈplɔːz] n applaudissements mpl

apple [ˈæpl] n pomme f; **~ tree** n pommier m

appliance [əˈplaɪəns] n appareil m

applicable [əˈplɪkəbl] adj (relevant): **to be ~ to** valoir pour

applicant [ˈæplɪkənt] n: **~ (for)** candidat(e) (à)

application [æplɪˈkeɪʃən] n application f; (for a job, a grant etc) demande f; candidature f; **~ form** n formulaire m de demande

applied [əˈplaɪd] adj appliqué(e)

apply [əˈplaɪ] vt: **to ~ (to)** (paint, ointment) appliquer (sur); (law etc) appliquer (à) ♦ vi: **to ~ to** (be suitable for, relevant to) s'appliquer à; (ask) s'adresser à; **to ~ (for)** (permit, grant) faire une demande (en vue d'obtenir); (job) poser sa candidature (pour), faire une demande d'emploi (concernant); **to ~ o.s. to** s'appliquer à

appoint [əˈpɔɪnt] vt nommer, engager; **~ed** adj: **at the ~ed time** à l'heure dite; **~ment** n nomination f; (meeting) rendez-vous m; **to make an ~ment (with)** prendre rendez-vous (avec)

appraisal [əˈpreɪzl] n évaluation f

appreciate [əˈpriːʃɪeɪt] vt (like) apprécier; (be grateful for) être reconnaissant(e) de; (understand) comprendre; se rendre compte de ♦ vi (FINANCE) prendre de la valeur

appreciation [əpriːʃɪˈeɪʃən] n appréciation f; (gratitude) reconnaissance f; (COMM) hausse f, valorisation f

appreciative [əˈpriːʃɪətɪv] adj (person) sensible; (comment) élogieux(-euse)

apprehensive [æprɪˈhensɪv] adj inquiet(-ète), appréhensif(-ive)

apprentice [əˈprentɪs] n apprenti m; **~ship** n apprentissage m

approach [əˈprəutʃ] vi approcher ♦ vt (come near) approcher de; (ask, apply to) s'adresser à; (situation, problem) aborder ♦ n approche f; (access) accès m; **~able** adj accessible

appropriate [adj əˈprəuprɪɪt, vb əˈprəuprɪeɪt] adj (moment, remark) opportun(e); (tool etc) approprié(e) ♦ vt (take) s'approprier

approval [əˈpruːvəl] n approbation f; **on ~** (COMM) à l'examen

approve [əˈpruːv] vt approuver; **~ of** vt fus approuver

approximate [adj əˈprɒksɪmɪt, vb əˈprɒksɪmeɪt] adj approximatif(-ive) ♦ vt se rapprocher de, être proche de; **~ly** adv approximativement

apricot [ˈeɪprɪkɒt] n abricot m

April [ˈeɪprəl] n avril m; **~ Fool's Day** le premier avril

apron [ˈeɪprən] n tablier m

apt [æpt] adj (suitable) approprié(e); (likely): **~ to do** susceptible de faire; qui a tendance à faire

Aquarius [əˈkweərɪəs] n le Verseau

Arab [ˈærəb] adj arabe ♦ n Arabe m/f; **~ian** [əˈreɪbɪən] adj arabe; **~ic** adj arabe ♦ n arabe m

arbitrary [ˈɑːbɪtrərɪ] adj arbitraire

arbitration [ɑːbɪˈtreɪʃən] n arbitrage m

arcade [ɑːˈkeɪd] n arcade f; (passage with shops) passage m, galerie marchande; (with video games) salle f de jeu

arch [ɑːtʃ] n arc m; (of foot) cambrure f, voûte f plantaire ♦ vt arquer, cambrer

archaeologist [ɑːkɪˈɒlədʒɪst] n archéologue m/f

archaeology [ɑːkɪˈɒlədʒɪ] n archéologie f

archbishop [ɑːtʃˈbɪʃəp] n archevêque m

archeology etc (US) [ɑːkɪˈɒlədʒɪ] = **archaeology** etc

archery [ˈɑːtʃərɪ] n tir m à l'arc

architect [ˈɑːkɪtekt] n architecte m; **~ure** n architecture f

archives [ˈɑːkaɪvz] npl archives fpl

Arctic [ˈɑːktɪk] adj arctique ♦ n Arctique m

ardent [ˈɑːdənt] adj fervent(e)

are [ɑːˈ] vb see **be**

area [ˈeərɪə] n (GEOM) superficie f; (zone) région f; (: smaller) secteur m, partie f; (in room) coin m; (knowledge, research) domaine m; **~ code** (US) n (TEL) indicatif m téléphonique

aren't [ɑːnt] = **are not**

Argentina [ɑːdʒənˈtiːnə] n Argentine f; **Argentinian** [ɑːdʒənˈtɪnɪən] adj argentin(e) ♦ n Argentin(e)

arguably [ˈɑːɡjuəblɪ] adv: **it is ~ ...** on peut soutenir que c'est ...

argue [ˈɑːɡjuː] vi (quarrel) se disputer; (reason) argumenter; **to ~ that** objecter or alléguer que

argument [ˈɑːɡjumənt] n (reasons) argument m; (quarrel) dispute f; **~ative** [ɑːɡjuˈmentətɪv] adj ergoteur(-euse), raisonneur(-euse)

Aries [ˈeərɪz] n le Bélier

arise [əˈraɪz] (pt **arose**, pp **arisen**) vi survenir, se présenter

aristocrat [ˈærɪstəkræt] n aristocrate m/f

arithmetic [əˈrɪθmətɪk] n arithmétique f

ark [ɑːk] n: **Noah's A~** l'Arche f de Noé

arm [ɑːm] *n* bras *m* ♦ *vt* armer; **~s** *npl* (*weapons*, HERALDRY) armes *fpl*; **~ in ~** bras dessus bras dessous

armaments ['ɑːməmənts] *npl* armement *m*

armchair ['ɑːmtʃɛəʳ] *n* fauteuil *m*

armed [ɑːmd] *adj* armé(e); **~ robbery** *n* vol *m* à main armée

armour ['ɑːməʳ] (*US* **armor**) *n* armure *f*; (MIL: *tanks*) blindés *mpl*; **~ed car** *n* véhicule blindé

armpit ['ɑːmpɪt] *n* aisselle *f*

armrest ['ɑːmrest] *n* accoudoir *m*

army ['ɑːmɪ] *n* armée *f*

A road (BRIT) *n* (AUT) route nationale

aroma [ə'rəumə] *n* arôme *m*; **~therapy** *n* aromathérapie *f*

arose [ə'rauz] *pt of* **arise**

around [ə'raund] *adv* autour; (*nearby*) dans les parages ♦ *prep* autour de; (*near*) près de; (*fig*: *about*) environ; (: *date, time*) vers

arouse [ə'rauz] *vt* (*sleeper*) éveiller; (*curiosity, passions*) éveiller, susciter; (*anger*) exciter

arrange [ə'reɪndʒ] *vt* arranger; **to ~ to do sth** prévoir de faire qch; **~ment** *n* arrangement *m*; **~ments** *npl* (*plans etc*) arrangements *mpl*, dispositions *fpl*

array [ə'reɪ] *n*: **~ of** déploiement *m* or étalage *m* de

arrears [ə'rɪəz] *npl* arriéré *m*; **to be in ~ with one's rent** devoir un arriéré de loyer

arrest [ə'rest] *vt* arrêter; (*sb's attention*) retenir, attirer ♦ *n* arrestation *f*; **under ~** en état d'arrestation

arrival [ə'raɪvl] *n* arrivée *f*; **new ~** nouveau venu, nouvelle venue; (*baby*) nouveau-né(e)

arrive [ə'raɪv] *vi* arriver

arrogant ['ærəgənt] *adj* arrogant(e)

arrow ['ærəu] *n* flèche *f*

arse [ɑːs] (BRIT: *inf!*) *n* cul *m* (!)

arson ['ɑːsn] *n* incendie criminel

art [ɑːt] *n* art *m*; **A~s** *npl* (SCOL) les lettres *fpl*

artery ['ɑːtərɪ] *n* artère *f*

art gallery *n* musée *m* d'art; (*small and private*) galerie *f* de peinture

arthritis [ɑː'θraɪtɪs] *n* arthrite *f*

artichoke ['ɑːtɪtʃəuk] *n* (*also*: **globe ~**) artichaut *m*; (*also*: **Jerusalem ~**) topinambour *m*

article ['ɑːtɪkl] *n* article *m*; **~s** *npl* (BRIT: LAW: *training*) ≈ stage *m*; **~ of clothing** vêtement *m*

articulate [*adj* ɑː'tɪkjulɪt, *vb* ɑː'tɪkjuleɪt] *adj* (*person*) qui s'exprime bien; (*speech*) bien articulé(e), prononcé(e) clairement ♦ *vt* exprimer; **~d lorry** (BRIT) *n* (camion *m*) semi-remorque *m*

artificial [ɑːtɪ'fɪʃəl] *adj* artificiel(le); **~ respiration** *n* respiration artificielle

artist ['ɑːtɪst] *n* artiste *m/f*; **~ic** [ɑː'tɪstɪk] *adj* artistique; **~ry** *n* art *m*, talent *m*

art school *n* ≈ école *f* des beaux-arts

as [æz, əz] *conj* **1** (*referring to time*) comme, alors que; à mesure que; **he came in as I was leaving** il est arrivé comme je partais; **as the years went by** à mesure que les années passaient; **as from tomorrow** à partir de demain

2 (*in comparisons*): **as big as** aussi grand que; **twice as big as** deux fois plus grand que; **as much** or **many as** autant que; **as much money/many books** autant d'argent/de livres que; **as soon as** dès que

3 (*since, because*) comme, puisque; **as he had to be home by 10** ... comme il or puisqu'il devait être de retour avant 10 h ...

4 (*referring to manner, way*) comme; **do as you wish** faites comme vous voudrez

5 (*concerning*): **as for** or **to that** quant à cela, pour ce qui est de cela

6: **as if** or **though** comme si; **he looked as if he was ill** il avait l'air d'être malade; *see also* **long**; **such**; **well**

♦ *prep*: **he works as a driver** il travaille comme chauffeur; **as chairman of the company, he ...** en tant que président de la société, il ...; **dressed up as a cowboy** déguisé en cowboy; **he gave me it as a present** il me l'a offert, il m'en a fait cadeau

a.s.a.p. *abbr* (= *as soon as possible*) dès que possible

asbestos [æz'bestəs] *n* amiante *m*

ascend [ə'send] *vt* gravir; (*throne*) monter sur

ascertain [æsə'teɪn] *vt* vérifier

ash [æʃ] *n* (*dust*) cendre *f*; (*also*: **~ tree**) frêne *m*

ashamed [ə'ʃeɪmd] *adj* honteux(-euse), confus(e); **to be ~ of** avoir honte de

ashore [ə'ʃɔːʳ] *adv* à terre

ashtray ['æʃtreɪ] *n* cendrier *m*

Ash Wednesday *n* mercredi *m* des cendres

Asia ['eɪʃə] *n* Asie *f*; **~n** *n* Asiatique *m/f* ♦ *adj* asiatique

aside [ə'saɪd] *adv* de côté; à l'écart ♦ *n* aparté *m*

ask [ɑːsk] *vt* demander; (*invite*) inviter; **to ~ sb sth/to do sth** demander qch à qn/à qn de faire qch; **to ~ sb about sth** questionner qn sur qch; se renseigner auprès de qn sur qch; **to ~ (sb) a question** poser une question (à qn); **to ~ sb out to dinner** inviter qn au restaurant; **~ after** *vt fus* demander des nouvelles de; **~ for** *vt fus* demander; (*trouble*) chercher

asking price ['ɑːskɪŋ-] *n*: **the ~** le prix de départ

asleep [ə'sliːp] *adj* endormi(e); **to fall ~** s'endormir

asparagus [əs'pærəgəs] n asperges fpl

aspect ['æspekt] n aspect m; (direction in which a building etc faces) orientation f, exposition f

aspire [əs'paɪəʳ] vi: **to ~ to** aspirer à

aspirin ['æsprɪn] n aspirine f

ass [æs] n âne m; (inf) imbécile m/f; (US: inf!) cul m (!)

assailant [ə'seɪlənt] n agresseur m; assaillant m

assassinate [ə'sæsɪneɪt] vt assassiner; **assassination** [əsæsɪ'neɪʃən] n assassinat m

assault [ə'sɔːlt] n (MIL) assaut m; (gen: attack) agression f ♦ vt attaquer; (sexually) violenter

assemble [ə'sembl] vt assembler ♦ vi s'assembler, se rassembler; **assembly** n assemblée f, réunion f; (institution) assemblée; (construction) assemblage m; **assembly line** n chaîne f de montage

assent [ə'sent] n assentiment m, consentement m

assert [ə'sɜːt] vt affirmer, déclarer; (one's authority) faire valoir; (one's innocence) protester de

assess [ə'ses] vt évaluer; (tax, payment) établir or fixer le montant de; (property etc: for tax) calculer la valeur imposable de; (person) juger la valeur de; **~ment** n évaluation f, fixation f, calcul m de la valeur imposable de, jugement m; **~or** n expert m (impôt et assurance)

asset ['æset] n avantage m, atout m; **~s** npl (FINANCE) capital m; avoir(s) m(pl); actif m

assign [ə'saɪn] vt (date) fixer; (task) assigner à; (resources) affecter à; **~ment** n tâche f, mission f

assist [ə'sɪst] vt aider, assister; **~ance** n aide f, assistance f; **~ant** n assistant(e), adjoint(e); (BRIT: also: **shop ~ant**) vendeur(-euse)

associate [n, adj ə'səuʃɪt, vb ə'səuʃɪeɪt] adj, n associé(e) ♦ vt associer ♦ vi: **to ~ with sb** fréquenter qn; **association** [əsəusɪ'eɪʃən] n association f

assorted [ə'sɔːtɪd] adj assorti(e)

assortment [ə'sɔːtmənt] n assortiment m

assume [ə'sjuːm] vt supposer; (responsibilities etc) assumer; (attitude, name) prendre, adopter; **assumption** [ə'sʌmpʃən] n supposition f, hypothèse f; (of power) assomption f, prise f

assurance [ə'ʃuərəns] n assurance f

assure [ə'ʃuəʳ] vt assurer

asthma ['æsmə] n asthme m

astonish [ə'stɔnɪʃ] vt étonner, stupéfier; **~ment** n étonnement m

astound [ə'staund] vt stupéfier, sidérer

astray [ə'streɪ] adv: **to go ~** s'égarer; (fig) quitter le droit chemin; **to lead ~** détourner

du droit chemin

astride [ə'straɪd] prep à cheval sur

astrology [əs'trɔlədʒɪ] n astrologie f

astronaut ['æstrənɔːt] n astronaute m/f

astronomy [əs'trɔnəmɪ] n astronomie f

asylum [ə'saɪləm] n asile m

KEYWORD
---

at [æt] prep 1 (referring to position, direction) à; **at the top** au sommet; **at home/school** à la maison or chez soi/à l'école; **at the baker's** à la boulangerie, chez le boulanger; **to look at sth** regarder qch

2 (referring to time): **at 4 o'clock** à 4 heures; **at Christmas** à Noël; **at night** la nuit; **at times** par moments, parfois

3 (referring to rates, speed etc) à; **at £1 a kilo** une livre le kilo; **two at a time** deux à la fois; **at 50 km/h** à 50 km/h

4 (referring to manner): **at a stroke** d'un seul coup; **at peace** en paix

5 (referring to activity): **to be at work** être au travail, travailler; **to play at cowboys** jouer aux cowboys; **to be good at sth** être bon en qch

6 (referring to cause): **shocked/surprised/annoyed at sth** choqué par/étonné de/agacé par qch; **I went at his suggestion** j'y suis allé sur son conseil

---

ate [eɪt] pt of eat

atheist ['eɪθɪɪst] n athée m/f

Athens ['æθɪnz] n Athènes

athlete ['æθliːt] n athlète m/f; **athletic** [æθ'letɪk] adj athlétique; **athletics** n athlétisme m

Atlantic [ət'læntɪk] adj atlantique ♦ n: **the ~ (Ocean)** l'(océan m) Atlantique m

atlas ['ætləs] n atlas m

ATM n abbr (= automated telling machine) guichet m automatique

atmosphere ['ætməsfɪəʳ] n atmosphère f

atom ['ætəm] n atome m; **~ic** [ə'tɔmɪk] adj atomique; **~(ic) bomb** n bombe f atomique; **~izer** n atomiseur m

atone [ə'təun] vi: **to ~ for** expier, racheter

atrocious [ə'trəuʃəs] adj (very bad) atroce, exécrable

attach [ə'tætʃ] vt attacher; (document, letter) joindre; **to be ~ed to sb/sth** être attaché à qn/qch

attaché case [ə'tæʃeɪ] n mallette f, attaché-case m

attachment [ə'tætʃmənt] n (tool) accessoire m; (love): **~ (to)** affection f (pour), attachement m (à)

attack [ə'tæk] vt attaquer; (task etc) s'attaquer à ♦ n attaque f; (also: **heart ~**) crise f cardiaque

attain [ə'teɪn] vt (also: **to ~ to**) parvenir à,

atteindre; (: *knowledge*) acquérir

attempt [ə'tɛmpt] *n* tentative f ♦ *vt* essayer, tenter; **to make an ~ on sb's life** attenter à la vie de qn; **~ed** *adj*: **~ed murder/suicide** tentative f de meurtre/suicide

attend [ə'tɛnd] *vt* (*course*) suivre; (*meeting, talk*) assister à; (*school, church*) aller à, fréquenter; (*patient*) soigner, s'occuper de; **~ to** *vt fus* (*needs, affairs etc*) s'occuper de; (*customer, patient*) s'occuper de; **~ance** *n* (*being present*) présence f; (*people present*) assistance f; **~ant** *n* employé(e) ♦ *adj* (*dangers*) inhérent(e), concomitant(e)

attention [ə'tɛnʃən] *n* attention f; **~!** (MIL) garde-à-vous!; **for the ~ of** (ADMIN) à l'attention de

attentive [ə'tɛntɪv] *adj* attentif(-ive); (*kind*) prévenant(e)

attest [ə'tɛst] *vi*: **to ~ to** (*demonstrate*) démontrer; (*confirm*) témoigner

attic ['ætɪk] *n* grenier *m*

attitude ['ætɪtjuːd] *n* attitude f; pose f, maintien *m*

attorney [ə'tɜːnɪ] *n* (US: *lawyer*) avoué *m*; **A~ General** *n* (BRIT) ≈ procureur général; (US) ≈ garde *m* des Sceaux, ministre *m* de la Justice

attract [ə'trækt] *vt* attirer; **~ion** *n* (*gen pl*: *pleasant things*) attraction f, attrait *m*; (PHYSICS) attraction f; (*fig: towards sb or sth*) attirance f; **~ive** *adj* attrayant(e); (*person*) séduisant(e)

attribute [*n* 'ætrɪbjuːt, *vb* ə'trɪbjuːt] *n* attribut *m* ♦ *vt*: **to ~ sth to** attribuer qch à

attrition [ə'trɪʃən] *n*: **war of ~** guerre f d'usure

aubergine ['əubəʒiːn] *n* aubergine f

auction ['ɔːkʃən] *n* (*also*: **sale by ~**) vente f aux enchères ♦ *vt* (*also*: **sell by ~**) vendre aux enchères; (*also*: **put up for ~**) mettre aux enchères; **~eer** [ɔːkʃə'nɪəʳ] *n* commissaire-priseur *m*

audience ['ɔːdɪəns] *n* (*people*) assistance f; public *m*; spectateurs *mpl*; (*interview*) audience f

audiovisual ['ɔːdɪəu'vɪzjuəl] *adj* audiovisuel(le); **~ aids** *npl* supports or moyens audiovisuels

audit ['ɔːdɪt] *vt* vérifier

audition [ɔː'dɪʃən] *n* audition f

auditor ['ɔːdɪtəʳ] *n* vérificateur *m* des comptes

augur ['ɔːgəʳ] *vi*: **it ~s well** c'est bon signe or de bon augure

August ['ɔːgəst] *n* août *m*

aunt [ɑːnt] *n* tante f; **~ie, ~y** ['ɑːntɪ] *n dimin of* **aunt**

au pair ['əu'pɛəʳ] *n* (*also*: **~ girl**) jeune fille f au pair

auspicious [ɔːs'pɪʃəs] *adj* de bon augure, propice

Australia [ɔs'treɪlɪə] *n* Australie f; **~n** *adj* australien(ne) ♦ *n* Australien(ne)

Austria ['ɔstrɪə] *n* Autriche f; **~n** *adj* autrichien(ne) ♦ *n* Autrichien(ne)

authentic [ɔː'θɛntɪk] *adj* authentique

author ['ɔːθəʳ] *n* auteur *m*

authoritarian [ɔːθɒrɪ'tɛərɪən] *adj* autoritaire

authoritative [ɔː'θɒrɪtətɪv] *adj* (*account*) digne de foi; (*study, treatise*) qui fait autorité; (*person, manner*) autoritaire

authority [ɔː'θɒrɪtɪ] *n* autorité f; (*permission*) autorisation (formelle); **the authorities** *npl* (*ruling body*) les autorités *fpl*, l'administration f

authorize ['ɔːθəraɪz] *vt* autoriser

auto ['ɔːtəu] *n* (US) auto f, voiture f

auto-: **~biography** [ɔːtəbaɪ'ɔgrəfɪ] *n* autobiographie f; **~graph** ['ɔːtəgrɑːf] *n* autographe *m* ♦ *vt* signer, dédicacer; **~mated** ['ɔːtəmeɪtɪd] *adj* automatisé(e), automatique; **~matic** [ɔːtə'mætɪk] *adj* automatique ♦ *n* (*gun*) automatique *m*; (*washing machine*) machine f à laver automatique; (BRIT: AUT) voiture f à transmission automatique; **~matically** *adv* automatiquement; **~mation** [ɔːtə'meɪʃən] *n* automatisation f (électronique); **~mobile** ['ɔːtəməbiːl] (US) *n* automobile f; **~nomy** [ɔː'tɒnəmɪ] *n* autonomie f

autumn ['ɔːtəm] *n* automne *m*; **in ~** en automne

auxiliary [ɔːg'zɪlɪərɪ] *adj* auxiliaire ♦ *n* auxiliaire *m/f*

avail [ə'veɪl] *vt*: **to ~ o.s. of** profiter de ♦ *n*: **to no ~** sans résultat, en vain, en pure perte

availability [əveɪlə'bɪlɪtɪ] *n* disponibilité f

available [ə'veɪləbl] *adj* disponible

avalanche ['ævəlɑːnʃ] *n* avalanche f

Ave *abbr* = **avenue**

avenge [ə'vɛndʒ] *vt* venger

avenue ['ævənjuː] *n* avenue f; (*fig*) moyen *m*

average ['ævərɪdʒ] *n* moyenne f; (*fig*) moyen *m* ♦ *adj* moyen(ne) ♦ *vt* (*a certain figure*) atteindre *or* faire *etc* en moyenne; **on ~** en moyenne; **~ out** *vi*: **to ~ out at** représenter en moyenne, donner une moyenne de

averse [ə'vɜːs] *adj*: **to be ~ to sth/doing sth** éprouver une forte répugnance envers qch/à faire qch

avert [ə'vɜːt] *vt* (*danger*) prévenir, écarter; (*one's eyes*) détourner

aviary ['eɪvɪərɪ] *n* volière f

avocado [ævə'kɑːdəu] *n* (BRIT: ~ **pear**) avocat *m*

avoid [ə'vɔɪd] *vt* éviter

await [ə'weɪt] *vt* attendre

awake [ə'weɪk] (*pt* **awoke**, *pp* **awoken**) *adj* éveillé(e) ♦ *vt* éveiller ♦ *vi* s'éveiller; **~ to**

(*dangers, possibilities*) conscient(e) de; **to be ~** être réveillé(e); **he was still ~** il ne dormait pas encore; **~ning** n réveil m

award [ə'wɔːd] n récompense f, prix m; (LAW: *damages*) dommages-intérêts mpl ♦ vt (*prize*) décerner; (LAW: *damages*) accorder

aware [ə'wɛəʳ] adj: **~ (of)** (*conscious*) conscient(e) (de); (*informed*) au courant (de); **to become ~ of/that** prendre conscience de/que; se rendre compte de/que; **~ness** n conscience f, connaissance f

away [ə'weɪ] adj, adv (au) loin; absent(e); **two kilometres ~** à (une distance de) deux kilomètres, à deux kilomètres de distance; **two hours ~ by car** à deux heures de voiture or de route; **the holiday was two weeks ~** il restait deux semaines jusqu'aux vacances; **~ from** loin de; **he's ~ for a week** il est parti (pour) une semaine; **to pedal/work/laugh ~** être en train de pédaler/travailler/rire; **to fade ~** (*sound*) s'affaiblir; (*colour*) s'estomper; **to wither ~** (*plant*) se dessécher; **to take ~** emporter; (*subtract*) enlever; **~ game** n (SPORT) match m à l'extérieur

awe [ɔː] n respect mêlé de crainte; **~-inspiring** ['ɔːɪnspaɪərɪŋ] adj impressionnant(e)

awful ['ɔːfəl] adj affreux(-euse); **an ~ lot (of)** un nombre incroyable (de); **~ly** adv (*very*) terriblement, vraiment

awkward ['ɔːkwəd] adj (*clumsy*) gauche, maladroit(e); (*inconvenient*) peu pratique; (*embarrassing*) gênant(e), délicat(e)

awning ['ɔːnɪŋ] n (*of tent*) auvent m; (*of shop*) store m; (*of hotel etc*) marquise f

awoke [ə'wəuk] pt of **awake**; **~n** [ə'wəukən] pp of **awake**

axe [æks] (US **ax**) n hache f ♦ vt (*project etc*) abandonner; (*jobs*) supprimer

axes¹ ['æksɪz] npl of **axe**

axes² ['æksiːz] npl of **axis**

axis ['æksɪs] (pl **axes**) n axe m

axle ['æksl] n (also: **~-tree**: AUT) essieu m

ay(e) [aɪ] excl (*yes*) oui

B, b

B [biː] n (MUS) si m; **~ road** (BRIT) route départementale

B.A. abbr = **Bachelor of Arts**

babble ['bæbl] vi bredouiller; (*baby, stream*) gazouiller

baby ['beɪbɪ] n bébé m; (US: inf: *darling*): **come on, ~!** viens ma belle/mon gars!; **~ carriage** (US) n voiture f d'enfant; **~ foods** aliments mpl pour bébé(s); **~-sit** vi garder les enfants; **~-sitter** n baby-sitter m/f; **~ wipe** n lingette f (*pour bébé*)

bachelor ['bætʃələʳ] n célibataire m; **B~ of Arts/Science** ≈ licencié(e) ès or en lettres/ sciences

back [bæk] n (*of person, horse, book*) dos m; (*of hand*) dos, revers m; (*of house*) derrière m; (*of car, train*) arrière m; (*of chair*) dossier m; (*of page*) verso m; (*of room, audience*) fond m; (SPORT) arrière m ♦ vt (*candidate*: also: **~ up**) soutenir, appuyer; (*horse*: at *races*) parier or miser sur; (*car*) (faire) reculer ♦ vi (also: **~ up**) reculer; (also: **~ up**: car etc) faire marche arrière ♦ adj (*in compounds*) de derrière, à l'arrière ♦ adv (*not forward*) en arrière; (*returned*): **he's ~** il est rentré, il est de retour; (*restitution*): **throw the ball ~** renvoie la balle; (*again*): **he called ~** il a rappelé; **~ seat/wheels** (AUT) sièges mpl/roues fpl arrière; **~ payments/rent** arriéré m de paiements/loyer; **he ran ~** il est revenu en courant; **~ down** vi rabattre de ses prétentions; **~ out** vi (*of promise*) se dédire; **~ up** vt (*candidate etc*) soutenir, appuyer; (COMPUT) sauvegarder; **~ache** n mal m de dos; **~bencher** (BRIT) n membre du parlement sans portefeuille; **~bone** n colonne vertébrale, épine dorsale; **~date** vt (*letter*) antidater; **~dated pay rise** augmentation f avec effet rétroactif; **~fire** vi (AUT) pétarader; (*plans*) mal tourner; **~ground** n arrière-plan m; (*of events*) situation f, conjoncture f; (*basic knowledge*) éléments mpl de base; (*experience*) formation f; **family ~ground** milieu familial; **~hand** n (TENNIS: also: **~hand stroke**) revers m; **~hander** (BRIT) n (*bribe*) pot-de-vin m; **~ing** n (*fig*) soutien m, appui m; **~lash** n contre-coup m, répercussion f; **~log** n: **~log of work** travail m en retard; **~ number** n (*of magazine etc*) vieux numéro; **~pack** n sac m à dos; **~packer** n randonneur(-euse); **~ pain** n mal m de dos; **~ pay** n rappel m de salaire; **~side** (inf) n derrière m, postérieur m; **~stage** adv ♦ n derrière la scène, dans la coulisse; **~stroke** n dos crawlé; **~up** adj (*train, plane*) supplémentaire, de réserve; (COMPUT) de sauvegarde ♦ n (*support*) appui m, soutien m; (also: **~up disk/file**) sauvegarde f; **~ward** adj (*movement*) en arrière; (*person, country*) arriéré(e); attardé(e); **~wards** adv (*move, go*) en arrière; (*read a list*) à l'envers, à rebours; (*fall*) à la renverse; (*walk*) à reculons; **~water** n (*fig*) coin reculé; bled perdu (*péj*); **~yard** n arrière-cour f

bacon ['beɪkən] n bacon m, lard m

bacteria [bæk'tɪərɪə] npl bactéries fpl

bad [bæd] adj mauvais(e); (*child*) vilain(e); (*mistake, accident etc*) grave; (*meat, food*) gâté(e), avarié(e); **his ~ leg** sa jambe malade; **to go ~** (*meat, food*) se gâter

badge [bædʒ] n insigne m; (of policeman) plaque f

badger ['bædʒə'] n blaireau m

badly ['bædlɪ] adv (work, dress etc) mal; ~ **wounded** grièvement blessé; **he needs it** ~ il en a absolument besoin; ~ **off** adj, adv dans la gêne

badminton ['bædmɪntən] n badminton m

bad-tempered ['bæd'tempəd] adj (person: by nature) ayant mauvais caractère; (: on one occasion) de mauvaise humeur

baffle ['bæfl] vt (puzzle) déconcerter

bag [bæg] n sac m ♦ vt (inf: take) empocher; s'approprier; ~**s** of (inf: lots of) des masses de; ~**gage** n bagages mpl; ~**gage allowance** n franchise f de bagages; ~**gage reclaim** n livraison f de bagages; ~**gy** adj avachi(e), qui fait des poches; ~**pipes** npl cornemuse f

bail [beɪl] n (payment) caution f; (release) mise f en liberté sous caution ♦ vt (prisoner: also: grant ~ to) mettre en liberté sous caution; (boat: also: ~ out) écoper; **on** ~ (prisoner) sous caution; see also **bale**; ~ **out** vt (prisoner) payer la caution de

bailiff ['beɪlɪf] n (BRIT) ≈ huissier m; (US) ≈ huissier-audiencier m

bait [beɪt] n appât m ♦ vt appâter; (fig: tease) tourmenter

bake [beɪk] vt (faire) cuire au four ♦ vi (bread etc) cuire (au four); (make cakes etc) faire de la pâtisserie; ~**d beans** npl haricots blancs à la sauce tomate; ~**d potato** n pomme f de terre en robe des champs; ~**r** n boulanger m; ~**ry** n boulangerie f; (dance) bal m; **to play** ~ **(with sb)** (fig) coopérer (avec qn)

baking n cuisson f; **baking powder** n levure f (chimique)

balance ['bæləns] n équilibre m; (COMM: sum) solde m; (remainder) reste m; (scales) balance f ♦ vt mettre or faire tenir en équilibre; (pros and cons) peser; (budget) équilibrer; (account) balancer; ~ **of trade/ payments** balance commerciale/des comptes or paiements; ~**d** adj (personality, diet) équilibré(e); (report) objectif(-ive); ~ **sheet** n bilan m

balcony ['bælkənɪ] n balcon m; (in theatre) deuxième balcon

bald [bɔːld] adj chauve; (tyre) lisse

bale [beɪl] n balle f, ballot m; ~ **out** vi (of a plane) sauter en parachute

ball [bɔːl] n boule f; (football) ballon m; (for tennis, golf) balle f; (of wool) pelote f; (of string) bobine f; (dance) bal m; **to play** ~ **(with sb)** (fig) coopérer (avec qn)

ballast ['bæləst] n lest m

ball bearings npl roulement m à billes

ballerina [bælə'riːnə] n ballerine f

ballet ['bæleɪ] n ballet m; (art) danse f

(classique); ~ **dancer** n danceur(-euse) m/f de ballet; ~ **shoe** n chausson m de danse

balloon [bə'luːn] n ballon m; (in comic strip) bulle f

ballot ['bælət] n scrutin m; ~ **paper** n bulletin m de vote

ballpoint (pen) ['bɔːlpɔɪnt(-)] n stylo m à bille

ballroom ['bɔːlrum] n salle f de bal

ban [bæn] n interdiction f ♦ vt interdire

banana [bə'nɑːnə] n banane f

band [bænd] n bande f; (at a dance) orchestre m; (MIL) musique f, fanfare f; ~ **together** vi se liguer

bandage ['bændɪdʒ] n bandage m, pansement m ♦ vt bander

Bandaid ® ['bændeɪd] (US) n pansement adhésif

bandit ['bændɪt] n bandit m

bandy-legged ['bændɪ'legɪd] adj aux jambes arquées

bang [bæŋ] n détonation f; (of door) claquement m; (blow) coup (violent) ♦ vt frapper (violemment); (door) claquer ♦ vi détoner; claquer ♦ excl pan!; ~**s** (US) npl (fringe) frange f

banish ['bænɪʃ] vt bannir

banister(s) ['bænɪstə(z)] n(pl) rampe f (d'escalier)

bank [bæŋk] n banque f; (of river, lake) bord m, rive f; (of earth) talus m, remblai m ♦ vi (AVIAT) virer sur l'aile; ~ **on** vt fus miser or tabler sur; ~ **account** n compte m en banque; ~ **card** n carte f d'identité bancaire; ~**er** n banquier m; ~**er's card** (BRIT) n = **bank card**; ~ **holiday** (BRIT) n jour férié (les banques sont fermées); ~**ing** n opérations fpl bancaires; profession f de banquier; ~**note** n billet m de banque; ~ **rate** n taux m de l'escompte

bankrupt ['bæŋkrʌpt] adj en faillite; **to go** ~ faire faillite; ~**cy** n faillite f

bank statement n relevé m de compte

banner ['bænə'] n bannière f

bannister(s) ['bænɪstə(z)] n(pl) = **banister(s)**

baptism ['bæptɪzəm] n baptême m

bar [bɑːr] n (pub) bar m; (counter: in pub) comptoir m, bar; (rod: of metal etc) barre f; (on window etc) barreau m; (of chocolate) tablette f, plaque f; (fig) obstacle m; (prohibition) mesure f d'exclusion; (MUS) mesure f ♦ vt (road) barrer; (window) munir de barreaux; (person) exclure; (activity) interdire; ~ **of soap** savonnette f; **the B~** (LAW) le barreau; **behind ~s** (prisoner) sous les verrous; ~ **none** sans exception

barbaric [bɑː'bærɪk] adj barbare

barbecue ['bɑːbɪkjuː] n barbecue m

barbed wire ['bɑːbd-] n fil m de fer barbelé
barber ['bɑːbə'] n coiffeur m (pour hommes)
bar code n (on goods) code m à barres
bare [beə'] adj nu(e) ♦ vt mettre à nu,
dénuder; (teeth) montrer; **the ~ necessities** le
strict nécessaire; **~back** adv à cru, sans selle;
~faced adj impudent(e), effronté(e); **~foot**
adj, adv nu-pieds, (les) pieds nus; **~ly** adv à
peine
bargain ['bɑːgɪn] n (transaction) marché m;
(good buy) affaire f, occasion f ♦ vi (haggle)
marchander; (negotiate): **to ~ (with sb)**
négocier (avec qn), traiter (avec qn); **into**
the ~ par-dessus le marché; **~ for** vt fus: **he**
got more than he ~ed for il ne s'attendait pas
à un coup pareil
barge [bɑːdʒ] n péniche f; **~ in** vi (walk in)
faire irruption; (interrupt talk) intervenir mal à
propos
bark [bɑːk] n (of tree) écorce f; (of dog)
aboiement m ♦ vi aboyer
barley ['bɑːlɪ] n orge f; **~ sugar** n sucre m
d'orge
bar: ~maid n serveuse f de bar, barmaid f;
~man (irreg) n barman m; **~ meal** n repas
m de bistrot; **to go for a ~ meal** aller manger
au bistrot
barn [bɑːn] n grange f
barometer [bə'rɒmɪtə'] n baromètre m
baron ['bærən] n baron m; **~ess** ['bærənɪs] n
baronne f
barracks ['bærəks] npl caserne f
barrage ['bærɑːʒ] n (MIL) tir m de barrage;
(dam) barrage m; (fig) pluie f
barrel ['bærəl] n tonneau m; (of oil) baril m;
(of gun) canon m
barren ['bærən] adj stérile
barricade [bærɪ'keɪd] n barricade f
barrier ['bærɪə'] n barrière f; (fig: to progress
etc) obstacle m
barring ['bɑːrɪŋ] prep sauf
barrister ['bærɪstə'] n (BRIT) avocat (plaidant)
barrow ['bærəu] n (wheelbarrow) charrette f à
bras
bartender ['bɑːtɛndə'] n (US) barman m
barter ['bɑːtə'] vt: **to ~ sth for** échanger qch
contre
base [beɪs] n base f; (of tree, post) pied m
♦ vt: **to ~ sth on** baser or fonder qch sur
♦ adj vil(e), bas(se)
baseball ['beɪsbɔːl] n base-ball m
basement ['beɪsmənt] n sous-sol m
bases[1] ['beɪsɪz] npl of **base**
bases[2] ['beɪsiːz] npl of **basis**
bash [bæʃ] (inf) vt frapper, cogner
bashful ['bæʃful] adj timide; modeste
basic ['beɪsɪk] adj fondamental(e), de base;
(minimal) rudimentaire; **~ally** adv
fondamentalement, à la base; (in fact) en fait,

au fond; **~s** npl: **the ~s** l'essentiel m
basil ['bæzl] n basilic m
basin ['beɪsn] n (vessel, also GEO) cuvette f,
bassin m; (also: **washbasin**) lavabo m
basis ['beɪsɪs] n (pl bases) base f; **on a trial ~**
à titre d'essai; **on a part-time ~** à temps partiel
bask [bɑːsk] vi: **to ~ in the sun** se chauffer au
soleil
basket ['bɑːskɪt] n corbeille f; (with handle)
panier m; **~ball** n basket-ball m
bass [beɪs] n (MUS) basse f; **~ drum** n grosse
caisse f
bassoon [bə'suːn] n (MUS) basson m
bastard ['bɑːstəd] n enfant naturel(le),
bâtard(e); (inf!) salaud m (!)
bat [bæt] n chauve-souris f; (for baseball etc)
batte f; (BRIT: for table tennis) raquette f ♦ vt:
he didn't ~ an eyelid il n'a pas sourcillé or
bronché
batch [bætʃ] n (of bread) fournée f; (of
papers) liasse f
bated ['beɪtɪd] adj: **with ~ breath** en retenant
son souffle
bath [bɑːθ] n bain m; (~tub) baignoire f ♦ vt
baigner, donner un bain à; **to have a ~**
prendre un bain; see also **baths**
bathe [beɪð] vi se baigner ♦ vt (wound) laver;
bathing n baignade f; **bathing costume**,
bathing suit (US) n maillot m (de bain)
bath: ~robe n peignoir m de bain; **~room** n
salle f de bains; **~s** npl (also: **swimming ~s**)
piscine f; **~ towel** n serviette f de bain
baton ['bætən] n bâton m; (MUS) baguette f;
(club) matraque f
batter ['bætə'] vt battre ♦ n pâte f à frire;
~ed ['bætəd] adj (hat, pan) cabossé(e)
battery ['bætərɪ] n batterie f; (of torch) pile f;
~ farming n élevage f en batterie
battle ['bætl] n bataille f, combat m ♦ vi se
battre, lutter; **~field** n champ m de bataille;
~ship n cuirassé m
Bavaria [bə'veərɪə] n Bavière f
bawl [bɔːl] vi hurler; (child) brailler
bay [beɪ] n (of sea) baie f; **to hold sb at ~** tenir
qn à distance or en échec; **~ leaf** n laurier m;
~ window n baie vitrée
bazaar [bə'zɑːʳ] n bazar m; vente f de charité
B & B n abbr = **bed and breakfast**
BBC n abbr (= British Broadcasting Corporation)
office de la radiodiffusion et télévision
britannique
B.C. adv abbr (= before Christ) av. J.-C.

KEYWORD
---

be [biː] (pt **was**, **were**, pp **been**) aux vb **1** (with
present participle: forming continuous tenses):
what are you doing? que faites-vous?; **they're**
coming tomorrow ils viennent demain; **I've**
been waiting for you for 2 hours je t'attends

depuis 2 heures

2 (*in film with pp: forming passives*) être; **to be killed** être tué(e); **he was nowhere to be seen** on ne le voyait nulle part

3 (*in tag questions*): **it was fun, wasn't it?** c'était drôle, n'est-ce pas?; **she's back, is she?** elle est rentrée, n'est-ce pas or alors?

4 (+*to* +*infinitive*): **the house is to be sold** la maison doit être vendue; **he's not to open it** il ne doit pas l'ouvrir

♦ *vb* + *complement* **1** (*gen*) être; **I'm English** je suis anglais(e); **I'm tired** je suis fatigué(e); **I'm hot/cold** j'ai chaud/froid; **he's a doctor** il est médecin; **2 and 2 are 4** 2 et 2 font 4

2 (*of health*) aller; **how are you?** comment allez-vous?; **he's fine now** il va bien maintenant; **he's very ill** il est très malade

3 (*of age*) avoir; **how old are you?** quel âge avez-vous?; **I'm sixteen (years old)** j'ai seize ans

4 (*cost*) coûter; **how much was the meal?** combien a coûté le repas?; **that'll be £5, please** ça fera 5 livres, s'il vous plaît

♦ *vi* **1** (*exist, occur etc*) être, exister; **the prettiest girl that ever was** la fille la plus jolie qui ait jamais existé; **be that as it may** quoi qu'il en soit; **so be it** soit

2 (*referring to place*) être, se trouver; **I won't be here tomorrow** je ne serai pas là demain; **Edinburgh is in Scotland** Édimbourg est or se trouve en Écosse

3 (*referring to movement*) aller; **where have you been?** où êtes-vous allé(s)?

♦ *impers vb* **1** (*referring to time, distance*) être; **it's 5 o'clock** il est 5 heures; **it's the 28th of April** c'est le 28 avril; **it's 10 km to the village** le village est à 10 km

2 (*referring to the weather*) faire; **it's too hot/cold** il fait trop chaud/froid; **it's windy** il y a du vent

3 (*emphatic*): **it's me/the postman** c'est moi/le facteur

beach [biːtʃ] *n* plage *f* ♦ *vt* échouer
beacon ['biːkən] *n* (*lighthouse*) fanal *m*; (*marker*) balise *f*
bead [biːd] *n* perle *f*
beak [biːk] *n* bec *m*
beaker ['biːkər] *n* gobelet *m*
beam [biːm] *n* poutre *f*; (*of light*) rayon *m* ♦ *vi* rayonner
bean [biːn] *n* haricot *m*; (*of coffee*) grain *m*; **runner ~** haricot *m* (à rames); **broad ~** fève *f*; **~sprouts** *npl* germes *mpl* de soja
bear [bɛər] (*pt bore, pp borne*) *n* ours *m* ♦ *vt* porter; (*endure*) supporter ♦ *vi*: **to ~ right/left** obliquer à droite/gauche, se diriger vers la droite/gauche; **~ out** *vt* corroborer, confirmer; **~ up** *vi* (*person*) tenir le coup

beard [bɪəd] *n* barbe *f*; **~ed** *adj* barbu(e)
bearer ['bɛərər] *n* porteur *m*; (*of passport*) titulaire *m/f*
bearing ['bɛərɪŋ] *n* maintien *m*, allure *f*; (*connection*) rapport *m*; **~s** *npl* (*also*: **ball ~s**) roulement (à billes); **to take a ~** faire le point
beast [biːst] *n* bête *f*; (*inf: person*) brute *f*; **~ly** *adj* infect(e)
beat [biːt] (*pt beat, pp beaten*) *n* battement *m*; (*MUS*) temps *m*, mesure *f*; (*of policeman*) ronde *f* ♦ *vt, vi* battre; **off the ~en track** hors des chemins or sentiers battus; **~ it!** (*inf*) fiche(-moi) le camp!; **~ off** *vt* repousser; **~ up** *vt* (*inf: person*) tabasser; (*eggs*) battre; **~ing** *n* raclée *f*
beautiful ['bjuːtɪful] *adj* beau (belle); **~ly** *adv* admirablement
beauty ['bjuːtɪ] *n* beauté *f*; **~ salon** *n* institut *m* de beauté; **~ spot** (*BRIT*) *n* (*TOURISM*) site naturel (d'une grande beauté)
beaver ['biːvər] *n* castor *m*
because [bɪ'kɒz] *conj* parce que; **~ of** *prep* à cause de
beck [bɛk] *n*: **to be at sb's ~ and call** être à l'entière disposition de qn
beckon ['bɛkən] *vt* (*also*: **~ to**) faire signe (de venir) à
become [bɪ'kʌm] (*irreg: like come*) *vi* devenir; **to ~ fat/thin** grossir/maigrir; **becoming** *adj* (*behaviour*) convenable, bienséant(e); (*clothes*) seyant(e)
bed [bɛd] *n* lit *m*; (*of flowers*) parterre *m*; (*of coal, clay*) couche *f*; (*of sea*) fond *m*; **to go to ~** aller se coucher; **~ and breakfast** *n* (*terms*) chambre et petit déjeuner; (*place*) ≈ chambre *f* d'hôte; **~clothes** *npl* couvertures *fpl* et draps *mpl*; **~ding** *n* literie *f*; **~ linen** *n* draps *mpl* de lit (et taies *fpl* d'oreillers), literie *f*
bedraggled [bɪ'drægld] *adj* (*person, clothes*) débraillé(e); (*hair: wet*) trempé(e)
bed: **~ridden** *adj* cloué(e) au lit; **~room** *n* chambre *f* (à coucher); **~side** *n*: **at sb's ~side** au chevet de qn; **~sit(ter)** *n* (*BRIT*) chambre meublée, studio *m*; **~spread** *n* couvre-lit *m*, dessus-de-lit *m inv*; **~time** *n* heure *f* du coucher
bee [biː] *n* abeille *f*
beech [biːtʃ] *n* hêtre *m*
beef [biːf] *n* bœuf *m*; **roast ~** rosbif *m*; **~burger** *n* hamburger *m*; **~eater** *n* hallebardier de la Tour de Londres
bee: **~hive** *n* ruche *f*; **~line** *n*: **to make a ~line for** se diriger tout droit vers
been [biːn] *pp of* be
beer [bɪər] *n* bière *f*
beet [biːt] *n* (*vegetable*) betterave *f*; (*US: also*: **red ~**) betterave (potagère)

beetle ['bi:tl] n scarabée m

beetroot ['bi:tru:t] (BRIT) n betterave f

before [bɪ'fɔ:'] prep (in time) avant; (in space) devant ♦ conj avant que +sub; avant de ♦ adv avant; devant; ~ going avant de partir; ~ she goes avant qu'elle ne parte; **the week ~** la semaine précédente or d'avant; **I've seen it ~** je l'ai déjà vu; ~hand adv au préalable, à l'avance

beg [beg] vi mendier ♦ vt mendier; (forgiveness, mercy etc) demander; (entreat) supplier; see also **pardon**

began [bɪ'gæn] pt of **begin**

beggar ['begə'] n mendiant(e)

begin [bɪ'gɪn] (pt **began**, pp **begun**) vt, vi commencer; **to ~ doing** or **to do sth** commencer à or de faire qch; ~**ner** n débutant(e); ~**ning** n commencement m, début m

behalf [bɪ'hɑ:f] n: **on ~ of**, (US) **in ~ of** (representing) de la part de; (for benefit of) pour le compte de; **on my/his ~** pour moi/lui

behave [bɪ'heɪv] vi se conduire, se comporter; (well: also: ~ o.s.) se conduire bien or comme il faut; **behaviour** (US **behavior**) [bɪ'heɪvjə'] n comportement m, conduite f

behead [bɪ'hed] vt décapiter

behind [bɪ'haɪnd] prep derrière; (time, progress) en retard sur; (work, studies) en retard dans ♦ adv derrière ♦ n derrière m; **to be ~ (schedule)** avoir du retard; ~ **the scenes** dans les coulisses

behold [bɪ'həuld] (irreg: like **hold**) vt apercevoir, voir

beige [beɪʒ] adj beige

Beijing ['beɪ'dʒɪŋ] n Beijing, Pékin

being ['bi:ɪŋ] n être m

Beirut [beɪ'ru:t] n Beyrouth

Belarus [belə'rus] n Bélarus f

belated [bɪ'leɪtɪd] adj tardif(-ive)

belch [beltʃ] vi avoir un renvoi, roter ♦ vt (also: ~ **out**: smoke etc) vomir, cracher

Belgian ['beldʒən] adj belge, de Belgique ♦ n Belge m/f

Belgium ['beldʒəm] n Belgique f

belie [bɪ'laɪ] vt démentir

belief [bɪ'li:f] n (opinion) conviction f; (trust, faith) foi f

believe [bɪ'li:v] vt, vi croire; **to ~ in** (God) croire en; (method, ghosts) croire à; ~**r** n (in idea, activity): ~**r** in partisan(e) de; (REL) croyant(e)

belittle [bɪ'lɪtl] vt déprécier, rabaisser

bell [bel] n cloche f; (small) clochette f, grelot m; (on door) sonnette f; (electric) sonnerie f

belligerent [bɪ'lɪdʒərənt] adj (person, attitude) agressif(-ive)

bellow ['beləu] vi (bull) meugler; (person) brailler

belly ['belɪ] n ventre m

belong [bɪ'lɒŋ] vi: **to ~ to** appartenir à; (club etc) faire partie de; **this book ~s here** ce livre va ici; ~**ings** npl affaires fpl, possessions fpl

beloved [bɪ'lʌvɪd] adj (bien-)aimé(e)

below [bɪ'ləu] prep sous, au-dessous de ♦ adv en dessous; **see ~** voir plus bas or plus loin or ci-dessous

belt [belt] n ceinture f; (of land) région f; (TECH) courroie f ♦ vt (thrash) donner une raclée à; ~**way** (US) n (AUT) route f de ceinture; (: motorway) périphérique m

bemused [bɪ'mju:zd] adj stupéfié(e)

bench [bentʃ] n (gen, also BRIT: POL) banc m; (in workshop) établi m; **the B~** (LAW: judge) le juge; (: judges collectively) la magistrature, la Cour

bend [bend] (pt, pp **bent**) vt courber; (leg, arm) plier ♦ vi se courber ♦ n (BRIT: in road) virage m, tournant m; (in pipe, river) coude m; ~ **down** vi se baisser; ~ **over** vi se pencher

beneath [bɪ'ni:θ] prep sous, au-dessous de; (unworthy of) indigne de ♦ adv dessous, au-dessous, en bas

benefactor ['benɪfæktə'] n bienfaiteur m

beneficial [benɪ'fɪʃəl] adj salutaire; avantageux(-euse); ~ **to the health** bon(ne) pour la santé

benefit ['benɪfɪt] n avantage m, profit m; (allowance of money) allocation f ♦ vt faire du bien à, profiter à ♦ vi: **he'll ~ from it** cela lui fera du bien, il y gagnera or s'en trouvera bien

Benelux ['benɪlʌks] n Bénélux m

benevolent [bɪ'nevələnt] adj bienveillant(e); (organization) bénévole

benign [bɪ'naɪn] adj (person, smile) bienveillant(e), affable; (MED) bénin(-igne)

bent [bent] pt, pp of **bend** ♦ n inclination f, penchant m; **to be ~ on** être résolu(e) à

bequest [bɪ'kwest] n legs m

bereaved [bɪ'ri:vd] n: **the ~** la famille du disparu

beret ['bereɪ] n béret m

Berlin [bə:'lɪn] n Berlin

berm [bə:m] (US) n (AUT) accotement m

Bermuda [bə:'mju:də] n Bermudes fpl

berry ['berɪ] n baie f

berserk [bə'sə:k] adj: **to go ~** (madman, crowd) se déchaîner

berth [bə:θ] n (bed) couchette f; (for ship) poste m d'amarrage, mouillage m ♦ vi (in harbour) venir à quai; (at anchor) mouiller

beseech [bɪ'si:tʃ] (pt, pp **besought**) vt implorer, supplier

beset [bɪ'set] (pt, pp **beset**) vt assaillir

beside [bɪ'saɪd] prep à côté de; **to be ~ o.s. (with anger)** être hors de soi; **that's ~ the**

point cela n'a rien à voir; **~s** *adv* en outre, de plus; (*in any case*) d'ailleurs ♦ *prep* (*as well as*) en plus de

besiege [bɪ'siːdʒ] *vt* (*town*) assiéger; (*fig*) assaillir

best [bɛst] *adj* meilleur(e) ♦ *adv* le mieux; **the ~ part of** (*quantity*) le plus clair de, la plus grande partie de; **at ~** au mieux; **to make the ~ of sth** s'accommoder de qch (du mieux que l'on peut); **to do one's ~** faire de son mieux; **to the ~ of my knowledge** pour autant que je sache; **to the ~ of my ability** du mieux que je pourrai; **~ before date** *n* date *f* de limite d'utilisation *or* de consommation; **~ man** *n* garçon *m* d'honneur

bestow [bɪ'stəu] *vt*: **to ~ sth on sb** accorder qch à qn; (*title*) conférer qch à qn

bet [bɛt] (*pt, pp* **bet** *or* **betted**) *n* pari *m* ♦ *vt, vi* parier

betray [bɪ'treɪ] *vt* trahir

better ['bɛtəʳ] *adj* meilleur(e) ♦ *adv* mieux ♦ *vt* améliorer ♦ *n*: **to get the ~ of** triompher de, l'emporter sur; **you had ~ do it** vous feriez mieux de le faire; **he thought ~ of it** il s'est ravisé; **to get ~** aller mieux; s'améliorer; **~ off** *adj* plus à l'aise financièrement; (*fig*): **you'd be ~ off this way** vous vous en trouveriez mieux ainsi

betting ['bɛtɪŋ] *n* paris *mpl*; **~ shop** (*BRIT*) *n* bureau *m* de paris

between [bɪ'twiːn] *prep* entre ♦ *adv*: (**in**) **~** au milieu; dans l'intervalle; (*in time*) dans l'intervalle

beverage ['bɛvərɪdʒ] *n* boisson *f* (*gén sans alcool*)

beware [bɪ'wɛəʳ] *vi*: **to ~ (of)** prendre garde (à); **"~ of the dog"** "(attention) chien méchant"

bewildered [bɪ'wɪldəd] *adj* dérouté(e), ahuri(e)

beyond [bɪ'jɔnd] *prep* (*in space, time*) au-delà de; (*exceeding*) au-dessus de ♦ *adv* au-delà; **~ doubt** hors de doute; **~ repair** irréparable

bias ['baɪəs] *n* (*prejudice*) préjugé *m*, parti pris; **~(s)ed** *adj* partial(e), montrant un parti pris

bib [bɪb] *n* bavoir *m*, bavette *f*

Bible ['baɪbl] *n* Bible *f*

bicarbonate of soda [baɪ'kɑːbənɪt-] *n* bicarbonate *m* de soude

bicker ['bɪkəʳ] *vi* se chamailler

bicycle ['baɪsɪkl] *n* bicyclette *f*

bid [bɪd] (*pt* **bid** *or* **bade**, *pp* **bid(den)**) *n* offre *f*; (*at auction*) enchère *f*; (*attempt*) tentative *f* ♦ *vi* faire une enchère *or* offre ♦ *vt* faire une enchère *or* offre de; **to ~ sb good day** souhaiter le bonjour à qn; **~der** *n*: **the highest ~der** le plus offrant; **~ding** *n* enchères *fpl*

bide [baɪd] *vt*: **to ~ one's time** attendre son heure

bifocals [baɪ'fəuklz] *npl* verres *mpl* à double foyer, lunettes bifocales

big [bɪg] *adj* grand(e); gros(se); **~-headed** *adj* prétentieux(-euse)

bigot ['bɪgət] *n* fanatique *m/f*, sectaire *m/f*; **~ed** *adj* fanatique, sectaire; **~ry** *n* fanatisme *m*, sectarisme *m*

big top *n* grand chapiteau

bike [baɪk] *n* vélo *m*, bécane *f*

bikini [bɪ'kiːni] *n* bikini ® *m*

bilingual [baɪ'lɪŋgwəl] *adj* bilingue

bill [bɪl] *n* note *f*, facture *f*; (*POL*) projet *m* de loi; (*US: banknote*) billet *m* (de banque); (*of bird*) bec *m*; (*THEATRE*): **on the ~** à l'affiche; **"post no ~s"** "défense d'afficher"; **to fit** *or* **fill the ~** (*fig*) faire l'affaire; **~board** *n* panneau *m* d'affichage

billet ['bɪlɪt] *n* cantonnement *m* (chez l'habitant)

billfold ['bɪlfəuld] (*US*) *n* portefeuille *m*

billiards ['bɪljədz] *n* (jeu *m* de) billard *m*

billion ['bɪljən] *n* (*BRIT*) billion *m* (*million de millions*); (*US*) milliard *m*

bimbo ['bɪmbəu] (*inf*) *n* ravissante idiote *f*, potiche *f*

bin [bɪn] *n* boîte *f*; (*also:* **dustbin**) poubelle *f*; (*for coal*) coffre *m*

bind [baɪnd] (*pt, pp* **bound**) *vt* attacher; (*book*) relier; (*oblige*) obliger, contraindre ♦ *n* (*inf: nuisance*) scie *f*; **~ing** *adj* (*contract*) constituant une obligation

binge [bɪndʒ] (*inf*) *n*: **to go on a/the ~** aller faire la bringue

bingo ['bɪŋgəu] *n* jeu de loto pratiqué dans des établissements publics

binoculars [bɪ'nɔkjuləz] *npl* jumelles *fpl*

bio *prefix*: **~chemistry** *n* biochimie *f*; **~degradable** *adj* biodégradable; **~graphy** *n* biographie *f*; **~logical** *adj* biologique; **~logy** *n* biologie *f*

birch [bəːtʃ] *n* bouleau *m*

bird [bəːd] *n* oiseau *m*; (*BRIT: inf: girl*) nana *f*; **~'s-eye view** *n* vue *f* à vol d'oiseau; (*fig*) vue d'ensemble *or* générale; **~-watcher** *n* ornithologue *m/f* amateur

Biro ® ['baɪərəu] *n* stylo *m* à bille

birth [bəːθ] *n* naissance *f*; **to give ~ to** (*subj: woman*) donner naissance à; (: *animal*) mettre bas; **~ certificate** *n* acte *m* de naissance; **~ control** *n* (*policy*) limitation *f* des naissances; (*method*) méthode(s) contraceptive(s); **~day** *n* anniversaire *m* ♦ *cpd* d'anniversaire; **~place** *n* lieu *m* de naissance; (*fig*) berceau *m*; **~ rate** *n* (taux *m* de) natalité *f*

biscuit ['bɪskɪt] *n* (*BRIT*) biscuit *m*; (*US*) petit pain au lait

bisect [baɪ'sɛkt] *vt* couper *or* diviser en deux

bishop ['bɪʃəp] n évêque m; (CHESS) fou m
bit [bɪt] pt of **bite** ♦ n morceau m; (of tool)
mèche f; (of horse) mors m; (COMPUT)
élément m binaire; **a ~ of** un peu de; **a ~ mad**
un peu fou; **~ by ~** petit à petit
bitch [bɪtʃ] n (dog) chienne f; (inf!) salope f
(!), garce f
bite [baɪt] (pt **bit**, pp **bitten**) vt, vi mordre;
(insect) piquer ♦ n (insect ~) piqûre f;
(mouthful) bouchée f; **let's have a ~ (to eat)**
(inf) mangeons un morceau; **to ~ one's nails**
se ronger les ongles
bitter ['bɪtəʳ] adj amer(-ère); (weather, wind)
glacial(e); (criticism) cinglant(e); (struggle)
acharné(e) ♦ n (BRIT: beer) bière f (forte);
~ness n amertume f; (taste) goût amer
black [blæk] adj noir(e) ♦ n (colour) noir m;
(person): **B~** noir(e) ♦ vt (BRIT: INDUSTRY)
boycotter; **to give sb a ~ eye** pocher l'œil à
qn, faire un œil au beurre noir à qn; **~ and
blue** couvert(e) de bleus; **to be in the ~** (in
credit) être créditeur(-trice); **~berry** n mûre
f; **~bird** n merle m; **~board** n tableau noir;
~ coffee n café noir; **~currant** n cassis m;
~en vt noircir; **~ ice** n verglas m; **~leg** (BRIT)
n briseur de grève, jaune m; **~list** n liste
noire; **~mail** n chantage m ♦ vt faire chanter,
soumettre au chantage; **~ market** n marché
noir; **~out** n panne d'électricité; (TV etc)
interruption f d'émission; (fainting) syncope f;
~ pudding n boudin (noir); **B~ Sea** n: **the
B~ Sea** la mer Noire; **~ sheep** n brebis
galeuse; **~smith** n forgeron m; **~ spot** (AUT)
n point noir
bladder ['blædəʳ] n vessie f
blade [bleɪd] n lame f; (of propeller) pale f;
~ of grass brin m d'herbe
blame [bleɪm] n faute f, blâme m ♦ vt: **to
~ sb/sth for sth** attribuer à qn/qch la
responsabilité de qch; reprocher qch à qn/
qch; **who's to ~?** qui est le fautif or coupable
or responsable?
bland [blænd] adj (taste, food) doux (douce),
fade
blank [blæŋk] adj blanc (blanche); (look) sans
expression, dénué(e) d'expression ♦ n espace
m vide, blanc m; (cartridge) cartouche f à
blanc; **his mind was a ~** il avait la tête vide;
~ cheque chèque m en blanc
blanket ['blæŋkɪt] n couverture f; (of snow,
cloud) couche f
blare [bleaʳ] vi beugler
blast [blɑːst] n souffle m; (of explosive)
explosion f ♦ vt faire sauter or exploser; **~-
off** n (SPACE) lancement m
blatant ['bleɪtənt] adj flagrant(e), criant(e)
blaze [bleɪz] n (fire) incendie m; (fig)
flamboiement m ♦ vi (fire) flamber; (fig: eyes)
flamboyer; (: guns) crépiter ♦ vt: **to ~ a trail**

(fig) montrer la voie
blazer ['bleɪzəʳ] n blazer m
bleach [bliːtʃ] n (also: **household ~**) eau f de
Javel ♦ vt (linen etc) blanchir; **~ed** adj (hair)
oxygéné(e), décoloré(e)
bleak [bliːk] adj morne; (countryside)
désolé(e)
bleat [bliːt] vi bêler
bleed [bliːd] (pt, pp **bled**) vt, vi saigner; **my
nose is ~ing** je saigne du nez
bleeper ['bliːpəʳ] n (device) bip m
blemish ['blemɪʃ] n défaut m; (on fruit,
reputation) tache f
blend [blend] n mélange m ♦ vt mélanger
♦ vi (colours etc: also: **~ in**) se mélanger, se
fondre; **~er** n mixeur m
bless [bles] (pt, pp **blessed** or **blest**) vt bénir;
~ you! (after sneeze) à vos souhaits!; **~ing** n
bénédiction f; (godsend) bienfait m
blew [bluː] pt of **blow**
blight [blaɪt] vt (hopes etc) anéantir; (life)
briser
blimey ['blaɪmɪ] (BRIT: inf) excl mince alors!
blind [blaɪnd] adj aveugle ♦ n (for window)
store m ♦ vt aveugler; **~ alley** n impasse f;
~ corner (BRIT) n virage m sans visibilité;
~fold n bandeau m ♦ adj, adv les yeux
bandés ♦ vt bander les yeux à; **~ly** adv
aveuglément; **~ness** n cécité f; **~ spot** n
(AUT etc) angle mort; **that is her ~ spot** (fig)
elle refuse d'y voir clair sur ce point
blink [blɪŋk] vi cligner des yeux; (light)
clignoter; **~ers** npl œillères fpl
bliss [blɪs] n félicité f, bonheur m sans
mélange
blister ['blɪstəʳ] n (on skin) ampoule f, cloque
f; (on paintwork, rubber) boursouflure f ♦ vi
(paint) se boursoufler, se cloquer
blizzard ['blɪzəd] n blizzard m, tempête f de
neige
bloated ['bləʊtɪd] adj (face) bouffi(e);
(stomach, person) gonflé(e)
blob [blɔb] n (drop) goutte f; (stain, spot)
tache f
block [blɔk] n bloc m; (in pipes) obstruction f;
(toy) cube m; (of buildings) pâté m (de
maisons) ♦ vt bloquer; (fig) faire obstacle à;
~ of flats (BRIT) immeuble (locatif); **mental ~**
trou m de mémoire; **~ade** [blɔ'keɪd] n blocus
m; **~age** n obstruction f; **~buster** n (film,
book) grand succès; **~ letters** npl majuscules
fpl
bloke [bləʊk] (BRIT: inf) n type m
blond(e) [blɔnd] adj, n blond(e)
blood [blʌd] n sang m; **~ donor** n don-
neur(-euse) de sang; **~ group** n groupe
sanguin; **~hound** n limier m; **~ poisoning** n
empoisonnement m du sang; **~ pressure** n
tension f (artérielle); **~shed** n effusion f de

sang, carnage m; **~ sports** npl sports mpl
sanguinaires; **~shot** adj: **~shot eyes** yeux
injectés de sang; **~ing** n sang m,
système sanguin; **~ test** n prise f de sang;
~thirsty adj sanguinaire; **~ vessel** n
vaisseau sanguin; **~y** adj sanglant(e); (nose)
en sang; (BRIT: inf!): **this ~y** ... ce foutu ... (!),
ce putain de ... (!); **~y strong/good**
vachement or sacrément fort/bon; **~y-
minded** (BRIT: inf) adj contrariant(e),
obstiné(e)

bloom [bluːm] n fleur f ♦ vi être en fleur

blossom ['blɒsəm] n fleur(s) f(pl) ♦ vi être
en fleurs; (fig) s'épanouir; **to ~ into** devenir

blot [blɒt] n tache f ♦ vt tacher; **~ out** vt
(memories) effacer; (view) cacher, masquer

blotchy ['blɒtʃɪ] adj (complexion) couvert(e)
de marbrures

blotting paper ['blɒtɪŋ-] n buvard m

blouse [blauz] n chemisier m, corsage m

blow [bləu] (pt **blew**, pp **blown**) n coup m
♦ vi souffler ♦ vt souffler; (fuse) faire sauter;
(instrument) jouer de; **to ~ one's nose** se
moucher; **to ~ a whistle** siffler; **~ away** vt
chasser, faire s'envoler; **~ down** vt faire
tomber, renverser; **~ off** vt emporter; **~ out**
vi (fire, flame) s'éteindre; **~ over** vi s'apaiser;
~ up vi faire sauter; (tyre) gonfler; (PHOT)
agrandir ♦ vi exploser, sauter; **~-dry** n
brushing m; **~lamp** (BRIT) n chalumeau m;
~-out n (of tyre) éclatement m; **~-torch** n
= blowlamp

blue [bluː] adj bleu(e); (fig) triste; **~s** n
(MUS): **the ~s** le blues; **~ film/joke** film m/
histoire f pornographique; **to come out of the
~** (fig) être complètement inattendu; **~bell** n
jacinthe f des bois; **~bottle** n mouche f à
viande; **~print** n (fig) projet m, plan
directeur

bluff [blʌf] vi bluffer ♦ n bluff m; **to call sb's ~**
mettre qn au défi d'exécuter ses menaces

blunder ['blʌndəʳ] n gaffe f, bévue f ♦ vi faire
une gaffe or une bévue

blunt [blʌnt] adj (person) brusque, ne
mâchant pas ses mots; (knife) émoussé(e),
peu tranchant(e); (pencil) mal taillé

blur [bləːʳ] n tache or masse floue or confuse
♦ vt brouiller

blush [blʌʃ] vi rougir ♦ n rougeur f

blustery ['blʌstərɪ] adj (weather) à
bourrasques

boar [bɔːʳ] n sanglier m

board [bɔːd] n planche f; (on wall) panneau
m; (for chess) échiquier m; (cardboard)
carton m; (committee) conseil m, comité m;
(in firm) conseil d'administration; (NAUT,
AVIAT): **on ~** à bord ♦ vt (ship) monter à bord
de; (train) monter dans; **full ~** (BRIT) pension
complète; **half ~** demi-pension f; **~ and**

lodging chambre f avec pension; **which goes
by the ~** (fig) qu'on laisse tomber, qu'on
abandonne; **~ up** vt (door, window) boucher;
~er n (SCOL) interne m/f, pensionnaire;
~ game n jeu m de société; **~ing card** n
= boarding pass; **~ing house** n pension f;
~ing pass n (AVIAT, NAUT) carte f
d'embarquement; **~ing school** n internat m,
pensionnat m; **~ room** n salle f du conseil
d'administration

boast [bəust] vi: **to ~ (about or of)** se vanter
(de)

boat [bəut] n bateau m; (small) canot m;
barque f; **~ train** n train m (qui assure
correspondance avec le ferry)

bob [bɒb] vi (boat, cork on water: also: **~ up
and down**) danser, se balancer

bobby ['bɒbɪ] (BRIT: inf) n ≈ agent m (de
police)

bobsleigh ['bɒbsleɪ] n bob m

bode [bəud] vi: **to ~ well/ill (for)** être de bon/
mauvais augure (pour)

bodily ['bɒdɪlɪ] adj corporel(le) ♦ adv dans ses
bras

body ['bɒdɪ] n corps m; (of car) carrosserie f;
(of plane) fuselage m; (fig: society) organe m,
organisme m; (: quantity) ensemble m, masse
f; (of wine) corps; **~-building** n culturisme
m; **~guard** n garde m du corps; **~work** n
carrosserie f

bog [bɒg] n tourbière f ♦ vt: **to get ~ged down**
(fig) s'enliser

bog-standard (inf) adj tout à fait ordinaire

bogus ['bəugəs] adj bidon inv; fantôme

boil [bɔɪl] vt (faire) bouillir ♦ vi bouillir ♦ n
(MED) furoncle m; **to come to the** (BRIT) **~ or
a** (US) **~** bouillir; **~ down to** vt fus (fig) se
réduire or ramener à; **~ over** vi déborder;
~ed egg n œuf m à la coque; **~ed
potatoes** npl pommes fpl à l'anglaise or à
l'eau; **~er** n chaudière f; **~ing point** n point
m d'ébullition

boisterous ['bɔɪstərəs] adj bruyant(e),
tapageur(-euse)

bold [bəuld] adj hardi(e), audacieux(-euse);
(peh) effronté(e); (outline, colour) franc
(franche), tranché(e), marqué(e); (pattern)
grand(e)

bollard ['bɒləd] (BRIT) n (AUT) borne
lumineuse or de signalisation

bolt [bəult] n (lock) verrou m; (with nut)
boulon m ♦ adv: **~ upright** droit(e) comme
un piquet ♦ vt verrouiller; (TECH: also: **~ on,
~ together**) boulonner; (food) engloutir ♦ vi
(horse) s'emballer

bomb [bɔm] n bombe f ♦ vt bombarder;
~ing n (by terrorist) attentat m à la bombe;
~ disposal unit n section f de déminage;
~er n (AVIAT) bombardier m; **~shell** n (fig)

bombe f

bond [bɔnd] n lien m; (binding promise) engagement m, obligation f; (COMM) obligation; **in ~** (of goods) en douane

bondage ['bɔndɪdʒ] n esclavage m

bone [bəun] n os m; (of fish) arête f ♦ vt désosser; ôter les arêtes de; **~ dry** adj complètement sec (sèche); **~ idle** adj fainéant(e); **~ marrow** n moelle f osseuse

bonfire ['bɔnfaɪəʳ] n feu m (de joie); (for rubbish) feu

bonnet ['bɔnɪt] n bonnet m; (BRIT: of car) capot m

bonus ['bəunəs] n prime f, gratification f

bony ['bəunɪ] adj (arm, face, MED: tissue) osseux(-euse); (meat) plein(e) d'os; (fish) plein d'arêtes

boo [bu:] excl hou!, peuh! ♦ vt huer

booby trap ['bu:bɪ-] n engin piégé

book [buk] n livre m; (of stamps, tickets) carnet m ♦ vt (ticket) prendre; (seat, room) réserver; (driver) dresser un procès-verbal à; (football player) prendre le nom de; **~s** npl (accounts) comptes mpl, comptabilité f; **~case** n bibliothèque f (meuble); **~ing office** (BRIT) n bureau m de location; **~-keeping** n comptabilité f; **~let** n brochure f; **~maker** n bookmaker m; **~seller** n libraire m/f; **~shelf** n (single) étagère f (à livres); **~shop** n librairie f; **~store** n librairie f

boom [bu:m] n (noise) grondement m; (in prices, population) forte augmentation ♦ vi gronder; prospérer

boon [bu:n] n bénédiction f, grand avantage

boost [bu:st] n stimulant m, remontant m ♦ vt stimuler; **~er** n (MED) rappel m

boot [bu:t] n botte f; (for hiking) chaussure f (de marche); (for football etc) soulier m; (BRIT: of car) coffre m ♦ vt (COMPUT) amorcer, initialiser; **to ~** (in addition) par-dessus le marché

booth [bu:ð] n (at fair) baraque (foraine); (telephone etc) cabine f; (also: **voting ~**) isoloir m

booze [bu:z] (inf) n boissons fpl alcooliques, alcool m

border ['bɔ:dəʳ] n bordure f; bord m; (of a country) frontière f ♦ vt border; (also: **~ on:** country) être limitrophe de; **the B~s** la région frontière entre l'Écosse et l'Angleterre; **~ on** vt fus être voisin(e) de, toucher à; **~line** n (fig) ligne f de démarcation; **~line case** cas m limite

bore [bɔ:ʳ] pt of bear ♦ vt (hole) percer; (oil well, tunnel) creuser; (person) ennuyer, raser ♦ n raseur(-euse); (of gun) calibre m; **to be ~d** s'ennuyer; **~dom** n ennui m; **boring** adj ennuyeux(-euse)

born [bɔ:n] adj: **to be ~** naître; **I was ~ in 1960** je suis né en 1960

borne [bɔ:n] pp of bear

borough ['bʌrə] n municipalité f

borrow ['bɔrəu] vt: **to ~ sth (from sb)** emprunter qch (à qn)

Bosnia (and) Herzegovina ['bɔznɪə(ənd)hɜːtsəgəu'vi:nə] n Bosnie-Herzégovine f; **Bosnian** adj bosniaque, bosnien(ne) ♦ n Bosniaque m/f

bosom ['buzəm] n poitrine f; (fig) sein m

boss [bɔs] n patron(ne) ♦ vt (also: **~ around/about**) mener à la baguette; **~y** adj autoritaire

bosun ['bəusn] n maître m d'équipage

botany ['bɔtənɪ] n botanique f

botch [bɔtʃ] vt (also: **~ up**) saboter, bâcler

both [bəuθ] adj les deux, l'un(e) et l'autre ♦ pron: **~ (of them)** les deux, tous (toutes) (les) deux, l'un(e) et l'autre; **they sell ~ the fabric and the finished curtains** ils vendent (et) le tissu et les rideaux (finis), ils vendent à la fois le tissu et les rideaux (finis); **~ of us went, we ~ went** nous y sommes allés (tous) les deux

bother ['bɔðəʳ] vt (worry) tracasser; (disturb) déranger ♦ vi (also: **~ o.s.**) se tracasser, se faire du souci ♦ n: **it is a ~ to do** c'est vraiment ennuyeux d'avoir à faire; **it's no ~** aucun problème; **to ~ doing** prendre la peine de faire

bottle ['bɔtl] n bouteille f; (baby's) biberon m ♦ vt mettre en bouteille(s); **~d beer** bière f en canette; **~d water** eau minérale; **~ up** vt refouler, contenir; **~ bank** n conteneur m à verre; **~neck** n étranglement m; **~-opener** n ouvre-bouteille m

bottom ['bɔtəm] n (of container, sea etc) fond m; (buttocks) derrière m; (of page, list) bas m ♦ adj du fond; du bas; **the ~ of the class** le dernier de la classe

bough [bau] n branche f, rameau m

bought [bɔ:t] pt, pp of buy

boulder ['bəuldəʳ] n gros rocher

bounce [bauns] vi (ball) rebondir; (cheque) être refusé(e) (étant sans provision) ♦ vt faire rebondir ♦ n (rebound) rebond m; **~r** (inf) n (at dance, club) videur m

bound [baund] pt, pp of bind ♦ n (gen pl) limite f; (leap) bond m ♦ vi (leap) bondir ♦ vt (limit) borner ♦ adj: **to be ~ to do sth** (obliged) être obligé(e) or avoir obligation de faire qch; **he's ~ to fail** (likely) il est sûr d'échouer, son échec est inévitable or assuré; **~ by** (law, regulation) engagé(e) par; **~ for** à destination de; **out of ~s** dont l'accès est interdit

boundary ['baundrɪ] n frontière f

bout [baut] n période f; (of malaria etc) accès m, crise f, attaque f; (BOXING etc) combat m, match m

bow¹ [bəu] n nœud m; (weapon) arc m; (MUS) archet m

bow² [bau] n (with body) révérence f, inclination f (du buste or corps); (NAUT: also: ~s) proue f ♦ vi faire une révérence, s'incliner; (yield): to ~ to or before s'incliner devant, se soumettre à

bowels ['bauəlz] npl intestins mpl; (fig) entrailles fpl

bowl [bəul] n (for eating) bol m; (ball) boule f ♦ vi (CRICKET, BASEBALL) lancer (la balle)

bow-legged ['bəu'lɛgɪd] adj aux jambes arquées

bowler ['bəulə'] n (CRICKET, BASEBALL) lanceur m (de la balle); (BRIT: also: ~ hat) (chapeau m) melon m

bowling ['bəulɪŋ] n (game) jeu m de boules; jeu m de quilles; ~ **alley** n bowling m; ~ **green** n terrain m de boules (gazonné et carré)

bowls [bəulz] n (game) (jeu m de) boules fpl

bow tie [bəu-] n nœud m papillon

box [bɔks] n boîte f; (also: **cardboard ~**) carton m; (THEATRE) loge f ♦ vt mettre en boîte; (SPORT) boxer avec ♦ vi boxer, faire de la boxe; ~**er** n (person) boxeur m; ~**er shorts** npl caleçon msg; ~**ing** n (SPORT) boxe f; **B~ing Day** (BRIT) n le lendemain de Noël; ~**ing gloves** npl gants mpl de boxe; ~**ing ring** n ring m; ~ **office** n bureau m de location; ~**room** n débarras m; chambrette f

boy [bɔɪ] n garçon m

boycott ['bɔɪkɔt] n boycottage m ♦ vt boycotter

boyfriend ['bɔɪfrɛnd] n (petit) ami

boyish ['bɔɪɪʃ] adj (behaviour) de garçon; (girl) garçonnier(-ière)

BR n abbr = **British Rail**

bra [brɑ:] n soutien-gorge m

brace [breɪs] n (on teeth) appareil m (dentaire); (tool) vilbrequin m ♦ vt (knees, shoulders) appuyer; ~s npl (BRIT: for trousers) bretelles fpl; to ~ o.s. (lit) s'arc-bouter; (fig) se préparer mentalement

bracelet ['breɪslɪt] n bracelet m

bracing ['breɪsɪŋ] adj tonifiant(e), tonique

bracket ['brækɪt] n (TECH) tasseau m, support m; (group) classe f, tranche f; (also: **brace ~**) accolade f; (also: **round ~**) parenthèse f; (also: **square ~**) crochet m ♦ vt mettre entre parenthèse(s); (fig: also: ~ **together**) regrouper

brag [bræg] vi se vanter

braid [breɪd] n (trimming) galon m; (of hair) tresse f

brain [breɪn] n cerveau m; ~s npl (intellect, CULIN) cervelle f; he's got ~s il est intelligent; ~**wash** vt faire subir un lavage de cerveau à;

~**wave** n idée géniale; ~**y** adj intelligent(e), doué(e)

braise [breɪz] vt braiser

brake [breɪk] n (on vehicle, also fig) frein m ♦ vi freiner; ~ **light** n feu m de stop

bran [bræn] n son m

branch [brɑ:ntʃ] n branche f; (COMM) succursale f ♦ vi bifurquer; ~ **out** vi (fig): to ~ **out into** étendre ses activités à

brand [brænd] n marque (commerciale) ♦ vt (cattle) marquer (au fer rouge); ~-**new** adj tout(e) neuf (neuve), flambant neuf (neuve)

brandy ['brændɪ] n cognac m, fine f

brash [bræʃ] adj effronté(e)

brass [brɑ:s] n cuivre m (jaune), laiton m; the ~ (MUS) les cuivres; ~ **band** n fanfare f

brat [bræt] n (pej) mioche m/f, môme m/f

brave [breɪv] adj courageux(-euse), brave ♦ n guerrier indien ♦ vt braver, affronter; ~**ry** n bravoure f, courage m

brawl [brɔ:l] n rixe f, bagarre f

brazen ['breɪzn] adj impudent(e), effronté(e) ♦ vt: to ~ **it out** payer d'effronterie, crâner

brazier ['breɪzɪə'] n brasero m

Brazil [brə'zɪl] n Brésil m

breach [bri:tʃ] vt ouvrir une brèche dans ♦ n (gap) brèche f; (breaking): ~ **of contract** rupture f de contrat; ~ **of the peace** attentat m à l'ordre public

bread [brɛd] n pain m; ~ **and butter** n tartines (beurrées); (fig) subsistance f; ~**bin** (BRIT) n boîte f à pain; (bigger) huche f à pain; ~**crumbs** npl miettes fpl de pain; (CULIN) chapelure f, panure f; ~**line** n: to be on the ~**line** être sans le sou or dans l'indigence

breadth [brɛtθ] n largeur f; (fig) ampleur f

breadwinner ['brɛdwɪnə'] n soutien m de famille

break [breɪk] (pt **broke**, pp **broken**) vt casser, briser; (promise) rompre; (law) violer ♦ vi (se) casser, se briser; (weather) tourner; (story, news) se répandre; (day) se lever ♦ n (gap) brèche f; (fracture) cassure f; (pause, interval) interruption f, arrêt m; (: short) pause f; (: at school) récréation f; (chance) chance f, occasion f favorable; to ~ **one's leg** etc se casser la jambe etc; to ~ **a record** battre un record; to ~ **the news to sb** annoncer la nouvelle à qn; ~ **even** rentrer dans ses frais; ~ **free** or **loose** se dégager, s'échapper; ~ **open** (door etc) forcer, fracturer; ~ **down** vt (figures, data) décomposer, analyser ♦ vi s'effondrer; (MED) faire une dépression (nerveuse); (AUT) tomber en panne; ~ **in** vt (horse etc) dresser ♦ vi (burglar) entrer par effraction; (interrupt) interrompre; ~ **into** vt fus (house) s'introduire or pénétrer par effraction dans; ~ **off** vi (speaker) s'interrompre; (*branch*) se rompre; **~ out** vi éclater, se déclarer; (*prisoner*) s'évader; **to ~ out in spots** or **a rash** avoir une éruption de boutons; **~ up** vi (*ship*) se disloquer; (*crowd, meeting*) se disperser, se séparer; (*marriage*) se briser; (*SCOL*) entrer en vacances ♦ vt casser; (*fight etc*) interrompre, faire cesser; **~age** n casse f; **~down** n (*AUT*) panne f; (*in communications, marriage*) rupture f; (*MED: also:* **nervous ~down**) dépression (nerveuse); (*of statistics*) ventilation f; **~down van** (*BRIT*) n dépanneuse f; **~er** n brisant m

breakfast ['brekfəst] n petit déjeuner

break: ~-in n cambriolage m; **~ing and entering** n (*LAW*) effraction f; **~through** n percée f; **~water** n brise-lames m inv, digue f

breast [brest] n (*of woman*) sein m; (*chest, of meat*) poitrine f; **~-feed** (*irreg: like* **feed**) vt, vi allaiter; **~stroke** n brasse f

breath [breθ] n haleine f; **out of ~** à bout de souffle, essoufflé(e); **B~alyser** ® ['breθəlaizər] n Alcootest ® m

breathe [bri:ð] vt, vi respirer; **~ in** vt, vi aspirer, inspirer; **~ out** vt, vi expirer; **~r** n moment m de repos or de répit; **breathing** n respiration f

breathless ['breθlɪs] adj essoufflé(e), haletant(e)

breathtaking ['breθteikɪŋ] adj stupéfiant(e)

breed [bri:d] (*pt, pp* **bred**) vt élever, faire l'élevage de ♦ vi se reproduire ♦ n race f, variété f; **~ing** n (*upbringing*) éducation f

breeze [bri:z] n brise f; **breezy** adj frais (fraîche); aéré(e); (*manner etc*) désinvolte, jovial(e)

brevity ['brevɪtɪ] n brièveté f

brew [bru:] vt (*tea*) faire infuser; (*beer*) brasser ♦ vi (*fig*) se préparer, couver; **~ery** n brasserie f (*fabrique*)

bribe [braɪb] n pot-de-vin m ♦ vt acheter; soudoyer; **~ry** n corruption f

brick [brik] n brique f; **~layer** n maçon m

bridal ['braɪdl] adj nuptial(e)

bride [braɪd] n mariée f, épouse f; **~groom** n marié m, époux m; **~smaid** n demoiselle f d'honneur

bridge [brɪdʒ] n pont m; (*NAUT*) passerelle f (de commandement); (*of nose*) arête f; (*CARDS, DENTISTRY*) bridge m ♦ vt (*fig: gap, gulf*) combler

bridle ['braɪdl] n bride f; **~ path** n piste or allée cavalière

brief [bri:f] adj bref (brève) ♦ n (*LAW*) dossier m, cause f; (*gen*) tâche f ♦ vt mettre au courant; **~s** npl (*undergarment*) slip m; **~case** n serviette f; porte-documents m inv; **~ly** adv brièvement

bright [braɪt] adj brillant(e); (*room, weather*) clair(e); (*clever: person, idea*) intelligent(e);

(*cheerful: colour, person*) vif (vive)

brighten ['braɪtn] (*also:* **~ up**) vt (*room*) éclaircir, égayer; (*event*) égayer ♦ vi s'éclaircir; (*person*) retrouver un peu de sa gaieté; (*face*) s'éclairer; (*prospects*) s'améliorer

brilliance ['brɪljəns] n éclat m

brilliant ['brɪljənt] adj brillant(e); (*sunshine, light*) éclatant(e); (*inf: holiday etc*) super

brim [brim] n bord m

brine [braɪn] n (*CULIN*) saumure f

bring [brɪŋ] (*pt, pp* **brought**) vt apporter; (*person*) amener; **~ about** vt provoquer, entraîner; **~ back** vt rapporter; ramener; (*restore: hanging*) réinstaurer; **~ down** vt (*price*) faire baisser; (*enemy plane*) descendre; (*government*) faire tomber; **~ forward** vt avancer; **~ off** vt (*task, plan*) réussir, mener à bien; **~ out** vt (*meaning*) faire ressortir; (*book*) publier; (*object*) sortir; **~ round** vt (*unconscious person*) ranimer; **~ up** vt (*child*) élever; (*carry up*) monter; (*question*) soulever; (*food: vomit*) vomir, rendre

brink [brɪŋk] n bord m

brisk [brɪsk] adj vif (vive)

bristle ['brɪsl] n poil m ♦ vi se hérisser

Britain ['brɪtən] n (*also:* **Great ~**) Grande-Bretagne f

British ['brɪtɪʃ] adj britannique ♦ npl: **the ~** les Britanniques mpl; **~ Isles** npl: **the ~ Isles** les Iles fpl Britanniques; **~ Rail** n compagnie ferroviaire britannique

Briton ['brɪtən] n Britannique m/f

Brittany ['brɪtənɪ] n Bretagne f

brittle ['brɪtl] adj cassant(e), fragile

broach [brəʊtʃ] vt (*subject*) aborder

broad [brɔ:d] adj large; (*general: outlines*) grand(e); (: *distinction*) général(e); (*accent*) prononcé(e); **in ~ daylight** en plein jour; **~cast** (*pt, pp* **broadcast**) n émission f ♦ vt radiodiffuser; téléviser ♦ vi émettre; **~en** vt élargir ♦ vi s'élargir; **to ~en one's mind** élargir ses horizons; **~ly** adv en gros, généralement; **~-minded** adj large d'esprit

broccoli ['brɒkəlɪ] n brocoli m

brochure ['brəʊʃjʊər] n prospectus m, dépliant m

broil [brɔɪl] vt griller

broke [brəʊk] pt of **break** ♦ adj (*inf*) fauché(e)

broken ['brəʊkn] pp of **break** ♦ adj cassé(e); (*machine: also:* **~ down**) fichu(e); **in ~ English/French** dans un anglais/français approximatif or hésitant; **~ leg etc** jambe etc cassée; **~-hearted** adj (ayant) le cœur brisé

broker ['brəʊkər] n courtier m

brolly ['brɒlɪ] (*BRIT: inf*) n pépin m, parapluie m

bronchitis [brɒŋ'kaɪtɪs] n bronchite f

bronze [brɒnz] *n* bronze *m*

brooch [brəutʃ] *n* broche *f*

brood [bru:d] *n* couvée *f* ♦ *vi* (*person*) méditer (sombrement), ruminer

broom [brum] *n* balai *m*; (*BOT*) genêt *m*; **~stick** *n* manche *m* à balai

Bros. *abbr* = **Brothers**

broth [brɒθ] *n* bouillon *m* de viande et de légumes

brothel [brɒθl] *n* maison close, bordel *m*

brother [brʌðər] *n* frère *m*; **~-in-law** *n* beau-frère *m*

brought [brɔ:t] *pt, pp of* **bring**

brow [brau] *n* front *m*; (*eyebrow*) sourcil *m*; (*of hill*) sommet *m*

brown [braun] *adj* brun(e), marron *inv*; (*hair*) châtain *inv*, brun; (*eyes*) marron *inv*; (*tanned*) bronzé(e) ♦ *n* (*colour*) brun *m* ♦ *vt* (*CULIN*) faire dorer; **~ bread** *n* pain *m* bis; **B~ie** *n* (*also*: **B~ie Guide**) jeannette *f*, éclaireuse (cadette); **~ie** (*US*) *n* (*cake*) gâteau *m* au chocolat et aux noix; **~ paper** *n* papier *m* d'emballage; **~ sugar** *n* cassonade *f*

browse [brauz] *vi* (*among books*) bouquiner, feuilleter les livres; **to ~ through a book** feuilleter un livre

browser [brauzər] *n* (*COMPUT*) navigateur *m*

bruise [bru:z] *n* bleu *m*, contusion *f* ♦ *vt* contusionner, meurtrir

brunette [bru:ˈnɛt] *n* (*femme*) brune

brunt [brʌnt] *n*: **the ~ of** (*attack, criticism etc*) le plus gros de

brush [brʌʃ] *n* brosse *f*; (*painting*) pinceau *m*; (*shaving*) blaireau *m*; (*quarrel*) accrochage *m*, prise *f* de bec ♦ *vt* brosser; (*also*: **~ against**) effleurer, frôler; **~ aside** *vt* écarter, balayer; **~ up** *vt* (*knowledge*) rafraîchir, réviser; **~wood** *n* broussailles *fpl*, taillis *m*

Brussels [brʌslz] *n* Bruxelles; **~ sprout** *n* chou *m* de Bruxelles

brutal [bru:tl] *adj* brutal(e)

brute [bru:t] *n* brute *f* ♦ *adj*: **by ~ force** par la force

BSc *abbr* = **Bachelor of Science**

BSE *n abbr* (= *bovine spongiform encephalopathy*) ESB *f*, BSE *f*

bubble [bʌbl] *n* bulle *f* ♦ *vi* bouillonner, faire des bulles; (*sparkle*) pétiller; **~ bath** *n* bain moussant; **~ gum** *n* bubblegum *m*

buck [bʌk] *n* mâle *m* (*d'un lapin, daim etc*); (*US*: *inf*) dollar *m* ♦ *vi* ruer, lancer une ruade; **to pass the ~ (to sb)** se décharger de la responsabilité (sur qn); **~ up** *vi* (*cheer up*) reprendre du poil de la bête, se remonter

bucket [bʌkɪt] *n* seau *m*

buckle [bʌkl] *n* boucle *f* ♦ *vt* (*belt etc*) boucler, attacher ♦ *vi* (*warp*) tordre, gauchir; (*: wheel*) se voiler; se déformer

bud [bʌd] *n* bourgeon *m*; (*of flower*) bouton *m* ♦ *vi* bourgeonner; (*flower*) éclore

Buddhism [budɪzəm] *n* bouddhisme *m*

Buddhist *adj* bouddhiste ♦ *n* Bouddhiste *m/f*

budding [bʌdɪŋ] *adj* (*poet etc*) en herbe; (*passion etc*) naissant(e)

buddy [bʌdɪ] (*US*) *n* copain *m*

budge [bʌdʒ] *vt* faire bouger; (*fig*: *person*) faire changer d'avis ♦ *vi* bouger; changer d'avis

budgerigar [bʌdʒərɪgɑ:ʳ] (*BRIT*) *n* perruche *f*

budget [bʌdʒɪt] *n* budget *m* ♦ *vi*: **to ~ for sth** inscrire qch au budget

budgie [bʌdʒɪ] (*BRIT*) *n* = **budgerigar**

buff [bʌf] *adj* (couleur *f*) chamois *m* ♦ *n* (*inf*: *enthusiast*) mordu(e); **he's a ... ~** c'est un mordu de ...

buffalo [bʌfələu] (*pl* **~** *or* **~es**) *n* buffle *m*; (*US*) bison *m*

buffer [bʌfəʳ] *n* tampon *m*; (*COMPUT*) mémoire *f* tampon

buffet¹ [bʌfɪt] *vt* secouer, ébranler

buffet² [bufeɪ] *n* (*food, BRIT*: *bar*) buffet *m*; **~ car** (*BRIT*) *n* (*RAIL*) voiture-buffet *f*

bug [bʌg] *n* (*insect*) punaise *f*; (: *gen*) insecte *m*, bestiole *f*; (*fig*: *germ*) virus *m*, microbe *m*; (*COMPUT*) erreur *f*; (*fig*: *spy device*) dispositif *m* d'écoute (électronique) ♦ *vt* garnir de dispositifs d'écoute; (*inf*: *annoy*) embêter; **~ged** *adj* sur écoute

bugle [bju:gl] *n* clairon *m*

build [bɪld] (*pt, pp* **built**) *n* (*of person*) carrure *f*, charpente *f* ♦ *vt* construire, bâtir; **~ up** *vt* accumuler, amasser; accroître; **~er** *n* entrepreneur *m*; **~ing** *n* (*trade*) construction *f*; (*house, structure*) bâtiment *m*, construction *f*; (*offices, flats*) immeuble *m*; **~ing society** (*BRIT*) *n* société *f* de crédit immobilier

built [bɪlt] *pt, pp of* **build**; **~-in** [bɪltˈɪn] *adj* (*cupboard, oven*) encastré(e); (*device*) incorporé(e); intégré(e); **~-up area** [bɪltʌp-] *n* zone urbanisée

bulb [bʌlb] *n* (*BOT*) bulbe *m*, oignon *m*; (*ELEC*) ampoule *f*

Bulgaria [bʌlˈgɛərɪə] *n* Bulgarie *f*

bulge [bʌldʒ] *n* renflement *m*, gonflement *m* ♦ *vi* (*pocket, file etc*) être plein(e) à craquer; (*cheeks*) être gonflé(e)

bulk [bʌlk] *n* masse *f*, volume *m*; (*of person*) corpulence *f*; **in ~** (*COMM*) en vrac; **the ~ of** la plus grande ou grosse partie de; **~y** *adj* volumineux(-euse), encombrant(e)

bull [bul] *n* taureau *m*; (*male elephant/whale*) mâle *m*; **~dog** *n* bouledogue *m*

bulldozer [buldəuzəʳ] *n* bulldozer *m*

bullet [bulɪt] *n* balle *f* (*de fusil etc*)

bulletin [bulɪtɪn] *n* bulletin *m*, communiqué *m*; (*news ~*) (bulletin d')informations *fpl*

bulletproof [bulɪtpru:f] *adj* (*car*) blindé(e); (*vest etc*) pare-balles *inv*

bullfight ['bulfaɪt] n corrida f, course f de taureaux; **~er** n torero m; **~ing** n tauromachie f

bullion ['buljən] n or m or argent m en lingots

bullock ['bulək] n bœuf m

bullring ['bulrɪŋ] n arènes fpl

bull's-eye ['bulzaɪ] n centre m (de la cible)

bully ['bulɪ] n brute f, tyran m ♦ vt tyranniser, rudoyer

bum [bʌm] n (inf: backside) derrière m; (esp US: tramp) vagabond(e), traîne-savates m/f inv

bumblebee ['bʌmblbiː] n bourdon m

bump [bʌmp] n (in car: minor accident) accrochage m; (jolt) cahot m; (on road etc, on head) bosse f ♦ vt heurter, cogner; **~ into** vt fus rentrer dans, tamponner; (meet) tomber sur; **~er** n pare-chocs m inv ♦ adj: **~er crop/harvest** récolte/moisson exceptionnelle; **~er cars** (US) npl autos tamponneuses; **~y** adj cahoteux(-euse)

bun [bʌn] n petit pain au lait; (of hair) chignon m

bunch [bʌntʃ] n (of flowers) bouquet m; (of keys) trousseau m; (of bananas) régime m; (of people) groupe m; **~es** npl (in hair) couettes fpl; **~ of grapes** grappe f de raisin

bundle ['bʌndl] n paquet m ♦ vt (also: **~ up**) faire un paquet de; (put): **to ~ sth/sb into** fourrer or enfourner qch/qn dans

bungalow ['bʌŋɡələu] n bungalow m

bungle ['bʌŋɡl] vt bâcler, gâcher

bunion ['bʌnjən] n oignon m (au pied)

bunk [bʌŋk] n couchette f; **~ beds** npl lits superposés

bunker ['bʌŋkər] n (coal store) soute f à charbon; (MIL, GOLF) bunker m

bunting ['bʌntɪŋ] n pavoisement m, drapeaux mpl

buoy [bɔɪ] n bouée f; **~ up** vt faire flotter; (fig) soutenir, épauler; **~ant** adj capable de flotter; (carefree) gai(e), plein(e) d'entrain; (economy) ferme, actif

burden ['bəːdn] n fardeau m ♦ vt (trouble) accabler, surcharger

bureau ['bjuərəu] (pl **~x**) n (BRIT: writing desk) bureau m, secrétaire m; (US: chest of drawers) commode f; (office) bureau, office m; **~cracy** [bjuə'rɔkrəsɪ] n bureaucratie f

burglar ['bəːɡlər] n cambrioleur m; **~ alarm** n sonnerie f d'alarme; **~y** n cambriolage m

Burgundy ['bəːɡəndɪ] n Bourgogne f

burial ['berɪəl] n enterrement m

burly ['bəːlɪ] adj de forte carrure, costaud(e)

Burma ['bəːmə] n Birmanie f

burn [bəːn] (pt, pp **burned** or **burnt**) vt, vi brûler ♦ n brûlure f; **~ down** vt incendier, détruire par le feu; **~er** n brûleur m; **~ing**

adj brûlant(e); (house) en flammes; (ambition) dévorant(e)

burrow ['bʌrəu] n terrier m ♦ vt creuser

bursary ['bəːsərɪ] (BRIT) n bourse f (d'études)

burst [bəːst] (pt, pp **burst**) vt crever; faire éclater; (subj: river: banks etc) rompre ♦ vi éclater; (tyre) crever ♦ n (of gunfire) rafale f (de tir); (also: **~ pipe**) rupture f; fuite f; **a ~ of enthusiasm/energy** un accès d'enthousiasme/ d'énergie; **to ~ into flames** s'enflammer soudainement; **to ~ out laughing** éclater de rire; **to ~ into tears** fondre en larmes; **to be ~ing with** être plein (à craquer) de; (fig) être débordant(e) de; **~ into** vt fus (room etc) faire irruption dans

bury ['berɪ] vt enterrer

bus [bʌs] (pl **~es**) n autobus m

bush [buʃ] n buisson m; (scrubland) brousse f; **to beat about the ~** tourner autour du pot; **~y** adj broussailleux(-euse), touffu(e)

busily ['bɪzɪlɪ] adv activement

business ['bɪznɪs] n (matter, firm) affaire f; (trading) affaires fpl; (job, duty) travail m; **to be away on ~** être en déplacement d'affaires; **it's none of my ~** cela ne me regarde pas, ce ne sont pas mes affaires; **he means ~** il ne plaisante pas, il est sérieux; **~like** adj (firm) sérieux(-euse); (method) efficace; **~man** (irreg) n homme m d'affaires; **~ trip** n voyage m d'affaires; **~woman** (irreg) n femme f d'affaires

busker ['bʌskər] (BRIT) n musicien ambulant

bus: **~ shelter** n abribus m; **~ station** n gare routière; **~ stop** n arrêt m d'autobus

bust [bʌst] n buste m; (measurement) tour m de poitrine ♦ adj (inf: broken) fichu(e), fini(e); **to go ~** faire faillite

bustle ['bʌsl] n remue-ménage m, affairement m ♦ vi s'affairer, se démener; **bustling** adj (town) bruyant(e), affairé(e)

busy ['bɪzɪ] adj occupé(e); (shop, street) très fréquenté(e) ♦ vt: **to ~ o.s.** s'occuper; **~body** n mouche f du coche, âme f charitable; **~ signal** (US) n (TEL) tonalité f occupé inv

---

KEYWORD

---

but [bʌt] conj mais; **I'd love to come, but I'm busy** j'aimerais venir mais je suis occupé ♦ prep (apart from, except) sauf, excepté; **we've had nothing but trouble** nous n'avons eu que des ennuis; **no-one but him can do it** lui seul peut le faire; **but for you/your help** sans toi/ton aide; **anything but that** tout sauf or excepté ça, tout mais pas ça ♦ adv (just, only) ne ... que; **she's but a child** elle n'est qu'une enfant; **had I but known** si seulement j'avais su; **all but finished** pratiquement terminé

butcher ['butʃəʳ] *n* boucher *m* ♦ *vt* massacrer; (*cattle etc for meat*) tuer; **~'s (shop)** *n* boucherie *f*

butler ['bʌtləʳ] *n* maître *m* d'hôtel

butt [bʌt] *n* (*large barrel*) gros tonneau; (*of gun*) crosse *f*; (*of cigarette*) mégot *m*; (*BRIT: fig: target*) cible *f* ♦ *vt* donner un coup de tête à; **~ in** *vi* (*interrupt*) s'immiscer dans la conversation

butter ['bʌtəʳ] *n* beurre *m* ♦ *vt* beurrer; **~cup** *n* bouton *m* d'or

butterfly ['bʌtəflaɪ] *n* papillon *m*; (*SWIMMING: also:* **~ stroke**) brasse *f* papillon

buttocks ['bʌtəks] *npl* fesses *fpl*

button ['bʌtn] *n* bouton *m*; (*US: badge*) pin *m* ♦ *vt* (*also:* **~ up**) boutonner ♦ *vi* se boutonner

buttress ['bʌtrɪs] *n* contrefort *m*

buy [baɪ] (*pt, pp* **bought**) *vt* acheter ♦ *n* achat *m*; **to ~ sb sth/sth from sb** acheter qch à qn; **to ~ sb a drink** offrir un verre *or* à boire à qn; **~er** *n* acheteur(-euse)

buzz [bʌz] *n* bourdonnement *m*; (*inf: phone call*): **to give sb a ~** passer un coup *m* de fil à qn ♦ *vi* bourdonner; **~er** *n* timbre *m* électrique; **~ word** *n* (*inf*) mot *m* à la mode

---

by [baɪ] *prep* **1** (*referring to cause, agent*) par, de; **killed by lightning** tué par la foudre; **surrounded by a fence** entouré d'une barrière; **a painting by Picasso** un tableau de Picasso
2 (*referring to method, manner, means*): **by bus/car** en autobus/voiture; **by train** par le *or* en train; **to pay by cheque** payer par chèque; **by saving hard, he ...** à force d'économiser, il ...
3 (*via, through*) par; **we came by Dover** nous sommes venus par Douvres
4 (*close to, past*) à côté de; **the house by the school** la maison à côté de l'école; **a holiday by the sea** des vacances au bord de la mer; **she sat by his bed** elle était assise à son chevet; **she went by me** elle est passée à côté de moi; **I go by the post office every day** je passe devant la poste tous les jours
5 (*with time: not later than*) avant; (*: during*): **by daylight** à la lumière du jour; **by night** la nuit, de nuit; **by 4 o'clock** avant 4 heures; **by this time tomorrow** d'ici demain à la même heure; **by the time I got here it was too late** lorsque je suis arrivé il était déjà trop tard
6 (*amount*) à; **by the kilo/metre** au kilo/au mètre; **paid by the hour** payé à l'heure
7 (*MATH, measure*): **to divide/multiply by 3** diviser/multiplier par 3; **a room 3 metres by 4** une pièce de 3 mètres sur 4; **it's broader by a metre** c'est plus large d'un mètre; **one by one** un à un; **little by little** petit à petit, peu à peu

8 (*according to*) d'après, selon; **it's 3 o'clock by my watch** il est 3 heures à ma montre; **it's all right by me** je n'ai rien contre
9: (**all**) **by oneself** *etc* tout(e) seul(e)
10: by the way au fait, à propos
♦ *adv* **1** *see* **go**; **pass** *etc*
2: by and by plus tard, bientôt; **by and large** dans l'ensemble

bye(-bye) ['baɪ('baɪ)] *excl* au revoir!, salut!

by(e)-law ['baɪlɔ:] *n* arrêté municipal

by: **~-election** (*BRIT*) *n* élection (législative) partielle; **~gone** *adj* passé(e) ♦ *n*: **let ~gones be ~gones** passons l'éponge, oublions le passé; **~pass** *n* (route *f* de) contournement *m*; (*MED*) pontage *m* ♦ *vt* éviter; **~-product** *n* sous-produit *m*, dérivé *m*; (*fig*) conséquence *f* secondaire, retombée *f*; **~stander** *n* spectateur(-trice), badaud(e)

byte [baɪt] *n* (*COMPUT*) octet *m*

byword ['baɪwə:d] *n*: **to be a ~ for** être synonyme de (*fig*)

C, c

C [si:] *n* (*MUS*) do *m*

CA *abbr* = **chartered accountant**

cab [kæb] *n* taxi *m*; (*of train, truck*) cabine *f*

cabaret ['kæbəreɪ] *n* (*show*) spectacle *m* de cabaret

cabbage ['kæbɪdʒ] *n* chou *m*

cabin ['kæbɪn] *n* (*house*) cabane *f*, hutte *f*; (*on ship*) cabine *f*; (*on plane*) compartiment *m*; **~ crew** *n* (*AVIAT*) équipage *m*; **~ cruiser** *n* cruiser *m*

cabinet ['kæbɪnɪt] *n* (*POL*) cabinet *m*; (*furniture*) petit meuble à tiroirs et rayons; (*also: display ~*) vitrine *f*, petite armoire vitrée

cable ['keɪbl] *n* câble *m* ♦ *vt* câbler, télégraphier; **~-car** *n* téléphérique *m*; **~ television** *n* télévision *f* par câble

cache [kæʃ] *n* stock *m*

cackle ['kækl] *vi* caqueter

cactus ['kæktəs] (*pl* **cacti**) *n* cactus *m*

cadet [kə'dɛt] *n* (*MIL*) élève *m* officier

cadge [kædʒ] (*inf*) *vt*: **to ~ (from** *or* **off)** se faire donner (par)

Caesarian [sɪ'zɛərɪən] *n* (*also: ~ section*) césarienne *f*

café ['kæfeɪ] *n* ≈ café(-restaurant) *m* (*sans alcool*)

cage [keɪdʒ] *n* cage *f*

cagey ['keɪdʒɪ] (*inf*) *adj* réticent(e); méfiant(e)

cagoule [kə'gu:l] *n* K-way ® *m*

Cairo ['kaɪərəu] *n* le Caire

cajole [kə'dʒəul] *vt* couvrir de flatteries *or* de gentillesses

cake [keɪk] n gâteau m; **~d** adj: **~d with** raidi(e) par, couvert(e) d'une croûte de
calculate ['kælkjuleɪt] vt calculer; (estimate: chances, effect) évaluer; **calculation** n calcul m; **calculator** n machine f à calculer, calculatrice f; (pocket) calculette f
calendar ['kæləndə'] n calendrier m; **~ year** n année civile
calf [kɑːf] (pl calves) n (of cow) veau m; (of other animals) petit m; (also: **~skin**) veau m, vachette f; (ANAT) mollet m
calibre ['kælɪbə'] (US **caliber**) n calibre m
call [kɔːl] vt appeler; (meeting) convoquer ♦ vi appeler; (visit: also: **~ in**, **~ round**) passer ♦ n (shout) appel m, cri m; (also: **telephone ~**) coup m de téléphone; (visit) visite f; **she's ~ed Suzanne** elle s'appelle Suzanne; **to be on ~** être de permanence; **~ back** vi (return) repasser; (TEL) rappeler; **~ for** vt fus (demand) demander; (fetch) passer prendre; **~ off** vt annuler; **~ on** vt fus (visit) rendre visite à, passer voir; (request): **to ~ on sb to do** inviter qn à faire; **~ out** vi pousser un cri or des cris; **~ up** vt (MIL) appeler, mobiliser; (TEL) appeler; **~box** (BRIT) n (TEL) cabine f téléphonique; **~ centre** n centre m d'appels; **~er** n (TEL) personne f qui appelle; (visitor) visiteur m; **~ girl** n call-girl f; **~-in** (US) n (RADIO, TV: phone-in) programme m à ligne ouverte; **~ing** n vocation f; (trade, occupation) état m; **~ing card** (US) n carte f de visite
callous ['kæləs] adj dur(e), insensible
calm [kɑːm] adj calme ♦ n calme m ♦ vt calmer, apaiser; **~ down** vi se calmer ♦ vt calmer, apaiser
Calor gas ® ['kælə'-] n butane m, butagaz m ®
calorie ['kælərɪ] n calorie f
calves [kɑːvz] npl of **calf**
camber ['kæmbə'] n (of road) bombement m
Cambodia [kæm'bəudɪə] n Cambodge m
camcorder ['kæmkɔːdə'] n caméscope m
came [keɪm] pt of **come**
camel ['kæməl] n chameau m
camera ['kæmərə] n (PHOT) appareil-photo m; (also: **cine-~**, **movie~**) caméra f; **in ~** à huis clos; **~man** (irreg) n caméraman m
camouflage ['kæməflɑːʒ] n camouflage m ♦ vt camoufler
camp [kæmp] n camp m ♦ vi camper ♦ adj (man) efféminé(e)
campaign [kæm'peɪn] n (MIL, POL etc) campagne f ♦ vi faire campagne
camp: **~bed** (BRIT) n lit m de camp; **~er** n campeur(-euse); (vehicle) camping-car m; **~ing** n camping m; **to go ~ing** faire du camping; **~ing gas** ® n butane m; **~site** n campement m, (terrain m de) camping m

campus ['kæmpəs] n campus m
can¹ [kæn] n (of milk, oil, water) bidon m; (tin) boîte f de conserve ♦ vt mettre en conserve

┌─────────────┐
│ **KEYWORD** │
└─────────────┘

can² [kæn] (negative **cannot**, **can't**, conditional and pt **could**) aux vb **1** (be able to) pouvoir; **you can do it if you try** vous pouvez le faire si vous essayez; **I can't hear you** je ne t'entends pas
2 (know how to) savoir; **I can swim/play tennis/drive** je sais nager/jouer au tennis/ conduire; **can you speak French?** parlez-vous français?
3 (may) pouvoir; **can I use your phone?** puis-je me servir de votre téléphone?
4 (expressing disbelief, puzzlement etc): **it can't be true!** ce n'est pas possible!; **what CAN he want?** qu'est-ce qu'il peut bien vouloir?
5 (expressing possibility, suggestion etc): **he could be in the library** il est peut-être dans la bibliothèque; **she could have been delayed** il se peut qu'elle ait été retardée

Canada ['kænədə] n Canada m; **Canadian** [kə'neɪdɪən] adj canadien(ne) ♦ n Canadien(ne)
canal [kə'næl] n canal m
canapé ['kænəpeɪ] n canapé m
canary [kə'nɛərɪ] n canari m, serin m
cancel ['kænsəl] vt annuler; (train) supprimer; (party, appointment) décommander; (cross out) barrer, rayer; **~lation** [kænsə'leɪʃən] n annulation f; suppression f
cancer ['kænsə'] n (MED) cancer m; **C~** (ASTROLOGY) le Cancer
candid ['kændɪd] adj (très) franc (franche), sincère
candidate ['kændɪdeɪt] n candidat(e)
candle ['kændl] n bougie f; (of tallow) chandelle f; (in church) cierge m; **~light** n: **by ~light** à la lumière d'une bougie; (dinner) aux chandelles; **~stick** n (also: **~ holder**) bougeoir m; (bigger, ornate) chandelier m
candour ['kændə'] (US **candor**) n (grande) franchise or sincérité
candy ['kændɪ] n sucre candi; (US) bonbon m; **~-floss** (BRIT) n barbe f à papa
cane [keɪn] n canne f; (for furniture, baskets etc) rotin m ♦ vt (BRIT: SCOL) administrer des coups de bâton à
canister ['kænɪstə'] n boîte f; (of gas, pressurized substance) bombe f
cannabis ['kænəbɪs] n (drug) cannabis m
canned [kænd] adj (food) en boîte, en conserve
cannon ['kænən] (pl ~ or ~s) n (gun) canon m

cannot ['kænɒt] = **can not**

canoe [kə'nu:] n pirogue f; (SPORT) canoë m; **~ing** n: to go **~ing** faire du canoë

canon ['kænən] n (clergyman) chanoine m; (standard) canon m

can-opener ['kænəupnəʳ] n ouvre-boîte m

canopy ['kænəpɪ] n baldaquin m; dais m

can't [kænt] = **cannot**

canteen [kæn'ti:n] n cantine f; (BRIT: of cutlery) ménagère f

canter ['kæntəʳ] vi (horse) aller au petit galop

canvas ['kænvəs] n toile f

canvass ['kænvəs] vi (POL): to **~ for** faire campagne pour ♦ vt (investigate: opinions etc) sonder

canyon ['kænjən] n cañon m, gorge (profonde)

cap [kæp] n casquette f; (of pen) capuchon m; (of bottle) capsule f; (contraceptive: also: Dutch **~**) diaphragme m; (for toy gun) amorce f ♦ vt (outdo) surpasser; (put limit on) plafonner

capability [keɪpə'bɪlɪtɪ] n aptitude f, capacité f

capable ['keɪpəbl] adj capable

capacity [kə'pæsɪtɪ] n capacité f; (capability) aptitude f; (of factory) rendement m

cape [keɪp] n (garment) cape f; (GEO) cap m

caper ['keɪpəʳ] n (CULIN: gen pl) câpre f; (prank) farce f

capital ['kæpɪtl] n (also: **~ city**) capitale f; (money) capital m; (also: **~ letter**) majuscule f; **~ gains tax** n (COMM) impôt m sur les plus-values; **~ism** n capitalisme m; **~ist** adj capitaliste ♦ n capitaliste m/f; **~ize** ['kæpɪtəlaɪz] vi: to **~ize on** tirer parti de; **~ punishment** n peine capitale

Capricorn ['kæprɪkɔ:n] n le Capricorne

capsize [kæp'saɪz] vt faire chavirer ♦ vi chavirer

capsule ['kæpsju:l] n capsule f

captain ['kæptɪn] n capitaine m

caption ['kæpʃən] n légende f

captive ['kæptɪv] adj, n captif(-ive)

capture ['kæptʃəʳ] vt capturer, prendre; (attention) capter; (COMPUT) saisir ♦ n capture f; (data **~**) saisie f de données

car [kɑ:ʳ] n voiture f, auto f; (RAIL) wagon m, voiture

caramel ['kærəməl] n caramel m

caravan ['kærəvæn] n caravane f; **~ning** n: to go **~ning** faire du caravaning; **~ site** (BRIT) n camping m pour caravanes

carbohydrate [kɑ:bəu'haɪdreɪt] n hydrate m de carbone; (food) féculent m

carbon ['kɑ:bən] n carbone m; **~ dioxide** n gaz m carbonique; **~ monoxide** n oxyde m de carbone; **~ paper** n papier m carbone

car boot sale n marché aux puces où les particuliers vendent des objets entreposés dans le coffre de leur voiture

carburettor [kɑ:bju'retəʳ] (US **carburetor**) n carburateur m

card [kɑ:d] n carte f; (material) carton m; **~board** n carton m; **~ game** n jeu m de cartes

cardiac ['kɑ:dɪæk] adj cardiaque

cardigan ['kɑ:dɪgən] n cardigan m

cardinal ['kɑ:dɪnl] adj cardinal(e) ♦ n cardinal m

card index n fichier m

cardphone n téléphone m à carte

care [kɛəʳ] n soin m, attention f; (worry) souci m; (charge) charge f, garde f ♦ vi: to **~ about** se soucier de, s'intéresser à; (person) être attaché(e) à; **~ of** chez, aux bons soins de; in sb's **~** à la garde de qn, confié(e) à qn; to take **~ (to do)** faire attention (à faire); to take **~ of** s'occuper de; I don't **~** ça m'est bien égal; I couldn't **~ less** je m'en fiche complètement (inf); **~ for** vt fus s'occuper de; (like) aimer

career [kə'rɪəʳ] n carrière f ♦ vi (also: **~ along**) aller à toute allure; **~ woman** (irreg) n femme ambitieuse

care: ~free adj sans souci, insouciant(e); **~ful** adj (thorough) soigneux(-euse); (cautious) prudent(e); **(be) ~ful!** (fais) attention!; **~fully** adv avec soin, soigneusement; prudemment; **~less** adj négligent(e); (heedless) insouciant(e); **~r** n (MED) aide f

caress [kə'res] n caresse f ♦ vt caresser

caretaker ['kɛəteɪkəʳ] n gardien(ne), concierge m/f

car-ferry ['kɑ:fɛrɪ] n (on sea) ferry(-boat) m

cargo ['kɑ:gəu] (pl **~es**) n cargaison f, chargement m

car hire n location f de voitures

Caribbean [kærɪ'bɪən] adj: the **~ (Sea)** la mer des Antilles or Caraïbes

caring ['kɛərɪŋ] adj (person) bienveillant(e); (society, organization) humanitaire

carnation [kɑ:'neɪʃən] n œillet m

carnival ['kɑ:nɪvl] n (public celebration) carnaval m; (US: funfair) fête foraine

carol ['kærəl] n: **(Christmas) ~** chant m de Noël

carp [kɑ:p] n (fish) carpe f

car park (BRIT) n parking m, parc m de stationnement

carpenter ['kɑ:pɪntəʳ] n charpentier m; **carpentry** n menuiserie f

carpet ['kɑ:pɪt] n tapis m ♦ vt recouvrir d'un tapis; **~ sweeper** n balai m mécanique

car phone n (TEL) téléphone m de voiture

car rental n location f de voitures

carriage ['kærɪdʒ] n voiture f; (of goods) transport m; (: cost) port m; **~way** (BRIT) n (*part of road*) chaussée f

carrier ['kærɪəʳ] n transporteur m, camionneur m; (*company*) entreprise f de transport; (*MED*) porteur(-euse); **~ bag** (*BRIT*) n sac m (en papier or en plastique)

carrot ['kærət] n carotte f

carry ['kærɪ] vt (*subj: person*) porter; (: *vehicle*) transporter; (*involve: responsibilities etc*) comporter, impliquer ♦ vi (*sound*) porter; **to get carried away** (*fig*) s'emballer, s'enthousiasmer; **~ on** vi: **to ~ on with sth/doing** continuer qch/de faire ♦ vt poursuivre; **~ out** vt (*orders*) exécuter; (*investigation*) mener; **~cot** (*BRIT*) n porte-bébé m; **~-on** (*inf*) n (*fuss*) histoires fpl

cart [kɑ:t] n charrette f ♦ vt (*inf*) transporter, trimballer (*inf*)

carton ['kɑ:tən] n (*box*) carton m; (*of yogurt*) pot m; (*of cigarettes*) cartouche f

cartoon [kɑ:'tu:n] n (*PRESS*) dessin m (humoristique), caricature f; (*BRIT: comic strip*) bande dessinée; (*CINEMA*) dessin animé

cartridge ['kɑ:trɪdʒ] n cartouche f

carve [kɑ:v] vt (*meat*) découper; (*wood, stone*) tailler, sculpter; **~ up** vt découper; (*fig: country*) morceler; **carving** n sculpture f; **carving knife** n couteau m à découper

car wash n station f de lavage (de voitures)

case [keɪs] n cas m; (*LAW*) affaire f, procès m; (*box*) caisse f, boîte f, étui m; (*BRIT: also:* **suitcase**) valise f; **in ~ of** en cas de; **in ~ he ...** au cas où il ...; **just in ~** à tout hasard; **in any ~** en tout cas, de toute façon

cash [kæʃ] n argent m; (*COMM*) argent liquide, espèces fpl ♦ vt encaisser; **to pay (in) ~** payer comptant; **~ on delivery** payable or paiement à la livraison; **~-book** n livre m de caisse; **~ card** (*BRIT*) n carte f de retrait; **~ desk** (*BRIT*) n caisse f; **~ dispenser** (*BRIT*) n distributeur m automatique de billets, billeterie f

cashew [kæ'ʃu:] n (*also:* **~ nut**) noix f de cajou

cashier [kæ'ʃɪəʳ] n caissier(-ère)

cashmere ['kæʃmɪəʳ] n cachemire m

cash register n caisse (enregistreuse)

casing ['keɪsɪŋ] n revêtement (protecteur), enveloppe (protectrice)

casino [kə'si:nəu] n casino m

casket ['kɑ:skɪt] n coffret m; (*US: coffin*) cercueil m

casserole ['kæsərəul] n (*container*) cocotte f; (*food*) ragoût m (en cocotte)

cassette [kæ'set] n cassette f, musicassette f; **~ player** n lecteur m de cassettes; **~ recorder** n magnétophone m à cassettes

cast [kɑ:st] (*pt, pp cast*) vt (*throw*) jeter; (*shed*) perdre; se dépouiller de; (*statue*) mouler; (*THEATRE*): **to ~ sb as Hamlet** attribuer

à qn le rôle de Hamlet ♦ n (*THEATRE*) distribution f; (*also:* **plaster ~**) plâtre m; **to ~ one's vote** voter; **~ off** vi (*NAUT*) larguer les amarres; (*KNITTING*) arrêter les mailles; **~ on** vi (*KNITTING*) monter les mailles

castaway ['kɑ:stəweɪ] n naufragé(e)

caster sugar ['kɑ:stə-] (*BRIT*) n sucre m semoule

casting vote (*BRIT*) n voix prépondérante (*pour départager*)

cast iron n fonte f

castle ['kɑ:sl] n château (fort); (*CHESS*) tour f

castor ['kɑ:stəʳ] n (*wheel*) roulette f; **~ oil** n huile f de ricin

castrate [kæs'treɪt] vt châtrer

casual ['kæʒju.l] adj (*by chance*) de hasard, fait(e) au hasard, fortuit(e); (*irregular: work etc*) temporaire; (*unconcerned*) désinvolte; **~ly** adv avec désinvolture, négligemment; (*dress*) de façon décontractée

casualty ['kæʒjultɪ] n accidenté(e), blessé(e); (*dead*) victime f, mort(e); (*MED: department*) urgences fpl

casual wear n vêtements mpl décontractés

cat [kæt] n chat m

catalogue ['kætəlɔg] (*US catalog*) n catalogue m ♦ vt cataloguer

catalyst ['kætəlɪst] n catalyseur m

catalytic converter [kætə'lɪtɪk kən'vɜ:təʳ] n pot m catalytique

catapult ['kætəpʌlt] (*BRIT*) n (*sling*) lance-pierres m inv, fronde M

catarrh [kə'tɑ:ʳ] n rhume m chronique, catarrhe m

catastrophe [kə'tæstrəfɪ] n catastrophe f

catch [kætʃ] (*pt, pp caught*) vt attraper; (*person: by surprise*) prendre, surprendre; (*understand, hear*) saisir ♦ vi (*fire*) prendre; (*become trapped*) se prendre, s'accrocher ♦ n prise f; (*trick*) attrape f; (*of lock*) loquet m; **to ~ sb's attention or eye** attirer l'attention de qn; **to ~ one's breath** retenir son souffle; **to ~ fire** prendre feu; **to ~ sight of** apercevoir; **~ on** vi saisir; (*grow popular*) prendre; **~ up** vi se rattraper, combler son retard ♦ vt (*also:* **~ up with**) rattraper; **~ing** adj (*MED*) contagieux(-euse); **~ment area** ['kætʃmənt-] (*BRIT*) n (*SCOL*) secteur m de recrutement; (*of hospital*) circonscription hospitalière; **~ phrase** n slogan m; expression f (à la mode); **~y** adj (*tune*) facile à retenir

category ['kætɪgərɪ] n catégorie f

cater ['keɪtəʳ] vi (*provide food*): **to ~ (for)** préparer des repas (pour), se charger de la restauration (pour); **~ for** (*BRIT*) vt fus (*needs*) satisfaire, pourvoir à; (*readers, consumers*) s'adresser à, pourvoir aux besoins de; **~er** n traiteur m; fournisseur m; **~ing** n restauration f; approvisionnement m,

ravitaillement m
caterpillar ['kætəpɪlə'] n chenille f
cathedral [kə'θiːdrəl] n cathédrale f
catholic ['kæθəlɪk] adj (tastes) éclectique, varié(e); **C~** adj catholique ♦ n catholique m/f
Catseye ® ['kætsˌaɪ] (BRIT) n (AUT) catadioptre m
cattle ['kætl] npl bétail m
catty ['kætɪ] adj méchant(e)
caucus ['kɔːkəs] n (POL: group) comité local d'un parti politique; (US: POL) comité électoral (pour désigner des candidats)
caught [kɔːt] pt, pp of **catch**
cauliflower ['kɒlɪflaʊə'] n chou-fleur m
cause [kɔːz] n cause f ♦ vt causer
caution ['kɔːʃən] n prudence f; (warning) avertissement m ♦ vt avertir, donner un avertissement à; **cautious** adj prudent(e)
cavalry ['kævəlrɪ] n cavalerie f
cave [keɪv] n caverne f, grotte f; **~ in** vi (roof etc) s'effondrer; **~man** ['keɪvmæn] (irreg) n homme m des cavernes
caviar(e) ['kævɪɑː'] n caviar m
CB n abbr (= Citizens' Band (Radio)) CB f
CBI n abbr (= Confederation of British Industries) groupement du patronat
cc abbr = **carbon copy; cubic centimetres**
CD n abbr (= compact disc (player)) CD m; **CDI** n abbr (= Compact Disk Interactive) CD-I m; **CD player** n platine f laser; **CD-ROM** [siːdiː'rɔm] n abbr (= compact disc read-only memory) CD-Rom m
cease [siːs] vt, vi cesser; **~fire** n cessez-le-feu m; **~less** adj incessant(e), continuel(le)
cedar ['siːdə'] n cèdre m
ceiling ['siːlɪŋ] n plafond m
celebrate ['sɛlɪbreɪt] vt, vi célébrer; **~d** adj célèbre; **celebration** [sɛlɪ'breɪʃən] n célébration f; **celebrity** [sɪ'lɛbrɪtɪ] n célébrité f
celery ['sɛlərɪ] n céleri m (à côtes)
cell [sɛl] n cellule f; (ELEC) élément m (de pile)
cellar ['sɛlə'] n cave f
cello ['tʃɛləʊ] n violoncelle m
cellphone ['sɛlfəʊn] n téléphone m cellulaire
Celt [kɛlt, sɛlt] n Celte m/f; **~ic** adj celte
cement [sə'mɛnt] n ciment m; **~ mixer** n bétonnière f
cemetery ['sɛmɪtrɪ] n cimetière m
censor ['sɛnsə'] n censeur m ♦ vt censurer; **~ship** n censure f
censure ['sɛnʃə'] vt blâmer, critiquer
census ['sɛnsəs] n recensement m
cent [sɛnt] n (US etc: coin) cent m (= un centième du dollar); see also **per**
centenary [sɛn'tiːnərɪ] n centenaire m
center ['sɛntə'] (US) n = **centre**
centigrade ['sɛntɪgreɪd] adj centigrade

centimetre ['sɛntɪmiːtə'] (US **centimeter**) n centimètre m
centipede ['sɛntɪpiːd] n mille-pattes m inv
central ['sɛntrəl] adj central(e); **C~ America** n Amérique centrale; **~ heating** n chauffage central; **~ reservation** (BRIT) n (AUT) terre-plein central
centre ['sɛntə'] (US **center**) n centre m ♦ vt centrer; **~-forward** n (SPORT) avant-centre m; **~-half** n (SPORT) demi-centre m
century ['sɛntjʊrɪ] n siècle m; **20th ~** XXe siècle
ceramic [sɪ'ræmɪk] adj céramique
cereal ['sɪːrɪəl] n céréale f
ceremony ['sɛrɪmənɪ] n cérémonie f; **to stand on ~** faire des façons
certain ['sɜːtən] adj certain(e); **for ~** certainement, sûrement; **~ly** adv certainement; **~ty** n certitude f
certificate [sə'tɪfɪkɪt] n certificat m
certified ['sɜːtɪfaɪd] adj: **by ~ mail** (US) en recommandé, avec avis de réception; **~ public accountant** (US) expert-comptable m
certify ['sɜːtɪfaɪ] vt certifier; (award diploma to) conférer un diplôme etc à; (declare insane) déclarer malade mental(e)
cervical ['sɜːvɪkl] adj: **~ cancer** cancer m du col de l'utérus; **~ smear** frottis vaginal
cervix ['sɜːvɪks] n col m de l'utérus
cf. abbr (= compare) cf., voir
CFC n abbr (= chlorofluorocarbon) CFC m (gen pl)
ch. abbr (= chapter) chap
chafe [tʃeɪf] vt irriter, frotter contre
chain [tʃeɪn] n chaîne f ♦ vt (also: **~ up**) enchaîner, attacher (avec une chaîne); **~ reaction** n réaction f en chaîne; **~-smoke** vi fumer cigarette sur cigarette; **~ store** n magasin m à succursales multiples
chair [tʃɛə'] n chaise f; (armchair) fauteuil m; (of university) chaire f; (of meeting, committee) présidence f ♦ vt (meeting) présider; **~lift** n télésiège m; **~man** (irreg) n président m
chalet ['ʃæleɪ] n chalet m
chalk [tʃɔːk] n craie f
challenge ['tʃælɪndʒ] n défi m ♦ vt défier; (statement, right) mettre en question, contester; **to ~ sb to do** mettre qn au défi de faire; **challenging** adj (tone, look) de défi, provocateur(-trice); (task, career) qui représente un défi ou une gageure
chamber ['tʃeɪmbə'] n chambre f; **~ of commerce** chambre de commerce; **~maid** n femme f de chambre; **~ music** n musique f de chambre
champagne [ʃæm'peɪn] n champagne m
champion ['tʃæmpɪən] n champion(ne); **~ship** n championnat m

chance [tʃɑːns] n (opportunity) occasion f, possibilité f; (hope, likelihood) chance f; (risk) risque m ♦ vt: to ~ it risquer (le coup), essayer ♦ adj fortuit(e), de hasard; to take a ~ prendre un risque; by ~ par hasard

chancellor ['tʃɑːnsələʳ] n chancelier m; C~ of the Exchequer (BRIT) n chancelier m de l'Échiquier; ≈ ministre m des Finances

chandelier [ʃændə'lɪəʳ] n lustre m

change [tʃeɪndʒ] vt (alter, replace, COMM: money) changer; (hands, trains, clothes, one's name) changer de; (transform): to ~ sb into changer or transformer qn en ♦ vi (gen) changer; (one's clothes) se changer; (be transformed): to ~ into se changer or transformer en ♦ n changement m; (money) monnaie f; (AUT) to ~ gear changer de vitesse; to ~ one's mind changer d'avis; a ~ of clothes des vêtements de rechange; for a ~ pour changer; ~able adj (weather) variable; ~ machine n distributeur m de monnaie; ~over n (to new system) changement m, passage m; **changing** adj changeant(e); **changing room** (BRIT) n (in shop) salon m d'essayage; (SPORT) vestiaire m

channel ['tʃænl] n (TV) chaîne f; (navigable passage) chenal m; (irrigation) canal m ♦ vt canaliser; the (English) C~ la Manche; the C~ Islands les îles de la Manche, les îles Anglo-Normandes; the C~ Tunnel le tunnel sous la Manche; ~-hopping n (TV) zapping m

chant [tʃɑːnt] n chant m; (REL) psalmodie f ♦ vt chanter, scander

chaos ['keɪɒs] n chaos m

chap [tʃæp] (BRIT: inf) n (man) type m

chapel ['tʃæpl] n chapelle f; (BRIT: nonconformist ~) église f

chaplain ['tʃæplɪn] n aumônier m

chapped [tʃæpt] adj (skin, lips) gercé(e)

chapter ['tʃæptəʳ] n chapitre m

char [tʃɑːʳ] vt (burn) carboniser

character ['kærɪktəʳ] n caractère m; (in novel, film) personnage m; (eccentric) numéro m, phénomène m; ~istic [kærɪktə'rɪstɪk] adj caractéristique ♦ n caractéristique f

charcoal ['tʃɑːkəul] n charbon m de bois; (for drawing) charbon m

charge [tʃɑːdʒ] n (cost) prix (demandé); (accusation) accusation f; (LAW) inculpation f ♦ vt: to ~ sb (with) inculper qn (de); (battery, enemy) charger; (customer, sum) faire payer ♦ vi foncer; ~s npl (costs) frais mpl; to reverse the ~s (TEL) téléphoner en P.C.V.; to take ~ of se charger de; to be in ~ of être responsable de, s'occuper de; how much do you ~? combien prenez-vous?; to ~ an expense (up) to sb mettre une dépense sur le compte de qn; ~ card n carte f de

client

charity ['tʃærɪtɪ] n charité f; (organization) institution f charitable or de bienfaisance, œuvre f (de charité)

charm [tʃɑːm] n charme m; (on bracelet) breloque f ♦ vt charmer, enchanter; ~ing adj charmant(e)

chart [tʃɑːt] n tableau m, diagramme m; graphique m; (map) carte marine ♦ vt dresser or établir la carte de; ~s npl (hit parade) hit-parade m

charter ['tʃɑːtəʳ] vt (plane) affréter ♦ n (document) charte f; ~ed accountant (BRIT) n expert-comptable m; ~ flight n charter m

chase [tʃeɪs] vt poursuivre, pourchasser; (also: ~ away) chasser ♦ n poursuite f, chasse f

chasm ['kæzəm] n gouffre m, abîme m

chat [tʃæt] vi (also: have a ~) bavarder, causer ♦ n conversation f; ~ show (BRIT) n causerie f télévisée

chatter ['tʃætəʳ] vi (person) bavarder; (animal) jacasser ♦ n bavardage m; jacassement m; my teeth are ~ing je claque des dents; ~box (inf) n moulin m à paroles

chatty ['tʃætɪ] adj (style) familier(-ère); (person) bavard(e)

chauffeur ['ʃəufəʳ] n chauffeur m (de maître)

chauvinist ['ʃəuvɪnɪst] n (male ~) phallocrate m; (nationalist) chauvin(e)

cheap [tʃiːp] adj bon marché inv, pas cher (chère); (joke) facile, d'un goût douteux; (poor quality) bon marché, de qualité médiocre ♦ adv à bon marché, pour pas cher; ~ day return billet m d'aller et retour réduit (valable pour la journée); ~er adj moins cher (chère); ~ly adv à bon marché, à bon compte

cheat [tʃiːt] vi tricher ♦ vt tromper, duper; (rob): to ~ sb out of sth escroquer qch à qn ♦ n tricheur(-euse); escroc m

check [tʃek] vt vérifier; (passport, ticket) contrôler; (halt) arrêter; (restrain) maîtriser ♦ n vérification f; contrôle m; (curb) frein m; (US: bill) addition f; (pattern: gen pl) carreaux mpl; (US) = cheque ♦ adj (pattern, cloth) à carreaux; ~ in vi (in hotel) remplir sa fiche (d'hôtel); (at airport) se présenter à l'enregistrement ♦ vt (luggage) (faire) enregistrer; ~ out vi (in hotel) régler sa note; ~ up vi: to ~ up (on sth) vérifier (qch); to ~ up on sb se renseigner sur le compte de qn; ~ered (US) adj = chequered; ~ers (US) npl jeu m de dames; ~-in (desk) n enregistrement m; ~ing account (US) n (current account) compte courant; ~mate n échec et mat m; ~out n (in shop) caisse f; ~point n contrôle m; ~room (US) n (left-luggage office) consigne f; ~up n (MED) examen médical, check-up m

cheek [tʃiːk] n joue f; (impudence) toupet m, culot m; **~bone** n pommette f; **~y** adj effronté(e), culotté(e)

cheep [tʃiːp] vi piauler

cheer [tʃɪəʳ] vt acclamer, applaudir; (gladden) réjouir, réconforter ♦ vi applaudir ♦ n (gen pl) acclamations fpl, applaudissements mpl; bravos mpl, hourras mpl; **~s!** à la vôtre!; **~ up** vi se dérider, reprendre courage ♦ vt remonter le moral à or de, dérider; **~ful** adj gai(e), joyeux(-euse)

cheerio [tʃɪərɪˈəu] (BRIT) excl salut!, au revoir!

cheese [tʃiːz] n fromage m; **~board** n plateau m de fromages

cheetah [ˈtʃiːtə] n guépard m

chef [ʃef] n chef (cuisinier)

chemical [ˈkemɪkl] adj chimique ♦ n produit m chimique

chemist [ˈkemɪst] n (BRIT: pharmacist) pharmacien(ne); (scientist) chimiste m/f; **~ry** n chimie f; **~'s (shop)** (BRIT) n pharmacie f

cheque [tʃek] (BRIT) n chèque m; **~book** n chéquier m, carnet m de chèques; **~ card** n carte f (d'identité) bancaire

chequered [ˈtʃekəd] (US **checkered**) adj (fig) varié(e)

cherish [ˈtʃerɪʃ] vt chérir

cherry [ˈtʃerɪ] n cerise f; (also: ~ **tree**) cerisier m

chess [tʃes] n échecs mpl; **~board** n échiquier m

chest [tʃest] n poitrine f; (box) coffre m, caisse f; **~ of drawers** n commode f

chestnut [ˈtʃesnʌt] n châtaigne f; (also: ~ **tree**) châtaignier m

chew [tʃuː] vt mâcher; **~ing gum** n chewing-gum m

chic [ʃiːk] adj chic inv, élégant(e)

chick [tʃɪk] n poussin m; (inf) nana f

chicken [ˈtʃɪkɪn] n poulet m; (inf: coward) poule mouillée; **~ out** (inf) vi se dégonfler; **~pox** n varicelle f

chicory [ˈtʃɪkərɪ] n (for coffee) chicorée f; (salad) endive f

chief [tʃiːf] n chef m ♦ adj principal(e); **~ executive** (US **chief executive officer**) n directeur(-trice) général(e); **~ly** adv principalement, surtout

chiffon [ˈʃɪfɔn] n mousseline f de soie

chilblain [ˈtʃɪlbleɪn] n engelure f

child [tʃaɪld] n (pl **~ren**) enfant m/f; **~birth** n accouchement m; **~hood** n enfance f; **~ish** adj puéril(e), enfantin(e); **~like** adj d'enfant, innocent(e); **~ minder** (BRIT) n garde f d'enfants; **~ren** [ˈtʃɪldrən] npl of **child**

Chile [ˈtʃɪlɪ] n Chili m

chill [tʃɪl] n (of water) froid m; (of air) fraîcheur f; (MED) refroidissement m, coup m de froid ♦ vt (person) faire frissonner; (CULIN)

mettre au frais, rafraîchir

chil(l)i [ˈtʃɪlɪ] n piment m (rouge)

chilly [ˈtʃɪlɪ] adj froid(e), glacé(e); (sensitive to cold) frileux(-euse); **to feel ~** avoir froid

chime [tʃaɪm] n carillon m ♦ vi carillonner, sonner

chimney [ˈtʃɪmnɪ] n cheminée f; **~ sweep** n ramoneur m

chimpanzee [tʃɪmpænˈziː] n chimpanzé m

chin [tʃɪn] n menton m

China [ˈtʃaɪnə] n Chine f

china [ˈtʃaɪnə] n porcelaine f; (crockery) (vaisselle f en) porcelaine

Chinese [tʃaɪˈniːz] adj chinois(e) ♦ n inv (person) Chinois(e); (LING) chinois m

chink [tʃɪŋk] n (opening) fente f, fissure f; (noise) tintement m

chip [tʃɪp] n (gen pl: CULIN: BRIT) frite f; (: US: potato ~) chip m; (of wood) copeau m; (of glass, stone) éclat m; (also: **microchip**) puce f ♦ vt (cup, plate) ébrécher

chiropodist [kɪˈrɔpədɪst] (BRIT) n pédicure m/f

chirp [tʃəːp] vi pépier, gazouiller

chisel [ˈtʃɪzl] n ciseau m

chit [tʃɪt] n mot m, note f

chitchat [ˈtʃɪttʃæt] n bavardage m

chivalry [ˈʃɪvəlrɪ] n esprit m chevaleresque, galanterie f

chives [tʃaɪvz] npl ciboulette f, civette f

chock-a-block [ˈtʃɔkəˈblɔk], **chock-full** [tʃɔkˈful] adj plein(e) à craquer

chocolate [ˈtʃɔklɪt] n chocolat m

choice [tʃɔɪs] n choix m ♦ adj de choix

choir [ˈkwaɪəʳ] n chœur m, chorale f; **~boy** n jeune choriste m

choke [tʃəuk] vi étouffer ♦ vt étrangler; étouffer ♦ n (AUT) starter m; **street ~d with traffic** rue engorgée or embouteillée

cholesterol [kəˈlestərɔl] n cholestérol m

choose [tʃuːz] (pt **chose**, pp **chosen**) vt choisir; **to ~ to do** décider de faire, juger bon de faire; **choosy** adj: **(to be) choosy** (faire le/la) difficile

chop [tʃɔp] vt (wood) couper (à la hache); (CULIN: also: ~ **up**) couper (fin), émincer, hacher (en morceaux) ♦ n (CULIN) côtelette f; **~s** npl (jaws) mâchoires fpl

chopper [ˈtʃɔpəʳ] n (helicopter) hélicoptère m, hélico m

choppy [ˈtʃɔpɪ] adj (sea) un peu agité(e)

chopsticks [ˈtʃɔpstɪks] npl baguettes fpl

chord [kɔːd] n (MUS) accord m

chore [tʃɔːʳ] n travail m de routine; **household ~s** travaux mpl du ménage

chortle [ˈtʃɔːtl] vi glousser

chorus [ˈkɔːrəs] n chœur m; (repeated part of song: also fig) refrain m

chose [tʃəuz] pt of **choose**; **~n** pp of **choose**

chowder ['tʃaudəʳ] n soupe f de poisson
Christ [kraɪst] n Christ m
christen ['krɪsn] vt baptiser
christening n baptême m
Christian ['krɪstɪən] adj, n chrétien(ne); **~ity**
[krɪstɪ'ænɪtɪ] n christianisme m; **~ name** n
prénom m
Christmas ['krɪsməs] n Noël m or f; Happy
or Merry **~**! joyeux Noël!; **~ card** n carte f de
Noël; **~ Day** n le jour de Noël; **~ Eve** n la
veille de Noël; la nuit de Noël; **~ tree** n
arbre m de Noël
chrome [krəum] n chrome m
chromium ['krəumɪəm] n chrome m
chronic ['krɒnɪk] adj chronique
chronicle ['krɒnɪkl] n chronique f
chronological [krɒnə'lɒdʒɪkl] adj
chronologique
chrysanthemum [krɪ'sænθəməm] n
chrysanthème m
chubby ['tʃʌbɪ] adj potelé(e), rondelet(te)
chuck [tʃʌk] (inf) vt (throw) lancer, jeter;
(BRIT: person) plaquer; (: also: **~ up**: job)
lâcher; **~ out** vt flanquer dehors or à la porte;
(rubbish) jeter
chuckle ['tʃʌkl] vi glousser
chug [tʃʌg] vi faire teuf-teuf; (also: **~ along**)
avancer en faisant teuf-teuf
chum [tʃʌm] n copain (copine)
chunk [tʃʌŋk] n gros morceau
church [tʃəːtʃ] n église f; **~yard** n cimetière
m
churn [tʃəːn] n (for butter) baratte f; (also:
milk **~**) (grand) bidon à lait; **~ out** vt débiter
chute [ʃuːt] n glissoire f; (also: **rubbish ~**)
vide-ordures m inv
chutney ['tʃʌtnɪ] n condiment m à base de
fruits au vinaigre
CIA n abbr (= Central Intelligence Agency) CIA f
CID (BRIT) n abbr (= Criminal Investigation
Department) P.J. f
cider ['saɪdəʳ] n cidre m
cigar [sɪ'gɑːʳ] n cigare m
cigarette [sɪgə'ret] n cigarette f; **~ case** n
étui m à cigarettes; **~ end** n mégot m
Cinderella [sɪndə'relə] n Cendrillon
cinders ['sɪndəz] npl cendres fpl
cine-camera ['sɪnɪ'kæmərə] (BRIT) n caméra
f
cinema ['sɪnəmə] n cinéma m
cinnamon ['sɪnəmən] n cannelle f
circle ['səːkl] n cercle m; (in cinema, theatre)
balcon m ♦ vi faire or décrire des cercles ♦ vt
(move round) faire le tour de, tourner autour
de; (surround) entourer, encercler
circuit ['səːkɪt] n circuit m; **~ous** [səː'kjuɪtəs]
adj indirect(e), qui fait un détour
circular ['səːkjulə'] adj circulaire ♦ n circulaire
f

circulate ['səːkjuleɪt] vi circuler ♦ vt faire
circuler; **circulation** [səːkju'leɪʃən] n
circulation f; (of newspaper) tirage m
circumflex ['səːkəmfleks] n (also: **~ accent**)
accent m circonflexe
circumstances ['səːkəmstənsɪz] npl
circonstances fpl; (financial condition) moyens
mpl, situation financière
circus ['səːkəs] n cirque m
CIS n abbr (= Commonwealth of Independent
States) CEI f
cistern ['sɪstən] n réservoir m (d'eau); (in
toilet) réservoir de la chasse d'eau
citizen ['sɪtɪzn] n citoyen(ne); (resident): the
~s of this town les habitants de cette ville;
~ship n citoyenneté f
citrus fruit ['sɪtrəs-] n agrume m
city ['sɪtɪ] n ville f, cité f; the **C~** la Cité de
Londres (centre des affaires); **~ technology
college** n établissement m d'enseignement
technologique
civic ['sɪvɪk] adj civique; (authorities)
municipal(e); **~ centre** (BRIT) n centre
administratif (municipal)
civil ['sɪvɪl] adj civil(e); (polite) poli(e),
courtois(e); (disobedience, defence) pas-
sif(-ive); **~ engineer** n ingénieur m des travaux publics; **~ian** [sɪ'vɪlɪən] adj, n civil(e)
civilization [sɪvɪlaɪ'zeɪʃən] n civilisation f
civilized ['sɪvɪlaɪzd] adj civilisé(e); (fig) où
règnent les bonnes manières
civil: ~ law n code civil; (study) droit civil;
~ servant n fonctionnaire m/f; **C~ Service**
n fonction publique, administration f; **~ war**
n guerre civile
clad [klæd] adj: **~ (in)** habillé(e) (de)
claim [kleɪm] vt revendiquer; (rights,
inheritance) demander, prétendre à; (assert)
déclarer, prétendre ♦ vi (for insurance) faire
une déclaration de sinistre ♦ n revendication
f; demande f; prétention f, déclaration f;
(right) droit m, titre m; **~ant** n (ADMIN, LAW)
requérant(e)
clairvoyant [kleə'vɔɪənt] n voyant(e), extra-
lucide m/f
clam [klæm] n palourde f
clamber ['klæmbəʳ] vi grimper, se hisser
clammy ['klæmɪ] adj humide (et froid(e)),
moite
clamour ['klæməʳ] (US clamor) vi: to **~ for**
réclamer à grands cris
clamp [klæmp] n agrafe f, crampon m ♦ vt
serrer; (sth to sth) fixer; (wheel) mettre un
sabot à; **~ down on** vt fus sévir or prendre
des mesures draconiennes contre
clan [klæn] n clan m
clang [klæŋ] vi émettre un bruit or fracas
métallique
clap [klæp] vi applaudir; **~ping** n

applaudissements *mpl*

claret ['klærət] *n* (vin *m* de) bordeaux *m* (rouge)

clarinet [klærɪ'net] *n* clarinette *f*

clarity ['klærɪtɪ] *n* clarté *f*

clash [klæʃ] *n* choc *m*; (*fig*) conflit *m* ♦ *vi* se heurter; être *or* entrer en conflit; (*colours*) jurer; (*two events*) tomber en même temps

clasp [klɑːsp] *n* (*of necklace, bag*) fermoir *m*; (*hold, embrace*) étreinte *f* ♦ *vt* serrer, étreindre

class [klɑːs] *n* classe *f* ♦ *vt* classer, classifier

classic ['klæsɪk] *adj* classique ♦ *n* (*author, work*) classique *m*; **~al** *adj* classique

classified ['klæsɪfaɪd] *adj* (*information*) secret(-ète); **~ advertisement** *n* petite annonce

classmate ['klɑːsmeɪt] *n* camarade *m/f* de classe

classroom ['klɑːsrum] *n* (salle *f* de) classe *f*

clatter ['klætə'] *n* cliquetis *m* ♦ *vi* cliqueter

clause [klɔːz] *n* clause *f*; (*LING*) proposition *f*

claw [klɔː] *n* griffe *f*; (*of bird of prey*) serre *f*; (*of lobster*) pince *f*

clay [kleɪ] *n* argile *f*

clean [kliːn] *adj* propre; (*clear, smooth*) net(te); (*record, reputation*) sans tache; (*joke, story*) correct(e) ♦ *vt* nettoyer; **~ out** *vt* nettoyer (à fond); **~ up** *vt* nettoyer; (*fig*) remettre de l'ordre dans; **~-cut** *adj* (*person*) net(te), soigné(e); **~er** *n* (*person*) nettoyeur(-euse), femme *f* de ménage; (*product*) détachant *m*; **~er's** *n* (*also:* **dry ~er's**) teinturier *m*; **~ing** *n* nettoyage *m*; **~liness** ['klɛnlɪnɪs] *n* propreté *f*

cleanse [klɛnz] *vt* nettoyer; (*purify*) purifier; **~r** *n* (*for face*) démaquillant *m*

clean-shaven ['kliːn'ʃeɪvn] *adj* rasé(e) de près

cleansing department ['klɛnzɪŋ-] (*BRIT*) *n* service *m* de voirie

clear [klɪə'] *adj* clair(e); (*glass, plastic*) transparent(e); (*road, way*) libre, dégagé(e); (*conscience*) net(te) ♦ *vt* (*room*) débarrasser; (*of people*) faire évacuer; (*cheque*) compenser; (*LAW: suspect*) innocenter; (*obstacle*) franchir *or* sauter sans heurter ♦ *vi* (*weather*) s'éclaircir; (*fog*) se dissiper ♦ *adv*: **~ of** à distance de, à l'écart de; **to ~ the table** débarrasser la table, desservir; **~ up** *vt* ranger, mettre en ordre; (*mystery*) éclaircir, résoudre; **~ance** *n* (*removal*) déblaiement *m*; (*permission*) autorisation *f*; **~-cut** *adj* clair(e), nettement défini(e); **~ing** *n* (*in forest*) clairière *f*; **~ing bank** (*BRIT*) *n* banque qui appartient à une chambre de compensation; **~ly** *adv* clairement; (*evidently*) de toute évidence; **~way** (*BRIT*) *n* route *f* à stationnement interdit

clef [klef] *n* (*MUS*) clé *f*

cleft [kleft] *n* (*in rock*) crevasse *f*, fissure *f*

clementine ['klemantaɪn] *n* clémentine *f*

clench [klentʃ] *vt* serrer

clergy ['klɜːdʒɪ] *n* clergé *m*; **~man** (*irreg*) *n* ecclésiastique *m*

clerical ['klerɪkl] *adj* de bureau, d'employé de bureau; (*REL*) clérical(e), du clergé

clerk [klɑːk, (*US*) klɜːrk] *n* employé(e) de bureau; (*US: salesperson*) vendeur(-euse)

clever ['klevə'] *adj* (*mentally*) intelligent(e); (*deft, crafty*) habile, adroit(e); (*device, arrangement*) ingénieux(-euse), astucieux(-euse)

click [klɪk] *vi* faire un bruit sec *or* un déclic

client ['klaɪənt] *n* client(e)

cliff [klɪf] *n* falaise *f*

climate ['klaɪmɪt] *n* climat *m*

climax ['klaɪmæks] *n* apogée *m*, point culminant; (*sexual*) orgasme *m*

climb [klaɪm] *vi* grimper, monter ♦ *vt* gravir, escalader, monter sur ♦ *n* montée *f*, escalade *f*; **~-down** *n* reculade *f*, dérobade *f*; **~er** *n* (*mountaineer*) grimpeur(-euse), varappeur(-euse); (*plant*) plante grimpante; **~ing** *n* (*mountaineering*) escalade *f*, varappe *f*

clinch [klɪntʃ] *vt* (*deal*) conclure, sceller

cling [klɪŋ] (*pt, pp* **clung**) *vi*: **to ~ (to)** se cramponner (à), s'accrocher (à); (*of clothes*) coller (à)

clinic ['klɪnɪk] *n* centre médical; **~al** *adj* clinique; (*attitude*) froid(e), détaché(e)

clink [klɪŋk] *vt* tinter, cliqueter

clip [klɪp] *n* (*for hair*) barrette *f*; (*also:* **paper ~**) trombone *m* ♦ *vt* (*fasten*) attacher; (*hair, nails*) couper; (*hedge*) tailler; **~pers** *npl* (*for hedge*) sécateur *m*; (*also:* **nail ~pers**) coupe-ongles *m inv*; **~ping** *n* (*from newspaper*) coupure *f* de journal

cloak [kləuk] *n* grande cape ♦ *vt* (*fig*) masquer, cacher; **~room** *n* (*for coats etc*) vestiaire *m*; (*BRIT: WC*) toilettes *fpl*

clock [klɔk] *n* (*large*) horloge *f*; (*small*) pendule *f*; **~ in** (*BRIT*) *vi* pointer (en arrivant); **~ off** (*BRIT*) *vi* pointer (en partant); **~ on** (*BRIT*) *vi* = **clock in**; **~ out** (*BRIT*) *vi* = **clock off**; **~wise** *adv* dans le sens des aiguilles d'une montre; **~work** *n* rouages *mpl*, mécanisme *m*; (*of clock*) mouvement *m* (d'horlogerie) ♦ *adj* mécanique

clog [klɔg] *n* sabot *m* ♦ *vt* boucher ♦ *vi* (*also:* **~ up**) se boucher

cloister ['klɔɪstə'] *n* cloître *m*

close[1] [kləus] *adj* (*near*) près, proche; (*contact, link*) étroit(e); (*contest*) très serré(e); (*watch*) étroit(e), strict(e); (*examination*) attentif(-ive), minutieux(-euse); (*weather*) lourd(e), étouffant(e) ♦ *adv* près, à proximité; **~ to** près de, proche de; **~ by** *adj* proche ♦ *adv* tout(e) près; **~ at hand** = **close by**; **a ~ friend** un ami intime; **to have a ~ shave** (*fig*) l'échapper belle

close² [kləuz] *vt* fermer ♦ *vi* (*shop etc*) fermer; (*lid, door etc*) se fermer; (*end*) se terminer, se conclure ♦ *n* (*end*) conclusion *f*, fin *f*; **~ down** *vt, vi* fermer (*définitivement*); **~d** *adj* fermé(e); **~d shop** *n* organisation *f* qui n'admet que des travailleurs syndiqués

close-knit ['kləus'nɪt] *adj* (*family, community*) très uni(e)

closely ['kləuslɪ] *adv* (*examine, watch*) de près

closet ['klɔzɪt] *n* (*cupboard*) placard *m*, réduit *m*

close-up ['kləusʌp] *n* gros plan

closure ['kləuʒə'] *n* fermeture *f*

clot [klɔt] *n* (*gen: blood ~*) caillot *m*; (*inf: person*) ballot *m* ♦ *vi* (*blood*) se coaguler; **~ted cream** crème fraîche très épaisse

cloth [klɔθ] *n* (*material*) tissu *m*, étoffe *f*; (*also: teacloth*) torchon *m*; lavette *f*

clothe [kləuð] *vt* habiller, vêtir; **~s** *npl* vêtements *mpl*, habits *mpl*; **~s brush** *n* brosse *f* à habits; **~s line** *n* corde *f* (à linge); **~s peg** (*US* **clothes pin**) *n* pince *f* à linge;

clothing *n* = **clothes**

cloud [klaud] *n* nuage *m*; **~burst** *n* grosse averse; **~y** *adj* nuageux(-euse), couvert(e); (*liquid*) trouble

clout [klaut] *vt* flanquer une taloche à

clove [kləuv] *n* (*CULIN: spice*) clou *m* de girofle; **~ of garlic** gousse *f* d'ail

clover ['kləuvə'] *n* trèfle *m*

clown [klaun] *n* clown *m* ♦ *vi* (*also: ~ about, ~ around*) faire le clown

cloying ['klɔɪɪŋ] *adj* (*taste, smell*) écœurant(e)

club [klʌb] *n* (*society, place: also: golf ~*) club *m*; (*weapon*) massue *f*, matraque *f* ♦ *vt* matraquer ♦ *vi*: **to ~ together** s'associer; **~s** *npl* (*CARDS*) trèfle *m*; **~ class** *n* (*AVIAT*) classe *f* club; **~house** *n* club *m*

cluck [klʌk] *vi* glousser

clue [klu:] *n* indice *m*; (*in crosswords*) définition *f*; **I haven't a ~** je n'en ai pas la moindre idée

clump [klʌmp] *n*: **~ of trees** bouquet *m* d'arbres

clumsy ['klʌmzɪ] *adj* gauche, maladroit(e)

clung [klʌŋ] *pt, pp of* **cling**

cluster ['klʌstə'] *n* (*of people*) (petit) groupe; (*of flowers*) grappe *f*; (*of stars*) amas *m* ♦ *vi* se rassembler

clutch [klʌtʃ] *n* (*grip, grasp*) étreinte *f*, prise *f*; (*AUT*) embrayage *m* ♦ *vt* (*grasp*) agripper; (*hold tightly*) serrer fort; (*hold on to*) se cramponner à

clutter ['klʌtə'] *vt* (*also: ~ up*) encombrer

CND *n abbr* (= Campaign for Nuclear Disarmament) mouvement pour le désarmement nucléaire

Co. *abbr* = **county**; **company**

c/o *abbr* (= care of) c/o, aux bons soins de

coach [kəutʃ] *n* (*bus*) autocar *m*; (*horse-drawn*) diligence *f*; (*of train*) voiture *f*, wagon *m*; (*SPORT: trainer*) entraîneur(-euse) *m*; (*SCOL: tutor*) répétiteur(-trice) ♦ *vt* entraîner; (*student*) faire travailler; **~ trip** *n* excursion *f* en car

coal [kəul] *n* charbon *m*; **~ face** *n* front *m* de taille; **~field** *n* bassin houiller

coalition [kəuə'lɪʃən] *n* coalition *f*

coalman ['kəulmən] (*irreg*) *n* charbonnier *m*, marchand *m* de charbon

coalmine ['kəulmaɪn] *n* mine *f* de charbon

coarse [kɔːs] *adj* grossier(-ère), rude

coast [kəust] *n* côte *f* ♦ *vi* (*car, cycle etc*) descendre en roue libre; **~al** *adj* côtier(-ère); **~guard** *n* garde-côte *m*; (*service*) gendarmerie *f* maritime; **~line** *n* côte *f*, littoral *m*

coat [kəut] *n* manteau *m*; (*of animal*) pelage *m*, poil *m*; (*of paint*) couche *f* ♦ *vt* couvrir; **~ hanger** *n* cintre *m*; **~ing** *n* couche *f*, revêtement *m*; **~ of arms** *n* blason *m*, armoiries *fpl*

coax [kəuks] *vt* persuader par des cajoleries

cobbler ['kɔblə'] *n* cordonnier *m*

cobbles ['kɔblz] (*also: ~tones*) *npl* pavés (ronds)

cobweb ['kɔbweb] *n* toile *f* d'araignée

cocaine [kə'keɪn] *n* cocaïne *f*

cock [kɔk] *n* (*rooster*) coq *m*; (*male bird*) mâle *m* ♦ *vt* (*gun*) armer; **~erel** *n* jeune coq *m*

cockle ['kɔkl] *n* coque *f*

cockney ['kɔknɪ] *n* cockney *m*, habitant des quartiers populaires de l'East End de Londres, ≈ faubourien(ne)

cockpit ['kɔkpɪt] *n* (*in aircraft*) poste *m* de pilotage, cockpit *m*

cockroach ['kɔkrəutʃ] *n* cafard *m*

cocktail ['kɔkteɪl] *n* cocktail *m*; (*fruit ~ etc*) salade *f*; **~ cabinet** *n* (*meuble-*)bar *m*; **~ party** *n* cocktail *m*

cocoa ['kəukəu] *n* cacao *m*

coconut ['kəukənʌt] *n* noix *f* de coco

COD *abbr* = **cash on delivery**

cod [kɔd] *n* morue fraîche, cabillaud *m*

code [kəud] *n* code *m*

cod-liver oil *n* huile *f* de foie de morue

coercion [kəu'ə:ʃən] *n* contrainte *f*

coffee ['kɔfɪ] *n* café *m*; **~ bar** *n* (*BRIT*) café *m*; **~ bean** *n* grain *m* de café; **~ break** *n* pause-café *f*; **~pot** *n* cafetière *f*; **~ table** *n* (petite) table basse

coffin ['kɔfɪn] *n* cercueil *m*

cog [kɔg] *n* dent *f* (d'engrenage); (*wheel*)

roue dentée

cogent ['kəudʒənt] adj puissant(e), convaincant(e)

coil [kɔɪl] n rouleau m, bobine f; (contraceptive) stérilet m ♦ vt enrouler

coin [kɔɪn] n pièce f de monnaie ♦ vt (word) inventer; ~**age** n monnaie f, système m monétaire; ~ **box** (BRIT) n cabine f téléphonique

coincide [kəun'saɪd] vi coïncider; ~**nce** [kəu'ɪnsɪdəns] n coïncidence f

Coke ® [kəuk] n coca m

coke [kəuk] n coke m

colander ['kɔləndər] n passoire f

cold [kəuld] adj froid(e) ♦ n froid m; (MED) rhume m; **it's ~** il fait froid; **to be or feel ~** (person) avoir froid; **to catch ~** prendre or attraper froid; **to catch a ~** attraper un rhume; **in ~ blood** de sang-froid; ~-**shoulder** vt se montrer froid(e) envers, snober; ~ **sore** n bouton m de fièvre

coleslaw ['kəulslɔː] n sorte de salade de chou cru

colic ['kɔlɪk] n colique(s) f(pl)

collapse [kə'læps] vi s'effondrer, s'écrouler ♦ n effondrement m, écroulement m; **collapsible** adj pliant(e); télescopique

collar ['kɔlər] n (of coat, shirt) col m; (for animal) collier m; ~**bone** n clavicule f

collateral [kə'lætərl] n nantissement m

colleague ['kɔliːg] n collègue m/f

collect [kə'lekt] vt rassembler; ramasser; (as a hobby) collectionner; (BRIT: call and pick up) (passer) prendre; (mail) faire la levée de, ramasser; (money owed) encaisser; (donations, subscriptions) recueillir ♦ vi (people) se rassembler; (things) s'amasser; **to call ~** (US: TEL) téléphoner en P.C.V.; ~**ion** n collection f; (of mail) levée f; (for money) collecte f, quête f; ~**or** n collectionneur m

college ['kɔlɪdʒ] n collège m

collide [kə'laɪd] vi entrer en collision

colliery ['kɔlɪərɪ] (BRIT) n mine f de charbon, houillère f

collision [kə'lɪʒən] n collision f

colloquial [kə'ləukwɪəl] adj familier(-ère)

colon ['kəulən] n (sign) deux-points m inv; (MED) côlon m

colonel ['kəːnl] n colonel m

colony ['kɔlənɪ] n colonie f

colour ['kʌlər] (US color) n couleur f ♦ vt (paint) peindre; (dye) teindre; (news) fausser, exagérer ♦ vi (blush) rougir; ~**s** npl (of party, club) couleurs fpl; ~ **bar** n colorier; ~ **bar** n discrimination raciale (dans un établissement); ~-**blind** adj daltonien(ne); ~**ed** adj (person) de couleur; (illustration) en couleur; ~ **film** n (for camera) pellicule f (en) couleur; ~**ful** adj coloré(e), vif(-vive); (personality) pittoresque,

haut(e) en couleurs; ~**ing** ['kʌlərɪŋ] n colorant m; (complexion) teint m; ~ **scheme** n combinaison f de(s) couleurs; ~ **television** n télévision f (en) couleur

colt [kəult] n poulain m

column ['kɔləm] n colonne f; ~**ist** ['kɔləmnɪst] n chroniqueur(-euse)

coma ['kəumə] n coma m

comb [kəum] n peigne m ♦ vt (hair) peigner; (area) ratisser, passer au peigne fin

combat ['kɔmbæt] n combat m ♦ vt combattre, lutter contre

combination [kɔmbɪ'neɪʃən] n combinaison f

combine [vb kəm'baɪn, n 'kɔmbaɪn] vt: **to ~ sth with sth** combiner qch avec qch; (one quality with another) joindre or allier qch à qch ♦ vi s'associer; (CHEM) se combiner ♦ n (ECON) trust m; ~ (**harvester**) n moissonneuse-batteuse(-lieuse) f

come [kʌm] (pt came, pp come) vi venir, arriver; **to ~ to** (decision etc) parvenir or arriver à; **to ~ undone/loose** se défaire/ desserrer; ~ **about** vi se produire, arriver; ~ **across** vt fus rencontrer par hasard, tomber sur; ~ **along** vi = come on; ~ **away** vi partir, s'en aller, se détacher; ~ **back** vi revenir; ~ **by** vt fus (acquire) obtenir, se procurer; ~ **down** vi descendre; (prices) baisser; (buildings) s'écrouler, être démoli(e); ~ **forward** vi s'avancer, se présenter, s'annoncer; ~ **from** vt fus être originaire de, venir de; ~ **in** vi entrer; ~ **in for** (criticism etc) être l'objet de; ~ **into** vt fus (money) hériter de; ~ **off** vi (button) se détacher; (stain) s'enlever; (attempt) réussir; ~ **on** vi (pupil, work, project) faire des progrès, s'avancer; (lights, electricity) s'allumer; (central heating) se mettre en marche; ~ **on!** viens!, allons!, allez!; ~ **out** vi sortir; (book) paraître; (strike) cesser le travail, se mettre en grève; ~ **round** vi (after faint, operation) revenir à soi, reprendre connaissance; ~ **to** vi revenir à soi; ~ **up** vi monter; ~ **up against** vt fus (resistance, difficulties) rencontrer; ~ **up with** vt fus: **he came up with an idea** il a eu une idée, il a proposé quelque chose; ~ **upon** vt fus tomber sur; ~**back** n (THEATRE etc) rentrée f

comedian [kə'miːdɪən] n (in music hall etc) comique m; (THEATRE) comédien m

comedy ['kɔmɪdɪ] n comédie f

comeuppance [kʌm'ʌpəns] n: **to get one's ~** recevoir ce que l'on mérite

comfort ['kʌmfət] n confort m, bien-être m; (relief) soulagement m, réconfort m ♦ vt consoler, réconforter; **the ~s of home** les commodités fpl de la maison; ~**able** adj confortable; (person) à l'aise; (patient) dont l'état est stationnaire; (*walk etc*) facile; **~ably** *adv* (*sit*) confortablement; (*live*) à l'aise; **~ station** (*US*) *n* toilettes *fpl*

comic ['kɔmɪk] *adj* (*also:* **~al**) comique ♦ *n* comique *m*; (*BRIT: magazine*) illustré *m*; **~ strip** *n* bande dessinée

coming ['kʌmɪŋ] *n* arrivée *f* ♦ *adj* prochain(e), à venir; **~(s) and going(s)** *n(pl)* va-et-vient *m inv*

comma ['kɔmə] *n* virgule *f*

command [kə'mɑ:nd] *n* ordre *m*, commandement *m*; (*MIL: authority*) commandement; (*mastery*) maîtrise *f* ♦ *vt* (*troops*) commander; **to ~ sb to do** ordonner à qn de faire; **~eer** [kɔmən'dɪə'] *vt* réquisitionner; **~er** *n* (*MIL*) commandant *m*

commando [kə'mɑ:ndəu] *n* commando *m*; membre *m* d'un commando

commemorate [kə'meməreɪt] *vt* commémorer

commence [kə'mɛns] *vt, vi* commencer

commend [kə'mɛnd] *vt* louer; (*recommend*) recommander

commensurate [kə'mɛnʃərɪt] *adj*: **~ with** or **to** en proportion de, proportionné(e) à

comment ['kɔmɛnt] *n* commentaire *m* ♦ *vi*: **to ~ (on)** faire des remarques (sur); **"no ~"** "je n'ai rien à dire"; **~ary** ['kɔməntəri] *n* commentaire *m*; (*SPORT*) reportage *m* (en direct); **~ator** ['kɔməntɛɪtə'] *n* commentateur *m*; reporter *m*

commerce ['kɔmə:s] *n* commerce *m*

commercial [kə'mə:ʃəl] *adj* commercial(e) ♦ *n* (*TV, RADIO*) annonce *f* publicitaire, spot *m* (publicitaire)

commiserate [kə'mɪzəreɪt] *vi*: **to ~ with sb** témoigner de la sympathie pour qn

commission [kə'mɪʃən] *n* (*order for work*) commande *f*; (*committee, fee*) commission *f* ♦ *vt* (*work of art*) commander, charger un artiste de l'exécution de; **out of ~** (*not working*) hors service; **~aire** [kəmɪʃə'nɛə'] (*BRIT*) *n* (*at shop, cinema etc*) portier *m* (en uniforme); **~er** *n* (*POLICE*) préfet *m* (de police)

commit [kə'mɪt] *vt* (*act*) commettre; (*resources*) consacrer; (*to sb's care*) confier (à); **to ~ o.s. (to do)** s'engager (à faire); **to ~ suicide** se suicider; **~ment** *n* engagement *m*; (*obligation*) responsabilité(s) *f(pl)*

committee [kə'mɪtɪ] *n* comité *m*

commodity [kə'mɔdɪtɪ] *n* produit *m*, marchandise *f*, article *m*

common ['kɔmən] *adj* commun(e); (*usual*) courant(e) ♦ *n* terrain communal; **the C~s** (*BRIT*) *npl* la chambre des Communes; **in ~** en commun; **~er** *n* roturier(-ière); **~ law** *n* droit coutumier; **~ly** *adv* communément, généralement; couramment; **C~ Market** *n*

Marché commun; **~place** *adj* banal(e), ordinaire; **~ room** *n* salle commune; **~ sense** *n* bon sens; **C~wealth** (*BRIT*) *n* Commonwealth *m*

commotion [kə'məuʃən] *n* désordre *m*, tumulte *m*

communal ['kɔmju:nl] *adj* (*life*) communautaire; (*for common use*) commun(e)

commune [*n* 'kɔmju:n, *vb* kə'mju:n] *n* (*group*) communauté *f* ♦ *vi*: **to ~ with** communier avec

communicate [kə'mju:nɪkeɪt] *vt, vi* communiquer; **communication** [kəmju:nɪ'keɪʃən] *n* communication *f*; **communication cord** (*BRIT*) *n* sonnette *f* d'alarme

communion [kə'mju:nɪən] *n* (*also:* **Holy C~**) communion *f*

communism ['kɔmjunɪzəm] *n* communisme *m*; **communist** *adj* communiste ♦ *n* communiste *m/f*

community [kə'mju:nɪtɪ] *n* communauté *f*; **~ centre** *n* centre *m* de loisirs; **~ chest** (*US*) *n* fonds commun

commutation ticket [kɔmju'teɪʃən-] (*US*) *n* carte *f* d'abonnement

commute [kə'mju:t] *vi* faire un trajet journalier pour se rendre à son travail ♦ *vt* (*LAW*) commuer; **~r** *n* banlieusard(e) (*qui fait un trajet journalier pour se rendre à son travail*)

compact [*adj* kəm'pækt, *n* 'kɔmpækt] *adj* compact(e) ♦ *n* (*also:* **powder ~**) poudrier *m*; **~ disc** *n* disque compact; **~ disc player** *n* lecteur *m* de disque compact

companion [kəm'pænjən] *n* compagnon (compagne); **~ship** *n* camaraderie *f*

company ['kʌmpənɪ] *n* compagnie *f*; **to keep sb ~** tenir compagnie à qn; **~ secretary** (*BRIT*) *n* (*COMM*) secrétaire général (*d'une société*)

comparative [kəm'pærətɪv] *adj* (*study*) comparatif(-ive); (*relative*) relatif(-ive); **~ly** *adv* (*relatively*) relativement

compare [kəm'pɛə'] *vt*: **to ~ sth/sb with/to** comparer qch/qn avec or et/à ♦ *vi*: **to ~ (with)** se comparer (à); être comparable (à); **comparison** [kəm'pærɪsn] *n* comparaison *f*

compartment [kəm'pɑ:tmənt] *n* compartiment *m*

compass ['kʌmpəs] *n* boussole *f*; **~es** *npl* (*GEOM: also:* **pair of ~es**) compas *m*

compassion [kəm'pæʃən] *n* compassion *f*; **~ate** *adj* compatissant(e)

compatible [kəm'pætɪbl] *adj* compatible

compel [kəm'pɛl] *vt* contraindre, obliger

compensate ['kɔmpənseɪt] *vt* indemniser, dédommager ♦ *vi*: **to ~ for** compenser;

compensation [kɒmpənˈseɪʃən] *n* compensation *f*; (*money*) dédommagement *m*, indemnité *f*

compère [ˈkɒmpɛəʳ] *n* (*TV*) animateur(-trice)

compete [kəmˈpiːt] *vi*: **to ~ (with)** rivaliser (avec), faire concurrence (à)

competent [ˈkɒmpɪtənt] *adj* compétent(e), capable

competition [kɒmpɪˈtɪʃən] *n* (*contest*) compétition *f*, concours *m*; (*ECON*) concurrence *f*

competitive [kəmˈpetɪtɪv] *adj* (*ECON*) concurrentiel(le); (*sport*) de compétition; (*person*) qui a l'esprit de compétition; **competitor** *n* concurrent(e)

complacency [kəmˈpleɪsnsɪ] *n* suffisance *f*, vaine complaisance

complain [kəmˈpleɪn] *vi*: **to ~ (about)** se plaindre (de); (*in shop etc*) réclamer (au sujet de); **to ~ of** (*pain*) se plaindre de; **~t** *n* plainte *f*; réclamation *f*; (*MED*) affection *f*

complement [*n* ˈkɒmplɪmənt, *vb* ˈkɒmplɪment] *n* complément *m*; (*especially of ship's crew etc*) effectif complet ♦ *vt* (*enhance*) compléter; **~ary** [kɒmplɪˈmentərɪ] *adj* complémentaire

complete [kəmˈpliːt] *adj* complet(-ète) ♦ *vt* achever, parachever; (*set, group*) compléter; (*a form*) remplir; **~ly** *adv* complètement; **completion** *n* achèvement *m*; (*of contract*) exécution *f*

complex [ˈkɒmpleks] *adj* complexe ♦ *n* complexe *m*

complexion [kəmˈplekʃən] *n* (*of face*) teint *m*

compliance [kəmˈplaɪəns] *n* (*submission*) docilité *f*; (*agreement*): **~ with** le fait de se conformer à; **in ~ with** en accord avec

complicate [ˈkɒmplɪkeɪt] *vt* compliquer; **~d** *adj* compliqué(e); **complication** [kɒmplɪˈkeɪʃən] *n* complication *f*

compliment [*n* ˈkɒmplɪmənt, *vb* ˈkɒmplɪment] *n* compliment *m* ♦ *vt* complimenter; **~s** *npl* (*respects*) compliments *mpl*, hommages *mpl*; **to pay sb a ~** faire *or* adresser un compliment à qn; **~ary** [kɒmplɪˈmentərɪ] *adj* flatteur(-euse); (*free*) (offert(e)) à titre gracieux; **~ary ticket** *n* billet *m* de faveur

comply [kəmˈplaɪ] *vi*: **to ~ with** se soumettre à, se conformer à

component [kəmˈpəʊnənt] *n* composant *m*, élément *m*

compose [kəmˈpəʊz] *vt* composer; (*form*): **to be ~d of** se composer de; **to ~ o.s.** se calmer, se maîtriser; prendre une contenance; **~d** *adj* calme, posé(e); **~r** *n* (*MUS*) compositeur *m*; **composition** [kɒmpəˈzɪʃən] *n* composition *f*; **composure** [kəmˈpəʊʒəʳ] *n*

calme *m*, maîtrise *f* de soi

compound [ˈkɒmpaʊnd] *n* composé *m*; (*enclosure*) enclos *m*, enceinte *f*; **~ fracture** fracture compliquée; **~ interest** *n* intérêt composé

comprehend [kɒmprɪˈhend] *vt* comprendre; **comprehension** *n* compréhension *f*

comprehensive [kɒmprɪˈhensɪv] *adj* (très) complet(-ète); **~ policy** *n* (*INSURANCE*) assurance *f* tous risques; **~ (school)** (*BRIT*) *n* école secondaire polyvalente; ≈ C.E.S. *m*

compress [*vb* kəmˈpres, *n* ˈkɒmpres] *vt* comprimer; (*text, information*) condenser ♦ *n* (*MED*) compresse *f*

comprise [kəmˈpraɪz] *vt* (*also*: **be ~d of**) comprendre; (*constitute*) constituer, représenter

compromise [ˈkɒmprəmaɪz] *n* compromis *m* ♦ *vt* compromettre ♦ *vi* transiger, accepter un compromis

compulsion [kəmˈpʌlʃən] *n* contrainte *f*, force *f*

compulsive [kəmˈpʌlsɪv] *adj* (*PSYCH*) compulsif(-ive); (*book, film etc*) captivant(e)

compulsory [kəmˈpʌlsərɪ] *adj* obligatoire

computer [kəmˈpjuːtəʳ] *n* ordinateur *m*; **~ game** *n* jeu *m* vidéo; **~-generated** *adj* de synthèse; **~ize** *vt* informatiser; **~ programmer** *n* programmeur(-euse); **~ programming** *n* programmation *f*; **~ science** *n* informatique *f*; **computing** *n* = computer science

comrade [ˈkɒmrɪd] *n* camarade *m/f*

con [kɒn] *vt* duper; (*cheat*) escroquer ♦ *n* escroquerie *f*

conceal [kənˈsiːl] *vt* cacher, dissimuler

conceit [kənˈsiːt] *n* vanité *f*, suffisance *f*, prétention *f*; **~ed** *adj* vaniteux(-euse), suffisant(e)

conceive [kənˈsiːv] *vt, vi* concevoir

concentrate [ˈkɒnsəntreɪt] *vi* se concentrer ♦ *vt* concentrer; **concentration** *n* concentration *f*; **concentration camp** *n* camp *m* de concentration

concept [ˈkɒnsept] *n* concept *m*

concern [kənˈsɜːn] *n* (*COMM*) affaire *f*; entreprise *f*, firme *f*; (*anxiety*) inquiétude *f*, souci *m* ♦ *vt* concerner; **to be ~ed (about)** s'inquiéter (de), être inquiet(-ète) (au sujet de); **~ing** *prep* en ce qui concerne, à propos de

concert [ˈkɒnsət] *n* concert *m*; **~ed** [kənˈsɜːtɪd] *adj* concerté(e); **~ hall** *n* salle *f* de concert

concerto [kənˈtʃɜːtəʊ] *n* concerto *m*

concession [kənˈseʃən] *n* concession *f*; **tax ~** dégrèvement fiscal

conclude [kənˈkluːd] *vt* conclure; **conclusion** [kənˈkluːʒən] *n* conclusion *f*;

conclusive [kən'klu:sɪv] adj concluant(e), définitif(-ive)

concoct [kən'kɔkt] vt confectionner, composer; (fig) inventer; **~ion** n mélange m

concourse ['kɔŋkɔ:s] n (hall) hall m, salle f des pas perdus

concrete ['kɔŋkri:t] n béton m ♦ adj concret(-ète); (floor etc) en béton

concur [kən'kə:ʳ] vi (agree) être d'accord

concurrently [kən'kʌrntlɪ] adv simultanément

concussion [kən'kʌʃən] n (MED) commotion (cérébrale)

condemn [kən'dɛm] vt condamner

condensation [kɔndɛn'seɪʃən] n condensation f

condense [kən'dɛns] vi se condenser ♦ vt condenser; **~d milk** n lait concentré (sucré)

condition [kən'dɪʃən] n condition f; (MED) état m ♦ vt déterminer, conditionner; **on ~ that** à condition que +sub, à condition de; **~al** adj conditionnel(le); **~er** n (for hair) baume après-shampooing m; (for fabrics) assouplissant m

condolences [kən'dəʊlənsɪz] npl condoléances fpl

condom ['kɔndəm] n préservatif m

condominium [kɔndə'mɪnɪəm] (US) n (building) immeuble m (en copropriété)

condone [kən'dəʊn] vt fermer les yeux sur, approuver (tacitement)

conducive [kən'dju:sɪv] adj: **~ to** favorable à, qui contribue à

conduct [n 'kɔndʌkt, vb kən'dʌkt] n conduite f ♦ vt conduire; (MUS) diriger; **to ~ o.s.** se conduire, se comporter; **~ed tour** n voyage organisé; (of building) visite guidée; **~or** n (of orchestra) chef m d'orchestre; (on bus) receveur m; (US: on train) chef m de train; (ELEC) conducteur m; **~ress** n (on bus) receveuse f

cone [kəʊn] n cône m; (for ice-cream) cornet m; (BOT) pomme f de pin, cône

confectioner [kən'fɛkʃənəʳ] n confiseur(-euse); **~'s (shop)** n confiserie f; **~y** n confiserie f

confer [kən'fə:ʳ] vt: **to ~ sth on** conférer qch à ♦ vi conférer, s'entretenir

conference ['kɔnfərəns] n conférence f

confess [kən'fɛs] vt confesser, avouer ♦ vi se confesser; **~ion** n confession f

confetti [kən'fɛtɪ] n confettis mpl

confide [kən'faɪd] vi: **to ~ in** se confier à

confidence ['kɔnfɪdns] n confiance f; (also: self-~) assurance f, confiance en soi; (secret) confidence f; **in ~** (speak, write) en confidence, confidentiellement; **~ trick** n escroquerie f; **confident** adj sûr(e), assuré(e); **confidential** [kɔnfɪ'dɛnʃəl] adj confidentiel(le)

confine [kən'faɪn] vt limiter, borner; (shut up) confiner, enfermer; **~d** adj (space) restreint(e), réduit(e); **~ment** n emprisonnement m, détention f; **~s** ['kɔnfaɪnz] npl confins mpl, bornes fpl

confirm [kən'fə:m] vt confirmer; (appointment) ratifier; **~ation** [kɔnfə'meɪʃən] n confirmation f; **~ed** adj invétéré(e), incorrigible

confiscate ['kɔnfɪskeɪt] vt confisquer

conflict [n 'kɔnflɪkt, vb kən'flɪkt] n conflit m, lutte f ♦ vi être ou entrer en conflit; (opinions) s'opposer, se heurter; **~ing** [kən'flɪktɪŋ] adj contradictoire

conform [kən'fɔ:m] vi: **to ~ (to)** se conformer (à)

confound [kən'faʊnd] vt confondre

confront [kən'frʌnt] vt confronter, mettre en présence; (enemy, danger) affronter, faire face à; **~ation** [kɔnfrən'teɪʃən] n confrontation f

confuse [kən'fju:z] vt (person) troubler; (situation) embrouiller; (one thing with another) confondre; **~d** adj (person) dérouté(e), désorienté(e); **confusing** adj peu clair(e), déroutant(e); **confusion** [kən'fju:ʒən] n confusion f

congeal [kən'dʒi:l] vi (blood) se coaguler; (oil etc) se figer

congenial [kən'dʒi:nɪəl] adj sympathique, agréable

congested [kən'dʒɛstɪd] adj (MED) congestionné(e); (area) surpeuplé(e); (road) bloqué(e); **congestion** n congestion f; (fig) encombrement m

congratulate [kən'grætjuleɪt] vt: **to ~ sb (on)** féliciter qn (de); **congratulations** [kəngrætju'leɪʃənz] npl félicitations fpl

congregate ['kɔngrɪgeɪt] vi se rassembler, se réunir; **congregation** [kɔngrɪ'geɪʃən] n assemblée f (des fidèles)

congress ['kɔngrɛs] n congrès m; **~man** (irreg) (US) n membre m du Congrès

conjunction [kən'dʒʌŋkʃən] n (LING) conjonction f

conjunctivitis [kəndʒʌŋktɪ'vaɪtɪs] n conjonctivite f

conjure ['kʌndʒəʳ] vi faire des tours de passe-passe; **~ up** vt (ghost, spirit) faire apparaître; (memories) évoquer; **~r** n prestidigitateur m, illusionniste m/f

con man (irreg) n escroc m

connect [kə'nɛkt] vt joindre, relier; (ELEC) connecter; (TEL: caller) mettre en connection (with avec); (: new subscriber) brancher; (fig) établir un rapport entre, faire un rapprochement entre ♦ vi (train): **to ~ with** assurer la correspondance avec; **to be ~ed with** (fig) avoir un rapport avec, avoir des rapports avec, être en relation avec; **~ion** n relation f, lien m; (ELEC) connexion f; (train, plane etc) correspondance f; (TEL) branchement m, communication f

connive [kə'naɪv] vi: **to ~ at** se faire le complice de

conquer ['kɒŋkər] vt conquérir; (feelings) vaincre, surmonter; **conquest** ['kɒŋkwest] n conquête f

cons [kɒnz] npl see **convenience; pro**

conscience ['kɒnʃəns] n conscience f; **conscientious** [kɒnʃɪ'enʃəs] adj consciencieux(-euse)

conscious ['kɒnʃəs] adj conscient(e); **~ness** n conscience f; (MED) connaissance f

conscript ['kɒnskrɪpt] n conscrit m

consent [kən'sent] n consentement m ♦ vi: **to ~ (to)** consentir (à)

consequence ['kɒnsɪkwəns] n conséquence f, suites fpl; (significance) importance f; **consequently** adv par conséquent, donc

conservation [kɒnsə'veɪʃən] n préservation f, protection f

conservative [kən'sə:vətɪv] adj conservateur(-trice); **at a ~ estimate** au bas mot; **C~** (BRIT) adj, n (POL) conservateur(-trice)

conservatory [kən'sə:vətrɪ] n (greenhouse) serre f

conserve [kən'sə:v] vt conserver, préserver; (supplies, energy) économiser ♦ n confiture f

consider [kən'sɪdər] vt (study) considérer, réfléchir à; (take into account) penser à, prendre en considération; (regard, judge) considérer, estimer; **to ~ doing sth** envisager de faire qch; **~able** adj considérable; **~ably** adv nettement; **~ate** adj prévenant(e), plein(e) d'égards; **~ation** [kənsɪdə'reɪʃən] n considération f; **~ing** prep étant donné

consign [kən'saɪn] vt expédier; (to sb's care) confier; (fig) livrer; **~ment** n arrivage m, envoi m

consist [kən'sɪst] vi: **to ~ of** consister en, se composer de

consistency [kən'sɪstənsɪ] n consistance f; (fig) cohérence f

consistent [kən'sɪstənt] adj logique, cohérent(e)

consolation [kɒnsə'leɪʃən] n consolation f

console¹ [kən'səul] vt consoler

console² ['kɒnsəul] n (COMPUT) console f

consonant ['kɒnsənənt] n consonne f

conspicuous [kən'spɪkjuəs] adj voyant(e), qui attire l'attention

conspiracy [kən'spɪrəsɪ] n conspiration f, complot m

constable ['kʌnstəbl] (BRIT) n ≈ agent m de police, gendarme m; **chief ~** ≈ préfet m de police; **constabulary** [kən'stæbjulərɪ] (BRIT)

n ≈ police f, gendarmerie f

constant ['kɒnstənt] adj constant(e); incessant(e); **~ly** adv constamment, sans cesse

constipated ['kɒnstɪpeɪtɪd] adj constipé(e); **constipation** [kɒnstɪ'peɪʃən] n constipation f

constituency [kən'stɪtjuənsɪ] n circonscription électorale

constituent [kən'stɪtjuənt] n (POL) électeur(-trice); (part) élément constitutif, composant m

constitution [kɒnstɪ'tju:ʃən] n constitution f; **~al** adj constitutionnel(le)

constraint [kən'streɪnt] n contrainte f

construct [kən'strʌkt] vt construire; **~ion** n construction f; **~ive** adj constructif(-ive); **~ive dismissal** démission forcée

consul ['kɒnsl] n consul m; **~ate** ['kɒnsjulɪt] n consulat m

consult [kən'sʌlt] vt consulter; **~ant** n (MED) médecin consultant; (other specialist) consultant m, (expert-)conseil m; **~ing room** (BRIT) n cabinet m de consultation

consume [kən'sju:m] vt consommer; **~r** n consommateur(-trice); **~r goods** npl biens mpl de consommation; **~r society** n société f de consommation

consummate ['kɒnsʌmeɪt] vt consommer

consumption [kən'sʌmpʃən] n consommation f

cont. abbr (= continued) suite

contact ['kɒntækt] n contact m; (person) connaissance f, relation f ♦ vt contacter, se mettre en contact or en rapport avec; **~ lenses** npl verres mpl de contact, lentilles fpl

contagious [kən'teɪdʒəs] adj contagieux(-euse)

contain [kən'teɪn] vt contenir; **to ~ o.s.** se contenir, se maîtriser; **~er** n récipient m; (for shipping etc) container m

contaminate [kən'tæmɪneɪt] vt contaminer

cont'd abbr (= continued) suite

contemplate ['kɒntəmpleɪt] vt contempler; (consider) envisager

contemporary [kən'tempərərɪ] adj contemporain(e); (design, wallpaper) moderne ♦ n contemporain(e)

contempt [kən'tempt] n mépris m, dédain m; **~ of court** (LAW) outrage m à l'autorité de la justice; **~uous** [kən'temptjuəs] adj dédaigneux(-euse), méprisant(e)

contend [kən'tend] vt: **to ~ that** soutenir or prétendre que ♦ vi: **to ~ with** (compete) rivaliser avec; (struggle) lutter avec; **~er** n concurrent(e); (POL) candidat(e)

content [adj, vb kən'tent, n 'kɒntent] adj content(e), satisfait(e) ♦ vt contenter, satisfaire ♦ n contenu m; (of fat, moisture) teneur f; **~s** npl (of container etc) contenu m; **(table of) ~s** table f des matières; **~ed** adj content(e), satisfait(e)

contention [kən'tɛnʃən] n dispute f, contestation f; (argument) assertion f, affirmation f

contest [n 'kɔntest, vb kən'test] n combat m, lutte f; (competition) concours m ♦ vt (decision, statement) contester, discuter; (compete for) disputer; **~ant** [kən'tɛstənt] n concurrent(e); (in fight) adversaire m/f

context ['kɔntɛkst] n contexte m

continent ['kɔntɪnənt] n continent m; **the C~** (BRIT) l'Europe continentale; **~al** [kɔntɪ'nɛntl] adj continental(e); **~al breakfast** n petit déjeuner m à la française; **~al quilt** (BRIT) n couette f

contingency [kən'tɪndʒənsɪ] n éventualité f, événement imprévu

continual [kən'tɪnjuəl] adj continuel(le)

continuation [kəntɪnju'eɪʃən] n continuation f; (after interruption) reprise f; (of story) suite f

continue [kən'tɪnjuː] vi, vt continuer; (after interruption) reprendre, poursuivre; **continuity** [kɔntɪ'njuːɪtɪ] n continuité f; (TV etc) enchaînement m; **continuous** [kən'tɪnjuəs] adj continu(e); (LING) progressif(-ive)

contort [kən'tɔːt] vt tordre, crisper

contour ['kɔntuər] n contour m, profil m; (on map: also: **~ line**) courbe f de niveau

contraband ['kɔntrəbænd] n contrebande f

contraceptive [kɔntrə'sɛptɪv] adj contraceptif(-ive), anticonceptionnel(le) ♦ n contraceptif m

contract [n 'kɔntrækt, vb kən'trækt] n contrat m ♦ vi (become smaller) se contracter, se resserrer; (COMM): **to ~ to do sth** s'engager (par contrat) à faire qch; **~ion** [kən'trækʃən] n contraction f; **~or** [kən'træktər] n entrepreneur m

contradict [kɔntrə'dɪkt] vt contredire

contraflow ['kɔntrəfləu] n (AUT): **~ lane** voie f à contresens; **there's a ~ system in operation on ...** une voie a été mise en sens inverse sur ...

contraption [kən'træpʃən] (pej) n machin m, truc m

contrary[1] ['kɔntrərɪ] adj contraire, opposé(e) ♦ n contraire m; **on the ~** au contraire; **unless you hear to the ~** sauf avis contraire

contrary[2] [kən'treərɪ] adj (perverse) contrariant(e), entêté(e)

contrast [n 'kɔntrɑːst, vb kən'trɑːst] n contraste m ♦ vt mettre en contraste, contraster; **in ~ to** or **with** contrairement à

contravene [kɔntrə'viːn] vt enfreindre, violer, contrevenir à

contribute [kən'trɪbjuːt] vi contribuer ♦ vt: **to ~ £10/an article to** donner 10 livres/un article à; **to ~ to** contribuer à; (newspaper) collaborer à; **contribution** [kɔntrɪ'bjuːʃən] n contribution f; **contributor** [kən'trɪbjutər] n (to newspaper) collaborateur(-trice)

contrive [kən'traɪv] vi: **to ~ to do** s'arranger pour faire, trouver le moyen de faire

control [kən'trəul] vt maîtriser, commander; (check) contrôler ♦ n contrôle m, autorité f; maîtrise f; **~s** npl (of machine etc) commandes fpl; (on radio, TV) boutons mpl de réglage; **~led substance** narcotique m; **everything is under ~** tout va bien, j'ai (or il a etc) la situation en main; **to be in ~ of** être maître de, maîtriser; **the car went out of ~** j'ai (or il a etc) perdu le contrôle du véhicule; **~ panel** n tableau m de commande; **~ room** n salle f des commandes; **~ tower** n (AVIAT) tour f de contrôle

controversial [kɔntrə'vəːʃl] adj (topic) discutable, controversé(e); (person) qui fait beaucoup parler de lui; **controversy** ['kɔntrəvəːsɪ] n controverse f, polémique f

convalesce [kɔnvə'lɛs] vi relever de maladie, se remettre (d'une maladie)

convector [kən'vɛktər] n (heater) radiateur m (à convexion)

convene [kən'viːn] vt convoquer, assembler ♦ vi se réunir, s'assembler

convenience [kən'viːnɪəns] n commodité f; **at your ~** quand or comme cela vous convient; **all modern ~s**, (BRIT) **all mod cons** avec tout le confort moderne, tout confort

convenient [kən'viːnɪənt] adj commode

convent ['kɔnvənt] n couvent m; **~ school** n couvent m

convention [kən'vɛnʃən] n convention f; **~al** adj conventionnel(le)

conversant [kən'vəːsnt] adj: **to be ~ with** s'y connaître en; être au courant de

conversation [kɔnvə'seɪʃən] n conversation f

converse [n 'kɔnvəːs, vb kən'vəːs] n contraire m, inverse m ♦ vi s'entretenir; **~ly** [kɔn'vəːslɪ] adv inversement, réciproquement

convert [vb kən'vəːt, n 'kɔnvəːt] vt (REL, COMM) convertir; (alter) transformer; (house) aménager ♦ n converti(e); **~ible** [kən'vəːtəbl] n (voiture f) décapotable f

convey [kən'veɪ] vt transporter; (thanks) transmettre; (idea) communiquer; **~or belt** n convoyeur m, tapis roulant

convict [vb kən'vɪkt, n 'kɔnvɪkt] vt déclarer (or reconnaître) coupable ♦ n forçat m, détenu m; **~ion** n (LAW) condamnation f; (belief) conviction f

convince [kən'vɪns] vt convaincre, persuader; **convincing** adj persuasif(-ive), convaincant(e)

convoluted ['kɒnvəlu:tɪd] adj (argument) compliqué(e)

convulse [kən'vʌls] vt: **to be ~d with laughter/pain** se tordre de rire/douleur

cook [kuk] vt (faire) cuire ♦ vi cuire; (person) faire la cuisine ♦ n cuisinier(-ière); **~book** n livre m de cuisine; **~er** n cuisinière f; **~ery** n cuisine f; **~ery book** (BRIT) n = **cookbook**; **~ie** (US) n biscuit m, petit gâteau sec; **~ing** n cuisine f

cool [ku:l] adj frais (fraîche); (calm, unemotional) calme; (unfriendly) froid(e) ♦ vt, vi rafraîchir, refroidir

coop [ku:p] n poulailler m; (for rabbits) clapier m ♦ vt: **to ~ up** (fig) cloîtrer, enfermer

cooperate [kəu'ɒpəreɪt] vi coopérer, collaborer; **cooperation** [kəuɒpə'reɪʃən] n coopération f, collaboration f; **cooperative** [kəu'ɒpərətɪv] adj coopératif(-ive) ♦ n coopérative f

coordinate [vb kəu'ɔ:dɪneɪt, n kəu'ɔ:dɪnət] vt coordonner ♦ n (MATH) coordonnée f; **~s** npl (clothes) ensemble m, coordonnés mpl

co-ownership [kəu'əunəʃɪp] n co-propriété f

cop [kɒp] (inf) n flic m

cope [kəup] vi: **to ~ with** faire face à; (solve) venir à bout de

copper ['kɒpər] n cuivre m; (BRIT: inf: policeman) flic m; **~s** npl (coins) petite monnaie

copy ['kɒpɪ] n copie f; (of book etc) exemplaire m ♦ vt copier; **~right** n droit m d'auteur, copyright m

coral ['kɒrəl] n corail m

cord [kɔ:d] n corde f; (fabric) velours côtelé; (ELEC) cordon m, fil m

cordial ['kɔ:dɪəl] adj cordial(e), chaleureux(-euse) ♦ n cordial m

cordon ['kɔ:dn] n cordon m; **~ off** vt boucler (par cordon de police)

corduroy ['kɔ:dərɔɪ] n velours côtelé

core [kɔ:r] n noyau m; (of fruit) trognon m, cœur m; (of building, problem) cœur ♦ vt enlever le trognon or le cœur de

cork [kɔ:k] n liège m; (of bottle) bouchon m; **~screw** n tire-bouchon m

corn [kɔ:n] n (BRIT: wheat) blé m; (US: maize) maïs m; (on foot) cor m; **~ on the cob** (CULIN) épi m de maïs; **~ed beef** n corned-beef m

corner ['kɔ:nər] n coin m; (AUT) tournant m, virage m; (FOOTBALL: also: **~ kick**) corner m ♦ vt acculer, mettre au pied du mur; coincer; (COMM: market) accaparer ♦ vi prendre un virage; **~stone** n pierre f angulaire

cornet ['kɔ:nɪt] n (MUS) cornet m à pistons; (BRIT: of ice-cream) cornet (de glace)

cornflakes ['kɔ:nfleɪks] npl corn-flakes mpl

cornflour ['kɔ:nflauər] (BRIT), **cornstarch** ['kɔ:nstɑ:tʃ] (US) n farine f de maïs, maïzena f ®

Cornwall ['kɔ:nwəl] n Cornouailles f

corny ['kɔ:nɪ] (inf) adj rebattu(e)

coronary ['kɒrənərɪ] n (also: **~ thrombosis**) infarctus m (du myocarde), thrombose f coronarienne

coronation [kɒrə'neɪʃən] n couronnement m

coroner ['kɒrənər] n officiel chargé de déterminer les causes d'un décès

corporal ['kɔ:pərl] n caporal m, brigadier m ♦ adj: **~ punishment** châtiment corporel

corporate ['kɔ:pərɪt] adj en commun, collectif(-ive); (COMM) de l'entreprise

corporation [kɔ:pə'reɪʃən] n (of town) municipalité f, conseil municipal; (COMM) société f

corps [kɔ:r] (pl **~**) n corps m

corpse [kɔ:ps] n cadavre m

correct [kə'rɛkt] adj (accurate) correct(e), exact(e); (proper) correct, convenable ♦ vt corriger; **~ion** n correction f

correspond [kɒrɪs'pɒnd] vi correspondre; **~ence** n correspondance f; **~ence course** n cours m par correspondance; **~ent** n correspondant(e)

corridor ['kɒrɪdɔ:r] n couloir m, corridor m

corrode [kə'rəud] vt corroder, ronger ♦ vi se corroder

corrugated ['kɒrəgeɪtɪd] adj plissé(e); ondulé(e); **~ iron** n tôle ondulée

corrupt [kə'rʌpt] adj corrompu(e) ♦ vt corrompre; **~ion** n corruption f

Corsica ['kɔ:sɪkə] n Corse f

cosmetic [kɒz'mɛtɪk] n produit m de beauté, cosmétique m

cost [kɒst] (pt, pp **cost**) n coût m ♦ vi coûter ♦ vt établir or calculer le prix de revient de; **~s** npl (COMM) frais mpl; (LAW) dépens mpl; **it ~s £5/too much** cela coûte cinq livres/c'est trop cher; **at all ~s** coûte que coûte, à tout prix

co-star ['kəustɑ:r] n partenaire m/f

cost: **~-effective** adj rentable; **~ly** adj coûteux(-euse); **~-of-living** adj: **~-of-living allowance** indemnité f de vie chère; **~-of-living index** index m du coût de la vie; **~ price** (BRIT) n prix coûtant or de revient

costume ['kɒstju:m] n costume m; (lady's suit) tailleur m; (BRIT: also: **swimming ~**) maillot m (de bain); **~ jewellery** n bijoux mpl fantaisie

cosy ['kəuzɪ] (US **cozy**) adj douillet(te); (person) à l'aise, au chaud

cot [kɒt] n (BRIT: child's) lit m d'enfant, petit lit; (US: campbed) lit de camp

cottage ['kɒtɪdʒ] n petite maison (à la campagne), cottage m; **~ cheese** n fromage blanc (*maigre*)

cotton ['kɔtn] n coton m; ~ **on** (*inf*) vi: to
~ **on to** piger; ~ **candy** (*US*) n barbe f à
papa; ~ **wool** (*BRIT*) n ouate f, coton m
hydrophile

couch [kautʃ] n canapé m; divan m

couchette [ku:'ʃet] n couchette f

cough [kɔf] vi tousser ♦ n toux f; ~ **sweet** n
pastille f pour or contre la toux

could [kud] pt of **can²**; ~**n't** = **could not**

council ['kaunsl] n conseil m; **city** or **town** ~
conseil municipal; ~ **estate** (*BRIT*) n (zone f
de) logements loués à/par la municipalité;
~ **house** (*BRIT*) n maison f (à loyer modéré)
louée par la municipalité; ~**lor** n conseil-
ler(-ère)

counsel ['kaunsl] n (*lawyer*) avocat(e);
(*advice*) conseil m, consultation f; ~**lor** n
conseiller(-ère); (*US: lawyer*) avocat(e)

count [kaunt] vt, vi compter ♦ n compte m;
(*nobleman*) comte m; ~ **on** vt fus compter
sur; ~**down** n compte m à rebours

countenance ['kauntinəns] n expression f
♦ vt approuver

counter ['kauntə'] n comptoir m; (*in post
office, bank*) guichet m; (*in game*) jeton m
♦ vt aller à l'encontre de, opposer ♦ adv: ~ **to**
contrairement à; ~**act** vt neutraliser,
contrebalancer; ~**feit** n faux m, contrefaçon f
♦ vt contrefaire ♦ adj faux (fausse); ~**foil** n
talon m, souche f; ~**part** n (*of person etc*)
homologue m/f

countess ['kauntis] n comtesse f

countless ['kauntlis] adj innombrable

country ['kʌntri] n pays m; (*native land*)
patrie f; (*as opposed to town*) campagne f;
(*region*) région f, pays; ~ **dancing** (*BRIT*) n
danse f folklorique; ~ **house** n manoir m,
(petit) château; ~**man** (*irreg*) n (*compatriot*)
compatriote m; (*country dweller*) habitant m
de la campagne, campagnard m; ~**side** n
campagne f

county ['kaunti] n comté m

coup [ku:] (*pl* ~**s**) n beau coup; (*also:
~ d'état*) coup d'État

couple ['kʌpl] n couple m; **a ~ of** deux; (*a
few*) quelques

coupon ['ku:pɔn] n coupon m, bon-prime m,
bon-réclame m; (*COMM*) coupon

courage ['kʌridʒ] n courage m

courier ['kuriə'] n messager m, courrier m;
(*for tourists*) accompagnateur(-trice), guide
m/f

course [kɔ:s] n cours m; (*of ship*) route f; (*for
golf*) terrain m; (*part of meal*) plat m; **first** ~
entrée f; **of** ~ bien sûr; ~ **of action** parti m,
ligne f de conduite; ~ **of treatment** (*MED*)
traitement m

court [kɔ:t] n cour·f; (*LAW*) cour, tribunal m;

(*TENNIS*) court m ♦ vt (*woman*) courtiser, faire
la cour à; **to take to** ~ actionner or poursuivre
en justice

courteous ['kɔ:tiəs] adj courtois(e), poli(e);
courtesy ['kɔ:təsi] n courtoisie f, politesse f;
(**by**) **courtesy of** avec l'aimable autorisation
de; **courtesy bus** or **coach** n navette
gratuite

court: ~**house** (*US*) n palais m de justice;
~**ier** n courtisan m, dame f de la cour;
~ **martial** (*pl* **courts martial**) n cour martiale,
conseil m de guerre; ~**room** n salle f de
tribunal; ~**yard** n cour f

cousin ['kʌzn] n cousin(e); **first** ~ cousin(e)
germain(e)

cove [kəuv] n petite baie, anse f

covenant ['kʌvənənt] n engagement m

cover ['kʌvə'] vt couvrir ♦ n couverture f; (*of
pan*) couvercle m; (*over furniture*) housse f;
(*shelter*) abri m; **to take** ~ se mettre à l'abri;
under ~ à l'abri; **under** ~ **of darkness** à la
faveur de la nuit; **under separate** ~ (*COMM*)
sous pli séparé; **to** ~ **up for sb** couvrir qn;
~**age** n (*TV, PRESS*) reportage m; ~ **charge** n
couvert m (*supplément à payer*); ~**ing** n
couche f; ~**ing letter** (*US* **cover letter**) n
lettre explicative; ~ **note** n (*INSURANCE*) police
f provisoire

covert ['kʌvət] adj (*threat*) voilé(e), caché(e);
(*glance*) furtif(-ive)

cover-up ['kʌvərʌp] n tentative f pour
étouffer une affaire

covet ['kʌvit] vt convoiter

cow [kau] n vache f ♦ vt effrayer, intimider

coward ['kauəd] n lâche m/f; ~**ice** n lâcheté
f; ~**ly** adj lâche

cowboy ['kaubɔi] n cow-boy m

cower ['kauə'] vi se recroqueviller

coy [kɔi] adj faussement effarouché(e) or
timide

cozy ['kəuzi] (*US*) adj = **cosy**

CPA (*US*) n abbr = **certified public accountant**

crab [kræb] n crabe m; ~ **apple** n pomme f
sauvage

crack [kræk] n (*split*) fente f, fissure f; (*in cup,
bone etc*) fêlure f; (*in wall*) lézarde f; (*noise*)
craquement m, coup (sec); (*drug*) crack m
♦ vt fendre, fissurer; fêler; lézarder; (*whip*)
faire claquer; (*nut*) casser; (*code*) déchiffrer;
(*problem*) résoudre ♦ adj (*athlete*) de
première classe, d'élite; ~ **down on** vt fus
mettre un frein à; ~ **up** vi être au bout du
rouleau, s'effondrer; ~**ed** adj (*cup, bone*)
fêlé(e); (*broken*) cassé(e); (*wall*) lézardé(e);
(*surface*) craquelé(e); (*inf: mad*) cinglé(e);
~**er** n (*Christmas cracker*) pétard m; (*biscuit*)
biscuit (salé)

crackle ['krækl] vi crépiter, grésiller

cradle ['kreidl] n berceau m

craft [krɑːft] n métier (artisanal); (pl inv: boat) embarcation f, barque f; (: plane) appareil m; **~sman** (irreg) n artisan m, ouvrier (qualifié); **~smanship** n travail m; **~y** adj rusé(e), malin(-igne)

crag [kræg] n rocher escarpé

cram [kræm] vt (fill): **to ~ sth with** bourrer qch de; (put): **to ~ sth into** fourrer qch dans ♦ vi (for exams) bachoter

cramp [kræmp] n crampe f ♦ vt gêner, entraver; **~ed** adj à l'étroit, très serré(e)

cranberry ['krænbəri] n canneberge f

crane [kreɪn] n grue f

crank [kræŋk] n manivelle f; (person) excentrique m/f

cranny ['kræni] n see nook

crash [kræʃ] n fracas m; (of car) collision f; (of plane) accident m ♦ vt avoir un accident avec ♦ vi (plane) s'écraser; (two cars) se percuter, s'emboutir; (COMM) s'effondrer; **to ~ into** se jeter or se fracasser contre; **~ course** n cours intensif; **~ helmet** n casque (protecteur); **~ landing** n atterrissage forcé or en catastrophe

crate [kreɪt] n cageot m; (for bottles) caisse f

cravat(e) [krə'væt] n foulard (noué autour du cou)

crave [kreɪv] vt, vi: **to ~ (for)** avoir une envie irrésistible de

crawl [krɔːl] vi ramper; (vehicle) avancer au pas ♦ n (SWIMMING) crawl m

crayfish ['kreɪfɪʃ] n inv (freshwater) écrevisse f; (saltwater) langoustine f

crayon ['kreɪən] n crayon m (de couleur)

craze [kreɪz] n engouement m

crazy ['kreɪzi] adj fou (folle)

creak [kriːk] vi grincer; craquer

cream [kriːm] n crème f ♦ adj (colour) crème inv; **~ cake** n (petit) gâteau à la crème; **~ cheese** n fromage m à la crème, fromage blanc; **~y** adj crémeux(-euse)

crease [kriːs] n pli m ♦ vt froisser, chiffonner ♦ vi se froisser, se chiffonner

create [kriː'eɪt] vt créer; **creation** n création f; **creative** adj (artistic) créatif(-ive); (ingenious) ingénieux(-euse)

creature ['kriːtʃə] n créature f

crèche [krɛʃ] n garderie f, crèche f

credence ['kriːdns] n: **to lend** or **give ~ to** ajouter foi à

credentials [krɪ'denʃlz] npl (references) références fpl; (papers of identity) pièce f d'identité

credit ['krɛdɪt] n crédit m; (recognition) honneur m ♦ vt (COMM) créditer; (believe: also: **give ~ to**) ajouter foi à, croire; **~s** npl (CINEMA, TV) générique m; **to be in ~** (person, bank account) être créditeur(-trice); **to ~ sb with** (fig) prêter or attribuer à qn; **~ card** n

carte f de crédit; **~or** n créancier(-ière)

creed [kriːd] n croyance f, credo m

creek [kriːk] n crique f, anse f; (US: stream) ruisseau m, petit cours d'eau

creep [kriːp] (pt, pp **crept**) vi ramper; **~er** n plante grimpante; **~y** adj (frightening) qui fait frissonner, qui donne la chair de poule

cremate [krɪ'meɪt] vt incinérer; **crematorium** [krɛmə'tɔːrɪəm] (pl **crematoria**) n four m crématoire

~crêpe [kreɪp] n crêpe m; **~ bandage** (BRIT) n bande f Velpeau ®

crept [krɛpt] pt, pp of creep

crescent ['krɛsnt] n croissant m; (street) rue f (en arc de cercle)

cress [krɛs] n cresson m

crest [krɛst] n crête f; **~fallen** adj déconfit(e), découragé(e)

Crete [kriːt] n Crète f

crevice ['krɛvɪs] n fissure f, lézarde f, fente f

crew [kruː] n équipage m; (CINEMA) équipe f; **~-cut** n: **to have a ~-cut** avoir les cheveux en brosse; **~-neck** n col ras du cou

crib [krɪb] n lit m d'enfant; (for baby) berceau m ♦ vt (inf) copier

crick [krɪk] n: **~ in the neck** torticolis m; **~ in the back** tour m de reins

cricket ['krɪkɪt] n (insect) grillon m, cri-cri m inv; (game) cricket m

crime [kraɪm] n crime m; **criminal** ['krɪmɪnl] adj, n criminel(le)

crimson ['krɪmzn] adj cramoisi(e)

cringe [krɪndʒ] vi avoir un mouvement de recul

crinkle ['krɪŋkl] vt froisser, chiffonner

cripple ['krɪpl] n boiteux(-euse), infirme m/f ♦ vt estropier

crisis ['kraɪsɪs] (pl **crises**) n crise f

crisp [krɪsp] adj croquant(e); (weather) vif (vive); (manner etc) brusque; **~s** (BRIT) npl (pommes) chips fpl

crisscross ['krɪskrɔs] adj entrecroisé(e)

criterion [kraɪ'tɪərɪən] (pl **criteria**) n critère m

critic ['krɪtɪk] n critique m; **~al** adj critique; **~ally** adv (examine) d'un œil critique; (speak etc) sévèrement; **~ally ill** gravement malade; **~ism** ['krɪtɪsɪzəm] n critique f; **~ize** ['krɪtɪsaɪz] vt critiquer

croak [krəuk] vi (frog) coasser; (raven) croasser; (person) parler d'une voix rauque

Croatia [krəu'eɪʃə] n Croatie f

crochet ['krəuʃeɪ] n travail m au crochet

crockery ['krɒkəri] n vaisselle f

crocodile ['krɒkədaɪl] n crocodile m

crocus ['krəukəs] n crocus m

croft [krɒft] (BRIT) n petite ferme

crony ['krəuni] (inf: pej) n copain (copine)

crook [kruk] n escroc m; (of shepherd) houlette f; **~ed** ['krukɪd] adj courbé(e),

tordu(e); (*action*) malhonnête
crop [krɔp] *n* (*produce*) culture *f*; (*amount produced*) récolte *f*; (*riding ~*) cravache *f* ♦ *vt* (*hair*) tondre; **~ up** *vi* surgir, se présenter, survenir

cross [krɔs] *n* croix *f*; (*BIO etc*) croisement *m* ♦ *vt* (*street etc*) traverser; (*arms, legs, BIO*) croiser; (*cheque*) barrer ♦ *adj* en colère, fâché(e); **~ out** *vt* barrer, biffer; **~ over** *vi* traverser; **~bar** *n* barre (transversale); **~-country** (*race*) *n* cross(-country) *m*; **~-examine** *vt* (*LAW*) faire subir un examen contradictoire à; **~-eyed** *adj* qui louche; **~fire** *n* feux croisés; **~ing** *n* (*sea passage*) traversée *f*; (*also*: **pedestrian ~ing**) passage clouté; **~ing guard** (*US*) *n* contractuel qui fait traverser la rue aux enfants; **~ purposes** *npl*: **to be at ~ purposes with sb** comprendre qn de travers; **~-reference** *n* renvoi *m*, référence *f*; **~roads** *n* carrefour *m*; **~ section** *n* (*of object*) coupe transversale; (*in population*) échantillon *m*; **~walk** (*US*) *n* passage clouté; **~wind** *n* vent *m* de travers; **~word** *n* mots *mpl* croisés

crotch [krɔtʃ] *n* (*ANAT, of garment*) entrejambes *m inv*

crouch [kraʊtʃ] *vi* s'accroupir; se tapir

crow [krəʊ] *n* (*bird*) corneille *f*; (*of cock*) chant *m* du coq, cocorico *m* ♦ *vi* (*cock*) chanter

crowbar [ˈkrəʊbɑːʳ] *n* levier *m*

crowd [kraʊd] *n* foule *f* ♦ *vt* remplir ♦ *vi* affluer, s'attrouper, s'entasser; **to ~ in** entrer en foule; **~ed** *adj* bondé(e), plein(e)

crown [kraʊn] *n* couronne *f*; (*of head*) sommet *m* de la tête; (*of hill*) sommet ♦ *vt* couronner; **~ jewels** *npl* joyaux *mpl* de la Couronne

crow's-feet [ˈkrəʊzfiːt] *npl* pattes *fpl* d'oie

crucial [ˈkruːʃl] *adj* crucial(e), décisif(-ive)

crucifix [ˈkruːsɪfɪks] *n* (*REL*) crucifix *m*; **~ion** [kruːsɪˈfɪkʃən] *n* (*REL*) crucifixion *f*

crude [kruːd] *adj* (*materials*) brut(e); non raffiné(e); (*fig: basic*) rudimentaire, sommaire; (: *vulgar*) cru(e), grossier(-ère); **~ (oil)** *n* (*pétrole*) brut *m*

cruel [ˈkruəl] *adj* cruel(le); **~ty** *n* cruauté *f*

cruise [kruːz] *n* croisière *f* ♦ *vi* (*ship*) croiser; (*car*) rouler; **~r** *n* croiseur *m*; (*motorboat*) yacht *m* de croisière

crumb [krʌm] *n* miette *f*

crumble [ˈkrʌmbl] *vt* émietter ♦ *vi* (*plaster etc*) s'effriter; (*land, earth*) s'ébouler; (*building*) s'effondrer, crouler; (*fig*) s'effondrer; **crumbly** *adj* friable

crumpet [ˈkrʌmpɪt] *n* petite crêpe (épaisse)

crumple [ˈkrʌmpl] *vt* froisser, friper

crunch [krʌntʃ] *vt* croquer; (*underfoot*) faire craquer *or* crisser, écraser ♦ *n* (*fig*) instant *m*

or moment *m* critique, moment de vérité; **~y** *adj* croquant(e), croustillant(e)

crusade [kruːˈseɪd] *n* croisade *f*

crush [krʌʃ] *n* foule *f*, cohue *f*; (*love*): **to have a ~ on sb** avoir le béguin pour qn (*inf*); (*drink*): **lemon ~** citron pressé ♦ *vt* écraser; (*crumple*) froisser; (*fig: hopes*) anéantir

crust [krʌst] *n* croûte *f*

crutch [krʌtʃ] *n* béquille *f*

crux [krʌks] *n* point crucial

cry [kraɪ] *vi* pleurer; (*shout: also*: **~ out**) crier ♦ *n* cri *m*; **~ off** (*inf*) *vi* se dédire; se décommander

cryptic [ˈkrɪptɪk] *adj* énigmatique

crystal [ˈkrɪstl] *n* cristal *m*; **~-clear** *adj* clair(e) comme de l'eau de roche

CSA *n abbr* (= *Child Support Agency*) *organisme pour la protection des enfants de parents séparés, qui contrôle le versement des pensions alimentaires*

CTC *n abbr* = **city technology college**

cub [kʌb] *n* petit *m* (*d'un animal*); (*also*: **C~ scout**) louveteau *m*

Cuba [ˈkjuːbə] *n* Cuba *m*

cube [kjuːb] *n* cube *m* ♦ *vt* (*MATH*) élever au cube; **cubic** *adj* cubique; **cubic metre** *etc* mètre *m etc* cube; **cubic capacity** *n* cylindrée *f*

cubicle [ˈkjuːbɪkl] *n* (*in hospital*) box *m*; (*at pool*) cabine *f*

cuckoo [ˈkʊkuː] *n* coucou *m*; **~ clock** *n* (*pendule f à*) coucou *m*

cucumber [ˈkjuːkʌmbəʳ] *n* concombre *m*

cuddle [ˈkʌdl] *vt* câliner, caresser ♦ *vi* se blottir l'un contre l'autre

cue [kjuː] *n* (*snooker ~*) queue *f* de billard; (*THEATRE etc*) signal *m*

cuff [kʌf] *n* (*BRIT: of shirt, coat etc*) poignet *m*, manchette *f*; (*US: of trousers*) revers *m*; (*blow*) tape *f*; **off the ~** à l'improviste; **~ links** *npl* boutons *mpl* de manchette

cul-de-sac [ˈkʌldəsæk] *n* cul-de-sac *m*, impasse *f*

cull [kʌl] *vt* sélectionner ♦ *n* (*of animals*) massacre *m*

culminate [ˈkʌlmɪneɪt] *vi*: **to ~ in** finir *or* se terminer par; (*end in*) mener à; **culmination** [kʌlmɪˈneɪʃən] *n* point culminant

culottes [kjuːˈlɔts] *npl* jupe-culotte *f*

culprit [ˈkʌlprɪt] *n* coupable *m/f*

cult [kʌlt] *n* culte *m*

cultivate [ˈkʌltɪveɪt] *vt* cultiver; **cultivation** [kʌltɪˈveɪʃən] *n* culture *f*

cultural [ˈkʌltʃərəl] *adj* culturel(le)

culture [ˈkʌltʃəʳ] *n* culture *f*; **~d** *adj* (*person*) cultivé(e)

cumbersome [ˈkʌmbəsəm] *adj* encombrant(e), embarrassant(e)

cunning [ˈkʌnɪŋ] *n* ruse *f*, astuce *f* ♦ *adj*

rusé(e), malin(-igne); (*device, idea*)
astucieux(-euse)

cup [kʌp] *n* tasse *f*; (*as prize*) coupe *f*; (*of bra*)
bonnet *m*

cupboard ['kʌbəd] *n* armoire *f*; (*built-in*)
placard *m*

cup tie (*BRIT*) *n* match *m* de coupe

curate ['kjuərɪt] *n* vicaire *m*

curator [kjuə'reɪtər] *n* conservateur *m* (*d'un
musée etc*)

curb [kə:b] *vt* refréner, mettre un frein à ♦ *n*
(*fig*) frein *m*, restriction *f*; (*US: kerb*) bord *m*
du trottoir

curdle ['kə:dl] *vi* se cailler

cure [kjuər] *vt* guérir; (*CULIN: salt*) saler;
(: *smoke*) fumer; (: *dry*) sécher ♦ *n* remède *m*

curfew ['kə:fju:] *n* couvre-feu *m*

curiosity [kjuərɪ'ɔsɪtɪ] *n* curiosité *f*

curious ['kjuərɪəs] *adj* curieux(-euse)

curl [kə:l] *n* boucle *f* (*de cheveux*) ♦ *vt, vi*
boucler; (*tightly*) friser; ~ **up** *vi* s'enrouler;
se pelotonner; **~er** *n* bigoudi *m*, rouleau *m*;
~y *adj* bouclé(e); frisé(e)

currant ['kʌrnt] *n* (*dried*) raisin *m* de
Corinthe, raisin sec; (*bush*) groseiller *m*;
(*fruit*) groseille *f*

currency ['kʌrnsɪ] *n* monnaie *f*; **to gain ~**
(*fig*) s'accréditer

current ['kʌrnt] *n* courant *m* ♦ *adj*
courant(e); ~ **account** (*BRIT*) *n* compte
courant; ~ **affairs** *npl* (*questions fpl*
d')actualité *f*; **~ly** *adv* actuellement

curriculum [kə'rɪkjuləm] (*pl* **~s** *or* **curricula**)
n programme *m* d'études; ~ **vitae** *n*
curriculum vitae *m*

curry ['kʌrɪ] *n* curry *m* ♦ *vt*: **to ~ favour with**
chercher à s'attirer les bonnes grâces de

curse [kə:s] *vi* jurer, blasphémer ♦ *vt* maudire
♦ *n* (*spell*) malédiction *f*; (*problem, scourge*)
fléau *m*; (*swearword*) juron *m*

cursor ['kə:sər] *n* (*COMPUT*) curseur *m*

cursory ['kə:sərɪ] *adj* superficiel(le), hâtif(-ive)

curt [kə:t] *adj* brusque, sec (sèche)

curtail [kə:'teɪl] *vt* (*visit etc*) écourter;
(*expenses, freedom etc*) réduire

curtain ['kə:tn] *n* rideau *m*

curts(e)y ['kə:tsɪ] *vi* faire une révérence

curve [kə:v] *n* courbe *f*; (*in the road*) tournant
m, virage *m* ♦ *vi* se courber; (*road*) faire une
courbe

cushion ['kuʃən] *n* coussin *m* ♦ *vt* (*fall,
shock*) amortir

custard ['kʌstəd] *n* (*for pouring*) crème
anglaise

custody ['kʌstədɪ] *n* (*of child*) garde *f*; **to
take sb into ~** (*suspect*) placer qn en
détention préventive

custom ['kʌstəm] *n* coutume *f*, usage *m*;
(*COMM*) clientèle *f*; **~ary** *adj* habituel(le)

customer ['kʌstəmər] *n* client(e)

customized ['kʌstəmaɪzd] *adj* (*car etc*)
construit(e) sur commande

custom-made ['kʌstəm'meɪd] *adj* (*clothes*)
fait(e) sur mesure; (*other goods*) hors série,
fait(e) sur commande

customs ['kʌstəmz] *npl* douane *f*; ~ **officer**
n douanier(-ière)

cut [kʌt] (*pt, pp* **cut**) *vt* couper; (*meat*)
découper; (*reduce*) réduire ♦ *vi* couper ♦ *n*
coupure *f*; (*of clothes*) coupe *f*; (*in salary etc*)
réduction *f*; (*of meat*) morceau *m*; **to ~ one's
hand** se couper la main; **to ~ a tooth** percer
une dent; ~ **down** *vt fus* (*tree etc*) couper,
abattre; (*consumption*) réduire; ~ **off** *vt*
couper; (*fig*) isoler; ~ **out** *vt* découper;
(*stop*) arrêter; (*remove*) ôter; ~ **up** *vt* (*paper,
meat*) découper; **~back** *n* réduction *f*

cute [kju:t] *adj* mignon(ne), adorable

cutlery ['kʌtlərɪ] *n* couverts *mpl*

cutlet ['kʌtlɪt] *n* côtelette *f*

cut: **~out** *n* (*switch*) coupe-circuit *m inv*;
(*cardboard cutout*) découpage *m*; **~price** (*US*
cut-rate) *adj* au rabais, à prix réduit; **~-
throat** *n* assassin *m* ♦ *adj* acharné(e); **~ting**
adj tranchant(e), coupant(e); (*fig*)
cinglant(e), mordant(e) ♦ *n* (*BRIT: from
newspaper*) coupure *f* (*de journal*); (*from
plant*) bouture *f*

CV *n abbr* = **curriculum vitae**

cwt *abbr* = **hundredweight(s)**

cyanide ['saɪənaɪd] *n* cyanure *m*

cybercafé ['saɪbəkæfeɪ] *n* cybercafé *m*

cyberspace ['saɪbəspeɪs] *n* cyberspace *m*

cycle ['saɪkl] *n* cycle *m*; (*bicycle*) bicyclette *f*,
vélo *m* ♦ *vi* faire de la bicyclette; ~ **hire** *n*
location *f* de vélos; ~ **lane** *or* **path** *n* piste *f*
cyclable; **cycling** *n* cyclisme *m*; **cyclist**
['saɪklɪst] *n* cycliste *m/f*

cygnet ['sɪgnɪt] *n* jeune cygne *m*

cylinder ['sɪlɪndər] *n* cylindre *m*; **~-head
gasket** *n* joint *m* de culasse

cymbals ['sɪmblz] *npl* cymbales *fpl*

cynic ['sɪnɪk] *n* cynique *m/f*; **~al** *adj* cynique;
~ism ['sɪnɪsɪzəm] *n* cynisme *m*

Cypriot ['sɪprɪət] *adj* cypriote, chypriote ♦ *n*
Cypriote *m/f*, Chypriote *m/f*

Cyprus ['saɪprəs] *n* Chypre *f*

cyst [sɪst] *n* kyste *m*

cystitis [sɪs'taɪtɪs] *n* cystite *f*

czar [zɑ:r] *n* tsar *m*

Czech [tʃɛk] *adj* tchèque ♦ *n* Tchèque *m/f*;
(*LING*) tchèque *m*

Czechoslovak [tʃɛkə'sləuvæk] *adj*
tchécoslovaque ♦ *n* Tchécoslovaque *m/f*

Czechoslovakia [tʃɛkəslə'vækɪə] *n*
Tchécoslovaquie *f*

D, d

D [di:] n (MUS) ré m

dab [dæb] vt (eyes, wound) tamponner; (paint, cream) appliquer (par petites touches or rapidement)

dabble ['dæbl] vi: **to ~ in** faire or se mêler or s'occuper un peu de

dad [dæd] n, **daddy** ['dædɪ] n papa m

daffodil ['dæfədɪl] n jonquille f

daft [dɑːft] adj idiot(e), stupide

dagger ['dægər] n poignard m

daily ['deɪlɪ] adj quotidien(ne), journalier(-ère) ♦ n quotidien m ♦ adv tous les jours

dainty ['deɪntɪ] adj délicat(e), mignon(ne)

dairy ['deərɪ] n (BRIT: shop) crémerie f, laiterie f; (on farm) laiterie; **~ products** npl produits laitiers; **~ store** (US) n crémerie f, laiterie f

daisy ['deɪzɪ] n pâquerette f

dale [deɪl] n vallon m

dam [dæm] n barrage m ♦ vt endiguer

damage ['dæmɪdʒ] n dégâts mpl, dommages mpl; (fig) tort m ♦ vt endommager, abîmer; (fig) faire du tort à; **~s** npl (LAW) dommages-intérêts mpl

damn [dæm] vt condamner; (curse) maudire ♦ n (inf): **I don't give a ~** je m'en fous ♦ adj (inf: also: **~ed**): **this ~** ... ce sacré or foutu ...; **~ (it)!** zut!; **~ing** adj accablant(e)

damp [dæmp] adj humide ♦ n humidité f ♦ vt (also: **~en**: cloth, rag) humecter; (: enthusiasm) refroidir

damson ['dæmzən] n prune f de Damas

dance [dɑːns] n danse f; (social event) bal m ♦ vi danser; **~ hall** n salle f de bal, dancing m; **~r** n danseur(-euse); **dancing** n danse f

dandelion ['dændɪlaɪən] n pissenlit m

dandruff ['dændrəf] n pellicules fpl

Dane [deɪn] n Danois(e)

danger ['deɪndʒər] n danger m; **there is a ~ of fire** il y a (un) risque d'incendie; **in ~** de tomber; **he was in ~ of falling** il risquait de tomber; **~ous** adj dangereux(-euse)

dangle ['dæŋgl] vt balancer ♦ vi pendre

Danish ['deɪnɪʃ] adj danois(e) ♦ n (LING) danois m

dare [deər] vt: **to ~ sb to do** défier qn de faire ♦ vi: **to ~ (to) do sth** oser faire qch; **I ~ say** (I suppose) il est probable (que); **daring** adj hardi(e), audacieux(-euse); (dress) osé(e) ♦ n audace f, hardiesse f

dark [dɑːk] adj (night, room) obscur(e), sombre; (colour, complexion) foncé(e), sombre ♦ n: **in the ~** dans le noir; **in the ~ about** (fig) ignorant tout de; **after ~** après la tombée de la nuit; **~en** vt obscurcir, assombrir ♦ vi s'obscurcir, s'assombrir;

~ glasses npl lunettes noires; **~ness** n obscurité f; **~room** n chambre noire

darling ['dɑːlɪŋ] adj chéri(e) ♦ n chéri(e); (favourite): **to be the ~ of** être la coqueluche de

darn [dɑːn] vt repriser, raccommoder

dart [dɑːt] n fléchette f; (sewing) pince f ♦ vi: **to ~ towards** (also: **make a ~ towards**) se précipiter or s'élancer vers; **to ~ away/along** partir/passer comme une flèche; **~board** n cible f (de jeu de fléchettes); **~s** n (jeu m de) fléchettes fpl

dash [dæʃ] n (sign) tiret m; (small quantity) goutte f, larme f ♦ vt (missile) jeter or lancer violemment; (hopes) anéantir ♦ vi: **to ~ towards** (also: **make a ~ towards**) se précipiter or se ruer vers; **~ away** vi partir à toute allure, filer; **~ off** vi = **dash away**

dashboard ['dæʃbɔːd] n (AUT) tableau m de bord

dashing ['dæʃɪŋ] adj fringant(e)

data ['deɪtə] npl données fpl; **~base** n (COMPUT) base f de données; **~ processing** n traitement m de données

date [deɪt] n date f; (with sb) rendez-vous m; (fruit) datte f ♦ vt dater; (person) sortir avec; **~ of birth** date de naissance; **to ~** (until now) à ce jour; **out of ~** (passport) périmé(e); (theory etc) dépassé(e); (clothes etc) démodé(e); **up to ~** moderne; (news) très récent; **~d** ['deɪtɪd] adj démodé(e); **~ rape** n viol m (à l'issue d'un rendez-vous galant)

daub [dɔːb] vt barbouiller

daughter ['dɔːtər] n fille f; **~-in-law** n belle-fille f, bru f

daunting ['dɔːntɪŋ] adj décourageant(e)

dawdle ['dɔːdl] vi traîner, lambiner

dawn [dɔːn] n aube f, aurore f ♦ vi (day) se lever, poindre; (fig): **it ~ed on him that** ... il lui vint à l'esprit que ...

day [deɪ] n jour m; (as duration) journée f; (period of time, age) époque f, temps m; **the ~ before** la veille, le jour précédent; **the ~ after, the following ~** le lendemain, le jour suivant; **the ~ after tomorrow** après-demain; **the ~ before yesterday** avant-hier; **by ~** de jour; **~break** n point m du jour; **~dream** vi rêver (tout éveillé); **~light** n (lumière f du) jour m; **~ return** (BRIT) n billet m d'aller-retour (valable pour la journée); **~time** n jour m, journée f; **~-to-~** adj quotidien(ne); (event) journalier(-ère)

daze [deɪz] vt (stun) étourdir ♦ n: **in a ~** étourdi(e), hébété(e)

dazzle ['dæzl] vt éblouir, aveugler

DC abbr (= direct current) courant continu

D-day ['diːdeɪ] n le jour J

dead [dɛd] adj mort(e); (numb) engourdi(e), insensible; (battery) à plat; (telephone): **the**

line is ~ la ligne est coupée ♦ adv absolument, complètement ♦ npl: **the** ~ les morts; **he was shot** ~ il a été tué d'un coup de revolver; ~ **on time** à l'heure pile; ~ **tired** éreinté(e), complètement fourbu(e); **to stop** ~ s'arrêter pile or net; ~**en** vt (blow, sound) amortir; (pain) calmer; ~ **end** n impasse f; ~ **heat** n (SPORT) to finish in a ~ heat terminer ex-æquo; ~**line** n date f or heure f limite; ~**lock** (fig) n impasse f; ~ **loss** n: **to be a ~ loss** (inf: person) n'être bon(ne) à rien; ~**ly** adj mortel(le); (weapon) meurtrier(-ère); (accuracy) extrême; ~**pan** adj impassible; **D~ Sea** n: **the D~ Sea** la mer Morte

deaf [dɛf] adj sourd(e); ~**en** vt rendre sourd; ~**ening** adj assourdissant(e); ~**-mute** n sourd(e)-muet(te); ~**ness** n surdité f

deal [di:l] n (pt, pp **dealt**) n affaire f, marché m ♦ vt (blow) porter; (cards) donner, distribuer; **a great ~ (of)** beaucoup (de); ~ **in** vt fus faire le commerce de; ~ **with** vt fus (person, problem) s'occuper or se charger de; (be about: book etc) traiter de; ~**er** n marchand m; ~**ings** npl (COMM) transactions fpl; (relations) relations fpl, rapports mpl

dean [di:n] n (REL, BRIT: SCOL) doyen m; (US: SCOL) conseiller(-ère) (principal(e)) d'éducation

dear [dɪəʳ] adj cher (chère); (expensive) cher, coûteux(-euse) ♦ n: **my** ~ mon cher/ma chère; ~ **me!** mon Dieu!; **D~ Sir/Madam** (in letter) Monsieur/Madame; **D~ Mr/Mrs X** Cher Monsieur/Chère Madame; ~**ly** adv (love) tendrement; (pay) cher

death [dɛθ] n mort f; (fatality) mort m; (ADMIN) décès m; ~ **certificate** n acte m de décès; ~**ly** adj de mort; ~ **penalty** n peine f de mort; ~ **rate** n (taux m de) mortalité f; ~ **toll** n nombre m de morts

debase [dɪ'beɪs] vt (value) déprécier, dévaloriser

debatable [dɪ'beɪtəbl] adj discutable

debate [dɪ'beɪt] n discussion f, débat m ♦ vt discuter, débattre

debit [dɛbɪt] n débit m ♦ vt: **to ~ a sum to sb** or **to sb's account** porter une somme au débit de qn, débiter qn d'une somme; see also **direct**

debt [dɛt] n dette f; **to be in** ~ avoir des dettes, être endetté(e); ~**or** n débiteur(-trice)

decade ['dɛkeɪd] n décennie f, décade f

decadence [dɛkədəns] n décadence f

decaff ['di:kæf] (inf) n déca m

decaffeinated [dɪ'kæfɪneɪtɪd] adj décaféiné(e)

decanter [dɪ'kæntəʳ] n carafe f

decay [dɪ'keɪ] n (of building) délabrement m; (also: **tooth ~**) carie f (dentaire) ♦ vi (rot) se décomposer, pourrir; (: teeth) se carier

deceased [dɪ'si:st] n défunt(e)

deceit [dɪ'si:t] n tromperie f, supercherie f; ~**ful** adj trompeur(-euse); **deceive** vt tromper

December [dɪ'sɛmbəʳ] n décembre m

decent ['di:sənt] adj décent(e), convenable

deception [dɪ'sɛpʃən] n tromperie f

deceptive [dɪ'sɛptɪv] adj trompeur(-euse)

decide [dɪ'saɪd] vt (person) décider; (question, argument) trancher, régler ♦ vi se décider, décider; **to ~ to do/that** décider de faire/que; **to ~ on** décider, se décider pour; ~**d** adj (resolute) résolu(e), décidé(e); (clear, definite) net(te), marqué(e); ~**dly** adv résolument; (distinctly) incontestablement, nettement

deciduous [dɪ'sɪdjuəs] adj à feuilles caduques

decimal ['dɛsɪməl] adj décimal(e) ♦ n décimale f; ~ **point** n ≈ virgule f

decipher [dɪ'saɪfəʳ] vt déchiffrer

decision [dɪ'sɪʒən] n décision f

decisive [dɪ'saɪsɪv] adj décisif(-ive); (person) décidé(e)

deck [dɛk] n (NAUT) pont m; (of bus): **top** ~ impériale f; (of cards) jeu m; (record ~) platine f; ~**chair** n chaise longue

declare [dɪ'klɛəʳ] vt déclarer

decline [dɪ'klaɪn] n (decay) déclin m; (lessening) baisse f ♦ vt refuser, décliner ♦ vi décliner; (business) baisser

decoder [di:'kəudəʳ] n (TV) décodeur m

decorate ['dɛkəreɪt] vt (adorn, give a medal to) décorer; (paint and paper) peindre et tapisser; **decoration** [dɛkə'reɪʃən] n (medal etc, adornment) décoration f; **decorator** n peintre-décorateur m

decoy ['di:kɔɪ] n piège m; (person) compère m

decrease [n 'di:kri:s, vb di:'kri:s] n: ~ **(in)** diminution f (de) ♦ vt, vi diminuer

decree [dɪ'kri:] n (POL, REL) décret m; (LAW) arrêt m, jugement m; ~ **nisi** [-'naɪsaɪ] n jugement m provisoire de divorce

dedicate ['dɛdɪkeɪt] vt consacrer; (book etc) dédier; ~**d** adj (person) dévoué(e); (COMPUT) spécialisé(e), dédié(e); **dedication** [dɛdɪ'keɪʃən] n (devotion) dévouement m; (in book) dédicace f

deduce [dɪ'dju:s] vt déduire, conclure

deduct [dɪ'dʌkt] vt: **to ~ sth (from)** déduire qch (de), retrancher qch (de); ~**ion** n (deducting, deducing) déduction f; (from wage etc) prélèvement m, retenue f

deed [di:d] n action f, acte m; (LAW) acte notarié, contrat m

deep [di:p] adj profond(e); (voice) grave ♦ adv: **spectators stood 20** ~ il y avait 20 rangs de spectateurs; **4 metres** ~ de 4 mètres de profondeur; ~ **end** (of swimming pool)

grand bain; **~en** vt approfondir ♦ vi (fig)
s'épaissir; **~freeze** n congélateur m; **~fry** vt
faire frire (en friteuse); **~ly** adv profondément; (interested) vivement; **~sea**
diver n sous-marin(e); **~sea diving** n
plongée sous-marine; **~sea fishing** n
grande pêche; **~seated** adj profond(e),
profondément enraciné(e)

deer [dɪəʳ] n inv: (red) ~ cerf m, biche f;
(fallow) ~ daim m; (roe) ~ chevreuil m; **~skin**
n daim

deface [dɪ'feɪs] vt dégrader; (notice, poster)
barbouiller

default [dɪ'fɔːlt] n (COMPUT: also: ~ value)
valeur f par défaut; **by ~** (LAW) par défaut, par
contumace; (SPORT) par forfait

defeat [dɪ'fiːt] n défaite f ♦ vt (team,
opponents) battre

defect [n 'diːfɛkt, vb dɪ'fɛkt] n défaut m ♦ vi:
to ~ to the enemy passer à l'ennemi; **~ive**
[dɪ'fɛktɪv] adj défectueux(-euse)

defence [dɪ'fɛns] (US **defense**) n défense f;
~less adj sans défense

defend [dɪ'fɛnd] vt défendre; **~ant** n
défendeur(-deresse); (in criminal case)
accusé(e), prévenu(e); **~er** n défenseur m

defer [dɪ'fəːʳ] vt (postpone) différer, ajourner

defiance [dɪ'faɪəns] n défi m; **in ~ of** au
mépris de; **defiant** adj provocant(e), de défi;
(person) rebelle, intraitable

deficiency [dɪ'fɪʃənsɪ] n insuffisance f,
déficience f; **deficient** adj (inadequate)
insuffisant(e); **to be deficient in** manquer de

deficit ['dɛfɪsɪt] n déficit m

define [dɪ'faɪn] vt définir

definite ['dɛfɪnɪt] adj (fixed) défini(e), (bien)
déterminé(e); (clear, obvious) net(te),
manifeste; (certain) sûr(e); **he was ~ about it**
il a été catégorique; **~ly** adv sans aucun
doute

definition [dɛfɪ'nɪʃən] n définition f;
(clearness) netteté f

deflate [diː'fleɪt] vt dégonfler

deflect [dɪ'flɛkt] vt détourner, faire dévier

deformed [dɪ'fɔːmd] adj difforme

defraud [dɪ'frɔːd] vt frauder; **to ~ sb of sth**
escroquer qch à qn

defrost [diː'frɔst] vt dégivrer; (food)
décongeler; **~er** (US) n (demister) dispositif m
anti-buée inv

deft [dɛft] adj adroit(e), preste

defunct [dɪ'fʌŋkt] adj défunt(e)

defuse [diː'fjuːz] vt désamorcer

defy [dɪ'faɪ] vt défier; (efforts etc) résister à

degenerate [vb dɪ'dʒɛnəreɪt, adj dɪ'dʒɛnərɪt]
vi dégénérer ♦ adj dégénéré(e)

degree [dɪ'griː] n degré m; (SCOL) diplôme m
(universitaire); **a (first) ~ in maths** une licence
en maths; **by ~s** (gradually) par degrés; **to**

some ~, to a certain ~ jusqu'à un certain
point, dans une certaine mesure

dehydrated [diːhaɪ'dreɪtɪd] adj
déshydraté(e); (milk, eggs) en poudre

de-ice ['diː'aɪs] vt (windscreen) dégivrer

deign [deɪn] vi: **to ~ to do** daigner faire

dejected [dɪ'dʒɛktɪd] adj abattu(e),
déprimé(e)

delay [dɪ'leɪ] vt retarder ♦ vi s'attarder ♦ n
délai m, retard m; **to be ~ed** être en retard

delectable [dɪ'lɛktəbl] adj délicieux(-euse)

delegate [n 'dɛlɪgɪt, vb 'dɛlɪgeɪt] n délé-
gué(e) ♦ vt déléguer

delete [dɪ'liːt] vt rayer, supprimer

deliberate [adj dɪ'lɪbərɪt, vb dɪ'lɪbəreɪt] adj
(intentional) délibéré(e); (slow) mesuré(e)
♦ vi délibérer, réfléchir; **~ly** [dɪ'lɪbərɪtlɪ] adv
(on purpose) exprès, délibérément

delicacy ['dɛlɪkəsɪ] n délicatesse f; (food)
mets fin or délicat, friandise f

delicate ['dɛlɪkɪt] adj délicat(e)

delicatessen [dɛlɪkə'tɛsn] n épicerie fine

delicious [dɪ'lɪʃəs] adj délicieux(-euse)

delight [dɪ'laɪt] n (grande) joie, grand plaisir
♦ vt enchanter; **to take (a) ~ in** prendre
grand plaisir à; **~ed** adj: **~ed (at or with/to
do)** ravi(e) (de/de faire); **~ful** adj (person)
adorable; (meal, evening) merveilleux(-euse)

delinquent [dɪ'lɪŋkwənt] adj, n délin-
quant(e)

delirious [dɪ'lɪrɪəs] adj: **to be ~** délirer

deliver [dɪ'lɪvəʳ] vt (mail) distribuer; (goods)
livrer; (message) remettre; (speech)
prononcer; (MED: baby) mettre au monde;
~y n distribution f; livraison f; (of speaker)
élocution f; (MED) accouchement m; **to take
~y of** prendre livraison de

delude [dɪ'luːd] vt tromper, leurrer; **delusion**
n illusion f

demand [dɪ'mɑːnd] vt réclamer, exiger ♦ n
exigence f; (claim) revendication f; (ECON)
demande f; **in ~** demandé(e), recherché(e);
on ~ sur demande; **~ing** adj (person)
exigeant(e); (work) astreignant(e)

demean [dɪ'miːn] vt: **to ~ o.s.** s'abaisser

demeanour [dɪ'miːnəʳ] (US **demeanor**) n
comportement m; maintien m

demented [dɪ'mɛntɪd] adj dément(e), fou
(folle)

demise [dɪ'maɪz] n mort f

demister [diː'mɪstəʳ] (BRIT) n (AUT) dispositif
m anti-buée inv

demo ['dɛməu] (inf) n abbr (= demonstration)
manif f

democracy [dɪ'mɔkrəsɪ] n démocratie f;
democrat ['dɛməkræt] n démocrate m/f;
democratic [dɛmə'krætɪk] adj démocratique

demolish [dɪ'mɔlɪʃ] vt démolir

demonstrate ['dɛmənstreɪt] vt démontrer,

prouver; (*show*) faire une démonstration de
♦ *vi*: **to ~ (for/against)** manifester (en faveur de/contre); **demonstration**
[deman'streɪʃən] *n* démonstration *f*,
manifestation *f*; **demonstrator** *n* (*POL*)
manifestant(e)

demote [dɪ'məut] *vt* rétrograder

demure [dɪ'mjuər] *adj* sage, réservé(e)

den [den] *n* tanière *f*, antre *m*

denial [dɪ'naɪəl] *n* démenti *m*; (*refusal*)
dénégation *f*

denim ['denɪm] *n* jean *m*; **~s** *npl* (*jeans*)
(blue-)jean(s) *m(pl)*

Denmark ['denmɑːk] *n* Danemark *m*

denomination [dɪnɔmɪ'neɪʃən] *n* (*of
money*) valeur *f*; (*REL*) confession *f*

denounce [dɪ'nauns] *vt* dénoncer

dense [dens] *adj* dense; (*stupid*) obtus(e),
bouché(e); **~ly** *adv*: **~ly populated** à forte
densité de population; **density** ['densɪtɪ] *n*
densité *f*; **double/high-density diskette**
disquette *f* double densité/haute densité

dent [dent] *n* bosse *f* ♦ *vt* (*also*: **make a ~ in**)
cabosser

dental ['dentl] *adj* dentaire; **~ surgeon** *n*
(chirurgien(ne)) dentiste

dentist ['dentɪst] *n* dentiste *m/f*

dentures ['dentʃəz] *npl* dentier *m sg*

deny [dɪ'naɪ] *vt* nier; (*refuse*) refuser

deodorant [diː'əudərənt] *n* déodorant *m*,
désodorisant *m*

depart [dɪ'pɑːt] *vi* partir; **to ~ from** (*fig: differ
from*) s'écarter de

department [dɪ'pɑːtmənt] *n* (*COMM*) rayon
m; (*SCOL*) section *f*; (*POL*) ministère *m*,
département *m*; **~ store** *n* grand magasin

departure [dɪ'pɑːtʃər] *n* départ *m*; **a new ~**
une nouvelle voie; **~ lounge** *n* (*at airport*)
salle *f* d'embarquement

depend [dɪ'pend] *vi*: **to ~ on** dépendre de;
(*rely on*) compter sur; **it ~s** cela dépend; **~ing
on the result** selon le résultat; **~able** *adj*
(*person*) sérieux(-euse), sûr(e); (*car, watch*)
solide, fiable; **~ant** *n* personne *f* à charge;
~ent *adj*: **to be ~ent (on)** dépendre (de) ♦ *n*
= **dependant**

depict [dɪ'pɪkt] *vt* (*in picture*) représenter; (*in
words*) (dé)peindre, décrire

depleted [dɪ'pliːtɪd] *adj* (considérablement)
réduit(e) ou diminué(e)

deport [dɪ'pɔːt] *vt* expulser

deposit [dɪ'pɔzɪt] *n* (*CHEM, COMM, GEO*) dépôt
m; (*of ore, oil*) gisement *m*; (*part payment*)
arrhes *fpl*, acompte *m*; (*on bottle etc*)
consigne *f*; (*for hired goods etc*)
cautionnement *m*, garantie *f* ♦ *vt* déposer;
~ account *n* compte *m* sur livret

depot ['depəu] *n* dépôt *m*; (*US: RAIL*) gare *f*

depress [dɪ'pres] *vt* déprimer; (*press down*)

appuyer sur, abaisser; (*prices, wages*) faire
baisser; **~ed** *adj* (*person*) déprimé(e); (*area*)
en déclin, touché(e) par le sous-emploi; **~ing**
adj déprimant(e); **~ion** *n* dépression *f*;
(*hollow*) creux *m*

deprivation [deprɪ'veɪʃən] *n* privation *f*;
(*loss*) perte *f*

deprive [dɪ'praɪv] *vt*: **to ~ sb of** priver qn de;
~d *adj* déshérité(e)

depth [depθ] *n* profondeur *f*; **in the ~s of
despair** au plus profond du désespoir; **to be
out of one's ~** avoir perdu pied, nager

deputize ['depjutaɪz] *vi*: **to ~ for** assurer
l'intérim de

deputy ['depjutɪ] *adj* adjoint(e) ♦ *n* (*second
in command*) adjoint(e); (*US: also*: **~ sheriff**)
shérif adjoint; **~ head** directeur adjoint, sous-
directeur *m*

derail [dɪ'reɪl] *vt*: **to be ~ed** dérailler

deranged [dɪ'reɪndʒd] *adj*: **to be (mentally) ~**
avoir le cerveau dérangé

derby ['dɑːrbɪ] (*US*) *n* (*bowler hat*) (chapeau
m) melon *m*

derelict ['derɪlɪkt] *adj* abandonné(e), à
l'abandon

derisory [dɪ'raɪsərɪ] *adj* (*sum*) dérisoire;
(*smile, person*) moqueur(-euse)

derive [dɪ'raɪv] *vt*: **to ~ sth from** tirer qch de;
trouver qch dans ♦ *vi*: **to ~ from** provenir de,
dériver de

derogatory [dɪ'rɔgətərɪ] *adj* désobligeant(e);
péjoratif(-ive)

descend [dɪ'send] *vt, vi* descendre; **to ~ from**
descendre de, être issu(e) de; **to ~ to (doing)
sth** s'abaisser à (faire) qch; **descent** *n*
descente *f*; (*origin*) origine *f*

describe [dɪs'kraɪb] *vt* décrire; **description**
[dɪs'krɪpʃən] *n* description *f*; (*sort*) sorte *f*,
espèce *f*

desecrate ['desɪkreɪt] *vt* profaner

desert [*n* 'dezət, *vb* dɪ'zəːt] *n* désert *m* ♦ *vt*
déserter, abandonner ♦ *vi* (*MIL*) déserter; **~s**
npl: **to get one's just ~s** n'avoir que ce qu'on
mérite; **~er** [dɪ'zəːtər] *n* déserteur *m*; **~ion**
[dɪ'zəːʃən] *n* (*MIL*) désertion *f*; (*LAW: of
spouse*) abandon *m* du domicile conjugal;
~ island *n* île déserte

deserve [dɪ'zəːv] *vt* mériter; **deserving** *adj*
(*person*) méritant(e); (*action, cause*) méritoire

design [dɪ'zaɪn] *n* (*sketch*) plan *m*, dessin *m*;
(*layout, shape*) conception *f*, ligne *f*; (*pattern*)
dessin *m*, motif(s) *m(pl)*; (*COMM, art*) design
m, stylisme *m*; (*intention*) dessein *m* ♦ *vt*
dessiner; élaborer; **~er** *n* (*TECH*) concepteur-
projeteur *m*; (*ART*) dessinateur(-trice),
designer *m*; (*fashion*) styliste *m/f*

desire [dɪ'zaɪər] *n* désir *m* ♦ *vt* désirer

desk [desk] *n* (*in office*) bureau *m*; (*for pupil*)
pupitre *m*; (*BRIT: in shop, restaurant*) caisse *f*;

(in hotel, at airport) réception f; **~-top publishing** *n* publication assistée par ordinateur, PAO f

desolate ['desəlɪt] *adj* désolé(e); *(person)* affligé(e)

despair [dɪs'peə'] *n* désespoir *m* ♦ *vi*: **to ~ of** désespérer de

despatch [dɪs'pætʃ] *n, vt* = **dispatch**

desperate ['despərɪt] *adj* désespéré(e); *(criminal)* prêt(e) à tout; **to be ~ for sth/to do sth** avoir désespérément besoin de qch/de faire qch; **~ly** *adv* désespérément; *(very)* terriblement, extrêmement; **desperation** [despə'reɪʃən] *n* désespoir *m*; **in (sheer) desperation** en désespoir de cause

despicable [dɪs'pɪkəbl] *adj* méprisable

despise [dɪs'paɪz] *vt* mépriser

despite [dɪs'paɪt] *prep* malgré, en dépit de

despondent [dɪs'pɔndənt] *adj* découragé(e), abattu(e)

dessert [dɪ'zə:t] *n* dessert *m*; **~spoon** *n* cuiller f à dessert

destination [destɪ'neɪʃən] *n* destination f

destined ['destɪnd] *adj*: **to be ~ to do/for sth** être destiné(e) à faire/à qch

destiny ['destɪnɪ] *n* destinée f, destin *m*

destitute ['destɪtju:t] *adj* indigent(e)

destroy [dɪs'trɔɪ] *vt* détruire; *(injured horse)* abattre; *(dog)* faire piquer; **~er** *n* (NAUT) contre-torpilleur *m*

destruction [dɪs'trʌkʃən] *n* destruction f

detach [dɪ'tætʃ] *vt* détacher; **~ed** *adj* *(attitude, person)* détaché(e); **~ed house** *n* pavillon *m*, maison(nette) (individuelle); **~ment** *n* (MIL) détachement *m*; *(fig)* détachement *m*, indifférence f

detail ['di:teɪl] *n* détail *m* ♦ *vt* raconter en détail, énumérer; **in ~** en détail; **~ed** *adj* détaillé(e)

detain [dɪ'teɪn] *vt* retenir; *(in captivity)* détenir; *(in hospital)* hospitaliser

detect [dɪ'tekt] *vt* déceler, percevoir; *(MED, POLICE)* dépister; *(MIL, RADAR, TECH)* détecter; **~ion** *n* découverte f; **~ive** *n* agent *m* de la sûreté, policier *m*; **private ~ive** détective privé; **~ive story** *n* roman policier

detention [dɪ'tenʃən] *n* détention f; *(SCOL)* retenue f, consigne f

deter [dɪ'tə:'] *vt* dissuader

detergent [dɪ'tə:dʒənt] *n* détergent *m*, détersif *m*

deteriorate [dɪ'tɪərɪəreɪt] *vi* se détériorer, se dégrader

determine [dɪ'tə:mɪn] *vt* déterminer; **to ~ to do** résoudre de faire, se déterminer à faire; **~d** *adj* *(person)* déterminé(e), décidé(e)

deterrent [dɪ'terənt] *n* effet *m* de dissuasion; force f de dissuasion

detest [dɪ'test] *vt* détester, avoir horreur de

detonate ['detəneɪt] *vt* faire détoner *or* exploser

detour ['di:tuə'] *n* détour *m*; *(US: AUT: diversion)* déviation f

detract [dɪ'trækt] *vt*: **to ~ from** *(quality, pleasure)* diminuer; *(reputation)* porter atteinte à

detriment ['detrɪmənt] *n*: **to the ~ of** au détriment de, au préjudice de; **~al** [detrɪ'mentl] *adj*: **~al to** préjudiciable *or* nuisible à

devaluation [dɪvælju'eɪʃən] *n* dévaluation f

devastate ['devəsteɪt] *vt* dévaster; **~d** *adj* *(fig)* anéanti(e); **devastating** *adj* dévastateur(-trice); *(news)* accablant(e)

develop [dɪ'veləp] *vt* (gen) développer; *(disease)* commencer à souffrir de; *(resources)* mettre en valeur, exploiter ♦ *vi* se développer; *(situation, disease: evolve)* évoluer; *(facts, symptoms: appear)* se manifester, se produire; **~ing country** pays *m* en voie de développement; **the machine has ~ed a fault** un problème s'est manifesté dans cette machine; **~er** [dɪ'veləpə'] *n* *(also: property ~er)* promoteur *m*; **~ment** [dɪ'veləpmənt] *n* développement *m*; *(of affair, case)* rebondissement *m*, fait(s) nouveau(x)

device [dɪ'vaɪs] *n* *(apparatus)* engin *m*, dispositif *m*

devil ['devl] *n* diable *m*; démon *m*

devious ['di:vɪəs] *adj* *(person)* sournois(e), dissimulé(e)

devise [dɪ'vaɪz] *vt* imaginer, concevoir

devoid [dɪ'vɔɪd] *adj*: **~ of** dépourvu(e) de, dénué(e) de

devolution [di:və'lu:ʃən] *n* (POL) décentralisation f

devote [dɪ'vaut] *vt*: **to ~ sth to** consacrer qch à; **~d** [dɪ'vautɪd] *adj* dévoué(e); **to be ~d to** *(book etc)* être consacré(e) à; *(person)* être très attaché(e) à; **~e** [devəu'ti:] *n* (REL) adepte *m/f*; *(MUS, SPORT)* fervent(e); **devotion** *n* dévouement *m*, attachement *m*; *(REL)* dévotion f, piété f

devour [dɪ'vauə'] *vt* dévorer

devout [dɪ'vaut] *adj* pieux(-euse), dévot(e)

dew [dju:] *n* rosée f

diabetes [daɪə'bi:ti:z] *n* diabète *m*; **diabetic** [daɪə'betɪk] *adj* diabétique ♦ *n* diabétique *m/f*

diabolical [daɪə'bɔlɪkl] *(inf) adj* *(weather)* atroce; *(behaviour)* infernal(e)

diagnosis [daɪəg'nəusɪs] *(pl diagnoses) n* diagnostic *m*

diagonal [daɪ'ægənl] *adj* diagonal(e) ♦ *n* diagonale f

diagram ['daɪəgræm] *n* diagramme *m*, schéma *m*

dial ['daɪəl] *n* cadran *m* ♦ *vt* *(number)* faire, composer

dialect ['daɪəlekt] *n* dialecte *m*

dialling code ['daɪəlɪŋ-] (*BRIT*) *n* indicatif *m* (téléphonique)

dialling tone (*BRIT*) *n* tonalité *f*

dialogue ['daɪəlɒg] *n* dialogue *m*

dial tone (*US*) *n* = **dialling tone**

diameter [daɪ'æmɪtə'] *n* diamètre *m*

diamond ['daɪəmənd] *n* diamant *m*; (*shape*) losange *m*; **~s** *npl* (*CARDS*) carreau *m*

diaper ['daɪəpə'] (*US*) *n* couche *f*

diaphragm ['daɪəfræm] *n* diaphragme *m*

diarrhoea [daɪə'riːə] (*US* **diarrhea**) *n* diarrhée *f*

diary ['daɪərɪ] *n* (*daily account*) journal *m*; (*book*) agenda *m*

dice [daɪs] *n inv* dé *m* ♦ *vt* (*CULIN*) couper en dés or en cubes

dictate [dɪk'teɪt] *vt* dicter; **dictation** *n* dictée *f*

dictator [dɪk'teɪtə'] *n* dictateur *m*; **~ship** *n* dictature *f*

dictionary ['dɪkʃənrɪ] *n* dictionnaire *m*

did [dɪd] *pt of* do; **~n't** = **did not**

die [daɪ] *vi* mourir; **to be dying for sth** avoir une envie folle de qch; **to be dying to do sth** mourir d'envie de faire qch; **~ away** *vi* s'éteindre; **~ down** *vi* se calmer, s'apaiser; **~ out** *vi* disparaître

diesel ['diːzl] *n* (*vehicle*) diesel *m*; (*also:* **~ oil**) carburant *m* diesel, gas-oil *m*; **~ engine** *n* moteur *m* diesel

diet ['daɪət] *n* alimentation *f*; (*restricted food*) régime *m* ♦ *vi* (*also:* **be on a ~**) suivre un régime

differ ['dɪfə'] *vi* (*be different*): **to ~ (from)** être différent (de); différer (de); (*disagree*): **to ~ (from sb over sth)** ne pas être d'accord (avec qn au sujet de qch); **~ence** *n* différence *f*; (*quarrel*) différend *m*, désaccord *m*; **~ent** *adj* différent(e); **~entiate** [dɪfə'renʃɪeɪt] *vi*: **to ~entiate (between)** faire une différence (entre)

difficult ['dɪfɪkəlt] *adj* difficile; **~y** *n* difficulté *f*

diffident ['dɪfɪdənt] *adj* qui manque de confiance or d'assurance

dig [dɪg] (*pt, pp dug*) *vt* (*hole*) creuser; (*garden*) bêcher ♦ *n* (*prod*) coup *m* de coude; (*fig*) coup de griffe or de patte; (*archeological*) fouilles *fpl*; **~ in** *vi* (*MIL: also:* **~ o.s. in**) se retrancher; **~ into** *vt fus* (*savings*) puiser dans; **to ~ one's nails into sth** enfoncer ses ongles dans qch; **~ up** *vt* déterrer

digest [*vb* daɪ'dʒest, *n* 'daɪdʒest] *vt* digérer ♦ *n* sommaire *m*, résumé *m*; **~ion** [dɪ'dʒestʃən] *n* digestion *f*

digit ['dɪdʒɪt] *n* (*number*) chiffre *m*; (*finger*) doigt *m*; **~al** *adj* digital(e), à affichage

numérique *or* digital; **~al computer** calculateur *m* numérique; **~al TV** *n* télévision *f* numérique; **~al watch** montre *f* à affichage numérique

dignified ['dɪgnɪfaɪd] *adj* digne

dignity ['dɪgnɪtɪ] *n* dignité *f*

digress [daɪ'gres] *vi*: **to ~ from** s'écarter de, s'éloigner de

digs [dɪgz] (*BRIT: inf*) *npl* piaule *f*, chambre meublée

dilapidated [dɪ'læpɪdeɪtɪd] *adj* délabré(e)

dilemma [daɪ'lemə] *n* dilemme *m*

diligent ['dɪlɪdʒənt] *adj* appliqué(e), assidu(e)

dilute [daɪ'luːt] *vt* diluer

dim [dɪm] *adj* (*light*) faible; (*memory, outline*) vague, indécis(e); (*figure*) vague, indistinct(e); (*room*) sombre; (*stupid*) borné(e), obtus(e) ♦ *vt* (*light*) réduire, baisser; (*US: AUT*) mettre en code

dime [daɪm] (*US*) *n* = **10 cents**

dimension [daɪ'menʃən] *n* dimension *f*

diminish [dɪ'mɪnɪʃ] *vt, vi* diminuer

diminutive [dɪ'mɪnjutɪv] *adj* minuscule, tout(e) petit(e)

dimmers ['dɪməz] (*US*) *npl* (*AUT*) phares *mpl* code *inv*; feux *mpl* de position

dimple ['dɪmpl] *n* fossette *f*

din [dɪn] *n* vacarme *m*

dine [daɪn] *vi* dîner; **~r** *n* (*person*) dîneur(-euse); (*US: restaurant*) petit restaurant

dinghy ['dɪŋgɪ] *n* youyou *m*; (*also:* **rubber ~**) canot *m* pneumatique; (*also:* **sailing ~**) voilier *m*, dériveur *m*

dingy ['dɪndʒɪ] *adj* miteux(-euse), minable

dining car (*BRIT*) *n* wagon-restaurant *m*

dining room *n* salle *f* à manger

dinner ['dɪnə'] *n* dîner *m*; (*lunch*) déjeuner *m*; (*public*) banquet *m*; **~ jacket** *n* smoking *m*; **~ party** *n* dîner *m*; **~ time** *n* heure *f* du dîner; (*midday*) heure du déjeuner

dinosaur ['daɪnəsɔː'] *n* dinosaure *m*

dip [dɪp] *n* déclivité *f*; (*in sea*) baignade *f*, bain *m*; (*CULIN*) ≈ sauce *f* ♦ *vt* tremper, plonger; (*BRIT: AUT: lights*) mettre en code, baisser ♦ *vi* plonger

diploma [dɪ'pləumə] *n* diplôme *m*

diplomacy [dɪ'pləuməsɪ] *n* diplomatie *f*

diplomat ['dɪpləmæt] *n* diplomate *m*; **~ic** [dɪplə'mætɪk] *adj* diplomatique

dipstick ['dɪpstɪk] *n* (*AUT*) jauge *f* de niveau d'huile

dipswitch ['dɪpswɪtʃ] (*BRIT*) *n* (*AUT*) interrupteur *m* de lumière réduite

dire [daɪə'] *adj* terrible, extrême, affreux(-euse)

direct [daɪ'rekt] *adj* direct(e) ♦ *vt* diriger, orienter; (*letter, remark*) adresser; (*film, programme*) réaliser; (*play*) mettre en scène; (*order*): **to ~ sb to do sth** ordonner à qn de

faire qch ♦ adv directement; **can you ~ me to
...?** pouvez-vous m'indiquer le chemin de ...?;
~ debit (BRIT) n prélèvement m automatique
direction [dɪˈrɛkʃən] n direction f; **~s** npl
(advice) indications fpl; **sense of ~** sens m de
l'orientation; **~s for use** mode m d'emploi
directly [dɪˈrɛktlɪ] adv (in a straight line)
directement, tout droit; (at once) tout de
suite, immédiatement
director [dɪˈrɛktəʳ] n directeur m; (THEATRE)
metteur m en scène; (CINEMA, TV)
réalisateur(-trice)
directory [dɪˈrɛktərɪ] n annuaire m; (COMPUT)
répertoire m; **~ enquiries** (US **directory
assistance**) n renseignements mpl
dirt [dɜːt] n saleté f; crasse f; (earth) terre f,
boue f; **~-cheap** adj très bon marché inv;
~y adj sale ♦ vt salir; **~y trick** coup tordu
disability [dɪsəˈbɪlɪtɪ] n invalidité f, infirmité f
disabled [dɪsˈeɪbld] adj infirme, invalide
♦ npl: **the ~** les handicapés
disadvantage [dɪsədˈvɑːntɪdʒ] n
désavantage m, inconvénient m
disagree [dɪsəˈgriː] vi (be different) ne pas
concorder; (be against, think otherwise): **to
~ (with)** ne pas être d'accord (avec); **~able**
adj désagréable; **~ment** n désaccord m,
différend m
disallow [ˈdɪsəˈlaʊ] vt rejeter
disappear [dɪsəˈpɪəʳ] vi disparaître; **~ance** n
disparition f
disappoint [dɪsəˈpɔɪnt] vt décevoir; **~ed** adj
déçu(e); **~ing** adj décevant(e); **~ment** n
déception f
disapproval [dɪsəˈpruːvəl] n désapprobation
f
disapprove [dɪsəˈpruːv] vi: **to ~ (of)**
désapprouver
disarmament [dɪsˈɑːməmənt] n
désarmement m
disarray [dɪsəˈreɪ] n: **in ~** (army) en déroute;
(organization) en désarroi; (hair, clothes) en
désordre
disaster [dɪˈzɑːstəʳ] n catastrophe f, désastre
m; **disastrous** adj désastreux(-euse)
disband [dɪsˈbænd] vt démobiliser; disperser
♦ vi se séparer; se disperser
disbelief [ˈdɪsbəˈliːf] n incrédulité f
disc [dɪsk] n disque m; (COMPUT) = **disk**
discard [dɪsˈkɑːd] vt (old things) se
débarrasser de; (fig) écarter, renoncer à
discern [dɪˈsɜːn] vt discerner, distinguer;
~ing adj perspicace
discharge [vb dɪsˈtʃɑːdʒ, n ˈdɪstʃɑːdʒ] vt
décharger; (duties) s'acquitter de; (patient)
renvoyer (chez lui); (employee) congédier,
licencier; (soldier) rendre à la vie civile,
réformer; (defendant) relaxer, élargir ♦ n
décharge f; (dismissal) renvoi m; licenciement

m; élargissement m; (MED) écoulement m
discipline [ˈdɪsɪplɪn] n discipline f
disc jockey n disc-jockey m
disclaim [dɪsˈkleɪm] vt nier
disclose [dɪsˈkləʊz] vt révéler, divulguer;
disclosure n révélation f
disco [ˈdɪskəʊ] n abbr = **discotheque**
discomfort [dɪsˈkʌmfət] n malaise m, gêne f;
(lack of comfort) manque m de confort
disconcert [dɪskənˈsɜːt] vt déconcerter
disconnect [dɪskəˈnɛkt] vt (ELEC, RADIO, pipe)
débrancher; (TEL, water) couper
discontent [dɪskənˈtɛnt] n mécontentement
m; **~ed** adj mécontent(e)
discontinue [dɪskənˈtɪnjuː] vt cesser,
interrompre; **"~d"** (COMM) "fin de série"
discord [ˈdɪskɔːd] n discorde f, dissension f;
(MUS) dissonance f
discotheque [ˈdɪskəʊtɛk] n discothèque f
discount [n ˈdɪskaʊnt, vb dɪsˈkaʊnt] n remise
f, rabais m ♦ vt (sum) faire une remise de;
(fig) ne pas tenir compte de
discourage [dɪsˈkʌrɪdʒ] vt décourager
discover [dɪsˈkʌvəʳ] vt découvrir; **~y** n
découverte f
discredit [dɪsˈkrɛdɪt] vt (idea) mettre en
doute; (person) discréditer
discreet [dɪsˈkriːt] adj discret(-ète)
discrepancy [dɪsˈkrɛpənsɪ] n divergence f,
contradiction f
discretion [dɪsˈkrɛʃən] n discrétion f; **use
your own ~** à vous de juger
discriminate [dɪsˈkrɪmɪneɪt] vi: **to
~ between** établir une distinction entre, faire
la différence entre; **to ~ against** pratiquer une
discrimination contre; **discriminating** adj
qui a du discernement; **discrimination**
[dɪskrɪmɪˈneɪʃən] n discrimination f;
(judgment) discernement m
discuss [dɪsˈkʌs] vt discuter de; (debate)
discuter; **~ion** n discussion f
disdain [dɪsˈdeɪn] n dédain m
disease [dɪˈziːz] n maladie f
disembark [dɪsɪmˈbɑːk] vi débarquer
disentangle [dɪsɪnˈtæŋgl] vt (wool, wire)
démêler, débrouiller; (from wreckage)
dégager
disfigure [dɪsˈfɪgəʳ] vt défigurer
disgrace [dɪsˈgreɪs] n honte f; (disfavour)
disgrâce f ♦ vt déshonorer, couvrir de honte;
~ful adj scandaleux(-euse), honteux(-euse)
disgruntled [dɪsˈgrʌntld] adj mécontent(e)
disguise [dɪsˈgaɪz] n déguisement m ♦ vt
déguiser; **in ~** déguisé(e)
disgust [dɪsˈgʌst] n dégoût m, aversion f ♦ vt
dégoûter, écœurer; **~ing** adj dégoûtant(e);
révoltant(e)
dish [dɪʃ] n plat m; **to do** or **wash the ~es** faire
la vaisselle; **~ out** vt servir, distribuer; **~ up**

vt servir; **~cloth** *n* (*for washing*) lavette *f*

dishearten [dɪs'hɑːtn] *vt* décourager

dishevelled [dɪ'ʃevəld] (*US* **disheveled**) *adj* ébouriffé(e); décoiffé(e); débraillé(e)

dishonest [dɪs'ɔnɪst] *adj* malhonnête

dishonour [dɪs'ɔnər] (*US* **dishonor**) *n* déshonneur *m*; **~able** *adj* (*behaviour*) déshonorant(e); (*person*) peu honorable

dishtowel ['dɪʃtauəl] (*US*) *n* torchon *m*

dishwasher ['dɪʃwɔʃər] *n* lave-vaisselle *m*

disillusion [dɪsɪ'luːʒən] *vt* désabuser, désillusionner

disinfect [dɪsɪn'fekt] *vt* désinfecter; **~ant** *n* désinfectant *m*

disintegrate [dɪs'ɪntɪgreɪt] *vi* se désintégrer

disinterested [dɪs'ɪntrəstɪd] *adj* désintéressé(e)

disjointed [dɪs'dʒɔɪntɪd] *adj* décousu(e), incohérent(e)

disk [dɪsk] *n* (*COMPUT*) disque *m*; (: *floppy ~*) disquette *f*; **single-/double-sided ~** simple/double face; **~ drive** *n* lecteur *m* de disquettes; **~ette** [dɪs'ket] *n* disquette *f*, disque *m* souple

dislike [dɪs'laɪk] *n* aversion *f*, antipathie *f* ♦ *vt* ne pas aimer

dislocate ['dɪsləkeɪt] *vt* disloquer; déboîter

dislodge [dɪs'lɔdʒ] *vt* déplacer, faire bouger

disloyal [dɪs'lɔɪəl] *adj* déloyal(e)

dismal ['dɪzml] *adj* lugubre, maussade

dismantle [dɪs'mæntl] *vt* démonter

dismay [dɪs'meɪ] *n* consternation *f*

dismiss [dɪs'mɪs] *vt* congédier, renvoyer; (*soldiers*) faire rompre les rangs à; (*idea*) écarter; (*LAW*): **to ~ a case** rendre une fin de non-recevoir; **~al** *n* renvoi *m*

dismount [dɪs'maunt] *vi* mettre pied à terre, descendre

disobedient [dɪsə'biːdɪənt] *adj* désobéissant(e)

disobey [dɪsə'beɪ] *vt* désobéir à

disorder [dɪs'ɔːdər] *n* désordre *m*; (*rioting*) désordres *mpl*; (*MED*) troubles *mpl*; **~ly** *adj* en désordre; désordonné(e)

disorientated [dɪs'ɔːrɪenteɪtɪd] *adj* désorienté(e)

disown [dɪs'əun] *vt* renier

disparaging [dɪs'pærɪdʒɪŋ] *adj* désobligeant(e)

dispassionate [dɪs'pæʃənət] *adj* calme, froid(e); impartial(e), objectif(-ive)

dispatch [dɪs'pætʃ] *vt* expédier, envoyer ♦ *n* envoi *m*, expédition *f*; (*MIL, PRESS*) dépêche *f*

dispel [dɪs'pel] *vt* dissiper, chasser

dispense [dɪs'pens] *vt* distribuer, administrer; **~ with** *vt fus* se passer de; **~r** *n* (*machine*) distributeur *m*; **dispensing chemist** (*BRIT*) *n* pharmacie *f*

disperse [dɪs'pəːs] *vt* disperser ♦ *vi* se disperser

dispirited [dɪs'pɪrɪtɪd] *adj* découragé(e), déprimé(e)

displace [dɪs'pleɪs] *vt* déplacer

display [dɪs'pleɪ] *n* étalage *m*; déploiement *m*; affichage *m*; (*screen*) écran *m*, visuel *m*; (*of feeling*) manifestation *f* ♦ *vt* montrer; (*goods*) mettre à l'étalage, exposer; (*results, departure times*) afficher; (*pej*) faire étalage de

displease [dɪs'pliːz] *vt* mécontenter, contrarier; **~d** *adj*: **~d with** mécontent(e) de; **displeasure** [dɪs'pleʒər] *n* mécontentement *m*

disposable [dɪs'pəuzəbl] *adj* (*pack etc*) jetable, à jeter; (*income*) disponible; **~ nappy** (*BRIT*) *n* couche *f* à jeter, couche-culotte *f*

disposal [dɪs'pəuzl] *n* (*of goods for sale*) vente *f*; (*of property*) disposition *f*, cession *f*; (*of rubbish*) enlèvement *m*; destruction *f*; **at one's ~** à sa disposition

dispose [dɪs'pəuz] *vt* disposer; **~ of** *vt fus* (*unwanted goods etc*) se débarrasser de, se défaire de; (*problem*) expédier; **to be ~d to do sth** être disposé(e) à faire qch; **disposition** [dɪspə'zɪʃən] *n* disposition *f*; (*temperament*) naturel *m*

disprove [dɪs'pruːv] *vt* réfuter

dispute [dɪs'pjuːt] *n* discussion *f*; (*also:* **industrial ~**) conflit *m* ♦ *vt* contester; (*matter*) discuter; (*victory*) disputer

disqualify [dɪs'kwɔlɪfaɪ] *vt* (*SPORT*) disqualifier; **to ~ sb for sth/from doing** rendre qn inapte à qch/à faire

disquiet [dɪs'kwaɪət] *n* inquiétude *f*, trouble *m*

disregard [dɪsrɪ'gɑːd] *vt* ne pas tenir compte de

disrepair ['dɪsrɪ'peər] *n*: **to fall into ~** (*building*) tomber en ruine

disreputable [dɪs'repjutəbl] *adj* (*person*) de mauvaise réputation; (*behaviour*) déshonorant(e)

disrespectful [dɪsrɪ'spektful] *adj* irrespectueux(-euse)

disrupt [dɪs'rʌpt] *vt* (*plans*) déranger; (*conversation*) interrompre

dissatisfied [dɪs'sætɪsfaɪd] *adj*: **~ (with)** insatisfait(e) (de)

dissect [dɪ'sekt] *vt* disséquer

dissent [dɪ'sent] *n* dissentiment *m*, différence *f* d'opinion

dissertation [dɪsə'teɪʃən] *n* mémoire *m*

disservice [dɪs'səːvɪs] *n*: **to do sb a ~** rendre un mauvais service à qn

dissimilar [dɪ'sɪmɪlər] *adj*: **~ (to)** dissemblable (à), différent(e) (de)

dissipate ['dɪsɪpeɪt] *vt* dissiper; (*money, efforts*) disperser

dissolute ['dɪsəluːt] *adj* débauché(e), dissolu(e)

dissolve [dɪ'zɔlv] *vt* dissoudre ♦ *vi* se dissoudre, fondre; **to ~ in(to) tears** fondre en larmes

distance ['dɪstns] *n* distance *f*; **in the ~** au loin

distant ['dɪstnt] *adj* lointain(e), éloigné(e); (*manner*) distant(e), froid(e)

distaste [dɪs'teɪst] *n* dégoût *m*; **~ful** *adj* déplaisant(e), désagréable

distended [dɪs'tɛndɪd] *adj* (*stomach*) dilaté(e)

distil [dɪs'tɪl] (*US* **distill**) *vt* distiller; **~lery** *n* distillerie *f*

distinct [dɪs'tɪŋkt] *adj* distinct(e); (*clear*) marqué(e); **as ~ from** par opposition à; **~ion** *n* distinction *f*; (*in exam*) mention *f* très bien; **~ive** *adj* distinctif(-ive)

distinguish [dɪs'tɪŋgwɪʃ] *vt* distinguer; **~ed** *adj* (*eminent*) distingué(e); **~ing** *adj* (*feature*) distinctif(-ive), caractéristique

distort [dɪs'tɔːt] *vt* déformer

distract [dɪs'trækt] *vt* distraire, déranger; **~ed** *adj* distrait(e); (*anxious*) éperdu(e), égaré(e); **~ion** *n* distraction *f*; égarement *m*

distraught [dɪs'trɔːt] *adj* éperdu(e)

distress [dɪs'trɛs] *n* détresse *f* ♦ *vt* affliger; **~ing** *adj* douloureux(-euse), pénible

distribute [dɪs'trɪbjuːt] *vt* distribuer; **distribution** [dɪstrɪ'bjuːʃən] *n* distribution *f*; **distributor** *n* distributeur *m*

district ['dɪstrɪkt] *n* (*of country*) région *f*; (*of town*) quartier *m*; (*ADMIN*) district *m*; **~ attorney** (*US*) *n* ≈ procureur *m* de la République; **~ nurse** (*BRIT*) *n* infirmière visiteuse

distrust [dɪs'trʌst] *n* méfiance *f* ♦ *vt* se méfier de

disturb [dɪs'tɜːb] *vt* troubler; (*inconvenience*) déranger; **~ance** *n* dérangement *m*; (*violent event, political etc*) troubles *mpl*; **~ed** *adj* (*worried, upset*) agité(e), troublé(e); **to be emotionally ~ed** avoir des problèmes affectifs; **~ing** *adj* troublant(e), inquiétant(e)

disuse [dɪs'juːs] *n*: **to fall into ~** tomber en désuétude; **~d** [dɪs'juːzd] *adj* désaffecté(e)

ditch [dɪtʃ] *n* fossé *m*; (*irrigation*) rigole *f* ♦ *vt* (*inf*) abandonner; (*person*) plaquer

dither ['dɪðə*] *vi* hésiter

ditto ['dɪtəu] *adv* idem

dive [daɪv] *n* plongeon *m*; (*of submarine*) plongée *f* ♦ *vi* plonger; **to ~ into** (*bag, drawer etc*) plonger la main dans; (*shop, car etc*) se précipiter dans; **~r** *n* plongeur *m*

diversion [daɪ'vɜːʃən] *n* (*BRIT: AUT*) déviation *f*; (*distraction, MIL*) diversion *f*

divert [daɪ'vɜːt] *vt* (*funds, BRIT: traffic*) dévier; (*river, attention*) détourner

divide [dɪ'vaɪd] *vt* diviser; (*separate*) séparer ♦ *vi* se diviser; **~d highway** (*US*) *n* route *f* à quatre voies

dividend ['dɪvɪdɛnd] *n* dividende *m*

divine [dɪ'vaɪn] *adj* divin(e)

diving ['daɪvɪŋ] *n* plongée (sous-marine); **~ board** *n* plongeoir *m*

divinity [dɪ'vɪnɪtɪ] *n* divinité *f*; (*SCOL*) théologie *f*

division [dɪ'vɪʒən] *n* division *f*

divorce [dɪ'vɔːs] *n* divorce *m* ♦ *vt* divorcer d'avec; (*dissociate*) séparer; **~d** *adj* divorcé(e); **~e** *n* divorcé(e)

D.I.Y. (*BRIT*) *n abbr* = **do-it-yourself**

dizzy ['dɪzɪ] *adj*: **to make sb ~** donner le vertige à qn; **to feel ~** avoir la tête qui tourne

DJ *n abbr* = **disc jockey**

DNA fingerprinting [-'fɪŋgəprɪntɪŋ] *n* technique *f* des empreintes génétiques

---

┌─────────────┐
│ KEYWORD   │
└─────────────┘

do [duː] (*pt* **did**, *pp* **done**) *n* (*inf: party etc*) soirée *f*, fête *f*

♦ *vb* **1** (*in negative constructions*) non traduit; **I don't understand** je ne comprends pas

2 (*to form questions*) non traduit; **didn't you know?** vous ne le saviez pas?; **why didn't you come?** pourquoi n'êtes-vous pas venu?

3 (*for emphasis, in polite expressions*): **she does seem rather late** je trouve qu'elle est bien en retard; **do sit down/help yourself** asseyez-vous/servez-vous je vous en prie

4 (*used to avoid repeating vb*): **she swims better than I do** elle nage mieux que moi; **do you agree? - yes, I do/no, I don't** vous êtes d'accord? - oui/non; **she lives in Glasgow - so do I** elle habite Glasgow - moi aussi; **who broke it? - I did** qui l'a cassé? - c'est moi

5 (*in question tags*): **he laughed, didn't he?** il a ri, n'est-ce pas?; **I don't know him, do I?** je ne crois pas le connaître

♦ *vt* (*gen: carry out, perform etc*) faire; **what are you doing tonight?** qu'est-ce que vous faites ce soir?; **to do the cooking/washing-up** faire la cuisine/la vaisselle; **to do one's teeth/hair/nails** se brosser les dents/se coiffer/se faire les ongles; **the car was doing 100** ≈ la voiture faisait du 160 (à l'heure)

♦ *vi* **1** (*act, behave*) faire; **do as I do** faites comme moi

2 (*get on, fare*) marcher; **the firm is doing well** l'entreprise marche bien; **how do you do?** comment allez-vous?; (*on being introduced*) enchanté(e)!

3 (*suit*) aller; **will it do?** est-ce que ça ira?

4 (*be sufficient*) suffire, aller; **will £10 do?** est-ce que 10 livres suffiront?; **that'll do** ça suffit, ça ira; **that'll do!** (*in annoyance*) ça va *or* suffit comme ça!; **to make do (with)** se contenter (de)

do away with vt fus supprimer

do up vt (laces, dress) attacher; (buttons) boutonner; (zip) fermer; (renovate: room) refaire; (: house) remettre à neuf

do with vt fus (need): **I could do with a drink/some help** quelque chose à boire/un peu d'aide ne serait pas de refus; (be connected): **that has nothing to do with you** cela ne vous concerne pas; **I won't have anything to do with it** je ne veux pas m'en mêler

do without vi s'en passer ♦ vt fus se passer de

dock [dɔk] n dock m; (LAW) banc m des accusés ♦ vi se mettre à quai; (SPACE) s'arrimer; **~er** n docker m; **~yard** n chantier m de construction navale

doctor ['dɔktər] n médecin m, docteur m; (PhD etc) docteur ♦ vt (drink) frelater; **D~ of Philosophy** n (degree) doctorat m; (person) Docteur m en Droit or Lettres etc, titulaire m/f d'un doctorat

document ['dɔkjumənt] n document m; **~ary** [dɔkju'mentərɪ] adj documentaire ♦ n documentaire m

dodge [dɔdʒ] n truc m; combine f ♦ vt esquiver, éviter

dodgems ['dɔdʒəmz] (BRIT) npl autos tamponneuses

doe [dəu] n (deer) biche f; (rabbit) lapine f

does [dʌz] vb see do; **~n't** = does not

dog [dɔg] n chien(ne) ♦ vt suivre de près; poursuivre, harceler; **~ collar** n collier m de chien; (fig) faux-col m d'ecclésiastique; **~-eared** adj corné(e); **~ged** ['dɔgɪd] adj obstiné(e), opiniâtre; **~sbody** n bonne f à tout faire, tâcheron m

doings ['duːɪŋz] npl activités fpl

do-it-yourself ['duːɪtjɔː'self] n bricolage m

doldrums ['dɔldrəmz] npl: **to be in the ~** avoir le cafard; (business) être dans le marasme

dole [dəul] n (BRIT: payment) allocation f de chômage; **on the ~** au chômage; **~ out** vt donner au compte-goutte

doll [dɔl] n poupée f

dollar ['dɔlər] n dollar m

dolled up [dɔld-] (inf) adj: **(all) ~** sur son trente et un

dolphin ['dɔlfɪn] n dauphin m

dome [dəum] n dôme m

domestic [də'mestɪk] adj (task, appliances) ménager(-ère); (of country: trade, situation etc) intérieur(e); (animal) domestique; **~ated** (animal) domestiqué(e); (husband) pantouflard(e)

dominate ['dɔmɪneɪt] vt dominer

domineering [dɔmɪ'nɪərɪŋ] adj dominateur(-trice), autoritaire

dominion [də'mɪnɪən] n (territory) territoire m; **to have ~ over** contrôler

domino ['dɔmɪnəu] (pl **~es**) n domino m; **~es** n (game) dominos mpl

don [dɔn] (BRIT) n professeur m d'université

donate [də'neɪt] vt faire don de, donner

done [dʌn] pp of do

donkey ['dɔŋkɪ] n âne m

donor ['dəunər] n (of blood etc) donneur(-euse); (to charity) donateur(-trice); **~ card** n carte f de don d'organes

don't [dəunt] vb = do not

donut ['dəunʌt] (US) n = doughnut

doodle ['duːdl] vi griffonner, gribouiller

doom [duːm] n destin m ♦ vt: **to be ~ed (to failure)** être voué(e) à l'échec

door [dɔːr] n porte f; (RAIL, car) portière f; **~bell** n sonnette f; **~handle** n poignée f de la porte; (car) poignée de portière; **~man** (irreg) n (in hotel) portier m; **~mat** n paillasson m; **~step** n pas m de (la) porte, seuil m; **~way** n (embrasure f de la) porte f

dope [dəup] n (inf: drug) drogue f; (: person) andouille f ♦ vt (horse etc) doper

dormant ['dɔːmənt] adj assoupi(e), en veilleuse

dormitory ['dɔːmɪtrɪ] n dortoir m; (US: building) résidence f universitaire

dormouse ['dɔːmaus] (pl dormice) n loir m

DOS [dɔs] n abbr (= disk operating system) DOS

dose [dəus] n dose f

dosh [dɔʃ] (inf) n fric m

doss house ['dɔs-] (BRIT) n asile m de nuit

dot [dɔt] n point m; (on material) pois m ♦ vt: **~ted with** parsemé(e) de; **on the ~** à l'heure tapante or pile; **~ted line** n pointillé(s) m(pl)

double ['dʌbl] adj double ♦ adv (twice): **to cost ~ (sth)** coûter le double (de qch) or deux fois plus (que qch) ♦ n double m ♦ vt doubler; (fold) plier en deux ♦ vi doubler; **~s** n (TENNIS) double m; **on** or (BRIT) **at the ~** au pas de course; **~ bass** (BRIT) n contrebasse f; **~ bed** n grand lit; **~ bend** (BRIT) n virage m en S; **~-breasted** adj croisé(e); **~-cross** vt doubler, trahir; **~-decker** n autobus m à impériale; **~ glazing** (BRIT) n double vitrage m; **~ room** n chambre f pour deux personnes; **doubly** adv doublement, deux fois plus

doubt [daut] n doute m ♦ vt douter de; **to ~ that** douter que; **~ful** adj douteux(-euse); (person) incertain(e); **~less** adv sans doute, sûrement

dough [dəu] n pâte f; **~nut** (US donut) n beignet m

dove [dʌv] n colombe f

Dover ['dəuvəʳ] n Douvres
dovetail ['dʌvteɪl] vi (fig) concorder
dowdy ['daudɪ] adj démodé(e); mal
fagoté(e) (inf)
down [daun] n (soft feathers) duvet m ♦ adv
en bas, vers le bas; (on the ground) par terre
♦ prep en bas de; (along) le long de ♦ vt (inf:
drink, food) s'envoyer; ~ **with X!** à bas X!; ~-
and-out n clochard(e); ~-**at-heel** adj
éculé(e); (fig) miteux(-euse); ~**cast** adj
démoralisé(e); ~**fall** n chute f; ruine f;
~**hearted** adj découragé(e); ~**hill** adv: **to
go** ~**hill** descendre; (fig) péricliter;
~ **payment** n acompte m; ~**pour** n pluie
torrentielle, déluge m; ~**right** adj (lie etc)
effronté(e); (refusal) catégorique; ~**size** vt
(ECON) réduire ses effectifs
Down's syndrome [daunz-] n (MED)
trisomie f
down: ~**stairs** adv au rez-de-chaussée; à
l'étage inférieur; ~**stream** adv en aval; ~-
to-earth adj terre à terre inv; ~**town** adv en
ville; ~ **under** adv en Australie/Nouvelle-
Zélande; ~**ward** adj, adv vers le bas;
~**wards** adv vers le bas
dowry ['dauri] n dot f
doz. abbr = dozen
doze [dauz] vi sommeiller; ~ **off** vi s'assoupir
dozen ['dʌzn] n douzaine f; **a** ~ **books** une
douzaine de livres; ~**s of** des centaines de
Dr. abbr = doctor; doctor
drab [dræb] adj terne, morne
draft [drɑ:ft] n ébauche f; (of letter, essay etc)
brouillon m; (COMM) traite f; (US: call-up)
conscription f ♦ vt faire le brouillon d'un
projet de; (MIL: send) détacher; see also
draught
draftsman ['drɑ:ftsmən] (irreg) (US) n
= draughtsman
drag [dræg] vt traîner; (river) draguer ♦ vi
traîner ♦ n (inf) casse-pieds m/f; (women's
clothing): **in** ~ (en) travesti; ~ **on** vi
s'éterniser
dragon ['drægn] n dragon m
dragonfly ['drægənflaɪ] n libellule f
drain [dreɪn] n égout m, canalisation f; (on
resources) saignée f ♦ vt (land, marshes etc)
drainer, assécher; (vegetables) égoutter;
(glass) vider ♦ vi (water) s'écouler; ~**age**
n drainage m; système m d'égouts or de
canalisations; ~**ing board** (US **drain board**) n
égouttoir m; ~**pipe** n tuyau m d'écoulement
drama ['drɑ:mə] n (art) théâtre m, art m
dramatique; (play) pièce f (de théâtre);
(event) drame m; ~**tic** [drə'mætɪk] adj
dramatique; spectaculaire; ~**tist** ['dræmətɪst]
n auteur m dramatique; ~**tize** ['dræmətaɪz] vt
(events) dramatiser; (adapt: for TV/cinema)
adapter pour la télévision/pour l'écran

drank [dræŋk] pt of **drink**
drape [dreɪp] vt draper; ~**s** (US) npl rideaux
mpl
drastic ['dræstɪk] adj sévère; énergique;
(change) radical(e)
draught [drɑ:ft] (US **draft**) n courant m d'air;
(NAUT) tirant m d'eau; **on** ~ (beer) à la
pression; ~**board** (BRIT) n damier m; ~**s**
(BRIT) n (jeu m de) dames fpl
draughtsman ['drɑ:ftsmən] (irreg) n
dessinateur(-trice) (industriel(le))
draw [drɔ:] (pt **drew**, pp **drawn**) vt tirer;
(tooth) arracher, extraire; (attract) attirer;
(picture) dessiner; (line, circle) tracer; (money)
retirer; (wages) toucher ♦ vi (SPORT) faire
match nul ♦ n match nul; (lottery) tirage m
au sort; loterie f; **to** ~ **near** s'approcher;
approcher; ~ **out** vi (lengthen) s'allonger ♦ vt
(money) retirer; ~ **up** vi (stop) s'arrêter ♦ vt
(chair) approcher; (document) établir,
dresser; ~**back** n inconvénient m,
désavantage m; ~**bridge** n pont-levis m
drawer [drɔ:ʳ] n tiroir m
drawing ['drɔ:ɪŋ] n dessin m; ~ **board** n
planche f à dessin; ~ **pin** (BRIT) n punaise f;
~ **room** n salon m
drawl [drɔ:l] n accent traînant
drawn [drɔ:n] pp of **draw**
dread [dred] n terreur f, effroi m ♦ vt
redouter, appréhender; ~**ful** adj
affreux(-euse)
dream [dri:m] (pt, pp **dreamed** or **dreamt**) n
rêve m ♦ vt, vi rêver; ~**y** adj rêveur(-euse);
(music) langoureux(-euse)
dreary ['drɪərɪ] adj morne; monotone
dredge [dredʒ] vt draguer
dregs [dregz] npl lie f
drench [drentʃ] vt tremper
dress [dres] n robe f; (no pl: clothing)
habillement m, tenue f ♦ vi s'habiller ♦ vt
habiller; (wound) panser; **to get** ~**ed**
s'habiller; ~ **up** vi s'habiller; (in fancy ~) se
déguiser; ~ **circle** (BRIT) n (THEATRE) premier
balcon; ~**er** n (furniture) vaisselier m; (: US)
coiffeuse f, commode f; ~**ing** n (MED)
pansement m; (CULIN) sauce f,
assaisonnement m; ~**ing gown** (BRIT) n robe
f de chambre; ~**ing room** n (THEATRE) loge f;
(SPORT) vestiaire m; ~**ing table** n coiffeuse f;
~**maker** n couturière f; ~ **rehearsal** n
(répétition) générale f
drew [dru:] pt of **draw**
dribble ['drɪbl] vi (baby) baver ♦ vt (ball)
dribbler
dried [draɪd] adj (fruit, beans) sec (sèche);
(eggs, milk) en poudre
drier ['draɪəʳ] n = **dryer**
drift [drɪft] n (of current etc) force f; direction
f, mouvement m; (of snow) rafale f; (: on

ground) congère f; *(general meaning)* sens (général) ♦ *vi (boat)* aller à la dérive, dériver; *(sand, snow)* s'amonceler, s'entasser; **~wood** *n* bois flotté

drill [drɪl] *n* perceuse f; *(~ bit)* foret *m*, mèche f; *(of dentist)* roulette f, fraise f; *(MIL)* exercice *m* ♦ *vt* percer; *(troops)* entraîner ♦ *vi (for oil)* faire un *or* des forage(s)

drink [drɪŋk] *(pt* **drank**, *pp* **drunk**) *n* boisson f; *(alcoholic)* verre *m* ♦ *vt, vi* boire; **to have a ~** boire quelque chose, boire un verre; **to have a ~ of water** un verre d'eau; **~er** *n* buveur(-euse); **~ing water** *n* eau f potable

drip [drɪp] *n* goutte f; *(MED)* goutte-à-goutte *m inv*, perfusion f ♦ *vi* tomber goutte à goutte; *(tap)* goutter; **~-dry** *adj (shirt)* sans repassage; **~ping** *n* graisse f (de rôti)

drive [draɪv] *(pt* **drove**, *pp* **driven**) *n* promenade f *or* trajet *m* en voiture; *(also: ~way)* allée f; *(energy)* dynamisme *m*, énergie f; *(push)* effort (concerté), campagne f; *(also: disk ~)* lecteur *m* de disquettes ♦ *vt* conduire; *(push)* chasser, pousser; *(TECH: motor, wheel)* faire fonctionner; entraîner; *(nail, stake etc)*: **to ~ sth into sth** enfoncer qch dans qch ♦ *vi (AUT: at controls)* conduire; *(: travel)* aller en voiture; **left-/right-hand ~** conduite f à gauche/droite; **to ~ sb mad** rendre qn fou (folle); **to ~ sb home/to the airport** reconduire qn chez lui/conduire qn à l'aéroport; **~-by shooting** *n* (tentative d')assassinat par coups de feu tirés d'un voiture

drivel ['drɪvl] *(inf) n* idioties *fpl*

driver ['draɪvəʳ] *n* conducteur(-trice); *(of taxi, bus)* chauffeur *m*; **~'s license** *(US) n* permis *m* de conduire

driveway ['draɪvweɪ] *n* allée f

driving ['draɪvɪŋ] *n* conduite f; **~ instructor** *n* moniteur *m* d'auto-école; **~ lesson** *n* leçon f de conduite; **~ licence** *(BRIT) n* permis *m* de conduire; **~ school** *n* auto-école f; **~ test** *n* examen *m* du permis de conduire

drizzle ['drɪzl] *n* bruine f, crachin *m*

drool [druːl] *vi* baver

droop [druːp] *vi (shoulders)* tomber; *(head)* pencher; *(flower)* pencher la tête

drop [drɔp] *n* goutte f; *(fall)* baisse f; *(also: parachute ~)* saut *m* ♦ *vt* laisser tomber; *(voice, eyes, price)* baisser; *(set down from car)* déposer ♦ *vi* tomber; **~s** *npl (MED)* gouttes; **~ off** *vi (sleep)* s'assoupir ♦ *vt (passenger)* déposer; **~ out** *vi (withdraw)* se retirer; *(student etc)* abandonner, décrocher; **~out** *n* marginal(e); **~per** *n* compte-gouttes *m inv*; **~pings** *npl* crottes *fpl*

drought [draut] *n* sécheresse f

drove [drəuv] *pt of* **drive**

drown [draun] *vt* noyer ♦ *vi* se noyer

drowsy ['drauzɪ] *adj* somnolent(e)

drug [drʌg] *n* médicament *m*; *(narcotic)* drogue f ♦ *vt* droguer; **to be on ~s** se droguer; **~ addict** *n* toxicomane *m/f*; **~gist** *(US) n* pharmacien(ne)-droguiste; **~store** *(US) n* pharmacie-droguerie f, drugstore *m*

drum [drʌm] *n* tambour *m*; *(for oil, petrol)* bidon *m*; **~s** *npl (kit)* batterie f; **~mer** *n* (joueur *m* de) tambour *m*

drunk [drʌŋk] *pp of* **drink** ♦ *adj* ivre, soûl(e) ♦ *n (also: ~ard)* ivrogne *m/f*; **~en** *adj (person)* ivre, soûl(e); *(rage, stupor)* ivrogne, d'ivrogne

dry [draɪ] *adj* sec (sèche); *(day)* sans pluie; *(humour)* pince-sans-rire *inv*; *(lake, riverbed, well)* à sec ♦ *vt* sécher; *(clothes)* faire sécher ♦ *vi* sécher; **~ up** *vi* tarir; **~-cleaner's** *n* teinturerie f; **~er** *n* séchoir *m*; *(spin-dryer)* essoreuse f; **~ness** *n* sécheresse f; **~ rot** *n* pourriture sèche *(du bois)*

DSS *n abbr (= Department of Social Security)* ≈ Sécurité sociale

DTP *n abbr (= desk-top publishing)* PAO f

dual ['djuəl] *adj* double; **~ carriageway** *(BRIT) n* route f à quatre voies *or* à chaussées séparées; **~-purpose** *adj* à double usage

dubbed [dʌbd] *adj (CINEMA)* doublé(e)

dubious ['djuːbɪəs] *adj* hésitant(e), incertain(e); *(reputation, company)* douteux(-euse)

duchess ['dʌtʃɪs] *n* duchesse f

duck [dʌk] *n* canard *m* ♦ *vi* se baisser vivement, baisser subitement la tête; **~ling** ['dʌklɪŋ] *n* caneton *m*

duct [dʌkt] *n* conduite f, canalisation f; *(ANAT)* conduit *m*

dud [dʌd] *n (object, tool)*: **it's a ~** c'est de la camelote, ça ne marche pas ♦ *adj*: **~ cheque** *(BRIT)* chèque sans provision

due [djuː] *adj* dû (due); *(expected)* attendu(e); *(fitting)* qui convient ♦ *n*: **to give sb his *(or her)* ~** être juste envers qn ♦ *adv*: **~ north** droit vers le nord; **~s** *npl (for club, union)* cotisation f; *(in harbour)* droits *mpl* (de port); **in ~ course** en temps utile *or* voulu; finalement; **to be ~ to** dû à; causé(e) par; **he's ~ to finish tomorrow** normalement il doit finir demain

duet [djuː'et] *n* duo *m*

duffel bag ['dʌfl-] *n* sac *m* marin

duffel coat *n* duffel-coat *m*

dug [dʌg] *pt, pp of* **dig**

duke [djuːk] *n* duc *m*

dull [dʌl] *adj* terne, morne; *(boring)* ennuyeux(-euse); *(sound, pain)* sourd(e); *(weather, day)* gris(e), maussade ♦ *vt (pain, grief)* atténuer; *(mind, senses)* engourdir

duly ['djuːlɪ] *adv (on time)* en temps voulu; *(as expected)* comme il se doit

dumb [dʌm] *adj* muet(te); *(stupid)* bête;

~founded adj sidéré(e)
dummy ['dʌmɪ] n (tailor's model) mannequin m; (mock-up) factice m, maquette f; (BRIT: for baby) tétine f ♦ adj faux (fausse), factice
dump [dʌmp] n (also: rubbish ~) décharge (publique); (pej) trou m ♦ vt (put down) déposer; déverser; (get rid of) se débarrasser de; (COMPUT: data) vider, transférer
dumpling ['dʌmplɪŋ] n boulette f (de pâte)
dumpy ['dʌmpɪ] adj boulot(te)
dunce [dʌns] n âne m, cancre m
dune [djuːn] n dune f
dung [dʌŋ] n fumier m
dungarees [dʌŋɡə'riːz] npl salopette f; bleu(s) m(pl)
dungeon ['dʌndʒən] n cachot m
duplex ['djuːpleks] (US) n maison jumelée; (apartment) duplex m
duplicate [n 'djuːplɪkət, vb 'djuːplɪkeɪt] n double m ♦ vt faire un double de; (on machine) polycopier; photocopier; **in ~** en deux exemplaires
durable ['djuərəbl] adj durable; (clothes, metal) résistant(e), solide
duration [djuə'reɪʃən] n durée f
during ['djuərɪŋ] prep pendant, au cours de
dusk [dʌsk] n crépuscule m
dust [dʌst] n poussière f ♦ vt (furniture) épousseter, essuyer; (cake etc) **to ~ with** saupoudrer de; **~bin** (BRIT) n poubelle f; **~er** n chiffon m; **~man** (BRIT) (irreg) n boueux m, éboueur m; **~y** adj poussiéreux(-euse)
Dutch [dʌtʃ] adj hollandais(e), néerlandais(e) ♦ n (LING) hollandais m ♦ adv (inf): **to go ~** partager les frais; **the ~** npl (people) les Hollandais; **~man** (irreg) n Hollandais; **~woman** (irreg) n Hollandaise f
duty ['djuːtɪ] n devoir m; (tax) droit m, taxe f; **on ~** de service; (at night etc) de garde; **off ~** libre, pas de service or de garde; **~-free** adj exempté(e) de douane, hors taxe inv
duvet ['duːveɪ] (BRIT) n couette f
dwarf [dwɔːf] (pl dwarves) n nain(e) ♦ vt écraser
dwell [dwel] (pt, pp dwelt) vi demeurer; **~ on** vt fus s'appesantir sur
dwindle ['dwɪndl] vi diminuer, décroître
dye [daɪ] n teinture f ♦ vt teindre
dying ['daɪɪŋ] adj mourant(e), agonisant(e)
dyke [daɪk] (BRIT) n digue f
dynamic [daɪ'næmɪk] adj dynamique
dynamite ['daɪnəmaɪt] n dynamite f
dynamo ['daɪnəməu] n dynamo f
dyslexia [dɪs'leksɪə] n dyslexie f

E, e

E [iː] n (MUS) mi m
each [iːtʃ] adj chaque ♦ pron chacun(e); **~ other** l'un(e) l'autre; **they hate ~ other** ils se détestent (mutuellement); **you are jealous of ~ other** vous êtes jaloux l'un de l'autre; **they have 2 books ~** ils ont 2 livres chacun
eager ['iːɡər] adj (keen) avide; **to be ~ to do sth** avoir très envie de faire qch; **to be ~ for** désirer vivement, être avide de
eagle ['iːɡl] n aigle m
ear [ɪər] n oreille f; (of corn) épi m; **~ache** n mal m aux oreilles; **~drum** n tympan m
earl [əːl] (BRIT) n comte m
earlier ['əːlɪər] adj (date etc) plus rapproché(e); (edition, fashion etc) plus ancien(ne), antérieur(e) ♦ adv plus tôt
early ['əːlɪ] adv très tôt, de bonne heure; (ahead of time) en avance; (near the beginning) au début ♦ adj qui se manifeste (or se fait) tôt or de bonne heure; (work) de jeunesse; (settler, Christian) premier(-ère); (reply) rapide; (death) prématuré(e); **to have an ~ night** se coucher tôt or de bonne heure; **in the ~** or **~ in the spring/19th century** au début du printemps/19ème siècle; **~ retirement** n: **to take ~ retirement** prendre sa retraite anticipée
earmark ['ɪəmɑːk] vt: **to ~ sth for** réserver or destiner qch à
earn [əːn] vt gagner; (COMM: yield) rapporter
earnest ['əːnɪst] adj sérieux(-euse); **in ~** ♦ adv sérieusement
earnings ['əːnɪŋz] npl salaire m; (of company) bénéfices mpl
ear: **~phones** npl écouteurs mpl; **~ring** n boucle f d'oreille; **~shot** n: **within ~shot** à portée de voix
earth [əːθ] n (gen, also BRIT: ELEC) terre f ♦ vt relier à la terre; **~enware** n poterie f; faïence f; **~quake** n tremblement m de terre, séisme m; **~y** adj (vulgar: humour) truculent(e)
ease [iːz] n facilité f, aisance f; (comfort) bien-être m ♦ vt (soothe) calmer; (loosen) relâcher, détendre; **to ~ sth in/out** faire pénétrer/sortir qch délicatement or avec douceur; faciliter la pénétration/la sortie de qch; **at ~!** (MIL) repos!; **~ off** or **up** vi diminuer; (slow down) ralentir
easel ['iːzl] n chevalet m
easily ['iːzɪlɪ] adv facilement
east [iːst] n est m ♦ adj (wind) d'est; (side) est inv ♦ adv à l'est, vers l'est; **the E~** l'Orient m; les pays mpl de l'Est
Easter ['iːstər] n Pâques fpl; **~ egg** n œuf m de Pâques
east: **~erly** ['iːstəlɪ] adj (wind) d'est;

(*direction*) est *inv*; (*point*) à l'est; **~ern** ['iːstən] *adj* de l'est, oriental(e); **~ward(s)** ['iːstwəd(z)] *adv* vers l'est, à l'est

easy ['iːzɪ] *adj* facile; (*manner*) aisé(e) ♦ *adv*: **to take it** *or* **things ~** ne pas se fatiguer; (*not worry*) ne pas (trop) s'en faire; (*chair*) ~ fauteuil *m*; **~-going** *adj* accommodant(e), facile à vivre

eat [iːt] (*pt* **ate**, *pp* **eaten**) *vt, vi* manger; **~ away at**, **~ into** *vt fus* ronger, attaquer; (*savings*) entamer

eaves [iːvz] *npl* avant-toit *m*

eavesdrop ['iːvzdrɔp] *vi*: **to ~ (on a conversation)** écouter (une conversation) de façon indiscrète

ebb [eb] *n* reflux *m* ♦ *vi* refluer; (*fig: also:* **~ away**) décliner

ebony ['ebənɪ] *n* ébène *f*

EC *n abbr* (= *European Community*) C.E. *f*

ECB *n abbr* (= *European Central Bank*) BCE *f*

eccentric [ɪk'sentrɪk] *adj* excentrique ♦ *n* excentrique *m/f*

echo ['ekəu] (*pl* **~es**) *n* écho *m* ♦ *vt* répéter ♦ *vi* résonner, faire écho

eclipse [ɪ'klɪps] *n* éclipse *f*

ecology [ɪ'kɔlədʒɪ] *n* écologie *f*

economic [iːkə'nɔmɪk] *adj* économique; (*business etc*) rentable; **~ refugee** réfugié *m* économique

economical [iːkə'nɔmɪkl] *adj* économique; (*person*) économe

economics [iːkə'nɔmɪks] *n* économie *f* politique ♦ *npl* (*of project, situation*) aspect *m* financier

economize [ɪ'kɔnəmaɪz] *vi* économiser, faire des économies

economy [ɪ'kɔnəmɪ] *n* économie *f*; **~ class** *n* classe *f* touriste; **~ size** *n* format *m* économique

ecstasy ['ekstəsɪ] *n* extase *f* (*drogue aussi*); **ecstatic** [eks'tætɪk] *adj* extatique

ECU ['eɪkjuː] *n abbr* (= *European Currency Unit*) ECU *m*

eczema ['eksɪmə] *n* eczéma *m*

edge [edʒ] *n* bord *m*; (*of knife etc*) tranchant *m*, fil *m* ♦ *vt* border; **on ~** (*fig*) crispé(e), tendu(e); **to ~ away from** s'éloigner furtivement de; **~ways** *adv*: **he couldn't get a word in ~ways** il ne pouvait pas placer un mot

edgy ['edʒɪ] *adj* crispé(e), tendu(e)

edible ['edɪbl] *adj* comestible

Edinburgh ['edɪnbərə] *n* Édimbourg

edit ['edɪt] *vt* (*text, book*) éditer; (*report*) préparer; (*film*) monter; (*broadcast*) réaliser; **~ion** [ɪ'dɪʃən] *n* édition *f*; **~or** *n* (*of column*) rédacteur(-trice); (*of newspaper*) rédacteur(-trice) en chef; (*of sb's work*) éditeur(-trice); **~orial** [edɪ'tɔːrɪəl] *adj* de la

rédaction, éditorial(e) ♦ *n* éditorial *m*

educate ['edjukeɪt] *vt* (*teach*) instruire; (*instruct*) éduquer; **~d** *adj* (*person*) cultivé(e); **education** [edju'keɪʃən] *n* éducation *f*; (*studies*) études *fpl*; (*teaching*) enseignement *m*, instruction *f*; **educational** *adj* (*experience, toy*) pédagogique; (*institution*) scolaire; (*policy*) d'éducation

eel [iːl] *n* anguille *f*

eerie ['ɪərɪ] *adj* inquiétant(e)

effect [ɪ'fekt] *n* effet *m* ♦ *vt* effectuer; **to take ~** (*law*) entrer en vigueur, prendre effet; (*drug*) agir, faire son effet; **in ~** en fait; **~ive** [ɪ'fektɪv] *adj* efficace; (*actual*) véritable; **~ively** *adv* efficacement; (*in reality*) effectivement; **~iveness** *n* efficacité *f*

effeminate [ɪ'femɪnɪt] *adj* efféminé(e)

effervescent [efə'vesnt] *adj* (*drink*) gazeux(-euse)

efficiency [ɪ'fɪʃənsɪ] *n* efficacité *f*; (*of machine*) rendement *m*

efficient [ɪ'fɪʃənt] *adj* efficace; (*machine*) qui a un bon rendement

effort ['efət] *n* effort *m*; **~less** *adj* (*style*) aisé(e); (*achievement*) facile

effusive [ɪ'fjuːsɪv] *adj* chaleureux(-euse)

e.g. *adv abbr* (= *exempli gratia*) par exemple, p. ex.

egg [eg] *n* œuf *m*; **hard-boiled/soft-boiled ~** œuf dur/à la coque; **~ on** *vt* pousser; **~cup** *n* coquetier *m*; **~plant** *n* (*esp US*) aubergine *f*; **~shell** *n* coquille *f* d'œuf

ego ['iːgəu] *n* (*self-esteem*) amour-propre *m*

egotism ['egəutɪzəm] *n* égotisme *m*

egotist ['egəutɪst] *n* égocentrique *m/f*

Egypt ['iːdʒɪpt] *n* Égypte *f*; **~ian** [ɪ'dʒɪpʃən] *adj* égyptien(ne) ♦ *n* Égyptien(ne)

eiderdown ['aɪdədaun] *n* édredon *m*

Eiffel Tower ['aɪfəl-] *n* tour *f* Eiffel

eight [eɪt] *num* huit; **~een** [eɪ'tiːn] *num* dix-huit; **~h** [eɪtθ] *num* huitième; **~y** ['eɪtɪ] *num* quatre-vingt(s)

Eire ['ɛərə] *n* République *f* d'Irlande

either ['aɪðə*r*] *adj* l'un ou l'autre; (*both, each*) chaque ♦ *pron*: **~ (of them)** l'un ou l'autre ♦ *adv* non plus ♦ *conj*: **~ good or bad** ou bon ou mauvais, soit bon soit mauvais; **on ~ side** de chaque côté; **I don't like ~** je n'aime ni l'un ni l'autre; **no, I don't ~** moi non plus

eject [ɪ'dʒekt] *vt* (*tenant etc*) expulser; (*object*) éjecter

elaborate [*adj* ɪ'læbərɪt, *vb* ɪ'læbəreɪt] *adj* compliqué(e), recherché(e) ♦ *vt* élaborer ♦ *vi*: **to ~ (on)** entrer dans les détails (de)

elastic [ɪ'læstɪk] *adj* élastique ♦ *n* élastique *m*; **~ band** *n* élastique *m*

elated [ɪ'leɪtɪd] *adj* transporté(e) de joie

elation [ɪ'leɪʃən] *n* allégresse *f*

elbow ['elbəu] *n* coude *m*

elder ['eldər] adj aîné(e) ♦ n (tree) sureau m; one's ~s ses aînés; ~ly adj âgé(e) ♦ npl: the ~ly les personnes âgées

eldest ['eldıst] adj, n: the ~ (child) l'aîné(e) (des enfants)

elect [ı'lekt] vt élire ♦ adj: the president ~ le président désigné; to ~ to do choisir de faire; ~ion n élection f; ~ioneering [ılekʃə'nıərıŋ] n propagande électorale, manœuvres électorales; ~or n électeur(-trice); ~orate n électorat m

electric [ı'lektrık] adj électrique; ~al adj électrique; ~ blanket n couverture chauffante; ~ fire (BRIT) n radiateur m électrique; ~ian [ılek'trıʃən] n électricien m; ~ity [ılek'trısıtı] n électricité f; **electrify** [ı'lektrıfaı] vt (RAIL, fence) électrifier; (audience) électriser

electronic [ılek'trɔnık] adj électronique; ~ mail n courrier m électronique; ~s n électronique f

elegant ['elıgənt] adj élégant(e)

element ['elımənt] n (gen) élément m; (of heater, kettle etc) résistance f; ~ary [elı'mentərı] adj élémentaire; (school, education) primaire

elephant ['elıfənt] n éléphant m

elevation [elı'veıʃən] n (raising, promotion) avancement m, promotion f; (height) hauteur f

elevator ['elıveıtər] n (in warehouse etc) élévateur m, monte-charge m inv; (US: lift) ascenseur m

eleven [ı'levn] num onze; ~ses [ı'levnzız] npl ≈ pause-café f; ~th num onzième

elicit [ı'lısıt] vt: to ~ (from) obtenir (de), arracher (à)

eligible ['elıdʒəbl] adj: to be ~ for remplir les conditions requises pour; an ~ young man/ woman un beau parti

elm [elm] n orme m

elongated ['i:lɔŋgeıtıd] adj allongé(e)

elope [ı'ləup] vi (lovers) s'enfuir (ensemble)

eloquent ['eləkwənt] adj éloquent(e)

else [els] adv d'autre; something ~ quelque chose d'autre, autre chose; somewhere ~ ailleurs, autre part; everywhere ~ partout ailleurs; nobody ~ personne d'autre; where ~? à quel autre endroit?; little ~ pas grand-chose d'autre; ~where adv ailleurs, autre part

elude [ı'lu:d] vt échapper à

elusive [ı'lu:sıv] adj insaisissable

emaciated [ı'meısıeıtıd] adj émacié(e), décharné(e)

e-mail ['i:meıl] n courrier m électronique ♦ vt (person) envoyer un message électronique à

emancipate [ı'mænsıpeıt] vt émanciper

embankment [ım'bæŋkmənt] n (of road, railway) remblai m, talus m; (of river) berge f, quai m

embark [ım'bɑ:k] vi embarquer; to ~ on (journey) entreprendre; (fig) se lancer or s'embarquer dans; ~ation [embɑ:'keıʃən] n embarquement m

embarrass [ım'bærəs] vt embarrasser, gêner; ~ed adj gêné(e); ~ing adj gênant(e), embarrassant(e); ~ment n embarras m, gêne f

embassy ['embəsı] n ambassade f

embedded [ım'bedıd] adj enfoncé(e)

embellish [ım'belıʃ] vt orner, décorer; (fig: account) enjoliver

embers ['embəz] npl braise f

embezzle [ım'bezl] vt détourner; ~ment n détournement m de fonds

embitter [ım'bıtər] vt (person) aigrir; (relations) envenimer

embody [ım'bɔdı] vt (features) réunir, comprendre; (ideas) formuler, exprimer

embossed [ım'bɔst] adj (metal) estampé(e); (leather) frappé(e); ~ wallpaper papier gaufré

embrace [ım'breıs] vt embrasser, étreindre; (include) embrasser ♦ vi s'étreindre, s'embrasser ♦ n étreinte f

embroider [ım'brɔıdər] vt broder; ~y n broderie f

emerald ['emərəld] n émeraude f

emerge [ı'mə:dʒ] vi apparaître; (from room, car) surgir; (from sleep, imprisonment) sortir

emergency [ı'mə:dʒənsı] n urgence f; in an ~ en cas d'urgence; ~ cord (US) sonnette f d'alarme; ~ exit n sortie f de secours; ~ landing n atterrissage forcé; ~ services npl: the ~ services (fire, police, ambulance) les services mpl d'urgence

emery board ['emərı-] n lime f à ongles (en carton émerisé)

emigrate ['emıgreıt] vi émigrer

eminent ['emınənt] adj éminent(e)

emissions [ı'mıʃənz] npl émissions fpl

emit [ı'mıt] vt émettre

emotion [ı'məuʃən] n émotion f; ~al adj (person) émotif(-ive), très sensible; (needs, exhaustion) affectif(-ive); (scene) émouvant(e); (tone, speech) qui fait appel aux sentiments; **emotive** adj chargé(e) d'émotion; (subject) sensible

emperor ['empərər] n empereur m

emphasis ['emfəsıs] (pl -ases) n (stress) accent m; (importance) insistance f

emphasize ['emfəsaız] vt (syllable, word, point) appuyer or insister sur; (feature) souligner, accentuer

emphatic [em'fætık] adj (strong) énergique, vigoureux(-euse); (unambiguous, clear) catégorique

empire ['empaıər] n empire m

employ [ım'plɔı] vt employer; ~ee n

employé(e); **~er** n employeur(-euse);
~ment n emploi m; **~ment agency** n
agence f or bureau m de placement
empower [ɪm'pauəʳ] vt: **to ~ sb to do**
autoriser or habiliter qn à faire
empress ['emprɪs] n impératrice f
emptiness ['emptɪnɪs] n (of area, region)
aspect m désertique; (of life) vide m,
vacuité f
empty ['emptɪ] adj vide; (threat, promise) en
l'air, vain(e) ♦ vt vider ♦ vi se vider; (liquid)
s'écouler; **~-handed** adj les mains vides
EMU n abbr (= economic and monetary union)
UME f
emulate ['emjuleɪt] vt rivaliser avec, imiter
emulsion [ɪ'mʌlʃən] n émulsion f; (also:
~ **paint**) peinture mate
enable [ɪ'neɪbl] vt: **to ~ sb to do** permettre à
qn de faire
enamel [ɪ'næməl] n émail m; (also: ~ **paint**)
peinture laquée
enchant [ɪn'tʃɑːnt] vt enchanter; **~ing** adj
ravissant(e), enchanteur(-teresse)
encl. abbr = **enclosed**
enclose [ɪn'kləuz] vt (land) clôturer; (space,
object) entourer; (letter etc): **to ~** (**with**)
joindre (à); **please find ~d** veuillez trouver ci-
joint; **enclosure** n enceinte f
encompass [ɪn'kʌmpəs] vt (include)
contenir, inclure
encore [ɔŋ'kɔːʳ] excl bis ♦ n bis m
encounter [ɪn'kauntəʳ] n rencontre f ♦ vt
rencontrer
encourage [ɪn'kʌrɪdʒ] vt encourager;
~ment n encouragement m
encroach [ɪn'krəutʃ] vi: **to ~** (**up**)**on** empiéter
sur
encyclop(a)edia [ensaɪkləu'piːdɪə] n
encyclopédie f
end [end] n (gen, also: aim) fin f; (of table,
street, rope etc) bout m, extrémité f ♦ vt
terminer; (also: **bring to an ~, put an ~ to**)
mettre fin à ♦ vi se terminer, finir; **in the ~**
finalement; **on ~** (object) debout, dressé(e);
to stand on ~ (hair) se dresser sur la tête; **for
hours on ~** pendant des heures et des heures;
~ up vi: **to ~ up in** (condition) finir or se
terminer par; (place) finir or aboutir à
endanger [ɪn'deɪndʒəʳ] vt mettre en danger;
an ~ed species une espèce en voie de
disparition
endearing [ɪn'dɪərɪŋ] adj attachant(e)
endeavour [ɪn'devəʳ] (US **endeavor**) n
tentative f, effort m ♦ vi: **to ~ to do** tenter or
s'efforcer de faire
ending ['endɪŋ] n dénouement m, fin f;
(LING) terminaison f
endive ['endaɪv] n chicorée f; (smooth)
endive f

endless ['endlɪs] adj sans fin, interminable
endorse [ɪn'dɔːs] vt (cheque) endosser;
(approve) appuyer, approuver, sanctionner;
~ment n (approval) appui m, aval m; (BRIT:
on driving licence) contravention portée au
permis de conduire
endure [ɪn'djuəʳ] vt supporter, endurer ♦ vi
durer
enemy ['enəmɪ] adj, n ennemi(e)
energetic [enə'dʒetɪk] adj énergique;
(activity) qui fait se dépenser (physiquement)
energy ['enədʒɪ] n énergie f
enforce [ɪn'fɔːs] vt (law) appliquer, faire
respecter
engage [ɪn'geɪdʒ] vt engager; (attention etc)
retenir ♦ vi (TECH) s'enclencher, s'engrener;
to ~ in se lancer dans; **~d** adj (BRIT: busy, in
use) occupé(e); (betrothed) fiancé(e); **to get
~d** se fiancer; **~d tone** n (TEL) tonalité f
occupé inv or pas libre; **~ment** n obligation
f, engagement m; rendez-vous m inv; (to
marry) fiançailles fpl; **~ment ring** n bague f
de fiançailles; **engaging** adj engageant(e),
attirant(e)
engine ['endʒɪn] n (AUT) moteur m; (RAIL)
locomotive f; **~ driver** n mécanicien m
engineer [endʒɪ'nɪəʳ] n ingénieur m; (BRIT:
repairer) dépanneur m; (NAVY, US RAIL)
mécanicien m; **~ing** n engineering m,
ingénierie f; (of bridges, ships) génie m; (of
machine) mécanique f
England ['ɪŋglənd] n Angleterre f; **English**
adj anglais(e) ♦ n (LING) anglais m; **the
English** npl (people) les Anglais; **the English
Channel** la Manche; **Englishman** (irreg) n
Anglais; **Englishwoman** (irreg) n Anglaise f
engraving [ɪn'greɪvɪŋ] n gravure f
engrossed [ɪn'grəust] adj: **~ in** absorbé(e)
par, plongé(e) dans
engulf [ɪn'gʌlf] vt engloutir
enhance [ɪn'hɑːns] vt rehausser, mettre en
valeur
enjoy [ɪn'dʒɔɪ] vt aimer, prendre plaisir à;
(have: health, fortune) jouir de; (: success)
connaître; **to ~ o.s.** s'amuser; **~able** adj
agréable; **~ment** n plaisir m
enlarge [ɪn'lɑːdʒ] vt accroître, (PHOT)
agrandir ♦ vi: **to ~ on** (subject) s'étendre sur;
~ment n (PHOT)
agrandissement m
enlighten [ɪn'laɪtn] vt éclairer; **~ed** adj
éclairé(e); **~ment** n: **the E~ment** (HISTORY) ≈
le Siècle des lumières
enlist [ɪn'lɪst] vt recruter; (support) s'assurer
♦ vi s'engager
enmity ['enmɪtɪ] n inimitié f
enormous [ɪ'nɔːməs] adj énorme
enough [ɪ'nʌf] adj, pron: **~ time/books** assez
or suffisamment de temps/livres ♦ adv: **big ~**

assez *or* suffisamment grand; **have you got ~** en avez-vous assez?; **he has not worked ~** il n'a pas assez *or* suffisamment travaillé; **~ to eat** assez à manger; **~!** assez!, ça suffit!; **that's ~**, thanks cela suffit *or* c'est assez, merci; **I've had ~ of him** j'en ai assez de lui; ... **which, funnily** *or* **oddly ~** ... qui, chose curieuse

enquire [ɪnˈkwaɪəʳ] *vt, vi* = **inquire**

enrage [ɪnˈreɪdʒ] *vt* mettre en fureur *or* en rage, rendre furieux(-euse)

enrol [ɪnˈrəʊl] (*US* **enroll**) *vt* inscrire ♦ *vi* s'inscrire; **~ment** (*US* **enrollment**) *n* inscription *f*

en suite [ɒnˈswiːt] *adj*: **with ~ bathroom** avec salle de bains en attenante

ensure [ɪnˈʃuəʳ] *vt* assurer; garantir; **to ~ that** s'assurer que

entail [ɪnˈteɪl] *vt* entraîner, occasionner

entangled [ɪnˈtæŋgld] *adj*: **to become ~ (in)** s'empêtrer (dans)

enter [ˈɛntəʳ] *vt* (*room*) entrer dans, pénétrer dans; (*club, army*) entrer à; (*competition*) s'inscrire à *or* pour; (*sb for a competition*) (faire) inscrire; (*write down*) inscrire, noter; (*COMPUT*) entrer, introduire ♦ *vi* entrer; **~ for** *vt fus* s'inscrire à, se présenter pour *or* à; **~ into** *vt fus* (*explanation*) se lancer dans; (*discussion, negotiations*) entamer; (*agreement*) conclure

enterprise [ˈɛntəpraɪz] *n* entreprise *f*; (*initiative*) (esprit *m* d')initiative *f*; **free ~** libre entreprise; **private ~** entreprise privée; **enterprising** *adj* entreprenant(e), dynamique; (*scheme*) audacieux(-euse)

entertain [ɛntəˈteɪn] *vt* amuser, distraire; (*invite*) recevoir (à dîner); (*idea, plan*) envisager; **~er** *n* artiste *m/f* de variétés; **~ing** *adj* amusant(e), distrayant(e); **~ment** *n* (*amusement*) divertissement *m*, amusement *m*; (*show*) spectacle *m*

enthralled [ɪnˈθrɔːld] *adj* captivé(e)

enthusiasm [ɪnˈθuːzɪæzəm] *n* enthousiasme *m*

enthusiast [ɪnˈθuːzɪæst] *n* enthousiaste *m/f*; **~ic** [ɪnˌθuːzɪˈæstɪk] *adj* enthousiaste; **to be ~ic about** être enthousiasmé(e) par

entire [ɪnˈtaɪəʳ] *adj* (tout) entier(-ère); **~ly** *adv* entièrement, complètement; **~ty** [ɪnˈtaɪərətɪ] *n*: **in its ~ty** dans sa totalité

entitle [ɪnˈtaɪtl] *vt*: **to ~ sb to sth** donner droit à qch à qn; **~d** [ɪnˈtaɪtld] *adj* (*book*) intitulé(e); **to be ~d to do** avoir le droit de *or* être habilité à faire

entrance [*n* ˈɛntrns, *vb* ɪnˈtrɑːns] *n* entrée *f* ♦ *vt* enchanter, ravir; **to gain ~ to** (*university etc*) être admis à; **~ examination** *n* examen *m* d'entrée; **~ fee** *n* (*to museum etc*) prix *m* d'entrée; (*to join club etc*) droit *m* d'inscription; **~ ramp** (*US*) *n* (*AUT*) bretelle *f*

d'accès; **entrant** *n* participant(e); concurrent(e); (*BRIT: in exam*) candidat(e)

entrenched [ɛnˈtrɛntʃt] *adj* retranché(e); (*ideas*) arrêté(e)

entrepreneur [ˈɒntrəprəˈnəːʳ] *n* entrepreneur *m*

entrust [ɪnˈtrʌst] *vt*: **to ~ sth to** confier qch à

entry [ˈɛntrɪ] *n* entrée *f*; (*in register*) inscription *f*; **no ~** défense d'entrer, entrée interdite; (*AUT*) sens interdit; **~ form** *n* feuille *f* d'inscription; **~ phone** (*BRIT*) *n* interphone *m*

envelop [ɪnˈvɛləp] *vt* envelopper

envelope [ˈɛnvələʊp] *n* enveloppe *f*

envious [ˈɛnvɪəs] *adj* envieux(-euse)

environment [ɪnˈvaɪrnmənt] *n* environnement *m*; (*social, moral*) milieu *m*; **~al** [ɪnvaɪərnˈmɛntl] *adj* écologique; du milieu; **~-friendly** *adj* écologique

envisage [ɪnˈvɪzɪdʒ] *vt* (*foresee*) prévoir

envoy [ˈɛnvɔɪ] *n* (*diplomat*) ministre *m* plénipotentiaire

envy [ˈɛnvɪ] *n* envie *f* ♦ *vt* envier; **to ~ sb sth** envier qch à qn

epic [ˈɛpɪk] *n* épopée *f* ♦ *adj* épique

epidemic [ɛpɪˈdɛmɪk] *n* épidémie *f*

epilepsy [ˈɛpɪlɛpsɪ] *n* épilepsie *f*; **epileptic** *n* épileptique *m/f*

episode [ˈɛpɪsəʊd] *n* épisode *m*

epitome [ɪˈpɪtəmɪ] *n* modèle *m*; **epitomize** *vt* incarner

equal [ˈiːkwl] *adj* égal(e) ♦ *n* égal(e) ♦ *vt* égaler; **~ to** (*task*) à la hauteur de; **~ity** [iːˈkwɒlɪtɪ] *n* égalité *f*; **~ize** *vi* (*SPORT*) égaliser; **~ly** *adv* également; (*just as*) tout aussi

equanimity [ɛkwəˈnɪmɪtɪ] *n* égalité *f* d'humeur

equate [ɪˈkweɪt] *vt*: **to ~ sth with** comparer qch à; assimiler qch à; **equation** *n* (*MATH*) équation *f*

equator [ɪˈkweɪtəʳ] *n* équateur *m*

equilibrium [iːkwɪˈlɪbrɪəm] *n* équilibre *m*

equip [ɪˈkwɪp] *vt*: **to ~ (with)** équiper (de); **to be well ~ped** être bien équipé(e); **~ment** *n* équipement *m*; (*electrical etc*) appareillage *m*, installation *f*

equities [ˈɛkwɪtɪz] (*BRIT*) *npl* (*COMM*) actions cotées en Bourse

equivalent [ɪˈkwɪvələnt] *adj*: **~ (to)** équivalent(e) (à) ♦ *n* équivalent *m*

era [ˈɪərə] *n* ère *f*, époque *f*

eradicate [ɪˈrædɪkeɪt] *vt* éliminer

erase [ɪˈreɪz] *vt* effacer; **~r** *n* gomme *f*

erect [ɪˈrɛkt] *adj* droit(e) ♦ *vt* construire; (*monument*) ériger, élever; (*tent etc*) dresser; **~ion** *n* érection *f*

ERM *n abbr* (= *Exchange Rate Mechanism*) MTC *m*

erode [ɪˈrəʊd] *vt* éroder; (*metal*) ronger

erotic [ı'rɔtık] *adj* érotique

errand ['ɛrənd] *n* course *f*, commission *f*

erratic [ı'rætık] *adj* irrégulier(-ère); inconstant(e)

error ['ɛrə*r*] *n* erreur *f*

erupt [ı'rʌpt] *vi* entrer en éruption; *(fig)* éclater; **~ion** *n* éruption *f*

escalate ['ɛskəleıt] *vi* s'intensifier

escalator ['ɛskəleıtə*r*] *n* escalier roulant

escapade [ɛskə'peıd] *n (misdeed)* fredaine *f*; *(adventure)* équipée *f*

escape [ıs'keıp] *n* fuite *f*; *(from prison)* évasion *f* ♦ *vi* s'échapper, fuir; *(from jail)* s'évader; *(fig)* s'en tirer; *(leak)* s'échapper ♦ *vt* échapper à; **to ~ from** *(person)* échapper à; *(place)* s'échapper de; *(fig)* fuir; **escapism** *n (fig)* évasion *f*

escort [*n* 'ɛskɔːt, *vb* ıs'kɔːt] *n* escorte *f* ♦ *vt* escorter

Eskimo ['ɛskıməu] *n* Esquimau(de)

especially [ıs'pɛʃlı] *adv (particularly)* particulièrement; *(above all)* surtout

espionage ['ɛspıənɑːʒ] *n* espionnage *m*

Esquire [ıs'kwaıə*r*] *n*: **J Brown, ~** Monsieur J. Brown

essay ['ɛseı] *n (SCOL)* dissertation *f*; *(LITERATURE)* essai *m*

essence ['ɛsns] *n* essence *f*

essential [ı'sɛnʃl] *adj* essentiel(le); *(basic)* fondamental(e) ♦ *n*: **~s** éléments essentiels; **~ly** *adv* essentiellement

establish [ıs'tæblıʃ] *vt* établir; *(business)* fonder, créer; *(one's power etc)* asseoir, affermir; **~ed** *adj* bien établi(e); **~ment** *n* établissement *m*; *(founding)* création *f*

estate [ıs'teıt] *n (land)* domaine *m*, propriété *f*; *(LAW)* biens *mpl*, succession *f*; *(BRIT: also:* **housing ~)** lotissement *m*, cité *f*; **~ agent** *n* agent immobilier; **~ car** *(BRIT)* *n* break *m*

esteem [ıs'tiːm] *n* estime *f*

esthetic [ıs'θɛtık] *(US)* *adj* = **aesthetic**

estimate [*n* 'ɛstımət, *vb* 'ɛstımeıt] *n* estimation *f*; *(COMM)* devis *m* ♦ *vt* estimer; **estimation** [ɛstı'meıʃən] *n* opinion *f*; *(calculation)* estimation *f*

estranged [ıs'treındʒd] *adj* séparé(e); dont on s'est séparé(e)

etc. *abbr* (= *et cetera*) etc

eternal [ı'təːnl] *adj* éternel(le)

eternity [ı'təːnıtı] *n* éternité *f*

ethical ['ɛθıkl] *adj* moral(e); **ethics** *n* éthique *f* ♦ *npl* moralité *f*

Ethiopia [iːθı'əupıə] *n* Éthiopie *f*

ethnic ['ɛθnık] *adj* ethnique; *(music etc)* folklorique; **~ minority** minorité *f* ethnique

ethos ['iːθɔs] *n* génie *m*

etiquette ['ɛtıkɛt] *n* convenances *fpl*, étiquette *f*

EU *n abbr* (= *European Union*) UE *f*

euro ['juərəu] *n (currency)* euro *m*

Euroland ['juərəulænd] *n* Eurolande *f*

Eurocheque ['juərəutʃɛk] *n* eurochèque *m*

Europe ['juərəp] *n* Europe *f*; **~an** [juərə'piːən] *adj* européen(ne) ♦ *n* Européen(ne); **~an Community** Communauté européenne

evacuate [ı'vækjueıt] *vt* évacuer

evade [ı'veıd] *vt* échapper à; *(question etc)* éluder; *(duties)* se dérober à; **to ~ tax** frauder le fisc

evaporate [ı'væpəreıt] *vi* s'évaporer; **~d milk** *n* lait condensé non sucré

evasion [ı'veıʒən] *n* dérobade *f*; **tax ~** fraude fiscale

eve [iːv] *n*: **on the ~ of** à la veille de

even ['iːvn] *adj (level, smooth)* régulier(-ère); *(equal)* égal(e); *(number)* pair(e) ♦ *adv* même; **~ if** même si +*indic*; **~ though** alors même que +*cond*; **~ more** encore plus; **~ so** quand même; **not ~** pas même; **to get ~ with sb** prendre sa revanche sur qn

evening ['iːvnıŋ] *n* soir *m*; *(as duration, event)* soirée *f*; **in the ~** le soir; **~ class** *n* cours *m* du soir; **~ dress** *n* tenue *f* de soirée

event [ı'vɛnt] *n* événement *m*; *(SPORT)* épreuve *f*; **in the ~ of** en cas de; **~ful** *adj* mouvementé(e)

eventual [ı'vɛntʃuəl] *adj* final(e); **~ity** [ıvɛntʃu'ælıtı] *n* possibilité *f*, éventualité *f*; **~ly** *adv* finalement

ever ['ɛvə*r*] *adv* jamais; *(at all times)* toujours; **the best ~** le meilleur qu'on ait jamais vu; **have you ~ seen it?** l'as-tu déjà vu?, as-tu eu l'occasion or t'est-il arrivé de le voir?; **why ~ not?** mais enfin, pourquoi pas?; **~ since** *adv* depuis ♦ *conj* depuis que; **~green** *n* arbre *m* à feuilles persistantes; **~lasting** *adj* éternel(le)

every ['ɛvrı] *adj* chaque; **~ day** tous les jours, chaque jour; **~ other/third day** tous les deux/ trois jours; **~ other car** une voiture sur deux; **~ now and then** de temps en temps; **~body** *pron* tout le monde, tous *pl*; **~day** *adj* quotidien(ne), de tous les jours; **~one** *pron* = **everybody**; **~thing** *pron* tout; **~where** *adv* partout

evict [ı'vıkt] *vt* expulser; **~ion** *n* expulsion *f*

evidence ['ɛvıdns] *n (proof)* preuve(s) *f(pl)*; *(of witness)* témoignage *m*; *(sign)*: **to show ~** of présenter des signes de; **to give ~** témoigner, déposer

evident ['ɛvıdnt] *adj* évident(e); **~ly** *adv* de toute évidence; *(apparently)* apparemment

evil ['iːvl] *adj* mauvais(e) ♦ *n* mal *m*

evoke [ı'vəuk] *vt* évoquer

evolution [iːvə'luːʃən] *n* évolution *f*

evolve [ı'vɔlv] *vt* élaborer ♦ *vi* évoluer

ewe [juː] *n* brebis *f*

ex- [ɛks] *prefix* ex-

exact [ɪgˈzækt] *adj* exact(e) ♦ *vt*: **to ~ sth (from)** extorquer qch (à); exiger qch (de); **~ing** *adj* exigeant(e); (*work*) astreignant(e); **~ly** *adv* exactement

exaggerate [ɪgˈzædʒəreɪt] *vt, vi* exagérer; **exaggeration** [ɪgzædʒəˈreɪʃən] *n* exagération *f*

exalted [ɪgˈzɔːltɪd] *adj* (*prominent*) élevé(e); (: *person*) haut placé(e)

exam [ɪgˈzæm] *n abbr* (*SCOL*) = **examination**

examination [ɪgzæmɪˈneɪʃən] *n* (*SCOL, MED*) examen *m*

examine [ɪgˈzæmɪn] *vt* (*gen*) examiner; (*SCOL*: *person*) interroger; **~r** *n* examinateur(-trice)

example [ɪgˈzɑːmpl] *n* exemple *m*; **for ~** par exemple

exasperate [ɪgˈzɑːspəreɪt] *vt* exaspérer; **exasperation** [ɪgzɑːspəˈreɪʃən] *n* exaspération *f*, irritation *f*

excavate [ˈɛkskəveɪt] *vt* excaver; **excavation** [ɛkskəˈveɪʃən] *n* fouilles *fpl*

exceed [ɪkˈsiːd] *vt* dépasser; (*one's powers*) outrepasser; **~ingly** *adv* extrêmement

excellent [ˈɛksələnt] *adj* excellent(e)

except [ɪkˈsɛpt] *prep* (*also*: **~ for, ~ing**) sauf, excepté ♦ *vt* excepter; **~ if/when** sauf si/ quand; **~ that** sauf que, si ce n'est que; **~ion** *n* exception *f*; **to take ~ion to** s'offusquer de; **~ional** *adj* exceptionnel(le)

excerpt [ˈɛksɜːpt] *n* extrait *m*

excess [ɪkˈsɛs] *n* excès *m*; **~ baggage** *n* excédent *m* de bagages; **~ fare** (*BRIT*) *n* supplément *m*; **~ive** *adj* excessif(-ive)

exchange [ɪksˈtʃeɪndʒ] *n* échange *m*; (*also*: **telephone ~**) central *m* ♦ *vt*: **to ~ (for)** échanger (contre); **~ rate** *n* taux *m* de change

Exchequer [ɪksˈtʃɛkəʳ] (*BRIT*) *n*: **the ~** l'Échiquier *m*, ≈ le ministère des Finances

excise [*n* ˈɛksaɪz, *vb* ɛkˈsaɪz] *n* taxe *f* ♦ *vt* exciser

excite [ɪkˈsaɪt] *vt* exciter; **to get ~d** s'exciter; **~ment** *n* excitation *f*; **exciting** *adj* passionnant(e)

exclaim [ɪksˈkleɪm] *vi* s'exclamer; **exclamation** [ɛkskləˈmeɪʃən] *n* exclamation *f*; **exclamation mark** *n* point *m* d'exclamation

exclude [ɪksˈkluːd] *vt* exclure; **exclusion zone** *n* zone interdite; **exclusive** *adj* exclusif(-ive); (*club, district*) sélect(e); (*item of news*) en exclusivité; **exclusive of VAT** TVA non comprise; **mutually exclusive** qui s'excluent l'un(e) l'autre

excruciating [ɪksˈkruːʃɪeɪtɪŋ] *adj* atroce

excursion [ɪksˈkɜːʃən] *n* excursion *f*

excuse [*n* ɪksˈkjuːs, *vb* ɪksˈkjuːz] *n* excuse *f*

♦ *vt* excuser; **to ~ sb from** (*activity*) dispenser qn de; **~ me!** excusez-moi, pardon!; **now if you will ~ me, ...** maintenant, si vous (le) permettez ...

ex-directory [ˈɛksdɪˈrɛktərɪ] (*BRIT*) *adj* sur la liste rouge

execute [ˈɛksɪkjuːt] *vt* exécuter; **execution** *n* exécution *f*

executive [ɪgˈzɛkjutɪv] *n* (*COMM*) cadre *m*; (*of organization, political party*) bureau *m* ♦ *adj* exécutif(-ive)

exemplify [ɪgˈzɛmplɪfaɪ] *vt* illustrer; (*typify*) incarner

exempt [ɪgˈzɛmpt] *adj*: **~ from** exempté(e) or dispensé(e) de ♦ *vt*: **to ~ sb from** exempter or dispenser qn de

exercise [ˈɛksəsaɪz] *n* exercice *m* ♦ *vt* exercer; (*patience etc*) faire preuve de; (*dog*) promener ♦ *vi* prendre de l'exercice; **~ book** *n* cahier *m*

exert [ɪgˈzɜːt] *vt* exercer, employer; **to ~ o.s.** se dépenser; **~ion** *n* effort *m*

exhale [ɛksˈheɪl] *vt* exhaler ♦ *vi* expirer

exhaust [ɪgˈzɔːst] *n* (*also*: **~ fumes**) gaz *mpl* d'échappement; (*also*: **~ pipe**) tuyau *m* d'échappement ♦ *vt* épuiser; **~ed** *adj* épuisé(e); **~ion** *n* épuisement *m*; **nervous ~ion** fatigue nerveuse; surmenage mental; **~ive** *adj* très complet(-ète)

exhibit [ɪgˈzɪbɪt] *n* (*ART*) pièce exposée, objet exposé; (*LAW*) pièce à conviction ♦ *vt* exposer; (*courage, skill*) faire preuve de; **~ion** [ɛksɪˈbɪʃən] *n* exposition *f*; (*of ill-temper, talent etc*) démonstration *f*

exhilarating [ɪgˈzɪləreɪtɪŋ] *adj* grisant(e); stimulant(e)

ex-husband *n* ex-mari *m*

exile [ˈɛksaɪl] *n* exil *m*; (*person*) exilé(e) ♦ *vt* exiler

exist [ɪgˈzɪst] *vi* exister; **~ence** *n* existence *f*; **~ing** *adj* actuel(le)

exit [ˈɛksɪt] *n* sortie *f* ♦ *vi* (*COMPUT, THEATRE*) sortir; **~ poll** *n* sondage *m* (fait à la sortie de l'isoloir); **~ ramp** *n* (*AUT*) bretelle *f* d'accès

exodus [ˈɛksədəs] *n* exode *m*

exonerate [ɪgˈzɒnəreɪt] *vt*: **to ~ from** disculper de

exotic [ɪgˈzɒtɪk] *adj* exotique

expand [ɪksˈpænd] *vt* agrandir; accroître ♦ *vi* (*trade etc*) se développer, s'accroître; (*gas, metal*) se dilater

expanse [ɪksˈpæns] *n* étendue *f*

expansion [ɪksˈpænʃən] *n* développement *m*, accroissement *m*

expect [ɪksˈpɛkt] *vt* (*anticipate*) s'attendre à, s'attendre à ce que +*sub*; (*count on*) compter sur, escompter; (*require*) demander, exiger; (*suppose*) supposer; (*await, also baby*) attendre ♦ *vi*: **to be ~ing** être enceinte;

~ancy n (anticipation) attente f; life ~ancy espérance f de vie; (fig) attente f; ~ant mother n future maman; ~ation [ɛkspɛk'teɪʃən] n attente f; espérance(s) f(pl)

expedient [ɪks'piːdɪənt] adj indiqué(e), opportun(e) ♦ n expédient m

expedition [ɛkspə'dɪʃən] n expédition f

expel [ɪks'pɛl] vt chasser, expulser; (SCOL) renvoyer

expend [ɪks'pɛnd] vt consacrer; (money) dépenser; ~iture [ɪks'pɛndɪtʃər] n dépense f; dépenses fpl

expense [ɪks'pɛns] n dépense f, frais mpl; (high cost) coût m; ~s npl (COMM) frais mpl; at the ~ of aux dépens de; ~ account n (note f de) frais mpl; **expensive** adj cher (chère), coûteux(-euse); **to be expensive** coûter cher

experience [ɪks'pɪərɪəns] n expérience f ♦ vt connaître, faire l'expérience de; (feeling) éprouver; ~d adj expérimenté(e)

experiment [ɪks'pɛrɪmənt] n expérience f ♦ vi faire une expérience; **to ~ with** expérimenter

expert ['ɛkspəːt] adj expert(e) ♦ n expert m; ~ise [ɛkspəː'tiːz] n (grande) compétence f

expire [ɪks'paɪər] vi expirer; **expiry** n expiration f

explain [ɪks'pleɪn] vt expliquer; **explanation** [ɛksplə'neɪʃən] n explication f; **explanatory** [ɪks'plænətrɪ] adj explicatif(-ive)

explicit [ɪks'plɪsɪt] adj explicite; (definite) formel(le)

explode [ɪks'pləud] vi exploser

exploit [n 'ɛksplɔɪt, vb ɪks'plɔɪt] n exploit m ♦ vt exploiter; ~ation [ɛksplɔɪ'teɪʃən] n exploitation f

exploratory [ɪks'plɔrətrɪ] adj (expedition) d'exploration; (fig: talks) préliminaire

explore [ɪks'plɔː] vt explorer; (possibilities) étudier, examiner; ~r n explorateur(-trice)

explosion [ɪks'pləuʒən] n explosion f; **explosive** [ɪks'pləusɪv] adj explosif(-ive) ♦ n explosif m

exponent [ɪks'pəunənt] n (of school of thought etc) interprète m, représentant m

export [vb ɛks'pɔːt, n 'ɛkspɔːt] vt exporter ♦ n exportation f ♦ cpd d'exportation; ~er n exportateur m

expose [ɪks'pəuz] vt exposer; (unmask) démasquer, dévoiler; ~d adj (position, house) exposé(e); **exposure** n exposition f; (publicity) couverture f; (PHOT) (temps m de) pose f; (: shot) pose; **to die from exposure** (MED) mourir de froid; **exposure meter** n posemètre m

express [ɪks'prɛs] adj (definite) formel(le), exprès(-esse); (BRIT: letter etc) exprès inv ♦ n (train) rapide m; (bus) car m express ♦ vt exprimer; ~ion n expression f; ~ly adv

expressément, formellement; ~way (US) n (urban motorway) voie f express (à plusieurs files)

exquisite [ɛks'kwɪzɪt] adj exquis(e)

extend [ɪks'tɛnd] vt (visit, street) prolonger; (building) agrandir; (offer) présenter, offrir; (hand, arm) tendre ♦ vi s'étendre;

extension n prolongation f; agrandissement m; (building) annexe f; (to wire, table) rallonge f; (telephone: in offices) poste m; (: in private house) téléphone m supplémentaire; **extensive** adj étendu(e), vaste; (damage, alterations) considérable; (inquiries) approfondi(e); **extensively** adv: **he's travelled extensively** il a beaucoup voyagé

extent [ɪks'tɛnt] n étendue f; **to some ~** dans une certaine mesure; **to what ~?** dans quelle mesure?, jusqu'à quel point?; **to the ~ of ...** au point de ...; **to such an ~ that ...** à tel point que ...

extenuating [ɪks'tɛnjueɪtɪŋ] adj: ~ circumstances circonstances atténuantes

exterior [ɛks'tɪərɪər] adj extérieur(e) ♦ n extérieur m; dehors m

external [ɛks'təːnl] adj externe

extinct [ɪks'tɪŋkt] adj éteint(e)

extinguish [ɪks'tɪŋgwɪʃ] vt éteindre

extort [ɪks'tɔːt] vt: **to ~ sth (from)** extorquer qch (à); ~ionate [ɪks'tɔːʃnət] adj exorbitant(e)

extra ['ɛkstrə] adj supplémentaire, de plus ♦ adv (in addition) en plus ♦ n supplément m; (perk) à-côté m; (THEATRE) figurant(e) ♦ prefix extra...

extract [vb ɪks'trækt, n 'ɛkstrækt] vt extraire; (tooth) arracher; (money, promise) soutirer ♦ n extrait m

extracurricular ['ɛkstrəkə'rɪkjulər] adj parascolaire

extradite ['ɛkstrədaɪt] vt extrader

extra...: ~marital ['ɛkstrə'mærɪtl] adj extra-conjugal(e); ~**mural** ['ɛkstrə'mjuərl] adj hors faculté inv; (lecture) public(-que); ~**ordinary** [ɪks'trɔːdnrɪ] adj extraordinaire

extravagance [ɪks'trævəgəns] n prodigalités fpl; (thing bought) folie f, dépense excessive; **extravagant** adj extravagant(e); (in spending: person) prodigue, dépensier(-ère); (: tastes) dispendieux(-euse)

extreme [ɪks'triːm] adj extrême ♦ n extrême m; ~**ly** adv extrêmement; **extremist** adj, n extrémiste m/f

extricate ['ɛkstrɪkeɪt] vt: **to ~ sth (from)** dégager qch (de)

extrovert ['ɛkstrəvəːt] n extraverti(e)

ex-wife n ex-femme f

eye [aɪ] n œil m (pl yeux); (of needle) trou m, chas m ♦ vt examiner; **to keep an ~ on** surveiller; ~**brow** n sourcil m; ~**drops** npl gouttes *fpl* pour les yeux; **~lash** *n* cil *m*; **~lid** *n* paupière *f*; **~liner** *n* eye-liner *m*; **~opener** *n* révélation *f*; **~shadow** *n* ombre *f* à paupières; **~sight** *n* vue *f*; **~sore** *n* horreur *f*; **~ witness** *n* témoin *m* oculaire

F, f

F [ɛf] *n* (MUS) fa *m*
fable ['feɪbl] *n* fable *f*
fabric ['fæbrɪk] *n* tissu *m*
fabulous ['fæbjuləs] *adj* fabuleux(-euse); (*inf*: *super*) formidable
face [feɪs] *n* visage *m*, figure *f*; (*expression*) expression *f*; (*of clock*) cadran *m*; (*of cliff*) paroi *f*; (*of mountain*) face *f*; (*of building*) façade *f* ♦ *vt* faire face à; **~ down** (*person*) à plat ventre; (*card*) face en dessous; **to lose/save ~** perdre/sauver la face; **to make** or **pull a ~** faire une grimace; **in the ~ of** (*difficulties etc*) face à, devant; **on the ~ of it** à première vue; **~ to ~** face à face; **~ up to** *vt fus* faire face à, affronter; **~ cloth** (BRIT) *n* gant *m* de toilette; **~ cream** *n* crème *f* pour le visage; **~ lift** *n* lifting *m*; (*of building etc*) ravalement *m*, retapage *m*; **~ powder** *n* poudre *f* de riz; **~ value** *n* (*of coin*) valeur nominale; **to take sth at ~ value** (*fig*) prendre qch pour argent comptant
facilities [fə'sɪlɪtɪz] *npl* installations *fpl*, équipement *m*; **credit ~ facilités** *fpl* de paiement
facing ['feɪsɪŋ] *prep* face à, en face de
facsimile [fæk'sɪmɪlɪ] *n* (*exact replica*) facsimilé *m*; (*fax*) télécopie *f*
fact [fækt] *n* fait *m*; **in ~** en fait
factor ['fæktə'] *n* facteur *m*
factory ['fæktərɪ] *n* usine *f*, fabrique *f*
factual ['fæktjuəl] *adj* basé(e) sur les faits
faculty ['fækəltɪ] *n* faculté *f*; (US: *teaching staff*) corps enseignant
fad [fæd] *n* (*craze*) engouement *m*
fade [feɪd] *vi* se décolorer, passer; (*light, sound*) s'affaiblir; (*flower*) se faner
fag [fæg] (BRIT: *inf*) *n* (*cigarette*) sèche *f*
fail [feɪl] *vt* (*exam*) échouer à; (*candidate*) recaler; (*subj: courage, memory*) faire défaut à ♦ *vi* échouer; (*brakes*) lâcher; (*eyesight, health, light*) baisser, s'affaiblir; **to ~ to do sth** (*neglect*) négliger de faire qch; (*be unable*) ne pas arriver or parvenir à faire qch; **without ~** à coup sûr; sans faute; **~ing** *n* défaut *m* ♦ *prep* faute de; **~ure** *n* échec *m*; (*person*) raté(e); (*mechanical etc*) défaillance *f*
faint [feɪnt] *adj* faible; (*recollection*) vague; (*mark*) à peine visible ♦ *n* évanouissement *m* ♦ *vi* s'évanouir; **to feel ~** défaillir
fair [fɛə'] *adj* équitable, juste, impartial(e);

(*hair*) blond(e); (*skin, complexion*) pâle, blanc (blanche); (*weather*) beau (belle); (*good enough*) assez bon(ne); (*sizeable*) considérable ♦ *adv*: **to play ~** jouer franc-jeu ♦ *n* foire *f*; (BRIT: *funfair*) fête (foraine); **~ly** *adv* équitablement; (*quite*) assez; **~ness** *n* justice *f*, équité *f*, impartialité *f*
fairy ['fɛərɪ] *n* fée *f*; **~ tale** *n* conte *m* de fées
faith [feɪθ] *n* foi *f*; (*trust*) confiance *f*; (*specific religion*) religion *f*; **~ful** *adj* fidèle; **~fully** *adv* see **yours**
fake [feɪk] *n* (*painting etc*) faux *m*; (*person*) imposteur *m* ♦ *adj* faux (fausse) ♦ *vt* simuler; (*painting*) faire un faux de
falcon ['fɔ:lkən] *n* faucon *m*
fall [fɔ:l] (*pt* **fell**, *pp* **fallen**) *n* chute *f*; (US: *autumn*) automne *m* ♦ *vi* tomber; (*price, temperature, dollar*) baisser; **~s** *npl* (*waterfall*) chute *f* d'eau, cascade *f*; **to ~ flat** (*on one's face*) tomber de tout son long, s'étaler; (*joke*) tomber à plat; (*plan*) échouer; **~ back** *vi* reculer, se retirer; **~ back on** *vt fus* se rabattre sur; **~ behind** *vi* prendre du retard; **~ down** *vi* (*person*) tomber; (*building*) s'effondrer, s'écrouler; **~ for** *vt fus* (*trick, story etc*) se laisser prendre à; (*person*) tomber amoureux de; **~ in** *vi* s'effondrer; (MIL) se mettre en rangs; **~ off** *vi* tomber; (*diminish*) baisser, diminuer; **~ out** *vi* (*hair, teeth*) tomber; (MIL) rompre les rangs; (*friends etc*) se brouiller; **~ through** *vi* (*plan, project*) tomber à l'eau
fallacy ['fæləsɪ] *n* erreur *f*, illusion *f*
fallout ['fɔ:laut] *n* retombées (radioactives)
fallow ['fæləu] *adj* en jachère; en friche
false [fɔ:ls] *adj* faux (fausse); **~ alarm** *n* fausse alerte; **~ pretences** *npl*: **under ~ pretences** sous un faux prétexte; **~ teeth** (BRIT) *npl* fausses dents
falter ['fɔ:ltə'] *vi* chanceler, vaciller
fame [feɪm] *n* renommée *f*, renom *m*
familiar [fə'mɪlɪə'] *adj* familier(-ère); **to be ~ with** (*subject*) connaître
family ['fæmɪlɪ] *n* famille *f* ♦ *cpd* (*business, doctor etc*) de famille; **has he any ~?** (*children*) a-t-il des enfants?
famine ['fæmɪn] *n* famine *f*
famished ['fæmɪʃt] (*inf*) *adj* affamé(e)
famous ['feɪməs] *adj* célèbre; **~ly** *adv* (*get on*) fameusement, à merveille
fan [fæn] *n* (*folding*) éventail *m*; (ELEC) ventilateur *m*; (*of person*) fan *m*, admirateur(-trice); (*of team, sport etc*) supporter *m/f* ♦ *vt* éventer; (*fire, quarrel*) attiser
fanatic [fə'nætɪk] *n* fanatique *m/f*
fan belt *n* courroie *f* de ventilateur
fancy ['fænsɪ] *n* fantaisie *f*, envie *f*, imagination *f* ♦ *adj* (de) fantaisie *inv* ♦ *vt* (*feel*

like, want) avoir envie de; *(imagine, think)* imaginer; **to take a ~ to** se prendre d'affection pour; s'enticher de; **he fancies her** *(inf)* elle lui plaît; **~ dress** *n* déguisement *m*, travesti *m*; **~-dress ball** *n* bal masqué *or* costumé

fang [fæŋ] *n* croc *m*; *(of snake)* crochet *m*

fantastic [fæn'tæstɪk] *adj* fantastique

fantasy ['fæntəzɪ] *n* imagination *f*, fantaisie *f*; *(dream)* chimère *f*

far [fɑːʳ] *adj* lointain(e), éloigné(e) ♦ *adv* loin; **~ away** *or* **off** au loin, dans le lointain; **at the ~ side/end** à l'autre côté/bout; **~ better** beaucoup mieux; **~ from** loin de; **by ~** de loin, de beaucoup; **go as ~ as the farm** allez jusqu'à la ferme; **as ~ as I know** pour autant que je sache; **how ~ is it to ...?** combien y a-t-il jusqu'à ...?; **how ~ have you got?** où en êtes-vous?; **~away** ['fɑːrəweɪ] *adj* lointain(e); *(look)* distrait(e)

farce [fɑːs] *n* farce *f*

fare [fɛəʳ] *n* *(on trains, buses)* prix *m* du billet; *(in taxi)* prix de la course; *(food)* table *f*, chère *f*; **half ~** demi-tarif; **full ~** plein tarif

Far East *n* Extrême-Orient *m*

farewell [fɛəˈwɛl] *excl* adieu ♦ *n* adieu *m*

farm [fɑːm] *n* ferme *f* ♦ *vt* cultiver; **~er** *n* fermier(-ère); cultivateur(-trice); **~hand** *n* ouvrier(-ère) agricole; **~house** *n* (maison *f* de) ferme *f*; **~ing** *n* agriculture *f*; *(of animals)* élevage *m*; **~land** *n* terres cultivées; **~ worker** *n* = **farmhand**; **~yard** *n* cour *f* de ferme

far-reaching ['fɑːˈriːtʃɪŋ] *adj* d'une grande portée

fart [fɑːt] *(inf!)* *vi* péter

farther ['fɑːðəʳ] *adv* plus loin ♦ *adj* plus éloigné(e), plus lointain(e)

farthest ['fɑːðɪst] *superl* of **far**

fascinate ['fæsɪneɪt] *vt* fasciner; **fascinating** *adj* fascinant(e)

fascism ['fæʃɪzəm] *n* fascisme *m*

fashion ['fæʃən] *n* mode *f*; *(manner)* façon *f*, manière *f* ♦ *vt* façonner; **in ~** à la mode; **out of ~** démodé(e); **~able** *adj* à la mode; **~ show** *n* défilé *m* de mannequins *or* de mode

fast [fɑːst] *adj* rapide; *(clock)*: **to be ~** avancer; *(dye, colour)* grand *or* bon teint *inv* ♦ *adv* vite, rapidement; *(stuck, held)* solidement ♦ *n* jeûne *m* ♦ *vi* jeûner; **~ asleep** profondément endormi

fasten ['fɑːsn] *vt* attacher, fixer; *(coat)* attacher, fermer ♦ *vi* se fermer, s'attacher; **~er**, **~ing** *n* attache *f*

fast food *n* fast food *m*, restauration *f* rapide

fastidious [fæsˈtɪdɪəs] *adj* exigeant(e), difficile

fat [fæt] *adj* gros(se) ♦ *n* graisse *f*; *(on meat)* gras *m*; *(for cooking)* matière grasse

fatal ['feɪtl] *adj* *(injury etc)* mortel(le); *(mistake)* fatal(e); **~ity** [fəˈtælɪtɪ] *n* *(road death etc)* victime *f*, décès *m*

fate [feɪt] *n* destin *m*; *(of person)* sort *m*; **~ful** *adj* fatidique

father ['fɑːðəʳ] *n* père *m*; **~-in-law** *n* beau-père *m*; **~ly** *adj* paternel(le)

fathom ['fæðəm] *n* brasse *f* (= 1828 mm) ♦ *vt* *(mystery)* sonder, pénétrer

fatigue [fəˈtiːg] *n* fatigue *f*

fatten ['fætn] *vt*, *vi* engraisser

fatty ['fætɪ] *adj* *(food)* gras(se) ♦ *n* *(inf)* gros(se)

fatuous ['fætjuəs] *adj* stupide

faucet ['fɔːsɪt] *(US)* *n* robinet *m*

fault [fɔːlt] *n* faute *f*; *(defect)* défaut *m*; *(GEO)* faille *f* ♦ *vt* trouver des défauts à; **it's my ~** c'est de ma faute; **to find ~ with** trouver à redire *or* à critiquer à; **at ~** fautif(-ive), coupable; **~y** *adj* défectueux(-euse)

fauna ['fɔːnə] *n* faune *f*

favour ['feɪvəʳ] *(US* favor*)* *n* faveur *f*; *(help)* service *m* ♦ *vt* *(proposition)* être en faveur de; *(pupil etc)* favoriser; *(team, horse)* donner gagnant; **to do sb a ~** rendre un service à qn; **to find ~ with** trouver grâce aux yeux de; **in ~ of** en faveur de; **~able** *adj* favorable; **~ite** ['feɪvrɪt] *adj*, *n* favori(te)

fawn [fɔːn] *n* faon *m* ♦ *adj* *(colour)* fauve ♦ *vi*: **to ~ (up)on** flatter servilement

fax [fæks] *n* *(document)* télécopie *f*; *(machine)* télécopieur *m* ♦ *vt* envoyer par télécopie

FBI *n abbr* (US: = *Federal Bureau of Investigation*) F.B.I. *m*

fear [fɪəʳ] *n* crainte *f*, peur *f* ♦ *vt* craindre; **for ~ of** de peur que +*sub*, de peur de +*infin*; **~ful** *adj* craintif(-ive); *(sight, noise)* affreux(-euse), épouvantable; **~less** *adj* intrépide

feasible ['fiːzəbl] *adj* faisable, réalisable

feast [fiːst] *n* festin *m*, banquet *m*; *(REL: also:* **~ day***)* fête *f* ♦ *vi* festoyer

feat [fiːt] *n* exploit *m*, prouesse *f*

feather ['fɛðəʳ] *n* plume *f*

feature ['fiːtʃəʳ] *n* caractéristique *f*; *(article)* chronique *f*, rubrique *f* ♦ *vt* *(subj: film)* avoir pour vedette(s) ♦ *vi*: **to ~ in** figurer (en bonne place) dans; *(in film)* jouer dans; **~s** *npl* *(of face)* traits *mpl*; **~ film** *n* long métrage *m*

February ['februərɪ] *n* février *m*

fed [fɛd] *pt*, *pp* of **feed**

federal ['fɛdərəl] *adj* fédéral(e)

fed up *adj*: **to be ~** en avoir marre, en avoir plein le dos

fee [fiː] *n* rémunération *f*; *(of doctor, lawyer)* honoraires *mpl*; *(for examination)* droits *mpl*; **school ~s** frais *mpl* de scolarité

feeble ['fiːbl] *adj* faible; *(pathetic: attempt, excuse)* pauvre; *(: joke)* piteux(-euse)

feed [fiːd] *(pt*, *pp* **fed***)* *n* *(of animal)* fourrage

m; pâture f; (on printer) mécanisme m
d'alimentation ♦ vt (person) nourrir; (BRIT:
baby) allaiter; (: with bottle) donner le
biberon à; (horse etc) donner à manger à;
(machine) alimenter; (data, information): to
~ **sth into** fournir qch à; ~ **on** vt fus se nourrir
de; **~back** n feed-back m inv

feel [fi:l] (pt, pp **felt**) n sensation f;
(impression) impression f ♦ vt toucher;
(explore) tâter, palper; (cold, pain) sentir;
(grief, anger) ressentir, éprouver; (think,
believe) trouver; **to ~ hungry/cold** avoir faim/
froid; **to ~ lonely/better** se sentir seul/mieux; **I
don't ~ well** je ne me sens pas bien; **it ~s soft**
c'est doux (douce) au toucher; **to ~ like**
(want) avoir envie de; ~ **about** vi fouiller,
tâtonner; **~er** n (of insect) antenne f; **~ing** n
(physical) sensation f; (emotional) sentiment
m

feet [fi:t] npl of **foot**
feign [fein] vt feindre, simuler
fell [fel] pt of **fall** ♦ vt (tree, person) abattre
fellow ['feləu] n type m; (comrade)
compagnon m; (of learned society) membre
m ♦ cpd: **their ~ prisoners/students** leurs
camarades prisonniers/d'étude; ~ **citizen** n
concitoyen(ne) m/f; ~ **countryman** (irreg) n
compatriote m; ~ **men** npl semblables mpl;
~ship n (society) association f; (comradeship)
amitié f, camaraderie f; (grant) sorte de bourse
universitaire

felony ['feləni] n crime m, forfait m
felt [felt] pt, pp of **feel** ♦ n feutre m; **~-tip
pen** n stylo-feutre m
female ['fi:meil] n (ZOOL) femelle f; (pej:
woman) bonne femme ♦ adj (BIO) femelle;
(sex, character) féminin(e); (vote etc) des
femmes

feminine ['feminin] adj féminin(e)
feminist ['feminist] n féministe m/f
fence [fens] n barrière f ♦ vt (also: ~ **in**)
clôturer ♦ vi faire de l'escrime; **fencing** n
escrime m
fend [fend] vi: **to ~ for o.s.** se débrouiller
(tout seul); ~ **off** vt (attack etc) parer
fender ['fendər] n garde-feu m inv; (on boat)
défense f; (US: of car) aile f
ferment [vb fə'ment, n 'fɜ:ment] vi fermenter
♦ n agitation f, effervescence f
fern [fɜ:n] n fougère f
ferocious [fə'rəuʃəs] adj féroce
ferret ['ferit] n furet m
ferry ['feri] n (small) bac m; (large: also:
~boat) ferry(-boat) m ♦ vt transporter
fertile ['fɜ:tail] adj fertile; (BIO) fécond(e);
fertilizer ['fɜ:tilaizə] n engrais m
fester ['festə] vi suppurer
festival ['festivəl] n (REL) fête f; (ART, MUS)
festival m

festive ['festiv] adj de fête; **the ~ season**
(BRIT: Christmas) la période des fêtes;
festivities npl réjouissances fpl
festoon [fes'tu:n] vt: **to ~ with** orner de
fetch [fetʃ] vt aller chercher; (sell for) se
vendre
fête [feit] n fête f, kermesse f
feud [fju:d] n dispute f, dissension f
fever ['fi:və] n fièvre f; **~ish** adj fiév-
reux(-euse), fébrile
few [fju:] adj (not many) peu de; **a ~** adj
quelques ♦ pron quelques-uns(-unes); **~er**
['fju:ə] adj moins de; moins (nombreux); **~-
est** ['fju:ist] adj le moins (de)
fiancé, e [fi'ɑ̃:ŋsei] n fiancé(e) m/f
fib [fib] n bobard m
fibre ['faibər] (US fiber) n fibre f; **~glass**
['faibəglɑ:s] (Fiberglass ® US) n fibre de verre
fickle ['fikl] adj inconstant(e), volage,
capricieux(-euse)
fiction ['fikʃən] n romans mpl, littérature f
romanesque; (invention) fiction f; **~al** adj
fictif(-ive)
fictitious adj fictif(-ive), imaginaire
fiddle ['fidl] n (MUS) violon m; (cheating)
combine f, escroquerie f ♦ vt (BRIT: accounts)
falsifier, maquiller; ~ **with** vt fus tripoter
fidget ['fidʒit] vi se trémousser, remuer
field [fi:ld] n champ m; (fig) domaine m,
champ; (SPORT: ground) terrain m; **~work** n
travaux mpl pratiques (sur le terrain)
fiend [fi:nd] n démon m
fierce [fiəs] adj (look, animal) féroce, sauvage;
(wind, attack, person) (très) violent(e);
(fighting, enemy) acharné(e)
fiery ['faiəri] adj ardent(e), brûlant(e);
(temperament) fougueux(-euse)
fifteen [fif'ti:n] num quinze
fifth [fifθ] num cinquième
fifty ['fifti] num cinquante; **~-fifty** adj: **a ~-
fifty chance** etc une chance etc sur deux ♦ adv
moitié-moitié
fig [fig] n figue f
fight [fait] (pt, pp **fought**) n (MIL) combat m;
(between persons) bagarre f; (against cancer
etc) lutte f ♦ vt se battre contre; (cancer,
alcoholism, emotion) combattre, lutter contre;
(election) se présenter à ♦ vi se battre; **~er** n
(fig) lutteur m; (plane) chasseur m; **~ing** n
combats mpl; (brawl) bagarres fpl
figment ['figmənt] n: **a ~ of the imagination**
une invention
figurative ['figjurətiv] adj figuré(e)
figure ['figə] n figure f; (number, cipher)
chiffre m; (body, outline) silhouette f; (shape)
ligne f, formes fpl ♦ vt (think: esp US)
supposer ♦ vi (appear) figurer; ~ **out** vt
(work out) calculer; **~head** n (NAUT) figure f
de proue; (pej) prête-nom m; ~ **of speech** n

figure f de rhétorique

file [faɪl] n (dossier) dossier m; (folder) dossier, chemise f; (: with hinges) classeur m; (COMPUT) fichier m; (row) file f; (tool) lime f ♦ vt (nails, wood) limer; (papers) classer; (LAW: claim) faire enregistrer; déposer ♦ vi: to ~ in/out entrer/sortir l'un derrière l'autre; to ~ for divorce faire une demande en divorce; **filing cabinet** n classeur m (meuble)

fill [fɪl] vt remplir; (need) répondre à ♦ n: to eat one's ~ manger à sa faim; to ~ with remplir de; ~ in vt (hole) boucher; (form) remplir; ~ up vt remplir; ~ it up, please (AUT) le plein, s'il vous plaît

fillet ['fɪlɪt] n filet m; ~ **steak** n filet m de bœuf, tournedos m

filling ['fɪlɪŋ] n (CULIN) garniture f, farce f; (for tooth) plombage m; ~ **station** n station-service f

film [fɪlm] n film m; (PHOT) pellicule f, film; (of powder, liquid) couche f, pellicule ♦ vt (scene) filmer ♦ vi tourner; ~ **star** n vedette f de cinéma

filter ['fɪltər] n filtre m ♦ vt filtrer; ~ **lane** n (AUT) voie f de sortie; ~**-tipped** adj à bout filtre

filth [fɪlθ] n saleté f; ~**y** adj sale, dégoûtant(e); (language) ordurier(-ère)

fin [fɪn] n (of fish) nageoire f

final ['faɪnl] adj final(e); (definitive) définitif(-ive) ♦ n (SPORT) finale f; ~**s** npl (SCOL) examens mpl de dernière année; ~**e** [fɪ'nɑːlɪ] n finale m; ~**ist** n finaliste m/f; ~**ize** vt mettre au point; ~**ly** adv (eventually) enfin, finalement; (lastly) en dernier lieu

finance [faɪ'næns] n finance f ♦ vt financer; ~**s** npl (financial position) finances fpl; **financial** [faɪ'nænʃəl] adj financier(-ère)

find [faɪnd] (pt, pp found) vt trouver; (lost object) retrouver ♦ n trouvaille f, découverte f; to ~ sb guilty (LAW) déclarer qn coupable; ~ **out** vt (truth, secret) découvrir; (person) démasquer ♦ vi: to ~ out about (make enquiries) se renseigner; (by chance) apprendre; ~**ings** npl (LAW) conclusions fpl, verdict m; (of report) conclusions

fine [faɪn] adj (excellent) excellent(e); (thin, not coarse, subtle) fin(e); (weather) beau (belle) ♦ adv (well) très bien ♦ n (LAW) amende f; contravention f ♦ vt (LAW) condamner à une amende; donner une contravention à; **to be ~** (person) aller bien; (weather) être beau; ~ **arts** npl beaux-arts mpl; ~**ry** n parure f

finger ['fɪŋgər] n doigt m ♦ vt palper, toucher; **little** ~ auriculaire m, petit doigt; **index** ~ index m; ~**nail** n ongle m (de la main); ~**print** n empreinte digitale; ~**tip** n bout m du doigt

finish ['fɪnɪʃ] n fin f; (SPORT) arrivée f; (polish etc) finition f ♦ vt finir, terminer ♦ vi finir, se terminer; to ~ **doing sth** finir de faire qch; to ~ **third** arriver or terminer troisième; ~ **up** vi, vt finir, terminer; (kill) achever; ~**ing line** n ligne f d'arrivée

finite ['faɪnaɪt] adj fini(e); (verb) conjugué(e)

Finland ['fɪnlənd] n Finlande f; **Finn** [fɪn] n Finlandais(e); **Finnish** adj finlandais(e) ♦ n (LING) finnois m

fir [fəːr] n sapin m

fire ['faɪər] n feu m; (accidental) incendie m; (heater) radiateur m ♦ vt (fig) enflammer, animer; (inf: dismiss) mettre à la porte, renvoyer; (discharge): to ~ **a gun** tirer un coup de feu ♦ vi (shoot) tirer, faire feu; **on** ~ en feu; ~ **alarm** n avertisseur m d'incendie; ~**arm** n arme à feu; ~ **brigade** n (sapeurs-)pompiers mpl; ~ **department** (US) n = fire brigade; ~ **engine** n (vehicle) voiture f des pompiers; ~ **escape** n escalier m de secours; ~ **extinguisher** n extincteur m; ~**man** n pompier m; ~**place** n cheminée f; ~**side** n foyer m, coin m du feu; ~ **station** n caserne f de pompiers; ~**wood** n bois m de chauffage; ~**works** npl feux mpl d'artifice; (display) feu(x) d'artifice

firing squad ['faɪərɪŋ-] n peloton m d'exécution

firm [fəːm] adj ferme ♦ n compagnie f, firme f

first [fəːst] adj premier(-ère) ♦ adv (before all others) le premier, la première; (before all other things) en premier, d'abord; (when listing reasons etc) en premier lieu, premièrement ♦ n (person: in race) premier(-ère); (BRIT: SCOL) mention f très bien; (AUT) première f; **at** ~ au commencement, au début; ~ **of all** tout d'abord, pour commencer; ~ **aid** n premiers secours or soins; ~**-aid kit** n trousse f à pharmacie; ~**-class** adj de première classe; (excellent) excellent(e), exceptionnel(le); ~**-hand** adj de première main; ~ **lady** n (US) femme f du président; ~**ly** adv premièrement, en premier lieu; ~ **name** n prénom m; ~**-rate** adj excellent(e)

fish [fɪʃ] n inv poisson m ♦ vt, vi pêcher; to go ~**ing** aller à la pêche; ~**erman** n pêcheur m; ~ **farm** n établissement m piscicole; ~ **fingers** (BRIT) npl bâtonnets de poisson (congelés); ~**ing boat** n barque f or bateau m de pêche; ~**ing line** n ligne f (de pêche); ~**ing rod** n canne f à pêche; ~**ing tackle** n attirail m de pêche; ~**monger's (shop)** n poissonnerie f; ~ **slice** n pelle f à poisson; ~ **sticks** (US) npl = fish fingers; ~**y** (inf) adj suspect(e), louche

fist [fɪst] n poing m

fit [fɪt] adj (healthy) en (bonne) forme;

(*proper*) convenable; approprié(e) ♦ *vt* (*subj: clothes*) aller à; (*put in, attach*) installer, poser; adapter; (*equip*) équiper, garnir, munir; (*suit*) convenir à ♦ *vi* (*clothes*) aller; (*parts*) s'adapter; (*in space, gap*) entrer, s'adapter ♦ *n* (*MED*) accès *m*, crise *f*; (*of anger*) accès; (*of hysterics, jealousy*) crise; ~ **to** en état de; ~ **for** digne de; apte à; ~ **of coughing** quinte *f* de toux; **a ~ of giggles** le fou rire; **this dress is a good ~** cette robe (me) va très bien; **by ~s and starts** par à-coups; ~ **in** *vi* s'accorder; s'adapter; **~ful** *adj* (*sleep*) agité(e); **~ment** *n* meuble encastré, élément *m*; **~ness** *n* (*MED*) forme *f* physique; **~ted carpet** moquette *f*; **~ted kitchen** (*BRIT*) *n* cuisine équipée; **~ter** *n* monteur *m*; **~ting** *adj* approprié(e) ♦ *n* (*of dress*) essayage *m*; (*of piece of equipment*) pose *f*, installation *f*; **~tings** *npl* (*in building*) installations *fpl*; **~ting room** *n* cabine *f* d'essayage

five [faɪv] *num* cinq; **~r** (*inf*) *n* (*BRIT*) billet *m* de cinq livres; (*US*) billet de cinq dollars

fix [fɪks] *vt* (*date, amount etc*) fixer; (*organize*) arranger; (*mend*) réparer; (*meal, drink*) préparer ♦ *n*: **to be in a ~** être dans le pétrin; ~ **up** *vt* (*meeting*) arranger; **to ~ sb up with sth** faire avoir qch à qn; **~ation** [fɪk'seɪʃən] *n* (*PSYCH*) fixation *f*; (*fig*) obsession *f*; **~ed** *adj* (*prices etc*) fixe; (*smile*) figé(e); **~ture** *n* installation *f* (fixe); (*SPORT*) rencontre *f* (au programme)

fizzy ['fɪzɪ] *adj* pétillant(e); gazeux(-euse)

flabbergasted ['flæbəgɑːstɪd] *adj* sidéré(e), ahuri(e)

flabby ['flæbɪ] *adj* mou (molle)

flag [flæg] *n* drapeau *m*; (*also*: **~stone**) dalle *f* ♦ *vi* faiblir; fléchir; ~ **down** *vt* héler, faire signe (de s'arrêter) à; **~pole** *n* mât *m*; **~ship** *n* vaisseau *m* amiral; (*fig*) produit *m* vedette

flair [fleə*r*] *n* flair *m*

flak [flæk] *n* (*MIL*) tir antiaérien; (*inf: criticism*) critiques *fpl*

flake [fleɪk] *n* (*of rust, paint*) écaille *f*; (*of snow, soap powder*) flocon *m* ♦ *vi* (*also*: ~ **off**) s'écailler

flamboyant [flæm'bɔɪənt] *adj* flamboyant(e), éclatant(e); (*person*) haut(e) en couleur

flame [fleɪm] *n* flamme *f*

flamingo [flə'mɪŋgəu] *n* flamant *m* (rose)

flammable ['flæməbl] *adj* inflammable

flan [flæn] (*BRIT*) *n* tarte *f*

flank [flæŋk] *n* flanc *m* ♦ *vt* flanquer

flannel ['flænl] *n* (*fabric*) flanelle *f*; (*BRIT: also*: **face ~**) gant *m* de toilette

flap [flæp] *n* (*of pocket, envelope*) rabat *m* ♦ *vt* (*wings*) battre (de) ♦ *vi* (*sail, flag*) claquer; (*inf: also*: **be in a ~**) paniquer

flare [fleə*r*] *n* (*signal*) signal lumineux; (*in skirt etc*) évasement *m*; ~ **up** *vi* s'embraser; (*fig: person*) se mettre en colère, s'emporter; (: *revolt etc*) éclater

flash [flæʃ] *n* éclair *m*; (*also*: **news ~**) flash *m* (d'information); (*PHOT*) flash ♦ *vt* (*light*) projeter; (*send: message*) câbler; (*look*) jeter; (*smile*) lancer ♦ *vi* (*light*) clignoter; **a ~ of lightning** un éclair; **in a ~** en un clin d'œil; **to ~ one's headlights** faire un appel de phares; **to ~ by** or **past** (*person*) passer (devant) comme un éclair; **~bulb** *n* ampoule *f* de flash; **~cube** *n* cube-flash *m*; **~light** *n* lampe *f* de poche; **~y** (*pej*) *adj* tape-à-l'œil *inv*, tapageur(-euse)

flask [flɑːsk] *n* flacon *m*, bouteille *f*; (*also*: **vacuum ~**) thermos ® *m* or *f*

flat [flæt] *adj* plat(e); (*tyre*) dégonflé(e), à plat; (*beer*) éventé(e); (*denial*) catégorique; (*MUS*) bémol *inv*; (: *voice*) faux (fausse); (*fee, rate*) fixe ♦ *n* (*BRIT: apartment*) appartement *m*; (*AUT*) crevaison *f*; (*MUS*) bémol *m*; **to work ~ out** travailler d'arrache-pied; **~ly** *adv* catégoriquement; **~ten** *vt* (*also*: **~ten out**) aplatir; (*crop*) coucher; (*building(s)*) raser

flatter ['flætə*r*] *vt* flatter; **~ing** *adj* flatteur(-euse); **~y** *n* flatterie *f*

flaunt [flɔːnt] *vt* faire étalage de

flavour ['fleɪvə*r*] (*US* **flavor**) *n* goût *m*, saveur *f*; (*of ice cream etc*) parfum *m* ♦ *vt* parfumer; **vanilla-~ed** à l'arôme de vanille, à la vanille; **~ing** *n* arôme *m*

flaw [flɔː] *n* défaut *m*; **~less** *adj* sans défaut

flax [flæks] *n* lin *m*

flea [fliː] *n* puce *f*

fleck [flek] *n* tacheture *f*, moucheture *f*

flee [fliː] (*pt, pp* **fled**) *vt* fuir ♦ *vi* fuir, s'enfuir

fleece [fliːs] *n* toison *f* ♦ *vt* (*inf*) voler, filouter

fleet [fliːt] *n* flotte *f*; (*of lorries etc*) parc *m*, convoi *m*

fleeting ['fliːtɪŋ] *adj* fugace, fugitif(-ive); (*visit*) très bref (brève)

Flemish ['flemɪʃ] *adj* flamand(e)

flesh [fleʃ] *n* chair *f*; ~ **wound** *n* blessure superficielle

flew [fluː] *pt of* **fly**

flex [fleks] *n* fil *m* or câble *m* électrique ♦ *vt* (*knee*) fléchir; (*muscles*) tendre; **~ible** *adj* flexible

flick [flɪk] *n* petite tape; chiquenaude *f*; (*of duster*) petit coup ♦ *vt* donner un petit coup à; (*switch*) appuyer sur; ~ **through** *vt fus* feuilleter

flicker ['flɪkə*r*] *vi* (*light*) vaciller; **his eyelids ~ed** il a cillé

flier ['flaɪə*r*] *n* aviateur *m*

flight [flaɪt] *n* vol *m*; (*escape*) fuite *f*; (*also*: ~ **of steps**) escalier *m*; ~ **attendant** (*US*) *n* steward *m*, hôtesse *f* de l'air; ~ **deck** *n*

(AVIAT) poste m de pilotage; (NAUT) pont m d'envol

flimsy ['flɪmzɪ] adj peu solide; (clothes) trop léger(-ère); (excuse) pauvre, mince

flinch [flɪntʃ] vi tressaillir; **to ~ from** se dérober à, reculer devant

fling [flɪŋ] (pt, pp flung) vt jeter, lancer

flint [flɪnt] n silex m; (in lighter) pierre f (à briquet)

flip [flɪp] vt (throw) lancer (d'une chiquenaude); **to ~ sth over** retourner qch

flippant ['flɪpənt] adj désinvolte, irrévérencieux(-euse)

flipper ['flɪpə'] n (of seal etc) nageoire f; (for swimming) palme f

flirt [flɜːt] vi flirter ♦ n flirteur(-euse) m/f

float [fləʊt] n flotteur m; (in procession) char m; (money) réserve f ♦ vi flotter

flock [flɒk] n troupeau m; (of birds) vol m; (REL) ouailles fpl ♦ vi: **to ~ to** se rendre en masse à

flog [flɒg] vt fouetter

flood [flʌd] n inondation f; (of letters, refugees etc) flot m ♦ vt inonder ♦ vi (people): **to ~ into** envahir; **~ing** n inondation f; **~light** n projecteur m

floor [flɔː'] n sol m; (storey) étage m; (of sea, valley) fond m ♦ vt (subj: question) déconcerter; (: blow) terrasser; **on the ~** par terre; **ground ~**, (US) **first ~** rez-de-chaussée m inv; **first ~**, (US) **second ~** premier étage; **~board** n planche f (du plancher); **~ show** n spectacle m de variétés

flop [flɒp] n fiasco m ♦ vi être un fiasco; (fall: into chair) s'affaler, s'effondrer; **~py** adj lâche, flottant(e) ♦ n (COMPUT: also: **~py disk**) disquette f

flora ['flɔːrə] n flore f

floral ['flɔːrl] adj (dress) à fleurs

florid ['flɒrɪd] adj (complexion) coloré(e); (style) plein(e) de fioritures

florist ['flɒrɪst] n fleuriste m/f; **~'s (shop)** n magasin m or boutique f de fleuriste

flounder ['flaʊndə'] vi patauger ♦ n (ZOOL) flet m

flour ['flaʊə'] n farine f

flourish ['flʌrɪʃ] vi prospérer ♦ n (gesture) moulinet m

flout [flaʊt] vt se moquer de, faire fi de

flow [fləʊ] n (ELEC, of river) courant m; (of blood in veins) circulation f; (of tide) flux m; (of orders, data) flot m ♦ vi couler; (traffic) s'écouler; (robes, hair) flotter; **the ~ of traffic** l'écoulement m de la circulation; **~ chart** n organigramme m

flower ['flaʊə'] n fleur f ♦ vi fleurir; **~ bed** n plate-bande f; **~pot** n pot m (de fleurs); **~y** adj fleuri(e)

flown [fləʊn] pp of fly

flu [fluː] n grippe f

fluctuate ['flʌktjʊeɪt] vi varier, fluctuer

fluent ['fluːənt] adj (speech) coulant(e), aisé(e); **he speaks ~ French, he's ~ in French** il parle couramment le français

fluff [flʌf] n duvet m; (on jacket, carpet) peluche f; **~y** adj duveteux(-euse); (toy) en peluche

fluid ['fluːɪd] adj fluide ♦ n fluide m

fluke [fluːk] (inf) n (luck) coup m de veine

flung [flʌŋ] pt, pp of fling

fluoride ['flʊəraɪd] n fluorure f; **~ toothpaste** dentifrice m au fluor

flurry ['flʌrɪ] n (of snow) rafale f, bourrasque f; **~ of activity/excitement** affairement m/ excitation f soudain(e)

flush [flʌʃ] n (on face) rougeur f; (fig: of youth, beauty etc) éclat m ♦ vt nettoyer à grande eau ♦ vi rougir ♦ adj: **~ with** au ras de, de niveau avec; **to ~ the toilet** tirer la chasse (d'eau); **~ed** adj (tout(e)) rouge

flustered ['flʌstəd] adj énervé(e)

flute [fluːt] n flûte f

flutter ['flʌtə'] n (of panic, excitement) agitation f; (of wings) battement m ♦ vi (bird) battre des ailes, voleter

flux [flʌks] n: **in a state of ~** fluctuant sans cesse

fly [flaɪ] (pt flew, pp flown) n (insect) mouche f; (on trousers: also: **flies**) braguette f ♦ vt piloter; (passengers, cargo) transporter (par avion); (distances) parcourir ♦ vi voler; (passengers) aller en avion; (escape) s'enfuir, fuir; (flag) se déployer; **~ away** vi (bird, insect) s'envoler; **~ off** vi = fly away; **~-drive** n formule f avion plus voiture; **~ing** n (activity) aviation f; (action) vol m ♦ adj: **a ~ing visit** une visite éclair; **with ~ing colours** haut la main; **~ing saucer** n soucoupe volante; **~ing start** n: **to get off to a ~ing start** prendre un excellent départ; **~over** (BRIT) n (bridge) saut-de-mouton m; **~sheet** n (for tent) double toit m

foal [fəʊl] n poulain m

foam [fəʊm] n écume f; (on beer) mousse f; (also: **~ rubber**) caoutchouc mousse m ♦ vi (liquid) écumer; (soapy water) mousser

fob [fɒb] vt: **to ~ sb off** se débarrasser de qn

focal point ['fəʊkl-] n (fig) point central

focus ['fəʊkəs] (pl **~es**) n foyer m; (of interest) centre m ♦ vt (field glasses etc) mettre au point ♦ vi: **to ~ (on)** (with camera) régler la mise au point (sur); (person) fixer son regard (sur); **out of/in ~** (picture) flou(e)/net(te); (camera) pas au point/au point

fodder ['fɒdə'] n fourrage m

foe [fəʊ] n ennemi m

fog [fɒg] n brouillard m; **~gy** adj: **it's ~gy** il y a du brouillard; **~ lamp** (US **fog light**) n (AUT)

phare *m* antibrouillard
foil [fɔɪl] *vt* déjouer, contrecarrer ♦ *n* feuille *f*
de métal; (*kitchen* ~) papier *m* alu(minium);
(*complement*) repoussoir *m*
fold [fəuld] *n* (*bend, crease*) pli *m*; (*AGR*) parc
m à moutons; (*fig*) bercail *m* ♦ *vt* plier;
(*arms*) croiser; ~ **up** *vi* (*map, table etc*) se
plier; (*business*) fermer boutique ♦ *vt* (*map,
clothes*) plier; ~**er** *n* (*for papers*) chemise *f*;
(: *with hinges*) classeur *m*; ~**ing** *adj* (*chair,
bed*) pliant(e)
foliage ['fəulɪɪdʒ] *n* feuillage *m*
folk [fəuk] *npl* gens *mpl* ♦ *cpd* folklorique; ~**s**
(*inf*) *npl* (*parents*) parents *mpl*; ~**lore**
['fəuklɔːʳ] *n* folklore *m*; ~ **song** *n* chanson *f*
folklorique
follow ['fɔləu] *vt* suivre ♦ *vi* suivre; (*result*)
s'ensuivre; **to** ~ **suit** (*fig*) faire de même;
~ **up** *vt* (*letter, offer*) donner suite à; (*case*)
suivre; ~**er** *n* disciple *m/f*, partisan(e); ~**ing**
adj suivant(e) ♦ *n* partisans *mpl*, disciples *mpl*
folly ['fɔlɪ] *n* inconscience *f*; folie *f*
fond [fɔnd] *adj* (*memory, look*) tendre; (*hopes,
dreams*) un peu fou (folle); **to be** ~ **of** aimer
beaucoup
fondle ['fɔndl] *vt* caresser
font [fɔnt] *n* (*in church: for baptism*) fonts
baptismaux; (*TYP*) fonte *f*
food [fuːd] *n* nourriture *f*; ~ **mixer** *n* mixer
m; ~ **poisoning** *n* intoxication *f* alimentaire;
~ **processor** *n* robot *m* de cuisine; ~**stuffs**
npl denrées *fpl* alimentaires
fool [fuːl] *n* idiot(e); (*CULIN*) mousse *f* de fruits
♦ *vt* berner, duper ♦ *vi* faire l'idiot *or*
l'imbécile; ~**hardy** *adj* téméraire,
imprudent(e); ~**ish** *adj* idiot(e), stupide;
(*rash*) imprudent(e); insensé(e); ~**proof** *adj*
(*plan etc*) infaillible
foot [fut] (*pl* feet) *n* pied *m*; (*of animal*) patte
f; (*measure*) pied (= 30,48 cm; 12 inches)
♦ *vt* (*bill*) payer; **on** ~ à pied; ~**age** *n*
(*CINEMA: length*) ≈ métrage *m*; (: *material*)
séquences *fpl*; ~**ball** *n* ballon *m* (de football);
(*sport: BRIT*) football *m*, foot *m*; (: *US*) football
américain; ~**ball player** (*BRIT*) *n* (*also:
~baller*) joueur *m* de football; ~**brake** *n* frein
m à pédale; ~**bridge** *n* passerelle *f*; ~**hills**
npl contreforts *mpl*; ~**hold** *n* prise *f* de
pied); ~**ing** *n* (*fig*) position *f*; **to lose one's
~ing** perdre pied; ~**lights** *npl* rampe *f*;
~**note** *n* note *f* (en bas de page); ~**path** *n*
sentier *m*; (*in street*) trottoir *m*; ~**print** *n*
trace *f* (de pas); ~**step** *n* pas *m*; ~**wear** *n*
chaussure(s) *f(pl)*

for [fɔːʳ] *prep* **1** (*indicating destination,
intention, purpose*) pour; **the train for London**
le train pour *or* (à destination) de Londres; **he**

went for the paper il est allé chercher le
journal; **it's time for lunch** c'est l'heure du
déjeuner; **what's it for?** ça sert à quoi?; **what
for?** (*why*) pourquoi?
2 (*on behalf of, representing*) pour; **the MP for
Hove** le député de Hove; **to work for sb/sth**
travailler pour qn/qch; **G for George** G
comme Georges
3 (*because of*) pour; **for this reason** pour
cette raison; **for fear of being criticized** de
peur d'être critiqué
4 (*with regard to*) pour; **it's cold for July** il fait
froid pour juillet; **a gift for languages** un don
pour les langues
5 (*in exchange for*): **I sold it for £5** je l'ai
vendu 5 livres; **to pay 50 pence for a ticket**
payer un billet 50 pence
6 (*in favour of*) pour; **are you for or against
us?** êtes-vous pour ou contre nous?
7 (*referring to distance*) pendant, sur; **there
are roadworks for 5 km** il y a des travaux sur
5 km; **we walked for miles** nous avons
marché pendant des kilomètres
8 (*referring to time*) pendant; depuis; pour;
he was away for 2 years il a été absent
pendant 2 ans; **she will be away for a month**
elle sera absente (pendant) un mois; **I have
known her for years** je la connais depuis des
années; **can you do it for tomorrow?** est-ce
que tu peux le faire pour demain?
9 (*with infinitive clauses*): **it is not for me to
decide** ce n'est pas à moi de décider; **it would
be best for you to leave** le mieux serait que
vous partiez; **there is still time for you to do it**
vous avez encore le temps de le faire; **for this
to be possible** ... pour que cela soit possible ...
10 (*in spite of*): **for all his work/efforts**
malgré tout son travail/tous ses efforts; **for all
his complaints, he's very fond of her** il a beau
se plaindre, il l'aime beaucoup
♦ *conj* (*since, as: rather formal*) car

forage ['fɔrɪdʒ] *vi* fourrager
foray ['fɔreɪ] *n* incursion *f*
forbid [fə'bɪd] (*pt* forbad(e), *pp* forbidden) *vt*
défendre, interdire; **to ~ sb to do** défendre *or*
interdire à qn de faire; ~**ding** *adj* sévère,
sombre
force [fɔːs] *n* force *f* ♦ *vt* forcer; (*push*)
pousser (de force); **the F~s** *npl* (*MIL*) l'armée
f; **in** ~ en vigueur; ~**-feed** *vt* nourrir de force;
~**ful** *adj* énergique, volontaire; **forcibly** *adv*
par la force, de force; (*express*)
énergiquement
ford [fɔːd] *n* gué *m*
fore [fɔːʳ] *n*: **to come to the ~** se faire
remarquer; ~**arm** *n* avant-bras *m inv*;
~**boding** *n* pressentiment *m* (néfaste); ~**cast**
(*irreg: like cast*) *n* prévision *f* ♦ *vt* prévoir;

~**court** n (of garage) devant m; ~**finger** n
index m; ~**front** n: **in the ~front of** au
premier rang or plan de
foregone ['fɔːɡɔn] adj: **it's a ~ conclusion**
c'est couru d'avance
foreground ['fɔːɡraund] n premier plan
forehead ['fɔrɪd] n front m
foreign ['fɔrɪn] adj étranger(-ère); (trade)
extérieur(-e); ~**er** n étranger(-ère);
~ **exchange** n change m; **F~ Office** (BRIT) n
ministère m des affaires étrangères;
F~ Secretary (BRIT) n ministre m des affaires
étrangères
fore: ~**leg** n (of cat, dog) patte f de devant;
(of horse) jambe antérieure; ~**man** (irreg) n
(of factory, building site) contremaître m, chef
m d'équipe; ~**most** adj le (la) plus en vue;
premier(-ère) ♦ adv: **first and ~most** avant
tout, tout d'abord
forensic [fəˈrɛnsɪk] adj: ~ **medicine** médecine
légale; ~ **scientist** médecin m légiste
fore: ~**runner** n précurseur m; ~**see** (irreg:
like see) vt prévoir; ~**seeable** adj prévisible;
~**shadow** vt présager, annoncer, laisser
prévoir; ~**sight** n prévoyance f
forest ['fɔrɪst] n forêt f; ~**ry** n sylviculture f
foretaste ['fɔːteɪst] n avant-goût m
foretell [fɔːˈtɛl] (irreg: like **tell**) vt prédire
forever [fəˈrɛvəʳ] adv pour toujours; (fig)
continuellement
foreword ['fɔːwəːd] n avant-propos m inv
forfeit ['fɔːfɪt] vt (lose) perdre
forgave [fəˈɡeɪv] pt of **forgive**
forge [fɔːdʒ] n forge f ♦ vt (signature)
contrefaire; (wrought iron) forger; **to ~ money**
(BRIT) fabriquer de la fausse monnaie;
~ **ahead** vi pousser de l'avant, prendre de
l'avance; ~**d** adj faux (fausse); ~**r** n faussaire
m; ~**ry** n faux m, contrefaçon f
forget [fəˈɡɛt] (pt **forgot**, pp **forgotten**) vt, vi
oublier; ~**ful** adj distrait(e), étourdi(e); ~-
me-not n myosotis m
forgive [fəˈɡɪv] (pt **forgave**, pp **forgiven**) vt
pardonner; **to ~ sb for sth/for doing sth**
pardonner qch à qn/à qn de faire qch;
~**ness** n pardon m
forgo [fɔːˈɡəu] (pt **forwent**, pp **forgone**) vt
renoncer à
fork [fɔːk] n (for eating) fourchette f; (for
gardening) fourche f; (of roads) bifurcation f;
(of railways) embranchement m ♦ vi (road)
bifurquer; ~ **out** (inf) allonger; ~-**lift
truck** n chariot élévateur
forlorn [fəˈlɔːn] adj (deserted) abandonné(e);
(attempt, hope) désespéré(e)
form [fɔːm] n forme f; (SCOL) classe f;
(questionnaire) formulaire m ♦ vt former;
(habit) contracter; **in top ~** en pleine forme
formal ['fɔːməl] adj (offer, receipt) en bonne

et due forme; (person) cérémonieux(-euse);
(dinner) officiel(le); (clothes) de soirée;
(garden) à la française; (education) à
proprement parler; ~**ly** adv officiellement;
cérémonieusement
format ['fɔːmæt] n format m ♦ vt (COMPUT)
formater
formation [fɔːˈmeɪʃən] n formation f
formative ['fɔːmətɪv] adj: ~ **years** années fpl
d'apprentissage or de formation
former ['fɔːməʳ] adj ancien(ne) (before n),
précédent(e); **the ~ ... the latter** le premier ...
le second, celui-là ... celui-ci; ~**ly** adv
autrefois
formidable ['fɔːmɪdəbl] adj redoutable
formula ['fɔːmjulə] (pl ~**s** or ~**e**) n formule f
forsake [fəˈseɪk] (pt **forsook**, pp **forsaken**) vt
abandonner
fort [fɔːt] n fort m
forte ['fɔːtɪ] n (point) fort m
forth [fɔːθ] adv en avant; **to go back and ~**
aller et venir; **and so ~** et ainsi de suite;
~**coming** adj (event) qui va avoir lieu
prochainement; (character) ouvert(e),
communicatif(-ive); (available) disponible;
~**right** adj franc (franche), direct(e); ~**with**
adv sur-le-champ
fortify ['fɔːtɪfaɪ] vt fortifier
fortitude ['fɔːtɪtjuːd] n courage m
fortnight ['fɔːtnaɪt] (BRIT) n quinzaine f,
quinze jours mpl; ~**ly** (BRIT) adj bimensuel(le)
♦ adv tous les quinze jours
fortunate ['fɔːtʃənɪt] adj heureux(-euse);
(person) chanceux(-euse); **it is ~ that** c'est
une chance que; ~**ly** adv heureusement
fortune ['fɔːtʃən] n chance f; (wealth) fortune
f; ~-**teller** n diseuse f de bonne aventure
forty ['fɔːtɪ] num quarante
forward ['fɔːwəd] adj (ahead of schedule) en
avance; (movement, position) en avant, vers
l'avant; (not shy) direct(e); effronté(e) ♦ n
(SPORT) avant m ♦ vt (letter) faire suivre;
(parcel, goods) expédier; (fig) promouvoir,
favoriser; ~(**s**) adv en avant; **to move ~**
avancer
fossil ['fɔsl] n fossile m
foster ['fɔstəʳ] vt encourager, favoriser; (child)
élever (sans obligation d'adopter); ~ **child** n
enfant adoptif(-ive)
fought [fɔːt] pt, pp of **fight**
foul [faul] adj (weather, smell, food) infect(e);
(language) ordurier(-ère) ♦ n (SPORT) faute f
♦ vt (dirty) salir, encrasser; **he's got a
~ temper** il a un caractère de chien; ~ **play** n
(LAW) acte criminel
found [faund] pt, pp of **find** ♦ vt (establish)
fonder; ~**ation** [faunˈdeɪʃən] n (act)
fondation f; (base) fondement m; (also:
~**ation cream**) fond m de teint; ~**ations** npl (of

building) fondations *fpl*

founder ['faundər] *n* fondateur *m* ♦ *vi* couler, sombrer

foundry ['faundrı] *n* fonderie *f*

fountain ['fauntın] *n* fontaine *f*; **~ pen** *n* stylo *m* (à encre)

four [fɔːʳ] *num* quatre; **on all ~s** à quatre pattes; **~-poster** *n* (*also*: **~-poster bed**) lit *m* à baldaquin; **~teen** *num* quatorze; **~th** *num* quatrième

fowl [faul] *n* volaille *f*

fox [fɔks] *n* renard *m* ♦ *vt* mystifier

foyer ['fɔɪeɪ] *n* (*hotel*) hall *m*; (*THEATRE*) foyer *m*

fraction ['frækʃən] *n* fraction *f*

fracture ['fræktʃəʳ] *n* fracture *f*

fragile ['frædʒaɪl] *adj* fragile

fragment ['frægmənt] *n* fragment *m*

fragrant ['freɪgrənt] *adj* parfumé(e), odorant(e)

frail [freɪl] *adj* fragile, délicat(e)

frame [freɪm] *n* charpente *f*; (*of picture, bicycle*) cadre *m*; (*of door, window*) encadrement *m*, chambranle *m*; (*of spectacles: also*: **~s**) monture *f* ♦ *vt* encadrer; **~ of mind** disposition *f* d'esprit; **~work** *n* structure *f*

France [frɑːns] *n* France *f*

franchise ['fræntʃaɪz] *n* (*POL*) droit *m* de vote; (*COMM*) franchise *f*

frank [fræŋk] *adj* franc (franche) ♦ *vt* (*letter*) affranchir; **~ly** *adv* franchement

frantic ['fræntık] *adj* (*hectic*) frénétique; (*distraught*) hors de soi

fraternity [frə'təːnıtı] *n* (*spirit*) fraternité *f*; (*club*) communauté *f*, confrérie *f*

fraud [frɔːd] *n* supercherie *f*, fraude *f*, tromperie *f*; (*person*) imposteur *m*

fraught [frɔːt] *adj*: **~ with** chargé(e) de, plein(e) de

fray [freɪ] *vi* s'effilocher

freak [friːk] *n* (*also cpd*) phénomène *m*, créature ou événement exceptionnel par sa rareté

freckle ['frekl] *n* tache *f* de rousseur

free [friː] *adj* libre; (*gratis*) gratuit(e) ♦ *vt* (*prisoner etc*) libérer; (*jammed object or person*) dégager; **~ (of charge), for ~** gratuitement; **~dom** *n* liberté *f*; **F~fone** ® *n* numéro vert; **~-for-all** *n* mêlée générale; **~ gift** *n* prime *f*; **~hold** *n* propriété foncière libre; **~ kick** *n* coup franc; **~lance** *adj* indépendant(e); **~ly** *adv* librement; (*liberally*) libéralement; **F~mason** *n* franc-maçon *m*; **F~post** ® *n* port payé; **~-range** *adj* (*hen, eggs*) de ferme; **~ trade** *n* libre-échange *m*; **~way** (*US*) *n* autoroute *f*; **~ will** *n* libre arbitre *m*; **of one's own ~ will** de son plein gré

freeze [friːz] (*pt* **froze**, *pp* **frozen**) *vi* geler ♦ *vt* geler; (*food*) congeler; (*prices, salaries*) bloquer, geler ♦ *n* gel *m*; (*fig*) blocage *m*; **~-dried** *adj* lyophilisé(e); **~r** *n* congélateur *m*, freezer *m*

freezing *adj*: **freezing (cold)** (*weather, water*) glacial(e) ♦ *n*: **3 degrees below freezing** 3 degrés au-dessous de zéro; **freezing point** *n* point *m* de congélation

freight [freɪt] *n* (*goods*) fret *m*, cargaison *f*; (*money charged*) fret, prix *m* du transport; **~ train** *n* train *m* de marchandises

French [frentʃ] *adj* français(e) ♦ *n* (*LING*) français *m*; **the ~** *npl* (*people*) les Français; **~ bean** *n* haricot vert; **~ fried (potatoes)** (*US* **~ fries**) *npl* (pommes de terre *fpl*) frites *fpl*; **~ horn** *n* (*MUS*) cor *m* (d'harmonie); **~ kiss** *n* baiser profond; **~ loaf** *n* baguette *f*; **~man** (*irreg*) *n* Français *m*; **~ window** *n* porte-fenêtre *f*; **~woman** (*irreg*) *n* Française *f*

frenzy ['frenzı] *n* frénésie *f*

frequency ['friːkwənsı] *n* fréquence *f*

frequent [*adj* 'friːkwənt, *vb* fri'kwent] *adj* fréquent(e) ♦ *vt* fréquenter; **~ly** *adv* fréquemment

fresh [freʃ] *adj* frais (fraîche); (*new*) nouveau (nouvelle); (*cheeky*) familier(-ère), culotté(e); **~en** *vi* (*wind, air*) fraîchir; **~en up** *vi* faire un brin de toilette; **~er** (*BRIT*: *inf*) *n* (*SCOL*) bizuth *m*, étudiant(e) de 1ère année; **~ly** *adv* nouvellement, récemment; **~man** (*US*) (*irreg*) *n* **= fresher**; **~ness** *n* fraîcheur *f*; **~water** *adj* (*fish*) d'eau douce

fret [fret] *vi* s'agiter, se tracasser

friar ['fraɪəʳ] *n* moine *m*, frère *m*

friction ['frıkʃən] *n* friction *f*

Friday ['fraɪdı] *n* vendredi *m*

fridge [frıdʒ] (*BRIT*) *n* frigo *m*, frigidaire ® *m*

fried [fraɪd] *adj* frit(e); **~ egg** œuf *m* sur le plat

friend [frend] *n* ami(e); **~ly** *adj* amical(e); gentil(le); (*place*) accueillant(e); **they were killed by ~ly fire** ils sont morts sous les tirs de leur propre camp; **~ship** *n* amitié *f*

frieze [friːz] *n* frise *f*

fright [fraɪt] *n* peur *f*, effroi *m*; **to take ~** prendre peur, s'effrayer; **~en** *vt* effrayer, faire peur à; **~ened** *adj*: **to be ~ened (of)** avoir peur (de); **~ening** *adj* effrayant(e); **~ful** *adj* affreux(-euse)

frigid ['frıdʒıd] *adj* frigide

frill [frıl] *n* (*on dress*) volant *m*; (*on shirt*) jabot *m*

fringe [frındʒ] *n* (*BRIT*: *of hair*) frange *f*; (*edge*: *of forest etc*) bordure *f*; **~ benefits** *npl* avantages sociaux *or* en nature

Frisbee ® ['frızbı] *n* Frisbee ® *m*

frisk [frısk] *vt* fouiller

fritter ['frıtəʳ] *n* beignet *m*; **~ away** *vt* gaspiller

frivolous ['frıvələs] *adj* frivole

frizzy ['frɪzɪ] adj crépu(e)
fro [frəu] adv: **to go to and ~** aller et venir
frock [frɔk] n robe f
frog [frɔg] n grenouille f; **~man** n homme-grenouille m
frolic ['frɔlɪk] vi folâtrer, batifoler

KEYWORD

from [frɔm] prep 1 (*indicating starting place, origin etc*) de; **where do you come from?, where are you from?** d'où venez-vous?; **from London to Paris** de Londres à Paris; **a letter from my sister** une lettre de ma sœur; **to drink from the bottle** boire à (même) la bouteille
2 (*indicating time*) (à partir) de; **from one o'clock to or until or till two** d'une heure à deux heures; **from January (on)** à partir de janvier
3 (*indicating distance*) de; **the hotel is one kilometre from the beach** l'hôtel est à un kilomètre de la plage
4 (*indicating price, number etc*) de; **the interest rate was increased from 9% to 10%** le taux d'intérêt est passé de 9 à 10%
5 (*indicating difference*) de; **he can't tell red from green** il ne peut pas distinguer le rouge du vert
6 (*because of, on the basis of*): **from what he says** d'après ce qu'il dit; **weak from hunger** affaibli par la faim

front [frʌnt] n (*of house, dress*) devant m; (*of coach, train*) avant m; (*promenade: also:* **sea ~**) bord m de mer; (*MIL, METEOROLOGY*) front m; (*fig: appearances*) contenance f, façade f ♦ adj de devant; (*seat*) avant inv; **in ~ (of)** devant; **~age** n (*of building*) façade f; **~ door** n porte f d'entrée; (*of car*) portière f avant; **~ier** ['frʌntɪə'] n frontière f; **~ page** n première page; **~ room** (*BRIT*) n pièce f de devant, salon m; **~-wheel drive** n traction f avant
frost [frɔst] n gel m, gelée f; (*also:* **hoarfrost**) givre m; **~bite** n gelures fpl; **~ed** adj (*glass*) dépoli(e); **~y** adj (*weather, welcome*) glacial(e)
froth [frɔθ] n mousse f; écume f
frown [fraun] vi froncer les sourcils
froze [frəuz] pt of **freeze**
frozen ['frəuzn] pp of **freeze**
fruit [fruːt] n inv fruit m; **~erer** n fruitier m, marchand(e) de fruits; **~ful** adj (*fig*) fructueux(-euse); **~ion** [fruːˈɪʃən] n: **to come to ~ion** se réaliser; **~ juice** n jus m de fruit; **~ machine** (*BRIT*) n machine f à sous; **~ salad** n salade f de fruits
frustrate [frʌsˈtreɪt] vt frustrer
fry [fraɪ] (*pt, pp* **fried**) vt (faire) frire; *see also*

small; **~ing pan** n poêle f (à frire)
ft. abbr = **foot; feet**
fudge [fʌdʒ] n (*CULIN*) caramel m
fuel ['fjuəl] n (*for heating*) combustible m; (*for propelling*) carburant m; **~ oil** n mazout m; **~ tank** n (*in vehicle*) réservoir m
fugitive ['fjuːdʒɪtɪv] n fugitif(-ive)
fulfil [fulˈfɪl] (*US* **fulfill**) vt (*function, condition*) remplir; (*order*) exécuter; (*wish, desire*) satisfaire, réaliser; **~ment** (*US* **fulfillment**) n (*of wishes etc*) réalisation f; (*feeling*) contentement m
full [ful] adj plein(e); (*details, information*) complet(-ète); (*skirt*) ample, large ♦ adv: **to know ~ well that** savoir fort bien que; **I'm ~ (up)** j'ai bien mangé; **a ~ two hours** deux bonnes heures; **at ~ speed** à toute vitesse; **in ~** (*reproduce, quote*) intégralement; (*write*) en toutes lettres; **~ employment** plein emploi; **to pay in ~** tout payer; **~-length** adj (*film*) long métrage; (*portrait, mirror*) en pied; (*coat*) long(ue); **~ moon** n pleine lune; **~-scale** adj (*attack, war*) complet(-ète), total(e); (*model*) grandeur nature inv; **~ stop** n point m; **~-time** adj, adv (*work*) à plein temps; **~y** adv entièrement, complètement; (*at least*) au moins; **~y licensed** (*hotel, restaurant*) autorisé(e) à vendre des boissons alcoolisées; **~-fledged** adj (*barrister etc*) diplômé(e); (*citizen, member*) à part entière
fumble ['fʌmbl] vi: **~ with** tripoter
fume [fjuːm] vi rager; **~s** npl vapeurs fpl, émanations fpl, gaz mpl
fun [fʌn] n amusement m, divertissement m; **to have ~** s'amuser; **for ~** pour rire; **to make ~ of** se moquer de
function ['fʌŋkʃən] n fonction f; (*social occasion*) cérémonie f, soirée officielle ♦ vi fonctionner; **~al** adj fonctionnel(le)
fund [fʌnd] n caisse f, fonds m; (*source, store*) source f, mine f; **~s** npl (*money*) fonds mpl
fundamental [fʌndəˈmɛntl] adj fondamental(e)
funeral ['fjuːnərəl] n enterrement m, obsèques fpl; **~ parlour** n entreprise f de pompes funèbres; **~ service** n service m funèbre
funfair ['fʌnfɛə'] (*BRIT*) n fête (foraine)
fungi ['fʌŋgaɪ] npl of **fungus**
fungus ['fʌŋgəs] (*pl* **fungi**) n champignon m; (*mould*) moisissure f
funnel ['fʌnl] n entonnoir m; (*of ship*) cheminée f
funny ['fʌnɪ] adj amusant(e), drôle; (*strange*) curieux(-euse), bizarre
fur [fəː'] n fourrure f; (*BRIT: in kettle etc*) (dépôt m de) tartre m
furious ['fjuərɪəs] adj furieux(-euse); (*effort*) acharné(e)

furlong ['fə:lɔŋ] n = 201,17 m

furnace ['fə:nıs] n fourneau m

furnish ['fə:nɪʃ] vt meubler; (supply): **to ~ sb with sth** fournir qch à qn; **~ings** npl mobilier m, ameublement m

furniture ['fə:nɪtʃə'] n meubles mpl, mobilier m; **piece of ~** meuble m

furrow ['fʌrəu] n sillon m

furry ['fə:rɪ] adj (animal) à fourrure; (toy) en peluche

further ['fə:ðə'] adj (additional) supplémentaire, autre; nouveau (nouvelle); (moreover) de plus ♦ vt faire avancer or progresser, promouvoir; **~ education** n enseignement m postscolaire; **~more** adv de plus, en outre

furthest ['fə:ðıst] superl of **far**

fury ['fjuərı] n fureur f

fuse [fju:z] (US **fuze**) n fusible m; (for bomb etc) amorce f, détonateur m ♦ vt, vi (metal) fondre; **to ~ the lights** (BRIT) faire sauter les plombs; **~ box** n boîte f à fusibles

fuss [fʌs] n (excitement) agitation f; (complaining) histoire(s) f(pl); **to make a ~** faire des histoires; **to make a ~ of sb** être aux petits soins pour qn; **~y** adj (person) tatillon(ne), difficile; (dress, style) tarabiscoté(e)

future ['fju:tʃə'] adj futur(e) ♦ n avenir m; (LING) futur m; **in ~** à l'avenir

fuze [fju:z] (US) n, vt, vi = **fuse**

fuzzy ['fʌzı] adj (PHOT) flou(e); (hair) crépu(e)

G, g

G [dʒi:] n (MUS) sol m

G8 n abbr (= Group of 8) le groupe des 8

gabble ['gæbl] vi bredouiller

gable ['geıbl] n pignon m

gadget ['gædʒıt] n gadget m

Gaelic ['geılık] adj gaélique ♦ n (LING) gaélique m

gag [gæg] n (on mouth) bâillon m; (joke) gag m ♦ vt bâillonner

gaiety ['geıtı] n gaieté f

gain [geın] n (improvement) gain m; (profit) gain, profit m; (increase): **~ (in)** augmentation f (de) ♦ vt gagner ♦ vi (watch) avancer; **to ~ 3 lbs (in weight)** prendre 3 livres; **to ~ on sb** (catch up) rattraper qn; **to ~ from/by** gagner de/à

gal. abbr = **gallon**

gale [geıl] n coup m de vent

gallant ['gælənt] adj vaillant(e), brave; (towards ladies) galant

gall bladder ['gɔ:l-] n vésicule f biliaire

gallery ['gælərı] n galerie f; (also: **art ~**) musée m; (: private) galerie

gallon ['gæln] n gallon m (BRIT = 4,5 l; US = 3,8 l)

gallop ['gæləp] n galop m ♦ vi galoper

gallows ['gæləuz] n potence f

gallstone ['gɔ:lstəun] n calcul m biliaire

galore [gə'lɔ:'] adv en abondance, à gogo

Gambia ['gæmbıə] n: **(The) ~** la Gambie

gambit ['gæmbıt] n (fig): **(opening) ~** manœuvre f stratégique

gamble ['gæmbl] n pari m, risque calculé ♦ vt, vi jouer; **to ~ on** (fig) miser sur; **~r** n joueur m; **gambling** n jeu m

game [geım] n jeu m; (match) match m; (strategy, scheme) plan m; projet m; (HUNTING) gibier m ♦ adj (willing): **to be ~ (for)** être prêt(e) (à or pour); **big ~** gros gibier; **~keeper** n garde-chasse m

gammon ['gæmən] n (bacon) quartier m de lard fumé; (ham) jambon fumé

gamut ['gæmət] n gamme f

gang [gæŋ] n bande f; (of workmen) équipe f; **~ up** vi: **to ~ up on sb** se liguer contre qn; **~ster** n gangster m; **~way** ['gæŋweı] n passerelle f; (BRIT: of bus, plane) couloir central; (: in cinema) allée centrale

gaol [dʒeıl] (BRIT) n = **jail**

gap [gæp] n trou m; (in time) intervalle m; (difference): **~ between** écart m entre

gape [geıp] vi (person) être or rester bouche bée; (hole, shirt) être ouvert(e); **gaping** adj (hole) béant(e)

garage ['gæra:ʒ] n garage m

garbage ['ga:bıdʒ] n (US: rubbish) ordures fpl, détritus mpl; (inf: nonsense) foutaises fpl; **~ can** (US) n poubelle f, boîte f à ordures

garbled ['ga:bld] adj (account, message) embrouillé(e)

garden ['ga:dn] n jardin m; **~s** npl jardin public; **~er** n jardinier m; **~ing** n jardinage m

gargle ['ga:gl] vi se gargariser

garish ['gɛərıʃ] adj criard(e), voyant(e); (light) cru(e)

garland ['ga:lənd] n guirlande f; couronne f

garlic ['ga:lık] n ail m

garment ['ga:mənt] n vêtement m

garrison ['gærısn] n garnison f

garter ['ga:tə'] n jarretière f; (US) jarretelle f

gas [gæs] n gaz m; (US: gasoline) essence f ♦ vt asphyxier; **~ cooker** (BRIT) n cuisinière f à gaz; **~ cylinder** n bouteille f de gaz; **~ fire** (BRIT) n radiateur m à gaz

gash [gæʃ] n entaille f; (on face) balafre f

gasket ['gæskıt] n (AUT) joint m de culasse

gas mask n masque m à gaz

gas meter n compteur m à gaz

gasoline ['gæsəli:n] (US) n essence f

gasp [ga:sp] vi haleter

gas: ~ **ring** n brûleur m; ~ **station** (US) n station-service f; ~ **tap** n bouton m (de cuisinière à gaz); (on pipe) robinet m à gaz

gastric ['gæstrɪk] adj gastrique; ~ **flu** grippe f intestinale

gate [geɪt] n (of garden) portail m; (of field) barrière f; (of building, at airport) porte f

gateau ['gætəu] n (pl ~x) (gros) gâteau à la crème

gatecrash vt s'introduire sans invitation dans

gateway n porte f

gather ['gæðər] vt (flowers, fruit) cueillir; (pick up) ramasser; (assemble) rassembler, réunir; recueillir; (understand) comprendre; (SEWING) froncer ♦ vi (assemble) se rassembler; **to ~ speed** prendre de la vitesse; **~ing** n rassemblement m

gaudy ['gɔːdɪ] adj voyant(e)

gauge [geɪdʒ] n (instrument) jauge f ♦ vt jauger

gaunt [gɔːnt] adj (thin) décharné(e); (grim, desolate) désolé(e)

gauntlet ['gɔːntlɪt] n (glove) gant m

gauze [gɔːz] n gaze f

gave [geɪv] pt of **give**

gay [geɪ] adj (homosexual) homosexuel(le); (cheerful) gai(e), réjoui(e); (colour etc) gai, vif (vive)

gaze [geɪz] n regard m fixe ♦ vi: **to ~ at** fixer du regard

gazump [gə'zʌmp] (BRIT) vi revenir sur une promesse de vente (pour accepter une offre plus intéressante)

GB abbr = **Great Britain**

GCE n abbr (BRIT) = **General Certificate of Education**

GCSE n abbr (BRIT) = **General Certificate of Secondary Education**

gear [gɪər] n matériel m, équipement m; (TECH) engrenage m; (AUT) vitesse f ♦ vt (fig: adapt): **to ~ sth to** adapter qch à; **top** or (US) **high ~** quatrième (or cinquième) vitesse; **low ~** première vitesse; **in ~** en prise; **~ box** n boîte f de vitesses; **~ lever** (US **gear shift**) n levier m de vitesse

geese [giːs] npl of **goose**

gel [dʒel] n gel m

gem [dʒem] n pierre précieuse

Gemini ['dʒemɪnaɪ] n les Gémeaux mpl

gender ['dʒendər] n genre m

gene [dʒiːn] n gène m

general ['dʒenərl] n général m ♦ adj général(e); **in ~** en général; **~ delivery** n poste restante; **~ election** n élection(s) législative(s); **~ knowledge** n connaissances générales; **~ly** adv généralement; **~ practitioner** n généraliste m/f

generate ['dʒenəreɪt] vt engendrer; (electricity etc) produire; **generation** n

génération f; (of electricity etc) production f; **generator** n générateur m

generosity [dʒenə'rɔsɪtɪ] n générosité f

generous ['dʒenərəs] adj généreux(-euse); (copious) copieux(-euse)

genetic [dʒɪ'netɪk] adj: ~ **engineering** ingéniérie f génétique; ~ **fingerprinting** système m d'empreinte génétique

genetics [dʒɪ'netɪks] n génétique f

Geneva [dʒɪ'niːvə] n Genève

genial ['dʒiːnɪəl] adj cordial(e), chaleureux(-euse)

genitals ['dʒenɪtlz] npl organes génitaux

genius ['dʒiːnɪəs] n génie m

genteel [dʒen'tiːl] adj de bon ton, distingué(e)

gentle ['dʒentl] adj doux (douce)

gentleman ['dʒentlmən] n monsieur m; (well-bred man) gentleman m

gently ['dʒentlɪ] adv doucement

gentry ['dʒentrɪ] n inv: **the ~** la petite noblesse

gents [dʒents] n W.-C. mpl (pour hommes)

genuine ['dʒenjuɪn] adj véritable, authentique; (person) sincère

geographical [dʒɪə'græfɪkl] adj géographique

geography [dʒɪ'ɔgrəfɪ] n géographie f

geology [dʒɪ'ɔlədʒɪ] n géologie f

geometric(al) [dʒɪə'metrɪk(l)] adj géométrique

geometry [dʒɪ'ɔmətrɪ] n géométrie f

geranium [dʒɪ'reɪnɪəm] n géranium m

geriatric [dʒerɪ'ætrɪk] adj gériatrique

germ [dʒəːm] n (MED) microbe m

German ['dʒəːmən] adj allemand(e) ♦ n Allemand(e); (LING) allemand m; ~ **measles** (BRIT) n rubéole f

Germany ['dʒəːmənɪ] n Allemagne f

gesture ['dʒestjər] n geste m

KEYWORD

get [get] (pt, pp **got**, pp **gotten** (US)) vi **1** (become, be) devenir; **to get old/tired** devenir vieux/fatigué, vieillir/se fatiguer; **to get drunk** s'enivrer; **to get killed** se faire tuer; **when do I get paid?** quand est-ce que je serai payé?; **it's getting late** il se fait tard

2 (go): **to get to/from** aller à/de; **to get home** rentrer chez soi; **how did you get here?** comment es-tu arrivé ici?

3 (begin) commencer or se mettre à; **I'm getting to like him** je commence à l'apprécier; **let's get going** or **started** allons-y

4 (modal aux vb): **you've got to do it** il faut que vous le fassiez; **I've got to tell the police** je dois le dire à la police

♦ vt **1**: **to get sth done** (do) faire qch; (have done) faire faire qch; **to get one's hair cut** se

faire couper les cheveux; **to get sb to do sth**
faire faire qch à qn; **to get sb drunk** enivrer
qn
2 (*obtain: money, permission, results*) obtenir,
avoir; (*find: job, flat*) trouver; (*fetch: person,
doctor, object*) aller chercher; **to get sth for sb**
procurer qch à qn; **get me Mr Jones, please**
(*on phone*) passez-moi Mr Jones, s'il vous
plaît; **can I get you a drink?** est-ce que je peux
vous servir à boire?
3 (*receive: present, letter*) recevoir, avoir;
(*acquire: reputation*) avoir; (: *prize*) obtenir;
what did you get for your birthday? qu'est-ce
que tu as eu pour ton anniversaire?
4 (*catch*) prendre, saisir, attraper; (*hit: target
etc*) atteindre; **to get sb by the arm/throat**
prendre *or* saisir *or* attraper qn par le bras/à la
gorge; **get him!** arrête-le!
5 (*take, move*) faire parvenir; **do you think
we'll get it through the door?** on arrivera à le
faire passer par la porte?; **I'll get you there
somehow** je me débrouillerai pour t'y
emmener
6 (*catch, take: plane, bus etc*) prendre
7 (*understand*) comprendre, saisir; (*hear*)
entendre; **I've got it!** j'ai compris!, je saisis!; **I
didn't get your name** je n'ai pas entendu
votre nom
8 (*have, possess*): **to have got** avoir; **how
many have you got?** vous en avez combien?
get about *vi* se déplacer; (*news*) se répandre
get along *vi* (*agree*) s'entendre; (*depart*)
s'en aller; (*manage*) = **get by**
get at *vt fus* (*attack*) s'en prendre à; (*reach*)
attraper, atteindre
get away *vi* partir, s'en aller; (*escape*)
s'échapper
get away with *vt fus* en être quitte pour; se
faire passer *or* pardonner
get back *vi* (*return*) rentrer ♦ *vt* récupérer,
recouvrer
get by *vi* (*pass*) passer; (*manage*) se
débrouiller
get down *vi, vt fus* descendre ♦ *vt*
descendre; (*depress*) déprimer
get down to *vt fus* (*work*) se mettre à
(faire)
get in *vi* rentrer; (*train*) arriver
get into *vt fus* entrer dans; (*car, train etc*)
monter dans; (*clothes*) mettre, enfiler,
endosser; **to get into bed/a rage** se mettre au
lit/en colère
get off *vi* (*from train etc*) descendre; (*depart:
person, car*) s'en aller; (*escape*) s'en tirer ♦ *vt*
(*remove: clothes, stain*) enlever ♦ *vt fus* (*train,
bus*) descendre de
get on *vi* (*at exam etc*) se débrouiller;
(*agree*): **to get on (with)** s'entendre (avec)
♦ *vt fus* monter dans; (*horse*) monter sur

get out *vi* sortir; (*of vehicle*) descendre ♦ *vt*
sortir
get out of *vt fus* sortir de; (*duty etc*)
échapper à, se soustraire à
get over *vt fus* (*illness*) se remettre de
get round *vt fus* contourner; (*fig: person*)
entortiller
get through *vi* (*TEL*) avoir la
communication; **to get through to sb**
atteindre qn
get together *vi* se réunir ♦ *vt* assembler
get up *vi* (*rise*) se lever ♦ *vt fus* monter
get up to *vt fus* (*reach*) arriver à; (*prank etc*)
faire

getaway ['gɛtəweɪ] *n*: **to make one's ~** filer
geyser ['giːzə^r] *n* (*GEO*) geyser *m*; (*BRIT: water
heater*) chauffe-eau *m inv*
Ghana ['gɑːnə] *n* Ghana *m*
ghastly ['gɑːstlɪ] *adj* atroce, horrible; (*pale*)
livide, blême
gherkin ['gəːkɪn] *n* cornichon *m*
ghetto blaster ['gɛtəʊˈblɑːstə^r] *n* stéréo *f*
portable
ghost [gəʊst] *n* fantôme *m*, revenant *m*
giant ['dʒaɪənt] *n* géant(e) ♦ *adj* géant(e),
énorme
gibberish ['dʒɪbərɪʃ] *n* charabia *m*
giblets ['dʒɪblɪts] *npl* abats *mpl*
Gibraltar [dʒɪˈbrɔːltə^r] *n* Gibraltar *m*
giddy ['gɪdɪ] *adj* (*dizzy*): **to be** *or* **feel ~** avoir
le vertige
gift [gɪft] *n* cadeau *m*; (*donation, ability*) don
m; **~ed** *adj* doué(e); **~ shop** *n* boutique *f* de
cadeaux; **~ token** *n* chèque-cadeau *m*
gigantic [dʒaɪˈgæntɪk] *adj* gigantesque
giggle ['gɪgl] *vi* pouffer (de rire), rire
sottement
gill [dʒɪl] *n* (*measure*) = 0.25 pints (*BRIT*
= 0.15 l, US = 0.12 l)
gills [gɪlz] *npl* (*of fish*) ouïes *fpl*, branchies *fpl*
gilt [gɪlt] *adj* doré(e) ♦ *n* dorure *f*; **~-edged**
adj (*COMM*) de premier ordre
gimmick ['gɪmɪk] *n* truc *m*
gin [dʒɪn] *n* (*liquor*) gin *m*
ginger ['dʒɪndʒə^r] *n* gingembre *m*; **~ ale**,
~ beer *n* boisson gazeuse au gingembre;
~bread *n* pain *m* d'épices
gingerly ['dʒɪndʒəlɪ] *adv* avec précaution
gipsy ['dʒɪpsɪ] *n* = **gypsy**
giraffe [dʒɪˈrɑːf] *n* girafe *f*
girder ['gəːdə^r] *n* poutrelle *f*
girl [gəːl] *n* fille *f*, fillette *f*; (*young unmarried
woman*) jeune fille; (*daughter*) fille; **an
English ~** une jeune Anglaise; **~friend** *n* (*of
girl*) amie *f*; (*of boy*) petite amie; **~ish** *adj* de
petite *or* de jeune fille; (*for a boy*)
efféminé(e)
giro ['dʒaɪrəʊ] *n* (*bank ~*) virement *m*

bancaire; (post office ~) mandat m; (BRIT: welfare cheque) mandat m d'allocation chômage

gist [dʒɪst] n essentiel m

give [gɪv] (pt **gave**, pp **given**) vt donner ♦ vi (break) céder; (stretch: fabric) se prêter; **to ~ sb sth, ~ sth to sb** donner qch à qn; **to ~ a cry/sigh** pousser un cri/un soupir; **~ away** vt donner; (~ free) faire cadeau de; (betray) donner, trahir; (disclose) révéler; (bride) conduire à l'autel; **~ back** vt rendre; **~ in** vi céder ♦ vt donner; **~ off** vt dégager; **~ out** vt distribuer; annoncer; **~ up** vi renoncer ♦ vt renoncer à; **to ~ up smoking** arrêter de fumer; **to ~ o.s. up** se rendre; **~ way** (BRIT) vi céder; (AUT) céder la priorité

glacier ['glæsɪəʳ] n glacier m

glad [glæd] adj content(e); **~ly** adv volontiers

glamorous ['glæmərəs] adj (person) séduisant(e); (job) prestigieux(-euse)

glamour ['glæməʳ] n éclat m, prestige m

glance [glɑːns] n coup m d'œil ♦ vi: **to ~ at** jeter un coup d'œil à; **glancing** adj (blow) oblique

gland [glænd] n glande f

glare [glɛəʳ] n (of anger) regard furieux, (of light) lumière éblouissante; (of publicity) feux mpl ♦ vi briller d'un éclat aveuglant; **to ~ at** lancer un regard furieux à; **glaring** adj (mistake) criant(e), qui saute aux yeux

glass [glɑːs] n verre m; **~es** npl (spectacles) lunettes fpl; **~house** (BRIT) n (for plants) serre f; **~ware** n verrerie f

glaze [gleɪz] vt (door, window) vitrer; (pottery) vernir ♦ n (on pottery) vernis m; **~d** adj (pottery) verni(e); (eyes) vitreux(-euse)

glazier ['gleɪzɪəʳ] n vitrier m

gleam [gliːm] vi luire, briller

glean [gliːn] vt (information) glaner

glee [gliː] n joie f

glib [glɪb] adj (person) qui a du bagou; (response) désinvolte, facile

glide [glaɪd] vi glisser; (AVIAT, birds) planer; **~r** n (AVIAT) planeur m; **gliding** n (SPORT) vol m à voile

glimmer ['glɪməʳ] n lueur f

glimpse [glɪmps] n vision passagère, aperçu m ♦ vt entrevoir, apercevoir

glint [glɪnt] vi étinceler

glisten ['glɪsn] vi briller, luire

glitter ['glɪtəʳ] vi scintiller, briller

gloat [gləut] vi: **to ~ (over)** jubiler (à propos de)

global ['gləubl] adj mondial(e); **~ warming** réchauffement de la planète

globe [gləub] n globe m

gloom [gluːm] n obscurité f; (sadness) tristesse f, mélancolie f; **~y** adj sombre, triste, lugubre

glorious ['glɔːrɪəs] adj glorieux(-euse); splendide

glory ['glɔːrɪ] n gloire f; splendeur f

gloss [glɔs] n (shine) brillant m, vernis m; **~ over** vt fus glisser sur

glossary ['glɔsərɪ] n glossaire m

glossy ['glɔsɪ] adj brillant(e); **~ magazine** magazine m de luxe

glove [glʌv] n gant m; **~ compartment** n (AUT) boîte f à gants, vide-poches m inv

glow [gləu] vi rougeoyer; (face) rayonner; (eyes) briller

glower ['glauəʳ] vi: **to ~ (at)** lancer des regards mauvais (à)

glucose ['gluːkəus] n glucose m

glue [gluː] n colle f ♦ vt coller

glum [glʌm] adj morose, morne

glut [glʌt] n surabondance f

glutton ['glʌtn] n glouton(ne); **a ~ for work** un bourreau de travail; **a ~ for punishment** un masochiste (fig)

GM abbr (= genetically modified) génétiquement modifié(e)

gnat [næt] n moucheron m

gnaw [nɔː] vt ronger

go [gəu] (pt **went**, pp **gone**, pl **~es**) vi aller; (depart) partir, s'en aller; (work) marcher; (break etc) céder; (be sold): **to ~ for £10** se vendre 10 livres; (fit, suit): **to ~ with** aller avec; (become): **to ~ pale/mouldy** pâlir/moisir ♦ n: **to have a ~ (at)** essayer (de faire); **to be on the ~** être en mouvement; **whose ~ is it?** à qui est-ce de jouer?; **he's ~ing to do it** il va faire, il est sur le point de faire; **to ~ for a walk** aller se promener; **to ~ dancing** aller danser; **how did it ~?** comment est-ce que ça s'est passé?; **to ~ round the back/by the shop** passer par derrière/devant le magasin; **~ about** vi (rumour) se répandre ♦ vt fus: **how do I ~ about this?** comment dois-je m'y prendre (pour faire ceci)?; **~ after** vt fus (pursue) poursuivre, courir après; (job, record etc) essayer d'obtenir; **~ ahead** vi (make progress) avancer; (get going) y aller; **~ along** vi aller, avancer ♦ vt fus longer, parcourir; **~ away** vi partir, s'en aller; **~ back** vi rentrer; revenir; (~ again) retourner; **~ back on** vt fus (promise) revenir sur; **~ by** vi (years, time) passer, s'écouler ♦ vt fus s'en tenir à; en croire; **~ down** vi descendre; (ship) couler; (sun) se coucher ♦ vt fus descendre; **~ for** vt fus (fetch) aller chercher; (like) aimer; (attack) s'en prendre à, attaquer; **~ in** vi entrer; **~ in for** vt fus (competition) se présenter à; (like) aimer; **~ into** vt fus entrer dans; (investigate) étudier, examiner; (embark on) se lancer dans; **~ off** vi partir, s'en aller; (food) se gâter; (explode) sauter; (event) se dérouler

♦ vt fus ne plus aimer; **the gun went off** le coup est parti; ~ **on** vt continuer; (happen) se passer; **to ~ on doing** continuer à faire; ~ **out** vi sortir; (fire, light) s'éteindre; ~ **over** vt fus (check) revoir, vérifier; ~ **past** vt fus: **to ~ past sth** passer devant qch; ~ **round** vi (circulate: news, rumour) circuler; (revolve) tourner; (suffice) suffire (pour tout le monde); **to ~ round to sb's** (visit) passer chez qn; **to ~ round (by)** (make a detour) faire un détour (par); ~ **through** vt fus (town etc) traverser; ~ **up** vi monter; (price) augmenter ♦ vt fus gravir; ~ **with** vt fus (suit) aller avec; ~ **without** vt fus se passer de

goad [gəʊd] vt aiguillonner

go-ahead ['gəʊəhɛd] adj dynamique, entreprenant(e) ♦ n feu vert

goal [gəʊl] n but m; ~**keeper** n gardien m de but; ~**post** n poteau m de but

goat [gəʊt] n chèvre f

gobble ['gɔbl] vt (also: ~ **down**, ~ **up**) engloutir

go-between ['gəʊbɪtwiːn] n intermédiaire m/f

god [gɔd] n dieu m; **G~** n Dieu m; ~**child** n filleul(e); ~**daughter** n filleule f; ~**dess** n déesse f; ~**father** n parrain m; ~**forsaken** adj maudit(e); ~**mother** n marraine f; ~**send** n aubaine f; ~**son** n filleul m

goggles ['gɔglz] npl (for skiing etc) lunettes protectrices

going ['gəʊɪŋ] n (conditions) état m du terrain ♦ adj: **the ~ rate** le tarif (en vigueur)

gold [gəʊld] n or m ♦ adj en or; (reserves) d'or; ~**en** adj (made of gold) en or; (gold in colour) doré(e); ~**fish** n poisson m rouge; ~**plated** adj plaqué(e) or inv; ~**smith** n orfèvre m

golf [gɔlf] n golf m; ~ **ball** n balle f de golf; (on typewriter) boule f; ~ **club** n club m de golf; (stick) club m, crosse f de golf; ~ **course** n (terrain m de) golf m; ~**er** n joueur(-euse) de golf

gone [gɔn] pp of **go**

gong [gɔŋ] n gong m

good [gʊd] adj bon(ne); (kind) gentil(le); (child) sage ♦ n bien m; ~**s** npl (COMM) marchandises fpl, articles mpl; ~! bon!, très bien!; **to be ~ at** être bon en; **to be ~ for** être bon pour; **would you be ~ enough to ...?** auriez-vous la bonté or l'amabilité de ...?; **a ~ deal (of)** beaucoup (de); **a ~ many** beaucoup (de); **to make ~** vi (succeed) faire son chemin, réussir ♦ vt (deficit) combler; (losses) compenser; **it's no ~ complaining** cela ne sert à rien de se plaindre; **for ~** pour de bon, une fois pour toutes; ~ **morning/afternoon!** bonjour!; ~ **evening!** bonsoir!; ~ **night!** bonsoir!; (on going to bed) bonne nuit!; ~**bye** excl au revoir!; **G~ Friday** n Vendredi saint; ~-**looking** adj beau (belle), bien inv; ~-**natured** adj (person) qui a un bon naturel; ~**ness** n (of person) bonté f; **for ~ness sake!** je vous en prie!; ~**ness gracious!** mon Dieu!; ~**s train** (BRIT) n train m de marchandises; ~**will** n bonne volonté

goose [guːs] (pl **geese**) n oie f

gooseberry ['gʊzbəri] n groseille f à maquereau; **to play ~** (BRIT) tenir la chandelle

gooseflesh ['guːsflɛʃ] n, **goose pimples** npl chair f de poule

gore [gɔːr] vt encorner ♦ n sang m

gorge [gɔːdʒ] n gorge f ♦ vt: **to ~ o.s. (on)** se gorger (de)

gorgeous ['gɔːdʒəs] adj splendide, superbe

gorilla [gə'rɪlə] n gorille m

gorse [gɔːs] n ajoncs mpl

gory ['gɔːrɪ] adj sanglant(e); (details) horrible

go-slow ['gəʊ'sləʊ] (BRIT) n grève perlée

gospel ['gɔspl] n évangile m

gossip ['gɔsɪp] n (chat) bavardages mpl; commérage m, cancans mpl; (person) commère f ♦ vi bavarder; (maliciously) cancaner, faire des commérages

got [gɔt] pt, pp of **get**; ~**ten** (US) pp of **get**

gout [gaʊt] n goutte f

govern ['gʌvən] vt gouverner; ~**ess** n gouvernante f; ~**ment** n gouvernement m; (BRIT: ministers) ministère m; ~**or** n (of state, bank) gouverneur m; (of school, hospital) ≈ membre m/f du conseil d'établissement; (BRIT: of prison) directeur(-trice)

gown [gaʊn] n robe f; (of teacher, BRIT: of judge) toge f

GP n abbr = **general practitioner**

grab [græb] vt saisir, empoigner ♦ vi: **to ~ at** essayer de saisir

grace [greɪs] n grâce f ♦ vt honorer; (adorn) orner; **5 days' ~** cinq jours de répit; ~**ful** adj gracieux(-euse), élégant(e); **gracious** ['greɪʃəs] adj bienveillant(e)

grade [greɪd] n (COMM) qualité f; (in hierarchy) catégorie f, grade m, échelon m; (SCOL) note f; (US: school class) classe f ♦ vt classer; ~ **crossing** (US) n passage m à niveau; ~ **school** (US) n école f primaire

gradient ['greɪdɪənt] n inclinaison f, pente f

gradual ['grædjʊəl] adj graduel(le), progressif(-ive); ~**ly** adv peu à peu, graduellement

graduate [n 'grædjuɪt, vb 'grædjueɪt] n diplômé(e), licencié(e); (US: of high school) bachelier(-ère) ♦ vi obtenir son diplôme; (US) obtenir son baccalauréat; **graduation** [grædju'eɪʃən] n (cérémonie f de) remise f des diplômes

graffiti [grə'fiːtɪ] npl graffiti mpl

graft [grɑːft] n (AGR, MED) greffe f; (bribery)

corruption f ♦ vt greffer; **hard ~** (BRIT: inf) boulot acharné

grain [greɪn] n grain m

gram [græm] n gramme m

grammar ['græmə^r] n grammaire f; **~ school** (BRIT) n ≈ lycée m; **grammatical** [grə'mætɪkl] adj grammatical(e)

gramme [græm] n = **gram**

grand [grænd] adj magnifique, splendide; (gesture etc) noble; **~children** npl petits-enfants mpl; **~dad** (inf) n grand-papa m; **~daughter** n petite-fille f; **~father** n grand-père m; **~ma** (inf) n grand-maman f; **~mother** n grand-mère f; **~pa** (inf) n = **granddad**; **~parents** npl grands-parents mpl; **~ piano** n piano m à queue; **~son** n petit-fils m; **~stand** n (SPORT) tribune f

granite ['grænɪt] n granit m

granny ['grænɪ] (inf) n grand-maman f

grant [grɑːnt] vt accorder; (a request) accéder à; (admit) concéder ♦ n (SCOL) bourse f; (ADMIN) subside m, subvention f; **to take it for ~ed** that trouver tout naturel que +sub; **to take sb for ~ed** considérer qn comme faisant partie du décor

granulated sugar ['grænjuleɪtɪd-] n sucre m en poudre

grape [greɪp] n raisin m

grapefruit ['greɪpfruːt] n pamplemousse m

graph [grɑːf] n graphique m; **~ic** ['græfɪk] adj graphique; (account, description) vivant(e); **~ics** n arts mpl graphiques; graphisme m ♦ npl représentations fpl

grapple ['græpl] vi: **to ~ with** être aux prises avec

grasp [grɑːsp] vt saisir ♦ n (grip) prise f; (understanding) compréhension f, connaissance f; **~ing** adj cupide

grass [grɑːs] n herbe f; (lawn) gazon m; **~hopper** n sauterelle f; **~-roots** adj de la base, du peuple

grate [greɪt] n grille f de cheminée ♦ vi grincer ♦ vt (CULIN) râper

grateful ['greɪtful] adj reconnaissant(e)

grater ['greɪtə^r] n râpe f

gratifying ['grætɪfaɪɪŋ] adj agréable

grating ['greɪtɪŋ] n (iron bars) grille f ♦ adj (noise) grinçant(e)

gratitude ['grætɪtjuːd] n gratitude f

gratuity [grə'tjuːɪtɪ] n pourboire m

grave [greɪv] n tombe f ♦ adj grave, sérieux(-euse)

gravel ['grævl] n gravier m

gravestone ['greɪvstəun] n pierre tombale

graveyard ['greɪvjɑːd] n cimetière m

gravity ['grævɪtɪ] n (PHYSICS) gravité f; pesanteur f; (seriousness) gravité

gravy ['greɪvɪ] n jus m (de viande); sauce f

gray [greɪ] (US) adj = **grey**

graze [greɪz] vi paître, brouter ♦ vt (touch lightly) frôler, effleurer; (scrape) écorcher ♦ n écorchure f

grease [griːs] n (fat) graisse f; (lubricant) lubrifiant m ♦ vt graisser; lubrifier; **~proof paper** (BRIT) n papier sulfurisé; **greasy** adj gras(se), graisseux(-euse)

great [greɪt] adj grand(e); (inf) formidable; **G~ Britain** n Grande-Bretagne f; **~grandfather** n arrière-grand-père m; **~grandmother** n arrière-grand-mère f; **~ly** adv très, grandement; (with verbs) beaucoup; **~ness** n grandeur f

Greece [griːs] n Grèce f

greed [griːd] n (also: **~iness**) avidité f; (for food) gourmandise f, gloutonnerie f; **~y** adj avide; gourmand(e), glouton(ne)

Greek [griːk] adj grec (grecque) ♦ n Grec (Grecque); (LING) grec m

green [griːn] adj vert(e); (inexperienced) (bien) jeune, naïf (naïve); (POL) vert(e), écologiste; (ecological) écologique ♦ n vert m; (stretch of grass) pelouse f; **~s** npl (vegetables) légumes verts; (POL): **the G~s** les Verts mpl; **the G~ Party** (BRIT: POL) le parti écologiste; **~ belt** n (round town) ceinture verte; **~ card** n (AUT) carte verte; (US) permis m de travail; **~ery** n verdure f; **~grocer's** (BRIT) n marchand m de fruits et légumes; **~house** n serre f; **~house effect** n effet m de serre; **~house gas** n gas m à effet de serre; **~ish** adj verdâtre

Greenland ['griːnlənd] n Groenland m

greet [griːt] vt accueillir; **~ing** n salutation f; **~ing(s) card** n carte f de vœux

gregarious [grə'geərɪəs] adj (person) sociable

grenade [grə'neɪd] n grenade f

grew [gruː] pt of **grow**

grey [greɪ] (US **gray**) adj gris(e); (dismal) sombre; **~-haired** adj grisonnant(e); **~hound** n lévrier m

grid [grɪd] n grille f; (ELEC) réseau m; **~lock** n (traffic jam) embouteillage m; **~locked** adj: **to be ~locked** (roads) être bloqué par un embouteillage; (talks etc) être suspendu

grief [griːf] n chagrin m, douleur f

grievance ['griːvəns] n doléance f, grief m

grieve [griːv] vi avoir du chagrin; se désoler ♦ vt faire de la peine à, affliger; **to ~ for sb** (dead person) pleurer qn; **grievous** adj (LAW): **grievous bodily harm** coups mpl et blessures fpl

grill [grɪl] n (on cooker) gril m; (food: also **mixed ~**) grillade(s) f(pl) ♦ vt (BRIT) griller; (inf: question) cuisiner

grille [grɪl] n grille f, grillage m; (AUT) calandre f

grim [grɪm] adj sinistre, lugubre; (serious, stern) sévère

grimace [grɪ'meɪs] n grimace f ♦ vi grimacer, faire une grimace

grime [graɪm] n crasse f, saleté f

grin [grɪn] n large sourire m ♦ vi sourire

grind [graɪnd] (pt, pp **ground**) vt écraser; (coffee, pepper etc) moudre; (US: meat) hacher; (make sharp) aiguiser ♦ n (work) corvée f

grip [grɪp] n (hold) prise f, étreinte f; (control) emprise f; (grasp) connaissance f; (handle) poignée f; (holdall) sac m de voyage ♦ vt saisir, empoigner; **to come to ~s with** en venir aux prises avec; **~ping** adj prenant(e), palpitant(e)

grisly ['grɪzlɪ] adj sinistre, macabre

gristle ['grɪsl] n cartilage m

grit [grɪt] n gravillon m; (courage) cran m ♦ vt (road) sabler; **to ~ one's teeth** serrer les dents

groan [grəʊn] n (of pain) gémissement m ♦ vi gémir

grocer ['grəʊsər] n épicier m; **~ies** npl provisions fpl; **~'s (shop)** n épicerie f

groin [grɔɪn] n aine f

groom [gruːm] n palefrenier m; (also: **bridegroom**) marié m ♦ vt (horse) panser; (fig): **to ~ sb for** former qn pour; **well-~ed** très soigné(e)

groove [gruːv] n rainure f

grope [grəʊp] vi: **to ~ for** chercher à tâtons

gross [grəʊs] adj grossier(-ère); (COMM) brut(e); **~ly** adv (greatly) très, grandement

grotto ['grɒtəʊ] n grotte f

grotty ['grɒtɪ] (inf) adj minable, affreux(-euse)

ground [graʊnd] pt, pp of **grind** ♦ n sol m, terre f; (land) terrain m, terres fpl; (SPORT) terrain m; (US: also: ~ **wire**) terre; (reason: gen pl) raison f ♦ vt (plane) empêcher de décoller, retenir au sol; (US: ELEC) équiper d'une prise de terre; **~s** npl (of coffee etc) marc m; (gardens etc) parc m, domaine m; **on the ~, to the ~** par terre; **to gain/lose ~** gagner/perdre du terrain; **~ cloth** (US) = **groundsheet**; **~ing** n (in education) connaissances fpl de base; **~less** adj sans fondement; **~sheet** (BRIT) n tapis m de sol; **~ staff** n personnel m au sol; **~work** n préparation f

group [gruːp] n groupe m ♦ vt (also: ~ **together**) grouper ♦ vi se grouper

grouse [graʊs] n inv (bird) grouse f ♦ vi (complain) rouspéter, râler

grove [grəʊv] n bosquet m

grovel ['grɒvl] vi (fig) ramper

grow [grəʊ] (pt **grew**, pp **grown**) vi pousser, croître; (person) grandir; (increase) augmenter, se développer; (become): **to ~ rich/weak** s'enrichir/s'affaiblir; (develop): **he's ~n out of his jacket** sa veste est

(devenue) trop petite pour lui ♦ vt cultiver, faire pousser; (beard) laisser pousser; **he'll ~ out of it!** ça lui passera!; **~ up** vi grandir; **~er** n producteur m; **~ing** adj (fear, amount) croissant(e), grandissant(e)

growl [graʊl] vi grogner

grown [grəʊn] pp of **grow**; **~-up** n adulte m/f, grande personne

growth [grəʊθ] n croissance f, développement m; (what has grown) pousse f; (MED) grosseur f, tumeur f

grub [grʌb] n larve f; (inf: food) bouffe f

grubby ['grʌbɪ] adj crasseux(-euse)

grudge [grʌdʒ] n rancune f ♦ vt: **to ~ sb sth** (in giving) donner qch à qn à contre-cœur; (resent) reprocher qch à qn; **to bear sb a ~ (for)** garder rancune or en vouloir à qn (de)

gruelling ['gruːəlɪŋ] (US **grueling**) adj exténuant(e)

gruesome ['gruːsəm] adj horrible

gruff [grʌf] adj bourru(e)

grumble ['grʌmbl] vi rouspéter, ronchonner

grumpy ['grʌmpɪ] adj grincheux(-euse)

grunt [grʌnt] vi grogner

G-string ['dʒiːstrɪŋ] n (garment) cache-sexe m inv

guarantee [gærən'tiː] n garantie f ♦ vt garantir

guard [gɑːd] n garde f; (one man) garde m; (BRIT: RAIL) chef m de train; (on machine) dispositif m de sûreté; (also: **fireguard**) garde-feu m ♦ vt garder, surveiller; (protect): **to ~ (against or from)** protéger (contre); **~ against** vt (prevent) empêcher, se protéger de; **~ed** adj (fig) prudent(e); **~ian** n gardien(ne); (of minor) tuteur(-trice); **~'s van** (BRIT) n (RAIL) fourgon m

guerrilla [gə'rɪlə] n guérillero m

guess [ges] vt deviner; (estimate) évaluer; (US) croire, penser ♦ vi deviner ♦ n supposition f, hypothèse f; **to take or have a ~** essayer de deviner; **~work** n hypothèse f

guest [gest] n invité(e); (in hotel) client(e); **~-house** n pension f; **~ room** n chambre f d'amis

guffaw [gʌ'fɔː] vi pouffer de rire

guidance ['gaɪdəns] n conseils mpl

guide [gaɪd] n (person, book) guide m; (BRIT: also: **girl ~**) guide f ♦ vt guider; **~book** n guide m; **~ dog** n chien m d'aveugle; **~lines** npl (fig) instructions (générales), conseils mpl

guild [gɪld] n corporation f; cercle m, association f

guillotine ['gɪlətiːn] n guillotine f

guilt [gɪlt] n culpabilité f; **~y** adj coupable

guinea pig ['gɪnɪ-] n cobaye m

guise [gaɪz] n aspect m, apparence f

guitar [gɪ'tɑːr] n guitare f

gulf [gʌlf] n golfe m; (abyss) gouffre m
gull [gʌl] n mouette f; (larger) goéland m
gullible ['gʌlɪbl] adj crédule
gully ['gʌlɪ] n ravin m; ravine f; couloir m
gulp [gʌlp] vi avaler sa salive ♦ vt (also: ~ down) avaler
gum [gʌm] n (ANAT) gencive f; (glue) colle f; (sweet: also ~drop) boule f de gomme; (also: chewing ~) chewing-gum m ♦ vt coller; **~boots** (BRIT) npl bottes fpl en caoutchouc
gun [gʌn] n (small) revolver m, pistolet m; (rifle) fusil m, carabine f; (cannon) canon m; **~boat** n canonnière f; **~fire** n fusillade f; **~man** n bandit armé; **~point** n: at ~point sous la menace du pistolet (or fusil); **~powder** n poudre f à canon; **~shot** n coup m de feu
gurgle ['gəːgl] vi gargouiller; (baby) gazouiller
gush [gʌʃ] vi jaillir; (fig) se répandre en effusions
gust [gʌst] n (of wind) rafale f; (of smoke) bouffée f
gusto ['gʌstəu] n enthousiasme m
gut [gʌt] n intestin m, boyau m; ~s npl (inf: courage) cran m
gutter ['gʌtəʳ] n (in street) caniveau m; (of roof) gouttière f
guy [gaɪ] n (inf: man) type m; (also: ~rope) corde f; (BRIT: figure) effigie de Guy Fawkes (brûlée en plein air le 5 novembre)
guzzle ['gʌzl] vt avaler gloutonnement
gym [dʒɪm] n (also: ~nasium) gymnase m; (also: ~nastics) gym f; **~nast** n gymnaste m/f; **~nastics** [dʒɪm'næstɪks] n, npl gymnastique f; ~ **shoes** npl chaussures fpl de gym; **~slip** (BRIT) n tunique f (d'écolière)
gynaecologist [gaɪnɪ'kɒlədʒɪst] (US **gynecologist**) n gynécologue m/f
gypsy ['dʒɪpsɪ] n gitan(e), bohémien(ne)

H, h

haberdashery [hæbə'dæʃərɪ] (BRIT) n mercerie f
habit ['hæbɪt] n habitude f; (REL: costume) habit m; **~ual** adj habituel(le); (drinker, liar) invétéré(e)
hack [hæk] vt hacher, tailler ♦ n (pej: writer) nègre m; **~er** n (COMPUT) pirate m (informatique); (: enthusiast) passionné(e) m/f des ordinateurs
hackneyed ['hæknɪd] adj usé(e), rebattu(e)
had [hæd] pt, pp of **have**
haddock ['hædək] (pl ~ or ~s) n églefin m; **smoked ~** haddock m
hadn't ['hædnt] = **had not**
haemorrhage ['hemərɪdʒ] (US **hemorrhage**) n hémorragie f

haemorrhoids ['hemərɔɪdz] (US **hemorrhoids**) npl hémorroïdes fpl
haggle ['hægl] vi marchander
Hague [heɪg] n: The ~ La Haye
hail [heɪl] n grêle f ♦ vt (call) héler; (acclaim) acclamer ♦ vi grêler; **~stone** n grêlon m
hair [heəʳ] n cheveux mpl; (of animal) pelage m; (single ~: on head) cheveu m; (: on body; of animal) poil m; **to do one's ~** se coiffer; **~brush** n brosse f à cheveux; **~cut** n coupe f (de cheveux); **~do** n coiffure f; **~dresser** n coiffeur(-euse); **~dresser's** n salon m de coiffure, coiffeur m; ~ **dryer** n sèche-cheveux m; ~ **gel** n gel m pour cheveux; **~grip** n pince f à cheveux; **~net** n filet m à cheveux; **~piece** n perruque f; **~pin** n épingle f à cheveux; **~pin bend** (US **hairpin curve**) n virage m en épingle à cheveux; **~-raising** adj à (vous) faire dresser les cheveux sur la tête; ~ **removing cream** n crème f dépilatoire; ~ **spray** n laque f (pour les cheveux); **~style** n coiffure f; **~y** adj poilu(e); (inf: fig) effrayant(e)
hake [heɪk] (pl ~ or ~s) n colin m, merlu m
half [hɑːf] (pl **halves**) n moitié f; (of beer: also: ~ pint) ≈ demi m; (RAIL, bus: also: ~ fare) demi-tarif m ♦ adj demi(e) ♦ adv (à) moitié, à demi; ~ **a dozen** une demi-douzaine; ~ **a pound** une demi-livre, ≈ 250 g; **two and a ~** deux et demi; **to cut sth in ~** couper qch en deux; **~-caste** ['hɑːfkɑːst] n métis(se); **~-hearted** adj tiède, sans enthousiasme; **~-hour** n demi-heure f; **~-mast** n: at ~-mast adv (flag) en berne; **~penny** (BRIT) n demi-penny m; **~-price** adj, adv: (at) ~-price à moitié prix; ~ **term** (BRIT) n (SCOL) congé m de demi-trimestre; **~-time** n mi-temps f; **~way** adv à mi-chemin
hall [hɔːl] n salle f; (entrance way) hall m, entrée f
hallmark ['hɔːlmɑːk] n poinçon m; (fig) marque f
hallo [hə'ləu] excl = **hello**
hall of residence (BRIT) (pl **halls of residence**) n résidence f universitaire
Hallowe'en ['hæləu'iːn] n veille f de la Toussaint
hallucination [həluːsɪ'neɪʃən] n hallucination f
hallway ['hɔːlweɪ] n vestibule m
halo ['heɪləu] n (of saint etc) auréole f
halt [hɔːlt] n halte f, arrêt m ♦ vt (progress etc) interrompre ♦ vi faire halte, s'arrêter
halve [hɑːv] vt (apple etc) partager or diviser en deux; (expense) réduire de moitié; **~s** npl of **half**
ham [hæm] n jambon m
hamburger ['hæmbɑːgəʳ] n hamburger m
hamlet ['hæmlɪt] n hameau m

hammer ['hæmə^r] *n* marteau *m* ♦ *vt* (*nail*) enfoncer; (*fig*) démolir ♦ *vi* (*on door*) frapper à coups redoublés; **to ~ an idea into sb** faire entrer de force une idée dans la tête de qn

hammock ['hæmək] *n* hamac *m*

hamper ['hæmpə^r] *vt* gêner ♦ *n* panier *m* (d'osier)

hamster ['hæmstə^r] *n* hamster *m*

hand [hænd] *n* main *f*; (*of clock*) aiguille *f*; (*~writing*) écriture *f*; (*worker*) ouvrier(-ère); (*at cards*) jeu *m* ♦ *vt* passer, donner; **to give** *or* **lend sb a ~** donner un coup de main à qn; **at ~** à portée de la main; **in ~** (*time*) à disposition; (*job, situation*) en main; **to be on ~** (*person*) être disponible; (*emergency services*) se tenir prêt(e) (à intervenir); **to ~** (*information etc*) sous la main, à portée de la main; **on the one ~ ...**, **on the other ~** d'une part ..., d'autre part; **~ in** *vt* remettre; **~ out** *vt* distribuer; **~ over** *vt* transmettre; céder; **~bag** *n* sac *m* à main; **~book** *n* manuel *m*; **~brake** *n* frein *m* à main; **~cuffs** *npl* menottes *fpl*; **~ful** *n* poignée *f*

handicap ['hændɪkæp] *n* handicap *m* ♦ *vt* handicaper; **mentally/physically ~ped** handicapé(e) mentalement/physiquement

handicraft ['hændɪkraːft] *n* (travail *m* d')artisanat *m*, technique artisanale; (*object*) objet artisanal

handiwork ['hændɪwəːk] *n* ouvrage *m*

handkerchief ['hæŋkətʃɪf] *n* mouchoir *m*

handle ['hændl] *n* (*of door etc*) poignée *f*; (*of cup etc*) anse *f*; (*of knife etc*) manche *m*; (*of saucepan*) queue *f*; (*for winding*) manivelle *f* ♦ *vt* toucher, manier; (*deal with*) s'occuper de; (*treat: people*) prendre; "**~ with care**" "fragile"; **to fly off the ~** s'énerver; **~bar(s)** *n(pl)* guidon *m*

hand: ~luggage *n* bagages *mpl* à main; **~made** *adj* fait(e) à la main; **~out** *n* (*from government, parents*) aide *f*, don *m*; (*leaflet*) documentation *f*, prospectus *m*; (*summary of lecture*) polycopié *m*; **~rail** *n* rampe *f*, main courante; **~set** *n* (*TEL*) combiné *m*; **please replace the ~set** raccrochez s'il vous plaît; **~shake** *n* poignée *f* de main

handsome ['hænsəm] *adj* beau (belle); (*profit, return*) considérable

handwriting ['hændraɪtɪŋ] *n* écriture *f*

handy ['hændɪ] *adj* (*person*) adroit(e); (*close at hand*) sous la main; (*convenient*) pratique

hang [hæŋ] (*pt, pp* **hung**) *vt* accrocher; (*criminal: pt, pp:* **~ed**) pendre ♦ *vi* pendre; (*hair, drapery*) tomber; **to get the ~ of (doing) sth** (*inf*) attraper le coup pour faire qch; **~ about** *vi* traîner; **~ around** *vi* = **hang about**; **~ on** *vi* (*wait*) attendre; **~ up** *vi* (*TEL*): **to ~ up (on sb)** raccrocher (au nez de qn) ♦ *vt* (*coat, painting etc*) accrocher, suspendre

hangar ['hæŋə^r] *n* hangar *m*

hanger ['hæŋə^r] *n* cintre *m*, portemanteau *m*; **~-on** *n* parasite *m*

hang: ~-gliding *n* deltaplane *m*, vol *m* libre; **~over** *n* (*after drinking*) gueule *f* de bois; **~-up** *n* complexe *m*

hanker ['hæŋkə^r] *vi*: **to ~ after** avoir envie de

hankie, hanky ['hæŋkɪ] *n abbr* = **handkerchief**

haphazard [hæp'hæzəd] *adj* fait(e) au hasard, fait(e) au petit bonheur

happen ['hæpən] *vi* arriver; se passer, se produire; **it so ~s that** il se trouve que; **as it ~s** justement; **~ing** *n* événement *m*

happily ['hæpɪlɪ] *adv* heureusement; (*cheerfully*) joyeusement

happiness ['hæpɪnɪs] *n* bonheur *m*

happy ['hæpɪ] *adj* heureux(-euse); **~ with** (*arrangements etc*) satisfait(e); **to be ~ to do** faire volontiers; **~ birthday!** bon anniversaire!; **~-go-lucky** *adj* insouciant(e); **~ hour** *n* heure pendant laquelle les consommations sont à prix réduit

harass ['hærəs] *vt* accabler, tourmenter; **~ment** *n* tracasseries *fpl*

harbour ['haːbə^r] (*US* **harbor**) *n* port *m* ♦ *vt* héberger, abriter; (*hope, fear etc*) entretenir

hard [haːd] *adj* dur(e); (*question, problem*) difficile, dur(e); (*facts, evidence*) concret(-ète) ♦ *adv* (*work*) dur; (*think, try*) sérieusement; **to look ~ at** regarder fixement; (*thing*) regarder de près; **no ~ feelings!** sans rancune!; **to be ~ of hearing** être dur(e) d'oreille; **to be ~ done by** être traité(e) injustement; **~back** *n* livre relié; **~ cash** *n* espèces *fpl*; **~ disk** *n* (*COMPUT*) disque dur; **~en** *vt* durcir; (*fig*) endurcir ♦ *vi* durcir; **~-headed** *adj* réaliste; décidé(e); **~ labour** *n* travaux forcés

hardly ['haːdlɪ] *adv* (*scarcely, no sooner*) à peine; **~ anywhere/ever** presque nulle part/ jamais

hard: ~ship *n* épreuves *fpl*; **~ shoulder** (*BRIT*) *n* (*AUT*) accotement stabilisé; **~ up** (*inf*) *adj* fauché(e); **~ware** *n* quincaillerie *f*; (*COMPUT, MIL*) matériel *m*; **~ware shop** *n* quincaillerie *f*; **~wearing** *adj* solide; **~-working** *adj* travailleur(-euse)

hardy ['haːdɪ] *adj* robuste; (*plant*) résistant(e) au gel

hare [hɛə^r] *n* lièvre *m*; **~-brained** *adj* farfelu(e)

harm [haːm] *n* mal *m*; (*wrong*) tort *m* ♦ *vt* (*person*) faire du mal *or* du tort à; (*thing*) endommager; **out of ~'s way** à l'abri du danger, en lieu sûr; **~ful** *adj* nuisible; **~less** *adj* inoffensif(-ive); sans méchanceté

harmony ['haːmənɪ] *n* harmonie *f*

harness ['haːnɪs] *n* harnais *m*; (*safety ~*)

harnais de sécurité ♦ vt (horse) harnacher; (resources) exploiter

harp [hɑ:p] n harpe f ♦ vi: **to ~ on about** rabâcher

harrowing ['hærəʊɪŋ] adj déchirant(e), très pénible

harsh [hɑ:ʃ] adj (hard) dur(e); (severe) sévère; (unpleasant: sound) discordant(e); (: light) cru(e)

harvest ['hɑ:vɪst] n (of corn) moisson f; (of fruit) récolte f; (of grapes) vendange f ♦ vt moissonner; récolter; vendanger

has [hæz] vb see **have**

hash [hæʃ] n (CULIN) hachis m; (fig: mess) gâchis m

hasn't ['hæznt] = **has not**

hassle ['hæsl] n (inf: bother) histoires fpl, tracas mpl

haste [heɪst] n hâte f; précipitation f; **~n** ['heɪsn] vt hâter, accélérer ♦ vi se hâter, s'empresser; **hastily** adv à la hâte; précipitamment; **hasty** adj hâtif(-ive); précipité(e)

hat [hæt] n chapeau m

hatch [hætʃ] n (NAUT: also: **~way**) écoutille f; (also: **service ~**) passe-plats m inv ♦ vi éclore; **~back** n (AUT) modèle m avec hayon arrière

hatchet ['hætʃɪt] n hachette f

hate [heɪt] vt haïr, détester ♦ n haine f; **~ful** adj odieux(-euse), détestable; **hatred** ['heɪtrɪd] n haine f

haughty ['hɔ:tɪ] adj hautain(e), arrogant(e)

haul [hɔ:l] vt traîner, tirer ♦ n (of fish) prise f; (of stolen goods etc) butin m; **~age** n transport routier; (costs) frais mpl de transport; **~ier** ['hɔ:lɪə*] (US **hauler**) n (company) transporteur (routier); (driver) camionneur m

haunch [hɔ:ntʃ] n hanche f; (of meat) cuissot m

haunt [hɔ:nt] vt (subj: ghost, fear) hanter; (: person) fréquenter ♦ n repaire m

KEYWORD

have [hæv] (pt, pp **had**) aux vb **1** (gen) avoir; être; **to have arrived/gone** être arrivé(e)/ allé(e); **to have eaten/slept** avoir mangé/ dormi; **he has been promoted** il a eu une promotion

2 (in tag questions): **you've done it, haven't you?** vous l'avez fait, n'est-ce pas?

3 (in short answers and questions): **no I haven't/yes we have!** mais non!/mais si!; **so I have!** ah oui!, oui c'est vrai!; **I've been there before, have you?** j'y suis déjà allé, et vous?

♦ modal aux vb (be obliged): **to have (got) to do sth** devoir faire qch; être obligé(e) de faire qch; **she has (got) to do it** elle doit le faire, il faut qu'elle le fasse; **you haven't to tell her**

vous ne devez pas le lui dire

♦ vt **1** (possess, obtain) avoir; **he has (got) blue eyes/dark hair** il a les yeux bleus/les cheveux bruns; **may I have your address?** puis-je avoir votre adresse?

2 (+noun: take, hold etc): **to have breakfast/a bath/a shower** prendre le petit déjeuner/un bain/une douche; **to have dinner/lunch** dîner/déjeuner; **to have a swim** nager; **to have a meeting** se réunir; **to have a party** organiser une fête

3: **to have sth done** faire faire qch; **to have one's hair cut** se faire couper les cheveux; **to have sb do sth** faire faire qch à qn

4 (experience, suffer) avoir; **to have a cold/flu** avoir un rhume/la grippe; **to have an operation** se faire opérer

5 (inf: dupe) avoir; **he's been had** il s'est fait avoir or rouler

have out vt: **to have it out with sb** (settle a problem etc) s'expliquer (franchement) avec qn

haven ['heɪvn] n port m; (fig) havre m

haven't ['hævnt] = **have not**

havoc ['hævək] n ravages mpl

hawk [hɔ:k] n faucon m

hay [heɪ] n foin m; **~ fever** n rhume m des foins; **~stack** n meule f de foin

haywire ['heɪwaɪə*] (inf) adj: **to go ~** (machine) se détraquer; (plans) mal tourner

hazard ['hæzəd] n (danger) danger m, risque m ♦ vt risquer, hasarder; **~ (warning) lights** npl (AUT) feux mpl de détresse

haze [heɪz] n brume f

hazelnut ['heɪzlnʌt] n noisette f

hazy ['heɪzɪ] adj brumeux(-euse); (idea) vague

he [hi:] pron il; **it is ~ who ...** c'est lui qui ...

head [hed] n tête f; (leader) chef m; (of school) directeur(-trice) ♦ vt (list) être en tête de; (group) être à la tête de; **~s (or tails)** pile (ou face); **~ first** la tête la première; **~ over heels in love** follement or éperdument amoureux(-euse); **to ~ a ball** faire une tête; **~ for** vt fus se diriger vers; **~ache** n mal m de tête; **~dress** (BRIT) n (of Red Indian etc) coiffure f; **~ing** n titre m; **~lamp** (BRIT) n = **headlight**; **~land** n promontoire m, cap m; **~light** n phare m; **~line** n titre m; **~long** adv (fall) la tête la première; (rush) tête baissée; **~master** n directeur m; **~mistress** n directrice f; **~ office** n bureau central, siège m; **~-on** adj (collision) de plein fouet; (confrontation) en face à face; **~phones** npl casque m (à écouteurs); **~quarters** npl bureau or siège central; (MIL) quartier général m; **~rest** n appui-tête m; **~room** n (in car) hauteur f de plafond; (under bridge)

hauteur limite; **~scarf** n foulard m; **~strong**
adj têtu(e), entêté(e); **~ teacher** n
directeur(-trice); (of secondary school)
proviseur m; **~way** n: **to make ~way** avancer, faire des
progrès; **~wind** n vent m contraire; (NAUT)
vent debout; **~y** adj capiteux(-euse),
enivrant(e); (experience) grisant(e)

heal [hi:l] vt, vi guérir

health [hɛlθ] n santé f; **~ food** n aliment(s)
naturel(s); **~ food shop** n magasin m
diététique; **H~ Service** (BRIT) n: **the
H~ Service** ≈ la Sécurité sociale; **~y** adj
(person) en bonne santé; (climate, food,
attitude etc) sain(e), bon(ne) pour la santé

heap [hi:p] n tas m ♦ vt: **to ~ (up)** entasser,
amonceler; **she ~ed her plate with cakes** elle a
chargé son assiette de gâteaux

hear [hɪəⁱ] (pt, pp heard) vt entendre; (news)
apprendre ♦ vi entendre; **to ~ about** entendre
parler de; avoir des nouvelles de; **to ~ from
sb** recevoir or avoir des nouvelles de qn; **~d**
[hɜːd] pt, pp of hear; **~ing** n (sense) ouïe f;
(of witnesses) audition f; (of a case) audience
f; **~ing aid** n appareil m acoustique; **~say**:
by ~say par ouï-dire m

hearse [hɜːs] n corbillard m

heart [hɑːt] n cœur m; **~s** npl (CARDS) cœur;
to lose/take ~ perdre/prendre courage; **at ~**
au fond; **by ~** (learn, know) par cœur; **~
attack** n crise f cardiaque; **~beat** n
battement m du cœur; **~breaking** adj
déchirant(e), qui fend le cœur; **~broken**
adj: **to be ~broken** avoir beaucoup de chagrin
or le cœur brisé; **~burn** n brûlures fpl
d'estomac; **~ failure** n arrêt m du cœur;
~felt adj sincère

hearth [hɑːθ] n foyer m, cheminée f

heartily ['hɑːtɪlɪ] adv chaleureusement;
(laugh) de bon cœur; (eat) de bon appétit;
to agree ~ être entièrement d'accord

hearty ['hɑːtɪ] adj chaleureux(-euse);
(appetite) robuste; (dislike) cordial(e)

heat [hi:t] n chaleur f; (fig) feu m, agitation f;
(SPORT: also: **qualifying ~**) éliminatoire f ♦ vt
chauffer; **~ up** vi (water) chauffer; (room) se
réchauffer ♦ vt réchauffer; **~ed** adj chauf-
fé(e); (fig) passionné(e), échauffé(e); **~er** n
appareil m de chauffage; radiateur m; (in car)
chauffage m; (water heater) chauffe-eau m

heath [hi:θ] (BRIT) n lande f

heather ['hɛðəⁱ] n bruyère f

heating ['hi:tɪŋ] n chauffage m

heatstroke ['hi:tstrəuk] n (MED) coup m de
chaleur

heat wave n vague f de chaleur

heave [hi:v] vt soulever (avec effort); (drag)
traîner ♦ vi se soulever; (retch) avoir un
haut-le-cœur; **to ~ a sigh** pousser un soupir

heaven ['hɛvn] n ciel m, paradis m; (fig)
paradis; **~ly** adj céleste, divin(e)

heavily ['hɛvɪlɪ] adv lourdement; (drink,
smoke) beaucoup; (sleep, sigh) profondément

heavy ['hɛvɪ] adj lourd(e); (work, sea, rain,
eater) gros(se); (snow) beaucoup de;
(drinker, smoker) grand(e); (breathing)
bruyant(e); (schedule, week) chargé(e);
~ goods vehicle n poids lourd; **~weight** n
(SPORT) poids lourd

Hebrew ['hi:bru:] adj hébraïque ♦ n (LING)
hébreu m

Hebrides ['hɛbrɪdɪz] npl: **the ~** les Hébrides
fpl

heckle ['hɛkl] vt interpeller (un orateur)

hectic ['hɛktɪk] adj agité(e), trépidant(e)

he'd [hi:d] = he would; he had

hedge [hɛdʒ] n haie f ♦ vi se dérober; **to
~ one's bets** (fig) se couvrir

hedgehog ['hɛdʒhɔg] n hérisson m

heed [hi:d] vt (also: **take ~ of**) tenir compte
de; **~less** adj insouciant(e)

heel [hi:l] n talon m ♦ vt retalonner

hefty ['hɛftɪ] adj (person) costaud(e); (parcel)
lourd(e); (profit) gros(se)

heifer ['hɛfəⁱ] n génisse f

height [haɪt] n (of person) taille f, grandeur f;
(of object) hauteur f; (of plane, mountain)
altitude f; (high ground) hauteur, éminence f;
(fig: of glory) sommet m; (: of luxury,
stupidity) comble m; **~en** vt (fig) augmenter

heir [ɛəⁱ] n héritier m; **~ess** n héritière f;
~loom n héritage m, meuble (or bijou m
or tableau m) de famille

held [hɛld] pt, pp of hold

helicopter ['hɛlɪkɔptəⁱ] n hélicoptère m

hell [hɛl] n enfer m; **~!** (inf!) merde!

he'll [hi:l] = he will; he shall

hellish ['hɛlɪʃ] (inf) adj infernal(e)

hello [hə'ləu] excl bonjour!; (to attract
attention) hé!; (surprise) tiens!

helm [hɛlm] n (NAUT) barre f

helmet ['hɛlmɪt] n casque m

help [hɛlp] n aide f; (charwoman) femme f de
ménage ♦ vt aider; **~!** au secours!; **~ yourself**
servez-vous; **he can't ~ it** il ne peut pas s'en
empêcher; **~er** n aide m/f, assistant(e); **~ful**
adj serviable, obligeant(e); (useful) utile;
~ing n portion f; **~less** adj impuissant(e);
(defenceless) faible

hem [hɛm] n ourlet m ♦ vt ourler; **~ in** vt
cerner

hemorrhage ['hɛmərɪdʒ] (US) n
= **haemorrhage**

hemorrhoids ['hɛmərɔɪdz] (US) npl
= **haemorrhoids**

hen [hɛn] n poule f

hence [hɛns] adv (therefore) d'où, de là; **2
years ~** d'ici 2 ans, dans 2 ans; **~forth** adv

dorénavant

her [həːʳ] *pron (direct)* la, l'; *(indirect)* lui; *(stressed, after prep)* elle ♦ *adj* son (sa), ses *pl; see also* **me**; **my**

herald ['herəld] *n* héraut *m* ♦ *vt* annoncer; **~ry** *n (study)* héraldique *f; (coat of arms)* blason *m*

herb [həːb] *n* herbe *f*

herd [həːd] *n* troupeau *m*

here [hɪəʳ] *adv (place); (time)* alors ♦ *excl* tiens!, tenez!; **~!** présent!; **~ is, ~ are** voici; **~ he/she is!** le/la voici!; **~after** *adv* après, plus tard; **~by** *adv (formal: in letter)* par la présente

hereditary [hɪ'redɪtrɪ] *adj* héréditaire

heresy ['herəsɪ] *n* hérésie *f*

heritage ['herɪtɪdʒ] *n (of country)* patrimoine *m*

hermit ['həːmɪt] *n* ermite *m*

hernia ['həːnɪə] *n* hernie *f*

hero ['hɪərəu] *(pl* **~es)** *n* héros *m*

heroin ['herəuɪn] *n* héroïne *f*

heroine ['herəuɪn] *n* héroïne *f*

heron ['herən] *n* héron *m*

herring ['herɪŋ] *n* hareng *m*

hers [həːz] *pron* le (la) sien(ne), les siens (siennes); *see also* **mine**[1]

herself [həː'self] *pron (reflexive)* se; *(emphatic)* elle-même; *(after prep)* elle; *see also* **oneself**

he's [hiːz] **= he is; he has**

hesitant ['hezɪtənt] *adj* hésitant(e), indécis(e)

hesitate ['hezɪteɪt] *vi* hésiter; **hesitation** [hezɪ'teɪʃən] *n* hésitation *f*

heterosexual ['hetərəu'seksjuəl] *adj, n* hétérosexuel(le)

heyday ['heɪdeɪ] *n:* **the ~ of** l'âge *m* d'or de, les beaux jours de

HGV *n abbr* **= heavy goods vehicle**

hi [haɪ] *excl* salut!; *(to attract attention)* hé!

hiatus [haɪ'eɪtəs] *n (gap)* lacune *f; (interruption)* pause *f*

hibernate ['haɪbəneɪt] *vi* hiberner

hiccough, hiccup ['hɪkʌp] *vi* hoqueter; **~s** *npl* hoquet *m*

hide [haɪd] *(pt* **hid**, *pp* **hidden)** *n (skin)* peau *f* ♦ *vt* cacher ♦ *vi:* **to ~ (from sb)** se cacher (de qn); **~-and-seek** *n* cache-cache *m*

hideous ['hɪdɪəs] *adj* hideux(-euse)

hiding ['haɪdɪŋ] *n (beating)* correction *f*, volée *f* de coups; **to be in ~** *(concealed)* se tenir caché(e)

hierarchy ['haɪərɑːkɪ] *n* hiérarchie *f*

hi-fi ['haɪfaɪ] *n* hi-fi *f inv* ♦ *adj* hi-fi *inv*

high [haɪ] *adj* haut(e); *(speed, respect, number)* grand(e); *(price)* élevé(e); *(wind)* fort(e), violent(e); *(voice)* aigu (aiguë) ♦ *adv* haut; **20 m ~** haut(e) de 20 m; **~brow** *adj, n* intellectuel(le); **~chair** *n (child's)* chaise

haute; **~er education** *n* études supérieures; **~-handed** *adj* très autoritaire; très cavalier(-ère); **~-heeled** *adj* à hauts talons; **~ jump** *n (SPORT)* saut *m* en hauteur; **~lands** *npl* Highlands *mpl*; **~light** *n (fig: of event)* point culminant ♦ *vt* faire ressortir, souligner; **~lights** *npl (in hair)* reflets *mpl*; **~ly** *adv* très, fort, hautement; **to speak/think ~ly of sb** dire/penser beaucoup de bien de qn; **~ly paid** *adj* très bien payé(e); **~ly strung** *adj* nerveux(-euse), toujours tendu(e); **~ness** *n*: **Her (or His) H~ness** Son Altesse *f*; **~-pitched** *adj* aigu (aiguë); **~-rise block, ~-rise flats** tour *f* (d'habitation); **~ school** *n* lycée *m*; *(US)* établissement *m* d'enseignement supérieur; **~ season** *(BRIT)* *n* haute saison; **~ street** *(BRIT)* *n* grand-rue *f*; **~way** *n* route nationale; **H~way Code** *(BRIT)* *n* code *m* de la route

hijack ['haɪdʒæk] *vt (plane)* détourner; **~er** *n* pirate *m* de l'air

hike [haɪk] *vi* aller *or* faire des excursions à pied ♦ *n* excursion *f* à pied, randonnée *f*; **~r** *n* promeneur(-euse), excursionniste *m/f*; **hiking** *n* excursions *fpl* à pied

hilarious [hɪ'lɛərɪəs] *adj (account, event)* désopilant(e)

hill [hɪl] *n* colline *f; (fairly high)* montagne *f; (on road)* côte *f*; **~side** *n (flanc m de)* coteau *m*; **~-walking** *n* randonnée *f* de basse montagne; **~y** *adj* vallonné(e); montagneux(-euse)

hilt [hɪlt] *n (of sword)* garde *f*; **to the ~** *(fig: support)* à fond

him [hɪm] *pron (direct)* le, l'; *(stressed, indirect, after prep)* lui; *see also* **me**; **~self** *pron (reflexive)* se; *(emphatic)* lui-même; *(after prep)* lui; *see also* **oneself**

hinder ['hɪndəʳ] *vt* gêner; *(delay)* retarder; **hindrance** *n* gêne *f*, obstacle *m*

hindsight ['haɪndsaɪt] *n*: **with ~** avec du recul, rétrospectivement

Hindu ['hɪnduː] *adj* hindou(e)

hinge [hɪndʒ] *n* charnière *f* ♦ *vi (fig):* **to ~ on** dépendre de

hint [hɪnt] *n* allusion *f; (advice)* conseil *m* ♦ *vt:* **to ~ that** insinuer que ♦ *vi:* **to ~ at** faire une allusion à

hip [hɪp] *n* hanche *f*

hippie ['hɪpɪ] *n* hippie *m/f*

hippo ['hɪpəu] *(pl* **~s)**, **hippopotamus** [hɪpə'pɒtəməs] *(pl* **~potamuses** *or* **~potami)** *n* hippopotame *m*

hire ['haɪəʳ] *vt (BRIT: car, equipment)* louer; *(worker)* embaucher, engager ♦ *n* location *f*; **for ~** à louer; *(taxi)* libre; **~(d) car** *n* voiture *f* de location; **~ purchase** *(BRIT)* *n* achat *m* (*or* vente *f*) à tempérament *or* crédit

his [hɪz] *pron* le (la) sien(ne), les siens

(siennes) ♦ *adj* son (sa), ses *pl*; *see also* **my; mine**[1]

hiss [hɪs] *vi* siffler

historic [hɪ'stɔrɪk] *adj* historique; **~al** *adj* historique

histor**y** [ˈhɪstərɪ] *n* histoire *f*

hit [hɪt] (*pt, pp* **hit**) *vt* frapper; (*reach: target*) atteindre, toucher; (*collide with: car*) entrer en collision avec, heurter; (*fig: affect*) toucher ♦ *n* coup *m*; (*success*) succès *m*; (: *song*) tube *m*; **to ~ it off with sb** bien s'entendre avec qn; **~-and-run driver** *n* chauffard *m* (coupable du délit de fuite)

hitch [hɪtʃ] *vt* (*fasten*) accrocher, attacher; (*also: ~ up*) remonter d'une saccade ♦ *n* (*difficulty*) anicroche *f*, contretemps *m*; **to ~ a lift** faire du stop; **~hike** *vi* faire de l'auto-stop; **~hiker** *n* auto-stoppeur(-euse)

hi-tech [ˈhaɪˈtɛk] *adj* de pointe

hitherto [hɪðə'tuː] *adv* jusqu'ici

hit man *n* tueur *m* à gages

HIV *n abbr*: **~-negative/-positive** *adj* séronégatif(-ive)/-positif(-ive)

hive [haɪv] *n* ruche *f*

HMS *abbr* = Her/His Majesty's Ship

hoard [hɔːd] *n* (*of food*) provisions *fpl*, réserves *fpl*; (*of money*) trésor *m* ♦ *vt* amasser; **~ing** (*BRIT*) *n* (*for posters*) panneau *m* d'affichage or publicitaire

hoarse [hɔːs] *adj* enroué(e)

hoax [həuks] *n* canular *m*

hob [hɔb] *n* plaque (chauffante)

hobble [ˈhɔbl] *vi* boitiller

hobby [ˈhɔbɪ] *n* passe-temps favori

hobo [ˈhəubəu] (*US*) *n* vagabond *m*

hockey [ˈhɔkɪ] *n* hockey *m*

hog [hɔg] *n* porc (châtré) ♦ *vt* (*fig*) accaparer; **to go the whole ~** aller jusqu'au bout

hoist [hɔɪst] *n* (*apparatus*) palan *m* ♦ *vt* hisser

hold [həuld] (*pt, pp* **held**) *vt* tenir; (*contain*) contenir; (*believe*) considérer; (*possess*) avoir; (*detain*) détenir ♦ *vi* (*withstand pressure*) tenir (bon); (*be valid*) valoir ♦ *n* (*also fig*) prise *f*; (*NAUT*) cale *f*; **~ the line!** (*TEL*) ne quittez pas!; **to ~ one's own** (*fig*) (bien) se défendre; **to catch** or **get (a) ~ of** saisir; **to get ~ of** (*fig*) trouver; **~ back** *vt* retenir; (*secret*) taire; **~ down** *vt* (*person*) maintenir à terre; (*job*) occuper; **~ off** *vt* tenir à distance; **~ on** *vi* tenir bon; (*wait*) attendre; **~ on!** (*TEL*) ne quittez pas!; **~ on to** *vt fus* se cramponner à; (*keep*) conserver, garder; **~ out** *vt* offrir ♦ *vi* (*resist*) tenir bon; **~ up** *vt* (*raise*) lever; (*support*) soutenir; (*delay*) retarder; (*rob*) braquer; **~all** (*BRIT*) *n* fourre-tout *m inv*; **~er** *n* (*of ticket, record*) détenteur(-trice); (*of office, title etc*) titulaire *m/f*; (*container*) support *m*; **~ing** *n* (*share*) intérêts *mpl*; (*farm*) ferme *f*; **~-up** *n* (*robbery*) hold-up *m*;

(*delay*) retard *m*; (*BRIT: in traffic*) bouchon *m*

hole [həul] *n* trou *m*; **~-in-the-wall** *n* (*cash dispenser*) distributeur *m* de billets

holiday [ˈhɔlɪdeɪ] *n* vacances *fpl*; (*day off*) jour *m* de congé; (*public*) jour férié; **on ~** en congé; **~ camp** *n* (*also:* **~ centre**) camp *m* de vacances; **~-maker** (*BRIT*) *n* vacancier(-ère); **~ resort** *n* centre *m* de villégiature or de vacances

Holland [ˈhɔlənd] *n* Hollande *f*

hollow [ˈhɔləu] *adj* creux(-euse) ♦ *n* creux *m* ♦ *vt*: **to ~ out** creuser, évider

holly [ˈhɔlɪ] *n* houx *m*

holocaust [ˈhɔləkɔːst] *n* holocauste *m*

holster [ˈhəulstər] *n* étui *m* de revolver

holy [ˈhəulɪ] *adj* saint(e); (*bread, water*) bénit(e); (*ground*) sacré(e); **H~ Ghost** *n* Saint-Esprit *m*

homage [ˈhɔmɪdʒ] *n* hommage *m*; **to pay ~ to** rendre hommage à

home [həum] *n* foyer *m*, maison *f*; (*country*) pays natal, patrie *f*; (*institution*) maison ♦ *adj* de famille; (*ECON, POL*) national(e), intérieur(e); (*SPORT: game*) sur leur (*or* notre) terrain; (*team*) qui reçoit ♦ *adv* chez soi, à la maison; au pays natal; (*right in: nail etc*) à fond; **at ~** chez soi, à la maison; **make yourself at ~** faites comme chez vous; **~ address** *n* domicile permanent; **~land** *n* patrie *f*; **~less** *adj* sans foyer; sans abri; **~ly** *adj* (*plain*) simple, sans prétention; **~-made** *adj* fait(e) à la maison; **~ match** *n* match *m* à domicile; **H~ Office** (*BRIT*) *n* ministère *m* de l'Intérieur; **~ page** *n* (*COMPUT*) page *f* d'accueil; **~ rule** *n* autonomie *f*; **H~ Secretary** (*BRIT*) *n* ministre *m* de l'Intérieur; **~sick** *adj*: **to be ~sick** avoir le mal du pays; s'ennuyer de sa famille; **~ town** *n* ville natale; **~ward** *adj* (*journey*) du retour; **~work** *n* devoirs *mpl*

homoeopathic [həumɪəu'pæθɪk] (*US* **homeopathic**) *adj* (*medicine, methods*) homéopathique; (*doctor*) homéopathe

homogeneous [hɔməu'dʒiːnɪəs] *adj* homogène

homosexual [hɔməu'sɛksjuəl] *adj, n* homosexuel(le)

honest [ˈɔnɪst] *adj* honnête; (*sincere*) franc (franche); **~ly** *adv* honnêtement; franchement; **~y** *n* honnêteté *f*

honey [ˈhʌnɪ] *n* miel *m*; **~comb** *n* rayon *m* de miel; **~moon** *n* lune *f* de miel, voyage *m* de noces; **~suckle** (*BOT*) *n* chèvrefeuille *m*

honk [hɔŋk] *vi* (*AUT*) klaxonner

honorary [ˈɔnərərɪ] *adj* honoraire; (*duty, title*) honorifique

honour [ˈɔnər] (*US* **honor**) *vt* honorer ♦ *n* honneur *m*; **hono(u)rable** *adj* honorable; **hono(u)rs degree** *n* (*SCOL*) licence avec mention

hood [hud] n capuchon m; (of cooker) hotte f; (AUT: BRIT) capote f; (: US) capot m

hoof [hu:f] (pl **hooves**) n sabot m

hook [huk] n crochet m; (on dress) agrafe f; (for fishing) hameçon m ♦ vt accrocher; (fish) prendre

hooligan ['hu:lɪɡən] n voyou m

hoop [hu:p] n cerceau m

hooray [hu:'reɪ] excl hourra

hoot [hu:t] vi (AUT) klaxonner; (siren) mugir; (owl) hululer; **~er** n (BRIT: AUT) klaxon m; (NAUT, factory) sirène f

Hoover ® ['hu:və'] n (BRIT) aspirateur m ♦ vt: **h~** passer l'aspirateur dans ou sur

hooves [hu:vz] npl of **hoof**

hop [hɔp] vi (on one foot) sauter à cloche-pied; (bird) sautiller

hope [həup] vt, vi espérer ♦ n espoir m; **I ~ so** je l'espère; **I ~ not** j'espère que non; **~ful** adj (person) plein(e) d'espoir; (situation) prometteur(-euse), encourageant(e); **~fully** adv (expectantly) avec espoir, avec optimisme; (one hopes) avec un peu de chance; **~less** adj désespéré(e); (useless) nul(le)

hops [hɔps] npl houblon m

horizon [hə'raɪzn] n horizon m; **~tal** [hɔrɪ'zɔntl] adj horizontal(e)

horn [hɔ:n] n corne f; (MUS: also: **French ~**) cor m; (AUT) klaxon m

hornet ['hɔ:nɪt] n frelon m

horoscope ['hɔrəskəup] n horoscope m

horrendous [hə'rendəs] adj horrible, affreux(-euse)

horrible ['hɔrɪbl] adj horrible, affreux(-euse)

horrid ['hɔrɪd] adj épouvantable

horrify ['hɔrɪfaɪ] vt horrifier

horror ['hɔrə'] n horreur f; **~ film** n film m d'épouvante

hors d'oeuvre [ɔ:'də:vrə] n (CULIN) hors-d'œuvre m inv

horse [hɔ:s] n cheval m; **~back** n: on **~back** à cheval; **~ chestnut** n marron m (d'Inde); **~man** (irreg) n cavalier m; **~power** n puissance f (en chevaux); **~-racing** n courses fpl de chevaux; **~radish** n raifort m; **~shoe** n fer m à cheval

hose [həuz] n (also: **~pipe**) tuyau m; (also: **garden ~**) tuyau d'arrosage

hospitable ['hɔspɪtəbl] adj hospitalier(-ère)

hospital ['hɔspɪtl] n hôpital m; **in ~** à l'hôpital

hospitality [hɔspɪ'tælɪtɪ] n hospitalité f

host [həust] n hôte m; (TV, RADIO) animateur(-trice) m; (REL) hostie f; (large number): **a ~ of** une foule de

hostage ['hɔstɪdʒ] n otage m

hostel ['hɔstl] n foyer m; (also: **youth ~**)

auberge f de jeunesse

hostess ['həustɪs] n hôtesse f; (TV, RADIO) animatrice f

hostile ['hɔstaɪl] adj hostile; **hostility** [hɔ'stɪlɪtɪ] n hostilité f

hot [hɔt] adj chaud(e); (as opposed to only warm) très chaud; (spicy) fort(e); (contest etc) acharné(e); (temper) passionné(e); **to be ~** (person) avoir chaud; (object) être (très) chaud; **it is ~** (weather) il fait chaud; **~bed** n (fig) foyer m, pépinière f; **~ dog** n hot-dog m

hotel [həu'tel] n hôtel m

hot: ~house n serre (chaude); **~line** n (POL) téléphone m rouge, ligne directe; **~ly** adv passionnément, violemment; **~plate** n (on cooker) plaque chauffante; **~pot** (BRIT) n ragoût m; **~-water bottle** n bouillotte f

hound [haund] vt poursuivre avec acharnement ♦ n chien courant

hour ['auə'] n heure f; **~ly** adj, adv toutes les heures; (rate) horaire

house [n haus, vb hauz] n maison f; (POL) chambre f; (THEATRE) salle f; auditoire m ♦ vt (person) loger, héberger; (objects) abriter; **on the ~** (fig) aux frais de la maison; **~ arrest** n assignation f à résidence; **~boat** n bateau m (aménagé en habitation); **~bound** adj confiné(e) chez soi; **~breaking** n cambriolage m (avec effraction); **~hold** n (persons) famille f, maisonnée f; (ADMIN etc) ménage m; **~keeper** n gouvernante f; **~keeping** n (work) ménage m; **~keeping (money)** argent m du ménage; **~-warming (party)** n pendaison f de crémaillère; **~wife** (irreg) n ménagère f; femme f au foyer; **~work** n (travaux mpl du) ménage m

housing ['hauzɪŋ] n logement m; **~ development, ~ estate** n lotissement m

hovel ['hɔvl] n taudis m

hover ['hɔvə'] vi planer; **~craft** n aéroglisseur m

how [hau] adv comment; **~ are you?** comment allez-vous?; **~ do you do?** bonjour; enchanté(e); **~ far is it to?** combien y a-t-il jusqu'à ...?; **~ long have you been here?** depuis combien de temps êtes-vous là?; **~ lovely!** que or comme c'est joli!; **~ many/much?** combien?; **~ many people/much milk?** combien de gens/lait?; **~ old are you?** quel âge avez-vous?

however [hau'evə'] adv de quelque façon ou manière que +subj; (+adj) quelque ou si ... que +subj; (in questions) comment ♦ conj pourtant, cependant

howl [haul] vi hurler

H.P. abbr = **hire purchase**

h.p. abbr = **horsepower**

HQ abbr = **headquarters**

hub [hʌb] n (of wheel) moyeu m; (fig) centre

m, foyer *m*; **~cap** *n* enjoliveur *m*
huddle ['hʌdl] *vi*: **to ~ together** se blottir les uns contre les autres
hue [hjuː] *n* teinte *f*, nuance *f*
huff [hʌf] *n*: **in a ~** fâché(e)
hug [hʌg] *vt* serrer dans ses bras; (*shore, kerb*) serrer
huge [hjuːdʒ] *adj* énorme, immense
hulk [hʌlk] *n* (*ship*) épave *f*; (*car, building*) carcasse *f*; (*person*) mastodonte *m*
hull [hʌl] *n* coque *f*
hullo [hə'ləu] *excl* = **hello**
hum [hʌm] *vt* (*tune*) fredonner ♦ *vi* fredonner; (*insect*) bourdonner; (*plane, tool*) vrombir
human ['hjuːmən] *adj* humain(e) ♦ *n*: **~ being** être humain; **~e** [hjuː'meɪn] *adj* humain(e), humanitaire; **~itarian** [hjuːmænɪ'tɛərɪən] *adj* humanitaire; **~ity** [hjuː'mænɪtɪ] *n* humanité *f*
humble ['hʌmbl] *adj* humble, modeste ♦ *vt* humilier
humdrum ['hʌmdrʌm] *adj* monotone, banal(e)
humid ['hjuːmɪd] *adj* humide
humiliate [hjuː'mɪlɪeɪt] *vt* humilier; **humiliation** [hjuːmɪlɪ'eɪʃən] *n* humiliation *f*
humorous ['hjuːmərəs] *adj* humoristique; (*person*) plein(e) d'humour
humour ['hjuːmə*] (*US* **humor**) *n* humour *m*; (*mood*) humeur *f* ♦ *vt* (*person*) faire plaisir à; se prêter aux caprices de
hump [hʌmp] *n* bosse *f*
hunch [hʌntʃ] *n* (*premonition*) intuition *f*; **~back** *n* bossu(e); **~ed** *adj* voûté(e)
hundred ['hʌndrəd] *num* cent; **~s of** des centaines de; **~weight** *n* (*BRIT*) 50.8 kg, 112 lb; (*US*) 45.3 kg, 100 lb
hung [hʌŋ] *pt, pp of* **hang**
Hungary ['hʌŋgərɪ] *n* Hongrie *f*
hunger ['hʌŋgə*] *n* faim *f* ♦ *vi*: **to ~ for** avoir faim de, désirer ardemment
hungry ['hʌŋgrɪ] *adj* affamé(e); (*keen*): **~ for** avide de; **to be ~** avoir faim
hunk [hʌŋk] *n* (*of bread etc*) gros morceau
hunt [hʌnt] *vt* chasser; (*criminal*) pourchasser ♦ *vi* chasser; (*search*): **to ~ for** chercher (partout) ♦ *n* chasse *f*; **~er** *n* chasseur *m*; **~ing** *n* chasse *f*
hurdle ['hɜːdl] *n* (*SPORT*) haie *f*; (*fig*) obstacle *m*
hurl [hɜːl] *vt* lancer (avec violence); (*abuse, insults*) lancer
hurrah [hu'rɑː] *excl* = **hooray**
hurray [hu'reɪ] *excl* = **hooray**
hurricane ['hʌrɪkən] *n* ouragan *m*
hurried ['hʌrɪd] *adj* pressé(e), précipité(e); (*work*) fait(e) à la hâte; **~ly** *adv* précipitamment, à la hâte

hurry ['hʌrɪ] (*vb: also:* **~ up**) *n* hâte *f*, précipitation *f* ♦ *vi* se presser, se dépêcher ♦ *vt* (*person*) faire presser, faire se dépêcher; (*work*) presser; **to be in a ~** être pressé(e); **to do sth in a ~** faire qch en vitesse; **to ~ in/out** entrer/sortir précipitamment
hurt [hɜːt] (*pt, pp* **hurt**) *vt* (*cause pain to*) faire mal à; (*injure, fig*) blesser ♦ *vi* faire mal ♦ *adj* blessé(e); **~ful** *adj* (*remark*) blessant(e)
hurtle ['hɜːtl] *vi*: **to ~ past** passer en trombe; **to ~ down** dégringoler
husband ['hʌzbənd] *n* mari *m*
hush [hʌʃ] *n* calme *m*, silence *m* ♦ *vt* faire taire; **~!** chut!; **~ up** *vt* (*scandal*) étouffer
husk [hʌsk] *n* (*of wheat*) balle *f*; (*of rice, maize*) enveloppe *f*
husky ['hʌskɪ] *adj* rauque ♦ *n* chien *m* esquimau *or* de traîneau
hustle ['hʌsl] *vt* pousser, bousculer ♦ *n*: **~ and bustle** tourbillon *m* (d'activité)
hut [hʌt] *n* hutte *f*; (*shed*) cabane *f*
hutch [hʌtʃ] *n* clapier *m*
hyacinth ['haɪəsɪnθ] *n* jacinthe *f*
hydrant ['haɪdrənt] *n* (*also*: **fire ~**) bouche *f* d'incendie
hydraulic [haɪ'drɔːlɪk] *adj* hydraulique
hydroelectric ['haɪdrəu'lektrɪk] *adj* hydro-électrique
hydrofoil ['haɪdrəfɔɪl] *n* hydrofoil *m*
hydrogen ['haɪdrədʒən] *n* hydrogène *m*
hyena [haɪ'iːnə] *n* hyène *f*
hygiene ['haɪdʒiːn] *n* hygiène *f*; **hygienic** *adj* hygiénique
hymn [hɪm] *n* hymne *m*; cantique *m*
hype [haɪp] (*inf*) *n* battage *m* publicitaire
hypermarket ['haɪpəmɑːkɪt] (*BRIT*) *n* hypermarché *m*
hypertext ['haɪpətekst] *n* (*COMPUT*) hypertexte *m*
hyphen ['haɪfn] *n* trait *m* d'union
hypnotize ['hɪpnətaɪz] *vt* hypnotiser
hypocrisy [hɪ'pɔkrɪsɪ] *n* hypocrisie *f*; **hypocrite** ['hɪpəkrɪt] *n* hypocrite *m/f*; **hypocritical** *adj* hypocrite
hypothesis [haɪ'pɔθɪsɪs] (*pl* **hypotheses**) *n* hypothèse *f*
hysterical [hɪ'sterɪkl] *adj* hystérique; (*funny*) hilarant(e); **~ laughter** fou rire *m*
hysterics [hɪ'sterɪks] *npl*: **to be in/have ~** (*anger, panic*) avoir une crise de nerfs; (*laughter*) attraper un fou rire

I, i

I [aɪ] *pron* je; (*before vowel*) j'; (*stressed*) moi
ice [aɪs] *n* glace *f*; (*on road*) verglas *m* ♦ *vt* (*cake*) glacer ♦ *vi* (*also*: **~ over, ~ up**) geler; (*window*) se givrer; **~berg** *n* iceberg *m*;

~box n (US) réfrigérateur m; (BRIT)
compartiment m à glace; (insulated box)
glacière f; **~ cream** n glace f; **~ cube** n
glaçon m; **~d** adj glacé(e); **~ hockey** n
hockey m sur glace; **Iceland** n Islande f;
~ lolly n (BRIT) esquimau m (glace); **~ rink** n
patinoire f; **~-skating** n patinage m (sur
glace)

icicle ['aɪsɪkl] n glaçon m (naturel)

icing ['aɪsɪŋ] n (CULIN) glace f; **~ sugar** (BRIT)
n sucre m glace

icy ['aɪsɪ] adj glacé(e); (road) verglacé(e);
(weather, temperature) glacial(e)

I'd [aɪd] = I would; I had

idea [aɪ'dɪə] n idée f

ideal [aɪ'dɪəl] n idéal m ♦ adj idéal(e)

identical [aɪ'dɛntɪkl] adj identique

identification [aɪdɛntɪfɪ'keɪʃən] n
identification f; **means of ~** pièce f d'identité

identify [aɪ'dɛntɪfaɪ] vt identifier

Identikit picture ® [aɪ'dɛntɪkɪt-] n
portrait-robot m

identity [aɪ'dɛntɪtɪ] n identité f; **~ card** n
carte f d'identité

ideology [aɪdɪ'ɔlədʒɪ] n idéologie f

idiom ['ɪdɪəm] n expression f idiomatique;
(style) style m

idiosyncrasy [ɪdɪəʊ'sɪŋkrəsɪ] n (of person)
particularité f, petite manie

idiot ['ɪdɪət] n idiot(e), imbécile m/f; **~ic**
[ɪdɪ'ɔtɪk] adj idiot(e), bête, stupide

idle ['aɪdl] adj sans occupation, désœuvré(e);
(lazy) oisif(-ive), paresseux(-euse);
(unemployed) au chômage; (question,
pleasures) vain(e), futile ♦ vi (engine) tourner
au ralenti; **to lie ~** être arrêté(e), ne pas
fonctionner

idol ['aɪdl] n idole f; **~ize** vt idolâtrer, adorer

i.e. adv abbr (= id est) c'est-à-dire

if [ɪf] conj si; **~ so** si c'est le cas; **~ not** sinon;
~ only si seulement

ignite [ɪg'naɪt] vt mettre le feu à, enflammer
♦ vi s'enflammer; **ignition** n (AUT) allumage
m; **to switch on/off the ignition** mettre/
couper le contact; **ignition key** n clé f de
contact

ignorant ['ɪgnərənt] adj ignorant(e); **to be
~ of** (subject) ne rien connaître à; (events) ne
pas être au courant de

ignore [ɪg'nɔːʳ] vt ne tenir aucun compte de;
(person) faire semblant de ne pas reconnaître,
ignorer; (fact) méconnaître

ill [ɪl] adj (sick) malade; (bad) mauvais(e) ♦ n
mal m ♦ adv: **to speak/think ~ of** dire/penser
du mal de; **~s** npl (misfortunes) maux mpl,
malheurs mpl; **to be taken ~** tomber malade;
~-advised adj (decision) peu judi-
cieux(-euse); (person) malavisé(e); **~-at-
ease** adj mal à l'aise

I'll [aɪl] = I will; I shall

illegal [ɪ'liːgl] adj illégal(e)

illegible [ɪ'lɛdʒɪbl] adj illisible

illegitimate [ɪlɪ'dʒɪtɪmət] adj illégitime

ill-fated [ɪl'feɪtɪd] adj malheureux(-euse);
(day) néfaste

ill feeling n ressentiment m, rancune f

illiterate [ɪ'lɪtərət] adj illettré(e); (letter)
plein(e) de fautes

ill: **~-mannered** adj (child) mal élevé(e);
~ness n maladie f; **~-treat** vt maltraiter

illuminate [ɪ'luːmɪneɪt] vt (room, street)
éclairer; (for special effect) illuminer;
illumination [ɪluːmɪ'neɪʃən] n éclairage m;
illumination f

illusion [ɪ'luːʒən] n illusion f

illustrate ['ɪləstreɪt] vt illustrer; **illustration**
[ɪlə'streɪʃən] n illustration f

ill will n malveillance f

I'm [aɪm] = I am

image ['ɪmɪdʒ] n image f; (public face) image
de marque; **~ry** n images fpl

imaginary [ɪ'mædʒɪnərɪ] adj imaginaire

imagination [ɪmædʒɪ'neɪʃən] n imagination
f

imaginative [ɪ'mædʒɪnətɪv] adj imagina-
tif(-ive); (person) plein(e) d'imagination

imagine [ɪ'mædʒɪn] vt imaginer, s'imaginer;
(suppose) imaginer, supposer

imbalance [ɪm'bæləns] n déséquilibre m

imitate ['ɪmɪteɪt] vt imiter; **imitation**
[ɪmɪ'teɪʃən] n imitation f

immaculate [ɪ'mækjulət] adj impeccable;
(REL) immaculé(e)

immaterial [ɪmə'tɪərɪəl] adj sans importance,
insignifiant(e)

immature [ɪmə'tjuəʳ] adj (fruit) (qui n'est)
pas mûr(e); (person) qui manque de maturité

immediate [ɪ'miːdɪət] adj immédiat(e); **~ly**
adv (at once) immédiatement; **~ly next to**
juste à côté de

immense [ɪ'mɛns] adj immense; énorme

immerse [ɪ'məːs] vt immerger, plonger;
immersion heater (BRIT) n chauffe-eau m
électrique

immigrant ['ɪmɪgrənt] n immigrant(e);
immigré(e); **immigration** [ɪmɪ'greɪʃən] n
immigration f

imminent ['ɪmɪnənt] adj imminent(e)

immoral [ɪ'mɔrl] adj immoral(e)

immortal [ɪ'mɔːtl] adj, n immortel(le)

immune [ɪ'mjuːn] adj: **~ (to)** immunisé(e)
(contre); (fig) à l'abri de; **immunity** n
immunité f

impact ['ɪmpækt] n choc m, impact m; (fig)
impact

impair [ɪm'pɛəʳ] vt détériorer, diminuer

impart [ɪm'pɑːt] vt communiquer,
transmettre; (flavour) donner

impartial [ɪmˈpɑːʃl] *adj* impartial(e)

impassable [ɪmˈpɑːsəbl] *adj* infranchissable; (*road*) impraticable

impassive [ɪmˈpæsɪv] *adj* impassible

impatience [ɪmˈpeɪʃəns] *n* impatience *f*

impatient [ɪmˈpeɪʃənt] *adj* impatient(e); **to get** *or* **grow ~** s'impatienter; **~ly** *adv* avec impatience

impeccable [ɪmˈpekəbl] *adj* impeccable, parfait(e)

impede [ɪmˈpiːd] *vt* gêner; **impediment** *n* obstacle *m*; (*also*: **speech impediment**) défaut *m* d'élocution

impending [ɪmˈpendɪŋ] *adj* imminent(e)

imperative [ɪmˈperətɪv] *adj* (*need*) urgent(e), pressant(e); (*tone*) impérieux(-euse) ♦ *n* (*LING*) impératif *m*

imperfect [ɪmˈpəːfɪkt] *adj* imparfait(e); (*goods etc*) défectueux(-euse)

imperial [ɪmˈpɪərɪəl] *adj* impérial(e); (*BRIT*: *measure*) légal(e)

impersonal [ɪmˈpəːsənl] *adj* impersonnel(le)

impersonate [ɪmˈpəːsəneɪt] *vt* se faire passer pour; (*THEATRE*) imiter

impertinent [ɪmˈpəːtɪnənt] *adj* impertinent(e), insolent(e)

impervious [ɪmˈpəːvɪəs] *adj* (*fig*): **~ to** insensible à

impetuous [ɪmˈpetjuəs] *adj* impétueux(-euse), fougueux(-euse)

impetus [ˈɪmpətəs] *n* impulsion *f*; (*of runner*) élan *m*

impinge [ɪmˈpɪndʒ]: **to ~ on** *vt fus* (*person*) affecter, toucher; (*rights*) empiéter sur

implement [*n* ˈɪmplɪmənt, *vb* ˈɪmplɪment] *n* outil *m*, instrument *m*; (*for cooking*) ustensile *m* ♦ *vt* exécuter

implicit [ɪmˈplɪsɪt] *adj* implicite; (*complete*) absolu(e), sans réserve

imply [ɪmˈplaɪ] *vt* suggérer, laisser entendre; indiquer, supposer

impolite [ɪmpəˈlaɪt] *adj* impoli(e)

import [*vb* ɪmˈpɔːt, *n* ˈɪmpɔːt] *vt* importer ♦ *n* (*COMM*) importation *f*

importance [ɪmˈpɔːtns] *n* importance *f*

important [ɪmˈpɔːtənt] *adj* important(e)

importer [ɪmˈpɔːtəʳ] *n* importateur(-trice)

impose [ɪmˈpəuz] *vt* imposer ♦ *vi*: **to ~ on sb** abuser de la gentillesse de qn; **imposing** *adj* imposant(e), impressionnant(e); **imposition** [ɪmpəˈzɪʃən] *n* (*of tax etc*) imposition *f*; **to be an imposition on** (*person*) abuser de la gentillesse *or* la bonté de

impossible [ɪmˈpɔsɪbl] *adj* impossible

impotent [ˈɪmpətnt] *adj* impuissant(e)

impound [ɪmˈpaund] *vt* confisquer, saisir

impoverished [ɪmˈpɔvərɪʃt] *adj* appauvri(e), pauvre

impractical [ɪmˈpræktɪkl] *adj* pas pratique;

(*person*) qui manque d'esprit pratique

impregnable [ɪmˈpregnəbl] *adj* (*fortress*) imprenable

impress [ɪmˈpres] *vt* impressionner, faire impression sur; (*mark*) imprimer, marquer; **to ~ sth on sb** faire bien comprendre qch à qn; **~ed** *adj* impressionné(e)

impression [ɪmˈpreʃən] *n* impression *f*; (*of stamp, seal*) empreinte *f*; (*imitation*) imitation *f*; **to be under the ~ that** avoir l'impression que; **~ist** *n* (*ART*) impressionniste *m/f*; (*entertainer*) imitateur(-trice) *m/f*

impressive [ɪmˈpresɪv] *adj* impressionnant(e)

imprint [ˈɪmprɪnt] *n* (*outline*) marque *f*, empreinte *f*

imprison [ɪmˈprɪzn] *vt* emprisonner, mettre en prison

improbable [ɪmˈprɔbəbl] *adj* improbable; (*excuse*) peu plausible

improper [ɪmˈprɔpəʳ] *adj* (*unsuitable*) déplacé(e), de mauvais goût; indécent(e); (*dishonest*) malhonnête

improve [ɪmˈpruːv] *vt* améliorer ♦ *vi* s'améliorer; (*pupil etc*) faire des progrès; **~ment** *n* amélioration *f* (*in de*); progrès *m*

improvise [ˈɪmprəvaɪz] *vt, vi* improviser

impudent [ˈɪmpjudnt] *adj* impudent(e)

impulse [ˈɪmpʌls] *n* impulsion *f*; **on ~** impulsivement, sur un coup de tête; **impulsive** *adj* impulsif(-ive)

KEYWORD

in [ɪn] *prep* **1** (*indicating place, position*) dans; **in the house/the fridge** dans la maison/le frigo; **in the garden** dans le *or* au jardin; **in town** en ville; **in the country** à la campagne; **in school** à l'école; **in here/there** ici/là

2 (*with place names: of town, region, country*): **in London** à Londres; **in England** en Angleterre; **in Japan** au Japon; **in the United States** aux États-Unis

3 (*indicating time: during*): **in spring** au printemps; **in summer** en été; **in May/1992** en mai/1992; **in the afternoon** (dans) l'après-midi; **at 4 o'clock in the afternoon** à 4 heures de l'après-midi

4 (*indicating time: in the space of*) en; (: *future*) dans; **I did it in 3 hours/days** je l'ai fait en 3 heures/jours; **I'll see you in 2 weeks** *or* **in 2 weeks' time** je te verrai dans 2 semaines

5 (*indicating manner etc*) à; **in a loud/soft voice** à voix haute/basse; **in pencil** au crayon; **in French** en français; **the boy in the blue shirt** le garçon à *or* avec la chemise bleue

6 (*indicating circumstances*): **in the sun** au soleil; **in the shade** à l'ombre; **in the rain** sous la pluie

7 (*indicating mood, state*): **in tears** en larmes;

in anger sous le coup de la colère; **in despair** au désespoir; **in good condition** en bon état; **to live in luxury** vivre dans le luxe
8 (with ratios, numbers): **1 in 10 (households)**, **1 (household) in 10** 1 (ménage) sur 10; **20 pence in the pound** 20 pence par livre sterling; **they lined up in twos** ils se mirent en rangs (deux) par deux; **in hundreds** par centaines
9 (referring to people, works) chez; **the disease is common in children** c'est une maladie courante chez les enfants; **in (the works of) Dickens** chez Dickens, dans (l'œuvre de) Dickens
10 (indicating profession etc) dans; **to be in teaching** être dans l'enseignement
11 (after superlative) de; **the best pupil in the class** le meilleur élève de la classe
12 (with present participle): **in saying this** en disant ceci
♦ adv: **to be in** (person: at home, work) être là; (train, ship, plane) être arrivé(e); (in fashion) être à la mode; **to ask sb in** inviter qn à entrer; **to run/limp etc in** entrer en courant/boitant etc
♦ n: **the ins and outs (of)** (of proposal, situation etc) les tenants et aboutissants (de)

in. abbr = **inch**
inability [ɪnəˈbɪlɪtɪ] n incapacité f
inaccurate [ɪnˈækjurət] adj inexact(e); (person) qui manque de précision
inadequate [ɪnˈædɪkwət] adj insuffisant(e), inadéquat(e)
inadvertently [ɪnədˈvəːtntlɪ] adv par mégarde
inadvisable [ɪnədˈvaɪzəbl] adj (action) à déconseiller
inane [ɪˈneɪn] adj inepte, stupide
inanimate [ɪnˈænɪmət] adj inanimé(e)
inappropriate [ɪnəˈprəʊprɪət] adj inopportun(e), mal à propos; (word, expression) impropre
inarticulate [ɪnɑːˈtɪkjulət] adj (person) qui s'exprime mal; (speech) indistinct(e)
inasmuch as [ɪnəzˈmʌtʃ-] adv (insofar as) dans la mesure où; (seeing that) attendu que
inauguration [ɪnɔːgjuˈreɪʃən] n inauguration f; (of president) investiture f
inborn [ɪnˈbɔːn] adj (quality) inné(e)
inbred [ɪnˈbred] adj inné(e), naturel(le); (family) consanguin(e)
Inc. abbr = **incorporated**
incapable [ɪnˈkeɪpəbl] adj incapable
incapacitate [ɪnkəˈpæsɪteɪt] vt: **to ~ sb from doing** rendre qn incapable de faire
incense [n ˈɪnsens, vb ɪnˈsens] n encens m
♦ vt (anger) mettre en colère
incentive [ɪnˈsentɪv] n encouragement m,

raison f de se donner de la peine
incessant [ɪnˈsesnt] adj incessant(e); **~ly** adv sans cesse, constamment
inch [ɪntʃ] n pouce m (= 25 mm; 12 in a foot); **within an ~ of** à deux doigts de; **he didn't give an ~** (fig) il n'a pas voulu céder d'un pouce
incident [ˈɪnsɪdnt] n incident m; **~al** [ɪnsɪˈdentl] adj (additional) accessoire; **~al to** qui accompagne; **~ally** adv (by the way) à propos
inclination [ɪnklɪˈneɪʃən] n (fig) inclination f
incline [n ˈɪnklaɪn, vb ɪnˈklaɪn] n pente f ♦ vt incliner ♦ vi (surface) s'incliner; **to be ~d to do** avoir tendance à faire
include [ɪnˈkluːd] vt inclure, comprendre; **including** prep y compris; **inclusive** adj inclus(e), compris(e); **inclusive of tax** etc taxes etc comprises
income [ˈɪnkʌm] n revenu m; **~ tax** n impôt m sur le revenu
incoming [ˈɪnkʌmɪŋ] adj qui arrive; (president) entrant(e); **~ mail** courrier m du jour; **~ tide** marée montante
incompetent [ɪnˈkɔmpɪtnt] adj incompétent(e), incapable
incomplete [ɪnkəmˈpliːt] adj incomplet(-ète)
incongruous [ɪnˈkɔŋgruəs] adj incongru(e)
inconsiderate [ɪnkənˈsɪdərət] adj (person) qui manque d'égards; (action) inconsidéré(e)
inconsistency [ɪnkənˈsɪstənsɪ] n (of actions etc) inconséquence f; (of work) irrégularité f; (of statement etc) incohérence f
inconsistent [ɪnkənˈsɪstnt] adj inconséquent(e); irrégulier(-ère); peu cohérent(e); **~ with** incompatible avec
inconspicuous [ɪnkənˈspɪkjuəs] adj qui passe inaperçu(e); (colour, dress) discret(-ète)
inconvenience [ɪnkənˈviːnjəns] n inconvénient m; (trouble) dérangement m ♦ vt déranger
inconvenient [ɪnkənˈviːnjənt] adj (house) malcommode; (time, place) mal choisi(e), qui ne convient pas; (visitor) importun(e)
incorporate [ɪnˈkɔːpəreɪt] vt incorporer; (contain) contenir; **~d company** (US) n ≈ société f anonyme
incorrect [ɪnkəˈrekt] adj incorrect(e)
increase [n ˈɪnkriːs, vb ɪnˈkriːs] n augmentation f ♦ vi, vt augmenter; **increasing** adj (number) croissant(e); **increasingly** adv de plus en plus
incredible [ɪnˈkredɪbl] adj incroyable
incubator [ˈɪnkjubeɪtər] n (for babies) couveuse f
incumbent [ɪnˈkʌmbənt] n (president) président m en exercice; (REL) titulaire m/f ♦ adj: **it is ~ on him to ...** il lui incombe or

appartient de ...

incur [ɪn'kəːʳ] vt (expenses) encourir; (anger, risk) s'exposer à; (debt) contracter; (loss) subir

indebted [ɪn'dɛtɪd] adj: **to be ~ to sb (for)** être redevable à qn (de)

indecent [ɪn'diːsnt] adj indécent(e), inconvenant(e); **~ assault** (BRIT) n attentat m à la pudeur; **~ exposure** n outrage m (public) à la pudeur

indecisive [ɪndɪ'saɪsɪv] adj (person) indécis(e)

indeed [ɪn'diːd] adv vraiment; en effet; (furthermore) d'ailleurs; **yes ~!** certainement!

indefinitely [ɪn'dɛfɪnɪtlɪ] adv (wait) indéfiniment

indemnity [ɪn'dɛmnɪtɪ] n (safeguard) assurance f, garantie f; (compensation) indemnité f

independence [ɪndɪ'pɛndns] n indépendance f

independent [ɪndɪ'pɛndnt] adj indépendant(e); (school) privé(e); (radio) libre

index ['ɪndɛks] n (pl: ~es: in book) index m; (: in library etc) catalogue m; (pl: indices: ratio, sign) indice m; **~ card** n fiche f; **~ finger** n index m; **~-linked** adj indexé(e) (sur le coût de la vie etc)

India ['ɪndɪə] n Inde f; **~n** adj indien(ne) ♦ n Indien(ne); **(American) ~n** Indien(ne) (d'Amérique); **~ Ocean** n océan Indien

indicate ['ɪndɪkeɪt] vt indiquer; **indication** [ɪndɪ'keɪʃən] n indication ᶘ signe m; **indicative** [ɪn'dɪkətɪv] adj: **indicative of** symptomatique de ♦ n (LING) indicatif m; **indicator** n (sign) indicateur m; (AUT) clignotant m

indices ['ɪndɪsiːz] npl of **index**

indictment [ɪn'daɪtmənt] n accusation f

indifferent [ɪn'dɪfrənt] adj indifférent(e); (poor) médiocre, quelconque

indigenous [ɪn'dɪdʒɪnəs] adj indigène

indigestion [ɪndɪ'dʒɛstʃən] n indigestion f, mauvaise digestion

indignant [ɪn'dɪgnənt] adj: **~ (at sth/with sb)** indigné(e) (de qch/contre qn)

indignity [ɪn'dɪgnɪtɪ] n indignité f, affront m

indirect [ɪndɪ'rɛkt] adj indirect(e)

indiscreet [ɪndɪs'kriːt] adj indiscret(-ète); (rash) imprudent(e)

indiscriminate [ɪndɪs'krɪmɪnət] adj (person) qui manque de discernement; (killings) commis(e) au hasard

indisputable [ɪndɪs'pjuːtəbl] adj incontestable, indiscutable

individual [ɪndɪ'vɪdjuəl] n individu m ♦ adj individuel(le); (characteristic) particulier(-ère), original(e)

indoctrination [ɪndɔktrɪ'neɪʃən] n endoctrinement m

Indonesia [ɪndə'niːzɪə] n Indonésie f

indoor ['ɪndɔːʳ] adj (plant) d'appartement; (swimming pool) couvert(e); (sport, games) pratiqué(e) en salle; **~s** adv à l'intérieur

induce [ɪn'djuːs] vt (persuade) persuader; (bring about) provoquer; **~ment** n (incentive) récompense f; (pej: bribe) pot-de-vin m

indulge [ɪn'dʌldʒ] vt (whim) céder à, satisfaire; (child) gâter ♦ vi: **to ~ in sth** (luxury) se permettre qch; (fantasies etc) se livrer à qch; **~nce** n fantaisie f (que l'on s'offre); (leniency) indulgence f; **~nt** adj indulgent(e)

industrial [ɪn'dʌstrɪəl] adj industriel(le); (injury) du travail; **~ action** n action revendicative; **~ estate** (BRIT) n zone industrielle; **~ist** n industriel m; **~ park** (US) n = **industrial estate**

industrious [ɪn'dʌstrɪəs] adj travailleur(-euse)

industry ['ɪndəstrɪ] n industrie f; (diligence) zèle m, application f

inebriated [ɪ'niːbrɪeɪtɪd] adj ivre

inedible [ɪn'ɛdɪbl] adj immangeable; (plant etc) non comestible

ineffective [ɪnɪ'fɛktɪv], **ineffectual** [ɪnɪ'fɛktjuəl] adj inefficace

inefficient [ɪnɪ'fɪʃənt] adj inefficace

inequality [ɪnɪ'kwɔlɪtɪ] n inégalité f

inescapable [ɪnɪ'skeɪpəbl] adj inéluctable, inévitable

inevitable [ɪn'ɛvɪtəbl] adj inévitable; **inevitably** adv inévitablement

inexpensive [ɪnɪk'spɛnsɪv] adj bon marché inv

inexperienced [ɪnɪk'spɪərɪənst] adj inexpérimenté(e)

infallible [ɪn'fælɪbl] adj infaillible

infamous ['ɪnfəməs] adj infâme, abominable

infancy ['ɪnfənsɪ] n petite enfance, bas âge

infant ['ɪnfənt] n (baby) nourrisson m; (young child) petit(e) enfant; **~ school** (BRIT) n classes fpl préparatoires (entre 5 et 7 ans)

infatuated [ɪn'fætjueɪtɪd] adj: **~ with** entiché(e) de; **infatuation** [ɪnfætju'eɪʃən] n engouement m

infect [ɪn'fɛkt] vt infecter, contaminer; **~ion** n infection f; (contagion) contagion f; **~ious** adj infectieux(-euse); (also fig) contagieux(-euse)

infer [ɪn'fəːʳ] vt conclure, déduire

inferior [ɪn'fɪərɪəʳ] adj inférieur(e); (goods) de qualité inférieure ♦ n inférieur(e); (in rank) subalterne m/f; **~ity** [ɪnfɪərɪ'ɔrɪtɪ] n infériorité f

infertile [ɪn'fəːtaɪl] adj stérile

infighting ['ɪnfaɪtɪŋ] n querelles fpl internes

infinite ['ɪnfɪnɪt] *adj* infini(e)
infinitive [ɪn'fɪnɪtɪv] *n* infinitif *m*
infinity [ɪn'fɪnɪtɪ] *n* infinité *f*; (*also* MATH) infini *m*
infirmary [ɪn'fə:mərɪ] *n* (*hospital*) hôpital *m*
inflamed [ɪn'fleɪmd] *adj* enflammé(e)
inflammable [ɪn'flæməbl] (*BRIT*) *adj* inflammable
inflammation [ɪnflə'meɪʃən] *n* inflammation *f*
inflatable [ɪn'fleɪtəbl] *adj* gonflable
inflate [ɪn'fleɪt] *vt* (*tyre, balloon*) gonfler; (*price*) faire monter; **inflation** *n* (ECON) inflation *f*; **inflationary** *adj* inflationniste
inflict [ɪn'flɪkt] *vt*: **to ~ on** infliger à
influence ['ɪnfluəns] *n* influence *f* ♦ *vt* influencer; **under the ~ of alcohol** en état d'ébriété; **influential** [ɪnflu'ɛnʃl] *adj* influent(e)
influenza [ɪnflu'ɛnzə] *n* grippe *f*
influx ['ɪnflʌks] *n* afflux *m*
infomercial ['ɪnfəuməːʃl] (*US*) *n* (*for product*) publi-information *f*; (POL) émission où un candidat présente son programme électoral
inform [ɪn'fɔːm] *vt*: **to ~ sb (of)** informer or avertir qn (de) ♦ *vi*: **to ~ on sb** dénoncer qn
informal [ɪn'fɔːml] *adj* (*person, manner, party*) simple; (*visit, discussion*) dénué(e) de formalités; (*announcement, invitation*) non officiel(le); (*colloquial*) familier(-ère); **~ity** [ɪnfɔː'mælɪtɪ] *n* simplicité *f*, absence *f* de cérémonie; caractère non officiel
informant [ɪn'fɔːmənt] *n* informateur(-trice)
information [ɪnfə'meɪʃən] *n* information *f*; renseignements *mpl*; (*knowledge*) connaissances *fpl*; **a piece of ~** un renseignement; **~ desk** *n* accueil *m*; **~ office** *n* bureau *m* de renseignements
informative [ɪn'fɔːmətɪv] *adj* instructif(-ive)
informer [ɪn'fɔːmə'] *n* (*also*: **police ~**) indicateur(-trice)
infringe [ɪn'frɪndʒ] *vt* enfreindre ♦ *vi*: **to ~ on** empiéter sur; **~ment** *n*: **~ment (of)** infraction *f* (à)
infuriating [ɪn'fjuərɪeɪtɪŋ] *adj* exaspérant(e)
ingenious [ɪn'dʒiːnjəs] *adj* ingénieux(-euse); **ingenuity** [ɪndʒɪ'njuːɪtɪ] *n* ingéniosité *f*
ingenuous [ɪn'dʒɛnjuəs] *adj* naïf (naïve), ingénu(e)
ingot ['ɪŋgət] *n* lingot *m*
ingrained [ɪn'greɪnd] *adj* enraciné(e)
ingratiate [ɪn'greɪʃɪeɪt] *vt*: **to ~ o.s. with** s'insinuer dans les bonnes grâces de, se faire bien voir de
ingredient [ɪn'griːdɪənt] *n* ingrédient *m*; (*fig*) élément *m*
inhabit [ɪn'hæbɪt] *vt* habiter; **~ant** *n* habitant(e)
inhale [ɪn'heɪl] *vt* respirer; (*smoke*) avaler ♦ *vi*

aspirer; (*in smoking*) avaler la fumée
inherent [ɪn'hɪərənt] *adj*: **~ (in or to)** inhérent(e) (à)
inherit [ɪn'hɛrɪt] *vt* hériter (de); **~ance** *n* héritage *m*
inhibit [ɪn'hɪbɪt] *vt* (PSYCH) inhiber; (*growth*) freiner; **~ion** [ɪnhɪ'bɪʃən] *n* inhibition *f*
inhuman [ɪn'hjuːmən] *adj* inhumain(e)
initial [ɪ'nɪʃl] *adj* initial(e) ♦ *n* initiale *f* ♦ *vt* parafer; **~s** *npl* (*letters*) initiales *fpl*; (*as signature*) parafe *m*; **~ly** *adv* initialement, au début
initiate [ɪ'nɪʃɪeɪt] *vt* (*start*) entreprendre, amorcer; (*entreprise*) lancer; (*person*) initier; **to ~ proceedings against sb** intenter une action à qn; **initiative** *n* initiative *f*
inject [ɪn'dʒɛkt] *vt* injecter; (*person*): **to ~ sb with sth** faire une piqûre de qch à qn; **~ion** *n* injection *f*, piqûre *f*
injure ['ɪndʒə'] *vt* blesser; (*reputation etc*) compromettre; **~d** *adj* blessé(e); **injury** *n* blessure *f*; **~ time** *n* (SPORT) arrêts *mpl* de jeu
injustice [ɪn'dʒʌstɪs] *n* injustice *f*
ink [ɪŋk] *n* encre *f*
inkling ['ɪŋklɪŋ] *n*: **to have an/no ~ of** avoir une (vague) idée de/n'avoir aucune idée de
inlaid ['ɪnleɪd] *adj* incrusté(e); (*table etc*) marqueté(e)
inland [*adj* 'ɪnlənd, *adv* ɪn'lænd] *adj* intérieur(e) ♦ *adv* à l'intérieur, dans les terres; **Inland Revenue** (*BRIT*) *n* fisc *m*
in-laws ['ɪnlɔːz] *npl* beaux-parents *mpl*; belle famille
inlet ['ɪnlɛt] *n* (GEO) crique *f*
inmate ['ɪnmeɪt] *n* (*in prison*) détenu(e); (*in asylum*) interné(e)
inn [ɪn] *n* auberge *f*
innate [ɪ'neɪt] *adj* inné(e)
inner ['ɪnə'] *adj* intérieur(e); **~ city** *n* centre *m* de zone urbaine; **~ tube** *n* (*of tyre*) chambre *f* à air
innings ['ɪnɪŋz] *n* (CRICKET) tour *m* de batte
innocent ['ɪnəsnt] *adj* innocent(e)
innocuous [ɪ'nɔkjuəs] *adj* inoffensif(-ive)
innuendo [ɪnju'ɛndəu] (*pl* **~es**) *n* insinuation *f*, allusion (malveillante)
innumerable [ɪ'njuːmrəbl] *adj* innombrable
inpatient ['ɪnpeɪʃənt] *n* malade hospitalisé(e)
input ['ɪnput] *n* (*resources*) ressources *fpl*; (COMPUT) entrée *f* (de données); (: *data*) données *fpl*
inquest ['ɪnkwɛst] *n* enquête *f*; (**coroner's**) **~** enquête judiciaire
inquire [ɪn'kwaɪə'] *vi* demander ♦ *vt* demander; **to ~ about** se renseigner sur; **~ into** *vt fus* faire une enquête sur; **inquiry** *n* demande *f* de renseignements; (*investigation*) enquête *f*, investigation *f*; **inquiries** *npl*: **the inquiries** (RAIL *etc*) les

renseignements; **inquiry** or **inquiries office** (BRIT) n bureau m des renseignements

inquisitive [ɪnˈkwɪzɪtɪv] adj curieux(-euse)

ins abbr = **inches**

insane [ɪnˈseɪn] adj fou (folle); (MED) aliéné(e); **insanity** [ɪnˈsænɪtɪ] n folie f; (MED) aliénation (mentale)

inscription [ɪnˈskrɪpʃən] n inscription f; (in book) dédicace f

inscrutable [ɪnˈskruːtəbl] adj impénétrable; (comment) obscur(e)

insect [ˈɪnsɛkt] n insecte m; **~icide** [ɪnˈsɛktɪsaɪd] n insecticide m; **~ repellent** n crème f anti-insecte

insecure [ɪnsɪˈkjuər] adj peu solide; peu sûr(e); (person) anxieux(-euse)

insensitive [ɪnˈsɛnsɪtɪv] adj insensible

insert [ɪnˈsɜːt] vt insérer; **~ion** n insertion f

in-service [ˈɪnˈsɜːvɪs] adj (training) continu(e), en cours d'emploi; (course) de perfectionnement, de recyclage

inshore [ˈɪnˈʃɔː] adj côtier(-ère) ♦ adv près de la côte; (move) vers la côte

inside [ˈɪnˈsaɪd] n intérieur m ♦ adj intérieur(e) ♦ adv à l'intérieur, dedans ♦ prep à l'intérieur de; (of time): **~ 10 minutes** en moins de 10 minutes; **~s** npl (inf) intestins mpl; **~ information** n renseignements obtenus à la source; (: in US, Europe etc) voie f de gauche; **~ lane** n (AUT: in Britain) voie f de gauche; (: in US, Europe etc) voie de droite; **~ out** adv à l'envers; (know) à fond; **~r dealing, ~r trading** n (St Ex) délit m d'initié

insight [ˈɪnsaɪt] n perspicacité f; (glimpse, idea) aperçu m

insignificant [ɪnsɪgˈnɪfɪknt] adj insignifiant(e)

insincere [ɪnsɪnˈsɪə] adj hypocrite

insinuate [ɪnˈsɪnjueɪt] vt insinuer

insist [ɪnˈsɪst] vi insister; **to ~ on doing** insister pour faire; **to ~ on sth** exiger qch; **to ~ that** insister pour que; (claim) maintenir or soutenir que; **~ent** adj insistant(e), pressant(e); (noise, action) ininterrompu(e)

insole [ˈɪnsəul] n (removable) semelle intérieure

insolent [ˈɪnsələnt] adj insolent(e)

insolvent [ɪnˈsɒlvənt] adj insolvable

insomnia [ɪnˈsɒmnɪə] n insomnie f

inspect [ɪnˈspɛkt] vt inspecter; (ticket) contrôler; **~ion** n inspection f; contrôle m; **~or** n inspecteur(-trice), (BRIT: on buses, trains) contrôleur(-euse)

inspire [ɪnˈspaɪə] vt inspirer

install [ɪnˈstɔːl] vt installer; **~ation** [ɪnstəˈleɪʃən] n installation f

instalment [ɪnˈstɔːlmənt] (US **installment**) n acompte m, versement partiel; (of TV serial etc) épisode m; **in ~s** (pay) à tempérament;

(receive) en plusieurs fois

instance [ˈɪnstəns] n exemple m; **for ~** par exemple; **in the first ~** tout d'abord, en premier lieu

instant [ˈɪnstənt] n instant m ♦ adj immédiat(e); (coffee, food) instantané(e), en poudre; **~ly** adv immédiatement, tout de suite

instead [ɪnˈstɛd] adv au lieu de cela; **~ of** au lieu de; **~ of sb** à la place de qn

instep [ˈɪnstɛp] n cou-de-pied m; (of shoe) cambrure f

instigate [ˈɪnstɪgeɪt] vt (rebellion) fomenter, provoquer; (talks etc) promouvoir

instil [ɪnˈstɪl] vt: **to ~ (into)** inculquer (à); (courage) insuffler (à)

instinct [ˈɪnstɪŋkt] n instinct m

institute [ˈɪnstɪtjuːt] n institut m ♦ vt instituer, établir; (inquiry) ouvrir; (proceedings) entamer

institution [ɪnstɪˈtjuːʃən] n institution f; (educational) établissement m (scolaire); (mental home) établissement (psychiatrique)

instruct [ɪnˈstrʌkt] vt: **to ~ sb in sth** enseigner qch à qn; **to ~ sb to do** charger qn or ordonner à qn de faire; **~ion** n instruction f; **~ions** npl (orders) directives fpl; **~ions (for use)** mode m d'emploi; **~or** n professeur m; (for skiing, driving) moniteur m

instrument [ˈɪnstrumənt] n instrument m; **~al** [ɪnstruˈmɛntl] adj: **to be ~al in** contribuer à; **~ panel** n tableau m de bord

insufficient [ɪnsəˈfɪʃnt] adj insuffisant(e)

insular [ˈɪnsjulə] adj (outlook) borné(e); (person) aux vues étroites

insulate [ˈɪnsjuleɪt] vt isoler; (against sound) insonoriser; **insulation** [ɪnsjuˈleɪʃən] n isolation f; insonorisation f

insulin [ˈɪnsjulɪn] n insuline f

insult [n ˈɪnsʌlt, vb ɪnˈsʌlt] n insulte f, affront m ♦ vt insulter, faire affront à

insurance [ɪnˈʃuərəns] n assurance f; **fire/life ~** assurance-incendie/-vie; **~ policy** n police f d'assurance

insure [ɪnˈʃuə] vt assurer; **to ~ (o.s.) against** (fig) parer à

intact [ɪnˈtækt] adj intact(e)

intake [ˈɪnteɪk] n (of food, oxygen) consommation f; (BRIT: SCOL): **an ~ of 200 a year** 200 admissions fpl par an

integral [ˈɪntɪgrəl] adj (part) intégrant(e)

integrate [ˈɪntɪgreɪt] vt intégrer ♦ vi s'intégrer

intellect [ˈɪntɪlɛkt] n intelligence f; **~ual** [ɪntəˈlɛktjuəl] adj, n intellectuel(le)

intelligence [ɪnˈtɛlɪdʒəns] n intelligence f; (MIL etc) informations fpl, renseignements mpl; **~ service** n services secrets; **intelligent** adj intelligent(e)

intend [ɪn'tɛnd] vt (gift etc): **to ~ sth for** destiner qch à; **to ~ to do** avoir l'intention de faire

intense [ɪn'tɛns] adj intense; (person) véhément(e); **~ly** adv intensément; profondément

intensive [ɪn'tɛnsɪv] adj intensif(-ive); **~ care unit** n service m de réanimation

intent [ɪn'tɛnt] n intention f ♦ adj attentif(-ive); (absorbed): **~ (on)** absorbé(e) (par); **to all ~s and purposes** en fait, pratiquement; **to be ~ on doing sth** être (bien) décidé à faire qch; **~ion** n intention f; **~ional** adj intentionnel(le), délibéré(e); **~ly** adv attentivement

interact [ɪntər'ækt] vi avoir une action réciproque; (people) communiquer; **~ive** adj (COMPUT) interactif(-ive)

interchange [n 'ɪntətʃeɪndʒ, vb ɪntə'tʃeɪndʒ] n (exchange) échange m; (on motorway) échangeur m; **~able** adj interchangeable

intercom ['ɪntəkɔm] n interphone m

intercourse ['ɪntəkɔːs] n (sexual) rapports mpl

interest ['ɪntrɪst] n intérêt m; (pastime): **my main ~** ce qui m'intéresse le plus; (COMM) intérêts mpl ♦ vt intéresser; **to be ~ed in sth** s'intéresser à qch; **I am ~ed in going** ça m'intéresse d'y aller; **~ing** adj intéressant(e); **~ rate** n taux m d'intérêt

interface ['ɪntəfeɪs] n (COMPUT) interface f

interfere [ɪntə'fɪə] vi: **to ~ in** (quarrel) s'immiscer dans; (other people's business) se mêler de; **to ~ with** (object) toucher à; (plans) contrecarrer; (duty) être en conflit avec; **~nce** n (in affairs) ingérance f; (RADIO, TV) parasites mpl

interim ['ɪntərɪm] adj provisoire ♦ n: **in the ~** dans l'intérim, entre-temps

interior [ɪn'tɪərɪə] n intérieur m ♦ adj intérieur(e); (minister, department) de l'Intérieur; **~ designer** n styliste m/f, designer m/f

interjection [ɪntə'dʒɛkʃən] n (interruption) interruption f; (LING) interjection f

interlock [ɪntə'lɔk] vi s'enclencher

interlude ['ɪntəluːd] n intervalle m; (THEATRE) intermède m

intermediate [ɪntə'miːdɪət] adj intermédiaire; (SCOL: course, level) moyen(ne)

intermission [ɪntə'mɪʃən] n pause f; (THEATRE, CINEMA) entracte m

intern [vb ɪn'təːn, n 'ɪntəːn] vt interner ♦ n (US) interne m/f

internal [ɪn'təːnl] adj interne; (politics) intérieur(e); **~ly** adv: **"not to be taken ~ly"** "pour usage externe"; **I~ Revenue Service** (US) n fisc m

international [ɪntə'næʃənl] adj international(e)

Internet ['ɪntənɛt] n Internet m

interplay ['ɪntəpleɪ] n effet m réciproque, interaction f

interpret [ɪn'təːprɪt] vt interpréter ♦ vi servir d'interprète; **~er** n interprète m/f

interrelated [ɪntərɪ'leɪtɪd] adj en corrélation, en rapport étroit

interrogate [ɪn'tɛrəʊgeɪt] vt interroger; (suspect etc) soumettre à un interrogatoire; **interrogation** [ɪntɛrəʊ'geɪʃən] n interrogation f; interrogatoire m

interrupt [ɪntə'rʌpt] vt, vi interrompre; **~ion** n interruption f

intersect [ɪntə'sɛkt] vi (roads) se croiser, se couper; **~ion** n (of roads) croisement m

intersperse [ɪntə'spəːs] vt: **to ~ with** parsemer de

intertwine [ɪntə'twaɪn] vi s'entrelacer

interval ['ɪntəvl] n intervalle m; (BRIT: THEATRE) entracte m; (: SPORT) mi-temps f; **at ~s** par intervalles

intervene [ɪntə'viːn] vi (person) intervenir; (event) survenir; (time) s'écouler (entre-temps); **intervention** n intervention f

interview ['ɪntəvjuː] n (RADIO, TV etc) interview f; (for job) entrevue f ♦ vt interviewer; avoir une entrevue avec; **~er** n (RADIO, TV) interviewer m

intestine [ɪn'tɛstɪn] n intestin m

intimacy ['ɪntɪməsɪ] n intimité f

intimate [adj 'ɪntɪmət, vb 'ɪntɪmeɪt] adj intime; (friendship) profond(e); (knowledge) approfondi(e) ♦ vt (hint) suggérer, laisser entendre

into ['ɪntu] prep dans; **~ pieces/French** en morceaux/français

intolerant [ɪn'tɔlərnt] adj: **~ (of)** intolérant(e) (de)

intoxicated [ɪn'tɔksɪkeɪtɪd] adj (drunk) ivre

intractable [ɪn'træktəbl] adj (child) indocile, insoumis(e); (problem) insoluble

intranet ['ɪntrənɛt] n intranet m

intransitive [ɪn'trænsɪtɪv] adj intransitif(-ive)

intravenous [ɪntrə'viːnəs] adj intraveineux(-euse)

in-tray ['ɪntreɪ] n courrier m "arrivée"

intricate ['ɪntrɪkət] adj complexe, compliqué(e)

intrigue [ɪn'triːg] n intrigue f ♦ vt intriguer; **intriguing** adj fascinant(e)

intrinsic [ɪn'trɪnsɪk] adj intrinsèque

introduce [ɪntrə'djuːs] vt introduire; (TV show, people to each other) présenter; **to ~ sb to** (pastime, technique) initier qn à; **introduction** n introduction f; (of person) présentation f; (to new experience) initiation f; **introductory** adj préliminaire, d'introduction; **introductory offer** n

(COMM) offre f de lancement

intrude [ɪn'truːd] vi (person) être importun(e); **to ~ on** (conversation etc) s'immiscer dans; **~r** n intrus(e)

intuition [ɪntjuː'ɪʃən] n intuition f

inundate ['ɪnʌndeɪt] vt: **to ~ with** inonder de

invade [ɪn'veɪd] vt envahir

invalid n ['ɪnvəlɪd, adj ɪn'vælɪd] n malade m/f; (with disability) invalide m/f ♦ adj (not valid) non valide or valable

invaluable [ɪn'væljuəbl] adj inestimable, inappréciable

invariably [ɪn'vɛərɪəblɪ] adv invariablement; toujours

invent [ɪn'vɛnt] vt inventer; **~ion** n invention f; **~ive** adj inventif(-ive); **~or** n inventeur(-trice)

inventory ['ɪnvəntrɪ] n inventaire m

invert [ɪn'vɜːt] vt intervertir; (cup, object) retourner; **~ed commas** (BRIT) npl guillemets mpl

invest [ɪn'vɛst] vt investir ♦ vi: **to ~ in sth** placer son argent dans qch; (fig) s'offrir qch

investigate [ɪn'vɛstɪgeɪt] vt (crime etc) faire une enquête sur; **investigation** [ɪnvɛstɪ'geɪʃən] n (of crime) enquête f

investment [ɪn'vɛstmənt] n investissement m, placement m

investor [ɪn'vɛstəʳ] n investisseur m; actionnaire m/f

invigilator [ɪn'vɪdʒɪleɪtəʳ] n surveillant(e)

invigorating [ɪn'vɪgəreɪtɪŋ] adj vivifiant(e); (fig) stimulant(e)

invisible [ɪn'vɪzɪbl] adj invisible

invitation [ɪnvɪ'teɪʃən] n invitation f

invite [ɪn'vaɪt] vt inviter; (opinions etc) demander; **inviting** adj engageant(e), attrayant(e)

invoice ['ɪnvɔɪs] n facture f

involuntary [ɪn'vɔləntrɪ] adj involontaire

involve [ɪn'vɔlv] vt (entail) entraîner, nécessiter; (concern) concerner; (associate): **to ~ sb (in)** impliquer qn (dans), mêler qn (à); faire participer qn (à); **~d** adj (complicated) complexe; **to be ~d in** participer à; **~ment** n: **~ment (in)** participation f (à); rôle m (dans); (enthusiasm) enthousiasme m (pour)

inward ['ɪnwəd] adj (thought, feeling) profond(e), intime; (movement) vers l'intérieur; **~(s)** adv vers l'intérieur

I/O abbr (COMPUT) (= input/output) E/S

iodine ['aɪəudiːn] n iode m

iota [aɪ'əutə] n (fig) brin m, grain m

IOU n abbr (= I owe you) reconnaissance f de dette

IQ n abbr (= intelligence quotient) Q.I. m

IRA n abbr (= Irish Republican Army) IRA m

Iran [ɪ'rɑːn] n Iran m

Iraq [ɪ'rɑːk] n Irak m

irate [aɪ'reɪt] adj courroucé(e)

Ireland ['aɪələnd] n Irlande f

iris ['aɪrɪs] (pl **~es**) n iris m

Irish ['aɪrɪʃ] adj irlandais(e) ♦ npl: **the ~** les Irlandais; **~man** (irreg) n Irlandais m; **~ Sea** n mer f d'Irlande; **~woman** (irreg) n Irlandaise f

iron ['aɪən] n fer m; (for clothes) fer m à repasser ♦ cpd de or en fer; (fig) de fer ♦ vt (clothes) repasser; **~ out** vt (fig) aplanir; faire disparaître

ironic(al) [aɪ'rɔnɪk(l)] adj ironique

ironing ['aɪənɪŋ] n repassage m; **~ board** n planche f à repasser

ironmonger's (shop) ['aɪənmʌŋgəz-] n quincaillerie f

irony ['aɪrənɪ] n ironie f

irrational [ɪ'ræʃənl] adj irrationnel(le)

irregular [ɪ'rɛgjuləʳ] adj irrégulier(-ère); (surface) inégal(e)

irrelevant [ɪ'rɛləvənt] adj sans rapport, hors de propos

irresistible [ɪrɪ'zɪstɪbl] adj irrésistible

irrespective [ɪrɪ'spɛktɪv]: **~ of** prep sans tenir compte de

irresponsible [ɪrɪ'spɔnsɪbl] adj (act) irréfléchi(e); (person) irresponsable, inconscient(e)

irrigate ['ɪrɪgeɪt] vt irriguer; **irrigation** [ɪrɪ'geɪʃən] n irrigation f

irritate ['ɪrɪteɪt] vt irriter

irritating adj irritant(e); **irritation** [ɪrɪ'teɪʃən] n irritation f

IRS n abbr = **Internal Revenue Service**

is [ɪz] vb see **be**

Islam ['ɪzlɑːm] n Islam m; **~ic** adj islamique; **~ic fundamentalists** intégristes mpl musulmans

island ['aɪlənd] n île f; **~er** n habitant(e) d'une île, insulaire m/f

isle [aɪl] n île f

isn't ['ɪznt] = **is not**

isolate ['aɪsəleɪt] vt isoler; **~d** adj isolé(e); **isolation** n isolation f

Israel ['ɪzreɪl] n Israël m; **~i** [ɪz'reɪlɪ] adj israélien(ne) ♦ n Israélien(ne)

issue ['ɪʃuː] n question f, problème m; (of book) publication f, parution f; (of banknotes etc) émission f; (of newspaper etc) numéro m ♦ vt (rations, equipment) distribuer; (statement) publier, faire; (banknotes etc) émettre, mettre en circulation; **at ~** en jeu, en cause; **to take ~ with sb (over)** exprimer son désaccord avec qn (sur); **to make an ~ of sth** faire une montagne de qch

---
KEYWORD
---

it [ɪt] pron **1** (specific: subject) il (elle); (: direct object) le (la) (l'); (: indirect object) lui; **it's**

on the table c'est or il (or elle) est sur la table; **about/from/of it** en; **I spoke to him about it** je lui en ai parlé; **what did you learn from it?** qu'est-ce que vous en avez retiré?; **I'm proud of it** j'en suis fier; **in/to it** y; **put the book in it** mettez-y le livre; **he agreed to it** il y a consenti; **did you go to it?** (party, concert etc) est-ce que vous y êtes allé(s)?
2 (impersonal) il; ce; **it's raining** il pleut; **it's Friday tomorrow** demain c'est vendredi or nous sommes vendredi; **it's 6 o'clock** il est 6 heures; **who is it? - it's me** qui est-ce? - c'est moi

Italian [ɪ'tæljən] adj italien(ne) ♦ n Italien(ne); (LING) italien m
italics [ɪ'tælɪks] npl italiques fpl
Italy ['ɪtəlɪ] n Italie f
itch [ɪtʃ] n démangeaison f ♦ vi (person) éprouver des démangeaisons; (part of body) démanger; **I'm ~ing to do** l'envie me démange de faire; **~y** adj qui démange; **to be ~y** avoir des démangeaisons
it'd ['ɪtd] = **it would; it had**
item ['aɪtəm] n article m; (on agenda) question f, point m; (also: news ~) nouvelle f; **~ize** vt détailler, faire une liste de
itinerary [aɪ'tɪnərərɪ] n itinéraire m
it'll ['ɪtl] = **it will; it shall**
its [ɪts] adj son (sa), ses pl
it's [ɪts] = **it is; it has**
itself [ɪt'sɛlf] pron (reflexive) se; (emphatic) lui-même (elle-même)
ITV n abbr (BRIT: Independent Television) chaîne privée
IUD n abbr (= intra-uterine device) DIU m, stérilet m
I've [aɪv] = **I have**
ivory ['aɪvərɪ] n ivoire m
ivy ['aɪvɪ] n lierre m

J, j

jab [dʒæb] vt: **to ~ sth into** enfoncer or planter qch dans ♦ n (inf: injection) piqûre f
jack [dʒæk] n (AUT) cric m; (CARDS) valet m; **~ up** vt soulever (au cric)
jackal ['dʒækl] n chacal m
jacket ['dʒækɪt] n veste f, veston m; (of book) jaquette f, couverture f; **~ potato** n pomme f de terre en robe des champs
jack: ~knife vi: **the lorry ~knifed** la remorque (du camion) s'est mise en travers; **~ plug** n (ELEC) prise jack mâle f; **~pot** n gros lot
jaded ['dʒeɪdɪd] adj éreinté(e), fatigué(e)
jagged ['dʒægɪd] adj dentelé(e)
jail [dʒeɪl] n prison f ♦ vt emprisonner, mettre

en prison
jam [dʒæm] n confiture f; (also: traffic ~) embouteillage m ♦ vt (passage etc) encombrer, obstruer; (mechanism, drawer etc) bloquer, coincer; (RADIO) brouiller ♦ vi se coincer, se bloquer; (gun) s'enrayer; **to be in a ~** (inf) être dans le pétrin; **to ~ sth into** entasser qch dans; enfoncer qch dans
Jamaica [dʒə'meɪkə] n Jamaïque f
jam: ~ jar n pot m à confiture; **~med** adj (window etc) coincé(e); **~-packed** adj: **~-packed (with)** bourré(e) (de)
jangle ['dʒæŋgl] vi cliqueter
janitor ['dʒænɪtə'] n concierge m
January ['dʒænjuərɪ] n janvier m
Japan [dʒə'pæn] n Japon m; **~ese** [dʒæpə'niːz] adj japonais(e) ♦ n inv Japonais(e); (LING) japonais m
jar [dʒɑː'] n (stone, earthenware) pot m; (glass) bocal m ♦ vi (sound discordant) produire un son grinçant or discordant; (colours etc) jurer
jargon ['dʒɑːgən] n jargon m
jaundice ['dʒɔːndɪs] n jaunisse f
javelin ['dʒævlɪn] n javelot m
jaw [dʒɔː] n mâchoire f
jay [dʒeɪ] n geai m; **~walker** n piéton indiscipliné
jazz [dʒæz] n jazz m; **~ up** vt animer, égayer
jealous ['dʒɛləs] adj jaloux(-ouse); **~y** n jalousie f
jeans [dʒiːnz] npl jean m
jeer [dʒɪə'] vi: **to ~ (at)** se moquer cruellement (de), railler
Jehovah's Witness [dʒɪ'həuvəz-] n témoin m de Jéhovah
jelly ['dʒɛlɪ] n gelée f; **~fish** ['dʒɛlɪfɪʃ] n méduse f
jeopardy ['dʒɛpədɪ] n: **to be in ~** être en danger or péril
jerk [dʒɔːk] n secousse f; saccade f; sursaut m, spasme m; (inf: idiot) pauvre type m ♦ vt (pull) tirer brusquement ♦ vi (vehicles) cahoter
jersey ['dʒɔːzɪ] n (pullover) tricot m; (fabric) jersey m
Jesus ['dʒiːzəs] n Jésus
jet [dʒɛt] n (gas, liquid) jet m; (AVIAT) avion m à réaction, jet m; **~-black** adj (d'un noir) de jais; **~ engine** n moteur m à réaction; **~ lag** n (fatigue due au) décalage m horaire
jettison ['dʒɛtɪsn] vt jeter par-dessus bord
jetty ['dʒɛtɪ] n jetée f, digue f
Jew [dʒuː] n Juif m
jewel ['dʒuːəl] n bijou m, joyau m; (in watch) rubis m; **~ler** (US **jeweler**) n bijoutier(-ère), joaillier m; **~ler's (shop)** n bijouterie f, joaillerie f; **~lery** (US **jewelry**) n bijoux mpl
Jewess ['dʒuːɪs] n Juive f

Jewish ['dʒuːɪʃ] *adj* juif (juive)

jibe [dʒaɪb] *n* sarcasme *m*

jiffy ['dʒɪfɪ] (*inf*) *n*: **in a ~** en un clin d'œil

jigsaw ['dʒɪgsɔː] *n* (*also*: ~ **puzzle**) puzzle *m*

jilt [dʒɪlt] *vt* laisser tomber, plaquer

jingle ['dʒɪŋgl] *n* (*for advert*) couplet *m* publicitaire ♦ *vi* cliqueter, tinter

jinx [dʒɪŋks] (*inf*) *n* (mauvais) sort

jitters ['dʒɪtəz] (*inf*) *npl*: **to get the ~** (*inf*) avoir la trouille or la frousse

job [dʒɒb] *n* (*chore, task*) travail *m*, tâche *f*; (*employment*) emploi *m*, poste *m*, place *f*; **it's a good ~ that** ... c'est heureux *or* c'est une chance que ...; **just the ~!** (c'est) juste *or* exactement ce qu'il faut!; **~ centre** (*BRIT*) *n* agence *f* pour l'emploi; **~less** *adj* sans travail, au chômage

jockey ['dʒɒkɪ] *n* jockey *m* ♦ *vi*: **to ~ for position** manœuvrer pour être bien placé

jog [dʒɒg] *vt* secouer ♦ *vi* (*SPORT*) faire du jogging; **to ~ sb's memory** rafraîchir la mémoire de qn; **~ along** *vi* cheminer, trotter; **~ging** *n* jogging *m*

join [dʒɔɪn] *vt* (*put together*) unir, assembler; (*become member of: club*) s'inscrire à; (*meet*) rejoindre, retrouver; (*queue*) se joindre à ♦ *vi* (*roads, rivers*) se rejoindre, se rencontrer ♦ *n* raccord *m*; **~ in** *vi* se mettre de la partie, participer ♦ *vt fus* participer à, se mêler à; **~ up** *vi* (*meet*) se rejoindre; (*MIL*) s'engager

joiner ['dʒɔɪnə*] (*BRIT*) *n* menuisier *m*

joint [dʒɔɪnt] *n* (*TECH*) jointure *f*; joint *m*; (*ANAT*) articulation *f*, jointure; (*BRIT: CULIN*) rôti *m*; (*inf: place*) boîte *f*; (: *of cannabis*) joint *m* ♦ *adj* commun(e); **~ account** *n* (*with bank etc*) compte joint

joke [dʒəʊk] *n* plaisanterie *f*; (*also*: **practical ~**) farce *f* ♦ *vi* plaisanter; **to play a ~ on** jouer un tour à, faire une farce à; **~r** *n* (*CARDS*) joker *m*

jolly ['dʒɒlɪ] *adj* gai(e), enjoué(e); (*enjoyable*) amusant(e), plaisant(e) ♦ *adv* (*BRIT: inf*) rudement, drôlement

jolt [dʒəʊlt] *n* cahot *m*, secousse *f*; (*shock*) choc *m* ♦ *vt* cahoter, secouer

Jordan ['dʒɔːdən] *n* (*country*) Jordanie *f*

jostle ['dʒɒsl] *vt* bousculer, pousser

jot [dʒɒt] *n*: **not one ~** pas un brin; **~ down** *vt* noter; **~ter** (*BRIT*) *n* cahier *m* (de brouillon); (*pad*) bloc-notes *m*

journal ['dʒɜːnl] *n* journal *m*; **~ism** *n* journalisme *m*; **~ist** *n* journaliste *m/f*

journey ['dʒɜːnɪ] *n* voyage *m*; (*distance covered*) trajet *m*

joy [dʒɔɪ] *n* joie *f*; **~ful** *adj* joyeux(-euse); **~rider** *n* personne qui fait une virée dans une voiture volée; **~stick** *n* (*AVIAT, COMPUT*) manche *m* à balai

JP *n abbr* = **Justice of the Peace**

Jr *abbr* = **junior**

jubilant ['dʒuːbɪlnt] *adj* triomphant(e); réjoui(e)

judge [dʒʌdʒ] *n* juge *m* ♦ *vt* juger; **judg(e)ment** *n* jugement *m*

judicial [dʒuː'dɪʃl] *adj* judiciaire; **judiciary** *n* (pouvoir *m*) judiciaire *m*

judo ['dʒuːdəʊ] *n* judo *m*

jug [dʒʌg] *n* pot *m*, cruche *f*

juggernaut ['dʒʌgənɔːt] *n* (*BRIT*) *n* (*huge truck*) énorme poids lourd

juggle ['dʒʌgl] *vi* jongler; **~r** *n* jongleur *m*

juice [dʒuːs] *n* jus *m*; **juicy** *adj* juteux(-euse)

jukebox ['dʒuːkbɒks] *n* juke-box *m*

July [dʒuː'laɪ] *n* juillet *m*

jumble ['dʒʌmbl] *n* fouillis *m* ♦ *vt* (*also*: ~ **up**) mélanger, brouiller; **~ sale** (*BRIT*) *n* vente *f* de charité

jumbo (jet) ['dʒʌmbəʊ-] *n* jumbo-jet *m*, gros porteur

jump [dʒʌmp] *vi* sauter, bondir; (*start*) sursauter; (*increase*) monter en flèche ♦ *vt* sauter, franchir ♦ *n* saut *m*, bond *m*; sursaut *m*; **to ~ the queue** (*BRIT*) passer avant son tour

jumper ['dʒʌmpə*] *n* (*BRIT: pullover*) pull-over *m*; (*US: dress*) robe-chasuble *f*

jumper cables (*US*), **jump leads** (*BRIT*) *npl* câbles *mpl* de démarrage

jumpy ['dʒʌmpɪ] *adj* nerveux(-euse), agité(e)

Jun. *abbr* = **junior**

junction ['dʒʌŋkʃən] (*BRIT*) *n* (*of roads*) carrefour *m*; (*of rails*) embranchement *m*

juncture ['dʒʌŋktʃə*] *n*: **at this ~** à ce moment-là, sur ces entrefaites

June [dʒuːn] *n* juin *m*

jungle ['dʒʌŋgl] *n* jungle *f*

junior ['dʒuːnɪə*] *adj, n*: **he's ~ to me (by 2 years)**, **he's my ~ (by 2 years)** il est mon cadet (de 2 ans), il est plus jeune que moi (de 2 ans); **he's ~ to me** (*seniority*) il est en dessous de moi (dans la hiérarchie), j'ai plus d'ancienneté que lui; **~ school** *n* ≈ école *f* primaire

junk [dʒʌŋk] *n* (*rubbish*) camelote *f*; (*cheap goods*) bric-à-brac *m inv*; **~ food** *n* aliments *mpl* sans grande valeur nutritive; **~ mail** *n* prospectus *mpl* (non sollicités); **~ shop** *n* (boutique *f* de) brocanteur *m*

Junr *abbr* = **junior**

juror ['dʒʊərə*] *n* juré *m*

jury ['dʒʊərɪ] *n* jury *m*

just [dʒʌst] *adj* juste ♦ *adv*: **he's ~ done it/left** il vient de le faire/partir; **~ right/two o'clock** exactement or juste ce qu'il faut/deux heures; **she's ~ as clever as you** elle est tout aussi intelligente que vous; **it's ~ as well (that) ...** heureusement que ...; **~ as he was leaving** au moment or à l'instant précis où il partait; **~ before/enough/here** juste avant/assez/ici; **it's ~ me/a mistake** ce n'est que moi/(rien)

qu'une erreur; ~ **missed/caught** manqué/
attrapé de justesse; ~ **listen to this!** écoutez
un peu ça!
justice ['dʒʌstɪs] n justice f; (US: judge) juge
m de la Cour suprême; **J~ of the Peace** n
juge m de paix
justify ['dʒʌstɪfaɪ] vt justifier
jut [dʒʌt] vi (also: ~ **out**) dépasser, faire saillie
juvenile ['dʒuːvənaɪl] adj juvénile; (court,
books) pour enfants ♦ n adolescent(e)

K, k

K abbr (= one thousand) K; (= kilobyte) Ko
kangaroo [kæŋgə'ruː] n kangourou m
karate [kə'rɑːtɪ] n karaté m
kebab [kə'bæb] n kébab m
keel [kiːl] n quille f; **on an even ~** (fig) à flot
keen [kiːn] adj (eager) plein(e)
d'enthousiasme; (interest, desire, competition)
vif (vive); (eye, intelligence) pénétrant(e);
(edge) effilé(e); **to be ~ to do** or **on doing sth**
désirer vivement faire qch, tenir beaucoup à
faire qch; **to be ~ on sth/sb** aimer beaucoup
qch/qn
keep [kiːp] (pt, pp **kept**) vt (retain, preserve)
garder; (detain) retenir; (shop, accounts,
diary, promise) tenir; (house) avoir; (support)
entretenir; (chickens, bees etc) élever ♦ vi
(remain) rester; (food) se conserver ♦ n (of
castle) donjon m; (food etc): **enough for his ~**
assez pour (assurer) sa subsistance; (inf): **for
~s** pour de bon, pour toujours; **to ~ doing sth**
ne pas arrêter de faire qch; **to ~ sb from
doing** empêcher qn de faire or que qn ne
fasse; **to ~ sb happy/a place tidy** faire que qn
soit content/qu'un endroit reste propre; **to
~ sth to o.s.** garder qch pour soi, tenir qch
secret; **to ~ sth (back) from sb** cacher qch à
qn; **to ~ time** (clock) être à l'heure, ne pas
retarder; **well kept** bien entretenu(e); ~ **on**
vi: **to ~ on doing** continuer à faire; **don't ~ on
about it!** arrête (d'en parler)!; ~ **out** vt
empêcher d'entrer; **"~ out"** "défense
d'entrer"; ~ **up** vt continuer, maintenir ♦ vi:
to ~ up with sb (in race etc) aller aussi vite
que qn; (in work etc) se maintenir au niveau
de qn; ~**er** n gardien(ne); ~**fit** n
gymnastique f d'entretien; ~**ing** n (care)
garde f; **in ~ing with** en accord avec; ~**sake**
n souvenir m
kennel ['kɛnl] n niche f; ~**s** npl (boarding ~s)
chenil m
kerb [kəːb] (BRIT) n bordure f du trottoir
kernel ['kəːnl] n (of nut) amande f; (fig)
noyau m
kettle ['kɛtl] n bouilloire f; ~**drum** n timbale f
key [kiː] n (gen, MUS) clé f; (of piano,

typewriter) touche f ♦ cpd clé ♦ vt (also: ~ **in**)
introduire (au clavier), saisir; ~**board** n
clavier m; ~**ed up** adj (person) surexcité(e);
~**hole** n trou m de la serrure; ~**hole
surgery** n chirurgie très minutieuse où
l'incision est minimale; ~**note** n (of speech)
note dominante; (MUS) tonique f; ~ **ring** n
porte-clés m
khaki ['kɑːkɪ] n kaki m
kick [kɪk] vt donner un coup de pied à ♦ vi
(horse) ruer ♦ n coup m de pied; (thrill): **he
does it for ~s** il le fait parce que ça l'excite, il
le fait pour le plaisir; **to ~ the habit** (inf)
arrêter; ~ **off** vi (SPORT) donner le coup
d'envoi
kid [kɪd] n (inf: child) gamin(e), gosse m/f;
(animal, leather) chevreau m ♦ vi (inf)
plaisanter, blaguer
kidnap ['kɪdnæp] vt enlever, kidnapper; ~**per**
n ravisseur(-euse); ~**ping** n enlèvement m
kidney ['kɪdnɪ] n (ANAT) rein m; (CULIN)
rognon m
kill [kɪl] vt tuer ♦ n mise f à mort; ~**er** n
tueur(-euse); meurtrier(-ère); ~**ing** n meurtre
m; (of group of people) tuerie f, massacre m;
to make a ~ing (inf) réussir un beau coup (de
filet); ~**joy** n rabat-joie m/f
kiln [kɪln] n four m
kilo ['kiːləu] n kilo m; ~**byte** n (COMPUT) kilo-
octet m; ~**gram(me)** n kilogramme m;
~**metre** (US **kilometer**) n kilomètre m; ~**watt**
n kilowatt m
kilt [kɪlt] n kilt m
kin [kɪn] n see next
kind [kaɪnd] adj gentil(le), aimable ♦ n sorte f,
espèce f, genre m; **to be two of a ~** se
ressembler; **in ~** (COMM) en nature
kindergarten ['kɪndəgɑːtn] n jardin m
d'enfants
kind-hearted [kaɪnd'hɑːtɪd] adj bon
(bonne)
kindle ['kɪndl] vt allumer, enflammer
kindly ['kaɪndlɪ] adj bienveillant(e), plein(e)
de gentillesse ♦ adv avec bonté; **will you ~ ...!**
auriez-vous la bonté or l'obligeance de ...?
kindness ['kaɪndnɪs] n bonté f, gentillesse f
king [kɪŋ] n roi m; ~**dom** n royaume m;
~**fisher** n martin-pêcheur m; ~**-size bed** n
grand lit (de 1,95 m de large); ~**-size(d)** adj
format géant inv; (cigarettes) long (longue)
kiosk ['kiːɔsk] n kiosque m; (BRIT: TEL) cabine f
(téléphonique)
kipper ['kɪpər] n hareng fumé et salé
kiss [kɪs] n baiser m ♦ vt embrasser; **to ~ (each
other)** s'embrasser; ~ **of life** (BRIT) bouche
à bouche m
kit [kɪt] n équipement m, matériel m; (set of
tools etc) trousse f; (for assembly) kit m
kitchen ['kɪtʃɪn] n cuisine f; ~ **sink** n évier m

kite [kaɪt] n (toy) cerf-volant m
kitten ['kɪtn] n chaton m, petit chat
kitty ['kɪtɪ] n (money) cagnotte f
km abbr = kilometre
knack [næk] n: **to have the ~ of doing** avoir le coup pour faire
knapsack ['næpsæk] n musette f
knead [niːd] vt pétrir
knee [niː] n genou m; **~cap** n rotule f
kneel [niːl] (pt, pp knelt) vi (also: ~ down) s'agenouiller
knew [njuː] pt of know
knickers ['nɪkəz] (BRIT) npl culotte f (de femme)
knife [naɪf] (pl knives) n couteau m ♦ vt poignarder, frapper d'un coup de couteau
knight [naɪt] n chevalier m; (CHESS) cavalier m; **~hood** (BRIT) n (title): **to get a ~hood** être fait chevalier
knit [nɪt] vt tricoter ♦ vi tricoter; (broken bones) se ressouder; **to ~ one's brows** froncer les sourcils; **~ting** n tricot m; **~ting needle** n aiguille f à tricoter; **~wear** n tricots mpl, lainages mpl
knives [naɪvz] npl of knife
knob [nɔb] n bouton m
knock [nɔk] vt frapper; (bump into) heurter; (inf) dénigrer ♦ vi (at door etc): **to ~ at** or **on** frapper à ♦ n coup m; ~ **down** vt renverser; ~ **off** vi (inf: finish) s'arrêter (de travailler) ♦ vt (from price) faire un rabais de; (inf: steal) piquer; ~ **out** vt assommer; (BOXING) mettre k.-o.; (defeat) éliminer; ~ **over** vt renverser, faire tomber; **~er** n (on door) heurtoir m; **~out** n (BOXING) knock-out m, K.-O. m; **~out competition** compétition f avec épreuves éliminatoires
knot [nɔt] n (gen) nœud m ♦ vt nouer
know [nəu] (pt knew, pp known) vt savoir; (person, place) connaître; **to ~ how to do** savoir (comment) faire; **to ~ how to swim** savoir nager; **to ~ about** or **of sth** être au courant de qch; **to ~ about** or **of sb** avoir entendu parler de qn; **~-all** (pej) n je-sais-tout m/f; **~-how** n savoir-faire m; **~ing** adj (look etc) entendu(e); **~ingly** adv sciemment; (smile, look) d'un air entendu
knowledge ['nɔlɪdʒ] n connaissance f; (learning) connaissances, savoir m; **~able** adj bien informé(e)
knuckle ['nʌkl] n articulation f (des doigts), jointure f
Koran [kɔ'rɑːn] n Coran m
Korea [kə'rɪə] n Corée f
kosher ['kəuʃər] adj kascher inv

L, l

L abbr (= lake, large) L; (= left) g; (BRIT: AUT: learner) signale un conducteur débutant
lab [læb] n abbr (= laboratory) labo m
label ['leɪbl] n étiquette f ♦ vt étiqueter
labor etc ['leɪbər] (US) = **labour** etc
laboratory [lə'bɔrətərɪ] n laboratoire m
labour ['leɪbər] (US labor) n (work) travail m; (workforce) main-d'œuvre f ♦ vi: **to ~ (at)** travailler dur (à), peiner (sur) ♦ vt: **to ~ a point** insister sur un point; **in ~** (MED) en travail, en train d'accoucher; **L~, the L~ party** (BRIT) le parti travailliste, les travaillistes mpl; **~ed** ['leɪbəd] adj (breathing) pénible, difficile; **~er** n manœuvre m; **farm ~er** ouvrier m agricole
lace [leɪs] n dentelle f; (of shoe etc) lacet m ♦ vt (shoe: also: ~ up) lacer
lack [læk] n manque m ♦ vt manquer de; **through** or **for ~ of** faute de, par manque de; **to be ~ing** manquer, faire défaut; **to be ~ing in** manquer de
lacquer ['lækər] n laque f
lad [læd] n garçon m, gars m
ladder ['lædər] n échelle f; (BRIT: in tights) maille filée
laden ['leɪdn] adj: ~ **(with)** chargé(e) (de)
ladle ['leɪdl] n louche f
lady ['leɪdɪ] n dame f; (in address): **ladies and gentlemen** Mesdames (et) Messieurs; **young ~** jeune fille f; (married) jeune femme f; **the ladies' (room)** les toilettes fpl (pour dames); **~bird** (US **ladybug**) n coccinelle f; **~like** adj distingué(e); **~ship** n: **your ~ship** Madame la comtesse/la baronne etc
lag [læg] n retard m ♦ vi (also: ~ **behind**) rester en arrière, traîner; (fig) rester en traîne ♦ vt (pipes) calorifuger
lager ['lɑːgər] n bière blonde
lagoon [lə'guːn] n lagune f
laid [leɪd] pt, pp of lay; **~-back** (inf) adj relaxe, décontracté(e); **~ up** adj alité(e)
lain [leɪn] pp of lie
lake [leɪk] n lac m
lamb [læm] n agneau m; ~ **chop** n côtelette f d'agneau
lame [leɪm] adj boiteux(-euse)
lament [lə'mɛnt] n lamentation f ♦ vt pleurer, se lamenter sur
laminated ['læmɪneɪtɪd] adj laminé(e); (windscreen) (en verre) feuilleté
lamp [læmp] n lampe f; **~post** (BRIT) n réverbère m; **~shade** n abat-jour m inv
lance [lɑːns] vt (MED) inciser
land [lænd] n (as opposed to sea) terre f (ferme); (soil) terre; terrain m; (estate)

terre(s), domaine(s) m(pl); (country) pays m
♦ vi (AVIAT) atterrir; (fig) (re)tomber ♦ vt
(passengers, goods) débarquer; **to ~ sb with
sth** (inf) coller qch à qn; **~ up** vi atterrir,
(finir par) se retrouver; **~fill site** n décharge
f; **~ing** n (AVIAT) atterrissage m; (of staircase)
palier m; (of troops) débarquement m; **~ing
strip** n piste f d'atterrissage; **~lady** n
propriétaire f, logeuse f; (of pub) patronne f;
~locked adj sans littoral; **~lord** n
propriétaire m, logeur m; (of pub etc) patron
m; **~mark** n (point m de) repère m; **to be a
~mark** (fig) faire date or époque; **~owner** n
propriétaire foncier or terrien; **~scape** n
paysage m; **~scape gardener** n jardin-
ier(-ère) paysagiste; **~slide** n (GEO)
glissement m (de terrain); (fig: POL) raz-de-
marée (électoral)

lane [leɪn] n (in country) chemin m; (AUT) voie
f; file f; (in race) couloir m; **"get in ~"** (AUT)
"mettez-vous dans or sur la bonne file"

language ['læŋgwɪdʒ] n langue f; (way one
speaks) langage m; **bad ~** grossièretés fpl,
langage grossier; **~ laboratory** n laboratoire
m de langues

lank [læŋk] adj (hair) raide et terne

lanky ['læŋkɪ] adj grand(e) et maigre,
efflanqué(e)

lantern ['læntən] n lanterne f

lap [læp] n (of track) tour m (de piste); (of
body): **in** or **on one's ~** sur les genoux ♦ vt
(also: **~ up**) laper ♦ vi (waves) clapoter; **~ up**
vt (fig) accepter béatement, gober

lapel [lə'pɛl] n revers m

Lapland ['læplænd] n Laponie f

lapse [læps] n défaillance f; (in behaviour)
écart m de conduite ♦ vi (LAW) cesser d'être
en vigueur; (contract) expirer; **~ into bad
habits** prendre de mauvaises habitudes; **~ of
time** laps m de temps, intervalle m

laptop (computer) ['læptɒp(-)] n portable
m

larceny ['lɑːsənɪ] n vol m

larch [lɑːtʃ] n mélèze m

lard [lɑːd] n saindoux m

larder ['lɑːdər] n garde-manger m inv

large [lɑːdʒ] adj grand(e); (person, animal)
gros(se); **at ~** (free) en liberté; (generally) en
général; see also **by**; **~ly** adv en grande
partie; (principally) surtout; **~-scale** adj
(action) d'envergure; (map) à grande échelle

lark [lɑːk] n (bird) alouette f; (joke) blague f,
farce f

laryngitis [lærɪn'dʒaɪtɪs] n laryngite f

laser ['leɪzər] n laser m; **~ printer** n
imprimante f laser

lash [læʃ] n coup m de fouet; (also: **eyelash**)
cil m ♦ vt fouetter; (tie) attacher; **~ out** vi: to
~ out at or **against** attaquer violemment

lass [læs] (BRIT) n (jeune) fille f

lasso [læ'suː] n lasso m

last [lɑːst] adj dernier(-ère) ♦ adv en dernier;
(finally) finalement ♦ vi durer; **~ week** la
semaine dernière; **~ night** (evening) hier soir;
(night) la nuit dernière; **at ~** enfin; **~ but one**
avant-dernier(-ère); **~-ditch** adj (attempt)
ultime, désespéré(e); **~ing** adj durable; **~ly**
adv en dernier lieu, pour finir; **~-minute** adj
de dernière minute

latch [lætʃ] n loquet m

late [leɪt] adj (not on time) en retard; (far on
in day etc) tardif(-ive); (edition, delivery)
dernier(-ère); (former) ancien(ne) ♦ adv tard;
(behind time, schedule) en retard; **of ~**
dernièrement; **in ~ May** vers la fin (du mois)
de mai, fin mai; **the ~ Mr X** feu M. X;
~comer n retardataire m/f; **~ly** adv
récemment; **~r** adj (date etc) ultérieur(e);
(version etc) plus récent(e) ♦ adv plus tard; **~r
on** plus tard; **~st** adj tout(e) dernier(-ère); **at
the ~st** au plus tard

lathe [leɪð] n tour m

lather ['lɑːðər] n mousse f (de savon) ♦ vt
savonner

Latin ['lætɪn] n latin m ♦ adj latin(e);
~ America n Amérique latine; **~ American**
adj latino-américain(e)

latitude ['lætɪtjuːd] n latitude f

latter ['lætər] adj deuxième, dernier(-ère) ♦ n:
the ~ ce dernier, celui-ci; **~ly** adv
dernièrement, récemment

laudable ['lɔːdəbl] adj louable

laugh [lɑːf] n rire m ♦ vi rire; **~ at** vt fus se
moquer de; rire de; **~ off** vt écarter par une
plaisanterie or par une boutade; **~able** adj
risible, ridicule; **~ing stock** n: **the ~ing stock
of** la risée de; **~ter** n rire m; rires mpl

launch [lɔːntʃ] n lancement m; (motorboat)
vedette f ♦ vt lancer; **~ into** vt fus se lancer
dans

Launderette ® [lɔːn'drɛt] (BRIT),
Laundromat ® ['lɔːndrəmæt] (US) n laverie
f (automatique)

laundry ['lɔːndrɪ] n (clothes) linge m;
(business) blanchisserie f; (room) buanderie f

laurel ['lɔrl] n laurier m

lava ['lɑːvə] n lave f

lavatory ['lævətərɪ] n toilettes fpl

lavender ['lævəndər] n lavande f

lavish ['lævɪʃ] adj (amount) copieux(-euse);
(person): **~ with** prodigue de ♦ vt: **to ~ sth
on sb** prodiguer qch à qn; (money) dépenser
qch sans compter pour qn/qch

law [lɔː] n loi f; (science) droit m; **~-abiding**
adj respectueux(-euse) des lois; **~ and order**
n l'ordre public; **~ court** n tribunal m, cour f
de justice; **~ful** adj légal(e); **~less** adj
(action) illégal(e)

lawn [lɔ:n] n pelouse f; **~mower** n tondeuse f à gazon; **~ tennis** n tennis m
law school (US) n faculté f de droit
lawsuit ['lɔ:su:t] n procès m
lawyer ['lɔ:jər] n (consultant, with company) juriste m; (for sales, wills etc) notaire m; (partner, in court) avocat m
lax [læks] adj relâché(e)
laxative ['læksətɪv] n laxatif m
lay [leɪ] (pt, pp **laid**) pt of **lie** ♦ adj laïque; (not expert) profane ♦ vt poser, mettre; (eggs) pondre; **to ~ the table** mettre la table; **~ aside** vt mettre de côté; **~ by** vt = **lay aside**; **~ down** vt poser; **to ~ down the law** faire la loi; **to ~ down one's life** sacrifier sa vie; **~ off** vt (workers) licencier; **~ on** vt (provide) fournir; **~ out** vt (display) disposer, étaler; **~about** (inf) n fainéant(e); **~-by** (BRIT) n aire f de stationnement (sur le bas-côté)
layer ['leɪər] n couche f
layman ['leɪmən] (irreg) n profane m
layout ['leɪaut] n disposition f, plan m, agencement m; (PRESS) mise f en page
laze [leɪz] vi (also: **~ about**) paresser
lazy ['leɪzɪ] adj paresseux(-euse)
lb abbr = **pound** (weight)
lead¹ [li:d] (pt, pp **led**) n (distance, time ahead) avance f; (clue) piste f; (THEATRE) rôle principal; (ELEC) fil m; (for dog) laisse f ♦ vt mener, conduire; (be ~er of) être à la tête de ♦ vi (street etc) mener, conduire; (SPORT) mener, être en tête; **in the ~** en tête; **to ~ the way** montrer le chemin; **~ away** vt emmener; **~ back** vt: **to ~ back to** ramener à; **~ on** vt (tease) faire marcher; **~ to** vt fus mener à; conduire à; **~ up to** vt fus conduire à
lead² [led] n (metal) plomb m; (in pencil) mine f; **~ed petrol** n essence f au plomb; **~en** adj (sky, sea) de plomb
leader ['li:dər] n chef m; dirigeant(e), leader m; (SPORT: in league) leader; (: in race) coureur m de tête; **~ship** n direction f; (quality) qualités fpl de chef
lead-free ['ledfri:] adj (petrol) sans plomb
leading ['li:dɪŋ] adj principal(e); de premier plan; (in race) de tête; **~ lady** n (THEATRE) vedette (féminine); **~ light** n (person) vedette f, sommité f; **~ man** (irreg) n vedette (masculine)
lead singer [li:d-] n (in pop group) (chanteur m) vedette f
leaf [li:f] (pl **leaves**) n feuille f ♦ vi: **to ~ through** feuilleter; **to turn over a new ~** changer de conduite or d'existence
leaflet ['li:flɪt] n prospectus m, brochure f; (POL, REL) tract m
league [li:g] n ligue f; (FOOTBALL)

championnat m; **to be in ~ with** avoir partie liée avec, être de mèche avec
leak [li:k] n fuite f ♦ vi (pipe, liquid etc) fuir; (shoes) prendre l'eau; (ship) faire eau ♦ vt (information) divulguer
lean [li:n] (pt, pp **leaned** or **leant**) adj maigre ♦ vt: **to ~ sth on sth** appuyer qch sur qch ♦ vi (slope) pencher; (rest): **to ~ against** s'appuyer contre; être appuyé(e) contre; **to ~ on** s'appuyer sur; **to ~ back/forward** se pencher en arrière/avant; **~ out** vi se pencher au dehors; **~ over** vi se pencher; **~ing** n: **~ing (towards)** tendance f (à), penchant m (pour); **~t** [lent] pt, pp of **lean**
leap [li:p] (pt, pp **leaped** or **leapt**) n bond m, saut m ♦ vi bondir, sauter; **~frog** n saute-mouton m; **~t** [lept] pt, pp of **leap**; **~ year** n année f bissextile
learn [lə:n] (pt, pp **learned** or **learnt**) vt, vi apprendre; **to ~ to do sth** apprendre à faire qch; **to ~ about** or **of sth** (hear, read) apprendre qch; **~ed** ['lə:nɪd] adj érudit(e), savant(e); **~er** (BRIT) n (also: **~er driver**) (conducteur(-trice)) débutant(e); **~ing** n (knowledge) savoir m; **~t** pt, pp of **learn**
lease [li:s] n bail m ♦ vt louer à bail
leash [li:ʃ] n laisse f
least [li:st] adj: **the ~** (+noun) le (la) plus petit(e), le (la) moindre; (: smallest amount of) le moins de ♦ adv (+verb) le moins; (+adj): **the ~** le (la) moins; **at ~** au moins; (or rather) du moins; **not in the ~** pas le moins du monde
leather ['leðər] n cuir m
leave [li:v] (pt, pp **left**) vt laisser; (go away from) quitter; (forget) oublier ♦ vi partir, s'en aller ♦ n (time off) congé m; (MIL also: consent) permission f; **to be left** rester; **there's some milk left over** il reste du lait; **on ~** en permission; **~ behind** vt (person, object) laisser; (forget) oublier; **~ out** vt oublier, omettre; **~ of absence** n congé exceptionnel; (MIL) permission spéciale
leaves [li:vz] npl of **leaf**
Lebanon ['lebənən] n Liban m
lecherous ['letʃərəs] (pej) adj lubrique
lecture ['lektʃər] n conférence f; (SCOL) cours m ♦ vi donner des cours; enseigner ♦ vt (scold) sermonner, réprimander; **to give a ~ on** faire une conférence sur; donner un cours sur; **~r** (BRIT) n (at university) professeur m (d'université)
led [led] pt, pp of **lead¹**
ledge [ledʒ] n (of window, on wall) rebord m; (of mountain) saillie f, corniche f
ledger ['ledʒər] n (COMM) registre m, grand livre
leech [li:tʃ] n (also fig) sangsue f
leek [li:k] n poireau m

leer [lɪəʳ] vi: **to ~ at sb** regarder qn d'un air mauvais or concupiscent

leeway ['liːweɪ] n (fig): **to have some ~** avoir une certaine liberté d'action

left [left] pt, pp of **leave** ♦ adj (not right) gauche ♦ n gauche f ♦ adv à gauche; **on the ~, to the ~** à gauche; **the L~** (POL) la gauche; **~-handed** adj gaucher(-ère); **~-hand side** n gauche f; **~-luggage locker** n (casier m à) consigne f automatique; **~-luggage (office)** (BRIT) n consigne f; **~overs** npl restes mpl; **~-wing** adj (POL) de gauche

leg [leg] n jambe f; (of animal) patte f; (of furniture) pied m; (CULIN: of chicken, pork) cuisse f; (: of lamb) gigot m; (of journey) étape f; **1st/2nd ~** (SPORT) match m aller/retour

legacy ['legəsɪ] n héritage m, legs m

legal ['liːgl] adj légal(e); **~ holiday** (US) n jour férié; **~ tender** n monnaie légale

legend ['ledʒənd] n légende f

leggings ['legɪŋz] npl caleçon m

legible ['ledʒəbl] adj lisible

legislation [ledʒɪs'leɪʃən] n législation f; **legislature** ['ledʒɪslətʃəʳ] n (corps m) législatif m

legitimate [lɪ'dʒɪtɪmət] adj légitime

leg-room ['legruːm] n place f pour les jambes

leisure ['leʒəʳ] n loisir m, temps m libre; loisirs mpl; **at ~** (tout) à loisir; à tête reposée; **~ centre** n centre m de loisirs; **~ly** adj tranquille; fait(e) sans se presser

lemon ['lemən] n citron m; **~ade** [lemə'neɪd] n limonade f; **~ tea** n thé m au citron

lend [lend] (pt, pp **lent**) vt: **to ~ sth (to sb)** prêter qch (à qn)

length [leŋθ] n longueur f; (section: of road, pipe etc) morceau m, bout m; (of time) durée f; **at ~** (at last) enfin, à la fin; (~ily) longuement; **~en** vt allonger, prolonger ♦ vi s'allonger; **~ways** adv dans le sens de la longueur, en long; **~y** adj (très) long (longue)

lenient ['liːnɪənt] adj indulgent(e), clément(e)

lens [lenz] n lentille f; (of spectacles) verre m; (of camera) objectif m

Lent [lent] n carême m

lent [lent] pt, pp of **lend**

lentil ['lentɪl] n lentille f

Leo ['liːəʊ] n le Lion

leotard ['liːətɑːd] n maillot m (de danseur etc), collant m

leprosy ['leprəsɪ] n lèpre f

lesbian ['lezbɪən] n lesbienne f

less [les] adj, pron, adv moins ♦ prep moins; **~ than that/you** moins que cela/vous; **~ than half** moins de la moitié; **~ than ever** moins que jamais; **~ and ~** de moins en moins; **the ~ he works ...** moins il travaille ...; **~en** vi diminuer, s'atténuer ♦ vt diminuer, réduire, atténuer; **~er** adj moindre; **to a ~er extent** à un degré moindre

lesson ['lesn] n leçon f; **to teach sb a ~** (fig) donner une bonne leçon à qn

let [let] (pt, pp **let**) vt laisser; (BRIT: lease) louer; **to ~ sb do sth** laisser qn faire qch; **to ~ sb know sth** faire savoir qch à qn, prévenir qn de qch; **~'s go** allons-y; **~ him come** qu'il vienne; **"to ~"** "à louer"; **~ down** vt (tyre) dégonfler; (person) décevoir, faire faux bond à; **~ go** vi lâcher prise ♦ vt lâcher; **~ in** vt laisser entrer; (visitor etc) faire entrer; **~ off** vt (culprit) ne pas punir; (firework etc) faire partir; (on (inf) vt dire; **~ out** vt laisser sortir; (scream) laisser échapper; **~ up** vi diminuer; (cease) s'arrêter

lethal ['liːθl] adj mortel(le), fatal(e)

letter ['letəʳ] n lettre f; **~ bomb** n lettre piégée; **~box** (BRIT) n boîte f aux or à lettres; **~ing** n caractères fpl; caractères mpl

lettuce ['letɪs] n laitue f, salade f

let-up ['letʌp] n répit m, arrêt m

leukaemia [luː'kiːmɪə] (US **leukemia**) n leucémie f

level ['levl] adj plat(e), plan(e), uni(e); horizontal(e) ♦ n niveau m ♦ vt niveler, aplanir; **to be ~ with** être au même niveau que; **to draw ~ with** (person, vehicle) arriver à la hauteur de; **"A" ~s** (BRIT) ≈ baccalauréat m; **"O" ~s** (BRIT) ≈ B.E.P.C.; **on the ~** (fig: honest) régulier(-ère); **~ off** vi (prices etc) se stabiliser; **~ out** vi = level off; **~ crossing** (BRIT) n passage à niveau; **~-headed** adj équilibré(e)

lever ['liːvəʳ] n levier m; **~age** n: **~age (on or with)** prise f (sur)

levy ['levɪ] n taxe f, impôt m ♦ vt prélever, imposer; percevoir

lewd [luːd] adj obscène, lubrique

liability [laɪə'bɪlɪtɪ] n responsabilité f; (handicap) handicap m; **liabilities** npl (on balance sheet) passif m

liable ['laɪəbl] adj (subject): **~ to** sujet(te) à; passible de; (responsible): **~ (for)** responsable (de); (likely): **~ to do** susceptible de faire

liaise [liː'eɪz] vi: **to ~ (with)** assurer la liaison avec; **liaison** n liaison f

liar ['laɪəʳ] n menteur(-euse)

libel ['laɪbl] n diffamation f; (document) écrit m diffamatoire ♦ vt diffamer

liberal ['lɪbərl] adj libéral(e); (generous): **~ with** prodigue de, généreux(-euse) avec; **the L~ Democrats** (BRIT) le parti libéral-démocrate

liberation [lɪbə'reɪʃən] n libération f

liberty ['lɪbətɪ] n liberté f; **to be at ~** to do être libre de faire

Libra ['li:brə] n la Balance
librarian [laɪ'brɛərɪən] n bibliothécaire m/f
library ['laɪbrərɪ] n bibliothèque f
libretto [lɪ'brɛtəu] n livret m
Libya ['lɪbɪə] n Libye f
lice [laɪs] npl of **louse**
licence ['laɪsns] (US **license**) n autorisation f, permis m, (RADIO, TV) redevance f; **driving ~**, (US) **driver's license** permis m (de conduire); **~ number** n numéro m d'immatriculation; **~ plate** n plaque f minéralogique
license ['laɪsns] n (US) = **licence ♦** vt donner une licence à; **~d** adj (car) muni(e) de la vignette; (to sell alcohol) patenté(e) pour la vente des spiritueux, qui a une licence de débit de boissons
lick [lɪk] vt lécher; (inf: defeat) écraser; **to ~ one's lips** (fig) se frotter les mains
licorice ['lɪkərɪs] (US) n = **liquorice**
lid [lɪd] n couvercle m; (eyelid) paupière f
lie [laɪ] (pt **lay**, pp **lain**) vi (rest) être étendu(e) or allongé(e) or couché(e); (in grave) être enterré(e), reposer; (be situated) se trouver, être; (be untruthful: pt, pp ~d) mentir ♦ n mensonge m; **to ~ low** (fig) se cacher; **~ about** vi traîner; **~ around** vi = **lie about**; **~down** (BRIT) n: **to have a ~down** s'allonger, se reposer; **~in** (BRIT) n: **to have a ~in** faire la grasse matinée
lieutenant [lef'tɛnənt, (US) lu:'tɛnənt] n lieutenant m
life [laɪf] (pl **lives**) n vie f; **to come to ~** (fig) s'animer; **~ assurance** (BRIT) n = **life insurance**; **~belt** (BRIT) n bouée f de sauvetage; **~boat** n canot m or chaloupe f de sauvetage; **~buoy** n bouée f de sauvetage; **~guard** n surveillant m de baignade; **~ insurance** n assurance-vie f; **~ jacket** n gilet m or ceinture f de sauvetage; **~less** adj sans vie, inanimé(e); (dull) qui manque de vie ou de vigueur; **~like** adj qui semble vrai(e) or vivant(e); (painting) réaliste; **~long** adj de toute une vie, de toujours; **~ preserver** (US) n = **lifebelt**; **life jacket**; **~-saving** n sauvetage m; **~ sentence** n condamnation f à perpétuité; **~-size(d)** adj grandeur nature inv; **~ span** n (durée f de) vie f; **~style** n style m or mode m de vie; **~-support system** n (MED) respirateur artificiel; **~time** n vie f; **in his ~time** de son vivant
lift [lɪft] vt soulever, lever; (end) supprimer, lever ♦ vi se lever ♦ n (BRIT: elevator) ascenseur m; **to give sb a ~** (BRIT: AUT) emmener or prendre qn en voiture; **~-off** n décollage m
light [laɪt] (pt, pp **lit**) n lumière f; (lamp) lampe f; (AUT: rear ~) feu m; (: headlight) phare m; (for cigarette etc): **have you got a ~?**

avez-vous du feu? ♦ vt (candle, cigarette, fire) allumer; (room) éclairer ♦ adj (room, colour) clair(e); (not heavy) léger(-ère); (not strenuous) peu fatigant(e); **~s** npl (AUT: traffic ~s) feux mpl; **to come to ~** être dévoilé(e) or découvert(e); **~ up** vi (face) s'éclairer ♦ vt (illuminate) éclairer, illuminer; **~ bulb** n ampoule f; **~en** vt (make less heavy) alléger; **~er** n (also: cigarette **~er**) briquet m; **~-headed** adj étourdi(e); (excited) grisé(e); **~-hearted** adj gai(e), joyeux(-euse), enjoué(e); **~house** n phare m; **~ing** n (on road) éclairage m; (in theatre) éclairages; **~ly** adv légèrement; **to get off ~ly** s'en tirer à bon compte; **~ness** n (in weight) légèreté f
lightning ['laɪtnɪŋ] n éclair m, foudre f; **~ conductor** (US **lightning rod**) n paratonnerre m
light pen n crayon m optique
lightweight ['laɪtweɪt] adj (suit) léger(-ère) ♦ n (BOXING) poids léger
like [laɪk] vt aimer (bien) ♦ prep comme ♦ adj semblable, pareil(le) ♦ n: **and the ~** et d'autres du même genre; **his ~s and dislikes** ses goûts mpl or préférences fpl; **I would ~**, **I'd ~** je voudrais, j'aimerais; **would you ~ a coffee?** voulez-vous du café?; **to be/look ~ sb/sth** ressembler à qn/qch; **what does it look ~?** de quoi est-ce que ça a l'air?; **what does it taste ~?** quel goût est-ce que ça a?; **that's just ~ him** c'est bien de lui, ça lui ressemble; **do it ~ this** fais-le comme ceci; **it's nothing ~ ...** ce n'est pas du tout comme ...; **~able** adj sympathique, agréable
likelihood ['laɪklɪhud] n probabilité f
likely ['laɪklɪ] adj probable; plausible; **he's ~ to leave** il va sûrement partir, il risque fort de partir; **not ~!** (inf) pas de danger!
likeness ['laɪknɪs] n ressemblance f; **that's a good ~** c'est très ressemblant
likewise ['laɪkwaɪz] adv de même, pareillement
liking ['laɪkɪŋ] n (for person) affection f; (for thing) penchant m, goût m
lilac ['laɪlək] n lilas m
lily ['lɪlɪ] n lis m; **~ of the valley** n muguet m
limb [lɪm] n membre m
limber up ['lɪmbə-] vi se dégourdir, faire des exercices d'assouplissement
limbo ['lɪmbəu] n: **to be in ~** (fig) être tombé(e) dans l'oubli
lime [laɪm] n (tree) tilleul m; (fruit) lime f, citron vert; (GEO) chaux f
limelight ['laɪmlaɪt] n: **in the ~** (fig) en vedette, au premier plan
limerick ['lɪmərɪk] n poème m humoristique (de 5 vers)
limestone ['laɪmstəun] n pierre f à chaux; (GEO) calcaire m

limit ['lɪmɪt] n limite f ♦ vt limiter; **~ed** adj limité(e), restreint(e); **to be ~ed to** se limiter à, ne concerner que; **~ed (liability) company** (BRIT) n ≈ société f anonyme

limousine ['lɪməzi:n] n limousine f

limp [lɪmp] n: **to have a ~** boiter ♦ vi boiter ♦ adj mou (molle)

limpet ['lɪmpɪt] n patelle f

line [laɪn] n ligne f; (stroke) trait m; (wrinkle) ride f; (rope) corde f; (wire) fil m; (of poem) vers m; (row, series) rangée f; (of people) file f, queue f; (railway track) voie f; (COMM: series of goods) article(s) m(pl); (work) métier m, type m d'activité; (attitude, policy) position f ♦ vt (subj: trees, crowd) border; **in a ~** aligné(e); **in his ~ of business** dans sa partie, dans son rayon; **in ~ with** en accord avec; **to ~ (with)** (clothes) doubler (de); (box) garnir or tapisser (de); **~ up** vi s'aligner, se mettre en rang(s) ♦ vt aligner; (event) prévoir, préparer; **~d** adj (face) ridé(e), marqué(e); (paper) réglé(e)

linen ['lɪnɪn] n linge m (de maison); (cloth) lin m

liner ['laɪnər] n paquebot m (de ligne); (for bin) sac m à poubelle

linesman ['laɪnzmən] (irreg) n juge m de touche; (TENNIS) juge m de ligne

line-up ['laɪnʌp] n (US: queue) file f; (SPORT) (composition f de l')équipe f

linger ['lɪŋgər] vi s'attarder; traîner; (smell, tradition) persister

linguist ['lɪŋgwɪst] n: **to be a good ~** être doué(e) par les langues; **~ics** [lɪŋ'gwɪstɪks] n linguistique f

lining ['laɪnɪŋ] n doublure f

link [lɪŋk] n lien m, rapport m; (of a chain) maillon m ♦ vt relier, lier, unir; **~s** npl (GOLF) (terrain m de) golf m; **~ up** vt relier ♦ vi se rejoindre; s'associer

lino ['laɪnəu] n = **linoleum**

linoleum [lɪ'nəulɪəm] n linoléum m

lion ['laɪən] n lion m; **~ess** n lionne f

lip [lɪp] n lèvre f

liposuction ['lɪpəusʌkʃən] n liposuccion f

lip: ~-read vi lire sur les lèvres; **~ salve** n pommade f rosat or pour les lèvres; **~ service** n: **to pay ~ service to sth** ne reconnaître le mérite de qch que pour la forme; **~stick** n rouge m à lèvres

liqueur [lɪ'kjuər] n liqueur f

liquid ['lɪkwɪd] adj liquide ♦ n liquide m; **~ize** vt (CULIN) passer au mixer; **~izer** n mixer m

liquor ['lɪkər] (US) n spiritueux m, alcool m

liquorice ['lɪkərɪs] (BRIT) n réglisse f

liquor store (US) n magasin m de vins et spiritueux

lisp [lɪsp] vi zézayer

list [lɪst] n liste f ♦ vt (write down) faire une or

la liste de; (mention) énumérer; **~ed building** (BRIT) n monument classé

listen ['lɪsn] vi écouter; **to ~** écouter; **~er** n auditeur(-trice)

listless ['lɪstlɪs] adj indolent(e), apathique

lit [lɪt] pt, pp of **light**

liter ['li:tər] (US) n = **litre**

literacy ['lɪtərəsɪ] n degré m d'alphabétisation, fait m de savoir lire et écrire

literal ['lɪtərəl] adj littéral(e); **~ly** adv littéralement; (really) réellement

literary ['lɪtərərɪ] adj littéraire

literate ['lɪtərət] adj qui sait lire et écrire, instruit(e)

literature ['lɪtrɪtʃər] n littérature f; (brochures etc) documentation f

lithe [laɪð] adj agile, souple

litigation [lɪtɪ'geɪʃən] n litige m; contentieux m

litre ['li:tər] (US **liter**) n litre m

litter ['lɪtər] n (rubbish) détritus mpl, ordures fpl; (young animals) portée f; **~ bin** (BRIT) n boîte f à ordures, poubelle f; **~ed** adj: **~ed with** jonché(e) de, couvert(e) de

little ['lɪtl] adj (small) petit(e) ♦ adv peu; **~ milk/time** peu de lait/temps; **a ~** un peu (de); **a ~ bit** un peu; **~ by ~** petit à petit, peu à peu

live[1] [laɪv] adj (animal) vivant(e), en vie; (wire) sous tension; (bullet, bomb) non explosé(e); (broadcast) en direct; (performance) en public

live[2] [lɪv] vi vivre; (reside) habiter; **~ down** vt faire oublier (avec le temps); **~ on** vt fus (food, salary) vivre de; **~ together** vi vivre ensemble, cohabiter; **~ up to** vt fus se montrer à la hauteur de

livelihood ['laɪvlɪhud] n moyens mpl d'existence

lively ['laɪvlɪ] adj vif (vive), plein(e) d'entrain; (place, book) vivant(e)

liven up ['laɪvn-] vt animer ♦ vi s'animer

liver ['lɪvər] n foie m

lives [laɪvz] npl of **life**

livestock ['laɪvstɔk] n bétail m, cheptel m

livid ['lɪvɪd] adj livide, blafard(e); (inf: furious) furieux(-euse), furibond(e)

living ['lɪvɪŋ] adj vivant(e), en vie ♦ n: **to earn** or **make a ~** gagner sa vie; **~ conditions** npl conditions fpl de vie; **~ room** n salle f de séjour; **~ standards** npl niveau m de vie; **~ wage** n salaire m permettant de vivre (décemment)

lizard ['lɪzəd] n lézard m

load [ləud] n (weight) poids m; (thing carried) chargement m, charge f ♦ vt (also: ~ **up**): **to ~ (with)** charger (de); (gun, camera) charger (avec); (COMPUT) charger; **a ~ of, ~s of** (fig) un or des tas de, des masses de; **to talk a ~ of**

rubbish dire des bêtises; **~ed** adj (question) insidieux(-euse); (inf: rich) bourré(e) de fric

loaf [ləʊf] (pl **loaves**) n pain m, miche f

loan [ləʊn] n prêt m ♦ vt prêter; **on ~** prêté(e), en prêt

loath [ləʊθ] adj: **to be ~ to do** répugner à faire

loathe [ləʊð] vt détester, avoir en horreur

loaves [ləʊvz] npl of **loaf**

lobby ['lɒbɪ] n hall m, entrée f; (POL) groupe m de pression, lobby m ♦ vt faire pression sur

lobster ['lɒbstə^r] n homard m

local ['ləʊkl] adj local(e) ♦ n (BRIT: pub) pub m or café m du coin; **the ~s** npl (inhabitants) les gens mpl du pays ou du coin; **~ anaesthetic** n anesthésie locale; **~ authority** n collectivité locale, municipalité f; **~ call** n communication urbaine; **~ government** n administration locale or municipale; **~ity** [ləʊ'kælɪtɪ] n région f, environs mpl; (position) lieu m

locate [ləʊ'keɪt] vt (find) trouver, repérer; (situate): **to be ~d in** être situé(e) à or en; **location** n emplacement m; **on location** (CINEMA) en extérieur

loch [lɒx] n lac m, loch m

lock [lɒk] n (of door, box) serrure f; (of canal) écluse f; (of hair) mèche f, boucle f ♦ vt (with key) fermer à clé ♦ vi (door etc) fermer à clé; (wheels) se bloquer; **~ in** vt enfermer; **~ out** vt enfermer dehors; (deliberately) mettre à la porte; **~ up** vt (person) enfermer; (house) fermer à clé ♦ vi tout fermer (à clé)

locker ['lɒkə^r] n casier m; (in station) consigne f automatique

locket ['lɒkɪt] n médaillon m

locksmith ['lɒksmɪθ] n serrurier m

lockup ['lɒkʌp] n (prison) prison f

locum ['ləʊkəm] n (MED) suppléant(e) (de médecin)

lodge [lɒdʒ] n pavillon m (de gardien); (hunting ~) pavillon de chasse ♦ vi (person): **to ~ (with)** être logé(e) (chez), être en pension (chez); (bullet) se loger ♦ vt: **to ~ a complaint** porter plainte; **~r** n locataire m/f; (with meals) pensionnaire m/f; **lodgings** npl chambre f; meublé m

loft [lɒft] n grenier m

lofty ['lɒftɪ] adj (noble) noble, élevé(e); (haughty) hautain(e)

log [lɒg] n (of wood) bûche f; (book) = **logbook** ♦ vt (record) noter; **~book** n (NAUT) livre m or journal m de bord; (AVIAT) carnet m de vol; (of car) ≈ carte grise

loggerheads ['lɒgəhedz] npl: **at ~ (with)** à couteaux tirés (avec)

logic ['lɒdʒɪk] n logique f; **~al** adj logique

loin [lɔɪn] n (CULIN) filet m, longe f

loiter ['lɔɪtə^r] vi traîner

loll [lɒl] vi (also: **~ about**) se prélasser, fainéanter

lollipop ['lɒlɪpɒp] n sucette f; **~ man/lady** (BRIT: irreg) n contractuel qui fait traverser la rue aux enfants

lolly ['lɒlɪ] (inf) n (lollipop) sucette f; (money) fric m

London ['lʌndən] n Londres m; **~er** n Londonien(ne)

lone [ləʊn] adj solitaire

loneliness ['ləʊnlɪnɪs] n solitude f, isolement m

lonely ['ləʊnlɪ] adj seul(e); solitaire, isolé(e)

long [lɒŋ] adj long (longue) ♦ adv longtemps ♦ vi: **to ~ for sth** avoir très envie de qch; attendre qch avec impatience; **so** or **as ~ as** pourvu que; **don't be ~!** dépêchez-vous!; **how ~ is this river/course?** quelle est la longueur de ce fleuve/la durée de ce cours?; **6 metres ~** (long) de 6 mètres; **6 months ~** qui dure 6 mois, de 6 mois; **all night ~** toute la nuit; **he no ~er comes** il ne vient plus; **they're no ~er going out together** ils ne sortent plus ensemble; **I can't stand it any ~er** je ne peux plus le supporter; **~ before/after** longtemps avant/après; **before ~** (+future) avant peu, dans peu de temps; (+past) peu de temps après; **at ~ last** enfin; **~-distance** adj (call) interurbain(e); **~er** ['lɒŋgə^r] adv see **long**; **~hand** n écriture normale or courante; **~ing** n désir m, envie f, nostalgie f

longitude ['lɒŋgɪtjuːd] n longitude f

long: ~ jump n saut m en longueur; **~-life** adj (batteries etc) longue durée inv; (milk) longue conservation; **~-lost** adj (person) perdu(e) de vue depuis longtemps; **~-range** adj à longue portée; **~-sighted** adj (MED) presbyte; **~-standing** adj de longue date; **~-suffering** adj empreint(e) d'une patience résignée; extrêmement patient(e); **~-term** adj à long terme; **~ wave** n grandes ondes; **~-winded** adj intarissable, interminable

loo [luː] (BRIT: inf) n W.-C. mpl, petit coin

look [lʊk] vi regarder; (seem) sembler, paraître, avoir l'air; (building etc): **to ~ south/(out) over the sea** donner au sud/sur la mer ♦ n regard m; (appearance) air m, allure f, aspect m; **~s** npl (good ~s) physique m, beauté f; **to have a ~** regarder; **~!** regarde!; **~ (here)!** (annoyance) écoutez!; **~ after** vt fus (care for, deal with) s'occuper de; **~ at** vt fus regarder; (problem etc) examiner; **~ back** vi: **to ~ back on** (event etc) évoquer, repenser à; **~ down on** vt fus (fig) regarder de haut, dédaigner; **~ for** vt fus chercher; **~ forward to** vt fus attendre avec impatience; **we ~ forward to hearing from you** (in letter) dans l'attente de vous lire; **~ into** vt fus examiner, étudier; **~ on** vi regarder (en spectateur); **~ out** vi (beware): **to ~ out (for)** prendre

garde (à), faire attention (à); **~ out for** vt
fus être à la recherche de; guetter; **~ round**
vi regarder derrière soi, se retourner; **~ to** vt
fus (rely on) compter sur; **~ up** vi lever les
yeux; (improve) s'améliorer ♦ vt (word, name)
chercher; **~ up to** vt fus avoir du respect
pour ♦ n poste m de guet; (person) guetteur
m; **to be on the ~ out (for)** guetter

loom [luːm] vi (also: **~ up**) surgir; (approach:
event etc) être imminent(e); (threaten)
menacer ♦ n (for weaving) métier m à tisser

loony ['luːnɪ] (inf) adj, n timbré(e), cinglé(e)

loop [luːp] n boucle f; **~hole** n (fig) porte f
de sortie; échappatoire f

loose [luːs] adj (knot, screw) desserré(e);
(clothes) ample, lâche; (hair) dénoué(e),
épars(e); (not firmly fixed) pas solide;
(morals, discipline) relâché(e) ♦ n: **on the ~** en
liberté; **~ change** n petite monnaie; **~ chippings** npl (on road) gravillons mpl; **~ end** n:
to be a ~ end or (US) **at ~ ends** ne pas trop
savoir quoi faire; **~ly** adv sans serrer; (impre-
cisely) approximativement; **~n** vt desserrer

loot [luːt] n (inf: money) pognon m, fric m
♦ vt piller

lopsided ['lɒp'saɪdɪd] adj de travers,
asymétrique

lord [lɔːd] n seigneur m; **L~ Smith** lord Smith;
the L~ le Seigneur; **good L~!** mon Dieu!; **the
(House of) L~s** (BRIT) la Chambre des lords;
my L~ = your Lordship; **L~ship** n: **your
L~ship** Monsieur le comte/le baron/le juge;
(to bishop) Monseigneur

lore [lɔːʳ] n tradition(s) f(pl)

lorry ['lɒrɪ] (BRIT) n camion m; **~ driver** (BRIT)
n camionneur m, routier m

lose [luːz] (pt, pp lost) vt, vi perdre; **to
~ (time)** (clock) retarder; **to get lost** ♦ vi se
perdre; **~r** n perdant(e)

loss [lɒs] n perte f; **to be at a ~** être perplexe
or embarrassé(e)

lost [lɒst] pt, pp of **lose** ♦ adj perdu(e); **~ and
found** (US), **~ property** n objets trouvés

lot [lɒt] n (set) lot m; **the ~** le tout; **a ~ (of)**
beaucoup (de); **~s of** des tas de; **to draw ~s
(for sth)** tirer (qch) au sort

lotion ['ləʊʃən] n lotion f

lottery ['lɒtərɪ] n loterie f

loud [laʊd] adj bruyant(e), sonore; (voice)
fort(e); (support, condemnation) vigou-
reux(-euse); (gaudy) voyant(e), tapa-
geur(-euse) ♦ adv (speak etc) fort; **out ~** tout
haut; **~-hailer** (BRIT) n porte-voix m inv; **~ly**
adv fort, bruyamment; **~speaker** n haut-
parleur m

lounge [laʊndʒ] n salon m; (at airport) salle f;
(BRIT: also: **~ bar**) (salle de) café m or bar m
♦ vi (also: **~ about** or **around**) se prélasser,
paresser; **~ suit** (BRIT) n complet m; (on

invitation) "tenue de ville"

louse [laʊs] (pl lice) n pou m

lousy ['laʊzɪ] (inf) adj infect(e), moche; **I feel
~** je suis mal fichu(e)

lout [laʊt] n rustre m, butor m

lovable ['lʌvəbl] adj adorable; très
sympathique

love [lʌv] n amour m ♦ vt aimer; (caringly,
kindly) aimer beaucoup; **"~ (from) Anne"**
"affectueusement, Anne"; **I ~ chocolate**
j'adore le chocolat; **to be/fall in ~ with** être/
tomber amoureux(-euse) de; **to make ~** faire
l'amour; **"15 ~"** (TENNIS) "15 à rien or zéro";
~ affair n liaison (amoureuse); **~ life** n vie
sentimentale

lovely ['lʌvlɪ] adj (très) joli(e), ravissant(e);
(delightful: person) charmant(e); (holiday etc)
(très) agréable

lover ['lʌvəʳ] n amant m; (person in love)
amoureux(-euse); (amateur): **a ~ of** un
amateur de; un(e) amoureux(-euse) de

loving ['lʌvɪŋ] adj affectueux(-euse), tendre

low [ləʊ] adj bas (basse); (quality)
mauvais(e), inférieur(e); (person: depressed)
déprimé(e); (: ill) bas (basse), affaibli(e)
♦ adv bas ♦ n (METEOROLOGY) dépression f; **to
be ~ on** être à court de; **to feel ~** se sentir
déprimé(e); **to reach an all-time ~** être au
plus bas; **~-alcohol** adj peu alcoolisé(e); **~-
calorie** adj hypocalorique; **~-cut** adj (dress)
décolleté(e); **~er** adj inférieur(e) ♦ vt
abaisser, baisser; **~er sixth** (BRIT) n (SCOL)
première f; **~-fat** adj maigre; **~lands** npl
(GEO) plaines fpl; **~ly** adj humble, modeste

loyal ['lɔɪəl] adj loyal(e), fidèle; **~ty** n loyauté
f, fidélité f; **~ty card** n carte f de fidélité

lozenge ['lɒzɪndʒ] n (MED) pastille f

LP n abbr = long-playing record

L-plates ['elpleɪts] (BRIT) npl plaques fpl
d'apprenti conducteur

Ltd abbr (= limited) ≈ S.A.

lubricant ['luːbrɪkənt] n lubrifiant m

lubricate ['luːbrɪkeɪt] vt lubrifier, graisser

luck [lʌk] n chance f; **bad ~** malchance f,
malheur m; **bad** or **hard** or **tough ~!** pas de
chance!; **good ~!** bonne chance!; **~ily** adv
heureusement, par bonheur; **~y** adj (person)
qui a de la chance; (coincidence, event)
heureux(-euse); (object) porte-bonheur inv

ludicrous ['luːdɪkrəs] adj ridicule, absurde

lug [lʌg] (inf) vt traîner, tirer

luggage ['lʌgɪdʒ] n bagages mpl; **~ rack** n
(on car) galerie f

lukewarm ['luːkwɔːm] adj tiède

lull [lʌl] n accalmie f; (in conversation) pause f
♦ vt: **to ~ sb to sleep** bercer qn pour qu'il
s'endorme; **to be ~ed into a false sense of
security** s'endormir dans une fausse sécurité

lullaby ['lʌləbaɪ] n berceuse f

lumbago [lʌm'beɪgəu] n lumbago m

lumber ['lʌmbəʳ] n (wood) bois m de charpente; (junk) bric-à-brac m inv; **~jack** n bûcheron m

luminous ['luːmɪnəs] adj lumineux(-euse)

lump [lʌmp] n morceau m; (swelling) grosseur f ♦ vt: **to ~ together** réunir, mettre en tas; **~ sum** n somme globale or forfaitaire; **~y** adj (sauce) avec des grumeaux; (bed) défoncé(e), peu confortable

lunar ['luːnəʳ] adj lunaire

lunatic ['luːnətɪk] adj fou (folle), cinglé(e) (inf)

lunch [lʌntʃ] n déjeuner m

luncheon ['lʌntʃən] n déjeuner m (chic); **~ meat** n sorte de mortadelle; **~ voucher** (BRIT) n chèque-repas m

lung [lʌŋ] n poumon m

lunge [lʌndʒ] vi (also: **~ forward**) faire un mouvement brusque en avant; **to ~ at** envoyer or assener un coup à

lurch [ləːtʃ] vi vaciller, tituber ♦ n écart m brusque; **to leave sb in the ~** laisser qn se débrouiller or se dépêtrer tout(e) seul(e)

lure [luəʳ] n (attraction) attrait m, charme m ♦ vt attirer or persuader par la ruse

lurid ['luərɪd] adj affreux(-euse), atroce; (pej: colour, dress) criard(e)

lurk [ləːk] vi se tapir, se cacher

luscious ['lʌʃəs] adj succulent(e); appétissant(e)

lush [lʌʃ] adj luxuriant(e)

lust [lʌst] n (sexual) désir m; (fig): **~ for** soif f de; **~y** adj vigoureux(-euse), robuste

Luxembourg ['lʌksəmbəːg] n Luxembourg m

luxurious [lʌg'zjuərɪəs] adj luxueux(-euse)

luxury ['lʌkʃərɪ] n luxe m ♦ cpd de luxe

lying ['laɪɪŋ] n mensonge(s) m(pl) ♦ vb see **lie**

lyrical ['lɪrɪkl] adj lyrique

lyrics ['lɪrɪks] npl (of song) paroles fpl

M, m

m. abbr = metre; mile; million

M.A. abbr = Master of Arts

mac [mæk] (BRIT) n imper(méable) m

macaroni [mækə'rəunɪ] n macaroni mpl

machine [mə'ʃiːn] n machine f ♦ vt (TECH) façonner à la machine; (dress etc) coudre à la machine; **~ gun** n mitrailleuse f; **~ language** n (COMPUT) langage-machine m; **~ry** n machinerie f, machines fpl; (fig) mécanisme(s) m(pl)

mackerel ['mækrl] n inv maquereau m

mackintosh ['mækɪntɔʃ] (BRIT) n imperméable m

mad [mæd] adj fou (folle); (foolish)

insensé(e); (angry) furieux(-euse); (keen): **to be ~ about** être fou (folle) de

madam ['mædəm] n madame f

madden ['mædn] vt exaspérer

made [meɪd] pt, pp of **make**

Madeira [mə'dɪərə] n (GEO) Madère f; (wine) madère m

made-to-measure ['meɪdtə'meʒəʳ] (BRIT) adj fait(e) sur mesure

madly ['mædlɪ] adv follement; **~ in love** éperdument amoureux(-euse)

madman ['mædmən] (irreg) n fou m

madness ['mædnɪs] n folie f

magazine [mægə'ziːn] n (PRESS) magazine m, revue f; (RADIO, TV: also: **~ programme**) magazine

maggot ['mægət] n ver m, asticot m

magic ['mædʒɪk] n magie f ♦ adj magique; **~al** adj magique; (experience, evening) merveilleux(-euse); **~ian** [mə'dʒɪʃən] n magicien(ne); (conjurer) prestidigitateur m

magistrate ['mædʒɪstreɪt] n magistrat m; juge m

magnet ['mægnɪt] n aimant m; **~ic** [mæg'netɪk] adj magnétique

magnificent [mæg'nɪfɪsnt] adj superbe, magnifique; (splendid: robe, building) somptueux(-euse), magnifique

magnify ['mægnɪfaɪ] vt grossir; (sound) amplifier; **~ing glass** n loupe f

magnitude ['mægnɪtjuːd] n ampleur f

magpie ['mægpaɪ] n pie f

mahogany [mə'hɔgənɪ] n acajou m

maid [meɪd] n bonne f; **old ~** (pej) vieille fille

maiden ['meɪdn] n jeune fille f ♦ adj (aunt etc) non mariée; (speech, voyage) inaugural(e); **~ name** n nom m de jeune fille

mail [meɪl] n poste f; (letters) courrier m ♦ vt envoyer (par la poste); **~box** (US) n boîte f aux lettres; **~ing list** n liste f d'adresses; **~-order** n vente f or achat m par correspondance

maim [meɪm] vt mutiler

main [meɪn] adj principal(e) ♦ n: **the ~(s)** ♦ n(pl) (gas, water) conduite principale, canalisation f; **the ~s** npl (ELEC) le secteur; **the ~ thing** l'essentiel; **in the ~** dans l'ensemble; **~frame** n (COMPUT) (gros) ordinateur, unité centrale; **~land** n continent m; **~ly** adv principalement, surtout; **~ road** n grand-route f; **~stay** n (fig) pilier m; **~stream** n courant principal

maintain [meɪn'teɪn] vt entretenir; (continue) maintenir; (affirm) soutenir; **maintenance** ['meɪntənəns] n entretien m; (alimony) pension f alimentaire

maize [meɪz] n maïs m

majestic [mə'dʒestɪk] adj majestueux(-euse)

majesty ['mædʒɪstɪ] n majesté f

major ['meɪdʒəʳ] n (MIL) commandant m
♦ adj (important) important(e); (most
important) principal(e); (MUS) majeur(e)
Majorca [məˈjɔːkə] n Majorque f
majority [məˈdʒɒrɪtɪ] n majorité f
make [meɪk] (pt, pp **made**) vt faire;
(manufacture) faire, fabriquer; (earn) gagner;
(cause to be): **to ~ sb sad** etc rendre qn triste
etc; (force): **to ~ sb do sth** obliger qn à faire
qch, faire faire qch à qn; (equal): **2 and 2 ~ 4**
2 et 2 font 4 ♦ n fabrication f; (brand)
marque f; **to ~ a fool of sb** (ridicule) ridiculiser
qn; (trick) avoir ou duper qn; **to ~ a profit**
faire un ou des bénéfice(s); **to ~ a loss** essuyer
une perte; **to ~ it** (arrive) arriver; (achieve sth)
parvenir à qch, réussir; **what time do you ~ it?**
quelle heure avez-vous?; **to ~ do with** se
contenter de; se débrouiller avec; **~ for** vt fus
(place) se diriger vers; **~ out** vt (write out:
cheque) faire; (decipher) déchiffrer;
(understand) comprendre; (see) distinguer;
~ up vt (constitute) constituer; (invent)
inventer, imaginer; (parcel, bed) faire ♦ vi se
réconcilier; (with cosmetics) se maquiller;
~ up for vt fus compenser; **~-believe** n: **it's
just ~-believe** (game) c'est pour faire
semblant; (invention) c'est de l'invention
pure; **~r** n fabricant m; **~shift** adj provisoire,
improvisé(e); **~-up** n maquillage m
making ['meɪkɪŋ] n (fig): **in the ~** en
formation or gestation; **to have the ~s of**
(actor, athlete etc) avoir l'étoffe de
malaria [məˈleərɪə] n malaria f
Malaysia [məˈleɪzɪə] n Malaisie f
male [meɪl] n (BIO) mâle m ♦ adj mâle; (sex,
attitude) masculin(e); (child etc) du sexe
masculin
malevolent [məˈlevələnt] adj malveillant(e)
malfunction [mælˈfʌŋkʃən] n
fonctionnement défectueux
malice ['mælɪs] n méchanceté f, malveillance
f; **malicious** [məˈlɪʃəs] adj méchant(e),
malveillant(e)
malignant [məˈlɪgnənt] adj (MED) ma-
lin(-igne)
mall [mɔːl] n (also: **shopping ~**) centre
commercial
mallet ['mælɪt] n maillet m
malpractice [mælˈpræktɪs] n faute
professionnelle; négligence f
malt [mɔːlt] n malt m ♦ cpd (also: **~ whisky**)
pur malt
Malta ['mɔːltə] n Malte f
mammal ['mæml] n mammifère m
mammoth ['mæməθ] n mammouth m ♦ adj
géant(e), monstre
man [mæn] (pl **men**) n homme m ♦ vt (NAUT:
ship) garnir d'hommes; (MIL: gun) servir;
(: post) être de service à; (machine) assurer le

fonctionnement de; **an old ~** un vieillard;
~ and wife mari et femme
manage ['mænɪdʒ] vi se débrouiller ♦ vt (be
in charge of) s'occuper de; (: business etc)
gérer; (control: ship) manier, manœuvrer;
(: person) savoir s'y prendre avec; **to ~ to do**
réussir à faire; **~able** adj (task) faisable;
(number) raisonnable; **~ment** n gestion f,
administration f, direction f; **~r** n directeur m;
administrateur m; (SPORT) manager m; (of
artist) impresario m; **~ress** [mænɪdʒəˈres] n
directrice f; gérante f; **~rial** [mænɪˈdʒɪərɪəl]
adj directorial(e); (skills) de cadre, de
gestion; **managing director** n directeur
général
mandarin ['mændərɪn] n (also: **~ orange**)
mandarine f; (person) mandarin m
mandatory ['mændətərɪ] adj obligatoire
mane [meɪn] n crinière f
maneuver [məˈnuːvəʳ] (US) vt, vi, n
= **manoeuvre**
manfully ['mænfəlɪ] adv vaillamment
mangle ['mæŋgl] vt déchiqueter; mutiler
mango ['mæŋgəu] (pl **~es**) n mangue f
mangy ['meɪndʒɪ] adj galeux(-euse)
man: ~handle vt malmener; **~hole** n trou m
d'homme; **~hood** n âge m d'homme; virilité
f; **~-hour** n heure f de main-d'œuvre; **~hunt**
n (POLICE) chasse f à l'homme
mania ['meɪnɪə] n manie f; **~c** ['meɪnɪæk] n
maniaque m/f; (fig) fou (folle) m/f; **manic**
['mænɪk] adj maniaque
manicure ['mænɪkjuəʳ] n manucure f
manifest ['mænɪfest] vt manifester ♦ adj
manifeste, évident(e); **~o** [mænɪˈfestəu] n
manifeste m
manipulate [məˈnɪpjuleɪt] vt manipuler;
(system, situation) exploiter
man: ~kind [mænˈkaɪnd] n humanité f, genre
humain; **~ly** adj viril(e); **~-made** adj
artificiel(le); (fibre) synthétique
manner ['mænəʳ] n manière f, façon f;
(behaviour) attitude f, comportement m;
(sort): **all ~ of** toutes sortes de; **~s** npl
(behaviour) manières; **~ism** n particularité f
de langage (or de comportement), tic m
manoeuvre [məˈnuːvəʳ] (US **maneuver**) vt
(move) manœuvrer; (manipulate: person)
manipuler; (: situation) exploiter ♦ vi
manœuvrer ♦ n manœuvre f
manor ['mænəʳ] n (also: **~ house**) manoir m
manpower ['mænpauəʳ] n main-d'œuvre f
mansion ['mænʃən] n château m, manoir m
manslaughter ['mænslɔːtəʳ] n homicide m
involontaire
mantelpiece ['mæntlpiːs] n cheminée f
manual ['mænjuəl] adj manuel(le) ♦ n
manuel m
manufacture [mænjuˈfæktʃəʳ] vt fabriquer

♦ *n* fabrication *f*; **~r** *n* fabricant *m*
manure [mə'njuər] *n* fumier *m*
manuscript ['mænjuskrɪpt] *n* manuscrit *m*
many ['mɛnɪ] *adj* beaucoup de, de
nombreux(-euses) ♦ *pron* beaucoup, un
grand nombre; **a great ~** un grand nombre
(de); **~ a ... bien des ...**, plus d'un(e) ...
map [mæp] *n* carte *f*; (*of town*) plan *m*; **~ out**
vt tracer; (*task*) planifier
maple ['meɪpl] *n* érable *m*
mar [mɑːr] *vt* gâcher, gâter
marathon ['mærəθən] *n* marathon *m*
marble ['mɑːbl] *n* marbre *m*; (*toy*) bille *f*
March [mɑːtʃ] *n* mars *m*
march [mɑːtʃ] *vi* marcher au pas; (*fig:
protesters*) défiler ♦ *n* marche *f*;
(*demonstration*) manifestation *f*
mare [mɛər] *n* jument *f*
margarine [mɑːdʒə'riːn] *n* margarine *f*
margin ['mɑːdʒɪn] *n* marge *f*; **~al (seat)** *n*
(*POL*) siège disputé
marigold ['mærɪɡəʊld] *n* souci *m*
marijuana [mærɪ'wɑːnə] *n* marijuana *f*
marina [mə'riːnə] *n* (*harbour*) marina *f*
marine [mə'riːn] *adj* marin(e) ♦ *n* fusilier
marin; (*US*) marine *m*
marital ['mærɪtl] *adj* matrimonial(e); **~ status**
situation *f* de famille
marjoram ['mɑːdʒərəm] *n* marjolaine *f*
mark [mɑːk] *n* marque *f*; (*of skid etc*) trace *f*;
(*BRIT: SCOL*) note *f*; (*currency*) mark *m* ♦ *vt*
marquer; (*stain*) tacher; (*BRIT: SCOL*) noter;
corriger; **to ~ time** marquer le pas; **~er** *n*
(*sign*) jalon *m*; (*bookmark*) signet *m*
market ['mɑːkɪt] *n* marché *m* ♦ *vt* (*COMM*)
commercialiser; **~ garden** (*BRIT*) *n* jardin
maraîcher; **~ing** *n* marketing *m*; **~place** *n*
place *f* du marché; (*COMM*) marché *m*;
~ research *n* étude *f* de marché
marksman ['mɑːksmən] (*irreg*) *n* tireur *m*
d'élite
marmalade ['mɑːməleɪd] *n* confiture *f*
d'oranges
maroon [mə'ruːn] *vt*: **to be ~ed** être
abandonné(e); (*fig*) être bloqué(e) ♦ *adj*
bordeaux *inv*
marquee [mɑː'kiː] *n* chapiteau *m*
marriage ['mærɪdʒ] *n* mariage *m*;
~ certificate *n* extrait *m* d'acte de mariage
married ['mærɪd] *adj* marié(e); (*life, love*)
conjugal(e)
marrow ['mærəʊ] *n* moelle *f*; (*vegetable*)
courge *f*
marry ['mærɪ] *vt* épouser, se marier avec;
(*subj: father, priest etc*) marier ♦ *vi* (*also*: **get
married**) se marier
Mars [mɑːz] *n* (*planet*) Mars *f*
marsh [mɑːʃ] *n* marais *m*, marécage *m*
marshal ['mɑːʃl] *n* maréchal *m*; (*US: fire,*

police) ≈ capitaine *m*; (*SPORT*) membre *m* du
service d'ordre ♦ *vt* rassembler
marshy ['mɑːʃɪ] *adj* marécageux(-euse)
martyr ['mɑːtər] *n* martyr(e); **~dom** *n*
martyre *m*
marvel ['mɑːvl] *n* merveille *f* ♦ *vi*: **to ~ (at)**
s'émerveiller (de); **~lous** (*US* **marvelous**) *adj*
merveilleux(-euse)
Marxist ['mɑːksɪst] *adj* marxiste ♦ *n* marxiste
m/f
marzipan ['mɑːzɪpæn] *n* pâte *f* d'amandes
mascara [mæs'kɑːrə] *n* mascara *m*
masculine ['mæskjulɪn] *adj* masculin(e)
mash [mæʃ] *vt* écraser, réduire en purée; **~ed
potatoes** *npl* purée *f* de pommes de terre
mask [mɑːsk] *n* masque *m* ♦ *vt* masquer
mason ['meɪsn] *n* (*also*: **stonemason**) maçon
m; (*also*: **freemason**) franc-maçon *m*; **~ry** *n*
maçonnerie *f*
masquerade [mæskə'reɪd] *vi*: **to ~ as** se faire
passer pour
mass [mæs] *n* multitude *f*, masse *f*; (*PHYSICS*)
masse; (*REL*) messe *f* ♦ *cpd* (*communication*)
de masse; (*unemployment*) massif(-ive) ♦ *vi*
se masser; **the ~es** les masses; **~es of** des tas
de
massacre ['mæsəkər] *n* massacre *m*
massage ['mæsɑːʒ] *n* massage *m* ♦ *vt* masser
massive ['mæsɪv] *adj* énorme, massif(-ive)
mass media *n inv* mass-media *mpl*
mass production *n* fabrication *f* en série
mast [mɑːst] *n* mât *m*; (*RADIO*) pylône *m*
master ['mɑːstər] *n* maître *m*; (*in secondary
school*) professeur *m*; (*title for boys*): **M~ X**
Monsieur X ♦ *vt* maîtriser; (*learn*) apprendre
à fond; **~ly** *adj* magistral(e); **~mind** *n* esprit
supérieur ♦ *vt* diriger, être le cerveau de;
M~ of Arts/Science ≈ maîtrise *f* en
lettres/sciences); **~piece** *n* chef-d'œuvre *m*;
~plan *n* stratégie *f* d'ensemble; **~y** *n* maîtrise
f; connaissance parfaite
mat [mæt] *n* petit tapis; (*also*: **doormat**)
paillasson *m*; (*also*: **tablemat**) napperon *m*
♦ *adj* = **matt**
match [mætʃ] *n* allumette *f*; (*game*) match *m*,
partie *f*; (*fig*) égal(e) ♦ *vt* (*also*: **~ up**)
assortir; (*go well with*) aller bien avec,
s'assortir à; (*equal*) égaler, valoir ♦ *vi* être
assorti(e); **to be a good ~** être bien assorti(e);
~box *n* boîte *f* d'allumettes; **~ing** *adj*
assorti(e)
mate [meɪt] *n* (*inf*) copain (copine); (*animal*)
partenaire *m/f*, mâle/femelle; (*in merchant
navy*) second *m* ♦ *vi* s'accoupler
material [mə'tɪərɪəl] *n* (*substance*) matière *f*,
matériau *m*; (*cloth*) tissu *m*, étoffe *f*;
(*information, data*) données *fpl* ♦ *adj*
matériel(le); (*relevant: evidence*) pertinent(e);
~s *npl* (*equipment*) matériaux *mpl*

maternal [mə'tə:nl] *adj* maternel(le)

maternity [mə'tə:nɪtɪ] *n* maternité *f*;
~ **dress** *n* robe *f* de grossesse; ~ **hospital** *n*
maternité *f*

mathematical [mæθə'mætɪkl] *adj*
mathématique

mathematics [mæθə'mætɪks] *n*
mathématiques *fpl*

maths [mæθs] (*US* **math**) *n* math(s) *fpl*

matinée ['mætɪneɪ] *n* matinée *f*

mating call *n* appel *m* du mâle

matrices ['meɪtrɪsi:z] *npl of* **matrix**

matriculation [mətrɪkju'leɪʃən] *n* inscription
f

matrimonial [mætrɪ'məunɪəl] *adj*
matrimonial(e), conjugal(e)

matrimony ['mætrɪmənɪ] *n* mariage *m*

matrix ['meɪtrɪks] (*pl* **matrices**) *n* matrice *f*

matron ['meɪtrən] *n* (*in hospital*) infirmière-
chef *f*; (*in school*) infirmière

mat(t) [mæt] *adj* mat(e)

matted ['mætɪd] *adj* emmêlé(e)

matter ['mætə*] *n* question *f*; (*PHYSICS*)
matière *f*; (*content*) contenu *m*, fond *m*;
(*MED: pus*) pus *m* ♦ *vi* importer; ~**s** *npl*
(*affairs, situation*) la situation; **it doesn't** ~ cela
n'a pas d'importance; (*I don't mind*) cela ne
fait rien; **what's the** ~? qu'est-ce qu'il y a?,
qu'est-ce qui ne va pas?; **no** ~ **what** quoiqu'il
arrive; **as a** ~ **of course** tout naturellement; **as
a** ~ **of fact** en fait; ~~**of-fact** *adj* terre à terre;
(*voice*) neutre

mattress ['mætrɪs] *n* matelas *m*

mature [mə'tjuə*] *adj* mûr(e); (*cheese*)
fait(e); (*wine*) arrivé(e) à maturité ♦ *vi*
(*person*) mûrir; (*wine, cheese*) se faire

maul [mɔ:l] *vt* lacérer

mauve [məuv] *adj* mauve

maximum ['mæksɪməm] (*pl* **maxima**) *adj*
maximum ♦ *n* maximum *m*

May [meɪ] *n* mai *m*; ~ **Day** *n* le Premier Mai;
see also **mayday**

may [meɪ] (*conditional* **might**) *vi* (*indicating
possibility*): **he** ~ **come** il se peut qu'il vienne;
(*be allowed to*): ~ **I smoke?** puis-je fumer?;
(*wishes*): ~ **God bless you!** (que) Dieu vous
bénisse!; **you** ~ **as well go** à votre place, je
partirais

maybe ['meɪbi:] *adv* peut-être; ~ **he'll** ...
peut-être qu'il ...

mayday ['meɪdeɪ] *n* SOS *m*

mayhem ['meɪhem] *n* grabuge *m*

mayonnaise [meɪə'neɪz] *n* mayonnaise *f*

mayor [mɛə*] *n* maire *m*; ~**ess** *n* épouse *f* du
maire

maze [meɪz] *n* labyrinthe *m*, dédale *m*

M.D. *n abbr* (= *Doctor of Medicine*) titre
universitaire; = **managing director**

me [mi:] *pron* me, m' +*vowel*; (*stressed, after*

prep) moi; **he heard** ~ il m'a entendu(e); **give**
~ **a book** donnez-moi un livre; **after** ~ après
moi

meadow ['medəu] *n* prairie *f*, pré *m*

meagre ['mi:gə*] (*US* **meager**) *adj* maigre

meal [mi:l] *n* repas *m*; (*flour*) farine *f*; ~**time**
n l'heure *f* du repas

mean [mi:n] (*pt, pp* **meant**) *adj* (*with money*)
avare, radin(e); (*unkind*) méchant(e);
(*shabby*) misérable; (*average*) moyen(ne)
♦ *vt* signifier, vouloir dire; (*refer to*) faire
allusion à, parler de; (*intend*): **to** ~ **to do** avoir
l'intention de faire ♦ *n* moyenne *f*; ~**s** *npl*
(*way, money*) moyens *mpl*; **by** ~**s of** par
l'intermédiaire de; au moyen de; **by all** ~**s!** je
vous en prie!; **to be** ~ **for sb/sth** être
destiné(e) à qn/qch; **do you** ~ **it?** vous êtes
sérieux?; **what do you** ~? que voulez-vous
dire?

meander [mɪ'ændə*] *vi* faire des méandres

meaning ['mi:nɪŋ] *n* signification *f*, sens *m*;
~**ful** *adj* significatif(-ive); (*relationship,
occasion*) important(e); ~**less** *adj* dénué(e)
de sens

meanness ['mi:nnɪs] *n* (*with money*) avarice
f; (*unkindness*) méchanceté *f*; (*shabbiness*)
médiocrité *f*

meant [ment] *pt, pp of* **mean**

meantime ['mi:ntaɪm] *adv* (*also:* **in the** ~)
pendant ce temps

meanwhile ['mi:nwaɪl] *adv* = **meantime**

measles ['mi:zlz] *n* rougeole *f*

measure ['meʒə*] *vt, vi* mesurer ♦ *n* mesure
f; (*ruler*) règle (graduée); ~**ments** *npl*
mesures *fpl*; **chest/hip** ~**ment(s)** tour *m* de
poitrine/hanches

meat [mi:t] *n* viande *f*; ~**ball** *n* boulette *f* de
viande

Mecca ['mekə] *n* La Mecque

mechanic [mɪ'kænɪk] *n* mécanicien *m*; ~**al**
adj mécanique; ~**s** *n* (*PHYSICS*) mécanique *f*
♦ *npl* (*of reading, government*) mécanisme
m

mechanism ['mekənɪzəm] *n* mécanisme *m*

medal ['medl] *n* médaille *f*; ~**lion** [mɪ'dælɪən]
n médaillon *m*; ~**list** (*US* **medalist**) *n* (*SPORT*)
médaillé(e)

meddle ['medl] *vi*: **to** ~ **in** se mêler de,
s'occuper de; **to** ~ **with** toucher à

media ['mi:dɪə] *npl* media *mpl*

mediaeval [medɪ'i:vl] *adj* = **medieval**

median ['mi:dɪən] (*US*) *n* (*also:* ~ **strip**)
bande médiane

mediate ['mi:dɪeɪt] *vi* servir d'intermédiaire

Medicaid ® ['medɪkeɪd] (*US*) *n* assistance
médicale aux indigents

medical ['medɪkl] *adj* médical(e) ♦ *n* visite
médicale

Medicare ® ['medɪkɛə*] (*US*) *n* assistance

médicale aux personnes âgées

medication [mɛdɪ'keɪʃən] *n* (*drugs*) médicaments *mpl*

medicine ['mɛdsɪn] *n* médecine *f*; (*drug*) médicament *m*

medieval [mɛdɪ'iːvl] *adj* médiéval(e)

mediocre [miːdɪ'əukəʳ] *adj* médiocre

meditate ['mɛdɪteɪt] *vi* méditer

Mediterranean [mɛdɪtə'reɪnɪən] *adj* méditerranéen(ne); **the ~ (Sea)** la (mer) Méditerranée

medium ['miːdɪəm] (*pl* media) *adj* moyen(ne) ♦ *n* (*means*) moyen *m*; (*pl* ~s: *person*) médium *m*; **the happy ~** le juste milieu; **~-sized** *adj* de taille moyenne; **~ wave** *n* ondes moyennes

medley ['mɛdlɪ] *n* mélange *m*; (*MUS*) pot-pourri *m*

meek [miːk] *adj* doux (douce), humble

meet [miːt] (*pt, pp* met) *vt* rencontrer; (*by arrangement*) retrouver, rejoindre; (*for the first time*) faire la connaissance de; (*go and fetch*): **I'll ~ you at the station** j'irai te chercher à la gare; (*opponent, danger*) faire face à; (*obligations*) satisfaire à ♦ *vi* (*friends*) se rencontrer, se retrouver; (*in session*) se réunir; (*join: lines, roads*) se rejoindre; **~ with** *vt fus* rencontrer; **~ing** *n* rencontre *f*; (*session: of club etc*) réunion *f*; (*POL*) meeting *m*; **she's at a ~ing** (*COMM*) elle est en conférence

mega ['mɛgə] (*inf*) *adv*: **he's ~ rich** il est hyper-riche; **~byte** *n* (*COMPUT*) méga-octet *m*; **~phone** *n* porte-voix *m inv*

melancholy ['mɛlənkəlɪ] *n* mélancolie *f* ♦ *adj* mélancolique

mellow ['mɛləu] *adj* velouté(e); doux (douce); (*sound*) mélodieux(-euse) ♦ *vi* (*person*) s'adoucir

melody ['mɛlədɪ] *n* mélodie *f*

melon ['mɛlən] *n* melon *m*

melt [mɛlt] *vi* fondre ♦ *vt* faire fondre; (*metal*) fondre; **~ away** *vi* fondre complètement; **~ down** *vt* fondre; **~down** *n* fusion *f* (du cœur d'un réacteur nucléaire); **~ing pot** *n* (*fig*) creuset *m*

member ['mɛmbəʳ] *n* membre *m*; **M~ of Parliament** (*BRIT*) député *m*; **M~ of the European Parliament** Eurodéputé *m*; **~ship** *n* adhésion *f*; statut *m* de membre; (*members*) membres *mpl*, adhérents *mpl*; **~ship card** *n* carte *f* de membre

memento [mə'mɛntəu] *n* souvenir *m*

memo ['mɛməu] *n* note *f* (de service)

memoirs ['mɛmwɑːz] *npl* mémoires *mpl*

memorandum [mɛmə'rændəm] (*pl* **memoranda**) *n* note *f* (de service)

memorial [mɪ'mɔːrɪəl] *n* mémorial *m* ♦ *adj* commémoratif(-ive)

memorize ['mɛməraɪz] *vt* apprendre par

cœur; retenir

memory ['mɛmərɪ] *n* mémoire *f*; (*recollection*) souvenir *m*

men [mɛn] *npl* of **man**

menace ['mɛnɪs] *n* menace *f*; (*nuisance*) plaie *f* ♦ *vt* menacer; **menacing** *adj* menaçant(e)

mend [mɛnd] *vt* réparer; (*darn*) raccommoder, repriser ♦ *n*: **on the ~** en voie de guérison; **to ~ one's ways** s'amender; **~ing** *n* réparation *f*; (*clothes*) raccommodage *m*

menial ['miːnɪəl] *adj* subalterne

meningitis [mɛnɪn'dʒaɪtɪs] *n* méningite *f*

menopause ['mɛnəupɔːz] *n* ménopause *f*

menstruation [mɛnstru'eɪʃən] *n* menstruation *f*

mental ['mɛntl] *adj* mental(e); **~ity** [mɛn'tælɪtɪ] *n* mentalité *f*

mention ['mɛnʃən] *n* mention *f* ♦ *vt* mentionner, faire mention de; **don't ~ it!** je vous en prie, il n'y a pas de quoi!

menu ['mɛnjuː] *n* (*set* ~, *COMPUT*) menu *m*; (*list of dishes*) carte *f*

MEP *n abbr* = **Member of the European Parliament**

mercenary ['mɜːsɪnərɪ] *adj* intéressé(e), mercenaire ♦ *n* mercenaire *m*

merchandise ['mɜːtʃəndaɪz] *n* marchandises *fpl*

merchant ['mɜːtʃənt] *n* négociant *m*, marchand *m*; **~ bank** (*BRIT*) *n* banque *f* d'affaires; **~ navy** (*US* **merchant marine**) *n* marine marchande

merciful ['mɜːsɪful] *adj* miséricordieux(-euse), clément(e); **a ~ release** une délivrance

merciless ['mɜːsɪlɪs] *adj* impitoyable, sans pitié

mercury ['mɜːkjurɪ] *n* mercure *m*

mercy ['mɜːsɪ] *n* pitié *f*, indulgence *f*; (*REL*) miséricorde *f*; **at the ~ of** à la merci de

mere [mɪəʳ] *adj* simple; (*chance*) pur(e); **a ~ two hours** seulement deux heures; **~ly** *adv* simplement, purement

merge [mɜːdʒ] *vt* unir ♦ *vi* (*colours, shapes, sounds*) se mêler; (*roads*) se joindre; (*COMM*) fusionner; **~r** *n* (*COMM*) fusion *f*

meringue [mə'ræŋ] *n* meringue *f*

merit ['mɛrɪt] *n* mérite *m*, valeur *f*

mermaid ['mɜːmeɪd] *n* sirène *f*

merry ['mɛrɪ] *adj* gai(e); **M~ Christmas!** joyeux Noël!; **~-go-round** *n* manège *m*

mesh [mɛʃ] *n* maille *f*

mesmerize ['mɛzməraɪz] *vt* hypnotiser; fasciner

mess [mɛs] *n* désordre *m*, fouillis *m*, pagaille *f*; (*muddle: of situation*) gâchis *m*; (*dirt*) saleté *f*; (*MIL*) mess *m*, cantine *f*; **~ about** (*inf*) *vi* perdre son temps; **~ about with** (*inf*) *vt fus* tripoter; **~ around** (*inf*) *vi* = **mess about**;

~ around with vt fus = **mess about with**; **~ up** vt (dirty) salir; (spoil) gâcher

message ['mesɪdʒ] n message m; **messenger** ['mesɪndʒəʳ] n messager m

Messrs ['mesəz] abbr (on letters) MM

messy ['mesɪ] adj sale; en désordre

met [met] pt, pp of **meet**

metal ['metl] n métal m; **~lic** [mɪ'tælɪk] adj métallique

meteorology [miːtɪə'rɒlədʒɪ] n météorologie f

meter ['miːtəʳ] n (instrument) compteur m; (also: **parking ~**) parcomètre m; (US: unit) = **metre**

method ['meθəd] n méthode f; **~ical** [mɪ'θɒdɪkl] adj méthodique; **M~ist** n méthodiste m/f

meths [meθs] (BRIT) n = **methylated spirit**

methylated spirit ['meθɪleɪtɪd-] (BRIT) n alcool m à brûler

metre ['miːtəʳ] (US **meter**) n mètre m; **metric** ['metrɪk] adj métrique

metropolitan [metrə'pɒlɪtn] adj métropolitain(e); **the M~ Police** (BRIT) la police londonienne

mettle ['metl] n: **to be on one's ~** être d'attaque

mew [mjuː] vi (cat) miauler

mews [mjuːz] (BRIT) n: **~ cottage** cottage aménagé dans une ancienne écurie

Mexico ['meksɪkəʊ] n Mexique m

miaow [miː'aʊ] vi miauler

mice [maɪs] npl of **mouse**

micro ['maɪkrəʊ] n (also: **~computer**) micro-ordinateur m; **~chip** n puce f; **~phone** n microphone m; **~scope** n microscope m; **~wave** n (also: **~wave oven**) four m à micro-ondes

mid [mɪd] adj: **in ~ May** à la mi-mai; **~ afternoon** le milieu de l'après-midi; **in ~ air** en plein ciel; **~day** n midi m

middle ['mɪdl] n milieu m; (waist) taille f ♦ adj du milieu; (average) moyen(ne); **in the ~ of the night** au milieu de la nuit; **~-aged** adj d'un certain âge; **M~ Ages** npl: **the M~ Ages** le moyen âge; **~-class** adj ≈ bourgeois(e); **~ class(es)** n(pl): **the ~ class(es)** ≈ les classes moyennes; **M~ East** n Proche-Orient m, Moyen-Orient m; **~man** (irreg) n intermédiaire m; **~ name** n deuxième nom m; **~-of-the-road** adj (politician) modéré(e); (music) neutre; **~weight** n (BOXING) poids moyen; **middling** adj moyen(ne)

midge [mɪdʒ] n moucheron m

midget ['mɪdʒɪt] n nain(e)

Midlands ['mɪdləndz] npl comtés du centre de l'Angleterre

midnight ['mɪdnaɪt] n minuit m

midriff ['mɪdrɪf] n estomac m, taille f

midst [mɪdst] n: **in the ~ of** au milieu de

mid [mɪd-]: **~summer** [mɪd'sʌməʳ] n milieu m de l'été; **~way** [mɪd'weɪ] adj, adv: **~ (between)** à mi-chemin (entre); **~ through** ... au milieu de ..., en plein(e) ...; **~week** [mɪd'wiːk] adj au milieu de la semaine

midwife ['mɪdwaɪf] (pl **midwives**) n sage-femme f

might [maɪt] vb see **may** ♦ n puissance f, force f; **~y** adj puissant(e)

migraine ['miːgreɪn] n migraine f

migrant ['maɪgrənt] adj (bird) migrateur(-trice); (worker) saisonnier(-ère)

migrate [maɪ'greɪt] vi émigrer

mike [maɪk] n abbr (= microphone) micro m

mild [maɪld] adj doux (douce); (reproach, infection) léger(-ère); (illness) bénin(-igne); (interest) modéré(e); (taste) peu relevé(e) ♦ n (beer) bière légère; **~ly** adv doucement; légèrement; **to put it ~ly** c'est le moins qu'on puisse dire

mile [maɪl] n mi(l)le m (= 1609 m); **~age** n distance f en milles; ≈ kilométrage m; **~ometer** [maɪ'lɒmɪtəʳ] n compteur m (kilométrique); **~stone** n borne f; (fig) jalon m

militant ['mɪlɪtnt] adj militant(e)

military ['mɪlɪtərɪ] adj militaire

militia [mɪ'lɪʃə] n milice(s) f(pl)

milk [mɪlk] n lait m ♦ vt (cow) traire; (fig: person) dépouiller, plumer; (: situation) exploiter à fond; **~ chocolate** n chocolat m au lait; **~man** (irreg) n laitier m; **~ shake** n milk-shake m; **~y** adj (drink) au lait; (colour) laiteux(-euse); **M~y Way** n voie lactée

mill [mɪl] n moulin m; (steel ~) aciérie f; (spinning ~) filature f; (flour ~) minoterie f ♦ vt moudre, broyer ♦ vi (also: **~ about**) grouiller; **~er** n meunier m

millennium bug [mɪ'lenɪəm-] n bogue m or bug m de l'an 2000

milligram(me) ['mɪlɪgræm] n milligramme m

millimetre ['mɪlɪmiːtəʳ] (US **millimeter**) n millimètre m

million ['mɪljən] n million m; **~aire** n millionnaire m

milometer [maɪ'lɒmɪtəʳ] n ≈ compteur m kilométrique

mime [maɪm] n mime m ♦ vt, vi mimer; **mimic** ['mɪmɪk] n imitateur(-trice) ♦ vt imiter, contrefaire

min. abbr = **minute(s)**; **minimum**

mince [mɪns] vt hacher ♦ n (BRIT: CULIN) viande hachée, hachis m; **~meat** n (fruit) hachis de fruits secs utilisé en pâtisserie; (US: meat) viande hachée, hachis; **~ pie** n (sweet) sorte de tarte aux fruits secs; **~r** n hachoir m

mind [maɪnd] n esprit m ♦ vt (attend to, look

after) s'occuper de; (*be careful*) faire attention à; (*object to*): **I don't ~ the noise** le bruit ne me dérange pas; **I don't ~** cela ne me dérange pas; **it is on my ~** cela me préoccupe; **to my ~** à mon avis or sens; **to be out of one's ~** ne plus avoir toute sa raison; **to keep** or **bear sth in ~** tenir compte de qch; **to make up one's ~** se décider; **~ you, ...** remarquez ...; **never ~** ça ne fait rien; (*don't worry*) ne vous en faites pas; **"~ the step"** "attention à la marche"; **~er** n (*child-minder*) gardienne f; (*inf: bodyguard*) ange gardien (*fig*); **~ful** *adj*: **~ful of** attentif(-ive) à, soucieux(-euse) de; **~less** *adj* irréfléchi(e); (*boring: job*) idiot(e)

mine¹ [maɪn] *pron* le (la) mien(ne), les miens (miennes) ♦ *adj*: **this book is ~** ce livre est à moi

mine² [maɪn] n mine f ♦ *vt* (*coal*) extraire; (*ship, beach*) miner; **~field** n champ m de mines; (*fig*) situation (très délicate); **~r** n mineur m

mineral ['mɪnərəl] *adj* minéral(e) ♦ n minéral m; **~s** npl (*BRIT: soft drinks*) boissons gazeuses; **~ water** n eau minérale

mingle ['mɪŋgl] *vi*: **to ~ with** se mêler à

miniature ['mɪnətʃər] *adj* (en) miniature ♦ n miniature f

minibus ['mɪnɪbʌs] n minibus m

minimal ['mɪnɪml] *adj* minime

minimize ['mɪnɪmaɪz] *vt* (*reduce*) réduire au minimum; (*play down*) minimiser

minimum ['mɪnɪməm] (*pl* **minima**) *adj*, n minimum m

mining ['maɪnɪŋ] n exploitation minière

miniskirt ['mɪnɪskəːt] n mini-jupe f

minister ['mɪnɪstər] n (*BRIT: POL*) ministre m; (*REL*) pasteur m ♦ *vi*: **to ~ to sb('s needs)** pourvoir aux besoins de qn; **~ial** [mɪnɪs'tɪərɪəl] (*BRIT*) *adj* (*POL*) ministériel(le); **ministry** n (*BRIT: POL*) ministère m; (*REL*): **to go into the ministry** devenir pasteur

mink [mɪŋk] n vison m

minor ['maɪnər] *adj* petit(e), de peu d'importance; (*MUS, poet, problem*) mineur(e) ♦ n (*LAW*) mineur(e)

minority [maɪ'nɔrɪtɪ] n minorité f

mint [mɪnt] n (*plant*) menthe f; (*sweet*) bonbon m à la menthe ♦ *vt* (*coins*) battre; **the (Royal) M~,** (*US*) **the (US) M~** ≈ l'Hôtel m de la Monnaie; **in ~ condition** à l'état de neuf

minus ['maɪnəs] n (*also:* **~ sign**) signe m moins ♦ *prep* moins

minute¹ [maɪ'njuːt] *adj* minuscule; (*detail, search*) minutieux(-euse)

minute² ['mɪnɪt] n minute f; **~s** npl (*official record*) procès-verbal, compte rendu

miracle ['mɪrəkl] n miracle m

mirage ['mɪrɑːʒ] n mirage m

mirror ['mɪrər] n miroir m, glace f; (*in car*) rétroviseur m

mirth [məːθ] n gaieté f

misadventure [mɪsəd'ventʃər] n mésaventure f

misapprehension ['mɪsæprɪ'henʃən] n malentendu m, méprise f

misappropriate [mɪsə'prəuprɪeɪt] *vt* détourner

misbehave [mɪsbɪ'heɪv] *vi* mal se conduire

miscalculate [mɪs'kælkjuleɪt] *vt* mal calculer

miscarriage ['mɪskærɪdʒ] n (*MED*) fausse couche; **~ of justice** erreur f judiciaire

miscellaneous [mɪsɪ'leɪnɪəs] *adj* (*items*) divers(es); (*selection*) varié(e)

mischief ['mɪstʃɪf] n (*naughtiness*) sottises fpl; (*fun*) farce f; (*playfulness*) espièglerie f; (*maliciousness*) méchanceté f; **mischievous** ['mɪstʃɪvəs] *adj* (*playful, naughty*) coquin(e), espiègle

misconception ['mɪskən'sepʃən] n idée fausse

misconduct [mɪs'kɔndʌkt] n inconduite f; **professional ~** faute professionnelle

misdemeanour [mɪsdɪ'miːnər] (*US* **misdemeanor**) n écart m de conduite; infraction f

miser ['maɪzər] n avare m/f

miserable ['mɪzərəbl] *adj* (*person, expression*) malheureux(-euse); (*conditions*) misérable; (*weather*) maussade; (*offer, donation*) minable; (*failure*) pitoyable

miserly ['maɪzəlɪ] *adj* avare

misery ['mɪzərɪ] n (*unhappiness*) tristesse f; (*pain*) souffrances fpl; (*wretchedness*) misère f

misfire [mɪs'faɪər] *vi* rater

misfit ['mɪsfɪt] n (*person*) inadapté(e)

misfortune [mɪs'fɔːtʃən] n malchance f, malheur m

misgiving [mɪs'gɪvɪŋ] n (*apprehension*) craintes fpl; **to have ~s about** avoir des doutes quant à

misguided [mɪs'gaɪdɪd] *adj* malavisé(e)

mishandle [mɪs'hændl] *vt* (*mismanage*) mal s'y prendre pour faire or résoudre *etc*

mishap ['mɪshæp] n mésaventure f

misinform [mɪsɪn'fɔːm] *vt* mal renseigner

misinterpret [mɪsɪn'təːprɪt] *vt* mal interpréter

misjudge [mɪs'dʒʌdʒ] *vt* méjuger

mislay [mɪs'leɪ] (*irreg: like* **lay**) *vt* égarer

mislead [mɪs'liːd] (*irreg: like* **lead**) *vt* induire en erreur; **~ing** *adj* trompeur(-euse)

mismanage [mɪs'mænɪdʒ] *vt* mal gérer

misplace [mɪs'pleɪs] *vt* égarer

misprint ['mɪsprɪnt] n faute f d'impression

Miss [mɪs] n Mademoiselle

miss [mɪs] *vt* (*fail to get, attend or see*) manquer, rater; (*regret the absence of*): **I**

~ **him/it** il/cela me manque ♦ *vi* manquer ♦ *n* (*shot*) coup manqué; ~ **out** (*BRIT*) *vt* oublier

misshapen [mɪs'ʃeɪpən] *adj* difforme

missile ['mɪsaɪl] *n* (*MIL*) missile *m*; (*object thrown*) projectile *m*

missing ['mɪsɪŋ] *adj* manquant(e); (*after escape, disaster: person*) disparu(e); **to go ~** disparaître; **to be ~** avoir disparu

mission ['mɪʃən] *n* mission *f*; **~ary** ['mɪʃənrɪ] *n* missionnaire *m/f*; **~ statement** *n* déclaration *f* d'intention

mist [mɪst] *n* brume *f* ♦ *vi* (*also:* ~ **over:** *eyes*) s'embuer; ~ **over** *vi* (*windows etc*) s'embuer; ~ **up** *vi* = **mist over**

mistake [mɪs'teɪk] (*irreg: like* **take**) *n* erreur *f*, faute *f* ♦ *vt* (*meaning, remark*) mal comprendre; se méprendre sur; **to make a ~** se tromper, faire une erreur; **by ~** par erreur, par inadvertance; **to ~ for** prendre pour; **~n** *pp of* **mistake** ♦ *adj* (*idea etc*) erroné(e); **to be ~n** faire erreur, se tromper

mister ['mɪstər] (*inf*) *n* Monsieur *m*; *see also* **Mr**

mistletoe ['mɪsltəʊ] *n* gui *m*

mistook [mɪs'tʊk] *pt of* **mistake**

mistress ['mɪstrɪs] *n* maîtresse *f*; (*BRIT: in primary school*) institutrice *f*; (: *in secondary school*) professeur *m*

mistrust [mɪs'trʌst] *vt* se méfier de

misty ['mɪstɪ] *adj* brumeux(-euse); (*glasses, window*) embué(e)

misunderstand [mɪsʌndə'stænd] (*irreg*) *vt, vi* mal comprendre; **~ing** *n* méprise *f*, malentendu *m*

misuse [*n* mɪs'juːs, *vb* mɪs'juːz] *n* mauvais emploi; (*of power*) abus *m* ♦ *vt* mal employer; abuser de; ~ **of funds** détournement *m* de fonds

mitigate ['mɪtɪgeɪt] *vt* atténuer

mitt(en) ['mɪt(n)] *n* mitaine *f*; moufle *f*

mix [mɪks] *vt* mélanger; (*sauce, drink etc*) préparer ♦ *vi* se mélanger; (*socialize*): **he doesn't ~ well** il est peu sociable ♦ *n* mélange *m*; **to ~ with** (*people*) fréquenter; ~ **up** *vt* mélanger; (*confuse*) confondre; **~ed** *adj* (*feelings, reactions*) contradictoire; (*salad*) mélangé(e); (*school, marriage*) mixte; **~ed grill** *n* assortiment *m* de grillades; **~ed-up** *adj* (*confused*) désorienté(e), embrouillé(e); **~er** *n* (*for food*) batteur *m*, mixer *m*; (*person*): **he is a good ~er** il est très liant; **~ture** *n* assortiment *m*, mélange *m*; (*MED*) préparation *f*; **~up** *n* confusion *f*

mm *abbr* (= *millimetre*) mm

moan [məʊn] *n* gémissement *m* ♦ *vi* gémir; (*inf: complain*): **to ~ (about)** se plaindre (de)

moat [məʊt] *n* fossé *m*, douves *fpl*

mob [mɔb] *n* foule *f*; (*disorderly*) cohue *f* ♦ *vt* assaillir

mobile ['məʊbaɪl] *adj* mobile ♦ *n* mobile *m*; ~ **home** *n* (grande) caravane; ~ **phone** *n* téléphone portatif

mock [mɔk] *vt* ridiculiser; (*laugh at*) se moquer de ♦ *adj* faux (fausse); ~ **exam** examen blanc; **~ery** *n* moquerie *f*, raillerie *f*; **to make a ~ery of** tourner en dérision; **~-up** *n* maquette *f*

mod [mɔd] *adj see* **convenience**

mode [məʊd] *n* mode *m*

model ['mɔdl] *n* modèle *m*; (*person: for fashion*) mannequin *m*; (: *for artist*) modèle ♦ *vt* (*with clay etc*) modeler ♦ *vi* travailler comme mannequin ♦ *adj* (*railway: toy*) modèle réduit *inv*; (*child, factory*) modèle; **to ~ clothes** présenter des vêtements; **to ~ o.s. on** imiter

modem ['məʊdem] *n* (*COMPUT*) modem *m*

moderate [*adj* 'mɔdərət, *vb* 'mɔdəreɪt] *adj* modéré(e); (*amount, change*) peu important(e) ♦ *vi* se calmer ♦ *vt* modérer

modern ['mɔdən] *adj* moderne; **~ize** *vt* moderniser

modest ['mɔdɪst] *adj* modeste; **~y** *n* modestie *f*

modify ['mɔdɪfaɪ] *vt* modifier

mogul ['məʊgl] *n* (*fig*) nabab *m*

mohair ['məʊhɛər] *n* mohair *m*

moist [mɔɪst] *adj* humide, moite; **~en** *vt* humecter, mouiller légèrement; **~ure** *n* humidité *f*; **~urizer** *n* produit hydratant

molar ['məʊlər] *n* molaire *f*

molasses [mə'læsɪz] *n* mélasse *f*

mold [məʊld] (*US*) *n, vt* = **mould**

mole [məʊl] *n* (*animal, fig: spy*) taupe *f*; (*spot*) grain *m* de beauté

molest [mə'lest] *vt* (*harass*) molester; (*LAW: sexually*) attenter à la pudeur de

mollycoddle ['mɔlɪkɔdl] *vt* chouchouter, couver

molt [məʊlt] (*US*) *vi* = **moult**

molten ['məʊltən] *adj* fondu(e); (*rock*) en fusion

mom [mɔm] (*US*) *n* = **mum**

moment ['məʊmənt] *n* moment *m*, instant *m*; **at the ~** en ce moment; **at that ~** à ce moment-là; **~ary** *adj* momentané(e), passager(-ère); **~ous** [məʊ'mentəs] *adj* important(e), capital(e)

momentum [məʊ'mentəm] *n* élan *m*, vitesse acquise; (*fig*) dynamique *f*; **to gather ~** prendre de la vitesse

mommy ['mɔmɪ] (*US*) *n* maman *f*

Monaco ['mɔnəkəʊ] *n* Monaco *m*

monarch ['mɔnək] *n* monarque *m*; **~y** *n* monarchie *f*

monastery ['mɔnəstərɪ] *n* monastère *m*

Monday ['mʌndɪ] *n* lundi *m*

monetary ['mʌnɪtərɪ] *adj* monétaire

money ['mʌnɪ] *n* argent *m*; **to make ~** gagner de l'argent; **~ belt** *n* ceinture-portefeuille *f*; **~ order** *n* mandat *m*; **~-spinner** (*inf*) *n* mine *f* d'or (*fig*)

mongrel ['mʌŋgrəl] *n* (*dog*) bâtard *m*

monitor ['mɒnɪtə*] *n* (*TV, COMPUT*) moniteur *m* ♦ *vt* contrôler; (*broadcast*) être à l'écoute de; (*progress*) suivre (de près)

monk [mʌŋk] *n* moine *m*

monkey ['mʌŋkɪ] *n* singe *m*; **~ nut** (*BRIT*) *n* cacahuète *f*

monopoly [mə'nɒpəlɪ] *n* monopole *m*

monotone ['mɒnətəun] *n* ton *m* (*or* voix *f*) monocorde; **monotonous** [mə'nɒtənəs] *adj* monotone

monsoon [mɒn'su:n] *n* mousson *f*

monster ['mɒnstə*] *n* monstre *m*; **monstrous** ['mɒnstrəs] *adj* monstrueux(-euse); (*huge*) gigantesque

month [mʌnθ] *n* mois *m*; **~ly** *adj* mensuel(le) ♦ *adv* mensuellement

monument ['mɒnjumənt] *n* monument *m*

moo [mu:] *vi* meugler, beugler

mood [mu:d] *n* humeur *f*, disposition *f*; **to be in a good/bad ~** être de bonne/mauvaise humeur; **~y** *adj* (*variable*) d'humeur changeante, lunatique; (*sullen*) morose, maussade

moon [mu:n] *n* lune *f*; **~light** *n* clair *m* de lune; **~lighting** *n* travail *m* au noir; **~lit** *adj*: **a ~lit night** une nuit de lune

moor [muə*] *n* lande *f* ♦ *vt* (*ship*) amarrer ♦ *vi* mouiller; **~land** *n* lande *f*

moose [mu:s] *n inv* élan *m*

mop [mɒp] *n* balai *m* à laver; (*for dishes*) lavette *f* (à vaisselle) ♦ *vt* essuyer; **~ of hair** tignasse *f*; **~ up** *vt* éponger

mope [məup] *vi* avoir le cafard, se morfondre

moped ['məuped] *n* cyclomoteur *m*

moral ['mɒrl] *adj* moral(e) ♦ *n* morale *f*; **~s** *npl* (*attitude, behaviour*) moralité *f*

morale [mɒ'rɑ:l] *n* moral *m*

morality [mə'rælɪtɪ] *n* moralité *f*

morass [mə'ræs] *n* marais *m*, marécage *m*

more [mɔ:*] *adj* **1** (*greater in number etc*) plus (de), davantage; **more people/work (than)** plus de gens/de travail (que)
2 (*additional*) encore (de); **do you want (some) more tea?** voulez-vous encore du thé?; **I have no** *or* **I don't have any more money** je n'ai plus d'argent; **it'll take a few more weeks** ça prendra encore quelques semaines
♦ *pron* plus, davantage; **more than 10** plus de 10; **it cost more than we expected** cela a coûté plus que prévu; **I want more** j'en veux plus *or* davantage; **is there any more?** est-ce

qu'il en reste?; **there's no more** il n'y en a plus; **a little more** un peu plus; **many/much more** beaucoup plus, bien davantage
♦ *adv*: **more dangerous/easily (than)** plus dangereux/facilement (que); **more and more expensive** de plus en plus cher; **more or less** plus ou moins; **more than ever** plus que jamais

moreover [mɔ:'rəuvə*] *adv* de plus

morning ['mɔ:nɪŋ] *n* matin *m*; matinée *f* ♦ *cpd* matinal(e); (*paper*) du matin; **in the ~** le matin; **7 o'clock in the ~** 7 heures du matin; **~ sickness** *n* nausées matinales

Morocco [mə'rɒkəu] *n* Maroc *m*

moron ['mɔ:rɒn] (*inf*) *n* idiot(e)

Morse [mɔ:s] *n*: **~ code** morse *m*

morsel ['mɔ:sl] *n* bouchée *f*

mortar ['mɔ:tə*] *n* mortier *m*

mortgage ['mɔ:gɪdʒ] *n* hypothèque *f*; (*loan*) prêt *m* (*or* crédit *m*) hypothécaire ♦ *vt* hypothéquer; **~ company** (*US*) *n* société *f* de crédit immobilier

mortuary ['mɔ:tjuərɪ] *n* morgue *f*

mosaic [məu'zeɪɪk] *n* mosaïque *f*

Moscow ['mɒskəu] *n* Moscou

Moslem ['mɒzləm] *adj, n* = **Muslim**

mosque [mɒsk] *n* mosquée *f*

mosquito [mɒs'ki:təu] (*pl* **~es**) *n* moustique *m*

moss [mɒs] *n* mousse *f*

most [məust] *adj* la plupart de; le plus de ♦ *pron* la plupart ♦ *adv* le plus; (*very*) très, extrêmement; **the ~** (*also*: **+ adjective**) le plus; **~ of** la plus grande partie de; **~ of them** la plupart d'entre eux; **I saw (the) ~** j'en ai vu la plupart; c'est moi qui en ai vu le plus; **at the (very) ~** au plus; **to make the ~ of** profiter au maximum de; **~ly** *adv* (*chiefly*) surtout; (*usually*) généralement

MOT *n abbr* (*BRIT*: = *Ministry of Transport*): **the MOT (test)** la visite technique (annuelle) obligatoire des véhicules à moteur

motel [məu'tel] *n* motel *m*

moth [mɒθ] *n* papillon *m* de nuit; (*in clothes*) mite *f*

mother ['mʌðə*] *n* mère *f* ♦ *vt* (*act as ~ to*) servir de mère à; (*pamper, protect*) materner; **~ country** mère patrie; **~hood** *n* maternité *f*; **~-in-law** *n* belle-mère *f*; **~ly** *adj* maternel(le); **~-of-pearl** *n* nacre *f*; **M~'s Day** *n* fête *f* des Mères; **~-to-be** *n* future maman; **~ tongue** *n* langue maternelle

motion ['məuʃən] *n* mouvement *m*; (*gesture*) geste *m*; (*at meeting*) motion *f* ♦ *vt, vi*: **~ (to) sb to do** faire signe à qn de faire; **~less** *adj* immobile, sans mouvement; **~ picture** *n* film *m*

motivated ['məutɪveɪtɪd] *adj* motivé(e);

motivation [məʊtɪ'veɪʃən] n motivation f
motive ['məʊtɪv] n motif m, mobile m
motley ['mɒtlɪ] adj hétéroclite
motor ['məʊtəʳ] n moteur m; (BRIT: inf: vehicle) auto f ♦ cpd (industry, vehicle) automobile; **~bike** n moto f; **~boat** n bateau m à moteur; **~car** (BRIT) n automobile f; **~cycle** n vélomoteur m; **~cycle racing** n course f de motos; **~cyclist** n motocycliste m/f; **~ing** (BRIT) n tourisme m automobile; **~ist** n automobiliste m/f; **~ mechanic** n mécanicien m garagiste; **~ racing** (BRIT) n course f automobile; **~ trade** n secteur m de l'automobile; **~way** (BRIT) n autoroute f
mottled ['mɒtld] adj tacheté(e), marbré(e)
motto ['mɒtəʊ] (pl **~es**) n devise f
mould [məʊld] (US **mold**) n moule m; (mildew) moisissure f ♦ vt mouler, modeler; (fig) façonner; **mo(u)ldy** adj moisi(e); (smell) de moisi
moult [məʊlt] (US **molt**) vi muer
mound [maʊnd] n monticule m, tertre m; (heap) monceau m, tas m
mount [maʊnt] n mont m, montagne f ♦ vt monter ♦ vi (inflation, tension) augmenter; (also: ~ up: problems etc) s'accumuler; ~ **up** vi (bills, costs, savings) s'accumuler
mountain ['maʊntɪn] n montagne f ♦ cpd de montagne; ~ **bike** n VTT m, vélo tout-terrain; **~eer** [maʊntɪ'nɪəʳ] n alpiniste m/f; **~eering** n alpinisme m; **~ous** adj montagneux(-euse); ~ **rescue team** n équipe f de secours en montagne; **~side** n flanc m or versant m de la montagne
mourn [mɔːn] vt pleurer ♦ vi: **to ~ (for)** (person) pleurer (la mort de); **~er** n parent(e) or ami(e) du défunt; personne f en deuil; **~ing** n deuil m; **in ~ing** en deuil
mouse [maʊs] (pl **mice**) n (also COMPUT) souris f; **~trap** n souricière f
mousse [muːs] n mousse f
moustache [məs'tɑːʃ] (US **mustache**) n moustache(s) f(pl)
mousy ['maʊsɪ] adj (hair) d'un châtain terne
mouth [maʊθ] (pl **~s**) n bouche f; (of dog, cat) gueule f; (of river) embouchure f; (of hole, cave) ouverture f; **~ful** n bouchée f; ~ **organ** n harmonica m; **~piece** n (of musical instrument) embouchure f; (spokesman) porte-parole m inv; **~wash** n eau f dentifrice; **~-watering** adj qui met l'eau à la bouche
movable ['muːvəbl] adj mobile
move [muːv] n (~ment) mouvement m; (in game) coup m; (: turn to play) tour m; (·change: of house) déménagement m; (: of job) changement m d'emploi ♦ vt déplacer, bouger; (emotionally) émouvoir; (POL: resolution etc) proposer; (in game) jouer ♦ vi

(gen) bouger, remuer; (traffic) circuler; (also: ~ house) déménager; (situation) progresser; **that was a good ~** bien joué!; **to get a ~ on** se dépêcher, se remuer; **to ~ sb to do sth** pousser or inciter qn à faire qch; ~ **about** vi (fidget) remuer; (travel) voyager, se déplacer; (change residence, job) ne pas rester au même endroit; ~ **along** vi se pousser; ~ **around** vi = move about; ~ **away** vi s'en aller; ~ **back** vi revenir, retourner; ~ **forward** vi avancer; ~ **in** vi (to a house) emménager; (police, soldiers) intervenir; ~ **on** vi se remettre en route; ~ **out** vi (of house) déménager; ~ **over** vi se pousser, se déplacer; ~ **up** vi (pupil) passer dans la classe supérieure; (employee) avoir de l'avancement; **~able** adj = movable
movement ['muːvmənt] n mouvement m
movie ['muːvɪ] n film m; **the ~s** le cinéma
moving ['muːvɪŋ] adj en mouvement; (emotional) émouvant(e)
mow [məʊ] (pt **mowed**, pp **mowed** or **mown**) vt faucher; (lawn) tondre; ~ **down** vt faucher; **~er** n (also: **lawnmower**) tondeuse f à gazon
MP n abbr = Member of Parliament
mph abbr = miles per hour
Mr ['mɪstəʳ] n: ~ **Smith** Monsieur Smith, M. Smith
Mrs ['mɪsɪz] n: ~ **Smith** Madame Smith, Mme Smith
Ms [mɪz] n (= Miss or Mrs): ~ **Smith** Madame Smith, Mme Smith
MSc abbr = Master of Science
much [mʌtʃ] adj beaucoup de ♦ adv, n, pron beaucoup; **how ~ is it?** combien est-ce que ça coûte?; **too ~** trop (de); **as ~ as** autant que
muck [mʌk] n (dirt) saleté f; ~ **about** or **around** (inf) vi faire l'imbécile; ~ **up** (inf) vt (exam, interview) se planter à (fam); **~y** adj (très) sale; (book, film) cochon(ne)
mud [mʌd] n boue f
muddle ['mʌdl] n (mess) pagaille f, désordre m; (mix-up) confusion f ♦ vt (also: ~ up) embrouiller; ~ **through** vi se débrouiller
muddy ['mʌdɪ] adj boueux(-euse)
mudguard ['mʌdgɑːd] n garde-boue m inv
muesli ['mjuːzlɪ] n muesli m
muffin ['mʌfɪn] n muffin m
muffle ['mʌfl] vt (sound) assourdir, étouffer; (against cold) emmitoufler; **~d** adj (sound) étouffé(e); (person) emmitouflé(e); **~r** (US) n (AUT) silencieux m
mug [mʌg] n (cup) grande tasse (sans soucoupe); (: for beer) chope f; (inf: face) bouille f; (: fool) poire f ♦ vt (assault) agresser; **~ger** n agresseur m; **~ging** n agression f
muggy ['mʌgɪ] adj lourd(e), moite

mule [mjuːl] n mule f
multi-level ['mʌltɪlevl] (US) adj
= **multistorey**
multiple ['mʌltɪpl] adj multiple ♦ n multiple
m; ~ **sclerosis** [-sklɪ'rəusɪs] n sclérose f en
plaques
multiplex cinema ['mʌltɪpleks-] n cinéma
m multisalles
multiplication [mʌltɪplɪ'keɪʃən] n
multiplication f; **multiply** ['mʌltɪplaɪ] vt
multiplier ♦ vi se multiplier
multistorey ['mʌltɪ'stɔːrɪ] (BRIT) adj
(building) à étages; (car park) à étages or
niveaux multiples ♦ n (car park) parking m à
plusieurs étages
mum [mʌm] (BRIT: inf) n maman f ♦ adj: **to
keep ~** ne pas souffler mot
mumble ['mʌmbl] vt, vi marmotter,
marmonner
mummy ['mʌmɪ] n (BRIT: mother) maman f;
(embalmed) momie f
mumps [mʌmps] n oreillons mpl
munch [mʌntʃ] vt, vi mâcher
mundane [mʌn'deɪn] adj banal(e), terre à
terre inv
municipal [mjuː'nɪsɪpl] adj municipal(e)
murder ['məːdər] n meurtre m, assassinat m
♦ vt assassiner; ~**er** n meurtrier m, assassin
m; ~**ous** ['məːdərəs] adj meurtrier(-ère)
murky ['məːkɪ] adj sombre, ténébreux(-euse);
(water) trouble
murmur ['məːmər] n murmure m ♦ vt, vi
murmurer
muscle ['mʌsl] n muscle m; (fig) force f; ~
in vi (on territory) envahir; (on success)
exploiter; **muscular** ['mʌskjulər] adj
musculaire; (person, arm) musclé(e)
muse [mjuːz] vi méditer, songer
museum [mjuː'zɪəm] n musée m
mushroom ['mʌʃrum] n champignon m ♦ vi
pousser comme un champignon
music ['mjuːzɪk] n musique f; ~**al** adj
musical(e); (person) musicien(ne) ♦ n (show)
comédie musicale; ~**al instrument** n
instrument m de musique; ~ **centre** n chaîne
compacte; ~**ian** [mjuː'zɪʃən] n musicien(ne)
Muslim ['mʌzlɪm] adj, n musulman(e)
muslin ['mʌzlɪn] n mousseline f
mussel ['mʌsl] n moule f
must [mʌst] aux vb (obligation): **I ~ do it** je
dois le faire, il faut que je le fasse;
(probability): **he ~ be there by now** il doit y
être maintenant, il y est probablement
maintenant; (suggestion, invitation): **you
~ come and see me** il faut que vous veniez me
voir; (indicating sth unwelcome): **why ~ he
behave so badly?** qu'est-ce qui le pousse à se
conduire si mal? ♦ n nécessité f, impératif m;
it's a ~ c'est indispensable

mustache ['mʌstæʃ] (US) n = **moustache**
mustard ['mʌstəd] n moutarde f
muster ['mʌstər] vt rassembler
mustn't ['mʌsnt] = **must not**
mute [mjuːt] adj muet(te); ~**d** adj (colour)
sourd(e); (reaction) voilé(e)
mutiny ['mjuːtɪnɪ] n mutinerie f ♦ vi se
mutiner
mutter ['mʌtər] vt, vi marmonner, marmotter
mutton ['mʌtn] n mouton m
mutual ['mjuːtʃuəl] adj mutuel(le),
réciproque; (benefit, interest) commun(e);
~**ly** adv mutuellement
muzzle ['mʌzl] n museau m; (protective
device) muselière f; (of gun) gueule f ♦ vt
museler
my [maɪ] adj mon (ma), mes pl; ~ **house/car/
gloves** ma maison/mon auto/mes gants; **I've
washed ~ hair/cut ~ finger** je me suis lavé les
cheveux/coupé le doigt; ~**self** [maɪ'self] pron
(reflexive) me; (emphatic) moi-même; (after
prep) moi; see also **oneself**
mysterious [mɪs'tɪərɪəs] adj mysté-
rieux(-euse)
mystery ['mɪstərɪ] n mystère m
mystify ['mɪstɪfaɪ] vt mystifier; (puzzle)
ébahir
myth [mɪθ] n mythe m; ~**ology** [mɪ'θɔlədʒɪ]
n mythologie f

N, n

n/a abbr = **not applicable**
naff [næf] (BRIT: inf) adj nul(le)
nag [næg] vt (scold) être toujours après,
reprendre sans arrêt; ~**ging** adj (doubt, pain)
persistant(e)
nail [neɪl] n (human) ongle m; (metal) clou m
♦ vt clouer; **to ~ sb down to a date/price**
contraindre qn à accepter or donner une
date/un prix; ~**brush** n brosse f à ongles;
~**file** n lime f à ongles; ~ **polish** n vernis m à
ongles; ~ **polish remover** n dissolvant m;
~ **scissors** npl ciseaux mpl à ongles;
~ **varnish** (BRIT) n = **nail polish**
naïve [naɪ'iːv] adj naïf(-ïve)
naked ['neɪkɪd] adj nu(e)
name [neɪm] n nom m; (reputation)
réputation f ♦ vt nommer; (identify:
accomplice etc) citer; (price, date) fixer,
donner; **by ~** par son nom; **in the ~ of** au
nom de; **what's your ~?** comment vous
appelez-vous?; ~**less** adj sans nom; (witness,
contributor) anonyme; ~**ly** adv à savoir;
~**sake** n homonyme m
nanny ['nænɪ] n bonne f d'enfants
nap [næp] n (sleep) (petit) somme ♦ vi: **to be
caught ~ping** être pris à l'improviste or en

défaut

nape [neɪp] n: ~ **of the neck** nuque f

napkin ['næpkɪn] n serviette f (de table)

nappy ['næpɪ] (BRIT) n couche f (gen pl);
~ **rash** n: **to have ~ rash** avoir les fesses
rouges

narcissus [nɑːˈsɪsəs] (pl **narcissi**) n narcisse
m

narcotic [nɑːˈkɒtɪk] n (drug) stupéfiant m;
(MED) narcotique m

narrative ['nærətɪv] n récit m

narrow ['nærəʊ] adj étroit(e); (fig)
restreint(e), limité(e) ♦ vi (road) devenir plus
étroit, se rétrécir; (gap, difference) se réduire;
to have a ~ escape l'échapper belle; **to ~ sth
down to** réduire qch à; ~**ly** adv: **he ~ly
missed injury/the tree** il a failli se blesser/
rentrer dans l'arbre; ~-**minded** adj à l'esprit
étroit, borné(e); (attitude) borné

nasty ['nɑːstɪ] adj (person: malicious)
méchant(e); (: rude) très désagréable;
(smell) dégoûtant(e); (wound, situation,
disease) mauvais(e)

nation ['neɪʃən] n nation f

national ['næʃənl] adj national(e) ♦ n
(abroad) ressortissant(e); (when home)
national(e); ~ **anthem** n hymne national;
~ **dress** n costume national; **N~ Health
Service** (BRIT) n service national de santé;
≈ Sécurité Sociale; **N~ Insurance** (BRIT) n
≈ Sécurité Sociale; ~**ism** n nationalisme m;
~**ist** adj nationaliste ♦ n nationaliste m/f;
~**ity** [næʃəˈnælɪtɪ] n nationalité f; ~**ize** vt
nationaliser; ~**ly** adv (as a nation) du point
de vue national; (nationwide) dans le pays
entier; ~ **park** n parc national

nationwide ['neɪʃənwaɪd] adj s'étendant à
l'ensemble du pays; (problem) à l'échelle du
pays entier ♦ adv à travers or dans tout le
pays

native ['neɪtɪv] n autochtone m/f, habitant(e)
du pays ♦ adj du pays, indigène; (country)
natal(e); (ability) inné(e); **a ~ of Russia** une
personne originaire de Russie; **a ~ speaker of
French** une personne de langue maternelle
française; **N~ American** n Indien(ne)
d'Amérique; ~ **language** n langue
maternelle

NATO ['neɪtəʊ] n abbr (= North Atlantic Treaty
Organization) OTAN f

natural ['nætʃrəl] adj naturel(le); ~ **gas** n
gaz naturel; ~**ist** n naturaliste m/f; ~**ly** adv
naturellement

nature ['neɪtʃəʳ] n nature f; **by ~** par
tempérament, de nature

naught [nɔːt] n = **nought**

naughty ['nɔːtɪ] adj (child) vilain(e), pas sage

nausea ['nɔːsɪə] n nausée f

naval ['neɪvl] adj naval(e); ~ **officer** n officier

m de marine

nave [neɪv] n nef f

navel ['neɪvl] n nombril m

navigate ['nævɪgeɪt] vt (steer) diriger; (plot
course) naviguer ♦ vi naviguer; **navigation**
[nævɪˈgeɪʃən] n navigation f

navvy ['nævɪ] (BRIT) n terrassier m

navy ['neɪvɪ] n marine f; ~(-**blue**) adj bleu
marine inv

Nazi ['nɑːtsɪ] n Nazi(e)

NB abbr (= nota bene) NB

near [nɪəʳ] adj proche ♦ adv près ♦ prep (also:
~ **to**) près de ♦ vt approcher de; ~**by**
[nɪəˈbaɪ] adj proche ♦ adv tout près, à
proximité; ~**ly** adv presque; **I ~ly fell** j'ai failli
tomber; ~ **miss** n (AVIAT) quasi-collision f;
that was a ~ miss (gen) il s'en est fallu de
peu; (of shot) c'est passé très près; ~**side** n
(AUT: in Britain) côté m gauche; (: in US,
Europe etc) côté droit; ~-**sighted** adj myope

neat [niːt] adj (person, work) soigné(e); (room
etc) bien tenu(e) or rangé(e); (skilful) habile;
(spirits) pur(e); ~**ly** adv avec soin or ordre;
habilement

necessarily ['nesɪsrɪlɪ] adv nécessairement

necessary ['nesɪsrɪ] adj nécessaire;
necessity [nɪˈsesɪtɪ] n nécessité f; (thing
needed) chose nécessaire or essentielle;
necessities npl nécessaire m

neck [nek] n cou m; (of animal, garment)
encolure f; (of bottle) goulot m ♦ vi (inf) se
peloter; ~ **and ~** à égalité; ~**lace** n collier m;
~**line** n encolure f; ~**tie** n cravate f

need [niːd] n besoin m ♦ vt avoir besoin de;
to ~ to do devoir faire; avoir besoin de faire;
you don't ~ to go vous n'avez pas besoin or
vous n'êtes pas obligé de partir

needle ['niːdl] n aiguille f ♦ vt asticoter,
tourmenter

needless ['niːdlɪs] adj inutile

needlework ['niːdlwɜːk] n (activity) travaux
mpl d'aiguille; (object(s)) ouvrage m

needn't ['niːdnt] = **need not**

needy ['niːdɪ] adj nécessiteux(-euse)

negative ['negətɪv] n (PHOT, ELEC) négatif m;
(LING) terme m de négation ♦ adj néga-
tif(-ive); ~ **equity** situation dans laquelle la valeur d'une maison est inférieure à celle de
l'emprunt-logement contracté pour la payer

neglect [nɪˈglekt] vt négliger ♦ n le fait de
négliger; (state of ~) abandon m; ~**ed** adj
négligé(e), à l'abandon

negligee ['neglɪʒeɪ] n déshabillé m

negotiate [nɪˈgəʊʃɪeɪt] vi, vt négocier;
negotiation [nɪgəʊʃɪˈeɪʃən] n négociation f,
pourparlers mpl

neigh [neɪ] vi hennir

neighbour ['neɪbəʳ] (US **neighbor**) n
voisin(e); ~**hood** n (place) quartier m;

(*people*) voisinage *m*; **~ing** *adj* voisin(e), avoisinant(e); **~ly** *adj* obligeant(e); (*action etc*) amical(e)

neither ['naɪðə*'*] *adj, pron* aucun(e) (des deux), ni l'un(e) ni l'autre ♦ *conj*: **I didn't move and ~ did Claude** je n'ai pas bougé, (et) Claude non plus ♦ *adv*: **~ good nor bad** ni bon ni mauvais; ..., **~ did I refuse** ..., (et or mais) je n'ai pas non plus refusé ...

neon ['niːɔn] *n* néon *m*; **~ light** *n* lampe *f* au néon

nephew ['nɛvjuː] *n* neveu *m*

nerve [nəːv] *n* nerf *m*; (*fig: courage*) sang-froid *m*, courage *m*; (: *impudence*) aplomb, toupet *m*; **to have a fit of ~s** avoir le trac; **~-racking** *adj* angoissant(e)

nervous ['nəːvəs] *adj* nerveux(-euse); (*anxious*) inquiet(-ète), plein(e) d'appréhension; (*timid*) intimidé(e); **~ breakdown** *n* dépression nerveuse

nest [nɛst] *n* nid *m* ♦ *vi* (se) nicher, faire son nid; **~ egg** *n* (*fig*) bas *m* de laine, magot *m*

nestle ['nɛsl] *vi* se blottir

net [nɛt] *n* filet *m*; **the N~** (*Internet*) le Net ♦ *adj* net(te) ♦ *vt* (*fish etc*) prendre au filet; (*profit*) rapporter; **~ball** *n* netball *m*

Netherlands ['nɛðələndz] *npl*: **the ~** les Pays-Bas *mpl*

nett [nɛt] *adj* = **net**

netting ['nɛtɪŋ] *n* (*for fence etc*) treillis *m*, grillage *m*

nettle ['nɛtl] *n* ortie *f*

network ['nɛtwəːk] *n* réseau *m*

neurotic [njuə'rɔtɪk] *adj* névrosé(e)

neuter ['njuːtə*'*] *adj* neutre ♦ *vt* (*cat etc*) châtrer, couper

neutral ['njuːtrəl] *adj* neutre ♦ *n* (*AUT*) point mort; **~ize** *vt* neutraliser

never ['nɛvə*'*] *adv* (ne ...) jamais; **~ again** plus jamais; **~ in my life** jamais de ma vie; *see also* **mind**; **~-ending** *adj* interminable; **~theless** *adv* néanmoins, malgré tout

new [njuː] *adj* nouveau (nouvelle); (*brand ~*) neuf (neuve); **N~ Age** *n* New Age *m*; **~born** *adj* nouveau-né(e); **~comer** *n* nouveau venu/nouvelle venue; **~-fangled** ['njuː'fæŋgld] (*pej*) ultramoderne (et farfelu(e)); **~-found** *adj* (*enthusiasm*) de fraîche date; (*friend*) nouveau (nouvelle); **~ly** *adv* nouvellement, récemment; **~ly-weds** *npl* jeunes mariés *mpl*

news [njuːz] *n* nouvelle(s) *f(pl)*; (*RADIO, TV*) informations *fpl*, actualités *fpl*; **a piece of ~** une nouvelle; **~ agency** *n* agence *f* de presse; **~agent** (*BRIT*) *n* marchand *m* de journaux; **~caster** *n* présentateur(-trice);

~ flash *n* flash *m* d'information; **~letter** *n* bulletin *m*; **~paper** *n* journal *m*; **~print** *n* papier *m* (de) journal; **~reader** *n*

= **newscaster**; **~reel** *n* actualités (filmées); **~ stand** *n* kiosque *m* à journaux

newt [njuːt] *n* triton *m*

New Year *n* Nouvel An; **~'s Day** *n* le jour de l'An; **~'s Eve** *n* la Saint-Sylvestre

New Zealand [-'ziːlənd] *n* la Nouvelle-Zélande; **~er** *n* Néo-zélandais(e)

next [nɛkst] *adj* (*seat, room*) voisin(e), d'à côté; (*meeting, bus stop*) suivant(e); (*in time*) prochain(e) ♦ *adv* (*place*) à côté; (*time*) la fois suivante, la prochaine fois; (*afterwards*) ensuite; **the ~ day** le lendemain, le jour suivant or d'après; **~ year** l'année prochaine; **~ time** la prochaine fois; **~ to** à côté de; **~ to nothing** presque rien; **~, please!** (*at doctor's etc*) au suivant!; **~ door** *adv* à côté ♦ *adj* d'à côté; **~-of-kin** *n* parent *m* le plus proche

NHS *n abbr* = **National Health Service**

nib [nɪb] *n* (*bec m de*) plume *f*

nibble ['nɪbl] *vt* grignoter

nice [naɪs] *adj* (*pleasant, likeable*) agréable; (*pretty*) joli(e); (*kind*) gentil(le); **~ly** *adv* agréablement; joliment; gentiment

niceties ['naɪsɪtɪz] *npl* subtilités *fpl*

nick [nɪk] *n* (*indentation*) encoche *f*; (*wound*) entaille *f* ♦ *vt* (*BRIT: inf*) faucher, piquer; **in the ~ of time** juste à temps

nickel ['nɪkl] *n* nickel *m*; (*US*) pièce *f* de 5 cents

nickname ['nɪkneɪm] *n* surnom *m* ♦ *vt* surnommer

nicotine patch ['nɪkətiːn-] *n* timbre *m* anti-tabac, patch *m*

niece [niːs] *n* nièce *f*

Nigeria [naɪ'dʒɪərɪə] *n* Nigéria *m* or *f*

niggling ['nɪglɪŋ] *adj* (*person*) tatillon(ne); (*detail*) insignifiant(e); (*doubts, injury*) persistant(e)

night [naɪt] *n* nuit *f*; (*evening*) soir *m*; **at ~** la nuit; **by ~** de nuit; **the ~ before last** avant-hier soir; **~cap** *n* boisson prise avant le coucher; **~ club** *n* boîte *f* de nuit; **~dress** *n* chemise *f* de nuit; **~fall** *n* tombée *f* de la nuit; **~gown** *n* chemise *f* de nuit; **~ie** ['naɪtɪ] *n* chemise *f* de nuit; **~ingale** ['naɪtɪŋgeɪl] *n* rossignol *m*; **~life** *n* vie *f* nocturne; **~ly** *adj* de chaque nuit or soir; (*by night*) nocturne ♦ *adv* chaque nuit or soir; **~mare** *n* cauchemar *m*; **~ porter** *n* gardien *m* de nuit, concierge *m* de service la nuit; **~ school** *n* cours *mpl* du soir; **~ shift** *n* équipe *f* de nuit; **~-time** *n* nuit *f*; **~ watchman** *n* veilleur *m* or gardien *m* de nuit

nil [nɪl] *n* rien *m*; (*BRIT: SPORT*) zéro *m*

Nile [naɪl] *n*: **the ~** le Nil

nimble ['nɪmbl] *adj* agile

nine [naɪn] *num* neuf; **~teen** ['naɪn'tiːn] *num* dix-neuf; **~ty** ['naɪntɪ] *num* quatre-vingt-dix;

ninth [naɪnθ] *num* neuvième

nip [nɪp] vt pincer

nipple ['nɪpl] n (ANAT) mamelon m, bout m du sein

nitrogen ['naɪtrədʒən] n azote m

KEYWORD
---

no [nəu] (pl noes) adv (opposite of "yes") non; are you coming? - no (I'm not) est-ce que vous venez? - non; would you like some more? - no thank you vous en voulez encore? - non merci
♦ adj (not any) pas de, aucun(e) (used with "ne"); I have no money/books je n'ai pas d'argent/de livres; no student would have done it aucun étudiant ne l'aurait fait; "no smoking" "défense de fumer"; "no dogs" "les chiens ne sont pas admis"
♦ n non m

nobility [nəu'bɪlɪtɪ] n noblesse f

noble ['nəubl] adj noble

nobody ['nəubədɪ] pron personne

nod [nɒd] vi faire un signe de tête (affirmatif ou amical); (sleep) somnoler ♦ vt: to ~ one's head faire un signe de (la) tête; (in agreement) faire signe que oui ♦ n signe m de (la) tête; ~ off vi s'assoupir

noise [nɔɪz] n bruit m; **noisy** adj bruyant(e)

nominal ['nɒmɪnl] adj symbolique

nominate ['nɒmɪneɪt] vt (propose) proposer; (appoint) nommer; **nominee** [nɒmɪ'ni:] n candidat agréé; personne nommée

non... [nɒn] prefix non-; ~**alcoholic** adj non-alcoolisé(e); ~**committal** adj évasif(-ive); ~**descript** adj quelconque, indéfinissable

none [nʌn] pron aucun(e); ~ **of you** aucun d'entre vous, personne parmi vous; **I've ~ left** je n'en ai plus; **he's ~ the worse for it** il ne s'en porte pas plus mal

nonentity [nɒ'nentɪtɪ] n personne insignifiante

nonetheless ['nʌnðə'les] adv néanmoins

non-existent [nɒnɪg'zɪstənt] adj inexistant(e)

non-fiction [nɒn'fɪkʃən] n littérature f non-romanesque

nonplussed [nɒn'plʌst] adj perplexe

nonsense ['nɒnsəns] n absurdités fpl, idioties fpl; ~! ne dites pas d'idioties!

non: ~**smoker** n non-fumeur m; ~**smoking** adj non-fumeur; ~**stick** adj qui n'attache pas; ~**stop** adj direct(e), sans arrêt (or escale) ♦ adv sans arrêt

noodles ['nu:dlz] npl nouilles fpl

nook [nuk] n: ~**s and crannies** recoins mpl

noon [nu:n] n midi m

no one ['nəuwʌn] pron = **nobody**

noose [nu:s] n nœud coulant; (hangman's)

corde f

nor [nɔ:r] conj = **neither** ♦ adv see **neither**

norm [nɔ:m] n norme f

normal adj normal(e); ~**ly** ['nɔ:məlɪ] adv normalement

Normandy ['nɔ:məndɪ] n Normandie f

north [nɔ:θ] n nord m ♦ adj du nord, nord inv ♦ adv au or vers le nord; **N~ America** n Amérique f du Nord; ~**east** n nord-est m; ~**erly** ['nɔ:ðəlɪ] adj du nord; ~**ern** ['nɔ:ðən] adj du nord, septentrional(e); **N~ern Ireland** n Irlande f du Nord; **N~ Pole** n pôle m Nord; **N~ Sea** n mer f du Nord; ~**ward(s)** adv vers le nord; ~**west** n nord-ouest m

Norway ['nɔ:weɪ] n Norvège f; **Norwegian** [nɔ:'wi:dʒən] adj norvégien(ne) ♦ n Norvégien(ne); (LING) norvégien m

nose [nəuz] n nez m; ~ **about, around** vi fouiner or fureter (partout); ~**bleed** n saignement m du nez; ~**dive** n (descente f en) piqué m; ~**y** (inf) adj = **nosy**

nostalgia [nɒs'tældʒɪə] n nostalgie f

nostril ['nɒstrɪl] n narine f; (of horse) naseau m

nosy ['nəuzɪ] (inf) adj curieux(-euse)

not [nɒt] adv (ne ...) pas; **he is ~ or isn't here** il n'est pas ici; **you must ~ or mustn't do that** tu ne dois pas faire ça; **it's too late, isn't it** or **is it ~?** c'est trop tard, n'est-ce pas?; ~ **yet/now** pas encore/maintenant; ~ **at all** pas du tout; see also **all; only**

notably ['nəutəblɪ] adv (particularly) en particulier; (markedly) spécialement

notary ['nəutərɪ] n notaire m

notch [nɒtʃ] n encoche f

note [nəut] n note f; (letter) mot m; (banknote) billet m ♦ vt (also: ~ **down**) noter; (observe) constater; ~**book** n carnet m; ~**d** adj réputé(e); ~**pad** n bloc-notes m; ~**paper** n papier m à lettres

nothing ['nʌθɪŋ] n rien m; **he does** ~ il ne fait rien; ~ **new** rien de nouveau; **for** ~ pour rien

notice ['nəutɪs] n (announcement, warning) avis m; (period of time) délai m; (resignation) démission f; (dismissal) congé m ♦ vt remarquer, s'apercevoir de; **to take ~ of** prêter attention à; **to bring sth to sb's ~** porter qch à la connaissance de qn; **at short ~** dans un délai très court; **until further ~** jusqu'à nouvel ordre; **to hand in one's ~** donner sa démission, démissionner; ~**able** adj visible; ~ **board** (BRIT) n panneau m d'affichage

notify ['nəutɪfaɪ] vt: **to ~ sth to sb** notifier qch à qn; **to ~ sb (of sth)** avertir qn (de qch)

notion ['nəuʃən] n idée f; (concept) notion f

notorious [nəu'tɔ:rɪəs] adj notoire (souvent en mal)

nought [nɔːt] n zéro m

noun [naun] n nom m

nourish ['nʌrɪʃ] vt nourrir; **~ing** adj nourrissant(e); **~ment** n nourriture f

novel ['nɔvl] n roman m ♦ adj nouveau (nouvelle), original(e); **~ist** n romancier m; **~ty** n nouveauté f

November [nəu'vɛmbəʳ] n novembre m

now [nau] adv maintenant ♦ conj: ~ **(that)** maintenant que; **right ~** tout de suite; **by ~** à l'heure qu'il est; **just ~**: that's the fashion just ~ c'est la mode en ce moment; **~ and then, ~ and again** de temps en temps; **from ~ on** dorénavant; **~adays** adv de nos jours

nowhere ['nəuwɛəʳ] adv nulle part

nozzle ['nɔzl] n (of hose etc) ajutage m; (of vacuum cleaner) suceur m

nuclear ['njuːklɪəʳ] adj nucléaire

nucleus ['njuːklɪəs] (pl nuclei) n noyau m

nude [njuːd] adj nu(e) ♦ n nu m; **in the ~** (tout(e)) nu(e)

nudge [nʌdʒ] vt donner un (petit) coup de coude à

nudist ['njuːdɪst] n nudiste m/f

nuisance ['njuːsns] n: **it's a ~** c'est (très) embêtant; **he's a ~** il est assommant or casse-pieds; **what a ~!** quelle barbe!

null [nʌl] adj: **~ and void** nul(le) et non avenu(e)

numb [nʌm] adj engourdi(e); (with fear) paralysé(e)

number ['nʌmbəʳ] n nombre m; (numeral) chiffre m; (of house, bank account etc) numéro m ♦ vt numéroter; (amount to) compter; **a ~ of** un certain nombre de; **they were seven in ~** ils étaient (au nombre de) sept; **to be ~ed among** compter parmi; **~ plate** n (AUT) plaque f minéralogique or d'immatriculation

numeral ['njuːmərəl] n chiffre m

numerate ['njuːmərɪt] (BRIT) adj: **to be ~** avoir des notions d'arithmétique

numerical [njuː'mɛrɪkl] adj numérique

numerous ['njuːmərəs] adj nombreux(-euse)

nun [nʌn] n religieuse f, sœur f

nurse [nəːs] n infirmière f ♦ vt (patient, cold) soigner

nursery ['nəːsərɪ] n (room) nursery f; (institution) crèche f; (for plants) pépinière f; **~ rhyme** n comptine f, chansonnette f pour enfants; **~ school** n école maternelle; **~ slope** n (SKI) piste f pour débutants

nursing ['nəːsɪŋ] n (profession) profession f d'infirmière; (care) soins mpl; **~ home** n clinique f; maison f de convalescence

nut [nʌt] n (of metal) écrou m; (fruit) noix f; noisette f; cacahuète f; **~crackers** npl casse-noix m inv, casse-noisette(s) pl m

nutmeg ['nʌtmɛg] n (noix f) muscade f

nutritious [njuː'trɪʃəs] adj nutritif(-ive), nourrissant(e)

nuts [nʌts] (inf) adj dingue

nutshell ['nʌtʃɛl] n: **in a ~** en un mot

nutter ['nʌtəʳ] (BRIT: inf) n: **he's a complete ~** il est complètement cinglé

nylon ['naɪlɔn] n nylon m ♦ adj de or en nylon

O, o

oak [əuk] n chêne m ♦ adj de or en (bois de) chêne

OAP (BRIT) n abbr = **old-age pensioner**

oar [ɔːʳ] n aviron m, rame f

oasis [əu'eɪsɪs] (pl oases) n oasis f

oath [əuθ] n serment m; (swear word) juron m; **under ~,** (BRIT) **on ~** sous serment

oatmeal ['əutmiːl] n flocons mpl d'avoine

oats [əuts] n avoine f

obedience [ə'biːdɪəns] n obéissance f; **obedient** adj obéissant(e)

obey [ə'beɪ] vt obéir à; (instructions) se conformer à

obituary [ə'bɪtjuərɪ] n nécrologie f

object [n 'ɔbdʒɪkt, vb əb'dʒɛkt] n objet m; (purpose) but m, objet; (LING) complément m d'objet ♦ vi: **to ~ to** (attitude) désapprouver; (proposal) protester contre; **expense is no ~** l'argent n'est pas un problème; **he ~ed that ...** il a fait valoir or a objecté que ...; **I ~!** je proteste!; **~ion** [əb'dʒɛkʃən] n objection f; **~ionable** adj très désagréable; (language) choquant(e); **~ive** n objectif m ♦ adj objectif(-ive)

obligation [ɔblɪ'geɪʃən] n obligation f, devoir m; **without ~** sans engagement; **obligatory** [ə'blɪgətərɪ] adj obligatoire

oblige [ə'blaɪdʒ] vt (force): **to ~ sb to do** obliger or forcer qn à faire; (do a favour) rendre service à, obliger; **to be ~d to sb for sth** être obligé(e) à qn de qch; **obliging** adj obligeant(e), serviable

oblique [ə'bliːk] adj oblique; (allusion) indirect(e)

obliterate [ə'blɪtəreɪt] vt effacer

oblivion [ə'blɪvɪən] n oubli m; **oblivious** adj: **oblivious of** oublieux(-euse) de

oblong ['ɔblɔŋ] adj oblong (oblongue) ♦ n rectangle m

obnoxious [əb'nɔkʃəs] adj odieux(-euse); (smell) nauséabond(e)

oboe ['əubəu] n hautbois m

obscene [əb'siːn] adj obscène

obscure [əb'skjuəʳ] adj obscur(e) ♦ vt obscurcir; (hide: sun) cacher

observant [əb'zəːvənt] adj observateur(-trice)

observation [ɔbzə'veɪʃən] n (remark) observation f; (watching) surveillance f
observatory [əb'zɜːvətrɪ] n observatoire m
observe [əb'zɜːv] vt observer; (remark) faire observer or remarquer; ~**r** n observateur(-trice)
obsess [əb'sɛs] vt obséder; ~**ive** adj obsédant(e)
obsolete ['ɔbsəliːt] adj dépassé(e); démodé(e)
obstacle ['ɔbstəkl] n obstacle m; ~ **race** n course f d'obstacles
obstinate ['ɔbstɪnɪt] adj obstiné(e)
obstruct [əb'strʌkt] vt (block) boucher, obstruer; (hinder) entraver
obtain [əb'teɪn] vt obtenir
obvious ['ɔbvɪəs] adj évident(e), manifeste; ~**ly** adv manifestement; ~**ly not!** bien sûr que non!
occasion [ə'keɪʒən] n occasion f; (event) événement m; ~**al** adj pris(e) or fait(e) etc de temps en temps; occasionnel(le); ~**ally** adv de temps en temps, quelquefois
occupation [ɔkju'peɪʃən] n occupation f; (job) métier m, profession f; ~**al hazard** n risque m du métier
occupier ['ɔkjupaɪə*] n occupant(e)
occupy ['ɔkjupaɪ] vt occuper; to ~ **o.s. in** or **with doing** s'occuper à faire
occur [ə'kɜː*] vi (event) se produire; (phenomenon, error) se rencontrer; to ~ **to sb** venir à l'esprit de qn; ~**rence** f (existence) présence f, existence f; (event) cas m, fait m
ocean ['əuʃən] n océan m
o'clock [ə'klɔk] adv: **it is 5** ~ il est 5 heures
OCR n abbr = optical character reader; optical character recognition
October [ɔk'təubə*] n octobre m
octopus ['ɔktəpəs] n pieuvre f
odd [ɔd] adj (strange) bizarre, curieux(-euse); (number) impair(e); (not of a set) dépareillé(e); **60-**~ 60 et quelques; **at** ~ **times** de temps en temps; **the** ~ **one out** l'exception f; ~**ity** n (person) excentrique m/f; (thing) curiosité f; ~**job man** n homme m à tout faire; ~ **jobs** npl petits travaux divers; ~**ly** adv bizarrement, curieusement; ~**ments** npl (COMM) fins fpl de série; ~**s** npl (in betting) cote f; **it makes no** ~**s** cela n'a pas d'importance; **at** ~**s** en désaccord; ~**s and ends** de petites choses
odour ['əudə*] (US **odor**) n odeur f

of [ɔv, əv] prep **1** (gen) de; **a friend of ours** un de nos amis; **a boy of 10** un garçon de 10 ans; **that was kind of you** c'était gentil de votre part
2 (expressing quantity, amount, dates etc) de;

a kilo of flour un kilo de farine; **how much of this do you need?** combien vous en faut-il?; **there were 3 of them** (people) ils étaient 3; (objects) il y en avait 3; **3 of us went** 3 d'entre nous y sont allé(e)s; **the 5th of July** le 5 juillet
3 (from, out of) en, de; **a statue of marble** une statue de or en marbre; **made of wood** (fait) en bois

off [ɔf] adj, adv (engine) coupé(e); (tap) fermé(e); (BRIT: food: bad) mauvais(e); (: milk: bad) tourné(e); (absent) absent(e); (cancelled) annulé(e) ♦ prep de; sur; to be ~ (to leave) partir, s'en aller; to be ~ **sick** être absent pour cause de maladie; **a day** ~ un jour de congé; to **have an** ~ **day** n'être pas en forme; **he had his coat** ~ il avait enlevé son manteau; **10%** ~ (COMM) 10% de rabais; ~ **the coast** au large de la côte; **I'm** ~ **meat** je ne mange plus de viande, je n'aime plus la viande; **on the** ~ **chance** à tout hasard
offal ['ɔfl] n (CULIN) abats mpl
off-colour ['ɔf'kʌlə*] (BRIT) adj (ill) malade, mal fichu(e)
offence [ə'fɛns] (US **offense**) n (crime) délit m, infraction f; to **take** ~ **at** se vexer de, s'offenser de
offend [ə'fɛnd] vt (person) offenser, blesser; ~**er** n délinquant(e)
offense [ə'fɛns] (US) n = **offence**
offensive [ə'fɛnsɪv] adj offensant(e), choquant(e); (smell etc) très déplaisant(e); (weapon) offensif(-ive) ♦ n (MIL) offensive f
offer ['ɔfə*] n offre f, proposition f ♦ vt offrir, proposer; **"on** ~**"** (COMM) "en promotion"; ~**ing** n offrande f
offhand [ɔf'hænd] adj désinvolte ♦ adv spontanément
office ['ɔfɪs] n (place, room) bureau m; (position) charge f, fonction f; **doctor's** ~ (US) cabinet (médical); to **take** ~ entrer en fonctions; ~ **automation** n bureautique f; ~ **block** (US **office building**) n immeuble m de bureaux; ~ **hours** npl heures fpl de bureau; (US: MED) heures de consultation
officer ['ɔfɪsə*] n (MIL etc) officier m; (also: **police** ~) agent m (de police); (of organization) membre m du bureau directeur
office worker n employé(e) de bureau
official [ə'fɪʃl] adj officiel(le) ♦ n officiel m; (civil servant) fonctionnaire m/f; employé(e)
officiate [ə'fɪʃɪeɪt] vi (REL) officier; to ~ **at a marriage** célébrer un mariage
officious [ə'fɪʃəs] adj trop empressé(e)
offing ['ɔfɪŋ] n: **in the** ~ (fig) en perspective
off: ~**-licence** (BRIT) n (shop) débit m de vins et de spiritueux; ~**-line** adj, adv (COMPUT) (en mode) autonome; (: switched off) non

connecté(e); **~-peak** adj aux heures creuses; (electricity, heating, ticket) au tarif heures creuses; **~-putting** (BRIT) adj (remark) rébarbatif(-ive); (person) rebutant(e), peu engageant(e); **~-road vehicle** n véhicule m tout-terrain; **~-season** adj, adv hors-saison inv; **~set** (irreg) vt (counteract) contrebalancer, compenser; **~shoot** n (fig) ramification f, antenne f; **~shore** adj (breeze) de terre; (fishing) côtier(-ère); **~side** adj (SPORT) hors jeu; (: in US, Europe) de gauche; **~spring** n inv progéniture f; **~stage** adv dans les coulisses; **~-the-peg** (US **off-the-rack**) adv en prêt-à-porter; **~-white** adj blanc cassé inv

Oftel ['ɔftɛl] n organisme qui supervise les télécommunications

often ['ɔfn] adv souvent; **how ~ do you go?** vous y allez tous les combien?; **how ~ have you gone there?** vous y êtes allé combien de fois?

Ofwat ['ɔfwɔt] n organisme qui surveille les activités des compagnies des eaux

oh [əu] excl oh!, oh!, ah!

oil [ɔɪl] n huile f; (petroleum) pétrole m; (for central heating) mazout m ♦ vt (machine) graisser; **~can** n burette f de graissage; (for storing) bidon m à huile; **~field** n gisement m de pétrole; **~ filter** n (AUT) filtre m à huile; **~ painting** n peinture f à l'huile; **~ refinery** n raffinerie f; **~ rig** n derrick m; (at sea) plate-forme pétrolière; **~ slick** n nappe f de mazout; **~ tanker** n (ship) pétrolier m; (truck) camion-citerne m; **~ well** n puits m de pétrole; **~y** adj huileux(-euse); (food) gras(se)

ointment ['ɔɪntmənt] n onguent m

O.K., okay ['əu'keɪ] excl d'accord! ♦ adj (average) pas mal ♦ vt approuver, donner son accord à; **is it ~?, are you ~?** ça va?

old [əuld] adj vieux (vieille); (person) vieux, âgé(e); (former) ancien(ne), vieux; **how ~ are you?** quel âge avez-vous?; **he's 10 years ~** il a 10 ans, il est âgé de 10 ans; **~er brother/sister** frère/sœur aîné(e); **~ age** n vieillesse f; **~ age pensioner** (BRIT) n retraité(e); **~-fashioned** adj démodé(e); (person) vieux jeu inv

olive ['ɔlɪv] n (fruit) olive f; (tree) olivier m ♦ adj (also: **~-green**) (vert) olive inv; **~ oil** n huile f d'olive

Olympic [əu'lɪmpɪk] adj olympique; **the ~ Games, the ~s** les Jeux mpl olympiques

omelet(te) ['ɔmlɪt] n omelette f

omen ['əumən] n présage m

ominous ['ɔmɪnəs] adj menaçant(e), inquiétant(e); (event) de mauvais augure

omit [əu'mɪt] vt omettre; **to ~ to do** omettre de faire

KEYWORD

on [ɔn] prep 1 (indicating position) sur; **on the table** sur la table; **on the wall** sur le or au mur; **on the left** à gauche
2 (indicating means, method, condition etc): **on foot** à pied; **on the train/plane** (be) dans le train/l'avion; (go) en train/avion; **on the telephone/radio/television** au téléphone/à la radio/à la télévision; **to be on drugs** se droguer; **on holiday** en vacances
3 (referring to time): **on Friday** vendredi; **on Fridays** le vendredi; **on June 20th** le 20 juin; **a week on Friday** vendredi en huit; **on arrival** à l'arrivée; **on seeing this** en voyant cela
4 (about, concerning) sur, de; **a book on Balzac/physics** un livre sur Balzac/de physique
♦ adv 1 (referring to dress, covering): **to have one's coat on** avoir (mis) son manteau; **to put one's coat on** mettre son manteau; **what's she got on?** qu'est-ce qu'elle porte?; **screw the lid on tightly** vissez bien le couvercle
2 (further, continuously): **to walk** etc **on** continuer à marcher etc; **and off and on** de temps à autre
♦ adj 1 (in operation: machine) en marche; (: radio, TV, light) allumé(e); (: tap, gas) ouvert(e); (: brakes) mis(e); **is the meeting still on?** (not cancelled) est-ce que la réunion a bien lieu?; (in progress) la réunion dure-t-elle encore?; **when is this film on?** quand passe ce film?
2 (inf): **that's not on!** (not acceptable) cela ne se fait pas!; (not possible) pas question!

once [wʌns] adv une fois; (formerly) autrefois ♦ conj une fois que; **~ he had left/it was done** une fois qu'il fut parti/que ce fut terminé; **at ~** tout de suite, immédiatement; (simultaneously) à la fois; **~ a week** une fois par semaine; **~ more** encore une fois; **~ and for all** une fois pour toutes; **~ upon a time** il y avait une fois, il était une fois

oncoming ['ɔnkʌmɪŋ] adj (traffic) venant en sens inverse

KEYWORD

one [wʌn] num un(e); **one hundred and fifty** cent cinquante; **one day** un jour
♦ adj 1 (sole) seul(e), unique; **the one book which** l'unique or le seul livre qui; **the one man who** le seul (homme) qui
2 (same) même; **they came in the one car** ils sont venus dans la même voiture
♦ pron 1: **this one** celui-ci (celle-ci); **that one** celui-là (celle-là); **I've already got one/a red one** j'en ai déjà un(e)/un(e) rouge; **one by one** un(e) à or par un(e)
2: **one another** l'un(e) l'autre; **to look at one**

another se regarder
3 (*impersonal*) on; **one never knows** on ne sait jamais; **to cut one's finger** se couper le doigt

one: ~-**day excursion** (*US*) *n* billet *m* d'aller-retour (valable pour la journée); ~-**man** *adj* (*business*) dirigé(e) *etc* par un seul homme; ~-**man band** *n* homme-orchestre *m*; ~-**off** (*BRIT: inf*) *n* exemplaire *m* unique

oneself [wʌn'self] *pron* (*reflexive*) se; (*after prep*) soi(-même); (*emphatic*) soi-même; **to hurt** ~ se faire mal; **to keep sth for** ~ garder qch pour soi; **to talk to** ~ se parler à soi-même

one: ~-**sided** *adj* (*argument*) unilatéral; ~-**to**-~ *adj* (*relationship*) univoque; ~-**way** *adj* (*street, traffic*) à sens unique

ongoing ['ɔngəuɪŋ] *adj* en cours; (*relationship*) suivi(e)

onion ['ʌnjən] *n* oignon *m*

on-line ['ɔnlaɪn] *adj, adv* (*COMPUT*) en ligne; (: *switched on*) connecté(e)

onlooker ['ɔnlukə*ʳ*] *n* spectateur(-trice)

only ['əunlɪ] *adv* seulement ♦ *adj* seul(e), unique ♦ *conj* seulement, mais; **an** ~ **child** un enfant unique; **not** ~ ... **but also** non seulement ... mais aussi

onset ['ɔnset] *n* début *m*; (*of winter, old age*) approche *f*

onshore ['ɔnʃɔːʳ] *adj* (*wind*) du large

onslaught ['ɔnslɔːt] *n* attaque *f*, assaut *m*

onto ['ɔntu] *prep* = **on to**

onward(s) ['ɔnwəd(z)] *adv* (*move*) en avant; **from that time** ~ à partir de ce moment

ooze [uːz] *vi* suinter

opaque [əu'peɪk] *adj* opaque

OPEC ['əupek] *n abbr* (= *Organization of Petroleum-Exporting Countries*) O.P.E.P. *f*

open ['əupn] *adj* ouvert(e); (*car*) découvert(e); (*road, view*) dégagé(e); (*meeting*) public(-ique); (*admiration*) manifeste ♦ *vt* ouvrir ♦ *vi* (*flower, eyes, door, debate*) s'ouvrir; (*shop, bank, museum*) ouvrir; (*book etc: commence*) commencer, débuter; **in the** ~ (**air**) en plein air; ~ **on to** *vt fus* (*subj: room, door*) donner sur; ~ **up** *vt* ouvrir; (*blocked road*) dégager ♦ *vi* s'ouvrir; ~**ing** *n* ouverture *f*; (*opportunity*) occasion *f* ♦ *adj* (*remarks*) préliminaire; ~**ing hours** *npl* heures *fpl* d'ouverture; ~**ly** *adv* ouvertement; ~-**minded** *adj* à l'esprit ouvert; ~-**necked** *adj* à col ouvert; ~-**plan** *adj* sans cloisons

opera ['ɔpərə] *n* opéra *m*; ~ **singer** *n* chanteur(-euse) d'opéra

operate ['ɔpəreɪt] *vt* (*machine*) faire marcher, faire fonctionner ♦ *vi* fonctionner; (*MED*): **to** ~ (**on sb**) opérer (qn)

operatic [ɔpə'rætɪk] *adj* d'opéra

operating table ['ɔpəreɪtɪŋ-] *n* table *f* d'opération

operating theatre *n* salle *f* d'opération

operation [ɔpə'reɪʃən] *n* opération *f*; (*of machine*) fonctionnement *m*; **to be in** ~ (*system, law*) être en vigueur; **to have an** ~ (*MED*) se faire opérer

operative ['ɔpərətɪv] *adj* (*measure*) en vigueur

operator ['ɔpəreɪtə*ʳ*] *n* (*of machine*) opérateur(-trice); (*TEL*) téléphoniste *m/f*

opinion [ə'pɪnjən] *n* opinion *f*, avis *m*; **in my** ~ à mon avis; ~**ated** *adj* aux idées bien arrêtées; ~ **poll** *n* sondage *m* (d'opinion)

opponent [ə'pəunənt] *n* adversaire *m/f*

opportunity [ɔpə'tjuːnɪtɪ] *n* occasion *f*; **to take the** ~ **of doing** profiter de l'occasion pour faire; en profiter pour faire

oppose [ə'pəuz] *vt* s'opposer à; ~**d to** opposé(e) à; **as** ~**d to** par opposition à; **opposing** *adj* (*side*) opposé(e)

opposite ['ɔpəzɪt] *adj* opposé(e); (*house etc*) d'en face ♦ *adv* en face ♦ *prep* en face de ♦ *n* opposé *m*, contraire *m*; **the** ~ **sex** l'autre sexe, le sexe opposé; **opposition** [ɔpə'zɪʃən] *n* opposition *f*

oppressive [ə'presɪv] *adj* (*political regime*) oppressif(-ive); (*weather*) lourd(e); (*heat*) accablant(e)

opt [ɔpt] *vi*: **to** ~ **for** opter pour; **to** ~ **to do** choisir de faire; ~ **out** *vi*: **to** ~ **out of** choisir de ne pas participer à *or* de ne pas faire

optical ['ɔptɪkl] *adj* optique; (*instrument*) d'optique; ~ **character recognition/reader** *n* lecture *f*/lecteur *m* optique

optician [ɔp'tɪʃən] *n* opticien(ne)

optimist ['ɔptɪmɪst] *n* optimiste *m/f*; ~**ic** [ɔptɪ'mɪstɪk] *adj* optimiste

option ['ɔpʃən] *n* choix *m*, option *f*; (*SCOL*) matière *f* à option; (*COMM*) option; ~**al** *adj* facultatif(-ive); (*COMM*) en option

or [ɔːʳ] *conj* ou; (*with negative*): **he hasn't seen** ~ **heard anything** il n'a rien vu ni entendu; ~ **else** sinon; ou bien

oral ['ɔːrəl] *adj* oral(e) ♦ *n* oral *m*

orange ['ɔrɪndʒ] *n* (*fruit*) orange *f* ♦ *adj* orange *inv*

orbit ['ɔːbɪt] *n* orbite *f* ♦ *vt* graviter autour de; ~**al** (**motorway**) *n* périphérique *m*

orchard ['ɔːtʃəd] *n* verger *m*

orchestra ['ɔːkɪstrə] *n* orchestre *m*; (*US: seating*) (fauteuils *mpl* d')orchestre

orchid ['ɔːkɪd] *n* orchidée *f*

ordain [ɔː'deɪn] *vt* (*REL*) ordonner

ordeal [ɔː'diːl] *n* épreuve *f*

order ['ɔːdə*ʳ*] *n* ordre *m*; (*COMM*) commande *f* ♦ *vt* ordonner; (*COMM*) commander; **in** ~ en ordre; (*document*) en règle; **in** (**working**) ~ en état de marche; **out of** ~ (*not in correct* ~) en désordre; (*not working*) en dérangement; **in ~ to do/that** pour faire/que +*sub*; **on ~** (COMM) en commande; **to ~ sb to do** ordonner à qn de faire; **~ form** *n* bon de commande; **~ly** *n* (MIL) ordonnance *f*; (MED) garçon *m* de salle ♦ *adj* (*room*) en ordre; (*person*) qui a de l'ordre

ordinary ['ɔːdnrɪ] *adj* ordinaire, normal(e); (*pej*) ordinaire, quelconque; **out of the ~** exceptionnel(le)

Ordnance Survey map ['ɔːdnəns-] *n* ≈ carte *f* d'Etat-Major

ore [ɔːʳ] *n* minerai *m*

organ ['ɔːgən] *n* organe *m*; (MUS) orgue *m*, orgues *fpl*; **~ic** [ɔː'gænɪk] *adj* organique; (*food*) biologique

organization [ɔːgənaɪ'zeɪʃən] *n* organisation *f*

organize ['ɔːgənaɪz] *vt* organiser; **~r** *n* organisateur(-trice)

orgasm ['ɔːgæzm] *n* orgasme *m*

Orient ['ɔːrɪənt] *n*: **the ~** l'Orient *m*; **o~al** [ɔːrɪ'ɛntl] *adj* oriental(e)

origin ['ɔrɪdʒɪn] *n* origine *f*

original [ə'rɪdʒɪnl] *adj* original(e); (*earliest*) originel(le) ♦ *n* original *m*; **~ly** *adv* (*at first*) à l'origine

originate [ə'rɪdʒɪneɪt] *vi*: **to ~ from** (*person*) être originaire de; (*suggestion*) provenir de; **to ~ in** prendre naissance dans; avoir son origine dans

Orkney ['ɔːknɪ] *n* (*also*: **the ~ Islands**) les Orcades *fpl*

ornament ['ɔːnəmənt] *n* ornement *m*; (*trinket*) bibelot *m*; **~al** [ɔːnə'mɛntl] *adj* décoratif(-ive); (*garden*) d'agrément

ornate [ɔː'neɪt] *adj* très orné(e)

orphan ['ɔːfn] *n* orphelin(e)

orthopaedic [ɔːθə'piːdɪk] (US **orthopedic**) *adj* orthopédique

ostensibly [ɔs'tɛnsɪblɪ] *adv* en apparence

ostentatious [ɔstɛn'teɪʃəs] *adj* prétentieux(-euse)

ostracize ['ɔstrəsaɪz] *vt* frapper d'ostracisme

ostrich ['ɔstrɪtʃ] *n* autruche *f*

other ['ʌðəʳ] *adj* autre ♦ *pron*: **the ~ (one)** l'autre; **~s** (~ *people*) d'autres; **~ than** autrement que; à part; **~wise** *adv*, *conj* autrement

otter ['ɔtəʳ] *n* loutre *f*

ouch [autʃ] *excl* aïe!

ought [ɔːt] (*pt* ought) *aux vb*: **I ~ to do it** je devrais le faire, il faudrait que je le fasse; **this ~ to have been corrected** cela aurait dû être corrigé; **he ~ to win** il devrait gagner

ounce [auns] *n* once *f* (= 28.35g; 16 in a pound)

our ['auəʳ] *adj* notre, nos *pl*; *see also* **my**; **~s** *pron* le (la) nôtre, les nôtres; *see also* **mine**[1]

~selves [auə'sɛlvz] *pron pl* (*reflexive, after preposition*) nous; (*emphatic*) nous-mêmes; *see also* **oneself**

oust [aust] *vt* évincer

out [aut] *adv* dehors; (*published, not at home etc*) sorti(e); (*light, fire*) éteint(e); **~ here** ici; **~ there** là-bas; **he's ~** (*absent*) il est sorti; (*unconscious*) il est sans connaissance; **to be ~ in one's calculations** s'être trompé dans ses calculs; **to run/back etc ~** sortir en courant/en reculant *etc*; **~ loud** à haute voix; **~ of** (~*side*) en dehors de; (*because of: anger etc*) par; (*from among*): **~ of 10** sur 10; (*without*): **~ of petrol** sans essence, à court d'essence; **~ of order** (*machine*) en panne; (TEL: *line*) en dérangement; **~-and-~** *adj* (*liar, thief etc*) véritable; **~back** *n* (*in Australia*): **the ~back** l'intérieur *m*; **~board** *n* (*also*: **~board motor**) (moteur *m*) hors-bord *m*; **~break** *n* (*of war, disease*) début *m*; (*of violence*) éruption *f*; **~burst** *n* explosion *f*, accès *m*; **~cast** *n* exilé(e); (*socially*) paria *m*; **~come** *n* issue *f*, résultat *m*; **~crop** *n* (*of rock*) affleurement *m*; **~cry** *n* tollé (général); **~dated** *adj* démodé(e); **~do** (*irreg*) *vt* surpasser; **~door** *adj* de or en plein air; **~doors** *adv* dehors; au grand air

outer ['autəʳ] *adj* extérieur(e); **~ space** *n* espace *m* cosmique

outfit ['autfɪt] *n* (*clothes*) tenue *f*

out: **~going** *adj* (*character*) ouvert(e), extraverti(e); (*departing*) sortant(e); **~goings** (BRIT) *npl* (*expenses*) dépenses *fpl*; **~grow** (*irreg*) *vt* (*clothes*) devenir trop grand(e) pour; **~house** *n* appentis *m*, remise *f*

outing ['autɪŋ] *n* sortie *f*; excursion *f*

out: **~law** *n* hors-la-loi *m inv* ♦ *vt* mettre hors-la-loi; **~lay** *n* dépenses *fpl*; (*investment*) mise *f* de fonds; **~let** *n* (*for liquid etc*) issue *f*, sortie *f*; (US: ELEC) prise *f* de courant; (*also*: **retail ~let**) point *m* de vente; **~line** *n* (*shape*) contour *m*; (*summary*) esquisse *f*, grandes lignes ♦ *vt* (*fig: theory, plan*) exposer à grands traits; **~live** *vt* survivre à; **~look** *n* perspective *f*; (*fig*) attitude *f*; **~lying** *adj* écarté(e); **~moded** *adj* démodé(e); dépassé(e); **~number** *vt* surpasser en nombre; **~-of-date** *adj* (*passport*) périmé(e); (*theory etc*) dépassé(e); (*clothes etc*) démodé(e); **~-of-the-way** *adj* (*place*) loin de tout; **~patient** *n* malade *m/f* en consultation externe; **~post** *n* avant-poste *m*; **~put** *n* rendement *m*, production *f*; (COMPUT) sortie *f*

outrage ['autreɪdʒ] *n* (*anger*) indignation *f*; (*violent act*) atrocité *f*; (*scandal*) scandale *m* ♦ *vt* outrager; **~ous** [aut'reɪdʒəs] *adj* atroce; scandaleux(-euse)

outright [*adv* aut'raɪt, *adj* 'autraɪt] *adv*

complètement; (*deny, refuse*)
catégoriquement; (*ask*) carrément; (*kill*) sur
le coup ♦ *adj* complet(-ète); catégorique

outset ['autset] *n* début *m*

outside [aut'said] *n* extérieur *m* ♦ *adj*
extérieur(e) ♦ *adv* (au) dehors, à l'extérieur
♦ *prep* hors de, à l'extérieur de; **at the ~** (*fig*)
au plus ou maximum; **~ lane** *n* (*AUT: in
Britain*) voie *f* de droite; (: *in US, Europe*) voie
de gauche; **~ line** *n* (*TEL*) ligne extérieure; **~r**
n (*stranger*) étranger(-ère)

out: **~size** ['autsaiz] *adj* énorme; (*clothes*)
grande taille *inv*; **~skirts** *npl* faubourgs *mpl*;
~spoken *adj* très franc (franche);
~standing *adj* remarquable,
exceptionnel(le); (*unfinished*) en suspens;
(*debt*) impayé(e); (*problem*) non réglé(e);
~stay *vt*: **to ~stay one's welcome** abuser de
l'hospitalité de son hôte; **~stretched**
[aut'strɛtʃt] *adj* (*hand*) tendu(e); **~strip**
[aut'strip] *vt* (*competitors, demand*) dépasser;
~ tray *n* courrier *m* "départ"

outward ['autwəd] *adj* (*sign, appearances*)
extérieur(e); (*journey*) (d')aller

outweigh [aut'wei] *vt* l'emporter sur

outwit [aut'wit] *vt* se montrer plus malin que

oval ['əuvl] *adj* ovale ♦ *n* ovale *m*

ovary ['əuvəri] *n* ovaire *m*

oven ['ʌvn] *n* four *m*; **~proof** *adj* allant au
four

over ['əuvər] *adv* (par-)dessus ♦ *adj* (*finished*)
fini(e), terminé(e); (*too much*) en plus ♦ *prep*
sur; par-dessus; (*above*) au-dessus de; (*on the
other side of*) de l'autre côté de; (*more than*)
plus de; (*during*) pendant; **~ here** ici; **~ there**
là-bas; **all ~** (*everywhere*) partout, fini(e);
~ and ~ (**again**) à plusieurs reprises; **~ and
above** en plus de; **to ask sb ~** inviter qn (à
passer)

overall [*adj, n* 'əuvərɔ:l, *adv* əuvər'ɔ:l] *adj*
(*length, cost etc*) total(e); (*study*) d'ensemble
♦ *n* (*BRIT*) blouse *f* ♦ *adv* dans l'ensemble, en
général; **~s** *npl* bleus *mpl* (de travail)

over: **~awe** *vt* impressionner; **~balance** *vi*
basculer; **~board** *adv* (*NAUT*) par-dessus
bord; **~book** *vt* faire du surbooking; **~cast**
adj couvert(e)

overcharge [əuvə'tʃɑ:dʒ] *vt*: **to ~ sb for sth**
faire payer qch trop cher à qn

overcoat ['əuvəkəut] *n* pardessus *m*

overcome [əuvə'kʌm] (*irreg*) *vt* (*defeat*)
triompher de; (*difficulty*) surmonter

over: **~crowded** *adj* bondé(e); **~do** (*irreg*)
vt exagérer; (*overcook*) trop cuire; **to ~do it**
(*work etc*) se surmener; **~dose** *n* dose
excessive; **~draft** *n* découvert *m*; **~drawn**
adj (*account*) à découvert; (*person*) dont le
compte est à découvert; **~due** *adj* en retard;
(*change, reform*) qui tarde; **~estimate** *vt*

surestimer

overflow [əuvə'fləu] *vi* déborder ♦ *n* (*also:
~ pipe*) tuyau *m* d'écoulement, trop-plein *m*

overgrown [əuvə'grəun] *adj* (*garden*)
envahi(e) par la végétation

overhaul [*vb* əuvə'hɔ:l, *n* 'əuvəhɔ:l] *vt* réviser
♦ *n* révision *f*

overhead [*adv* əuvə'hɛd, *adj, n* 'əuvəhɛd]
adv au-dessus ♦ *adj* aérien(ne); (*lighting*)
vertical(e) ♦ *n* (*US*) = **overheads**; **~s** *npl*
(*expenses*) frais généraux; **~ projector** *n*
rétroprojecteur *m*

over: **~hear** (*irreg*) *vt* entendre (par hasard);
~heat *vi* (*engine*) chauffer; **~joyed** *adj*:
~joyed (at) ravi(e) (de), enchanté(e) (de)

overland ['əuvəlænd] *adj, adv* par voie de
terre

overlap [əuvə'læp] *vi* se chevaucher

over: **~leaf** *adv* au verso; **~load** *vt*
surcharger; **~look** *vt* (*have view of*) donner
sur; (*miss: by mistake*) oublier; (*forgive*)
fermer les yeux sur

overnight [*adv* əuvə'nait, *adj* 'əuvənait] *adv*
(*happen*) durant la nuit; (*fig*) soudain ♦ *adj*
d'une (*or* de) nuit; **he stayed there ~** il y a
passé la nuit

overpass ['əuvəpɑ:s] *n* pont autoroutier

overpower [əuvə'pauər] *vt* vaincre; (*fig*)
accabler; **~ing** *adj* (*heat, stench*) suffocant(e)

over: **~rate** *vt* surestimer; **~ride** (*irreg: like
ride*) *vt* (*order, objection*) passer outre à;
~riding *adj* prépondérant(e); **~rule** *vt*
(*decision*) annuler; (*claim*) rejeter; (*person*)
rejeter l'avis de; **~run** (*irreg: like run*) *vt*
(*country*) occuper; (*time limit*) dépasser

overseas [əuvə'si:z] *adv* outre-mer; (*abroad*)
à l'étranger ♦ *adj* (*trade*) extérieur(e);
(*visitor*) étranger(-ère)

overshadow [əuvə'ʃædəu] *vt* (*fig*) éclipser

oversight ['əuvəsait] *n* omission *f*, oubli *m*

oversleep [əuvə'sli:p] (*irreg*) *vi* se réveiller
(trop) tard

overstep [əuvə'stɛp] *vt*: **to ~ the mark**
dépasser la mesure

overt [əu'vɜ:t] *adj* non dissimulé(e)

overtake [əuvə'teik] (*irreg*) *vt* (*AUT*) dépasser,
doubler

over: **~throw** (*irreg*) *vt* (*government*)
renverser; **~time** *n* heures *fpl*
supplémentaires; **~tone** *n* (*also: ~tones*)
note *f*, sous-entendus *mpl*

overture ['əuvətʃuər] *n* (*MUS, fig*) ouverture *f*

over: **~turn** *vt* renverser ♦ *vi* se retourner;
~weight *adj* (*person*) trop gros(se);
~whelm *vt* (*subj: emotion*) accabler; (*enemy,
opponent*) écraser; **~whelming** *adj* (*victory,
defeat*) écrasant(e); (*desire*) irrésistible

overwrought [əuvə'rɔ:t] *adj* excédé(e)

owe [əu] *vt*: **to ~ sb sth, to ~ sth to sb** devoir

qch à qn; **owing to** prep à cause de, en
raison de
owl [aul] n hibou m
own [əun] vt posséder ♦ adj propre; **a room
of my ~** une chambre à moi, ma propre
chambre; **to get one's ~ back** prendre sa
revanche; **on one's ~** tout(e) seul(e); **~ up** vi
avouer; **~er** n propriétaire m/f; **~ership** n
possession f
ox [ɔks] (pl **~en**) n bœuf m; **~tail** n: **~tail soup**
soupe f à la queue de bœuf
oxygen ['ɔksɪdʒən] n oxygène m
oyster ['ɔɪstə'] n huître f
oz. abbr = **ounce(s)**
ozone ['əuzəun] n: **~-friendly** adj qui
n'attaque pas or qui préserve la couche
d'ozone; **~ hole** n trou m d'ozone; **~ layer**
n couche f d'ozone

P, p

p abbr = **penny**; **pence**
PA n abbr = **personal assistant**; **public address
system**
pa [pɑː] (inf) n papa m
p.a. abbr = **per annum**
pace [peɪs] n pas m; (speed) allure f; vitesse f
♦ vi: **to ~ up and down** faire les cent pas; **to
keep ~ with** aller à la même vitesse que;
~maker n (MED) stimulateur m cardiaque;
(SPORT; also: **~setter**) meneur(-euse) de train
Pacific [pə'sɪfɪk] n: **the ~ (Ocean)** le Pacifique,
l'océan m Pacifique
pack [pæk] n (~et, US: of cigarettes) paquet m;
(of hounds) meute f; (of thieves etc) bande f;
(back ~) sac m à dos; (of cards) jeu m ♦ vt
(goods) empaqueter, emballer; (box) remplir;
(cram) entasser; **to ~ one's suitcase** faire sa
valise; **to ~ (one's bags)** faire ses bagages; **to
~ sb off** expédier qn à; **~ it in!** laisse
tomber!, écrase!
package ['pækɪdʒ] n paquet m; (also: **~ deal**)
forfait m; **~ tour** (BRIT) n voyage organisé
packed adj (crowded) bondé(e); **~ lunch**
(BRIT) n repas froid
packet ['pækɪt] n paquet m
packing ['pækɪŋ] n emballage m; **~ case** n
caisse f (d'emballage)
pact [pækt] n pacte m, traité m
pad [pæd] n bloc-notes m; (to prevent
friction) tampon m; (inf: home) piaule f ♦ vt
rembourrer; **~ding** n rembourrage m
paddle ['pædl] n (oar) pagaie f; (US: for table
tennis) raquette f de ping-pong ♦ vt: **to ~ a
canoe** etc pagayer ♦ vi barboter, faire
trempette; **paddling pool** (BRIT) n petit
bassin
paddock ['pædək] n enclos m; (RACING)

paddock m
padlock ['pædlɔk] n cadenas m
paediatrics [piːdɪ'ætrɪks] (US **pediatrics**) n
pédiatrie f
pagan ['peɪgən] adj, n païen(ne)
page [peɪdʒ] n (of book) page f; (also: **~ boy**)
groom m, chasseur m; (at wedding) garçon m
d'honneur ♦ vt (in hotel etc) (faire) appeler
pageant ['pædʒənt] n spectacle m historique;
~ry n apparat m, pompe f
pager ['peɪdʒə'], **paging device** n (TEL)
récepteur m d'appels
paid [peɪd] pt, pp of **pay** ♦ adj (work, official)
rémunéré(e); (holiday) payé(e); **to put ~ to**
(BRIT) mettre fin à, régler
pail [peɪl] n seau m
pain [peɪn] n douleur f; **to be in ~** souffrir,
avoir mal; **to take ~s to do** se donner du mal
pour faire; **~ed** adj peiné(e), chagrin(e);
~ful adj douloureux(-euse); (fig) difficile,
pénible; **~fully** adv (fig: very) terriblement;
~killer n analgésique m; **~less** adj indolore;
~staking ['peɪnzteɪkɪŋ] adj (person)
soigneux(-euse); (work) soigné(e)
paint [peɪnt] n peinture f ♦ vt peindre; **to
~ the door blue** peindre la porte en bleu;
~brush n pinceau m; **~er** n peintre m; **~ing**
n peinture f; (picture) tableau m; **~work** n
peinture f
pair [peə'] n (of shoes, gloves etc) paire f; (of
people) couple m; **~ of scissors** (paire de)
ciseaux mpl; **~ of trousers** pantalon m
pajamas [pə'dʒɑːməz] (US) npl pyjama(s)
m(pl)
Pakistan [pɑːkɪ'stɑːn] n Pakistan m; **~i** adj
pakistanais(e) ♦ n Pakistanais(e)
pal [pæl] (inf) n copain (copine)
palace ['pæləs] n palais m
palatable ['pælɪtəbl] adj bon (bonne),
agréable au goût
palate ['pælɪt] n palais m (ANAT)
pale [peɪl] adj pâle ♦ n: **beyond the ~**
(behaviour) inacceptable; **to grow ~** pâlir
Palestine ['pælɪstaɪn] n Palestine f;
Palestinian [pælɪs'tɪnɪən] adj palestinien(ne)
♦ n Palestinien(ne)
palette ['pælɪt] n palette f
pall [pɔːl] n (of smoke) voile m ♦ vi devenir
lassant(e)
pallet ['pælɪt] n (for goods) palette f
pallid ['pælɪd] adj blême
palm [pɑːm] n (of hand) paume f; (also:
~ tree) palmier m ♦ vt: **to ~ sth off on sb** (inf)
refiler qch à qn; **P~ Sunday** n le dimanche
des Rameaux
paltry ['pɔːltrɪ] adj dérisoire
pamper ['pæmpə'] vt gâter, dorloter
pamphlet ['pæmflət] n brochure f
pan [pæn] n (also: **saucepan**) casserole f;

(*also:* frying ~) poêle f; ~**cake** n crêpe f

panda ['pændə] n panda m

pandemonium [pændɪ'məunɪəm] n tohu-bohu m

pander ['pændər] vi: **to ~ to** flatter bassement; obéir servilement à

pane [peɪn] n carreau m, vitre f

panel ['pænl] n (of wood, cloth etc) panneau m; (RADIO, TV) experts mpl; (for interview, exams) jury m; ~**ling** (US **paneling**) n boiseries fpl

pang [pæŋ] n: ~**s of remorse/jealousy** affres mpl du remords/de la jalousie; ~**s of hunger/ conscience** tiraillements mpl d'estomac/de la conscience

panic ['pænɪk] n panique f, affolement m ♦ vi s'affoler, paniquer; ~**ky** adj (person) qui panique or s'affole facilement; ~-**stricken** adj affolé(e)

pansy ['pænzɪ] n (BOT) pensée f; (inf: pej) tapette f, pédé m

pant [pænt] vi haleter

panther ['pænθər] n panthère f

panties ['pæntɪz] npl slip m

pantomime ['pæntəmaɪm] (BRIT) n spectacle m de Noël

pantry ['pæntrɪ] n garde-manger m inv

pants [pænts] npl (BRIT: woman's) slip m; (: man's) slip, caleçon m; (US: trousers) pantalon m

pantyhose ['pæntɪhəuz] (US) npl collant m

paper ['peɪpər] n papier m; (also: **wallpaper**) papier peint; (also: **newspaper**) journal m; (academic essay) article m; (exam) épreuve écrite ♦ adj en or de papier ♦ vt tapisser (de papier peint); ~**s** npl (also: **identity ~s**) papiers (d'identité); ~**back** n livre m de poche; livre broché or non relié; ~ **bag** n sac m en papier; ~ **clip** n trombone m; ~ **hankie** n mouchoir m en papier; ~**weight** n presse-papiers m inv; ~**work** n papiers mpl; (pej) paperasserie f

par [pɑːr] n pair m; (GOLF) normale f du parcours; **on a ~ with** à égalité avec, au même niveau que

parachute ['pærəʃuːt] n parachute m

parade [pə'reɪd] n défilé m ♦ vt (fig) faire étalage de ♦ vi défiler

paradise ['pærədaɪs] n paradis m

paradox ['pærədɔks] n paradoxe m; ~**ically** [pærə'dɔksɪklɪ] adv paradoxalement

paraffin ['pærəfɪn] (BRIT) n (also: ~ **oil**) pétrole (lampant)

paragon ['pærəgən] n modèle m

paragraph ['pærəgrɑːf] n paragraphe m

parallel ['pærəlɛl] adj parallèle; (fig) semblable ♦ n (line) parallèle f; (fig, GEO) parallèle m

paralyse ['pærəlaɪz] (BRIT) vt paralyser;

paralysis [pə'rælɪsɪs] n paralysie f; **paralyze** (US) vt = **paralyse**

paramount ['pærəmaunt] adj: **of ~ importance** de la plus haute or grande importance

paranoid ['pærənɔɪd] adj (PSYCH) paranoïaque

paraphernalia [pærəfə'neɪlɪə] n attirail m

parasol ['pærəsɔl] n ombrelle f; (over table) parasol m

paratrooper ['pærətruːpər] n parachutiste m (soldat)

parcel ['pɑːsl] n paquet m, colis m ♦ vt (also: ~ **up**) empaqueter

parchment ['pɑːtʃmənt] n parchemin m

pardon ['pɑːdn] n pardon m; grâce f ♦ vt pardonner à; ~ **me!**, **I beg your ~!** pardon!, je suis désolé!; (**I beg your**) ~?, (US) ~ **me?** pardon?

parent ['pɛərənt] n père m or mère f; ~**s** npl parents mpl

Paris ['pærɪs] n Paris

parish ['pærɪʃ] n paroisse f; (BRIT: civil) ≈ commune f

Parisian [pə'rɪzɪən] adj parisien(ne) ♦ n Parisien(ne)

park [pɑːk] n parc m, jardin public ♦ vt garer ♦ vi se garer

parking ['pɑːkɪŋ] n stationnement m; "**no ~**" "stationnement interdit"; ~ **lot** (US) n parking m, parc m de stationnement; ~ **meter** n parcomètre m; ~ **ticket** n P.V. m

parliament ['pɑːləmənt] n parlement m; ~**ary** [pɑːlə'mɛntərɪ] adj parlementaire

parlour ['pɑːlər] (US **parlor**) n salon m

parochial [pə'rəukɪəl] (pej) adj à l'esprit de clocher

parole [pə'rəul] n: **on ~** en liberté conditionnelle

parrot ['pærət] n perroquet m

parry ['pærɪ] vt (blow) esquiver

parsley ['pɑːslɪ] n persil m

parsnip ['pɑːsnɪp] n panais m

parson ['pɑːsn] n ecclésiastique m; (Church of England) pasteur m

part [pɑːt] n partie f; (of machine) pièce f; (THEATRE etc) rôle m; (of serial) épisode m; (US: in hair) raie f ♦ adv = **partly** ♦ vt séparer ♦ vi (people) se séparer; (crowd) s'ouvrir; **to take ~ in** participer à, prendre part à; **to take sth in good ~** prendre qch du bon côté; **to take sb's ~** prendre le parti de qn, prendre parti pour qn; **for my ~** en ce qui me concerne; **for the most ~** dans la plupart des cas; ~ **with** vt fus se séparer de; ~ **exchange** (BRIT) n: **in ~ exchange** en reprise

partial ['pɑːʃl] adj (not complete) partiel(le); **to be ~ to** avoir un faible pour

participate [pɑːˈtɪsɪpeɪt] *vi:* **to ~ (in)** participer (à), prendre part (à);
participation [pɑːtɪsɪˈpeɪʃən] *n* participation *f*

participle [ˈpɑːtɪsɪpl] *n* participe *m*

particle [ˈpɑːtɪkl] *n* particule *f*

particular [pəˈtɪkjʊləʳ] *adj* particulier(-ère); (*special*) spécial(e); (*fussy*) difficile; méticuleux(-euse); **~s** *npl* (*details*) détails *mpl*; (*personal*) nom, adresse *etc*; **in ~** en particulier; **~ly** *adv* particulièrement

parting [ˈpɑːtɪŋ] *n* séparation *f*; (*BRIT: in hair*) raie *f* ♦ *adj* d'adieu

partisan [pɑːtɪˈzæn] *n* partisan(e) ♦ *adj* partisan(e); de parti

partition [pɑːˈtɪʃən] *n* (*wall*) cloison *f*; (*POL*) partition *f*, division *f*

partly [ˈpɑːtlɪ] *adv* en partie, partiellement

partner [ˈpɑːtnəʳ] *n* partenaire *m/f*; (*in marriage*) conjoint(e); (*boyfriend, girlfriend*) ami(e); (*COMM*) associé(e); (*at dance*) cavalier(-ère); **~ship** *n* association *f*

partridge [ˈpɑːtrɪdʒ] *n* perdrix *f*

part-time [ˈpɑːtˈtaɪm] *adj, adv* à mi-temps, à temps partiel

party [ˈpɑːtɪ] *n* (*POL*) parti *m*; (*group*) groupe *m*; (*LAW*) partie *f*; (*celebration*) réception *f*; soirée *f*; fête *f* ♦ *cpd* (*POL*) de ou du parti; **~ dress** *n* robe habillée

pass [pɑːs] *vt* passer; (*place*) passer devant; (*friend*) croiser; (*overtake*) dépasser; (*exam*) être reçu(e) à, réussir; (*approve*) approuver, accepter ♦ *vi* passer; (*SCOL*) être reçu(e) or admis(e), réussir ♦ *n* (*permit*) laissez-passer *m inv*; carte *f* d'accès or d'abonnement; (*in mountains*) col *m*; (*SPORT*) passe *f*; (*SCOL: also: ~ mark*): **to get a ~** être reçu(e) (sans mention); **to make a ~ at sb** (*inf*) faire des avances à qn; **~ away** *vi* mourir; **~ by** *vi* passer ♦ *vt* négliger; **~ on** *vt* (*news, object*) transmettre; (*illness*) passer; **~ out** *vi* s'évanouir; **~ up** *vt* (*opportunity*) laisser passer; **~able** *adj* (*road*) praticable; (*work*) acceptable

passage [ˈpæsɪdʒ] *n* (*also: ~way*) couloir *m*; (*gen, in book*) passage *m*; (*by boat*) traversée *f*

passbook [ˈpɑːsbʊk] *n* livret *m*

passenger [ˈpæsɪndʒəʳ] *n* passager(-ère)

passer-by [pɑːsəˈbaɪ] (*pl* **~s-~**) *n* passant(e)

passing [ˈpɑːsɪŋ] *adj* (*fig*) passager(-ère); **in ~** en passant; **~ place** *n* (*AUT*) aire *f* de croisement

passion [ˈpæʃən] *n* passion *f*; **~ate** *adj* passionné(e)

passive [ˈpæsɪv] *adj* (*also LING*) passif(-ive); **~ smoking** *n* tabagisme *m* passif

Passover [ˈpɑːsəʊvəʳ] *n* Pâque *f* (*juive*)

passport [ˈpɑːspɔːt] *n* passeport *m*;

~ control *n* contrôle *m* des passeports; **~ office** *n* bureau *m* de délivrance des passeports

password [ˈpɑːswɜːd] *n* mot *m* de passe

past [pɑːst] *prep* (*in front of*) devant; (*further than*) au delà de, plus loin que; après; (*later than*) après ♦ *adj* passé(e); (*president etc*) ancien(ne) ♦ *n* passé *m*; **he's ~ forty** il a dépassé la quarantaine, il a plus de or passé quarante ans; **for the ~ few/3 days** depuis quelques/3 jours; ces derniers/3 derniers jours; **ten/quarter ~ eight** huit heures dix/un or et quart

pasta [ˈpæstə] *n* pâtes *fpl*

paste [peɪst] *n* pâte *f*; (*meat ~*) pâté *m* (à tartiner); (*tomato ~*) purée *f*, concentré *m*; (*glue*) colle *f* (de pâte) ♦ *vt* coller

pasteurized [ˈpæstʃəraɪzd] *adj* pasteurisé(e)

pastille [ˈpæstɪl] *n* pastille *f*

pastime [ˈpɑːstaɪm] *n* passe-temps *m inv*

pastry [ˈpeɪstrɪ] *n* pâte *f*; (*cake*) pâtisserie *f*

pasture [ˈpɑːstʃəʳ] *n* pâturage *m*

pasty [*n* ˈpæstɪ, *adj* ˈpeɪstɪ] *n* petit pâté (en croûte) ♦ *adj* (*complexion*) terreux(-euse)

pat [pæt] *vt* tapoter; (*dog*) caresser

patch [pætʃ] *n* (*of material*) pièce *f*; (*eye ~*) cache *m*; (*spot*) tache *f*; (*on tyre*) rustine *f* ♦ *vt* (*clothes*) rapiécer; (*to go through*) **a bad ~** (passer par) une période difficile; **~ up** *vt* réparer (grossièrement); **to ~ up a quarrel** se raccommoder; **~y** *adj* inégal(e); (*incomplete*) fragmentaire

pâté [ˈpæteɪ] *n* pâté *m*, terrine *f*

patent [ˈpeɪtnt] *n* brevet *m* (d'invention) ♦ *vt* faire breveter ♦ *adj* patent(e), manifeste; **~ leather** *n* cuir verni

paternal [pəˈtɜːnl] *adj* paternel(le)

path [pɑːθ] *n* chemin *m*, sentier *m*; (*in garden*) allée *f*; (*trajectory*) trajectoire *f*

pathetic [pəˈθetɪk] *adj* (*pitiful*) pitoyable; (*very bad*) lamentable, minable

pathological [pæθəˈlɒdʒɪkl] *adj* pathologique

pathway [ˈpɑːθweɪ] *n* sentier *m*, passage *m*

patience [ˈpeɪʃns] *n* patience *f*; (*BRIT: CARDS*) réussite *f*

patient [ˈpeɪʃnt] *n* malade *m/f*; (*of dentist etc*) patient(e) ♦ *adj* patient(e)

patio [ˈpætɪəʊ] *n* patio *m*

patriotic [pætrɪˈɒtɪk] *adj* patriotique; (*person*) patriote

patrol [pəˈtrəʊl] *n* patrouille *f* ♦ *vt* patrouiller dans; **~ car** *n* voiture *f* de police; **~man** (*irreg*) (*US*) *n* agent *m* de police

patron [ˈpeɪtrən] *n* (*in shop*) client(e); (*of charity*) patron(ne); **~ of the arts** mécène *m*; **~ize** [ˈpætrənaɪz] *vt* (*pej*) traiter avec condescendance; (*shop, club*) être (un) client or un habitué de

patter ['pætər] n crépitement m, tapotement m; (sales talk) boniment m

pattern ['pætən] n (design) motif m; (SEWING) patron m

pauper ['pɔ:pər] n indigent(e)

pause [pɔ:z] n pause f, arrêt m ♦ vi faire une pause, s'arrêter

pave [peɪv] vt paver, daller; **to ~ the way for** ouvrir la voie à

pavement ['peɪvmənt] (BRIT) n trottoir m

pavilion [pə'vɪlɪən] n pavillon m; tente f

paving ['peɪvɪŋ] n (material) pavé m, dalle f; **~ stone** n pavé m

paw [pɔ:] n patte f

pawn [pɔ:n] n (CHESS, also fig) pion m ♦ vt mettre en gage; **~broker** n prêteur m sur gages; **~shop** n mont-de-piété m

pay [peɪ] (pt, pp **paid**) n salaire m; paie f ♦ vt payer ♦ vi payer; (be profitable) être rentable; **to ~ attention (to)** prêter attention (à); **to ~ sb a visit** rendre visite à qn; **to ~ one's respects to sb** présenter ses respects à qn; **~ back** vt rembourser; **~ for** vt fus payer; **~ in** vt verser; **~ off** vt régler, acquitter; (person) rembourser ♦ vi (scheme, decision) se révéler payant(e); **~ up** vt (money) payer; **~able** adj: **~able to sb** (cheque) à l'ordre de qn; **~ee** [peɪ'i:] n bénéficiaire m/f; **~ envelope** (US) n = pay packet; **~ment** n paiement m; règlement m; monthly **~ment** mensualité f; **~ packet** (BRIT) n paie f; **~ phone** n cabine f téléphonique, téléphone public; **~roll** n registre m du personnel; **~ slip** n bulletin m de paie; **~ television** n chaînes fpl payantes

PC n abbr = **personal computer**

p.c. abbr = **per cent**

pea [pi:] n (petit) pois

peace [pi:s] n paix f; (calm) calme m, tranquillité f; **~ful** adj paisible, calme

peach [pi:tʃ] n pêche f

peacock ['pi:kɔk] n paon m

peak [pi:k] n (mountain) pic m, cime f; (of cap) visière f; (fig: highest level) maximum m; (: of career, fame) apogée m; **~ hours** npl heures fpl de pointe

peal [pi:l] n (of bells) carillon m; **~ of laughter** éclat m de rire

peanut ['pi:nʌt] n arachide f, cacahuète f; **~ butter** n beurre m de cacahuète

pear [peər] n poire f

pearl [pə:l] n perle f

peasant ['peznt] n paysan(ne)

peat [pi:t] n tourbe f

pebble ['pebl] n caillou m, galet m

peck [pek] vt (also: **~ at**) donner un coup de bec à ♦ n coup m de bec; (kiss) bise f; **~ing order** n ordre m des préséances; **~ish** (BRIT: inf) adj: **I feel ~ish** je mangerais bien quelque chose

peculiar [pɪ'kju:lɪər] adj étrange, bizarre, curieux(-euse); **~ to** particulier(-ère) à

pedal ['pedl] n pédale f ♦ vi pédaler

pedantic [pɪ'dæntɪk] adj pédant(e)

peddler ['pedlər] n (of drugs) revendeur(-euse)

pedestal ['pedəstl] n piédestal m

pedestrian [pɪ'destrɪən] n piéton m; **~ crossing** (BRIT) n passage clouté; **~ized** adj: **a ~ized street** une rue piétonne

pediatrics [pi:dɪ'ætrɪks] (US) n = **paediatrics**

pedigree ['pedɪgri:] n ascendance f; (of animal) pedigree m ♦ cpd (animal) de race

pee [pi:] (inf) vi faire pipi, pisser

peek [pi:k] vi jeter un coup d'œil (furtif)

peel [pi:l] n pelure f, épluchure f; (of orange, lemon) écorce f ♦ vt peler, éplucher ♦ vi (paint etc) s'écailler; (wallpaper) se décoller; (skin) peler

peep [pi:p] n (BRIT: look) coup d'œil furtif; (sound) pépiement m ♦ vi (BRIT) jeter un coup d'œil (furtif); **~ out** (BRIT) vi se montrer (furtivement); **~hole** n judas m

peer [pɪər] vi: **to ~ at** regarder attentivement, scruter ♦ n (noble) pair m; (equal) pair, égal(e); **~age** ['pɪərɪdʒ] n pairie f

peeved [pi:vd] adj irrité(e), fâché(e)

peg [peg] n (for coat etc) patère f; (BRIT: also: clothes **~**) pince f à linge

Pekin(g)ese [pi:kɪ'ni:z] n (dog) pékinois m

pelican ['pelɪkən] n pélican m; **~ crossing** (BRIT) n (AUT) feu m à commande manuelle

pellet ['pelɪt] n boulette f; (of lead) plomb m

pelt [pelt] vt: **to ~ sb (with)** bombarder qn (de) ♦ vi (rain) tomber à seaux; (inf: run) courir à toutes jambes ♦ n peau f

pelvis ['pelvɪs] n bassin m

pen [pen] n (for writing) stylo m; (for sheep) parc m

penal ['pi:nl] adj pénal(e); (system, colony) pénitentiaire; **~ize** ['pi:nəlaɪz] vt pénaliser

penalty ['penltɪ] n pénalité f; sanction f; (fine) amende f; (SPORT) pénalisation f; (FOOTBALL) penalty m; (RUGBY) pénalité f

penance ['penəns] n pénitence f

pence [pens] (BRIT) npl of **penny**

pencil ['pensl] n crayon m; **~ case** n trousse f (d'écolier); **~ sharpener** n taille-crayon(s) m inv

pendant ['pendnt] n pendentif m

pending ['pendɪŋ] prep en attendant ♦ adj en suspens

pendulum ['pendjuləm] n (of clock) balancier m

penetrate ['penɪtreɪt] vt pénétrer dans; pénétrer

penfriend ['penfrend] (BRIT) n correspondant(e)

penguin ['peŋgwin] n pingouin m
penicillin [peni'sılın] n pénicilline f
peninsula [pə'nınsjulə] n péninsule f
penis ['piːnɪs] n pénis m, verge f
penitentiary [penɪ'tenʃərɪ] n prison f
penknife ['pennaɪf] n canif m
pen name n nom m de plume, pseudonyme m
penniless ['penɪlɪs] adj sans le sou
penny ['penɪ] n (pl pennies or (BRIT) pence) n penny m
penpal ['penpæl] n correspondant(e)
pension ['penʃən] n pension f; (from company) retraite f; **~er** (BRIT) n retraité(e); **~ fund** n caisse f de pension; **~ plan** n plan m de retraite
pentathlon [pen'tæθlən] n pentathlon m
Pentecost ['pentıkɔst] n Pentecôte f
penthouse ['penthaus] n appartement m (de luxe) (en attique)
pent-up ['pentʌp] adj (feelings) refoulé(e)
penultimate [pe'nʌltımət] adj avant-dernier(-ère)
people ['piːpl] npl gens mpl; personnes fpl; (inhabitants) population f; (POL) peuple m ♦ n (nation, race) peuple m; **several ~ came** plusieurs personnes sont venues; **~ say that ...** on dit que ...
pep up ['pep-] (inf) vt remonter
pepper ['pepər] n poivre m; (vegetable) poivron m ♦ vt (fig): **to ~ with** bombarder de; **~ mill** n moulin à poivre; **~mint** n (sweet) pastille f de menthe
peptalk ['peptɔːk] (inf) n (petit) discours d'encouragement
per [pəːr] prep par; **~ hour** (miles etc) à l'heure; (fee) (de) l'heure; **~ kilo** etc le kilo etc; **~ annum** par an; **~ capita** par personne, par habitant
perceive [pə'siːv] vt percevoir; (notice) remarquer, s'apercevoir de
per cent adv pour cent; **percentage** n pourcentage m
perception [pə'sepʃən] n perception f; (insight) perspicacité f
perceptive [pə'septıv] adj pénétrant(e); (person) perspicace
perch [pəːtʃ] n (fish) perche f; (for bird) perchoir m ♦ vi: **to ~ on** se percher sur
percolator ['pəːkəleɪtər] n cafetière f (électrique)
percussion [pə'kʌʃən] n percussion f
perennial [pə'renıəl] adj perpétuel(le); (BOT) vivace
perfect [adj, n 'pəːfıkt, vb pə'fɛkt] adj parfait(e) ♦ n (also: **~ tense**) parfait m ♦ vt parfaire; mettre au point; **~ly** adv parfaitement
perforate ['pəːfəreɪt] vt perforer, percer;

perforation [pəːfə'reɪʃən] n perforation f
perform [pə'fɔːm] vt (carry out) exécuter; (concert etc) jouer, donner ♦ vi jouer; **~ance** n représentation f, spectacle m; (of an artist) interprétation f; (SPORT) performance f; (of car, engine) fonctionnement m; (of company, economy) résultats mpl; **~er** n artiste m/f, interprète m/f
perfume ['pəːfjuːm] n parfum m
perhaps [pə'hæps] adv peut-être
peril ['perıl] n péril m
perimeter [pə'rımıtər] n périmètre m
period ['pıərıəd] n période f; (of history) époque f; (SCOL) cours m; (full stop) point m; (MED) règles fpl ♦ adj (costume, furniture) d'époque; **~ic(al)** [pıərı'ɔdık(l)] adj périodique; **~ical** [pıərı'ɔdıkl] n périodique m
peripheral [pə'rıfərəl] adj périphérique ♦ n (COMPUT) périphérique m
perish ['perıʃ] vi périr; (decay) se détériorer; **~able** adj périssable
perjury ['pəːdʒərɪ] n parjure m, faux serment
perk [pəːk] n avantage m accessoire, à-côté m; **~ up** vi (cheer up) se ragaillardir; **~y** adj (cheerful) guilleret(te)
perm [pəːm] n (for hair) permanente f
permanent ['pəːmənənt] adj permanent(e)
permeate ['pəːmıeıt] vi s'infiltrer ♦ vt s'infiltrer dans; pénétrer
permissible [pə'mısıbl] adj permis(e), acceptable
permission [pə'mıʃən] n permission f, autorisation f
permissive [pə'mısıv] adj tolérant(e), permissif(-ive)
permit [n 'pəːmıt, vb pə'mıt] n permis m ♦ vt permettre
perpendicular [pəːpən'dıkjulər] adj perpendiculaire
perplex [pə'pleks] vt (person) rendre perplexe
persecute ['pəːsıkjuːt] vt persécuter
persevere [pəːsı'vıər] vi persévérer
Persian ['pəːʃən] adj persan(e) ♦ n (LING) persan m; **the ~ Gulf** le golfe Persique
persist [pə'sıst] vi: **to ~ (in doing)** persister or s'obstiner (à faire); **~ent** [pə'sıstənt] adj persistant(e), tenace; **~ent vegetative state** état m végétatif persistant
person ['pəːsn] n personne f; **in ~** en personne; **~al** adj personnel(le); **~al assistant** n secrétaire privé(e); **~al column** n annonces personnelles; **~al computer** n ordinateur personnel; **~ality** [pəːsə'nælıtı] n personnalité f; **~ally** adv personnellement; **to take sth ~ally** se sentir visé(e) (par qch); **~al organizer** n filofax m ®; **~al stereo** n Walkman ® m, baladeur m
personnel [pəːsə'nel] n personnel m
perspective [pə'spektıv] n perspective f; **to**

get things into ~ faire la part des choses

Perspex ® ['pəːspeks] n plexiglas ® m

perspiration [pəːspɪ'reɪʃən] n transpiration f

persuade [pə'sweɪd] vt: to ~ sb to do sth
persuader qn de faire qch; **persuasion**
[pə'sweɪʒən] n persuasion f; (creed) religion f

perverse [pə'vəːs] adj pervers(e); (contrary)
contrariant(e); **pervert** [n 'pəːvəːt, vb
pə'vəːt] n perverti(e) ♦ vt pervertir; (words)
déformer

pessimist ['pesɪmɪst] n pessimiste m/f; ~**ic**
[pesɪ'mɪstɪk] adj pessimiste

pest [pest] n animal m (or insecte m) nuisible;
(fig) fléau m

pester ['pestə'] vt importuner, harceler

pet [pet] n animal familier ♦ cpd (favourite)
favori(te) ♦ vt (stroke) caresser, câliner;
teacher's ~ chouchou m du professeur; ~ **hate**
bête noire

petal ['petl] n pétale m

peter out ['piːtə-] vi (stream, conversation)
tarir; (meeting) tourner court; (road) se
perdre

petite [pə'tiːt] adj menu(e)

petition [pə'tɪʃən] n pétition f

petrified ['petrɪfaɪd] adj (fig) mort(e) de peur

petrol ['petrəl] (BRIT) n essence f; **four-star** ~
super m; ~ **can** n bidon m à essence

petroleum [pə'trəʊlɪəm] n pétrole m

petrol: ~ **pump** (BRIT) n pompe f à essence;
~ **station** (BRIT) n station-service f; ~ **tank**
(BRIT) n réservoir m d'essence

petticoat ['petɪkəʊt] n combinaison f

petty ['petɪ] adj (mean) mesquin(e);
(unimportant) insignifiant(e), sans
importance; ~ **cash** n caisse f des dépenses
courantes; ~ **officer** n second-maître m

petulant ['petjulənt] adj boudeur(-euse),
irritable

pew [pjuː] n banc m (d'église)

pewter ['pjuːtə'] n étain m

phantom ['fæntəm] n fantôme m

pharmacy ['fɑːməsɪ] n pharmacie f

phase [feɪz] n phase f ♦ vt: to ~ sth in/out
introduire/supprimer qch progressivement

PhD abbr = Doctor of Philosophy ♦ n abbr
(title) ≈ docteur m (en droit ou lettres etc), ≈
doctorat m; (person) titulaire m/f d'un
doctorat

pheasant ['feznt] n faisan m

phenomenon [fə'nɔmɪnən] (pl **phenomena**)
n phénomène m

philosophical [fɪlə'sɔfɪkl] adj philosophique

philosophy [fɪ'lɔsəfɪ] n philosophie f

phobia ['fəʊbjə] n phobie f

phone [faun] n téléphone m ♦ vt téléphoner;
to be on the ~ avoir le téléphone; (be calling)
être au téléphone; ~ **back** vt, vi rappeler;
~ **up** vt téléphoner à ♦ vi téléphoner; ~ **bill**

n facture f de téléphone; ~ **book** n annuaire
m; ~ **booth**, ~ **box** (BRIT) n cabine f
téléphonique; ~ **call** n coup m de fil or de
téléphone; ~**card** n carte f de téléphone; ~-
in (BRIT) n (RADIO, TV) programme m à ligne
ouverte; ~ **number** n numéro m de
téléphone

phonetics [fə'netɪks] n phonétique f

phoney ['fəʊnɪ] adj faux (fausse), factice;
(person) pas franc (franche), poseur(-euse)

photo ['fəʊtəʊ] n photo f; ~**copier** n
photocopieuse f; ~**copy** n photocopie f ♦ vt
photocopier; ~**graph** n photographie f ♦ vt
photographier; ~**grapher** [fə'tɔɡrəfə'] n
photographe m/f; ~**graphy** [fə'tɔɡrəfɪ] n
photographie f

phrase [freɪz] n expression f; (LING) locution f
♦ vt exprimer; ~ **book** n recueil m
d'expressions (pour touristes)

physical ['fɪzɪkl] adj physique; ~ **education**
n éducation f physique; ~**ly** adv
physiquement

physician [fɪ'zɪʃən] n médecin m

physicist ['fɪzɪsɪst] n physicien(ne)

physics ['fɪzɪks] n physique f

physiotherapist [fɪzɪəʊ'θerəpɪst] n
kinésithérapeute m/f

physiotherapy [fɪzɪəʊ'θerəpɪ] n
kinésithérapie f

physique [fɪ'ziːk] n physique m; constitution
f

pianist ['piːənɪst] n pianiste m/f

piano [pɪ'ænəʊ] n piano m

pick [pɪk] n (tool: also: ~**axe**) pic m, pioche f
♦ vt choisir; (fruit etc) cueillir; (remove)
prendre; (lock) forcer; **take your** ~ faites votre
choix; **the** ~ **of** le (la) meilleur(e) de; **to**
~ **one's nose** se mettre les doigts dans le nez;
to ~ **one's teeth** se curer les dents; **to** ~ **a
quarrel with sb** chercher noise à qn; ~ **at** vt
fus: **to** ~ **at one's food** manger du bout des
dents, chipoter; ~ **on** vt fus (person) harceler;
~ **out** vt choisir; (distinguish) distinguer;
~ **up** vi (improve) s'améliorer ♦ vt ramasser;
(collect) passer prendre; (AUT: give lift to)
prendre, emmener; (learn) apprendre;
(RADIO) capter; **to** ~ **up speed** prendre de la
vitesse; **to** ~ **o.s. up** se relever

picket ['pɪkɪt] n (in strike) piquet m de grève
♦ vt mettre un piquet de grève devant

pickle ['pɪkl] n (also: ~**s**: as condiment) pickles
mpl; petits légumes macérés dans du vinaigre
♦ vt conserver dans du vinaigre or dans de la
saumure; **to be in a** ~ (mess) être dans le
pétrin

pickpocket ['pɪkpɔkɪt] n pickpocket m

pick-up ['pɪkʌp] n (small truck) pick-up m inv

picnic ['pɪknɪk] n pique-nique m

picture ['pɪktʃə'] n image f; (painting)

peinture f, tableau m; (*etching*) gravure f;
(*photograph*) photo(graphie) f; (*drawing*)
dessin m; (*film*) film m; (*fig*) description f;
tableau m ♦ vt se représenter; **the ~s** (*BRIT:
inf*) le cinéma; **~ book** n livre m d'images
picturesque [pɪktʃə'resk] *adj* pittoresque
pie [paɪ] n tourte f; (*of fruit*) tarte f; (*of meat*)
pâté m en croûte
piece [piːs] n morceau m; (*item*): **a ~ of
furniture/advice** un meuble/conseil ♦ vt: **to
~ together** rassembler; **to take to ~s**
démonter; (*bit by bit*) par bouts; **~work** n
travail m aux pièces
pie chart n graphique m circulaire,
camembert m
pier [pɪə'] n jetée f
pierce [pɪəs] vt percer, transpercer; **~d** *adj*
(*ears etc*) percé(e)
pig [pɪg] n cochon m, porc m
pigeon ['pɪdʒən] n pigeon m; **~hole** n casier
m
piggy bank ['pɪgɪ-] n tirelire f
pig: ~headed *adj* entêté(e), têtu(e); **~let** n
porcelet m, petit cochon; **~skin** n peau m de
porc; **~sty** n porcherie f; **~tail** n natte f,
tresse f
pike [paɪk] n (*fish*) brochet m
pilchard ['pɪltʃəd] n pilchard m (*sorte de
sardine*)
pile [paɪl] n (*pillar, of books*) pile f; (*heap*) tas
m; (*of carpet*) poils mpl ♦ vt (*also: ~ up*)
empiler, entasser ♦ vi (*also: ~ up*) s'entasser,
s'accumuler; **~ into** (*car*) s'entasser dans;
~s npl hémorroïdes fpl; **~-up** n (*AUT*)
télescopage m, collision f en série
pilfering ['pɪlfərɪŋ] n chapardage m
pilgrim ['pɪlgrɪm] n pèlerin m
pill [pɪl] n pilule f
pillage ['pɪlɪdʒ] vt piller
pillar ['pɪlə'] n pilier m; **~ box** (*BRIT*) n boîte f
aux lettres (*publique*)
pillion ['pɪljən] n: **to ride ~** (*on motorcycle*)
monter derrière
pillow ['pɪləʊ] n oreiller m; **~case** n taie f
d'oreiller
pilot ['paɪlət] n pilote m ♦ cpd (*scheme etc*)
pilote, expérimental(e) ♦ vt piloter; **~ light** n
veilleuse f
pimp [pɪmp] n souteneur m, maquereau m
pimple ['pɪmpl] n bouton m
pin [pɪn] n épingle f; (*TECH*) cheville f ♦ vt
épingler; **~s and needles** fourmis fpl; **to ~ sb
down** (*fig*) obliger qn à répondre; **to ~ sth on
sb** (*fig*) mettre qch sur le dos de qn
PIN n *abbr* (= *personal identification
number*) numéro m d'identification personnel
pinafore ['pɪnəfɔː'] n tablier m
pinball ['pɪnbɔːl] n flipper m

pincers ['pɪnsəz] npl tenailles fpl; (*of crab etc*)
pinces fpl
pinch [pɪntʃ] n (*of salt etc*) pincée f ♦ vt
pincer; (*inf: steal*) piquer, chiper; **at a ~** à la
rigueur
pincushion ['pɪnkʊʃən] n pelote f à épingles
pine [paɪn] n (*also: ~ tree*) pin m ♦ vi: **to ~ for**
s'ennuyer de, désirer ardemment; **~ away** vi
dépérir
pineapple ['paɪnæpl] n ananas m
ping [pɪŋ] n (*noise*) tintement m; **~-pong** ®
n ping-pong ® m
pink [pɪŋk] *adj* rose ♦ n (*colour*) rose m; (*BOT*)
œillet m, mignardise f
PIN (number) ['pɪn(-)] n code m
confidentiel
pinpoint ['pɪnpɔɪnt] vt indiquer or localiser
(avec précision); (*problem*) mettre le doigt
sur
pint [paɪnt] n pinte f (*BRIT = 0.57l; US = 0.47l*);
(*BRIT: inf*) ≈ demi m
pioneer [paɪə'nɪə'] n pionnier m
pious ['paɪəs] *adj* pieux(-euse)
pip [pɪp] n (*seed*) pépin m; **the ~s** npl (*BRIT:
time signal on radio*) le(s) top(s) sonore(s)
pipe [paɪp] n tuyau m, conduite f; (*for
smoking*) pipe f ♦ vt amener par tuyau; **~s** npl
(*also: bagpipes*) cornemuse f; **~ cleaner** n
cure-pipe m; **~ dream** n chimère f, château
m en Espagne; **~line** n pipe-line m; **~r** n
joueur(-euse) de cornemuse
piping ['paɪpɪŋ] *adv*: **~ hot** très chaud(e)
pique ['piːk] n dépit m
pirate ['paɪərət] n pirate m; **~d** *adj* pirate
Pisces ['paɪsiːz] n les Poissons mpl
piss [pɪs] (*inf!*) vi pisser; **~ed** (*inf!*) *adj* (*drunk*)
bourré(e)
pistol ['pɪstl] n pistolet m
piston ['pɪstən] n piston m
pit [pɪt] n trou m, fosse f; (*also: coal ~*) puits
m de mine; (*quarry*) carrière f ♦ vt: **to ~ one's
wits against sb** se mesurer à qn; **~s** npl (*AUT*)
aire f de service
pitch [pɪtʃ] n (*MUS*) ton m; (*BRIT: SPORT*)
terrain m; (*tar*) poix f; (*fig*) degré m; point m
♦ vt (*throw*) lancer ♦ vi (*fall*) tomber; **to ~ a
tent** dresser une tente; **~-black** *adj* noir(e)
(comme du cirage); **~ed battle** n bataille
rangée
pitfall ['pɪtfɔːl] n piège m
pith [pɪθ] n (*of orange etc*) intérieur m de
l'écorce; **~y** *adj* piquant(e)
pitiful ['pɪtɪful] *adj* (*touching*) pitoyable
pitiless ['pɪtɪlɪs] *adj* impitoyable
pittance ['pɪtns] n salaire m de misère
pity ['pɪtɪ] n pitié f ♦ vt plaindre; **what a ~!**
quel dommage!
pizza ['piːtsə] n pizza f
placard ['plækɑːd] n affiche f; (*in march*)

pancarte f
placate [plə'keɪt] vt apaiser, calmer
place [pleɪs] n endroit m, lieu m; (proper position, job, rank, seat) place f; (home): **at/to his ~** chez lui ♦ vt (object) placer, mettre; (identify) situer; reconnaître; **to take ~** avoir lieu; **out of ~** (not suitable) déplacé(e), inopportun(e); **to change ~s with sb** changer de place avec qn; **in the first ~** d'abord, en premier
plague [pleɪg] n fléau m; (MED) peste f ♦ vt (fig) tourmenter
plaice [pleɪs] n inv carrelet m
plaid [plæd] n tissu écossais
plain [pleɪn] adj (in one colour) uni(e); (simple) simple; (clear) clair(e), évident(e); (not handsome) quelconque, ordinaire ♦ adv franchement, carrément ♦ n plaine f; **~ chocolate** n chocolat m à croquer; **~ clothes** adj (police officer) en civil; **~ly** adv clairement; (frankly) carrément, sans détours
plaintiff ['pleɪntɪf] n plaignant(e)
plait [plæt] n tresse f, natte f
plan [plæn] n plan m; (scheme) projet m ♦ vt (think in advance) projeter; (prepare) organiser; (house) dresser les plans de, concevoir ♦ vi faire des projets; **to ~ to do** prévoir de faire
plane [pleɪn] n (AVIAT) avion m; (ART, MATH etc) plan m; (fig) niveau m, plan; (tool) rabot m; (also: **~ tree**) platane m ♦ vt raboter
planet ['plænɪt] n planète f
plank [plæŋk] n planche f
planner ['plænər] n planificateur(-trice); (town ~) urbaniste m/f
planning ['plænɪŋ] n planification f; **family ~** planning familial; **~ permission** n permis m de construire
plant [plɑːnt] n plante f; (machinery) matériel m; (factory) usine f ♦ vt planter; (bomb) poser; (microphone, incriminating evidence) cacher
plaster ['plɑːstər] n plâtre m; (also: **~ of Paris**) plâtre à mouler; (BRIT: also: **sticking ~**) pansement adhésif ♦ vt plâtrer; (cover): **to ~ with** couvrir de; **~ed** (inf) adj soûl(e)
plastic ['plæstɪk] n plastique m ♦ adj (made of ~) en plastique; **~ bag** n sac m en plastique
Plasticine ® ['plæstɪsiːn] n pâte f à modeler
plastic surgery n chirurgie f esthétique
plate [pleɪt] n (dish) assiette f; (in book) gravure f, planche f; (dental ~) dentier m
plateau ['plætəʊ] n (pl **~s** or **~x**) plateau m
plate glass n verre m (de vitrine)
platform ['plætfɔːm] n plate-forme f; (at meeting) tribune f; (stage) estrade f; (RAIL) quai m
platinum ['plætɪnəm] n platine m
platter ['plætər] n plat m

plausible ['plɔːzɪbl] adj plausible; (person) convaincant(e)
play [pleɪ] n (THEATRE) pièce f (de théâtre) ♦ vt (game) jouer à; (team, opponent) jouer contre; (instrument) jouer de; (part, piece of music, note) jouer; (record etc) passer ♦ vi jouer; **to ~ safe** ne prendre aucun risque; **~ down** vt minimiser; **~ up** vi (cause trouble) faire des siennes; **~boy** n playboy m; **~er** n joueur(-euse); (THEATRE) acteur(-trice); (MUS) musicien(ne); **~ful** adj enjoué(e); **~ground** n cour f de récréation; (in park) aire f de jeux; **~group** n garderie f; **~ing card** n carte f à jouer; **~ing field** n terrain m de sport; **~mate** n camarade m/f, copain (copine); **~-off** n (SPORT) belle f; **~pen** n parc m (pour bébé); **~thing** n jouet m; **~time** n récréation f; **~wright** n dramaturge m
plc abbr (= public limited company) SARL f
plea [pliː] n (request) appel m; (LAW) défense f
plead [pliːd] vt plaider; (give as excuse) invoquer ♦ vi (LAW) plaider; (beg): **to ~ with sb** implorer qn
pleasant ['plɛznt] adj agréable; **~ries** npl (polite remarks) civilités fpl
please [pliːz] excl s'il te (or vous) plaît ♦ vt plaire à ♦ vi plaire; (think fit): **do as you ~** faites comme il vous plaira; **~ yourself!** à ta (or votre) guise!; **~d** adj: **~d (with)** content(e) (de); **~d to meet you** enchanté (de faire votre connaissance); **pleasing** adj plaisant(e), qui fait plaisir
pleasure ['plɛʒər] n plaisir m; **"it's a ~"** "je vous en prie"
pleat [pliːt] n pli m
pledge [plɛdʒ] n (promise) promesse f ♦ vt engager; promettre
plentiful ['plɛntɪful] adj abondant(e), copieux(-euse)
plenty ['plɛntɪ] n: **~ of** beaucoup de; (bien) assez de
pliable ['plaɪəbl] adj flexible; (person) malléable
pliers ['plaɪəz] npl pinces fpl
plight [plaɪt] n situation f critique
plimsolls ['plɪmsəlz] (BRIT) npl chaussures fpl de tennis, tennis mpl
plinth [plɪnθ] n (of statue) socle m
P.L.O. n abbr (= Palestine Liberation Organization) OLP f
plod [plɒd] vi avancer péniblement; (fig) peiner
plonk [plɒŋk] (inf) n (BRIT: wine) pinard m, piquette f ♦ vt: **to ~ sth down** poser brusquement qch
plot [plɒt] n complot m, conspiration f; (of story, play) intrigue f; (of land) lot m de terrain, lopin m ♦ vt (sb's downfall)

comploter; (*mark out*) pointer; relever, déterminer ♦ *vi* comploter

plough [plaʊ] (*US* **plow**) *n* charrue *f* ♦ *vt* (*earth*) labourer; **to ~ money into** investir dans; **~ through** *vt fus* (*snow etc*) avancer péniblement dans; **~man's lunch** (*BRIT*) *n* assiette froide avec du pain, du fromage et des pickles

ploy [plɔɪ] *n* stratagème *m*

pluck [plʌk] *vt* (*fruit*) cueillir; (*musical instrument*) pincer; (*bird*) plumer; (*eyebrow*) épiler ♦ *n* courage *m*, cran *m*; **to ~ up courage** prendre son courage à deux mains

plug [plʌg] *n* (*ELEC*) prise *f* de courant; (*stopper*) bouchon *m*, bonde *f*; (*AUT: also:* **spark(ing) ~**) bougie *f* ♦ *vt* (*hole*) boucher; (*inf: advertise*) faire du battage pour; **~ in** *vt* (*ELEC*) brancher

plum [plʌm] *n* (*fruit*) prune *f* ♦ *cpd*: **~ job** (*inf*) travail *m* en or

plumb [plʌm] *vt*: **to ~ the depths** (*fig*) toucher le fond (du désespoir)

plumber ['plʌmər] *n* plombier *m*

plumbing ['plʌmɪŋ] *n* (*trade*) plomberie *f*; (*piping*) tuyauterie *f*

plummet ['plʌmɪt] *vi*: **to ~ (down)** plonger, dégringoler

plump [plʌmp] *adj* rondelet(te), dodu(e), bien en chair ♦ *vi*: **to ~ for** (*inf: choose*) se décider pour

plunder ['plʌndər] *n* pillage *m*; (*loot*) butin *m* ♦ *vt* piller

plunge [plʌndʒ] *n* plongeon *m*; (*fig*) chute *f* ♦ *vt* plonger ♦ *vi* (*dive*) plonger; (*fall*) tomber, dégringoler; **to take the ~** se jeter à l'eau; **plunging** ['plʌndʒɪŋ] *adj*: **plunging neckline** décolleté plongeant

pluperfect [pluː'pɜːfɪkt] *n* plus-que-parfait *m*

plural ['plʊərl] *adj* pluriel(le) ♦ *n* pluriel *m*

plus [plʌs] *n* (*also:* **~ sign**) signe *m* plus ♦ *prep* plus; **ten/twenty ~** plus de dix/vingt

plush [plʌʃ] *adj* somptueux(-euse)

ply [plaɪ] *vt* (*a trade*) exercer ♦ *vi* (*ship*) faire la navette ♦ *n* (*of wool, rope*) fil *m*, brin *m*; **to ~ sb with drink** donner continuellement à boire à qn; **to ~ sb with questions** presser qn de questions; **~wood** *n* contre-plaqué *m*

PM *abbr* = **Prime Minister**

p.m. *adv abbr* (= *post meridiem*) de l'après-midi

pneumatic drill [njuː'mætɪk-] *n* marteau-piqueur *m*

pneumonia [njuː'məʊnɪə] *n* pneumonie *f*

poach [pəʊtʃ] *vt* (*cook*) pocher; (*steal*) pêcher (*or* chasser) sans permis ♦ *vi* braconner; **~ed egg** *n* œuf poché; **~er** *n* braconnier *m*

P.O. box *n abbr* = **post office box**

pocket ['pɔkɪt] *n* poche *f* ♦ *vt* empocher; **to be out of ~** (*BRIT*) en être de sa poche;

~book (*US*) *n* (*wallet*) portefeuille *m*; **~ calculator** *n* calculette *f*; **~ knife** *n* canif *m*; **~ money** *n* argent *m* de poche

pod [pɔd] *n* cosse *f*

podgy ['pɔdʒɪ] *adj* rondelet(te)

podiatrist [pɔ'diːətrɪst] (*US*) *n* pédicure *m/f*, podologue *m/f*

poem ['pəʊɪm] *n* poème *m*

poet ['pəʊɪt] *n* poète *m/f*; **~ic** [pəʊ'etɪk] *adj* poétique; **~ry** ['pəʊɪtrɪ] *n* poésie *f*

poignant ['pɔɪnjənt] *adj* poignant(e); (*sharp*) vif (vive)

point [pɔɪnt] *n* point *m*; (*tip*) pointe *f*; (*in time*) moment *m*; (*in space*) endroit *m*; (*subject, idea*) point, sujet *m*; (*purpose*) sens *m*; (*ELEC*) prise *f*; (*also:* **decimal ~**): **2 ~ 3 (2.3)** 2 virgule 3 (2,3) ♦ *vt* (*show*) indiquer; (*gun etc*): **to ~ sth at** braquer *or* diriger qch sur ♦ *vi*: **to ~ at** montrer du doigt; **~s** *npl* (*AUT*) vis platinées; (*RAIL*) aiguillage *m*; **to be on the ~ of doing sth** être sur le point de faire qch; **to make a ~ of doing** ne pas manquer de faire; **to get the ~** comprendre, saisir; **to miss the ~** ne pas comprendre; **to come to the ~** en venir au fait; **there's no ~ (in doing)** cela ne sert à rien (de faire); **~ out** *vt* faire remarquer, souligner; **~ to** *vt fus* (*fig*) indiquer; **~-blank** *adv* (*fig*) catégoriquement; (*also:* **at ~-blank range**) à bout portant; **~ed** *adj* (*shape*) pointu(e); (*remark*) plein(e) de sous-entendus; **~er** *n* (*needle*) aiguille *f*; (*piece of advice*) conseil *m*; (*clue*) indice *m*; **~less** *adj* inutile, vain(e); **~ of view** *n* point *m* de vue

poise [pɔɪz] *n* (*composure*) calme *m*

poison ['pɔɪzn] *n* poison *m* ♦ *vt* empoisonner; **~ous** *adj* (*snake*) venimeux(-euse); (*plant*) vénéneux(-euse); (*fumes etc*) toxique

poke [pəʊk] *vt* (*fire*) tisonner; (*jab with finger, stick etc*) piquer; pousser du doigt; (*put*): **to ~ sth in(to)** fourrer *or* enfoncer qch dans; **~ about** *vi* fureter; **~r** *n* tisonnier *m*; (*CARDS*) poker *m*

poky ['pəʊkɪ] *adj* exigu(ë)

Poland ['pəʊlənd] *n* Pologne *f*

polar ['pəʊlər] *adj* polaire; **~ bear** *n* ours blanc

Pole [pəʊl] *n* Polonais(e)

pole [pəʊl] *n* poteau *m*; (*of wood*) mât *m*, perche *f*; (*GEO*) pôle *m*; **~ bean** (*US*) *n* haricot *m* (à rames); **~ vault** *n* saut *m* à la perche

police [pə'liːs] *npl* police *f* ♦ *vt* maintenir l'ordre dans; **~ car** *n* voiture *f* de police; **~man** (*irreg*) *n* agent *m* de police, policier *m*; **~ station** *n* commissariat *m* de police; **~woman** (*irreg*) *n* femme-agent *f*

policy ['pɔlɪsɪ] *n* politique *f*; (*also:* **insurance**

~) police f (d'assurance)

polio ['pəʊlɪəʊ] n polio f

Polish ['pəʊlɪʃ] adj polonais(e) ♦ n (LING) polonais m

polish ['pɒlɪʃ] n (for shoes) cirage m; (for floor) cire f, encaustique f; (shine) éclat m, poli m; (fig: refinement) raffinement m ♦ vt (put ~ on shoes, wood) cirer; (make shiny) astiquer, faire briller; ~ **off** (inf) vt (food) liquider; **~ed** adj (fig) raffiné(e)

polite [pə'laɪt] adj poli(e); **in ~ society** dans la bonne société; **~ly** adv poliment; **~ness** n politesse f

political [pə'lɪtɪkl] adj politique; **~ly correct** adj politiquement correct(e)

politician [pɒlɪ'tɪʃən] n homme m/femme f politique

politics ['pɒlɪtɪks] npl politique f

poll [pəʊl] n scrutin m, vote m; (also: **opinion ~**) sondage m (d'opinion) ♦ vt obtenir

pollen ['pɒlən] n pollen m

polling day ['pəʊlɪŋ-] (BRIT) n jour m des élections

polling station (BRIT) n bureau m de vote

pollute [pə'luːt] vt polluer; **pollution** n pollution f

polo ['pəʊləʊ] n polo m; **~-necked** adj à col roulé; **~ shirt** n polo m

polyester [pɒlɪ'estər] n polyester m

polystyrene [pɒlɪ'staɪriːn] n polystyrène m

polythene ['pɒlɪθiːn] n polyéthylène m; **~ bag** n sac m en plastique

pomegranate ['pɒmɪɡrænɪt] n grenade f

pomp [pɒmp] n pompe f, faste f, apparat m; **~ous** adj pompeux(-euse)

pond [pɒnd] n étang m; mare f

ponder ['pɒndər] vt considérer, peser; **~ous** adj pesant(e), lourd(e)

pong [pɒŋ] (BRIT: inf) n puanteur f

pony ['pəʊnɪ] n poney m; **~tail** n queue f de cheval; **~ trekking** (BRIT) n randonnée f à cheval

poodle ['puːdl] n caniche m

pool [puːl] n (of rain) flaque f; (pond) mare f; (also: **swimming ~**) piscine f; (billiards) poule f ♦ vt mettre en commun; **~s** npl (football ~s) ≈ loto sportif

poor [puər] adj pauvre; (mediocre) médiocre, faible, mauvais(e) ♦ npl: **the ~** les pauvres mpl; **~ly** adj souffrant(e), malade ♦ adv mal; médiocrement

pop [pɒp] n (MUS) musique f pop; (drink) boisson gazeuse; (US: inf: father) papa m; (noise) bruit sec ♦ vt (put) mettre (rapidement) ♦ vi éclater; (cork) sauter; **~ in** vi entrer en passant; **~ out** vi sortir (brièvement); **~ up** vi apparaître, surgir; **~corn** n pop-corn m

pope [pəʊp] n pape m

poplar ['pɒplər] n peuplier m

popper ['pɒpər] (BRIT: inf) n bouton-pression m

poppy ['pɒpɪ] n coquelicot m; pavot m

Popsicle ® ['pɒpsɪkl] (US) n esquimau m (glace)

popular ['pɒpjʊlər] adj populaire; (fashionable) à la mode

population [pɒpjʊ'leɪʃən] n population f

porcelain ['pɔːslɪn] n porcelaine f

porch [pɔːtʃ] n porche m; (US) véranda f

porcupine ['pɔːkjʊpaɪn] n porc-épic m

pore [pɔːr] n pore m ♦ vi: **to ~ over** s'absorber dans, être plongé(e) dans

pork [pɔːk] n porc m

porn [pɔːn] (inf) adj, n porno m

pornographic [pɔːnə'ɡræfɪk] adj pornographique

pornography [pɔː'nɒɡrəfɪ] n pornographie f

porpoise ['pɔːpəs] n marsouin m

porridge ['pɒrɪdʒ] n porridge m

port [pɔːt] n (harbour) port m; (NAUT: left side) bâbord m; (wine) porto m; **~ of call** escale f

portable ['pɔːtəbl] adj portatif(-ive)

porter ['pɔːtər] n (for luggage) porteur m; (doorkeeper) gardien(ne); portier m

portfolio [pɔːt'fəʊlɪəʊ] n portefeuille m; (of artist) portfolio m

porthole ['pɔːthəʊl] n hublot m

portion ['pɔːʃən] n portion f, part f

portrait ['pɔːtreɪt] n portrait m

portray [pɔː'treɪ] vt faire le portrait de; (in writing) dépeindre, représenter; (subj: actor) jouer

Portugal ['pɔːtjʊɡl] n Portugal m; **Portuguese** [pɔːtjʊ'ɡiːz] adj portugais(e) ♦ n inv Portugais(e); (LING) portugais m

pose [pəʊz] n pose f ♦ vi (pretend): **to ~ as** se poser en ♦ vt poser; (problem) créer

posh [pɒʃ] (inf) adj chic inv

position [pə'zɪʃən] n position f; (job) situation f ♦ vt placer

positive ['pɒzɪtɪv] adj positif(-ive); (certain) sûr(e), certain(e); (definite) formel(le), catégorique

possess [pə'zes] vt posséder; **~ion** n possession f

possibility [pɒsɪ'bɪlɪtɪ] n possibilité f; éventualité f

possible ['pɒsɪbl] adj possible; **as big as ~** aussi gros que possible; **possibly** adv (perhaps) peut-être; **if you possibly can** si cela vous est possible; **I cannot possibly come** il m'est impossible de venir

post [pəʊst] n poste f; (BRIT: letters, delivery) courrier m; (job, situation, MIL) poste m; (pole) poteau m ♦ vt (BRIT: send by ~) poster; (: appoint): **to ~ to** affecter à; **~age** n tarifs mpl d'affranchissement; **~al order** n mandat(-poste) m; **~box** (BRIT) n boîte f aux lettres; ~**card** n carte postale; ~**code** (BRIT) n code postal

poster ['pəustər] n affiche f

poste restante [pəust'restɑ̃:nt] (BRIT) n poste restante

postgraduate ['pəust'grædjuət] n ≈ étudiant(e) de troisième cycle

posthumous ['pɒstjuməs] adj posthume

postman ['pəustmən] (irreg) n facteur m

postmark ['pəustmɑ:k] n cachet m (de la poste)

postmortem [pəust'mɔ:təm] n autopsie f

post office n (building) poste f; (organization): **the P~ O~** les Postes; ~ ~ **box** n boîte postale

postpone [pəus'pəun] vt remettre (à plus tard)

posture ['pɒstʃər] n posture f; (fig) attitude f

postwar [pəust'wɔ:r] adj d'après-guerre

postwoman ['pəustwumən] n factrice f

posy ['pəuzɪ] n petit bouquet

pot [pɒt] n pot m; (for cooking) marmite f; casserole f; (teapot) théière f; (coffee pot) cafetière f; (inf: marijuana) herbe f ♦ vt (plant) mettre en pot; **to go to ~** (inf: work, performance) aller à vau-l'eau

potato [pə'teɪtəu] (pl ~**es**) n pomme f de terre; ~ **peeler** n épluche-légumes m inv

potent ['pəutnt] adj puissant(e); (drink) fort(e), très alcoolisé(e); (man) viril

potential [pə'tenʃl] adj potentiel(le) ♦ n potentiel m

pothole ['pɒthəul] n (in road) nid m de poule; (BRIT: underground) gouffre m, caverne f; (BRIT) ~**ing** n: **to go potholing** faire de la spéléologie

potluck [pɒt'lʌk] n: **to take ~** tenter sa chance

pot plant n plante f d'appartement

potted ['pɒtɪd] adj (food) en conserve; (plant) en pot; (abbreviated) abrégé(e)

potter ['pɒtər] n potier m ♦ vi: **to ~ around, ~ about** (BRIT) bricoler; ~**y** n poterie f

potty ['pɒtɪ] adj (inf: mad) dingue ♦ n (child's) pot m

pouch [pautʃ] n (ZOOL) poche f; (for tobacco) blague f; (for money) bourse f

poultry ['pəultrɪ] n volaille f

pounce [pauns] vi: **to ~ (on)** bondir (sur), sauter (sur)

pound [paund] n (unit of money) livre f; (unit of weight) livre ♦ vt (beat) bourrer de coups, marteler; (crush) piler, pulvériser ♦ vi (heart) battre violemment, taper

pour [pɔ:r] vt verser ♦ vi couler à flots; **to ~ (with rain)** pleuvoir à verse; **to ~ sb a drink** verser or servir à boire à qn; ~ **away** vt vider; ~ **in** vi (people) affluer, se précipiter; (news, letters etc) arriver en masse; ~ **off** vt = pour

away; ~ **out** vi (people) sortir en masse ♦ vt vider; (fig) déverser; (serve: a drink) verser; ~**ing** ['pɔ:rɪŋ] adj: ~**ing rain** pluie torrentielle

pout [paut] vi faire la moue

poverty ['pɒvətɪ] n pauvreté f, misère f; ~-**stricken** adj pauvre, déshérité(e)

powder ['paudər] n poudre f ♦ vt: **to ~ one's face** se poudrer; ~ **compact** n poudrier m; ~**ed milk** n lait m en poudre; ~ **room** n toilettes fpl (pour dames)

power ['pauər] n (strength) puissance f, force f; (ability, authority) pouvoir m; (of speech, thought) faculté f; (ELEC) courant m; **to be in ~** (POL etc) être au pouvoir; ~ **cut** (BRIT) n coupure f de courant; ~**ed** adj: ~**ed by** actionné(e) par, fonctionnant à; ~ **failure** n panne f de courant; ~**ful** adj puissant(e); ~**less** adj impuissant(e); ~ **point** (BRIT) n prise f de courant; ~ **station** n centrale f électrique; ~ **struggle** n lutte f pour le pouvoir

p.p. abbr (= per procurationem): **p.p. J. Smith** pour M. J. Smith

PR n abbr = **public relations**

practical ['præktɪkl] adj pratique; ~**ity** [præktɪ'kælɪtɪ] (no pl) n (of person) sens m pratique; ~**ities** npl (of situation) aspect m pratique; ~ **joke** n farce f; ~**ly** adv (almost) pratiquement

practice ['præktɪs] n pratique f; (of profession) exercice m; (at football etc) entraînement m; (business) cabinet m ♦ vt, vi (US) = **practise**; **in ~** (in reality) en pratique; **out of ~** rouillé(e)

practise ['præktɪs] (US **practice**) vt (musical instrument) travailler; (train for: sport) s'entraîner à; (a sport, religion) pratiquer; (profession) exercer ♦ vi s'exercer, travailler; (train) s'entraîner; (lawyer, doctor) exercer; **practising** adj (Christian etc) pratiquant(e); (lawyer) en exercice

practitioner [præk'tɪʃənər] n praticien(ne)

prairie ['preərɪ] n steppe f, prairie f

praise [preɪz] n éloge(s) m(pl), louange(s) f(pl) ♦ vt louer, faire l'éloge de; ~**worthy** adj digne d'éloges

pram [præm] (BRIT) n landau m, voiture f d'enfant

prance [prɑ:ns] vi (also: ~ **about**: person) se pavaner

prank [præŋk] n farce f

prawn [prɔ:n] n crevette f (rose); ~ **cocktail** n cocktail m de crevettes

pray [preɪ] vi prier; ~**er** [preər] n prière f

preach [pri:tʃ] vt, vi prêcher

precaution [prɪ'kɔ:ʃən] n précaution f

precede [prɪ'si:d] vt précéder

precedent ['presɪdənt] n précédent m

preceding [prɪsi:dɪŋ] adj qui précède/

précédait *etc*

precinct ['pri:sɪŋkt] *n* (*US*) circonscription *f*, arrondissement *m*; **~s** *npl* (*neighbourhood*) alentours *mpl*, environs *mpl*; **pedestrian ~** (*BRIT*) zone piétonnière *or* piétonne; **shopping ~** (*BRIT*) centre commercial

precious ['prɛʃəs] *adj* précieux(-euse)

precipitate [prɪ'sɪpɪteɪt] *vt* précipiter

precise [prɪ'saɪs] *adj* précis(e); **~ly** *adv* précisément

precocious [prɪ'kəʊʃəs] *adj* précoce

precondition ['pri:kən'dɪʃən] *n* condition *f* nécessaire

predecessor ['pri:dɪsesər] *n* prédécesseur *m*

predicament [prɪ'dɪkəmənt] *n* situation *f* difficile

predict [prɪ'dɪkt] *vt* prédire; **~able** *adj* prévisible

predominantly [prɪ'dɒmɪnəntlɪ] *adv* en majeure partie; surtout

pre-empt [prɪ'ɛmt] *vt* anticiper, devancer

preen [pri:n] *vt*: **to ~ itself** (*bird*) se lisser les plumes; **to ~ o.s.** s'admirer

prefab ['pri:fæb] *n* bâtiment préfabriqué

preface ['prɛfəs] *n* préface *f*

prefect ['pri:fɛkt] (*BRIT*) *n* (*in school*) élève chargé(e) de certaines fonctions de discipline

prefer [prɪ'fɜ:r] *vt* préférer; **~ably** ['prɛfrəblɪ] *adv* de préférence; **~ence** ['prɛfrəns] *n* préférence *f*; **~ential** [prɛfə'rɛnʃəl] *adj*: **~ential treatment** traitement *m* de faveur *or* préférentiel

prefix ['pri:fɪks] *n* préfixe *m*

pregnancy ['prɛgnənsɪ] *n* grossesse *f*

pregnant ['prɛgnənt] *adj* enceinte; (*animal*) pleine

prehistoric ['pri:hɪs'tɔrɪk] *adj* préhistorique

prejudice ['prɛdʒʊdɪs] *n* préjugé *m*; **~d** *adj* (*person*) plein(e) de préjugés; (*in a matter*) partial(e)

premarital ['pri:'mærɪtl] *adj* avant le mariage

premature ['prɛmətʃuər] *adj* prématuré(e)

premenstrual syndrome [pri:'mɛnstruəl-] *n* syndrome prémenstruel

premier ['prɛmɪər] *adj* premier(-ère), principal(e) ♦ *n* (*POL*) Premier ministre

première ['prɛmɪɛər] *n* première *f*

Premier League *n* première division

premise ['prɛmɪs] *n* prémisse *f*; **~s** *npl* (*building*) locaux *mpl*; **on the ~s** sur les lieux; sur place

premium ['pri:mɪəm] *n* prime *f*; **to be at a ~** faire prime; **~ bond** (*BRIT*) *n* bon *m* à lot, obligation *f* à prime

premonition [prɛmə'nɪʃən] *n* prémonition *f*

preoccupied [pri:'ɔkjupaɪd] *adj* préoccupé(e)

prep [prɛp] *n* (*SCOL*) étude *f*

prepaid [pri:'peɪd] *adj* payé(e) d'avance

preparation [prɛpə'reɪʃən] *n* préparation *f*; **~s** *npl* (*for trip, war*) préparatifs *mpl*

preparatory [prɪ'pærətərɪ] *adj* préliminaire; **~ school** (*BRIT*) *n* école primaire privée

prepare [prɪ'pɛər] *vt* préparer ♦ *vi*: **to ~ for** se préparer à; **~d to** prêt(e) à

preposition [prɛpə'zɪʃən] *n* préposition *f*

preposterous [prɪ'pɔstərəs] *adj* absurde

prep school *n* = **preparatory school**

prerequisite [pri:'rɛkwɪzɪt] *n* condition *f* préalable

Presbyterian [prɛzbɪ'tɪərɪən] *adj, n* presbytérien(ne) *m/f*

prescribe [prɪ'skraɪb] *vt* prescrire; **prescription** [prɪ'skrɪpʃən] *n* (*MED*) ordonnance *f*; (: *medicine*) médicament (obtenu sur ordonnance)

presence ['prɛzns] *n* présence *f*; **~ of mind** présence d'esprit

present [*adj, n* 'prɛznt, *vb* prɪ'zɛnt] *adj* présent(e) ♦ *n* (*gift*) cadeau *m*; (*actuality*) présent *m* ♦ *vt* présenter; (*prize, medal*) remettre; (*give*): **to ~ sb with sth** *or* **sth to sb** offrir qch à qn; **to give sb a ~** offrir un cadeau à qn; **at ~** en ce moment; **~ation** [prɛzn'teɪʃən] *n* présentation *f*; (*ceremony*) remise *f* du cadeau (*or* de la médaille *etc*); **~-day** *adj* contemporain(e), actuel(le); **~er** *n* (*RADIO, TV*) présentateur(-trice); **~ly** *adv* (*with verb in past*) peu après; (*soon*) tout à l'heure, bientôt; (*at present*) en ce moment

preservative [prɪ'zə:vətɪv] *n* agent *m* de conservation

preserve [prɪ'zə:v] *vt* (*keep safe*) préserver, protéger; (*maintain*) conserver, garder; (*food*) mettre en conserve ♦ *n* (*often pl*: *jam*) confiture *f*

president ['prɛzɪdənt] *n* président(e); **~ial** [prɛzɪ'dɛnʃl] *adj* présidentiel(le)

press [prɛs] *n* presse *f*; (*for wine*) pressoir *m* ♦ *vt* (*squeeze*) presser, serrer; (*push*) appuyer sur; (*clothes: iron*) repasser; (*put ~ure on*) faire pression sur; (*insist*): **to ~ sth on sb** presser qn d'accepter qch ♦ *vi* appuyer, peser; **to ~ for sth** faire pression pour obtenir qch; **we are ~ed for time/money** le temps/ l'argent nous manque; **~ on** *vi* continuer; **~ conference** *n* conférence *f* de presse; **~ing** *adj* urgent(e), pressant(e); **~ stud** (*BRIT*) *n* bouton-pression *m*; **~-up** (*BRIT*) *n* traction *f*

pressure ['prɛʃər] *n* pression *f*; (*stress*) tension *f*; **to put ~ on sb (to do)** faire pression sur qn (pour qu'il/elle fasse); **~ cooker** *n* cocotte-minute *f*; **~ gauge** *n* manomètre *m*; **~ group** *n* groupe *m* de pression

prestige [prɛs'ti:ʒ] *n* prestige *m*; **prestigious** [prɛs'tɪdʒəs] *adj* prestigieux(-euse)

presumably [prɪ'zju:məblɪ] *adv* vraisemblablement

presume [prɪ'zju:m] *vt* présumer, supposer

pretence [prɪ'tɛns] (*US* **pretense**) *n* (*claim*) prétention *f*; **under false ~s** sous des prétextes fallacieux

pretend [prɪ'tɛnd] *vt* (*feign*) feindre, simuler ♦ *vi* faire semblant

pretext ['pri:tɛkst] *n* prétexte *m*

pretty ['prɪtɪ] *adj* joli(e) ♦ *adv* assez

prevail [prɪ'veɪl] *vi* (*be usual*) avoir cours; (*win*) l'emporter, prévaloir; **~ing** *adj* dominant(e); **prevalent** ['prɛvələnt] *adj* répandu(e), courant(e)

prevent [prɪ'vɛnt] *vt*: **to ~ (from doing)** empêcher (de faire); **prevention** [prɪ'vɛntɪv], **~ive** [prɪ'vɛntɪv] *adj* préventif(-ive)

preview ['pri:vju:] *n* (*of film etc*) avant-première *f*

previous ['pri:vɪəs] *adj* précédent(e); antérieur(e); **~ly** *adv* précédemment, auparavant

prewar [pri:'wɔ:ᵊ] *adj* d'avant-guerre

prey [preɪ] *n* proie *f* ♦ *vi*: **to ~ on** s'attaquer à; **it was ~ing on his mind** cela le travaillait

price [praɪs] *n* prix *m* ♦ *vt* (*goods*) fixer le prix de; **~less** *adj* sans prix, inestimable; **~ list** *n* liste *f* des prix, tarif *m*

prick [prɪk] *n* piqûre *f* ♦ *vt* piquer; **to ~ up one's ears** dresser *ou* tendre l'oreille

prickle ['prɪkl] *n* (*of plant*) épine *f*; (*sensation*) picotement *m*; **prickly** *adj* piquant(e), épineux(-euse); **prickly heat** *n* fièvre *f* miliaire

pride [praɪd] *n* orgueil *m*; fierté *f* ♦ *vt*: **to ~ o.s. on** se flatter de; s'enorgueillir de

priest [pri:st] *n* prêtre *m*; **~hood** *n* prêtrise *f*, sacerdoce *m*

prim [prɪm] *adj* collet monté *inv*, guindé(e)

primarily ['praɪmərɪlɪ] *adv* principalement, essentiellement

primary ['praɪmərɪ] *adj* (*first in importance*) premier(-ère), primordial(e), principal(e) ♦ *n* (*US: election*) (élection *f*) primaire *f*; **~ school** (*BRIT*) *n* école primaire *f*

prime [praɪm] *adj* primordial(e), fondamental(e); (*excellent*) excellent(e) ♦ *n*: **in the ~ of life** dans la fleur de l'âge ♦ *vt* (*wood*) apprêter; (*fig*) mettre au courant; **P~ Minister** *n* Premier ministre *m*

primeval *adj* primitif(-ive); **~ forest** forêt *f* vierge

primitive ['prɪmɪtɪv] *adj* primitif(-ive)

primrose ['prɪmrəuz] *n* primevère *f*

primus (stove) ® ['praɪməs-] (*BRIT*) *n* réchaud *m* de camping

prince [prɪns] *n* prince *m*

princess [prɪn'sɛs] *n* princesse *f*

principal ['prɪnsɪpl] *adj* principal(e) ♦ *n*

(*headmaster*) directeur(-trice), principal *m*

principle ['prɪnsɪpl] *n* principe *m*; **in/on ~** en/par principe

print [prɪnt] *n* (*mark*) empreinte *f*; (*letters*) caractères *mpl*; (*ART*) gravure *f*, estampe *f*; (: *photograph*) photo *f* ♦ *vt* imprimer; (*publish*) publier; (*write in block letters*) écrire en caractères d'imprimerie; **out of ~** épuisé(e); **~ed matter** *n* imprimé(s) *m(pl)*; **~er** *n* imprimeur *m*; (*machine*) imprimante *f*; **~ing** *n* impression *f*; **~-out** *n* copie *f* papier

prior ['praɪəᵊ] *adj* antérieur(e), précédent(e); (*more important*) prioritaire ♦ *adv*: **~ to doing** avant de faire; **~ity** [praɪ'ɔrɪtɪ] *n* priorité *f*

prise [praɪz] *vt*: **to ~ open** forcer

prison ['prɪzn] *n* prison *f* ♦ *cpd* pénitentiaire; **~er** *n* prisonnier(-ère)

pristine ['prɪsti:n] *adj* parfait(e)

privacy ['prɪvəsɪ] *n* intimité *f*, solitude *f*

private ['praɪvɪt] *adj* privé(e); (*personal*) personnel(le); (*house, lesson*) particulier(-ère); (*quiet: place*) tranquille; (*reserved: person*) secret(-ète) ♦ *n* soldat *m* de deuxième classe; **"~"** (*on envelope*) "personnelle"; **in ~** en privé; **~ detective** *n* détective privé *m*; **~ enterprise** *n* l'entreprise privée, **~ property** *n* propriété privée;

privatize *vt* privatiser

privet ['prɪvɪt] *n* troène *m*

privilege ['prɪvɪlɪdʒ] *n* privilège *m*

privy ['prɪvɪ] *adj*: **to be ~ to** être au courant de

prize [praɪz] *n* prix *m* ♦ *adj* (*example, idiot*) parfait(e); (*bull, novel*) primé(e) ♦ *vt* priser, faire grand cas de; **~-giving** *n* distribution *f* des prix; **~winner** *n* gagnant(e)

pro [prəu] *n* (*SPORT*) professionnel(le); **the ~s and cons** le pour et le contre

probability [prɔbə'bɪlɪtɪ] *n* probabilité *f*

probable ['prɔbəbl] *adj* probable; **probably** *adv* probablement

probation [prə'beɪʃən] *n*: **on ~** (*LAW*) en liberté surveillée, en sursis; (*employee*) à l'essai

probe [prəub] *n* (*MED, SPACE*) sonde *f*; (*enquiry*) enquête *f*, investigation *f* ♦ *vt* sonder, explorer

problem ['prɔbləm] *n* problème *m*

procedure [prə'si:dʒəᵊ] *n* (*ADMIN, LAW*) procédure *f*; (*method*) marche *f* à suivre, façon *f* de procéder

proceed [prə'si:d] *vi* continuer; (*go forward*) avancer; **to ~ (with)** continuer, poursuivre; **to ~ to do** se mettre à faire; **~ings** *npl* (*LAW*) poursuites *fpl*; (*meeting*) réunion *f*, séance *f*; **~s** ['prəusi:dz] *npl* produit *m*, recette *f*

process ['prɔsɛs] *n* processus *m*; (*method*) procédé *m* ♦ *vt* traiter; **~ing** *n* (*PHOT*) développement *m*; **~ion** [prə'sɛʃən] *n* défilé m, cortège m; (REL) procession f; **funeral ~ion** (on foot) cortège m funèbre; (in cars) convoi m mortuaire

proclaim [prə'kleɪm] vt déclarer, proclamer

procrastinate [prəu'kræstɪneɪt] vi faire traîner les choses, vouloir tout remettre au lendemain

procure [prə'kjuər] vt obtenir

prod [prɒd] vt pousser

prodigal ['prɒdɪgl] adj prodigue

prodigy ['prɒdɪdʒɪ] n prodige m

produce [n 'prɒdjuːs, vb prə'djuːs] n (AGR) produits mpl ♦ vt produire; (to show) présenter; (cause) provoquer, causer; (THEATRE) monter, mettre en scène; **~r** n producteur m; (THEATRE) metteur m en scène

product ['prɒdʌkt] n produit m

production [prə'dʌkʃən] n production f; (THEATRE) mise f en scène; **~ line** n chaîne f (de fabrication)

productivity [prɒdʌk'tɪvɪtɪ] n productivité f

profession [prə'feʃən] n profession f; **~al** n professionnel(le) ♦ adj professionnel(le); (work) de professionnel; **~ally** adv professionnellement; (SPORT: play) en professionnel; **she sings ~ally** c'est une chanteuse professionnelle; **I only know him ~ally** je n'ai avec lui que des relations de travail

professor [prə'fesər] n professeur m (titulaire d'une chaire)

proficiency [prə'fɪʃənsɪ] n compétence f, aptitude f

profile ['prəufaɪl] n profil m

profit ['prɒfɪt] n bénéfice m; profit m ♦ vi: **to ~ (by or from)** profiter (de); **~able** adj lucratif(-ive), rentable

profound [prə'faund] adj profond(e)

profusely [prə'fjuːslɪ] adv abondamment; avec effusion

prognosis [prɒg'nəusɪs] n (pl **prognoses**) n pronostic m

programme ['prəugræm] (US **program**) n programme m; (RADIO, TV) émission f ♦ vt programmer; **~r** (US **programer**) n programmeur(-euse); **programming** (US **programing**) n programmation f

progress [n 'prəugres, vb prə'gres] n progrès m(pl) ♦ vi progresser, avancer; **in ~** en cours; **~ive** [prə'gresɪv] adj progressif(-ive); (person) progressiste

prohibit [prə'hɪbɪt] vt interdire, défendre

project [n 'prɒdʒekt, vb prə'dʒekt] n (plan) projet m, plan m; (venture) opération f, entreprise f; (research) étude f, dossier m ♦ vt projeter ♦ vi faire saillie, s'avancer; **~ion** n projection f; (overhang) saillie f; **~or** n projecteur m

prolong [prə'lɒŋ] vt prolonger

prom [prɒm] n abbr = **promenade**; (US: ball) bal m d'étudiants

promenade [prɒmə'nɑːd] n (by sea) esplanade f, promenade f; **~ concert** (BRIT) n concert m populaire (de musique classique)

prominent ['prɒmɪnənt] adj (standing out) proéminent(e); (important) important(e)

promiscuous [prə'mɪskjuəs] adj (sexually) de mœurs légères

promise ['prɒmɪs] n promesse f ♦ vt, vi promettre; **promising** adj prometteur(-euse)

promote [prə'məut] vt promouvoir; (new product) faire la promotion de; **~r** n (of event) organisateur(-trice); (of cause, idea) promoteur(-trice); **promotion** n promotion f

prompt [prɒmpt] adj rapide ♦ adv (punctually) à l'heure ♦ n (COMPUT) message m (de guidage) ♦ vt provoquer; (person) inciter, pousser; (THEATRE) souffler (son rôle or ses répliques) à; **~ly** adv rapidement, sans délai; ponctuellement

prone [prəun] adj (lying) couché(e) (face contre terre); **~ to** enclin(e) à

prong [prɒŋ] n (of fork) dent f

pronoun ['prəunaun] n pronom m

pronounce [prə'nauns] vt prononcer; **pronunciation** [prənʌnsɪ'eɪʃən] n prononciation f

proof [pruːf] n preuve f; (TYP) épreuve f ♦ adj: **~ against** à l'épreuve de

prop [prɒp] n support m, étai m; (fig) soutien m ♦ vt (also: **~ up**) étayer, soutenir; (lean): **to ~ sth against** appuyer qch contre or à

propaganda [prɒpə'gændə] n propagande f

propel [prə'pel] vt propulser, faire avancer; **~ler** n hélice f

propensity [prə'pensɪtɪ] n: **a ~ for** or **to/to do** une propension à/à faire

proper ['prɒpər] adj (suited, right) approprié(e), bon (bonne); (seemly) correct(e), convenable; (authentic) vrai(e), véritable; (referring to place): **the village ~** le village proprement dit; **~ly** adv correctement, convenablement; **~ noun** n nom m propre

property ['prɒpətɪ] n propriété f; (things owned) biens mpl; propriété(s) f(pl); (land) terres fpl

prophecy ['prɒfɪsɪ] n prophétie f

prophesy ['prɒfɪsaɪ] vt prédire

prophet ['prɒfɪt] n prophète m

proportion [prə'pɔːʃən] n proportion f; (share) part f; partie f; **~al, ~ate** adj proportionnel(le)

proposal [prə'pəuzl] n proposition f, offre f; (plan) projet m; (of marriage) demande f en mariage

propose [prə'pəuz] vt proposer, suggérer ♦ vi faire sa demande en mariage; **to ~ to do** avoir l'intention de faire; **proposition** [prɒpə'-

zɪʃən] n proposition f
proprietor [prə'praɪətə'] n propriétaire m/f
propriety [prə'praɪətɪ] n (seemliness)
bienséance f, convenance f
prose [prəuz] n (not poetry) prose f
prosecute ['prɔsɪkjuːt] vt poursuivre;
prosecution [prɔsɪ'kjuːʃən] n poursuites fpl
judiciaires; (accusing side) partie plaignante;
prosecutor n (US: plaintiff) plaignant(e);
(also: **public prosecutor**) procureur m,
ministère public
prospect [n 'prɔspekt, vb prə'spekt] n
perspective f ♦ vt, vi prospecter; **~s** npl (for
work etc) possibilités fpl d'avenir, débouchés
mpl; **~ing** n (for gold, oil etc) prospection f;
~ive adj (possible) éventuel(le); (future)
futur(e)
prospectus [prə'spektəs] n prospectus m
prosperity [prɔ'sperɪtɪ] n prospérité f
prostitute ['prɔstɪtjuːt] n prostitué(e)
protect [prə'tekt] vt protéger; **~ion**
protection f; **~ive** adj protecteur(-trice);
(clothing) de protection
protein ['prəutiːn] n protéine f
protest [n 'prəutest, vb prə'test] n
protestation f ♦ vi, vt: to ~ (that) protester
(que)
Protestant ['prɔtɪstənt] adj, n protestant(e)
protester [prə'testə'] n manifestant(e)
protracted [prə'træktɪd] adj prolongé(e)
protrude [prə'truːd] vi avancer, dépasser
proud [praud] adj fier(-ère); (pej)
orgueilleux(-euse)
prove [pruːv] vt prouver, démontrer ♦ vi: to
~ (to be) correct etc s'avérer juste etc; to
~ o.s. montrer ce dont on est capable
proverb ['prɔvəːb] n proverbe m
provide [prə'vaɪd] vt fournir; to ~ sb with sth
fournir qch à qn; ~ for vt fus (person)
subvenir aux besoins de; (future event)
prévoir; **~d (that)** conj à condition que
+sub; **providing (that)** conj à
condition que +sub
province ['prɔvɪns] n province f; (fig)
domaine m; **provincial** [prə'vɪnʃəl] adj
provincial(e)
provision [prə'vɪʒən] n (supplying) fourniture
f; approvisionnement m; (stipulation)
disposition f; **~s** npl (food) provisions fpl; **~al**
adj provisoire
proviso [prə'vaɪzəu] n condition f
provocative [prə'vɔkətɪv] adj provoca-
teur(-trice), provocant(e)
provoke [prə'vəuk] vt provoquer
prowess ['prauɪs] n prouesse f
prowl [praul] vi (also: ~ about, ~ around)
rôder ♦ n: on the ~ à l'affût; **~er** n rô-
deur(-euse)
proxy ['prɔksɪ] n procuration f

prudent ['pruːdnt] adj prudent(e)
prune [pruːn] n pruneau m ♦ vt élaguer
pry [praɪ] vi: to ~ into fourrer son nez dans
PS n abbr (= postscript) p.s.
psalm [sɑːm] n psaume m
pseudonym ['sjuːdənɪm] n pseudonyme m
psyche ['saɪkɪ] n psychisme m
psychiatrist [saɪ'kaɪətrɪst] n psychiatre m/f
psychic ['saɪkɪk] adj (also: ~al)
(méta)psychique; (person) doué(e) d'un
sixième sens
psychoanalyst [saɪkəu'ænəlɪst] n
psychanalyste m/f
psychological [saɪkə'lɔdʒɪkl] adj
psychologique
psychologist [saɪ'kɔlədʒɪst] n psychologue
m/f
psychology [saɪ'kɔlədʒɪ] n psychologie f
PTO abbr (= please turn over) T.S.V.P.
pub [pʌb] n (public house) pub m
public ['pʌblɪk] adj public(-ique) ♦ n public
m; in ~ en public; to make ~ rendre public;
~ **address system** n (système m de)
sonorisation f; hauts-parleurs mpl
publican ['pʌblɪkən] n patron de pub
public: ~ **company** n société f anonyme
(cotée en Bourse); ~ **convenience** (BRIT)
toilettes fpl; ~ **holiday** n jour férié; ~ **house**
(BRIT) n pub m
publicity [pʌb'lɪsɪtɪ] n publicité f
publicize ['pʌblɪsaɪz] vt faire connaître,
rendre public(-ique)
public: ~ **opinion** n opinion publique;
~ **relations** n relations publiques; ~ **school**
n (BRIT) école (secondaire) privée; (US) école
publique; **~-spirited** adj qui fait preuve de
civisme; ~ **transport** n transports mpl en
publish ['pʌblɪʃ] vt publier; **~er** n éditeur m;
~ing n édition f
pub lunch n repas m de bistrot
pucker ['pʌkə'] vt plisser
pudding ['pudɪŋ] n pudding m; (BRIT: sweet)
dessert m, entremets m; black ~, (US) blood ~
boudin (noir)
puddle ['pʌdl] n flaque f (d'eau)
puff [pʌf] n bouffée f ♦ vt: to ~ one's pipe tirer
sur sa pipe ♦ vi (pant) haleter; ~ out vt (fill
with air) gonfler; ~ **pastry** (US puff paste) n
pâte feuilletée; **~y** adj bouffi(e),
boursouflé(e)
pull [pul] n (tug): to give sth a ~ tirer sur qch
♦ vt tirer; (trigger) presser ♦ vi tirer; to ~ to
pieces mettre en morceaux; to ~ one's
punches ménager son adversaire; to ~ one's
weight faire sa part (du travail); to ~ o.s.
together se ressaisir; to ~ sb's leg (fig) faire
marcher qn; ~ **apart** vt (break) mettre en
pièces, démantibuler; ~ **down** vt (house)

démolir; ~ **in** vi (AUT) entrer; (RAIL) entrer en gare; ~ **off** vt enlever, ôter; (deal etc) mener à bien, conclure; ~ **out** vi démarrer, partir ♦ vt sortir; arracher; ~ **over** vi (AUT) se ranger; ~ **through** vi s'en sortir; ~ **up** vi (stop) s'arrêter ♦ vt remonter; (uproot) déraciner, arracher

pulley ['puli] n poulie f

pullover ['puləuvə⁺] n pull(-over) m, tricot m

pulp [pʌlp] n (of fruit) pulpe f

pulpit ['pulpit] n chaire f

pulsate [pʌl'seit] vi battre, palpiter; (music) vibrer

pulse [pʌls] n (of blood) pouls m; (of heart) battement m; (of music, engine) vibrations fpl; (BOT, CULIN) légume sec

pump [pʌmp] n pompe f; (shoe) escarpin m ♦ vt pomper; ~ **up** vt gonfler

pumpkin ['pʌmpkin] n potiron m, citrouille f

pun [pʌn] n jeu m de mots, calembour m

punch [pʌntʃ] n (blow) coup m de poing; (tool) poinçon m; (drink) punch m ♦ vt (hit): **to** ~ **sb/sth** donner un coup de poing à qn/ sur qch; ~**line** n (of joke) conclusion f; ~-**up** (BRIT: inf) n bagarre f

punctual ['pʌŋktjuəl] adj ponctuel(le)

punctuation [pʌŋktju'eiʃən] n ponctuation f

puncture ['pʌŋktʃə⁺] n crevaison f

pundit ['pʌndit] n individu m qui pontifie, pontife m

pungent ['pʌndʒənt] adj piquant(e), âcre

punish ['pʌniʃ] vt punir; ~**ment** n punition f, châtiment m

punk [pʌŋk] n (also: ~ **rocker**) punk m/f; (also: ~ **rock**) le punk rock; (US: inf: hoodlum) voyou m

punt [pʌnt] n (boat) bachot m

punter ['pʌntə⁺] n (BRIT: gambler) parieur(-euse); (inf): **the** ~s le public

puny ['pjuːni] adj chétif(-ive); (effort) piteux(-euse)

pup [pʌp] n chiot m

pupil ['pjuːpl] n (SCOL) élève m/f; (of eye) pupille f

puppet ['pʌpit] n marionnette f, pantin m

puppy ['pʌpi] n chiot m, jeune chien(ne)

purchase ['pəːtʃis] n achat m ♦ vt acheter; ~**r** n acheteur(-euse)

pure [pjuə⁺] adj pur(e); ~**ly** adv purement

purge [pəːdʒ] n purge f ♦ vt purger

purple ['pəːpl] adj violet(te); (face) cramoisi(e)

purpose ['pəːpəs] n intention f, but m; **on** ~ exprès; ~**ful** adj déterminé(e), résolu(e)

purr [pəː⁺] vi ronronner

purse [pəːs] n (BRIT: for money) porte-monnaie m inv; (US: handbag) sac m à main ♦ vt serrer, pincer

purser ['pəːsə⁺] n (NAUT) commissaire m du bord

pursue [pə'sjuː] vt poursuivre; **pursuit** [pə'sjuːt] n poursuite f; (occupation) occupation f, activité f

push [puʃ] n poussée f ♦ vt pousser; (button) appuyer sur; (product) faire de la publicité pour; (thrust): **to** ~ **sth (into)** enfoncer qch (dans) ♦ vi pousser; (demand): **to** ~ **for** exiger, demander avec insistance; ~ **aside** vt écarter; ~ **off** (inf) vi filer, ficher le camp; ~ **on** vi (continue) continuer; ~ **through** vi se frayer un chemin ♦ vt (measure) faire accepter; ~ **up** vt (total, prices) faire monter; ~**chair** (BRIT) n poussette f; ~**er** n (drug pusher) revendeur(-euse) (de drogue), ravitailleur(-euse) (en drogue); ~**over** (inf) n: **it's a** ~**over** c'est un jeu d'enfant; ~-**up** (US) n traction f; ~**y** (pej) n arriviste

puss [pus], **pussy (cat)** ['pusi(kæt)] (inf) n minet m

put [put] (pt, pp **put**) vt mettre, poser, placer; (say) dire, exprimer; (a question) poser; (case, view) exposer, présenter; (estimate) estimer; ~ **about** (rumour) faire courir; ~ **across** vt (ideas etc) communiquer; ~ **away** vt (store) ranger; ~ **back** vt (replace) remettre, replacer; (postpone) remettre; (delay) retarder; ~ **by** vt (money) mettre de côté, économiser; ~ **down** vt (parcel etc) poser, déposer; (in writing) mettre par écrit, inscrire; (suppress: revolt etc) réprimer, faire cesser; (animal) abattre; (dog, cat) faire piquer; (attribute) attribuer; ~ **forward** vt (ideas) avancer; ~ **in** vt (gas, electricity) installer; (application, complaint) soumettre; (time, effort) consacrer; ~ **off** vt (light etc) éteindre; (postpone) remettre à plus tard, ajourner; (discourage) dissuader; ~ **on** vt (clothes, lipstick, record) mettre; (light etc) allumer; (play etc) monter; (food: cook) mettre à cuire or à chauffer; (gain): **to** ~ **on weight** prendre du poids, grossir; **to** ~ **the brakes on** freiner; **to** ~ **the kettle on** mettre l'eau à chauffer; ~ **out** vt (take out) mettre dehors; (one's hand) tendre; (light etc) éteindre; (person: inconvenience) déranger, gêner; ~ **through** vt (TEL: call) passer; (: person) mettre en communication; (plan) faire accepter; ~ **up** vt (raise) lever, relever, remonter; (pin up) afficher; (hang) accrocher; (build) construire, ériger; (tent) monter; (umbrella) ouvrir; (increase) augmenter; (accommodate) loger; ~ **up with** vt fus supporter

putt [pʌt] n coup roulé; ~**ing green** n green m

putty ['pʌti] n mastic m

put-up ['putʌp] (BRIT) adj: ~-~ **job** coup monté

puzzle ['pʌzl] n énigme f, mystère m; (jigsaw)

puzzle m ♦ vt intriguer, rendre perplexe ♦ vi se creuser la tête; ~d adj perplexe; **puzzling** adj déconcertant(e)

pyjamas [pə'dʒɑːməz] (BRIT) npl pyjama(s) m(pl)

pylon ['paɪlən] n pylône m

pyramid ['pɪrəmɪd] n pyramide f

Pyrenees [pɪrə'niːz] npl: **the ~** les Pyrénées fpl

Q, q

quack [kwæk] n (of duck) coin-coin m inv; (pej: doctor) charlatan m

quad [kwɒd] n abbr = **quadrangle**; **quadruplet**

quadrangle ['kwɒdræŋgl] n (courtyard) cour f

quadruple [kwɒ'druːpl] vt, vi quadrupler; **~ts** npl quadruplés

quail [kweɪl] n (ZOOL) caille f ♦ vi: **to ~ at** or **before** reculer devant

quaint [kweɪnt] adj bizarre; (house, village) au charme vieillot, pittoresque

quake [kweɪk] vi trembler

qualification [kwɒlɪfɪ'keɪʃən] n (often pl: degree etc) diplôme m; (training) qualification(s) f(pl), expérience f; (ability) compétence(s) f(pl); (limitation) réserve f, restriction f

qualified ['kwɒlɪfaɪd] adj (trained) qualifié(e); (professionally) diplômé(e); (fit, competent) compétent(e), qualifié(e); (limited) conditionnel(le)

qualify ['kwɒlɪfaɪ] vt qualifier; (modify) atténuer, nuancer ♦ vi: **to ~ (as)** obtenir son diplôme (de); **to ~ (for)** remplir les conditions requises (pour); (SPORT) se qualifier (pour)

quality ['kwɒlɪtɪ] n qualité f; **~ time** n moments privilégiés

qualm [kwɑːm] n doute m; scrupule m

quandary ['kwɒndrɪ] n: **in a ~** devant un dilemme, dans l'embarras

quantity ['kwɒntɪtɪ] n quantité f; **~ surveyor** n métreur m vérificateur

quarantine ['kwɒrntiːn] n quarantaine f

quarrel ['kwɒrl] n querelle f, dispute f ♦ vi se disputer, se quereller

quarry ['kwɒrɪ] n (for stone) carrière f; (animal) proie f, gibier m

quart [kwɔːt] n ≈ litre m

quarter ['kwɔːtər] n quart m; (US: coin: 25 cents) quart de dollar; (of year) trimestre m; (district) quartier m ♦ vt (divide) partager en quartiers or en quatre; **~s** npl (living ~) logement m; (MIL) quartiers mpl, cantonnement m; **a ~ of an hour** un quart d'heure; **~ final** n quart m de finale; **~ly** adj trimestriel(le) ♦ adv tous les trois mois

quartet(te) [kwɔː'tɛt] n quatuor m; (jazz players) quartette m

quartz [kwɔːts] n quartz m

quash [kwɒʃ] vt (verdict) annuler

quaver ['kweɪvər] vi trembler

quay [kiː] n (also: **~side**) quai m

queasy ['kwiːzɪ] adj: **to feel ~** avoir mal au cœur

queen [kwiːn] n reine f; (CARDS etc) dame f; **~ mother** n reine mère f

queer [kwɪər] adj étrange, curieux(-euse); (suspicious) louche ♦ n (inf!) homosexuel m

quell [kwɛl] vt réprimer, étouffer

quench [kwɛntʃ] vt: **to ~ one's thirst** se désaltérer

query ['kwɪərɪ] n question f ♦ vt remettre en question, mettre en doute

quest [kwɛst] n recherche f, quête f

question ['kwɛstʃən] n question f ♦ vt (person) interroger; (plan, idea) remettre en question, mettre en doute; **beyond ~** sans aucun doute; **out of the ~** hors de question; **~able** adj discutable; **~ mark** n point m d'interrogation; **~naire** [kwɛstʃə'nɛər] n questionnaire m

queue [kjuː] (BRIT) n queue f, file f ♦ vi (also: **~ up**) faire la queue

quibble ['kwɪbl] vi: **~ (about)** or (**over**) or (**with sth**) ergoter (sur qch)

quick [kwɪk] adj rapide; (agile) agile, vif (vive) ♦ n: **cut to the ~** (fig) touché(e) au vif; **be ~!** dépêche-toi!; **~en** vt accélérer, presser ♦ vi s'accélérer, devenir plus rapide; **~ly** adv vite, rapidement; **~sand** n sables mouvants; **~-witted** adj à l'esprit vif

quid [kwɪd] (BRIT: inf) n, pl inv livre f

quiet ['kwaɪət] adj tranquille, calme; (voice) bas(se); (ceremony, colour) discret(-ète) ♦ n tranquillité f, calme m; (silence) silence m ♦ vt, vi (US) = **quieten**; **keep ~!** tais-toi!; **~en** vi (also: **~en down**) se calmer, s'apaiser ♦ vt calmer, apaiser; **~ly** adv tranquillement, calmement; (silently) silencieusement; **~ness** n tranquillité f, calme m; (silence) silence m

quilt [kwɪlt] n édredon m; (continental ~) couette f

quin [kwɪn] n abbr = **quintuplet**

quintuplets [kwɪn'tjuːplɪts] npl quintuplé(e)s

quip [kwɪp] n remarque piquante or spirituelle, pointe f

quirk [kwɜːk] n bizarrerie f

quit [kwɪt] (pt, pp **quit** or **quitted**) vt quitter; (smoking, grumbling) arrêter de ♦ vi (give up) abandonner, renoncer; (resign) démissionner

quite [kwaɪt] adv (rather) assez, plutôt; (entirely) complètement, tout à fait; (following a negative = almost): **that's not ~ big enough** ce n'est pas tout à fait assez grand; **I**

~ **understand** je comprends très bien; ~ **a few of them** un assez grand nombre d'entre eux; ~ **(so)!** exactement!

quits [kwɪts] *adj:* ~ **(with)** quitte (envers); **let's call it** ~ restons-en là

quiver ['kwɪvər] *vi* trembler, frémir

quiz [kwɪz] *n (game)* jeu-concours *m* ♦ *vt* interroger; **~zical** *adj* narquois(e)

quota ['kwəʊtə] *n* quota *m*

quotation [kwəʊ'teɪʃən] *n* citation *f*; *(estimate)* devis *m*; ~ **marks** *npl* guillemets *mpl*

quote [kwəʊt] *n* citation *f*; *(estimate)* devis *m* ♦ *vt* citer; *(price)* indiquer; **~s** *npl* guillemets *mpl*

R, r

rabbi ['ræbaɪ] *n* rabbin *m*

rabbit ['ræbɪt] *n* lapin *m*; ~ **hutch** *n* clapier *m*

rabble ['ræbl] *(pej) n* populace *f*

rabies ['reɪbiːz] *n* rage *f*

RAC *n abbr (BRIT)* = **Royal Automobile Club**

rac(c)oon [rə'kuːn] *n* raton laveur

race [reɪs] *n (species)* race *f*; *(competition, rush)* course *f* ♦ *vt (horse)* faire courir ♦ *vi (compete)* faire la course, courir; *(hurry)* aller à toute vitesse, courir; *(engine)* s'emballer; *(pulse)* augmenter; ~ **car** *(US) n* = **racing car**; ~ **car driver** *n (US)* = **racing driver**; **~course** *n* champ *m* de courses; **~horse** *n* cheval *m* de course; **~r** *n (bike)* vélo *m* de course; **~track** *n* piste *f*

racial ['reɪʃl] *adj* racial(e)

racing ['reɪsɪŋ] *n* courses *fpl*; ~ **car** *(BRIT) n* voiture *f* de course; ~ **driver** *(BRIT) n* pilote *m* de course

racism ['reɪsɪzəm] *n* racisme *m*; **racist** *adj* raciste ♦ *n* raciste *m/f*

rack [ræk] *n (for guns, tools)* râtelier *m*; *(also: luggage ~)* porte-bagages *m inv*, filet *m* à bagages; *(also: roof ~)* galerie *f*; *(dish ~)* égouttoir *m* ♦ *vt* tourmenter; **to** ~ **one's brains** se creuser la cervelle

racket ['rækɪt] *n (for tennis)* raquette *f*; *(noise)* tapage *m*; vacarme *m*; *(swindle)* escroquerie *f*

racquet ['rækɪt] *n* raquette *f*

racy ['reɪsɪ] *adj* plein(e) de verve; *(slightly indecent)* osé(e)

radar ['reɪdɑːr] *n* radar *m*

radial ['reɪdɪəl] *adj (also: ~-ply)* à carcasse radiale

radiant ['reɪdɪənt] *adj* rayonnant(e)

radiate ['reɪdɪeɪt] *vt (heat)* émettre, dégager; *(emotion)* rayonner de ♦ *vi (lines)* rayonner; **radiation** [reɪdɪ'eɪʃən] *n* rayonnement *m*;

(radioactive) radiation *f*; **radiator** ['reɪdɪeɪtər] *n* radiateur *m*

radical ['rædɪkl] *adj* radical(e)

radii ['reɪdɪaɪ] *npl of* **radius**

radio ['reɪdɪəʊ] *n* radio *f* ♦ *vt* appeler par radio; **on the** ~ à la radio; **~active** ['reɪdɪəʊ'æktɪv] *adj* radioactif(-ive); ~ **cassette** *n* radiocassette *m*; **~-controlled** *adj* téléguidé(e); ~ **station** *n* station *f* de radio

radish ['rædɪʃ] *n* radis *m*

radius ['reɪdɪəs] *(pl* **radii)** *n* rayon *m*

RAF *n abbr* = **Royal Air Force**

raffle ['ræfl] *n* tombola *f*

raft [rɑːft] *n (craft; also: life ~)* radeau *m*

rafter ['rɑːftər] *n* chevron *m*

rag [ræg] *n* chiffon *m*; *(pej: newspaper)* feuille *f* de chou, torchon *m*; *(student ~)* attractions organisées au profit d'œuvres de charité; **~s** *npl (torn clothes etc)* haillons *mpl*; ~ **doll** *n* poupée *f* de chiffon

rage [reɪdʒ] *n (fury)* rage *f*, fureur *f* ♦ *vi (person)* être fou (folle) de rage; *(storm)* faire rage, être déchaîné(e); **it's all the** ~ cela fait fureur

ragged ['rægɪd] *adj (edge)* inégal(e); *(clothes)* en loques; *(appearance)* déguenillé(e)

raid [reɪd] *n (attack, also: MIL)* raid *m*; *(criminal)* hold-up *m inv*; *(by police)* descente *f*, rafle *f* ♦ *vt* faire un raid sur or un hold-up or une descente dans

rail [reɪl] *n (on stairs)* rampe *f*; *(on bridge, balcony)* balustrade *f*; *(of ship)* bastingage *m*; **~s** *npl (track)* rails *mpl*, voie ferrée; **by** ~ par chemin de fer, en train; **~ing(s)** *n(pl)* grille *f*; **~road** *(US)*, **~way** *(BRIT) n (track)* voie ferrée; *(company)* chemin *m* de fer; **~way line** *(BRIT) n* ligne *f* de chemin de fer; **~wayman** *(BRIT) (irreg)* *n* cheminot *m*; **~way station** *(BRIT) n* gare *f*

rain [reɪn] *n* pluie *f* ♦ *vi* pleuvoir; **in the** ~ sous la pluie; **it's ~ing** il pleut; **~bow** *n* arc-en-ciel *m*; **~coat** *n* imperméable *m*; **~drop** *n* goutte *f* de pluie; **~fall** *n* chute *f* de pluie; *(measurement)* hauteur *f* des précipitations; **~forest** *n* forêt *f* tropicale humide; **~y** *adj* pluvieux(-euse)

raise [reɪz] *n* augmentation *f* ♦ *vt (lift)* lever; hausser; *(increase)* augmenter; *(morale)* remonter; *(standards)* améliorer; *(question, doubt)* provoquer, soulever; *(cattle, family)* élever; *(crop)* faire pousser; *(funds)* rassembler; *(loan)* obtenir; *(army)* lever; **to** ~ **one's voice** élever la voix

raisin ['reɪzn] *n* raisin sec

rake [reɪk] *n (tool)* râteau *m* ♦ *vt (garden, leaves)* ratisser

rally ['rælɪ] *n (POL etc)* meeting *m*, rassemblement *m*; *(AUT)* rallye *m*; *(TENNIS)* échange *m* ♦ *vt* (*support*) gagner ♦ *vi* (*sick person*) reprendre; ~ **round** *vt fus* venir en aide à

RAM [ræm] *n abbr* (= random access memory) mémoire vive

ram [ræm] *n* bélier *m* ♦ *vt* enfoncer; (*crash into*) emboutir; percuter

ramble ['ræmbl] *n* randonnée *f* ♦ *vi* (*walk*) se promener, faire une randonnée; (*talk: also:* ~ **on**) discourir, pérorer; ~**r** *n* promeneur(-euse), randonneur(-euse); (*BOT*) rosier grimpant; **rambling** *adj* (*speech*) décousu(e); (*house*) plein(e) de coins et de recoins; (*BOT*) grimpant(e)

ramp [ræmp] *n* (*incline*) rampe *f*; dénivellation *f*; **on ~**, **off ~** (*US: AUT*) bretelle *f* d'accès

rampage [ræm'peɪdʒ] *n*: **to be on the ~** se déchaîner

rampant ['ræmpənt] *adj* (*disease etc*) qui sévit

ram raiding [-reɪdɪŋ] *n* pillage d'un magasin en enfonçant la vitrine avec une voiture

ramshackle ['ræmʃækl] *adj* (*house*) délabré(e); (*car etc*) déglingué(e)

ran [ræn] *pt of* **run**

ranch [rɑːntʃ] *n* ranch *m*; ~**er** *n* propriétaire *m* de ranch

rancid ['rænsɪd] *adj* rance

rancour ['ræŋkəʳ] (*US* rancor) *n* rancune *f*

random ['rændəm] *adj* fait(e) or établi(e) au hasard; (*MATH*) aléatoire ♦ *n*: **at ~** au hasard; ~ **access** *n* (*COMPUT*) accès sélectif

randy ['rændɪ] (*BRIT: inf*) *adj* excité(e); lubrique

rang [ræŋ] *pt of* **ring**

range [reɪndʒ] *n* (*of mountains*) chaîne *f*; (*of missile, voice*) portée *f*; (*of products*) choix *m*, gamme *f*; (*MIL: also:* **shooting ~**) champ *m* de tir; (*indoor*) stand *m* de tir; (*also:* **kitchen ~**) fourneau *m* (de cuisine) ♦ *vt* (*place in a line*) mettre en rang, ranger ♦ *vi*: **to ~ over** (*extend*) couvrir; **to ~ from ... to** aller de ... à; **a ~ of** (*series: of proposals etc*) divers(e)

ranger ['reɪndʒəʳ] *n* garde forestier

rank [ræŋk] *n* rang *m*; (*MIL*) grade *m*; (*BRIT: also:* **taxi ~**) station *f* de taxis ♦ *vi*: **to ~ among** compter or se classer parmi ♦ *adj* (*stinking*) fétide, puant(e); **the ~ and file** (*fig*) la masse, la base

ransack ['rænsæk] *vt* fouiller (à fond); (*plunder*) piller

ransom ['rænsəm] *n* rançon *f*; **to hold to ~** (*fig*) exercer un chantage sur

rant [rænt] *vi* fulminer

rap [ræp] *vt* frapper sur or à; taper sur ♦ *n*: ~ **music** rap *m*

rape [reɪp] *n* viol *m*; (*BOT*) colza *m* ♦ *vt* violer; ~**(seed) oil** *n* huile *f* de colza

rapid ['ræpɪd] *adj* rapide; ~**s** *npl* (*GEO*)

rapides *mpl*

rapist ['reɪpɪst] *n* violeur *m*

rapport [ræ'pɔːr] *n* entente *f*

rapturous ['ræptʃərəs] *adj* enthousiaste, frénétique

rare [reəʳ] *adj* rare; (*CULIN: steak*) saignant(e)

raring ['reərɪŋ] *adj*: ~ **to go** (*inf*) très impatient(e) de commencer

rascal ['rɑːskl] *n* vaurien *m*

rash [ræʃ] *adj* imprudent(e), irréfléchi(e) ♦ *n* (*MED*) rougeur *f*, éruption *f*; (*spate: of events*) série (noire)

rasher ['ræʃəʳ] *n* fine tranche (de lard)

raspberry ['rɑːzbərɪ] *n* framboise *f*; ~ **bush** *n* framboisier *m*

rasping ['rɑːspɪŋ] *adj*: ~ **noise** grincement *m*

rat [ræt] *n* rat *m*

rate [reɪt] *n* taux *m*; (*speed*) vitesse *f*, rythme *m*; (*price*) tarif *m* ♦ *vt* classer; évaluer; ~**s** *npl* (*BRIT: tax*) impôts locaux; (*fees*) tarifs *mpl*; **to ~ sb/sth as** considérer qn/qch comme; ~**able value** (*BRIT*) *n* valeur locative imposable; ~**payer** ['reɪtpeɪəʳ] (*BRIT*) *n* contribuable *m/f* (*payant les impôts locaux*)

rather ['rɑːðəʳ] *adv* plutôt; **it's ~ expensive** c'est assez cher; (*too much*) c'est un peu cher; **there's ~ a lot** il y en a beaucoup; **I would** or **I'd ~ go** j'aimerais mieux or je préférerais partir

rating ['reɪtɪŋ] *n* (*assessment*) évaluation *f*; (*score*) classement *m*; ~**s** *npl* (*RADIO, TV*) indice *m* d'écoute

ratio ['reɪʃɪəʊ] *n* proportion *f*

ration ['ræʃən] *n* (*gen pl*) ration(s) *f(pl)*

rational ['ræʃənl] *adj* raisonnable, sensé(e); (*solution, reasoning*) logique; ~**e** [ræʃə'nɑːl] *n* raisonnement *m*; ~**ize** *vt* rationaliser; (*conduct*) essayer d'expliquer *or* de motiver

rat race *n* foire *f* d'empoigne

rattle ['rætl] *n* (*of door, window*) battement *m*; (*of coins, chain*) cliquetis *m*; (*of train, engine*) bruit *m* de ferraille; (*object: for baby*) hochet *m* ♦ *vi* cliqueter; (*car, bus*): **to ~ along** rouler dans un bruit de ferraille ♦ *vt* agiter (bruyamment); (*unnerve*) décontenancer; ~**snake** *n* serpent *m* à sonnettes

raucous ['rɔːkəs] *adj* rauque; (*noisy*) bruyant(e), tapageur(-euse)

rave [reɪv] *vi* (*in anger*) s'emporter; (*with enthusiasm*) s'extasier; (*MED*) délirer ♦ *n* (*BRIT: inf: party*) rave *f*, soirée *f* techno

raven ['reɪvən] *n* corbeau *m*

ravenous ['rævənəs] *adj* affamé(e)

ravine [rə'viːn] *n* ravin *m*

raving ['reɪvɪŋ] *adj*: ~ **lunatic** ♦ *n* fou (folle) furieux(-euse)

ravishing ['rævɪʃɪŋ] *adj* enchanteur(-eresse)

raw [rɔː] *adj* (*uncooked*) cru(e); (*not processed*) brut(e); (*sore*) à vif, irrité(e);

(*inexperienced*) inexpérimenté(e); (*weather, day*) froid(e) et humide; ~ **deal** (*inf*) *n* sale coup *m*; ~ **material** *n* matière première

ray [reɪ] *n* rayon *m*; ~ **of hope** lueur *f* d'espoir

raze [reɪz] *vt* (*also:* ~ **to the ground**) raser, détruire

razor *n* rasoir *m*; ~ **blade** *n* lame *f* de rasoir

Rd *abbr* = **road**

RE *n abbr* = **religious education**

re [riː] *prep* concernant

reach [riːtʃ] *n* portée *f*, atteinte *f*; (*of river etc*) étendue *f* ♦ *vt* atteindre; (*conclusion, decision*) parvenir à ♦ *vi* s'étendre, étendre le bras; **out of/within** ~ hors de/à portée; **within** ~ **of the shops** pas trop loin des or à proximité des magasins; ~ **out** *vt* tendre ♦ *vi*: **to** ~ **out (for)** allonger le bras (pour prendre)

react [riːˈækt] *vi* réagir; ~**ion** *n* réaction *f*

reactor [riːˈæktə*] *n* réacteur *m*

read [riːd, *pt, pp* red] (*pt, pp* **read**) *vi* lire ♦ *vt* lire; (*understand*) comprendre, interpréter; (*study*) étudier; (*meter*) relever; ~ **out** *vt* lire à haute voix; ~**able** *adj* facile or agréable à lire; (*writing*) lisible; ~**er** *n* lecteur(-trice); (*BRIT: at university*) chargé(e) d'enseignement; ~**ership** *n* (*of paper etc*) (nombre *m* de) lecteurs *mpl*

readily [ˈrɛdɪlɪ] *adv* volontiers, avec empressement; (*easily*) facilement

readiness [ˈrɛdɪnɪs] *n* empressement *m*; **in** ~ (*prepared*) prêt(e)

reading [ˈriːdɪŋ] *n* lecture *f*; (*understanding*) interprétation *f*; (*on instrument*) indications *fpl*

ready [ˈrɛdɪ] *adj* prêt(e); (*willing*) prêt, disposé(e); (*available*) disponible ♦ *n*: **at the** ~ (*MIL*) prêt à faire feu; **to get** ~ *vi* se préparer ♦ *vt* préparer; ~**-made** *adj* tout(e) fait(e); ~**-to-wear** *adj* prêt(e) à porter

real [rɪəl] *adj* véritable; réel(le); **in** ~ **terms** dans la réalité; ~ **estate** *n* biens fonciers or immobiliers; ~**istic** [rɪəˈlɪstɪk] *adj* réaliste; ~**ity** [riːˈælɪtɪ] *n* réalité *f*

realization [rɪəlaɪˈzeɪʃən] *n* (*awareness*) prise *f* de conscience; (*fulfilment; also: of asset*) réalisation *f*

realize [ˈrɪəlaɪz] *vt* (*understand*) se rendre compte de; (*a project, COMM: asset*) réaliser

really [ˈrɪəlɪ] *adv* vraiment; ~**?** vraiment?, c'est vrai?

realm [rɛlm] *n* royaume *m*; (*fig*) domaine *m*

realtor ® [ˈrɪəltɔː*] (*US*) *n* agent immobilier

reap [riːp] *vt* moissonner; (*fig*) récolter

reappear [riːəˈpɪə*] *vi* réapparaître, reparaître

rear [rɪə*] *adj* de derrière, arrière *inv*; (*AUT: wheel etc*) arrière ♦ *n* arrière *m* ♦ *vt* (*cattle, family*) élever ♦ *vi* (*also:* ~ **up**: *animal*) se cabrer; ~**guard** *n* (*MIL*) arrière-garde *f*; ~**view mirror** *n* (*AUT*) rétroviseur *m*

reason [ˈriːzn] *n* raison *f* ♦ *vi*: **to** ~ **with sb** raisonner qn, faire entendre raison à qn; **to have** ~ **to think** avoir lieu de penser; **it stands to** ~ **that** il va sans dire que; ~**able** *adj* raisonnable; (*not bad*) acceptable; ~**ably** *adv* raisonnablement; ~**ing** *n* raisonnement *m*

reassurance [riːəˈʃʊərəns] *n* réconfort *m*; (*factual*) assurance *f*, garantie *f*

reassure [riːəˈʃʊə*] *vt* rassurer

rebate [ˈriːbeɪt] *n* (*on tax etc*) dégrèvement *m*

rebel [*n* ˈrɛbl, *vb* rɪˈbɛl] *n* rebelle *m/f* ♦ *vi* se rebeller, se révolter; ~**lious** [rɪˈbɛljəs] *adj* rebelle

rebound [*vb* rɪˈbaʊnd, *n* ˈriːbaʊnd] *vi* (*ball*) rebondir ♦ *n* rebond *m*; **to marry on the** ~ se marier immédiatement après une déception amoureuse

rebuff [rɪˈbʌf] *n* rebuffade *f*

rebuke [rɪˈbjuːk] *vt* réprimander

rebut [rɪˈbʌt] *vt* réfuter

recall [*vb* rɪˈkɔːl, *n* ˈriːkɔl] *vt* rappeler; (*remember*) se rappeler, se souvenir de ♦ *n* rappel *m*; (*ability to remember*) mémoire *f*

recant [rɪˈkænt] *vi* se rétracter; (*REL*) abjurer

recap [ˈriːkæp], **recapitulate** [riːkəˈpɪtjuleɪt] *vt, vi* récapituler

rec'd *abbr* = **received**

recede [rɪˈsiːd] *vi* (*tide*) descendre; (*disappear*) disparaître peu à peu; (*memory, hope*) s'estomper; **receding** *adj* (*chin*) fuyant(e); **receding hairline** front dégarni

receipt [rɪˈsiːt] *n* (*document*) reçu *m*; (*for parcel etc*) accusé *m* de réception; (*act of receiving*) réception *f*; ~**s** *npl* (*COMM*) recettes *fpl*

receive [rɪˈsiːv] *vt* recevoir; ~**r** *n* (*TEL*) récepteur *m*, combiné *m*; (*RADIO*) récepteur *m*; (*of stolen goods*) receleur *m*; (*LAW*) administrateur *m* judiciaire

recent [ˈriːsnt] *adj* récent(e); ~**ly** *adv* récemment

receptacle [rɪˈsɛptɪkl] *n* récipient *m*

reception [rɪˈsɛpʃən] *n* réception *f*; (*welcome*) accueil *m*, réception; ~ **desk** *n* réception *f*; ~**ist** *n* réceptionniste *m/f*

recess [rɪˈsɛs] *n* (*in room*) renfoncement *m*, alcôve *f*; (*secret place*) recoin *m*; (*POL etc: holiday*) vacances *fpl*

recession [rɪˈsɛʃən] *n* récession *f*

recipe [ˈrɛsɪpɪ] *n* recette *f*

recipient [rɪˈsɪpɪənt] *n* (*of payment*) bénéficiaire *m/f*; (*of letter*) destinataire *m/f*

recital [rɪˈsaɪtl] *n* récital *m*

recite [rɪˈsaɪt] *vt* (*poem*) réciter

reckless [ˈrɛkləs] *adj* (*driver etc*) imprudent(e)

reckon [ˈrɛkən] *vt* (*count*) calculer, compter; (*think*): **I** ~ **that ...** je pense que ...; ~ **on** *vt* fus compter sur, s'attendre à; ~**ing** *n* compte *m*, calcul *m*; estimation *f*

reclaim [rɪ'kleɪm] vt (*demand back*) réclamer (le remboursement *or* la restitution de); (*land: from sea*) assécher; (*waste materials*) récupérer

recline [rɪ'klaɪn] vi être allongé(e) *or* étendu(e); **reclining** *adj* (*seat*) à dossier réglable

recluse [rɪ'kluːs] *n* reclus(e), ermite *m*

recognition [rɛkəg'nɪʃən] *n* reconnaissance *f*; **to gain** ~ être reconnu(e); **transformed beyond** ~ méconnaissable

recognizable ['rɛkəgnaɪzəbl] *adj*: ~ (**by**) reconnaissable (à)

recognize ['rɛkəgnaɪz] vt: **to** ~ (**by/as**) reconnaître (à/comme étant)

recoil [vb rɪ'kɔɪl, n 'riːkɔɪl] vi (*person*): **to** ~ (**from sth/doing sth**) reculer (devant qch/ l'idée de faire qch) ♦ *n* (*of gun*) recul *m*

recollect [rɛkə'lɛkt] vt (*two people*) se rappeler, se souvenir de; ~**ion** *n* souvenir *m*

recommend [rɛkə'mɛnd] vt recommander

reconcile ['rɛkənsaɪl] vt (*two people*) réconcilier; (*two facts*) concilier, accorder; **to** ~ **o.s. to** se résigner à

recondition [riːkən'dɪʃən] vt remettre à neuf; réviser entièrement

reconnoitre [rɛkə'nɔɪtər] (*US* **reconnoiter**) vt (*MIL*) reconnaître

reconsider [riːkən'sɪdər] vt reconsidérer

reconstruct [riːkən'strʌkt] vt (*building*) reconstruire; (*crime, policy, system*) reconstituer

record [n 'rɛkɔːd, vb rɪ'kɔːd] *n* rapport *m*, récit *m*; (*of meeting etc*) procès-verbal *m*; (*register*) registre *m*; (*file*) dossier *m*; (*also*: **criminal** ~) casier *m* judiciaire; (*MUS: disc*) disque *m*; (*SPORT*) record *m*; (*COMPUT*) article *m* ♦ vt (*set down*) noter; (*MUS: song etc*) enregistrer; **in** ~ **time** en un temps record *inv*; **off the** ~ *adj* officieux(-euse) ♦ *adv* officieusement; ~ **card** *n* (*in file*) fiche *f*; ~**ed delivery** *n* (*BRIT: POST*): ~**ed delivery letter etc** lettre *etc* recommandée; ~**er** *n* (*MUS*) flûte *f* à bec; ~ **holder** *n* (*SPORT*) détenteur(-trice) du record; ~**ing** *n* (*MUS*) enregistre- ment *m*; ~ **player** *n* tourne-disque *m*

recount [rɪ'kaunt] vt raconter

re-count ['riːkaunt] *n* (*POL: of votes*) deuxième compte *m*

recoup [rɪ'kuːp] vt: **to** ~ **one's losses** récupérer ce qu'on a perdu, se refaire

recourse [rɪ'kɔːs] *n*: **to have** ~ **to** avoir recours à

recover [rɪ'kʌvər] vt récupérer ♦ vi: **to** ~ (**from**) (*illness*) se rétablir (de); (*from shock*) se remettre (de); ~**y** *n* récupération *f*; rétablissement *m*; (*ECON*) redressement *m*

recreation [rɛkrɪ'eɪʃən] *n* récréation *f*,

détente *f*; ~**al** *adj* pour la détente, récréa-tif(-ive)

recruit [rɪ'kruːt] *n* recrue *f* ♦ vt recruter

rectangle ['rɛktæŋgl] *n* rectangle *m*; **rectangular** [rɛk'tæŋgjulər] *adj* rectangulaire

rectify ['rɛktɪfaɪ] vt (*error*) rectifier, corriger

rector ['rɛktər] *n* (*REL*) pasteur *m*

recuperate [rɪ'kjuːpəreɪt] vi récupérer; (*from illness*) se rétablir

recur [rɪ'kəːr] vi se reproduire; (*symptoms*) réapparaître; ~**rence** *n* répétition *f*; réapparition *f*; ~**rent** *adj* périodique, fréquent(e)

recycle [riː'saɪkl] vt recycler; **recycling** *n* recyclage *m*

red [rɛd] *n* rouge *m*; (*POL: pej*) rouge *m/f* ♦ *adj* rouge; (*hair*) roux (rousse); **in the** ~ (*account*) à découvert; (*business*) en déficit; ~ **carpet treatment** *n* réception *f* en grande pompe; **R~ Cross** *n* Croix-Rouge *f*; ~**currant** *n* groseille *f* (rouge); ~**den** vt, vi rougir

redecorate [riː'dɛkəreɪt] vi (*with wallpaper*) retapisser; (*with paint*) refaire les peintures

redeem [rɪ'diːm] vt (*debt*) rembourser; (*sth in pawn*) dégager; (*fig, also REL*) racheter; ~**ing** *adj* (*feature*) qui sauve, qui rachète (le reste)

redeploy [riːdɪ'plɔɪ] vt (*resources*) réorganiser

red: ~**-haired** *adj* roux (rousse); ~**-handed** *adj*: **to be caught** ~**-handed** être pris(e) en flagrant délit *or* la main dans le sac; ~**head** *n* roux (rousse); ~ **herring** *n* (*fig*) diversion *f*, fausse piste; ~**-hot** *adj* chauffé(e) au rouge, brûlant(e)

redirect [riːdaɪ'rɛkt] vt (*mail*) faire suivre

red light *n*: **to go through a** ~ (*AUT*) brûler un feu rouge; **red-light district** *n* quartier *m* des prostituées

redo [riː'duː] (*irreg*) vt refaire

redress [rɪ'drɛs] *n* réparation *f* ♦ vt redresser

red: **R~ Sea** *n* mer Rouge *f*; ~**skin** *n* Peau-Rouge *m/f*; ~ **tape** *n* (*fig*) paperasserie (administrative)

reduce [rɪ'djuːs] vt réduire; (*lower*) abaisser; "~ **speed now**" (*AUT*) "ralentir"; **reduction** [rɪ'dʌkʃən] *n* réduction *f*; (*discount*) rabais *m*

redundancy [rɪ'dʌndənsɪ] (*BRIT*) *n* licenciement *m*, mise *f* au chômage

redundant [rɪ'dʌndnt] *adj* (*BRIT: worker*) mis(e) au chômage, licencié(e); (*detail, object*) superflu(e); **to be made** ~ être licencié(e), mis(e) au chômage

reed [riːd] *n* (*BOT*) roseau *m*; (*MUS: of clarinet etc*) hanche *f*

reef [riːf] *n* (*at sea*) récif *m*, écueil *m*

reek [riːk] vi: **to** ~ (**of**) puer, empester

reel [riːl] *n* bobine *f*; (*FISHING*) moulinet *m*; (*CINEMA*) bande *f*; (*dance*) quadrille écossais

♦ vi (sway) chanceler; ~ **in** vt (fish, line)
ramener
ref [ref] (inf) n abbr (= referee) arbitre m
refectory [rɪ'fektərɪ] n réfectoire m
refer [rɪ'fɜ:ʳ] vt: **to ~ sb to** (inquirer: for
information, patient: to specialist) adresser qn
à; (reader: to text) renvoyer qn à; (dispute,
decision): **to ~ sth to** soumettre qch à ♦ vi:
~ **to** (allude to) parler de, faire allusion à;
(consult) se reporter à
referee [refə'ri:] n arbitre m; (BRIT: for job
application) répondant(e)
reference ['refrəns] n référence f, renvoi m;
(mention) allusion f, mention f; (for job
application: letter) références, lettre f de
recommandation; **with ~ to** (COMM: in letter)
me référant à, suite à; **~ book** n ouvrage m
de référence
refill [vb ri:'fɪl, n 'ri:fɪl] vt remplir à nouveau;
(pen, lighter etc) recharger ♦ n (for pen etc)
recharge f
refine [rɪ'faɪn] vt (sugar, oil) raffiner; (taste)
affiner; (theory, idea) fignoler (inf); **~d** adj
(person, taste) raffiné(e); **~ry** n raffinerie f
reflect [rɪ'flekt] vt (light, image) réfléchir,
refléter; (fig) refléter ♦ vi (think) réfléchir,
méditer; **it ~s badly on him** cela le discrédite;
it ~s well on him c'est tout à son honneur;
~ion n réflexion f; (image) reflet m;
(criticism): **~ion on** critique f de; atteinte f à;
on ~ion réflexion faite
reflex ['ri:fleks] adj réflexe ♦ n réflexe m; **~ive**
[rɪ'fleksɪv] adj (LING) réfléchi(e)
reform [rɪ'fɔ:m] n réforme f ♦ vt réformer;
~atory [rɪ'fɔ:mətərɪ] (US) n ≈ centre m
d'éducation surveillée
refrain [rɪ'freɪn] vi: **to ~ from doing** s'abstenir
de faire ♦ n refrain m
refresh [rɪ'freʃ] vt rafraîchir; (subj: sleep)
reposer; **~er course** (BRIT) n cours m de
recyclage; **~ing** adj (drink) rafraîchissant(e);
(sleep) réparateur(-trice); **~ments** npl
rafraîchissements mpl
refrigerator [rɪ'frɪdʒəreɪtəʳ] n réfrigérateur
m, frigidaire ® m
refuel [ri:'fjuəl] vi se ravitailler en carburant
refuge ['refju:dʒ] n refuge m; **to take ~ in** se
réfugier dans; **~e** [refju'dʒi:] n réfugié(e)
refund [n 'ri:fʌnd, vb ri'fʌnd] n
remboursement m ♦ vt rembourser
refurbish [ri:'fɜ:bɪʃ] vt remettre à neuf
refusal [rɪ'fju:zəl] n refus m; **to have first ~
on** avoir droit de préemption sur
refuse¹ [rɪ'fju:z] vt, vi refuser
refuse² ['refju:s] n ordures fpl, détritus mpl;
~ collection n ramassage m d'ordures
regain [rɪ'geɪn] vt regagner; retrouver
regal ['ri:gl] adj royal(e)
regard [rɪ'gɑ:d] n respect m, estime f,

considération f ♦ vt considérer; **to give one's
~s to** faire ses amitiés à; **"with kindest ~s"**
"bien amicalement"; **as ~s, with ~ to**
= **regarding**; **~ing** prep en ce qui concerne;
~less adv quand même; **~less of** sans se
soucier de
régime [reɪ'ʒi:m] n régime m
regiment ['redʒɪmənt] n régiment m; **~al**
[redʒɪ'mentl] adj d'un ou du régiment
region ['ri:dʒən] n région f; **in the ~ of** (fig)
aux alentours de; **~al** adj régional(e)
register ['redʒɪstəʳ] n registre m; (also:
electoral ~) liste électorale ♦ vt enregistrer;
(birth, death) déclarer; (vehicle) immatriculer;
(POST: letter) envoyer en recommandé; (subj:
instrument) marquer ♦ vi s'inscrire; (at hotel)
signer le registre; (make impression) être
(bien) compris(e); **~ed** adj (letter, parcel)
recommandé(e); **~ed trademark** n marque
déposée; **registrar** ['redʒɪstrɑ:ʳ] n officier m
de l'état civil; **registration** [redʒɪs'treɪʃən] n
enregistrement m; (BRIT: AUT: also:
registration number) numéro m
d'immatriculation
registry ['redʒɪstrɪ] n bureau m de
l'enregistrement; **~ office** (BRIT) n bureau m
de l'état civil; **to get married in a ~ office** ≈ se
marier à la mairie
regret [rɪ'gret] n regret m ♦ vt regretter;
~fully adv à ou avec regret
regular ['regjuləʳ] adj régulier(-ère); (usual)
habituel(le); (soldier) de métier ♦ n (client
etc) habitué(e); **~ly** adv régulièrement
regulate ['regjuleɪt] vt régler; **regulation**
[regju'leɪʃən] n (rule) règlement m;
(adjustment) réglage m
rehabilitation ['ri:əbɪlɪ'teɪʃən] n (of
offender) réinsertion f; (of addict)
réadaptation f
rehearsal [rɪ'hɜ:səl] n répétition f
rehearse [rɪ'hɜ:s] vt répéter
reign [reɪn] n règne m ♦ vi régner
reimburse [ri:ɪm'bɜ:s] vt rembourser
rein [reɪn] n (for horse) rêne f
reindeer ['reɪndɪəʳ] n, pl inv renne m
reinforce [ri:ɪn'fɔ:s] vt renforcer; **~d
concrete** n béton armé; **~ments** npl (MIL)
renfort(s) m(pl)
reinstate [ri:ɪn'steɪt] vt rétablir, réintégrer
reject [n 'ri:dʒekt, vb rɪ'dʒekt] n (COMM)
article m de rebut ♦ vt refuser; (idea) rejeter;
~ion n rejet m, refus m
rejoice [rɪ'dʒɔɪs] vi: **to ~ (at** or **over)** se réjouir
(de)
rejuvenate [rɪ'dʒu:vəneɪt] vt rajeunir
relapse [rɪ'læps] n (MED) rechute f
relate [rɪ'leɪt] vt (tell) raconter; (connect)
établir un rapport entre ♦ vi: **this ~s to** cela se
rapporte à; **to ~ to sb** entretenir des rapports

avec qn; **~d** adj apparenté(e); **relating to** prep concernant

relation [rɪ'leɪʃən] n (person) parent(e); (link) rapport m, lien m; **~ship** n rapport m, lien m; (personal ties) relations fpl, rapports; (also: **family ~ship**) lien de parenté

relative ['relətɪv] n parent(e) ♦ adj relatif(-ive); **all her ~s** toute sa famille; **~ly** adv relativement

relax [rɪ'læks] vi (muscle) se relâcher; (person: unwind) se détendre ♦ vt relâcher; (mind, person) détendre; **~ation** [riːlæk'seɪʃən] n relâchement m; (of mind) détente f, relaxation f; (recreation) détente, délassement m; **~ed** adj détendu(e); **~ing** adj délassant(e)

relay [n 'riːleɪ, vb rɪ'leɪ] n (SPORT) course f de relais ♦ vt (message) retransmettre, relayer

release [rɪ'liːs] n (from prison, obligation) libération f; (of gas etc) émission f; (of film etc) sortie f; (new recording) disque m ♦ vt (prisoner) libérer; (gas etc) émettre, dégager; (free: from wreckage etc) dégager; (TECH: catch, spring etc) faire jouer; (book, film) sortir; (report, news) rendre public, publier

relegate ['relǝgeɪt] vt reléguer; (BRIT: SPORT): **to be ~d** descendre dans une division inférieure

relent [rɪ'lent] vi se laisser fléchir; **~less** adj implacable; (unceasing) continuel(le)

relevant ['relǝvǝnt] adj (question) pertinent(e); (fact) significatif(-ive); (information) utile; **~ to** ayant rapport à, approprié à

reliable [rɪ'laɪǝbl] adj (person, firm) sérieux(-euse), fiable; (method, machine) fiable; (news, information) sûr(e); **reliably** adv: **to be reliably informed** savoir de source sûre

reliance [rɪ'laɪǝns] n: **~ (on)** (person) confiance f (en); (drugs, promises) besoin m (de), dépendance f (de)

relic ['relɪk] n (REL) relique f; (of the past) vestige m

relief [rɪ'liːf] n (from pain, anxiety etc) soulagement m; (help, supplies) secours m(pl); (ART, GEO) relief m

relieve [rɪ'liːv] vt (pain, patient) soulager; (fear, worry) dissiper; (bring help) secourir; (take over from: gen) relayer; (: guard) relever; **to ~ sb of sth** débarrasser qn de qch; **to ~ o.s.** se soulager

religion [rɪ'lɪdʒǝn] n religion f; **religious** adj religieux(-euse); (book) de piété

relinquish [rɪ'lɪŋkwɪʃ] vt abandonner; (plan, habit) renoncer à

relish ['relɪʃ] n (CULIN) condiment m; (enjoyment) délectation f ♦ vt (food etc) savourer; **to ~ doing** se délecter à faire

relocate [riːlǝu'keɪt] vt installer ailleurs ♦ vi déménager, s'installer ailleurs

reluctance [rɪ'lʌktǝns] n répugnance f

reluctant [rɪ'lʌktǝnt] adj peu disposé(e), qui hésite; **~ly** adv à contrecœur

rely on [rɪ'laɪ-] vt fus (be dependent) dépendre de; (trust) compter sur

remain [rɪ'meɪn] vi rester; **~der** n reste m; **~ing** adj qui reste; **~s** npl restes mpl

remake ['riːmeɪk] n (CINEMA) remake m

remand [rɪ'mɑːnd] n: **on ~** en détention préventive ♦ vt: **to be ~ed in custody** être placé(e) en détention préventive

remark [rɪ'mɑːk] n remarque f, observation f ♦ vt (faire) remarquer, dire; **~able** adj remarquable; **~ably** adv remarquablement

remarry [riː'mærɪ] vi se remarier

remedial [rɪ'miːdɪǝl] adj (tuition, classes) de rattrapage; **~ exercises** gymnastique corrective

remedy ['remǝdɪ] n: **~ (for)** remède m (contre or à) ♦ vt remédier à

remember [rɪ'membǝʳ] vt se rappeler, se souvenir de; (send greetings): **~ me to him** saluez-le de ma part; **remembrance** n souvenir m; mémoire f; **Remembrance Day** n le jour de l'Armistice

remind [rɪ'maɪnd] vt: **to ~ sb of** rappeler à qn; **to ~ sb to do** faire penser à qn à faire, rappeler à qn qu'il doit faire; **~er** n (souvenir) souvenir m; (letter) rappel m

reminisce [remɪ'nɪs] vi: **to ~ (about)** évoquer ses souvenirs (de); **~nt** adj: **to be ~nt of** rappeler, faire penser à

remiss [rɪ'mɪs] adj négligent(e); **~ion** n (of illness, sins) rémission f; (of debt, prison sentence) remise f

remit [rɪ'mɪt] vt (send: money) envoyer; **~tance** n paiement m

remnant ['remnǝnt] n reste m, restant m; (of cloth) coupon m; **~s** npl (COMM) fins fpl de série

remorse [rɪ'mɔːs] n remords m; **~ful** adj plein(e) de remords; **~less** adj (fig) impitoyable

remote [rɪ'mǝut] adj éloigné(e), lointain(e); (person) distant(e); (possibility) vague; **~ control** n télécommande f; **~ly** adv au loin; (slightly) très vaguement

remould ['riːmǝuld] (BRIT) n (tyre) pneu rechapé

removable [rɪ'muːvǝbl] adj (detachable) amovible

removal [rɪ'muːvǝl] n (taking away) enlèvement m; suppression f; (BRIT: from house) déménagement m; (from office: dismissal) renvoi m; (of stain) nettoyage m; (MED) ablation f; **~ van** (BRIT) n camion m de déménagement

remove [rɪ'muːv] vt enlever, retirer; (*employee*) renvoyer; (*stain*) faire partir; (*abuse*) supprimer; (*doubt*) chasser

render ['rɛndər] vt rendre; **~ing** n (MUS etc) interprétation f

rendezvous ['rɒndɪvuː] n rendez-vous m inv

renew [rɪ'njuː] vt renouveler; (*negotiations*) reprendre; (*acquaintance*) renouer; **~able** adj (*energy*) renouvelable; **~al** n renouvellement m; reprise f

renounce [rɪ'nauns] vt renoncer à

renovate ['rɛnəveɪt] vt rénover; (*art work*) restaurer

renown [rɪ'naun] n renommée f; **~ed** adj renommé(e)

rent [rɛnt] n loyer m ♦ vt louer; **~al** n (for television, car) (prix m de) location f

reorganize [riːˈɔːɡənaɪz] vt réorganiser

rep [rɛp] n abbr = **representative**; **repertory**

repair [rɪ'pɛər] n réparation f ♦ vt réparer; **in good/bad ~** en bon/mauvais état; **~ kit** n trousse f de réparation

repatriate [riːˈpætrɪeɪt] vt rapatrier

repay [riːˈpeɪ] vt (*irreg*) vt (money, creditor) rembourser; (sb's efforts) récompenser; **~ment** n remboursement m

repeal [rɪ'piːl] n (of law) abrogation f ♦ vt (law) abroger

repeat [rɪ'piːt] n (RADIO, TV) reprise f ♦ vt répéter; (COMM: order) renouveler; (SCOL: a class) redoubler ♦ vi répéter; **~edly** adv souvent, à plusieurs reprises

repel [rɪ'pɛl] vt repousser; **~lent** adj repoussant(e) ♦ n: **insect ~lent** insectifuge m

repent [rɪ'pɛnt] vi: **to ~ (of)** se repentir (de); **~ance** n repentir m

repertory ['rɛpətərɪ] n (also: **~ theatre**) théâtre m de répertoire

repetition [rɛpɪ'tɪʃən] n répétition f

repetitive [rɪ'pɛtɪtɪv] adj (movement, work) répétitif(-ive); (speech) plein(e) de redites

replace [rɪ'pleɪs] vt (put back) remettre, replacer; (take the place of) remplacer; **~ment** n (substitution) remplacement m; (person) remplaçant(e)

replay ['riːpleɪ] n (of match) match rejoué; (of tape, film) répétition f

replenish [rɪ'plɛnɪʃ] vt (glass) remplir (de nouveau); (stock etc) réapprovisionner

replica ['rɛplɪkə] n réplique f, copie exacte

reply [rɪ'plaɪ] n réponse f ♦ vi répondre

report [rɪ'pɔːt] n rapport m; (PRESS etc) reportage m; (BRIT: also: **school ~**) bulletin m (scolaire); (of gun) détonation f ♦ vt rapporter, faire un compte rendu de; (PRESS etc) faire un reportage sur; (bring to notice: occurrence) signaler ♦ vi (make a ~) faire un rapport (or un reportage); (present o.s.): **to ~ (to sb)** se présenter (chez qn); (be

responsible to): **to ~ to sb** être sous les ordres de qn; **~ card** n (US, SCOTTISH) n bulletin m scolaire; **~edly** adv: **she is ~edly living in ...** elle habiterait ...; **he ~edly told them to ...** il leur aurait ordonné de ...; **~er** n reporter m

repose [rɪ'pəuz] n: **in ~** en or au repos

represent [rɛprɪ'zɛnt] vt représenter; (view, belief) présenter, expliquer; (describe): **to ~ sth as** présenter or décrire qch comme; **~ation** [rɛprɪzɛn'teɪʃən] n représentation f; **~ations** npl (protest) démarche f; **~ative** [rɛprɪ'zɛntətɪv] n représentant(e); (US: POL) député m ♦ adj représentatif(-ive), caractéristique

repress [rɪ'prɛs] vt réprimer; **~ion** n répression f

reprieve [rɪ'priːv] n (LAW) grâce f; (fig) sursis m, délai m

reprisal [rɪ'praɪzl] n: **~s** npl représailles fpl

reproach [rɪ'prəutʃ] vt: **to ~ sb with sth** reprocher qch à qn; **~ful** adj de reproche

reproduce [riːprə'djuːs] vt reproduire ♦ vi se reproduire; **reproduction** [riːprə'dʌkʃən] n reproduction f

reproof [rɪ'pruːf] n reproche m

reptile ['rɛptaɪl] n reptile m

republic [rɪ'pʌblɪk] n république f; **~an** adj républicain(e)

repudiate [rɪ'pjuːdɪeɪt] vt répudier, rejeter

repulsive [rɪ'pʌlsɪv] adj repoussant(e), répulsif(-ive)

reputable ['rɛpjutəbl] adj de bonne réputation; (occupation) honorable

reputation [rɛpju'teɪʃən] n réputation f

reputed [rɪ'pjuːtɪd] adj (supposed) supposé(e); **~ly** adv d'après ce qu'on dit

request [rɪ'kwɛst] n demande f; (formal) requête f ♦ vt: **to ~ (of or from sb)** demander (à qn); **~ stop** (BRIT) n (for bus) arrêt facultatif

require [rɪ'kwaɪər] vt (need: subj: person) avoir besoin de; (: thing, situation) demander; (want) exiger; (order): **to ~ sb to do sth/sth of sb** exiger que qn fasse qch/qch de qn; **~ment** n exigence f; besoin m; condition requise

requisition [rɛkwɪ'zɪʃən] n: **~ (for)** demande f (de) ♦ vt (MIL) réquisitionner

rescue ['rɛskjuː] n (from accident) sauvetage m; (help) secours mpl ♦ vt sauver; **~ party** n équipe f de sauvetage; **~r** n sauveteur m

research [rɪ'sɜːtʃ] n recherche(s) f(pl) ♦ vt faire des recherches sur

resemblance [rɪ'zɛmbləns] n ressemblance f

resemble [rɪ'zɛmbl] vt ressembler à

resent [rɪ'zɛnt] vt être contrarié(e) par; **~ful** adj irrité(e), plein(e) de ressentiment; **~ment** n ressentiment m

reservation [rɛzə'veɪʃən] n (booking)

réservation f; (*doubt*) réserve f; (*for tribe*) réserve; **to make a ~ (in a hotel/a restaurant/on a plane)** réserver or retenir une chambre/une table/une place

reserve [rɪ'zɜːv] *n* réserve f; (*SPORT*) remplaçant(e) ♦ *vt* (*seats etc*) réserver, retenir; **~s** *npl* (*MIL*) réservistes *mpl*; **in ~** en réserve; **~d** *adj* réservé(e)

reshuffle [riː'ʃʌfl] *n*: **Cabinet ~** (*POL*) remaniement ministériel

residence ['rezɪdəns] *n* résidence f; **~ permit** (*BRIT*) *n* permis *m* de séjour

resident ['rezɪdənt] *n* résident(e) ♦ *adj* résidant(e); **~ial** [rezɪ'denʃəl] *adj* résidentiel(le); (*course*) avec hébergement sur place; **~ial school** *n* internat *m*

residue ['rezɪdjuː] *n* reste *m*; (*CHEM, PHYSICS*) résidu *m*

resign [rɪ'zaɪn] *vt* (*one's post*) démissionner de ♦ *vi* démissionner; **to ~ o.s. to** se résigner à; **~ation** [rezɪg'neɪʃən] *n* (*of post*) démission f; (*state of mind*) résignation f; **~ed** *adj* résigné(e)

resilient [rɪ'zɪlɪənt] *adj* (*material*) élastique; (*person*) qui réagit, qui a du ressort

resist [rɪ'zɪst] *vt* résister à; **~ance** *n* résistance f

resit [riː'sɪt] *vt* (*exam*) repasser ♦ *n* deuxième session f (*d'un examen*)

resolution [rezə'luːʃən] *n* résolution f

resolve [rɪ'zɒlv] *n* résolution f ♦ *vt* (*problem*) résoudre ♦ *vi*: **to ~ to do** résoudre or décider de faire

resort [rɪ'zɔːt] *n* (*seaside town*) station f balnéaire; (*ski ~*) station de ski; (*recourse*) recours *m* ♦ *vi*: **to ~ to** avoir recours à; **in the last ~** en dernier ressort

resounding [rɪ'zaundɪŋ] *adj* retentissant(e)

resource [rɪ'sɔːs] *n* ressource f; **~s** *npl* (*supplies, wealth etc*) ressources *fpl*; **~ful** *adj* ingénieux(-euse), débrouillard(e)

respect [rɪs'pekt] *n* respect *m* ♦ *vt* respecter; **~s** *npl* (*compliments*) respects, hommages *mpl*; **with ~ to** en ce qui concerne; **in this ~** à cet égard; **~able** *adj* respectable; **~ful** *adj* respectueux(-euse); **~ively** *adv* respectivement

respite ['respaɪt] *n* répit *m*

respond [rɪs'pɒnd] *vi* répondre; (*react*) réagir; **response** *n* réponse f; réaction f

responsibility [rɪspɒnsɪ'bɪlɪtɪ] *n* responsabilité f

responsible [rɪs'pɒnsɪbl] *adj* (*liable*): **~ (for)** responsable (de); (*person*) digne de confiance; (*job*) qui comporte des responsabilités

responsive [rɪs'pɒnsɪv] *adj* qui réagit; (*person*) qui n'est pas réservé(e) or indifférent(e)

rest [rest] *n* repos *m*; (*stop*) arrêt *m*, pause f; (*MUS*) silence *m*; (*support*) support *m*, appui *m*; (*remainder*) reste *m*, restant *m* ♦ *vi* se reposer; (*be supported*): **to ~ on** appuyer sur or reposer sur; (*remain*) rester ♦ *vt* (*lean*): **to ~ sth on/against** appuyer qch sur/contre; **the ~ of them** les autres; **it ~s with him to ...** c'est à lui de ...

restaurant ['restərɒŋ] *n* restaurant *m*; **~ car** (*BRIT*) *n* wagon-restaurant *m*

restful ['restful] *adj* reposant(e)

restive ['restɪv] *adj* agité(e), impatient(e); (*horse*) rétif(-ive)

restless ['restlɪs] *adj* agité(e)

restoration [restə'reɪʃən] *n* restauration f; restitution f; rétablissement *m*

restore [rɪ'stɔːr] *vt* (*building*) restaurer; (*sth stolen*) restituer; (*peace, health*) rétablir; **to ~ to** (*former state*) ramener à

restrain [rɪs'treɪn] *vt* contenir; (*person*): **to ~ (from doing)** retenir (de faire); **~ed** *adj* (*style*) sobre; (*manner*) mesuré(e); **~t** *n* (*restriction*) contrainte f; (*moderation*) retenue f

restrict [rɪs'trɪkt] *vt* restreindre, limiter; **~ion** *n* restriction f, limitation f

rest room (*US*) *n* toilettes *fpl*

result [rɪ'zʌlt] *n* résultat *m* ♦ *vi*: **to ~ in** aboutir à, se terminer par; **as a ~ of** à la suite de

resume [rɪ'zjuːm] *vt, vi* (*work, journey*) reprendre

résumé ['reɪzjuːmeɪ] *n* résumé *m*; (*US*) curriculum vitae *m*

resumption [rɪ'zʌmpʃən] *n* reprise f

resurgence [rɪ'sɜːdʒəns] *n* (*of energy, activity*) regain *m*

resurrection [rezə'rekʃən] *n* résurrection f

resuscitate [rɪ'sʌsɪteɪt] *vt* (*MED*) réanimer

retail ['riːteɪl] *adj* de ou au détail ♦ *adv* au détail; **~er** *n* détaillant(e); **~ price** *n* prix *m* de détail

retain [rɪ'teɪn] *vt* (*keep*) garder, conserver; **~er** *n* (*fee*) acompte *m*, provision f

retaliate [rɪ'tælɪeɪt] *vi*: **to ~ (against)** se venger (de); **retaliation** [rɪtælɪ'eɪʃən] *n* représailles *fpl*, vengeance f

retarded [rɪ'tɑːdɪd] *adj* retardé(e)

retch [retʃ] *vi* avoir des haut-le-cœur

retentive [rɪ'tentɪv] *adj*: **~ memory** excellente mémoire

retina ['retɪnə] *n* rétine f

retire [rɪ'taɪər] *vi* (*give up work*) prendre sa retraite; (*withdraw*) se retirer, partir; (*go to bed*) (aller) se coucher; **~d** *adj* (*person*) retraité(e); **~ment** *n* retraite f; **retiring** *adj* (*shy*) réservé(e); (*leaving*) sortant(e)

retort [rɪ'tɔːt] *vi* riposter

retrace [riː'treɪs] *vt*: **to ~ one's steps** revenir

sur ses pas
retract [rɪˈtrækt] vt (*statement, claws*) rétracter; (*undercarriage, aerial*) rentrer, escamoter
retrain [riːˈtreɪn] vt (*worker*) recycler
retread [ˈriːtrɛd] n (*tyre*) pneu rechapé
retreat [rɪˈtriːt] n retraite f ♦ vi battre en retraite
retribution [rɛtrɪˈbjuːʃən] n châtiment m
retrieval [rɪˈtriːvəl] n (*see vb*) récupération f; réparation f
retrieve [rɪˈtriːv] vt (*sth lost*) récupérer; (*situation, honour*) sauver; (*error, loss*) réparer; **~r** n chien m d'arrêt
retrospect [ˈrɛtrəspɛkt] n: **in ~** rétrospectivement, après coup; **~ive** [rɛtrəˈspɛktɪv] adj rétrospectif(-ive); (*law*) rétroactif(-ive)
return [rɪˈtɜːn] n (*going or coming back*) retour m; (*of sth stolen etc*) restitution f; (*FINANCE: from land, shares*) rendement m, rapport m ♦ cpd (*journey*) de retour; (*BRIT: ticket*) aller et retour; (*match*) retour ♦ vi (*come back*) revenir; (*go back*) retourner ♦ vt rendre; (*bring back*) rapporter; (*send back; also: ball*) renvoyer; (*put back*) remettre; (*POL: candidate*) élire; **~s** npl (*COMM*) recettes fpl; (*FINANCE*) bénéfices mpl; **in ~ (for)** en échange (de); **by ~ (of post)** par retour (du courrier); **many happy ~s (of the day)!** bon anniversaire!
reunion [riːˈjuːnɪən] n réunion f
reunite [riːjuːˈnaɪt] vt réunir
reuse [riːˈjuːz] vt réutiliser
rev [rɛv] n abbr (*AUT*: = *revolution*) tour m ♦ vt (*also*: **rev up**) emballer
revamp [riːˈvæmp] vt (*firm, system etc*) réorganiser
reveal [rɪˈviːl] vt (*make known*) révéler; (*display*) laisser voir; **~ing** adj révélateur(-trice); (*dress*) au décolleté généreux or suggestif
revel [ˈrɛvl] vi: **to ~ in sth/in doing** se délecter de qch/à faire
revenge [rɪˈvɛndʒ] n vengeance f; **to take ~ on** (*enemy*) se venger sur
revenue [ˈrɛvənjuː] n revenu m
reverberate [rɪˈvɜːbəreɪt] vi (*sound*) retentir, se répercuter; (*fig: shock etc*) se propager
reverence [ˈrɛvərəns] n vénération f, révérence f
Reverend [ˈrɛvərənd] adj (*in titles*): **the ~ John Smith** (*Anglican*) le révérend John Smith; (*Catholic*) l'abbé (John) Smith; (*Protestant*) le pasteur (John) Smith
reversal [rɪˈvɜːsl] n (*of opinion*) revirement m; (*of order*) renversement m; (*of direction*) changement m
reverse [rɪˈvɜːs] n contraire m, opposé m;

(*back*) dos m, envers m; (*of paper*) verso m; (*of coin; also: setback*) revers m; (*AUT: also:* **~ gear**) marche f arrière ♦ adj (*order, direction*) opposé(e), inverse ♦ vt (*order, position*) changer, inverser; (*direction, policy*) changer complètement de; (*decision*) annuler; (*roles*) renverser; (*car*) faire marche arrière avec ♦ vi (*BRIT: AUT*) faire marche arrière; **he ~d (the car) into a wall** il a embouti un mur en marche arrière; **~d charge call** (*BRIT*) n (*TEL*) communication f en PCV; **reversing lights** (*BRIT*) npl (*AUT*) feux mpl de marche arrière or de recul
revert [rɪˈvɜːt] vi: **to ~ to** revenir à, retourner à
review [rɪˈvjuː] n revue f; (*of book, film*) critique f, compte rendu; (*of situation, policy*) examen m, bilan m ♦ vt passer en revue; faire la critique de; examiner; **~er** n critique m
revise [rɪˈvaɪz] vt réviser, modifier; (*manuscript*) revoir, corriger ♦ vi (*study*) réviser; **revision** [rɪˈvɪʒən] n révision f
revival [rɪˈvaɪvəl] n reprise f; (*recovery*) rétablissement m; (*of faith*) renouveau m
revive [rɪˈvaɪv] vt (*person*) ranimer; (*economy*) relancer; (*hope, courage*) raviver, faire renaître; (*play*) reprendre ♦ vi (*person*) reprendre connaissance; (*: from ill health*) se rétablir; (*hope etc*) renaître; (*activity*) reprendre
revoke [rɪˈvəuk] vt révoquer; (*law*) abroger
revolt [rɪˈvəult] n révolte f ♦ vi se révolter, se rebeller ♦ vt révolter, dégoûter; **~ing** adj dégoûtant(e)
revolution [rɛvəˈluːʃən] n révolution f; (*of wheel etc*) tour m, révolution; **~ary** adj révolutionnaire ♦ n révolutionnaire m/f
revolve [rɪˈvɔlv] vi tourner
revolver [rɪˈvɔlvər] n revolver m
revolving [rɪˈvɔlvɪŋ] adj tournant(e); (*chair*) pivotant(e); **~ door** n (*porte f à*) tambour m
revulsion [rɪˈvʌlʃən] n dégoût m, répugnance f
reward [rɪˈwɔːd] n récompense f ♦ vt: **to ~ (for)** récompenser (de); **~ing** adj (*fig*) qui (en) vaut la peine, gratifiant(e)
rewind [riːˈwaɪnd] (*irreg*) vt (*tape*) rembobiner
rewire [riːˈwaɪər] vt (*house*) refaire l'installation électrique de
rheumatism [ˈruːmətɪzəm] n rhumatisme m
Rhine [raɪn] n Rhin m
rhinoceros [raɪˈnɔsərəs] n rhinocéros m
Rhone [rəun] n Rhône m
rhubarb [ˈruːbɑːb] n rhubarbe f
rhyme [raɪm] n rime f; (*verse*) vers mpl
rhythm [ˈrɪðm] n rythme m
rib [rɪb] n (*ANAT*) côte f
ribbon [ˈrɪbən] n ruban m; **in ~s** (*torn*) en lambeaux

rice [raɪs] *n* riz *m*; ~ **pudding** *n* riz au lait
rich [rɪtʃ] *adj* riche; (*gift, clothes*) somptu-
eux(-euse) ♦ *npl*: **the ~** les riches *mpl*; ~**es**
npl richesses *fpl*; ~**ly** *adv* richement;
(*deserved, earned*) largement
rickets [ˈrɪkɪts] *n* rachitisme *m*
rid [rɪd] (*pt, pp* **rid**) *vt*: **to ~ sb of** débarrasser
qn de; **to get ~ of** se débarrasser de
riddle [ˈrɪdl] *n* (*puzzle*) énigme *f* ♦ *vt*: **to be**
~d with être criblé(e) de; (*fig: guilt,*
corruption, doubts) être en proie à
ride [raɪd] (*pt* **rode**, *pp* **ridden**) *n* promenade *f*,
tour *m*; (*distance covered*) trajet *m* ♦ *vi* (*as*
sport) monter (à cheval), faire du cheval; (*go*
somewhere: on horse, bicycle) aller (à cheval
or bicyclette *etc*); (*journey: on bicycle,*
motorcycle, bus) rouler ♦ *vt* (*a certain horse*)
monter; (*distance*) parcourir, faire; **to take sb**
for a ~ (*fig*) faire marcher qn; **to ~ a horse/**
bicycle monter à cheval/à bicyclette; **~r** *n*
cavalier(-ère); (*in race*) jockey *m*; (*on bicycle*)
cycliste *m/f*; (*on motorcycle*) motocycliste *m/f*
ridge [rɪdʒ] *n* (*of roof, mountain*) arête *f*; (*of*
hill) faîte *m*; (*on object*) strie *f*
ridicule [ˈrɪdɪkjuːl] *n* ridicule *m*; dérision *f*
ridiculous [rɪˈdɪkjuləs] *adj* ridicule
riding [ˈraɪdɪŋ] *n* équitation *f*; ~ **school** *n*
manège *m*, école *f* d'équitation
rife [raɪf] *adj* répandu(e); **~ with** abondant(e)
en, plein(e) de
riffraff [ˈrɪfræf] *n* racaille *f*
rifle [ˈraɪfl] *n* fusil *m* (à canon rayé) ♦ *vt* vider,
dévaliser; **~ through** *vt* (*belongings*) fouiller;
(*papers*) feuilleter; **~ range** *n* champ *m* de
tir; (*at fair*) stand *m* de tir
rift [rɪft] *n* fente *f*, fissure *f*; (*fig: disagreement*)
désaccord *m*
rig [rɪg] *n* (*also: **oil ~**: at sea*) plate-forme
pétrolière ♦ *vt* (*election etc*) truquer; **~ out**
(*BRIT*) *vt*: **to ~ out as/in** habiller en/de; **~ up**
vt arranger, faire avec des moyens de fortune;
~ging *n* (*NAUT*) gréement *m*
right [raɪt] *adj* (*correctly chosen: answer, road*
etc) bon (bonne); (*true*) juste, exact(e);
(*suitable*) approprié(e), convenable; (*just*)
juste, équitable; (*morally good*) bien *inv*; (*not*
left) droit(e) ♦ *n* (*what is morally ~*) bien *m*;
(*title, claim*) droit *m*; (*not left*) droite *f* ♦ *adv*
(*answer*) correctement, juste; (*treat*) bien,
comme il faut; (*not on the left*) à droite ♦ *vt*
redresser ♦ *excl* bon!; **to be ~** (*person*) avoir
raison; (*answer*) être juste or correct(e);
(*clock*) être à l'heure (juste); **by ~s** en toute
justice; **on the ~** à droite; **to be in the ~** avoir
raison; **~ now** en ce moment même; tout de
suite; **~ in the middle** en plein milieu; **~ away**
immédiatement; **~ angle** *n* (*MATH*) angle
droit; **~eous** [ˈraɪtʃəs] *adj* droit(e),
vertueux(-euse); (*anger*) justifié(e); **~ful** *adj*

légitime; **~-handed** *adj* (*person*) droi-
tier(-ère); **~-hand man** *n* bras droit (*fig*);
~-hand side *n* la droite; **~ly** *adv* (*with reason*)
à juste titre; **~ of way** *n* droit *m* de passage;
(*AUT*) priorité *f*; **~-wing** *adj* (*POL*) de droite
rigid [ˈrɪdʒɪd] *adj* rigide; (*principle, control*)
strict(e)
rigmarole [ˈrɪgmərəul] *n* comédie *f*
rigorous [ˈrɪgərəs] *adj* rigoureux(-euse)
rile [raɪl] *vt* agacer
rim [rɪm] *n* bord *m*; (*of spectacles*) monture *f*;
(*of wheel*) jante *f*
rind [raɪnd] *n* (*of bacon*) couenne *f*; (*of lemon*
etc) écorce *f*, zeste *m*; (*of cheese*) croûte *f*
ring [rɪŋ] (*pt* **rang**, *pp* **rung**) *n* anneau *m*; (*on*
finger) bague *f*; (*also: **wedding ~**) alliance *f*;
(*of people, objects*) cercle *m*; (*of spies*) réseau
m; (*of smoke etc*) rond *m*; (*arena*) piste *f*,
arène *f*; (*for boxing*) ring *m*; (*sound of bell*)
sonnerie *f* ♦ *vi* (*telephone, bell*) sonner;
(*person: by telephone*) téléphoner; (*also:*
~ out: *voice, words*) retentir; (*ears*)
bourdonner ♦ *vt* (*BRIT: TEL: also: **~ up**)
téléphoner à, appeler; (*bell*) faire sonner; **to**
~ the bell sonner; **to give sb a ~** (*BRIT: TEL*)
appeler qn; **~ back** (*BRIT*) *vt, vi* (*TEL*)
rappeler; **~ off** (*BRIT*) *vi* (*TEL*) raccrocher;
~ up (*BRIT*) *vt* (*TEL*) appeler; **~ binder** *n*
classeur *m* à anneaux; **~ing** [ˈrɪŋɪŋ] *n* (*of*
telephone) sonnerie *f*; (*of bell*) tintement *m*;
(*in ears*) bourdonnement *m*; **~ing tone**
(*BRIT*) *n* (*TEL*) sonnerie *f*; **~leader** *n* (*of gang*)
chef *m*, meneur *m*; **~lets** *npl* anglaises *fpl*;
~ road (*BRIT*) *n* route *f* de ceinture;
(*motorway*) périphérique *m*
rink [rɪŋk] *n* (*also: **ice ~**) patinoire *f*
rinse [rɪns] *vt* rincer
riot [ˈraɪət] *n* émeute *f*; (*of flowers, colour*)
profusion *f* ♦ *vi* faire une émeute, manifester
avec violence; **to run ~** se déchaîner; **~ous**
adj (*mob, assembly*) séditieux(-euse),
déchaîné(e); (*living, behaviour*) débauché(e);
(*party*) très animé(e); (*welcome*) délirant(e)
rip [rɪp] *n* déchirure *f* ♦ *vt* déchirer ♦ *vi* se
déchirer; **~cord** *n* poignée *f* d'ouverture
ripe [raɪp] *adj* (*fruit*) mûr(e); (*cheese*) fait(e);
~n *vt* mûrir ♦ *vi* mûrir
rip-off [ˈrɪpɔf] (*inf*) *n*: **it's a ~~!** c'est de
l'arnaque!
ripple [ˈrɪpl] *n* ondulation *f*; (*of applause,*
laughter) cascade *f* ♦ *vi* onduler
rise [raɪz] (*pt* **rose**, *pp* **risen**) *n* (*slope*) côte *f*,
pente *f*; (*hill*) hauteur *f*; (*increase: in wages:*
BRIT) augmentation *f*; (: *in prices,*
temperature) hausse *f*, augmentation; (*fig: to*
power etc) ascension *f* ♦ *vi* s'élever, monter;
(*prices, numbers*) augmenter; (*waters*)
monter; (*sun; person: from chair, bed*) se
lever; (*also: **~ up**: tower, building*) s'élever; (:

rebel) se révolter; se rebeller; (*in rank*) s'élever; **to give ~ to** donner lieu à; **to ~ to the occasion** se montrer à la hauteur; **~r** *n*: **to be an early ~r** être matinal(e); **rising** *adj* (*number, prices*) en hausse; (*tide*) montant(e); (*sun, moon*) levant(e)

risk [rɪsk] *n* risque *m* ♦ *vt* risquer; **at ~** en danger; **at one's own ~** à ses risques et périls; **~y** *adj* risqué(e)

rissole [ˈrɪsəʊl] *n* croquette *f*

rite [raɪt] *n* rite *m*; **last ~s** derniers sacrements

ritual [ˈrɪtjuəl] *adj* rituel(le) ♦ *n* rituel *m*

rival [ˈraɪvl] *adj, n* rival(e); (*in business*) concurrent(e) ♦ *vt* (*match*) égaler; **~ry** [ˈraɪvlrɪ] *n* rivalité *f*, concurrence *f*

river [ˈrɪvəˀ] *n* rivière *f*; (*major, also fig*) fleuve *m* ♦ *cpd* (*port, traffic*) fluvial(e); **up/down ~** en amont/aval; **~bank** *n* rive *f*, berge *f*; **~bed** *n* lit *m* (de rivière *or* de fleuve)

rivet [ˈrɪvɪt] *n* rivet *m* ♦ *vt* (*fig*) river, fixer

Riviera [rɪvɪˈeərə] *n*: **the (French) ~** la Côte d'Azur; **the Italian ~** la Riviera (italienne)

road [rəʊd] *n* route *f*; (*in town*) rue *f*; (*fig*) chemin, voie *f*; **major/minor ~** route principale or à priorité/voie secondaire; **~ accident** *n* accident *m* de la circulation; **~block** *n* barrage routier; **~hog** *n* chauffard *m*; **~ map** *n* carte routière; **~ rage** *n* comportement très agressif de certains usagers de la route; **~ safety** *n* sécurité routière; **~side** *n* bord *m* de la route, bas-côté *m*; **~ sign** *n* panneau *m* de signalisation; **~way** *n* chaussée *f*; **~ works** *npl* travaux *mpl* (de réfection des routes); **~worthy** *adj* en bon état de marche

roam [rəʊm] *vi* errer, vagabonder

roar [rɔːˀ] *n* rugissement *m*; (*of crowd*) hurlements *mpl*; (*of vehicle, thunder, storm*) grondement *m* ♦ *vi* rugir; hurler; gronder; **to ~ with laughter** éclater de rire; **to do a ~ing trade** faire des affaires d'or

roast [rəʊst] *n* rôti *m* ♦ *vt* (*faire*) rôtir; (*coffee*) griller, torréfier; **~ beef** *n* rôti *m* de bœuf, rosbif *m*

rob [rɔb] *vt* (*person*) voler; (*bank*) dévaliser; **to ~ sb of sth** voler *or* dérober qch à qn; (*fig: deprive*) priver qn de qch; **~ber** *n* bandit *m*, voleur *m*; **~bery** *n* vol *m*

robe [rəʊb] *n* (*for ceremony etc*) robe *f*; (*also: bathrobe*) peignoir *m*; (*US*) couverture *f*

robin [ˈrɔbɪn] *n* rouge-gorge *m*

robot [ˈrəʊbɔt] *n* robot *m*

robust [rəʊˈbʌst] *adj* robuste; (*material, appetite*) solide

rock [rɔk] *n* (*substance*) roche *f*, roc *m*; (*boulder*) rocher *m*; (*US: small stone*) caillou *m*; (*BRIT: sweet*) ≈ sucre *m* d'orge ♦ *vt* (*swing gently: cradle*) balancer; (: *child*) bercer; (*shake*) ébranler, secouer ♦ *vi* (se) balancer; être ébranlé(e) *or* secoué(e); **on the ~s** (*drink*) avec des glaçons; (*marriage etc*) en train de craquer; **~ and roll** *n* rock (and roll) *m*, rock'n'roll *m*; **~-bottom** *adj* (*fig: prices*) sacrifié(e); **~ery** *n* (*jardin m de*) rocaille *f*

rocket [ˈrɔkɪt] *n* fusée *f*; (*MIL*) fusée, roquette *f*

rocking chair [ˈrɔkɪŋ-] *n* fauteuil *m* à bascule

rocking horse *n* cheval *m* à bascule

rocky [ˈrɔkɪ] *adj* (*hill*) rocheux(-euse); (*path*) rocailleux(-euse)

rod [rɔd] *n* (*wooden*) baguette *f*; (*metallic*) tringle *f*; (*TECH*) tige *f*; (*also: fishing ~*) canne *f* à pêche

rode [rəʊd] *pt of* **ride**

rodent [ˈrəʊdnt] *n* rongeur *m*

rodeo [ˈrəʊdɪəʊ] (*US*) *n* rodéo *m*

roe [rəʊ] *n* (*species: also: ~ deer*) chevreuil *m*; (*of fish: also: hard ~*) œufs *mpl* de poisson; **soft ~** laitance *f*

rogue [rəʊg] *n* coquin(e)

role [rəʊl] *n* rôle *m*; **~ play** *n* jeu *m* de rôle

roll [rəʊl] *n* rouleau *m*; (*of banknotes*) liasse *f*; (*also: bread ~*) petit pain; (*register*) liste *f*; (*sound: of drums etc*) roulement *m* ♦ *vt* rouler; (*also: ~ up: string*) enrouler; (: *sleeves*) retrousser; (*also: ~ out: pastry*) étendre au rouleau, abaisser ♦ *vi* rouler; **~ about** *vi* rouler ça et là; (*person*) se rouler par terre; **~ around** *vi* = **roll about**; **~ by** *vi* (*time*) s'écouler, passer; **~ over** *vi* se retourner; **~ up** *vi* (*inf: arrive*) àrriver, s'amener ♦ *vt* rouler; **~ call** *n* appel *m*; **~er** *n* rouleau *m*; (*wheel*) roulette *f*; (*for road*) rouleau compresseur; **~er blade** *n* patin *m* en ligne; **~er coaster** *n* montagnes *fpl* russes; **~er skates** *npl* patins *mpl* à roulettes; **~er skating** *n* patin *m* à roulettes; **~ing** *adj* (*landscape*) onduleux(-euse); **~ing pin** *n* rouleau *m* à pâtisserie; **~ing stock** *n* (*RAIL*) matériel roulant

ROM [rɔm] *n abbr* (= *read only memory*) mémoire morte

Roman [ˈrəʊmən] *adj* romain(e); **~ Catholic** *adj, n* catholique *m/f*

romance [rəˈmæns] *n* (*love affair*) idylle *f*; (*charm*) poésie *f*; (*novel*) roman *m* à l'eau de rose

Romania [rəʊˈmeɪnɪə] *n* Roumanie *f*; **~n** *adj* roumain(e) ♦ *n* Roumain(e); (*LING*) roumain *m*

Roman numeral *n* chiffre romain

romantic [rəˈmæntɪk] *adj* romantique; sentimental(e)

Rome [rəʊm] *n* Rome

romp [rɔmp] *n* jeux bruyants ♦ *vi* (*also: ~ about*) s'ébattre, jouer bruyamment; **~ers** *npl* barboteuse *f*

roof [ruːf] (*pl* **~s**) *n* toit *m* ♦ *vt* couvrir (d'un toit); **the ~ of the mouth** la voûte du palais;

~ing n toiture f; **~ rack** n (AUT) galerie f
rook [ruk] n (bird) freux m; (CHESS) tour f
room [ru:m] n (in house) pièce f; (also:
bedroom) chambre f (à coucher); (in school
etc) salle f; (space) place f; **~s** npl (lodging)
meublé m; **"~s to let"** (BRIT) or **"~s for rent"**
(US) "chambres à louer"; **single/double ~**
chambre pour une personne/deux personnes;
there is ~ for improvement cela laisse à
désirer; **~ing house** (US) n maison f or
immeuble m de rapport; **~mate** n camarade
m/f de chambre; **~ service** n service m des
chambres (dans un hôtel); **~y** adj spa-
cieux(-euse); (garment) ample
roost [ru:st] vi se jucher
rooster ['ru:stə'] n (esp US) coq m
root [ru:t] n (BOT, MATH) racine f; (fig: of
problem) origine f, fond m ♦ vi (plant)
s'enraciner; **~ about** vi (fig) fouiller; **~ for** vt
fus encourager, applaudir; **~ out** vt (find)
dénicher
rope [rəup] n corde f; (NAUT) cordage m ♦ vt
(tie up or together) attacher; (climbers: also:
~ together) encorder; (area: **~ off**) interdire
l'accès de; (: divide off) séparer; **to know the
~s** (fig) être au courant, connaître les ficelles;
~ in vt (fig: person) embringuer
rosary ['rəuzəri] n chapelet m
rose [rəuz] pt of **rise** ♦ n rose f; (also: **~bush**)
rosier m; (on watering can) pomme f
rosé ['rəuzei] n rosé m
rosebud ['rəuzbʌd] n bouton m de rose
rosemary ['rəuzməri] n romarin m
roster ['rɒstə'] n: **~ duty** n tableau m de service
rostrum ['rɒstrəm] n tribune f (pour un
orateur etc)
rosy ['rəuzi] adj rose; **a ~ future** un bel avenir
rot [rɒt] n (decay) pourriture f; (fig: pej)
idioties fpl ♦ vt, vi pourrir
rota ['rəutə] n liste f, tableau m de service; **on
a ~ basis** par roulement
rotary ['rəutəri] adj rotatif(-ive)
rotate [rəu'teit] vt (revolve) faire tourner;
(change round: jobs) faire à tour de rôle ♦ vi
(revolve) tourner; **rotating** adj (movement)
tournant(e)
rotten ['rɒtn] adj (decayed) pourri(e);
(dishonest) corrompu(e); (inf: bad)
mauvais(e), moche; **to feel ~** (ill) être mal
fichu(e)
rotund [rəu'tʌnd] adj (person) rondelet(te)
rough [rʌf] adj (cloth, skin) rêche, ru-
gueux(-euse); (terrain) accidenté(e); (path)
rocailleux(-euse); (voice) rauque, rude;
(person, manner: coarse) rude, fruste;
(: violent) brutal(e); (district, weather)
mauvais(e); (sea) houleux(-euse); (plan etc)
ébauché(e); (guess) approximatif(-ive) ♦ n
(GOLF) rough m ♦ vt: **to ~ it** vivre à la dure;

to sleep ~ (BRIT) coucher à la dure; **~age** n
fibres fpl alimentaires; **~-and-ready** adj
rudimentaire; **~ copy, ~ draft** n brouillon m;
~ly adv (handle) rudement, brutalement;
(speak) avec brusquerie; (make)
grossièrement; (approximately) à peu près, en
gros
roulette [ru:'let] n roulette f
Roumania [ru:'meiniə] n = Romania
round [raund] adj rond(e) ♦ n (BRIT: of toast)
tranche f; (duty: of policeman, milkman etc)
tournée f; (: of doctor) visites fpl; (game: of
cards, in competition) partie f; (BOXING) round
m; (of talks) série f ♦ vt (corner) tourner
♦ prep autour de ♦ adv: **all ~** tout autour; **the
long way ~** (par) le chemin le plus long; **all
the year ~** toute l'année; **it's just ~ the corner**
(fig) c'est tout près; **~ the clock** 24 heures sur
24; **to go ~ to sb's (house)** aller chez qn; **go
~ the back** passez par derrière; **enough to go
~** assez pour tout le monde; **~ of ammunition**
cartouche f; **~ of applause** ban m,
applaudissements mpl; **~ of drinks** tournée f;
~ of sandwiches sandwich m; **~ off** vt (speech
etc) terminer; **~ up** vt rassembler; (criminals)
effectuer une rafle de; (price, figure) arrondir
(au chiffre supérieur); **~about** n (BRIT: AUT)
rond-point m (à sens giratoire); (: at fair)
manège m (de chevaux de bois) ♦ adj (route,
means) détourné(e); **~ers** n (game) sorte de
baseball; **~ly** adv (fig) tout net, carrément;
~ trip n (voyage m) aller et retour m; **~up** n
rassemblement m; (of criminals) rafle f
rouse [rauz] vt (wake up) réveiller; (stir up)
susciter; provoquer; éveiller; **rousing** adj
(welcome) enthousiaste
route [ru:t] n itinéraire m; (of bus) parcours
m; (of trade, shipping) route f
routine [ru:'ti:n] adj (work) ordinaire,
courant(e); (procedure) d'usage ♦ n (habits)
habitudes fpl; (pej) train-train m; (THEATRE)
numéro m
rove [rəuv] vt (area, streets) errer dans
row¹ [rəu] n (line) rangée f; {of people, seats,
KNITTING) rang m; (behind one another: of
cars, people) file f ♦ vi (in boat) ramer; (as
sport) faire de l'aviron ♦ vt (boat) faire aller à
la rame or à l'aviron; **in a ~** (fig) d'affilée
row² [rau] n (noise) vacarme m; (dispute)
dispute f, querelle f; (scolding) réprimande f,
savon m ♦ vi se disputer, se quereller
rowboat ['rəubəut] (US) n canot m (à rames)
rowdy ['raudi] adj chahuteur(-euse);
(occasion) tapageur(-euse)
rowing ['rəuiŋ] n canotage m; (as sport)
aviron m; **~ boat** (BRIT) n canot m (à rames)
royal ['rɔiəl] adj royal(e); **R~ Air Force** (BRIT)
n armée de l'air britannique; **~ty** n (royal
persons) (membres mpl de la) famille royale;

(*payment: to author*) droits *mpl* d'auteur; (: *to inventor*) royalties *fpl*

rpm *abbr* (*AUT*) (= *revolutions per minute*) tr/mn

RSVP *abbr* (= *répondez s'il vous plaît*) R.S.V.P.

Rt Hon. *abbr* (*BRIT*: = *Right Honourable*) titre donné aux députés de la Chambre des communes

rub [rʌb] *vt* frotter; frictionner; (*hands*) se frotter ♦ *n* (*with cloth*) coup *m* chiffon *or* de torchon; **to give sth a ~** donner un coup de chiffon *or* de torchon à; **to ~ sb up** (*BRIT*) *or* **to ~ sb** (*US*) **the wrong way** prendre qn à rebrousse-poil; **~ off** *vi* partir; **~ off on** *vt fus* déteindre sur; **~ out** *vt* effacer

rubber [ˈrʌbəʳ] *n* caoutchouc *m*; (*BRIT*: *eraser*) gomme *f* (à effacer); **~ band** *n* élastique *m*; **~ plant** *n* caoutchouc *m* (*plante verte*)

rubbish [ˈrʌbɪʃ] *n* (*from household*) ordures *fpl*; (*fig: pej*) camelote *f*; (: *nonsense*) bêtises *fpl*, idioties *fpl*; **~ bin** (*BRIT*) *n* poubelle *f*; **~ dump** *n* décharge publique, dépotoir *m*

rubble [ˈrʌbl] *n* décombres *mpl*; (*smaller*) gravats *mpl*; (*CONSTR*) blocage *m*

ruby [ˈruːbɪ] *n* rubis *m*

rucksack [ˈrʌksæk] *n* sac *m* à dos

rudder [ˈrʌdəʳ] *n* gouvernail *m*

ruddy [ˈrʌdɪ] *adj* (*face*) coloré(e); (*inf: damned*) sacré(e), fichu(e)

rude [ruːd] *adj* (*impolite*) impoli(e); (*coarse*) grossier(-ère); (*shocking*) indécent(e), inconvenant(e)

ruffle [ˈrʌfl] *vt* (*hair*) ébouriffer; (*clothes*) chiffonner; (*fig: person*): **to get ~d** s'énerver

rug [rʌg] *n* petit tapis; (*BRIT: blanket*) couverture *f*

rugby [ˈrʌgbɪ] *n* (*also: ~ football*) rugby *m*

rugged [ˈrʌgɪd] *adj* (*landscape*) accidenté(e); (*features, character*) rude

ruin [ˈruːɪn] *n* ruine *f* ♦ *vt* ruiner; (*spoil, clothes*) abîmer; (*event*) gâcher; **~s** *npl* (*of building*) ruine(s)

rule [ruːl] *n* règle *f*; (*regulation*) règlement *m*; (*government*) autorité *f*, gouvernement *m* ♦ *vt* (*country*) gouverner; (*person*) dominer ♦ *vi* commander; (*LAW*) statuer; **as a ~** normalement, en règle générale; **~ out** *vt* exclure; **~d** *adj* (*paper*) réglé(e); **~r** *n* (*sovereign*) souverain(e); (*for measuring*) règle *f*; **ruling** *adj* (*party*) au pouvoir; (*class*) dirigeant(e) ♦ *n* (*LAW*) décision *f*

rum [rʌm] *n* rhum *m*

Rumania [ruːˈmeɪnɪə] *n* = **Romania**

rumble [ˈrʌmbl] *vi* gronder; (*stomach, pipe*) gargouiller

rummage [ˈrʌmɪdʒ] *vi* fouiller

rumour [ˈruːməʳ] (*US* **rumor**) *n* rumeur *f*, bruit *m* (qui court) ♦ *vt*: **it is ~ed that** le bruit court que

rump [rʌmp] *n* (*of animal*) croupe *f*; (*inf: of person*) postérieur *m*; **~ steak** *n* rumsteck *m*

rumpus [ˈrʌmpəs] (*inf*) *n* tapage *m*, chahut *m*

run [rʌn] (*pt* **ran**, *pp* **run**) *n* (*fast pace*) (pas *m* de) course *f*; (*outing*) tour *m or* promenade *f* (en voiture); (*distance travelled*) parcours *m*, trajet *m*; (*series*) suite *f*, série *f*; (*THEATRE*) série de représentations; (*SKI*) piste *f*; (*CRICKET, BASEBALL*) point *m*; (*in tights, stockings*) maille filée, échelle *f* ♦ *vt* (*operate: business*) diriger; (: *competition, course*) organiser; (: *hotel, house*) tenir; (*race*) participer à; (*COMPUT*) exécuter; (*to pass: hand, finger*) passer; (*water, bath*) faire couler; (*PRESS: feature*) publier ♦ *vi* courir; (*flee*) s'enfuir; (*work: machine, factory*) marcher; (*bus, train*) circuler; (*continue: play*) se jouer; (: *contract*) être valide; (*flow: river, bath; nose*) couler; (*colours, washing*) déteindre; (*in election*) être candidat, se présenter; **to go for a ~** faire un peu de course à pied; **there was a ~ on ...** (*meat, tickets*) les gens se sont rués sur ...; **in the long ~** à longue échéance; à la longue; en fin de compte; **on the ~** en fuite; **I'll ~ you to the station** je vais vous emmener *or* conduire à la gare; **to ~ a risk** courir un risque; **~ about** *vi* (*children*) courir çà et là; **~ across** *vt fus* (*find*) trouver par hasard; **~ around** *vi* = **run about**; **~ away** *vi* s'enfuir; **~ down** *vt* (*production*) réduire progressivement; (*factory*) réduire progressivement la production de; (*AUT*) renverser; (*criticize*) critiquer, dénigrer; **to be ~ down** (*person: tired*) être fatigué(e) *or* à plat; **~ in** (*BRIT*) *vt* (*car*) roder; **~ into** *vt fus* (*meet: person*) rencontrer par hasard; (*trouble*) se heurter à; (*collide with*) heurter; **~ off** *vi* s'enfuir ♦ *vt* (*water*) laisser s'écouler; (*copies*) tirer; **~ out** *vi* (*person*) sortir en courant; (*liquid*) couler; (*lease*) expirer; (*money*) être épuisé(e); **~ out of** *vt fus* se trouver à court de; **~ over** *vt* (*AUT*) écraser ♦ *vt fus* (*revise*) revoir, reprendre; **~ through** *vt fus* (*recapitulate*) reprendre; (*play*) répéter; **~ up** *vt*: **to ~ up against** (*difficulties*) se heurter à; **to ~ up a debt** s'endetter; **~away** *adj* (*horse*) emballé(e); (*truck*) fou (folle); (*person*) fugitif(-ive); (*teenager*) fugueur(-euse)

rung [rʌŋ] *pp of* **ring** ♦ *n* (*of ladder*) barreau *m*

runner [ˈrʌnəʳ] *n* (*in race: person*) coureur(-euse); (: *horse*) partant *m*; (*on sledge*) patin *m*; (*for drawer etc*) coulisseau *m*; **~ bean** (*BRIT*) *n* haricot *m* (à rames); **~-up** *n* second(e)

running [ˈrʌnɪŋ] *n* course *f*; (*of business, organization*) gestion *f*, direction *f* ♦ *adj* (*water*) courant(e); **to be in/out of the ~ for sth** être/ne pas être sur les rangs pour qch; **6**

days ~ 6 jours de suite; ~ **commentary** n commentaire détaillé; ~ **costs** npl frais mpl d'exploitation

runny ['rʌnɪ] adj qui coule

run-of-the-mill ['rʌnəvðə'mɪl] adj ordinaire, banal(e)

runt [rʌnt] n avorton m

run-up ['rʌnʌp] n: ~-~ **to sth** (election etc) période f précédant qch

runway ['rʌnweɪ] n (AVIAT) piste f

rupture ['rʌptʃə'] n (MED) hernie f

rural ['ruərl] adj rural(e)

rush [rʌʃ] n (hurry) hâte f, précipitation f; (of crowd, COMM: sudden demand) ruée f; (current) flot m; (of emotion) vague f; (BOT) jonc m ♦ vt (hurry) transporter or envoyer d'urgence ♦ vi se précipiter; ~ **hour** n heures fpl de pointe

rusk [rʌsk] n biscotte f

Russia ['rʌʃə] n Russie f; ~**n** adj russe ♦ n Russe m/f; (LING) russe m

rust [rʌst] n rouille f ♦ vi rouiller

rustic ['rʌstɪk] adj rustique

rustle ['rʌsl] vi bruire, produire un bruissement ♦ vt froisser

rustproof ['rʌstpru:f] adj inoxydable

rusty ['rʌstɪ] adj rouillé(e)

rut [rʌt] n ornière f; (ZOOL) rut m; **to be in a ~** suivre l'ornière, s'encroûter

ruthless ['ru:θlɪs] adj sans pitié, impitoyable

rye [raɪ] n seigle m

S, s

Sabbath ['sæbəθ] n (Jewish) sabbat m; (Christian) dimanche m

sabotage ['sæbətɑ:ʒ] n sabotage m ♦ vt saboter

saccharin(e) ['sækərɪn] n saccharine f

sachet ['sæʃeɪ] n sachet m

sack [sæk] n (bag) sac m ♦ vt (dismiss) renvoyer, mettre à la porte; (plunder) piller, mettre à sac; **to get the ~** être renvoyé(e), être mis(e) à la porte; ~**ing** n (material) toile f à sac; (dismissal) renvoi m

sacrament ['sækrəmənt] n sacrement m

sacred ['seɪkrɪd] adj sacré(e)

sacrifice ['sækrɪfaɪs] n sacrifice m ♦ vt sacrifier

sad [sæd] adj triste; (deplorable) triste, fâcheux(-euse)

saddle ['sædl] n selle f ♦ vt (horse) seller; **to be ~d with sth** (inf) avoir qch sur les bras; ~**bag** n sacoche f

sadistic [sə'dɪstɪk] adj sadique

sadly ['sædlɪ] adv tristement; (unfortunately) malheureusement; (seriously) fort

sadness ['sædnɪs] n tristesse f

s.a.e. n abbr = stamped addressed envelope

safe [seɪf] adj (out of danger) hors de danger, en sécurité; (not dangerous) sans danger; (cautious) prudent(e); (sure: bet etc) assuré(e) ♦ n coffre-fort m; ~ **from** à l'abri de; ~ **and sound** sain(e) et sauf (sauve); (just) **to be on the ~ side** pour plus de sûreté, par précaution; ~ **journey!** bon voyage!; ~-**conduct** n sauf-conduit m; ~-**deposit** n (vault) dépôt m de coffres-forts; (box) coffre-fort m; ~**guard** n sauvegarde f, protection f ♦ vt sauvegarder, protéger; ~**keeping** n bonne garde; ~**ly** adv (assume, say) sans risque d'erreur; (drive, arrive) sans accident; ~ **sex** n rapports mpl sexuels sans risque

safety ['seɪftɪ] n sécurité f; ~ **belt** n ceinture f de sécurité; ~ **pin** n épingle f de sûreté or de nourrice; ~ **valve** n soupape f de sûreté

sag [sæg] vi s'affaisser; (hem, breasts) pendre

sage [seɪdʒ] n (herb) sauge f; (person) sage m

Sagittarius [sædʒɪ'tɛərɪəs] n le Sagittaire

Sahara [sə'hɑːrə] n: **the ~ (Desert)** le (désert du) Sahara

said [sed] pt, pp of **say**

sail [seɪl] n (on boat) voile f; (trip): **to go for a ~** faire un tour en bateau ♦ vt (boat) manœuvrer, piloter ♦ vi (travel: ship) avancer, naviguer; (set off) partir, prendre la mer; (SPORT) faire de la voile; **they ~ed into Le Havre** ils sont entrés dans le port du Havre; ~ **through** vi, vt fus (fig) réussir haut la main; ~**boat** (US) n bateau m à voiles, voilier m; ~**ing** n (SPORT) voile f; **to go ~ing** faire de la voile; ~**ing boat** n bateau m à voiles, voilier m; ~**ing ship** n grand voilier m; ~**or** n marin m, matelot m

saint [seɪnt] n saint(e)

sake [seɪk] n: **for the ~ of** pour (l'amour de), dans l'intérêt de; par égard pour

salad ['sæləd] n salade f; ~ **bowl** n saladier m; ~ **cream** (BRIT) n (sorte f de) mayonnaise f; ~ **dressing** n vinaigrette f

salami [sə'lɑːmɪ] n salami m

salary ['sælərɪ] n salaire m

sale [seɪl] n vente f; (at reduced prices) soldes mpl; "**for ~**" "à vendre"; **on ~** en vente; **on ~ or return** vendu(e) avec faculté de retour; ~**room** n salle f des ventes; ~**s assistant** (US **sales clerk**) n vendeur(-euse); ~**sman** (irreg) n vendeur m; (representative) représentant m; ~**s rep** n (COMM) représentant(e) m/f; ~**swoman** (irreg) n vendeuse f; (representative) représentante f

salmon ['sæmən] n inv saumon m

salon ['sælɔn] n salon m

saloon [sə'luːn] n (US) bar m; (BRIT: AUT) berline f; (ship's lounge) salon m

salt [sɔːlt] n sel m ♦ vt saler; ~**cellar** n salière f; ~**water** adj de mer; ~**y** adj salé(e)

salute [sə'luːt] n salut m ♦ vt saluer

salvage ['sælvɪdʒ] n (saving) sauvetage m; (things saved) biens sauvés or récupérés ♦ vt sauver, récupérer

salvation [sæl'veɪʃən] n salut m; **S~ Army** n armée f du Salut

same [seɪm] adj même ♦ pron: **the ~** le (la) même, les mêmes; **the ~ book as** le même livre que; **at the ~ time** en même temps; **all or just the ~** tout de même, quand même; **to do the ~** faire de même, en faire autant; **to do the ~ as sb** faire comme qn; **the ~ to you!** à vous de même!; (after insult) toi-même!

sample ['sɑːmpl] n échantillon m; (blood) prélèvement m ♦ vt (food, wine) goûter

sanction ['sæŋkʃən] n approbation f, sanction f

sanctity ['sæŋktɪtɪ] n sainteté f, caractère sacré

sanctuary ['sæŋktjuərɪ] n (holy place) sanctuaire m; (refuge) asile m; (for wild life) réserve f

sand [sænd] n sable m ♦ vt (furniture: also: ~ down) poncer

sandal ['sændl] n sandale f

sand: ~box n (US) n tas m de sable; **~castle** n château m de sable; **~paper** n papier m de verre; **~pit** n (BRIT) n (for children) tas m de sable; **~stone** n grès m

sandwich ['sændwɪtʃ] n sandwich m; **cheese/ham ~** sandwich au fromage/jambon; **~ course** n (BRIT) n cours m de formation professionnelle

sandy ['sændɪ] adj sablonneux(-euse); (colour) sable inv, blond roux inv

sane [seɪn] adj (person) sain(e) d'esprit; (outlook) sensé(e), sain(e)

sang [sæŋ] pt of **sing**

sanitary ['sænɪtərɪ] adj (system, arrangements) sanitaire; (clean) hygiénique; **~ towel** (US **sanitary napkin**) n serviette f hygiénique

sanitation [sænɪ'teɪʃən] n (in house) installations fpl sanitaires; (in town) système m sanitaire; **~ department** (US) n service m de voirie

sanity ['sænɪtɪ] n santé mentale; (common sense) bon sens

sank [sæŋk] pt of **sink**

Santa Claus [sæntə'klɔːz] n le père Noël

sap [sæp] n (of plants) sève f ♦ vt (strength) saper, miner

sapling ['sæplɪŋ] n jeune arbre m

sapphire ['sæfaɪəʳ] n saphir m

sarcasm ['sɑːkæzm] n sarcasme m, raillerie f; **sarcastic** [sɑːˈkæstɪk] adj sarcastique

sardine [sɑːˈdiːn] n sardine f

Sardinia [sɑːˈdɪnɪə] n Sardaigne f

sash [sæʃ] n écharpe f

sat [sæt] pt, pp of **sit**

satchel ['sætʃl] n cartable m

satellite ['sætəlaɪt] n satellite m; **~ dish** n antenne f parabolique; **~ television** n télévision f par câble

satin ['sætɪn] n satin m ♦ adj en or de satin, satiné(e)

satire ['sætaɪəʳ] n satire f

satisfaction [sætɪs'fækʃən] n satisfaction f

satisfactory [sætɪs'fæktərɪ] adj satisfaisant(e)

satisfied ['sætɪsfaɪd] adj satisfait(e)

satisfy ['sætɪsfaɪ] vt satisfaire, contenter; (convince) convaincre, persuader; **~ing** adj satisfaisant(e)

Saturday ['sætədɪ] n samedi m

sauce [sɔːs] n sauce f; **~pan** n casserole f

saucer ['sɔːsəʳ] n soucoupe f

Saudi ['saudi-]: **~ Arabia** n Arabie Saoudite; **~ (Arabian)** adj saoudien(ne)

sauna ['sɔːnə] n sauna m

saunter ['sɔːntəʳ] vi: **to ~ along/in/out** etc marcher/entrer/sortir etc d'un pas nonchalant

sausage ['sɔsɪdʒ] n saucisse f; (cold meat) saucisson m; **~ roll** n ≈ friand m

savage ['sævɪdʒ] adj (cruel, fierce) brutal(e), féroce; (primitive) primitif(-ive), sauvage ♦ n sauvage m/f

save [seɪv] vt (person, belongings) sauver; (money) mettre de côté, économiser; (time) (faire) gagner; (keep) garder; (COMPUT) sauvegarder; (SPORT: stop) arrêter; (avoid: trouble) éviter ♦ vi (also: ~ up) mettre de l'argent de côté ♦ n (SPORT) arrêt m (du ballon) ♦ prep sauf, à l'exception de

saving ['seɪvɪŋ] n économie f ♦ adj: **the ~ grace of sth** ce qui rachète qch; **~s** npl (money saved) économies fpl; **~s account** n compte m d'épargne; **~s bank** n caisse f d'épargne

saviour ['seɪvjəʳ] (US **savior**) n sauveur m

savour ['seɪvəʳ] (US **savor**) vt savourer; **~y** (US **savory**) adj (dish: not sweet) salé(e)

saw [sɔː] (pt **sawed**, pp **sawed** or **sawn**) vt scier ♦ n (tool) scie f ♦ pt of **see**; **~dust** n sciure f; **~mill** n scierie f; **~-off** adj: **~-off shotgun** carabine f à canon scié

sax [sæks] (inf) n saxo m

saxophone ['sæksəfəun] n saxophone m

say [seɪ] (pt, pp **said**) n: **to have one's ~** dire ce qu'on a à dire ♦ vt dire; **to have** or **some ~ in sth** avoir voix au chapitre; **could you ~ that again?** pourriez-vous répéter ce que vous venez de dire?; **that goes without ~ing** cela va sans dire, cela va de soi; **~ing** n dicton m, proverbe m

scab [skæb] n croûte f; (pej) jaune m

scaffold ['skæfəld] n échafaud m; **~ing** n échafaudage m

scald [skɔːld] n brûlure f ♦ vt ébouillanter

scale [skeɪl] n (of fish) écaille f; (MUS) gamme

f; (of ruler, thermometer etc) graduation f, échelle (graduée); (of salaries, fees etc) barème m; (of map, also size, extent) échelle ♦ vt (mountain) escalader; **~s** npl (for weighing) balance f; (also: **bathroom ~**) pèse-personne m inv; **on a large ~** sur une grande échelle, en grand; **~ of charges** tableau m des tarifs; **~ down** vt réduire

scallop ['skɔləp] n coquille f Saint-Jacques; (SEWING) feston m

scalp [skælp] n cuir chevelu ♦ vt scalper

scampi ['skæmpɪ] npl langoustines (frites), scampi mpl

scan [skæn] vt scruter, examiner; (glance at quickly) parcourir; (TV, RADAR) balayer ♦ n (MED) scanographie f

scandal ['skændl] n scandale m; (gossip) ragots mpl

Scandinavia [skændɪ'neɪvɪə] n Scandinavie f; **~n** adj scandinave

scant [skænt] adj insuffisant(e); **~y** ['skæntɪ] adj peu abondant(e), insuffisant(e); (underwear) minuscule

scapegoat ['skeɪpgəut] n bouc m émissaire

scar [skɑː] n cicatrice f ♦ vt marquer (d'une cicatrice)

scarce [skɛəs] adj rare, peu abondant(e); **to make o.s. ~** (inf) se sauver; **~ly** adv à peine; **scarcity** n manque m, pénurie f

scare [skɛə] n peur f, panique f ♦ vt effrayer, faire peur à; **to ~ sb stiff** faire une peur bleue à qn; **bomb ~** alerte f à la bombe; **~ away** vt faire fuir; **~ off** vt = scare away; **~crow** n épouvantail m; **~d** adj: **to be ~d** avoir peur

scarf [skɑːf] (pl **~s** or **scarves**) n (long) écharpe f; (square) foulard m

scarlet ['skɑːlɪt] adj écarlate; **~ fever** n scarlatine f

scary ['skɛərɪ] (inf) adj effrayant(e)

scathing ['skeɪðɪŋ] adj cinglant(e), acerbe

scatter ['skætə'] vt éparpiller, répandre; (crowd) disperser ♦ vi se disperser; **~brained** adj écervelé(e), étourdi(e)

scavenger ['skævəndʒə'] n (person: in bins etc) pilleur m de poubelles

scene [siːn] n scène f; (of crime, accident) lieu(x) m(pl); (sight, view) spectacle m, vue f; **~ry** ['siːnərɪ] n (THEATRE) décor(s) m(pl); (landscape) paysage m; **scenic** adj (picturesque) offrant de beaux paysages or panoramas

scent [sɛnt] n parfum m, odeur f; (track) piste f

sceptical ['skɛptɪkl] (US **skeptical**) adj sceptique

schedule ['ʃɛdjuːl, (US) 'skɛdjuːl] n programme m, plan m; (of trains) horaire m; (of prices etc) barème m, tarif m ♦ vt prévoir; **on ~** à l'heure (prévue); à la date prévue; **to**

be ahead of/behind ~ avoir de l'avance/du retard; **~d flight** n vol régulier

scheme [skiːm] n plan m, projet m; (dishonest plan, plot) complot m, combine f; (arrangement) arrangement m, classification f; (pension ~ etc) régime m ♦ vi comploter, manigancer; **scheming** adj rusé(e), intrigant(e) ♦ n manigances fpl, intrigues fpl

scholar ['skɔlə'] n érudit(e); (pupil) boursier(-ère); **~ship** n (knowledge) érudition f; (grant) bourse f (d'études)

school [skuːl] n école f; (secondary ~) collège m, lycée m; (US: university) université f; (in university) faculté f ♦ cpd scolaire; **~book** n livre m scolaire or de classe; **~boy** n écolier m; collégien m, lycéen m; **~children** npl écoliers mpl; collégiens mpl, lycéens mpl; **~girl** n écolière f; collégienne f, lycéenne f; **~ing** n instruction f, études fpl; **~master** n (primary) instituteur m; (secondary) professeur m; **~mistress** n institutrice f; professeur m; **~teacher** n instituteur(-trice); professeur m

science ['saɪəns] n science f; **~ fiction** n science-fiction f; **scientific** [saɪən'tɪfɪk] adj scientifique; **scientist** n scientifique m/f; (eminent) savant m

scissors ['sɪzəz] npl ciseaux mpl

scoff [skɔf] vt (BRIT: inf: eat) avaler, bouffer ♦ vi: **to ~ (at)** (mock) se moquer (de)

scold [skəuld] vt gronder

scone [skɔn] n sorte de petit pain rond au lait

scoop [skuːp] n pelle f (à main); (for ice cream) boule f à glace; (PRESS) scoop m; **~ up** vt évider, creuser; **~ up** vt ramasser

scooter ['skuːtə'] n (also: **motor ~**) scooter m; (toy) trottinette f

scope [skəup] n (capacity: of plan, undertaking) portée f, envergure f; (: of person) compétence f, capacités fpl; (opportunity) possibilités fpl; **within the ~ of** dans les limites de

scorch [skɔːtʃ] vt (clothes) brûler (légèrement), roussir; (earth, grass) dessécher, brûler

score [skɔː'] n score m, décompte m des points; (MUS) partition f; (twenty) vingt ♦ vt (goal, point) marquer; (success) remporter ♦ vi marquer des points; (FOOTBALL) marquer un but; (keep ~) compter les points; **~s of** (very many) beaucoup de, un tas de (fam); **on that ~** sur ce chapitre, à cet égard; **to ~ 6 out of 10** obtenir 6 sur 10; **~ out** vt rayer, barrer, biffer; **~board** n tableau m

scorn [skɔːn] n mépris m, dédain m

Scorpio ['skɔːpɪəu] n le Scorpion

Scot [skɔt] n Écossais(e)

Scotch [skɔtʃ] n whisky m, scotch m

scot-free ['skɔt'friː] adv: **to get off ~~** s'en

tirer sans être puni(e)

Scotland ['skɔtlənd] n Écosse f; **Scots** adj écossais(e); **Scotsman** (irreg) n Écossais; **Scotswoman** (irreg) n Écossaise f; **Scottish** adj écossais(e)

scoundrel ['skaundrl] n vaurien m

scour ['skauə'] vt (search) battre, parcourir

scout [skaut] n (MIL) éclaireur m; (also: **boy** ~) scout m; **girl** ~ (US) guide f; ~ **around** vi explorer, chercher

scowl [skaul] vi se renfrogner, avoir l'air maussade; **to** ~ **at** regarder de travers

scrabble ['skræbl] vi (also: ~ **around**: search) chercher à tâtons; (claw): **to** ~ **(at)** gratter ♦ n: **S~** ® Scrabble ® m

scram [skræm] (inf) vi ficher le camp

scramble ['skræmbl] n (rush) bousculade f, ruée f ♦ vi: **to** ~ **up/down** grimper/descendre tant bien que mal; **to** ~ **out** sortir or descendre à toute vitesse; **to** ~ **through** se frayer un passage (à travers); **to** ~ **for** se bousculer or se disputer pour (avoir); ~**d eggs** npl œufs brouillés

scrap [skræp] n bout m, morceau m; (fight) bagarre f; (also: ~ **iron**) ferraille f ♦ vt jeter, mettre au rebut; (fig) abandonner, laisser tomber ♦ vi (fight) se bagarrer; ~**s** npl (waste) déchets mpl; ~**book** n album m; ~ **dealer** n marchand m de ferraille

scrape [skreɪp] vt, vi gratter, racler ♦ n: **to get into a** ~ s'attirer des ennuis; **to** ~ **through** réussir de justesse; ~ **together** vt (money) racler ses fonds de tiroir pour réunir

scrap: ~ **heap** n: **on the** ~ **heap** (fig) au rancart or rebut; ~ **merchant** (BRIT) n marchand m de ferraille; ~ **paper** n papier m brouillon

scratch [skrætʃ] n égratignure f, rayure f; éraflure f; (from claw) coup m de griffe ♦ cpd: ~ **team** équipe de fortune or improvisée ♦ vt (rub) (se) gratter; (record) rayer; (paint etc) érafler; (with claw, nail) griffer ♦ vi (se) gratter; **to start from** ~ partir de zéro; **to be up to** ~ être à la hauteur

scrawl [skrɔːl] vi gribouiller

scrawny ['skrɔːnɪ] adj décharné(e)

scream [skriːm] n cri perçant, hurlement m ♦ vi crier, hurler

screech [skriːtʃ] vi hurler; (tyres) crisser; (brakes) grincer

screen [skriːn] n écran m; (in room) paravent m; (fig) écran, rideau m ♦ vt (conceal) masquer, cacher; (from the wind etc) abriter, protéger; (film) projeter; (candidates etc) filtrer; ~**ing** n (MED) test m (or tests) de dépistage; ~**play** n scénario m

screw [skruː] n vis f ♦ vt (also: ~ **in**) visser; ~ **up** vt (paper etc) froisser; **to** ~ **up one's eyes** plisser les yeux; ~**driver** n tournevis m

scribble ['skrɪbl] vt, vi gribouiller, griffonner

script [skrɪpt] n (CINEMA etc) scénario m, texte m; (system of writing) (écriture f) script m

Scripture(s) ['skrɪptʃə'(-əz)] n(pl) (Christian) Écriture sainte; (other religions) écritures saintes

scroll [skrəul] n rouleau m

scrounge [skraundʒ] (inf) vt: **to** ~ **sth off** or **from sb** taper qn de qch; ~**r** (inf) n parasite m

scrub [skrʌb] n (land) broussailles fpl ♦ vt (floor) nettoyer à la brosse; (pan) récurer; (washing) frotter; (inf: cancel) annuler

scruff [skrʌf] n: **by the** ~ **of the neck** par la peau du cou

scruffy ['skrʌfɪ] adj débraillé(e)

scrum(mage) ['skrʌm(ɪdʒ)] n (RUGBY) mêlée f

scruple ['skruːpl] n scrupule m

scrutiny ['skruːtɪnɪ] n examen minutieux

scuff [skʌf] vt érafler

scuffle ['skʌfl] n échauffourée f, rixe f

sculptor ['skʌlptə'] n sculpteur m

sculpture ['skʌlptʃə'] n sculpture f

scum [skʌm] n écume f, mousse f; (pej: people) rebut m, lie f

scurry ['skʌrɪ] vi filer à toute allure; **to** ~ **off** détaler, se sauver

scuttle ['skʌtl] n (also: **coal** ~) seau m (à charbon) ♦ vt (ship) saborder ♦ vi (scamper): **to** ~ **away** or **off** détaler

scythe [saɪð] n faux f

SDP n abbr (= Social Democratic Party) parti m social-démocrate

sea [siː] n mer f ♦ cpd marin(e), de (la) mer; **by** ~ (travel) par mer, en bateau; **on the** ~ (boat) en mer; (town) au bord de la mer; **to be all at** ~ (fig) nager complètement; **out to** ~ au large; (out) **at** ~ en mer; ~**board** n côte f; ~**food** n fruits mpl de mer; ~**front** n bord de mer; ~**going** adj (ship) de mer; ~**gull** n mouette f

seal [siːl] n (animal) phoque m; (stamp) sceau m, cachet m ♦ vt sceller; (envelope) coller; (: with ~) cacheter; ~ **off** vt (forbid entry to) interdire l'accès de

sea level n niveau m de la mer

sea lion n otarie f

seam [siːm] n couture f; (of coal) veine f, filon m

seaman ['siːmən] (irreg) n marin m

seance ['seɪɔns] n séance f de spiritisme

seaplane ['siːpleɪn] n hydravion m

search [səːtʃ] n (for person, thing, COMPUT) recherche(s) f(pl); (LAW: at sb's home) perquisition f ♦ vt fouiller; (examine) examiner minutieusement; scruter ♦ vi: **to** ~ **for** chercher; **in** ~ **of** à la recherche de; ~ **through** vt fus fouiller; ~**ing** adj pénétrant(e); ~**light** n projecteur m; ~ **party** n *n* expédition *f* de secours; ~ **warrant** *n* mandat *m* de perquisition

sea: ~**shore** *n* rivage *m*, plage *f*, bord *m* de (la) mer; ~**sick** *adj*: **to be ~sick** avoir le mal de mer; ~**side** *n* bord *m* de la mer; ~**side resort** *n* station *f* balnéaire

season ['siːzn] *n* saison *f* ♦ *vt* assaisonner, relever; **to be in/out of ~** être/ne pas être de saison; ~**al** *adj* (*work*) saisonnier(-ère); ~**ed** *adj* (*fig*) expérimenté(e); ~ **ticket** *n* carte *f* d'abonnement

seat [siːt] *n* siège *m*; (*in bus, train: place*) place *f*; (*buttocks*) postérieur *m*; (*of trousers*) fond *m* ♦ *vt* faire asseoir, placer; (*have room for*) avoir des places assises pour, pouvoir accueillir; ~ **belt** *n* ceinture *f* de sécurité

sea: ~ **water** *n* eau *f* de mer; ~**weed** *n* algues *fpl*; ~**worthy** *adj* en état de naviguer

sec. *abbr* = **second(s)**

secluded [sɪ'kluːdɪd] *adj* retiré(e), à l'écart

seclusion [sɪ'kluːʒən] *n* solitude *f*

second[1] [sɪ'kɒnd] (*BRIT*) *vt* (*employee*) affecter provisoirement

second[2] ['sekənd] *adj* deuxième, second(e) ♦ *adv* (*in race etc*) en seconde position ♦ *n* (*unit of time*) seconde *f*; (*AUT*: ~ **gear**) seconde; (*COMM*: *imperfect*) article *m* de second choix; (*BRIT*: *UNIV*) licence *f* avec mention ♦ *vt* (*motion*) appuyer; ~**ary** *adj* secondaire; ~**ary school** *n* collège *m*, lycée *m*; ~-**class** *adj* de deuxième classe; (*RAIL*) de seconde (classe); (*POST*) au tarif réduit; (*pej*) de qualité inférieure ♦ *adv* (*RAIL*) en seconde; (*POST*) au tarif réduit; ~-**hand** *adj* d'occasion; de seconde main; ~ **hand** *n* (*on clock*) trotteuse *f*; ~-**ly** *adv* deuxièmement; ~**ment** [sɪ'kɒndmənt] (*BRIT*) *n* détachement *m*; ~-**rate** *adj* de deuxième ordre, de qualité inférieure; ~ **thoughts** *npl* doutes *mpl*; **on** ~ **thoughts** *or* (*US*) **thought** à la réflexion

secrecy ['siːkrəsɪ] *n* secret *m*

secret ['siːkrɪt] *adj* secret(-ète) ♦ *n* secret *m*; **in** ~ en secret, secrètement, en cachette

secretary ['sekrətərɪ] *n* secrétaire *m/f*; (*COMM*) secrétaire général; **S~ of State (for)** (*BRIT*: *POL*) ministre *m* (de)

secretive ['siːkrətɪv] *adj* dissimulé(e)

secretly ['siːkrɪtlɪ] *adv* en secret, secrètement

sectarian [sek'teərɪən] *adj* sectaire

section ['sekʃən] *n* section *f*; (*of document*) section, article *m*, paragraphe *m*; (*cut*) coupe *f*

sector ['sektəᵊ] *n* secteur *m*

secular ['sekjuləᵊ] *adj* profane; laïque; séculier(-ère)

secure [sɪ'kjuəᵊ] *adj* (*free from anxiety*) sans inquiétude, sécurisé(e); (*firmly fixed*) solide, bien attaché(e) (*or* fermé(e) *etc*); (*in safe place*) en lieu sûr, en sûreté ♦ *vt* (*fix*) fixer,

attacher; (*get*) obtenir, se procurer

security [sɪ'kjuərɪtɪ] *n* sécurité *f*, mesures *fpl* de sécurité; (*for loan*) caution *f*, garantie *f*; ~ **guard** *n* garde chargé de la sécurité; (*when transporting money*) convoyeur *m* de fonds

sedate [sɪ'deɪt] *adj* calme; posé(e) ♦ *vt* (*MED*) donner des sédatifs à

sedative ['sedɪtɪv] *n* calmant *m*, sédatif *m*

seduce [sɪ'djuːs] *vt* séduire; **seduction** [sɪ'dʌkʃən] *n* séduction *f*; **seductive** *adj* séduisant(e); (*smile*) séducteur(-trice); (*fig*: *offer*) alléchant(e)

see [siː] (*pt* **saw**, *pp* **seen**) *vt* voir; (*accompany*): **to ~ sb to the door** reconduire *or* raccompagner qn jusqu'à la porte ♦ *vi* voir ♦ *n* évêché *m*; **to ~ that** (*ensure*) veiller à ce que +*sub*, faire en sorte que +*sub*, s'assurer que; ~ **you soon!** à bientôt!; ~ **about** *vt fus* s'occuper de; ~ **off** *vt* accompagner (à la gare *or* à l'aéroport *etc*); ~ **through** *vt* mener à bonne fin ♦ *vt fus* voir clair dans; ~ **to** *vt fus* s'occuper de, se charger de

seed [siːd] *n* graine *f*; (*sperm*) semence *f*; (*fig*) germe *m*; (*TENNIS etc*) tête *f* de série; **to go to** ~ monter en graine; (*fig*) se laisser aller; ~**ling** *n* jeune plant *m*, semis *m*; ~**y** *adj* (*shabby*) minable, miteux(-euse)

seeing ['siːɪŋ] *conj*: ~ (**that**) vu que, étant donné que

seek [siːk] (*pt*, *pp* **sought**) *vt* chercher, rechercher

seem [siːm] *vi* sembler, paraître; **there ~s to be** ... il semble qu'il y a ...; on dirait qu'il y a ...; ~**ingly** *adv* apparemment

seen [siːn] *pp* of **see**

seep [siːp] *vi* suinter, filtrer

seesaw ['siːsɔː] *n* (jeu *m* de) bascule *f*

seethe [siːð] *vi* être en effervescence; **to ~ with anger** bouillir de colère

see-through ['siːθruː] *adj* transparent(e)

segment ['segmənt] *n* segment *m*; (*of orange*) quartier *m*

segregate ['segrɪgeɪt] *vt* séparer, isoler

seize [siːz] *vt* saisir, attraper; (*take possession of*) s'emparer de; (*opportunity*) saisir; ~ **up** *vi* (*TECH*) se gripper; ~ (**up**)**on** *vt fus* saisir, sauter sur

seizure ['siːʒəᵊ] *n* (*MED*) crise *f*, attaque *f*; (*of power*) prise *f*

seldom ['seldəm] *adv* rarement

select [sɪ'lekt] *adj* choisi(e), d'élite ♦ *vt* sélectionner, choisir; ~**ion** *n* sélection *f*, choix *m*

self [self] (*pl* **selves**) *n*: **the** ~ le moi *inv* ♦ *prefix* auto-; ~-**assured** *adj* sûr(e) de soi; ~-**catering** (*BRIT*) *adj* avec cuisine, où l'on peut faire sa cuisine; ~-**centred** (*US* self-**centered**) *adj* égocentrique; ~-**confidence** *n* confiance f en soi; **~-conscious** adj timide, qui manque d'assurance; **~-contained** (BRIT) adj (flat) avec entrée particulière, indépendant(e); **~-control** n maîtrise f de soi; **~-defence** (US **self-defense**) n autodéfense f; (LAW) légitime défense f; **~-discipline** n discipline personnelle; **~-employed** adj qui travaille à son compte; **~-evident** adj: **to be ~-evident** être évident(e), aller de soi; **~-governing** adj autonome; **~-indulgent** adj qui ne se refuse rien; **~-interest** n intérêt personnel; **~ish** adj égoïste; **~ishness** n égoïsme m; **~less** adj désintéressé(e); **~-pity** n apitoiement m sur soi-même; **~-possessed** adj assuré(e); **~-preservation** n instinct m de conservation; **~-respect** n respect m de soi, amour-propre m; **~-righteous** adj suffisant(e); **~-sacrifice** n abnégation f; **~-satisfied** adj content(e) de soi, suffisant(e); **~-service** adj libre-service, self-service; **~-sufficient** adj autosuffisant(e); (person: independent) indépendant(e); **~-taught** adj (artist, pianist) qui a appris par lui-même

sell [sɛl] (pt, pp **sold**) vt vendre ♦ vi se vendre; **to ~ at** or **for 10 F** se vendre 10 F; **~ off** vt liquider; **~ out** vi: **to ~ out (of sth)** (use up stock) vendre tout son stock (de qch); **the tickets are all sold out** il ne reste plus de billets; **~-by date** n date f limite de vente; **~er** n vendeur(-euse), marchand(e); **~ing price** n prix m de vente

Sellotape ® ['sɛləʊteɪp] (BRIT) n papier m collant, scotch ® m

selves [sɛlvz] npl of **self**

semblance ['sɛmblns] n semblant m

semen ['siːmən] n sperme m

semester [sɪ'mɛstəʳ] (esp US) n semestre m

semi ['sɛmɪ] prefix semi-, demi-; à demi, à moitié; **~circle** n demi-cercle m; **~colon** n point-virgule m; **~detached (house)** (BRIT) n maison jumelée or jumelle; **~final** n demi-finale f

seminar ['sɛmɪnɑːʳ] n séminaire m; **~y** n (REL: for priests) séminaire m

semiskilled [sɛmɪ'skɪld] adj: **~ worker** ouvrier(-ère) spécialisé(e)

semi-skimmed milk [sɛmɪ'skɪmd-] n lait m demi-écrémé

senate ['sɛnɪt] n sénat m; **senator** n sénateur m

send [sɛnd] (pt, pp **sent**) vt envoyer; **~ away** vt (letter, goods) envoyer, expédier; (unwelcome visitor) renvoyer; **~ away for** vt fus commander par correspondance, se faire envoyer; **~ back** vt renvoyer; **~ for** vt fus envoyer chercher; faire venir; **~ off** vt (goods) envoyer, expédier; (BRIT: SPORT: player) expulser or renvoyer du terrain; **~ out** vt

(invitation) envoyer (par la poste); (light, heat, signal) émettre; **~ up** vt faire monter; (BRIT: parody) mettre en boîte, parodier; **~er** n expéditeur(-trice); **~-off** n: **a good ~-off** des adieux chaleureux

senior ['siːnɪəʳ] adj (high-ranking) de haut niveau; (of higher rank): **to be ~ to sb** être le supérieur de qn ♦ n (older): **she is 15 years his ~** elle est son aînée de 15 ans, elle est plus âgée que lui de 15 ans; **~ citizen** n personne âgée; **~ity** [siːnɪ'ɔrɪtɪ] n (in service) ancienneté f

sensation [sɛn'seɪʃən] n sensation f; **~al** adj qui fait sensation; (marvellous) sensationnel(le)

sense [sɛns] n sens m; (feeling) sentiment m; (meaning) sens, signification f; (wisdom) bon sens ♦ vt sentir, pressentir; **it makes ~** c'est logique; **~less** adj insensé(e), stupide; (unconscious) sans connaissance

sensible ['sɛnsɪbl] adj sensé(e), raisonnable; sage

sensitive ['sɛnsɪtɪv] adj sensible

sensual ['sɛnsjʊəl] adj sensuel(le)

sensuous ['sɛnsjʊəs] adj voluptueux(-euse) / sensuel(le)

sent [sɛnt] pt, pp of **send**

sentence ['sɛntns] n (LING) phrase f; (LAW: judgment) condamnation f, sentence f; (: punishment) peine f ♦ vt: **to ~ sb to death/to 5 years in prison** condamner qn à mort/à 5 ans de prison

sentiment ['sɛntɪmənt] n sentiment m; (opinion) opinion f, avis m; **~al** [sɛntɪ'mɛntl] adj sentimental(e)

sentry ['sɛntrɪ] n sentinelle f

separate [adj 'sɛprɪt, vb 'sɛpəreɪt] adj séparé(e), indépendant(e), différent(e) ♦ vt séparer; (make a distinction between) distinguer ♦ vi se séparer; **~ly** adv séparément; **~s** npl (clothes) coordonnés mpl; **separation** [sɛpə'reɪʃən] n séparation f

September [sɛp'tɛmbəʳ] n septembre m

septic ['sɛptɪk] adj (wound) infecté(e); **~ tank** n fosse f septique

sequel ['siːkwl] n conséquence f; séquelles fpl; (of story) suite f

sequence ['siːkwəns] n ordre m, suite f; (film ~) séquence f; (dance ~) numéro m

sequin ['siːkwɪn] n paillette f

Serbia ['sɜːbɪə] n Serbie f

serene [sɪ'riːn] adj serein(e), calme, paisible

sergeant ['sɑːdʒənt] n sergent m; (POLICE) brigadier m

serial ['sɪərɪəl] n feuilleton m; **~ killer** n meurtrier m tuant en série; **~ number** n numéro m de série

series ['sɪərɪz] n inv série f; (PUBLISHING) collection f

serious ['sɪərɪəs] *adj* sérieux(-euse); (*illness*) grave; **~ly** *adv* sérieusement; (*hurt*) gravement

sermon ['sɜːmən] *n* sermon *m*

serrated [sɪ'reɪtɪd] *adj* en dents de scie

servant ['sɜːvənt] *n* domestique *m/f*; (*fig*) serviteur/servante

serve [sɜːv] *vt* (*employer etc*) servir, être au service de; (*purpose*) servir à; (*customer, food, meal*) servir; (*subj: train*) desservir; (*apprenticeship*) faire, accomplir; (*prison term*) purger ♦ *vi* servir; (*be useful*): **to ~ as/for/to do** servir de/à/à faire ♦ *n* (*TENNIS*) service *m*; **it ~s him right** c'est bien fait pour lui; **~ out, ~ up** *vt* (*food*) servir

service ['sɜːvɪs] *n* service *m*; (*AUT: maintenance*) révision *f* ♦ *vt* (*car, washing machine*) réviser; **the S~s** les forces armées; **to be of ~ to sb** rendre service à qn; **15% ~ included** service 15% compris; **~ not included** service non compris; **~able** *adj* pratique, commode; **~ area** *n* (*on motorway*) aire *f* de services; **~ charge** (*BRIT*) *n* service *m*; **~man** (*irreg*) *n* militaire *m*; **~ station** *n* station-service *f*

serviette [sɜːvɪ'et] (*BRIT*) *n* serviette *f* (de table)

session ['seʃən] *n* séance *f*

set [set] (*pt, pp* set) *n* série *f*, assortiment *m*; (*of tools etc*) jeu *m*; (*RADIO, TV*) poste *m*; (*TENNIS*) set *m*; (*group of people*) cercle *m*, milieu *m*; (*THEATRE: stage*) scène *f*; (: *scenery*) décor *m*; (*MATH*) ensemble *m*; (*HAIRDRESSING*) mise *f* en plis ♦ *adj* (*fixed*) fixe, déterminé(e); (*ready*) prêt(e) ♦ *vt* (*place*) poser, placer; (*fix, establish*) fixer; (: *record*) établir; (*adjust*) régler; (*decide: rules etc*) fixer, choisir; (*task*) donner; (*exam*) composer ♦ *vi* (*sun*) se coucher; (*jam, jelly, concrete*) prendre; (*bone*) se ressouder; **to be ~ on doing** être résolu à faire; **to ~ the table** mettre la table; **to ~ (to music)** mettre en musique; **to ~ on fire** mettre le feu à; **to ~ free** libérer; **to ~ sth going** déclencher qch; **to ~ sail** prendre la mer; **~ about** *vt fus* (*task*) entreprendre, se mettre à; **~ aside** *vt* mettre de côté; (*time*) garder; **~ back** *vt* (*in time*): **to ~ back (by)** retarder (de); (*cost*): **to ~ sb back £5** coûter 5 livres à qn; **~ off** *vi* se mettre en route, partir ♦ *vt* (*bomb*) faire exploser; (*cause to start*) déclencher; (*show up well*) mettre en valeur, faire valoir; **~ out** *vi* se mettre en route, partir ♦ *vt* (*arrange*) disposer; (*arguments*) présenter, exposer; **to ~ out to do** entreprendre de faire, avoir pour but *or* intention de faire; **~ up** *vt* (*organization*) fonder, créer; **~back** *n* (*hitch*) revers *m*, contretemps *m*; **~ menu** *n* menu *m*

settee [se'tiː] *n* canapé *m*

setting ['setɪŋ] *n* cadre *m*; (*of jewel*) monture *f*; (*position: of controls*) réglage *m*

settle ['setl] *vt* (*argument, matter, account*) régler; (*problem*) résoudre; (*MED: calm*) calmer ♦ *vi* (*bird, dust etc*) se poser; (*also: ~ down*) s'installer, se fixer; (*calm down*) se calmer; **to ~ for sth** accepter qch, se contenter de qch; **to ~ on sth** opter *or* se décider pour qch; **~ in** *vi* s'installer; **~ up** *vi*: **to ~ up with sb** régler (ce que l'on doit à) qn; **~ment** *n* (*payment*) règlement *m*; (*agreement*) accord *m*; (*village etc*) établissement *m*; hameau *m*; **~r** *n* colon *m*

setup ['setʌp] *n* (*arrangement*) manière *f* dont les choses sont organisées; (*situation*) situation *f*

seven ['sevn] *num* sept; **~teen** *num* dix-sept; **~th** *num* septième; **~ty** *num* soixante-dix

sever ['sevər] *vt* couper, trancher; (*relations*) rompre

several ['sevrəl] *adj, pron* plusieurs *m/fpl*; **~ of us** plusieurs d'entre nous

severance ['sevərəns] *n* (*of relations*) rupture *f*; **~ pay** *n* indemnité *f* de licenciement

severe [sɪ'vɪər] *adj* (*stern*) sévère, strict(e); (*serious*) grave, sérieux(-euse); (*plain*) sévère, austère; **severity** [sɪ'verɪtɪ] *n* sévérité *f*; gravité *f*; rigueur *f*

sew [səu] (*pt* sewed, *pp* sewn) *vt, vi* coudre; **~ up** *vt* (re)coudre

sewage ['suːɪdʒ] *n* vidange(s) *f(pl)*

sewer ['suːər] *n* égout *m*

sewing ['səuɪŋ] *n* couture *f*; (*item(s)*) ouvrage *m*; **~ machine** *n* machine *f* à coudre

sewn [səun] *pp* of **sew**

sex [seks] *n* sexe *m*; **to have ~ with** avoir des rapports (sexuels) avec; **~ism** *n* sexisme *m*; **~ist** *adj* sexiste; **~ual** ['seksjuəl] *adj* sexuel(le); **~uality** [seksju'ælɪtɪ] *n* sexualité *f*; **~y** *adj* sexy *inv*

shabby ['ʃæbɪ] *adj* miteux(-euse); (*behaviour*) mesquin(e), méprisable

shack [ʃæk] *n* cabane *f*, hutte *f*

shackles ['ʃæklz] *npl* chaînes *fpl*, entraves *fpl*

shade [ʃeɪd] *n* ombre *f*; (*for lamp*) abat-jour *m inv*; (*of colour*) nuance *f*, ton *m* ♦ *vt* abriter du soleil, ombrager; **in the ~** à l'ombre; **a ~ too large/more** un tout petit peu trop grand(e)/plus

shadow ['ʃædəu] *n* ombre *f* ♦ *vt* (*follow*) filer; **~ cabinet** (*BRIT*) *n* (*POL*) cabinet parallèle formé par l'Opposition; **~y** *adj* ombragé(e); (*dim*) vague, indistinct(e)

shady ['ʃeɪdɪ] *adj* ombragé(e); (*fig: dishonest*) louche, véreux(-euse)

shaft [ʃɑːft] *n* (*of arrow, spear*) hampe *f*; (*AUT, TECH*) arbre *m*; (*of mine*) puits *m*; (*of lift*) cage *f*; (*of light*) rayon *m*, trait *m*

shaggy ['ʃægɪ] *adj* hirsute; en broussaille

shake [ʃeɪk] (pt **shook**, pp **shaken**) vt secouer; (bottle, cocktail) agiter; (house, confidence) ébranler ♦ vi trembler; **to ~ one's head** (in refusal) dire or faire non de la tête; (in dismay) secouer la tête; **to ~ hands with sb** serrer la main à qn; **~ off** vt secouer; (pursuer) se débarrasser de; **~ up** vt secouer; **~n** pp of shake; **shaky** adj (hand, voice) tremblant(e); (building) branlant(e), peu solide

shall [ʃæl] aux vb: **I ~ go** j'irai; **~ I open the door?** j'ouvre la porte?; **I'll get the coffee, ~ I?** je vais chercher le café, d'accord?

shallow ['ʃæləʊ] adj peu profond(e); (fig) superficiel(le)

sham [ʃæm] n frime f ♦ vt simuler

shambles ['ʃæmblz] n (muddle) confusion f, pagaïe f, fouillis m

shame [ʃeɪm] n honte f ♦ vt faire honte à; **it is a ~ (that/to do)** c'est dommage (que +sub/de faire); **what a ~!** quel dommage!; **~ful** adj honteux(-euse), scandaleux(-euse); **~less** adj éhonté(e), effronté(e)

shampoo [ʃæm'puː] n shampooing m ♦ vt faire un shampooing à; **~ and set** n shampooing m (et) mise f en plis

shamrock ['ʃæmrɔk] n trèfle m (emblème de l'Irlande)

shandy ['ʃændɪ] n bière panachée

shan't [ʃɑːnt] = shall not

shanty town ['ʃæntɪ-] n bidonville m

shape [ʃeɪp] n forme f ♦ vt façonner, modeler; (sb's ideas) former; (sb's life) déterminer ♦ vi (also: **~ up:** events) prendre tournure; (: person) faire des progrès, s'en sortir; **to take ~** prendre forme or tournure; **-~d** suffix: **heart-~d** en forme de cœur; **~less** adj informe, sans forme; **~ly** adj bien proportionné(e), beau (belle)

share [ʃeəʳ] n part f; (COMM) action f ♦ vt partager; (have in common) avoir en commun; **~ out** vi partager; **~holder** n actionnaire m/f

shark [ʃɑːk] n requin m

sharp [ʃɑːp] adj (razor, knife) tranchant(e), bien aiguisé(e); (point, voice) aigu(-guë); (nose, chin) pointu(e); (outline, increase) net(te); (cold, pain) vif (vive); (taste) piquant(e), âcre; (MUS) dièse; (person: quick-witted) vif (vive), éveillé(e); (: unscrupulous) malhonnête ♦ n (MUS) dièse m ♦ adv (precisely): **at 2 o'clock ~** à 2 heures pile or précises; **~en** vt aiguiser; (pencil) tailler; **~ener** n (also: **pencil ~ener**) taille-crayon(s) m inv; **~-eyed** adj à qui rien n'échappe; **~ly** adv (turn, stop) brusquement; (stand out) nettement; (criticize, retort) sèchement, vertement

shatter ['ʃætəʳ] vt briser; (fig: upset) bouleverser; (: ruin) briser, ruiner ♦ vi voler en éclats, se briser

shave [ʃeɪv] vt raser ♦ vi se raser ♦ n: **to have a ~** se raser; **~r** n (also: **electric ~r**) rasoir m électrique

shaving ['ʃeɪvɪŋ] (action) rasage m; **~s** npl (of wood etc) copeaux mpl; **~ brush** n blaireau m; **~ cream** n crème f à raser; **~ foam** n mousse f à raser

shawl [ʃɔːl] n châle m

she [ʃiː] pron elle ♦ prefix: **~-cat** chatte f; **~-elephant** éléphant m femelle

sheaf [ʃiːf] (pl **sheaves**) n gerbe f; (of papers) liasse f

shear [ʃɪəʳ] (pt **sheared**, pp **shorn**) vt (sheep) tondre; **~s** npl (for hedge) cisaille(s) f(pl)

sheath [ʃiːθ] n gaine f, fourreau m, étui m; (contraceptive) préservatif m

shed [ʃed] (pt, pp **shed**) n remise f, resserre f ♦ vt perdre; (tears) verser, répandre; (workers) congédier

she'd [ʃiːd] = she had; she would

sheen [ʃiːn] n lustre m

sheep [ʃiːp] n inv mouton m; **~dog** n chien m de berger; **~skin** n peau f de mouton

sheer [ʃɪəʳ] adj (utter) pur(e), pur et simple; (steep) à pic, abrupt(e); (almost transparent) extrêmement fin(e) ♦ adv à pic, abruptement

sheet [ʃiːt] n (on bed) drap m; (of paper) feuille f; (of glass, metal etc) feuille, plaque f

sheik(h) [ʃeɪk] n cheik m

shelf [ʃelf] (pl **shelves**) n étagère f, rayon m

shell [ʃel] n (on beach) coquillage m; (of egg, nut etc) coquille f; (explosive) obus m; (of building) carcasse f ♦ vt (peas) écosser; (MIL) bombarder (d'obus)

she'll [ʃiːl] = she will; she shall

shellfish ['ʃelfɪʃ] n inv (crab etc) crustacé m; (scallop etc) coquillage m ♦ npl (as food) fruits mpl de mer

shell suit n survêtement m (en synthétique froissé)

shelter ['ʃeltəʳ] n abri m, refuge m ♦ vt abriter, protéger; (give lodging to) donner asile à ♦ vi s'abriter, se mettre à l'abri; **~ed housing** n foyers mpl (pour personnes âgées ou handicapées)

shelve [ʃelv] vt (fig) mettre en suspens or en sommeil; **~s** npl of shelf

shepherd ['ʃepəd] n berger m ♦ vt (guide) guider, escorter; **~'s pie** (BRIT) n ≈ hachis m Parmentier

sheriff ['ʃerɪf] (US) n shérif m

sherry ['ʃerɪ] n xérès m, sherry m

she's [ʃiːz] = she is; she has

Shetland ['ʃetlənd] n (also: **the ~ Islands**) les îles fpl Shetland

shield [ʃiːld] n bouclier m; (protection) écran m de protection ♦ vt: **to ~ (from)** protéger

(de or contre)

shift [ʃɪft] n (change) changement m; (work period) période f de travail; (of workers) équipe f, poste m ♦ vt déplacer, changer de place; (remove) enlever ♦ vi changer de place, bouger; ~ **work** n travail m en équipe or par relais or par roulement; **~y** adj sournois(e); (eyes) fuyant(e)

shimmer [ʃɪmər] vi miroiter, chatoyer

shin [ʃɪn] n tibia m

shine [ʃaɪn] n (pt, pp **shone**) n éclat m, brillant m ♦ vi briller ♦ vt (torch etc): **to ~ on** braquer sur; (polish: pt, pp ~d) faire briller or reluire

shingle [ʃɪŋgl] n (on beach) galets mpl; **~s** n (MED) zona m

shiny [ʃaɪnɪ] adj brillant(e)

ship [ʃɪp] n bateau m; (large) navire m ♦ vt transporter (par mer); (send) expédier (par mer); **~building** n construction navale; **~ment** n cargaison f; **~ping** n (ships) navires mpl; (the industry) industrie navale; (transport) transport m; **~wreck** n (ship) épave f; (event) naufrage m ♦ vt: **to be ~wrecked** faire naufrage; **~yard** n chantier naval

shire [ʃaɪər] (BRIT) n comté m

shirt [ʃɜːt] n (man's) chemise f; (woman's) chemisier m; **in (one's) ~ sleeves** en bras de chemise

shit [ʃɪt] (inf!) n, excl merde f (!)

shiver [ʃɪvər] n frisson m ♦ vi frissonner

shoal [ʃəʊl] n (of fish) banc m; (fig: also: ~s) masse f, foule f

shock [ʃɒk] n choc m; (ELEC) secousse f; (MED) commotion f, choc ♦ vt (offend) choquer, scandaliser; (upset) bouleverser; ~ **absorber** n amortisseur m; **~ing** adj (scandalizing) choquant(e), scandaleux(-euse); (appalling) épouvantable

shoddy [ʃɒdɪ] adj de mauvaise qualité, mal fait(e)

shoe [ʃuː] n (pt, pp **shod**) n chaussure f, soulier m; (also: **horseshoe**) fer m à cheval ♦ vt (horse) ferrer; **~lace** n lacet m (de soulier); ~ **polish** n cirage m; ~ **shop** n magasin m de chaussures; **~string** n (fig): **on a ~string** avec un budget dérisoire

shone [ʃɒn] pt, pp of **shine**

shook [ʃʊk] pt of **shake**

shoot [ʃuːt] (pt, pp **shot**) n (on branch, seedling) pousse f ♦ vt (game) chasser; tirer; abattre; (person) blesser (or tuer) d'un coup de fusil (or de revolver); (execute) fusiller; (arrow) tirer; (gun) tirer un coup de; (film) tourner ♦ vi (with gun, bow): **to ~ (at)** tirer (sur); (FOOTBALL) shooter, tirer; ~ **down** vt (plane) abattre; ~ **in** vi entrer comme une flèche; ~ **out** vi sortir comme une flèche; ~ **up** vi (fig) monter en flèche; **~ing** n

(shots) coups mpl de feu, fusillade f; (HUNTING) chasse f; **~ing star** n étoile filante

shop [ʃɒp] n magasin m; (workshop) atelier m ♦ vi (also: **go ~ping**) faire ses courses or ses achats; ~ **assistant** (BRIT) n vendeur(-euse); ~ **floor** (BRIT) n (INDUSTRY: fig) ouvriers mpl; **~keeper** n commerçant(e); **~lifting** n vol m à l'étalage; **~per** n personne f qui fait ses courses, acheteur(-euse); **~ping** n (goods) achats mpl, provisions fpl; **~ping bag** n sac m (à provisions); **~ping centre** (US **shopping center**) n centre commercial; **~-soiled** adj défraîchi(e), qui a fait la vitrine; ~ **steward** (BRIT) n (INDUSTRY) délégué(e) syndical(e); ~ **window** n vitrine f

shore [ʃɔːr] n (of sea, lake) rivage m, rive f ♦ vt: **to ~ (up)** étayer; **on ~** à terre

shorn [ʃɔːn] pp of **shear**

short [ʃɔːt] adj (not long) court(e); (soon finished) court, bref (brève); (person, step) petit(e); (curt) brusque, sec (sèche); (insufficient) insuffisant(e); **to be/run ~ of sth** être à court de or manquer de qch; **in ~** bref; en bref; ~ **of doing** ... à moins de faire ...; **everything ~ of** tout sauf; **it is ~ for** c'est l'abréviation or le diminutif de; **to cut ~** (speech, visit) abréger, écourter; **to fall ~ of** ne pas être à la hauteur de; **to run ~ of** arriver à court de, venir à manquer de; **to stop ~** s'arrêter net; **to stop ~ of** ne pas aller jusqu'à; **~age** n manque m, pénurie f; **~bread** n ≈ sablé m; **~change** vt ne pas rendre assez à; **~circuit** n court-circuit m; **~coming** n défaut m; **~(crust) pastry** (BRIT) n pâte brisée; **~cut** n raccourci m; **~en** vt raccourcir; (text, visit) abréger; **~fall** n déficit m; **~hand** n (BRIT) sténo(graphie) f; **~hand typist** (BRIT) n sténodactylo m/f; **~list** (BRIT) n (for job) liste f des candidats sélectionnés; **~ly** adv bientôt, sous peu; ~ **notice** n: **at ~ notice** au dernier moment; **~s** npl: **(a pair of) ~s** un short; **~-sighted** adj (BRIT) myope; (fig) qui manque de clairvoyance; **~-staffed** adj à court de personnel; **~-stay** adj (car park) de courte durée; ~ **story** n nouvelle f; **~-tempered** adj qui s'emporte facilement; **~-term** adj (effect) à court terme; ~ **wave** n (RADIO) ondes courtes

shot [ʃɒt] pt, pp of **shoot** ♦ n coup m (de feu); (try) coup, essai m; (injection) piqûre f; (PHOT) photo f; **he's a good/poor ~** il tire bien/mal; **like a ~** comme une flèche; (very readily) sans hésiter; **~gun** n fusil m de chasse

should [ʃʊd] aux vb: **I ~ go now** je devrais partir maintenant; **he ~ be there now** il devrait être arrivé maintenant; **I ~ go if I were you** si j'étais vous, j'irais; **I ~ like to** j'aimerais bien, volontiers

shoulder ['ʃəʊldər] n épaule f ♦ vt (fig) endosser, se charger de; ~ **bag** n sac m à bandoulière; ~ **blade** n omoplate f

shouldn't ['ʃʊdnt] = should not

shout [ʃaʊt] n cri m ♦ vt crier ♦ vi (also: ~ out) crier, pousser des cris; ~ **down** vt huer; ~**ing** n cris mpl

shove [ʃʌv] vt pousser; (inf: put): **to** ~ **sth in** fourrer or ficher qch dans; ~ **off** (inf) vi ficher le camp

shovel ['ʃʌvl] n pelle f

show [ʃəʊ] (pt showed, pp shown) n (of emotion) manifestation f, démonstration f; (semblance) semblant m, apparence f; (exhibition) exposition f, salon m; (THEATRE, TV) spectacle m ♦ vt montrer; (film) donner; (courage etc) faire preuve de, manifester; (exhibit) exposer ♦ vi se voir, être visible; **for** ~ pour l'effet; **on** ~ (exhibits etc) exposé(e); ~ **in** vt (person) faire entrer; ~ **off** vi (pej) crâner ♦ vt (display) faire valoir; ~ **out** vt (person) reconduire (jusqu'à la porte); ~ **up** vi (stand out) ressortir; (inf: turn up) se montrer ♦ vt (flaw) faire ressortir; ~ **business** n le monde du spectacle; ~**down** n épreuve f de force

shower ['ʃaʊər] n (rain) averse f; (of stones etc) pluie f, grêle f; (~bath) douche f ♦ vi prendre une douche, se doucher ♦ vt: **to** ~ **sb with** (gifts etc) combler qn de; **to have** or **take a** ~ prendre une douche; ~**proof** adj imperméabilisé(e)

showing ['ʃəʊɪŋ] n (of film) projection f

show jumping [-dʒʌmpɪŋ] n concours m hippique

shown [ʃəʊn] pp of **show**

show: ~-**off** (inf) n (person) crâneur(-euse), m'as-tu-vu(e); ~**piece** n (of exhibition) trésor m; ~**room** n magasin m or salle f d'exposition

shrank [ʃræŋk] pt of **shrink**

shrapnel ['ʃræpnl] n éclats mpl d'obus

shred [ʃred] n (gen pl) lambeau m, petit morceau ♦ vt mettre en lambeaux, déchirer; (CULIN: grate) râper; (: lettuce etc) couper en lanières; ~**der** n (for vegetables) râpeur m; (for documents) déchiqueteuse f

shrewd [ʃruːd] adj astucieux(-euse), perspicace; (businessman) habile

shriek [ʃriːk] vi hurler, crier

shrill [ʃrɪl] adj perçant(e), aigu(-guë), strident(e)

shrimp [ʃrɪmp] n crevette f

shrine [ʃraɪn] n (place) lieu m de pèlerinage

shrink [ʃrɪŋk] (pt shrank, pp shrunk) vi rétrécir; (fig) se réduire, diminuer; (move: also: ~ away) reculer ♦ vt (wool) (faire) rétrécir ♦ n (inf: pej) psychiatre m/f, psy m/f; **to** ~ **from** (doing) sth reculer devant (la pensée de faire) qch; ~**wrap** vt emballer sous film plastique

shrivel ['ʃrɪvl] vt (also: ~ up) ratatiner, flétrir ♦ vi se ratatiner, se flétrir

shroud [ʃraʊd] n linceul m ♦ vt: ~**ed in mystery** enveloppé(e) de mystère

Shrove Tuesday ['ʃrəʊv-] n (le) Mardi gras

shrub n arbuste m; ~**bery** n massif m d'arbustes

shrug [ʃrʌg] vt, vi: **to** ~ (**one's shoulders**) hausser les épaules; ~ **off** vt faire fi de

shrunk [ʃrʌŋk] pp of **shrink**

shudder ['ʃʌdər] vi frissonner, frémir

shuffle ['ʃʌfl] vt (cards) battre; **to** ~ (**one's feet**) traîner les pieds

shun [ʃʌn] vt éviter, fuir

shunt [ʃʌnt] vt (RAIL) aiguiller

shut [ʃʌt] (pt, pp shut) vt fermer ♦ vi (se) fermer; ~ **down** vt, vi fermer définitivement; ~ **off** vt couper, arrêter; ~ **up** vi (inf: keep quiet) se taire ♦ vt (close) fermer; (silence) faire taire; ~**ter** n volet m; (PHOT) obturateur m

shuttle ['ʃʌtl] n navette f; (also: ~ **service**) (service m de) navette f; ~**cock** n volant m (de badminton); ~ **diplomacy** n navettes fpl diplomatiques

shy [ʃaɪ] adj timide

Siberia [saɪ'bɪərɪə] n Sibérie f

Sicily ['sɪsɪlɪ] n Sicile f

sick [sɪk] adj (ill) malade; (vomiting): **to be** ~ vomir; (humour) noir(e), macabre; **to feel** ~ avoir envie de vomir, avoir mal au cœur; **to be** ~ **of** (fig) en avoir assez de; ~ **bay** n infirmerie f; ~**en** vt écœurer; ~**ening** adj (fig) écœurant(e), dégoûtant(e)

sickle ['sɪkl] n faucille f

sick: ~ **leave** n congé m de maladie; ~**ly** adj maladif(-ive), souffreteux(-euse); (causing nausea) écœurant(e); ~**ness** n maladie f; (vomiting) vomissement(s) m(pl); ~ **note** n (from parents) mot m d'absence; (from doctor) certificat médical; ~ **pay** n indemnité f de maladie

side [saɪd] n côté m; (of lake, road) bord m; (team) camp m, équipe f ♦ adj (door, entrance) latéral(e) ♦ vi: **to** ~ **with sb** prendre le parti de qn, se ranger du côté de qn; **by the** ~ **of** au bord de; ~ **by** ~ côte à côte; **from** ~ **to** ~ d'un côté à l'autre; **to take** ~**s (with)** prendre parti (pour); ~**board** n buffet m; ~**boards** (BRIT), ~**burns** npl (whiskers) pattes fpl; ~ **drum** n tambour plat; ~ **effect** n effet m secondaire; ~**light** n (AUT) veilleuse f; ~**line** n (SPORT) (ligne f de) touche f; (fig) travail m secondaire; ~**long** adj oblique; ~**show** n attraction f; ~**step** vt (fig) éluder; éviter; ~ **street** n (petite) rue transversale; ~**track** vt (fig) faire dévier de son sujet; ~**walk** (US) n trottoir m; ~**ways** adv de côté

siding ['saɪdɪŋ] n (RAIL) voie f de garage

siege [si:dʒ] n siège m

sieve [sɪv] n tamis m, passoire f

sift [sɪft] vt (fig: also: ~ **through**) passer en revue; (lit: flour etc) passer au tamis

sigh [saɪ] n soupir m ♦ vi soupirer, pousser un soupir

sight [saɪt] n (faculty) vue f; (spectacle) spectacle m; (on gun) mire f ♦ vt apercevoir; **in ~** visible; **out of ~** hors de vue; **~seeing** n tourisme m; **to go ~seeing** faire du tourisme

sign [saɪn] n signe m; (with hand etc) signe, geste m; (notice) panneau m, écriteau m ♦ vt signer; **~ on** (as unemployed) s'inscrire au chômage; (for course) s'inscrire ♦ vt (employee) embaucher; **~ over** vt: **to ~ sth over to sb** céder qch par écrit à qn; **~ up** vi (MIL) s'engager; (for course) s'inscrire

signal ['sɪgnl] n signal m ♦ vi (AUT) mettre son clignotant ♦ vt (person) faire signe à; (message) communiquer par signaux; **~man** (irreg) n (RAIL) aiguilleur m

signature ['sɪgnətʃəʳ] n signature f; **~ tune** n indicatif musical

signet ring ['sɪgnət-] n chevalière f

significance [sɪg'nɪfɪkəns] n signification f; importance f

significant [sɪg'nɪfɪkənt] adj significatif(-ive); (important) important(e), considérable

sign language n langage m per signes

signpost ['saɪnpəust] n poteau indicateur

silence ['saɪləns] n silence m ♦ vt faire taire, réduire au silence; **~r** n (on gun, BRIT: AUT) silencieux m

silent ['saɪlənt] adj silencieux(-euse); (film) muet(te); **to remain ~** garder le silence, ne rien dire; **~ partner** n (COMM) bailleur m de fonds, commanditaire m

silhouette [sɪlu:'et] n silhouette f

silicon chip ['sɪlɪkən-] n puce f électronique

silk [sɪlk] n soie f ♦ cpd de or en soie; **~y** adj soyeux(-euse)

silly ['sɪlɪ] adj stupide, sot(te), bête

silt [sɪlt] n vase f; limon m

silver ['sɪlvəʳ] n argent m; (money) monnaie f (en pièces d'argent); (also: ~**ware**) argenterie f ♦ adj d'argent, en argent; **~ paper** (BRIT) n papier m d'argent or d'étain; **~-plated** adj plaqué(e) argent inv; **~smith** n orfèvre m/f; **~y** adj argenté(e)

similar ['sɪmɪləʳ] adj: **~ (to)** semblable (à); **~ly** adv de la même façon, de même

simmer ['sɪməʳ] vi cuire à feu doux, mijoter

simple ['sɪmpl] adj simple; **simplicity** [sɪm'plɪsɪtɪ] n simplicité f; **simply** adv (without fuss) avec simplicité

simultaneous [sɪməl'teɪnɪəs] adj simultané(e)

sin [sɪn] n péché m ♦ vi pécher

since [sɪns] adv, prep depuis ♦ conj (time) depuis que; (because) puisque, étant donné que, comme; **~ then, ever ~** depuis ce moment-là

sincere [sɪn'sɪəʳ] adj sincère; **~ly** adv see **yours**; **sincerity** [sɪn'serɪtɪ] n sincérité f

sinew ['sɪnju:] n tendon m

sing [sɪŋ] (pt **sang**, pp **sung**) vt, vi chanter

Singapore [sɪŋgə'pɔ:ʳ] n Singapour m

singe [sɪndʒ] vt brûler légèrement; (clothes) roussir

singer ['sɪŋəʳ] n chanteur(-euse)

singing ['sɪŋɪŋ] n chant m

single ['sɪŋgl] adj seul(e), unique; (unmarried) célibataire; (not double) simple ♦ n (BRIT: also: ~ **ticket**) aller m (simple); (record) 45 tours m; **~ out** vt choisir; (distinguish) distinguer; **~ bed** n lit m d'une personne; **~-breasted** adj droit(e); **~ file** n: **in ~ file** en file indienne; **~-handed** adv tout(e) seul(e), sans (aucune) aide; **~-minded** adj résolu(e), tenace; **~ parent** n parent m unique; **~ room** n chambre f à un lit or pour une personne; **~s** n (TENNIS) simple m; **~-track road** n route f à voie unique; **singly** adv séparément

singular ['sɪŋgjuləʳ] adj singulier(-ère), étrange; (outstanding) remarquable; (LING) (au) singulier, du singulier ♦ n singulier m

sinister ['sɪnɪstəʳ] adj sinistre

sink [sɪŋk] (pt **sank**, pp **sunk**) n évier m ♦ vt (ship) (faire) couler, faire sombrer; (foundations) creuser ♦ vi couler, sombrer; (ground etc) s'affaisser; (also: ~ **back**, ~ **down**) s'affaisser, se laisser retomber; **to ~ sth into** enfoncer qch dans; **my heart sank** j'ai complètement perdu courage; **~ in** vi (fig) pénétrer, être compris(e)

sinner ['sɪnəʳ] n pécheur(-eresse)

sinus ['saɪnəs] n sinus m inv

sip [sɪp] n gorgée f ♦ vt boire à petites gorgées

siphon ['saɪfən] n siphon m; **~ off** vt siphonner; (money: illegally) détourner

sir [sɜ:ʳ] n monsieur m; **S~ John Smith** sir John Smith; **yes ~** oui, Monsieur

siren ['saɪərn] n sirène f

sirloin ['sɜ:lɔɪn] n (also: ~ **steak**) aloyau m

sissy ['sɪsɪ] (inf) n (coward) poule mouillée

sister ['sɪstəʳ] n sœur f; (nun) religieuse f, sœur; (BRIT: nurse) infirmière f en chef; **~-in-law** n belle-sœur f

sit [sɪt] (pt, pp **sat**) vi s'asseoir; (be ~ting) être assis(e); (assembly) être en séance, siéger; (for painter) poser ♦ vt (exam) passer, se présenter à; **~ down** vi s'asseoir; **~ in on** vt fus assister à; **~ up** vi s'asseoir; (straight) se redresser; (not go to bed) rester debout, ne pas se coucher

sitcom ['sɪtkɔm] n abbr (= situation comedy) comédie f de situation

site [saɪt] n emplacement m, site m; (also: **building ~**) chantier m ♦ vt placer

sit-in ['sɪtɪn] n (demonstration) sit-in m inv, occupation f (de locaux)

sitting ['sɪtɪŋ] n (of assembly etc) séance f; (in canteen) service m; **~ room** n salon m

situated ['sɪtjueɪtɪd] adj situé(e)

situation [sɪtju'eɪʃən] n situation f; "**~s vacant**" (BRIT) "offres d'emploi"

six [sɪks] num six; **~teen** num seize; **~th** num sixième; **~ty** num soixante

size [saɪz] n taille f; dimensions fpl; (of clothing) taille; (of shoes) pointure f; (fig) ampleur f; (glue) colle f; **~ up** vt juger, jauger; **~able** adj assez grand(e); assez important(e)

sizzle ['sɪzl] vi grésiller

skate [skeɪt] n patin m; (fish: pl inv) raie f ♦ vi patiner; **~board** n skateboard m, planche f à roulettes; **~boarding** n skateboard m; **~r** n patineur(-euse); **skating** n patinage m; **skating rink** n patinoire f

skeleton ['skelɪtn] n squelette m; (outline) schéma m; **~ staff** n effectifs réduits

skeptical ['skeptɪkl] (US) adj = sceptical

sketch [sketʃ] n (drawing) croquis m, esquisse f; (THEATRE) sketch m, saynète f ♦ vt esquisser, faire un croquis or une esquisse de; **~ book** n carnet m à dessin; **~y** adj incomplet(-ète), fragmentaire

skewer ['skjuːəʳ] n brochette f

ski [skiː] n ski m ♦ vi skier, faire du ski; **~ boot** n chaussure f de ski

skid [skɪd] vi déraper

ski: **~er** n skieur(-euse); **~ing** n ski m; **~ jump** n saut m à skis

skilful ['skɪlful] (US **skillful**) adj habile, adroit(e)

ski lift n remonte-pente m inv

skill [skɪl] n habileté f, adresse f, talent m; (requiring training: gen pl) compétences fpl; **~ed** adj habile, adroit(e); (worker) qualifié(e)

skim [skɪm] vt (milk) écrémer; (glide over) raser, effleurer ♦ vi: **to ~ through** (fig) parcourir; **~med milk** n lait écrémé

skimp [skɪmp] vt (also: **~ on:** work) bâcler, faire à la va-vite; (: cloth etc) lésiner sur; **~y** adj (skirt) étriqué(e)

skin [skɪn] n peau f ♦ vt (fruit etc) éplucher; (animal) écorcher; **~ cancer** n cancer m de la peau; **~-deep** adj superficiel(le); **~-diving** n plongée sous-marine; **~head** n skinhead m/f; **~ny** adj maigre, maigrichon(ne); **~tight** adj (jeans etc) moulant(e), ajusté(e)

skip [skɪp] n petit bond or saut; (BRIT: container) benne f ♦ vi gambader, sautiller; (with rope) sauter à la corde ♦ vt sauter

ski pass n forfait-skieur(s) m

ski pole n bâton m de ski

skipper ['skɪpəʳ] n capitaine m; (in race) skipper m

skipping rope ['skɪpɪŋ-] (BRIT) n corde f à sauter

skirmish ['skɜːmɪʃ] n escarmouche f, accrochage m

skirt [skɜːt] n jupe f ♦ vt longer, contourner; **~ing board** (BRIT) n plinthe f

ski: **~ slope** n piste f de ski; **~ suit** n combinaison f (de ski); **~ tow** n remonte-pente m inv

skittle ['skɪtl] n quille f; **~s** n (game) (jeu de) quilles fpl

skive [skaɪv] (BRIT: inf) vi tirer au flanc

skull [skʌl] n crâne m

skunk [skʌŋk] n mouffette f

sky [skaɪ] n ciel m; **~light** n lucarne f; **~scraper** n gratte-ciel m inv

slab [slæb] n (of stone) dalle f; (of food) grosse tranche

slack [slæk] adj (loose) lâche, desserré(e); (slow) stagnant(e); (careless) négligent(e), peu sérieux(-euse) or consciencieux(-euse); **~s** npl (trousers) pantalon m; **~en** vi ralentir, diminuer ♦ vt (speed) réduire; (grip) relâcher; (clothing) desserrer

slag heap [slæg-] n crassier m

slag off (BRIT: inf) vt dire du mal de

slam [slæm] vt (door) (faire) claquer; (throw) jeter violemment, flanquer (fam); (criticize) démolir ♦ vi claquer

slander ['slɑːndəʳ] n calomnie f; diffamation f

slang [slæŋ] n argot m

slant [slɑːnt] n inclinaison f; (fig) angle m, point m de vue; **~ed** adj = **slanting**; **~ing** adj en pente, incliné(e); **~ing eyes** yeux bridés

slap [slæp] n claque f, gifle f; tape f ♦ vt donner une claque or une gifle or une tape à; (paint) appliquer rapidement ♦ adv (directly) tout droit, en plein; **~dash** adj fait(e) sans soin or à la va-vite; (person) insouciant(e), négligent(e); **~stick** n (comedy) grosse farce, style m tarte à la crème; **~up** (BRIT) adj: **a ~-up meal** un repas extra or fameux

slash [slæʃ] vt entailler, tailladder; (fig: prices) casser

slat [slæt] n latte f, lame f

slate [sleɪt] n ardoise f ♦ vt (fig: criticize) éreinter, démolir

slaughter ['slɔːtəʳ] n carnage m, massacre m ♦ vt (animal) abattre; (people) massacrer; **~house** n abattoir m

slave [sleɪv] n esclave m/f ♦ vi (also: **~ away**) trimer, travailler comme un forçat; **~ry** n esclavage m

slay [sleɪ] (pt **slew**, pp **slain**) vt tuer

sleazy ['sliːzɪ] adj miteux(-euse), minable

sledge [slɛdʒ] n luge f ♦ vi: **to go sledging** faire de la luge

sledgehammer ['slɛdʒhæmə^r] n marteau m de forgeron

sleek [sliːk] adj (hair, fur etc) brillant(e), lisse; (car, boat etc) aux lignes pures or élégantes

sleep [sliːp] (pt, pp **slept**) n sommeil m ♦ vi dormir; (spend night) dormir, coucher; **to go to ~** s'endormir; **~ around** vi coucher à droite et à gauche; **~ in** vi (oversleep) se réveiller trop tard; **~er** (BRIT) n (RAIL: train) train-couchettes m; (ː berth) couchette f; **~ing bag** n sac m de couchage; **~ing car** n (RAIL) wagon-lit m, voiture-lit f; **~ing partner** (BRIT) n = **silent partner**; **~ing pill** n somnifère m; **~less** adj: **a ~less night** une nuit blanche; **~walker** n somnambule m/f; **~y** adj qui a sommeil; (fig) endormi(e)

sleet [sliːt] n neige fondue

sleeve [sliːv] n manche f; (of record) pochette f

sleigh [sleɪ] n traîneau m

sleight [slaɪt] n: **~ of hand** tour m de passe-passe

slender ['slɛndə^r] adj svelte, mince; (fig) faible, ténu(e)

slept [slɛpt] pt, pp of **sleep**

slew [sluː] vi (also: **~ around**) virer, pivoter ♦ pt of **slay**

slice [slaɪs] n tranche f; (round) rondelle f; (utensil) spatule f, truelle f ♦ vt couper en tranches (or en rondelles)

slick [slɪk] adj (skilful) brillant(e) (en apparence); (salesman) qui a du bagout ♦ n (also: **oil ~**) nappe f de pétrole, marée noire

slide [slaɪd] (pt, pp **slid**) n (in playground) toboggan m; (PHOT) diapositive f; (BRIT: also: **hair ~**) barrette f; (in prices) chute f, baisse f ♦ vt (faire) glisser ♦ vi glisser; **sliding** adj (door) coulissant(e); **sliding scale** n échelle f mobile

slight [slaɪt] adj (slim) mince, menu(e); (frail) frêle; (trivial) faible, insignifiant(e); (small) petit(e), léger(-ère) (before n) ♦ n offense f, affront m; **not in the ~est** pas le moins du monde, pas du tout; **~ly** adv légèrement, un peu

slim [slɪm] adj mince ♦ vi maigrir; (diet) suivre un régime amaigrissant

slime [slaɪm] n (mud) vase f; (other substance) substance visqueuse

slimming ['slɪmɪŋ] adj (diet, pills) amaigrissant(e); (foodstuff) qui ne fait pas grossir

sling [slɪŋ] (pt, pp **slung**) n (MED) écharpe f; (for baby) porte-bébé m; (weapon) fronde f, lance-pierre m ♦ vt lancer, jeter

slip [slɪp] n faux pas m; (mistake) erreur f; étourderie f; bévue f; (underskirt) combinaison f; (of paper) petite feuille, fiche f ♦ vt (slide) glisser ♦ vi glisser; (decline) baisser; (move smoothly): **to ~ into/out of** se glisser or se faufiler dans/hors de; **to ~ sth on/off** enfiler/enlever qch; **to give sb the ~** fausser compagnie à qn; **a ~ of the tongue** un lapsus; **~ away** vi s'esquiver; **~ in** vt glisser ♦ vi (errors) s'y glisser; **~ out** vi sortir; **~ up** vi faire une erreur, gaffer; **~ped disc** n déplacement m de vertèbre

slipper ['slɪpə^r] n pantoufle f

slippery ['slɪpərɪ] adj glissant(e)

slip: **~ road** (BRIT) n (to motorway) bretelle f d'accès; **~-up** n bévue f; **~way** n cale f (de construction or de lancement)

slit [slɪt] (pt, pp **slit**) n fente f; (cut) incision f ♦ vt fendre; couper; inciser

slither ['slɪðə^r] vi glisser; (snake) onduler

sliver ['slɪvə^r] n (of glass, wood) éclat m; (of cheese etc) petit morceau, fine tranche

slob [slɔb] (inf) n rustaud(e)

slog [slɔg] (BRIT) vi travailler très dur ♦ n gros effort; tâche fastidieuse

slogan ['sləʊgən] n slogan m

slope [sləʊp] n pente f, côte f; (side of mountain) versant m; (slant) inclinaison f ♦ vi: **to ~ down** être or descendre en pente; **to ~ up** monter; **sloping** adj en pente; (writing) penché(e)

sloppy ['slɔpɪ] adj (work) peu soigné(e), bâclé(e); (appearance) négligé(e), débraillé(e)

slot [slɔt] n fente f ♦ vt: **to ~ sth into** encastrer or insérer qch dans

sloth [sləʊθ] n (laziness) paresse f

slouch [slaʊtʃ] vi avoir le dos rond, être voûté(e)

slovenly ['slʌvənlɪ] adj sale, débraillé(e); (work) négligé(e)

slow [sləʊ] adj lent(e); (watch): **to be ~** retarder ♦ adv lentement ♦ vt, vi (also: **~ down, ~ up**) ralentir; **"~"** (road sign) "ralentir"; **~ly** adv lentement; **~ motion** n: **in ~ motion** au ralenti

sludge [slʌdʒ] n boue f

slug [slʌg] n limace f; (bullet) balle f

sluggish ['slʌgɪʃ] adj (person) mou (molle), lent(e); (stream, engine, trading) lent

sluice [sluːs] n (also: **~ gate**) vanne f

slum [slʌm] n (house) taudis m

slump [slʌmp] n baisse soudaine, effondrement m; (ECON) crise f ♦ vi s'effondrer, s'affaisser

slung [slʌŋ] pt, pp of **sling**

slur [slə:^r] n (fig: smear): **~ (on)** atteinte f (à); insinuation f (contre) ♦ vt mal articuler

slush [slʌʃ] n neige fondue

slut [slʌt] (pej) n souillon f

sly [slaɪ] adj (person) rusé(e); (smile, expression, remark) sournois(e)

smack [smæk] n (slap) tape f; (on face) gifle f
♦ vt donner une tape à; (on face) gifler; (on
bottom) donner la fessée à ♦ vi: **to ~ of** avoir
des relents de, sentir

small [smɔ:l] adj petit(e); **~ ads** (BRIT) npl
petites annonces; **~ change** n petite or
menue monnaie; **~holder** (BRIT) n petit
cultivateur; **~ hours** npl: **in the ~ hours** au
petit matin; **~pox** n variole f; **~ talk** n
menus propos

smart [smɑ:t] adj (neat, fashionable)
élégant(e), chic inv; (clever) intelligent(e),
astucieux(-euse), futé(e); (quick) rapide, vif
(vive), prompt(e) ♦ vi faire mal, brûler; (fig)
être piqué(e) au vif; **~ card** n carte f à puce;
~en up vi devenir plus élégant(e), se faire
beau (belle) ♦ vt rendre plus élégant(e)

smash [smæʃ] n (also: **~-up**) collision f,
accident m; (also: ~ **hit**) succès foudroyant
♦ vt casser, briser, fracasser; (opponent)
écraser; (SPORT: record) pulvériser ♦ vi se
briser, se fracasser; s'écraser; **~ing** (inf) adj
formidable

smattering ['smætərɪŋ] n: **a ~ of** quelques
notions de

smear [smɪəʳ] n tache f, salissure f; trace f;
(MED) frottis m ♦ vt enduire; (make dirty)
salir; **~ campaign** n campagne f de
diffamation

smell [smel] (pt, pp smelt or smelled) n odeur
f; (sense) odorat m ♦ vt sentir ♦ vi (food etc):
to ~ (of) sentir (de); (pej) sentir mauvais; **~y**
adj qui sent mauvais, malodorant(e)

smile [smaɪl] n sourire m ♦ vi sourire

smirk [smɜ:k] n petit sourire suffisant or
affecté

smock [smɔk] n blouse f

smog [smɔg] n brouillard mêlé de fumée,
smog m

smoke [sməʊk] n fumée f ♦ vt, vi fumer; **~d**
adj (bacon, glass) fumé(e); **~r** n (person)
fumeur(-euse); (RAIL) wagon m fumeurs;
~ screen n rideau m or écran m de fumée;
(fig) paravent m; **smoking** n tabagisme m;
"no smoking" (sign) "défense de fumer"; **to
give up smoking** arrêter de fumer; **smoking
compartment** (US **smoking car**) n wagon m
fumeurs; **smoky** adj enfumé(e); (taste)
fumé(e)

smolder ['sməʊldəʳ] (US) vi = **smoulder**

smooth [smu:ð] adj lisse; (sauce) onctu-
eux(-euse); (flavour, whisky) moelleux(-euse);
(movement) régulier(-ère), sans à-coups or
heurts; (pej: person) doucereux(-euse),
mielleux(-euse) ♦ vt (also: ~ **out**): skirt, paper)
lisser, défroisser; (: creases, difficulties) faire
disparaître

smother ['smʌðəʳ] vt étouffer

smoulder ['sməʊldəʳ] (US **smolder**) vi couver

smudge [smʌdʒ] n tache f, bavure f ♦ vt
salir, maculer

smug [smʌg] adj suffisant(e)

smuggle ['smʌgl] vt passer en contrebande
or en fraude; **~r** n contrebandier(-ère);
smuggling n contrebande f

smutty ['smʌtɪ] adj (fig) grossier(-ère),
obscène

snack [snæk] n casse-croûte m inv; **~ bar** n
snack(-bar) m

snag [snæg] n inconvénient m, difficulté f

snail [sneɪl] n escargot m

snake [sneɪk] n serpent m

snap [snæp] n (sound) claquement m, bruit
sec; (photograph) photo f, instantané m ♦ adj
subit(e); fait(e) sans réfléchir ♦ vt (break)
casser net; (fingers) faire claquer ♦ vi se
casser net or avec un bruit sec; (speak
sharply) parler d'un ton brusque; **to ~ shut** se
refermer brusquement; **~ at** vt fus (subj: dog)
essayer de mordre; **~ off** vi (break) casser
net; **~ up** vt sauter sur, saisir; **~py** (inf) adj
prompt(e); (slogan) qui a du punch; **make it
~py!** grouille-toi, et que ça saute!; **~shot** n
photo f, instantané m

snare [snɛəʳ] n piège m

snarl [snɑ:l] vi gronder

snatch [snætʃ] n (small amount): **~es of** des
fragments mpl or bribes fpl de ♦ vt saisir (d'un
geste vif); (steal) voler

sneak [sni:k] vi: **to ~ in/out** entrer/sortir
furtivement or à la dérobée ♦ n (inf: pej:
informer) faux jeton; **to ~ up on sb**
s'approcher de qn sans faire de bruit; **~ers**
npl tennis mpl, baskets mpl

sneer [snɪəʳ] vi ricaner; **to ~ at** traiter avec
mépris

sneeze [sni:z] vi éternuer

sniff [snɪf] vi renifler ♦ vt renifler, flairer; (glue,
drugs) sniffer, respirer

snigger ['snɪgəʳ] vi ricaner; pouffer de rire

snip [snɪp] n (cut) petit coup; (BRIT: inf:
bargain) (bonne) occasion or affaire f ♦ vt
couper

sniper ['snaɪpəʳ] n tireur embusqué

snippet ['snɪpɪt] n bribe(s) f(pl)

snob [snɔb] n snob m/f; **~bish** adj snob inv

snooker ['snu:kəʳ] n sorte de jeu de billard

snoop [snu:p] vi: **to ~ about** fureter

snooze [snu:z] n petit somme ♦ vi faire un
petit somme

snore [snɔ:ʳ] vi ronfler

snorkel ['snɔ:kl] n (of swimmer) tuba m

snort [snɔ:t] vi grogner; (horse) renâcler

snout [snaʊt] n museau m

snow [snəʊ] n neige f ♦ vi neiger; **~ball** n
boule f de neige; **~bound** adj enneigé(e),
bloqué(e) par la neige; **~drift** n congère f;
~drop n perce-neige m or f; **~fall** n chute f

de neige; **~flake** n flocon m de neige; **~man**
(irreg) n bonhomme m de neige; **~plough**
(US **snowplow**) n chasse-neige m inv; **~shoe**
n raquette f (pour la neige); **~storm** n
tempête f de neige
snub [snʌb] vt repousser, snober ♦ n
rebuffade f; **~-nosed** adj au nez retroussé
snuff [snʌf] n tabac m à priser
snug [snʌg] adj douillet(te), confortable;
(person) bien au chaud
snuggle ['snʌgl] vi: **to ~ up to sb** se serrer ou
se blottir contre qn

KEYWORD

so [səu] adv **1** (thus, likewise) ainsi; **if so** si oui;
so do ou **have I** moi aussi; **it's 5 o'clock – so it
is!** il est 5 heures – en effet! or c'est vrai!; **I
hope/think so** je l'espère/le crois; **so far**
jusqu'ici, jusqu'à maintenant; (in past)
jusque-là
2 (in comparisons etc: to such a degree) si,
tellement; **so big (that)** si ou tellement grand
(que); **she's not so clever as her brother** elle
n'est pas aussi intelligente que son frère
3: so many ♦ adj, adv tant (de); **I've got so much work**
j'ai tant de travail; **I love you so much** je vous
aime tant; **so many** tant (de)
4 (phrases): **10 or so** à peu près or environ
10; **so long!** (inf: goodbye) au revoir!, à un de
ces jours!
♦ conj **1** (expressing purpose): **so as to do**
pour faire, afin de faire; **so (that)** pour que ou
afin que +sub
2 (expressing result) donc, par conséquent; **so
that** si bien que, de (telle) sorte que

soak [səuk] vt faire tremper; (drench) tremper
♦ vi tremper; **~ in** être absorbé(e); **~ up**
vt absorber; **~ing** adj trempé(e)
soap [səup] n savon m; **~flakes** npl paillettes
fpl de savon; **~ opera** n feuilleton télévisé;
~ powder n lessive f; **~y** adj savon-
neux(-euse)
soar [sɔ:r] vi monter (en flèche), s'élancer;
(building) s'élancer
sob [sɔb] n sanglot m ♦ vi sangloter
sober ['səubər] adj qui n'est pas (or plus) ivre;
(serious) sérieux(-euse), sensé(e); (colour,
style) sobre, discret(-ète); **~ up** vt dessoûler
(inf) ♦ vi dessoûler (inf)
so-called ['səu'kɔ:ld] adj soi-disant inv
soccer ['sɔkər] n football m
social ['səuʃl] adj social(e); (sociable) sociable
♦ n (petite) fête; **~ club** n amicale f, foyer
m; **~ism** n socialisme m; **~ist** adj socialiste
♦ n socialiste m/f; **~ize** vi: **to ~ize (with)** lier
connaissance (avec); parler (avec);
~ security (BRIT) n aide sociale; **~ work** n

assistance sociale, travail social; **~ worker** n
assistant(e) social(e)
society [sə'saiəti] n société f; (club) société,
association f; (also: **high ~**) (haute) société,
grand monde
sociology [səusi'ɔlədʒi] n sociologie f
sock [sɔk] n chaussette f
socket ['sɔkit] n cavité f; (BRIT: ELEC: also: **wall
~**) prise f de courant
sod [sɔd] n (of earth) motte f; (BRIT: inf!) con
m (!); salaud m (!)
soda ['səudə] n (CHEM) soude f; (also: **~ water**) eau f de Seltz; (US: also: **~ pop**) soda m
sofa ['səufə] n sofa m, canapé m
soft [sɔft] adj (not rough) doux (douce); (not
hard) doux; mou (molle); (not loud) doux,
léger(-ère); (kind) doux, gentil(le); **~ drink**
n boisson non alcoolisée; **~en** vt (r)amollir;
(fig) adoucir; atténuer ♦ vi se ramollir;
s'adoucir; s'atténuer; **~ly** adv doucement;
gentiment; **~ness** n douceur f; **~ware** n
(COMPUT) logiciel m, software m
soggy ['sɔgi] adj trempé(e); détrempé(e)
soil [sɔil] n (earth) sol m, terre f ♦ vt salir; (fig)
souiller
solar ['səulər] adj solaire; **~ panel** n panneau
m solaire; **~ power** n énergie solaire
sold [səuld] pt, pp of **sell**
solder ['səuldər] vt souder (au fil à souder)
♦ n soudure f
soldier ['səuldʒər] n soldat m, militaire m
sole [səul] n (of foot) plante f; (of shoe)
semelle f; (fish: pl inv) sole f ♦ adj seul(e),
unique
solemn ['sɔləm] adj solennel(le); (person)
sérieux(-euse), grave
sole trader n (COMM) chef m d'entreprise
individuelle
solicit [sə'lisit] vt (request) solliciter ♦ vi
(prostitute) racoler
solicitor [sə'lisitər] n (for wills etc) ≈ notaire
m; (in court) ≈ avocat m
solid ['sɔlid] adj solide; (not hollow) plein(e),
compact(e), massif(-ive); (entire): **3 ~ hours**
3 heures entières ♦ n solide m
solidarity [sɔli'dæriti] n solidarité f
solitary ['sɔlitəri] adj solitaire;
~ confinement n (LAW) isolement m
solo ['səuləu] n solo m ♦ adv (fly) en solitaire;
~ist n soliste m/f
soluble ['sɔljubl] adj soluble
solution [sə'lu:ʃən] n solution f
solve [sɔlv] vt résoudre
solvent ['sɔlvənt] adj (COMM) solvable ♦ n
(CHEM) (dis)solvant m

KEYWORD

some [sʌm] adj **1** (a certain amount or
number of): **some tea/water/ice cream** du

thé/de l'eau/de la glace; **some children/
apples** des enfants/pommes
2 (*certain: in contrasts*): **some people say that
...** il y a des gens qui disent que ...; **some
films were excellent, but most ...** certains films
étaient excellents, mais la plupart ...
3 (*unspecified*): **some woman was asking for
you** il y avait une dame qui vous demandait;
he was asking for some book (or other) il
demandait un livre quelconque; **some day** un
de ces jours; **some day next week** un jour de la
semaine prochaine
♦ *pron* **1** (*a certain number*) quelques-un(e)s,
certain(e)s; **I've got some** (*books etc*) j'en ai
(quelques-uns); **some (of them) have been
sold** certains ont été vendus
2 (*a certain amount*) un peu; **I've got some**
(*money, milk*) j'en ai (un peu)
♦ *adv*: **some 10 people** quelque 10 personnes,
10 personnes environ

some: ~body ['sʌmbədɪ] *pron* = **someone**;
~how *adv* d'une façon ou d'une autre; (*for
some reason*) pour une raison ou une autre;
~one *pron* quelqu'un; **~place** (*US*) *adv*
= **somewhere**
somersault ['sʌməsɔːlt] *n* culbute *f*, saut
périlleux ♦ *vi* faire la culbute *or* un saut
périlleux; (*car*) faire un tonneau
some: ~thing *pron* quelque chose; **~thing
interesting** quelque chose d'intéressant;
~time *adv* (*in future*) un de ces jours, un
jour ou l'autre; (*in past*): **~time last month** au
cours du mois dernier; **~times** *adv*
quelquefois, parfois; **~what** *adv* quelque
peu, un peu; **~where** *adv* quelque part
son [sʌn] *n* fils *m*
song [sɒŋ] *n* chanson *f*; (*of bird*) chant *m*
son-in-law ['sʌnɪnlɔː] *n* gendre *m*, beau-fils
m
soon [suːn] *adv* bientôt; (*early*) tôt;
~ afterwards peu après; *see also* **as**; **~er** *adv*
(*time*) plus tôt; (*preference*): **I would ~er do**
j'aimerais autant *or* je préférerais faire; **~er or
later** tôt ou tard
soot [sut] *n* suie *f*
soothe [suːð] *vt* calmer, apaiser
sophisticated [sə'fɪstɪkeɪtɪd] *adj* raffiné(e);
sophistiqué(e); (*machinery*) hautement
perfectionné(e), très complexe
sophomore ['sɒfəmɔːr] (*US*) *n* étudiant(e)
de seconde année
sopping ['sɒpɪŋ] *adj* (*also*: **~ wet**)
complètement trempé(e)
soppy ['sɒpɪ] (*pej*) *adj* sentimental(e)
soprano [sə'prɑːnəu] *n* (*singer*) soprano
m/f
sorcerer ['sɔːsərər] *n* sorcier *m*
sore [sɔːr] *adj* (*painful*) douloureux(-euse),

sensible ♦ *n* plaie *f*; **~ly** ['sɔːlɪ] *adv* (*tempted*)
fortement
sorrow ['sɒrəu] *n* peine *f*, chagrin *m*
sorry ['sɒrɪ] *adj* désolé(e); (*condition, excuse*)
triste, déplorable; **~!** pardon!, excusez-moi!;
~? pardon?; **to feel ~ for sb** plaindre qn
sort [sɔːt] *n* genre *m*, espèce *f*, sorte *f* ♦ *vt*
(*also*: **~ out**) trier; classer; ranger; (: *problems*) résoudre, régler; **~ing office** ['sɔːtɪŋ-]
n bureau *m* de tri
SOS *n* S.O.S. *m*
so-so ['səusəu] *adv* comme ci comme ça
sought [sɔːt] *pt, pp of* **seek**
soul [səul] *n* âme *f*; **~ful** ['səulful] *adj*
sentimental(e); (*eyes*) expressif(-ive)
sound [saund] *adj* (*healthy*) en bonne santé,
sain(e); (*safe, not damaged*) solide, en bon
état; (*reliable, not superficial*) sérieux(-euse),
solide; (*sensible*) sensé(e) ♦ *adv*: **~ asleep**
profondément endormi(e) ♦ *n* son *m*; bruit
m; (GEO) détroit *m*, bras *m* de mer ♦ *vt*
(*alarm*) sonner ♦ *vi* sonner, retentir; (*fig:
seem*) sembler (être); **to ~ like** ressembler à;
~ out *vt* sonder; **~ barrier** *n* mur *m* du son;
~ bite *n* phrase *f* toute faite (*pour être citée
dans les médias*); **~ly** *adv* (*sleep*) profondément; (*beat*)
complètement, à plate couture; **~proof** *adj*
insonorisé(e); **~track** *n* (*of film*) bande *f*
sonore
soup [suːp] *n* soupe *f*, potage *m*; **~ plate** *n*
assiette creuse *or* à soupe; **~spoon** *n* cuiller *f*
à soupe
sour ['sauər] *adj* aigre; **it's ~ grapes** (*fig*) c'est
du dépit
source [sɔːs] *n* source *f*
south [sauθ] *n* sud *m* ♦ *adj* sud *inv*, du sud
♦ *adv* au sud, vers le sud; **S~ Africa** *n*
Afrique *f* du Sud; **S~ African** *adj* sud-
africain(e) ♦ *n* Sud-Africain(e); **S~ America**
n Amérique *f* du Sud; **S~ American** *adj*
sud-américain(e) ♦ *n* Sud-Américain(e); **~
east** *n* sud-est *m*; **~erly** ['sʌðəlɪ] *adj* du sud;
au sud; **~ern** ['sʌðən] *adj* (du) sud; méridio-
nal(e); **S~ Pole** *n* Pôle *m* Sud; **S~ Wales** *n*
sud *m* du Pays de Galles; **~ward(s)** *adv* vers
le sud; **~-west** *n* sud-ouest *m*
souvenir [suːvə'nɪər] *n* (*objet*) souvenir *m*
sovereign ['sɒvrɪn] *n* souverain(e)
soviet ['səuvɪət] *adj* soviétique; **the S~ Union**
l'Union *f* soviétique
sow¹ [sau] *n* truie *f*
sow² [səu] (*pt* **sowed**, *pp* **sown**) *vt* semer
sown [səun] *pp of* **sow²**
soya ['sɔɪə] (*US* **soy**) *n*: **~ bean** graine *f* de soja;
soy(a) sauce sauce *f* au soja
spa [spɑː] *n* (*town*) station thermale; (*US: also*:
health ~) établissement *m* de cure de
rajeunissement *etc*

space [speɪs] n espace m; (room) place f;
espace; (length of time) laps m de temps
♦ cpd spatial(e) ♦ vt (also: ~ out) espacer;
~**craft** n engin spatial; ~**man** (irreg) n
astronaute m, cosmonaute m; ~**ship** n
= **spacecraft**; **spacing** n espacement m;
spacious ['speɪʃəs] adj spacieux(-euse),
grand(e)

spade [speɪd] n (tool) bêche f, pelle f;
(child's) pelle; ~s npl (CARDS) pique m

Spain [speɪn] n Espagne f

span [spæn] n (of bird, plane) envergure f; (of
arch) portée f; (in time) espace m de temps,
durée f ♦ vt enjamber, franchir; (fig) couvrir,
embrasser

Spaniard ['spænjəd] n Espagnol(e)

spaniel ['spænjəl] n épagneul m

Spanish ['spænɪʃ] adj espagnol(e) ♦ n (LING)
espagnol m; the ~ npl les Espagnols mpl

spank [spæŋk] vt donner une fessée à

spanner ['spænə^r] (BRIT) n clé f (de
mécanicien)

spare [speə^r] adj de réserve, de rechange;
(surplus) de or en trop, de reste ♦ n (part)
pièce f de rechange, pièce détachée ♦ vt (do
without) se passer de; (afford to give) donner,
accorder; (refrain from hurting) épargner; **to**
~ (surplus) en surplus, de trop; ~ **part** n
pièce f de rechange, pièce détachée; ~ **time**
n moments mpl de loisir, temps m libre;
~ **wheel** n (AUT) roue f de secours;
sparingly adv avec modération

spark [spɑːk] n étincelle f; ~(**ing**) **plug** n
bougie f

sparkle ['spɑːkl] n scintillement m, éclat m
♦ vi étinceler, scintiller; **sparkling** adj (wine)
mousseux(-euse), pétillant(e); (water)
pétillant(e); (fig: conversation, performance)
étincelant(e), pétillant(e)

sparrow ['spærəu] n moineau m

sparse [spɑːs] adj clairsemé(e)

spartan ['spɑːtən] adj (fig) spartiate

spasm ['spæzəm] n (MED) spasme m; ~**odic**
[spæz'mɔdɪk] adj (fig) intermittent(e)

spastic ['spæstɪk] n handicapé(e) moteur

spat [spæt] pt, pp of **spit**

spate [speɪt] n (fig): **a** ~ **of** une avalanche or
un torrent de

spawn [spɔːn] vi frayer ♦ n frai m

speak [spiːk] (pt **spoke**, pp **spoken**) vt parler;
(truth) dire ♦ vi parler; (make a speech)
prendre la parole; **to** ~ **to sb/of** or **about sth**
parler à qn/de qch; ~ **up!** parle plus fort!;
~**er** n (in public) orateur m; (also:
loudspeaker) haut-parleur m; **the S~er** (BRIT:
POL) le président de la chambre des Communes;
(US: POL) le président de la chambre des
Représentants

spear [spɪə^r] n lance f ♦ vt transpercer;

~**head** vt (attack etc) mener

spec [spɛk] (inf) n: **on** ~ à tout hasard

special ['spɛʃl] adj spécial(e); ~**ist** n
spécialiste m/f; ~**ity** [spɛʃɪ'ælɪtɪ] n spécialité f;
~**ize** vi: **to** ~**ize (in)** se spécialiser (dans); ~**ly**
adv spécialement, particulièrement; ~**ty** (esp
US) n = **speciality**

species ['spiːʃiːz] n inv espèce f

specific [spə'sɪfɪk] adj précis(e); particu-
lier(-ère); (BOT, CHEM etc) spécifique; ~**ally**
adv expressément, explicitement; ~**ation**
[spɛsɪfɪ'keɪʃən] n (TECH) spécification f;
(requirement) stipulation f

specimen ['spɛsɪmən] n spécimen m,
échantillon m; (of blood) prélèvement m

speck [spɛk] n petite tache, petit point;
(particle) grain m

speckled ['spɛkld] adj tacheté(e),
moucheté(e)

specs [spɛks] (inf) npl lunettes fpl

spectacle ['spɛktəkl] n spectacle m; ~**s** npl
(glasses) lunettes fpl; **spectacular**
[spɛk'tækjulə^r] adj spectaculaire

spectator [spɛk'teɪtə^r] n spectateur(-trice)

spectrum ['spɛktrəm] (pl **spectra**) n spectre m

speculation [spɛkju'leɪʃən] n spéculation f

speech [spiːtʃ] n (faculty) parole f; (talk)
discours m, allocution f; (manner of speaking)
façon f de parler, langage m; (enunciation)
élocution f; ~**less** adj muet(te)

speed [spiːd] n vitesse f; (promptness) rapidité
f ♦ vi: **to** ~ **along/past** etc aller/passer etc à
toute vitesse or allure; **at full** or **top** ~ à toute
vitesse or allure; ~ **up** vi aller plus vite,
accélérer ♦ vt accélérer; ~**boat** n vedette f,
hors-bord m inv; ~**ily** adv rapidement,
promptement; ~**ing** n (AUT) excès m de
vitesse; ~ **limit** n limitation f de vitesse,
vitesse maximale permise; ~**ometer**
[spɪ'dɔmɪtə^r] n compteur m (de vitesse);
~**way** n (SPORT: also: ~**way racing**)
épreuve(s) f(pl) de vitesse de motos; ~**y** adj
rapide, prompt(e)

spell [spɛl] (pt, pp **spelt** or **spelled**) n (also:
magic ~) sortilège m, charme m; (period of
time) (courte) période f ♦ vt (in writing) écrire,
orthographier; (aloud) épeler; (fig) signifier;
to cast a ~ **on sb** jeter un sort à qn; **he can't** ~
il fait des fautes d'orthographe; ~**bound** adj
envoûté(e), subjugué(e); ~**ing** n
orthographe f

spend [spɛnd] (pt, pp **spent**) vt (money)
dépenser; (time, life) passer; consacrer;
~**thrift** n dépensier(-ère)

sperm [spɜːm] n sperme m

sphere [sfɪə^r] n sphère f

spice [spaɪs] n épice f; **spicy** adj épicé(e),
relevé(e); (fig) piquant(e)

spider ['spaɪdəʳ] n araignée f

spike [spaɪk] n pointe f; (BOT) épi m

spill [spɪl] (pt, pp spilt or spilled) vt renverser; répandre ♦ vi se répandre; ~ **over** vi déborder

spin [spɪn] (pt spun or span, pp spun) n (revolution of wheel) tour m; (AVIAT) (chute en) vrille f; (trip in car) petit tour, balade f ♦ vt (wool etc) filer; (wheel) faire tourner ♦ vi filer; (turn) tourner, tournoyer

spinach ['spɪnɪtʃ] n épinard m; (as food) épinards

spinal ['spaɪnl] adj vertébral(e), spinal(e); ~ **cord** n moelle épinière

spin doctor n personne enployée pour présenter un parti politique sous un jour favorable

spin-dryer [spɪn'draɪəʳ] (BRIT) n essoreuse f

spine [spaɪn] n colonne vertébrale; (thorn) épine f; **~less** adj (fig) mou (molle)

spinning ['spɪnɪŋ] n (of thread) filature f; ~ **top** n toupie f

spin-off ['spɪnɔf] n avantage inattendu; sous-produit m

spinster ['spɪnstəʳ] n célibataire f; vieille fille (péj)

spiral ['spaɪərl] n spirale f ♦ vi (fig) monter en flèche; ~ **staircase** n escalier m en colimaçon

spire ['spaɪəʳ] n flèche f, aiguille f

spirit ['spɪrɪt] n esprit m; (mood) état m d'esprit; (courage) courage m, énergie f; **~s** npl (drink) spiritueux mpl, alcool m; **in good ~s** de bonne humeur; **~ed** adj vif (vive), fougueux(-euse), plein(e) d'allant; **~ual** adj spirituel(le); (religious) religieux(-euse)

spit [spɪt] (pt, pp spat) n (for roasting) broche f; (saliva) salive f ♦ vi cracher; (sound) crépiter

spite [spaɪt] n rancune f, dépit m ♦ vt contrarier, vexer; **in ~ of** en dépit de, malgré; **~ful** adj méchant(e), malveillant(e)

spittle ['spɪtl] n salive f; (of animal) bave f; (spat out) crachat m

splash [splæʃ] n (sound) plouf m; (of colour) tache f ♦ vt éclabousser ♦ vi (also: ~ about) barboter, patauger

spleen [spli:n] n (ANAT) rate f

splendid ['splendɪd] adj splendide, superbe, magnifique

splint [splɪnt] n attelle f, éclisse f

splinter ['splɪntəʳ] n (wood) écharde f; (glass) éclat m ♦ vi se briser, se fendre

split [splɪt] (pt, pp split) n fente f, déchirure f; (fig: POL) scission f ♦ vt diviser; (work, profits) partager, répartir ♦ vi (divide) se diviser; ~ **up** vi (couple) se séparer, rompre; (meeting) se disperser

spoil [spɔɪl] (pt, pp spoilt or spoiled) vt

(damage) abîmer; (mar) gâcher; (child) gâter; **~s** npl butin m; (fig: profits) bénéfices npl; **~sport** n trouble-fête m, rabat-joie m

spoke [spəuk] pt of speak ♦ n (of wheel) rayon m

spoken ['spəukn] pp of speak

spokesman ['spəuksmən], **spokeswoman** ['spəukswumən] (irreg) n porte-parole m inv

sponge [spʌndʒ] n éponge f; (also: ~ **cake**) ≈ biscuit m de Savoie ♦ vt éponger ♦ vi: to ~ **off** or **on** vivre aux crochets de; ~ **bag** (BRIT) n trousse f de toilette

sponsor ['spɔnsəʳ] n (RADIO, TV, SPORT) sponsor m; (for application) parrain m, marraine f; (BRIT: for fund-raising event) donateur(-trice) ♦ vt sponsoriser; parrainer; faire un don à; **~ship** n sponsoring m; parrainage m; dons mpl

spontaneous [spɔn'teɪnɪəs] adj spontané(e)

spooky ['spu:kɪ] (inf) adj qui donne la chair de poule

spool [spu:l] n bobine f

spoon [spu:n] n cuiller f; **~-feed** vt nourrir à la cuiller; (fig) mâcher le travail à; **~ful** n cuillerée f

sport [spɔ:t] n sport m; (person) chic type (fille) ♦ vt arborer; **~ing** adj sportif(-ive); to **give sb a ~ing chance** donner sa chance à qn; ~ **jacket** (US) = sports jacket; **~s car** n voiture f de sport; **~s jacket** (BRIT) n veste f de sport; **~sman** (irreg) n sportif m; **~smanship** n esprit sportif, sportivité f; **~swear** n vêtements mpl de sport; **~swoman** (irreg) n sportive f; **~y** adj sportif(-ive)

spot [spɔt] n tache f; (dot: on pattern) pois m; (pimple) bouton m; (place) endroit m, coin m; (RADIO, TV: in programme: for person) numéro m; (: for activity) rubrique f; (small amount): **a ~ of** un peu de ♦ vt (notice) apercevoir, repérer; **on the ~** sur place, sur les lieux; (immediately) sur-le-champ; (in difficulty) dans l'embarras; ~ **check** n sondage m, vérification ponctuelle; **~less** adj immaculé(e); **~light** n projecteur m; **~ted** adj (fabric) à pois; **~ty** adj (face, person) boutonneux(-euse)

spouse [spaus] n époux (épouse)

spout [spaut] n (of jug) bec m; (of pipe) orifice m ♦ vi jaillir

sprain [spreɪn] n entorse f, foulure f ♦ vt: to ~ **one's ankle** etc se fouler or se tordre la cheville etc

sprang [spræŋ] pt of spring

sprawl [sprɔ:l] vi s'étaler

spray [spreɪ] n jet m (en fines gouttelettes); (from sea) embruns mpl, vaporisateur m; (for garden) pulvérisateur m; (aerosol) bombe f; (of flowers) petit bouquet ♦ vt vaporiser, pulvériser; (*crops*) traiter

spread [sprɛd] (*pt, pp* **spread**) *n* (*distribution*) répartition *f*; (*CULIN*) pâte *f* à tartiner; (*inf: meal*) festin *m* ♦ *vt* étendre, étaler; répandre; (*wealth, workload*) distribuer ♦ *vi* (*disease, news*) se propager; (*also:* **~ out**: *stain*) s'étaler; **~ out** *vi* (*people*) se disperser; **~-eagled** *adj* étendu(e) bras et jambes écartés; **~sheet** *n* (*COMPUT*) tableur *m*

spree [spri:] *n*: **to go on a ~** faire la fête

sprightly ['spraɪtlɪ] *adj* alerte

spring [sprɪŋ] (*pt* **sprang**, *pp* **sprung**) *n* (*leap*) bond *m*, saut *m*; (*coiled metal*) ressort *m*; (*season*) printemps *m*; (*of water*) source *f* ♦ *vi* (*leap*) bondir, sauter; **in ~** au printemps; **to ~ from** provenir de; **~ up** *vi* (*problem*) se présenter, surgir; (*plant, buildings*) surgir de terre; **~board** *n* tremplin *m*; **~-clean(ing)** *n* grand nettoyage de printemps; **~time** *n* printemps *m*

sprinkle ['sprɪŋkl] *vt*: **to ~ water** *etc* **on**, **~ with water** *etc* asperger d'eau *etc*; **to ~ sugar** *etc* **on**, **~ with sugar** *etc* saupoudrer de sucre *etc*; **~r** *n* (*for lawn*) arroseur *m*; (*to put out fire*) diffuseur *m* d'extincteur automatique d'incendie

sprint [sprɪnt] *n* sprint *m* ♦ *vi* courir à toute vitesse; (*SPORT*) sprinter; **~er** *n* sprinteur(-euse)

sprout [spraut] *vi* germer, pousser; **~s** *npl* (*also:* **Brussels ~s**) choux *mpl* de Bruxelles

spruce [spru:s] *n inv* épicéa *m* ♦ *adj* net(te), pimpant(e)

sprung [sprʌŋ] *pp of* **spring**

spun [spʌn] *pt, pp of* **spin**

spur [spə:r] *n* éperon *m*; (*fig*) aiguillon *m* ♦ *vt* (*also:* **~ on**) éperonner; aiguillonner; **on the ~ of the moment** sous l'impulsion du moment

spurious ['spjʊərɪəs] *adj* faux (fausse)

spurn [spə:n] *vt* repousser avec mépris

spurt [spə:t] *n* (*of blood*) jaillissement *m*; (*of energy*) regain *m*, sursaut *m* ♦ *vi* jaillir, gicler

spy [spaɪ] *n* espion(ne) ♦ *vi*: **to ~ on** espionner, épier; (*see*) apercevoir; **~ing** *n* espionnage *m*

sq. *abbr* = **square**

squabble ['skwɔbl] *vi* se chamailler

squad [skwɔd] *n* (*MIL, POLICE*) escouade *f*, groupe *m*; (*FOOTBALL*) contingent *m*

squadron ['skwɔdrn] *n* (*MIL*) escadron *m*; (*AVIAT, NAUT*) escadrille *f*

squalid ['skwɔlɪd] *adj* sordide

squall [skwɔ:l] *n* rafale *f*, bourrasque *f*

squalor ['skwɔlər] *n* conditions *fpl* sordides

squander ['skwɔndər] *vt* gaspiller, dilapider

square [skwɛər] *n* carré *m*; (*in town*) place *f* ♦ *adj* carré(e); (*inf: ideas, tastes*) vieux jeu *inv* ♦ *vt* (*arrange*) régler; arranger; (*MATH*) élever au carré ♦ *vi* (*reconcile*) concilier; **all ~** quitte;

à égalité; **a ~ meal** un repas convenable; **2 metres ~ (de)** 2 mètres sur 2; **2 ~ metres** 2 mètres carrés; **~ly** *adv* carrément

squash [skwɔʃ] *n* (*BRIT: drink*): **lemon/orange ~** citronnade *f*/orangeade *f*; (*US: marrow*) courge *f*; (*SPORT*) squash *m* ♦ *vt* écraser

squat [skwɔt] *adj* petit(e) et épais(se), ramassé(e) ♦ *vi* (*also:* **~ down**) s'accroupir; **~ter** *n* squatter *m*

squeak [skwi:k] *vi* grincer, crier; (*mouse*) pousser un petit cri

squeal [skwi:l] *vi* pousser un or des cri(s) aigu(s) or perçant(s); (*brakes*) grincer

squeamish ['skwi:mɪʃ] *adj* facilement dégoûté(e)

squeeze [skwi:z] *n* pression *f*; (*ECON*) restrictions *fpl* de crédit ♦ *vt* presser; (*hand, arm*) serrer; **~ out** *vt* exprimer

squelch [skwɛltʃ] *vi* faire un bruit de succion

squid [skwɪd] *n* calmar *m*

squiggle ['skwɪgl] *n* gribouillis *m*

squint [skwɪnt] *vi* loucher ♦ *n*: **he has a ~** il louche, il souffre de strabisme

squirm [skwə:m] *vi* se tortiller

squirrel ['skwɪrəl] *n* écureuil *m*

squirt [skwə:t] *vi* jaillir, gicler

Sr *abbr* = **senior**

St *abbr* = **saint**; **street**

stab [stæb] *n* (*with knife etc*) coup *m* (de couteau *etc*); (*of pain*) lancée *f*; (*inf: try*): **to have a ~ at (doing) sth** s'essayer à (faire) qch ♦ *vt* poignarder

stable ['steɪbl] *n* écurie *f* ♦ *adj* stable

stack [stæk] *n* tas *m*, pile *f* ♦ *vt* (*also:* **~ up**) empiler, entasser

stadium ['steɪdɪəm] (*pl* **stadia** *or* **~s**) *n* stade *m*

staff [sta:f] *n* (*workforce*) personnel *m*; (*BRIT: SCOL*) professeurs *mpl* ♦ *vt* pourvoir en personnel

stag [stæg] *n* cerf *m*

stage [steɪdʒ] *n* scène *f*; (*platform*) estrade *f* ♦ *n* (*point*) étape *f*, stade *m*; (*profession*): **the ~** le théâtre ♦ *vt* (*play*) monter, mettre en scène; (*demonstration*) organiser; **in ~s** par étapes, par degrés; **~coach** *n* diligence *f*; **~ manager** *n* régisseur *m*

stagger ['stægər] *vi* chanceler, tituber ♦ *vt* (*person: amaze*) stupéfier; (*hours, holidays*) étaler, échelonner; **~ing** *adj* (*amazing*) stupéfiant(e), renversant(e)

stagnate [stæg'neɪt] *vi* stagner, croupir

stag party *n* enterrement *m* de vie de garçon

staid [steɪd] *adj* posé(e), rassis(e)

stain [steɪn] *n* tache *f*; (*colouring*) colorant *m* ♦ *vt* tacher; (*wood*) teindre; **~ed glass window** *n* vitrail *m*; **~less steel** *n* acier *m* inoxydable, inox *m*; **~ remover** *n* détachant *m*

stair [stɛəʳ] *n* (*step*) marche *f*; **~s** *npl* (*flight of steps*) escalier *m*; **~case**, **~way** *n* escalier *m*

stake [steɪk] *n* pieu *m*, poteau *m*; (*BETTING*) enjeu *m*; (*COMM*: *interest*) intérêts *mpl* ♦ *vt* risquer, jouer; **to be at ~** être en jeu; **to ~ one's claim (to)** revendiquer

stale [steɪl] *adj* (*bread*) rassis(e); (*food*) pas frais (fraîche); (*beer*) éventé(e); (*smell*) de renfermé; (*air*) confiné(e)

stalemate ['steɪlmeɪt] *n* (*CHESS*) pat *m*; (*fig*) impasse *f*

stalk [stɔːk] *n* tige *f* ♦ *vt* traquer ♦ *vi*: **to ~ out/off** sortir/partir d'un air digne

stall [stɔːl] *n* (*BRIT*: *in street, market etc*) éventaire *m*, étal *m*; (*in stable*) stalle *f* ♦ *vt* (*AUT*) caler; (*delay*) retarder ♦ *vi* (*AUT*) caler; (*fig*) essayer de gagner du temps; **~s** *npl* (*BRIT*: *in cinema, theatre*) orchestre *m*

stallion ['stæljən] *n* étalon *m* (*cheval*)

stamina ['stæmɪnə] *n* résistance *f*, endurance *f*

stammer ['stæməʳ] *n* bégaiement *m* ♦ *vi* bégayer

stamp [stæmp] *n* timbre *m*; (*rubber ~*) tampon *m*; (*mark, also fig*) empreinte *f* ♦ *vi* (*also*: **~ one's foot**) taper du pied ♦ *vt* (*letter*) timbrer; (*with rubber ~*) tamponner; **~ album** *n* album *m* de timbres(-poste); **~ collecting** *n* philatélie *f*

stampede [stæm'piːd] *n* ruée *f*

stance [stæns] *n* position *f*

stand [stænd] (*pt, pp stood*) *n* (*position*) position *f*; (*for taxis*) station *f* (de taxis); (*music ~*) pupitre *m* à musique; (*COMM*) étalage *m*, stand *m*; (*SPORT: also*: **~s**) tribune *f* ♦ *vi* être ou se tenir (debout); (*rise*) se lever, se mettre debout; (*be placed*) se trouver; (*remain: offer etc*) rester valable; (*BRIT: in election*) être candidat(e), se présenter ♦ *vt* (*place*) mettre, poser; (*tolerate, withstand*) supporter; (*treat, invite to*) offrir, payer; **to make** *ou* **take a ~** prendre position; **to ~ at** (*score, value etc*) être de; **to ~ for parliament** (*BRIT*) se présenter aux élections législatives; **~ by** *vi* (*be ready*) se tenir prêt(e) ♦ *vt fus* (*opinion*) s'en tenir à; (*person*) ne pas abandonner, soutenir; **~ down** *vi* (*withdraw*) se retirer; **~ for** *vt fus* (*signify*) représenter, signifier; (*tolerate*) supporter, tolérer; **~ in for** *vt fus* remplacer; **~ out** *vi* (*be prominent*) ressortir; **~ up** *vi* (*rise*) se lever, se mettre debout; **~ up for** *vt fus* défendre; **~ up to** *vt fus* tenir tête à, résister à

standard ['stændəd] *n* (*level*) niveau (voulu); (*norm*) norme *f*, étalon *m*; (*criterion*) critère *m*; (*flag*) étendard *m* ♦ *adj* (*size etc*) ordinaire, normal(e); courant(e); (*text*) de base; **~s** *npl* (*morals*) morale *f*, principes *mpl*;

~ lamp (*BRIT*) *n* lampadaire *m*; **~ of living** *n* niveau *m* de vie

stand-by ['stændbaɪ] *n* remplaçant(e); **to be on ~~** se tenir prêt(e) (à intervenir); être de garde; **~~ ticket** *n* (*AVIAT*) billet *m* stand-by

stand-in ['stændɪn] *n* remplaçant(e)

standing ['stændɪŋ] *adj* debout *inv*; (*permanent*) permanent(e) ♦ *n* réputation *f*, rang *m*, standing *m*; **of many years' ~** qui dure *ou* existe depuis longtemps; **~ joke** *n* vieux sujet de plaisanterie; **~ order** (*BRIT*) *n* (*at bank*) virement *m* automatique, prélèvement *m* bancaire; **~ room** *n* places *fpl* debout

standpoint ['stændpɔɪnt] *n* point *m* de vue

standstill ['stændstɪl] *n*: **at a ~** paralysé(e); **to come to a ~** s'immobiliser, s'arrêter

stank [stæŋk] *pt of* **stink**

staple ['steɪpl] *n* (*for papers*) agrafe *f* ♦ *adj* (*food etc*) de base ♦ *vt* agrafer; **~r** *n* agrafeuse *f*

star [stɑːʳ] *n* étoile *f*; (*celebrity*) vedette *f* ♦ *vi*: **to ~ (in)** être la vedette (de) ♦ *vt* (*CINEMA etc*) avoir pour vedette; **the ~s** *npl* l'horoscope *m*

starboard ['stɑːbəd] *n* tribord *m*

starch [stɑːtʃ] *n* amidon *m*; (*in food*) fécule *f*

stardom ['stɑːdəm] *n* célébrité *f*

stare [stɛəʳ] *n* regard *m* fixe ♦ *vi*: **to ~ at** regarder fixement

starfish ['stɑːfɪʃ] *n* étoile *f* de mer

stark [stɑːk] *adj* (*bleak*) désolé(e), morne ♦ *adv*: **~ naked** complètement nu(e)

starling ['stɑːlɪŋ] *n* étourneau *m*

starry ['stɑːrɪ] *adj* étoilé(e); **~-eyed** *adj* (*innocent*) ingénu(e)

start [stɑːt] *n* commencement *m*, début *m*; (*of race*) départ *m*; (*sudden movement*) sursaut *m*; (*advantage*) avance *f*, avantage *m* ♦ *vt* commencer; (*found*) créer; (*engine*) mettre en marche ♦ *vi* partir, se mettre en route; (*jump*) sursauter; **to ~ doing** *ou* **to do sth** se mettre à faire qch; **~ off** *vi* commencer; (*leave*) partir; **~ up** *vi* commencer; (*car*) démarrer ♦ *vt* (*business*) créer; (*car*) mettre en marche; **~er** *n* (*AUT*) démarreur *m*; (*SPORT: official*) starter *m*; (*BRIT: CULIN*) entrée *f*; **~ing point** *n* point *m* de départ

startle ['stɑːtl] *vt* faire sursauter; donner un choc à; **startling** *adj* (*news*) surprenant(e)

starvation [stɑː'veɪʃən] *n* faim *f*, famine *f*

starve [stɑːv] *vi* mourir de faim; être affamé(e) ♦ *vt* affamer

state [steɪt] *n* état *m*; (*POL*) État *m* ♦ *vt* déclarer, affirmer; **the S~s** *npl* (*America*) les États-Unis *mpl*; **to be in a ~** être dans tous ses états; **~ly** *adj* majestueux(-euse), imposant(e); **~ly home** *n* château *m*; **~ment** *n* déclaration *f*; **~sman** (*irreg*) *n* homme *m* d'État

static ['stætɪk] n (RADIO, TV) parasites mpl
♦ adj statique

station ['steɪʃən] n gare f; (police ~) poste m
de police ♦ vt placer, poster

stationary ['steɪʃnərɪ] adj à l'arrêt, immobile

stationer ['steɪʃənəʳ] n papetier(-ère); ~'s
(shop) n papeterie f; ~**y** n papier m à
lettres, petit matériel de bureau

stationmaster ['steɪʃənmɑːstəʳ] n (RAIL)
chef m de gare

station wagon (US) n break m

statistic [stə'tɪstɪk] n statistique f; ~**s** [stə'tɪstɪks] n
(science) statistique f

statue ['stætjuː] n statue f

status ['steɪtəs] n position f, situation f;
(official) statut m; (prestige) prestige m;
~ **symbol** n signe extérieur de richesse

statute ['stætjuːt] n loi f, statut m; **statutory**
adj statutaire, prévu(e) par un article de loi

staunch [stɔːntʃ] adj sûr(e), loyal(e)

stay [steɪ] n (period of time) séjour m ♦ vi
rester; (reside) loger; (spend some time)
séjourner; to ~ **put** ne pas bouger; to ~ **with**
friends loger chez des amis; to ~ **the night**
passer la nuit; ~ **behind** vi rester en arrière;
~ **in** vi (at home) rester à la maison; ~ **on** vi
rester; ~ **out** vi (of house) ne pas rentrer;
~ **up** vi (at night) ne pas se coucher; ~**ing**
power n endurance f

stead [sted] n: **in sb's** ~ à la place de qn; **to**
stand sb in good ~ être très utile à qn

steadfast ['stedfɑːst] adj ferme, résolu(e)

steadily ['stedɪlɪ] adv (regularly)
progressivement; (firmly) fermement; (: walk)
d'un pas ferme; (fixedly: look) sans détourner
les yeux

steady ['stedɪ] adj stable, solide, ferme;
(regular) constant(e), régulier(-ère); (person)
calme, pondéré(e) ♦ vt stabiliser; (nerves)
calmer; **a** ~ **boyfriend** un petit ami

steak [steɪk] n (beef) bifteck m, steak m; (fish,
pork) tranche f

steal [stiːl] (pt **stole**, pp **stolen**) vt voler ♦ vi
voler; (move secretly) se faufiler, se déplacer
furtivement

stealth [stelθ] n: **by** ~ furtivement

steam [stiːm] n vapeur f ♦ vt (CULIN) cuire à
la vapeur ♦ vi fumer; ~ **engine** n locomotive
f à vapeur; ~**er** n (bateau m à) vapeur m;
~**ship** n = steamer; ~**y** adj embué(e),
humide

steel [stiːl] n acier m ♦ adj d'acier; ~**works** n
aciérie f

steep [stiːp] adj raide, escarpé(e); (price)
excessif(-ive)

steeple ['stiːpl] n clocher m

steer [stɪəʳ] vt diriger; (boat) gouverner;
(person) guider, conduire ♦ vi tenir le
gouvernail; ~**ing** n (AUT) conduite f; ~**ing**

wheel n volant m

stem [stɛm] n (of plant) tige f; (of glass) pied
m ♦ vt contenir, arrêter, juguler; ~ **from** vt
fus provenir de, découler de

stench [stɛntʃ] n puanteur f

stencil ['stɛnsl] n stencil m; (pattern used)
pochoir m ♦ vt polycopier

stenographer [stɛ'nɔgrəfəʳ] (US) n
sténographe m/f

step [stɛp] n pas m; (stair) marche f; (action)
mesure f, disposition f ♦ vi: **to** ~ **forward/back**
faire un pas en avant/arrière, avancer/reculer;
~**s** npl (BRIT) = **stepladder**; **to be in/out of**
~ **(with)** (fig) aller dans le sens (de)/être
déphasé(e) (par rapport à); ~ **down** vi (fig)
se retirer, se désister; ~ **up** vt augmenter;
intensifier; ~**brother** n demi-frère m;
~**daughter** n belle-fille f; ~**father** n beau-
père m; ~**ladder** (BRIT) n escabeau m;
~**mother** n belle-mère f; ~**ping stone** n
pierre f de gué; (fig) tremplin m; ~**sister** n
demi-sœur f; ~**son** n beau-fils m

stereo ['stɛrɪəu] n (sound) stéréo f; (hi-fi)
chaîne f stéréo inv ♦ adj (also: ~**phonic**)
stéréo(phonique)

sterile ['stɛraɪl] adj stérile; **sterilize** ['stɛrɪlaɪz]
vt stériliser

sterling ['stɜːlɪŋ] adj (silver) de bon aloi,
fin(e) ♦ n (ECON) livre fpl sterling inv; **a**
pound ~ une livre sterling

stern [stɜːn] adj sévère ♦ n (NAUT) arrière m,
poupe f

stew [stjuː] n ragoût m ♦ vt, vi cuire (à la
casserole)

steward ['stjuːəd] n (on ship, plane, train)
steward m; ~**ess** n hôtesse f (de l'air)

stick [stɪk] n (pt, pp **stuck**) n bâton m; (walking
~) canne f ♦ vt (glue) coller; (inf: put)
mettre, fourrer; (: tolerate) supporter;
(thrust): **to** ~ **sth into** planter or enfoncer qch
dans ♦ vi (become attached) rester collé(e) or
fixé(e); (be unmoveable: wheels etc) se
bloquer; (remain) rester; ~ **out** vi dépasser,
sortir; ~ **up** vi = stick out; ~ **up for** vt fus
défendre; ~**er** n auto-collant m; ~**ing**
plaster n sparadrap m, pansement adhésif

stick-up ['stɪkʌp] (inf) n braquage m, hold-
up m inv

sticky ['stɪkɪ] adj poisseux(-euse); (label)
adhésif(-ive); (situation) délicat(e)

stiff [stɪf] adj raide; rigide; dur(e); (difficult)
difficile, ardu(e); (cold) froid(e), distant(e);
(strong, high) fort(e), élevé(e) ♦ adv: **to be**
bored/scared/frozen ~ s'ennuyer à mort/être
mort(e) de peur/froid; ~**en** vi se raidir;
~ **neck** n torticolis m

stifle ['staɪfl] vt étouffer, réprimer

stigma ['stɪgmə] n stigmate m

stile [staɪl] n échalier m

stiletto [stɪˈlɛtəu] (BRIT) n (also: ~ **heel**) talon m aiguille

still [stɪl] adj immobile ♦ adv (up to this time) encore, toujours; (even) encore; (nonetheless) quand même, tout de même; ~**born** adj mort-né(e); ~ **life** n nature morte

stilt [stɪlt] n (for walking on) échasse f; (pile) pilotis m

stilted [ˈstɪltɪd] adj guindé(e), emprunté(e)

stimulate [ˈstɪmjuleɪt] vt stimuler

stimuli [ˈstɪmjulaɪ] npl of **stimulus**

stimulus [ˈstɪmjuləs] (pl **stimuli**) n stimulant m; (BIOL, PSYCH) stimulus m

sting [stɪŋ] (pt, pp **stung**) n piqûre f; (organ) dard m ♦ vt, vi piquer

stingy [ˈstɪndʒɪ] adj avare, pingre

stink [stɪŋk] (pt **stank**, pp **stunk**) n puanteur f ♦ vi puer, empester; ~**ing** (inf) adj (fig) infect(e), vache; **a ~ing ...** un(e) foutu(e) ...

stint [stɪnt] n part f de travail ♦ vi: **to ~ on** lésiner sur, être chiche de

stir [stəːʳ] n agitation f, sensation f ♦ vt remuer ♦ vi remuer, bouger; ~ **up** vt (trouble) fomenter, provoquer

stirrup [ˈstɪrəp] n étrier m

stitch [stɪtʃ] n (SEWING) point m; (KNITTING) maille f; (MED) point de suture; (pain) point de côté ♦ vt coudre, piquer; (MED) suturer

stoat [stəut] n hermine f (avec son pelage d'été)

stock [stɔk] n réserve f, provision f; (COMM) stock m; (AGR) cheptel m, bétail m; (CULIN) bouillon m; (descent, origin) souche f; (FINANCE) valeurs fpl, titres mpl ♦ adj (fig: reply etc) classique ♦ vt (have in ~) avoir, vendre; ~**s and shares** valeurs (mobilières), titres; **in/out of ~** en stock ou en magasin/ épuisé(e); **to take ~ of** (fig) faire le point de; ~ **up** vi: **to ~ up (with)** s'approvisionner (en); ~**broker** n agent m de change; ~ **cube** n bouillon-cube m; ~ **exchange** n Bourse f

stocking [ˈstɔkɪŋ] n bas m

stock: ~ **market** n Bourse f, marché financier; ~**pile** n stock m, réserve f ♦ vt stocker, accumuler; ~**taking** (BRIT) n (COMM) inventaire m

stocky [ˈstɔkɪ] adj trapu(e), râblé(e)

stodgy [ˈstɔdʒɪ] adj bourratif(-ive), lourd(e)

stoke [stəuk] vt (fire) garnir, entretenir; (boiler) chauffer

stole [stəul] pt of **steal** ♦ n étole f

stolen [ˈstəuln] pp of **steal**

stomach [ˈstʌmək] n estomac m; (abdomen) ventre m ♦ vt digérer, supporter; ~**ache** n mal m à l'estomac ou au ventre

stone [stəun] n pierre f; (pebble) caillou m, galet m; (in fruit) noyau m; (MED) calcul m; (BRIT: weight) 6,348 kg ♦ adj de ou en pierre ♦ vt (person) lancer des pierres sur, lapider;

~**cold** adj complètement froid(e); ~**deaf** adj sourd(e) comme un pot; ~**work** n maçonnerie f

stood [stud] pt, pp of **stand**

stool [stuːl] n tabouret m

stoop [stuːp] vi (also: **have a ~**) être voûté(e); (also: ~ **down**: bend) se baisser

stop [stɔp] n arrêt m; halte f; (in punctuation: also: **full ~**) point m ♦ vt arrêter, bloquer; (break off) interrompre; (also: **put a ~ to**) mettre fin à ♦ vi s'arrêter; (rain, noise etc) cesser, s'arrêter; **to ~ doing sth** cesser or arrêter de faire qch; ~ **dead** vi s'arrêter net; ~ **off** vi faire une courte halte; ~ **up** vt (hole) boucher; ~**gap** n (person) bouche-trou m; (measure) mesure f intérimaire; ~**over** n halte f; (AVIAT) escale f; ~**page** n (strike) arrêt de travail; (blockage) obstruction f; ~**per** n bouchon m; ~ **press** n nouvelles fpl de dernière heure; ~**watch** n chronomètre m

storage [ˈstɔːrɪdʒ] n entreposage m; ~ **heater** n radiateur m électrique par accumulation

store [stɔːʳ] n (stock) provision f, réserve f; (depot) entrepôt m; (BRIT: large shop) grand magasin m; (US) magasin m ♦ vt emmagasiner; (information) enregistrer; ~**s** npl (food) provisions; **in ~** en réserve; ~ **up** vt mettre en réserve; accumuler; ~**room** n réserve f, magasin m

storey [ˈstɔːrɪ] (US **story**) n étage m

stork [stɔːk] n cigogne f

storm [stɔːm] n tempête f; (thunderstorm) orage m ♦ vi (fig) fulminer ♦ vt prendre d'assaut; ~**y** adj orageux(-euse)

story [ˈstɔːrɪ] n histoire f; récit m; (US) = **storey**; ~**book** n livre m d'histoires or de contes

stout [staut] adj solide; (fat) gros(se), corpulent(e) ♦ n bière brune

stove [stəuv] n (for cooking) fourneau m; (: small) réchaud m; (for heating) poêle m

stow [stəu] vt (also: ~ **away**) ranger; ~**away** n passager(-ère) clandestin(e)

straddle [ˈstrædl] vt enjamber, être à cheval sur

straggle [ˈstrægl] vi être (or marcher) en désordre

straight [streɪt] adj droit(e); (hair) raide; (frank) honnête, franc (franche); (simple) simple ♦ adv (tout) droit; (drink) sec, sans eau; **to put** or **get ~** (fig) mettre au clair; ~ **away**, ~ **off** (at once) tout de suite; ~**en** vt ajuster; (bed) arranger; ~**en out** vt (fig) débrouiller; ~-**faced** adj impassible; ~**forward** adj simple; (honest) honnête, direct(e)

strain [streɪn] n tension f; pression f; (physical) effort m; (mental) tension (nerveuse); (*breed*) race f ♦ vt (*stretch: resources etc*) mettre à rude épreuve, grever; (*hurt: back etc*) se faire mal à; (*vegetables*) égoutter; **~s** npl (MUS) accords mpl, accents mpl; **back ~** tour m de rein; **~ed** adj (*muscle*) froissé(e); (*laugh etc*) forcé(e), contraint(e); (*relations*) tendu(e); **~er** n passoire f

strait [streɪt] n (GEO) détroit m; **~s** npl: **to be in dire ~s** avoir de sérieux ennuis (d'argent); **~jacket** n camisole f de force; **~-laced** [streɪt'leɪst] adj collet monté *inv*

strand [strænd] n (*of thread*) fil m, brin m; (*of rope*) toron m; (*of hair*) mèche f; **~ed** adj en rade, en plan

strange [streɪndʒ] adj (*not known*) inconnu(e); (*odd*) étrange, bizarre; **~ly** adv étrangement, bizarrement; *see also* **enough**; **~r** n inconnu(e); (*from another area*) étranger(-ère)

strangle ['stræŋgl] vt étrangler; **~hold** n (*fig*) emprise totale, mainmise f

strap [stræp] n lanière f, courroie f, sangle f; (*of slip, dress*) bretelle f

strategic [strə'tiːdʒɪk] adj stratégique; **strategy** ['strætɪdʒɪ] n stratégie f

straw [strɔː] n paille f; **that's the last ~!** ça, c'est le comble!

strawberry ['strɔːbərɪ] n fraise f

stray [streɪ] adj (*animal*) perdu(e), errant(e); (*scattered*) isolé(e) ♦ vi s'égarer; **~ bullet** n balle perdue

streak [striːk] n bande f, filet m; (*in hair*) raie f ♦ vt zébrer, strier ♦ vi: **to ~ past** passer à toute allure

stream [striːm] n (*brook*) ruisseau m; (*current*) courant m, flot m; (*of people*) défilé ininterrompu, flot ♦ vt (SCOL) répartir par niveau ♦ vi ruisseler; **to ~ in/out** entrer/sortir à flots

streamer ['striːmər] n serpentin m; (*banner*) banderole f

streamlined ['striːmlaɪnd] adj aérodynamique; (*fig*) rationalisé(e)

street [striːt] n rue f; **~car** (US) n tramway m; **~ lamp** n réverbère m; **~ plan** n plan m (des rues); **~wise** (*inf*) adj futé(e), réaliste

strength [streŋθ] n force f; (*of girder, knot etc*) solidité f; **~en** vt (*muscle etc*) fortifier; (*nation, case etc*) renforcer; (*building, ECON*) consolider

strenuous ['strenjuəs] adj vigoureux(-euse), énergique

stress [stres] n (*force, pressure*) pression f; (*mental strain*) tension (nerveuse), stress m; (*accent*) accent m ♦ vt insister sur, souligner

stretch [stretʃ] n (*of sand etc*) étendue f ♦ vi s'étirer; (*extend*): **to ~ to** or **as far as** s'étendre jusqu'à ♦ vt tendre, étirer; (*fig*) pousser (au maximum); **~ out** vi s'étendre

♦ vt (*arm etc*) allonger, tendre; (*spread*) étendre

stretcher ['stretʃər] n brancard m, civière f

stretchy ['stretʃɪ] adj élastique

strewn [struːn] adj: **~ with** jonché(e) de

stricken ['strɪkən] adj (*person*) très éprouvé(e); (*city, industry etc*) dévasté(e); **~ with** (*disease etc*) frappé(e) or atteint(e) de

strict [strɪkt] adj strict(e)

stride [straɪd] (*pt* **strode**, *pp* **stridden**) n grand pas, enjambée ♦ vi marcher à grands pas

strife [straɪf] n conflit m, dissensions fpl

strike [straɪk] (*pt, pp* **struck**) n grève f; (*of oil etc*) découverte f; (*attack*) raid m ♦ vt frapper; (*oil etc*) trouver, découvrir; (*deal*) conclure ♦ vi faire grève; (*attack*) attaquer; (*clock*) sonner; **on ~** (*workers*) en grève; **to ~ a match** frotter une allumette; **~ down** vt terrasser; **~ up** vt (MUS) se mettre à jouer; **to ~ up a friendship with** se lier d'amitié avec; **to ~ up a conversation (with)** engager une conversation (avec); **~r** n gréviste m/f; (SPORT) buteur m; **striking** adj frappant(e), saisissant(e); (*attractive*) éblouissant(e)

string [strɪŋ] (*pt, pp* **strung**) n ficelle f; (*row: of beads*) rang m; (: *of onions*) chapelet m; (MUS) corde f ♦ vt: **to ~ out** échelonner; **the ~s** npl (MUS) les instruments mpl à cordes; **to ~ together** enchaîner; **to pull ~s** (*fig*) faire jouer le piston; **~(ed) instrument** n (MUS) instrument m à cordes

stringent ['strɪndʒənt] adj rigoureux(-euse)

strip [strɪp] n bande f ♦ vt (*undress*) déshabiller; (*paint*) décaper; (*also*: **~ down**: *machine*) démonter ♦ vi se déshabiller; **~ cartoon** n bande dessinée

stripe [straɪp] n raie f, rayure f; (MIL) galon m; **~d** adj rayé(e), à rayures

strip: ~ lighting (BRIT) n éclairage m au néon or fluorescent; **~per** n strip-teaseur(-euse) f; **~ search** n fouille corporelle (*en faisant se déshabiller la personne*) ♦ vt: **he was ~ searched** on l'a fait se déshabiller et soumis à une fouille corporelle

stripy ['straɪpɪ] adj rayé(e)

strive [straɪv] (*pt* **strove**, *pp* **striven**) vi: **to ~ to do/for sth** s'efforcer de faire/d'obtenir qch

strode [strəud] pt of **stride**

stroke [strəuk] n coup m; (SWIMMING) nage f; (MED) attaque f ♦ vt caresser; **at a ~** d'un (seul) coup

stroll [strəul] n petite promenade ♦ vi flâner, se promener nonchalamment; **~er** (US) n (*pushchair*) poussette f

strong [strɒŋ] adj fort(e); vigoureux(-euse); (*heart, nerves*) solide; **they are 50 ~** ils sont au nombre de 50; **~hold** n bastion m; **~ly** adv fortemente, avec force; vigoureusement; solidement; **~room** n chambre forte

strove [strəuv] pt of **strive**

struck [strʌk] pt, pp of **strike**

structural ['strʌktʃrəl] adj structural(e); (CONSTR: defect) de construction; (damage) affectant les parties portantes

structure ['strʌktʃəʳ] n structure f; (building) construction f

struggle ['strʌgl] n lutte f ♦ vi lutter, se battre

strum [strʌm] vt (guitar) jouer (en sourdine) de

strung [strʌŋ] pt, pp of **string**

strut [strʌt] n étai m, support m ♦ vi se pavaner

stub [stʌb] n (of cigarette) bout m, mégot m; (of cheque etc) talon m ♦ vt: **to ~ one's toe** se cogner le doigt de pied; **~ out** vt écraser

stubble ['stʌbl] n chaume m; (on chin) barbe f de plusieurs jours

stubborn ['stʌbən] adj têtu(e), obstiné(e), opiniâtre

stuck [stʌk] pt, pp of **stick** ♦ adj (jammed) bloqué(e), coincé(e); **~-up** (inf) adj prétentieux(-euse)

stud [stʌd] n (on boots etc) clou m; (on collar) bouton de col; (earring) petite boucle d'oreille; (of horses: also: ~ **farm**) écurie f, haras m; (also: ~ **horse**) étalon m ♦ vt (fig): **~ded with** parsemé(e) or criblé(e) de

student ['stju:dənt] n étudiant(e) ♦ adj estudiantin(e); d'étudiant; ~ **driver** (US) n (conducteur(-trice)) débutant(e)

studio ['stju:dɪəu] n studio m, atelier m; (TV etc) studio

studious ['stju:dɪəs] adj studieux(-euse), appliqué(e); (attention) soutenu(e); **~ly** adv (carefully) soigneusement

study ['stʌdɪ] n étude f; (room) bureau m ♦ vt étudier; (examine) examiner ♦ vi étudier, faire ses études

stuff [stʌf] n chose(s) f(pl); affaires fpl, trucs mpl; (substance) substance f ♦ vt rembourrer; (CULIN) farcir; (inf: push) fourrer; **~ing** n bourre f, rembourrage m; (CULIN) farce f; **~y** adj (room) mal ventilé(e) or aéré(e); (ideas) vieux jeu inv

stumble ['stʌmbl] vi trébucher; **to ~ across or on** (fig) tomber sur; **stumbling block** n pierre f d'achoppement

stump [stʌmp] n souche f; (of limb) moignon m ♦ vt: **to be ~ed** sécher, ne pas savoir que répondre

stun [stʌn] vt étourdir; (fig) abasourdir

stung [stʌŋ] pt, pp of **sting**

stunk [stʌŋk] pp of **stink**

stunned [stʌnd] adj sidéré(e)

stunning ['stʌnɪŋ] adj (news etc)

stupéfiant(e); (girl etc) éblouissant(e)

stunt [stʌnt] n (in film) cascade f, acrobatie f; (publicity ~) truc m publicitaire ♦ vt retarder, arrêter; **~man** ['stʌntmæn] (irreg) n cascadeur m

stupendous [stju:'pɛndəs] adj prodigieux(-euse), fantastique

stupid ['stju:pɪd] adj stupide, bête; **~ity** [stju:'pɪdɪtɪ] n stupidité f, bêtise f

sturdy ['stə:dɪ] adj robuste; solide

stutter ['stʌtəʳ] vi bégayer

sty [staɪ] n (for pigs) porcherie f

stye [staɪ] n (MED) orgelet m

style [staɪl] n style m; (distinction) allure f, cachet m, style; **stylish** adj élégant(e), chic inv

stylus ['staɪləs] (pl styli or ~es) n (of record player) pointe f de lecture

suave [swɑ:v] adj doucereux(-euse), onctueux(-euse)

sub... [sʌb] prefix sub..., sous-; **~conscious** adj subconscient(e); **~contract** vt sous-traiter

subdue [səb'dju:] vt subjuguer, soumettre; **~d** adj (light) tamisé(e); (person) qui a perdu de son entrain

subject [n 'sʌbdʒɪkt, vb səb'dʒɛkt] n sujet m; (SCOL) matière f ♦ vt: **to ~ to** soumettre à; exposer à; **to be ~ to** (law) être soumis(e) à; (disease) être sujet(te) à; **~ive** [sʌb'dʒɛktɪv] adj subjectif(-ive); **~ matter** n (content) contenu m

sublet [sʌb'lɛt] vt sous-louer

submarine [sʌbmə'ri:n] n sous-marin m

submerge [səb'mə:dʒ] vt submerger ♦ vi plonger

submission [səb'mɪʃən] n soumission f; **submissive** adj soumis(e)

submit [səb'mɪt] vt soumettre ♦ vi se soumettre

subnormal [sʌb'nɔ:ml] adj au-dessous de la normale

subordinate [sə'bɔ:dɪnət] adj subalterne ♦ n subordonné(e)

subpoena [səb'pi:nə] n (LAW) citation f, assignation f

subscribe [səb'skraɪb] vi cotiser; **to ~ to** (opinion, fund) souscrire à; (newspaper) s'abonner à; être abonné(e) à; **~r** n (to periodical, telephone) abonné(e); **subscription** [səb'skrɪpʃən] n (to magazine etc) abonnement m

subsequent ['sʌbsɪkwənt] adj ultérieur(e), suivant(e); consécutif(-ive); **~ly** adv par la suite

subside [səb'saɪd] vi (flood) baisser; (wind, feelings) tomber; **~nce** [səb'saɪdns] n affaissement m

subsidiary [səb'sɪdɪərɪ] adj subsidiaire;

accessoire ♦ n filiale f

subsidize ['sʌbsɪdaɪz] vt subventionner; **subsidy** ['sʌbsɪdɪ] n subvention f

substance ['sʌbstəns] n substance f

substantial [səb'stænʃl] adj substantiel(le); (fig) important(e); **~ly** adv considérablement; (in essence) en grande partie

substantiate [səb'stænʃɪeɪt] vt étayer, fournir des preuves à l'appui de

substitute ['sʌbstɪtjuːt] n (person) remplaçant(e); (thing) succédané m ♦ vt: to ~ sth/sb for substituer qch/qn à, remplacer par qch/qn

subterranean [sʌbtə'reɪnɪən] adj souterrain(e)

subtitle ['sʌbtaɪtl] n (CINEMA, TV) sous-titre m; **~d** adj sous-titré(e)

subtle ['sʌtl] adj subtil(e)

subtotal [sʌb'təʊtl] n total partiel

subtract [səb'trækt] vt soustraire, retrancher; **~ion** n soustraction f

suburb ['sʌbəːb] n faubourg m; **the ~s** npl la banlieue; **~an** [sə'bəːbən] adj de banlieue, suburbain(e); **~ia** [sə'bəːbɪə] n la banlieue

subway ['sʌbweɪ] n (US: railway) métro m; (BRIT: underpass) passage souterrain

succeed [sək'siːd] vi réussir ♦ vt succéder à; **to ~ in doing** réussir à faire; **~ing** adj (following) suivant(e)

success [sək'ses] n succès m; réussite f; **~ful** adj (venture) couronné(e) de succès; **to be ~ful (in doing)** réussir (à faire); **~fully** adv avec succès

succession [sək'seʃən] n succession f; **3 days in ~** 3 jours de suite

successive [sək'sesɪv] adj successif(-ive); consécutif(-ive)

such [sʌtʃ] adj tel (telle); (of that kind): ~ a book un livre de ce genre, un livre pareil, un tel livre; (so much): ~ courage un tel courage ♦ adv si; ~ books des livres de ce genre, des livres pareils, de tels livres; ~ a long trip un si long voyage; ~ a lot of tellement or tant de; ~ as (like) tel que, comme; as ~ en tant que tel, à proprement parler; **~-and-~** adj tel ou tel

suck [sʌk] vt sucer; (breast, bottle) téter; **~er** n ventouse f; (inf) poire f

suction ['sʌkʃən] n succion f

sudden ['sʌdn] adj soudain(e), subit(e); **all of a ~** soudain, tout à coup; **~ly** adv brusquement, tout à coup, soudain

suds [sʌdz] npl eau savonneuse

sue [suː] vt poursuivre en justice, intenter un procès à

suede [sweɪd] n daim m

suet ['sʊɪt] n graisse f de rognon

suffer ['sʌfər] vt souffrir, subir; (bear) tolérer,

supporter ♦ vi souffrir; **~er** n (MED) malade m/f; **~ing** n souffrance(s) f(pl)

sufficient [sə'fɪʃənt] adj suffisant(e); ~ **money** suffisamment d'argent; **~ly** adv suffisamment, assez

suffocate ['sʌfəkeɪt] vi suffoquer; étouffer

sugar ['ʃʊgər] n sucre m ♦ vt sucrer; ~ **beet** n betterave sucrière; ~ **cane** n canne f à sucre

suggest [sə'dʒest] vt suggérer, proposer; (indicate) dénoter; **~ion** n suggestion f

suicide ['sʊɪsaɪd] n suicide m; see also **commit**

suit [suːt] n (man's) costume m, complet m; (woman's) tailleur m, ensemble m; (LAW) poursuite(s) f(pl), procès m; (CARDS) couleur f ♦ vt aller à; convenir à; (adapt): **to ~ sth to** adapter or approprier qch à; **well ~ed** (well matched) faits l'un pour l'autre, très bien assortis; **~able** adj qui convient; approprié(e); **~ably** adv comme il se doit (or se devait etc), convenablement

suitcase ['suːtkeɪs] n valise f

suite [swiːt] n (of rooms, also MUS) suite f; (furniture): **bedroom/dining room ~** (ensemble m de) chambre f à coucher/salle f à manger

suitor ['suːtər] n soupirant m, prétendant m

sulfur ['sʌlfər] (US) n = **sulphur**

sulk [sʌlk] vi bouder; **~y** adj boudeur(-euse), maussade

sullen ['sʌlən] adj renfrogné(e), maussade

sulphur ['sʌlfər] (US **sulfur**) n soufre m

sultana [sʌl'tɑːnə] n (CULIN) raisin (sec) de Smyrne

sultry ['sʌltrɪ] adj étouffant(e)

sum [sʌm] n somme f; (SCOL etc) calcul m; ~ **up** vt, vi résumer

summarize ['sʌməraɪz] vt résumer

summary ['sʌmərɪ] n résumé m

summer ['sʌmər] n été m ♦ adj d'été, estival(e); **~house** n (in garden) pavillon m; **~time** n été m; ~ **time** n (by clock) heure f d'été

summit ['sʌmɪt] n sommet m

summon ['sʌmən] vt appeler, convoquer; ~ **up** vt rassembler, faire appel à; **~s** n citation f, assignation f

sun [sʌn] n soleil m; **in the ~** au soleil; **~bathe** vi prendre un bain de soleil; **~block** n écran m total; **~burn** n coup m de soleil; **~burned**, **~burnt** adj (tanned) bronzé(e)

Sunday ['sʌndɪ] n dimanche m; ~ **school** n ≈ catéchisme m

sundial ['sʌndaɪəl] n cadran m solaire

sundown ['sʌndaʊn] n coucher m du (or de) soleil

sundries ['sʌndrɪz] npl articles divers

sundry ['sʌndrɪ] adj divers(e), différent(e) ♦ n: **all and ~** tout le monde, n'importe qui

sunflower ['sʌnflaʊər] n tournesol m

sung [sʌŋ] pp of **sing**
sunglasses ['sʌŋglɑːsɪz] npl lunettes fpl de soleil
sunk [sʌŋk] pp of **sink**
sun: ~**light** n (lumière f du) soleil m; ~**lit** adj ensoleillé(e); ~**ny** adj ensoleillé(e); ~**rise** n lever m du (or de) soleil; ~ **roof** n (AUT) toit ouvrant; ~**screen** n crème f solaire; ~**set** n coucher m du (or de) soleil; ~**shade** n (over table) parasol m; ~**shine** n (lumière f du) soleil m; ~**stroke** n insolation f; ~**tan** n bronzage m; ~**tan lotion** n lotion f or lait m solaire; ~**tan oil** n huile f solaire
super ['suːpəʳ] (inf) adj formidable
superannuation [suːpərænjuˈeɪʃən] n (contribution) cotisations fpl pour la pension
superb [suːˈpəːb] adj superbe, magnifique
supercilious [suːpəˈsɪlɪəs] adj hautain(e), dédaigneux(-euse)
superficial [suːpəˈfɪʃəl] adj superficiel(le)
superimpose ['suːpərɪmˈpəuz] vt superposer
superintendent [suːpərɪnˈtɛndənt] n directeur(-trice); (POLICE) ≈ commissaire m
superior [suˈpɪərɪəʳ] adj, n supérieur(e); ~**ity** [supɪərɪˈɔrɪtɪ] n supériorité f
superlative [suˈpəːlətɪv] n (LING) superlatif m
superman ['suːpəmæn] (irreg) n surhomme m
supermarket ['suːpəmɑːkɪt] n supermarché m
supernatural [suːpəˈnætʃərəl] adj surnaturel(le)
superpower ['suːpəpauəʳ] n (POL) superpuissance f
supersede [suːpəˈsiːd] vt remplacer, supplanter
superstitious [suːpəˈstɪʃəs] adj superstitieux(-euse)
supervise ['suːpəvaɪz] vt surveiller; diriger; **supervision** [suːpəˈvɪʒən] n surveillance f; contrôle m; **supervisor** n surveillant(e); (in shop) chef m de rayon
supper ['sʌpəʳ] n dîner m; (late) souper m
supple ['sʌpl] adj souple
supplement [n 'sʌplɪmənt, vb sʌplɪˈmɛnt] n supplément m ♦ vt compléter; ~**ary** [sʌplɪˈmɛntərɪ] adj supplémentaire; ~**ary benefit** (BRIT) n allocation f (supplémentaire) d'aide sociale
supplier [səˈplaɪəʳ] n fournisseur m
supply [səˈplaɪ] vt (provide) fournir; (equip): **to ~ (with)** approvisionner or ravitailler (en); fournir (en) ♦ n provision f, réserve f; (~ing) approvisionnement m; **supplies** npl (food) vivres mpl; (MIL) subsistances fpl; ~ **teacher** (BRIT) n suppléant(e)
support [səˈpɔːt] n (moral, financial etc) soutien m, appui m; (TECH) support m,

soutien ♦ vt soutenir, supporter; (financially) subvenir aux besoins de; (uphold) être pour, être partisan de, appuyer; ~**er** n (POL etc) partisan(e); (SPORT) supporter m
suppose [səˈpəuz] vt supposer; imaginer; **to be ~d to do** être censé(e) faire; ~**dly** [səˈpəuzɪdlɪ] adv soi-disant; **supposing** conj si, à supposer que +sub
suppress [səˈprɛs] vt (revolt) réprimer; (information) supprimer; (yawn) étouffer; (feelings) refouler
supreme [suˈpriːm] adj suprême
surcharge ['səːtʃɑːdʒ] n surcharge f
sure [ʃuəʳ] adj sûr(e); (definite, convinced) sûr, certain(e); ~! (of course) bien sûr!; ~ **enough** effectivement; **to make ~ of sth** s'assurer de or vérifier qch; **to make ~ that** s'assurer or vérifier que; ~**ly** adv sûrement; certainement
surf [səːf] n (waves) ressac m
surface ['səːfɪs] n surface f ♦ vt (road) poser un revêtement sur ♦ vi remonter à la surface; faire surface; ~ **mail** n courrier m par voie de terre (or maritime)
surfboard ['səːbɔːd] n planche f de surf
surfeit ['səːfɪt] n: **a ~ of** un excès de; une indigestion de
surfing ['səːfɪŋ] n surf m
surge [səːdʒ] n vague f, montée f ♦ vi déferler
surgeon ['səːdʒən] n chirurgien m
surgery ['səːdʒərɪ] n chirurgie f; (BRIT: room) cabinet m (de consultation); (: also: ~ **hours**) heures fpl de consultation
surgical ['səːdʒɪkl] adj chirurgical(e); ~ **spirit** (BRIT) n alcool m à 90°
surname ['səːneɪm] n nom m de famille
surplus ['səːpləs] n surplus m, excédent m ♦ adj en surplus, de trop; (COMM) excédentaire
surprise [səˈpraɪz] n surprise f; (astonishment) étonnement m ♦ vt surprendre; (astonish) étonner; **surprising** adj surprenant(e), étonnant(e); **surprisingly** adv (easy, helpful) étonnamment
surrender [səˈrɛndəʳ] n reddition f, capitulation f ♦ vi se rendre, capituler
surreptitious [sʌrəpˈtɪʃəs] adj subreptice, furtif(-ive)
surrogate ['sʌrəgɪt] n substitut m; ~ **mother** n mère porteuse or de substitution
surround [səˈraund] vt entourer; (MIL etc) encercler; ~**ing** adj environnant(e); ~**ings** npl environs mpl, alentours mpl
surveillance [səːˈveɪləns] n surveillance f
survey [n 'səːveɪ, vb səːˈveɪ] n enquête f, étude f; (in housebuying etc) inspection f, (rapport m d')expertise f; (of land) levé m ♦ vt enquêter sur; inspecter; (look at) embrasser du regard; ~**or** n (of house) expert m; (of land) (arpenteur m) géomètre m
survival [səˈvaɪvl] n survie f; (relic) vestige m

survive [sə'vaɪv] vi survivre; (custom etc) subsister ♦ vt survivre à; **survivor** n survivant(e); (fig) battant(e)

susceptible [sə'sɛptəbl] adj: ~ (to) sensible (à); (disease) prédisposé(e) (à)

suspect [adj, n 'sʌspɛkt, vb səs'pɛkt] adj, n suspect(e) ♦ vt soupçonner, suspecter

suspend [səs'pɛnd] vt suspendre; ~ed **sentence** n condamnation f avec sursis; ~er **belt** n porte-jarretelles m inv; ~ers npl (BRIT) jarretelles fpl; (US) bretelles fpl

suspense [səs'pɛns] n attente f, incertitude f; (in film etc) suspense m

suspension [səs'pɛnʃən] n suspension f; (of driving licence) retrait m provisoire; ~ **bridge** n pont suspendu

suspicion [səs'pɪʃən] n soupçon(s) m(pl); **suspicious** adj (suspecting) soupçonneux(-euse), méfiant(e); (causing suspicion) suspect(e)

sustain [səs'teɪn] vt soutenir; (food etc) nourrir, donner des forces à; (suffer) subir; recevoir; ~**able** adj (development, growth etc) viable; ~**ed** adj (effort) soutenu(e), prolongé(e); **sustenance** ['sʌstɪnəns] n nourriture f; (money) moyens mpl de subsistance

swab [swɔb] n (MED) tampon m

swagger ['swægə*] vi plastronner

swallow ['swɔləu] n (bird) hirondelle f ♦ vt avaler; ~ **up** vt engloutir

swam [swæm] pt of swim

swamp [swɔmp] n marais m, marécage m ♦ vt submerger

swan [swɔn] n cygne m

swap [swɔp] vt: to ~ (for) échanger (contre), troquer (contre)

swarm [swɔ:m] n essaim m ♦ vi fourmiller, grouiller

swastika ['swɔstɪkə] n croix gammée

swat [swɔt] vt écraser

sway [sweɪ] vi se balancer, osciller ♦ vt (influence) influencer

swear [swɛə*] (pt swore, pp sworn) vt, vi jurer; ~**word** n juron m, gros mot

sweat [swɛt] n sueur f, transpiration f ♦ vi suer

sweater ['swɛtə*] n tricot m, pull m

sweaty ['swɛtɪ] adj en sueur, moite or mouillé(e) de sueur

Swede [swi:d] n Suédois(e)

swede [swi:d] n (BRIT) rutabaga m

Sweden ['swi:dn] n Suède f; **Swedish** adj suédois(e) ♦ n (LING) suédois m

sweep [swi:p] (pt, pp swept) n (also: chimney ~) ramoneur m ♦ vt balayer; (subj: current) emporter; ~ **away** vt balayer; entraîner; emporter; ~ **past** vi passer majestueusement or rapidement; ~ **up** vt, vi balayer; ~**ing** adj (gesture) large; circulaire; **a ~ing statement** une généralisation hâtive

sweet [swi:t] n (candy) bonbon m; (BRIT: pudding) dessert m ♦ adj doux (douce); (not savoury) sucré(e); (fig: kind) gentil(le); (baby) mignon(ne); ~**corn** ['swi:tkɔ:n] n maïs m; ~**en** vt adoucir; (with sugar) sucrer; ~**heart** n amoureux(-euse); ~**ness** n goût sucré; douceur f; ~ **pea** n pois m de senteur

swell [swɛl] (pt **swelled**, pp **swollen** or **swelled**) n (of sea) houle f ♦ adj (US: inf: excellent) chouette ♦ vi grossir, augmenter; (sound) s'enfler; (MED) enfler; ~**ing** n (MED) enflure f; (lump) grosseur f

sweltering ['swɛltərɪŋ] adj étouffant(e), oppressant(e)

swept [swɛpt] pt, pp of sweep

swerve [swə:v] vi faire une embardée or un écart; dévier

swift [swɪft] n (bird) martinet m ♦ adj rapide, prompt(e)

swig [swɪg] (inf) n (drink) lampée f

swill [swɪl] vt (also: ~ out, ~ down) laver à grande eau

swim [swɪm] (pt swam, pp swum) n: to go **for a ~** aller nager or se baigner ♦ vi nager; (SPORT) faire de la natation; (head, room) tourner ♦ vt traverser (à la nage); (a length) faire (à la nage); ~**mer** n nageur(-euse); ~**ming** n natation f; ~**ming cap** n bonnet m de bain; ~**ming costume** (BRIT) n maillot m (de bain); ~**ming pool** n piscine f; ~**ming trunks** npl caleçon m or slip m de bain; ~**suit** n maillot m (de bain)

swindle ['swɪndl] n escroquerie f

swine [swaɪn] (inf!) n inv salaud m (!)

swing [swɪŋ] (pt, pp swung) n balançoire f; (movement) balancement m, oscillations fpl; (change: in opinion etc) revirement m ♦ vt balancer, faire osciller; (also: ~ round) tourner, faire virer ♦ vi se balancer, osciller; (also: ~ round) virer, tourner; **to be in full ~** battre son plein; ~ **bridge** n pont tournant; ~ **door** (US **swinging door**) n porte battante

swingeing ['swɪndʒɪŋ] (BRIT) adj écrasant(e); (cuts etc) considérable

swipe [swaɪp] (inf) vt (steal) piquer

swirl [swə:l] vi tourbillonner, tournoyer

Swiss [swɪs] adj suisse ♦ n inv Suisse m/f

switch [swɪtʃ] n (for light, radio etc) bouton m; (change) changement m, revirement m ♦ vt changer; ~ **off** vt éteindre; (engine) arrêter; ~ **on** vt allumer; (engine, machine) mettre en marche; ~**board** n (TEL) standard m

Switzerland ['swɪtsələnd] n Suisse f

swivel ['swɪvl] vi (also: ~ round) pivoter, tourner

swollen ['swəulən] pp of swell

swoon [swu:n] *vi* se pâmer

swoop [swu:p] *n* (*by police*) descente *f* ♦ *vi* (*also:* ~ **down**) descendre en piqué, piquer

swop [swɔp] *vt* = **swap**

sword [sɔːd] *n* épée *f*; ~**fish** *n* espadon *m*

swore [swɔːˀ] *pt of* **swear**

sworn [swɔːn] *pp of* **swear** ♦ *adj* (*statement, evidence*) donné(e) sous serment

swot [swɔt] *vi* bûcher, potasser

swum [swʌm] *pp of* **swim**

swung [swʌŋ] *pt, pp of* **swing**

syllable ['sɪləbl] *n* syllabe *f*

syllabus ['sɪləbəs] *n* programme *m*

symbol ['sɪmbl] *n* symbole *m*

symmetry ['sɪmɪtrɪ] *n* symétrie *f*

sympathetic [sɪmpə'θetɪk] *adj* compatissant(e); bienveillant(e), compréhensif(-ive); (*likeable*) sympathique; ~ **towards** bien disposé(e) envers

sympathize ['sɪmpəθaɪz] *vi*: to ~ **with sb** plaindre qn; (*in grief*) s'associer à la douleur de qn; to ~ **with sth** comprendre qch; ~**r** *n* (*POL*) sympathisant(e)

sympathy ['sɪmpəθɪ] *n* (*pity*) compassion *f*; **sympathies** *npl* (*support*) soutien *m*; **left-wing** *etc* **sympathies** penchants *mpl* à gauche *etc*; **in ~ with** (*strike*) en or par solidarité avec; **with our deepest ~** en vous priant d'accepter nos sincères condoléances

symphony ['sɪmfənɪ] *n* symphonie *f*

symptom ['sɪmptəm] *n* symptôme *m*; indice *m*

syndicate ['sɪndɪkɪt] *n* syndicat *m*, coopérative *f*

synopsis [sɪ'nɔpsɪs] (*pl* **synopses**) *n* résumé *m*

synthetic [sɪn'θetɪk] *adj* synthétique

syphon ['saɪfən] *n, vb* = **siphon**

Syria ['sɪrɪə] *n* Syrie *f*

syringe [sɪ'rɪndʒ] *n* seringue *f*

syrup ['sɪrəp] *n* sirop *m*; (*also:* **golden ~**) mélasse raffinée

system ['sɪstəm] *n* système *m*; (*ANAT*) organisme *m*; ~**atic** [sɪstə'mætɪk] *adj* systématique; méthodique; ~ **disk** *n* (*COMPUT*) disque *m* système; ~**s analyst** *n* analyste fonctionnel(le)

T, t

ta [tɑː] (*BRIT: inf*) *excl* merci!

tab [tæb] *n* (*label*) étiquette *f*; (*on drinks can etc*) languette *f*; **to keep ~s on** (*fig*) surveiller

tabby ['tæbɪ] *n* (*also:* ~ **cat**) chat(te) tigré(e)

table ['teɪbl] *n* table *f* ♦ *vt* (*BRIT: motion etc*) présenter; **to lay** or **set the ~** mettre le couvert or la table; ~**cloth** *n* nappe *f*; ~ **d'hôte** [tɑːbl'dəut] *adj* (*meal*) à prix fixe; ~ **lamp** *n*

lampe *f* de table; ~**mat** *n* (*for plate*) napperon *m*, set *m*; (*for hot dish*) dessous-de-plat *m inv*; ~ **of contents** *n* table *f* des matières; ~**spoon** *n* cuiller *f* de service; (*also:* ~**spoonful:** *as measurement*) cuillerée *f* à soupe

tablet ['tæblɪt] *n* (*MED*) comprimé *m*

table tennis *n* ping-pong ® *m*, tennis *m* de table

table wine *n* vin *m* de table

tabloid ['tæblɔɪd] *n* quotidien *m* populaire

tack [tæk] *n* (*nail*) petit clou ♦ *vt* clouer; (*fig*) direction *f*; (*BRIT: stitch*) faufiler ♦ *vi* tirer un or des bord(s)

tackle ['tækl] *n* matériel *m*, équipement *m*; (*for lifting*) appareil *m* de levage; (*RUGBY*) plaquage *m* ♦ *vt* (*difficulty, animal, burglar etc*) s'attaquer à; (*person: challenge*) s'expliquer avec; (*RUGBY*) plaquer

tacky ['tækɪ] *adj* collant(e); (*pej: of poor quality*) miteux(-euse)

tact [tækt] *n* tact *m*; ~**ful** *adj* plein(e) de tact

tactical ['tæktɪkl] *adj* tactique

tactics ['tæktɪks] *npl* tactique *f*

tactless ['tæktlɪs] *adj* qui manque de tact

tadpole ['tædpəul] *n* têtard *m*

tag [tæg] *n* étiquette *f*; ~ **along** *vi* suivre

tail [teɪl] *n* queue *f*; (*of shirt*) pan *m* ♦ *vt* (*follow*) suivre, filer; ~**s** *npl* habit *m*; ~ **away**, ~ **off** *vi* (*in size, quality etc*) baisser peu à peu; ~**back** (*BRIT*) *n* (*AUT*) bouchon *m*; ~ **end** *n* bout *m*, fin *f*; ~**gate** *n* (*AUT*) hayon *m* arrière

tailor ['teɪləˀ] *n* tailleur *m*; ~**ing** *n* (*cut*) coupe *f*; ~**-made** *adj* fait(e) sur mesure; (*fig*) conçu(e) spécialement

tailwind ['teɪlwɪnd] *n* vent *m* arrière *inv*

tainted ['teɪntɪd] *adj* (*food*) gâté(e); (*water, air*) infecté(e); (*fig*) souillé(e)

take [teɪk] (*pt* **took**, *pp* **taken**) *vt* prendre; (*gain: prize*) remporter; (*require: effort, courage*) demander; (*tolerate*) accepter, supporter; (*hold: passengers etc*) contenir; (*accompany*) emmener, accompagner; (*bring, carry*) apporter, emporter; (*exam*) passer, se présenter à; **to ~ sth from** (*drawer etc*) prendre qch dans; (*person*) prendre qch à; **I ~ it that ...** je suppose que ...; ~ **after** *vt fus* ressembler à; ~ **apart** *vt* démonter; ~ **away** *vt* enlever; (*carry off*) emporter; ~ **back** *vt* (*return*) rendre, rapporter; (*one's words*) retirer; ~ **down** *vt* (*building*) démolir; (*letter etc*) prendre, écrire; ~ **in** *vt* (*deceive*) tromper, rouler; (*understand*) comprendre, saisir; (*include*) comprendre, inclure; (*lodger*) prendre; ~ **off** *vi* (*AVIAT*) décoller ♦ *vt* (*go away*) s'en aller; (*remove*) enlever; ~ **on** *vt* (*work*) accepter, se charger de; (*employee*) prendre, embaucher; (*opponent*) accepter de se battre contre; ~ **out** *vt* (*invite*) emmener, sortir; (*remove*) enlever; **to ~ sth out of sth** (*drawer, pocket etc*) prendre qch dans qch; **~ over** *vt* (*business*) reprendre ♦ *vi*: **to ~ over from sb** prendre la relève de qn; **~ to** *vt fus* (*person*) se prendre d'amitié pour; (*thing*) prendre goût à; **~ up** *vt* (*activity*) se mettre à; (*dress*) raccourcir; (*occupy: time, space*) prendre, occuper; **to ~ sb up on an offer** accepter la proposition de qn; **~away** (*BRIT*) *adj* (*food*) à emporter ♦ *n* (*shop, restaurant*) café *m* qui vend de plats à emporter; **~off** *n* (*AVIAT*) décollage *m*; **~over** *n* (*COMM*) rachat *m*; **takings** *npl* (*COMM*) recette *f*

talc [tælk] *n* (*also*: **~um powder**) talc *m*

tale [teɪl] *n* (*story*) conte *m*, histoire *f*; (*account*) récit *m*; **to tell ~s** (*fig*) rapporter

talent ['tælnt] *n* talent *m*, don *m*; **~ed** *adj* doué(e), plein(e) de talent

talk [tɔːk] *n* (*a speech*) causerie *f*, exposé *m*; (*conversation*) discussion *f*, entretien *m*; (*gossip*) racontars *mpl* ♦ *vi* parler; **~s** *npl* (*POL etc*) entretiens *mpl*; **to ~ about** parler de; **to ~ sb into/out of doing** persuader qn de faire/ ne pas faire; **to ~ shop** parler métier or affaires; **~ over** *vt* discuter (de); **~ative** *adj* bavard(e); **~ show** *n* causerie (télévisée or radiodiffusée)

tall [tɔːl] *adj* (*person*) grand(e); (*building, tree*) haut(e); **to be 6 feet ~** ≈ mesurer 1 mètre 80; **~ story** *n* histoire *f* invraisemblable

tally ['tælɪ] *n* compte *m* ♦ *vi*: **to ~ (with)** correspondre (à)

talon ['tælən] *n* griffe *f*; (*of eagle*) serre *f*

tame [teɪm] *adj* apprivoisé(e); (*fig: story, style*) insipide

tamper ['tæmpər] *vi*: **to ~ with** toucher à

tampon ['tæmpɔn] *n* tampon *m* (hygiénique or périodique)

tan [tæn] *n* (*also*: **suntan**) bronzage *m* ♦ *vt, vi* bronzer ♦ *adj* (*colour*) brun roux *inv*

tang [tæŋ] *n* odeur (or saveur) piquante

tangent ['tændʒənt] *n* (*MATH*) tangente *f*; **to go off at a ~** (*fig*) changer de sujet

tangerine [tændʒə'riːn] *n* mandarine *f*

tangle ['tæŋgl] *n* enchevêtrement *m*; **to get in(to) a ~** s'embrouiller

tank [tæŋk] *n* (*water ~*) réservoir *m*; (*for fish*) aquarium *m*; (*MIL*) char *m* d'assaut, tank *m*

tanker ['tæŋkər] *n* (*ship*) pétrolier *m*, tanker *m*; (*truck*) camion-citerne *m*

tantalizing ['tæntəlaɪzɪŋ] *adj* (*smell*) extrêmement appétissant(e); (*offer*) terriblement tentant(e)

tantamount ['tæntəmaunt] *adj*: **~ to** qui équivaut à

tantrum ['tæntrəm] *n* accès *m* de colère

tap [tæp] *n* (*on sink etc*) robinet *m*; (*gentle blow*) petite tape ♦ *vt* frapper or taper légèrement; (*resources*) exploiter, utiliser;

(*telephone*) mettre sur écoute; **on ~** (*fig: resources*) disponible; **~-dancing** *n* claquettes *fpl*

tape [teɪp] *n* ruban *m*; (*also*: **magnetic ~**) bande *f* (magnétique); (*cassette*) cassette *f*; (*sticky*) scotch *m* ♦ *vt* (*record*) enregistrer; (*stick with ~*) coller avec du scotch; **~ deck** *n* platine *f* d'enregistrement; **~ measure** *n* mètre *m* à ruban

taper ['teɪpər] *vi* s'effiler

tape recorder *n* magnétophone *m*

tapestry ['tæpɪstrɪ] *n* tapisserie *f*

tar [tɑː] *n* goudron *m*

target ['tɑːgɪt] *n* cible *f*; (*fig*) objectif *m*

tariff ['tærɪf] *n* (*COMM*) tarif *m*; (*taxes*) tarif douanier

tarmac ['tɑːmæk] *n* (*BRIT: on road*) macadam *m*; (*AVIAT*) piste *f*

tarnish ['tɑːnɪʃ] *vt* ternir

tarpaulin [tɑːˈpɔːlɪn] *n* bâche (goudronnée)

tarragon ['tærəgən] *n* estragon *m*

tart [tɑːt] *n* (*CULIN*) tarte *f*; (*BRIT: inf: prostitute*) putain *f* ♦ *adj* (*flavour*) âpre, aigrelet(te); **~ up** (*BRIT: inf*) *vt* (*object*) retaper; **to ~ o.s. up** se faire beau (belle), s'attifer (*pej*)

tartan ['tɑːtn] *n* tartan *m* ♦ *adj* écossais(e)

tartar ['tɑːtər] *n* (*on teeth*) tartre *m*; **~(e) sauce** *n* sauce *f* tartare

task [tɑːsk] *n* tâche *f*; **to take sb to ~** prendre qn à partie; **~ force** *n* (*MIL, POLICE*) détachement spécial

tassel ['tæsl] *n* gland *m*; pompon *m*

taste [teɪst] *n* goût *m*; (*fig: glimpse, idea*) idée *f*, aperçu *m* ♦ *vt* goûter ♦ *vi*: **to ~ of** or **like** (*fish etc*) avoir le or un goût de; **you can ~ the garlic (in it)** on sent bien l'ail; **can I have a ~ of this wine?** puis-je goûter un peu de ce vin?; **in good/bad ~** de bon/mauvais goût; **~ful** *adj* de bon goût; **~less** *adj* (*food*) fade; (*remark*) de mauvais goût; **tasty** *adj* savoureux(-euse), délicieux(-euse)

tatters ['tætəz] *npl*: **in ~** en lambeaux

tattoo [təˈtuː] *n* tatouage *m*; (*spectacle*) parade *f* militaire ♦ *vt* tatouer

tatty ['tætɪ] (*BRIT: inf*) *adj* (*clothes*) frippé(e); (*shop, area*) délabré(e)

taught [tɔːt] *pt, pp* of **teach**

taunt [tɔːnt] *n* raillerie *f* ♦ *vt* railler

Taurus ['tɔːrəs] *n* le Taureau

taut [tɔːt] *adj* tendu(e)

tax [tæks] *n* (*on goods etc*) taxe *f*; (*on income*) impôts *mpl*, contributions *fpl* ♦ *vt* taxer; imposer; (*fig: patience etc*) mettre à l'épreuve; **~able** *adj* (*income*) imposable; **~ation** [tækˈseɪʃən] *n* taxation *f*; impôts *mpl*, contributions *fpl*; **~ avoidance** *n* dégrèvement fiscal; **~ disc** (*BRIT*) *n* (*AUT*) vignette *f* (automobile); **~ evasion** *n* fraude fiscale; **~-free** adj exempt(e) d'impôts

taxi ['tæksı] n taxi m ♦ vi (AVIAT) rouler (lentement) au sol; **~ driver** n chauffeur m de taxi; **~ rank** (BRIT) n station f de taxis; **~ stand** n = taxi rank

tax: **~ payer** n contribuable m/f; **~ relief** n dégrèvement fiscal; **~ return** n déclaration f d'impôts or de revenus

TB n abbr = **tuberculosis**

tea [ti:] n thé m; (BRIT: snack: for children) goûter m; **high** **~** collation combinant goûter et dîner; **~ bag** n sachet m de thé; **~ break** (BRIT) n pause-thé f

teach [ti:tʃ] (pt, pp taught) vt: to **~ sb sth**, **~ sth to sb** apprendre qch à qn; (in school etc) enseigner qch à qn ♦ vi enseigner; **~er** n (in secondary school) professeur m; (in primary school) instituteur(-trice); **~ing** n enseignement m

tea: **~ cloth** n torchon m; **~ cosy** n cloche f à thé; **~cup** n tasse f à thé

teak [ti:k] n teck m

tea leaves npl feuilles fpl de thé

team [ti:m] n équipe f; (of animals) attelage m; **~work** n travail m d'équipe

teapot ['ti:pɔt] n théière f

tear[1] [tɛəʳ] (pt tore, pp torn) n déchirure f ♦ vt déchirer ♦ vi se déchirer; **~ along** vi (rush) aller à toute vitesse; **~ up** vt (sheet of paper etc) déchirer, mettre en morceaux or pièces

tear[2] [tıəʳ] n larme f; **in ~s** en larmes; **~ful** adj larmoyant(e); **~ gas** n gaz m lacrymogène

tearoom ['tı:ru:m] n salon m de thé

tease [ti:z] vt taquiner; (unkindly) tourmenter

tea set n service m à thé

teaspoon ['ti:spu:n] n petite cuiller; (also: **~ful**: as measurement) ≈ cuillerée f à café

teat [ti:t] n tétine f

teatime ['ti:taım] n l'heure f du thé

tea towel (BRIT) n torchon m (à vaisselle)

technical ['teknıkl] adj technique; **~ity** [teknı'kælıtı] n (detail) détail m technique; (point of law) vice m de forme; **~ly** adv techniquement; (strictly speaking) en théorie

technician [tek'nıʃən] n technicien(ne)

technique [tek'ni:k] n technique f

techno ['teknəu] n (music) techno f

technological [teknə'lɔdʒıkl] adj technologique

technology [tek'nɔlədʒı] n technologie f

teddy (bear) ['tedı(-)] n ours m en peluche

tedious ['ti:dıəs] adj fastidieux(-euse)

tee [ti:] n (GOLF) tee m

teem [ti:m] vi: to **~ (with)** grouiller (de); **it is ~ing (with rain)** il pleut à torrents

teenage ['ti:neıdʒ] adj (fashions etc) pour jeunes, pour adolescents; (children) adolescent(e); **~r** n adolescent(e)

teens [ti:nz] npl: **to be in one's ~** être

adolescent(e)

tee-shirt ['ti:ʃə:t] n = T-shirt

teeter ['ti:təʳ] vi chanceler, vaciller

teeth [ti:θ] npl of **tooth**

teethe [ti:ð] vi percer ses dents

teething troubles ['ti:ðıŋ-] npl (fig) difficultés initiales

teetotal ['ti:'təutl] adj (person) qui ne boit jamais d'alcool

tele ['telı-]: **~communications** npl télécommunications fpl; **~conferencing** n téléconférence(s) f(pl); **~gram** n télégramme m; **~graph** n télégraphe m; **~graph pole** n poteau m télégraphique

telephone ['telıfəun] n téléphone m ♦ vt (person) téléphoner à; (message) téléphoner; **on the ~** au téléphone; **to be on the ~** (BRIT: have a ~) avoir le téléphone; **~ booth**, **~ box** (BRIT) n cabine f téléphonique; **~ call** n coup m de téléphone, appel m téléphonique; **~ directory** n annuaire m (du téléphone); **~ number** n numéro m de téléphone; **telephonist** [tə'lefənıst] (BRIT) n téléphoniste m/f

telescope ['telıskəup] n télescope m

television ['telıvıʒən] n télévision f; **on ~** à la télévision; **~ set** n (poste f de) télévision m

telex ['teleks] n télex m

tell [tel] (pt, pp told) vt dire; (relate: story) raconter; (distinguish): to **~ sth from** distinguer qch de ♦ vi (talk): **~ to (of)** parler (de); (have effect) se faire sentir, se voir; to **~ sb to do** dire à qn de faire; **~ off** vt réprimander, gronder; **~er** n (in bank) caissier(-ère); **~ing** adj (remark, detail) révélateur(-trice); **~tale** adj (sign) éloquent(e), révélateur(-trice)

telly ['telı] (BRIT: inf) n abbr (= television) télé f

temp [temp] n abbr (= temporary) (secrétaire f) intérimaire f

temper ['tempəʳ] n (nature) caractère m; (mood) humeur f; (fit of anger) colère f ♦ vt (moderate) tempérer, adoucir; **to be in a ~** être en colère; **to lose one's ~** se mettre en colère

temperament ['temprəmənt] n (nature) tempérament m; **~al** [temprə'mentl] adj capricieux(-euse)

temperate ['temprət] adj (climate, country) tempéré(e)

temperature ['temprətʃəʳ] n température f; **to have** or **run a ~** avoir de la fièvre

temple ['templ] n (building) temple m; (ANAT) tempe f

temporary ['tempərərı] adj temporaire, provisoire; (job, worker) temporaire

tempt [tempt] vt tenter; **to ~ sb into doing** persuader qn de faire; **~ation** [temp'teıʃən] n tentation f; **~ing** adj tentant(e)

ten [tɛn] num dix
tenacity [tə'næsɪtɪ] n ténacité f
tenancy ['tɛnənsɪ] n location f; état m de
locataire
tenant ['tɛnənt] n locataire m/f
tend [tɛnd] vt s'occuper de ♦ vi: **to ~ to do**
avoir tendance à faire; **~ency** ['tɛndənsɪ] n
tendance f
tender ['tɛndər] adj tendre; (delicate)
délicat(e); (sore) sensible ♦ n (COMM: offer)
soumission f ♦ vt offrir
tenement ['tɛnəmənt] n immeuble m
tennis ['tɛnɪs] n tennis m; **~ ball** n balle f de
tennis; **~ court** n (court m de) tennis;
~ player n joueur(-euse) de tennis; **~ racket**
n raquette f de tennis; **~ shoes** npl
(chaussures fpl de) tennis mpl
tenor ['tɛnər] n (MUS) ténor m
tenpin bowling ['tɛnpɪn-] (BRIT) n bowling
m (à dix quilles)
tense [tɛns] adj tendu(e) ♦ n (LING) temps m
tension ['tɛnʃən] n tension f
tent [tɛnt] n tente f
tentative ['tɛntətɪv] adj timide, hésitant(e);
(conclusion) provisoire
tenterhooks ['tɛntəhuks] npl: **on ~** sur des
charbons ardents
tenth [tɛnθ] num dixième
tent peg n piquet m de tente
tent pole n montant m de tente
tenuous ['tɛnjuəs] adj ténu(e)
tenure ['tɛnjuər] n (of property) bail m; (of
job) période f de jouissance
tepid ['tɛpɪd] adj tiède
term [tə:m] n terme m; (SCOL) trimestre m
♦ vt appeler; **~s** npl (conditions) conditions
fpl; (COMM) tarif m; **in the short/long ~** à
court/long terme; **to come to ~s with**
(problem) faire face à
terminal ['tə:mɪnl] adj (disease) dans sa
phase terminale; (patient) incurable ♦ n
(ELEC) borne f; (for oil, ore etc, COMPUT)
terminal m; (also: **air ~**) aérogare f; (BRIT:
also: **coach ~**) gare routière; **~ly** adv: **to be**
~ly ill être condamné(e)
terminate ['tə:mɪneɪt] vt mettre fin à;
(pregnancy) interrompre
termini ['tə:mɪnaɪ] npl of **terminus**
terminus ['tə:mɪnəs] (pl termini) n terminus
m inv
terrace ['tɛrəs] n terrasse f; (BRIT: row of
houses) rangée f de maisons (attenantes); **the**
~s npl (BRIT: SPORT) les gradins mpl; **~d** adj
(garden) en terrasses
terracotta ['tɛrə'kɔtə] n terre cuite
terrain [tɛ'reɪn] n terrain m (sol)
terrible ['tɛrɪbl] adj terrible, atroce; (weather,
conditions) affreux(-euse), épouvantable;
terribly adv terriblement; (very badly)

affreusement mal
terrier ['tɛrɪər] n terrier m (chien)
terrific [tə'rɪfɪk] adj fantastique, incroyable,
terrible; (wonderful) formidable,
sensationnel(le)
terrify ['tɛrɪfaɪ] vt terrifier
territory ['tɛrɪtərɪ] n territoire m
terror ['tɛrər] n terreur f; **~ism** n terrorisme
m; **~ist** n terroriste m/f
test [tɛst] n (trial, check) essai m; (of courage
etc) épreuve f; (MED) examen m; (CHEM)
analyse f; (SCOL) interrogation f; (also: **driving**
~) (examen du) permis m de conduire ♦ vt
essayer; mettre à l'épreuve; examiner;
analyser; faire subir une interrogation à
testament ['tɛstəmənt] n testament m; **the**
Old/New T~ l'Ancien/le Nouveau Testament
testicle ['tɛstɪkl] n testicule m
testify ['tɛstɪfaɪ] vi (LAW) témoigner, déposer;
to ~ to sth attester qch
testimony ['tɛstɪmənɪ] n témoignage m;
(clear proof): **to be (a) ~ to** être la preuve de
test match n (CRICKET, RUGBY) match
international
test tube n éprouvette f
tetanus ['tɛtənəs] n tétanos m
tether ['tɛðər] vt attacher ♦ n: **at the end of**
one's ~ à bout (de patience)
text [tɛkst] n texte m; **~book** n manuel m
textile ['tɛkstaɪl] n textile m
texture ['tɛkstʃər] n texture f; (of skin, paper
etc) grain m
Thailand ['taɪlænd] n Thaïlande f
Thames [tɛmz] n: **the ~** la Tamise
than [ðæn, ðən] conj que; (with numerals):
more ~ 10/once plus de 10/d'une fois; **I have**
more/less ~ you j'en ai plus/moins que toi;
she has more apples ~ pears elle a plus de
pommes que de poires
thank [θæŋk] vt remercier, dire merci à; **~s**
npl (gratitude) remerciements mpl ♦ excl
merci!; **~ you (very much)** merci (beaucoup);
~s to grâce à; **~ God!** Dieu merci!; **~ful** adj:
~ful (for) reconnaissant(e) (de); **~less** adj
ingrat(e); **T~sgiving (Day)** n jour m
d'action de grâce (fête américaine)

KEYWORD

that [ðæt] adj (demonstrative: pl those) ce, cet
+vowel or h mute, cette f; that **man/woman/**
book cet homme/cette femme/ce livre; (not
"this") cet homme-là/cette femme-là/ce
livre-là; **that one** celui-là (celle-là)
♦ pron 1 (demonstrative: pl those) ce; (not
"this one") cela, ça; **who's that?** qui est-ce?;
what's that? qu'est-ce que c'est?; **is that you?**
c'est toi?; **I prefer this to that** je préfère ceci à
cela or ça; **that's what he said** c'est or voilà ce
qu'il a dit; **that is (to say)** c'est-à-dire, à savoir

2 (*relative: subject*) qui; (: *object*) que; (: *indirect*) lequel (laquelle), lesquels (lesquelles) *pl*; **the book that I read** le livre que j'ai lu; **the books that are in the library** les livres qui sont dans la bibliothèque; **all that I have** tout ce que j'ai; **the box that I put it in** la boîte dans laquelle je l'ai mis; **the people that I spoke to** les gens auxquels or à qui j'ai parlé
3 (*relative: of time*) où; **the day that he came** le jour où il est venu
♦ *conj* que; **he thought that I was ill** il pensait que j'étais malade
♦ *adv* (*demonstrative*): **I can't work that much** je ne peux pas travailler autant que cela; **I didn't know it was that bad** je ne savais pas que c'était si *or aussi* mauvais; **it's about that high** c'est à peu près de cette hauteur

thatched [θætʃt] *adj* (*roof*) de chaume; **~ cottage** chaumière *f*

thaw [θɔː] *n* dégel *m* ♦ *vi* (*ice*) fondre; (*food*) dégeler ♦ *vt* (*food: also: ~ out*) (faire) dégeler

KEYWORD

the [ðiː, ðə] *def art* 1 (*gen*) le, la *f*, l' +*vowel or h mute*, les *pl*; **the boy/girl/ink** le garçon/la fille/l'encre; **the children** les enfants; **the history of the world** l'histoire du monde; **give it to the postman** donne-le au facteur; **to play the piano/flute** jouer du piano/de la flûte; **the rich and the poor** les riches et les pauvres
2 (*in titles*): **Elizabeth the First** Elisabeth première; **Peter the Great** Pierre le Grand
3 (*in comparisons*): **the more he works, the more he earns** plus il travaille, plus il gagne de l'argent

theatre ['θɪətər] *n* théâtre *m*; (*also: lecture ~*) amphi(théâtre) *m*; (*MED: also: operating ~*) salle *f* d'opération; **~-goer** *n* habitué(e) *f* du théâtre; **theatrical** [θɪˈætrɪkl] *adj* théâtral(e)

theft [θɛft] *n* vol *m* (*larcin*)

their [ðɛər] *adj* leur; (*pl*) leurs; *see also* **my**; **~s** *pron* le (la) leur; (*pl*) les leurs; *see also* **mine**[1]

them [ðɛm, ðəm] *pron* (*direct*) les; (*indirect*) leur; (*stressed, after prep*) eux (elles); *see also* **me**

theme [θiːm] *n* thème *m*; **~ park** *n* parc *m* (d'attraction) à thème; **~ song** *n* chanson principale

themselves [ðəmˈsɛlvz] *pl pron* (*reflexive*) se; (*emphatic, after prep*) eux-mêmes (elles-mêmes); *see also* **oneself**

then [ðɛn] *adv* (*at that time*) alors, à ce moment-là; (*next*) puis, ensuite; (*and also*) et puis ♦ *conj* (*therefore*) alors, dans ce cas ♦ *adj*: **the ~ president** le président d'alors or de l'époque; **by ~** (*past*) à ce moment-là; (*future*) d'ici là; **from ~ on** dès lors

theology [θɪˈɒlədʒɪ] *n* théologie *f*

theoretical [θɪəˈrɛtɪkl] *adj* théorique

theory ['θɪərɪ] *n* théorie *f*

therapy ['θɛrəpɪ] *n* thérapie *f*

KEYWORD

there [ðɛər] *adv* 1: **there is, there are** il y a; **there are 3 of them** (*people, things*) il y en a 3; **there has been an accident** il y a eu un accident
2 (*referring to place*) là, là-bas; **it's there** c'est là(-bas); **in/on/up/down there** là-dedans/là-dessus/là-haut/en bas; **he went there on Friday** il y est allé vendredi; **I want that book there** je veux ce livre-là; **there he is!** le voilà!
3: **there, there** (*esp to child*) allons, allons!

there: ~abouts *adv* (*place*) par là, près de là; (*amount*) environ, à peu près; **~after** *adv* par la suite; **~by** *adv* ainsi; **~fore** *adv* donc, par conséquent; **~'s = there is; there has**

thermal ['θɜːml] *adj* (*springs*) thermal(e); (*underwear*) en thermolactyl ®; (*COMPUT: paper*) thermosensible; (: *printer*) thermique

thermometer [θəˈmɒmɪtər] *n* thermomètre *m*

Thermos ® ['θɜːməs] *n* (*also: ~ flask*) thermos ® *m or f inv*

thermostat ['θɜːməustæt] *n* thermostat *m*

thesaurus [θɪˈsɔːrəs] *n* dictionnaire *m* des synonymes

these [ðiːz] *pl adj* ces; (*not "those"*): **~ books** ces livres-ci ♦ *pl pron* ceux-ci (celles-ci)

thesis ['θiːsɪs] (*pl* **theses**) *n* thèse *f*

they [ðeɪ] *pl pron* ils (elles); (*stressed*) eux (elles); **~ say that ...** (*it is said that*) on dit que ...; **~'d = they had; they would**; **~'ll = they shall; they will**; **~'re = they are**; **~'ve = they have**

thick [θɪk] *adj* épais(se); (*stupid*) bête, borné(e) ♦ *n*: **in the ~ of** au beau milieu de, en plein cœur de; **it's 20 cm ~** il/elle a 20 cm d'épaisseur; **~en** *vi* s'épaissir ♦ *vt* (*sauce etc*) épaissir; **~ness** *n* épaisseur *f*; **~set** *adj* trapu(e), costaud(e)

thief [θiːf] (*pl* **thieves**) *n* voleur(-euse)

thigh [θaɪ] *n* cuisse *f*

thimble ['θɪmbl] *n* dé *m* (à coudre)

thin [θɪn] *adj* mince; (*skinny*) maigre; (*soup, sauce*) peu épais(se), clair(e); (*hair, crowd*) clairsemé(e) ♦ *vt*: **to ~ (down)** (*sauce, paint*) délayer

thing [θɪŋ] *n* chose *f*; (*object*) objet *m*; (*contraption*) truc *m*; (*mania*): **to have a ~ about** être obsédé(e) par; **~s** *npl* (*belongings*) affaires *fpl*; **poor ~!** le (la) pauvre!; **the best ~ would be to** le mieux serait de; **how are ~s?** comment ça va?

think [θɪŋk] (*pt, pp* **thought**) *vi* penser,

réfléchir; (*believe*) penser ♦ vt (*imagine*)
imaginer; **what did you ~ of them?** qu'avez-
vous pensé d'eux?; **to ~ about sth/sb** penser
à qch/qn; **I'll ~ about it** je vais y réfléchir; **to
~ of doing** avoir l'idée de faire; **I ~ so/not** je
crois or pense que oui/non; **to ~ well of** avoir
une haute opinion de; **~ over** vt bien
réfléchir à; **~ up** vt inventer, trouver; **~ tank**
n groupe m de réflexion

thinly ['θɪnlɪ] adv (*cut*) en fines tranches;
(*spread*) en une couche mince

third [θəːd] num troisième ♦ n (*fraction*) tiers
m; (*AUT*) troisième (vitesse) f; (*BRIT: SCOL:
degree*) ≈ licence f sans mention; **~ly** adv
troisièmement; **~ party insurance** (*BRIT*) n
assurance f au tiers; **~-rate** adj de qualité
médiocre; **the T~ World** n le tiers monde

thirst [θəːst] n soif f; **~y** adj (*person*) qui a
soif, assoiffé(e); (*work*) qui donne soif; **to
be ~y** avoir soif

thirteen [θəː'tiːn] num treize

thirty ['θəːtɪ] num trente

⌐ **KEYWORD** ¬

this [ðɪs] adj (*demonstrative: pl these*) ce, cet
+vowel or h mute, cette f; **this man/woman/
book** cet homme/cette femme/ce livre; (*not
"that"*) cet homme-ci/cette femme-ci/ce
livre-ci; **this one** celui-ci (celle-ci)
♦ pron (*demonstrative: pl these*) ce; (*not "that
one"*) celui-ci (celle-ci), ceci; **who's this?** qui
est-ce?; **what's this?** qu'est-ce que c'est?; **I
prefer this to that** je préfère ceci à cela; **this is
what he said** voici ce qu'il a dit; **this is Mr
Brown** (*in introductions*) je vous présente Mr
Brown; (*in photo*) c'est Mr Brown; (*on
telephone*) ici Mr Brown
♦ adv (*demonstrative*): **it was about this big**
c'était à peu près de cette grandeur or grand
comme ça; **I didn't know it was this bad** je ne
savais pas que c'était si or aussi mauvais

---

thistle ['θɪsl] n chardon m

thorn [θɔːn] n épine f

thorough ['θʌrə] adj (*search*) minu-
tieux(-euse); (*knowledge, research*) appro-
fondi(e); (*work, person*) consciencieux
(-euse); (*cleaning*) à fond; **~bred** n (*horse*)
pur-sang m inv; **~fare** n route f; **"no ~fare"**
"passage interdit"; **~ly** adv minutieusement;
en profondeur; à fond; (*very*) tout à fait

those [ðəuz] pl adj ces; (*not "these"*): **~ books**
ces livres-là ♦ pl pron ceux-là (celles-là)

though [ðəu] conj bien que +sub, quoique
+sub ♦ adv pourtant

thought [θɔːt] pt, pp of **think** ♦ n pensée f;
(*idea*) idée f; (*opinion*) avis m; **~ful** adj (*deep
in thought*) pensif(-ive); (*serious*) réfléchi(e);
(*considerate*) prévenant(e); **~less** adj

étourdi(e); qui manque de considération

thousand ['θauzənd] num mille; **two ~** deux
mille; **~s of** des milliers de; **~th** num millième

thrash [θræʃ] vt rouer de coups; donner une
correction à; (*defeat*) battre à plate couture;
~ about, **~ around** vi se débattre; **~ out** vt
débattre de

thread [θred] n fil m; (*TECH*) pas m, filetage m
♦ vt (*needle*) enfiler; **~bare** adj râpé(e),
élimé(e)

threat [θret] n menace f; **~en** vi menacer
♦ vt: **to ~en sb with sth/to do** menacer qn de
qch/de faire

three [θriː] num trois; **~-dimensional** adj à
trois dimensions; **~-piece suit** n complet m
(avec gilet); **~-piece suite** n salon m
comprenant un canapé et deux fauteuils
assortis; **~-ply** adj (*wool*) trois fils inv

threshold ['θreʃhəuld] n seuil m

threw [θruː] pt of **throw**

thrifty ['θrɪftɪ] adj économe

thrill [θrɪl] n (*excitement*) émotion f, sensation
forte; (*shudder*) frisson m ♦ vt (*audience*)
électriser; **to be ~ed** (*with gift etc*) être
ravi(e); **~er** n film m (or roman m or pièce f)
à suspense; **~ing** adj saisissant(e),
palpitant(e)

thrive [θraɪv] (*pt, pp* thrived) vi pousser, se
développer; (*business*) prospérer; **he ~s on it**
cela lui réussit; **thriving** adj (*business,
community*) prospère

throat [θrəut] n gorge f; **to have a sore ~**
avoir mal à la gorge

throb [θrɔb] vi (*heart*) palpiter; (*engine*)
vibrer; **my head is ~bing** j'ai des élancements
dans la tête

throes [θrəuz] npl: **in the ~ of** au beau milieu
de

throne [θrəun] n trône m

throng ['θrɔŋ] n foule f ♦ vt se presser dans

throttle ['θrɔtl] n (*AUT*) accélérateur m ♦ vt
étrangler

through [θruː] prep à travers; (*time*)
pendant, durant; (*by means of*) par, par
l'intermédiaire de; (*owing to*) à cause de
♦ adj (*ticket, train, passage*) direct(e) ♦ adv à
travers; **to put sb ~ to sb** (*BRIT: TEL*) passer qn
à qn; **to be ~** (*BRIT: TEL*) avoir la
communication; (*esp US: have finished*) avoir
fini; **to be ~ with sb** (*relationship*) avoir
rompu avec qn; **"no ~ road"** (*BRIT*)
"impasse"; **~out** prep (*place*) partout dans;
(*time*) durant tout(e) le (la) ♦ adv partout

throw [θrəu] (*pt threw, pp thrown*) n jet m;
(*SPORT*) lancer m ♦ vt lancer, jeter; (*SPORT*)
lancer; (*rider*) désarçonner; (*fig*)
décontenancer; **to ~ a party** donner une
réception; **~ away** vt jeter; **~ off** vt se
débarrasser de; **~ out** vt jeter; (*reject*) rejeter;

(*person*) mettre à la porte; ~ **up** *vi* vomir; **~away** *adj* à jeter; (*remark*) fait(e) en passant; **~-in** *n* (*SPORT*) remise *f* en jeu

thru [θru:] (*US*) = **through**

thrush [θrʌʃ] *n* (*bird*) grive *f*

thrust [θrʌst] (*pt, pp* **thrust**) *n* (*TECH*) poussée *f* ♦ *vt* pousser brusquement; (*push in*) enfoncer

thud [θʌd] *n* bruit sourd

thug [θʌg] *n* voyou *m*

thumb [θʌm] *n* (*ANAT*) pouce *m* ♦ *vt*: **to ~ a lift** faire de l'auto-stop, arrêter une voiture; **~ through** *vt* (*book*) feuilleter; **~tack** (*US*) *n* punaise *f* (*clou*)

thump [θʌmp] *n* grand coup; (*sound*) bruit sourd ♦ *vt* cogner sur ♦ *vi* cogner, battre fort

thunder ['θʌndər] *n* tonnerre *m* ♦ *vi* tonner; (*train etc*): **to ~ past** passer dans un grondement *or* un bruit de tonnerre; **~bolt** *n* foudre *f*; **~clap** *n* coup *m* de tonnerre; **~storm** *n* orage *m*; **~y** *adj* orageux(-euse)

Thursday ['θə:zdɪ] *n* jeudi *m*

thus [ðʌs] *adv* ainsi

thwart [θwɔ:t] *vt* contrecarrer

thyme [taɪm] *n* thym *m*

tiara [tɪ'ɑ:rə] *n* diadème *m*

tick [tɪk] *n* (*sound: of clock*) tic-tac *m*; (*mark*) coche *f*; (*ZOOL*) tique *f*; (*BRIT: inf*): **in a ~** dans une seconde ♦ *vi* faire tic-tac ♦ *vt* (*item on list*) cocher; **~ off** *vt* (*item on list*) cocher; (*person*) réprimander, attraper; **~ over** *vi* (*engine*) tourner au ralenti; (*fig*) aller *or* marcher doucettement

ticket ['tɪkɪt] *n* billet *m*; (*for bus, tube*) ticket *m*; (*in shop: on goods*) étiquette *f*; (*for library*) carte *f*; (*parking ~*) papillon *m*, p.-v. *m*; **~ collector**, **~ inspector** *n* contrôleur(-euse); **~ office** *n* guichet *m*, bureau *m* de vente des billets

tickle ['tɪkl] *vt, vi* chatouiller; **ticklish** *adj* (*person*) chatouilleux(-euse); (*problem*) épineux(-euse)

tidal ['taɪdl] *adj* (*force*) de la marée; (*estuary*) à marée; **~ wave** *n* raz-de-marée *m inv*

tidbit ['tɪdbɪt] (*US*) *n* = **titbit**

tiddlywinks ['tɪdlɪwɪŋks] *n* jeu *m* de puce

tide [taɪd] *n* marée *f*; (*fig: of events*) cours *m* ♦ *vt*: **to ~ sb over** dépanner qn; **high/low ~** marée haute/basse

tidy ['taɪdɪ] *adj* (*room*) bien rangé(e); (*dress, work*) net(te), soigné(e); (*person*) ordonné(e), qui a de l'ordre ♦ *vt* (*also: ~ up*) ranger

tie [taɪ] *n* (*string etc*) cordon *m*; (*BRIT: also: necktie*) cravate *f*; (*fig: link*) lien *m*; (*SPORT: draw*) égalité *f* de points; match nul ♦ *vt* (*parcel*) attacher; (*ribbon, shoelaces*) nouer ♦ *vi* (*SPORT*) faire match nul; finir à égalité de points; **to ~ sth in a bow** faire un nœud à *or*

avec qch; **to ~ a knot in sth** faire un nœud à qch; **~ down** *vt* (*fig*): **to ~ sb down (to)** contraindre qn (à accepter); **to be ~d down** (*by relationship*) se fixer; **~ up** *vt* (*parcel*) ficeler; (*dog, boat*) attacher; (*prisoner*) ligoter; (*arrangements*) conclure; **to be ~d up** (*busy*) être pris(e) *or* occupé(e)

tier [tɪər] *n* gradin *m*; (*of cake*) étage *m*

tiger ['taɪgər] *n* tigre *m*

tight [taɪt] *adj* (*rope*) tendu(e), raide; (*clothes*) étroit(e), très juste; (*budget, programme, bend*) serré(e); (*control*) strict(e), sévère; (*inf: drunk*) ivre, rond(e) ♦ *adv* (*squeeze*) très fort; (*shut*) hermétiquement, bien; **~en** *vt* (*rope*) tendre; (*screw*) resserrer; (*control*) renforcer ♦ *vi* se tendre, se resserrer; **~fisted** *adj* avare; **~ly** *adv* (*grasp*) bien, très fort; **~rope** *n* corde *f* raide; **~s** (*BRIT*) *npl* collant *m*

tile [taɪl] *n* (*on roof*) tuile *f*; (*on wall or floor*) carreau *m*; **~d** *adj* en tuiles; carrelé(e)

till [tɪl] *n* caisse (enregistreuse) ♦ *vt* (*land*) cultiver ♦ *prep, conj* = **until**

tiller ['tɪlər] *n* (*NAUT*) barre *f* (du gouvernail)

tilt [tɪlt] *vt* pencher, incliner ♦ *vi* pencher, être incliné(e)

timber ['tɪmbər] *n* (*material*) bois *m* (de construction); (*trees*) arbres *mpl*

time [taɪm] *n* temps *m*; (*epoch: often pl*) époque *f*, temps *m*; (*by clock*) heure *f*; (*moment*) moment *m*; (*occasion, also MATH*) fois *f*; (*MUS*) mesure *f* ♦ *vt* (*race*) chronométrer; (*programme*) minuter; (*visit*) fixer; (*remark etc*) choisir le moment de; **a long ~** un long moment, longtemps; **for the ~ being** pour le moment; **4 at a ~** 4 à la fois; **from ~ to ~** de temps en temps; **at ~s** parfois; **in ~** (*soon enough*) à temps; (*after some ~*) avec le temps, à la longue; (*MUS*) en mesure; **in a week's ~** dans une semaine; **in no ~** en un rien de temps; **any ~** n'importe quand; **on ~** à l'heure; **5 ~s 5** 5 fois 5; **what ~ is it?** quelle heure est-il?; **to have a good ~** bien s'amuser; **~ bomb** *n* bombe *f* à retardement; **~ lag** (*BRIT*) *n* décalage *m*; (*in travel*) décalage horaire; **~less** *adj* éternel(le); **~ly** *adj* opportun(e); **~ off** *n* temps *m* libre; **~r** *n* (*TECH*) minuteur *m*; (*in kitchen*) compte-minutes *m inv*; **~scale** *n* délais *mpl*; **~-share** *n* maison *f*/appartement *m* en multipropriété; **~ switch** (*BRIT*) *n* minuteur *m*; (*for lighting*) minuterie *f*; **~table** *n* (*RAIL*) (indicateur *m*) horaire *m*; (*SCOL*) emploi *m* du temps; **~ zone** *n* fuseau *m* horaire

timid ['tɪmɪd] *adj* timide; (*easily scared*) peureux(-euse)

timing ['taɪmɪŋ] *n* minutage *m*; chronométrage *m*; **the ~ of his resignation** le moment choisi pour sa démission

timpani ['tɪmpənɪ] *npl* timbales *fpl*

tin [tɪn] *n* étain *m*; (*also:* ~ **plate**) fer-blanc *m*; (*BRIT: can*) boîte *f* (de conserve); (*for storage*) boîte *f*; ~**foil** *n* papier *m* d'étain *or* aluminium

tinge [tɪndʒ] *n* nuance *f* ♦ *vt:* ~**d with** teinté(e) de

tingle ['tɪŋgl] *vi* picoter; (*person*) avoir des picotements

tinker ['tɪŋkə*] *n* (*gipsy*) romanichel *m*; ~ **with** *vt fus* bricoler, rafistoler

tinkle ['tɪŋkl] *vi* tinter

tinned [tɪnd] (*BRIT*) *adj* (*food*) en boîte, en conserve

tin opener [-'əupnə*] (*BRIT*) *n* ouvre-boîte(s) *m*

tinsel ['tɪnsl] *n* guirlandes *fpl* de Noël (*argentées*)

tint [tɪnt] *n* teinte *f*; (*for hair*) shampooing colorant; ~**ed** *adj* (*hair*) teint(e); (*spectacles, glass*) teinté(e)

tiny ['taɪnɪ] *adj* minuscule

tip [tɪp] *n* (*end*) bout *m*; (*gratuity*) pourboire *m*; (*BRIT: for rubbish*) décharge *f*; (*advice*) tuyau *m* ♦ *vt* (*waiter*) donner un pourboire à; (*tilt*) incliner; (*overturn: also:* ~ **over**) renverser; (*empty: also:* ~ **out**) déverser; ~**off** *n* (*hint*) tuyau *m*; ~**ped** (*BRIT*) *adj* (*cigarette*) (à bout) filtre *inv*

tipsy ['tɪpsɪ] (*inf*) *adj* un peu ivre, éméché(e)

tiptoe ['tɪptəu] *n:* **on** ~ sur la pointe des pieds

tiptop [tɪp'tɒp] *adj:* **in** ~ **condition** en excellent état

tire ['taɪə*] *n* (*US*) = **tyre** ♦ *vt* fatiguer ♦ *vi* se fatiguer; ~**d** *adj* fatigué(e); **to be** ~**d of** en avoir assez de, être las (lasse) de; ~**less** *adj* (*person*) infatigable; (*efforts*) inlassable; ~**some** *adj* ennuyeux(-euse); **tiring** *adj* fatigant(e)

tissue ['tɪʃuː] *n* tissu *m*; (*paper handkerchief*) mouchoir *m* en papier, kleenex ® *m*; ~ **paper** *n* papier *m* de soie

tit [tɪt] *n* (*bird*) mésange *f*; **to give** ~ **for tat** rendre la pareille

titbit ['tɪtbɪt] *n* (*food*) friandise *f*; (*news*) potin *m*

title ['taɪtl] *n* titre *m*; ~ **deed** *n* (*LAW*) titre (constitutif) de propriété; ~ **role** *n* rôle principal

TM *abbr* = **trademark**

KEYWORD

to [tuː, tə] *prep* **1** (*direction*) à; **to go to France/Portugal/London/school** aller en France/au Portugal/à Londres/à l'école; **to go to Claude's/the doctor's** aller chez Claude/le docteur; **the road to Edinburgh** la route d'Édimbourg

2 (*as far as*) (jusqu')à; **to count to 10** compter jusqu'à 10; **from 40 to 50 people** de 40 à 50 personnes

3 (*with expressions of time*): **a quarter to 5** 5 heures moins le quart; **it's twenty to 3** il est 3 heures moins vingt

4 (*for, of*): **the key to the front door** la clé de la porte d'entrée; **a letter to his wife** une lettre (adressée) à sa femme

5 (*expressing indirect object*) à; **to give sth to sb** donner qch à qn; **to talk to sb** parler à qn

6 (*in relation to*) à; **3 goals to 2** 3 (buts) à 2; **30 miles to the gallon** 9,4 litres aux cent (km)

7 (*purpose, result*): **to come to sb's aid** venir au secours de qn, porter secours à qn; **to sentence sb to death** condamner qn à mort; **to my surprise** à ma grande surprise

♦ *with vb* **1** (*simple infinitive*): **to go/eat** aller/manger

2 (*following another vb*): **to want/try/start to do** vouloir/essayer de/commencer à faire

3 (*with vb omitted*): **I don't want to** je ne veux pas

4 (*purpose, result*) pour; **I did it to help you** je l'ai fait pour vous aider

5 (*equivalent to relative clause*): **I have things to do** j'ai des choses à faire; **the main thing is to try** l'important est d'essayer

6 (*after adjective etc*): **ready to go** prêt(e) à partir; **too old/young to ...** trop vieux/jeune pour ...

♦ *adv:* **push/pull the door to** tirez/poussez la porte

toad [təud] *n* crapaud *m*

toadstool ['təudstuːl] *n* champignon (vénéneux)

toast [təust] *n* (*CULIN*) pain grillé, toast *m*; (*drink, speech*) toast ♦ *vt* (*CULIN*) faire griller; (*drink to*) porter un toast à; ~**er** *n* grille-pain *m inv*

tobacco [tə'bækəu] *n* tabac *m*; ~**nist** *n* marchand(e) de tabac; ~**nist's (shop)** *n* (bureau *m* de) tabac *m*

toboggan [tə'bɒgən] *n* toboggan *m*; (*child's*) luge *f* ♦ *vi:* **to go** ~**ing** faire de la luge

today [tə'deɪ] *adv* (*also fig*) aujourd'hui ♦ *n* aujourd'hui *m*

toddler ['tɒdlə*] *n* enfant *m/f* qui commence à marcher, bambin *m*

toe [təu] *n* doigt *m* de pied, orteil *m*; (*of shoe*) bout *m* ♦ *vt:* **to** ~ **the line** (*fig*) obéir, se conformer; ~**nail** *n* ongle *m* du pied

toffee ['tɒfɪ] *n* caramel *m*; ~ **apple** (*BRIT*) *n* pomme caramélisée

together [tə'geðə*] *adv* ensemble; (*at same time*) en même temps; ~ **with** avec

toil [tɔɪl] *n* dur travail, labeur *m* ♦ *vi* peiner

toilet ['tɔɪlət] *n* (*BRIT: lavatory*) toilettes *fpl* ♦ *cpd* (*accessories etc*) de toilette; ~ **bag** *n* nécessaire *m* de toilette; ~ **paper** *n* papier *m* hygiénique; ~**ries** *npl* articles *mpl* de toilette;

~ roll n rouleau m de papier hygiénique

token ['təukən] n (sign) marque f, témoignage m; (metal disc) jeton m ♦ adj (strike, payment etc) symbolique; **book/record ~** (BRIT) chèque-livre/-disque m; **gift ~** bon-cadeau m

told [təuld] pt, pp of tell

tolerable ['tɔlərəbl] adj (bearable) tolérable; (fairly good) passable

tolerant ['tɔlərnt] adj: **~ (of)** tolérant(e) (à l'égard de)

tolerate ['tɔləreɪt] vt supporter, tolérer

toll [təul] n (tax, charge) péage m ♦ vi (bell) sonner; **the accident ~ on the roads** le nombre des victimes de la route

tomato [tə'mɑːtəu] (pl **~es**) n tomate f

tomb [tuːm] n tombe f

tomboy ['tɔmbɔɪ] n garçon manqué

tombstone ['tuːmstəun] n pierre tombale

tomcat ['tɔmkæt] n matou m

tomorrow [tə'mɔrəu] adv (also fig) demain ♦ n demain m; **the day after ~** après-demain; **~ morning** demain matin

ton [tʌn] n tonne f (BRIT = 1016kg; US = 907kg); (metric) tonne (= 1000 kg); **~s of** (inf) des tas de

tone [təun] n ton m ♦ vi (also: **~ in**) s'harmoniser; **~ down** vt (colour, criticism) adoucir; (sound) baisser; **~ up** vt (muscles) tonifier; **~-deaf** adj qui n'a pas d'oreille

tongs [tɔŋz] npl (for coal) pincettes fpl; (for hair) fer m à friser

tongue [tʌŋ] n langue f; **~ in cheek** ironiquement; **~-tied** adj (fig) muet(te); **~ twister** n phrase f très difficile à prononcer

tonic ['tɔnɪk] n (MED) tonique m; (also: **~ water**) tonic m, Schweppes ® m

tonight [tə'naɪt] adv, n cette nuit; (this evening) ce soir

tonsil ['tɔnsl] n amygdale f; **~litis** [tɔnsɪ'laɪtɪs] n angine f

too [tuː] adv (excessively) trop; (also) aussi; **~ much** adv trop ♦ adj trop de; **~ many** trop de; **~ bad!** tant pis!

took [tuk] pt of take

tool [tuːl] n outil m; **~ box** n boîte f à outils

toot [tuːt] n (of car horn) coup m de klaxon; (of whistle) coup de sifflet ♦ vi (with car horn) klaxonner

tooth [tuːθ] (pl **teeth**) n (ANAT, TECH) dent f; **~ache** n mal m de dents; **~brush** n brosse f à dents; **~paste** n (pâte f) dentifrice m; **~pick** n cure-dent m

top [tɔp] n (of mountain, head) sommet m; (of page, ladder, garment) haut m; (of box, cupboard, table) dessus m; (lid: of box, jar) couvercle m; (: of bottle) bouchon m; (toy) toupie f ♦ adj du haut; (in rank) pre-mier(-ère); (best) meilleur(e) ♦ vt (exceed)

dépasser; (be first in) être en tête de; **on ~ of** sur; (in addition to) en plus de; **from ~ to bottom** de fond en comble; **~ up** (US **~ off**) vt (bottle) remplir; (salary) compléter; **~ floor** n dernier étage; **~ hat** n haut-de-forme m; **~-heavy** adj (object) trop lourd(e) du haut

topic ['tɔpɪk] n sujet m, thème m; **~al** adj d'actualité

top: ~less adj (bather etc) aux seins nus; **~level** adj (talks) au plus haut niveau; **~most** adj le (la) plus haut(e)

topple ['tɔpl] vt renverser, faire tomber ♦ vi basculer; tomber

top-secret ['tɔp'siːkrɪt] adj top secret(-ète)

topsy-turvy ['tɔpsɪ'tɜːvɪ] adj, adv sens dessus dessous

torch [tɔːtʃ] n torche f; (BRIT: electric) lampe f de poche

tore [tɔːr] pt of tear[1]

torment [n 'tɔːment, vb tɔː'ment] n tourment m ♦ vt tourmenter; (fig: annoy) harceler

torn [tɔːn] pp of tear[1]

tornado [tɔː'neɪdəu] (pl **~es**) n tornade f

torpedo [tɔː'piːdəu] (pl **~es**) n torpille f

torrent ['tɔrnt] n torrent m; **~ial** [tɔ'renʃl] adj torrentiel(le)

tortoise ['tɔːtəs] n tortue f; **~shell** adj en écaille

torture ['tɔːtʃər] n torture f ♦ vt torturer

Tory ['tɔːrɪ] (BRIT: POL) adj, n tory (m/f), conservateur(-trice)

toss [tɔs] vt lancer, jeter; (pancake) faire sauter; (head) rejeter en arrière; **to ~ a coin** jouer à pile ou face; **to ~ up for sth** jouer qch à pile ou face; **to ~ and turn** (in bed) se tourner et se retourner

tot [tɔt] n (BRIT: drink) petit verre; (child) bambin m

total ['təutl] adj total(e) ♦ n total m ♦ vt (add up) faire le total de, additionner; (amount to) s'élever à; **~ly** adv totalement

totter ['tɔtər] vi chanceler

touch [tʌtʃ] n contact m, toucher m; (sense, also skill: of pianist etc) toucher ♦ vt toucher; (tamper with) toucher à; **a ~ of** (fig) un petit peu de; une touche de; **to get in ~ with** prendre contact avec; **to lose ~** (friends) se perdre de vue; **~ on** vt fus (topic) effleurer, aborder; **~ up** vt (paint) retoucher; **~-and-go** adj incertain(e); **~down** n atterrissage m; (on sea) amerrissage m; (US: FOOTBALL) touché-en-but m; **~ed** adj (moved) touché(e); **~ing** adj touchant(e), attendrissant(e); **~line** n (SPORT) (ligne f de) touche f; **~y** adj (person) susceptible

tough [tʌf] adj dur(e); (resistant) résistant(e), solide; (meat) dur, coriace; (firm) inflexible; (task) dur, pénible; **~en** vt (character) endurcir; (glass etc) renforcer

toupee ['tu:peɪ] n postiche m

tour [tʊəʳ] n voyage m; (also: **package ~**) voyage organisé; (of town, museum) tour m, visite f; (by artist) tournée f ♦ vt visiter; **~ guide** n (person) guide m/f

tourism ['tʊərɪzm] n tourisme m

tourist ['tʊərɪst] n touriste m/f ♦ cpd touristique; **~ office** n syndicat m d'initiative

tournament ['tʊənəmənt] n tournoi m

tousled ['taʊzld] adj (hair) ébouriffé(e)

tout [taʊt] vi: **to ~** for essayer de raccrocher, racoler ♦ n (also: **ticket ~**) revendeur m de billets

tow [təʊ] vt remorquer; (caravan, trailer) tracter; "**on ~**" (BRIT) or "**in ~**" (US) (AUT) "véhicule en remorque"

toward(s) [tə'wɔ:d(z)] prep vers; (of attitude) envers, à l'égard de; (of purpose) pour

towel ['taʊəl] n serviette f (de toilette); **~ling** n (fabric) tissu éponge m; **~ rail** (US **towel rack**) n porte-serviettes m inv

tower ['taʊəʳ] n tour f; **~ block** (BRIT) n tour f (d'habitation); **~ing** adj très haut(e), imposant(e)

town [taʊn] n ville f; **to go to ~** aller en ville; (fig) y mettre le paquet; **~ centre** n centre m de la ville, centre-ville m; **~ council** n conseil municipal; **~ hall** n ≈ mairie f; **~ plan** n plan m de ville; **~ planning** n urbanisme m

towrope ['təʊrəʊp] n (câble m de) remorque f

tow truck (US) n dépanneuse f

toy [tɔɪ] n jouet m; **~ with** vt fus jouer avec; (idea) caresser

trace [treɪs] n trace f ♦ vt (draw) tracer, dessiner; (follow) suivre la trace de; (locate) retrouver; **tracing paper** n papier-calque m

track [træk] n (mark) trace f; (path: gen) chemin m, piste f; (: of bullet etc) trajectoire f; (: of suspect, animal) piste f; (RAIL) voie ferrée, rails mpl; (on tape, SPORT) piste; (on record) plage f ♦ vt suivre la trace or la piste de; **to keep ~** of suivre; **~ down** vt (prey) trouver et capturer; (sth lost) finir par retrouver; **~suit** n survêtement m

tract [trækt] n (of land) étendue f

traction ['trækʃən] n traction f; (MED): **in ~** en extension

tractor ['træktəʳ] n tracteur m

trade [treɪd] n commerce m; (skill, job) métier m ♦ vi faire du commerce ♦ vt (exchange): **to ~ sth (for sth)** échanger qch (contre qch); **~ in** vt (old car etc) faire reprendre; **~ fair** n foire(-exposition) commerciale; **~-in price** n prix m à la reprise; **~mark** n marque f de fabrique; **~ name** n nom m de marque; **~r** n commerçant(e), négociant(e); **~sman** (irreg)

n (shopkeeper) commerçant; **~ union** n syndicat m; **~ unionist** n syndicaliste m/f

tradition [trə'dɪʃən] n tradition f; **~al** adj traditionnel(le)

traffic ['træfɪk] n trafic m; (cars) circulation f ♦ vi: **to ~ in** (pej: liquor, drugs) faire le trafic de; **~ calming** n ralentissement m de la circulation; **~ circle** (US) n rond-point m; **~ jam** n embouteillage m; **~ lights** npl feux mpl (de signalisation); **~ warden** n contractuel(le)

tragedy ['trædʒədɪ] n tragédie f

tragic ['trædʒɪk] adj tragique

trail [treɪl] n (tracks) trace f, piste f; (path) chemin m, piste; (of smoke etc) traînée f ♦ vt traîner, tirer; (follow) suivre ♦ vi traîner; (in game, contest) être en retard; **~ behind** vi traîner, être à la traîne; **~er** n (AUT) remorque f; (US) caravane f; (CINEMA) bande-annonce f; **~er truck** (US) n (camion m) semi-remorque m

train [treɪn] n train m; (in underground) rame f; (of dress) traîne f ♦ vt (apprentice, doctor etc) former; (sportsman) entraîner; (dog) dresser; (memory) exercer; (point: gun etc): **to ~ sth on** braquer qch sur ♦ vi suivre une formation; (SPORT) s'entraîner; **~ of thought** le fil de sa pensée; **~ed** adj qualifié(e), qui a reçu une formation; (animal) dressé(e); **~ee** [treɪ'ni:] n stagiaire m/f; (in trade) apprenti(e); **~er** n (SPORT: coach) entraîneur(-euse); (: shoe) chaussure f de sport; (of dogs etc) dresseur(-euse); **~ing** n formation f; entraînement m; **in ~ing** (SPORT) à l'entraînement; (fit) en forme; **~ing college** n école professionnelle; (for teachers) ≈ école normale; **~ing shoes** npl chaussures fpl de sport

trait [treɪt] n trait m (de caractère)

traitor ['treɪtəʳ] n traître m

tram [træm] (BRIT) n (also: **~car**) tram(way) m

tramp [træmp] n (person) vagabond(e), clochard(e); (inf: pej: woman): **to be a ~** être coureuse ♦ vi marcher d'un pas lourd

trample ['træmpl] vt: **to ~ (underfoot)** piétiner

trampoline ['træmpəli:n] n trampoline m

tranquil ['træŋkwɪl] adj tranquille; **~lizer** (US **tranquilizer**) n (MED) tranquillisant m

transact [træn'zækt] vt (business) traiter; **~ion** n transaction f

transatlantic ['trænzət'læntɪk] adj transatlantique

transfer [n 'trænsfəʳ, vb træns'fə:ʳ] n (gen, also SPORT) transfert m; (POL: of power) passation f; (picture, design) décalcomanie f; (: stick-on) autocollant m ♦ vt transférer; passer; **to ~ the charges** (BRIT: TEL) téléphoner en P.C.V.; **~ desk** n (AVIAT) guichet m de transit

transform [træns'fɔ:m] vt transformer

transfusion [træns'fju:ʒən] n transfusion f

transient ['trænzıənt] adj transitoire, éphémère

transistor [træn'zıstər] n (~ radio) transistor m

transit ['trænzıt] n: **in ~** en transit

transitive ['trænzıtıv] adj (LING) transitif(-ive)

transit lounge n salle f de transit

translate [trænz'leıt] vt traduire; **translation** n traduction f; **translator** n traducteur(-trice)

transmission [trænz'mıʃən] n transmission f

transmit [trænz'mıt] vt transmettre; (RADIO, TV) émettre

transparency [træns'peərnsı] n (of glass etc) transparence f; (BRIT: PHOT) diapositive f

transparent [træns'pærnt] adj transparent(e)

transpire [træns'paıər] vi (turn out): **it ~d that ...** on a appris que ...; (happen) arriver

transplant [vb træns'plɑ:nt, n 'trænsplɑ:nt] vt transplanter; (seedlings) repiquer ♦ n (MED) transplantation f

transport [n 'trænspɔ:t, vb træns'pɔ:t] n transport m; (car) moyen m de transport, voiture f ♦ vt transporter; **~ation** ['trænspɔ:'teıʃən] n transport m; (means of transportation) moyen m de transport; **~ café** (BRIT) n ≈ restaurant m de routiers

trap [træp] n (snare, trick) piège m; (carriage) cabriolet m ♦ vt prendre au piège; (confine) coincer; **~ door** n trappe f

trapeze [trə'pi:z] n trapèze m

trappings ['træpıŋz] npl ornements mpl; attributs mpl

trash [træʃ] (pej) n (goods) camelote f; (nonsense) sottises fpl; **~ can** (US) n poubelle f; **~y** (inf) adj de camelote; (novel) de quatre sous

trauma ['trɔ:mə] n traumatisme m; **~tic** [trɔ:'mætık] adj traumatisant(e)

travel ['trævl] n voyage(s) m(pl) ♦ vi voyager; (news, sound) circuler, se propager ♦ vt (distance) parcourir; **~ agency** n agence f de voyages; **~ agent** n agent m de voyages; **~ler** (US traveler) n voyageur(-euse); **~ler's cheque** (US traveler's check) n chèque m de voyage; **~ling** (US traveling) n voyage(s) m(pl); **~ sickness** n mal m de la route (or de mer or de l'air)

trawler ['trɔ:lər] n chalutier m

tray [treı] n (for carrying) plateau m; (on desk) corbeille f

treacherous ['tretʃərəs] adj (person, look) traître(-esse); (ground, tide) dont il faut se méfier

treacle ['tri:kl] n mélasse f

tread [tred] (pt trod, pp trodden) n pas m; (sound) bruit m de pas; (of tyre) chape f, bande f de roulement ♦ vi marcher; **~ on** vt fus marcher sur

treason ['tri:zn] n trahison f

treasure ['treʒər] n trésor m ♦ vt (value) tenir beaucoup à; **~r** n trésorier(-ère); **treasury** n: **the Treasury, (US) the Treasury Department** le ministère des Finances

treat [tri:t] n petit cadeau, petite surprise ♦ vt traiter; **to ~ sb to sth** offrir qch à qn

treatment ['tri:tmənt] n traitement m

treaty ['tri:tı] n traité m

treble ['trebl] adj triple ♦ vt, vi tripler; **~ clef** n (MUS) clé f de sol

tree [tri:] n arbre m

trek [trek] n (long) voyage; (on foot) (longue) marche, tirée f

tremble ['trembl] vi trembler

tremendous [trı'mendəs] adj (enormous) énorme, fantastique; (excellent) formidable

tremor ['tremər] n tremblement m; (also: **earth ~**) secousse f sismique

trench [trentʃ] n tranchée f

trend [trend] n (tendency) tendance f; (of events) cours m; (fashion) mode f; **~y** adj (idea, person) dans le vent; (clothes) dernier cri inv

trespass ['trespəs] vi: **to ~ on** s'introduire sans permission dans; **"no ~ing"** "propriété privée", "défense d'entrer"

trestle ['tresl] n tréteau m

trial ['traıəl] n (LAW) procès m, jugement m; (test: of machine etc) essai m; **~s** npl (unpleasant experiences) épreuves fpl; **to be on ~** (LAW) passer en jugement; **by ~ and error** par tâtonnements; **~ period** n période f d'essai

triangle ['traıæŋgl] n (MATH, MUS) triangle m; **triangular** [traı'æŋgjulər] adj triangulaire

tribe [traıb] n tribu f; **~sman** (irreg) n membre m d'une tribu

tribunal [traı'bju:nl] n tribunal m

tributary ['trıbjutərı] n (river) affluent m

tribute ['trıbju:t] n tribut m, hommage m; **to pay ~ to** rendre hommage à

trick [trık] n (magic ~) tour m; (joke, prank) tour, farce f; (skill, knack) astuce f, truc m; (CARDS) levée f ♦ vt attraper, rouler; **to play a ~ on sb** jouer un tour à qn; **that should do the ~** ça devrait faire l'affaire; **~ery** n ruse f

trickle ['trıkl] n (of water etc) filet m ♦ vi couler en un filet or goutte à goutte

tricky ['trıkı] adj difficile, délicat(e)

tricycle ['traısıkl] n tricycle m

trifle ['traıfl] n bagatelle f; (CULIN) ≈ diplomate m ♦ adv: **a ~ long** un peu long; **trifling** adj insignifiant(e)

trigger ['trıgər] n (of gun) gâchette f; **~ off** vt

déclencher

trim [trɪm] adj (house, garden) bien tenu(e); (figure) svelte ♦ n (haircut etc) légère coupe; (on car) garnitures fpl ♦ vt (cut) couper légèrement; (NAUT: a sail) gréer; (decorate): **to ~ (with)** décorer (de); **~mings** npl (CULIN) garniture f

trinket ['trɪŋkɪt] n bibelot m; (piece of jewellery) colifichet m

trip [trɪp] n voyage m; (excursion) excursion f; (stumble) faux pas ♦ vi faire un faux pas, trébucher; **on a ~** en voyage; **~ up** vi trébucher ♦ vt faire un croc-en-jambe à

tripe [traɪp] n (CULIN) tripes fpl; (pej: rubbish) idioties fpl

triple ['trɪpl] adj triple; **~ts** npl triplés(-ées)

triplicate ['trɪplɪkət] n: **in triplicate** en trois exemplaires

tripod ['traɪpɔd] n trépied m

trite [traɪt] (pej) adj banal(e)

triumph ['traɪʌmf] n triomphe m ♦ vi: **to ~ (over)** triompher (de)

trivia ['trɪvɪə] (pej) npl futilités fpl; **~l** adj insignifiant(e); (commonplace) banal(e)

trod [trɔd] pt of **tread**; **~den** pp of **tread**

trolley ['trɔlɪ] n chariot m

trombone [trɔm'bəun] n trombone m

troop [truːp] n bande f, groupe m ♦ vi: **~ in/out** entrer/sortir en groupe; **~s** npl (MIL) troupes fpl; (: men) hommes mpl, soldats mpl; **~ing the colour** (BRIT) (ceremony) le salut au drapeau

trophy ['trəufɪ] n trophée m

tropic ['trɔpɪk] n tropique m; **~al** adj tropical(e)

trot [trɔt] n trot m ♦ vi trotter; **on the ~** (BRIT: fig) d'affilée

trouble ['trʌbl] n difficulté(s) f(pl), problème(s) m(pl); (worry) ennuis mpl, soucis mpl; (bother, effort) peine f; (POL) troubles mpl; (MED): **stomach etc ~** troubles gastriques etc ♦ vt (disturb) déranger, gêner; (worry) inquiéter ♦ vi: **to ~ to do** prendre la peine de faire; **~s** npl (POL etc) troubles mpl; (personal) ennuis, soucis; **to be in ~** avoir des ennuis; (ship, climber etc) être en difficulté; **what's the ~?** qu'est-ce qui ne va pas?; **~d** adj (person) inquiet(-ète); (epoch, life) agité(e); **~maker** n élément perturbateur, fauteur m de troubles; **~shooter** n (in conflict) médiateur m; **~some** adj (child) fatigant(e), difficile; (cough etc) gênant(e)

trough [trɔf] n (also: drinking ~) abreuvoir m; (also: feeding ~) auge f; (depression) creux m

trousers ['trauzəz] npl pantalon m; **short ~** culottes courtes

trout [traut] n inv truite f

trowel ['trauəl] n truelle f; (garden tool) déplantoir m

truant ['truənt] (BRIT) n: **to play ~** faire l'école buissonnière

truce [truːs] n trêve f

truck [trʌk] n camion m; (RAIL) wagon m à plate-forme; **~ driver** n camionneur m; **~ farm** (US) n jardin maraîcher

true [truː] adj vrai(e); (accurate) exact(e); (genuine) vrai, véritable; (faithful) fidèle; **to come ~** se réaliser

truffle ['trʌfl] n truffe f

truly ['truːlɪ] adv vraiment, réellement; (truthfully) sans mentir; see also **yours**

trump [trʌmp] n (also: **~ card**) atout m

trumpet ['trʌmpɪt] n trompette f

truncheon ['trʌntʃən] (BRIT) n bâton m (d'agent de police); matraque f

trundle ['trʌndl] vt, vi: **to ~ along** rouler lentement (et bruyamment)

trunk [trʌŋk] n (of tree, person) tronc m; (of elephant) trompe f; (case) malle f; (US: AUT) coffre m; **~s** npl (also: **swimming ~s**) maillot m or slip m de bain

truss [trʌs] vt: **to ~ (up)** ligoter

trust [trʌst] n confiance f; (responsibility) charge f; (LAW) fidéicommis m ♦ vt (rely on) avoir confiance en; (hope) espérer; (entrust): **to ~ sth to sb** confier qch à qn; **to take sth on ~** accepter qch les yeux fermés; **~ed** adj en qui l'on a confiance; **~ee** [trʌs'tiː] n (LAW) fidéicommissaire m/f; (of school etc) administrateur(-trice); **~ful, ~ing** adj confiant(e); (answer) sincère

truth [truːθ] n vérité f; **~ful** adj (person) qui dit la vérité; (answer) sincère

try [traɪ] n essai m, tentative f; (RUGBY) essai ♦ vt (attempt) essayer, tenter; (test: sth new: also: **~ out**) essayer, tester; (LAW: person) juger; (strain) éprouver ♦ vi essayer; **to have a ~** essayer; **to ~ to do** essayer de faire; (seek) chercher à faire; **~ on** vt (clothes) essayer; **~ing** adj pénible

T-shirt ['tiːʃəːt] n tee-shirt m

T-square ['tiːskwɛə'] n équerre f en T, té m

tub [tʌb] n cuve f; (for washing clothes) baquet m; (bath) baignoire f

tubby ['tʌbɪ] adj rondelet(te)

tube [tjuːb] n tube m; (BRIT: underground) métro m; (for tyre) chambre f à air

tuberculosis [tjubəːkju'ləusɪs] n tuberculose f

TUC n abbr (BRIT: Trades Union Congress) confédération des syndicats britanniques

tuck [tʌk] vt (put) mettre; **~ away** vt cacher, ranger; **~ in** vt rentrer; (child) border ♦ vi (eat) manger (de bon appétit); **~ up** vt (child) border; **~ shop** (BRIT) n boutique f à provisions (dans une école)

Tuesday ['tjuːzdɪ] n mardi m

tuft [tʌft] n touffe f

tug [tʌg] n (ship) remorqueur m ♦ vt tirer (sur); **~-of-war** n lutte f à la corde; (fig) lutte acharnée

tuition [tjuːˈɪʃən] n (BRIT) leçons fpl; (: private ~) cours particuliers; (US: school fees) frais mpl de scolarité

tulip [ˈtjuːlɪp] n tulipe f

tumble [ˈtʌmbl] n (fall) chute f, culbute f ♦ vi tomber, dégringoler; **to ~ to sth** (inf) réaliser qch; **~down** adj délabré(e); **~ dryer** (BRIT) n séchoir m à air chaud

tumbler [ˈtʌmblər] n (glass) verre (droit), gobelet m

tummy [ˈtʌmɪ] (inf) n ventre m; **~ upset** n maux mpl de ventre

tumour [ˈtjuːmər] (US tumor) n tumeur f

tuna [ˈtjuːnə] n inv (also: ~ fish) thon m

tune [tjuːn] n (melody) air m ♦ vt (MUS) accorder; (RADIO, TV, AUT) régler; **to be in/out of ~** (instrument) être accordé/désaccordé; (singer) chanter juste/faux; **to be in/out of ~ with** (fig) être en accord/désaccord avec; **~ in** vi (RADIO, TV): **to ~ in (to)** se mettre à l'écoute (de); **~ up** vi (musician) accorder son instrument; **~ful** adj mélodieux(-euse); **~r** n: **piano ~r** accordeur m (de pianos)

tunic [ˈtjuːnɪk] n tunique f

Tunisia [tjuːˈnɪzɪə] n Tunisie f

tunnel [ˈtʌnl] n tunnel m; (in mine) galerie f ♦ vi percer un tunnel

turbulence [ˈtɜːbjʊləns] n (AVIAT) turbulence f

tureen [təˈriːn] n (for soup) soupière f; (for vegetables) légumier m

turf [tɜːf] n gazon m; (clod) motte f (de gazon) ♦ vt gazonner; **~ out** (inf) vt (person) jeter dehors

Turk [tɜːk] n Turc (Turque)

Turkey [ˈtɜːkɪ] n Turquie f

turkey [ˈtɜːkɪ] n dindon m, dinde f

Turkish [ˈtɜːkɪʃ] adj turc (turque) ♦ n (LING) turc m

turmoil [ˈtɜːmɔɪl] n trouble m, bouleversement m; **in ~** en émoi, en effervescence

turn [tɜːn] n tour m; (in road) tournant m; (of mind, events) tournure f; (performance) numéro m; (MED) crise f, attaque f ♦ vt tourner; (collar, steak) retourner; (change): **to ~ sth into** changer qch en ♦ vi (object, wind, milk) tourner; (person: look back) se (re)tourner; (reverse direction) faire demi-tour; (become) devenir; (age) atteindre; **to ~ into** se changer en; **a good ~** un service; **it gave me quite a ~** ça m'a fait un coup; **"no left ~"** (AUT) "défense de tourner à gauche"; **it's your ~** c'est (à) votre tour; **in ~** à son tour; à tour de rôle; **to take ~s (at)** se relayer (pour or à); **~ away** vi se détourner ♦ vt

(applicants) refuser; **~ back** vi revenir, faire demi-tour ♦ vt (person, vehicle) faire faire demi-tour à; (clock) reculer; **~ down** vt (refuse) rejeter, refuser; (reduce) baisser; (fold) rabattre; **~ in** vi (inf: go to bed) aller se coucher ♦ vt (fold) rentrer; **~ off** vi (from road) tourner ♦ vt (light, radio etc) éteindre; (tap) fermer; (engine) arrêter; **~ on** vt (light, radio etc) allumer; (tap) ouvrir; (engine) mettre en marche; **~ out** vt (light, gas) éteindre; (produce) produire ♦ vi (voters, troops etc) se présenter; **to ~ out to be ...** s'avérer ..., se révéler ...; **~ over** vi (person) se retourner ♦ vt (object) retourner; (page) tourner; **~ round** vi (person) faire demi-tour; (rotate) tourner; **~ up** vi (person) arriver, se pointer (inf); (lost object) être retrouvé(e) ♦ vt (collar) remonter; (radio, heater) mettre plus fort; **~ing** n (in road) tournant m; **~ing point** n (fig) tournant m, moment décisif

turnip [ˈtɜːnɪp] n navet m

turn: ~out n (of voters) taux m de participation; **~over** n (COMM: amount of money) chiffre m d'affaires; (: of goods) roulement m; (of staff) renouvellement m, changement m; **~pike** (US) n autoroute f à péage; **~stile** n tourniquet m (d'entrée); **~table** n (on record player) platine f; **~-up** (BRIT) n (on trousers) revers m

turpentine [ˈtɜːpəntaɪn] n (also: turps) (essence f de) térébenthine f

turquoise [ˈtɜːkwɔɪz] n (stone) turquoise f ♦ adj turquoise inv

turret [ˈtʌrɪt] n tourelle f

turtle [ˈtɜːtl] n tortue marine or d'eau douce; **~neck (sweater)** n (BRIT) pullover m à col montant; (US) pullover m à col roulé

tusk [tʌsk] n défense f

tutor [ˈtjuːtər] n (in college) directeur(-trice) d'études; (private teacher) précepteur(-trice); **~ial** [tjuːˈtɔːrɪəl] n (SCOL) (séance f de) travaux mpl pratiques

tuxedo [tʌkˈsiːdəu] (US) n smoking m

TV n abbr (= television) télé f

twang [twæŋ] n (of instrument) son vibrant; (of voice) ton nasillard

tweed [twiːd] n tweed m

tweezers [ˈtwiːzəz] npl pince f à épiler

twelfth [twelfθ] num douzième

twelve [twelv] num douze; **at ~ (o'clock)** à midi; (midnight) à minuit

twentieth [ˈtwentɪɪθ] num vingtième

twenty [ˈtwentɪ] num vingt

twice [twaɪs] adv deux fois; **~ as much** deux fois plus

twiddle [ˈtwɪdl] vt, vi: **to ~ (with) sth** tripoter qch; **to ~ one's thumbs** (fig) se tourner les pouces

twig [twɪg] n brindille f ♦ vi (inf) piger

twilight ['twaɪlaɪt] n crépuscule m

twin [twɪn] adj, n jumeau(-elle) ♦ vt jumeler; **~(-bedded) room** n chambre f à deux lits; **~ beds** npl lits jumeaux

twine [twaɪn] n ficelle f ♦ vi (plant) s'enrouler

twinge [twɪndʒ] n (of pain) élancement m; **a ~ of conscience** un certain remords; **a ~ of regret** un pincement au cœur

twinkle ['twɪŋkl] vi scintiller; (eyes) pétiller

twirl [twə:l] vt faire tournoyer ♦ vi tournoyer

twist [twɪst] n torsion f, tour m; (in road) virage m; (in wire, flex) tortillon m; (in story) coup m de théâtre ♦ vt tordre; (weave) entortiller; (roll around) enrouler; (fig) déformer ♦ vi (road, river) serpenter

twit [twɪt] (inf) n crétin(e)

twitch [twɪtʃ] n (pull) coup sec, saccade f; (nervous) tic m ♦ vi se convulser; avoir un tic

two [tu:] num deux; **to put ~ and ~ together** (fig) faire le rapprochement; **~-door** adj (AUT) à deux portes; **~-faced** (pej) adj (person) faux (fausse); **~fold** adv: **to increase ~fold** doubler; **~-piece (suit)** n (man's) costume m (deux-pièces); (woman's) (tailleur m) deux-pièces m inv; **~-piece (swimsuit)** n (maillot m de bain) deux-pièces m inv; **~some** n (people) couple m; **~-way** adj (traffic) dans les deux sens

tycoon [taɪ'ku:n] n: **(business) ~** gros homme d'affaires

type [taɪp] n (category) type m, genre m, espèce f; (model, example) type m, modèle m; (TYP) type, caractère m ♦ vt (letter etc) taper (à la machine); **~cast** adj (actor) condamné(e) à toujours jouer le même rôle; **~face** n (TYP) œil m de caractère; **~script** n texte dactylographié; **~writer** n machine f à écrire; **~written** adj dactylographié(e)

typhoid ['taɪfɔɪd] n typhoïde f

typical ['tɪpɪkl] adj typique, caractéristique

typing ['taɪpɪŋ] n dactylo(graphie) f

typist ['taɪpɪst] n dactylo m/f

tyrant ['taɪərnt] n tyran m

tyre ['taɪər] (US **tire**) n pneu m; **~ pressure** n pression f (de gonflage)

U, u

U-bend ['ju:bɛnd] n (in pipe) coude m

ubiquitous [ju:'bɪkwɪtəs] adj omniprésent(e)

udder ['ʌdər] n pis m, mamelle f

UFO ['ju:fəu] n abbr (= unidentified flying object) OVNI m

Uganda [ju:'gændə] n Ouganda m

ugh [ə:h] excl pouah!

ugly ['ʌglɪ] adj laid(e), vilain(e); (situation) inquiétant(e)

UHT abbr (= ultra heat treated): **UHT milk** lait m UHT or longue conservation

UK n abbr = **United Kingdom**

ulcer ['ʌlsər] n ulcère m; (also: **mouth ~**) aphte f

Ulster ['ʌlstər] n Ulster m; (inf: Northern Ireland) Irlande f du Nord

ulterior [ʌl'tɪərɪər] adj: **~ motive** arrière-pensée f

ultimate ['ʌltɪmət] adj ultime, final(e); (authority) suprême; **~ly** adv (at last) en fin de compte; (fundamentally) finalement

ultrasound ['ʌltrəsaund] n ultrason m

umbilical cord [ʌm'bɪlɪkl-] n cordon ombilical

umbrella [ʌm'brɛlə] n parapluie m; (for sun) parasol m

umpire ['ʌmpaɪər] n arbitre m

umpteen [ʌmp'ti:n] adj je ne sais combien de; **~th** adj: **for the ~th time** pour la nième fois

UN n abbr = **United Nations**

unable [ʌn'eɪbl] adj: **to be ~ to** ne pas pouvoir, être dans l'impossibilité de; (incapable) être incapable de

unacceptable [ʌnək'sɛptəbl] adj (behaviour) inadmissible; (price, proposal) inacceptable

unaccompanied [ʌnə'kʌmpənɪd] adj (child, lady) non accompagné(e); (song) sans accompagnement

unaccustomed [ʌnə'kʌstəmd] adj: **to be ~ to sth** ne pas avoir l'habitude de qch

unanimous [ju:'nænɪməs] adj unanime; **~ly** adv à l'unanimité

unarmed [ʌn'ɑ:md] adj (without a weapon) non armé(e); (combat) sans armes

unattached [ʌnə'tætʃt] adj libre, sans attaches; (part) non attaché(e), indépendant(e)

unattended [ʌnə'tɛndɪd] adj (car, child, luggage) sans surveillance

unattractive [ʌnə'træktɪv] adj peu attrayant(e); (character) peu sympathique

unauthorized [ʌn'ɔ:θəraɪzd] adj non autorisé(e), sans autorisation

unavoidable [ʌnə'vɔɪdəbl] adj inévitable

unaware [ʌnə'wɛər] adj: **to be ~ of** ignorer, être inconscient(e) de; **~s** adv à l'improviste, au dépourvu

unbalanced [ʌn'bælənst] adj déséquilibré(e); (report) peu objectif(-ive)

unbearable [ʌn'bɛərəbl] adj insupportable

unbeatable [ʌn'bi:təbl] adj imbattable

unbeknown(st) [ʌnbɪ'nəun(st)] adv: **~ to me/Peter** à mon insu/l'insu de Peter

unbelievable [ʌnbɪ'li:vəbl] adj incroyable

unbend [ʌn'bɛnd] (irreg) vi se détendre ♦ vt (wire) redresser, détordre

unbiased [ʌn'baɪəst] adj impartial(e)

unborn [ʌn'bɔ:n] adj à naître, qui n'est pas

encore né(e)

unbreakable [ʌn'breɪkəbl] adj incassable

unbroken [ʌn'brəukən] adj intact(e); (fig) continu(e), ininterrompu(e)

unbutton [ʌn'bʌtn] vt déboutonner

uncalled-for [ʌn'kɔːldfɔːʳ] adj déplacé(e), injustifié(e)

uncanny [ʌn'kænɪ] adj étrange, troublant(e)

unceremonious [ʌnserɪ'məunɪəs] adj (abrupt, rude) brusque

uncertain [ʌn'sɜːtn] adj incertain(e); (hesitant) hésitant(e); **in no ~ terms** sans équivoque possible; **~ty** n incertitude f, doute(s) m(pl)

uncivilized [ʌn'sɪvɪlaɪzd] adj (gen) non civilisé(e); (fig: behaviour etc) barbare; (hour) indu(e)

uncle ['ʌŋkl] n oncle m

uncomfortable [ʌn'kʌmfətəbl] adj inconfortable, peu confortable; (uneasy) mal à l'aise, gêné(e); (situation) désagréable

uncommon [ʌn'kɔmən] adj rare, singulier(-ère), peu commun(e)

uncompromising [ʌn'kɔmprəmaɪzɪŋ] adj intransigeant(e), inflexible

unconcerned [ʌnkən'sɜːnd] adj: **to be ~ (about)** ne pas s'inquiéter (de)

unconditional [ʌnkən'dɪʃənl] adj sans conditions

unconscious [ʌn'kɔnʃəs] adj sans connaissance, évanoui(e); (unaware): **~ of** inconscient(e) de ♦ n: **the ~** l'inconscient m; **~ly** adv inconsciemment

uncontrollable [ʌnkən'trəuləbl] adj indiscipliné(e); (temper, laughter) irrépressible

unconventional [ʌnkən'venʃənl] adj peu conventionnel(le)

uncouth [ʌn'kuːθ] adj grossier(-ère), fruste

uncover [ʌn'kʌvəʳ] vt découvrir

undecided [ʌndɪ'saɪdɪd] adj indécis(e), irrésolu(e)

under ['ʌndəʳ] prep sous; (less than) (de) moins de; au-dessous de; (according to) selon, en vertu de ♦ adv au-dessous; en dessous; **~ there** là-dessous; **~ repair** en (cours de) réparation; **~age** adj (person) qui n'a pas l'âge réglementaire; **~carriage** n (AVIAT) train m d'atterrissage; **~charge** vt ne pas faire payer assez à; **~coat** n (paint) couche f de fond; **~cover** adj secret(-ète), clandestin(e); **~current** n courant or sentiment sous-jacent; **~cut** (irreg) vt vendre moins cher que; **~dog** n opprimé m; **~done** adj (CULIN) saignant(e); (pej) pas assez cuit(e); **~estimate** vt sous-estimer; **~fed** adj sous-alimenté(e); **~foot** adv sous les pieds; **~go** (irreg) vt subir; (treatment) suivre; **~graduate** n étudiant(e) (qui prépare la licence); **~ground** n (BRIT:

railway) métro m; (POL) clandestine f ♦ adj souterrain(e); (fig) clandestin(e) ♦ adv dans la clandestinité, clandestinement; **~growth** n broussailles fpl, sous-bois m; **~hand(ed)** adj (fig: behaviour, method etc) en dessous; **~lie** (irreg) vt être à la base de; **~line** vt souligner; **~mine** vt saper, miner; **~neath** adv (en) dessous ♦ prep sous, au-dessous de; **~paid** adj sous-payé(e); **~pants** npl caleçon m, slip m; **~pass** (BRIT) n passage souterrain; (on motorway) passage inférieur; **~privileged** adj défavorisé(e), économiquement faible; **~rate** vt sous-estimer; **~shirt** (US) n tricot m de corps; **~shorts** (US) npl caleçon m, slip m; **~side** n dessous m; **~skirt** (BRIT) n jupon m

understand [ʌndə'stænd] (irreg: like **stand**) vt, vi comprendre; **I ~ that ...** je me suis laissé dire que ...; je crois comprendre que ...; **~able** adj compréhensible; **~ing** adj compréhensif(-ive) ♦ n compréhension f; (agreement) accord m

understatement ['ʌndəsteɪtmənt] n: **that's an ~** c'est (bien) peu dire, le terme est faible

understood [ʌndə'stud] pt, pp of **understand** ♦ adj entendu(e); (implied) sous-entendu(e)

understudy ['ʌndəstʌdɪ] n doublure f

undertake [ʌndə'teɪk] (irreg) vt entreprendre; se charger de; **to ~ to do sth** s'engager à faire qch

undertaker [ʌndə'teɪkəʳ] n entrepreneur m des pompes funèbres, croque-mort m

undertaking ['ʌndəteɪkɪŋ] n entreprise f; (promise) promesse f

under: ~tone n: **in an ~tone** à mi-voix; **~water** adv sous l'eau ♦ adj sous-marin(e); **~wear** n sous-vêtements mpl; (women's only) dessous mpl; **~world** n (of crime) milieu m, pègre f; **~write** n (INSURANCE) assureur m

undies ['ʌndɪz] (inf) npl dessous mpl, lingerie f

undiplomatic ['ʌndɪplə'mætɪk] adj peu diplomatique

undo [ʌn'duː] (irreg) vt défaire; **~ing** n ruine f, perte f

undoubted [ʌn'dautɪd] adj indubitable, certain(e); **~ly** adv sans aucun doute

undress [ʌn'dres] vi se déshabiller

undue [ʌn'djuː] adj indu(e), excessif(-ive)

undulating ['ʌndjuleɪtɪŋ] adj ondoyant(e), onduleux(-euse)

unduly [ʌn'djuːlɪ] adv trop, excessivement

unearth [ʌn'ɜːθ] vt déterrer; (fig) dénicher

unearthly [ʌn'ɜːθlɪ] adj (hour) indu(e), impossible

uneasy [ʌn'iːzɪ] adj mal à l'aise, gêné(e); (worried) inquiet(-ète); (feeling) désagréable; (peace, truce) fragile

uneconomic(al) ['ʌniːkə'nɔmɪk(l)] adj peu

économique

uneducated [ʌn'edjukeɪtɪd] *adj* (*person*) sans instruction

unemployed [ʌnɪm'plɔɪd] *adj* sans travail, en *or* au chômage ♦ *n*: **the ~** les chômeurs *mpl*; **unemployment** *n* chômage *m*

unending [ʌn'endɪŋ] *adj* interminable, sans fin

unerring [ʌn'ɜːrɪŋ] *adj* infaillible, sûr(e)

uneven [ʌn'iːvn] *adj* inégal(e); (*quality, work*) irrégulier(-ère)

unexpected [ʌnɪks'pektɪd] *adj* inattendu(e), imprévu(e); **~ly** [ʌnɪks'pektɪdlɪ] *adv* (*arrive*) à l'improviste; (*succeed*) contre toute attente

unfailing [ʌn'feɪlɪŋ] *adj* inépuisable; (*remedy*) infaillible

unfair [ʌn'feər] *adj*: **~ (to)** injuste (envers)

unfaithful [ʌn'feɪθful] *adj* infidèle

unfamiliar [ʌnfə'mɪlɪər] *adj* étrange, inconnu(e); **to be ~ with** mal connaître

unfashionable [ʌn'fæʃnəbl] *adj* (*clothes*) démodé(e); (*place*) peu chic *inv*

unfasten [ʌn'fɑːsn] *vt* défaire; détacher; (*open*) ouvrir

unfavourable [ʌn'feɪvrəbl] (*US* **unfavorable**) *adj* défavorable

unfeeling [ʌn'fiːlɪŋ] *adj* insensible, dur(e)

unfinished [ʌn'fɪnɪʃt] *adj* inachevé(e)

unfit [ʌn'fɪt] *adj* en mauvaise santé; pas en forme; (*incompetent*): **~ (for)** impropre (à); (*work, service*) inapte (à)

unfold [ʌn'fəuld] *vt* déplier ♦ *vi* se dérouler

unforeseen ['ʌnfɔː'siːn] *adj* imprévu(e)

unforgettable [ʌnfə'getəbl] *adj* inoubliable

unfortunate [ʌn'fɔːtʃənət] *adj* malheureux(-euse); (*event, remark*) malencontreux(-euse); **~ly** *adv* malheureusement

unfounded [ʌn'faundɪd] *adj* sans fondement

unfriendly [ʌn'frendlɪ] *adj* inamical(e), peu aimable

ungainly [ʌn'geɪnlɪ] *adj* gauche, dégingandé(e)

ungodly [ʌn'gɒdlɪ] *adj* (*hour*) indu(e)

ungrateful [ʌn'greɪtful] *adj* ingrat(e)

unhappiness [ʌn'hæpɪnɪs] *n* tristesse *f*, peine *f*

unhappy [ʌn'hæpɪ] *adj* triste, malheureux(-euse); **~ about** *or* **with** (*arrangements etc*) mécontent(e) de, peu satisfait(e) de

unharmed [ʌn'hɑːmd] *adj* indemne, sain(e) et sauf (sauve)

UNHCR *n abbr* (= *United Nations High Commission for refugees*) HCR *m*

unhealthy [ʌn'helθɪ] *adj* malsain(e); (*person*) maladif(-ive)

unheard-of [ʌn'hɜːdɔv] *adj* inouï(e), sans précédent

unhurt [ʌn'hɜːt] *adj* indemne

unidentified [ʌnaɪ'dentɪfaɪd] *adj* non

identifié(e); *see also* **UFO**

uniform ['juːnɪfɔːm] *n* uniforme *m* ♦ *adj* uniforme

uninhabited [ʌnɪn'hæbɪtɪd] *adj* inhabité(e)

unintentional [ʌnɪn'tenʃənəl] *adj* involontaire

union ['juːnjən] *n* union *f*; (*also:* **trade ~**) syndicat *m* ♦ *cpd* du syndicat, syndical(e); **U~ Jack** *n* drapeau du Royaume-Uni

unique [juː'niːk] *adj* unique

UNISON ['juːnɪsn] *n grand syndicat des services publics en Grande-Bretagne*

unison ['juːnɪsn] *n*: **in ~** (*sing*) à l'unisson; (*say*) en chœur

unit ['juːnɪt] *n* unité *f*; (*section: of furniture etc*) élément *m*, bloc *m*; **kitchen ~** élément de cuisine

unite [juː'naɪt] *vt* unir ♦ *vi* s'unir; **~d** *adj* uni(e); unifié(e); (*effort*) conjugué(e); **U~d Kingdom** *n* Royaume-Uni *m*; **U~d Nations (Organization)** *n* (Organisation *f* des) Nations unies; **U~d States (of America)** *n* États-Unis *mpl*

unit trust (*BRIT*) *n* fonds commun de placement

unity ['juːnɪtɪ] *n* unité *f*

universal [juːnɪ'vɜːsl] *adj* universel(le)

universe ['juːnɪvɜːs] *n* univers *m*

university [juːnɪ'vɜːsɪtɪ] *n* université *f*

unjust [ʌn'dʒʌst] *adj* injuste

unkempt [ʌn'kempt] *adj* négligé(e), débraillé(e); (*hair*) mal peigné(e)

unkind [ʌn'kaɪnd] *adj* peu gentil(le), méchant(e)

unknown [ʌn'nəun] *adj* inconnu(e)

unlawful [ʌn'lɔːful] *adj* illégal(e)

unleaded ['ʌn'ledɪd] *adj* (*petrol, fuel*) sans plomb

unleash [ʌn'liːʃ] *vt* (*fig*) déchaîner; déclencher

unless [ʌn'les] *conj*: **he leaves** à moins qu'il ne parte

unlike [ʌn'laɪk] *adj* dissemblable, différent(e) ♦ *prep* contrairement à

unlikely [ʌn'laɪklɪ] *adj* (*happening*) improbable; (*explanation*) invraisemblable

unlimited [ʌn'lɪmɪtɪd] *adj* illimité(e)

unlisted ['ʌn'lɪstɪd] (*US*) *adj* (*TEL*) sur la liste rouge

unload [ʌn'ləud] *vt* décharger

unlock [ʌn'lɔk] *vt* ouvrir

unlucky [ʌn'lʌkɪ] *adj* (*person*) malchanceux(-euse); (*object, number*) qui porte malheur; **to be ~** (*person*) ne pas avoir de chance

unmarried [ʌn'mærɪd] *adj* célibataire

unmistak(e)able [ʌnmɪs'teɪkəbl] *adj* indubitable; qu'on ne peut pas ne pas reconnaître

unmitigated [ʌnˈmɪtɪɡeɪtɪd] *adj* non mitigé(e), absolu(e), pur(e)

unnatural [ʌnˈnætʃrəl] *adj* non naturel(le); (*habit*) contre nature

unnecessary [ʌnˈnesəsərɪ] *adj* inutile, superflu(e)

unnoticed [ʌnˈnəʊtɪst] *adj*: (to go *or* pass) ~ (passer) inaperçu(e)

UNO *n abbr* = United Nations Organization

unobtainable [ʌnəbˈteɪnəbl] *adj* impossible à obtenir

unobtrusive [ʌnəbˈtruːsɪv] *adj* discret(-ète)

unofficial [ʌnəˈfɪʃl] *adj* (*news*) officieux(-euse); (*strike*) sauvage

unorthodox [ʌnˈɔːθədɒks] *adj* peu orthodoxe; (*REL*) hétérodoxe

unpack [ʌnˈpæk] *vi* défaire sa valise ♦ *vt* (*suitcase*) défaire; (*belongings*) déballer

unpalatable [ʌnˈpælətəbl] *adj* (*meal*) mauvais(e); (*truth*) désagréable (à entendre)

unparalleled [ʌnˈpærəleld] *adj* incomparable, sans égal

unpleasant [ʌnˈpleznt] *adj* déplaisant(e), désagréable

unplug [ʌnˈplʌɡ] *vt* débrancher

unpopular [ʌnˈpɒpjʊlər] *adj* impopulaire

unprecedented [ʌnˈpresɪdəntɪd] *adj* sans précédent

unpredictable [ʌnprɪˈdɪktəbl] *adj* imprévisible

unprofessional [ʌnprəˈfeʃənl] *adj*: ~ **conduct** manquement *m* aux devoirs de la profession

UNPROFOR *n abbr* (= *United Nations Protection Force*) FORPRONU *f*

unqualified [ʌnˈkwɒlɪfaɪd] *adj* (*teacher*) non diplômé(e), sans titres; (*success, disaster*) sans réserve, total(e)

unquestionably [ʌnˈkwestʃənəblɪ] *adv* incontestablement

unravel [ʌnˈrævl] *vt* démêler

unreal [ʌnˈrɪəl] *adj* irréel(le); (*extraordinary*) incroyable

unrealistic [ʌnrɪəˈlɪstɪk] *adj* irréaliste; peu réaliste

unreasonable [ʌnˈriːznəbl] *adj* qui n'est pas raisonnable

unrelated [ʌnrɪˈleɪtɪd] *adj* sans rapport; sans lien de parenté

unreliable [ʌnrɪˈlaɪəbl] *adj* sur qui (*or* quoi) on ne peut pas compter, peu fiable

unremitting [ʌnrɪˈmɪtɪŋ] *adj* inlassable, infatigable, acharné(e)

unreservedly [ʌnrɪˈzɜːvɪdlɪ] *adv* sans réserve

unrest [ʌnˈrest] *n* agitation f, troubles *mpl*

unroll [ʌnˈrəʊl] *vt* dérouler

unruly [ʌnˈruːlɪ] *adj* indiscipliné(e)

unsafe [ʌnˈseɪf] *adj* (*in danger*) en danger; (*journey, car*) dangereux(-euse)

unsaid [ʌnˈsed] *adj*: to leave sth ~ passer qch sous silence

unsatisfactory [ˈʌnsætɪsˈfæktərɪ] *adj* peu satisfaisant(e)

unsavoury [ʌnˈseɪvərɪ] (*US* **unsavory**) *adj* (*fig*) peu recommandable

unscathed [ʌnˈskeɪðd] *adj* indemne

unscrew [ʌnˈskruː] *vt* dévisser

unscrupulous [ʌnˈskruːpjʊləs] *adj* sans scrupules

unsettled [ʌnˈsetld] *adj* perturbé(e); instable

unshaven [ʌnˈʃeɪvn] *adj* non *or* mal rasé(e)

unsightly [ʌnˈsaɪtlɪ] *adj* disgracieux(-euse), laid(e)

unskilled [ʌnˈskɪld] *adj*: ~ **worker** manœuvre *m*

unspeakable [ʌnˈspiːkəbl] *adj* indicible; (*awful*) innommable

unstable [ʌnˈsteɪbl] *adj* instable

unsteady [ʌnˈstedɪ] *adj* mal assuré(e), chancelant(e), instable

unstuck [ʌnˈstʌk] *adj*: to come ~ se décoller; (*plan*) tomber à l'eau

unsuccessful [ʌnsəkˈsesful] *adj* (*attempt*) infructueux(-euse), vain(e); (*writer, proposal*) qui n'a pas de succès; **to be** ~ (*in attempting sth*) ne pas réussir; ne pas avoir de succès; (*application*) ne pas être retenu(e)

unsuitable [ʌnˈsuːtəbl] *adj* qui ne convient pas, peu approprié(e); inopportun(e)

unsure [ʌnˈʃʊər] *adj* pas sûr(e); **to be** ~ **of o.s.** manquer de confiance en soi

unsuspecting [ʌnsəsˈpektɪŋ] *adj* qui ne se doute de rien

unsympathetic [ˈʌnsɪmpəˈθetɪk] *adj* (*person*) antipathique; (*attitude*) peu compatissant(e)

untapped [ʌnˈtæpt] *adj* (*resources*) inexploité(e)

unthinkable [ʌnˈθɪŋkəbl] *adj* impensable, inconcevable

untidy [ʌnˈtaɪdɪ] *adj* (*room*) en désordre; (*appearance, person*) débraillé(e); (*person: in character*) sans ordre, désordonné

untie [ʌnˈtaɪ] *vt* (*knot, parcel*) défaire; (*prisoner, dog*) détacher

until [ənˈtɪl] *prep* jusqu'à; (*after negative*) avant ♦ *conj* jusqu'à ce que +*sub*; (*in past, after negative*) avant que +*sub*; ~ **he comes** jusqu'à ce qu'il vienne, jusqu'à son arrivée; ~ **now** jusqu'à présent, jusqu'ici; ~ **then** jusque-là

untimely [ʌnˈtaɪmlɪ] *adj* inopportun(e); (*death*) prématuré(e)

untold [ʌnˈtəʊld] *adj* (*story*) jamais raconté(e); (*wealth*) incalculable; (*joy, suffering*) indescriptible

untoward [ʌntəˈwɔːd] *adj* fâcheux(-euse), malencontreux(-euse)

unused¹ [ʌnˈjuːzd] adj (clothes) neuf (neuve)
unused² [ʌnˈjuːst] adj: **to be ~ to sth/to doing sth** ne pas avoir l'habitude de qch/de faire qch
unusual [ʌnˈjuːʒuəl] adj insolite, exceptionnel(le), rare
unveil [ʌnˈveɪl] vt dévoiler
unwanted [ʌnˈwɔntɪd] adj (child, pregnancy) non désiré(e); (clothes etc) à donner
unwelcome [ʌnˈwɛlkəm] adj importun(e); (news) fâcheux(-euse)
unwell [ʌnˈwɛl] adj souffrant(e); **to feel ~** ne pas se sentir bien
unwieldy [ʌnˈwiːldɪ] adj (object) difficile à manier; (system) lourd(e)
unwilling [ʌnˈwɪlɪŋ] adj: **to be ~ to do** ne pas vouloir faire; **~ly** adv à contrecœur, contre son gré
unwind [ʌnˈwaɪnd] (irreg) vt dérouler ♦ vi (relax) se détendre
unwise [ʌnˈwaɪz] adj irréfléchi(e), imprudent(e)
unwitting [ʌnˈwɪtɪŋ] adj involontaire
unworkable [ʌnˈwəːkəbl] adj (plan) impraticable
unworthy [ʌnˈwəːðɪ] adj indigne
unwrap [ʌnˈræp] vt défaire; ouvrir
unwritten [ʌnˈrɪtn] adj (agreement) tacite

KEYWORD
---

up [ʌp] prep: **he went up the stairs/the hill** il a monté l'escalier/la colline; **the cat was up a tree** le chat était dans un arbre; **they live further up the street** ils habitent plus haut dans la rue
♦ adv **1** (upwards, higher): **up in the sky/the mountains** (là-haut) dans le ciel/les montagnes; **put it a bit higher up** mettez-le un peu plus haut; **up there** là-haut; **up above** au-dessus
2: **to be up** (out of bed) être levé(e); (prices) avoir augmenté or monté
3: **up to** (as far as) jusqu'à; **up to now** jusqu'à présent
4: **to be up to** (depending on): **it's up to you** c'est à vous de décider; (equal to): **he's not up to it** (job, task etc) il n'en est pas capable; (inf: be doing): **what is he up to?** qu'est-ce qu'il peut bien faire?
♦ n: **ups and downs** hauts et bas mpl

---

up-and-coming [ʌpəndˈkʌmɪŋ] adj plein(e) d'avenir or de promesses
upbringing [ˈʌpbrɪŋɪŋ] n éducation f
update [ʌpˈdeɪt] vt mettre à jour
upgrade [ʌpˈgreɪd] vt (house) moderniser; (job) revaloriser; (employee) promouvoir
upheaval [ʌpˈhiːvl] n bouleversement m; branle-bas m

uphill [ˈʌpˈhɪl] adj qui monte; (fig: task) difficile, pénible ♦ adv (face, look) en amont; **to go ~** monter
uphold [ʌpˈhəuld] (irreg) vt (law, decision) maintenir
upholstery [ʌpˈhəulstərɪ] n rembourrage m; (cover) tissu m d'ameublement; (of car) garniture f
upkeep [ˈʌpkiːp] n entretien m
upon [əˈpɔn] prep sur
upper [ˈʌpəʳ] adj supérieur(e); du dessus ♦ n (of shoe) empeigne f; **~-class** adj de la haute société, aristocratique; **~ hand** n: **to have the ~ hand** avoir le dessus; **~most** adj le (la) plus haut(e); **what was ~most in my mind** ce à quoi je pensais surtout; **~ sixth** n terminale f
upright [ˈʌpraɪt] adj droit(e); vertical(e); (fig) droit, honnête
uprising [ˈʌpraɪzɪŋ] n soulèvement m, insurrection f
uproar [ˈʌprɔːʳ] n tumulte m; (protests) tempête f de protestations
uproot [ʌpˈruːt] vt déraciner
upset [n ˈʌpsɛt, vb, adj ʌpˈsɛt] (irreg: like set) n bouleversement m; (stomach) indigestion f ♦ vt (glass etc) renverser; (plan) déranger; (person: offend) contrarier; (: grieve) faire de la peine à; bouleverser ♦ adj contrarié(e); peiné(e); (stomach) dérangé(e)
upshot [ˈʌpʃɔt] n résultat m
upside-down [ʌpsaɪdˈdaun] adv à l'envers; **to turn ~ ~** mettre sens dessus dessous
upstairs [ʌpˈstɛəz] adv en haut ♦ adj (room) du dessus, d'en haut ♦ n: **the ~** l'étage m
upstart [ˈʌpstaːt] n (pej) parvenu(e) m
upstream [ʌpˈstriːm] adv en amont
uptake [ˈʌpteɪk] n: **to be quick/slow on the ~** comprendre vite/être lent à comprendre
uptight [ʌpˈtaɪt] (inf) adj très tendu(e), crispé(e)
up-to-date [ˈʌptəˈdeɪt] adj moderne; (information) très récent(e)
upturn [ˈʌptəːn] n (in luck) retournement m; (COMM: in market) hausse f
upward [ˈʌpwəd] adj ascendant(e); vers le haut; **~(s)** adv vers le haut; **~(s) of 200** 200 et plus
urban [ˈəːbən] adj urbain(e); **~ clearway** n rue f à stationnement interdit
urbane [əːˈbeɪn] adj urbain(e), courtois(e)
urchin [ˈəːtʃɪn] n polisson m
urge [əːdʒ] n besoin m; envie f; forte envie, désir m ♦ vt: **to ~ sb to do** exhorter qn à faire, pousser qn à faire; recommander vivement à qn de faire
urgency [ˈəːdʒənsɪ] n urgence f; (of tone) insistance f
urgent [ˈəːdʒənt] adj urgent(e); (tone) insistant(e), pressant(e)

urinal ['juərɪnl] *n* urinoir *m*

urine ['juərɪn] *n* urine *f*

urn [əːn] *n* urne *f*; (*also*: **tea ~**) fontaine *f* à thé

US *n abbr* = **United States**

us [ʌs] *pron* nous; *see also* **me**

USA *n abbr* = **United States of America**

use [*n* juːs, *vb* juːz] *n* emploi *m*, utilisation *f*; usage *m*; (*~fulness*) utilité *f* ♦ *vt* se servir de, utiliser, employer; **in ~** en usage; **out of ~** hors d'usage; **to be of ~** servir, être utile; **it's no ~** ça ne sert à rien; **she ~d to do it** elle le faisait (autrefois), elle avait coutume de le faire; **~d to: to be ~d to** avoir l'habitude de, être habitué(e) à; **~ up** *vt* finir, épuiser; consommer; **~d** [juːzd] *adj* (*car*) d'occasion; **~ful** ['juːsful] *adj* utile; **~fulness** *n* utilité *f*; **~less** ['juːslɪs] *adj* inutile; (*person: hopeless*) nul(le); **~r** ['juːzəʳ] *n* utilisateur(-trice), usager *m*; **~r-friendly** *adj* (*computer*) convivial(e), facile d'emploi

usher ['ʌʃəʳ] *n* (*at wedding ceremony*) placeur *m*; **~ette** [ʌʃəˈrɛt] *n* (*in cinema*) ouvreuse *f*

usual ['juːʒuəl] *adj* habituel(le); **as ~** comme d'habitude; **~ly** ['juːʒuəlɪ] *adv* d'habitude, d'ordinaire

utensil [juːˈtɛnsl] *n* ustensile *m*

uterus ['juːtərəs] *n* utérus *m*

utility [juːˈtɪlɪtɪ] *n* utilité *f*; (*also*: **public ~**) service public; **~ room** *n* buanderie *f*

utmost ['ʌtməʊst] *adj* extrême, le (la) plus grand(e) ♦ *n*: **to do one's ~** faire tout son possible

utter ['ʌtəʳ] *adj* total(e), complet(-ète) ♦ *vt* (*words*) prononcer, proférer; (*sounds*) émettre; **~ance** *n* paroles *fpl*; **~ly** *adv* complètement, totalement

U-turn ['juːˈtəːn] *n* demi-tour *m*

V, v

v. *abbr* = **verse**; **versus**; **volt**; (= *vide*) **voir**

vacancy ['veɪkənsɪ] *n* (*BRIT: job*) poste vacant; (*room*) chambre *f* disponible; **"no vacancies"** "complet"

vacant ['veɪkənt] *adj* (*seat etc*) libre, disponible; (*expression*) distrait(e)

vacate [vəˈkeɪt] *vt* quitter

vacation [vəˈkeɪʃən] *n* vacances *fpl*

vaccinate ['væksɪneɪt] *vt* vacciner

vacuum ['vækjum] *n* vide *m*; **~ cleaner** *n* aspirateur *m*; **~-packed** *adj* emballé(e) sous vide

vagina [vəˈdʒaɪnə] *n* vagin *m*

vagrant ['veɪgrənt] *n* vagabond(e)

vague [veɪg] *adj* vague, imprécis(e); (*blurred: photo, outline*) flou(e); **~ly** *adv* vaguement

vain [veɪn] *adj* (*useless*) vain(e); (*conceited*) vaniteux(-euse); **in ~** en vain

valentine ['væləntaɪn] *n* (*also*: **~ card**) carte *f* de la Saint-Valentin; (*person*) bien-aimé(e) (*le jour de la Saint-Valentin*); **V~'s day** *n* Saint-Valentin *f*

valiant ['væliənt] *adj* vaillant(e)

valid ['vælɪd] *adj* valable; (*document*) valable, valide

valley ['vælɪ] *n* vallée *f*

valour ['væləʳ] (*US* **valor**) *n* courage *m*

valuable ['væljuəbl] *adj* (*jewel*) de valeur; (*time, help*) précieux(-euse); **~s** *npl* objets *mpl* de valeur

valuation [væljuˈeɪʃən] *n* (*price*) estimation *f*; (*quality*) appréciation *f*

value ['væljuː] *n* valeur *f* ♦ *vt* (*fix price*) évaluer, expertiser; (*appreciate*) apprécier; **~ added tax** (*BRIT*) *n* taxe *f* à la valeur ajoutée; **~d** *adj* (*person*) estimé(e); (*advice*) précieux(-euse)

valve [vælv] *n* (*in machine*) soupape *f*, valve *f*; (*MED*) valve, valvule *f*

van [væn] *n* (*AUT*) camionnette *f*

vandal ['vændl] *n* vandale *m/f*; **~ism** *n* vandalisme *m*; **~ize** *vt* saccager

vanguard ['vænɡɑːd] *n* (*fig*): **in the ~ of** à l'avant-garde de

vanilla [vəˈnɪlə] *n* vanille *f*

vanish ['vænɪʃ] *vi* disparaître

vanity ['vænɪtɪ] *n* vanité *f*

vantage point ['vɑːntɪdʒ-] *n* bonne position

vapour ['veɪpəʳ] (*US* **vapor**) *n* vapeur *f*; (*on window*) buée *f*

variable ['vɛərɪəbl] *adj* variable; (*mood*) changeant(e)

variance ['vɛərɪəns] *n*: **to be at ~ (with)** être en désaccord (avec); (*facts*) être en contradiction (avec)

varicose ['værɪkəʊs] *adj*: **~ veins** varices *fpl*

varied ['vɛərɪd] *adj* varié(e), divers(e)

variety [vəˈraɪətɪ] *n* variété *f*; (*quantity*) nombre *m*, quantité *f*; **~ show** *n* (spectacle *m* de) variétés *fpl*

various ['vɛərɪəs] *adj* divers(e), différent(e); (*several*) divers, plusieurs

varnish ['vɑːnɪʃ] *n* vernis *m* ♦ *vt* vernir

vary ['vɛərɪ] *vt*, *vi* varier, changer

vase [vɑːz] *n* vase *m*

Vaseline ® ['væsɪliːn] *n* vaseline *f*

vast [vɑːst] *adj* vaste, immense; (*amount, success*) énorme

VAT [væt] *n abbr* (= *value added tax*) TVA *f*

vat [væt] *n* cuve *f*

vault [vɔːlt] *n* (*of roof*) voûte *f*; (*tomb*) caveau *m*; (*in bank*) salle *f* des coffres; chambre forte ♦ *vt* (*also*: **~ over**) sauter (d'un bond)

vaunted ['vɔːntɪd] *adj*: **much-~** tant vanté(e)

VCR *n abbr* = **video cassette recorder**

VD *n abbr* = **venereal disease**

VDU *n abbr* = **visual display unit**

veal [viːl] n veau m

veer [vɪəʳ] vi tourner; virer

vegan ['viːgən] n végétalien(ne)

vegeburger ['vedʒɪbəːgəʳ] n burger végétarien

vegetable ['vedʒtəbl] n légume m ♦ adj végétal(e)

vegetarian [vedʒɪ'teərɪən] adj, n végétarien(ne)

vehement ['viːɪmənt] adj violent(e), impétueux(-euse); (impassioned) ardent(e)

vehicle ['viːɪkl] n véhicule m

veil [veɪl] n voile m

vein [veɪn] n veine f; (on leaf) nervure f

velocity [vɪ'lɔsɪtɪ] n vitesse f

velvet ['velvɪt] n velours m

vending machine ['vendɪŋ-] n distributeur m automatique

veneer [və'nɪəʳ] n (on furniture) placage m; (fig) vernis m

venereal [vɪ'nɪərɪəl] adj: ~ **disease** maladie vénérienne

Venetian blind [vɪ'niːʃən-] n store vénitien

vengeance ['vendʒəns] n vengeance f; **with a ~** (fig) vraiment, pour de bon

venison ['venɪsn] n venaison f

venom ['venəm] n venin m

vent [vent] n conduit m d'aération; (in dress, jacket) fente f ♦ vt (fig: one's feelings) donner libre cours à

ventilator ['ventɪleɪtəʳ] n ventilateur m

ventriloquist [ven'trɪləkwɪst] n ventriloque m/f

venture ['ventʃəʳ] n entreprise f ♦ vt risquer, hasarder ♦ vi s'aventurer, se risquer

venue ['venjuː] n lieu m

verb [vəːb] n verbe m; ~**al** adj verbal(e); (translation) littéral(e)

verbatim [vəː'beɪtɪm] adj, adv mot pour mot

verdict ['vəːdɪkt] n verdict m

verge [vəːdʒ] n (BRIT) bord m, bas-côté m; **"soft ~s"** (BRIT: AUT) "accotement non stabilisé"; **on the ~ of doing** sur le point de faire; **~ on** vt fus approcher de

verify ['verɪfaɪ] vt vérifier; (confirm) confirmer

vermin ['vəːmɪn] npl animaux mpl nuisibles; (insects) vermine f

vermouth ['vəːməθ] n vermouth m

versatile ['vəːsətaɪl] adj polyvalent(e)

verse [vəːs] n (poetry) vers mpl; (stanza) strophe f; (in Bible) verset m

version ['vəːʃən] n version f

versus ['vəːsəs] prep contre

vertical ['vəːtɪkl] adj vertical(e) ♦ n verticale f

vertigo ['vəːtɪgəu] n vertige m

verve [vəːv] n brio m, enthousiasme m

very ['verɪ] adv très ♦ adj: **the ~ book which** le livre même que; **the ~ last** le tout dernier; **at the ~ least** tout au moins; **~ much** beaucoup

vessel ['vesl] n (ANAT, NAUT) vaisseau m; (container) récipient m

vest [vest] n (BRIT) tricot m de corps; (US: waistcoat) gilet m

vested interest ['vestɪd-] n (COMM) droits acquis

vet [vet] n abbr (BRIT: veterinary surgeon) vétérinaire m/f ♦ vt examiner soigneusement

veteran ['vetərn] n vétéran m; (also: **war ~**) ancien combattant

veterinary surgeon ['vetrɪnərɪ-] (BRIT), **veterinarian** [vetrɪ'neərɪən] (US) n vétérinaire m/f

veto ['viːtəu] (pl **~es**) n veto m ♦ vt opposer son veto à

vex [veks] vt fâcher, contrarier; **~ed** adj (question) controversé(e)

via ['vaɪə] prep par, via

viable ['vaɪəbl] adj viable

vibrate [vaɪ'breɪt] vi vibrer

vicar ['vɪkəʳ] n pasteur m (de l'Église anglicane); **~age** n presbytère m

vicarious [vɪ'keərɪəs] adj indirect(e)

vice [vaɪs] n (evil) vice m; (TECH) étau m

vice- [vaɪs] prefix vice-

vice squad n ≈ brigade mondaine

vice versa ['vaɪsɪ'vəːsə] adv vice versa

vicinity [vɪ'sɪnɪtɪ] n environs mpl, alentours mpl

vicious ['vɪʃəs] adj (remark) cruel(le), méchant(e); (blow) brutal(e); (dog) méchant(e), dangereux(-euse); (horse) vicieux(-euse); **~ circle** n cercle vicieux

victim ['vɪktɪm] n victime f

victor ['vɪktəʳ] n vainqueur m

Victorian [vɪk'tɔːrɪən] adj victorien(ne)

victory ['vɪktərɪ] n victoire f

video ['vɪdɪəu] cpd vidéo inv ♦ n (~ film) vidéo f; (also: **~ cassette**) vidéocassette f; (also: **~ cassette recorder**) magnétoscope m; **~ tape** n bande f vidéo inv; (cassette) vidéocassette f; **~ wall** n mur m d'images vidéo

vie [vaɪ] vi: **to ~ with** rivaliser avec

Vienna [vɪ'enə] n Vienne

Vietnam ['vjet'næm] n Viêt-Nam m, Vietnam m; **~ese** [vjetnə'miːz] adj vietnamien(ne) ♦ n inv Vietnamien(ne); (LING) vietnamien m

view [vjuː] n vue f; (opinion) avis m, vue ♦ vt voir, regarder; (situation) considérer; (house) visiter; **in full ~ of** sous les yeux de; **in ~ of the weather/the fact that** étant donné le temps/ que; **in my ~** à mon avis; **~er** n (TV) téléspectateur(-trice); **~finder** n viseur m; **~point** n point m de vue

vigorous ['vɪgərəs] adj vigoureux(-euse)

vile [vaɪl] adj (action) vil(e); (smell, food) abominable; (temper) massacrant(e)

villa ['vɪlə] n villa f

village ['vɪlɪdʒ] n village m; **~r** n villageois(e)

villain ['vɪlən] n (scoundrel) scélérat m; (BRIT: criminal) bandit m; (in novel etc) traître m

vindicate ['vɪndɪkeɪt] vt (person) innocenter; (action) justifier

vindictive [vɪn'dɪktɪv] adj vindicatif(-ive), rancunier(-ère)

vine [vaɪn] n vigne f; (climbing plant) plante grimpante

vinegar ['vɪnɪɡəʳ] n vinaigre m

vineyard ['vɪnjɑːd] n vignoble m

vintage ['vɪntɪdʒ] n (year) année f, millésime m; ~ **car** n voiture f d'époque; ~ **wine** n vin m de grand cru

viola [vɪ'əulə] n (MUS) alto m

violate ['vaɪəleɪt] vt violer

violence ['vaɪələns] n violence f

violent ['vaɪələnt] adj violent(e)

violet ['vaɪələt] adj violet(te) ♦ n (colour) violet m; (plant) violette f

violin [vaɪə'lɪn] n violon m; ~**ist** [vaɪə'lɪnɪst] n violoniste m/f

VIP n abbr (= very important person) V.I.P. m

virgin ['vɜːdʒɪn] n vierge f ♦ adj vierge

Virgo ['vɜːɡəu] n la Vierge

virile ['vɪraɪl] adj viril(e)

virtually ['vɜːtjuəlɪ] adv (almost) pratiquement

virtual reality ['vɜːtjuəl-] n (COMPUT) réalité virtuelle

virtue ['vɜːtjuː] n vertu f; (advantage) mérite m, avantage m; by ~ of en vertu or en raison de; **virtuous** adj vertueux(-euse)

virus ['vaɪərəs] n (COMPUT) virus m

visa ['viːzə] n visa m

visibility [vɪzɪ'bɪlɪtɪ] n visibilité f

visible ['vɪzəbl] adj visible

vision ['vɪʒən] n (sight) vue f, vision f; (foresight, in dream) vision

visit ['vɪzɪt] n visite f; (stay) séjour m ♦ vt (person) rendre visite à; (place) visiter; ~**ing hours** npl (in hospital etc) heures fpl de visite; ~**or** n visiteur(-euse); (to one's house) visite f, invité(e); ~**or centre** n hall m or centre m d'accueil

visor ['vaɪzəʳ] n visière f

vista ['vɪstə] n vue f

visual ['vɪzjuəl] adj visuel(le); ~ **aid** n support visuel; ~ **display unit** n console f de visualisation, visuel m; ~**ize** vt se représenter, s'imaginer; ~**ly-impaired** adj malvoyant(e)

vital ['vaɪtl] adj vital(e); (person) plein(e) d'entrain; ~**ly** adv (important) absolument; ~ **statistics** npl (fig) mensurations fpl

vitamin ['vɪtəmɪn] n vitamine f

vivacious [vɪ'veɪʃəs] adj animé(e), qui a de la vivacité

vivid ['vɪvɪd] adj (account) vivant(e); (light, imagination) vif (vive); ~**ly** adv (describe) d'une manière vivante; (remember) de façon

précise

V-neck ['viːnɛk] n décolleté m en V

vocabulary [vəu'kæbjulərɪ] n vocabulaire m

vocal ['vəukl] adj vocal(e); (articulate) qui sait s'exprimer; ~ **cords** npl cordes vocales

vocation [vəu'keɪʃən] n vocation f; ~**al** adj professionnel(le)

vociferous [və'sɪfərəs] adj bruyant(e)

vodka ['vɔdkə] n vodka f

vogue [vəuɡ] n: in ~ en vogue f

voice [vɔɪs] n voix f ♦ vt (opinion) exprimer, formuler; ~**mail** n (system) messagerie f vocale; (device) boîte f vocale

void [vɔɪd] n vide m ♦ adj nul(le); ~ **of** vide de, dépourvu(e) de

volatile ['vɔlətaɪl] adj volatil(e); (person) versatile; (situation) explosif(-ive)

volcano [vɔl'keɪnəu] (pl ~**es**) n volcan m

volition [və'lɪʃən] n: of one's own ~ de son propre gré

volley ['vɔlɪ] n (of gunfire) salve f; (of stones etc) grêle f, volée f; (of questions) multitude f, série f; (TENNIS etc) volée f; ~**ball** n volley(-ball) m

volt [vəult] n volt m; ~**age** n tension f, voltage m

volume ['vɔljuːm] n volume m

voluntarily ['vɔləntrɪlɪ] adv volontairement

voluntary ['vɔləntərɪ] adj volontaire; (unpaid) bénévole

volunteer [vɔlən'tɪəʳ] n volontaire m/f ♦ vi (MIL) s'engager comme volontaire; to ~ to do se proposer pour faire

vomit ['vɔmɪt] vt, vi vomir

vote [vəut] n vote m, suffrage m; (cast) voix f, vote; (franchise) droit m de vote ♦ vt (elect): to be ~d chairman etc être élu président etc; (propose): to ~ that proposer que ♦ vi voter; ~ of thanks discours m de remerciement; ~**r** n électeur(-trice); **voting** n scrutin m, vote m

voucher ['vautʃəʳ] n (for meal, petrol, gift) bon m

vouch for ['vautʃ-] vt fus se porter garant de

vow [vau] n vœu m, serment m ♦ vi jurer

vowel ['vauəl] n voyelle f

voyage ['vɔɪdʒ] n voyage m par mer, traversée f; (by spacecraft) voyage

vulgar ['vʌlɡəʳ] adj vulgaire

vulnerable ['vʌlnərəbl] adj vulnérable

vulture ['vʌltʃəʳ] n vautour m

W, w

wad [wɔd] n (of cotton wool, paper) tampon m; (of banknotes etc) liasse f

waddle ['wɔdl] vi se dandiner

wade [weɪd] vi: to ~ **through** marcher dans, patauger dans; (fig: book) s'évertuer à lire

wafer ['weɪfə⁺] n (CULIN) gaufrette f

waffle ['wɒfl] n (CULIN) gaufre f; (inf) verbiage m, remplissage m ♦ vi parler pour ne rien dire, faire du remplissage

waft [wɒft] vt porter ♦ vi flotter

wag [wæg] vt agiter, remuer ♦ vi remuer

wage [weɪdʒ] n (also: ~s) salaire m, paye f ♦ vt: to ~ war faire la guerre; ~ **earner** n salarié(e); ~ **packet** n (enveloppe f de) paye f

wager ['weɪdʒə⁺] n pari m

wag(g)on ['wægən] n (horse-drawn) chariot m; (BRIT: RAIL) wagon m (de marchandises)

wail [weɪl] vi gémir; (siren) hurler

waist [weɪst] n taille f; ~**coat** (BRIT) n gilet m; ~**line** n (tour m de) taille f

wait [weɪt] n attente f ♦ vi attendre; to keep sb ~ing faire attendre qn; to ~ for attendre; I can't ~ to ... (fig) je meurs d'envie de ...; ~ **behind** vi rester (à attendre); ~ **on** vt fus servir; ~**er** n garçon m (de café), serveur m; ~**ing** n: "no ~ing" (BRIT: AUT) "stationnement interdit"; ~**ing list** n liste f d'attente; ~**ing room** n salle f d'attente; ~**ress** n serveuse f

waive [weɪv] vt renoncer à, abandonner

wake [weɪk] (pt **woke**, **waked**, pp **woken**, **waked**) vt (also: ~ **up**) réveiller ♦ vi (also: ~ **up**) se réveiller ♦ n (for dead person) veillée f mortuaire; (NAUT) sillage m

Wales [weɪlz] n pays m de Galles; **the Prince of ~** le prince de Galles

walk [wɔːk] n promenade f; (short) petit tour; (gait) démarche f; (path) chemin m; (in park etc) allée f ♦ vi marcher; (for pleasure, exercise) se promener ♦ vt (distance) faire à pied; (dog) promener; **10 minutes' ~ from** à 10 minutes à pied de; **from all ~s of life** de toutes conditions sociales; ~ **out** vi (audience) sortir, quitter la salle; (workers) se mettre en grève; ~ **out on** (inf) vt fus quitter, plaquer; ~**er** n (person) marcheur(-euse); ~**ie-talkie** n talkie-walkie m; ~**ing** n marche f à pied; ~**ing shoes** npl chaussures fpl de marche; ~**ing stick** n canne f; **W~man** ® n Walkman ® m; ~**out** n (of workers) grève-surprise f; ~**over** (inf) n victoire f ou examen m etc facile; ~**way** n promenade f

wall [wɔːl] n mur m; (of tunnel, cave etc) paroi m; ~**ed** adj (city) fortifié(e); (garden) entouré(e) d'un mur, clos(e)

wallet ['wɒlɪt] n portefeuille m

wallflower ['wɔːlflaʊə⁺] n giroflée f; **to be a ~** (fig) faire tapisserie

wallow ['wɒləʊ] vi se vautrer

wallpaper ['wɔːlpeɪpə⁺] n papier peint ♦ vt tapisser

walnut ['wɔːlnʌt] n noix f; (tree, wood) noyer m

walrus ['wɔːlrəs] (pl ~ or ~es) n morse m⚬⚬

waltz [wɔːlts] n valse f ♦ vi valser

wand [wɒnd] n (also: **magic ~**) baguette f (magique)

wander ['wɒndə⁺] vi (person) errer; (thoughts) vagabonder, errer ♦ vt errer dans

wane [weɪn] vi (moon) décroître; (reputation) décliner

wangle ['wæŋgl] (BRIT: inf) vt se débrouiller pour avoir; carotter

want [wɒnt] vt vouloir; (need) avoir besoin de ♦ n: **for ~ of** par manque de, faute de; ~**s** npl (needs) besoins mpl; **to ~ to do** vouloir faire; **to ~ sb to do** vouloir que qn fasse; ~**ed** adj (criminal) recherché(e) par la police; "**cook ~ed**" "on recherche un cuisinier"; ~**ing** adj: **to be found ~ing** ne pas être à la hauteur

war [wɔː⁺] n guerre f; **to make ~ (on)** faire la guerre (à)

ward [wɔːd] n (in hospital) salle f; (POL) canton m; (LAW: child) pupille m/f; ~ **off** vt (attack, enemy) repousser, éviter

warden ['wɔːdn] n gardien(ne); (BRIT: of institution) directeur(-trice); (: also: **traffic ~**) contractuel(le); (of youth hostel) père m ou mère f aubergiste

warder ['wɔːdə⁺] (BRIT) n gardien m de prison

wardrobe ['wɔːdrəʊb] n (cupboard) armoire f; (clothes) garde-robe f; (THEATRE) costumes mpl

warehouse ['wɛəhaʊs] n entrepôt m

wares [wɛəz] npl marchandises fpl

warfare ['wɔːfɛə⁺] n guerre f

warhead ['wɔːhɛd] n (MIL) ogive f

warily ['wɛərɪlɪ] adv avec prudence

warm [wɔːm] adj chaud(e); (thanks, welcome, applause, person) chaleureux(-euse); **it's ~** il fait chaud; **I'm ~** j'ai chaud; ~ **up** vi (person, room) se réchauffer; (water) chauffer; (athlete) s'échauffer ♦ vt (food) (faire) réchauffer, (faire) chauffer; (engine) faire chauffer; ~**-hearted** adj affectueux(-euse); ~**ly** adv chaudement, chaleureusement; ~**th** n chaleur f

warn [wɔːn] vt avertir, prévenir; **to ~ sb (not) to do** conseiller à qn de (ne pas) faire; ~**ing** n avertissement m; (notice) avis m; (signal) avertisseur m; ~**ing light** n avertisseur lumineux; ~**ing triangle** n (AUT) triangle m de présignalisation

warp [wɔːp] vi (wood) travailler, se déformer ♦ vt (fig: character) pervertir

warrant ['wɒrnt] n (guarantee) garantie f; (LAW: to arrest) mandat m d'arrêt; (: to search) mandat de perquisition; ~**y** n garantie f

warren ['wɒrən] n (of rabbits) terrier m; (fig: of streets etc) dédale m

warrior ['wɒrɪə⁺] n guerrier(-ère)

Warsaw ['wɔːsɔː] *n* Varsovie
warship ['wɔːʃɪp] *n* navire *m* de guerre
wart [wɔːt] *n* verrue *f*
wartime ['wɔːtaɪm] *n*: **in ~** en temps de guerre
wary ['wɛərɪ] *adj* prudent(e)
was [wɔz] *pt of* **be**
wash [wɔʃ] *vt* laver ♦ *vi* se laver; (*sea*): **to ~ over/against sth** inonder/baigner qch ♦ *n* (*clothes*) lessive *f*; (*~ing programme*) lavage *m*; (*of ship*) sillage *m*; **to have a ~** se laver, faire sa toilette; **to give sth a ~** laver qch; **~ away** *vt* (*stain*) enlever au lavage; (*subj: river etc*) emporter; **~ off** *vi* partir au lavage; **~ up** *vi* (*BRIT*) faire la vaisselle; (*US*) se débarbouiller; **~able** *adj* lavable; **~basin** (*US* **washbowl**) *n* lavabo *m*; **~cloth** (*US*) *n* gant *m* de toilette; **~er** *n* (*TECH*) rondelle *f*, joint *m*; **~ing** (*dirty*) linge *m*; (*clean*) lessive *f*; **~ing machine** *n* machine *f* à laver; **~ing powder** (*BRIT*) *n* lessive *f* (en poudre); **~ing-up** *n* vaisselle *f*; **~ing-up liquid** *n* produit *m* pour la vaisselle; **~-out** (*inf*) *n* désastre *m*; **~room** (*US*) *n* toilettes *fpl*
wasn't ['wɔznt] = **was not**
wasp [wɔsp] *n* guêpe *f*
wastage ['weɪstɪdʒ] *n* gaspillage *m*; (*in manufacturing, transport etc*) pertes *fpl*, déchets *mpl*; **natural ~** départs naturels
waste [weɪst] *n* gaspillage *m*; (*of time*) perte *f*; (*rubbish*) déchets *mpl*; (*also: household ~*) ordures *fpl* ♦ *adj* (*land, ground: in city*) à l'abandon; (*leftover*): **~ material** déchets *mpl* ♦ *vt* gaspiller; (*time, opportunity*) perdre; **~s** *npl* (*area*) étendue *f* désertique; **~ away** *vi* dépérir; **~ disposal unit** (*BRIT*) *n* broyeur *m* d'ordures; **~ful** *adj* gaspilleur(-euse); (*process*) peu économique; **~ ground** (*BRIT*) *n* terrain *m* vague; **~paper basket** *n* corbeille *f* à papier
watch [wɔtʃ] *n* montre *f*; (*act of ~ing*) surveillance *f*; guet *m*; (*MIL: guards*) garde *f*; (*NAUT: guards, spell of duty*) quart *m* ♦ *vt* (*look at*) observer; (: *match, programme, TV*) regarder; (*spy on, guard*) surveiller; (*be careful of*) faire attention à ♦ *vi* regarder; (*keep guard*) monter la garde; **~ out** *vi* faire attention; **~dog** *n* chien *m* de garde; (*fig*) gardien(ne); **~ful** *adj* attentif(-ive), vigilant(e); **~maker** *n* horloger(-ère); **~man** (*irreg*) *n* see **night**; **~strap** *n* bracelet *m* de montre
water ['wɔːtə'] *n* eau *f* ♦ *vt* (*plant, garden*) arroser ♦ *vi* (*eyes*) larmoyer; (*mouth*): **it makes my mouth ~** j'en ai l'eau à la bouche; **in British ~s** dans les eaux territoriales britanniques; **~ down** *vt* (*milk*) couper d'eau; (*fig: story*) édulcorer; **~colour** (*US* **watercolor**) *n* aquarelle *f*; **~cress** *n* cresson *m*

(*de fontaine*); **~fall** *n* chute *f* d'eau; **~ heater** *n* chauffe-eau *m*; **~ing can** *n* arrosoir *m*; **~ lily** *n* nénuphar *m*; **~line** *n* (*NAUT*) ligne *f* de flottaison; **~logged** *adj* (*ground*) détrempé(e); **~ main** *n* canalisation *f* d'eau; **~melon** *n* pastèque *f*; **~proof** *adj* imperméable; **~shed** *n* (*GEO*) ligne *f* de partage des eaux; (*fig*) moment *m* critique, point décisif; **~-skiing** *n* ski *m* nautique; **~tight** *adj* étanche; **~way** *n* cours *m* d'eau navigable; **~works** *n* (*building*) station *f* hydraulique; **~y** *adj* (*coffee, soup*) trop faible; (*eyes*) humide, larmoyant(e)
watt [wɔt] *n* watt *m*
wave [weɪv] *n* vague *f*; (*of hand*) geste *m*, signe *m*; (*RADIO*) onde *f*; (*in hair*) ondulation *f* ♦ *vi* faire signe de la main; (*flag*) flotter au vent; (*grass*) ondoyer ♦ *vt* (*handkerchief*) agiter; (*stick*) brandir; **~length** *n* longueur *f* d'ondes
waver ['weɪvə'] *vi* vaciller; (*voice*) trembler; (*person*) hésiter
wavy ['weɪvɪ] *adj* (*hair, surface*) ondulé(e); (*line*) onduleux(-euse)
wax [wæks] *n* cire *f*; (*for skis*) fart *m* ♦ *vt* cirer; (*car*) lustrer; (*skis*) farter ♦ *vi* (*moon*) croître; **~works** *npl* personnages *mpl* de cire ♦ *n* musée *m* de cire
way [weɪ] *n* chemin *m*, voie *f*; (*distance*) distance *f*; (*direction*) chemin *m*, direction *f*; (*manner*) façon *f*, manière *f*; (*habit*) habitude *f*, façon; **which ~? - this ~** par où? - par ici; **on the ~** (*en route*) en route; **to be on one's ~** être en route; **to go out of one's ~ to do** (*fig*) se détourner du mal pour faire; **to be in the ~** bloquer le passage; (*fig*) gêner; **to lose one's ~** perdre son chemin; **under ~** en cours; **in a ~** dans un sens; **in some ~s** à certains égards; **no ~!** (*inf*) pas question!; **by the ~** ... à propos ...; **"~ in"** (*BRIT*) "entrée"; **"~ out"** (*BRIT*) "sortie"; **the ~ back** le chemin du retour; **"give ~"** (*BRIT: AUT*) "cédez le passage"; **~lay** (*irreg*) *vt* attaquer
wayward ['weɪwəd] *adj* capricieux(-euse), entêté(e)
W.C. *n abbr* w.c. *mpl*, waters *mpl*
we [wiː] *pl pron* nous
weak [wiːk] *adj* faible; (*health*) fragile; (*beam etc*) peu solide; **~en** *vi* faiblir, décliner ♦ *vt* affaiblir; **~ling** *n* (*physically*) gringalet *m*; (*morally etc*) faible *m/f*; **~ness** *n* faiblesse *f*; (*fault*) point *m* faible; **to have a ~ness for** avoir un faible pour
wealth [wɛlθ] *n* (*money, resources*) richesse(s) *f(pl)*; (*of details*) profusion *f*; **~y** *adj* riche
wean [wiːn] *vt* sevrer
weapon ['wɛpən] *n* arme *f*
wear [wɛə'] (*pt* **wore**, *pp* **worn**) *n* (*use*) usage *m*; (*deterioration through use*) usure *f*;

(clothing): **sports/babywear** vêtements mpl de sport/pour bébés ♦ vt (clothes) porter; (put on) mettre; (damage: through use) user ♦ vi (last) faire de l'usage; (rub etc through) s'user; **town/evening** ~ tenue f de ville/soirée; ~ **away** vt user, ronger ♦ vi (inscription) s'effacer; ~ **down** vt user; (strength, person) épuiser; ~ **off** vi disparaître; ~ **out** vt user; (person, strength) épuiser; ~ **and tear** n usure f

weary ['wɪərɪ] adj (tired) épuisé(e); (dispirited) las (lasse), abattu(e) ♦ vi: **to ~ of** se lasser de

weasel ['wiːzl] n (ZOOL) belette f

weather ['weðər] n temps m ♦ vt (tempest, crisis) essuyer, réchapper à, survivre à; **under the ~** (fig: ill) mal fichu(e); **~-beaten** adj (person) hâlé(e); (building) dégradé(e) par les intempéries; **~cock** n girouette f; **~ forecast** n prévisions fpl météorologiques, météo f; **~ man** (irreg) (inf) n météorologue m; **~ vane** n = weathercock

weave [wiːv] (pt **wove**, pp **woven**) vt (cloth) tisser; (basket) tresser; **~r** n tisserand(e)

web [web] n (of spider) toile f; (on foot) palmure f; (fabric, also fig) tissu m; **the (World Wide) W~** le Web

website ['websaɪt] n (COMPUT) site m Web

wed [wed] (pt, pp **wedded**) vt épouser ♦ vi se marier

we'd [wiːd] = we had; we would

wedding [wedɪŋ] n mariage m; **silver/golden ~ (anniversary)** noces fpl d'argent/d'or; **~ day** n jour du mariage; **~ dress** n robe f de mariée; **~ ring** n alliance f

wedge [wedʒ] n (of wood etc) coin m, cale f; (of cake) part f ♦ vt (fix) caler; (pack tightly) enfoncer

Wednesday ['wednzdɪ] n mercredi m

wee [wiː] adj (SCOTTISH) adj (tout(e)) petit(e)

weed [wiːd] n mauvaise herbe ♦ vt désherber; **~killer** n désherbant m; **~y** adj (~: man) gringalet

week [wiːk] n semaine f; **a ~ today/on Friday** aujourd'hui/vendredi en huit; **~day** n jour m de semaine; (COMM) jour ouvrable; **~end** n week-end m; **~ly** adv une fois par semaine, chaque semaine ♦ adj hebdomadaire

weep [wiːp] (pt, pp **wept**) vi (person) pleurer; **~ing willow** n saule pleureur

weigh [weɪ] vt, vi peser; **to ~ anchor** lever l'ancre; ~ **down** vt (person, animal) écraser; (fig: with worry) accabler; ~ **up** vt examiner

weight [weɪt] n poids m; **to lose/put on ~** maigrir/grossir; **~ing** n (allowance) indemnité f, allocation f; **~lifter** n haltérophile m; **~lifting** n haltérophilie f; **~y** adj lourd(e); (important) de poids, important(e)

weir [wɪər] n barrage m

weird [wɪəd] adj bizarre

welcome ['welkəm] adj bienvenu(e) ♦ n accueil m ♦ vt accueillir; (also: **bid ~**) souhaiter la bienvenue à; (be glad of) se réjouir de; **thank you - you're ~!** merci - de rien or il n'y a pas de quoi!

welder [weldər] n soudeur(-euse)

welfare ['welfeər] n (wellbeing) bien-être m; (social aid) assistance sociale; **~ state** n État-providence m

well [wel] n puits m ♦ adv bien ♦ adj: **to be ~** aller bien ♦ excl eh bien!; (relief also) bon!; (resignation) enfin!; **as ~** aussi, également; **as ~ as** en plus de; ~ **done!** bravo!; **get ~ soon** remets-toi vite!; **to do ~** bien réussir; (business) prospérer; ~ **up** vi monter

we'll [wiːl] = we will; we shall

well: ~-behaved adj sage, obéissant(e); **~-being** n bien-être m; **~-built** adj (person) bien bâti(e); **~-deserved** adj (bien) mérité(e); **~-dressed** adj bien habillé(e); **~-heeled** (inf) adj (wealthy) nanti(e)

wellingtons ['welɪŋtənz] npl (also: **wellington boots**) bottes fpl de caoutchouc

well: ~-known adj (person) bien connu(e); **~-mannered** adj bien élevé(e); **~-meaning** adj bien intentionné(e); **~-off** adj aisé(e); **~-read** adj cultivé(e); **~-to-do** adj aisé(e); **~-wishers** npl amis mpl et admirateurs mpl; (friends) amis mpl

Welsh [welʃ] adj gallois(e) ♦ n (LING) gallois m; **the ~** npl (people) les Gallois mpl; **~man** (irreg) n Gallois m; **~woman** (irreg) n Galloise f

went [went] pt of go

wept [wept] pt, pp of weep

were [wɜːr] pt of be

we're [wɪər] = we are

weren't [wɜːnt] = were not

west [west] n ouest m ♦ adj ouest inv, de or à l'ouest ♦ adv à or vers l'ouest; **the W~** l'Occident m, l'Ouest; **the W~ Country** (BRIT) ♦ n le sud-ouest de l'Angleterre; **~erly** adj (wind) d'ouest; (point) à l'ouest; **~ern** adj occidental(e), de or à l'ouest ♦ n (CINEMA) western m; **W~ Indian** adj antillais(e) ♦ n Antillais(e); **W~ Indies** npl Antilles fpl; **~ward(s)** adv vers l'ouest

wet [wet] adj mouillé(e); (damp) humide; (soaked) trempé(e); (rainy) pluvieux(-euse) ♦ n (BRIT: POL) modéré m du parti conservateur; **to get ~** se mouiller; "**~ paint**" "attention peinture fraîche"; ~ **suit** n combinaison f de plongée

we've [wiːv] = we have

whack [wæk] vt donner un grand coup à

whale [weɪl] n (ZOOL) baleine f

wharf [wɔːf] n (pl **wharves**) n quai m

what [wɔt] *adj* quel(le); **what size is he?**
quelle taille fait-il?; **what colour is it?** de
quelle couleur est-ce?; **what books do you
need?** quels livres vous faut-il?; **what a mess!**
quel désordre!

♦ *pron* **1** (*interrogative*) que, *prep* +quoi;
what are you doing? que faites-vous?, qu'est-
ce que vous faites?; **what is happening?**
qu'est-ce qui se passe?, que se passe-t-il?;
what are you talking about? de quoi parlez-
vous?; **what is it called?** comment est-ce que
ça s'appelle?; **what about me?** et moi?; **what
about doing ...?** et si on faisait ...?
2 (*relative: subject*) ce qui; (*: direct object*) ce
que; (*: indirect object*) ce +*prep* +quoi, ce
dont; **I saw what you did/was on the table**
j'ai vu ce que vous avez fait/ce qui était sur la
table; **tell me what you remember** dites-moi
ce dont vous vous souvenez

♦ *excl* (*disbelieving*) quoi!, comment!

whatever [wɔt'evər] *adj*: ~ **book** quel que
soit le livre que (*or* qui) +*sub*; n'importe quel
livre ♦ *pron*: **do** ~ **is necessary** faites (tout) ce
qui est nécessaire; ~ **happens** quoi qu'il
arrive; **no reason** ~ pas la moindre raison;
nothing ~ rien du tout

whatsoever [wɔtsəu'evər] *adj* = **whatever**

wheat [wiːt] *n* blé *m*, froment *m*

wheedle ['wiːdl] *vt*: **to** ~ **sb into doing sth**
cajoler *or* enjôler qn pour qu'il fasse qch; **to**
~ **sth out of sb** obtenir qch de qn par des
cajoleries

wheel [wiːl] *n* roue *f*; (*also*: **steering** ~) volant
m; (NAUT) gouvernail *m* ♦ *vt* (*pram etc*)
pousser ♦ *vi* (*birds*) tournoyer; (*also*: ~ **round**:
person) virevolter; ~**barrow** *n* brouette *f*;
~**chair** *n* fauteuil roulant; ~ **clamp** *n* (AUT)
sabot *m* (de Denver)

wheeze [wiːz] *vi* respirer bruyamment

when [wɛn] *adv* quand; **when did he go?**
quand est-ce qu'il est parti?

♦ *conj* **1** (*at, during, after the time that*)
quand, lorsque; **she was reading when I came
in** elle lisait quand *or* lorsque je suis entré
2 (*on, at which*): **on the day when I met him**
le jour où je l'ai rencontré
3 (*whereas*) alors que; **I thought I was wrong
when in fact I was right** j'ai cru que j'avais
tort alors qu'en fait j'avais raison

whenever [wɛn'evər] *adv* quand donc ♦ *conj*
quand; (*every time that*) chaque fois que

where [wɛər] *adv, conj* où; **this is** ~ c'est là
que; ~**abouts** ['wɛərəbauts] *adv* où donc

♦ *n*: **nobody knows his** ~**abouts** personne ne
sait où il se trouve; ~**as** [wɛər'æz] *conj* alors
que; ~**by** *adv* par lequel (*or* laquelle *etc*);
wherever [wɛər'evər] *adv* où donc ♦ *conj* où
que +*sub*; ~**withal** ['wɛəwɪðɔːl] *n* moyens
mpl

whether ['wɛðər] *conj* si; **I don't know** ~ **to
accept or not** je ne sais pas si je dois accepter
ou non; **it's doubtful** ~ il est peu probable
que +*sub*; ~ **you go or not** que vous y alliez
ou non

which [wɪtʃ] *adj* (*interrogative: direct, indirect*)
quel(le); **which picture do you want?** quel
tableau voulez-vous?; **which one?** lequel
(laquelle)?; **in which case** auquel cas

♦ *pron* **1** (*interrogative*) lequel (laquelle),
lesquels (lesquelles) *pl*; **I don't mind which**
peu importe lequel; **which (of these) are
yours?** lesquels sont à vous?; **tell me which
you want** dites-moi lesquels *or* ceux que vous
voulez
2 (*relative: subject*) qui; (*: object*) que, *prep*
+lequel (laquelle); **the apple which you ate/
which is on the table** la pomme que vous
avez mangée/qui est sur la table; **the chair on
which you are sitting** la chaise sur laquelle
vous êtes assis; **the book of which you spoke**
le livre dont vous avez parlé; **he knew, which
is true/I feared** il le savait, ce qui est vrai/ce
que je craignais; **after which** après quoi

whichever [wɪtʃ'evər] *adj*: **take** ~ **book you
prefer** prenez le livre que vous préférez, peu
importe lequel; ~ **book you take** quel que soit
le livre que vous preniez

while [waɪl] *n* moment *m* ♦ *conj* pendant
que; (*as long as*) tant que; (*whereas*) alors
que; bien que +*sub* ♦ *vt* ~ **away** ~ **a while**
temps; ~ **away** *vt* (*time*) (faire) passer

whim [wɪm] *n* caprice *m*

whimper ['wɪmpər] *vi* geindre

whimsical ['wɪmzɪkəl] *adj* (*person*)
capricieux(-euse); (*look, story*) étrange

whine [waɪn] *vi* gémir, geindre

whip [wɪp] *n* fouet *m*; (*for riding*) cravache *f*;
(POL: *person*) chef de file assurant la discipline
dans son groupe parlementaire ♦ *vt* fouetter;
(*eggs*) battre; (*move quickly*) enlever/sortir
brusquement; ~**ped cream** *n* crème
fouettée; ~**round** (BRIT) *n* collecte *f*

whirl [wɜːl] *vi* tourbillonner; (*dancers*)
tournoyer ♦ *vt* faire tourbillonner; faire
tournoyer; ~**pool** *n* tourbillon *m*; ~**wind** *n*
tornade *f*

whirr [wɜːr] *vi* (*motor etc*) ronronner;
(*: louder*) vrombir

whisk [wɪsk] *n* (CULIN) fouet *m* ♦ *vt* fouetter;

(*eggs*) battre; **to ~ sb away** *or* **off** emmener qn rapidement

whiskers ['wɪskəz] *npl* (*of animal*) moustaches *fpl*; (*of man*) favoris *mpl*

whisky ['wɪskɪ] (*IRELAND, US* **whiskey**) *n* whisky *m*

whisper ['wɪspər] *vt, vi* chuchoter

whistle ['wɪsl] *n* (*sound*) sifflement *m*; (*object*) sifflet *m* ♦ *vi* siffler

white [waɪt] *adj* blanc (blanche); (*with fear*) blême ♦ *n* blanc *m*; (*person*) blanc (blanche); **~ coffee** (*BRIT*) *n* café *m* au lait, (café) crème *m*; **~-collar worker** *n* employé(e) de bureau; **~ elephant** *n* (*fig*) objet dispendieux et superflu; **~ lie** *n* pieux mensonge; **~ paper** *n* (*POL*) livre blanc; **~wash** *vt* blanchir à la chaux; (*fig*) blanchir ♦ *n* (*paint*) blanc *m* de chaux

whiting ['waɪtɪŋ] *n inv* (*fish*) merlan *m*

Whitsun ['wɪtsn] *n* la Pentecôte

whizz [wɪz] *vi*: **to ~ past** *or* **by** passer à toute vitesse; **~ kid** (*inf*) *n* petit prodige

who [huː] *pron* qui; **~dunit** [huːˈdʌnɪt] (*inf*) *n* roman policier

whoever [huːˈevər] *pron*: **~ finds it** celui (celle) qui le trouve; **ask ~ you like** demandez à qui vous voulez; **~ he marries** quelle que soit la personne qu'il épouse; **~ told you that?** qui a bien pu vous dire ça?

whole [həʊl] *adj* (*complete*) entier(-ère), tout(e); (*not broken*) intact(e), complet(-ète) ♦ *n* (*all*): **the ~ of** la totalité de, tout(e) le (la); (*entire unit*) tout *m*; **the ~ of the town** la ville tout entière; **on the ~, as a ~** dans l'ensemble; **~food(s)** *n(pl)* aliments complets; **~hearted** *adj* sans réserve(s); **~meal** (*BRIT*) *adj* (*bread, flour*) complet(-ète); **~sale** *n* (*vente f en*) gros *m* ♦ *adj* (*price*) de gros; (*destruction*) systématique ♦ *adv* en gros; **~saler** *n* grossiste *m/f*; **~some** *adj* sain(e); **~wheat** *adj* = **wholemeal**; **wholly** ['həʊlɪ] *adv* entièrement, tout à fait

KEYWORD

whom [huːm] *pron* **1** (*interrogative*) qui; **whom did you see?** qui avez-vous vu?; **to whom did you give it?** à qui l'avez-vous donné?

2 (*relative*) que, *prep* +qui; **the man whom I saw/to whom I spoke** l'homme que j'ai vu/à qui j'ai parlé

whooping cough ['huːpɪŋ-] *n* coqueluche *f*

whore [hɔːr] (*inf: pej*) *n* putain *f*

KEYWORD

whose [huːz] *adj* **1** (*possessive: interrogative*): **whose book is this?** à qui est ce livre?; **whose**

pencil have you taken? à qui est le crayon que vous avez pris?, c'est le crayon de qui que vous avez pris?; **whose daughter are you?** de qui êtes-vous la fille?

2 (*possessive: relative*): **the man whose son you rescued** l'homme dont *or* de qui vous avez sauvé le fils; **the girl whose sister you were speaking to** la fille à la sœur de qui *or* de laquelle vous parliez; **the woman whose car was stolen** la femme dont la voiture a été volée

♦ *pron* à qui; **whose is this?** à qui est ceci?; **I know whose it is** je sais à qui c'est

why [waɪ] *adv* pourquoi ♦ *excl* eh bien!, tiens!; **the reason ~** la raison pour laquelle; **tell me ~** dites-moi pourquoi; **~ not?** pourquoi pas?

wicked ['wɪkɪd] *adj* mauvais(e), méchant(e); (*crime*) pervers(e); (*mischievous*) malicieux(-euse)

wicket ['wɪkɪt] *n* (*CRICKET*) guichet *m*; terrain *m* (*entre les deux guichets*)

wide [waɪd] *adj* large; (*area, knowledge*) vaste, très étendu(e); (*choice*) grand(e) ♦ *adv*: **to open ~** ouvrir tout grand; **to shoot ~** tirer à côté; **~-awake** *adj* bien éveillé(e); **~ly** *adv* (*differing*) radicalement; (*spaced*) sur une grande étendue; (*believed*) généralement; (*travel*) beaucoup; **~n** *vt* élargir ♦ *vi* s'élargir; **~ open** *adj* grand(e) ouvert(e); **~spread** *adj* (*belief etc*) très répandu(e)

widow ['wɪdəʊ] *n* veuve *f*; **~ed** *adj* veuf (veuve); **~er** *n* veuf *m*

width [wɪdθ] *n* largeur *f*

wield [wiːld] *vt* (*sword*) manier; (*power*) exercer

wife [waɪf] (*pl* **wives**) *n* femme *f*, épouse *f*

wig [wɪg] *n* perruque *f*

wiggle ['wɪgl] *vt* agiter, remuer

wild [waɪld] *adj* sauvage; (*sea*) déchaîné(e); (*idea, life*) fou (folle); (*behaviour*) extravagant(e), déchaîné(e); **to make a ~ guess** émettre une hypothèse à tout hasard; **~erness** ['wɪldənɪs] *n* désert *m*, région *f* sauvage; **~life** *n* (*animals*) faune *f*; **~ly** *adv* (*behave*) de manière déchaînée; (*applaud*) frénétiquement; (*hit, guess*) au hasard; (*happy*) follement; **~s** *npl* (*remote area*) régions *fpl* sauvages

wilful ['wɪlfʊl] (*US* **willful**) *adj* (*person*) obstiné(e); (*action*) délibéré(e)

KEYWORD

will [wɪl] (*vt: pt, pp* **willed**) *aux vb* **1** (*forming future tense*): **I will finish it tomorrow** je le finirai demain; **I will have finished it by tomorrow** je l'aurai fini d'ici demain; **will you do it? - yes I will/no I won't** le ferez-vous? -

oui/non

2 (*in conjectures, predictions*): **he will** or **he'll be there by now** il doit être arrivé à l'heure qu'il est; **that will be the postman** ça doit être le facteur

3 (*in commands, requests, offers*): **will you be quiet!** voulez-vous bien vous taire!; **will you help me?** est-ce que vous pouvez m'aider?; **will you have a cup of tea?** voulez-vous une tasse de thé?; **I won't put up with it!** je ne le tolérerai pas!

♦ *vt*: **to will sb to do** souhaiter ardemment que qn fasse; **he willed himself to go on** par un suprême effort de volonté, il continua
♦ *n* volonté *f*; testament *m*

willing ['wɪlɪŋ] *adj* de bonne volonté, serviable; **he's ~ to do it** il est disposé à le faire, il veut bien le faire; **~ly** *adv* volontiers; **~ness** *n* bonne volonté
willow ['wɪləu] *n* saule *m*
willpower ['wɪl'pauə'] *n* volonté *f*
willy-nilly ['wɪlɪ'nɪlɪ] *adv* bon gré mal gré
wilt [wɪlt] *vi* dépérir; (*flower*) se faner
win [wɪn] (*pt, pp* **won**) *n* (*in sports etc*) victoire *f* ♦ *vt* gagner; (*prize*) remporter; (*popularity*) acquérir ♦ *vi* gagner; **~ over** *vt* convaincre; **~ round** (*BRIT*) *vt* = **win over**
wince [wɪns] *vi* tressaillir
winch [wɪntʃ] *n* treuil *m*
wind[1] [wɪnd] *n* (*also MED*) vent *m*; (*breath*) souffle *m* ♦ *vt* (*take breath*) couper le souffle à
wind[2] [waɪnd] (*pt, pp* **wound**) *vt* enrouler; (*wrap*) envelopper; (*clock, toy*) remonter ♦ *vi* (*road, river*) serpenter; **~ up** *vt* (*clock*) remonter; (*debate*) terminer, clôturer
windfall ['wɪndfɔːl] *n* coup *m* de chance
winding ['waɪndɪŋ] *adj* (*road*) sinueux(-euse); (*staircase*) tournant(e)
wind instrument ['wɪnd-] *n* (*MUS*) instrument *m* à vent
windmill ['wɪndmɪl] *n* moulin *m* à vent
window ['wɪndəu] *n* fenêtre *f*; (*in car, train, also:* ~ *pane*) vitre *f*; (*in shop etc*) vitrine *f*; **~ box** *n* jardinière *f*; **~ cleaner** *n* (*person*) laveur(-euse) de vitres; **~ ledge** *n* rebord *m* de la fenêtre; **~ pane** *n* vitre *f*, carreau *m*; **~-shopping** *n*: **to go ~-shopping** faire du lèche-vitrines; **~sill** ['wɪndəusɪl] *n* (*inside*) appui *m* de la fenêtre; (*outside*) rebord *m* de la fenêtre
windpipe ['wɪndpaɪp] *n* trachée *f*
wind power ['wɪnd-] *n* énergie éolienne
windscreen ['wɪndskriːn] *n* pare-brise *m inv*; **~ washer** *n* lave-glace *m inv*; **~ wiper** *n* essuie-glace *m inv*
windshield ['wɪndʃiːld] (*US*) *n* = **windscreen**
windswept ['wɪndswept] *adj* balayé(e) par

le vent; (*person*) ébouriffé(e)
windy ['wɪndɪ] *adj* venteux(-euse); **it's ~** il y a du vent
wine [waɪn] *n* vin *m*; **~ bar** *n* bar *m* à vin; **~ cellar** *n* cave *f* à vin; **~ glass** *n* verre *m* à vin; **~ list** *n* carte *f* des vins; **~ waiter** *n* sommelier *m*
wing [wɪŋ] *n* aile *f*; **~s** *npl* (*THEATRE*) coulisses *fpl*; **~er** *n* (*SPORT*) ailier *m*
wink [wɪŋk] *n* clin *m* d'œil ♦ *vi* faire un clin d'œil; (*blink*) cligner des yeux
winner ['wɪnə'] *n* gagnant(e)
winning ['wɪnɪŋ] *adj* (*team*) gagnant(e); (*goal*) décisif(-ive); **~s** *npl* gains *mpl*
winter ['wɪntə'] *n* hiver *m*; **in ~** en hiver; **~ sports** *npl* sports *mpl* d'hiver; **wintry** *adj* hivernal(e)
wipe [waɪp] *n*: **to give sth a ~** donner un coup de torchon/de chiffon/d'éponge à qch ♦ *vt* essuyer; (*erase: tape*) effacer; **~ off** *vt* enlever; **~ out** *vt* (*debt*) éteindre, amortir; (*memory*) effacer; (*destroy*) anéantir; **~ up** *vt* essuyer
wire ['waɪə'] *n* fil *m* (de fer); (*ELEC*) fil électrique; (*TEL*) télégramme *m* ♦ *vt* (*house*) faire l'installation électrique de; (*also:* ~ *up*) brancher; (*person: send telegram to*) télégraphier à; **~less** (*BRIT*) *n* poste *m* de radio; **wiring** *n* installation *f* électrique; **wiry** *adj* noueux(-euse), nerveux(-euse); (*hair*) dru(e)
wisdom ['wɪzdəm] *n* sagesse *f*; (*of action*) prudence *f*; **~ tooth** *n* dent *f* de sagesse
wise [waɪz] *adj* sage, prudent(e); (*remark*) judicieux(-euse) ♦ *suffix*: **...wise**: **timewise** *etc* en ce qui concerne le temps *etc*
wish [wɪʃ] *n* (*desire*) désir *m*; (*specific desire*) souhait *m*, vœu *m* ♦ *vt* souhaiter, désirer, vouloir; **best ~es** (*on birthday etc*) meilleurs vœux; **with best ~es** (*in letter*) bien amicalement; **to ~ sb goodbye** dire au revoir à qn; **he ~ed me well** il m'a souhaité bonne chance; **to ~ to do/sb to do** désirer *or* vouloir faire/que qn fasse; **to ~ for** souhaiter; **~ful** *adj*: **it's ~ful thinking** c'est prendre ses désirs pour des réalités
wistful ['wɪstful] *adj* mélancolique
wit [wɪt] *n* (*gen pl*) intelligence *f*, esprit *m*; (*presence of mind*) présence *f* d'esprit; (*wittiness*) esprit; (*person*) homme/femme d'esprit
witch [wɪtʃ] *n* sorcière *f*; **~craft** *n* sorcellerie *f*

┌─────────────┐
│ KEYWORD │
└─────────────┘

with [wɪð, wɪθ] *prep* **1** (*in the company of*) avec; (*at the home of*) chez; **we stayed with friends** nous avons logé chez des amis; **I'll be with you in a minute** je suis à vous dans un instant

2 (*descriptive*): **a room with a view** une chambre avec vue; **the man with the grey hat/blue eyes** l'homme au chapeau gris/aux yeux bleus

3 (*indicating manner, means, cause*): **with tears in her eyes** les larmes aux yeux; **to walk with a stick** marcher avec une canne; **red with anger** rouge de colère; **to shake with fear** trembler de peur; **to fill sth with water** remplir qch d'eau

4: I'm with you (*I understand*) je vous suis; **to be with it** (*inf: up-to-date*) être dans le vent

withdraw [wɪθ'drɔː] (*irreg*) vt retirer ♦ vi se retirer; **~al** n retrait m; **~al symptoms** npl (MED): **to have ~al symptoms** être en état de manque; **~n** adj (*person*) renfermé(e)

wither ['wɪðə'] vi (*plant*) se faner

withhold [wɪθ'həuld] (*irreg*) vt (*money*) retenir; **to ~ (from)** (*information*) cacher (à); (*permission*) refuser (à)

within [wɪð'ɪn] prep à l'intérieur de ♦ adv à l'intérieur; **~ his reach** à sa portée; **~ sight of** en vue de; **~ a kilometre of** à moins d'un kilomètre de; **~ the week** avant la fin de la semaine

without [wɪð'aut] prep sans; **~ a coat** sans manteau; **~ speaking** sans parler; **to go ~ sth** se passer de qch

withstand [wɪθ'stænd] (*irreg*) vt résister à

witness ['wɪtnɪs] n (*person*) témoin m ♦ vt (*event*) être témoin de; (*document*) attester l'authenticité de; **to bear ~ (to)** (*fig*) attester; **~ box** (US **witness stand**) n barre f des témoins

witty ['wɪtɪ] adj spirituel(le), plein(e) d'esprit

wives [waivz] npl of **wife**

wizard ['wɪzəd] n magicien m

wk abbr = **week**

wobble ['wɔbl] vi trembler; (*chair*) branler

woe [wəu] n malheur m

woke [wəuk] pt of **wake**; **~n** pp of **wake**

wolf [wulf] (*pl* **wolves**) n loup m

woman ['wumən] (*pl* **women**) n femme f; **~ doctor** n femme f médecin; **~ly** adj féminin(e)

womb [wuːm] n (ANAT) utérus m

women ['wɪmɪn] npl of **woman**; **~'s lib** (*inf*) n MLF m; **W~'s (Liberation) Movement** n mouvement m de libération de la femme

won [wʌn] pt, pp of **win**

wonder ['wʌndə'] n merveille f, miracle m; (*feeling*) émerveillement m ♦ vi: **to ~ whether/why** se demander si/pourquoi; **to ~ at** (*marvel*) s'émerveiller de; **to ~ about** songer à; **it's no ~ (that)** il n'est pas étonnant (que +sub); **~ful** adj merveilleux(-euse)

won't [wəunt] = **will not**

wood [wud] n (*timber, forest*) bois m;

~ carving n sculpture f en or sur bois; **~ed** adj boisé(e); **~en** adj en bois; (*fig*) raide; inexpressif(-ive); **~pecker** n pic m (*oiseau*); **~wind** n (MUS): **the ~wind** les bois mpl; **~work** n menuiserie f; **~worm** n ver m du bois

wool [wul] n laine f; **to pull the ~ over sb's eyes** (*fig*) en faire accroire à qn; **~len** (US **woolen**) adj de or en laine; (*industry*) lainier(-ère); **~lens** npl (*clothes*) lainages mpl; **~ly** (US **wooly**) adj laineux(-euse); (*fig: ideas*) confus(e)

word [wəːd] n mot m; (*promise*) parole f; (*news*) nouvelles fpl ♦ vt rédiger, formuler; **in other ~s** d'autres termes; **to break/keep one's ~** manquer à sa parole/tenir parole; **~ing** n termes mpl; libellé m; **~ processing** n traitement m de texte; **~ processor** n machine f de traitement de texte

wore [wɔː'] pt of **wear**

work [wəːk] n travail m; (ART, LITERATURE) œuvre f ♦ vi travailler; (*mechanism*) marcher, fonctionner; (*plan etc*) marcher; (*medicine*) agir ♦ vt (*clay, wood etc*) travailler; (*mine etc*) exploiter; (*machine*) faire marcher or fonctionner; (*miracles, wonders etc*) faire; **to be out of ~** être sans emploi; **to ~ loose** se défaire, se desserrer; **~ on** vt fus travailler à; (*influence*) (essayer d')influencer; **~ out** vi (*plans etc*) marcher ♦ vt (*problem*) résoudre; (*plan*) élaborer; **it ~s out at £100** ça fait 100 livres; **~ up** vt: **to get ~ed up** se mettre dans tous ses états; **~able** adj (*solution*) réalisable; **~aholic** [wəːkə'hɔlɪk] n bourreau m de travail; **~er** n travailleur(-euse), ouvrier(-ère); **~ experience** n stage m; **~force** n main-d'œuvre f; **~ing class** n classe f ouvrière; **~ing-class** adj ouvrier(-ère); **~ing order** n: **in ~ing order** en état de marche; **~man** (*irreg*) n ouvrier m; **~manship** (*skill*) n métier m, habileté f; **~s** n (BRIT: *factory*) usine f ♦ npl (*of clock, machine*) mécanisme m; **~ sheet** n (COMPUT) feuille f de programmation; **~shop** n atelier m; **~ station** n poste m de travail; **~-to-rule** (BRIT) n grève f du zèle

world [wəːld] n monde m ♦ cpd (*champion*) du monde; (*power, war*) mondial(e); **to think the ~ of sb** (*fig*) ne jurer que par qn; **~ly** adj de ce monde; (*knowledgeable*) qui a l'expérience du monde; **~wide** adj universel(le); **W~-Wide Web** n Web n.

worm [wəːm] n ver m

worn [wɔːn] pp of **wear** ♦ adj usé(e); **~-out** adj (*object*) complètement usé(e); (*person*) épuisé(e)

worried ['wʌrɪd] adj inquiet(-ète)

worry ['wʌrɪ] n souci m ♦ vt inquiéter ♦ vi s'inquiéter, se faire du souci

worse [wəːs] adj pire, plus mauvais(e) ♦ adv plus mal ♦ n pire m; **a change for the ~** une détérioration; **~n** vt, vi empirer; **~ off** adj moins à l'aise financièrement; (fig): **you'll be ~ off this way** ça ira moins bien de cette façon

worship ['wəːʃɪp] n culte m ♦ vt (God) rendre un culte à; (person) adorer; **Your W~** (BRIT: to mayor) Monsieur le maire; (: to judge) Monsieur le juge

worst [wəːst] adj le (la) pire, le (la) plus mauvais(e) ♦ adv le plus mal ♦ n pire m; **at ~** au pis aller

worth [wəːθ] n valeur f ♦ adj: **to be ~** valoir; **it's ~ it** cela en vaut la peine, ça vaut la peine; **it is ~ one's while (to do)** on gagne à (faire); **~less** adj qui ne vaut rien; **~while** adj (activity, cause) utile, louable

worthy [wəːðɪ] adj (person) digne; (motive) louable; **~ of** digne de

---
KEYWORD
---

would [wud] aux vb **1** (conditional tense): **if you asked him he would do it** si vous le lui demandiez, il le ferait; **if you had asked him he would have done it** si vous le lui aviez demandé, il l'aurait fait

2 (in offers, invitations, requests): **would you like a biscuit?** voulez-vous un biscuit?; **would you close the door please?** voulez-vous fermer la porte, s'il vous plaît?

3 (in indirect speech): **I said I would do it** j'ai dit que je le ferais

4 (emphatic): **it WOULD have to snow today!** naturellement il neige aujourd'hui! or il fallait qu'il neige aujourd'hui!

5 (insistence): **she wouldn't do it** elle n'a pas voulu or elle a refusé de le faire

6 (conjecture): **it would have been midnight** il devait être minuit

7 (indicating habit): **he would go there on Mondays** il y allait le lundi

would-be ['wudbiː] (pej) adj soi-disant
wouldn't ['wudnt] = **would not**
wound[1] [wuːnd] n blessure f ♦ vt blesser
wound[2] [waund] pt, pp of **wind**[2]
wove [wəuv] pt of **weave**; **~n** pp of **weave**
wrap [ræp] vt (also: **~ up**) envelopper, emballer; (wind) enrouler; **~per** n (BRIT: of book) couverture f; (on chocolate) emballage m, papier m; **~ping paper** n papier m d'emballage; (for gift) papier cadeau

wreak [riːk] vt: **to ~ havoc (on)** avoir un effet désastreux (sur)

wreath [riːθ] (pl **~s**) n couronne f

wreck [rɛk] n (ship) épave f; (vehicle) véhicule accidenté; (pej: person) loque humaine ♦ vt démolir; (fig) briser, ruiner;

~age n débris mpl; (of building) décombres mpl; (of ship) épave f

wren [rɛn] n (ZOOL) roitelet m

wrench [rɛntʃ] n (TECH) clé f (à écrous); (tug) violent mouvement de torsion; (fig) déchirement m ♦ vt tirer violemment sur, tordre; **to ~ sth from** arracher qch à or de

wrestle ['rɛsl] vi: **to ~ (with sb)** lutter (avec qn); **~r** n lutteur(-euse); **wrestling** n lutte f; (also: **all-in wrestling**) catch m, lutte f libre

wretched ['rɛtʃɪd] adj misérable; (inf) maudit(e)

wriggle ['rɪgl] vi (also: **~ about**) se tortiller

wring [rɪŋ] (pt, pp **wrung**) vt tordre; (wet clothes) essorer; (fig): **to ~ sth out of sb** arracher qch à qn

wrinkle ['rɪŋkl] n (on skin) ride f; (on paper etc) pli m ♦ vt plisser ♦ vi se plisser; **~d** adj (skin, face) ridé(e)

wrist [rɪst] n poignet m; **~watch** n montre-bracelet f

writ [rɪt] n acte m judiciaire

write [raɪt] (pt **wrote**, pp **written**) vt, vi écrire; (prescription) rédiger; **~ down** vt noter; (put in writing) mettre par écrit; **~ off** vt (debt) passer aux profits et pertes; (project) mettre une croix sur; **~ out** vt écrire; **~ up** vt rédiger; **~-off** n perte totale; **~r** n auteur m, écrivain m

writhe [raɪð] vi se tordre

writing ['raɪtɪŋ] n écriture f; (of author) œuvres fpl; **in ~** par écrit; **~ paper** n papier m à lettres

wrong [rɔŋ] adj (incorrect) faux (fausse); (morally) mauvais(e); (wicked) mal; (unfair) injuste ♦ adv mal ♦ n tort m ♦ vt faire du tort à, léser; **you are ~ to do it** tu as tort de le faire; **you are ~ about that, you've got it ~** tu te trompes; **what's ~?** qu'est-ce qui ne va pas?; **you've got the ~ number** vous vous êtes trompé de numéro; **to go ~** (person) se tromper; (plan) mal tourner; (machine) tomber en panne; **to be in the ~** avoir tort; **~ful** adj injustifié(e); **~ly** adv mal, incorrectement; **~ side** n (of material) envers m

wrote [rəut] pt of **write**
wrought iron [rɔːt] n fer forgé
wrung [rʌŋ] pt, pp of **wring**
wt. abbr = **weight**
WWW n abbr (= World Wide Web): **the ~** le Web

X, x

Xmas ['ɛksməs] n abbr = **Christmas**
X-ray ['ɛksreɪ] n (ray) rayon m X; (photo) radio(graphie) f

xylophone ['zaɪləfəun] n xylophone m

Y, y

yacht [jɔt] n yacht m; voilier m; **~ing** n yachting m, navigation f de plaisance; **~sman** (irreg) n plaisancier m

Yank [jæŋk], **Yankee** ['jæŋkɪ] (pej) n Amerloque m/f

yap [jæp] vi (dog) japper

yard [jɑːd] n (of house etc) cour f; (measure) yard m (= 91,4 cm); **~stick** n (fig) mesure f, critères mpl

yarn [jɑːn] n fil m; (tale) longue histoire

yawn [jɔːn] n bâillement m ♦ vi bâiller; **~ing** adj (gap) béant(e)

yd. abbr = **yard(s)**

yeah [jɛə] (inf) adv ouais

year [jɪə'] n an m, année f; **to be 8 ~s old** avoir 8 ans; **an eight-~-old child** un enfant de huit ans; **~ly** adj annuel(le) ♦ adv annuellement

yearn [jəːn] vi: **to ~ for sth** aspirer à qch, languir après qch

yeast [jiːst] n levure f

yell [jɛl] vi hurler

yellow ['jɛləu] adj jaune

yelp [jɛlp] vi japper; glapir

yes [jɛs] adv oui; (answering negative question) si ♦ n oui m; **to say/answer ~** dire/répondre oui

yesterday ['jɛstədɪ] adv hier ♦ n hier m; **~ morning/evening** hier matin/soir; **all day ~** toute la journée d'hier

yet [jɛt] adv encore; déjà ♦ conj pourtant, néanmoins; **it is not finished ~** ce n'est pas encore fini or toujours pas fini; **the best ~** le meilleur jusqu'ici or jusque-là; **as ~** jusqu'ici, encore

yew [juː] n if m

yield [jiːld] n production f, rendement m; rapport m ♦ vt produire, rendre, rapporter; (surrender) céder ♦ vi céder; (US: AUT) céder la priorité

YMCA n abbr (= Young Men's Christian Association) YMCA m

yob [jɔb] (BRIT: inf) n loubar(d) m

yoghourt ['jəugət] n yaourt m

yog(h)urt ['jəugət] n = **yoghourt**

yoke [jəuk] n joug m

yolk [jəuk] n jaune m (d'œuf)

KEYWORD

---

you [juː] pron 1 (subject) tu; (polite form) vous; (plural) vous; **you French enjoy your food** vous autres Français, vous aimez bien manger; **you and I will go** toi et moi or vous et moi, nous irons

2 (object: direct, indirect) te, t' +vowel, vous;

I know you je te or vous connais; **I gave it to you** je vous l'ai donné, je te l'ai donné

3 (stressed) toi; vous; **I told YOU to do it** c'est à toi or vous que j'ai dit de le faire

4 (after prep, in comparisons) toi; vous; **it's for you** c'est pour toi or vous; **she's younger than you** elle est plus jeune que toi or vous

5 (impersonal: one) on; **fresh air does you good** l'air frais fait du bien; **you never know** on ne sait jamais

---

you'd [juːd] = **you had**; **you would**

you'll [juːl] = **you will**; **you shall**

young [jʌŋ] adj jeune ♦ npl (of animal) petits mpl; (people): **the ~** les jeunes, la jeunesse; **~er** [jʌŋgə'] adj (brother etc) cadet(te); **~ster** n jeune m (garçon m); (child) enfant m/f

your [jɔː'] adj ton (ta), tes pl; (polite form, pl) votre, vos pl; see also **my**

you're [juə'] = **you are**

yours [jɔːz] pron le (la) tien(ne), les tiens (tiennes); (polite form, pl) le (la) vôtre, les vôtres; **~ sincerely/faithfully/truly** veuillez agréer l'expression de mes sentiments les meilleurs; see also **mine**[1]

yourself [jɔː'sɛlf] pron (reflexive) te; (: polite form) vous; (after prep) toi; vous; (emphatic) toi-même; vous-même; see also **oneself**;

yourselves pl pron vous; (emphatic) vous-mêmes

youth [juːθ] n jeunesse f; (young man: pl ~s) jeune homme m; **~ club** n centre m de jeunes; **~ful** adj jeune; (enthusiasm) de jeunesse, juvénile; **~ hostel** n auberge f de jeunesse

you've [juːv] = **you have**

YTS n abbr (BRIT: Youth Training Scheme) ≈ TUC m

Yugoslav ['juːgəuslɑːv] adj yougoslave ♦ n Yougoslave m/f

Yugoslavia ['juːgəu'slɑːvɪə] n Yougoslavie f

yuppie ['jʌpɪ] (inf) n yuppie m/f

YWCA n abbr (= Young Women's Christian Association) YWCA m

Z, z

zany ['zeɪnɪ] adj farfelu(e), loufoque

zap [zæp] vt (COMPUT) effacer

zeal [ziːl] n zèle m, ferveur f; empressement m

zebra ['ziːbrə] n zèbre m; **~ crossing** (BRIT) n passage clouté or pour piétons

zero ['zɪərəu] n zéro m

zest [zɛst] n entrain m, élan m; (of orange) zeste m

zigzag ['zɪgzæg] n zigzag m

Zimbabwe [zɪm'bɑːbwɪ] n Zimbabwe m

Zimmer frame ['zɪmə-] *n* déambulateur *m*

zinc [zɪŋk] *n* zinc *m*

zip [zɪp] *n* fermeture *f* éclair ® ♦ *vt* (*also:* ~ **up**) fermer avec une fermeture éclair ®; ~ **code** (*US*) *n* code postal; **~per** (*US*) *n* = **zip**

zit [zɪt] (*inf*) *n* bouton *m*

zodiac ['zəudɪæk] *n* zodiaque *m*

zone [zəun] *n* zone *f*

zoo [zu:] *n* zoo *m*

zoom [zu:m] *vi*: **to ~ past** passer en trombe; ~ **lens** *n* zoom *m*

zucchini [zu:'ki:nɪ] (*US*) *n(pl)* courgette(s) *f(pl)*

VERB TABLES

1 Participe présent 2 Participe passé 3 Présent 4 Imparfait 5 Futur 6 Conditionnel 7 Subjonctif présent

acquérir 1 acquérant 2 acquis 3 acquiers, acquérons, acquièrent 4 acquérais 5 acquerrai 7 acquière
ALLER 1 allant 2 allé 3 vais, vas, va, allons, allez, vont 4 allais 5 irai 6 irais 7 aille
asseoir 1 asseyant 2 assis 3 assieds, asseyons, asseyez, asseyent 4 asseyais 5 assiérai 7 asseye
atteindre 1 atteignant 2 atteint 3 atteins, atteignons 4 atteignais 7 atteigne
AVOIR 1 ayant 2 eu 3 ai, as, a, avons, avez, ont 4 avais 5 aurai 6 aurais 7 aie, aies, ait, ayons, ayez, aient
battre 1 battant 2 battu 3 bats, bat, battons 4 battais 7 batte
boire 1 buvant 2 bu 3 bois, buvons, boivent 4 buvais 7 boive
bouillir 1 bouillant 2 bouilli 3 bous, bouillons 4 bouillais 7 bouille
conclure 1 concluant 2 conclu 3 conclus, concluons 4 concluais 7 conclue
conduire 1 conduisant 2 conduit 3 conduis, conduisons 4 conduisais 7 conduise
connaître 1 connaissant 2 connu 3 connais, connaît, connaissons 4 connaissais 7 connaisse
coudre 1 cousant 2 cousu 3 couds, cousons, cousez, cousent 4 cousais 7 couse
courir 1 courant 2 couru 3 cours, courons, courais 5 courrai 7 coure
couvrir 1 couvrant 2 couvert 3 couvre, couvrons 4 couvrais 7 couvre
craindre 1 craignant 2 craint 3 crains, craignons 4 craignais 7 craigne
croire 1 croyant 2 cru 3 crois, croyons, croient 4 croyais 7 croie
croître 1 croissant 2 crû, crue, crus, crues 3 croîs, croissons 4 croissais 7 croisse
cueillir 1 cueillant 2 cueilli 3 cueille, cueillons 4 cueillais 5 cueillerai 7 cueille
devoir 1 devant 2 dû, due, dus, dues 3 dois, devons, doivent 4 devais 5 devrai 7 doive
dire 1 disant 2 dit 3 dis, disons, dites, disent 4 disais 7 dise
dormir 1 dormant 2 dormi 3 dors, dormons 4 dormais 7 dorme
écrire 1 écrivant 2 écrit 3 écris, écrivons 4 écrivais 7 écrive
ÊTRE 1 étant 2 été 3 suis, es, est, sommes, êtes, sont 4 étais 5 serai 6 serais 7 sois, sois, soit, soyons, soyez, soient
FAIRE 1 faisant 2 fait 3 fais, fais, fait, faisons, faites, font 4 faisais 5 ferai 6 ferais 7 fasse
falloir 2 fallu 3 faut 4 fallait 5 faudra 7 faille
FINIR 1 finissant 2 fini 3 finis, finis, finit, finissons, finissez, finissent 4 finissais 5 finirai 6 finirais 7 finisse
fuir 1 fuyant 2 fui 3 fuis, fuyons, fuient 4 fuyais 7 fuie
joindre 1 joignant 2 joint 3 joins, joignons 4 joignais 7 joigne
lire 1 lisant 2 lu 3 lis, lisons 4 lisais 7 lise
luire 1 luisant 2 lui 3 luis, luisons 4 luisais 7 luise
maudire 1 maudissant 2 maudit 3 maudis, maudissons 4 maudissait 7 maudisse
mentir 1 mentant 2 menti 3 mens, mentons 4 mentais 7 mente
mettre 1 mettant 2 mis 3 mets, mettons 4 mettais 7 mette

mourir 1 mourant 2 mort 3 meurs, mourons, meurent 4 mourais 5 mourrai 7 meure

naître 1 naissant 2 né 3 nais, naît, naissons 4 naissais 7 naisse

offrir 1 offrant 2 offert 3 offre, offrons 4 offrais 7 offre

PARLER 1 parlant 2 parlé 3 parle, parles, parle, parlons, parlez, parlent 4 parlais, parlais, parlait, parlions, parliez, parlaient 5 parlerai, parleras, parlera, parlerons, parlerez, parleront 6 parlerais, parlerais, parlerait, parlerions, parleriez, parleraient 7 parle, parles, parle, parlions, parliez, parlent *impératif* parle! parlez!

partir 1 partant 2 parti 3 pars, partons 4 partais 7 parte

plaire 1 plaisant 2 plu 3 plais, plaît, plaisons 4 plaisais 7 plaise

pleuvoir 1 pleuvant 2 plu 3 pleut, pleuvent 4 pleuvait 5 pleuvra 7 pleuve

pourvoir 1 pourvoyant 2 pourvu 3 pourvois, pourvoyons, pourvoient 4 pourvoyais 7 pourvoie

pouvoir 1 pouvant 2 pu 3 peux, peut, pouvons, peuvent 4 pouvais 5 pourrai 7 puisse

prendre 1 prenant 2 pris 3 prends, prenons, prennent 4 prenais 7 prenne

prévoir *like voir* 5 prévoirai

RECEVOIR 1 recevant 2 reçu 3 reçois, reçois, reçoit, recevons, recevez, reçoivent 4 recevais 5 recevrai 6 recevrais 7 reçoive

RENDRE 1 rendant 2 rendu 3 rends, rends, rend, rendons, rendez, rendent 4 rendais 5 rendrai

6 rendrais 7 rende

résoudre 1 résolvant 2 résolu 3 résous, résolvons 4 résolvais 7 résolve

rire 1 riant 2 ri 3 ris, rions 4 riais 7 rie

savoir 1 sachant 2 su 3 sais, savons, savent 4 savais 5 saurai 7 sache *impératif* sache, sachons, sachez

servir 1 servant 2 servi 3 sers, servons 4 servais 7 serve

sortir 1 sortant 2 sorti 3 sors, sortons 4 sortais 7 sorte

souffrir 1 souffrant 2 souffert 3 souffre, souffrons 4 souffrais 7 souffre

suffire 1 suffisant 2 suffi 3 suffis, suffisons 4 suffisais 7 suffise

suivre 1 suivant 2 suivi 3 suis, suivons 4 suivais 7 suive

taire 1 taisant 2 tu 3 tais, taisons 4 taisais 7 taise

tenir 1 tenant 2 tenu 3 tiens, tenons, tiennent 4 tenais 5 tiendrai 7 tienne

vaincre 1 vainquant 2 vaincu 3 vaincs, vainc, vainquons 4 vainquais 7 vainque

valoir 1 valant 2 valu 3 vaux, vaut, valons 4 valais 5 vaudrai 7 vaille

venir 1 venant 2 venu 3 viens, venons, viennent 4 venais 5 viendrai 7 vienne

vivre 1 vivant 2 vécu 3 vis, vivons 4 vivais 7 vive

voir 1 voyant 2 vu 3 vois, voyons, voient 4 voyais 5 verrai 7 voie

vouloir 1 voulant 2 voulu 3 veux, veut, voulons, veulent 4 voulais 5 voudrai 7 veuille *impératif* veuillez

VERBES IRRÉGULIERS

present	pt	pp	present	pt	pp
arise	arose	arisen	draw	drew	drawn
awake	awoke	awaked	dream	dreamed,	dreamed,
be (am,	was, were	been		dreamt	dreamt
is, are;			drink	drank	drunk
being)			drive	drove	driven
bear	bore	born(e)	dwell	dwelt	dwelt
beat	beat	beaten	eat	ate	eaten
become	became	become	fall	fell	fallen
begin	began	begun	feed	fed	fed
behold	beheld	beheld	feel	felt	felt
bend	bent	bent	fight	fought	fought
beset	beset	beset	find	found	found
bet	bet,	bet,	flee	fled	fled
	betted	betted	fling	flung	flung
bid	bid, bade	bid,	fly (flies)	flew	flown
		bidden	forbid	forbade	forbidden
bind	bound	bound	forecast	forecast	forecast
bite	bit	bitten	forget	forgot	forgotten
bleed	bled	bled	forgive	forgave	forgiven
blow	blew	blown	forsake	forsook	forsaken
break	broke	broken	freeze	froze	frozen
breed	bred	bred	get	got	got, (US)
bring	brought	brought			gotten
build	built	built	give	gave	given
burn	burnt,	burnt,	go (goes)	went	gone
	burned	burned	grind	ground	ground
burst	burst	burst	grow	grew	grown
buy	bought	bought	hang	hung,	hung,
can	could	(been		hanged	hanged
		able)	have	had	had
cast	cast	cast	(has;		
catch	caught	caught	having)		
choose	chose	chosen	hear	heard	heard
cling	clung	clung	hide	hid	hidden
come	came	come	hit	hit	hit
cost	cost	cost	hold	held	held
creep	crept	crept	hurt	hurt	hurt
cut	cut	cut	keep	kept	kept
deal	dealt	dealt	kneel	knelt,	knelt,
dig	dug	dug		kneeled	kneeled
do (3rd	did	done	know	knew	known
person;			lay	laid	laid
he/she/			lead	led	led
it/does)			lean	leant,	leant,

present	pt	pp	present	pt	pp
	leaned	leaned	shrink	shrank	shrunk
leap	leapt,	leapt,	shut	shut	shut
	leaped	leaped	sing	sang	sung
learn	learnt,	learnt,	sink	sank	sunk
	learned	learned	sit	sat	sat
leave	left	left	slay	slew	slain
lend	lent	lent	sleep	slept	slept
let	let	let	slide	slid	slid
lie (lying)	lay	lain	sling	slung	slung
light	lit,	lit,	slit	slit	slit
	lighted	lighted	smell	smelt,	smelt,
lose	lost	lost		smelled	smelled
make	made	made	sow	sowed	sown,
may	might	—			sowed
mean	meant	meant	speak	spoke	spoken
meet	met	met	speed	sped,	sped,
mistake	mistook	mistaken		speeded	speeded
mow	mowed	mown,	spell	spelt,	spelt,
		mowed		spelled	spelled
must	(had to)	(had to)	spend	spent	spent
pay	paid	paid	spill	spilt,	spilt,
put	put	put		spilled	spilled
quit	quit,	quit,	spin	spun	spun
	quitted	quitted	spit	spat	spat
read	read	read	split	split	split
rid	rid	rid	spoil	spoiled,	spoiled,
ride	rode	ridden		spoilt	spoilt
ring	rang	rung	spread	spread	spread
rise	rose	risen	spring	sprang	sprung
run	ran	run	stand	stood	stood
saw	sawed	sawn	steal	stole	stolen
say	said	said	stick	stuck	stuck
see	saw	seen	sting	stung	stung
seek	sought	sought	stink	stank	stunk
sell	sold	sold	stride	strode	stridden
send	sent	sent	strike	struck	struck,
set	set	set			stricken
shake	shook	shaken	strive	strove	striven
shall	should	—	swear	swore	sworn
shear	sheared	shorn,	sweep	swept	swept
		sheared	swell	swelled	swollen,
shed	shed	shed			swelled
shine	shone	shone	swim	swam	swum
shoot	shot	shot	swing	swung	swung
show	showed	shown	take	took	taken

present	pt	pp	present	pt	pp
teach	taught	taught	weave	wove,	woven,
tear	tore	torn		weaved	weaved
tell	told	told	wed	wedded,	wedded,
think	thought	thought		wed	wed
throw	threw	thrown	weep	wept	wept
thrust	thrust	thrust	win	won	won
tread	trod	trodden	wind	wound	wound
wake	woke,	woken,	wring	wrung	wrung
	waked	waked	write	wrote	written
wear	wore	worn			